THE PRESS AND THE STATE

"The mass communications of this country
have more effect upon the American mind
than all the schools and universities combined."

—James Reston, columnist and
vice-president,
The New York Times

The Press and The State:

Sociohistorical and Contemporary Studies

Walter M. Brasch
Dana R. Ulloth

UNIVERSITY PRESS OF AMERICA
LANHAM • NEW YORK • LONDON

University Press of America,® Inc.

4720 Boston Way
Lanham, MD 20706

3 Henrietta Street
London WC2E 8LU England

Library of Congress Cataloging in Publication Data

Brasch, Walter M., 1945-
   The press and the state.

   Includes bibliographies and index.
   1. Government and the press—United States.
2. Government and the press.   I. Ulloth, Dana Royal.
II. Title.
PN4738.B73   1986   302.2'32'0973   86-15855
ISBN 0-8191-5502-0 (alk. paper)
ISBN 0-8191-5272-2 (pbk. : alk. paper)

All University Press of America books are produced on acid-free
paper which exceeds the minimum standards set by the National
Historical Publications and Records Commission.

Acknowledgements

The development of a work of this magnitude required the assistance of several persons who influenced our thinking about press and State relationships and assisted in its production.

Among our many friends and colleagues at the Schools of Journalism of the Ohio University and the University of Missouri who stimulated our thinking were Dr. Hugh Culbertson, Dr. Norman H. Dohn, and Dr. Ralph Izard, at Ohio; and Ed Lambert, Dr. William Stephenson, and Dr. G. Joseph Wolfe at Missouri. Among many others who challenged us were Dr. Leo Barrile, Dr. Craig Newton, and Dr. James Sperry, Bloomsburg University; Dr. John C. Merrill, Louisiana State University; and Dr. Karlen Mooradian, Gilgamesh Press. Dr. Sperry reviewed the book for historical accuracy; Dr. Peter Bohling reviewed parts of the book dealing with political economics.

The unselfish assistance of the people at the Freedom of Information Center of the School of Journalism, University of Missouri, is appreciated; they answered all our questions and provided stacks of information.

The librarians at the Bloomsburg University of Pennsylvania library provided us with many interlibrary loan materials, and assisted in data retrieval and materials acquisition.

Our wives, Rosemary Renn Brasch and Sara S. Ulloth, endured much the past two years while we each taught four classes a semester, served on or chaired innumerable (and often seemingly inconsequential) committees, directed programs, developed curricula, *and* researched and wrote a major journalism text. We deeply appreciate their encouragement, advice, and understanding.

We are also indebted to the many professionals of the University Press of America who have stood behind this project and worked with us for more than a year, and will be there to support us—and the book—for what we know will be a very long time. Elizabeth M. (Beth) Carnes, president of UPA's two major trade divisions, brought our unfinished manuscript to the attention of the entire UPA staff, fought hard for its acceptance and publication, and became our first cheerleader. Helen B. Hudson, production editor, provided constant advice and symbolically held our hands, calming our fears, keeping our spirits high, and supporting us in numerous ways. Sheila Dell, promotion director, and David Little, publicity assistant, are providing marketing guidance for this project. Mary Gonzalez and Joyce Culley supervised parts of pre-press and press preparation; Debra Grasley provided competent indexing. Jeff Lund, programmer, directed the composition, assuring that the computer typesetting and laser print system did not eat too many bytes. Printing was done at Edwards Brothers (Ann Arbor, Mich.). James E. (Jed) Lyons, vice-president and publisher, took a risk on this book, moving UPA into an even stronger commitment to media studies; a book of this size, scope, and complexity requires a financial as well as emotional commitment; Jed made a commitment to bring out this book that presents a different way at looking at the media, and one that fills a major hole in journalism education.

—Walter M. Brasch, Ph.D.
Dana R. Ulloth, Ph.D.

January 1986

Contents

Zenger (1735)   71-76

PART II:
The Framework for the Media:
Contemporary Perspectives

Introduction

Press libertarianism is "pure" . . . if it is uncontrolled, full, unregulated laissez-faire journalism–with a separation of State and press. Admittedly, a pure system has really never existed, for various degrees of governmental control have always undermined and distorted it.

John C. Merrill, *The Imperative of Freedom* (1974)

From the birth of civilization, tension has existed between the rulers and the masses, especially individuals who challenge the established and accepted order. Interested in protecting the "truth" and their authority, the powerful have gone to great lengths to limit the expression of contrary views. Leaders have universally believed that dissidents would weaken their authority.

To maintain their existence, the perservation of the established society and, more importantly, the "truth"—as they have accepted and taught it to the masses, these leaders have developed a wide range of tools—including licensing of the press, torture, and massacre—to enforce conformity and to discourage open discussion of issues.

In contrast, those who argue for the absence of governmental controls soon recognize that without any controls, anarchy would result. As John Merrill points out, complete freedom has never existed; all analyses of the inter-relationships of the press and the State must, therefore, determine the appropriate limitation of the independence that the press should have in the interest of "greater" societal or individual rights. Limitations grow out of the inherent fear that some "right" or "good" will be damaged or destroyed. Fear that the heretic will defame the god or gods of the accepted and established church, and possibly bring upon civilization a "wrath of the gods," leads to laws of heresy; fear that the State will collapse under the weight of criticism leads to laws of sedition; in most societies, an attack upon one is an attack upon both. Fear also leads the State to create laws protecting the individual from other individuals, as well as from a capricious press.

The Press and the State; Sociohistorical and Contemporary Interpretations presents a new political philosophy to help explain the concepts that define the limits of expression within the State. The focus is on the reason for the controls placed upon the media, and upon events and the laws as they shape the role of the State in controlling freedom of expression. In developing this philosophy, the history of the media, media law, and political philosophy are explored only as they relate to the philosophy.

Part I—"The Framework For the Media: Sociohistorical and Philosophical Perspectives"—is a brief review of five thousand years of the controls placed by government and religion upon expression, and of the major political philosophies that helped shape those controls. The relationship between State and press can be characterized by government's desire to exercise the most authoritarian restraints and by the conflicting demands of independent thinkers to loosen by some degree those controls. However, the history of civilization also shows that those in power wish to retain power, and those out of power wish to attain it. Once attained, those who formerly argued for the limitless right of free expression develop reasons for limiting that expression. The philosophy discussed in this book is based upon historical developments in Western civilization and upon the concepts created by thinkers usually thought of as "Western." While the philosphy thus developed may be relevant in any part of the world, no attempt has been made to explore its universality.

Part II—"The Framework for the Media: Contemporary Perspectives"— examines the political values and institutions the United States has established to assure that the press "responsibly" functions as a part of the society and not for the destruction of the State.

In its relationship to the press, the State can assume three distinct roles. The State can limit the elements that permit freedom of expression, as well as restrain expression it finds offensive or threatening; it can encourage an environment within which freedom of expression can flourish, within the boundaries of serving the State's own interest; and it can use the media to promote its own goals and interest. These three State-press relationships are discussed in Part II as "Section 1: The State as Suppressor: Arguments for Limiting Expression"; "Section 2: The State as Facilitator: Arguments for Promoting Expression"; and "Section 3: The State as Manipulator: The Right to Influence."

The articles that are a part of Part II reflect the analyses of some of the foremost writers in mass media, government, and politics, the military, education, and law who have made substantial contributions to the philosophy of State-press relationships. However, in a book of this length, it would be impossible to include an exhaustive treatment of all authors who have added to the understanding of this important field. We have tried to select a reasonable representation of views from people who have made the policies now in effect and the critics of those policies. To supplement the readings, bibliographies representing samples of additional views are included at the end of most chapters.

The chapters in Part II were created to include content that continues to develop and provide a depth to the theoretical foundation presented in Part I, with specific application to the nature and status of the mass media in the United

States. The theoretical model guided the commissioning of special articles and the selection of several previously published works, many of which were updated and revised for this book. Articles and commentary not identified with bylines are those of the authors of this book.

Part I

The Framework for the Media: Sociohistorical and Philosophical Perspectives

"When a nation goes down . . . or a society perishes, one condition may always be found. They forgot where they came from. They lost sight of what had brought them along."

—Carl Sandburg

Chapter 1

A History of Fear

No greater calamity could come upon the people than the privation of free speech.

Demosthenes

The history of any civilization is a history of oppression, of the subjugation of the people to the control of rulers. Whether they rule by "divine birth right," popular election, or conquest; whether they are despotic and tyrannical, benevolent and caring; whether wise or stupid, hedonistic, stoic, or puritanical; whether their people are nomadic or sedentary; whether their governments are called oligarchies, autocracies, theocracies, republics, or democracies, they are still rulers, and their subjects are still being ruled. It makes no difference if they are preliterate kinship groups, neolithic villages, or the ancient civilizations which developed in the lands of the world we call Mesopotamia, Egypt, Greece, Rome, Mesoamerica, Peru, the Indus River Valley, or Chang-Chou; it makes no difference if they are the great empires we call the Holy Roman, Byzantine, Ottoman, British, and Spanish, or modern societies we label as industrial, agrarian, or tribal, and sub-divide into ethnic and geographical regions we call "Western," Slavic, Amerindian, Judaic, African, Asian, Hispanic, or any of half-a-hundred others. All civilizations have the same threads of life in them, the people having the same emotions, wants, and needs—and all have the history of oppression.

Underlying the oppression is a history of fear. In legend, it could have begun with a universal Spirit's fear of creating a universe or in placing life on earth. Perhaps, according to myth, the dinosaurs were not destroyed by the ice age or a meteorite of destruction, but by the universal spirit who became afraid of the power unleashed by animals with small brains and large teeth and claws. In the expulsion from the Garden of Eden of the first two humans on earth, the Spirit showed a fear that mankind would be able to become immortal and understand in its own rationality "good" and "evil," thus threatening the uniqueness of that universal Spirit called Yahweh, Jehovah, or God.

3

The ancient peoples were so awed by the universe, by the sun, the moon, and the stars, by the seasons, by rain, wind, and thunder, by the mountains, rivers, and lakes, by the plants and trees, by animals of all kinds, that they knew that no mere human beings could create such a magnificent universe. To them it was created by that which was supernatural, not human. And so to the spirit they called gods, they worshipped, in awe as much as in fear of the power that could create such a universe. And, yet, it was difficult to worship that which could not be seen, could not be heard, could not be touched. The spirit of the gods was everywhere, yet nowhere. By the dawn of civilization, the people had to have created a priest class, those few among them who understood at least a portion of the universe, could even do what we today call "illusions" or "magic." The leaders were believed to have talked with the gods, had descended from the heavens, placed on earth to communicate that knowledge with the people. To better the people's existence on earth, the priests were willing to give the people both security and a spiritual freedom—but at a cost of all other freedoms. To speak in opposition, thus, was not even considered, for it would bring about the wrath of the gods. As society developed, the collective interests of the people now required a subordination of the people to the good of the society.

It is impossible, if no more than one opinion is uttered, to make choice of the best: a man is forced then to follow whatever advice may have been given him; but if opposite speeches are delivered, then choice can be exercised. In like manner, pure gold is not recognized by itself; but when we test it along with baser ore, we perceive which is the better.

Artabanus, about 480 B.C.

The Development of the State

In all societies, it is the people who initially adopt the values of "right" and "wrong," values accepted, institutionalized, then enforced by the form of governmental control they assume was divinely-inspired. In time, the people forget that it is they who have created the state, and accept the belief that the state was created for them by divine intervention, and accept the authority of the ruler as absolute. It is these absolute values that may keep a society or civilization from continual anarchy or destruction; it is these values that the ruler must now defend.

To gain protection and services, and to reduce their fear of sustaining life entirely on their own, the people transfer some or all of their liberties to the responsibility of centralized government; thus, not only is the state essential, according to the Authoritarian Theory,* but primary, for the state, as the enbodiment of God and, as representative of the people, provides the framework through which mankind advances, and individuals achieve their ends. The need for the State becomes greater as the societies increase in size; the larger and more complex it becomes, the greater the need for the State.

The people chose to worship that universal Spirit as much out of a fear of the wrath of God or the gods and the need to preserve their lands and cultures as out of a necessity for a greater explanation for their existence. On this basis, the Jews formed the Covenant with God, a pact that would guarantee the survival of the people of Israel; for their part, they were required to put their complete obedience into the God of Israel, and to worship no other gods before Him.

To fulfill their part of the contract, rulers must not only provide for the spiritual health of their people provide protection and essential services, but must also try to maintain their rule against a multitude. To protect the existing order and cover their own anxieties and fears, rulers, whether secular or temporal, must induce fear into the people, assuring them that as long as the state and theology, represented by the ruler, is strong and unchallenged from within, services will continue to be provided, and the state will not be destroyed by conquest, its people killed or placed into bondage.

Because the ruler represents the "right," the collective conscience of the people, attacks against a ruler are not only attacks against the people, but against society as well. In defending the people and providing services, the rulers must assume that they alone possess "truth," and are, therefore, "right." If others with differing viewpoints are allowed to exist, then the ruler must assume that these views threaten the existing order and could, if they became accepted by the people, lead not only to his overthrow, but to the overthrow of the existing society as well. In fear of a destruction of their society, the people give the ruler the power to threaten them with imprisonment and torture, or a loss of position, property, or life should they not accept the "righteousness" of the ruler, thus assuring the preservation of the foundations of their society. Thus, the state assumes the authority of not only providing for the needs of the people, but also of suppressing dissent, prosecuting those suspected of sedition, writing or speaking against a government; and for treason, the attempt to overthrow a government.

Ironically, although the overthrow of the State can occur only when it is not sufficient to provide for the needs and protection of the people, the decline of almost every great civilization has occurred not by a decisive war, but during a time when there is little threat of invasion, when the people have become content that the state is providing all their needs—and when they lose the fear that has created the State.

---

*In *Four Theories of the Press* (1956), Fred S. Siebert, Theodore Peterson, and Wilbur Schramm outlined the Authoritarian, Libertarian, Soviet Communist, and Social Responsibility theories. Although a major study which provided a strong focus for media historians to better understand the concepts of press–state relationships, the study does not critically accept the premise that there are many theories, and that one society can have elements of all four theories. In the United States, for example, elements of the Authoritarian, Libertarian, and Social Responsibility theories operate in both combination and opposition to each other.

The Birth of Writing

The first known written language was developed sometime after 3500 B.C. in Sumeria, the southern district of Babylonia, in the region known as Mesopotamia; surviving are several articles and histories attesting to the development of literature. The Sumerians are also credited with the development of a system of mathematics, architecture, engineering, corporate business practices, and the creation of a specialized society in which people developed vocational specialities to divide the common work.

The Sumerians had looked to their gods for guidance and inspiration, creating a priest class which was able to convince the people that they could do nothing without the help of the gods. And so the people gave freely to the gods, in the process becoming poorer, while the priests became richer and more powerful, suppressing all freedoms in the names of the gods. The gods could cause destruction of cities, could wreak vengeance upon the people by floods, famine, or storms, all of which the people might not understand the reasons for, but accepted as the will of the gods.

In the 24th century, B.C., King Urukagina, of the Sumerian city-state of Lagash, acting in the name of the god Ningirsu, abolished not only the tax collectors, but also broke the power of the priests, thus giving his people a restoration of earlier freedoms, including the freedom of speech. Urukagina's reforms, however, lasted only a decade, for his government was overthrown by a rival city-state.

About 2113 B.C., the Third Dynasty of Ur, founded by Urnammu, restored freedoms to the people and led to the renaissance of the arts and sciences. The Sumerian civilization eventually died out about 1500 B.C.

Pharaohs and Gods

In Egypt, like Babylonia, the welfare of the people depended upon the gods, one of whom was the pharaoh, son of a mortal woman and of Re, the Sun god. The State was an extension of the gods; the pharaohs were the caretakers of the gods' land. There was no political or religious dissent; since the people understood and accepted the power and wisdom of the gods, they also understood and accepted the power and wisdom of the pharaoh; because the gods so willed it, they would allow themselves to be subjugated to what today appear to be unjust laws and practices.

About 1350 B.C., the pharaoh, Ikhnaton, declared that the sun god, Aton, was one god, that there were no other gods but him. Amon-Re had required secret ceremonies and ritualistic passages. Aton, however, did not wish only priests to know and communicate his power; thus, Ikhnaton ordered the closed and mysterious temples of Amon to be destroyed, and new temples be built "open to the sky," so that all people should be able to worship and understand Aton's commands, as interpreted by the pharaoh. Ikhnaton further ordered the destruction of all references to Amon. However, rulers, no matter how divine the people believed them to be, can not just change theology and expect everyone to accept it as a will of God or gods. To force compliance, Ikhnaton unleashed a brutality of force that brought enslavement, torture and death to those who did not accept the god, Aton, as the one god of the universe. Upon Ikhnaton's death about 1400 B.C., his son-in-law, became pharaoh, restored Amon as the principal god of Egypt, and to show the people the strength of the bond between the god and the pharaoh, took the name Tutankhamon, or Tut-Ankh-Amon.

The Greek Civilization

Like other civilizations before them, the Greeks had a fear of their gods; however, unlike other civilizations, neither the gods nor the Greeks despaired for mankind's existence on earth.

The gods of ancient Greece were human-like, playful with human frailties, needs, wants, and desires. Homer, author of the "Odyssey," portrayed Zeus, the leader of the gods, "the Father of Gods and Men," as a kind, jovial, and adulterous god; Aeschylus, in *Promethius Bound*, saw Zeus as a raging tyrant determined to destroy mankind; Hesiod thought of Zeus as a guardian of the rights of the poor and oppressed. Greece had no divine "sons of gods," no prophets, and no "god-like" individuals, such as Buddha, Confucius, or Moses. Other religions, both ancient and modern, would suppress views that ascribed human characteristics to gods. But, in ancient Greece, public discussion, even dissent, was not only tolerated, it was encouraged.

The Greek writers, scientists, and philosophers disregarded "magic," and tried to find rational, reasonable explanations for the nature of the universe,

---

Preserving Confucius

The creation of a different form of government usually necessitates not only the destruction of the previous form of government but also its culture.

Shih Huang Ti (259 B.C.-210 B.C.), who unified China after centuries as a series of feudal societies, and under whose direction the Great Wall and numerous social improvements were made, was also Asia's first great suppressor of literature. To effect the creation of a strong centralized government, he ordered all literature of the Chou dynasty, including the works of Confucius, to be destroyed.

Some were able to hide the works of the great writers and philosophers; but many, afraid of torture and possible death should the works be discovered, forced themselves to memorize long sections of the written philosophy and literature.

Nevertheless, the Ch'in dynasty provided the base for the Han dynasty (206 B.C.-220 A.D.), during which China expanded her territories and developed a stronger base of literature and philosophy, requiring all government officials to pass examinations to test their knowledge of China's literature and philosophies.

seeking wisdom to understand nature. From the quest for understanding, in an aura of tolerance, there developed the great writers, philosophers, scientists, and political leaders, their works still read in schools throughout the world—historian-journalists Herodotus (484 B.C.-425 B.C.), Thucydides (460 B.C.-395 B.C.), and Xenophon (430 B.C. -355 B.C.); poets Homer (8th century B.C.), Archillochus (about 650 B.C.), and Hesiod (about 1700 B.C.); dramatists Aeschylus (525 B.C. - 456 B.C.), Sophocles (496 B.C. - 406 B.C.), Euripides (480 B.C.-406 B.C.), and Aristophanes (450 B.C. - 388 B.C.); statesmen Solon (630 B.C. - 560 B.C.) who gave the Greeks a system of laws, and Pericles (495 B.C. - 429 B.C.); military genius Alexander the Great (356 B.C. - 323 B.C.) who expanded the Greek empire; scientists Archimedes, Pythagorus, Euclid, Apollonius, Herophilus, Erasistratus, Aristarchus, and Eratosthenes; and the great philosophers Socrates (470 B.C. - 399 B.C.), Plato (428 B.C. - 348 B.C.), and Aristotle (384 B.C.- 322 B.C.), Epicurus, and Xenophanes. All of them, and thousands more in Greece's one millenium history, used the freedom they had as property-owning adult males to look at Greek society, and to help all people understand the basic nature of the human spirit.

Under the political leadership of Solon, the Athenian laws were rewritten to give greater freedom to the people; included was the requirement that all non-slave adult males, even those not owning land, be allowed to participate in the State's decision-making process. Exceptions were those citizens convicted of crimes, who were unable to pay legal debts, or whom a body of elected citizens had determined to be "unworthy" (e.g., those who committed unethical, though not necessarily illegal, acts). Although dictatorships were sandwiched in the governance of Athens during the next century, Cleisthenes and Pericles both expanded freedom of expression. Nevertheless, Athenian law also called for the punishment of those who were found guilty of defamation, sedition, the attempted creation of legislation that would be unconstitutional, knowingly gave bad advice or use the rights of free expression to deceive people.

But, as in all civilizations, there would come an era in which religious and political dissent would no longer be tolerated; the end of toleration would come not from invaders, but from within the people. Within Greece, three of mankind's greatest scholars—Socrates, Plato, and Aristophanes—would be a part of the beginning of the decline of Greece's "golden age."

Most Athenians though of Socrates as a brilliant scholar and teacher—perhaps eccentric, maybe a pest, but a man worthy of respect; to a few, he was a radical, injecting false ideas into the minds of the young.

Like most Greeks, Socrates had believed in the system of participatory democracy, but as he saw the masses continue to make inept, unwise, or even stupid decisions—or no decisions at all—he argued that "wise men," few in number, must be allowed to be the leaders of the people. The quest for what is "good," and what is "right," said Socrates, could not come from a group process that includes those who were not trained in the specialty known as philosophy.

In 404 B.C., Critias, a former pupil of Socrates, returned to Athens after banishment by the Greek democracy. With the help of Sparta, he overthrew the democracy, became leader during the "Reign of the Thirty Tyrants," and launched a bloodbath of terror, resulting in the execution of 1,500 Athenians, and the exile of another 5,000. A year later, he was killed in a civil war that restored democracy to Athens. But, Athenians would remember that Socrates was the teacher of Critias, and had taught him that governance should be by a few wise men.

Sometime about 399 B.C., Socrates was brought to trial in Athens, charged with both atheism and creating false gods—"trumped up" charges with no basis of fact—and with corrupting the young. In his defense, Socrates, as quoted by Plato, argued:

> As long as I have breath and strength, I will not give up philosophy and exhorting you and declaring the truth to everyone of you and whom I meet saying, as I am accustomed, "My good friend, you are a citizen of Athens, a city which is very great and very famous for its wisdom and power—are you not ashamed of caring so much for the making of money and for fame and prestige, when you neither think nor care about wisdom and truth and the improvement of your soul? . . . Whether you acquit me or not, I shall not change my way of life; no, not if I have to die for it many times."

Nevertheless, the government of Athens, threatened by a philosopher/teacher who was considered to be both an eccentric and a leader of a "free thinking" movement which had challenged conventional views sentenced him to death by a vote of 281-220, offering him the option of exile. Socrates chose death. The government leaders were now upset, for they did not wish Socrates dead, only that he should stop "corrupting the young" by telling them that there were other ways to look at a government and a universe. However, the leaders did not panic, for they knew that the friends of Socrates would bribe his jailers and arrange for his escape, as other prisoners had done before him. But Socrates would not allow others to arrange his escape, arguing that he would accept death to show the conviction of his principles, and that wise men must be allowed to search for truth, no matter how many obstacles are put into their paths.

In life, Socrates influenced a generation of Greeks to look at different ways to understand the universe. Ironically, it would be his death that would bring about a revolution of thought, and result in an even greater restriction of free speech than what his tormentors had undertaken against him.

Plato, shaken by the death of his "older friend" and mentor, now took Socrates's beliefs of governance even further, bitterly arguing that the death of Socrates proved that the masses were incapable of governing themselves. The ideal State, said Plato, was a benevolent oligarchy, ruled by philosopher-kings, wise but powerful men who would be able to unify and co-ordinate life. The State, wrote Plato, is safe "only in the hands of wiser men . . . who are governed by moral authority and who use this authority to keep the baser elements in line." The "baser elements," said Plato, are the other two classes of society—the guardians of civilization (armies and police forces) and the workers. Only the greatest intellectuals would be allowed to become the philosopher-kings, for during their training they would have learned not only the arts and sciences, but also the values of what is "good" and "right," and what is "evil" and "wrong." The intellectual strength of the philosopher-kings, said Plato, will control their emotions and their greed, protecting civilization from selfish and materialistic encroachments inherent in the guardians and workers, the lesser intelligent and capable.

Because of the necessity of protecting the "right"—which Plato called the Form of the Good, and from which all knowledge is disseminated—the kingdoms must regulate all areas that would inject a "wrong." All writing must be regulated in order to preserve the public good, wrote Plato, thus preserving the knowledge that a society needs in which to function. Magistrates would determine if there was anything in the works that opposed the public good, and whether the work itself was good for the spiritual health of the people. Violators would be exiled. Likewise, any attack upon the rulers would be considered to be an attack upon the people, and the cause for exile.

Plato would also have required the magistrates to suppress all forms of fiction—drama, stories, and poetry—since they do not elevate people's minds, but subject them to lies (untruths), and therefore are "wrong." Plato would have banished all such writers, calling them enemies of the State, to prevent the people from becoming further depraved by exposure to these fictions.

Anger had formed the base for Plato's philosophical conviction, for it was a work of fiction that had led to the arrest and death of the man Plato held to be one of his closest friends. In Aristophanes's biting comedic satire, *Clouds,* Socrates is ridiculed and portrayed as a subversive whose teachings undermined the moral and intellectual fiber of Athens. Almost all Athenians knew that *Clouds* was an exaggeration; certainly, Aristophanes never thought of it as factually accurate, although he could reasonably argue that it did present truth. In an age of toleration, both Socrates and Aristophanes were allowed to say what they pleased. But the play, first performed in 423 B.C., when Plato was only five years old, continued to be performed, showing contempt for Socrates, pointing out his "radicalism," and showing the Athenians what Socrates was saying to "undermine" the authority of the government. Plato, Socrates' pupil, thought it was a vicious play. And then, with a new government—one that was believed to be more democratic than the old—Socrates was charged with corrupting the morals of the young, a major theme of *Clouds* . . . And then he was dead, and Plato would not tolerate what had happened.

And so it was the words of Socrates, after receiving the sentence of death, now recorded by Plato, that would come to haunt the Greek civilization:

> There will be more men who will call you to account, whom I have held back, though you did not recognize it. And they will be harsher toward you than I have been, for they will be younger, and you will be more indignant with them. For if you think you will restrain men from reproaching you for not living as you should, by putting them to death, you are very much mistaken. That way of escape is neither possible nor

Plato didn't like drama => no intellectual stimulation

honorable. It is much more honorable and much easier not to suppress others, but to make yourselves as good as you can. This is my parting prophecy to you who have condemned me.

By the time of Plato's own death in 348 B.C., magistrates had begun a systematic censorship of plays and poetry; soon there was minimal discussion of politics, and all sexually-suggestive plays, such as Aristophanes' *Lysistra*, in which women conspired to refuse to have sexual intercourse with their husbands if wars continued, were forbidden from performance. Meander, a dramatist, in response to the regulation of fiction, wrote, "We live not as we choose, but as we can."

The Roman Civilization

The death of Socrates, and the vindictiveness of Plato and the younger generation of Greeks, became a part of the culture of the nation that would conquer Greece. The Roman civilization, reported Scipio, as recorded by Cicero, "considered comedy and all theatrical performances as disgraceful, and therefore not only barred players from offices and honors open to ordinary citizens, but also decreed that their names shall be branded by the censor, and erased from the roll of their tribe."

Further, within the Roman civilization, attacks upon individuals, such as that directed against Socrates by Aristophanes, were not only forbidden, but were also capital crimes. Scipio, as quoted by Cicero, noted:

Though our Twelve Tables [of law] attach the penalty of death only to a very few offenses, yet among these few this was one: if any man should have sung a pasquinade, or composed a satire calculated to bring infamy or disgrace on another person. [It is] wisely decreed. For it is by decisions of magistrates, and by a well-informed justice, that our lives ought to be judged, and not by the flighty fancies of poets; neither ought we be exposed to her calunmies, save where we have the liberty of replying, and defending ourselves before an adequate tribunal.

It would be more than two centuries before Rome would produce some of the greatest writers in history—Lucretius (99 B.C.-55 B.C), Catullus (84 B.C.-54 B.C.), Vergil (70 B.C.-19 B.C.), and Horace (65 B.C.-8 B.C.); and the journalist-historians Cicero (106 B.C.-43 B.C.), Livy (59 B.C.-17 A.D.), Plutarch (46 A.D.?-127 A.D.), and Tacitus (55 A.D.-120 A.D.).

The glory that was Rome's was the glory that was Caesar's (100 B.C.-44 B.C.). Julius Caesar, a brilliant writer and military leader, ruled the Roman empire less than five years, but brought a unification to the peoples of Rome, created a major system of roads and aquaducts, provided for the betterment of the people, and ordered widespread amnesty for his former enemies, at a time when he could have ordered their slaughter, as had military leaders done for millenia. But, he was also a dictator who ordered the building of temples, created lavish patriotic displays, and infuriated many by having his image placed on coinage and in all parts of the empire. Claiming opposition to tyranny, and claiming they represented libertarian interests, some members of the Roman senate assassinated him in the Forum.

Cicero, one of Caesar's most bitter rivals, later killed in a counter-revolt, had argued that the people, not the generals or gods, created the commonwealth and gave it its authority, and that the emperor, therefore, was subject to the will of the people. The emperor's authority, thus, was only as great as the people allowed. Cicero further argued that not only the gods possessed reason, as had all civilizations believed, but that mankind also possessed the power of reason:

> Since there is nothing better than reason, and since it exists in both man and God, the first common possession of man and God is reason, but those who have reason in common must also have right reason in common. And since right reason is Law, we must believe that men have Law also in common with the gods. Further, those who share Law must also share Justice . . .

For these beliefs, Cicero knew that tyranny had to be ended, no matter how benevolent the dictatorship. His views would continue to thread their way through Western civilization, forming a base for the develoment of the Libertarian theory in the Renaissance.

Many of the caesars of the first two centuries, A.D.—among them Augustus, Tiberius, Caligula, Claudius, and Vespasian—allowed dissent. However, Caligula soon was was stung so often by criticism that he undertook a brutal campaign that resulted in the execution of opponents. Nero, who followed Claudius, and Domitian, who followed Vespasian, instituted repressive measures, including torture and death.

Like the early years of Greece, Rome allowed a freedom of worship, inviting the gods of conquered nations to share a place in the Pantheon. Within a couple centuries, however, during Rome's golden age, the people were required to pray to the caesar, now considered to be ascribed with divine traits. Only the monotheistic Jews were exempt, although they were required to pray *for* the caesar, and to help pay for the maintenance of the Roman temples.

To many in contemporary Western society, it would not be the great poets, historians, or military leaders, or the tolerance to Jews and peoples with differing religions for which Rome would be remembered, but for its intolerance, its crucifixion of one Jew, and the persecution of the religions known as Judaism and Christianity.

Essay on Freedom

by Montaigne

There was one Labienus at Rome, a man of great worth and authority, and, amongst other qualities, excellent in all sorts of literature; who was, as I take it, the son of that great Labienus, the chief of Caesar's captains in the wars of Gaul; and who, afterwards, siding with Pompey the great, so valiantly maintained his cause, till he was by Caesar defeated in Spain. This Labienus, of whom I am now speaking, had several enemies envious of his virtue, and 'tis likely, the courtiers and minions of the emperors of his time who were very angry at his freedom and the paternal humour which he yet retained against tyranny, with which it is to be supposed he had tinctured his books and writings. His adversaries prosecuted several pieces he had published before the magistrate at Rome, and prevailed so far against him, as to have them condemned to the fire. It was in him that this new example of punishment was begun, which was afterwards continued against others at Rome, to punish even writing and studies with death. There would not be means and matter enough of cruelty, did we not mix with them things that nature has exempted from all sense and suffering, as reputation and the products of the mind, and did we not communicate corporal punishments to the teachings and monuments of the Muses. Now Labienus could not suffer this loss, nor survive these his so dear issue; and therefore caused himself to be conveyed and shut up alive in the monument of his ancestors, where he made shift to kill and bury himself at once. 'Tis hard to show a more vehement paternal affection than this.

Cassius Severus, a man of great eloquence and his very intimate friend, seeing his books burned, cried out that by the same sentence they should as well condemn him to the fire too, seeing that he carried in his memory all that they contained. The like accident befel Cremutius Cordus, who being accused of having in his books commended Brutus and Cassius, that dirty, servile, and corrupt senate, and worthy a worse master than Tiberius, condemned his writings to the flame. He was willing to bear them company and killed himself with fasting. The good Lucan, being condemned by that rascal Nero, at the last gasp of his life when the greater part of his blood was already spent through the veins of his arms which he had caused his physician to open to make him die, and when the cold had seized upon all his extremities, and began to approach his vital parts, the last thing he had in his memory was some of the verses of his Battle of Pharsalia, which he recited, dying with them in his mouth. What was this, but taking a tender and paternal leave of his children, in imitation of the valedictions and embraces wherewith we part from ours, when we come to die, and an effect of that natural inclination, that suggests to our remembrance in this extremity those things which were dearest to us during the time of our life?

Can we believe that Epicurus, who, as he says himself, dying of the intolerable pain of the stone, had all his consolation in the beauty of the doctrine he left behind him, could have received the same satisfaction from many children, though never so well-conditioned and brought up, had he had them, as he did from the production of so many rich writings? Or that, had it been in his choice to have left behind him a deformed and untoward child, or a foolish and ridiculous book, he or any other man of his understanding, would not rather have chosen to have run the first misfortune than the other? It had been, for example, peradventure, an impiety in St. Augustine, if on the one hand, it had been proposed to him to bury his writings, from which religion has received so great fruit, or on the other, to bury his children, had he had them, had he not rather chosen to bury his children. And I know not whether I had not much rather have begot a very beautiful one, through society with the Muses, than by lying with my wife to this, such as it is, what I give it, I give absolutely and irrevocably, as men do to their bodily children. That little I have done for it, is no more at my own disposal; it may know many things that are gone from me, and from me hold that which I have not retained; and which, as well, a stranger, I should borrow thence, should I stand in need. If I am wiser than my book, it is richer than I. There are few men addicted to poetry who would not be much prouder to be fathers to the Aenid than to the handsomest youth in Rome; and who would not much better bear the loss of the one than of the other.

Histories

by Tacitus

At the close of the year [20 A.D.], Caius Lutorius Priscus, a Roman knight, who, after writing a popular poem bewailing the death of Germanicus, had received a reward in money from the emperor, was fastened on by an informer, and charged with having composed another during the illness of Drusus, which, in the event of the prince's death, might be published with even greater profit to himself. He had in his vanity read it in the house of Publius Petronius before Vitellia, Petronius's mother-in-law, and several ladies of rank. As soon as the accuser appeared, all but Vitellia were frightened into giving evidence. She alone swore that she had heard not a word. But those who criminated him fatally were rather believed, and on the motion of Haterius Agrippa, the consul-elect, the last penalty was invoked on the accused.

Marcus Lepidus spoke against the sentence as follows—"Senators, if we look to the single fact of the infamous utterance with which Lutorius has polluted his own mind and the ears of the public, neither dungeon not halter nor tortures fit for a slave would be punishment enough for him. But though vice and wicked deeds have no limit, penalties and correctives are moderated by the clemency of the sovereign and by the precedents of your ancestors and yourselves. Folly differs from wickedness; evil words from evil deeds, and thus there is room for a sentence by which this offense may not go unpunished, while we shall have no cause to regret either leniency or severity. Often have I heard our emperor complain when any one has anticipated his mercy by a self-inflicted death. Lutorius's life is still safe; if spared, he will be no danger to the State; if put to death he will be no warning to others. His productions are as empty and ephemeral as they are replete with folly. Nothing serious or alarming is to be apprehended from the man who is the betrayer of his own shame and works on the imaginations not of men but of silly women. However, let him leave Rome, lose his property, and be outlawed. That is my proposal, just as though he were convicted under the law of treason."

Only one of the ex-consuls, Rubellius Blandus, supported Lepidus. The rest voted with Agrippa. Priscus was dragged off to prison and instantly put to death. Of this Tiberius complained to the Senate with his usual ambiguity, extolling their loyalty in so sharply avenging the very slightest insults to the sovereign, though he deprecated such hasty punishment of mere words, praising Lepidus and not censuring Agrippa. So the Senate passed a resolution that their decrees should not be registered in the treasury till nine days had expired, and so much respite was to be given to condemned persons. Still the Senate had not liberty to alter their purpose, and lapse of time never softened Tiberius.

Chapter 2

A Massacre of Mankind

Each religion creates its own government, based upon what the people think their gods wish. However, to protect the religion, one's basic values and beliefs, most religions establish themselves as the one "true" religion, excluding all other doctrine as being false, even harmful. The "true" religion is encumbered with helping—shepherding—mankind in its earthly existence, giving comfort and protecting it from evil. If "false" doctrine is allowed to exist, then the religion would have failed in its mission. Dissent—in kin groups, in villages, in civilizations, ancient or modern—has met with swift retribution. Upon their need to have all peoples accept the "true" religion, mankind has massacred itself.

The Jewish Experience

The faith of Abraham and Job, and the leadership of Moses, had given the Jews a base for accepting a theocracy for their government. Against the most powerful adversaries, the Jews have been given strength by their faith that serves as the basis for their love of wisdom, their compelling spirit of freedom and tolerance, their pursuit of justice, and their charity and kindness to all people. Although theirs was a merciful God, a caring and compassionate God, He was also a jealous God, and defiance was met by death. It was God's vengeance that gave Moses, (the Moses who led the Jews out of slavery) the authority to order the deaths of almost three thousand people for worshipping a golden calf. It was God's vengeance that gave King Jehu the "right" to lure thousands of recalcitrant Jews and "non-believers" into a temple, then had them massacred. And it was in the name of God that the Jews, under King Herod in the first century, B.C., in a grand attempt to extend their territory, forced the Idumeans either to convert to Judaism or be killed or exiled.

Nevertheless, throughout their history, the Jews have been one of the most persecuted of all religions. In the eighth century, B.C., their northern kingdom of Israel was destroyed; in the sixth century, B.C., Judah, their southern kingdom, was destroyed by the Babylonian armies. Most Jews were killed or forced into assimilation with their conquerors. With their temples to the God they called Yahweh destroyed, the Jews realized that it was not temples that united the people, nor allowed the worship of the God they called Yahweh; the love of God was not in the worldly materialism, but in the heart. The

17

few thousand Jews who held onto their religion became even more dedicated to its preservation, creating, in the fifth century, B.C., the *Torah*, the written documents of their laws and traditions. From the *Torah*, there developed the *Talmud*, the discussions and explanations for the laws of God.

In the fourth century, B.C., Alexander the Great, of Greece, conquered most of what was then the civilized world. With a millenium of their faith for support, the Jewish people resisted all attempts to convert them to the faith of the peoples of Greece; the greater the attempts to convert the Jews, whether by kindness or brutality, the greater the resistance. In 175 B.C., Antiochus Epiphanes, seeing Judaism as a "false" religion that directly threatened the people of Greece, forbid all Jewish worship upon penalty of death, then ordered all Jews to worship the Greek gods. The greater the oppression, the greater the resistance, and the attempt to oppress all Jewish worship led the Jews to renew their faith and strike out against their persecutors. The Maccabean revolt united the Jewish people, gave them a cause for the overthrow of an oppressive nation, and led to their independence in 142 B.C.

Under the Roman empire, the Jews were given a limited right of worship, the caesars recognizing that attempts to suppress a world population that now exceeded seven million would lead to their own destruction. But even then, Jews were persecuted by the Roman citizens—and by other Jews.

The influence that Greece had upon Rome had transcended geographical and cultural boundaries, eventually influencing Jewish thought. In intolerance, there arose a radical Jewish organization, the Zealots, which demanded strict, fundamental, observation of the laws of Judaism, pointing out that the word of God, as recorded in the *Torah*, was Law, and any attempt to accept other cultures was a direct disobedience to God. By 6 A.D., the Zealots had begun terroristic attacks against all non-Jews, as well as Jews who accepted part of the Greek culture. As the brutality of the Zealots became better known— several thousand non-Jews and several hundred Jews would die in the terroristic campaigns—Rome responded with fury, destroying Jerusalem in 70 A.D., effectively ending the Zealot's revolt against Roman persecution. Then, about 170 A.D., Hadrian ordered the Jewish temple in Jerusalem to be rebuilt—as a temple to Jupiter, king of the Roman gods. The Jews, observant and non-observant, zealous or liberal, all of whom had seem their holy city destroyed several times in their history, now organized their hatred of the Romans, launching a massive revolt. By the time it was over, more than a million Jews were killed or enslaved; Judaism would continue, but the Jewish civilization would die, not to be resurrected for almost two millenia.

Christianity Persecuted

Sometime about 64 A.D., Rome was torched. No one knows whether it was set deliberately, perhaps by Christians, or through an accident; some historians claim that it may have been Nero (37 A.D.-68 A.D.), a psychotic ruler, who burned his capital city, perhaps to blame the emerging Christian sect. Whatever the truth, Nero initiated a systematic persecution of Christians, accusing them not of "false worship" or heresy, but for being arsonists; their punishment was to be burned alive. Trajan (53 A.D.-117 A.D., reign 98 A.D.-117 A.D.) increased the persecution of Christians, declaring them to be outlaws and "enemies of mankind," subject to execution without a trial. Following the death of Trajan, persecution diminished, then was renewed in 250 A.D. during the rule of Decius who ordered Christian writings burned, the churches destroyed, and all Roman citizens, with the exception of the Jews, to pledge their loyalty to the official state religion. Those who refused were assumed to be Christians and were summarily executed, charged with high treason. The persecution succeeded only in reducing the number of Christians, not the intensity of their beliefs.

Tertullian (155 A.D. - 230 A.D.), whom many Christians accept as one of the great early theologians, preached toleration at a time when Christians were subject to Roman persecution. But his views changed when he saw that there were still many who did not wish to become Christians. "It is a fundamental human right, a privilege of nature, that every man should worship according to his own convictions," he wrote. "One man's religion neither helps nor harms another man . . . It is not in the nature of religion to coerce religion which must be adopted freely and not by force." Later, however, believing that truth, and thus redemption lay only in the hands of Christianity, Tertullian looked caustically at the increasing secularism of the church, and the toleration he had earlier preached, proclaiming, "Heretics may properly be compelled, not enticed to duty. Obstinacy must be corrected not coaxed."

---

*For the sake of common worship, they've slain each other
with the sword. They have set up gods and challenged one
another to 'Put away your gods and come and worship
ours, or we will kill you and your gods!' And so it will be
to the end of the world, even when gods disappear from
earth; they will fall down before their idols just the same.*

—Fedor Dostoyefsky, "The Grand Inquisitor,"
in *The Brothers Karamazov* (1880)

Then, in 311 A.D., Constantine, Galerius, and Licinus, co-rulers of the empire, perhaps recognizing that a people who are oppressed have nothing to lose and could initiate revolution, ordered a "toleration" of Christians; a year later, the Edict of Milan guaranteed freedom of worship for all peoples:

> . . . [L]iberty of worship shall not be denied to any, but that the mind and will of every individual shall be free to manage divine affairs according to his choice . . .[E]very person who cherishes the desire to serve the Christian religion shall freely and unconditionally proceed to observe the same without . . . hindrance . . . [T]he same free and open power to follow their own religion or worship is granted also to others,

in accordance with the tranquility of our times, in order that every living person may have free opportunity to worship the object of his choice.

Christian Persecutors

A young religion, Christianity was fearful of its existence, but determined to let the world know what is considered to be the truth. As in most religions, the persecuted became the persecutors; the intensity of the Christian persecution of non-Christians would establish it as one of the most oppressive of all religions; it would dominate not only what we call Western civilization, but the nature and development of the press.

During the next five hundred years, numerous popes and kings launched numerous campaigns against the non-believers of Christianity, torturing hundreds of thousands to change their beliefs, killing those who didn't. During these centuries, a dark age in Western civilization, freedom of speech was only as free as a ruler permitted.

Less than two decades after declaring freedom of worship to be a universal right, Constantine, who had become a Christian, declared that Christianity represented law and order, and that any attack upon Christianity was heresy. By 346 A.D., all non-Christian temples and churches were ordered closed. Theodosius I (346 A.D.-395 A.D.) declared heretics (all non-Christians) to be enemies of the empire, subject to execution and confiscation of property, thus reducing opposition, while increasing the financial base of both church and State. In the name of "true faith," Theodosius lured as many as fifteen thousand "pagans" into a circus in Salonika, making them believe that they were to be part of a religious celebration—then ordered them killed. However, the bishop of Milan, later to be known as St. Ambrose, ordered Theodosius to do penance, establishing a precedent for the State being subsurvient to the church. In what we call Western Civilization, that status would not change for more than a millenium; in many parts of the contemporary world, it would continue into the present.

With the destruction of the Roman empire by the Goths and Vandals during the fifth and sixth centuries, the power of the Christian church increased until Rome became known not as the center of the greatest empire in history, but as the center of the Christian Church, later the Roman Catholic Church.

Pope Gelasius I, about 496 A.D., described the direction the Christian church was taking in world affairs:

> There are two things . . . by which this world is chiefly ruled: the sacred authority of the priesthood and the royal power. Of these two, the priests carry the greater weight, because they will have to render account in the divine judgement even for kings of men.

On Christmas Day, 800 A.D., Pope Leo III crowned Charlemagne (742 A.D.-814 A.D., reign 768-814) the first emperor of the Holy Roman Empire, returning the seat of government to Rome from Byzantium after more than three centuries. The crowning helped Charlemagne unify his vast kingdom, while also allowing the Pope to claim that it was the church that crowned kings, and matters of State were subservient to that of religion.

Nevertheless, not all rulers, possibly not even Charlemagne, accepted the Church's position, putting the Church in an awkward position of defending its claims or threats. For several decades, the rulers of the Holy Roman Empire, usually by bribes or influence peddling, had determined not only those who should be named priests and bishops, but also those whom they decided should be the pope. In the eleventh century, Pope Gregory VII declared that the pope alone can create or dissolve "empires, kingdoms, duchies, countships, and the possessions of all men." Henry IV, emperor of the Holy Roman Empire, disagreed; his council of appointed nobles and bishops supported him. However, when the pope excommunicated Henry, thus giving all persons of the kingdom complete freedom from any loyalty to him, the nobles ordered Henry to do penance and return to the Church. Henry, in humiliation, once again became a member of the Church, only to be excommunicated three years later. This time, he launched a military campaign that drove the pope from Rome, and established a "rival pope." Other rulers at other times also determined that the church should not have supremacy over the State.

About 1198, Pope Innocent III reaffirmed the Church's position that not only was the authority of the Pope greater than that of the secular monarchs, but that any attack upon the Pope was also an attack upon the Christian Church. For justification, he claimed that God had "left to Peter [believed by many Christians to have been the first pope] the government not only of the church, but of the whole world."

About 1205, Innocent III had to enforce his claims against King John of England who had challenged the Church's right to install the Archbishop of Canterbury, claiming to have been a secular right as by past custom. The threat to the Church ended when Innocent III excommunicated John and threatened to have the French invade England to restore "Christianity to the throne."

Less than a century later, Thomas Aquinas, a Christian theologian who would be canonized, wrote:

The highest aim of mankind is eternal happiness. To this chief aim of mankind all earthly claims must be subordinated. This chief aim can not be realized through human direction alone, but must obtain divine assistance which is only to be obtained through the Church. Therefore, the State, through which earthly aims are obtained, must be subordinated to the Church. The Church and State are as two swords which God has given Christendom for protection. Both of these, however, are given by Him to the Pope and the temporal sword by Him handed to the rulers of the State.

The Sword of Conversion

The Christian Church a millenium after its founding was still one of the world's youngest religions, but also one of the most concerned about either converting "non-believers" or in eliminating them from any opposition. With a missionary zeal to rid the earthly existence of what they determined to be "heretics," the Church launched crusades of vengeance.

The First Crusade, 1096-1099, was launched to take the land from the "infidel" Moslems in Asia Minor and Jerusalem, and to reclaim the land in behalf of Christianity. In the name of religion, the Christian invaders massacred the heretics of Antioch, and "reclaimed" Jerusalem. Other crusades—all marked by religious intolerance, their participants shouting, "God Wills It!"—occurred in 1144-1153, 1190-1193, and 1198-1204. During the Crusades, the Christians destroyed numerous temples and cities, including

Constantinople, one of the greatest cities, in the world, and a center for the Islamic faith. Two Children's Crusades about 1212 resulted in thousands of children being captured while on their mission to try to recapture the Holy Land from the Moslems.

During the thirteenth century, many of Europe's monarchs, under Papal threats of being removed from their kingdoms, declared that all heretics were subject to excommunication and death. In 1324, however, Marsilius, in *Defensor pacis*, argued that the State, not the church, must have dominance, even to the point of seizure of church property. According to Marsilius:

> Laws derive their authority from the State, and are invalid without its consent . . .The monarch, who is instituted by the people [legislature] to execute its will, ought to be armed by a force sufficient to coerce individuals [to comply with the laws], but not sufficient to control the majority of the people. [The monarch] is responsible to the nation, and [like the people] subject to the law. The nation that appoints him and assigns him [their rights], has to see to it that he obeys [the laws created by the people], and should dismiss him if he does not.

With blatant church corruption, including the selling of clerical titles, Marsilius' argument would begin to gain some acceptance on the European continent. And, it would lead the Christian church to impose even stronger restrictions against freedom of the press.

Chapter 3

An Inquisition of Knowledge

The Middle Ages established the three-tiered society of nobility, clergy, and peasants, with land becoming the centralized institution. Ownership of land gave social and political power to the nobility and clergy who were able to grant and receive favors from each other depending upon the land to be given, sold, or purchased. Protection of the clergy in the feudal societies prior to the Renaissance had come from the organization of knighthood whose members swore to protect not only their rulers and countries, but the religion as well. Knighthood led to the reinstitution of large-scale armies not seen on the European continent since the fall of Rome.

The dissemination of information to a large number of people has existed throughout history. As populations increase, and as an empire spreads over a larger territory, the need for the distribution of information becomes more obvious. Each major social change has brought with it a different form of information distribution, from writings on cave walls to the hand-lettering of notices posted in a common marketplace and the printing of bound sheaves.

However, the system of information dissemination during the Middle Ages was little different from the systems used at the height of the Roman empire. Then, about 1450, in Germany, Johann Gutenberg Gensfleisch invented a typesetting/printing system that used metal moveable type; each letter was on its own base, cast in molds. Previously, type was hand-carved in wood; if a letter was chipped, or worn down by heat or constant useage, a new letter had to be carved. Now, printer could pour metal into a previously-created mold, creating a new letter, to make a set of type as needed for printing.

The printing system reached England about 1476 when William Caxton set up a press in the abbey of Westminster. For the next fifteen years, he printed or reprinted almost one hundred books, many of them now considered to be classics. The Gutenberg press improved the ease and efficiency of printing, increasing the number of books, pamphlets, broadsheets, and news-sheets that could be published. The greater dissemination of information led to greater unity of people. Once, the clergy had forbidden the masses to read, fearing that with literacy would come "misinterpretations" of the scriptures—possibly even rebellion. Later, the clergy allowed the masses to read and write in the "vulgar tongue"—English—but they were still forbidden to learn Latin, the

language of scholarship and of the Christian religion. With a knowledge of both English and Latin, although the illiteracy rate was still extremely high, the masses had a means to communicate with each other, to learn how others lived, to identify common problems. The invention of the metal moveable type, combined with the Caxton Press, provided the base that increased the threat of the destruction of European authoritarian regimes, both secular and temporal. As printing developed, the clergy increased its efforts to prevent mankind from being influenced by "incorrect" or dangerous thoughts.

The Rise Of Mass Censorship

About 496 A.D., Pope Gelasius I had issued the first catalogue of censored books; persons reading any of those books were subject to excommunication. In the late tenth century, the Pope ordered his bishops to search for, and to bring to trial, all persons whose spoken or written words could be construed as heresy. The only appeal was directly to the Pope. Within decades, the process of inquisition—the searching and bringing to trial of heretics—was formalized with the establishment of the priest-inquisitors of the Domenican order who had full power to sit in judgment of those who spoke against the tenets of the Church. In 1252, Pope Innocent IV gave the inquisitors permission to use torture to gain evidence from witnesses; further, even those attempting to defend someone accused of heresy were believed to be heretics, subject to torture and death. During the eleventh through fifteenth centuries, several thousand dissenters and heretics were burned at the stake or strangled.

So powerful was the Church by the early fifteenth century that it could order the bones of the popular religious leader John Wycliffe (1330?-1384) dug up, burned, and thrown into England's Thames River. Wycliffe's two major offenses were his belief that all men were equal and priests in God's dominion, and his "incorrect" translation of the Bible from Latin into English, the "vulgar" language of the masses. Under the rigid control of the Church, others had translated the Bible, but Wycliffe's translation was not approved and, therefore, a threat to Christian dogma. The clergy feared that if there were no control over the translations, no matter how literal, the masses, by reading the Bible in English, would form "incorrect," even dangerous, opinions about religion; they might even challenge the authority of the clergy itself.

The Council of Lateran, formed by the Church in 1515, ordered that "no book may be printed in any town or diocese unless previously inspected by the bishop." The word "Imprimatur" in a book indicated Papal approval; persons writing, printing, selling, or reading any book not approved were subject to excommunication and removal from secular office.

church censorship ...

A Theological Reformation

Martin Luther (1483-1546), a German monk, nailed his "Ninety-Five Theses" to the door of Castle Church, Wittenberg, two years after the Council of Lateran. These "theses" protested the financial exploitation of the German people by the Roman church, and declared that God, not the Pope, had authority over the condemnation of humanity's souls. Pope Leo X issued a brutal reply, followed by Luther's declaration that the Pope was not infallible, an attack against one of the most basic of the Church's beliefs. Luther was spared death only by Frederick the Wise, of Germany, who was recently appointed emperor of the Holy Roman Empire.

At first, Luther's followers were known as Evangelicals, later Protestants. But, like the Roman Catholic Church, the Protestant religion would be as intolerant as the religion it broke from. Luther had once argued that all religions must show a tolerance for those who had different beliefs, that the heretics must be converted by tolerance and faith, not by intolerance and the sword:

> Neither pope nor bishop nor any man whatever has the right of making one syllable binding upon Christian man, unless it be done with his own consent. Whatever is done otherwise is done in the spirit of tyranny . . . I cry aloud in behalf of liberty and conscience, and I proclaim with confidence that no kind of law can with any justice be imposed upon Christians, except so far as they themselves will; for we are free from all.

However, as with almost all of mankind's leaders, once a certain liberty is attained, and they no longer are a fully oppressed minority, it becomes mandatory to impose one's will upon others. Luther was no exception, and the brutality of his attacks upon Jews, "heretics," and those who did not believe as he did is a tribute only to mankind's brutality against itself:

> Heretics are not to be disputed with, but to be condemned unheard, and whilst they perish by fire, the faithful ought to pursue the evil to its source, and bathe their hands in the blood of Catholic bishops, and of the Pope, who is a devil in disguise.

John Calvin (1509-1564), like Luther, was tolerant of opposing beliefs—until he became a ruler. In 1536, he was welcomed into Geneva as a professor of theology. For two years, he bitterly attacked the Roman Catholic Church, then was exiled in 1538 when the people objected to his rigid demands of discipline. Yet, three years later, the people again welcomed him back, realizing they needed discipline in their lives. Establishing a theocracy, Calvin required attendance at sermons, strict obedience to scripture, and ruled that any criticism of the clergy was blasphemy, punishable by death.

In opposition, the Anabaptists, Unitarians, Society of Friends (Quakers), and others argued for toleration, only to be persecuted and sentenced to death.

via Luther - Calvin

A Diffusion of Terror

Throughout Western civilization, the Inquisition continued, injecting fear and threatening lives.

In France, the Inquisition continued under Francis I and Catherine de Medici. In 1535, Francis I, readily accepting the will of Pope Paulus III, ordered the death penalty for writers and printers of unauthorized books. To assist the people to know what was acceptable—even reading unauthorized books was blasphemy—the Church, beginning in 1564, issued lists of banned books, authors, printers, and booksellers. Such lists would continue to be published by various churches and governments into the present.

. . .[M]an prefers peace, and even death, to freedom of choice in the knowledge of good and evil . . . Nothing is more seductive for man than his freedom of conscience, but nothing is a greater cause of suffering.

—The Grand Inquisitor, in Fedor Dostoyefsky's
The Brothers Karamazov (1880)

In 1572, Catherine de Medici, using deception and treachery, lured the French Hugenots into believing that France was declaring peace with them, and unleashed a mob of more than sixty thousand Catholics on a holocaust of annihilation. However, in 1598, Henry IV, who had converted from Protestantism to Catholicism, in the Edict of Nantes ordered toleration for the Hugenots, and allowed them to hold public office; the declaration was condemned by Pope Clement VIII. After Henry's murder in 1610, the Edict gradually lost its force until Louis XIV, ruling by "divine right," and declaring, "L'etat c'est moi"—"I am the State"—revoked it in 1685, forcing the non-Catholic citizens of France into exile. With revisions, France continued suppression of minority religions until the eve of the French Revolution in 1787.

By the mid-sixteenth century, the suppression of freedom of worship, speech, and the press had extended into Portugal which used the Inquisition to initiate a genocide against the Jews. Pope Paul III, furious at the methods of the Portuguese Inquisition, revoked the grant he had originally issued to John III. Nevertheless, the Inquisition continued in the vast Portuguese empire that included large land masses in the "New World," the result of Pope Alexander VI creating the Treaty of Tordesillas to divide all land in the "New World" between Spain and Portugal. In Italy, the Government used the Inquisition to solidify its opposition to Protestantism.

Whether it was a Catholic Inquisition protecting Catholic doctrine and denying freedom of speech to Protestants, Jews, Muslims, pagans, and heretics, or Anglican kings denying freedom of speech to Catholics, Jews, Muslims, pagans,

More Christian laters:

and heretics, the penalties were the same. To make the suspected heretic recant, to accept Jesus and the one "true religion," and the one "true" science, the inquisitors broke the bodies of the accused, hoping also to break their resistance, and to crush the Devil from their souls.

The sadism of the inquisitor knew no limits. To break the unrepentent, the authorities locked them into small cages—too small in which to sit—for hours or days; dunked them into rivers until moments before drowning; locked metal traps onto the limbs until the skin, muscle, and bone were crushed; pulled bones from their sockets, arms from the body; drove nails into sensitive bodies; burned skin with white hot irons; tore eyes from their sockets; sliced ears off; and ripped tongues from mouths. All of it was designed to break the body and spirit; the result would be a complacent populace that had no views other than what they were told to have.

The Spanish Inquisition

The greatest threat to freedom of speech in the Western world was in Spain. By the end of the fourteenth century, Spain, which had driven the Moors from the country, now looked to the Jews, forcing them to be baptized in the Christian faith; those who would not convert—or say they converted—were driven into exile or executed. During the late fifteenth century, more than two thousand persons—Jews, Muslims, and other "heretics"—were burned at the stake, and several thousand more were fined, tortured, and imprisoned, their lands and property confiscated. More than ninety thousand were imprisoned, most of them not even knowing the charges until days or months after arrest, and then were not allowed to face their accusers.

By the end of the fifteenth century, Thomas de Torquemada, the inquisitor general who ruled by terror, had as much authority over the people of the Spanish empire as did the monarchs, Ferdinand and Isabella, who had allowed the torture and Inquisition in their empire, having recognized the advantages that a reign of terror could have in keeping dissent suppressed.

Charles V (1500-1558), Holy Roman emperor who was launching a massacre of "non-believers" in the Netherlands, sent Hernando Cortes and Francisco Pizarro to the "New World" at the beginning of the sixteenth century. Cortes and Pizarro, believing they were acting under the will of God and Church to rid civilization of heretics, and knowing the riches of the land, massacred large numbers of the Indian populations. In Peru, Pizarro exterminated virtually all the great Incan civilization; in Mexico, Cortes virtually exterminated the Aztec civilization. Their victories were cheered in Europe by kings and popes, and by large segments of the population who greedily took the wealth of the "New World" and who also knew—they just absolutely *knew*—that there must be neither freedom of speech, nor of life, for those whose religious views differed from their own.

Although the Inquisition in all countries was originally established to search for and bring to trial persons who the Church determined were heretics, so widespreading had been the terror that the Inquisition also took under its authority

even more barbarism (w. all the gory details)

numerous "crimes against the State." Among the other crimes were adultery, incest, and theft, as well as the writing and printing of non-approved theological arguments, and any writing which questioned any action of the monarch. So vicious was the Inquisition that several priests were brought before it, and charged with heresy.

A Repeal of Natural Laws

The scientific revolution of the sixteenth and seventeenth centuries strengthened the views of liberal thinkers, giving them a unity in the scientific discovery of the nature of mankind. But the Church blocked dissemination of knowledge. Nicolaus Copernicus (1473-1543), about 1530, developed the theory that all planets rotate around the sun, a view directly in conflict with Church dogma that held earth and man central to the universe. From fear, Copernicus withheld publication for almost thirteen years. When the theory was eventually set in type, Copernicus had become ill from dysentery, suffered a stroke, and died within hours of receiving the bound copy of the book.

The conviction of the existence of absolute truth led the Church to arrest Galileo Galilei (1564-1642) and charge him with heresy for his studies of the universe. Among Galileo's observations, which had earned him prestige among mathematicians and philosophers, was that the universe could be infinite; that not only did the earth rotate around the sun but also upon its own axis; and that the nature of gravity causes all objects, no matter what size or weight, to fall at the same speed in a vacuum. In 1616, Pope Paul V ordered Galileo to answer the Dominican order accusations that such writing not only contradicted Aristotle and Ptolemy, but violated Church dogma. The Pope "proved" Galileo wrong, and dismissed him with a warning never to preach such heresy again. In 1618, Galileo challenged the theory of comets, advanced by Orazio Grassi, one of the most learned of the Jesuit priests, and brought the wrath of the Church upon him once more. In 1633, Pope Urban VIII, who had not challenged Galileo previously, now brought him to the Inquisition to answer for his writings. Now, sixty-nine years old, faced by conflict between his science and his religion, Galileo recanted his beliefs, was sentenced to life imprisonment, and then heard the Pope commute the sentence. Galileo retired, writing other great works—all published in the Netherlands—and died at the age of seventy-eight, four years after becoming blind.

Simon Stevin (1548-1620) also disagreed with Aristotelian concepts, and proved the impossibility of perpetual motion. Stevin improved the mathematics systems by using letters to represent quantities, and by inventing logarithms. Johann Kepler (1571-1630), René Descartes (1596-1650), and Isaac Newton (1642-1727) also helped disprove several Aristotelian concepts held by the Church as correct explanations for the nature of the universe. Kepler developed three major laws to help explain planetary motion; Descartes, philosopher and mathematician, developed analytical geometry and the concepts that knowledge comes from within the mind, not from a "feeling." In *Philosophiae Naturalis Principia Mathematicia* (1687), Newton established a philosophical framework for scientific discovery for more than two centuries, eclipsed only by Einsteinian philosophy:

> I wish I could derive all phenomena of nature by some kind of reasoning from mechanical principles; for I have many reasons to suspect that they all depend upon certain forces by which the particles of bodies are either mutually attracted and cohere in regular figures or are repelled and recede from each other.

Although the terror of the Inquisition diminished after the seventeenth century, it wasn't until 1834 that the Spanish Inquisition officially ended.

Chapter 4

The Star Chamber—and Beyond:
From Protection to Persecution

In England, which had a large non-Catholic population, the Inquisition was not as organized as in Italy, France, Portugal, Germany, and Spain. However, the suppression of personal liberty, and the crushing of the concepts of freedom of speech and the press, were just as severe.

In 1481, Henry VII (1457-1509, reign 1485-1509) gave his Privy Council authority in several secular and ecclesiastical matters. The Council, when sitting in judgment, was popularly known as the Star Chamber, named for a room in Westminster Hall where it met. The concept of the Star Chamber was that all subjects of the King would receive protection since the Star Chamber was greater than any other court, and was free of influence from the nobility; a person, no matter how lowly in the British hierarchy, no matter how uneducated or impoverished, who was libeled or wronged by even a baron or earl would be able to have justice on his side. For Henry VII, the Star Chamber helped re-establish the power of the Crown over the nobility following Henry's victory over Richard III in the Battle of Bosworth Field, ending the War of the Roses.

In 1215, on a battlefield in Runnymede, King John had signed the Magna Charta, England's first document guaranteeing the people a number of civil rights, including the rights of an impartial justice system. The Magna Charta, a "bill of rights," would be copied by many countries of the Commonwealth, including the American colonies after their successful revolution. But, the implementation and enforcement of many of the provisions of the Magna Charta were often arbitrary, based upon the personal beliefs of the rulers of England.

1275 Sixty years later, King Edward I and Parliament enacted what is now believed to be Western civilization's first written law against sedition, a broadly-based law that effectively silenced any opposition to the monarchy—communication of "any false newes or tales whereby discord or occasion of discord or slander may grow between the king and His people or great mean of the realm." The law was re-enacted 104 years later.

The Star Chamber, however, also served to bring to trial persons accused of sedition, heresy, and treason, the greatest threats to the preservation of the monarchy. The Star Chamber had the authority to levy fines, and to order torture or imprisonment for those judged to be guilty. However, it also had the

31

(see underlines)

authority to find an accused innocent, and to order the imprisonment, for life, of those found to have "brought false witness" to the court.

For the first two decades of the rule of Henry VIII (1491-1547, reign 1509-1547) the Star Chamber continued to function much in the manner that Henry VII had originally determined for it. After 1529, however, it also served as a chamber where Henry VIII could persecute his enemies, and the enemies of the newly-established Church of England.

Henry VIII, like his father, was a brilliant scholar and administrator who encouraged the development of the arts while also expanding England's military base. However, he was also an unpredictable ruler who allowed freedom of dissent as long as it wasn't directed against the State. To assure compliance with the Crown's need to have a non-threatening press, Henry created a system of patents (licenses) and monopolies. The State would allow a few persons the rights of establishing print shops, and give them, by a monopoly, assured financial success, but in return the printers would print nothing contrary to the wishes of the State, represented by Henry's staff and ministers.

However, it wasn't enforced compliance to the State's philosophy that would lead to an internal revolution in England, but Henry's insistence upon a divorce. It would be a revolution that would threaten the State and result in a tightening of freedom of expression.

In 1529, Pope Clement VII refused to grant Henry, a devout Catholic, a divorce of his twenty year marriage to Catherine of Aragon. Furious that the Church would not grant his request and allow him to marry Anne Boleyn—whom he would eventually order beheaded—Henry declared that the Crown itself would be the head of the Church of England, and that it would be independent of Rome. The failure of Thomas Wolsey to convince the Pope to grant Henry a divorce, as well as to establish some political alliances that had been promised by Wolsey, cost Wolsey the Lord Chancellorship—the second most powerful position in England. However, others suffered even greater losses. Henry ordered Sir Thomas More, one of his best friends, and Cardinal John Fisher to be executed for opposition to the establishment of a separate church.

Now divorced under the newly-established rules of the Church of England, Henry began a systematic campaign of persecutions not only against Catholics loyal to the Pope, but also against non-Catholics who refused to accept Henry as the head of the Church. Between 1536 and 1539, he ordered the Catholic monasteries in England to be seized for the Crown, thus gaining an estimated £100,000 a year. During the last two decades of Henry's reign, the nation's presses fell silent—except for official orders and tracts that either praised the monarchy or the advantages of an independent church.

Henry VIII persecuted Catholics + non Anglicans

A Repeal of Rights

Upon the death of Henry in 1547, Henry's eldest son became king. However, because Edward VI was only ten at the time of his father's death, Edward Seymour, his uncle, was appointed Protector of England. During the next two years, Seymour, with Edward's consent, revoked all heresy laws, most laws of sedition and treason, and encouraged freedom of speech and of the press. But, in 1549 he was forced out of the Protectorate by a coalition under John Dudley, a greedy and ambitious man who would, in 1552, order Seymour's execution, then arrange for the marriage of his own son, Guildford Dudley to Lady Jane Grey, granddaughter of Henry VII.

Edward VI, upon his deathbed in 1554, at the insistence of Dudley, willed that his half-sisters, Mary and Elizabeth, daughters of Henry VIII, be denied the throne. John Dudley then forced Parliament to proclaim Lady Jane queen. However, Mary (1516-1558, reign 1553-1558) moved into London, and was proclaimed queen nine days after Lady Jane's coronation, and hours after Lady Jane had voluntarily given up the throne. Although Mary realized that Lady Jane was only an innocent pawn in John Dudley's avaricious struggle to control the English crown, she was fearful of the possibility that supporters of Lady Jane would try to seize the throne. Within six months, Mary ordered the arrest of Jane's sister, Lady Catherine Grey, who would be imprisoned for seven years; and the executions of Guildford and John Dudley; Jane's father, Henry, who had allied himself in a military conspiracy against the queen; and Lady Jane Grey who was beheaded at the age of seventeen.

In the first year of her five-year reign, Mary had Parliament repeal all of Edward's orders regarding the rights of worship and freedom of speech. In 1555, she had Parliament repeal her father's orders that established a separate church, then declared that England once again had accepted the doctrine of Catholicism. During the next three years, she ordered the execution of more than three hundred persons she, or the Church, had determined were "heretics," and effectively silenced freedom of speech and the press by controlling the Stationers' Company.

The Stationers' Company had existed in England since 1357 as a guild of writers; later, it admitted both illustrators and printers. Now, under Mary's control, its purpose was to act as a monopoly on the issuance of pamphlets and books. The political advantages to the Crown were significant—Mary could claim that an "independent" guild of writers, illustrators, and printers—not she—was the "watchdog" of the quality of the press, knowing that this "independent" monopoly would do absolutely nothing they thought would displease her.

Edward VI revoked those + ordered freedom

Mary revoked those + ordered persecution of enemies
↳ brought UK back to Catholicism

A Re-establishment of Power

Upon Mary's death, Elizabeth (1533-1603) became queen, and during her forty-five year reign, re-established the power of the Crown, sending her armies and navies against the French and Spanish empires, and allowing her pirate ships to raid ships of other countries, while at the same time establishing England as a leader in world trade. The continual wars had cost Elizabeth most of her inheritance, savings, and lands, and threw the nation into several economic crises.

Shortly after her coronation in 1558, Elizabeth, like her father in 1529, required anyone holding office in England—secular or ecclesiastic—to swear allegiance to the crown, and to renounce any ties, spiritual or temporal, to any foreign ruler or spiritual leader. For a nation living almost in pathological fear of a Catholic rule, Elizabeth—although making a few gestures of religious toleration—now forbade Catholics from saying or hearing mass, upon penalties of heavy fines and imprisonment. The Crown, acting through the Anglican church, ordered mandatory attendance at Sunday services of the church, thus establishing an effective system of communication while also lessening the influence of the non-authorized religions. Persons physically able to attend the Anglican church, but unwilling to do so, were fined by civil authorities. The first fines were one shilling for each weekly service missed. Later, it was increased to £20 a month, at a time when most payments to the people and merchants were in the form of trade, rather than cash; only the nobility had money.

In 1586, Anglican archbishop John Whitgrift ordered all manuscripts to be approved by the Church prior to publication. In response, Martin Marprelate (believed to be the pseudonymn of John Perry, a Welsh Puritan) wrote a series of pamphlets, now regarded as the finest satiric prose of the Elizabethan age. Perry was hanged in 1593.

Between 1574 and 1603, Elizabeth ordered the execution of more than two hundred Catholics, many of them convicted of plots to assassinate the queen and bring Mary, Queen of Scots, a Catholic, to the Crown. A year after Mary's execution in 1587 on charges of treason, Phillip II of Spain (who had been king of England when married to Queen Mary Tudor, and those genocide against Jews, Moors, and other "heretics" established him as one of the most barbaric of European leaders) launched the Spanish Armada of 120 ships against England. He had hoped to avenge the death of a wife he probably did not love, and to destroy Protestantism in the only European country in which it was the dominant religious belief. The Armada, however, was defeated by Sir Francis Drake's ships—and by a brutal wind.

Although Elizabeth's fury at the invasion led her to rage against the nation's Catholics—a large number of whom had fought for England and against the Armada—it is believed that the only writer or printer she ordered to be executed was William Carter who had written an incendiary pro-Catholic pamphlet; he was tortured in 1580, then hanged four years later.

During her reign, Elizabeth increased the restrictions against the press, established a formal mechanism to censor books, and imposed heavy fines and imprisonment upon those whose works could be construed as containing anything that was heresy. Under an Anglican administration, heresy would include any-thing that denied the existence of God, accepted any tenets of the Catholic religion, or which attacked, no matter how innocently or unknowingly, the Queen or any of her ministers. Nevertheless, Elizabeth did permit discussion of political issues—as long as there were no challenges against her or her government.

Freedom of speech for the Speaker of the House of Commons had been established, after numerous battles, during the Middle Ages. Yet, members were often imprisoned or tortured for their comments. Elizabeth I had little desire to change this. At the opening of Parliament in 1593, she declared that "Freedom of speech is granted, but you must know what privilege you have; not to speak everyone what he listeth, or what cometh in his brain to utter that; but your privilege is [to cast a vote] *Aye* for *No*."

In 1586, the Star Chamber re-established the Stationers' Company, and entrusted it with the responsibility to regulate printing. By creating a private monopoly, Elizabeth was able to convince the public that there was no overt governmental intrusion upon the rights of the people. A government that creates a monopoly, however, can also dissolve it; thus, the Crown could maintain a distant control by veiled threats which, if enacted, would threaten the economic base for a large number of printers. The creation of this private monopoly had, as a side effect, the exploitation of the apprentice and journeymen printers who were given three choices—accept the working conditions and wages offered by the twenty master printers, find employment in other regulated crafts, or become "outlaw" printers. Just as the master printers would do nothing to upset the Crown, which through the Star Chamber gave it authority and economic survival, apprentice and journeymen printers would do nothing to upset the master printer who gave them the right to work, and their wages; the creation of blacklists by crafts masters was not uncommon. Nevertheless, the Stationers' Company provided a common base for the twenty master printers to discuss printing problems with each other, learn of newer and better techniques to set and print type, and handle their business affairs. Although a monopoly, subject to the abuses inherent in a monopolistic system, the Company was also a Guild, designed to protect its members.

Upon Elizabeth's death in 1603, James (1566-1625), Protestant son of Mary, Queen of Scots, became King of England; he retained his throne as king of Scotland, which he had held since shortly after birth. Under James I, England and Scotland became allies, and colonies were established in North America. However, his twenty-two year reign as king of England was marked by both internal and external wars fought largely for religious reasons. By the end of the Thirty Years War (1618-1648) most of the European countries were brought into armed conflict as participants in either the Protestant Reformation or the Catholic Counter–Reformation.

At home, James became involved in bitter feuds with Parliament which, following the Elizabethan era, was trying to re-establish its credibility. Like most monarchs, as well as most of the masses and nobility, James believed that he ruled by "divine right." In his role as the Anglican Church's "defender of the faith," James increased the persecution of the Puritan, Quaker, and other non-Anglican theologies, and tightened England's restrictions upon freedom of speech and of the press.

② charles I contol Anglian Chuch from James I

① James I contol Anglican church
   "   Persecuted non Anglicans
   "   contd restrictions of freedom

Chapter 5

Preservation Through Suppression

During an era in which freedom of expression was squeezed, newspapers began to appear on a periodic basis. The first newspaper may have been one printed in Antwerp in 1605; the earliest newspaper known to have survived, however, was probably the *Aviso* of Wolfenbuetal, Germany, founded in 1609. Within a decade, newspapers were founded in Frankfurt, Berlin, Hamburg, Basel, Vienna, and Amsterdam.

The first English language newspapers were probably printed in Amsterdam by George Veseler and Broer Jonson, December 2, 1620 through September 18, 1621. The newspapers were generically known as *corrantos*, possibly from now-extinct Latin words meaning *current* and *put together*. They were one-sheet papers about eight inches by ten inches, printed on one side, and featured almost exclusively news of what was later to become known as the Thirty Years War.

The *corrantos*, about twenty-five or thirty, were imported into England by Nathaniel Butter in 1621. By the middle of the year, Butter and printer Thomas Archer pirated much of the news from the Amsterdam *corrantos*, added some of their own, and put out a similar newspaper. However, James I issued a proclamation opposing not only the *corrantos*, but many of the pamphlets and news-sheets about the Thirty Years War, claiming that their printers and editors bred sedition for accusing him of vacillation in foreign policy during the war, and also arguing that the general public was better served by not being led into either false security or fear by news of the war. The security of the State was threatened by the newspapers, said James. When Archer refused to suspend publication, James ordered him imprisoned. In 1624, Butter and Nicholas Bourne received permission from James to resume publication as a weekly newspaper—*The Continuation of Our Weekly Newes*—provided all articles were submitted first to the State for approval. When Archer was released from prison, he became the newspaper's printer.

Upon the death of James I, his son, Charles I (1600-1649, reign 1625-1649), became king. Charles, like his father, continued the policies of suppression against religious minorities and against freedom of speech and of the press. Like most other rulers of the era, Charles had believed that he had a God-given mandate to preserve the faith, through suppression if necessary.

37

(see moderline)

To assure the preservation and domination of Anglican religious thought, and to suppress dissent, Charles increased the jurisdiction and power of the Star Chamber. To facilitate his policies, Charles appointed William Laud to be privy counsel, then bishop of London, and finally, archbishop of Canterbury. Laud used the Star Chamber to eliminate opposition to Charles and the Anglican church, as well as to eliminate his own enemies and to preserve his own political power base. In 1633, while bishop of London, Laud brought William Prynne (1600-1669)—lawyer, theologian, and author—to the Star Chamber, charging him with a series of offenses, including heresy and sedition.

Prynne, a Puritan, had written several tracts and pamphlets opposing a liberalization of social customs, including opposition to long hair and all forms of alcohol. However, the publication of *Histrio-Mastix* angered the Anglican leaders into taking action. In this pamphlet, Prynne attacked the arts, writing viciously against actresses whom he called little better than whores. He also called the English stage—the same one upon which William Shakespeare's plays were then being performed—the source of all evil and immorality in England.

The book was seen as an attack upon Charles, who was a patron of the arts, and upon Queen Henrietta Marie, who was in the rehearsal of a play. Furious, Laud had the Star Chamber order Prynne to be sent to the pillory, have parts of his ear lobes cut off, be fined, then sentenced to prison. When sentence was carried out the following year, there were very few in the kingdom who sympathized with Prynne. Even John Milton, who like Prynne was a Puritan and subject to persecution, had no sympathy, and wrote, anonymously, *Comus*, a thinly-disguised poem as vicious in its attack upon Prynne as was Prynne's attack upon the arts.

While in prison, Prynne continued to write against the church, king, and especially Laud who had determined that the best way to bring unity to England was by forced conformity to the dictates of the Anglican church and to Laud himself. When some of Laud's ministers began talking about the possible introduction of altars and saints into the Anglican church, the Protestants were positive that there was a Catholic plot to overthrow the Protestant religion in England.

Then, in 1637, Laud brought to the Star Chamber Prynne, Henry Burton, and John Bastwick—all of whom had written against him, calling him a "papist," an "innovator" in religion, and with being corrupt in the awarding of monopolies to inept and corrupt companies. Following trial, the three were sentenced to the pillory, to have their noses slit, their ears cut off, fined £5,000, and then sent to prison. In prison, Prynne would have the letters *S.L.*, for seditious libeller, burned onto his cheeks. However, this time, Prynne had the sympathy of the people, who almost surrounded him, Bastwick, and Burton, cheering them as they were led to the pillories. The people were appalled at the brutality of the sentences against members of the gentry. Although most of them did not agree with Prynne's views on the arts and other theological matters, by supporting Prynne they found a way to express their fears of a Catholic plot; in acts of civil disobedience they showed their hatred of Charles I and William Laud.

Prior to 1637, only printers had to be licensed. Now, with what was believed to be increased dissent, although most of the publications were quite innocuous, the Star Chamber—under Laud's direction, and with the approval of Charles I—decreed that all books must be licensed, and then registered by the Stationers' Company, by now an association of approved printers which exercised monopoly control over printing.

During 1640 and 1641, Parliament abolished the Star Chamber, reduced the power of the king, and took a stronger control over the nation's financial state. Then, in 1642, civil war broke out, following an intricate series of political, legal, and religious maneuvers by Charles I, various factions in Parliament, and the ministry. Charles I personally led the royalists; Oliver Cromwell, a Puritan, led the opposition. Like so many other wars, this was a religious war, but one which would also decide the form of English government, and the direction of freedom of the press.

A Defense of Freedom of Expression

It was during this war, with Parliament in session, that John Milton (1608-1674), the poet who had opposed William Prynne, delivered what many now regard as history's greatest defense for freedom of speech and the press. Between 1640 and 1642, Milton had written five pamphlets, none licensed, attacking the Presbyterian hierarchy in the Church of England. He had argued that for the Protestant Reformation to succeed in England, the Church must be purged of all "Romanism," and be returned to the simplicity first envisioned during Elizabeth's reign. During 1643 and 1644, Milton wrote four additional pamphlets, also unlicensed, attacking the Church's concepts of marriage and divorce, arguing that there were better reasons for a divorce than adultery, the only recognized grounds for divorce in England at that time. According to Milton, a marriage must be consumed by love and a mutual respect for each other; he claimed that incompatibility, not adultery, may be a greater crime against God and humanity. He pointed out that religious tradition placed women in an inferior role to men, that as long as women were denied formal education they would remain inferior to men, and treated as such. In June 1644, Milton's pamphlet, *On Education*, was published. It was a brilliant plan for a new kind of educational system in England, one based on the principles of Puritanism, but without the Puritans' mistrust of the arts and classics. (It, like Milton's other works, was also unlicensed.)

Following the abolishment of the Star Chamber in 1641, numerous unlicensed tracts and pamphlets appeared in England. On June 14, 1643, the Presbyterian-controlled Parliament passed an act strengthening the licensing of books. In August 1644, the Stationers' Company demanded strict enforcements of the act, citing John Milton as one of the worst violators. On November 24, 1644, John Milton came before the Parliament to deliver what became known as the *Areopagitica*.*

---

*The *areopagitica* (from the Greek *Ares*, the god of war; *pagos*, hill) was a hill in Athens where the supreme tribunal, the Court of Areopagus, met. Milton took his title for his defense of free expression from the Triubnal and from the *Areopagitic discourse* of Isocrates (436 B.C.-338 B.C.). In this speech, Isocrates called for a reform of the general assembly of Athens.

In an impassioned and inflammatory speech, Milton cited historical precedents against licensing and attacked the authoritarian beliefs that mankind was irrational and would be swayed by emotional argument. Mankind, said Milton, was given by God the virtue of reason, and is, thus, able to make reasonable decisions. Because mankind is not infallible, argued Milton, "final truth" is never obtainable, but if all views were presented, then mankind, a "rational creature [in] God's image" would be able to derive a "close truth" suitable for his own existence. Only God possessed "absolute truth," argued Milton. "Let [truth] and falsehood grapple . . . in a free and open encounter," he argued, for truth will eventually become known by all mankind:

> . . . [Licensing] will be primely [used] to the discouragement of all learning, and the stop of Truth, not only by the disexercising and blunting our abilities in what we already know, but by hindering and cropping the discovery that might be yet further made both in religious and civil wisdom . . .
>
> Unless wariness be used, as good almost kill a man as kill a good book; who kills a Man kills a reasonable creature, God's image; but he who destroys a good book, kills reason itself, kills the image of God, as it were in the eye. Many a Man lives a burden to the Earth; but a good book is a precious life-blood of a master spirit, embalmed and treasured up on purpose to a life beyond light . . .
>
> . . . And though all the winds of doctrine were let loose to prey upon the earth, so truth be in the field, we do injuriously by licensing and prohibiting to misdoubt her strength. Let her and falsehood grapple; who ever knew truth put to the worse in a free and open encounter . . . [Truth] is strong next to the Almighty; she needs no policies, no strategems, no licensings to make her victorious . . . [G]ive her but room, and do not bind her when she sleep, for then she speaks not true . . .

Milton, however, also spoke against the licentiousness of the Press, asking that the writers take care not to defame honest and decent people, and agreeing with the monarchy that there must be a registration of the names of the writers and authors of books:

> As for regulating the Press, let no man think of having the honor of advising you better than yourselves have done in that order published next before this, that no book be printed, unless the printer's and author's name, or at least printers, be registered. Those which otherwise come forth, if they be found mischevious and libelous, the fire and the executioner will be the timeliest and most effectual remedy, that man's prevention can use. ["The Areopagitica," by John Milton, 1644]

Later libertarians would argue that the duty of an open society is to freedom, not only to freedom of expression, but also to the creation of a way of life that would yield that freedom of expression. Yet, freedom carries with it limits,

Milton speech = give people a choice + they will come through, but be fair in portrayal

and all libertarians have recognized the need to establish restrictive laws, such as libel, copyright, and treason; libertarians, like those who accept limited authoritarian doctrine, recognize that the State must intervene when the public peace and security are threatened. Nevertheless, libertarian doctrine maintains that because mankind *is* rational, their rights to a diversity of opinion must be maintained at all costs—something even Milton did not believe.

Milton established very narrow boundaries as to whom should be granted freedom of speech. Included were "intellectuals," Puritans and very few others; excluded were the "common people" (Milton urged that Latin, not English, be used in matters of learning in order to exclude the lower classes), Catholics, Jews, "heretics," pagans, and almost all of mankind's religions. Throughout his life, Milton argued for free expression for some—and the subjugation of many. In *True Religion, Heresie, Schism, and Toleration* (1673), Milton unleashed another series of invectives against those whose views were theologically different from his:

> Popery [Catholicism], as being Idolatrous, is not to be tolerated in either Public or Private; it must now be thought how to remove it and hinder the growth thereof . . .

But, for the present, in November 1644, the members of parliament listened politely to *The Areopagitica*; Milton's words, even with their restrictions on freedom of speech, infuriated many, but had little effect, for England was in a civil war debating matters of not only religious direction of the country, but whether to continue the monarchy. Parliament would warn Milton about having his works printed without a license, but would not fine or imprison him since his loyalties lay with Cromwell's army, itself supported by Parliament. *The Areopagitica* would be printed—without license—and become one of the greatest pleas for freedom of the press.

Not until 1649, a year after Cromwell's army marched into London, and shortly after the execution of Charles I, did the Protectorate government of Oliver Cromwell abolish all forms of licensing.

Shortly after the execution of Charles I, Milton wrote *The Tenure of Kings and Magistrates*, arguing that the people, not the leader, hold the power, and the people may, if oppressed, overthrow or execute a leader. Later, he would say that he had written the pamphlet to help people understand why Charles I had to have been killed. Nevertheless, Milton still had doubts about the necessity for the execution.

The year after Cromwell took London, abolished licensing, and executed a king, he reinstated licensing. By 1655, he had suppressed all newspapers but two, both of them official publications. Ironically, in 1651, Milton, who had pleaded so eloquently for the abolishment of all licensing, became the censor and supervisory editor of the *Mercurius Politicus*, one of the two official publications. Milton had been a vigorous supporter of both the Revolution and Cromwell, writing several sonnets in praise of the Puritan leaders of the newly-formed Commonwealth. Milton also served Cromwell as secretary of foreign languages, from 1649 through 1651 when he lost his eyesight; afterwards, he was translator of State letters and documents, using aides to read and transcribe his words.

Cromwell's decade-long Commonwealth was marked by a greater tolerance of religious differences than had previously existed in the British empire. But, it was also marked by a continual struggle between the army, the houses of Parliament, and Cromwell on matters of religion and the nature of governance of England.

1660 Charles I comes back → proof for Pyrenne + L'estrange —
　　　　　　NG for Milton or 'Cromwellites'
　(Cromwell dies 1658).
　UK turns against Milton + Cromwell'

Chapter 6

The Restoration of Monarchy— and Suppression of the People

Following Oliver Cromwell's death in 1658, and the forced abdication of his son, Richard, after eight months, the monarchy was restored in 1660 by Parliament when it brought back from exile Charles II, son of the by-now martyred Charles I. The new king entered London to the enthusiastic warmth of a nation which had tired of living under a quasi-military rule, and was now ready for a restoration of the monarchy that accepted and respected the wishes of Parliament.

Although Charles II was generally respected as a wise and merciful king, the nation he ruled had turned against many whose liberties were encouraged under the Commonwealth, and who had supported Cromwell, "the usurper." Cromwell's body was dug up and officially hanged for what Parliament said were crimes against the people. Within two years, hundreds of books were seized by the soldiers of the Cavalier Parliament, then burned in public ceremony, their authors tortured or hanged, their bodies drawn and quartered. The books and poems of John Dryden were ordered burned, and Milton himself was forced into hiding during the Summer and Fall of 1660, his liberty threatened by Sir William Prynne, again a Parliament leader. For two decades, Prynne had lived with Milton's attacks upon him and his theological beliefs; for two decades, Prynne had believed that Milton's theological ideas were wrong, dangerous, and perhaps even heretical; for the past decade, Prynne had blamed Milton and Cromwell for his imprisonment between 1650 and 1653. This was the same Prynne who was tortured, mutilated, and imprisoned during the reign of Charles I, and who continued to write Puritan tracts while in prison. This was the same Prynne who had bitterly lashed out at the tyranny of Archbishop Laud (who was executed in 1655 during the Commonwealth). And this was the same Prynne who became a Royalist during his prison term under the Commonwealth.

With the monarchy restored, Prynne would unleash all the power of Parliament to bring to trial those whose writings and speeches had brought dissention and religious liberalism to the people, who caused the English to question their own faith—their *God-given* faith. In late Fall 1660, John Milton was taken into custody and brought to trial. Among those who spoke in favor of Milton were poet Andrew Marvel, a close friend who was now a member of Parliament; and

43

William Davenant, a Royalist playwright whose life Milton had saved during the Commonwealth.

The Court issued a sharp warning to Milton, then released him, possibly believing that Milton was no longer any danger to the Crown or that to sentence the popular blind poet would make him a martyr and bring a threat to the Crown once again.

'A Matter of Public Care . . .'

In 1662, Parliament enacted a much more stringent licensing act, declaring that "the well-government and regulating of printers and printing presses [is] a matter of public care and concernment, and one that by the general licentiousness of the late times many evilly disposed persons had been encouraged to bring and sell heretical and seditious books." The act forbade the printing of any publications outside of London, York, or the university cities of Oxford and Cambridge. It also required a surety bond from each of the twenty master printers, and upon demand of the courts or Crown, release of the names of authors published.

During the Commonwealth, Roger L'Estrange (1616-1704), a Royalist Catholic in a country fearful of Royalists and Catholics, had been imprisoned by Cromwell for four years, on charges of treason following an abortive attempt to reclaim land for the King. In 1660, out of prison, and weeks before the arrival of Charles II and the Restoration, L'Estrange wrote *No Blinde Guides Wanted,* a vicious attack upon Milton. Like Prynne, L'Estrange believed that Milton was a least partially responsible for his imprisonment.

Now, in 1663, L'Estrange, a writer who never let facts cloud his vitriolic arguments, was made, by Charles II, the country's first Surveyor of the Press, with "the sole privilege of writing, printing, and publishing of narratives, advertisements, mercuries, intelligencies, diurnals, and other book of public intelligence, with power to search for and seize unlicensed and treasonable, schismatic and scandalous books and papers." Shortly after his appointment, L'Estrange issued a thirty-four page pamphlet recommending to the King and Parliament, which later approved, a philosophy and set of rules and penalties for the conduct of the press.

L'Estrange opened his argument with what he assumed was an accepted fact, then proposed a solution:

> I think no man denies the necessity of suppressing licentious and unlawful pamphlets, and of regulating the press; but in what manner, and by what means this may be effected is the question.
>
> One great evil is the multiplicity of private presses, and consequently of printers, who for want of public, and warrantable employment, are forced either to play the knaves in corners, or want bread.
>
> The remedy is to reduce all printers, and presses, that are now in employment, to a limited number; and then to provide against private printing for the time to come . . . [*Considerations and Proposals in Order to the Regulation of the Press.*]

Milton got off w. a warning

L'Estrange first outlined exactly what must be prohibited— most of which dealt with writings against the monarchy—and then outlined the penalties, from death and multilation to imprisonment and fines.

The orders of the King and Parliament approving L'Estrange's proposal would affect every person in England and would significantly diminish all religious and political dissent.

Throughout civilization, some of the greatest literature was written during times of oppression. It was no different under the censorship of England. Two years after Parliament tightened the control of printing, John Milton completed his epic poem, "Paradise Lost," now considered to be the greatest poem written in the English language—and for which he received £10. During the last fourteen years of his life, Milton wrote textbooks of Latin grammar and logic, a history of Great Britain, the epic poems "Paradise Regained" and "Samson Agonistes," a revised edition of "Paradise Lost," several collections of poems, and most of a dictionary of Latin—all of them dictated without written notes to transcribers.

A Time of Growing Freedoms

During the twenty-five year reign of Charles II (1660-1685), Parliament consolidated its determination to separate the church from matters of state. It was a determination that had brought with it prosecutions for heresy of those who believed otherwise. The plague in 1665 and a fire that destroyed most of London the following year almost broke England's spirit. However, wars, plots to overthrow the government, torture and imprisonment of writers, printers, and booksellers, and the execution of Catholic priests (many of whom he knew to be innocent) kept England and the freedom of the press in turmoil.

The Licensing Act, which had been suspended in 1679, was renewed in 1685 after the death of Charles II and the accession of James II, son of Charles I. Upon his deathbed, Charles II had declared his belief in Catholicism; now, James II, a life-long Catholic whom many in the kingdom had earlier tried to prevent from taking the throne, tried to solidify the absolute power of the monarch, and give the Catholic Church domination over the social and political lives of the English. Much of the reign of James II was marked by the persecution of all who were not Catholics, with a vengeance for Puritans. While king of Scotland, James had enjoyed watching his victims being tortured. Now that he was king of England, he would be able to watch even more torture as he ordered the boot—a metal device which could crush a person's leg—put on those whose views differed from his own or those of the Catholic Church. Under James, Sir William Williams, speaker of the House of Commons, was fined £10,000 for comments made in the House.

In 1688, influential members of Parliament asked William of Orange, husband of Mary, eldest daughter of James II, to invade England, drive James II from the throne, and restore England to being a nation under laws. Among the laws, established after the invasion, was a Bill of Rights, drafted by Parliament, and approved by William and Mary. The Bill of Rights abolished the

Crown's power to suspend laws drafted by Parliament, required free elections to Parliament, and prohibited an army during peacetime.

Although the Bill of Rights granted freedom of expression to members of Parliament while Parliament was in session, it did not extend to the public, a provision readily agreeed upon by members of Parliament, fearful of attacks upon its authority. During the next two decades, Parliament would order the arrests of several persons for having commented upon Parliamentary actions, or upon individual members. Penalties could include, if the attack was against the House of Lords, lifetime imprisonment; if against the House of Commons, imprisonment for the session of Commons. The Bill of Rights also violated a religious right—it forbade Roman Catholics from the throne.

Under the Protestant leadership of William and Mary, John Dryden (1631-1700), a Catholic and one of England's finest poets and playwrights, who belived that poetry must tell the social history of a people, was removed first as poet laureate (in 1668) then as the royal historiographer (in 1670). However, by William and Mary's direction, censorship laws ended, and several newspapers were begun—including the first one in the North American colonies.

The Sentencing of John Twyn

On Friday afternoon, February 20, 1664, in London's Old Bayley courtroom, printer John Twyn stood before Lord Chief Justice Hide, awaiting judgment on his plea of not guilty to high treason. Twyn was accused of having printed a pamphlet that advocated the overthrow of an absolute monarch if the policies prove to be oppressive to the people.

At the beginning of the trial, Twyn had asked for counsel, but because he was charged with high treason, Hide informed him that the justices before him would be his counsel, stating:

> We are bound to be counsel with you, in point of *Law;* that is, the Court, my Brethren, my Self, are to see that you suffer nothing for your want of knowledge, in matter of Law; I say, we are to be of counsel with you; but for this horrid Crime, (I will hope in Charity you are not Guilty of it, but if you are) it is the most abominable and barbarous treason that I ever heard of, or any man else; the very *Title* of the *Book* (if there were no more) is as perfectly treason as possibly can be: the whole book through; all that is read in the indictment; not one sentence, but is as absolute High Treason, as ever I yet heard of. A company of mad brains, under pretense of the worship and service of God to bring in all vallainies and atheism, (as is seen in that *Book*) what a horrid thing is this! But you shall have free liberty of defending yourself to the matter of *Fact;* whether it be *So* or *No;* in this case, the law does not allow you counsel to plead for you;

but in matter of *Law,* we are of counsel with you, and it whall be our care to see that you have no wrong donc you.

Throughout the trial, Twyn seemed unable to fully understand all that was happening to him, claiming that he was a poor printer who agreed to print the pamphlet because he and his family needed the money; he said he did not share the view of the author whom he would not identify, consistenly claiming the right of a printer to protect the identity of his client.

Although several sheets of the pamphlet were printed, the work itself was not complete when Roger L'Estrange, the Commonwealth licensor, acting upon a tip, entered Twyn's house and seized the printing equipment and unfinished sheets. Throughout the trial Twyn had maintained that he did not read the sheets, but was found guilty by the justices who refused to believe that a man setting type would not know the content of what he was printing. Now, before the Chief Justice, John Twyn awaited sentencing:

Clerk. Are you all agreed of your verdict?

Jury. Yes.

Clerk. Who shall say for you?

Jury. The foreman.

Clerk. Set John Twyn to the bar. Look upon him my masters; how say you, is he *Guilty* of the High Treason whereof he stands indicted or *not guilty?*

Foreman. Guilty . . .

Clerk. Hearken to your verdict as the Court hath recorded it. You say that John Twyn is guilty of the high treason whereof he stood indicted, and at the time of committing the said treason, or any time since, he had no goods, chattles, lands nor tenements to your knowledge, and so you say all.

Jury. Yes.

Clerk. John Twyn, you hast been arraigned for high treason and there unto hast pleaded Not Guilty, and for thy trial hast put thy self upon God and the Country, and the Country hath found thee Guilty; what canst thou now say for thy self, why the Court should not proceed to judgment, and thereupon award execution of death against thee according to the Law?

John Twyn. I humbly beg mercy; I am a poor man, and have three small children; I never read a word of it.

Lord Hide. I'll tell you what you shall do. Ask mercy of them that can give it; that is of God and the King.

John Twyn. I humbly beseech you to intercede with His Majesty for mercy.

Clerk. Tie him up, Executioner.

Cryer. Oh yes, my Lords, and the King's Justices command all manner of persons to keep silence while judgment is in giving, upon pain of imprisonment.

Lord Hide. John Twyn ... I am heartily that your carriages and grievous offenses should draw me to give that judgement upon you that I must. It is the Law pronounces it, God knows it is full force against my inclination to do it; I will not trouble my self towards or you with repeating what you have done, but only this in the general, John Twyn, for you. Yours is the most grievous and highest treason, and the most complicated of all wickedness that ever I knew;

for you have as much as possibly lay in you, so reproached and reviled the King, the dead King, and his posterity, on purpose to endeavor to root them out from off the face of the earth. I speak it from my soul, I think we have the greatest happiness of the world, in enjoying what we do under so gracious and good a King. Yet you in the rancor of your heart thus to abuse him! I will be so charitable to think you are misled. There's nothing that pretends to religion that will avow or justify the killing of Kings ...; indeed it is a desperate and dangerous doctrine, fermented by divers of your temper, and it's high time some be made examples for it. I shall not spend my time in discourse to you to prepare you for death; I see a grave person whose office it is, and I leave it to him. Do not think of any time here; make your peace with God, which must be done by confession, and by the discovery of those that are guilty of the same crime with you. God have mercy upon you; and if you so do, He will have mercy upon you. But for as much as you John Twyn have been indicted of High Treason, you have put your Self upon God and the Country to try you; and the Country have found you guilty; therefore the judgment of the court is, and the court doth award . . . that you be led back to the place from whence you came, and from thence to be drawn upon an hurdle [a sled] to the place of execution, and there you shall be hanged by the neck, and being alive shall be cut down, and your privy members shall be cut off, your entrails shall be taken out of your body, and you living, the same to be burnt before your eyes; your head to be cut off, your body to be divided into four quarters, and your head and quarters to be disposed of the pleasure of the King's Majesty and the Lord have mercy upon your soul.

John Twyn. I most humbly beseech your Lordship to remember my condition, and intercede for me.

Lord Hide. I would not intercede for my own father in this case if he were alive.

Chapter 7

The American Colonies: Absence of Toleration

In the North American colonies, news was often disseminated by letter-carriers, balladeers, tavern owners who posted notices, and by people spreading gossip, rumor, hearsay and—occasionally—news.

The philosophical unification of church and State in the North American colonies, however, formed the base for a formal American media system, one in which freedom of expression was not tolerated on matters of church or State, and in which strict obedience to religious dogma was required. Virginia, in 1612, proscribed the death penalty for those who were convicted of blasphemy, as defined by the State. In the Massachusetts Bay Colony, the Puritans, many of whom had fled England because of religious persecution, now began a systematic persecution of other religions, forcing compliance not only to the creed of Christianity, but also to Puritanism. In 1646, the Massachusetts Act Against Heresy made it a crime against the State for denying the belief of the immortality of the soul, the resurrection of Jesus, or the need for repentence.

However, two American colonies, the only ones in the British empire, were established with provisions for complete religious freedom. In 1632, George Calvert, known as Lord Baltimore, established Maryland; in 1636, the Rev. Roger Williams, who had been banished from the Massachusetts Bay Colony for expressing religious opinion different from the doctrine of the official Puritan religion, established Rhode Island.

Maryland's Act of Toleration, written in 1649, however, tolerated only Christians, and proscribed the death penalty and forfeiture of property to the State for anyone who "shall hence forth blaspheme God . . . or deny our Savior Jesus Christ to be the Son of God, or shall deny the Holy Trinity . . . or shall use or utter any reproachful speeches, words, or language concerning the Holy Trinity."

Centuries later, in *Emerson* v. *Board of Education* (1947), Justice Hugo Black, of the Supreme Court of the United States, looked at the American experience of toleration, and concluded:

> Catholics found themselves hounded and proscribed because of their faith; Quakers who followed their conscience went to jail; Baptists were peculiarly obnoxious to certain dominant Protestant sects; men and women

49

of varied faiths who happened to be in a minority in a particular locality were persecuted because they steadfastly persisted in worshipping God only as their own consciences dictated. And all of these dissenters were compelled to pay tithes and taxes to support Government-sponsored churches whose ministers preached inflammatory sermons designed to strengthen and consolidate the established faith by generating a burning hatred against dissenters.

The animosities the various Christian religions and sects directed against each other were eventually blunted by their combined hatreds of the Jews who underwent a two century inquisition of fear within the United States and became subject to more intolerance and hatred than any other religion.

The first printing press in the Colonies had been established in 1639, the second in 1656; both were unlicensed, but at a time when licensing was not yet a law in the Colonies. The first document printed in the Colonies was a Loyalty Oath; other printed materials were either official notices and documents or religious tracts, pamphlets, and books. In 1662, a handful of books on religious matters were printed and declared to be "dangerous" by the Puritan leaders of Massachusetts. Later that year, Massachusetts enacted the Colonies' first licensing act, repealed it the following year, then re-enacted it a year later. Several prosecutions followed for printers of books that varied from the established Puritan theology. In 1668, a pamphlet written by Thomas á Kempis was approved by the official censor, then banned by the Massachusetts Bay Colony governor because Kempis was a "popish minister."

In 1681, William Penn established the colony now known as Pennsylvania as a refuge for persons of all religions. However, Penn's Frame of Government, written in 1682, required all residents to attend church; toleration extended only to the Christian religion—atheists, agnostics, and heretics (those who had religions other than Christianity) were persecuted.

When men have once taught their beasts to restrain [from] trespassing upon their neighbor's land, then they may expect to teach their fellow-creatures to cease from sin.

—John Asgill, 1712

Throughout the Colonies, the laws became so strict that in 1682 John Bucknew was imprisoned for printing, without authority, the official laws of Virginia.

Then in 1690, in Boston, the Colonies had their first newspaper. Benjamin Harris, a bold but occasionally inaccurate publisher, printer and bookseller had been imprisoned in London for two years on charges of sedition and libel under the reign of Charles II. Eventually, Harris fled to the Colonies and established *Publick Occurances, Both Foreign and Domestick,* which he intended to publish monthly.* In the first issue, he reported that the American Indians were "miserable savages, in whom we have too much confided"—the colonial governments were trying to have the people accept the Indians as allies in England's wars against the French. Harris reported on a smallpox epidemic— although most government officials didn't wish to "alarm" the colonists or those in England who might be thinking of visiting or perhaps establishing residence in the colonies. Harris also reported an adulterous affair between the Regent of France and the wife of one of the princes—almost everyone, not just the colonial government, was scandalized by such a blatant reporting of a sexual topic. The first issue of *Publick Occurances* was its last; the Massachusetts colonial government suppressed it because it was not licensed. Harris eventually returned to England where he again entered business, but now as the seller of medicines of dubious quality or value. It would be several years before another newspaper was published.

---

*Some media historians argue that *Public Occurences* cannot be the first newspaper in the American colonies; by only being published once, it did not meet the requirements of periodicity. However, the definition of what a newspaper is was established long after *Public Occurences* first appeared, and by the standards already established, it was by all accounts a newspaper.

Chapter 8

Philosophy and Free Expression

In the Colonies, there had been little discussion of freedom of the press issues, and the suppression of Harris's paper was seen as a just act for a scandalous publication. However, in Europe, there was much discussion about the rights of mankind and the philosophies of freedom of speech and of the press.

Communication [is] the natural right of mankind [and] the suppressing of either of these is 'taking away the Children's Bread'. It pleased God in his own time to have dictated to Man the invention of printing . . . [and] though several errors have and will be vented by the occasion of this invention, this is no more an argument against the invention itself than the growing of tares among wheat is an argument against growing of corn.

—John Asgill, 1712

In Holland, Baruch Spinoza (1632-1677), a Jew whose family had fled the Inquisition, challenged established beliefs by writing that the highest good is for the individual to be aware of the bonds to the whole of Nature. God, said Spinoza, is a "being absolutely infinite—that is, a substance consisting of infinite essentiality." Through a carefully worked out philosophical theorem, with a mathematical base, Spinoza declared that the primal being is an infinite substance which appears throughout nature, and not what Christians or Jews saw as a personalized or transcendent identity. For these views, Spinoza's writings were forbidden, by law, in Protestant nations, and the Roman Catholic Church placed his works on its Index of Forbidden Books. Spinoza's views of the nature of mankind within society shook even the secular monarchs. According to Spinoza, mankind is essentially anti-social, but establishes social organization only to further individual needs; mankind creates its rulers, but should a ruler abuse the privilege given, then power should revert to the people.

John Locke (1632-1704), one of England's greatest philosophers, argued that the people create government, that the mass of humanity is permanent, but that

53

rulers are only transient. Rulers, said Locke, are neither the product of divine
selection, nor do they rule by "divine right." This was a direct attack upon
the dominant beliefs throughout much of Europe. The people, said Locke,
allow rulers to exist; therefore, the rulers must be subservient to the people
who have surrendered some rights to achieve direction. In *A Letter Concerning
Toleration*, Locke suggested:

> The commonwealth seems to me to be a society of men constituted only
> for the procuring, preserving, and advancing their own civil interests.
> Civil interests I call life, liberty, health, and indolency of the body; and
> the possession of outward things, such as money, lands, houses, furniture,
> and the like.
> It is the duty of the civil magistrate, by the impartial execution of equal
> laws, to secure unto all the people in general and to every one of his
> subjects in particular the just possession of these things belonging to his
> life.
> [Similarly, on matters of religion] toleration [is] the chief characteristic
> mark of the true Church. For whatsoever some people boast of the
> antiquity of places and names, or of the pomp of their outward worship;
> others, of the reformation of their discipline; all, of the orthodoxy of their
> faith—for everyone is orthodox to himself—these things, and all others of
> this nature, are much rather marks of men striving for power and empire
> over one another than of the Church of Christ . . .
> No private person has any right in any manner to prejudice another
> person in his civil enjoyments because he is of another church or religion.
> All the rights and franchises that belong to him as a man, or as a denizen,
> are inviolably to be preserved to him. These are not the business of
> religion.

In *Two Treatises on Government* (1690), Locke refuted the divine right
argument by pointing out that political activity was valid only if it genuinely
served the public good. Consequently, a ruler lost the right to rule when he
or she ignored community needs—the right to lead, therefore, was conditional.
Locke further argued that a citizen who entered a regulated society did not give
up the right to think, worship, or write.

Also among those who argued for a greater freedom of expression was Matthew Tindal (1653?-1733), who combined much of the philosophies of Milton
and Locke to argue for an unrestrained press. Although mankind was given the
gift of reason, "the only light God has given him," wrote Tindal in 1698, it
is impossible to make any reasonable and logical decision without all available
information. Therefore, wrote Tindal, because mankind has knowledge, "God
has obligated mankind to share its knowledge." Attacking the "popish clergy,"
the Catholic church, Tindal claimed that the church "lost ground every where
. . . the press was either more or less free." Because of that, wrote Tindal, the
Catholic church *had* to restrict freedom of the press. However, turning to the
Protestant religion, which also restricted freedom of the press, Tindal argued:

But what pretense can the Protestants have for restraining it, who as they owe their religion to its liberty, so they cannot hinder it without destroying that religion which has no other foundation than that of every one's having a right to examine those reasons that are for or against any opinion, in order to make a true and impartial judgment?

The freedom of the people is based upon freedom of the press, Tindal wrote, arguing that it is the nature of the State to enslave the people, and that it is the press which has the capacity to give them the knowledge that they may choose their freedom:

But the arts of State, in most countries, being to enslave the people, or to keep them in slavery, it became a crime to talk, much more to write about political matters: and ever since printing has been invented, there have been, in most places, State-licensors, to hinder men from freely writing about government; for which there can be no other reason, but to prevent the defects of either the government, or the management of it, from being discovered and amended . . .

It's wholly owing to printing . . . that knowledge is become . . . not only more diffusive, but a great deal of more useful knowledge has been discovered in a short time since that invention than in many ages before.

The call for liberty and the free discourse of conflicting opinion came from those out of power; and, for every call for freedom of speech and of the press, there was usually a rebuttal from someone in authority. In August 1698, Francis Gregory, rector of Hambleden in Bucks County, England, replied to Matthew Tindal's philosophy on the necessity for freedom of the press. In a fifty-four page pamphlet, *A Modest Plea for the Regulation of the Press*, Gregory acknowledged that the invention of printing had "done a great deal of *good*," but that it also had the capacity to do "a great deal of *mischief*," and that the potential for this "mischief" required regulation:

When the press tends to promote religion and virtue, 'tis well employed, and ought to be encouraged; but when the press tends to promote vice and irreligion, it ought to be discountenanced and restrained. 'Tis evident that the press has been used to publish a great number of such papers, as to debauch the lives, and corrupt the judgments of men; such are our obscene poems, our profane and wanton stage-plays, where vice is not only represented but so promoted, that we may justly fear, that as all their spectators lose their time, so many of them may lose their innocence too. For since the hearts of men are so prone to evil, and become so like to tinder, apt to take fire from every little spark, 'tis hard to see those vices, which are pleasing to flesh and blood, represented upon a public stage, and yet not be infected by them.

Gregory also argued that because books contain "arguments so plausible, so seemingly strong," they need to be licensed because the people are "in no capacity to discover the fallacies that lie in them." To license the press, Gregory used a concept enunciated by Plato—"Men of integrity, learning and judgment . . . are able, at first view, to distinguish vice from virtue, and truth from error." Only those of the Church of England possessed such qualifications, wrote Gregory who, reflecting the beliefs of both church and State, explained his reasons for having a few judge the works directed to so many:

> 'When several interpretations are given of any texts, when doubts are raised, when arguments are produced to defend both parts of a contradiction; there is a vast number of men, who are no more able to judge which is *true*, and which is *false*, then a *blind* man is to distinguish betwixt a *good* color and a *bad* one.
>
> 'Tis the great unhappiness of such persons, that in matters of controversy they cannot rely upon their own weak reason; but must either suspend their judgments, or else give it up to the conduct of some other person, and who is so fit to be trusted with it, as their own ministers? provided they be, as every minister should be, men of piety and parts, able to satisfy doubts, remove scruples, and convince gainsayers . . .
>
> Suppose two persons are engaged in a doubtful controversy about an estate claimed by both, these persons being of themselves unable to determine the case, appeal to the King's judges, but do they thereby make those judges the lords of that estate which is contended for? surely no, the judge doth no more than according to evidence and law, declare to which person that estate doth justly belong.
>
> So it is in our present case, several parties of men lay claim to truth as theirs, and produce evidences for it: Now, a man unable to satisfy himself which side truth is to be found, consults his minister, who, by evidence of scripture, which in this case is the only law, assures his neighbor the truth lieth here or there . . .
>
> Since this unlimited liberty of the press would certainly be, as this author himself doth not deny, an in-let to schisms, heresies, and a great variety of opinions and practices in matters of religion; the allowance of it can never consist with that command of God, contend earnestly for the faith once delivered to the saints.
>
> This text supposeth that the true faith, or which is all one, the true religion, is but one; and that for that one, we are to *contend*, and that *earnestly* too: Now, to allow an unlimited liberty to the press, which will open a wide gap to introduce false religions, is so far from a contending *for* the one true faith, that it is indeed a contending *against* it; and therefore such an allowance is a direct breach of this command.
>
> Since this unlimited liberty of the press would certainly prove an in-let to schisms, heresies, and false religions, the allowance of it would be contradictory to the judgment and practice of the universal Church in all ages . . .
>
> I plead for the regulation of the press, as to such books only, as concern morality, faith, and religious worship, of which, our learned ecclesiastical

governours are the most proper judges. But as to policy and State affairs, they fall under the cognizance of the civil magistrate, whose province it is, and whose care it should be, to prevent the publishing of all such pamphlets as tend to promote popular tumults, sedition, treason, and rebellion. And had this been carefully done some years ago, it might have happily prevented those dreadful confusions, under which our church and State now do, and still are too like to groan.

Queen Mary died in 1694, King William in 1702, a year after the death of James II, the king whom Parliament had forced off the throne in 1688. The reign of William and Mary had been marked by wars and treaties, battles with Parliament, and the fear of what James II would do to recapture the throne.

Chapter 9

The Greater the Oppression,
the Greater the Resistance

The death of William brought Anne, Mary's sister, to the throne. Three days after Queen Anne was crowned, E. Mallet published the *Daily Courant* which, on March 11, 1702, became the first daily newspaper. But, under Queen Anne (1665-1714, reign 1702-1714) supression of dissent and severe censorship of the press again spread throughout England, bringing with it the public burning of books, and the ruthless imprisonment and torture of writers, printers, and booksellers.

Chief Justice J. Holt, in ruling against a defendant in a trial for sedition, gave the official version of why sedition must be a crime with severe penalties:

> [If speakers and writers] should not be called to account for possessing the people with an ill opinion of the government, no government can subsist. For it is very necessary for all governments that the people should have a good opinion of it.

By Queen Anne's direction, England enacted the Stamp Act in 1711, with the intended effect of crushing the smaller newspapers. The Stamp Act required all newspapers to pay a tax, receiving a taxation stamp upon payment. This tax, part of the economic power of a government, made prices of newspapers artifically high, causing several to go out of business, and succeeded in keeping the masses from purchasing newspapers.

During Queen Anne's reign, numerous presses, with the basic licensing law having been allowed to lapse, began publishing the writings of dissent, challenging the British to look at different views, different interpretations.

During this era—an era that saw England's Lord Marlborough defeat the great French armies, and the unification of England and Scotland—some of the greatest writers developed. Jonathan Swift, one of England's most accomplished writers, wrote numerous pamphlets in support of the Tory government, and of Queen Anne. But, it was for his devastating satire that Swift would be remembered best as he dug into the foibles of mankind to create Lemuel Gulliver and place him in different nations—all of them sub-species of England and of humanity itself. *Gulliver's Travels* (1726) solidified Swift's position as a brilliant writer—who hated mankind. His pamphlet, *Modest Proposal for Preventing the Children of Poor People in Ireland From Becoming a Burden to Their Parents* (1729)—in which he sugggested that to alleviate poverty, Irish families could raise and sell children to be butchered for food—is one of the English language's most savage pieces of ironical satire.

Alexander Pope (1688-1744), a Catholic, who because of anti-Catholic laws was denied the same kind of education as Protestants, became one of England's greatest poets, and a master of the heroic couplet form. Pope wrote his first great poem, *Pastorals*, in 1709 at the age of twenty-one, then *Essay on Criticism* (1711), and *The Rape of the Lock* (1712, 1714). His translations into English, from Latin, of Homer's *Iliad* (1720) and *Odyssey* (1726), earned him financial independence.

Satirical writings are hardly known in despotic governments, where dejection of mind on the one hand, and ignorance on the other, afford neither abilities nor will to write. In democracies they are not hindered, for the very same reason which causes them to be prohibited in monarchies; being generally levelled against men of power and authority, they flatter the malignancy of the people, who are the governing party. In monarchies they are forbidden, but rather as a subject of civil animadversion than as a capital crime. They may amuse the general malevolence, please the malcontents, diminish the envy against public employments, give the people patience to suffer, and make them laugh at their sufferings. But no government is so averse to satirical writings as the aristocratic. There the magistrates are petty sovereigns, but not great enough to despise affronts. If in a monarchy a satirical stroke is designed against the prince, he is placed on such an eminence that it does not reach him; but an aristocratic lord is pierced to the very heart. Hence the decemvirs, who formed an aristocracy, punished satirical writings with death.

—Charles De Secondat, Baron de Montesquieu, in *The Spirit of Laws* (1748) [The book was banned by the Catholic church]

The 'Father' of Modern Journalism

Daniel Defoe (1660-1731) is usually remembered as the author of *Robinson Crusoe* (1719) and *Moll Flanders* (1722), two of the finest books in English literature. Although he wrote ten novels—all of them published between 1719 and 1724 when he was in his sixties—fiction was only a small part of his life. During his seventy-one years, he was acknowledged as the "father of modern journalism," writing more than five hundred pamphlets or books, most of them on social issues. He also served as editor, publisher, or chief writer of twenty-six magazines, during a time when the magazine, essentially a collection of essays and articles, was a new medium. Defoe was also an economist, merchant, and one of Queen Anne's, and later George I's, major dissenters—as well as one of their strongest supporters.

Defoe was barred from attending England's universities since he was a Nonconformist, a person who refused to accept much of the doctrine of the Church of England during the reign of Charles II. Nevertheless, he received a good education in private schools, and in 1683, at the age of twenty-three, became a merchant, successfully dealing in the commodities market. However, when he began insuring ships—many of which were destroyed during a war with France—he went bankrupt, and spent much of his life trying to pay off a £17,000 debt. During that time, a shadow of immorality was cast over debtors, and this enabled his enemies to block the influence of many of his writings, but also placed an added burden upon him since his supporters in Parliament could only guarantee his freedom as long as he did not become "too radical" in his writings.

Defoe opposed the reign of James II, and went into exile, returning in 1688 to welcome the conquering armies of William of Orange, eventually becoming one of William's most trusted allies. In 1701, he wrote *The True-Born Englishman*, a biting satiric poem about racial prejudice, written following a particularly vicious attack upon William. Later that year, in *The Succession to the Crown, Considered*, Defoe argued that all political power belongs to the people who create both their rulers and Parliament to serve their needs. *The True-Born Englishman*, like *The Succession to the Crown, Considered*, became a controversial as well as highly-popular work.

That same year, with a religious war with Spain imminent, the House of Commons ordered imprisoned five individuals who had written a petition asking for increased defense preparedness. To the speaker of the House, Defoe presented *Legion's Memorial*, a vigorous defense for freedom of speech, containing the phrase, "Englishmen are no more to be slaves to Parliaments than to a King." With the release of the prisoners, Defoe became one of England's most popular heroes.

In May 1703, with Queen Anne on the throne, Defoe was arrested for seditious libel following publication of *The Shortest Way With the Dissenters*, a satire of the customs of the Church of England, written by Defoe as if it were written by a minister of the Church. Defoe was fined two hundred marks, sentenced to the pillory three times, and ordered to make a surety bond for seven years—"for good behavior." But, once again the people came to his side, giving him flowers and drinking to his health while he was in the pillory—and reading out loud his satiric poem, "Hymn to a Pillory." Later that year, he was released following the financial collapse of his once-successful brick-and-tile factory, the recognition that his wife and eight children needed an income, and the belief that he could be useful as a pamphleteer.

Upon his release, Defoe wrote *An Essay Upon the Regulation of the Press*, an attack against a proposed tax and further licensing of the press. In this twenty-two page pamphlet, Defoe argued that the proposed tax and the enforcement of licensing makes the press "a slave to a [political] party," and that "It cannot be proved that any one party has more right . . . to publish any thing than another, and therefore cannot in justice have more liberty given them to do it: For no man can justly demand an exclusive power where he had no precedent right . . ."

According to Defoe:

[An] absolute submitting the press to the will of the licensor . . . is bringing the whole trade of books, and the whole body of learning, under the power of mercenary men . . .

I know of no nation in the world, whose government is not perfectly despotic, that ever makes preventive laws; 'tis enough to make laws to punish crimes when they are committed, and not to put it in the power of any single man, on pretence of preventing offenses.

Defoe did agree that "licentiousness of all sorts ought to be restrained," but that "to regulate this evil by an evil [licensing] ten times more pernicious is doing us no service at all."

In 1704, about the time his essay on freedom of the press appeared, Daniel Defoe created the *Review*, an official newspaper of Queen Anne's government. The newspaper—Defoe wrote almost every article—appeared three times a week through 1713. The *Review* included relatively objective discussions about all political and social points of view, as well as numerous features about London and the English nation.

With George I now on the throne, Defoe again switched political parties—he was originally a Whig, then, under Anne, a Tory, now a Whig once again—and continued to write pamphlets and articles. This time he supported the Hanoverian monarchy, justifying his work as being a "moderating influence." Defoe died in 1731, probably in hiding from his creditors, but also one of the most respected people in the kingdom.

Attacking the Pope

In 1706, with three other editions within three years, Matthew Tindal wrote, *The Rights of the Christian Church Asserted Against Romish and Other Priests who Claim an Independent Power Over It*. The book was one of the nation's strongest attacks upon the Papacy. Although Tindal opposed the Catholic doctrine, an "acceptable" topic at the time, he also argued against much of the doctrine of the Anglican Church, and opposed the commonly-held doctrine that the Church should have supremacy over the State. In 1710, the pamphlet, one of the most controversial printed in England, was finally banned. In 1730, at the age of about seventy-seven, Tindal wrote, against much opposition, *Christianity as Old As Creation*, a brilliantly organized pamphlet which argued that God has created everything necessary for mankind, and that everything necessary for the study of theology or the practice of religion has been given outside a formal system of religion.

Addison and Steele and The Tatler

Queen Anne's Parliament, sometime about 1711, began requiring printers to identify, on the title page, the names of all authors, thus providing a battleground between the Tories, who favored regulation, and the Whigs, who opposed. The Whigs believed that by omitting the name of the author, authors could write the truth as they saw it, without fear of retaliation by the Crown. The Tories, however, believed that the anonymous author could hide behind that anonymity to libel others, or to write words of sedition. In a pamphlet, *The Thoughts of a Tory Author*, (1712) Joseph Addison explained the reasons why such action was needed:

> The great objection [to a truly free press] is the scandalous practices of the pirate printers and their hawkers [booksellers] which will be removed when all printers are obliged to put their names, and register their presses.
> We propose by our restraint . . . to put a stop to the mischiefs that arise by the difficulties of proof against printers and booksellers who being obliged to answer for whatever faults their authors commit . . . will take effectual care to bring them [authors] out, if there is a clause to indemnify them [booksellers and printers] on so doing . . .

Joseph Addison (1672-1719) and Richard Steele (1672-1729), like Defoe and Swift, were pamphleteers and journalists. In 1709, Steele began publication of *The Tatler*, a magazine of political and social essays, to which Addison, Steele's friend from childhood, had contributed several essays while a member of Parliament. However, in 1710, with the Tories taking over parliament, Addison, who had once been undersecretary of state, lost his government post.

The next year, he and Steele initiated *The Spectator*, a much better-edited and produced publication than *The Tatler*. During its almost two-year publication, *The Spectator* published numerous articles and essays—many written by Addison and Steele, individually or collectively—about theology, ethics, philosophy, and aesthetics, but little about politics. With the death of Queen Anne in 1714, and the accession of George I, Addison was again returned to high political offices, and became secretary of state in 1717, retiring a year later because of ill health. He died in 1719. Steele was elected to Parliament in 1713, but expelled the following year because of anti-Tory views; in 1714, George I knighted him, and ordered him returned to Parliament where he remained until 1718, when again he was expelled. He continued writing plays, but saw his financial resources dwindle to the point where he died almost impoverished, after being one of the most honored journalists in England.

George I (1660-1727, reign 1714-1727), a German whose claim to the throne was weak, had to survive an invasion of England by the son of James II who had secured support througout the European continent. With the failure of the invasion in 1715, the Tory party was left decimated by charges of treason, many of them true. Although there were minor skirmishes regarding freedom of speech issues, there was no significant oppression.

The 'Cato Letters'

Into this environment came Cato, pen-name for John Trenchard (1662-1723) and Thomas Gordon (1685?-1750) who would become two of the most popular, and controversial, authors in England. Trenchard and Gordon had selected the name to honor Cato the Younger who had committed suicide rather than live under the rule of Julius Caesar; Cato was also the title character in Joseph Addison's play, first performed about eight years earlier. The 197 "Cato Letters" appeared first in the *Independent Whig*, then in the *London Journal* and *British Journal* between 1720 and 1723. The essays were written in opposition to Sir Robert Walpole, England's prime minister. Amost one-fourth of the letters, most of them published in 1720, dealt with religious and personal freedom; 144 letters focused upon the rights of all citizens, and upon the responsibilities of government in the protection of its citizens. Trenchard and Gordon, while vigorously defending the rights of all people to criticize government, nevertheless believed that libels against the government—as opposed to libels against those who govern—were "always base and unlawful." Nevertheless, they also argued that the best way for a ruler to deal with an "undeserved libel" was to "laugh at them, and to despise them," but not to prosecute. The fifteenth article-essay, probably written by Gordon and assisted by Trenchard, was published February 4, 1720, and focused upon freedom of the press issues:

> Without freedom of thought, there can be no such thing as wisdom; and no such thing as public liberty, without freedom of speech: Which is the right of every man, as far as by it he does not hurt and control the right of another; and this is the only check which it ought to suffer, the only bounds which it ought to know.
>
> This sacred privilege is so essential to free government, that the security of property; and the freedom of speech, always go together; and in those wretched countries where a man cannot call his tongue his own, he can scarce call any thing else his own. Whoever would overthrow the liberty of the nation, must begin by subduing the freedom of speech; a thing terrible to public traitors.
>
> This secret was so well known to the court of King Charles I that his wicked ministry procured a proclamation to forbid the people to talk of parliaments, which those traitors had laid aside. To assert the undoubted right of the subject, and defend his majesty's legal prerogative, was called

disaffection, and punished as sedition. Nay, people were forbid to talk of religion in their families: For the priests had combined with the ministers to cook up tyranny, and suppress truth and the law. While the late King James, when Duke of York, went avowedly to Mass; men were fined, imprisoned, and undone, for saying that he was a papist: And, that King Charles II might live more securely a papist, there was an act of Parliament made, declaring it treason to say that he was one.

That men ought to speak well of their governors, is true, while their governors deserve to be well spoken of; but to do public mischief, without hearing of it, is only the prerogative and felicity of tyranny: A free people will be showing that they are so, by their freedom of speech.

The administration of government is nothing else, but the attendance of the trustees of the people upon the interest and affairs of the people. And as it is the part and business of the people, for whose sake alone all public matters are, or ought to be, transacted, to see whether they be well or ill transacted; so it is the interest, and ought to be the ambition, of all honest magistrates, to have their deeds openly examined, and publicly scanned: Only the wicked governors of men dread what is said of them.

Freedom of speech is ever the symptom, as well as the effect, of good government. In old Rome, all was left to the judgment and pleasure of the people; who examined the public proceedings with such discretion, and censured those who administered them with such equity and mildness, that in the space of three hundred years, not five public ministers suffered unjustly. Indeed, whenever the commons proceed to violence, the great ones had been the aggressors.

Guilt only dreads liberty of speech, which drags it out of its lurking holes, and exposes its deformity and horror to day-light. *Horatius, Valerious, Cincinnatus,* and other virtuous and undesigning magistrates of the Roman Commonwealth, had nothing to fear from liberty of speech. Their virtuous administration, the more it was examined, the more it brightened and gained by enquiry. When *Valerius,* in particular, was accused, upon some slight grounds, of affecting the Diadem; he, who was the first minister of Rome, did not accuse the people for examining his conduct, but approved his innocence in a speech to them; he gave such satisfaction to them, and gained such popularity to himself, that they gave him a new name . . .

But things afterwards took another turn: Rome, with the loss of its liberty, lost also its freedom of speech; then men's words began to be feared and watched; then first began the poisonous race of informers, banished indeed under the righteous administration of *Titus, Nerva, Trajan, Aurelius, &c.* but encouraged and enriched under the vile ministry of *Sejanus, Tigellinus, and others* . . .

The best princes have ever encouraged and promoted fredom of speech; they knew that upright measures would defend themselves, and that all upright men would defend them. *Tacitus,* speaking of the reigns of some of the princes above-mentioned, says with ecstasy, *Rara temporum felicitate, ubi sentire quae velis, & quae sentias dicere liceat:* A blessed time, when you might think what you would and speak what you thought!

The same was the opinion and practice of the wise and virtuous *Timoleon,* the deliverer of the great city of *Syracuse* from slavery. He being accused by *Demaenetus,* a popular orator, in a full assembly of the people, of several misdemeanors committed by him while he was General, gave no other answer, than that *He was highly obliged to the Gods for granting him a request that he had often made to them;* namely, *That he might live to see the* Syracusians *enjoy that liberty of speech which they now seemed to be masters of.*

And that great Commander, *M. Marcellus,* who won more battles than any Roman captain of his age, being accused by the *Syracusians,* while he was now a fourth time consul, of having done them indignities and hostile wrongs, contrary to the league, rose from his seat in the Senate, as soon as the charge against him was opened, and passing (as a private man) into the place where the accused were wont to make their defence, gave free liberty to the *Syracusians* to impeach him: Which, when they had done, he and they went out of the court together to attend the issue of the cause: Nor did he express the least ill-will or resentment towards these his accusers; but being acquitted, received their city into his protection. Had he been guilty, he would neither have shown such temper nor courage.

I doubt not but on *Spencer* and his Son, who were the chief ministers and betrayers of *Edward* II would have been very glad to have stopped the mouths of all the honest men in *England.* They dreaded to be called traitors, because they were traitors. And I dare say, Queen Elizabeth's Walsingham, who deserved no reproaches, feared none. Misrepresentation of public measures is easily overthrown, by representing public measures truly: When they are honest, they ought to be publicly known, that they may be publicly commended; but if they be knavish or pernicious, they ought to be publicly exposed, in order to be publicly detested.

To assert, that King *James* was a papist and a tyrant, was only so far hurtful to him, as it was true of him; and if the Earl of *Strafford* had not deserved to be impeached, he need not have feared a Bill of Attainder. If our directors and their confederates be not such knaves as the world thinks them, let them prove to all the world, that the world thinks wrong, and that they are guilty of none of those villainies which all the world lays to their charge. Others too, who would be thought to have no part of their guilt, must, before they are thought innocent, show that they did all that was in their power to prevent that guilt, and to check their proceedings.

Freedom of speech is the great bulwark of liberty; they prosper and die together: And it is the terror of traitors and oppressors, and a barrier against them. It produces excellent writers, and encourages men of fine genius. *Tacitus* tells us, that the *Roman* commonwealth bred great and numerous authors, who wrote with equal boldness and eloquence: But when it was enslaved, those great wits were no more . . . Tyranny had usurped the place of equality, which is the soul of liberty, and destroyed public courage. The minds of men, terrified by unjust power, degenerated into all the vileness and methods of servitude: Abject sycophancy and blind submission grew the only means of preferment, and indeed of safety; men do not open their mouths, but to flatter.

Pliny the Younger observes, that this dread of tyranny had such effect, that the Senate, the great *Roman* Senate, became at last stupid and dumb . . . Hence, says he, our spirit and genius are stupified, broken, and sunk for ever. And in one of his epistles, speaking of the works of his uncle, he makes an apology for eight of them, as not written with the same vigor which was to be found in the rest; for that these eight were written in the reign of *Nero*, when the spirit of writing was cramped by fear . . .

All ministers, therefore, who were oppressors, or intended to be oppressors, have been loud in their complaints against freedom of speech, and the license of the press; and always restrained, or endeavoured to restrain, both. In consequence of this, they have brow-beaten writers, punished them violently, and against law, and burnt their works. By all which they showed how much truth alarmed them, and how much they were at enmity with truth.

There is a famous instance of this in *Tacitus*: He tells us, that *Cremutius Cordus*, having in his annals praised *Brutus* and *Cassius*, gave offense to *Sejanus*, first minister, and to some inferior sycophants in the court of *Tiberius*; who, conscious of their own characters, took the praise bestowed on every worthy *Roman*, to be so many reproaches pointed at themselves: They therefore complain of the book to the senate; which, being now only the machine of tyranny, condemned it to be burnt. But this did not prevent its spreading . . .

Being censured, it was the more sought after. *From hence*, says *Tacitus, we may wonder at the stupidity of those statesmen, who hope to extinguish, by the terror of their power, the memory of their action;* for quite otherwise, *the punishment of good writers gains credit to their writings* . . . Nor did ever any government, who practiced impolitic severity, get any thing by it, but injury to themselves, and renown to those who suffered under it . . .

Freedom of speech, therefore, being of such infinite importance to the preservation of liberty, every one who loves liberty ought to encourage freedom of speech. Hence it is that I, living in a country of liberty, and under the best prince upon earth, shall take this very favorable opportunity of serving mankind, by warning them of the hideous mischiefs that they will suffer, if ever corrupt and wicked men shall hereafter get possession of any State, and the power of betraying their master: And, in order to do this, I will show them by what steps they will probably proceed to accomplish their traiterous ends. This may be the subject of my next.

Valerius Maximus tells us, that *Lentulus Marcellinus*, the *Roman* consul, having complained, in a popular assembly, of the overgrown power of *Pompey*; the whole people answered him with a shout of approbation: Upon which the consul told them, *Shout on, Gentlemen, shout on, and use those bold signs of liberty while you may; for I do not know how long they will be allowed you.*

God be thanked, we *Englishmen* have neither lost our liberties, nor are in danger of losing them. Let us always cherish this matchless blessing, almost peculiar to ourselves; that our posterity may, many ages hence, ascribe their freedom to our zeal. The defense of liberty is a noble, a heavenly office; which can only be performed where liberty is: For, as the same *Valerius Maximus* observes, *Quid ergo Libertas sine* Catone? *Non magis quam* Catofine *Libertate.* [What liberty would there be without Cato? Just as much, what would Cato be without liberty?]

There are many ways to silence opposition, yet not infuriate a citizenry. To effectively silence the opposition, Walpole arranged for subsidies to newspapers, secretly placed journalists on his payroll, and alternated threats with bribes to gain a compliant press. Trenchard and Gordon became victims of the power of greed. There had been several attempts to suppress the newspapers and to arrest the writers of the "Cato Letters." When those efforts proved unsuccessful, Walpole bought the co-operation of the editor of the *London Journal*, forcing Tranchard and Gordon to write their column in the weaker *British Journal*, effectively ending their immediate influence. Trenchard died at the end of 1723. Gordon, without Trenchard's inspiration, became less caustic, more conciliatory, and even accepted a government position—commissioner of wine licenses—from Walpole; he wrote against the Catholic Church (which pleased Walpole), and translated Tacitus's histories from the Latin, receiving critical acclaim for both the translation and the commentary, but was still hounded by the sarcasm of many of England's writers, including Alexander Pope. Yet, the influence of Cato was wide, eventually spreading to the American colonies.

Chapter 10

From Compliance to Dissent

In the American colonies, John Campbell, postmaster of Boston, established *The Boston News-Letter* in 1704, making sure that before publication, the Governor or one of his representatives had seen all the articles. The memory of what had happened to Benjamin Harris fourteen years earlier, combined with the ruling on sedition by Chief Justice Holt, helped guarantee a compliant press. No articles in Campbell's paper could offend anyone since most were summaries of the already-censored news of Europe, shipping and trade notices, obituaries, and official notices. For fourteen years, Campbell was postmaster, and accepted government subsidy to publish his newspaper and to print the official notices of Massachusetts. So weak was the financial base of the colonies' first continuing newspaper that the Commonwealth of Massachusetts twice had to save the three-hundred circulation newspaper from bankruptcy.

Then in 1719, Campbell was dismissed as postmaster, and ordered to give his newspaper to William Brooker, the new postmaster. Campbell, who had edited his newspaper, the only one in the colonies for fourteen years, refused, forcing Brooker to establish the *Boston Gazette*, the colonies' third newspaper which was now in direct competition with the *News-Letter*. The *Gazette*, at first, was competition only in an economic sense. As postmaster, Brooker received paid official notices, advertising, and circulation from the colonial government; and advertising and circulation from the citizens who were careful to advertise in, and subscribe to, the "official" publication. Brooker also had another advantage—he didn't have to pay as much as Campbell to mail his newspaper. However, like Campbell, Brooker, too, lost his political support, was dismissed as postmaster, and forced to turn over the *Gazette* to the new postmaster. Unlike Campbell, Brooker chose not to stay in journalism.

By 1721, James Franklin, former printer for Brooker, established the *New England Courant* in Boston. Franklin began the *Courant* in opposition to the *Gazette*, now under new ownership. However, Franklin was in trouble almost from the first issue. Although the licensing act had expired, all other newspaper and book publishers printed "by authority" on their works. Franklin refused, and began printing articles that infuriated local religious and secular leaders, especially Increase and Cotton Mather, father and son dictators of Puritan theology and customs. Increase Mather was president of Harvard; both of them were brilliant scholars, writers, and ministers, who commanded respect in England—which had policies against Puritans—and in the colonies—which were subjected to Puritan "righteousness." Most colonists accepted the views of the Mathers, for they believed that the highly-educated ministers spoke the truth of God, and were blessed by the wisdom of God.

Many citizens may have inwardly rebelled at the edicts of oppression issued by the Mathers, but outwardly they too meekly accepted what the Mathers said as truth, for offending the Mathers was somewhat like offending a king—and often with similar response. Franklin boldly dashed into attacks upon the Puritan leaders and scholars, and launched the colonies' first newspaper crusade, and attack upon the Mathers for advocating the use of a method of vaccination—learned from West African slaves—for the control of small pox. Ironically, it was this procedure that later led Edward Jenner to develop a more sophisticated method of smallpox innoculation.

Nevertheless, the Mathers not only maintained what was "right," but imposed their will—what they considered to be God's will, God's Truth—upon others. Franklin argued that not only are there many sides to every issue, but that not even the clergy was able to agree on their interpretations of the Bible. In the *Courant*, Franklin argued why dissent must be allowed:

> As, in controversies of religion, noting is more frequent than for divines themselves to press the same texts for opposing tenets, they cannot fairly condemn a man for dissenting from them in matters of religion; much less can any man be thought to hinder the success of the work of a minister, by opposing him in that which is not properly a minister's work . . . Even errors made publick, and afterwards publickly expos'd, less endanger the constitution of church or State, than when they are (without exception) industriously propagated in private conversation. Hence, to anathemize a printer for publishing the different opinions of men, is as injudicious as it is wicked.

Among the writers who were part of Franklin's Hell-Fire Club of satirists, dissidents, and future radicals was James' brother, fifteen-year-old Benjamin Franklin, writing under the name Silence Dogood. Franklin contributed several vicious satiric attacks on religious intolerance and on governmental policies. In 1722, when James Franklin launched a fusillade against the Massachusetts governor, he was brought before a Council, spoke his mind, and was thrown into prison. The General Court then quickly drew up an order forbidding Franklin from printing any newspaper or pamphlet without first receiving clearance on all the articles he planned to use. An attempt to name his younger brother, Benjamin, an apprentice, to the editorship to avoid the quasi-licensing law, failed when young Ben broke his promise and moved to Philadelphia. Before the censorship ruling, the *Courant* had been brightly written and edited, reflecting Franklin's knowledge of literature and the other arts; Franklin not only wrote outstanding article-essays, but also had introduced Addison and Steele, Defoe, and Cato to the colonial settlers. However now, with restrictions, the paper began a four year decline that resulted in its death about 1726.

Benjamin Franklin, meanwhile, was learning his trade as a printer, and in 1729, he and Hugh Meredith took over the *Pennsylvania Gazette*. A year later, Franklin bought out Meredith's share, became sole proprietor of the newspaper, and within the year had made it the best, most profitable, of the colonial newspapers.

In 1731, in the *Gazette*, Franklin published "An Apology for Printers," his views of the nature of libertarian doctrine as it should apply to the colonies. The "Apology," although widely reprinted during the next 250 years, added little that Cato—and numerous others—had not already written in England. In his "Apology," Franklin argued that diverse opinions must be presented to the public, that printers print all views, often without endorsing any, and that printers "do continually discourage the Printing of great Numbers of bad things, and Stifle them at Birth." Nevertheless, Franklin was in a position that could now be considered to be a conflict of interest; he was a public official—a postmaster entitled to free distribution of his newspaper—and a printer/journalist; most of what he published would entertain, but not offend anyone.

In 1692, William Bradford, who had established the first printing press in Pennsylvania seven years earlier, was arrested by the Quakers on charges of seditious libel. When Bradford announced that he was tired of harrassment, and was going to move to New York, the Pennsylvania authorities dropped charges and offered him a yearly fee and all the printing he could handle. However, in 1693, he moved to New York where he became the official printer. In 1725, Bradford founded the *New York Gazette*, first newspaper in that Colony. Because of economic ties to the New York colonial government, which had given him almost exclusive rights for all its printing needs, Bradford never challenged the jurisdiction, rights, actions, or decisions of that government. In supporting the administration, Bradford was often forced to neglect or slant his reporting against the emerging Whig class, the merchants and commercial businessmen who had already begun to dominate England's Parliament.

Zenger: "The Cause of Liberty"

Eight years after Bradford established the *New York Gazette*, several political opponents of Sir William Cosby, newly-appointed governor of New York, established the *New York Weekly Journal* as a medium for the Whigs, and in opposition to Bradford's Tory-supported newspaper. As their front, they selected John Peter Zenger, a master craftsman, who would be presented to the readers as the editor/publisher/owner, although his only responsibility was to print the newspaper. For almost nine years, Zenger had been a printer's apprentice to Bradford, and was later his partner before opening a printing shop in New York.

James Alexander would be one of those who words would dominate the editorial content of the *Journal*. Alexander was an engineer and mathematician, as well as lawyer, statesman, and journalist. During his career, he would be surveyor general of New York and New Jersey, attorney general of New Jersey, and a member of the General Assembly of New York. But, he was also a libertarian, knowledgeable in the philosophy that Milton had expounded less than a century earlier. In the November 12 and 19, 1733, issues of the *New York Weekly Journal*, the second and third issues printed by Zenger, Alexander presented what may be the first published American philosophy of the press, a powerful plea for absolute freedom:

> ... In an absolute Monarchy, the Will of the Prince being the Law, a Liberty of the Press to complain of Grievances would be complaining against the Law and the Constitution, to which they have submitted to have been obliged to submit; and therefore, in one Sense, may be said to deserve Punishment; so that under an absolute Monarchy, I say, such a Liberty is inconsistent with the Constitution, having no proper Subject to Politics on which it might ne exercis'd, and if exercis'd would incur a certain Penalty.
>
> But in a limited Monarchy, as England is, our Laws are known, fixed, and established. They are the streight Rule and sure Guide to direct the King, the Ministers, and other his Subjects: And therefore an Offense against the Laws is such an Offense against the Constitution as ought to receive a proper adequate Punishment; the several Constituents of the Government, the Ministry, and all subordinate Magistrates, having their certain, known, and limited Sphere in which they move; one part may certainly err, misbehave, and become criminal, without involving the rest or any of them in the Crime or Punishment . . .
>
> [The] Advantage of Exposing the exorbitant Crimes of wicked Ministers under a limited Monarchy makes the Liberty of the Press not only consistent with, but a necessary Part of, the Constitution itself.
>
> It is indeed urged, that the Liberty of the Press ought to be restrained, because not only the Actions of evil Ministers may be exposed, but the Character of good ones traduced. Admit it in the strongest Light that Calumny and Lies would prevail, and blast the Character of a great and good Minister; yet that is a less Evil than the Advantages we reap from the Liberty of the Press, as it is a Curb, a Bridle, a Terror, a Shame, and Restraint to evil Ministers; and it may be the only punishment, especially for a Time. But when did Calumnies and Lies ever destroy the Character of one good Minister? Their benign Influences are known, tasted, and felt by every body; Or if their Characters have been clouded for a Time, yet they have generally shined forth in greater Luster: Truth will always prevail over Falsehood.
>
> The Facts exposed are not to be believed, because said or published; but it draws People's Attention, directs their View, and fixes the Eye in a proper Position that everyone may judge for himself whether those Facts are true or not. People will recollect, enquire and search, before they condemn; and therefore very few good Ministers can be hurt by Falsehood, but many wicked Ones by seasonable Truth: But however the Mischief that a few may possibly, but improbably, suffer by the Freedom of the Press is not to be put in Competition with the Danger which the KING and the people may suffer by a shameful, cowardly Silence under the Tyranny of an insolent, rapacious, infamous Minister . . .

The Loss of Liberty in general would soon follow the Suppression of the Liberty of the Press; for as it is an essential Branch of Liberty, so perhaps it is the best Preservation of the whole. Even a Restraint of the Press would have a fatal Influence. No Nation Ancient or Modern ever lost the Liberty of freely Speaking, Writing, or Publishing their Sentiments, but forthwith lost their Liberty in general and became Slaves. LIBERTY and SLAVERY! how amiable is one! how odious and abominable the other! Liberty is universal Redemption, Joy, and Happiness; but Servitude is absolute Reprobation and everlasting Perdition in Politics.

All the venal Supporters of wicked Ministers are aware of the great use of the Liberty of the Press in a limited free Monarchy: They know how vain it would be to attack it openly, and therefore endeavor to puzzle the Case with Words, Inconsistencies, and Nonsense; but if the Opinion of the most numerous, unprejudiced and impartial Part of Mankind is an Argument of Truth, the Liberty of the Press has that as well as Reason on its Side. I believe every honest Britton of whatever Denomination, who loves his Country, if left to his own free and unbiased Judgment, is a Friend to the Liberty of the Press, and an Enemy to any Restraint upon it . . .

If Men in Power were always Men of Integrity, we might venture to trust them with the Direction of the Press, and there would be no Occasion to plead against the Restraint of it; but as they have Vices like their Fellows, so it very often happens that the best intended and the most valuable Writings are the Objects of their Resentment, because opposite to their own Tempers or Designs. In short, I think, every Man of common Sense will judge that he is an Enemy to his King and Country who pleads for any Restraints upon the Press; but by the Press, when Nonsense, Inconsistencies, or personal Reflections are writ, if despised, they die of Course; if Truth, solid Arguments, and elegant, just Sentiments are published, they should meet with Applause rather than Censure; if Sense and Nonsense are blended, then, by the free Use of the Press, which is open to all, the Inconsistencies of the Writer may be made apparent; but to grant a Liberty only for Praise, Flattery, and Panegyric, with a Restraint on every Thing which happens to be offensive and disagreeable to those who are at any Time in Power, is absurd, servile, and ridiculous; upon which I beg Leave to quote one Observation of the ingenious [Thomas] Gordon, in his excellent Discourses upon Tacitus. "In truth," says he, where no Liberty is allowed to speak of Governours besides that of praising them, their praises will be little believed; their Tenderness and Aversion to have their Conduct examined will be apt to prompt people to think their conduct guilty or weak, to suspect their Management and Designs to be worse perhaps than they are, and to become turbulent and seditious, rather than be forced to be silent. . .

During the next year, Gov. Cosby, by willful and capricious actions, many of them seen by the Whigs as motivated by personal greed, ruled New York as if he were a dictator, rather than a governor. William Bradford, of the *Gazette*, had chosen not to speak out against the governor; Zenger's *Journal*, however, forcefully pointed out "excesses" and greed on the part of the governor, and charged Cosby with numerous offenses against the rights of the citizenry. Further, by printing numerous articles and essays by Alexander, and by reprinting many of Cato's columns from England, the *Journal* had challenged not only English common law, but the very foundation of the existence of the State.

Finally, a year after the first issue of the *Journal* appeared, Zenger was arrested and charged with sedition on an indictment prepared by a council picked by Gov. Cosby—after both the Grand Jury and the General Assembly refused to indict the printer. It is probable that Zenger, who spoke German and was semi-literate in English, wrote none of the articles that offended Cosby. Nevertheless, since Zenger's name was the only one listed in the newspaper, and neither he not his writers revealed their identities, it would be Zenger who faced imprisonment. For almost a year, he was imprisoned—while Alexander, former Chief Justice Lewis Morris (whom Cosby removed from office in 1733), Rip Van Dam (a wealthy businessman who had served as an interim governor for a year before Cosby arrived), and others planned Zenger's defense while also continuing to write and edit the *Journal*, making it an even stronger voice against the government.

In July 1735, Zenger was finally brought to trial after Cosby disbarred both of Zenger's attorneys. In a courtroom in which the presiding judges were appointed by Cosby, it was accepted that Zenger would lose—and Cosby "vindicated." However, such was not to be. At the back of the courtroom, Andrew Hamilton, one of the most distinguished lawyers in the colonies—speaker of the Pennsylvania Assembly, former attorney general of Pennsylvania—rose to defend Zenger and the concept of freedom of the press. Hamilton would use the strategy outlined by Alexander, itself somewhat based upon the writings of Cato. In 1721, Cato had written:

> The exposing . . . of public Wickedness, as it is a Duty which every man owes to Truth and his Country, can never be a Libel in the Nature of Things; and they who call it so, make themselves no Complement; he who is affronted at the reading of the Ten Commandments would make the Decalogue a Libel, if he durst, but he Tempts us at the same Time to form a Judgment of his Life and Morals, not at all to his Advantage.
>
> . . . the People often Judge better than their Superiors, and have not so many Biasses to Judge wrong, and Politicians often rail at the People, chiefly because they have given the people occasion to rail: Those Ministers who cannot make the People their Friends, it is to be shrewdly suspected, do not deserve their Friendship . . .

Hamilton would use that concept to bring about an acquittal for his client. "I confess," said Hamilton, "that he printed and published two Papers set forth in the Information." With those words, Cosby knew that Zenger had to be found guilty of sedition and criminal libel. At the time, in the colonies, as in England, truth was not a defense for charges of libel. Since attacks upon the government and of the people who administer that government often led to public unrest and mistrust, and could threaten the entire existence of the "duly-constituted" government, any written or spoken attack would be considered to be cause for indictment. The only function of a court and jury, therefore, would be to determine authorship of the indictable offenses. By admitting that Zenger wrote the words—and preserving the identities of the actual authors—Hamilton seemed to conclude the case. But, he was not through. In an impassioned speech to the jury, Hamilton said that the case was *not* over, for the jury "will have something more to do before you make my client a libeller. For the words themselves must be libelous—that is *false, malicious, and seditious*—or else we are not guilty." Hamilton cited numerous instances to support his claims, but the judges struck them down, citing English law that truth is not a defense to libel since the statutes of libel were enacted to *protect* society from attacks upon itself. Hamilton agreed, but argued that the law was meant to protect the king and the preservation of the State and *not* to shield a bad or corrupt governor.

Turning to the jury, Hamilton argued that the people have the right to live without fear of an intolerable governor:

Men who injure and oppress the people under their administration provoke them to cry out and complain; and then make that very complaint the foundation for new oppressions and prosecutions . . .

[This] is not the case of the poor printer, nor of New York alone . . . It may in its consequence affect every freeman that lives under a British government on the main in *America*. It is the best cause. It is the cause of liberty, and I make no doubt but your upright conduct this day will not only entitle you to the love and esteem of your fellow citizens, but *every* man who prefers freedom to a life of slavery will bless and honor you as men who have baffled the attempt of tyranny; . . . by an impartial and uncorrupt verdict [you will] have laid a mobile foundation for securing to ourselves, our posterity, and our neighbors, that, which to nature and the laws of our country have given us a right—the liberty—both of exposing and opposing arbitrary power—in these parts of the world at least—by speaking and writing—TRUTH!

Under the laws of New York and England, the jury had to bring in a verdict of guilty—Zenger had admitted authorship, and the attack was seditious libel. But, the jury, knowing about the excesses of the governor, and with a spirit of rebellion, disregarded the law, and found Zenger to be innocent of all charges; the judge could have ordered the verdict vacated, arguing that it did not agree with the facts of the case. But Cosby reluctantly decided not to pursue the fight, knowing that his own political future was already tenuous.

Ironically, Hamilton believed that people *should* be arrested for seditious libel if they wrote falsehoods or against a "good" government. In the Zenger defense, Hamilton saw a way of attacking what he believed to be a corrupt government—and therefore one with no rights to charge its citizens with seditious libel.

Even with Hamilton's brilliant closing argument, even with a verdict of not guilty, the Zenger case was not adopted as legal precedent—it would be more than seven decades before truth would be a defense against libel. But it did serve to awaken the colonies' conscience to the power a jury might have, and, more importantly, the necessity for an unrestrained press.

Liberty Within The Bounds of Law

Andrew Bradford, William Bradford's son, had been another of the most vigorous supporters of the libertarian concept of the press. However, his words in defense of liberty of the press have been muted by his hatred of Hamilton (whom Bradford believed was responsible for his earlier imprisonment) and his rivalry with Benjamin Franklin who was revered by both the people and the colonial governments. Bradford had established the *American Weekly Mercury* in Philadelphia in 1719. Shortly after that, the colonial government ordered Bradford not to print anything about the government without first receiving permission. For transgressions, he was censured twice and imprisoned once. Bradford was fiercely independent, but believed that although the press must be free of government control, it must still, as a part of the society that governs it, be responsive to the needs and sensibilities of its citizens. On April 25, 1734, "Sentiments on the Liberty of the Press," an anonymously-attributed article– essay, probably written by Bradford, appeared in the *American Weekly Mercury* of Philadelphia. It is one of the most eloquent pleas for a freedom of the press within the bounds of law—a much narrower view than that of James Alexander. And, it is an argument that Alexander and Hamilton were familiar with when they planned their defense of Zenger:

In this as in all other Cases where the Subject of Liberty, is treated, we must carefully distinguish, between Liberty and Licentiousness . . .

The Caprice and Fury of a Mob undisciplined and under no Restraints from Law, may be as pernicious as the uncontrolable Edicts of an absolute Tyrant, —The Extremes that separate Liberty from License, are closer than most Men imagine; they ought therefore to be carefully distinguished.

By the Liberty of the Press then, I am far from understanding, (as I hope every Englishman is) a treasonable License, of calling into Question his most Sacred Majesty's undoubted Title, to the Realm of Great-Britain, or any of his Dominions thereunto belonging. Nor do I think that his Conduct in private or public Life ought to be arraigned. That the King can do no wrong is a Maxim (a just Maxim too) in the English Law. His Ministers indeed are accountable to the Public for their Male Administration, and have frequently felt the Resentment of a good natured but an injured People.

Nor, by the Liberty of the Press, do I mean that unwarrantable License, which some People of much Fire, but little judgment have taken of endeavouring to subvert the Fundamental Points of Religion or Morality. Religion ought to be treated with Veneration, and without Morality whose Doctrines true Religion always recommends and strengthens, Societies could not subsist. I have been astonished to hear some Men, who make high Pretences to Wit and Learning advance these and the like Stupidities; that Virtue and Vice are mere Words: That in the Nature of things there is no Distinction between the one and the other, that all Mankind are Villains; That what we call beautiful and generous in Life proceeds only from the sordid Motives of Pride or Self Interest; that Patriotism is a Word without Meaning, and Public Virtue a thing to be laughed at. I must confess I don't know any Business such unnatural Wretches have in Society, to whom by their own avowed Principles, they publicly disclaim all manner of Relation . . .

Nor, by the Liberty of the Press do I understand a License of traducing the Conduct of those Gentlemen who are appointed our Lawful Governors: When they behave themselves well, they ought to be treated with all the Respect and Gratitude that's due from an obliged People; should they behave themselves ill, their Measures are to be remonstrated against in Terms of Decency, and Moderation not of Fury or Scurrility . . .

We have a Governour, who hath deservedly gained the Hearts of the People under his Care; to whom he hath been always willing to Grant any Favours, proper for them to ask.

But, should it please God, as a Punishment for our Sins, to visit us with a Governor, so far intoxicated with Pride and Ambition, as to endeavour to set himself above the Laws, and affect an independent Sway: Should he remove from Places of the highest Trust those Persons who had discharged them with unquestioned Abilities and Integrity, in Order to promote the immediate Creatures of his own Will; should he presume to erect Arbitrary Courts, unknown to an English Constitution, and to Stop or Poison the streams of Justice. In such a Case, I doubt not in the least, but there would be found Men of Spirit, and Honesty enough, to let that Governor know that Such a Conduct did not become him.

Nor, under the Colour of this Liberty, ought such Doctrines to be published, as tend to lessen or take away, that sacred Veneration, which is due to the upright Dispensers of the Laws. Nor, should the Press be made use of as an Engine, to insult Personal Deformities, Frailities or Misfortunes, much less to expose the secrets of Families. This is mean, and unbecoming a Writer. And indeed all such irregular Sallies are sufficiently provided against by the Laws in being.

But by the Freedom of the Press, I mean a Liberty, within the Bounds of Law, for any Man to communicate to the Public his Sentiments on the Important Points of Religion and Government; of proposing any Laws, which he apprehends may be for the Good of his Country, and of applying for the Repeal of such, as he Judges pernicious. I mean a Liberty of detecting the wicked and destructive Measures of certain Politicians; of dragging Villainy out of its obscure lurking Holes, and exposing it in its full Deformity to open Day; of attacking Wickedness in high Places, of disentangling the intricate Folds of a wicked and corrupt Administration, and pleading freely for a Redress of Grievances: I mean a Liberty of examining the great Articles of our Faith, by the Lights of Scripture and Reason, a Privilege derived to us in its fullest Latitude, from our most excellent Charter.

This is the Liberty of the Press, the great Palladium of all our other Liberties, which I hope the good People of this Province, will forever enjoy; and that every Pennsylvanian, will resent with Scorn and Indignation, the least Attempt to weaken or subvert it. For, it may be demonstrated from numerous Instances in History, that whenever this inestimable Jewel was lost, Slavery, Desolation and Ruin ensued . . .

Cato's, Alexander's, and Bradford's arguments for a freedom that allows publication of many views and the rejection of a despotic or evil governor, while also recognizing the sovereignty of the State, were popular though not highly influential. The people still feared the chaos that could result from the mass distribution of information; the State still held the control, exercising it frequently to suppress non-licensed publication. After having determined in 1747 that it was the "undoubted Right of the People of this Colony to know the Proceedings of their Representatives", in 1753, ordered the arrest of Hugh Gaine, editor/printer of *The New York Mercury*. Gaine's offense? He published, without permission, proceedings of the Assembly. Humbling himself before the Assembly, Gaine was allowed to avoid jail—after being formally censured and paying court costs.

An Excuse for Suppression

In England, wars were the excuse for the government to argue for the suppression of information, claiming the right of a State for self-preservation. Under George II (1683–1760, reign 1727–1760), England was still at war with its neighbors and other nations in Europe, and still had severe restrictions against Nonconformists and Jews. In 1745–1746, England had brutally crushed a revolution launched in Scotland by Prince Charles Edward, grandson of James II and son of James Stuart. The Monarchy broke the power of the highland chieftains and forbade clans or tartans. France had provided Prince Charles, a Scot, with ships and supplies; after his defeat, he escaped to France.

In 1753, on the eve of what would be the Seven Years War, many writers, often without adequate information, attacked numerous government decisions, many of which involved the conduct of England's foreign policies. William Livingston pleaded for the Press to show restraint, to be responsible, for the lack of responsibility could challenge the freedom of press itself. In *Of the Use, Abuse, and Liberty of the Press*, Livingston wrote:

No nation in Europe is more jealous of the *Liberty of the Press* than the *English*, nor is there a people, among whom it is so grossly abused. With us, the most unbound licentiousness prevails. We are so besotted with the love of liberty, that running into extremes [sic] we even tolerate those things which naturally lead to its subversion. And what is still more surprising, an author justly chargeable with principles destructive of our

Constitution, with doctrines the most abject and slavish, may proceed even with inveterate malice to vilify, burlesque, and deny our great immunities and privileges, and yet shall be suffered to justify himself under the unrestrainable rights of the press. An absurdity grossly stupid and mischevous. What! sap the Constitution, disturb the public tranquility, and ruin the State, and yet plead a right to such liberty derived from the law of the State! The *Liberty of the Press*, like civil liberty, is talked of by the many, and understood but by few; the latter is taken by multitudes, for an irrestrainable license of acting at pleasure; and equal unrestraint in writing is often argued from the former, but both are fake and equally dangerous to our Constitution. Civil liberty is built upon a surrender of so much of our natural liberty as is necessary for the good ends of government; and the liberty of the press is always to be restricted from becoming a prejudice to the public weal. The design of entering into a state of society is to promote and secure the happiness of its individuals. Whatever tends to this end is politically lawful, and no State can permit any practice detrimental to the public tranquility, but in direct opposition to its fundamental principles. Agreeable to this doctrine, I lay it down as a rule that when the Press is prejudicial to the public weal, it is abused: and that the prohibition of printing any thing not repugnant to the prosperity of the State is an unjustifiable and tyrannical usurpation.

The growing tension between England and France escalated into war in 1754, and was fought first on the North American continent, then spread throughout the European continent, into Western Africa, and the British empire in India. The Seven Years War, known in North America as the French and Indian War, left England, once decimated by internal problems, as the world trade leader— and also strengthened its position on the control of free expression in order to preserve the State and public order.

Attacks and Counter-attacks

In England, Dr. Samuel Johnson (1709–1784)—poet, journalist, writer, and editor of the dictionary that became the standard reference for several decades— spoke for a majority of American colonials and English citizens in his argument for the necessity of press restrictions. According to Johnson (quoted by James Boswell, his biographer):

Every society has a right to preserve publick peace and order, and therefore has a good right to prohibit the propagation of opinions which have a dangerous tendency. To say the *magistrate* has this right, is an inadequate word: it is the *society* for which the magistrate is agent. He may be morally or theologically wrong in restraining the propogation of opinions which he thinks dangerous, but he is politically right . . . Everyman has a right to liberty of conscience, and with that the magistrate can not interfere. People confound liberty of thinking with liberty of talking; nay, with liberty of preaching. Every man has a physical right to think as he pleases; for it can not be discovered how he thinks. He has not a moral right, for he ought to inform himself, and think justly. But . . . no matter of a society has a right to teach any doctrine contrary to what the society holds to be true. The magistrate, I think, may be wrong in what he thinks: but while he thinks himself right, he may and ought to enforce what he thinks . . . The only method by which religious truth can be established is by martyrdom. The magistrate has a right to enforce what he thinks; and he who is conscious of the truth has a right suffer. I am afraid there is no other way of ascertaining the truth, but by persecution on the one hand and enduring it on the other . . . If mankind can not defend their own way of thinking, I can not defend it.

A Number for the People

John Wilkes (1727–1797) also accepted the premise that the greater good of society must take precedence over other matters, but he believed that the greater good would be served by a completely unrestrained press that had the audacity to attack, even if wrong. Because of this belief, he almost became a martyr to press freedom.

Wilkes was elected to Parliament in 1757—and expelled more times than any other member in its history. In 1762, he and Charles Churchill founded *The North Briton*, a general circulation newspaper, but one which Wilkes would use to launch his attacks upon the prime minister. In Issue No. 45, he attacked not only two of King George III's closest advisors, but the king himself, calling them "untruthful" for statements made about, and concessions to, the peace of 1763 in which England gave up large chunks of land it had taken in the Seven Years War. Wilkes was arrested for seditious libel; between one hundred and two hundred other persons were arrested on a variety of charges, most being sedition. Wilkes successfully argued that as a member of Parliament he was given the rights of free speech, and not subject to the provisions of the Court's general warrant; eventually, most of the charges against the others were dropped—after the Crown had sufficiently alerted the public that it would tolerate no further dissent.

The following year, on publication of his poem, "An Essay on Women," he was arrested on charges of obscene libel. At that time, Parliament had voted that members charged with seditious libel did not have the protection of Parliament. Wilkes fled to France, and was expelled from the House and convicted of libel. Throughout England, the number 45 became a symbol for freedom of the press, and for the rights of the free English to express their views against all opposition.

Wilkes returned to England in 1768, was re-elected to Parliament, turned himself in to the authorities, and served a two year prison sentence for criminal libel; while in prison, he was once again expelled from Parliament. Twice more he was re-elected, twice more expelled. On the third re-election, his opponent was seated. Finally, after four expulsions—all based upon his writings—Wilkes was finally seated in 1774, the year he was also elected Lord Mayor of London. Wilkes remained in Parliament through 1790, and was one of the more vocal supporters of American independence.

A Tax Not Accepted

In 1711, Queen Anne's government had enacted the Stamp Act as a means not only to raise revenue, but also to eliminate many newspapers. Now, in 1765, the government of King George III enacted England's second Stamp Act. This one, however, was primarily to raise revenue following the Seven Years War that left England nearly bankrupt, but having expanded its empire in North America. The Stamp Act of 1765 required the payment of taxes on paper used for legal documents and in printing. Although most editors in England paid the special tax, American colonials did not. Sam Adams had said that local stamp taxes in Massachusetts and New York had been determined by people elected in those colonies. The English tax, said Adams, was discriminatory and levied by persons who lived an ocean away, and was directed against a people not even represented in Parliament.

The tax further cut at an important concept of Libertarian philosophy; the media should survive or fail from an economic base—revenue from advertising and circulation—not from a restrictive governmental action. The stamp tax had threatened not only the editorial base of free expression, but also the always tenuous economic base.

By now, a small segment of colonists had begun protesting many of England's laws and the lack of colonial representation. Many newspapers suspended publication; others were still published, but without the mastheads—and the names of the editors; others were printed, without the stamp, but noted that because of mobs which had blocked entrance to governmental areas where stamps were being sold, none could be obtained. A few editors who tried to pay the tax found that the large mobs of dissidents could keep people out of buildings as easily as it could destroy a newspaper's building and press. Throughout the colonies, the cry of "No taxation without representation" was heard.

The following year, Parliament repealed the tax as unenforceable. But, the Americans had learned two important lessons—that taxation could be used to force compliance to governmental authority; *and*, an oppressed group, when united, has the strength to modify or overturn oppressive laws.

Chapter 11

The Libertarian Base for Revolution

From the philosophies developed by Milton and Locke, seven major principles of libertarianism emerged—1) mankind is a rational animal; 2) as a rational animal, mankind is governed by truth and by the laws of nature; 3) every individual has certain inalienable rights; 4) there must be an "open marketplace of ideas" in which all ideas could compete openly and fairly; 5) there is a "self-righting process"—as long as truth is in the marketplace, the people will eventually recognize it, although they might first be deceived by false doctrine and make initial decisions that could be of harm to them; 6) government exists to further the needs of the individual; and 7) and all media should be free to compete not with government but with themselves in an economic enterprise.

By the mid-eighteenth century, the libertarian philosophy became the foundation for media development in the American colonies. The basic functions of the media, argued the libertarians, must be to inform and to entertain. To carry out these functions, the media must be given a wide latitude to search for and present truth as they saw it. Because truth can be an elusive entity, no one—neither individual, nor the State—has the right to prevent any information from reaching the public, which will make the ultimate decisions as to how information affects their lives.

To the libertarian view established by Milton, Spinoza, and Locke, Voltaire, Rousseau, Hume, and Blackstone added their views of the relationship of mankind with the State, all of which would help unite the colonies in justifying reasons for a revolution.

Voltaire (1694-1774; born Francois-Marie Arouet) was active in his pursuit of justice against both rulers and the clergy who would deny freedom to others. Like most persons who were willing to challenge authority, he was persecuted and imprisoned for four months in the Bastille in 1718 for writing satiric verses against the regency of Louis XV; in 1746, however, he was appointed Royal Historiographer.

Voltaire amassed a fortune in business, but used much of it to fight for the rights of mankind and for a free and unbounded press, defending numerous persons accused of heresy and sedition, and those who were denied their civil liberties—liberties that Voltaire said could not be denied by any man.

The concept of a social contract between ruler and those being ruled has existed in political theory probably as long as there have been people. Niccholo

Machiavelli (1469-1527) had believed that the security of the ruler, and thus the security of the State, was paramount, and that a ruler could use any means possible to preserve the State. However, Machiavelli also recognized a certain contract between ruler and the ones being ruled. In *The Prince*, a political handbook for rulers, Machiavelli wrote:

> A principality is created either by the people or by the nobles, accordingly as one or another of them has the opportunity; for the nobles, seeing they cannot withstand the people, begin to cry up the reputation of one of themselves, and they make him a prince, so that under his shadow they can give vent to their ambitions. The people, finding they cannot resist the nobles, also cry up the reputation of one of themselves, and make him a prince so as to be defended by his authority. He who obtains sovereignty by the assistance of the nobles maintains himself with more difficulty than he who comes to it by the aid of the people, because the former finds himself with the many around him who consider themselves his equals, and because of this he can neither rule nor manage them to his liking. But he who reaches sovereignty by popular favor finds himself alone, and has none around him, or few, who are not prepared to obey him.

In *Leviathan*, one of the greatest philosophical documents, English philosopher Thomas Hobbes (1588-1679) gave one of the most brilliant arguments in modern philosophy for the existence of a strong State, under the direction of a strong ruler:

> The obligation of subjects to the sovereign is understood to last as long, and no longer, than the power lasteth by which he is able to protect them. For the right men have by nature to protect themselves, when none else can protect them can by no covenant be relinquished.
>
> Fear and liberty are consistent: as when a man throweth his goods into the sea for fear the ship would sink, he doth it nevertheless very willingly, and may refuse to do it if he will; it is therefore the action of one that was free. So a man sometimes pays his debt, only for fear of imprisonment which, because no body hindered him from detaining, was the action of a man at liberty. And generally, all actions which men do in Commonwealths, for fear of the law, are actions which the doers had the liberty to omit.

Jean Jacques Rousseau (1712-1778), a French Swiss, extended the concepts of a social contract further. According to Rousseau, mankind establishes with the State a Social Contract that requires it to give up certain liberties in order to gain civil and moral liberty, but the State should exist only within the parameters mankind determines for its existence. *The Social Contract* (1762) infuriated the monarchies of most European countries, but it wasn't until Rousseau challenged the concept of God that a warrant was issued for his arrest in 1762. He was forced to flee to Motiers, then Prussia and England, returning to France in 1767 where he wandered around for three years, disguised by an assumed name. In

1770, with the threat of imprisonment past, he again identified himself by his own name.

During his wanderings around Europe, avoiding imprisonment yet seeking to lead a simple life, Rousseau was invited to England by David Hume (1711-1776) who became his benefactor for about a year. Hume, a brilliant philosopher-historian, spoke out forcefully for the libertarian concepts of allowing mankind the right to seek out the facts, then make a rational decision based upon those facts. Hume argued that only a free and unrestricted press could help mankind in its search for truth:

> Since . . . the liberty of the press is so essential to the support of our . . . government, this sufficiently decides . . . whether this liberty be advantageous or prejudicial, there being nothing of greater importance in every State than the preservation of the ancient government, especially if it be a free one. But I would fain go a step further and assert that such a liberty is attended with so few inconveniences that it may be claimed as the common right of mankind and ought to be indulged them almost in every government except the ecclesiastical, to which, indeed, it would be fatal. We need not dread from this liberty any such ill consequences as followed from the harrangues of the popular demogogues of Athens and tribunes of Rome. A man reads a book or pamphlet alone and cooly. There is none present from whom he can catch the passion by contagion. He is not hurried away by the force and energy of action. And should he be wrought up to never so seditious a humor, there is no violent resolution presented to him by which he can immediately vent his passion. The liberty of the press, therefore, however abused, can scarce ever excite popular tumults or rebellion. And as to those murmurs or secret discontents it may occasion, it is better they should get vent in words, that they may come to the knowledge of the magistrate before it be too late, in order to his providing a remedy against them. Mankind, it is true, have always a greater propension to believe what is said to the disadvantage of their governors than the contrary; but this inclination is inseparable from them whether they have liberty or not. A whisper may fly as quick and be as pernicious as a pamphlet. Nay, it will be more pernicious where men are not accustomed to think freely or distinguish betwixt truth and falsehood.
>
> It has also been found, as the experience of mankind increases, that the people are no such dangerous monsters as they have been represented, and that it is in every respect better to guide them like rational creatures than to lead or drive them like brute beasts . . . It is to be hoped that men, being every day more accustomed to the free discussion of public affairs, will improve in their judgment of them and be with greater difficulty seduced by every idle rumor and popular clamor.

At the time that many American colonials were uniting against the Stamp Act, Sir William Blackstone (1723-1780) was writing about English law. His

Commentaries, published between 1765 and 1769, and based upon his lectures as a professor of law at Oxford University, became the first major analysis and interpretation of English law, and served as a text in law schools for almost a century. Blackstone's commentaries about the law also helped further some libertarian concepts of the press.

In his first volume, published in 1765, Blackstone outlined the absolute and relative rights of mankind. According to Blackstone, there are certain relative rights that are determined by the needs of society; other rights, however, are absolute—inviolable—and should be enjoyed by all persons, no matter what society they are living in, no matter what historical age. Upon the base established by Locke, Blackstone noted that "the principal aim of society is to protect individuals in the enjoyment of those absolute rights, which are vested in them by the immutable laws of nature." Elaborating, Blackstone argued:

> The absolute rights of man, considered as a free agent, endowed with discernment to know good from evil, and with power of choosing those measures which appear to him to be most desirable, are usually summed up in one general appellation, and denominated the natural liberty of mankind. This natural liberty consists properly in a power of acting as one thinks fit, without any restraint or control, unless by the law of nature; being a right inherent in us by birth, and one of the gifts of God to man at his creation, when he endued him with the faculty of free will. But every man, when he enters into society, gives up a part of his natural liberty, as the price of so valuable a purchase; and, in consideration of receiving the advantages of mutual commerce, obliges himself to conform to those laws, which the community has thought proper to establish. And this species of legal obedience and conformity is infinitely more desirable than that wild and savage liberty which is sacrificed to obtain it . . .
>
> No man, that considers a moment, would wish to retain the absolute and uncontrolled power of doing whatever he pleases: the consequence of which is, that every other man would also have the same power; and then there would be no security to individuals in any of the enjoyments of life. Political, therefore, or civil liberty, which is that of a member of society, is no other than natural liberty so far restrained by human laws (and no farther) as is necessary and expedient for the general advantage of the public. Hence we may collect that the law, which restrains a man from doing mischief to his fellow-citizens, though it diminishes the natural, inreases the civil liberty of mankind; but that every wanton and causeless restraint of the will of the subject, whether practiced by a monarch, a nobility, or a popular assembly, is a degree of tyranny: nay, that even laws themselves, whether made with or without our consent, if they regulate and constrain our conduct in matters of mere indifference, without any good end in view, are regulations destructive of liberty; whereas, if any public advantage can arise from observing such precepts, the control of our private inclinations, in one or two particular points, will conduce to preserve our general freedom in others of more importance; by supporting that state of society, which alone can secure our independence . . .

Laws, when prudently framed, are by no means subversive, but rather introductive of liberty; for as John Locke has well observed, where there is no law there is no freedom . . . [The] spirit of liberty is so deeply implanted in our constitution, and rooted even in our very soil, that a slave or negro, the moment he lands in England, falls under the protection of the laws, and so far becomes a freeman; though the master's right to his service may *possibly* still continue . . .

At some times we have seen the [the rights] depressed by overbearing and tyrannical princes; at others so luxuriant as even to tend to anarchy, a worse state than tyranny itself, as any government is better than none at all. But the vigor of our free constitution has always delivered the nation from these embarrassments: and, as soon as the convulsions consequent on the struggle have been over, the balance of our rights and liberties has settled to its proper level.

In the third volume of *Commentaries*, published in 1767, Blackstone discussed the issues of freedom of the press, concluding that a press is only free when there is an absence of prior restraint.

The liberty of the press is indeed essential to the nature of a free state but this consists in laying no *previous* restraints upon publication, and not in freedom from censure for criminal matter when published. Every freeman has an undoubted right to lay what sentiments he pleases before the public; to forbid this, is to destroy the freedom of the press; but if he publishes what is improper, mischievious, or illegal, he must take the consequences of his own temerity.

Blackstone's commentaries were attacked by legal scholars for being "superficial" and for several errors of historical and legal fact. But, as a foundation for the understanding of the nature of English law as well as for its sheer beauty of language the *Commentaries* are unsurpassed.

The liberty of the press is that a man may print what he pleases without a licensor . . . subject to the consequences of law; so long as it remains so, the liberty of the press is not restrained. [However], the 'licentiousness' of the press is a 'Pandora's' box, the source of every evil.

—Lord Mansfield

Jeremy Bentham (1748-1832), who would become one of the great libertarian philosophers, used Blackstone's commentaries as the foundation for his first important work, *A Fragment on Government* (1776). Bentham attacked Blackstone for an "antipathy to reform," arguing that freedom of expression must go beyond Blackstone's concept of the absence of prior restraint as the criterion for freedom of expression. Benthan argued that all persons must also be able to "communicate their sentiments, concert their plans, and practice every mode of opposition short of actual revolt, before the executive power can be legally justified in disturbing them."

In the American colonies, several newspaper articles about freedom of expression kept the libertarian philosophy at the forefront of what would lead to a revolution, the Radicals knowing that by fusing the arguments about inherent rights with those of the economic survival of the merchants, it was possible to create at least some doubt in the minds of many about England's ability to govern a people an ocean away. In 1766, the year that England repealed the Stamp Tax, William Bollan, advocate-general of Massachusetts, published *The Freedom of Speech and Writing Upon Public Affairs, Considered, With an Historical View*. The book was a well written and researched definitive history of libertarian thought, and presented a coherent argument both for the absence of prior restraint and freedom of expression, but also for the concepts that truth must be a defense to libel, that attacks upon the government and its politicians should be tolereated if truth of the accusations could be proven.

Nevertheless, most American colonists, although upset with some aspects of British rule, were still loyal to the crown, believing that the problems were not inherent in the monarchy, but in the monarch. As the Radicals began systematic campaigns to overthrow British rule, John Dickinson, a lawyer-farmer, contributed "Letters From a Farmer in Pennsylvania," a series of columns published in the *Pennsylvania Chronicle*, 1767-1768. In these short essays, Dickinson outlined problems with England, but argued that in a libertarian society, the only viable solution to problems with government must be in the "free marketplace of ideas," not in revolution—at least not until every possible means was tried.

The Massachusetts House of Representatives, under the leadership of Sam Adams, had blocked several attempts by the governor to bring charges against persons accused of seditious libel. Then, in 1768, it approved a resolution of a free press:

> The Liberty of the Press is a great Bulwark of the Liberty of the People: It is, therefore, the incumbent duty of those who are constituted the Guardians of the People's Rights to defend and maintain it.

By the end of the Revolutionary War, nine of the eleven states that had constitutions would also have freedom of the press clauses, most of them using the "bulwark of liberty" phrase, probably first popularized by Cato a century earlier.

Chapter 12

The Seeds of Revolution

Mankind, in its collective conscience, is not a revolutionary, nor are more than handfuls of people willing to speak out against social injustice, against the "wrongs" of their various societies, or to lead revolts. To accept rather than challenge, to yield rather than attack, has been a trait not only of Western civilization but of all civilization. In 1765, when the Stamp Act was passed, there were few radicals in the American colonies, and their refusal to accept the tax was more a matter of fear of retaliation by a few radicals than fear of the Crown, an ocean away. The preservation of the State and the protection given by the State were greater forces than the overthrow of a government. But, it would be a radical who would be the cause of a newer energy. Even a decade later, after the Battles of Lexington and Concord on the eve of the Declaration of Independence, the majority of American colonials were Whigs or Tories. The preservation of the State and the protection given by the State were greater forces than the overthrow of a government.

It was now 1769, and with the writings of Milton, Spinoza, Locke, Rousseau, Hume, Voltaire, and Blackstone, a few colonists spoke out on a freedom of the press issue as great to the colonies as was the John Wilkes case in England only five years before; the case would help mold colonial opinion against the English and, perhaps, become one of the major reasons why revolution became inevitable.

The man who became known as "America's John Wilkes" was Alexander McDougall, a leader of the Sons of Liberty, a radical organization dedicated to the overthrow of the bonds to England. McDougall had written a letter-essay protesting the actions of the New York Assembly. Several hundred flyers were distributed, bringing about not only public discussion of the governor's actions, but a reward, issued by the governor's office, at the request of the Assembly, for information leading to the arrest of the person who signed the flyer, "A Son of Liberty." An employee of the printer turned in his boss and collected the reward. The printer was James Parker, former editor of the *Independent Reflector*, a major libertarian newspaper, who was arrested several times on charges of seditious libel. Threatened with imprisonment, loss of his shop, and position as comptroller of the Post Office, Parker finally revealed the name of the author. McDougall was arrested and imprisoned for almost three months when he refused to pay an excessive bail. Parker then used his newspaper, *The New-York Gazette; or, The Post-Boy*, as a forum to attack the suppression of ideas and call for McDougall's release. What the *Post-Boy* and mobs of supporters could not do was done by death; when Parker, the state's key witness, died before the trial, the charges were dropped.

By the end of 1770, McDougall was again imprisoned. According to court documents, he was threatened with torture when he refused to plead guilty or not guilty. When he wrote out his reasons why he chose not to plead, thus not allowing trial to begin, the state filed additional libel charges on McDougall's statement. Finally, at the end of the legislative session, he was released from custody, having awakened New England to one of the more serious threats to their freedom. (During the Revolutionary War, he would become a major general; after the war, a prosperous banker and civic leader.)

England revered Cato, Blackstone, and Locke, but America took their words and made them speak for the rights of the colonists, the radical journalists citing section after section about the universal rights of mankind. In 1774, the First Continental Congress outlined five rights of mankind, including the right for a nation to have a free and unemcumbered press. In "A Summary View of the Rights of Mankind" (1774), Thomas Jefferson argued that just because the colonies were settled by people from England, it did not give England any rights over the colonies. Few on either side of the Atlantic accepted Jefferson's views—nor were they ready to eliminate "ancient or future aristocracy" from their lives. After all, the problem was not the system, they believed, but in the people who controlled the system. Revolution was still a last resort to gain those rights.

The Necessity of Revolt

In 1765, when the Stamp Act was passed, there were few radicals in the American colonies. Even a decade later, after the Battles of Lexington and Concord on the eve of the Declaration of Independence, the majority of American colonials were Whigs or Tories. The preservation of the State and the protection given by the State were greater forces than the overthrow of a government.

The radical press, a press forged by political conviction, would force the nation to accept the necessity for revolt. With the development of the radical American newspaper, a collective consciousness for separation evolved. In the mid-eighteenth century, there were only twelve newspapers in the colonies; by 1775, there were forty-eight, a few of them radical. Benjamin Edes and John Gill, editors of the *Boston Gazette*, Isaiah Thomas, editor of *The Massachusetts Spy*, and many other journalists would bring their voices, their newspapers, to the cutting edge of revolution, giving the people the knowledge that there were problems throughout the colonies, not just in isolated areas. Thus, it was not too unusual that Sam Adams and his Boston Tea Party organized at the *Boston Gazette* for their protest of the Stamp Act. During the decade following the Stamp Act, Adams would use newspapers and pamphlets to inform and try to radicalize a population that had felt more comfortable with a known government and with laws it clearly understood.

Throughout history, persons crying for freedom of speech and of the press have often denied those same rights to those who did not agree with their political, social, or religious philosophies. While believing in the right of mankind to live free of governmental restraint, and convinced that true freedom rests upon freedom of speech and of the press, the American Radicals, like radicals everywhere, believed that the "righteousness" of their beliefs must eventually triumph over the "wrongfulness"—perhaps even "harmfulness"—of other views, even if it meant resorting to suppression and violence. In the name of freedom, the Radicals initiated a campaign of terror. Quickly, the colonies learned that Radical "justice" was not much different than the excesses of British justice. The Radicals—still a minority in the American colonies—burned newspapers, and destroyed presses and printing plants of Tories, driving most out of business.

Suppression by Libertarians

In New York, the Sons of Liberty, led by Alexander McDougall, smashed several Tory presses. In Boston, in 1770, the radicals had mobbed John Mein, editor of the *Boston Chronicle*, a Tory newspaper. The *Boston Evening Post* of Thomas Fleet was eventually forced to suspend operations in 1775. The *Boston News-Letter*, the same one that became, in 1704, the second newspaper in America, was closed in 1776 by mob action.

The editor who may have suffered the most as the Radicals prepared to break from England was James Rivington, editor of *The New York Gazeteer*. For several decades, Rivington's family was the official printer for the Church of England. Rivington had come to the colonies in 1762 to avoid financial problems, the result of having become nearly bankrupt because of gambling losses. In the colonies, he founded the first chain bookstore; in 1773, he became a newspaper editor. He was widely respected by most political factions. A Tory, he was loyal to England, a believer in the inherent rights of the monarchy. In the eyes of the world, he was a patriot; in the eyes of the Radicals, who called themselves "Patriots," Rivington was a traitor. For two years, Rivington had tried to be objective; for two years, the Radicals, shouting their epithets of freedom, tried to shut him down, mobbing him, hanging and burning him in effigy, and raiding his newspaper. Rivington reacted, viciously printing innuendo and lies about the Radicals. Ironically, Rivington believed that the government had a right to suppress publication of views contrary to its own. Thus, he understood why the Sons of Liberty, although claiming they were fighting for freedom, had to try to shut down his printing plant—it was just the nature of the irrational mankind to suppress that which could threaten.

Even with the terrorism, most colonists were still undecided about whether a revolution was necessary. Then, in January 1776, Thomas Paine (1737-1809), who had moved to the colonies from England only two years before, completed his seventy-nine page pamphlet, *Common Sense*, a brilliant, well-reasoned, but inflammatory plea of the necessity for the separation of the colonies from England. "Society in every state is a blessing," wrote Paine, "but government even in its best state is but a necessary evil, in its worst state an intolerable one." He challenged "the warmest advocate for the reconciliation to show a single advantage that this continent can reap by being connected with Great Britain . . . The authority of Great Britain over this continent is a form of government which sooner or later must have an end."

Within weeks, about 100,000 copies were sold; parts of the essay were reprinted in almost every radical newspaper; half the nation of almost two and a half million people quickly became aware of Paine's call for freedom. The fury of Paine's words, the plea for freedom, helped unify a large number of the American people, giving a cohesion of thought necessary for a social movement to begin.

In March 1776, the Radicals intensified their efforts, saturating New York with flyers:

> Sir, if you print, or suffer to be printed in your press anything against the rights and liberties of America, or in favor of our inveterate foes, the king, the Ministry, and parliament of Great Britain, death and destruction, ruin and perdition, shall be your portion.

Numerous persons, including John Adams, now argued that freedom of the press could be guaranteed only as long as the newspaper editors swore allegiance to the Radical cause.

Chapter 13

A Flowering of the Revolution

As the colonies made plans to terminate their bonds to England, Thomas Jefferson, James Madison, James Monroe, Elbridge Gerry, Patrick Henry, and many others, took the words of Cato, Locke, and Blackstone, and the doctrine of the newly-emerging Libertarian theory, and made them part of the Declaration of Independence; later, they would be a base for the Constitution and Bill of Rights.

The "self-righting process" envisioned by John Milton had argued that falsehood and evil may at first triumph, but if the audience is exposed to all the facts, truth will eventually survive. The American colonies no longer could wait for good to triumph; in Philadelphia, one hot July afternoon in 1776, the delegates decided that time was not the benefit that Milton saw, but an enemy; it would be a revolution, not reason, that would change the political structure— the delegates would pledge "our lives, our honors, and our sacred fortunes" in their move to overthrow the bonds of England.

In the Declaration of Independence, an explanation of why revolt was the only recourse for the colonies, Thomas Jefferson outlined the fundamental political philosophy that would guide what they hoped would become a new country:

> We hold these truths to be self-evident, that all men are created equal, that they are endowed by their Creator with certain unalienable Rights, that among these are Life, Liberty and the pursuit of Happiness. That to secure these rights, Governments are instituted among Men, deriving their just powers from the consent of the governed. That whenever any Form of Government becomes destructive of these ends, it is the Right of the People to alter or to abolish it, and to institute new Government, laying its foundation on such principles and organizing its powers in such form, as to them shall seem most likely to effect their Safety and Happiness.

The Words of A Soldier

During the Revolution, Thomas Paine was a soldier, but it was his words, not his rifle, that helped mold the solidarity of thought, that gave the soldier and merchant, farmer and laborer, reasons to continue the struggle. During one of the greatest crises in America's history, a time when it appeared that the merchants would not sacrifice their goods any longer, when there was little food and Washington's rag-clothed soldiers were facing winter snows, Paine's first *Crises* paper gave courage to the Revolutionary Army; its opening lines may be one of the best known of any in American journalism:

> These are the times that try men's souls. The summer soldier and the sunshine patriot will, in this crises, shrink from the service of their country, but he that stands it now deserves the love and thanks of man and woman. Tyranny, like hell, is not easily conquered; yet we have this consolation with us that, the harder the conflict, the more glorious the triumph. What we obtain too cheap, we esteem too lightly; it is dearness only that gives everything its value. Heaven knows how to put a proper price upon its goods, and it would be strange indeed if so celestial an article as freedom should not be highly rated. Britain, with an army to enforce its tyranny, has declared that she has a right (*not only to tax*) but *to bind us in all cases whatsoever*; and if being *bound in that manner* is not slavery, then is there not such a thing as slavery upon earth . . .

Washington read the essay to his troops, Revolutionary leaders read it in the streets, and every time it was read, it stirred the passions of the people, reminding them of the reasons why the Revolution must be won.

During the Revolution, the individual states passed legislation or adopted clauses to their constitutions guaranteeing freedom of the press; but, these same states also passed legislation every bit as restrictive of free speech as that passed by England. The concepts of sedition were broad, and the penalties severe. In Virginia, the penalty was a maximum five years prison sentence and £20,000 fine; by the end of the war, the fine had increased to £100,000 for any person convicted of advocating that the colonies were, in any way, dependent upon England. By 1778, the states required loyalty oaths; those who refused were given additional American taxes and denied many basic rights. Several states forced those who did not sign the loyalty oaths to move away from population centers; many Tories were imprisoned for months without even knowing what the charges were.

As the Revolution continued, the Sons of Liberty and other radical organizations continued destruction of Tory property. As Washington's armies began to show that they could match those of England, more Tories and Whigs became neutral, and more neutrals became Radicals. By the end of the war, almost all surviving American newspapers were Radical, their editors having used truth, mixed with lies, distortion, and personal invective to propagandize against the British; the newspapers were at the cutting edge of the Revolution—a place they would never again be in American history.

Chapter 14

Radicals as Statesmen

An eight year revolution that had left more than 15,000 dead—American, British, and mercenary—had also left the new country struggling to determine an adequate form of government. With a new nation, a constitution would have to be created by the same people who had only months before been revolutionaries, often in opposition as much to each other as to the British. Most Americans, still fearful of the power of a monarch, wanted a decentralized government with extremely limited powers. The farmers and businessmen, artisans and professionals, had wished to be left alone, to farm or sell their goods or services as they wished without imposition of the State upon their lives.

In a letter to a friend in 1787, Thomas Jefferson outlined American thinking:

> I am persuaded that the good sense of the people will always be found to be the best army. They may be led astray for a moment, but will soon correct themselves. The people are the only censors of their governors; and even their errors will tend to keep these to the true principles of their institution. To punish these errors too severely would be to suppress the only safeguard of the public liberty. The way to prevent these irregular interpositions of the people is to give them full information of their affairs through the channel of the public papers, and to contrive that those papers should penetrate the whole mass of the people. The basis of our government being the opinion of the people, the very first object should be to keep that right; and were it left to me to decide whether we should have a government without newspapers, or newspapers without a government, I should not hesitate a moment to prefer the latter.

Others believed that only a strong central government could maintain the security of the State, while also providing for their welfare. In a series of eighty-five newspaper articles known today as the Federalist Papers, Alexander Hamilton, John Jay, and James Madison carefully outlined the needs for a strong centralized government, and also tried to eliminate the fears that most Americans had against what could have been regarded as imposition of an authority not unlike that exercised by England. The articles first appeared in the *New York Independent Journal*, October 1787 through April 1788, and were quickly reprinted throughout the country, then published in book form; the success of the Federalist Papers eventually led to establishment of the Federalist Party—and a strong central government.

Whether or not there should be a federal "bill of rights," guaranteeing the rights of free expression would become one of the major debates in establishing the Constitution. Alexander Hamilton and the Federalists argued that the protection of human rights was already included within the proposed constitution. Thomas Jefferson, James Madison, and several others, argued that a bill of rights was a necessity.

What signifies a declaration, that the liberty of the press shall be inviolably preserved? What is the liberty of the press? Who can give it any definition which would not leave the utmost latitude for evasion? I hold it to be impracticable; and from this I infer, that its security, whatever fine declartions may be inserted in any constitution respecting it, must altogether depend on public opinion, and on the general spirit of the people and of the government.

—Alexander Hamilton

Madison proposed several sections to include the specific rights to be protected, among them freedom of religion, of speech and the press, and the right of assembly:

> The civil rights of none shall be abridged on account of religious belief or worship, nor shall any national religion be established, nor shall the full and equal rights of conscience be in any manner, or on any pretext, infringed.
>
> The people shall not be deprived or abridged of their right to speak, to write, or to publish their sentiments; and the freedom of the press, as one of the great bulwarks of liberty, shall be inviolable.
>
> The people shall not be restrained from peaceably assembling and consulting for their common good; nor from applying to the legislature by petitions, or remonstrances, for redress of their grievances . . .
>
> [Further,] no state shall violate equal rights of conscience, or the freedom of the press, or the trial by jury in criminal cases.

Jefferson argued that only with a free press could the public be informed of the activities of their government and make decisions regarding its action; education, in complementing the press, would provide the people who could provide the leadership that an enlightened government needs. One of Jefferson's strongest statements regarding the necessity for the liberty of the press had appeared in the Virginia constitution, approved shortly before the Declaration of Independence: "Whereas, Almighty God hath created the mind free; that all attempts to influence it by temporal punishments or burthens, or by civil incapacitations, tend only to begat habits of hypocrisy and meanness."

I entertain a high ideal of the utility of periodical publications, insomuch that I could heartily desire, copies of . . . magazines as well as common gazettes [newspapers], might be spread through every city, town and village in America. I consider such easy vehicles of knowledge, more happily calculated than any other, to preserve liberty, stimulate the industry and meliorate the morals of an enlightened and free people.

—George Washington

Now, in the late 1780s, Jefferson argued that if the individual states considered freedom of the press issues so important, so should the federal government. The Anti-Federalists now realized that if they could focus upon an absence of the bill of rights, they could bring about substantial changes in the constitution that could either defeat it or modify it to reflect a weak central government. But still, there were not enough strong supporters of James Madison, Thomas Jefferson, Parick Henry, Elbridge Gerry, George Mason, and many others. The federal Constitutional Convention rejected a bill of rights, forcing the public to demand its inclusion when it heard about the proposed constitution. The memory of the persecutions of "heretics," the suppression of speech and writing by formal licensing and censorship, the John Peter Zenger trial, the Stamp Act, and the distasteful English rule remained in the minds of many, memories stirred up by the press which had a very personal reason to see a definitive bill of rights to protect freedom of speech and of the press. After considerable debate, the revised bill of rights was added to the Constitution on December 15, 1791, four years after the Constitution was ratified.

The First Amendment, not designed to be any more important than any other amendemnt, guaranteed:

Congress shall make no law respecting the establishment of religion, or prohibiting the free exercise thereof; or abridging the freedom of speech, or of the press; or the right of the people peaceably to assemble, and to petition the Government for a redress of grievances.

During the remainder of the life of the country, the First Amendment would be given myriad interpretations, creating philosophical difficulties for the courts and the people. Nevertheless, the country had a constitution, with a guarantee for freedom of speech and of the press. How it chose to use that guarantee left a "dark age" in America.

Chapter 15

A Dark Age

For the seven years of the Revolution, Benjamin Edes and John Gill through the *Boston Gazette*, Isaiah Thomas of the *Massachusetts Spy*, pamphleteer Thomas Paine, and many other journalists, carried the message of Revolution. For most of the seven years of the Revolution, almost all newspapers accepted their role to keep the Revolution alive. But now after the Revolution, with the creation of a new government, and the election of a president, the newspapers continued to attack authority or conflicting views, aligning themselves with either the Federalist party (George Washington, John Adams, Alexander Hamilton)—which had largely opposed the establishment of a separate Bill of Rights; or the Anti-Federalist (Republican) party (Thomas Jefferson, and James Madison).

Just as all revolutions bring about both vacillation and an abuse of authority as the new nation tries to determine its own parameters, and just as the post-revolutionary era of any nation includes a "Dark Ages," America had its "Dark Ages", a time when the governments of the thirteen states brought arrests of many persons for violating the "public peace"—and numerous editors and printers increased their attacks upon public officials.

To support their views, the journalists quoted the words of Junius Wilkes. Near the end of the Revolution, Wilkes had argued that public officials were completely accountable to the public, that because individuals choose to become public officials they accepted a greater degree of accountability, and that the public's right to learn about the activities of all facets of their government is far greater than defamation of a public official.

However, the propagandistic techniques of a revolution were no longer appropriate to a nation. During the eight years that George Washington was president, 1789-1797, he was unmercifully attacked by much of the nation's press which, having been socialized into believing that by attacking government and social injustice, believed it was leading the American people towards greater liberty. Given the First Amendment to the Constitution, the press was now testing that freedom. All governmental decisions were open for attack; all attacks were fair; all politicians fair game. For eight years, Washington, who had been an advocate of press freedom, took these attacks, many of them brutal and vicious, then upon his retirement in 1797 swore not to read newspapers again; he said that he was tired of being "buffeted in the public prints by a set of infamous scribblers."

*Allow your opponent to say what he thinks reasonable, and
combat him only with the weapons of reason. Have no
anxiety for the practical interests of humanity—these are
never imperiled in a purely speculative dispute. Such a
dispute serves merely to disclose the antinomy of reason,
which, as it has its source in the nature of reason, ought
to be thoroughly investigated. Reason is benefited by the
examination of a subject on both sides, and its judgments
are corrected by being limited. It is not the matter that
may give occasion to dispute, but the manner. For it is
perfectly permissible to employ, in the presence of reason,
the language of a firmly-rooted faith, even after we have
been obliged to renounce all pretensions to knowledge.
What is to be done to provide against the danger which seems
in the present case to menace the best interests of humanity?
The course to be pursued in reference to this subject is a perfectly plain and natural one. Let each thinker pursue his own
path; if he shows talent, if he gives evidence of profound
thought, in one word, if he shows that he possesses the power
of reasoning—reason is always the gainer. If you have recourse
to other means, if you attempt to coerce reason, if you raise
the cry of treason to humanity, if you excite the feelings of
the crowd, which can neither understand nor sympathize with
such subtle speculations—you will only make yourselves
ridiculous. For the question does not concern the advantage
or disadvantage which we are expected to reap from such inquiries; the question is merely how far reason can advance
in the field of speculation, apart from all kinds of interest,
and whether we may depend upon the exertions of speculative reason, or must renounce all reliance on it . . .
It is absurd to expect to be enlightened by Reason, and at the
same time to prescribe to her what side of the question she
must adopt. Moreover, reason is sufficiently held in check
by its own power, the limits imposed on it by its own nature
are sufficient; it is unnecessary for you to place over it additional guards, as if its power were dangerous to the constitution of the intellectual state . . .*

—Immanuel Kant, *The Critique of Pure Reason (1781)*

John Adams, Washington's vice-president, was now president, and experienced the same political attacks. Like Washington, Adams was a Federalist; however, Thomas Jefferson, his vice-president was a Republican, an Anti-Federalist.* The Federalists were politically allied with England, and were trying to work out a treaty to bring an end to all hostilities between the two countries; the Republicans were allied with France, the Colonies' ally during the Revolution. England and France were at war once again, and France was hostile to the American overtures to England. France demanded loans from America just to negotiate. This was a condition that the American administration would not tolerate. The Republican press launched vicious attacks upon Adams, secure in its belief that a constitutionally-given guarantee of freedom of the press protected its right to attack with impunity. Adams and the Federalists didn't think so, claiming that the actions of the opposition were destroying anything that the government was trying to do to assure peace.

The leaders of the American Revolution had looked to the libertarian thinkers to give them a philosophy for the revolution. It is the nature of those *out* of power to cite libertarian concepts to justify an attack on government; it is the nature of those *in* power to cite authoritarian concepts as reason to protect the people form insurrection and destruction of the State. It was no different in 1798 than in 1776. But now, the government argued that continual investigation into, and sniping at, a fragile government could cause its collapse at a time when building the nation, not its destruction, was needed. It would be an argument used by all young governments at all times in history. And, in America, there had been several instances in which local and state governments had caused the arrest of persons who had spoken out against them.

Alien and Sedition Laws

Against strong opposition, the Federalist majority in the House of Representatives passed a series of acts known as the Alien and Sedition Laws; the acts were signed into law by John Adams who had been a strong supporter of truth being permitted as a defense to libel. The alien and naturalization acts extended the waiting time for citizenship from five to fourteen years, and provided for the deportation of any alien who spoke out against the country. The Sedition Act stated that:

> . . . if any person shall write, print, utter or publish, or shall cause to procure to be written, printed, or uttered or published, or shall knowingly and willingly assist or aid in writing, printing, uttering or publishing any false, scandalous and malicious writing or writings against the government of the United States, or either house of the Congress of the United States, or the President of the United States, with intent to defame the said

*The party was officially known as the Democratic-Republican Party. It was not the same party as the Democratic party, developed by Andrew Jackson in the early nineteenth century, nor the Republican party developed under Lincoln in the mid-nineteenth century

government, or either house of the said congress, or the said President, or to bring them, or either of them, the hatred of the good people of the United States . . . shall be punished by a fine not exceeding two thousand dollars and by imprisonment not exceeding two years.

[I have] often heard in [Congress], and elsewhere, harrangues on the liberty of the press, as if it were to swallow up all other liberties; as if all law and reason and every right, human and divine, was to fall prostrate before the liberty of the Press; whereas, the true meaning of it no more than a man shall be at liberty to print what he pleases, provided he does not offend against the laws, and that no law shall be passed to regulate this liberty of the press.

—Rep. Robert Harper, South Carolina, 1798, in support of the Alien and Sedition Laws

---

If there was ever a nation which required a law of this kind, it is this. Let gentlemen look at certain papers printed in this city and elsewhere, and ask themselves whether any unwarranted and dangerous combination does not exist to overturn and ruin the Government by publishing the most shameless falsehoods against the Representatives of the people of all denominations, that they are hostile to free Government and genuine liberty, and of course to the welfare of this country; that they ought, therefore, to be displaced, and that the people ought to raise in insurrection against the Government.

—Rep. John Allen, Connecticut, 1798, in support for the the Alien and Sedition Laws

---

The Act, however, also provided for truth as a defense for libel, and allowed the jury to determine both law and fact, provisions urged by Alexander Hamilton, and based upon Fox's Libel Act that six years earlier had given England the same protections. The Federalists were willing to give the people greater individual freedoms in exchange for the preservation of the government. Nevertheless, the nation that had brought about a Revolution partially on the basis

The Sedition Act

An Act in addition to the act, entitled "An act for the punishment of certain crimes against the United States."

Sec. 1. *Be it enacted . . .* , That if any persons shall unlawfully combine or conspire together, with intent to oppose any measure or measures of the government of the United States, which are or shall be directed by proper authority, or to impede the operation of any law of the United States, or to intimidate or prevent any person holding a place or office in or under the government of the United States, from undertaking, performing or executing his trust or duty; and if any person or persons, with intent as aforesaid, shall counsel, advise or attempt to procure any insurrection, riot, unlawful assembly, or combination, whether such conspiracy, threatening, counsel, advice, or attempt shall have the proposed effect or not, he or they shall be deemed guilty of a high misdemeanor, and on conviction, before any court of the United States having jurisdiction thereof, shall be punished by a fine not exceeding five thousand dollars, and by imprisonment during a term not less than six months nor exceeding five years; and further, at the discretion of the court may be holden to find sureties for his good behaviour in such sum, and for such time, as the said court may direct.

Sec. 2. That if any person shall write, print, utter, or publish, or shall cause or procure to be written, printed, uttered or published, or shall knowingly and willingly assist or aid in writing, printing, uttering or publishing any false, scandalous and malicious writing or writings against the government of the United States, or either house of the Congress of the United States, or the President of the United States, with intent to defame the said government, or either house of the said Congress, or the said President, or to bring them, or either of them, into contempt or disrepute; or to exciteagainst them, or either or any of them, the hatred of the good people of the United States, or to stir up sedition within the United States, or to excite any unlawful combinations therein, for opposing or resisting any law of the United States, or any act of the President of the United States, done in pursuance of any such law, or of the powers in him vested by the constitiuion of the United States, or to resist, oppose, or defeat any such law or act, or to aid, encourage or abet any hostile designs of any foreign nation against the United States, their people or government, then such person, being thereof convicted before any court of the United States having jurisdiction thereof, shall be punished by a fine not exceeding two thousand dollars, and by imprisonment not exceeding two years.

Sec. 3. That if any person shall be prosecuted under this act, for the writing or publishing any libel aforesaid, it shall be lawful for the defendant, upon the trial of the cause, to give in evidence in his defence, the truth of the matter contained in the publication charged as a libel. And the jury who shall try the cause, shall have a right to determine the law and the fact, under the direction of the court, as in other cases.

Sec. 4. That this act shall continue to be in force until March 3, 1801, and no longer . . .

of opposition to suppression now enacted a law that could be seen to be just as severe as any that had existed in England. Ironically, most American newspapers strongly supported the Alien and Sedition Laws, but most American newspapers were Federalist.

The first person convicted under the Sedition Act was Matthew Lyon, a Republican representative from Vermont, and former colonel in the Revolutionary Army. Lyon had written a letter-to-the-editor, claiming that " . . . every consideration of the public welfare [by Adams was] swallowed up in a continual grasp for power, in an unbounded thirst for ridiculous [sic] pomp, foolish adulation, and selfish avarice." A Federalist judge fined Lyon $1,100 and sentenced him to four months in a filthy jail in Vergennes, Vermont. Although thousands of people signed petitions supporting Lyon, parole was not granted. Two months after he was jailed, Lyon was overwhelmingly re-elected to the Congress. When finally released in February 1799, Lyon returned to Philadelphia, site of the nation's capital, followed by a procession estimated to be more than ten miles long.

The second conviction was Anthony Haswell, editor of the *Vermont Gazette*. Haswell was found guilty of "aiding and abetting a criminal" when he pleaded for money to pay Lyon's fine, and for sedition for writing that Lyon was "holden by the oppressive hand of usurped power in a loathsome prison, deprived almost of the right of reason, and suffering all the indignities which can be heaped upon him by a hard-hearted savage [Marshall Fitch]."

Also convicted under the Act was James Callender, editor of the *Richmond Examiner*. Callender, a not-too-principled editor, had written, possibly with the encouragement of Thomas Jefferson, *The Prospect Before Us*. The pamphlet was one of the press's most vicious attacks upon Washington and Adams, calling Adams a "professed aristocrat [who] proved faithful and serviceable to the British interest," concluding that not Adams, who represented "war and beggary," but Jefferson, who represented "peace and competence," should be the president. However, no matter how spurious the claims by Callender, no matter how vicious the attack, under the provisions of the Bill of Rights, Callender should have been free from governmental actions. Nevertheless, he was arrested, fined, and jailed by a court that denied even the basics of justice in Callender's defense.*

Twenty-five years earlier, in the Declaration of Independence, Americans declared that "whenever any Form of Government becomes destructive of these ends [of Life, Liberty, and the pursuit of Happiness], it is the Right of the People to alter or to abolish it, and to institute new Government . . ." Within America, a few now considered that it would take a counter-revolution to curb the excesses of the Alien and Sedition Laws, restore the principles of libertarianism and to

---

*Ironically, Callender became a strong Federalist and launched vicious attacks against Jefferson after Jefferson, as president, refused to appoint Callender postmaster of Richmond and repay his $200 fine; Jefferson did pay $100, and had indicated that he was working out arrangements to pay the rest.

overthrow the believed tyranny of the Federalists. However, the Declaration of Independence also cautioned that "Governments long established should not be changed for light and transient causes." A nation with a constitution less than fifteen years could not be considered as "long established," but most Americans were willing to fight their battles in an established political forum than in a military campaign.

By now, freedom of the press and of speech was an issue that could be used for political advantage by Thomas Jefferson and the Republicans. In November 1798, Jefferson drew up a series of resolutions, passed by the Kentucky legislature, that declared the Alien and Sedition Laws to be unconstitutional and, thus, null and void within Kentucky. The Virginia legislature, a month later, passed a similar set of resolutions drawn up by James Madison, principal writer of the Constitution. Together, the Virginia and Kentucky resolutions were printed in Republican newspapers throughout the country, bringing the issues before the public.

In 1799, the Republicans tried to get the House of Representatives to repeal the Sedition Act, but failed, 52-28. Rep. Chauncey Goodrich presented the Federalist views of why the Sedition Act was necessary:

> . . . A law to punish false, scandalous, and malicious writings against the Government, with intent to stir up sedition, is a law necessary for carrying into effect the power vested by the Constitution . . . Because the direct tendency of [seditious] writings is to obstruct the acts of the Government by exciting opposition to them, to endanger its existence by rendering it odious and contemptible in the eyes of the people, and to produce seditious combinations against the laws, the power to punish . . . has never been questioned . . . It would be manifestly absurd to suppose that a Government might punish sedition, and yet be void of power to prevent it by punishing those acts which plainly and necessarily lead to it . . . [There are many laws which are not] expressly authorized, but which have been considered as Constitutional, because they are necessary and proper for carrying into effect certain powers expressly given to Congress . . .
>
> The act in question is said to be "an abridgement of the liberty of the press," and therefore unconstitutional . . . The liberty of the press consists not in license for every man to publish what he pleases without being liable to punishment, if he should abuse this license to the injury of others, but in a permission to publish, without previous restraint, whatever he may think proper, being answerable to the public and individuals, for any abuse of this permission to their prejudice. In like manner, as the liberty of speech does not authorize a man to speak malicious slanders against his neighbor, nor the liberty of action justify him in going, by violence, into another man's house, or in assaulting any person whom he may meet in the streets. In the several States the liberty of the press has always been understood in this manner, and no other; and the Constitution of every State which has been framed and adopted since the Declaration

of Independence, asserts "the liberty of the press;" while in several, if not all, their laws provide for the punishment of libellous publications, which would be a manifest absurdity and contradiction, if the liberty of the press meant to publish any and everything, without being amenable to the laws for the abuse of this license. According to this just, legal, and universally admitted definition of "the liberty of the press," a law to restrain its licentiousness, in publishing false, scandalous, and malicious libels against the Government, cannot be considered as "an abridgment" of its "liberty."

. . . The liberty of the press never did extend, . . . to the publication of false, scandalous, and malicious writings against the Government, written or published with intent to do mischief, such publications being unlawful, and punishable in every State . . .

In rebuttal, Rep. John Nicholas, using classic libertarian philosophy, argued, that it is difficult to determine what is true and what is false, especially when it comes to opinion. "The trial of the truth of opinions, in the best state of society," said Nicholas, "would be altogether precarious; and, perhaps, a jury of twelve men could never be found to agree in any one opinion." The Anti-Federalists further questioned the right of Congress or the administration to enact such laws or "to have control over the persons who alone can give information throughout a country."

Many wrote against the Alien and Sedition Acts, but with the First Amendment interpreted as forbidding prior restraint, and the Sedition Act now providing for truth as a defense to libel, the Anti-Federalists had to stretch the concepts of libertarianism, and develop a stronger philosophical base in order to further their support of a free press—and to attack Federalists on freedom of expression issues. Within a two year period, major philosophical arguments were written by George Hay, Thomas Cooper, and Tunis Wortman.

George Hay, writing under the pseudonym Hortensius in 1799, pushed the argument that the First Amendment provided that "Congress shall make no law" with regard to the press and exercise of free speech and religion, and that by establishing the Sedition Act, Congress had written an unconstitutional law.

"If all power originally belongs to the people," Hay wrote, "those who exercise any portion of power must derive their authority from the people, and can possess no power . . . that is not given, expressly, or by fair and necessary implication." Hay then briefly delineated a legal history of the country, establishing a syllogism:

I. Congress possesses no power unless it be expressly given, or necessary to carry a given power into effect . . .

II. The power of prescribing a punishment for libels [i.e., sedition] is not expressly given, nor necessary to carry a given power into effect.

III. Conclusion. Therefore so much of the sedition Bill as prescribes a punishment for libels . . . is not warranted by the Federal Constitution

Censors, Governments, and Individual Rights

. . . The people are the only censors of their governors;
and even their errors will tend to keep these to the true
principles of their institution. To punish these errors too
severely would be to suppress the only safeguard of the
public liberty. The way to prevent these irregular interposi-
tions of the people [such as Shays's Rebellion] is to give
them full information of their affairs through the channel of
the public papers, and to contrive that those papers should
penetrate the whole mass of the people. The basis of our
governments being the opinion of the people, the first object
should be to keep that right; and were it left to me to decide
whether we should have a government without newspapers,
or newspapers without a government, I should not hesitate
a moment to prefer the latter. But I should mean that
every man should receive those papers, and be capable
of reading them. I am convinced that those societies (as
the Indians) which live without government, enjoy in their
general mass an infinitely greater degree of happiness than
those who live under the European governments. Among
the former, public opinion is the place of law, and restrains
morals as powerfully as laws ever did anywhere. Among
the latter, under pretence of governing, they have divided
their nations into two classes, wolves and sheep . . . This
is a true picture of Europe. Cherish, therefore, the spirit
of our people, and keep alive their attention. Do not be too
severe upon their errors, but reclaim them by elightening
them.

—Thomas Jefferson, letter to Edward Carrington,
January 16, 1787

The Constitution having declared, that the freedom of the press shall not be abridged, has in fact, pronounced that no line of discrimination shall be drawn. For if the freedom of the press is not to be abridged, and if no man can tell where freedom stops, and licentiousness begins, it is obvious that no man can say, to what extent a law against licentiousness shall be carried. It follows, then that *no law can* be made to restrain the licentousness of the press.

The words, "freedom of the press," like most other words, having a
meaning, a clear, precise, and definite meaning, which the times require,
should be unequivocally ascertained. That this has not been done before,
is a wonderful and melancholy evidence of the imbecility of the human
mind, and of the slow progress which it makes, in acquiring knowledge
even on subjects the most useful and interesting.

It will, I presume, be admitted, that the words in question have a
meaning, and that the framers of the amendment containing these words,
meant something when they declared, that the freedom of the press should
not be abridged.

To ascertain what the "freedom of the press" is, we have only to
ascertain what freedom itself is. For, surely, it will be conceded, that
freedom applied to one subject, means the same as freedom applied to
another subject.

Now freedom is of two kinds, and of two kinds only: one is, that
absolute freedom which belongs to man, previous to any social institution;
and the other, that qualified or abridged freedom, which he is content to
enjoy, for the sake of government and society. I believe there is no other
sort of freedom in which man is concerned.

Absolute freedom [is] . . . the freedom belonging to man before any
social compact, [and] is the power uncontrolled by law, of doing what
he pleases, *provided he does no injury to any other individual.* If this
definition of freedom be applied to the press, as surely it ought to be, the
press . . . may do whatever it pleases to do, uncontrolled by any law,
taking care however to do no injury to any individual. This injury can
only be by slander or defamation, and reparation should be made for it in
a state of nature as well as in society.

But freedom in society, or what is called civil liberty, is defined to be,
natural liberty, so far, restrained by law as the public good requires, and no
farther. This is the definition given by a writer, particularly distinguished
for the accuracy of his definitions, and which, perhaps, cannot be mended.
Now let freedom, under this definition, be applied to the press, and what
will the freedom of the press amount to? It will amount precisely to the
privilege of publishing, as far as the legislative power shall say, the public
good requires: that is to say, the freedom of the press will be regulated
by law. If the word freedom was used in this sense, by the framers of
the amendment, they meant to say, Congress shall make no law abridging
the freedom of the press, which freedom, however, is to be regulated by
law. Folly itself does not speak such language.

The framers of the amendment meant that the power granted to Congress, did not authorise any control over the press, but they knew that
its freedom could not be too cautiously guarded from invasion. The
amendment in question was therefore introduced. Now if they used the
word "freedom" under the first definition, they did mean something, and
something of infinite importance in all free countries, the total exemption of the press from any kind of legislative control. But if they used

the word freedom under the second definition they meant nothing; for if they supposed that the freedom of the press, was absolute freedom, so far restrained by law as the public good required, and no farther, the amendment left the legislative power of the government on this subject, precisely where it was before. But it has been already admitted that the amendment had a meaning: the construction therefore which allows it no meaning is absurd and must be rejected.

This argument may be summed up in a few words. The word "freedom" has meaning. It is either absolute, that is exempt from all law, or it is qualified, that is, regulated by law. If it be exempt from the control of law, the Sedition Bill which controls the "freedom of the press" is unconstitutional. But if it is to be regulated by law, the amendment which declares that Congress shall make no law to abridge the freedom of the press, which freedom however may be regulated by law, is the grossest absurdity that ever was conceived by the human mind.

Hay later became U.S. District Attorney in Virginia, the government's prosecutor of Vice-President Aaron Burr on charges of treason, and in 1825 a federal judge.

Dr. Thomas Cooper, who left England in 1793 to settle in Northumberland, Pennsylvania, also became a victim of the Sedition Act when he criticized John Adams. Cooper had written several articles in the *Northumberland Gazette* about press-government relations, and in *Political Essays* (1800), he asked, "Who is to be the judge of truth and falsehood? The lawgivers who sedulously screen their own conduct from the public eye?" However, Cooper went further than many libertarian thinkers by arguing that without the means of knowledge, there is no freedom:

> The most effectual way to keep the people ignorant, if they are so, is to perpetuate those restrictions on freedom of enquiry . . . Diffuse knowledge—enable the people to read, and incite them to think . . . [E]very man may and *ought* to be taught to read, to write, and to be familiar with the common operations of arithmetic; he ought to have the *means* of knowledge put in his power . . .
>
> It is the general diffusion of knowledge—it is the free discussion, that eradicates the prejudices of the people . . . [P]eople will be governed by their passions, if they are not governed by their reason. What is the cure for this evil? Surely to call their reason into play—to incite them to reflect—to teach them that every question has two sides—that as their neighbor is not infallible, so neither are they. In short, to accustom them to free enquiry on all subjects. [*Political Essays* (1800)]

Within American universities, in classes in journalism and history, political science and philosophy, the works of Milton and Locke, Rousseau, Bentham, Mill, and numerous other libertarians, are read and analyzed, the professors, and their professors before them, having studied the great philosophers. But almost no one—not journalists nor historians, political scientists nor philosophers—knows about Tunis Wortman, his works largely unknown and unread. Whether deliberately or through negligence, the people have chosen to forget Wortman, to relegate him to unmapped catacombs of history. Unlike John Milton more than a century earlier, Tunis Wortman wrote no great literature that would increase the public acceptance and recognition of his earlier works, thus assuring the recognition of the *Areopagitica*; unlike John Stuart Mill, a half century later, he wrote no masses of philosophical doctrine. Tunis Wortman, a leader of New York's Tammany Hall, wrote only a couple articles and only one book, *A Treatise Concerning Political Enquiry and the Liberty of the Press.* Published in 1800, the work was promoted by the Anti-Federalists, and quickly became America's most important statement about the historical concepts of libertarian thought. Within the 276-page work, Wortman re-emphasized the basic libertarian concepts. "Man [is] a moral and intellectual Being . . . inseparably possessed of certain absolute and perfect rights," Wortman wrote, emphasizing that "Truth may be considered the property of every Intellectual Being: it is the vital principle of mind, and the only element in which our percipient powers can maintain a healthful existence."

Using Locke and Rousseau, Wortman vigorously argued that people create their society, "and government [is] its necessary consequence . . . derived from the pre-existing *rights* of society . . . an organ of the general will [of the people]," when government fails to respond to the people, they have the right to create a new government—exactly what had happened about twenty-five years earlier, a revolution now threatened by the Alien and Sedition laws.

The press, wrote Wortman, must have liberty, for it is through the press that mankind is represented and its wants and needs advanced:

> Next to the invention of language and of letters, that of printing may be justly considered as the most powerful benefactor of mankind. Before this important and valuable discovery, whatever may have been the attainments of a few distinguished individuals, the great majority of the human race were destined to remain unenlightened and uninformed . . .
>
> The press is undeniably possessed of extensive influence upon the government, manners, and morals. Every exertion should, therefore, be employed to render it subservient to liberty, truth, and virtue. While society is furnished with so powerful a vehicle of political information [as the press], the conduct of administration [of government] will be more cautious and deliberate.
>
> . . . Ambition cannot fail to dread that vigilant guardian of public liberty, whose eye can pentrate, and whose voice can be heard . . . in every quarter of the State.

To re-emphasize his argument for the necessity of an unrestrained press, Wortman looked at the counter-argument, one that had led to the enactment of the Alien and Sedition laws:

The licentiousness of the press has of late become a theme of fashionable invective: but those who have been most clamorous in their phillipies . . . have in general been most hostile to its liberty. The press is undoubtedly a powerful instrument; and, when left to itself, its natural direction will be towards truth and virtue. It is by no means surprising that ambition [of government leaders] should always be jealous of so formidible and discerning an opponent. Under arbitrary governments, it is a practice to prohibit every publication that has not been previously perused and sanctioned by some of its officers. By this means, every writing, which is friendly to the spirit of freedom, is suppressed; and nothing can appear but what is on the side of government. By such regulations it is obvious that the press, instead of being a guardian of public liberty, is rendered a dangerous and servile slave to despotism . . . In such case [writes] Lord Lyttelton . . . there should be "An inspector for the people as well as one for the court. But if nothing is to be licensed on the one side, and everything on the other, it would be vastly better for us to . . . allow no printing at all, than to leave it under such partial direction."

Wortman also argued against the Blackstonian concepts that freedom of the press meant the absence of prior restraint by arguing that the absence of prior restraint is only a small portion of what is necessary for a free press, and that, among other things, truth must be a defense to all libel:

Our natural liberty terminates at the precise point at which our conduct becomes injurious. Independent of the sanctions of civil institution, we could never claim the right of inflicting evil upon others. It is the principal end of society to prevent and redress our wrongs, to protect us in the enjoyment of our natural rights, and not to abolish or destroy them . . .

[However, for most instances,] of what use is the liberty of doing that for which I am punishable afterwards?

In ascertaining the rights I possess, it is not to be enquired what I may do, and be punished; but what I am entitled to perform without being subjected to punishment. The preceding explanation of the legal Liberty of the Press is fallacious in the extreme. It amounts to nothing definite. It cannot be said that any Liberty of the Press is established by law, unless the publication of Truth is expressly sanctioned, and it is particularly ascertained what species of writings shall be comprehended under the title of Libels . . .

To criminal prosecutions for Libels there will always exist the most serious objections. They are invariably, more formidable than the evil they are intended to prevent. As a security to a virtuous administration, they can never be necessary. In the hand of a vicious minister, they will be prostituted to the most pernicious purposes . . .

A year after Tunis Wortman's book was published, John Thomson completed *An Enquiry, Concerning the Liberty and Licentiousness of the Press, and the Uncontrollable Nature of the Human Mind* (1801), an overview of both libertarian thought and an attack upon the Alien and Sedition laws:

... Men of science have differed, and still differ in many of their opinions; and it is to this very difference, that mankind are indebted for those discussions which have from time to time agitated the scientific world, and to which are justly to be ascribed, the gratitude of mankind for the superlative scientific advantages they now enjoy. No danger is ever apprehended from discussions of this kind; and if the same unrestrained freedom were permitted in political and all other investigations, the same beneficial effects would follow. If all political opinions, and discussions upon those opinions had been thus viewed, then neither sedition nor alien laws would ever have disgraced the American code.

Government then ought no more to interfere with the discussion of politics, than with that of any other art or science. Were this maxim adopted, all such discussions would be equally harmless ...

One of the most prominent forerunners of violent revolution, is a total suppression of the Liberty of Speech and Press; the Government usurping the sole direction of public opinion. This is dangerous in every kind of Government; but more preposterous, as well as more dangerous in a republican country, than in any other. If in a democratic republic, the people are prevented from a free investigation of the actions of their public servants, it will inevitably be productive of the following effects.

Either it will drive the people into immediate acts of violence against the Government; or, if they silently submit, it will ultimately deprive the people of that free energy of thought, word, and action, which the consciousness of liberty and independence never fail to inspire. The Government will then cease to direct the public conerns of free men; and they will rule over a nation of degraded slaves. Both of these events ought to be equally dreaded by the good politician; because both, in the end, must terminate in violent and tumultuous revolution ...

Every Government however constituted, or whatever be its form, is always possessed of an extensive influence among the people. Although it be true, that Government depends for its chief, if not its only support, upon public opinion; yet it will always have a very considerable share in the formation, and direction thereof. This arises from the unavoidable patronage which it seems necessary to confer upon it; or at least, which *seems pretty generally thought so to be*. It may thence be obvious, that throwing any additional weight into this already preponderating scale, must be extremely improper, and highly dangerous. To guard the Government by Sedition laws, is giving to it the power of at least attempting to direct the opinions of the people. It gives to it the authority of determining what the people shall say concerning them. It is not *falsehood* that it will guard against; otherwise *flattery* would be equally punishable; equally a libel. The flattering sycophant will always escape the censure of Government; while the honest man who boldly speaks disagreeable truths, will fall a victim to his sincerity, and patriotism. Not unfrequently, the flatterer will be rewarded for his falsehood . . .

All the opponents of the Liberty of the Press, have sheltered themselves behind the specious veil of preserving the public peace. They say, licentiousness must be suppressed. Dangerous opinions in politics and religion must be guarded against, otherwise the social order of society will be endangered. What, it may be asked, would have been the situation of mankind, at this moment, had the subjects of religion and politics never been investigated? . . . Those who are in the administration of Government, will always defend its principles, and its actions; whether it be that of a Turkish Bashaw, or a Prime Minister of England. Investigation is equally dreaded by both. Both are sufficiently aware that many imperfections exist in their systems of Government, and that many abuses are committed under them. It is however to be hoped, that the officers of Government on this side of the Atlantic will not again follow such pernicious examples . . .

If newspapers, and other publications, have lately teemed with misrepresentation, or with undeserved abuse of private or public character: If calumnies and invective dressed up in the language of billingsgate have been profusely dealt abroad instead of argument; what is to be done? Does it follow that we ought to be deprived of LIBERTY because it may be, or has been abused? . . .

Truth is at all times sufficiently powerful. Coercion may *silence*, but it never can *convince* . . .

Let the whig and tory, the royalist and aristocrat, the republican and democrat, or by whatever other name the partisans of political parties are designated; let them, I say, be allowed to express their opinions, whether by speech or press, with the same unconstrained freedom with which men of science discuss their subjects of investigation. No more danger will result from the one discussion, than arises from the other.

The most violent advocate for the sedition law will surely acknowledge, that had it not been for *discussion*, these states had never been in a situation to have asserted and gained their independence. Had it not been for *discussion*, the Federal Government never would have existed. Certain it is, that the convention who framed this instrument, either were, or appeared to be, fully impressed with the importance of unrestrained discussion.

If we allow our terrors or prejudices so far to conquer our reason as again silently to acquiesce in the renewal of the Sedition Law; or tacitly give our consent to any abridgment of the Liberty of the Press. This is the palladium of freedom, which if once destroyed, Liberty is no more.

I think I hear some worthy but mistaken individuals exclaim, "Why all this declamation? we wish not to destroy the Liberty of the Press, we only wish to correct and suppress its licentiousness. By this the barriers of liberty will be strengthened." True, they will be strengthened, but it will be a fortification from which her sons will be forever shut out; unless they storm it at the expense of oceans of human blood . . .

Under the Alien Acts, no one was deported, but the potential enforcement of the acts was substantial enough that dissent was significantly diminished. Under the Sedition Act, at least two newspapers were forced to cease publication because of harrassment, one was forced to suspend publication for five months while its editor was in jail. However, only twenty-five persons, most of them journalists or politicians, were arrested; only ten of them convicted. Nevertheless, it was enough to give Thomas Jefferson a campaign issue to unite the Republican party, and to bring about his election as president in 1800. The victory effectively ended Federalist domination of the twelve-year old country; no other Federalist would ever be elected to the presidency. Nevertheless, America's "Dark Age of Journalism" continued, with Federalist and Anti-Federalist (Republican) editors resorting to lies and innuendoes in their attacks against each other, and against opposition leaders.

The Sedition Act expired on March 3, 1801, and Jefferson immediately upon his inauguration, ordered the release of all prisoners held under provisions of the Act. In his inaugural speech, Jefferson outlined his argument for a free press—"Error of opinion may be tolerated when reason is left free to combat it." Later, in a letter to Abigail Adams, wife of John Adams, Jefferson wrote:

> I discharged every prisoner under punishment or prosecution under the sedition law, because I considered . . . that law to be a nullity, as absolute and as palpable as if Congress had ordered us to fall down and worship a golden image; and that it was as much my duty to arrest its execution in every stage, as it would have been to have rescued from the fiery furnace those who should have been cast into it for refusing to worship the image. It was accordingly done in every instance, without asking what the offenders had done, or against whom they had offended, but whether the pains they were suffering were infliceted under the pretended sedition law.

A Change of Perspectives

All minority parties assume it is their right to criticize the majority, even to print "selected facts" and distorted truth, expecting the protection of the Constitution. Many minority charges are done "for the good of the country;" many more are done so that the minority party can become the majority party, it finds that being attacked hurts deeper than it thought and, therefore, argues that there must be responsibility in the press to print only the truth—at least the truth that the newly-elected majority party sees. Against Washington and Adams, the Republican newspapers had been brutal, forcing Adams to request the Sedition Act to attempt to silence the newspapers' attempts to influence policy by publishing falsehoods. During Jefferson's Republican presidency (1801-1809), the Federalists mounted just as vicious a campaign, leading Jefferson, author of the Declaration of Independence, one of the greatest libertarian documents in Western civilization, to write:

> So abandoned are the tory presses that . . . even the least informed of the people have learnt that nothing in a newspaper is to be believed. This

is a dangerous state of things, and the press ought to be restored to its credibility if possible. The restraints provided by the laws of the states are sufficient for this if applied. And I have therefore long thought that a few prosecutions of the most prominent offenders would have a wholesome effect in restoring the integrity of the presses.

Jefferson was trying to protect himself and his party against a petty lie-monger, Harry Croswell, Federalist editor of the *Wasp*, of Hudson, New York.

Croswell had reprinted gossip that Jefferson, while vice-president under Adams, had paid Callender to call Washington and Adams traitors and per-jurers. Just as the Federalists brought the Republican Callender to trial, so the Republicans now brought the Federalist Croswell to trial. Croswell was found guilty in 1804. On appeal, he was represented by one of the nation's most respected politicians, Alexander Hamilton, leader of the Federalist party. Hamilton argued that the press "has the right to publish with impunity truth, with good motives, for justifiable ends, though reflecting upon government, magistracy, or individuals."

The Zenger trial in 1735 had established the question of admitting truth as a defense, but set no precedent. The Constitution and the First Amendment had established an almost limitless boundary for the press to publish unrestricted; the Sedition Act had closed those boundaries, but Hamilton's arguments led the courts to establish truth as a defense and the right of a jury to determine both law and facts. However, the Sedition Act had expired, and Hamilton was now forced to ask the New York Court of Appeals to re-establish truth as a defense and the rights of the press to speak out with impunity on most matters. Although Hamilton and Jefferson were bitter political rivals, Hamilton probably was repulsed by the accusations and charges of Croswell, his client; nevertheless, Hamilton defended him because of the greater issues of the rights of the press, and for the future rights of the Federalist party. The Court, by a 2-2 vote, rejected Hamilton's arguments. However, the brilliance of Hamilton's remarks, as well as prevailing common opinion, led the New York legislature to enact a bill declaring that truth shall be a defense in all libel trials, and that the jury could determine both the law and the facts of a case. Soon, the other states also enacted similar legislation, and the arguments of Andrew Hamilton in 1735 and Alexander Hamilton in 1804 finally became law.

Restraint and Misinformation

by Thomas Jefferson

. . . To your request of my opinion of the manner in which a newspaper should be conducted, so as to be most useful, I should answer, "by restraining it to true facts and sound principles only." Yet I fear such a paper would find few subscribers. It is a melancholy truth, that a suppression of the press could not more completely deprive the nation of its benefits, than is done by its abandoned prostitution to falsehood. Nothing can now be believed which is seen in a newspaper. Truth itself becomes suspicious by being put into that polluted vehicle. The real extent of this state of misinformation is known only to those who are in situations to confront facts within their knowledge with the lies of the day. I really look with commiseration over the great body of my fellow citizens, who, reading newspapers, live and die in the belief that they have known something of what has been passing in the world in their time; whereas the accounts they have read in newspapers are just as true a history of any other period of the world as of the present, except that the real names of the day are affixed to their fables. General facts may indeed be collected from them, such as that Europe is now at war, that Bonaparte has been a successful warrior, that he has subjected a great portion of Europe to his will, etc., etc.; but no details can be relied on. I will add, that the man who never looks into a newspaper is better informed than he who reads them; in as much as he who knows nothing is nearer to truth than he whose mind is filled with falsehoods and errors. He who reads nothing will still learn the great facts, and the details are all false.

Perhaps an editor might begin a reformation in some such way as this. Divide his paper into four chapters, heading the 1st, Truths. 2d, Probabilities. 3d, Possibilities. 4th, Lies. The first chapter would be very short, as it would contain little more than authentic papers, and information from such sources, as the editor would be willing to risk his own reputation for their truth. The second would contain what, from a mature consideration of all circumstances, his judgment should conclude to be probably true. This, however, should rather contain too little than too much. The third and fourth should be professedly for those readers who would rather have lies for their money than the blank paper they would occupy.

Such an editor, too, would have to set his face against the demoralizing practice of feeding the public mind habitually on slander, and the depravity of taste which this nauseous ailment induces. Defamation is becoming a necessary of life; insomuch, that a dish of tea in the morning or evening cannot be digested without this stimulant. Even those who do not believe these abominations, still read them with complaisance to their auditors, and instead of the abhorrence and indignation which should fill a virtuous mind, betray a secret pleasure in the possibility that some may believe them, though they do not themselves. It seems to escape them, that it is not he who prints, but he who pays for printing a slander, who is its real author.

These thoughts on the subjects of your letter are hazarded at your request. Repeated instances of the publication of what has not been intended for the public eye, and the malignity with which political enemies torture every sentence from me into meanings imagined by their own wickedness only, justify my expressing a solicitude, that this hasty communication may in no wise be permitted to find its way into the public papers. Not fearing these political bulldogs, I yet avoid putting myself in the way of being baited by them, and do not wish to volunteer away that portion of tranquility, which a firm execution of my duties will permit me to enjoy.

[letter to John Nowell, June 11, 1807]

Chapter 16

No Longer Concerned . . .

Prior to, and during the Revolution, the Sons of Liberty had destroyed Tory newspapers, believing that by destroying physical property, they could silence the opposition to revolution. In doing so, of course, they had threatened the extremely tenuous nature of freedom of the press. After the revolution, the Alien and Sedition acts, the blatant propagandizing of the press, and the trials of Callender and Croswell had threatened the freedom of the press. But now, in 1812, a mob once again placed freedom of the press in jeopardy by its actions that suggested there may be a greater good to the preservation of society than by allowing a free and unrestricted press. America was engaged once again in a controversial war against Great Britain.

In Baltimore, Jacob Wagner and Alexander Hanson, publishers of the *Federal Republican* spoke out against President Madison and the war policies. Several vehement editorials and articles opposing the war brought a mob, with cannon, against the newspaper office. The publishers, and several of their supporters, were "escorted" to jail for their "protection" while the mob destroyed the newspaper plant. That completed, the mob moved to the jail where several contributing writers and supporters of the *Federal Republican* had escaped— nine were brutally attacked. In its violence and blind dedication to "punishing" those with views opposed to their own, and furious with those who had written against war and Madison's policies, the mob killed Revolutionary War Gen. James Lingan, and crippled for life Revolutionary War Lt. Col. "Light Horse Harry" Lee, former governor of Virginia and father of Robert E. Lee.

Lingan and Lee would not be the only journalists to confront the issue that freedom of the press can be suppressed by a mob and by America's utter fascination with the "public will." Nor would Lingan be the only American to lose his life in defense of the constitutional rights to present views that may be contrary to that "public will."

In American society, few are willing to risk anything in defense of their principles, in defense of their views. Many may claim to be "outspoken," but few truly are willing to accept the risks involved in being outspoken. To maintain peace and order, and to avoid confrontation, most Americans accept what either the majority want, or what they think the majority want, risking their views only when they think others have similar views. Even most of today's journalists who have studied the history of freedom of the press and are able to spout out epithets about "the public's right to know" and "freedom of the press is paramount in American society," are still unwilling to risk more than a few days in jail, if even that, to present views that may be contrary to the public will. The "collective society," ruled by "group think," has always taken a precedence over the "individual" society, for the masses are unwilling to lead, and are willing to accept a "majority" view, as explained by those who they have entrusted their leadership. It was no different in the ancient civilizations that accepted dictators and philospher-kings, or in the Middle Ages when knighthood protected the nobility and the clergy, or in England when citizens switched religions, usually without hesitation, when directed to do so by new rulers. It was no different in colonial America when the majority accepted the Puritan will or when they acknowledged that there were injustices in the British system, but that it wasn't worth a revolution. And, it was also important when Tories became Whigs or even Radicals as the Revolution progressed.

A Vulgar Turn of Mind

Alexis De Tocqueville, a French government official, spent a year in the United States, beginning in 1831, to study the American penal system. His observations about American culture and of the press were compiled into *Democracy in America*, one of history's better insights into the nature of the American people and their institutions.

The Price of Sedition

Lord Henry Cockburn (1779-1854), in his *Memorials of His Time* (1856), wrote eloquently of the effect of the sedition trials conducted during 1793 and 1794 in the Scotish Supreme Criminal court, trials that left their marks on the minds of many. Cockburn's observations point out the problem of prosecuting people, rather than trying to solve the underlying problem:

It has been said, in defence of [the court], that the times were dangerous. So they were. But these are the very times in which the torch of justice should burn most purely. It has also been said that the prisoners were all guilty. Holding this to be true, had they not a right to be fairly tried? And lastly, it has been said, that after these trials there was no more sedition. The same thing might be said though they had been tried by the boot, [a device of torture] and punished by the fire. Jeffreys and Kirke put down sedition, for the day, by their bloody assizes. But our exhibitions of judicial vigor, instead of eradicating the seditious propensity prolonged its inward vitality. Future outbreaks were only avoided by the course of events, which turned men's passions into other channels.

These trials, however, sunk deep not merely into the popular mind, but into the minds of all men who thought. It was by these proceedings, more than by any other wrong, that the spirit of discontent justified itself throughout the rest of that age.

Reviewing the nature of government and the media, DeTocqueville wrote:

> In countries where the doctrine of the sovereignty of the people ostensibly prevails, the censorship of the press is not only dangerous, but absurd. When the right of every citizen to a share in the government of society is acknowledged, everyone must be presumed to be able to choose between the various opinions of his contemporaries and to appreciate the different facts from which inferences may be drawn. The sovereignty of the people and the liberty of the press may therefore be regarded as correlative, just as the censorship of the press and universal suffrage are two things which are irreconcilably opposed and which cannot long be retained among the institutions of the same people.
>
> [The] influence [of the press] in America is immense. It causes political life to circulate through all the parts of that vast territory. Its eye is constantly open to detect the secret springs of political designs and to summon the leaders of all parties in turn to the bar of public opinion. It rallies the interests of the community round certain principles and draws up the creed of every party; for it affords a means of intercourse between those who hear and address each other without ever coming into immediate contact. When many organs of the press adopt the same line of conduct, their influence in the long run becomes irresistible, and public opinion, perpetually assailed from the same side, eventually yields to the attack. In the United States each separate journal exercises but little authority; but the power of the periodical press is second only to that of the people
> . . .

Although praising the press and American journalism, De Tocqueville had little praise for American journalists, claiming:

> The journalists of the United States are generally in a very humble position, with a scanty education and a vulgar turn of mind. The will of the majority is the most general of laws, and it establishes certain habits to which everyone must then conform . . .
>
> The characteristics of the American journalist consist in an open and coarse appeal to the passions of his readers; he abandons principles to assail the characters of individuals, to track them into private life and disclose all their weaknesses and vices.

However, De Tocqueville, whose own country had undergone a revolution a decade earlier, looked around at the American people, and of their professed love of liberty, and concluded that because the press was given so much freedom, that, "America is perhaps, at this moment, the country of the whole world that contains the fewest germs of revolution . . ."

By the late 1830s, the spirit of the American Revolution was over. The journalists and clergy had been at the front of the revolution, leading the masses to understand the reasons why revolution was inevitable, uniting them in common thought, propagandizing them into action, keeping the revolution alive. But now, as De Tocqueville had pointed out, America no longer was concerned with the Revolution. Trails were being blazed, roads were being laid down; and there was still half a continent to claim, and a race of people to move. It was the beginning of what would be America's "Manifest Destiny."

Chapter 17

A Manifest Destiny

A new direction in the nature of American journalism was set in the rise of the middle class, an increase in population, an increased literacy, industrialization, and the development of businesses, roads, and transportation to service newly-built towns, giving newspapers both an advertising and circulation base.

Although newspapers were being established throughout the eastern United States, the emergence of New York City as a business center for the country gave New York papers a greater influence. In the early 1830s, newspapers were targeted for the elite and merchant classes. They were heavily political, sold for six cents an issue, payable by yearly subscription only, and usually accepted advertising only on yearly contracts. The writing was verbose and dull, and much of the news, when not about politics, was of interest only to merchants, business owners, and the rich. At the time, there were eleven newspapers, with an aggregate circulation of about 30,000 in New York, a city of about 250,000.

Dr. Horatio Sheppard, about 1832, recognized that the working class did not have access to newspapers because of the newspapers' editorial content, and their extraordinarily high charges for advertising and subscriptions. Reasoning that merchants needed to present their ads to the "common man," and that a newspaper aimed to the middle class, could be profitable, Sheppard started the *New York Morning Post*, and priced it at a penny an issue, available one issue at a time instead of by yearly subscription. Within a few weeks it failed, possibly the result of Sheppard being a better physician than businessman.

However, the next "penny paper," the *New York Sun* became the most successful paper in New York, attaining a circulation of 30,000 within a year of its premiere issue. Benjamin Day gave it a business sense; George Wisner gave it a journalistic sense. *The Sun* emphasized stories of interest to the middle class which gladly paid a penny a copy to read not only about themselves, but of things that mattered to them. When the merchants saw the *Sun's* large circulation, and when they could purchase ads by the issue rather than on long-term subscription, they added the economic base a newspaper needs.

The other newspapers in New York, however, tore into the *Sun*, calling it a disgrace to journalism—for printing police news about "common drunks," and for catering to the masses. Wisner didn't have time to listen—he was busy establishing a code of ethics that did not allow the *Sun* to accept bribes to print—or not to print—news, something almost every other newspaper considered to be acceptable practice. Wisner argued that either a newspaper prints all the news, or none of the news, but it can not print some of the news and not print some of the news; nor, said Wisner, could a newspaper show favoritism in the printing of news.

More than fifty years after the Declaration of Independence, the bureaucrats of America's municipal governments still saw the concepts of the libertarian thinking as a hinderance. The people *can* be harmed by some truths, they argued—and many newspaper editors complied willingly. When the Board of Health of New York City lied about a possible cholera epidemic, most newspaper editors accepted the lies without investigating. When they learned that there were cases of cholera, and that an epidemic could be imminent, the editors accepted the Board's explanation that the lies were necessary to prevent a panic among the people—that the greater "public good" was done by not informing the people. Truth will eventually emerge, said Wisner; a newspaper that prints only some facts, some stories, can only lose its credibility. Wisner showed the other editors that they didn't have to listen to government officials for "truth," for what is good for society is not what elected officials say is "good," but by the presentation of all the facts to the public. Society is ultimately harmed not by knowing certain truths, but by not being given the right to inspect all facts, all truths, before making a decision.

George Wisner, a libertarian in a society that retained the seeds of authoritarianism yet believed it was libertarian, argued that an enlightened public would be able to determine for itself the truth, and how best to accept or react to it. *Not* to inform the public, said Wisner, would be tantamount to accepting the doctrine that mankind is irrational and needs governmental controls. Wisner's and Day's gamble paid off, and a new era in the nature of news began.

In 1835, James Gordon Bennett (1795-1872) added the *New York Herald* to penny press journalism; in 1841, Horace Greeley (1811-1872) began the *New York Tribune*. Both came into journalism from poverty. Bennett came to America in 1822, having been trained in economics, but without any lasting employment; Greeley had been ostracised as a child because of physical deformities, and had to drop out of school; but, he spent several years as one of New York's finest job printers. He was praised by his foremen, despised by owners who were repulsed by people who didn't conform to what *they* thought people should look like, and dress the way *they* thought people should dress. But, James Gordon Bennett became known as the "Great Innovator," an editor who gave the newspaper most of the elements and sections that today distinguish a newspaper. And, Horace Greeley gave the newspaper a "soul," an editorial page that was widely respected—even by those who disagreed with it. Wisner, Bennett, and Greeley, in the space of less than a decade, proved De Tocqueville wrong about the nature of the American journalist. By focusing upon the great emerging middle class, the media had elevated the nature of journalism and gave it a form that every American newspaper today follows.

Chapter 18

'If All Mankind Minus One . . .'

The Revolutionary War, War of 1812, and Mexican-American War had made the nation aware of the conflict not only in economic and political ideology, but in the philosophy of free expression. If there is to be a strict observance of First Amendment rights, and of the concepts enunciated by Milton, Locke, Rousseau, Blackstone, and Jefferson, then how could there be censorship, even in times of war, many asked. But, in times of war, must not certain liberties be suppressed, asked others, and isn't the good of all society better served by the suppression of certain information than by its transmission to the people? The libertarians, countered that if you suppress information because of the "greater public good" in times of war, could not a government then suppress dissent in times of peace, citing such dissent to be disruptive of the public good. The authoritarian philosophy counters that if the society itself is destroyed, whether from within or by external war, there will *never* be freedom.

Bringing strength to the authoritarian argument was German philosopher Georg Hegel (1770-1831) who expanded the original concepts of Plato to suggest a closer relationship between the State and church:

> The State is embodied Morality. It is the ethical spirit which has clarified itself and has taken substantial shape as Will, a Will which is manifest before the world, which is self conscious and knows its purposes and carries through that which it knows to the extent of its knowledge. Custom and capital morality are the outward and visible form of the inner essence of the State; the self consciousness of the individual citizen, his knowledge of the activity, are the outward and visible form of the indirect existence of the State. The self consciousness of the individual finds the substance of its freedom in the attitude of the citizen which is the essence, purpose, and achievement of its self consciousness.
>
> The State is Mind, per se. This is due to the fact that it is the embodiment of the substantial Will, which is nothing else than the individual self consciousness conceived in its abstract form and raised to the universal plane. This substantial and massive unity is an absolute and fixed end in itself. In it freedom attains to the maximum of its rights: but at the same time the State, being an end in itself, is provided with the maximum of rights over against the individual citizens, whose highest duty it is to be members of the State . . .

To define freedom of the press as freedom to say and write whatever we please is parallel to the assertion that freedom as such means freedom to do as we please. Talk of this kind is due to wholly uneducated, crude, and superficial ideas . . .

According to Hegel, the spirit that had created the world had become alienated from it; in this new age it had again sought a closeness with the world, and placed itself into the nature of the State, the people; thus, it was the State that was an embodied morality of the spirit which created the world. Hegel argued that there was an "absolute idea" manifested in the State, but history adn society progressively both help people to recognize the limits of freedom.

Karl Marx: Libertarian

The debate continued into the latter part of the nineteenth century. Only now, the libertarians had the carefully-constructed words of political philosophers Karl Marx (1818-1883) and John Stuart Mill (1806-1873) to give them a stronger base.

Marx, who had studied under Hegel, received a doctorate in philosophy in 1841 from the University of Jena. Upon graduation, he began a career as a journalist, becoming editor of the *Rheinische Zeitung*, published in Cologne. Later, he would edit other German-language newspapers, and become London correspondent for Horace Greeley's *New York Tribune*. As as journalist, Marx was a social critic of the nature of the media, particularly the "conservative press," which often were stung by censorship rulings, yet accepted them as necessary for the existence of society. Marx, a libertarian who later developed concepts of socialism that would revolutionize political philosophy, opposed censorship, arguing, "The essence of the free press if the characterful, rational, moral essence of freedom. The character of the censored press is the characterless monster of unfreedom; it is a civilised monster, a perfumed abortion . . . Censorship holds us all in subjugation . . . ."

Although subject to some of the most severe forms of censorship in the Western world, Marx accepted an existence of impoverishment and struggle, recognizing that financial security seldom comes to those who speak out in opposition to the established order. In May 1842, Shortly after the announcement of a new Prussian censorship order, Marx wrote against censorship, and for a freedom of the press:

Thus the [censorship] instruction forbids writers to cast suspicion on the frame of mind of individuals or whole classes, and in the same breath it bids the censor divide all citizens into suspicious and unsuspicious, into well-intentioned and evil-intentioned. The press is deprived of the right to criticise, but criticism becomes the daily duty of the governmental critic. This reversal, however, does not end the matter. Within the press what was anti-State as regards content appeared as something particular, but from the aspect of its form it was something universal, that is to say, subject to universal appraisal . . .

From the standpoint of the idea, it is self-evident that freedom of the press has a justification quite different from that of censorship because it is itself an embodiment of the idea, an embodiment of freedom, a positive good, whereas censorship is an embodiment of unfreedom, the polemic of a world outlook of semblance against the world outlook of essence; it has a merely negative nature.

No! No! No! our speaker breaks in. I do not find fault with the semblance, but with the essence. Freedom is the wicked feature of freedom of the press. Freedom creates the possibility of evil. Therefore freedom is evil.

Evil freedom! . . .

But does not freedom of the press exist in the land of censorship? The press in general is a realisation of human freedom. Consequently, where is a press there is freedom of the press.

True, in the land of censorship the State has no freedom of the press, but one organ of the State has it, viz., the *government*. Apart from the fact that official government documents enjoy perfect freedom of the press, does not the censor exercise daily an unconditional freedom of the press, if not directly, then indirectly?

Writers are, as it were, his secretaries, When the secretary does not express the opinion of his chief, the latter strikes out the botch. Hence the censorship makes the press. . .

Freedom is so much the essence of man that even its opponents implement it while combating its reality; they want to appropriate for themselves as a most precious ornament what they have rejected as an ornament of human nature.

No man combats freedom; at most he combats the freedom of others. Hence, every kind of freedom has always existed, only at one time as a special privilege, at another as a universal right.

The question has now for the first time been given a consistent *meaning*. It is not a question whether freedom of the press ought to exist, for it always exists. The question is whether freedom of the press is a privilege of particular individuals or whether it is a privilege of the human mind. The question is whether a right of one side ought to be a wrong for the other side. The question is whether *freedom of the mind* has more right than *freedom against the mind* . . .

You think it wrong to put birds in cages. Is not the cage a preventive measure against birds of prey, bullets and storms? You think it barbaric to blind nightingales, but it does not seem to you at all barbaric to put out the eyes of the press with the sharp pens of the censorship. You regard it as despotic to cut a free person's hair against his will, but the censorship daily cuts into the flesh of thinking people and allows only bodies without hearts, submissive bodies which show no reaction, to pass as healthy!

The censorship law, therefore, is not a law, it is a police measure; but it is a *bad police measure*, for it does not achieve what it intends, and it does not intend what it achieves . . .

Lack of freedom is the real mortal danger for mankind. For the time being, leaving aside the moral consequences, bear in mind that you cannot enjoy the advantages of a free press without putting up with its inconveniences. You cannot pluck the rose without its thorns! And what do you lose with a free press?

The free press is the ubiquitous vigilant eye of a people's soul, the embodiment of a people's faith in itself, the eloquent link that connects the individual with the State and the world, the embodied culture that transforms material struggles into intellectual struggles and idealises their crude material form. It is a people's frank confession to itself, and the redeeming power of confession is well known. It is the spiritual mirror in which a people can see itself, and self-examination is the first condition of wisdom. It is the spirit of the State, which can be delivered into every cottage, cheaper than coal gas. It is all-sided, ubiquitous, omniscient. It is the ideal world which always wells up out of the real world and flows back into it with ever greater spiritual riches and renews its soul . . .

Censorship holds us all in subjection, just as under a despotic regime all are equal, if not in value, then in absence of value; that kind of freedom of the press seeks to introduce oligarchy in the sphere of intellectual life. The censorship declares that an author is at most inconvenient, unsuitable within the bounds of its realm. That kind of freedom of the press claims to anticipate world history, to know in advance the voice of the people, which hitherto has been the sole judge as to which writer has "authority" and which is "without authority". Whereas Solon did not venture to judge a man until *after* his life was over, after his death, this view presumes to judge a writer even before his birth.

The press is the most general way by which individuals can communicate their intellectual being. It knows no respect for persons, but only respect for intelligence. Do you want ability for intellectual communication to be determined officially by special external signs? What I cannot be for others, I am not and cannot be for myself. If I am not allowed to be a spiritual force for others, then I have no right to be a spiritual force for myself; and do you want to give certain individuals the privilege of being spiritual forces? Just as everyone learns to read and write, so everyone must have the right to read and write.

However, like most persons who believe in the freedom of the press, Karl Marx had a blemish, one not unlike that which afflicted many libertarian thinkers. He could speak out against censorship while his newspaper was being censored; he could argue against the suppresison of political thought while he was of the minority. But, freedom did not extend to all thought, all beliefs— certain people, said Marx, couldn't be "trusted." He and those who later claimed to be Marxists would never be able to erase the fact that Marx, born a Jew, the descendant of rabbis, would become anti-Semitic, arguing for the suppression of much Jewish literature.

John Stuart Mill: Capitalist Libertarian

John Stuart Mill's father, James, a brilliant philosopher, economist, and historian, believed strongly in an intense education for his children. For that reason, he kept John out of school so he could devote more time to reading the works of Herodotus, Lucian, Diogenes, Isocrates, and Plato—all of whom he had read, in the original Greek or Latin, by the age of eight.

John Stuart Mill's career began in 1823 with service to the India House where he worked as an examiner, and eventually became chief of the examiner's office in 1856. It would be this salaried position which gave Mill the financial security to develop the strongest libertarian theory since Milton two centuries earlier. Mill's early years became a period of intense self examination during which he rejected many of the values held by contemporary society—and by his father whom he held in the highest respect. A visit to Paris in 1830 gave Mill the perspective of the French liberals to consider.

The 1830s became a time of intense writing for Mill, and in 1835, he became editor of the newly-founded *London Review*. His essays during that decade reflected his training in history, literature, and philosophy. In *The System of Logic* (1843), Mill tried to join a new system with a traditional system of logic to formulate a scientific method. A year later, he completed *Essays on Some Unsettled Questions in Political Economy*, in which he tried to deal with the economic problems related to the profits from international comerce, the relationship of consumption and production, and the ratio of profits to wages. These essays represented the first stage of Mill's development in which he dealt with technological problems that had been discussed, debated, but not solved by the economists.

The second stage of Mill's thinking appeared as *Principles of Political Economy* (1848), a two-volume work in which Mill began to show his independence from the traditional economic arguments. Mill was not satisfied with the system that had developed in England and Europe that permitted the landed classes to enjoy an excessive portion of the return on production while the laborers lived in poverty and sometimes starvation. Mill held many of the views of the socialists, but remained a capitalist. The mature individuals, said Mill, should be given the right of choice, as long as they don't interfere of harm anyone else's rights; the greatest good of society, Mill argued, was that in which the greatest number of people individually enjoyed the greatest amount of happiness. It was an idealism, nurtured by his friends, mentors, and by Harriet Hardy, whom he married in 1851, that led him to look at social issues even deeper than before. This was his third stage of development, a time when he tried to fuse his economic theories with philosophies with an underlying base of idealism, cast by tragedy. In 1858, the East India Company was dissolved, and Mill, at the age of fifty-two, sadly retired from public life; soon after, his wife died. The first significant work after his personal losses was *On Liberty* (1859), the most enduring of his philosophy, and the work which helped establish him as the greatest libertarian thinker since Milton. "We can never be sure," wrote Mill, "that the opinion we are endeavoring to stifle is a false opinion, and if we were sure, stifling it would be an evil still." Although Mill

expressed much enthusiasm for democratic government, he seemed pessimistic
about the likelihood of much success coming from it. *On Liberty* reflects his
fundamental support of the individual, and of the inherent rights of mankind—
but it also recognizes that libertarianism had to develop from an authoritarian
base, one that still exists:

> . . . Let us suppose, therefore, that the government is entirely at one
> with the people, and never thinks of exerting any power of coercion unless
> in agreement with what it conceives to be their voice. But I deny the right
> of the people to exercise such coercion, either by themselves or by their
> government. The power itself is illegitimate. The best government has
> no more title to it than the worst. It is as noxious, or more noxious, when
> exerted in accordance with public opinion, than when in opposition to it.
> If all mankind minus one were of one opinion, and only one person were of
> the contrary opinion, mankind would be no more justified in silencing that
> one person, than he, if he had the power, would be justified in silencing
> mankind. Were an opinion a personal possession of no value except to
> the owner; if to be obstructed in the enjoyment of it were simply a private
> injury, it would make some difference whether the injury was inflicted
> only on a few persons or on many. But the peculiar evil of silencing the
> expression of an opinion is, that it is robbing the human race; posterity as
> well as the existing generation; those who dissent from the opinion, still
> more than those who hold it. If the opinion is right, they are deprived of
> the opportunity of exchanging error for truth: if wrong, they lose, what
> is almost as great a benefit, the clearer perception and livelier impression
> of truth, produced by its collision with error . . .

> Absolute princes, or others who are accustomed to unlimited deference,
> usually feel this complete confidence in their own opinions on nearly all
> subjects. People more happily situated, who sometimes hear their opinions
> disputed, and are not wholly unused to be set right when they are wrong,
> place the same unbounded reliance only on such of their opinions as are
> shared by all who surround them, or to whom they habitually defer; for
> in proportion to a man's want of confidence in his own solitary judgment,
> does he usually repose, with implicit trust, on the infallibility of "the
> world" in general. And the world, to each individual, means the part of it
> with which he comes in contact; his party, his sect, his church, his class
> of society; the man may be called, by comparison, almost liberal and
> large-minded to whom it means anything so comprehensive as his own
> country or his own age.

Chapter 19

Freedom, Suppression, and Slavery: The Antebellum Era

All the philosophies and all the epithets about freedom of speech, all the laws written and all the decisions issued, cannot change attitudes. The United States had shown an underlying mistrust of libertarian thinking by its enactment of the Alien and Sedition acts which were later declared unconstitutional; by extensive editorial campaigns that advocated suppression of opposition; and by mob actions against those with unpopular views.

How antebellum America handled the slavery issue suggested that America could wrap itself in libertarianism, yet never truly become a libertarian country; at best, it would be a country that accepted libertarian philosophy only as long as the philosophy did not get in the way of its own self-interest.

Stolen from homes, bound in chains, starved into submission, Black slaves were brought to America from Western Africa more than a century before the Declaration of Independence was written. Now, more than a half-century after the "Bill of Rights," most Blacks were still slaves, bound to slave codes that forbade all freedom of expression, including the right to assemble, worship, and speak without slave owners or other Whites present; they were forbidden to talk with free Blacks, and with rare exceptions, were forbidden from learning to read or write, the Whites recognizing that access to mass communication could unify the Blacks and lead to a possible overthrow of slavery.

Thomas Jefferson had tried to get an anti-slavery clause put into the Constitution, but was thoroughly defeated. In the fifty years after the Constitution was approved, America was too busy fighting through its "Dark Ages," building and expanding a nation, to care too much about the problems of the slaves. It is a "Southern problem," said the North, "and up to the South to decide what to do." But there were people—North and South—who would speak out against slavery. The abolitionists united into anti-slavery societies whose purposes were to use the media to bring the terror of slavery to the attention of the country. On minimal budgets, these societies printed tracts and pamphlets to flood the North; upon almost-retired hand-presses, they printed slave narratives, autobiographies of fugitive and freed slaves. They brought the authors to public meetings to tell the truth about the "contented Darkey and magnanimous Southern gentleman," and sold the narratives for a few pennies.

On March 16, 1827, the Rev. Samuel Cornish and John D. Russwurm published the first issue of *Freedom's Journal*, explaining, "We wish to plead our own case. Too long have others spoken for us." Cornish had edited weeklies in New York, but now the nation would have its first newspaper with editorial content directed to the abolition of slavery. The newspaper ceased after almost three years, but it forced northeastern America to take a closer look at the nature of slavery, and of the abolitionist movement.

William Lloyd Garrison, a White editor, added his voice to the abolition movement after serving seven months in jail for refusing to recant statements that one of the more prominent citizens of Massachusetts was a slave importer. Garrison had been introduced to the abolition movement by Benjamin Lundy, Quaker editor of an abolitionist newspaper; this friendship, combined with what the authorities saw as Garrison's unyielding beliefs that slavery must be abolished, led to his arrest on libel charges. During his jail term, Garrison became more radical, more bitter. Impoverished, Garrison used whatever money he could make as a printer to start, and keep alive, *The Liberator*, a weekly newspaper that would become the voice of unification for the abolitionist movement in the North. The goal of the *Liberator*, said Garrison in 1831, was "to educate, not preach revolt."

Abolition infuriated the South, but upset the North for it challenged America's self-image as a land of liberty. To all political factions, Garrison argued, "He who opposes the public liberty overthrows his own." The more that people tried to silence his press—which usually put out no more than a couple thousand copies a week—the more fanatic Garrison became, soon advocating the overthrow of slavery by violence. Garrison was threatened, harassed, and once forced by a mob to run nearly naked through the streets of Boston—but he still refused to allow his voice to be silenced.

Postal Controls

A country that had fought a revolution upon libertarian principles now looked at the abolitionist literature and decided that there *are* certain views that need to be suppressed for the greater public good.

Amos Kendall, a journalist, one of President Andrew Jackson's closest advisors, and Postmaster General of the United States, allowed his mail clerks to "lose" *The Liberator* and other abolitionist newspapers being mailed to southern states. In 1835, a mob in Charleston, S.C., seized, then burned a sack of mail containing abolitionist literature. The postmaster at Charleston asked for the right to officially seize such mail, citing the literature as seditious. On August 4, 1835, Kendall wrote the postmaster that the federal government had "no legal authority to exclude newspapers from the mail." However, he also pointed out that "the post office department was created to serve the people of *each* and *all* of the *United States*, and not to be used as an instrument of their *destruction* . . . We owe an obligation to the laws, but a higher one to the communities in which we live, and if the *former* be perverted to disregard the *latter*, it is patriotism to disregard them." Thus, Kendall, using the argument that the greater good of society must always take precedence, essentially authorized postmasters to seize mail that could be considered seditious.

In 1835, President Andrew Jackson asked Congress to officially ban distribution in the South, by mail, of all publications which advocated the abolition of slavery. The ensuing controversy would pit three of America's outstanding statesmen in opposition. Sens. Daniel Webster and Henry Clay argued that such a law would be not only a threat to the freedom of the press, but would also be unconstitutional; Sen. John C. Calhoun argued for its passage. The following year, the Senate, by a vote of 29-19, rejected the President's request, and passed legislation that established severe penalties for any postmaster who withheld any mail from delivery.

Post office department, August 4th, 1835
P.M. Charleston, S.C.

Sir:

In your letter of the 29th . . . just received, you inform me that by the steamboat mail from New York your office had been filled with pamphlets and tracts upon slavery; that the public mind was highly excited upon the subject; that you doubted the safety of the mail itself out of your possession; that you had determined, as the wisest course, to detain these papers; and now you ask instructions from the department.

Upon a careful examination of the law, I am satisfied that the postmaster general has no legal authority to exclude newspapers from the mail, nor prohibit their carriage or delivery on account of their character or tendency, real or supposed. Probably, it was not thought safe to confer on the head of an executive department a power over the press, which might be perverted and abused.

But I am not prepared to direct you to forward or deliver the papers of which you speak. The post office department was created to serve the people of *each* and *all* of the *United States*, and not to be used as the instrument of their *destruction*. None of the papers detained have been forwarded to me, and I cannot judge for myself of their character and tendency but you inform me that they are, in character, "the most inflammatory and incendiary—and insurrectionary in the highest degree."

By no act, or direction of mine, official or private, could I be induced to aid, knowingly, in giving circulation to papers of this description, directly or indirectly. We owe an obligation to the laws, but a higher one to the communities in which we live, and if the *former* be perverted to destroy the *latter*, it is patriotism to disregard them. Entertaining these views, I cannot sanction, and will not condemn the step you have taken.

Your justification must be looked for in the character of the papers detained, and circumstances by which you are surrounded.

—Amos Kendall
Postmaster General

Strangling American Freedoms

Fear dictates the acceptance of authoritarian doctrine, and fear led the South to place severe restrictions upon the civil liberties of all its citizens. Stung by the Nat Turner slave rebellion in 1831, during which more than sixty Whites were killed, the South had reacted as one afraid for its own life, and began a random supression of all abolitionist literature. The refusal of Congress in 1835 to allow the suppression of abolitionist literature, and its subsequent enactment of laws to prevent suppression, led Southern legislatures to enact their own laws. In 1835, Georgia passed legislation that set the death penalty for anyone convicted of the "tendency to incite insurrection," with the understanding that publication of articles about the abolition movement would be held to be in violation of the law. Other states quickly followed the pattern. By the Civil War, in all Southern states, persons subscribing to, or in possession of, any abolitionist literature, were in violation of law, subject to imprisonment or, in extreme cases, death; although many Southern editors did speak out against the curtailing of First Amendment liberties, they were usually seen as traitors.

The South had tried to suppress abolitionist argument, but it was the North that gave the country a martyr. Elijah Lovejoy, editor of the *St. Louis Observer*, was a militant abolitionist who faced a mob which had determined that the *Observer* was threatening the peace of the community by printing numerous articles in opposition to slavery. The First Amendment, believed the mob, surely could not protect someone whose views were so contrary to, so damaging to, those of the people. Tyranny of the majority forced Lovejoy to move his newspaper plant a few miles away, to Alton, Illinois—where his presses were destroyed by another mob.

Like the people of St. Louis, the people of Alton knew—they just absolutely *knew*—that they had *right* on their side, and that it was justifiable to destroy

---

Russian Repression

In April 1849, all the members of the Petrashevsky Circle, a social-political discussion group in Russia, were arrested, tried, convicted, lined up before a firing squad and shot—though with blanks. The government planned to scare the people, by using the Petrashevsky Circle as an example, into an even deeper submission to the State.

Among those arrested was Feodor Dostoyefsky (1821-1881), author of *The Poor People* (1846), a highly popular novel about the poor and oppressed in Russia. For four years, after the terror of the "execution," Dostoyefsky lived in a Siberian prison; for six more years, he served in the Army, first as a private, then as an officer.

In the two decades left of his life, Dostoyefsky edited a popular journal (which was suppressed by the government), and wrote several of the world's greatest novels, among them *Crime and Punishment* (1866), *The Gambler* (1866), *The Idiot* (1867), and *The Brothers Karamazov* (1880).

views that were "not in the public interest." With contributions from friends, Lovejoy reestablished his newspaper. And again a mob destroyed it. Then, in this Northern city, the people called a meeting to decide what to do about an editor who would not be silent as he was directed by the *people*, who refused to accept the "public will," who dared to claim that slavery was a social evil that threatened the foundations of the country. Lovejoy attended that meeting to express his views about freedom of the press, was shouted down, and returned to a building that housed his newspaper press. Within minutes, the mob—no one knows how many—moved to the warehouse. On November 7, 1837, the day that a mob again decided that freedom must have limitations, Elijah Lovejoy, theology graduate of Princeton University, former teacher and minister, and now editor of the *Alton Observer*, died at the age of thirty-five, defending the rights of all people to a free and unmuzzled press.

Nineteen persons would be brought to trial . . . Nineteen of thousands would be charged not with murder but with rioting . . . None would be convicted.

Soon, the North used the media to solidify its position against the South. Slave narratives, many now written by Whites, spread distortions of slavery; reporters' stories became fictional accounts of what the North *thought* was happening in the South. It would become a moral crusade, one that would propagandize, then manipulate, a nation.

Women: The Suppressed

The Emancipation Proclamation and three constitutional amendments gave philosophical base to allow all people, no matter what their race, ethnicity, or beliefs, an equal opportunity in America with Whites. Nevertheless, Blacks, American Indians, Jews, Mexican-Americans and other minorities who "looked different" or "believed strange things" were still enslaved by a racist society unable and incapable of toleration. And women of all races and beliefs were denied the rights of citizenship. Colleges refused to admit them; the professions refused to certify them; public legislative bodies refused to allow them to speak. And the State, run by men, declared that it was State policy to deny freedom of expresion to women, citing the Bible for some of the justification. In 1855, Elizabeth Cady Stanton wrote Susan B. Anthony:

To think that all in me of which my father would have felt a proper pride had I been a male is deeply mortifying to him because I am a woman . . . [My husband] and friends are not willing that I should write even on the woman question. But I will both write and speak.

In 1920, by a constitutional amendment, women were given the right of voting; four years later, by legislation, the Indians were told that they were now American citizens.

Harriet Beecher Stowe's *Uncle Tom's Cabin*, a powerful but highly distorted view of plantation life and of slavery, was first serialized from June 5, 1851, to April 1, 1852, in *The National Era*, an abolitionist weekly. Even with distribution in the South suppressed, *Uncle Tom's Cabin* became the most influential novel in the history of the country. Within a year, more than 200,000 copies had been sold in the United States alone; by the end of 1855, more than half a million copies were in print. Eventually, there would be more than a million copies in print, with twenty-five separate translations for the international market. *Uncle Tom's Cabin* was propoganda designed to infuriate the North, to awaken it to the terror of slavery. The South, as a body, forbade its distribution or sale, claiming that it violated the laws of sedition and "inciting to riot." As "false doctrine," the South believed it had a duty to suppress the book in the greater interest of the society.

As the economic and political differences—and now the issue of slavery—continued to widen the split between the North and the South, U.S. Attorney General Caleb Cushing, in 1857, and Postmaster General J. Holt, in 1859, approved the censoring of mail in the South. This time, the censorship was not only to prevent abolition papers from furthering sedition, but to assure the federal government that military and political secrets were not being transmitted outside their lawful channels.

As the differences widened, the North began pouring abolitionist literature into the South, holding slavery to be the critical issue; the South responded by pointing to the economic and political actions of the North were choking the South. The South saw the country not much different than the colonists saw England in 1776; the North saw the country being torn apart, a *united* states now becoming a confederation of ideologies that would tear it apart. Neither side wished war, yet the bloodiest war to be fought on American soil became inevitable.

Chapter 20

Libertarianism, Censorship, and a Nation in Pain

War, perhaps more than almost any other time, opens the way for the believers of the authoritarian philosophy to assert themselves. Military officials and the civilian leadership need to maintain secrecy of battle strategy in order to surprise the enemy; but they also place a veil of silence over many other areas in order to keep the morale of the people high, and not to give "aid and comfort" to the enemy. Yet, at the same time, government needs to use the media to promote its points–of–view so that the electorate will continue to support the war effort. One method for gaining the desired behavior from the people involves trying to establish a cooperative agreement between the media and the government, the government emphasizing that the media are part of, not separate from, a nation at war.

The Civil War provided the opportunity to test the will of the government regarding control of the media. Shortly after the war began, and possibly because Northern editors pointed it out, the federal government refused to deliver any mail to the South, and placed severe restrictions upon the use of the telegraph. In the early battles of the war, several newspaper correspondents found their accounts were either not sent by telegraph lines, or had been censored by the military leadership to prevent disclosure of battle plans.

The first order calling for voluntary censorship during the Civil War came from a meeting between Maj. Gen. George B. McClellan and editors of several newspapers. The resolution of August 2, 1861, unanimously accepted by the press, proposed that editors would "refrain from publishing, either as editorial, or as correspondence of any description, or form any point, any matter that may furnish aid and comfort to the enemy." For his part, McClellan indicated he would open the lines of communication, assuring reporters they would receive news of public interest. The resolution lasted but a short time when the federal censor, employed by the Department of State, ordered that all communication by reporters on either military or civilian government operations be blocked.

In February 1862, censorship was taken from the Department of State and transferred to the War Department. Correspondents were now required to submit all articles to the provost marshals prior to transmission, but they also knew that the only censorship would be of areas directly affecting military operations.

In the South, Gen. P.G.T. Beauregard, recognizing the objectivity of the Press Association (PA), the South's wire service, ordered that the PA "should have every facility for early access to intelligence compatible with the public interests." Throughout the war, the PA confined its reporting to news and, unlike many Northern papers, refused to file dispatches that contained speculation and rumor. Giving the South a philosophical guidance was the First Amendment to the Constitution of the United States—now copied and a part of the Constitution of the Confederate States of America.

Abraham Lincoln, although suspending the constitutional guarantee of a writ of *habeus corpus*, did not want the newspapers suppressed. However, the strong Copperhead press in the North took on an anti-war, anti-Lincoln position; their views often led to wide–spread draft riots. And, as those who could neither buy their way out of the Army, nor find a suitable replacement, marched upon the government, the Copperhead press magnified the opposition to Lincoln's government. The *New York World* and the *New York Journal of Commerce*, two of the nation's larger newspapers, and numerous smaller newspapers throughout the North used whatever influence they had to disagree with the Lincoln administration on almost every issue regarding the war effort. Of the seventeen New York daily newspapers, only a half-dozen, led by Horace Greeley's *Tribune*, were loyal to Lincoln. Even James Gordon Bennett and his *Herald*, the *Tribune's* major competitor, was pro-South until a mob descended upon the building, and Bennett decided that he would confine his policies to attacks upon the Republican administration rather than upon the war effort.

In the South, an almost universal consensus of opinion, as well as extensive peer pressure, left little need for any form of governmental or extralegal censorship. However, in the North, where all shades of opinion existed, the Copperhead newspapers continued with their strong attacks upon Lincoln and the war effort.

The *Dayton* (Ohio) *Empire* became so violent in its attacks upon the government that Gen. Ambrose Burnside, commanding general of the district that included Ohio, issued General Order No. 38 warning Copperhead papers against giving "aid and comfort" to the enemy. Clement L. Vallandingham, editor of the *Empire*, and a former U.S. congressman and speaker of the Ohio House of Representatives, continued his anti-Lincoln, anti-abolitionist, and pro-seccession attacks; he was tried by military court, and sentenced to prison; Lincoln, however, ordered Vallandingham escorted into the South.

But, even Lincoln's patience had its limits. When the *New York World* and *Journal of Commerce* printed a bogus presidential proclamation on May 18, 1864, calling for the draft of 400,000 men, Lincoln became infuriated. Although both newspapers were anti-Lincoln, their printing of the proclamation was a hoax played upon them as much as upon the public by a greedy editor for the *Brooklyn Eagle* who planned to "buy low" after the inevitable drop in the stock market. Under considerable pressure from Secretary of State William H. Seward, Lincoln ordered the two newspapers, and a telegraph service that transmitted the message, closed. When they reopened two days later, federal officials were in the buildings to monitor the operations.

Lincoln's views of the rights of the press remained unchanged throughout the Civil War. In 1863, in response to a request by Gen. Ambrose Burnside to close the *Chicago Times*, a Copperhead newspaper which had viciously attacked Lincoln, the war effort, the Emancipation Proclamation, and which had also printed numerous articles that could have given aid and comfort to the South, Lincoln wrote, "I fear that you do not fully comprehend the danger of abridging the liberties of the people. A government had better go to the very extreme of toleration than to do aught that could be construed into an interference with or jeopardize in any degree the rights of the people."

However, the attacks of the *Times* continued, and Burnside forced the issue of suppression, issuing a general order closing the *Times*, citing the "repeated expression of disloyal and incendiary sentiments." Burnside had consistently warned the publisher of the *Times* about numerous articles that had transmitted information to the South, and ordered the paper closed in order to protect both the government and the security of the military forces. At the same time, Burnside also prohibited the circulation of the *New York World* in areas under his military control; the *World*, like the *Times*, had also published numerous vicious articles, many filled with lies, about the President. Upon learning of the order, Lincoln, torn between the issues of freedom of the press and the need to protect a nation torn by a civil war, finally asked Secretary of War Edwin M. Stanton to direct Burnside to reverse the order. Stanton relayed the President's order on June 1, 1863:

[The President] directs me to say that in his judgment it would be better for you to take an early occasion to revoke that order. The irritation produced by such acts is in his opinion likely to do more harm than the publication would do. The Government approves of your motives and desires to give you cordial and efficient support. But while military movements are left to your judgment, upon administrative questions such as the arrest of civilians and the suppression of newspapers not requiring immediate action, the President desires to be previously consulted.

In his diary of June 3, 1863, Gideon Welles, Lincoln's secretary of the navy and close personal advisor, wrote, "The President—and I think every member of the Cabinet—regrets what has been done [by Gen. Burnside]." Almost a year later, Lincoln wrote:

I can only say I was embarrassed with the question between what was due to the military service on the one hand, and the liberty of the press on the other . . . I am far from certain to-day that the revocation was not right.

Chapter 21

The Moral Suppresser

The Civil War had torn the United States apart and left two hundred thousand Americans dead. The North had continued to develop an industrial base during the war, and with peace was now ready to move into a new and rapid period of growth. The South, however, was devastated. The great plantations lay in ruin, the region's economy destroyed. For the ten years after the Civil War, the South was occupied by federal troops, military governors, and carpetbagers. Black citizens now had the right to vote, gained through the passage of the thirteenth, fourteenth, and fifteenth amendments to the Constitution between 1865 and 1870. Many were elected to local and state governing bodies, in an era now known as Reconstruction.

With the election of Rutherford B. Hayes (1822-1893) in 1876 (he took office on March 5, 1877), the troops began to leave the South and segregation emerged again. All-white legislatures appeared and passed "Jim Crow" laws relegating Blacks to second status citizenship again. The North did not have the offensive laws of the South, but discrimination existed in employment and social circles.

The years from the end of the war until the twentieth century saw the greatest expansion the nation had yet enjoyed, helped considerably by grant assistance from the federal government and the expansion into the West. Speculation and the building of fortunes during the late 1860s and early 1870s became commonplace. Oil found in Pennsylvania and Ohio, gold and silver mined farther west, iron smelted in Pittsburgh, lumber harvested in many places, copper mined for commercial use, and exports sent to much of the world characterized the era. But President Ulysses S. Grant's (1822-1885, president 1869-1877) helpful posture opened the way to fraud and abuse and eventually to failure with a depression that lasted throughout the final years of his administration.

The economic depression of the 1870s turned to better times by 1878 and the nation entered a period when the total value of manufactured goods rose from $5.4 billion in 1879 to $13 billion in 1899. The production of iron and steel rose from 1.25 million long tons to 10 million during the last twenty years of the nineteenth century.

The last third of the century saw a number of new inventions, including the telephone, typewriter, linotype, phonograph, electric light, cash register, air brake, refrigerator car, and automobile, and the widespread growth of the railroad. Some of these inventions would increase the demand for petroleum

139

Post 1865 — manufacturing

*Since primitive times virtually all religious or social sys-
tems have attempted to maintain themselves by forbidding
free criticism and analysis either of existing institutions or
of the doctrine that sustains them; of democracy alone is
it the cardinal principle that free criticism and analysis
by all and sundry is the highest virtue. In its inception
modern democracy was, therefore, a stupendous gamble
for the highest stakes. It offered long odds on the capacity
and integrity of the human mind. It wagered all it had
that the freest exercise of the human reason would never
disprove the proposition that only by the freest exercise of
the human reason can a tolerably just and rational society
ever be created.*

—Carl Becker, *Freedom and Responsibility
in the American Way of Life* (1949).

products in industry, business, and home; all would help existing or new
businesses develop to larger sizes.

The newspapers of New York City, Boston, and other cities flourished with
the new printing technologies that appeared over the next thirty years. The
speed of producing newspapers became faster, the number of magazines rose
from seven hundred at the end of the Civil War to more than four thousand at
century's end. The penny press that had emerged in the 1830s was growing into
large businesses and would eventually appear in the form of Joseph Pulitzer's
and William Randolph Hearst's newspapers. Circulations would exceed one
million per day before the end of the century. Newspapers would become big
business, just as oil, railroads, and steel were becoming. And there was work
for the censor.

Pornography: Controlling 'The Flood'

After the Civil War, the nation was concerned with restoring the rights of
its citizens and with the control of obscene materials—potentially conflicting
values. The constitutional amendment process became the battle ground for
making slavery illegal. The thirteenth amendment (1865) prohibited slavery,
but while the Constitution acquired a new amendment protecting citizens from
slavery, Congress created a new law to protect citizens from receiving certain
kinds of mail.

Although Anthony Comstock (1844-1915) became perhaps the best known
opponent of obscene literature in the world during the nineteenth century, he
hardly created the obsession for policing the promoters of "smut." Neither

did the United States become the originator of laws to supress the flow of pornography or other offensive literature. Many centuries ago, Shih Huang Ti, the architect of the Great Wall of China, destroyed the works of Confucius; Plato wanted the *Odyssey* removed from Greek society. Throughout history, church councils have produced lists of forbidden books and authors.

England had its problems with offensive sexual behavior when, in 1663, Sir Charles Sydlyes dared stand on a public balcony in London—nude, drunk, and noisy—while a crowd gathered below him. This case had little to do with the development of common law concepts of pornography and obscenity; however, more was to come.

With the publication of *Venus in the Cloister; Or, the Nun in Her Smock*— a crude attack upon the Catholic Church—there developed a common law regarding morality. In *Rex* v. *Curl* (1727), the court concluded that the publication "jeopardized" public morality and the publisher could be punished under English common law. Earlier prosecutions for obscenity had been done by ecclesiastical courts, but this case was tried in a public court establishing the practice of governmental prosecutions. A concurrent development in England saw the growth of societies committed to banning obscenity from English publication; but, as the societies grew, so did the popularity of obscenity; by the nineteenth century, England had emerged into its pornographic period.

The colonies had little interest in dealing with obscene or pornographic materials. In the United States, the first evidence of judicial concern with obscenity occured in 1821, *Commonwealth* v. *Holmes*. Fanny Hill was the heroine in *Memoirs of a Woman of Pleasure*, John Cleland's book first published in London, 1748-49. Two itinerate booksellers were punished as a result of a Massachusetts court decision for selling the book that both the United States Post Office and the Customs Bureau had banned. The American history of the work was little different from the English history where it had an underground existance for seventy years; eventually *Fanny Hill* would figure prominently in a major constitutional case in 1966.

In 1842, with the passage of the Tariff Act, Congress created a tool to prohibit the importing of "all indecent and obscene prints, paintings, lithographs, engravings, and transparencies." The law passed Congress with but the faintest sign of debate. There was no discussion about First Amendment implications regarding the control of the press or the right to read. Evidently, the legislators saw no harm in a law that would permit the seizure of pictures or prints. Despite the lack of controversy, the law had significant ramifications because customs officials could take obscene materials from anyone entering the country.

In 1865, the United States Postmaster General approached Congress with the information that "great numbers [of] obscene books and pictures [were reaching] the Army." Because of this trend, some postal officials had taken matters into their own hands and confiscated publications they thought obscene. Now they wanted a law to protect them in their work. The debate in Congress was short and vague, with little discussion of censorship or of possible First Amendment violations. However, Maryland's Sen. Reverdy Johnson, a lawyer

US didn't elect anti-porno laws

Early crackdowns on porno lit (incl Fanny Hill)

of considerable reputation, had some fear about postal officials breaking too many seals in their quest to save the nation from offensive material. Although Johnson said nothing about censorship, he did fear the Post Office might invade people's privacy in its quest to find contraband.

The resulting statute read: "No obscene book, pamphlet . . . shall be admitted into the mails." The law permitted the postmaster to examine the outside of packages to determine if they might be obscene, but in the interest of protecting citizens, did not permit the breaking of seals. The statute allowed a postmaster to refuse mail if the packages appeared to contain material in violation of the law. As passed, the law did not define obscenity, nor did it set up a specific administrative structure or procedure for policing the mails.

Only three years after Congress passed its postal law regarding obscene materials, an amendment to the Constitution of the United States provided protections involved in any legal proceeding. The Fourteenth Amendment (1868) promised:

> All persons born or naturalized in the United States and subject to the jurisdiction thereof, are citizens of the United States and of the State wherein they reside. No State shall make or enforce any law which shall abridge the privileges or immunities of citizens of the United States; nor shall any State deprive any person of life, liberty, or property, without due process of law; nor deny to any person within its jurisdiction the equal protection of the laws.

Two years later, the right to vote was guaranteed in the Fifteenth Amendment (1870). The "due process" provision of the Fourteenth Amendment would provide the ground upon which some important cases would transfer First Amendment rights to states.

The Hicklin Rule

By some irony, England was evolving a standard for identifying obscene material during the same years that the Fourteenth Amendment was added to the United States Constitution—a standard that would be used in a number of cases by judges in the United States.

Laws passed in the United States before the Civil War and shortly afterwards had declared it to be illegal to mail obscene materials, but Congress seemed unable or unwilling to create a standard for defining obscenity. The English were to help out, in *Regina* v. *Hicklin* (1868), by creating a standard for obscenity adopted by the United States courts when they could not evolve their own concepts. Hicklin had been arrested for selling a strongly worded pamphlet, *The Confessional Unmasked,* which was directed at the Catholics as part of a campaign of the Protestant Electoral Union to keep Catholics out of Parliament. The writing was not the typical pornography that had been prosecuted in England in the past, and Hicklin's attorney argued that the author had the right to point out the offenses of the confessional by any means he chose, including the relating of porongraphic conversations described as taking place during confession.

Posd.. len via #17
US standard for obscenity set by UK via Hicklin
= if any part is NG, it all NG (143)

Lord Chief Justice Henry Cockburn (1779-1854) disagreed. In writing the court opinion, he indicated what constituted obscenity that could be punished:

> Whether the tendency of the matter charged as obscene is to deprave and corrupt those whose minds are open to such immoral influences and into whose hands a publication of this sort might fall.

This standard was important first because Cockburn permitted the examination of selected parts of the questionable pamphlet to determine if isolated parts had a tendency to corrupt or deprave. If any part failed the test, then the entire work would be deemed to be obscene.

Secondly, the test required that the work be judged against the susceptibility of those most disposed to fall under the corrupting influence of a work. This meant that if the young or feeble might be adversely affected, then the work should be out of reach for all citizens. The "Hicklin rule," as it was known, would become the standard in American cases into the mid-twentieth century.

Corruption in High Places

During the 1860s and 1870s, a period just after the Civil War, many events were taking place which led Americans to fear for their country; corruption in government seemed to be everywhere. William M. "Boss" Tweed (1823-1878) of Tammany Hall was remembered for corruption in New York City government where he served in a number of municipal positions after 1856. Estimates suggest that Tweed's friends, the "Tweed Ring," plundered $30 million to $200 million of public funds. The *New York Times* found much to quarrel with in the Tweed circle, including a painter who was paid $2,807,464.06 for a modest paint job. The *Times* supposed the painter should give the six cents to charity. Thomas Nast had created the Tammany Tiger in a cartoon that appeared in *Harper's Weekly* in 1871. The tiger was shown destroying people, and appeared with the line "The Tammany tiger loose." Samuel J. Tilden (1814-1886) helped get Tweed tried and convicted on forgery and larceny charges. Tweed was sent to prison in 1873, but was released in 1875 and later tried on other charges. Tilden was governor of New York State and Democratic presidential candidate in 1876, a contest in which fraud may have occurred leading to the election of Rutherford B. Hayes.

Meanwhile, Black Friday, September 24, 1869, came about because James Fisk (1834-1872), a flamboyant financier, and Jay Gould (1836-1892), U. S. railroad executive and financier, tried to gain control over the nation's gold supply.

In 1873, the nation went into an economic collapse initiated by the failure of Jay Cooke and Company, an American financial concern; Grant, who had been popular with the electorate, became the one to criticize. The Credit Mobilier scandal—a company controlled by Union Pacific stockholders that apparently had given members of Congress gifts of stock—led to a congressional investigation. Other problems in the Grant administration included fraud in handling of whiskey by the Internal Revenue Department and the growth of the famous "whiskey ring" made public in 1875, and the improper handling of Indian affairs that led to the resignation of Secretary of War William W. Belnap to avoid impeachment. By 1876, the Grant administration was in disarray along with the economy. And reports filtering back from the South declared extensive fraud and many problems with Reconstruction. The average voter must have felt that the nation was collapsing. Meanwhile, the flow of pornography seemed to be increasing everywhere.

Comstock: Suppressor of Vice

Into this enviroment it was easy for Anthony Comstock (1844- 1915) to become the chief advocate in the fight against obscenity. Comstock became a zealous opponent of all the "filthy" and "depraved" literature he thought he saw spreading across the nation, with no concern whatever over the First Amendment rights of the nation's writers, publishers, and other citizens. The nation must be purified of this evil, he argued.

Comstock had spent his early life as a clerk for a Connecticut regiment during the Civil War—a post from which he was later discharged. About 1871, he went to work as a salesman, but again lost his job. During this time, he was on the staff of the Young Men's Christian Association (YMCA); the job permitted him to develop a new organization named The New York Society for the Suppression of Vice; set up by the YMCA in 1873, it followed the pattern of a similar society in London.

Although some thinkers had reservations about societies for the suppression of vice, the public either approved or passively accepted their work. Sydney Smith (1771-1845), the British scholar, reflecting upon the London society, observed, "It is hardly possible that a society for the suppression of vice can ever be kept within the bounds of good sense and moderation."

While Comstock was getting his society incorporated, a number of stories that appeared in the press, pointing to "improper" sexual activities, aroused Comstock's anger. In Fall 1872, a story appearing in *Woodhull & Claffin's Weekly* suggested that the Rev. Henry Ward Beecher (1813-1887), highly-respected American clergyman and author of several books, had had an affair with another man's wife. Comstock swore out a warrant to get the government to take action against the publication for printing obscenity. Although they had proven themselves to be competent journalists and activists, Victoria Woodhull and Tennessee Claffin were arrested for publishing allegedly obscene materials. The federal commissioner who heard the arguments for both sides could not decide how to proceed, so no federal trial came out of the incident. Comstock became convinced of the need for a stronger law.

George Francis Train, a wealthy financial businessman, became so disgusted at the events that had befallen Claffin and Woodhull that he produced a pamphlet entitled *The Train Lique*, more obscene than anything Claffin and Woodhull had published. The attorney who had defended the two women had used quotations from the Old Testament as comparison with the words in the *Weekly*. Train used the same line of thinking, quoting obscene passages from the Bible in his publication. Train later wrote:

Comstock started crusade against porno lit

I was immediately arrested on a charge of obscenity, and taken to the Tombs [New York City jail]. I was never tried on this charge, but was kept in jail as a lunatic, and then dismissed, under the ban of declared lunacy, and have so remained for thirty years. Although the public pretended to be against me, it was very eager to buy the edition of my paper that gave them extracts from the Bible. The price of the paper rose from five cents a copy to twenty, forty, sixty cents, and even to one dollar. In a few days it was selling surreptitiously for two dollars a copy.

During the winter of 1873, Comstock traveled to Washington, D. C., frequently with a case full of exhibits of books, bogus sex literature, and "objects"—birth control devices and abortion tools—that he believed had sexual implications. According to Comstock, these objects could be obtained through the mail; to every member of Congress who would listen to his pitch, he would decry the "moral decay" of the country. Many other groups saw what Comstock was doing, and gave him their support. Soon, he became a regular figure in Washington pushing for "his bill" in order to get the law through Congress before President Grant's second term started. During the first two months of 1873, Comstock and his supporters fought objections raised by several members of Congress. Eventually, the law was passed on March 3, 1873, only hours before the closing of the 42nd session of Congress, a time when many of the members were drunk and waiting for the close of business. Along with the Comstock law (a long verbose bill), 260 acts were hurried through passage, the contents of many unknown to those voting. When all those bills came to Grant's desk, he signed them as fast as an assistant could give them to him—probably with little or no knowledge of their content. The resulting law, reflecting the carelessness and rushed circumstances under which it was written, contained excessive language, poor writing, and imprecise explanations—but it was law.

The new law gave the U. S. Post Office power to appoint special agents to carry out the law's intentions. This was just what Comstock wanted, and he became a special agent for the Post Office in charge of censoring the mails of obscene materials.

While the New York Society for the Suppression of Vice concentrated on the federal legislature, it also secured a law in the State of New York on May 16, 1873, insuring that obscenity would not be purveyed there. The success with anti-obscenity statutes continued into the twentieth century until all fifty of the United States had their own laws controlling the flow of obscenity and fifty or more nations participated in an international agreement for its control.

The federal obscenity law of 1873 did not satisfy some, so Congress began tinkering with the wording again in 1876. The 1873 law specified a long list of "articles and things," the mailing of which would be a crime; but the act failed to say that writings and pictures were also criminal offenses. Congress, it seemed, wished to correct the oversight; the new act included writings and pictures along with the already extensive list of "non-mailable matter." The new law apparently approved of the Post Office censoring printed items—notwithstanding the First Amendment prohibition against government making laws restricting free expression. In fact, Joseph Gurney Cannon (1836-1926; in Congress 1873-1891, 1893-1913, 1915-1923), chairman of the House Post Office Committee, observed; "This bill [does not] give any right to any postmaster to open or interfere with anybody's mail. It is like anything else, before you can convict you must offer and make proof." Evidently, Cannon saw the bill enforced as any criminal law would—through the courts.

The federal law, with several revisions, remains part of the laws of the United States into the 1980s. The modern law provides the following:

> Every obscene, lewd, lascivious, indecent, filthy or vile article, matter, thing, device or substance; and . . . Every written or printed card, letter, circular, book, pamphlet, advertisement, or notice of any kind giving information, directly or indirectly, where, or how, or from whom, may be obtained . . . Is declared to be nonmailable matter and shall not be conveyed in the mails or delivered from any post office or by any letter carrier.

Although the law passed, fifty thousand people signed a petition asking for the repeal of the Comstock Act; for the most part, they were free-thinking groups or members of organizations such as the National Liberal League which recognized the threat the new law had for free expression. Their concern over civil liberties did not change the prevailing climate or stop the passage of the new law.

By 1877, Comstock's organization was successfully prosecuting Charles Bradlaugh and Annie Besant because they published *Fruits of Philosophy*, by Charles Knowlton. That success led to other court fights including one against Edward Truelove, an 86-year-old publisher for the offense of publishing *Moral Physiology*, a well-recognized work available in both England and the United States.

Case of James Sullivan, Bookseller

In 1873, Anthony Comstock entered Sullivan's book store, 113 Fulton Street, Brooklyn, and tried to purchase a copy of *The Lustful Turk* for $3, but was told that the store did not carry that kind of literature. Later, Comstock asked for the arrest of Sullivan on the grounds that Comstock, under the name of Jerry Baxter Sullivan, had written asking for a list of obscene books and places to purchase them.

In court, Comstock produced a copy of the list of books and an envelope mailed to Baxter. Neither had Sullivan's name, but the court told the jury that the list and envelope received by Comstock and his testimony or receipt was *prima facie* evidence of guilt. Although Sullivan swore he had never sent the information in question, he was fined $500 and imprisoned for a year.

Stronger Obscenity Suppression

The passage of the new federal anti-obscenity law in 1876 opened the way for a series of tests of the law in which the Hicklin standard became more entrenched as the basis for determining if a publication was obscene. The first test, however, was of the postal right to censorship in *Ex parte Jackson* (1878), which prohibited a publisher from mailing information regarding a lottery. A. Orlando Jackson mailed a circular advertising a lottery on February 23, 1877, to J. Ketcham of Gloversville, New York, in violation of the postal provisions. Subsequently, the Circuit Court of the United States for the Southern District of New York found Jackson guilty of violating the statute. Jackson was fined $100 and sentenced to jail; but he asked for a writ of *habeas corpus* from the Supreme Court, citing the constitutional prohibition against censorship. The Supreme Court's opinion held that the government, by owning the mails, had the right to set rates and control content. The opinion cited the Comstock Act as an example of that power.

Justice Stephen Field (1816-1899), who wrote the opinion for the Court, believed:

> The power possessed by Congress enbraces the regulation of the entire postal system of the country. The right to designate what shall be carried necessarily involves the right to determine what shall be excluded.

There were no First Amendment violations by the Post Office as long as other avenues of disseminating information remained uncensored; therefore, government by not censoring all forms of communication had not improperly abused the First Amendment limitations. However, Field did say that the Fourth Amendment prevented any opening of sealed packages or letters for search unless the postal official first secured a search warrant—obligations that had never been seriously questioned by Congress or the Post Office. Jackson, however, remained in jail. The Court also noted:

> Nor can any regulations be enforced against the transportation of printed matter in the mail, which is open to examination, so as to interfere in any manner with the freedom of the press. Liberty of circulating is as essential to that freedom as liberty of publishing; indeed, without the circulation, the publication would be of little value. If, therefore, printed matter be excluded from the mails, its transportation in any other way cannot be forbidden by Congress.

In 1878, Comstock filed a case against D. M. Bennett, a free thought and free love tract publisher in Princeton, Mass., over the publication and mailing of *Cupid's Yokes*. The case is important because the *Hicklin* standard was applied in determining if the pamphlet was obscene. The court would not allow the reading of the full work into the legal record, relying solely on passages marked as obscene. The jurors were told to decide that the work was obscene if any part was obscene, or if the work might be obscene to those with tendencies

1878 = No Lotto mail

towards obscenity. Although Bennett's lawyers appealed to the United States Court of Appeals, Bennett lost and went to prison. *United States* v. *Bennett* (1879) became a precedent for many future cases and was quoted approvingly by the Supreme Court of the United States in some of its later cases.

Other cases followed quickly, including *United States* v. *Chesman* (1881), declaring that a book on the physiology of sex was obscene and could not be mailed, except to physicians; *United States* v. *Comerford* (1885) decided that obscenity cases must be tried in the district where the publication was mailed; and *United States* v. *Harmon* (1888) provided an extensive and approving discussion on the *Hicklin* test. The Hicklin standard as a test for the obscenity law continued to be found in court opinions as late as *Commonwealth* v. *Friede* (1930) when the court thought Radclyffe Hall's *The Well of Loneliness* was obscene.

According to Comstock, in his own book, *Death Traps by Mail* (1884), by the end of 1882, 258 people had been arrested under federal laws, and 442 under state laws. The arrests led to 311 convictions or guilty pleadings and 273 sentencings. A total of $65,256.97 in fines and 155 years of imprisonment had been imposed.

Comstock's friends also confiscated 27,586 pounds of books and materials from dealers and others. In addition to the total weight, Comstock noted that his people had acquired 204,539 obscene pictures and photos along with large quantities of engraved steel and copper, negative plates, letters (opened while in the hands of the post office), figures, circulars, books, and articles. In addition, the group found 4,185 boxes "of pills, powders, etc., used by abortionists."

The campaign to stamp out vice led to the closing of four plays or places of amusement and the compilation of 979,010 names and addresses of people who might buy or be interested in obscene materials. In this effort, agents traveled 190,098 miles to destroy "evil." According to Comstock, printing plates for 163 books had been seized and destroyed in New York and Brooklyn, at the time two separate cities that were centers of the publishing of obscene materials.

In *Traps for the Young* (Third edition, 1884), Comstock delineated his philosophy attempting to justify why he had to work so hard to clean up the evils of the nation and to protect the morals of the young:

> Night and day this evil has been pursued by the agents of the society . . . Eternal vigilance is the price of moral purity. Let the efforts of this society be relaxed, or allow it to be known that its efforts will cease, and there are hundreds of villains ready to embark in this soul-destroying business . . .

Comstock's thinking had a religious zeal that prevented him from considering any alternatives. Comstock was on a "righteous" crusade, one not unlike the religious crusades of the middle ages. The first sentence of the book, designed to touch the sensitive nerves of parents, showed the author's zeal: "It is in the home that we must look for first impressions. Here the foundation of the character of the future man or woman is laid." From that innocent opening,

Comstock went on to talk about the joys and responsibilities of parenthood. *Traps for the Young* got to its point quickly:

> Evil thoughts, like bees, go in swarms. A single one may present itself before the mind. If entertainment be extended, or place be given it, at once this vile fellow is found to have an immense following. I repeat: their approach may be so secret and insidious, that but one may be discerned at first, and yet from all sides they will flock, darkening the eyes of the understanding, filling the ears of reason, until the danger signals can no longer be seen nor heard, and the poor victim swiftly becomes insensible to purity and virtue.

Comstock set out to explain the many hazards of anything sensational from sex to crime. His powerfully worded appeals have not lost their passion more than a century later:

> Satan is permitted to place his traps where they will do him most good and the children most harm. The sickening details of crimes, infidel scoffings, cheap works of ficion, newspaper advertisements, "blood-and-thunder" story papers—all are freely admitted around the hearthstones and under the roof-trees of the land.
>
> We now come to a class that is thrust upon the youth in secret. The favorite method is under the sanctity of the seal in the United States mail. By means of it the most infamous scoundrel may send the vilest matter to the purest boy or girl. And *this is being done systematically.* If the facts of the business of obscene publications and indecent articles could be published here a shock would be given to the sensitive and decent in the community that would make their blood run cold, while a wave of indignation would roll over the country that would sweep away any person found engaging in the business. The evils we have been considering travel openly, and are seen on all sides. But here comes a more subtle and insidious snare. To one acquainted with the history, the variety, and extent of this evil, it does not seem possible that man could sink so low as to edit such foulness, while it appears impossible for the human mind to invent the variety of indecencies which formerly existed before the actual efforts of the New York Society for the Suppression of Vice has suppressed them.
>
> Secrecy marks these operations. In the darkness of attic-room, of basement or celler, is the favorite salesroom. The message of these evil things is death—socially, morally, physically, and spiritually.
>
> This moral vulture steals upon our youth in the home, school, and college, silently striking its terrrible talons into their vitals, and forcibly bearing them away on hideous wings to shame and death. Like a cancer, it fastens itself upon the imagination, and sends down for the future life thousands of roots, poisoning the nature . . . destroying self-respect, fettering the will-power, defiling the mind, corrupting the thoughts, leading

to secret practices of most foul and revolting character, until the victim tires of life, and existence is scarcely endurable. It sears the conscience, hardens the heart, and damns the soul. It leads to lust and lust breeds unhallowed living, and sinks men made in the image of God, below the level of the beasts. There is no force at work in the community more insidious, more constant in its demands, or more powerful and far-reaching than lust. *It is the constant companion of all other crimes.* It is honeycombing society. Like a frightful monster, it stands peering over the sleeping child, to catch its first thoughts on awakening. This is especially true where the eye of youth has been defiled with the scenes of lasciviousness in the weekly criminal papers or by their offsprings, obscene books and pictures. The peace of the family is wrecked, homes desolated, and society degraded while it curses more and more each generation born into the world.

Think of the homes that are wrecked by unbridled passion, of the curse that falls upon any community when there is spread before the eyes of all classes by the newspaper gossip, the inner secrets of those whited sepulchres, those moral monsters, who, stripped of all sense of same, parade their foul living in the courts.

From the first impure thought till the close of the loathsome life of the victim of lust, there is a succession of sickening, offensive, and disgusting scenes before the mind, until life, to such a one, must be made up of disease, wounds, and putrefying sores. Suicide dances before his vision in his moments of despondency as the only means by which to hide his shame, and the sole cure for his wretched condition. The turgid waters speak louder with the death stillness which they promise than does hope, with its beckonings to a better life. Turn as he will, the chains of habit permit him to go but a short distance before they clank their hold upon him. The brightest sun over his head seems scarcely able to penetrate the gloom of despair that youthful indiscretions have often woven into his life. His one cry is, "Who shall deliver me from the body of this death?"

As the jackal follows in the wake of its equally ferocious yet stronger foe, so murder haunts the pathway of lust. There are in a neighboring city, at this writing, three youths on trial for murder. It is charged that after a most monstrous conspiracy, a young and beautiful maiden was ruined and then murdered to hide their shame. Lust has but to whistle, and red-handed murder quickly responds, obedient to his master.

I repeat, *lust is the boon companion of all other crimes.* There is no evil so extensive, none doing more to destroy the institutions of free America. It sets aside the laws of God and morality; marriage bonds are broken, most sacred ties severed, State laws ignored, and dens of infamy plant themselves in almost every community, and then reaching out like immense cuttlefish, draw in, from all sides, our youth to destruction.

Obscene literature may be said to be the favorite agency of the evil one to recruit these dens. City houses of ill-fame, in many instances, are filled with the daughters of country homes. Often children are scarcely able to walk before a curse and blight has been attempted by some foul-minded nurse upon these buds of humanity. Scarcely have they become able to observe what is passing about them before the seeds of impurity meet their eyes in the licentious papers that line their pathway. Then when the critical period approaches when they emerge from youth to manhood or womanhood, when those mysterious changes in nature take place, and they become aware of new emotions within, then the wily one stands ready to capture and pervert them to his own hellish purposes.

Consider some of his devices in this respect. Many a parent, before sending the child away from home to school, canvasses the country over for a proper and desirable institution where the child shall have all the comforts and advantages of home and culture. All the details are inquired into with greatest care. At last the child reaches the school, and his or her name appears upon the roll and is printed in the catalogue. These catalogues are sought for by those who send circulars through the mails advertising obscene and unlawful wares.

The obscenity dealer, the quacks, the lottery managers, and the frauds all adopt the same method of advertising, to wit, either as above, or by buying old letters from other dealers for the sake of the names, or by sending circulars to postal clerks and others through the country, offering prizes for a list of the names of youth of both sexes under twenty-one years of age, or by purchasing addressed envelopes of those who make a business of collecting names, and then addressing envelopes to supply parties doing business through the mails. These are some of the devices in vogue to secure names.

In one instance a professor of a female seminary of great prominence informed me that some party had obtained surreptitously of one of his assistants some fifteen or more catalogues of other female seminaries and colleges. After a long search I discovered the party, and when I called for the catalogues he brought out a pile of about one hundred different ones, and we selected the ones he had borrowed. I wrote immediately to each of the heads of these institutions, and before the close of that year I received complaints from more than one half of the number written to, who had detected noxious matter sent to the students. From two of these came almost direct replies, containing circulars of death-dealing articles of a most infamous character sent to young ladies. These are unfit for description. One lady teacher wrote, "Not only must this scoundrel have the catalogue of the present, but of the last term as well, as he has sent to the graduates of last term, besides sending to those of the present."

These catalogues then are directories for the venders of obscene matter, etc., which furnish them the names of our boys and girls. *Children have thrust upon them, unsolicited, these death-traps.* Their curiosity is piqued, and unconscious of danger, they often send for the matter advertised, simply to gratify inquisitiveness . . . Intemperance marks its victim by the bleared eye, bloated face, red nose, tainted breath, reeling form, and tottering step. The effects of this evil are not so easily discerned. *Its most*

*deadly effects are felt by the victims in the habit of secret vices, before
their course is marked by external appearances.*

While Comstock proclaimed himself to be the protector of Christian morality
and virtue, he also used his office to satisfy his own lust. On the evening of June
14, 1878, Comstock and five of his associates entered a house of prostitution
and paid three women $14 to take off all of their clothes. After the six men
had satisfied their need to gaze at the women, Comstock pulled out a revolver,
declared that he was Anthony Comstock, and arrested them.

In time, some people began to question Comstock's tactics. Oliver Johnson
of the *Orange* (N.J.) *Journal* believed that Comstock had done some good
for society, but also noted, "It is not for Mr. Comstock to make himself a
doctrinaire, to suppress by violence the right of speech and of printing upon
such subjects."

By the 1890s, the censorship power of the Post Office under the Comstock
Act was clearly affirmed by Attorney General Charles J. Bonaparte (1851-
1921). In an opinion about a postal action against a newspaper telling it to
stop carrying a serialized version of Leo Tolstoy's (1828-1910), *The Kreutzer
Sonata* (1891), Bonaparte decided that the Post Office had the right to stop
the mailing of any publication that carried anything considered to be obscene.
Tolstoy's work was a statement about jealousy and society's sexual education
of young people, which Bonaparte thought to be obscene. The decision upheld
censorship powers of the Post Office.

The Post Office: Champion of Comstock Censorship

Although some people believed that the Post Office had gained too much
power to censor the mails, the success of the Comstock law permitted the
Post Office to gain more censorship powers throughout the remainder of the
century. By 1900, a hundred or more cases were in the courts, and the cases
were becoming increasingly general in the types of communications deemed
unmailable. Envelopes or postcards containing anything that defamed were
judged unmailable. Even private correspondence between husband and wife
that contained statements or images a postal official thought to be filthy or
vulgar came under the purview of the Comstock Act.

One of the cases, *William Grimm* v. *U. S.* (1895), arose because Grimm, a
photographer living in St. Louis, Missouri, sent a letter to Herman Huntress on
July 22, 1890, offering to sell pictures and negatives of actresses that might be
"obscene, lewd, and lascivious" under provisions of the postal laws. Grimm's
letter was in response to a inquiry from Huntress about availabilities and quantity
prices.

During the case, Grimm's lawyer pointed out that Grimm had not sent
obscene pictures, only information on how and where to acquire them, and
that possession of obscene pictures was not an offense. Secondly, Grimm's
defense pointed out that no proof of the obscenity or lewdness of the pictures
had been shown in the indictment, nor had pictures been included for review by

Books & mail censored

the jury. Justice David J. Brewer (1837-1910) rejected both claims by noting regarding the first:

> However innocent on its face it may appear, if it conveyed, and was intended to convey, information in respect to the place or person where, or of whom such objectionable matters could be obtained, it is within the statute.

Regarding the second claim, Brewer noted:

> We do not think this objection is well taken. The charge is not of sending obscene matter through the mails, in which case some description might be necessary, both for identification of the offense and to enable the court to determine whether the matter was obscene, and, therefore, nonmailable. Even in such cases it is held that it is unnecessary to spread the obscene matter in all its filthiness upon the record; it is enough to so far describe it that its obnoxious character may be discerned.

Brewer and the majority seemed content to review the matter without benefit of the material that might be the source of concern. Grimm was found to be guilty and the sentence of one year and one day in prison was allowed to stand.

In *Arthur D. Andrews* v. *U. S.* (1896), Andrews was found guilty of mailing obscene materials at the Post Office in Los Angeles, although he used a sealed letter with nothing obscene on the envelope. The letter was sent to postal inspector M. H. Flint, posing under the name of Mrs. Susan Budlong, who had opened the letter and found the obscene materials. Andrews was declared guilty in the case.

Justice George Shiras (1832-1924), writing the majority opinion, rejected the contention that a postal inspector opening a letter mailed to him under the assumed name did not discredit the case. Although the envelope contained nothing obscene, the fact that the contents were obscene meant that the law had been violated and that the government detective had a proper right to bring the case to trial. Thus, Andrews' guilt was sustained.

In the case of *Lew Rosen* v. *U. S.* (1896), Rosen underwent a trial for mailing a publication on April 24, 1893, from New York which contained pictures of the female figure and detailed descriptions, as the court said, "which . . . would be offensive to the court and improper to spread upon the records of the court, because of their obscene, lewd, and indecent matters." Rosen had been tried and found guilty of mailing obscene materials, but he asked for a retrial on the grounds of errors he alleged to exist in the first trial. The second trial sustained the original findings, so an appeal was taken to the Supreme Court, where the finding of guilt was upheld. Rosen, as publisher, knew the content of the publication, but he did not regard it obscene within the definition of the law. Justice John M. Harlan (1833-1911), writing for the majority, concluded Rosen's inability to determine that he was mailing an obscene publication did not free him from the sanctions of the court.

Effect of Comstock

Censorship: The Cutting Power of the Cut Rate

Over the years, the Post Office built up an organization and policies that made censoring the mails common practice. The most potent power that the Post Office had was second class mail privilege, the cut rate given to magazines and newspapers for mailing their publications. Although George Washington believed that any postal charge on newspapers and periodicals might be too much, the Post Office has always charged something.

Congress had the power, and used it, to establish the conditions for cut rate publications. These qualifications were changed from time to time until during the administration of Woodrow Wilson, postal interpretations considered content in determining the eligibility of a publisher to use the reduced rate in a sedition case.

The nineteenth century became the proving ground upon which the varied restrictions on the First Amendment were found, tested, and developed. The twentieth century would take the ideas of the earlier century in many directions.

Chapter 22

The U. S. Post Office:
The Censor's Stamp

The problems of censorship did not disappear with the beginning of the twentieth century. If anything, the arm of government became stronger. One of the most powerful agencies of suppression continued to be the U. S. Post Office, and one of its most effective tools was the selective administration of the second-class mail permit. Because the permit allowed holders to send their periodicals for a small fraction of the next lowest postal rate, any publisher denied the use of second-class mailing privileges stood the strong chance of being driven out of business because of the higher distribution costs. A series of cases in the early years of the twentieth century provided answers regarding the views of the Supreme Court of the United States in who should have access to the reduced rates. The Supreme Court had to decide what classes of users could enjoy the second-class permit, what content could be excluded from the mails, and if the postmaster general could use permit power indiscriminately.

In *Bates & Guild Co.* v. *Henry C. Payne, Postmaster General* (1904), the Supreme Court of the United States was called upon to decide if a musical publication, complete in each issue but produced monthly, could be denied the second class mailing permit. Each issue of the magazine concentrated on a single composer and included a biographical essay, a picture, and "thirty-two pages of engraved piano music" reflecting the best of the composer's work. The first issue of the new Masters in Music series appeared in January 1903. The Postmaster General refused the second-class permit because he thought the publication to be sheet music disguised as a periodical.

In deciding the case, the Supreme Court sustained the Postmaster General, with uncertainty:

> While, as already observed, the question is one of doubt, we think the decision of the Postmaster General, who is vested by Congress with the power to exercise his judgment and discretion in the matter, should be accepted as final.

This decision agreed with cases in which the Court had held that serial books could not enjoy the benefits of the second-class permit.

The Supreme Court had the opportunity to review other postal restrictions on what could be mailed in *Public Clearing House* v. *Frederick E. Coyne, Postmaster* (1904), a case that involved a lottery rather than obscene materials. *Public Clearing House* had purchased a large number of names and address cards from the League of Educators for the purpose of promoting the sale of "co-operator" memberships in Public Clearing House's scheme to make money. Co-operators paid an admission fee of $3 and monthly investments for five years. At the end of the five years, members would receive a single payment based on the number of new members joining during the term of membership. Since repayment was based solely upon payments from new members joining the organization, and not from investments, the Postmaster of Chicago concluded that the organization was engaging in a lottery and issued a fraud order prohibiting Public Clearing House from using the mails.

Public Clearing House went to court to regain its mailing privileges. The Postmaster had exercised authority given him by a statute passed by Congress in 1890:

> The Postmaster General may, upon evidence satisfactory to him that a person or company is engaged in conducting any lottery . . . instruct postmasters at any postoffice at which *registered* letters arrive directed to any such person or company . . . to return all such registered letters to the postmaster at the office at which they were originally mailed, with the word 'fraudulent' plainly written or stamped upon the outside.

The court concluded that the due process of law protections are not destroyed when an administrative or regulatory agency performs a "judicial" act in the line of the agency's normal statutory duties–thus, the postmaster general can conduct a hearing and deny mailing privileges to a sender whom the postmaster general has properly decided is violating the statute. Moreover, when the Post Office refuses to handle letters or other mailable objects, it is not depriving owners of their money or title to property, only refusing to let them use the mails. (All questionable materials were returned to the sender so that Public Clearing House did not receive its mail, with checks.)

The Supreme Court also had to decide the right of the postmaster to return the mail undelivered. Justice Henry B. Brown (1836-1913) wrote the majority opinion and showed little concern for constitutional protections of publishers:

> We find no difficulty in sustaining the constitutionality of these sections. The postal service is by no means an indispensable adjunct to a civil government, and for hundreds, if not for thousands, of years the transmission of private letters was either intrusted to the hands of friends or to private enterprise. Indeed, it is only within the last three hundred years that governments have undertaken the work of transmitting intelligence as a branch of their general administration . . .
>
> It is not, however, a necessary part of the civil government in the same sense in which the protection of life, liberty, and property, the

defense of the government against insurrection and foreign invasion, and the administration of public justice are; but is a public function, assumed and established by Congress for the general welfare.

Justice Brown also declared that Congress "might designate what might be carried in the mails and what excluded." The Court believed that Congress could choose to exclude categories of printed matter as "newspapers, magazines, pamphlets, and other printed matter." Justice Brown continued:

> It may also refuse to include in its mails such printed matter or merchandise as may seem objectionable to it upon the ground of public policy, as dangerous to its employees or injurious to other mail matter carried in the same packages . . .

Excluding certain classes of matter from the mails based on content, type of publication, or public policy would seem to raise serious free expression issues since the Post Office Department would be censoring by preventing the mailing. Justice Brown dealt with this question by noting that any publication was free to use other means of distribution when the postal channels were closed. As long as the alternate channels were available, such as having young children riding their bicycles, deliver publications, the Supreme Court could see no reason to conclude that anyone's right of free expression was being denied.

Because the Supreme Court was not requiring that disputed administrative decisions of the postmaster be open to appeal to the courts, the post office was the "court of last resort" for publishers denied access to the mails. Since the postmaster was now empowered to exclude *classes* of publications on the basis of their serial nature, content, public policy considerations and since the postmaster could make the final decision on the mailability of a product, he and those designated by him, had virtually the same power to censor as the English licensors.

This became particularly apparent because the postal channels were the only economical means for distributing publications that had to travel considerable distances to reach subscribers. Since many publications operated on a very narrow financial margin, access to the least expensive postal rates could mean the difference between success or failure.

Even the fact that the postmaster could set standards that would permit one publisher to use the second-class rate and deny another publisher the permit through classifying one publication serial and another as periodic books insured that some would survive and others would die.

The postal authorities had gained great power during the last half of the nineteenth century and the beginning of the twentieth century to suppress publications through both economic (second class permit) and content (obscenity and lottery) means. But the press was growing too, through evolving technologies and changing business practices. The first half of the twentieth century would become the testing grounds on which some of the most significant battles over suppression and free expression would be fought.

Chapter 23

A Growing Economy,
A Growing Suppression

The late nineteenth century was a period of growth, a time when newspapers were experimenting with new styles and techniques for reaching their audiences, and newspaper and magazine reporters felt compelled to become the channel for exposing excesses in the growth industries. Many reporters, editors, and publishers were seeking means for meeting the new demands created by increased publishing costs and the need for circulation gains. Others had something to say about the unfairness they saw in business, government, and social institutions.

As the industrial output of the nation grew, so did the size of corporations. John D. Rockefeller's Standard Oil Company became the first of a group of business trusts, large companies that controlled not only other companies, but prices in their industry. Other trusts developed in sugar, whiskey, lead, cottonseed oil, and salt. But in 1887, a recession frightened the nation into concern over monopolies, and, in 1890, Congress passed the Sherman Antitrust Act.

The large companies also created a concern among labor over the way powerful industrial leaders treated their employees. Although the first strong labor organization had been the Knights of Labor (1869), many other labor groups came into being; but the depression (1873-1878) during the Grant administration caused problems for the labor unions. While labor unions survived the period, they grew at a reduced rate, if at all, and eventually the movement began to loose membership. Not until the American Federation of Labor gained considerable power by 1900 did union membership regain its strength.

Newspaper Growth

The revolutionary growth of newspapers during the last half of the nineteenth century can be traced to a number of inventions. In 1884, Otto Mergenthaler patented the Linotype, or line of type, machine which greatly increased the speed with which newspaper type could be set—opening the way for publishers to add more soft news sections and advertising without adding more typesetters.

The stereotype, a process for making duplicate printing plates by casting hot metal against original type, opened the way for making as many printing plates as needed. A Scottish goldsmith, William Ged, invented an early version of the

159

process in 1725; but it did not have much success until the nineteenth century when Charles Craske, in 1854, developed a method for producing plates in a curve for the rotary printing surfaces of the web press.

The web-fed rotary contributed to the speed with which a newspaper could be produced. An 1866 invention developed at the *Times* of London and named the Walter Press, after publisher John Walter III, created a technique for feeding paper from a number of supply rolls through a web to several printing drums. Guide rollers then brought the printed pages together where they were cut into pages and folded into complete sections. The press could achieve a speed of 25,000 impressions per hour. With the addition of half-tone engraving— a process for reproducing a photograph for printing—color printing methods, and improved paper, newspaper printing entered an era of massive circulation gains.

Related inventions such as Alexander Graham Bell's (1847-1922) telephone (1876) and the typewriter helped reporters in their news gathering responsibilities. Christopher Latham Sholes had constructed the first usable typewriter in 1867; and, working with others, improved it enough to get E. Remington and Sons to manufacture the commercial model in 1874.

The technology of the nineteenth century had converted newspapers from enterprises carried on by small printers who often supported themselves by other occupations such as postmaster and contract printer to large firms that rivaled big companies in other businesses.

Yellow Journalism

The growing costs of producing a newspaper and expanding circulation placed new demands on editors and publishers to create a product that would appeal to an ever increasing audience. To make their papers more popular, some newspapers resorted to bigger headlines, color, many pictures, and easier to read stories–and, in some cases sensationalized coverage. Many of the new devices improved the quality of journalism, but the potential for abuse was too great for some. There arose a new "journalism without a soul" called yellow journalism.

The term "yellow journalism" developed out of a cartoon strip which created some competition between William Randolph Hearst (1863-1951), owner of the *New York Journal* and the *San Francisco Examiner*, and Joseph Pulitzer (1847-1911), owner of the *St. Louis Post-Dispatch* and the *New York World*. (Both men acquired other newspapers also.) Hearst hired a cartoonist who produced a strip called "Yellow Kid" away from Pulitzer, but Pulitzer found another person to produce a similar strip. Other large circulation newspapers liked the "Yellow Kid" and began adding similar cartoons to their pages. The term "yellow journals" arose to describe the newspapers, and "yellow journalism" to describe the content of the newspapers. Yellow journalism demonstrated the success of the formula—sex, sin, and violence. But many of the yellow newspapers became crusaders for working people, searching out illegal, unethical, and unfair practices in government, industry, business, and social institutions. Although they were sometimes inaccurate, the yellow newspapers provided a necessary service to the powerless in society. Yellow journalism helped publishers increase circulation of their newspapers at a time when technology had pushed the circulation breakeven point to high figures.

Both Hearst and Pulitzer enjoyed huge circulation gains from their exploits— in 1892 the *New York World* was selling 374,000 newspapers in its morning and evening editions. Although the era of yellow journalism may have its roots in the technology that required circulation gains, Hearst, Pulitzer, and others saw an opportunity to sell more newspapers and make more money—a business judgment. The low point in yellow journalism, but its high point in circulation, came during the Spanish-American War of 1898.

The Spanish-American War developed out of a struggle between Cuba and Spain beginning in 1895. Cuba was trying to gain independence from Spain. The United States had an interest in the conflict because of the $100 million in annual trade with Cuba and the $50 million in investments in the country. Hearst at the *New York Journal* covered human suffering in the war by sometimes telling the individual stories of people who suffered, thus increasing circulation by appealing to human sympathy.

But the technological innovations had their benefits—benefits often over- looked when evaluating the late nineteenth century journalism. Although Pulit- zer used sensationalism to build circulation, he also concentrated on accurate and thorough reporting and clear, concise writing. Pulitzer's concern over ac- curacy remains legendary. Often Pulitzer supported causes others would not have the time or energy to take seriously, such as when he helped raise funds to pay for a site for the Statue of Liberty after Congress refused support. He also purchased food for earthquake victims.

Muckraking

The abuse of labor by the trusts, corruption in government, and acquisition of small businesses by the large trusts (including small coal and oil interests that were swallowed up in Pennsylvania), combined with the growing power of the press—particularly the magazine press—led to the appearance of a group of reporters who sought to expose the problems of society. Publishers John B. Walker, Cyrus H. K. Curtis, S. S. McClure, Frank A. Munsey, and Peter F. Collier, among others, provided the forum for the new writing. Jacob Riis, John Phillips, Burton J. Hendrick, Will Irwin, David Graham Phillips, Alfred Henry Lewis, Lincoln Steffens, Ray Stannard Baker, Frank Norris, Upton Sinclair, and Ida M. Tarbell, among many others, kept up a stream of writing for the publications. The new muckraking arose out of reaction to corruption in government and big business and the need to fight back for the individual citizen.

McClure's Magazine in January 1903, published the "The Shame of Minne- apolis: The Rescue and Redemption of a City that was Sold Out," by Lin- coln Steffens as one of the treatments of government corruption. In time, a variety of writings in form ranging from Brand Whitlock's novel about capital punishment, *The Turn of the Balance* (1907), to Thomas W. Lawson's study of corporate irresponsibility, "Frenzied Finance" in *Everybody's* (1904-1905), exposed every type of abuse. Ida Tarbell wrote a detailed "History of the Standard Oil Company," *McClure's* (1904), exposing unfair business practices used by Rockefeller designed to squeeze out competitors. Rockefeller, for example, had put many Pennsylvania oil and coal companies out of business through price cutting that made it impossible for them to continue. But it was David Graham Phillips' study of the U. S. Senate, "The Treason of the Senate," appearing in *Cosmopolitan* (1906) that influenced President Theodore Roosevelt to name the movement "muckrakers" after the "the Man with the Muckrake" in *Pilgrim's Progress*—a man who only looked down and saw the dirt of life. As Roosevelt saw it, this was the problem with the journalists who seemed solely interested in the ills of society.

Upton Sinclair wrote *The Jungle* (1906) as a novel intended to expose the terrible working conditions of immigrant workers in the meat packing houses of Chicago, but the novel also exposed unsanitary packing practices and the use of excessive chemicals and artificial dyes in food preparation. Dr. Harvey H. Wiley, chief chemist in the Department of Agriculture and others had proven the practices that Sinclair's novel discussed. The result was the passage of the Pure Food and Drugs Act of 1906.

Muckraking was a response to the traumatic times created by the rapid industrial growth and econmic corruption and change during the latter part of the nineteenth century. As the nineteenth century ended, prosecutions for criminal libel, obscenity, and contempt reached a high point. State and federal courts, legislatures at all levels, and citizen groups entered the area. Yet, the press seemed to be enjoying new importance in several areas.

Freedom—Some For, Some Against

While the muckrakers were describing the ills of society, others were discussing the degree of freedom writers, editors, and publishers should have. One person was Theodore Schroeder (1865-1953) who had a prolific career advocating free speech. Schroeder produced a steady stream of articles from the 1890s through mid-twentieth century—writings that focused on every aspect of the control of expression—sociological, cultural, and legal. One of his most famous was "Liberty of Conscience, Speech and Press" published in the August and September 1906 issues of *The Liberal Review*:

> . . . The desire to persecute, even for mere opinion's sake, seems to be an eternal inheritance of humans. We naturally and as a matter of course encourage others in doing and believing whatever for any reason, or without reason, we deem proper. Even though we have a mind fairly well disciplined in the duty of toleration, we quite naturally discourage others and feel a sense of outraged propriety, whenever they believe and act radically different from ourselves. Our resentment becomes vehement just in proportion as our reason is impotent and our nerves diseasedly sensitive. That is why it is said that "man is naturally, instinctively intolerant and a persecutor."

From this necessity of our undisciplined nature comes the stealthy but inevitable recurrence of legalized bigotry, and its rehabilitation of successive inquisitions. From the days of pagan antiquity to the present hour, there has never been a time or country wherein mankind could claim immunity from all persecution for intellectual differences. This cruel intolerance has always appealed to a "sacred and patroitic duty," and masked behind an ignorantly made and unwarranted pretense of "morality."

Persecution has not been the outgrowth of any one age, nationality or creed; it has been the ill-favored progeny of all. Thus, under the disguise of new names and new pretensions, again and again we punish unpopular, though wholly self-regarding, non-moral conduct, imprison men for expressing honest intellectual differences, deny the duty of toleration, destroy a proper liberty of thought and conduct, and always under the same old false pretenses of "morality," "law and order" . . .

The concurrence of many in like emotions, associated with and centered upon the same focus of irritation, makes the effective majority of the state view the toleration of their opponents as a crime, and their heresy, whether political, religious, ethical or sexual, is denounced as a danger to civil order, and the heretic must be judicially silenced. Thus all bigots have reasoned in all past ages. Thus do those afflicted with our present sex superstition again defend their moral censorship of literature and art . . .

Men of strong passions and weak intellects seldom see the expedience of encouraging others to disagree. Thence came all of those terrible presecutions for heresy, witchcraft, sedition, etc., which have prolonged the midnight of superstition into "dark ages" . . .

Such egomania always resulted in the persecution of those who furnished the common people with the materials upon which they might base a different opinion, or outgrow their slave-virtues.

So now we have many who likewise esteem it to be of immoral tendency for others than themselves to secure such information as may lead to a personal and different opinion about the physiology, psychology, hygiene, or ethics of sex, and by law, we make it a crime to distribute any specific and detailed information upon the subject, especially if it be unprudish in the manner of its presentation or is accompanied with unorthodox opinions about marriage or sexual ethics. This is repeating the old folly that the adult masses cannot be trusted to form an opinion of their own. The "free" people of the United States cannot be allowed to have the information which might lead to a change of their own statute laws upon sex.

There will always be those thoughtless enough to believe that truth may be properly suppressed for considerations of expediency. I prefer to believe with Professor Max Muller, that "The truth is always safe, and nothing else is safe," and with Drummond that "He that will not reason, is a bigot; he that cannot reason is a fool, and he that dares not reason is a slave;" and with Thomas Jefferson when in his inaugural address he wrote "Error of opinion may be tolerated, when reason is left free to combat it"; and I believe these are still truisms even though the subject is sex.

But if Schroeder wrote of the need for liberty and toleration, the president of the United States was arguing differently. Theodore Roosevelt (1858-1919; president, 1901-1909), the president who coined the name muckrakers for reporters concerned with the ills of society, chose to strike out against two newspapers that criticized his handling of the Panama Canal during 1908-1909. Joseph Pulitzer's *New York World* editorials and editorial remarks in the *Indianapolis News* suggested corruption had been involved in the purchase of the canal. The Department of Justice brought two separate legal charges against the two newspapers on the grounds of "criminal libel," but the reality was that the cases were based on the fact that the two newspapers had attacked government and its officials—seditious libel. The objective was to make the newspapers pay for their believed inaccuracies. The first case filed in Indianapolis anticipated bringing officials of both newspapers to Washington for trial, but District Judge A. B. Anderson rejected the government's position. A second appeal to the court in New York rested on the fact that twenty-nine copies of the *World* had been distributed on federal property at West Point. The federal courts, including the Supreme Court, supported a motion to quash the action against the *World* on the grounds that the federal government did not have jurisdiction.

While Roosevelt was appealing his case to the courts, he also asked Congress to intervene on December 15, 1908:

> In view of the constant reiteration of the assertion that there was some corrupt action by or on behalf of the United States Government in connection with the acquisition of the title of the French Company to the Panama Canal, and of the repetition of the story that a syndicate of American citizens owned either one or both of the Panama companies, I deem it wise to submit to the Congress all the information I have on the subject. These stories were first brought to my attention as published in a paper in Indianapolis, call "The News," edited by Mr. Delavan Smith. The stories were scurrilous and libelous in character and false in every essential particular. Mr. Smith shelters himself behind the excuse that he merely accepted the statements which had appeared in a paper published in New York, "The World," owned by Mr. Joseph Pulitzer. It is idle to say that the known character of Mr. Pulitzer and his newspaper are such that the statements in that paper will be believed by nobody; unfortunately, thousands of persons are ill informed in this respect and believe the statements they see in print, even though they appear in a newspaper published by Mr. Pulitzer. A Member of the Congress has actually introduced a resolution in reference to these charges. I therefore lay all the facts before you.
>
> The story repeated at various times by the World and by its followers in the newspaper press is substantially as follows: That there was corruption by or on behalf of the Government of the United States in the transaction by which the Panama Canal property was acquired from its French owners; that there were improper dealings of some kind between agents of the Government and outside persons, representing or acting for an

American syndicate, who had gotten possession of the French Company; that among these persons, who it was alleged made "huge profits," were Mr. Charles P. Taft, a brother of Mr. William H. Taft, then candidate for the Presidency, and Mr. Douglas Robinson, my brother-in-law; that Mr. Cromwell, the counsel for the Panama Canal Company in the negotiations, was in some way implicated with the United States governmental authorities in these improper transactions, that the Government has concealed the true facts, and has destroyed, or procured or agreed to the destruction of, certain documents; that Mr. W.H. Taft was Secretary of War at the time that be an agreement between the United States Government and the beneficiaries of the deal all traces thereof were "wiped out" by transferring all the archives and "secrets" to the American Government, just before the holding of the convention but June at which Mr. Taft was nominated [for vice-president].

These statements sometimes appeared in the editorials, sometimes in the news columns, sometimes in the shape of contributions from individuals either unknown or known to be of bad character. They are false in every particular from beginning to end.

The real offender is Mr. Joseph Pulitzer, editor and proprietor of the World. While the criminal offense of which Mr. Pulitzer has been guilty is in form a libel upon individuals, the great injury done is in blackening the good name of the American people. It should not be left to a private citizen to sue Mr. Pulitzer for libel. He should be prosecuted for libel by the governmental authorities. In point of encouragement of iniquity, in point of infamy, of wrongdoing, there is nothing to choose between a public servant who betrays his trust; a public servant who is guilty of blackmail, or theft, or financial dishonesty of any kind, and a man guilty as Mr. Joseph Pulitzer has been guilty in this instance. It is therefore a high national duty to bring to justice this vilifier of the American people, this man who wantonly and wickedly and without one shadow of justification seeks to blacken the character of reputable private citizens and to convict the Government of his own country in the eyes of the civilized world of wrongdoing of the basest and foulest kind, when he has not one shadow of justification of any sort or description for the charge he has made.

In light of Roosevelt's appeal to Congress, Judge A. B. Anderson's rejection of the government's position (United States v. Smith, 1909) is of special interest.

In this case Judge A.B. Anderson was asked to direct that the case be transferred to Washington for trial (where presumably) the government could find a court supportive of its opinion. Judge Anderson used this opportunity to reject the government's claim and to support expression:

To my mind that man has read the history of our institutions to little purpose who does not look with grave apprehension upon the possibility of the success of a proceeding such as this. If the history of liberty means anything, this proceeding must fail.

If the prosecuting officers have the authority to select the tribunal, if there be more than one tribunal to select from, if the government has that power, and can drag citizens from distant states to the capital of the nation, there to be tried, then, as Judge Cooley says, this is a strange result of a revolution where one of the grievances complained of was the assertion of the right to send parties abroad for trial.

Free Enterprise v. Free Expression

Big Business, which had been spouting libertarian epithets trying to force Big Government out of their lives, also tried to gag free expression when free expression threatened its economic existence.

One of the major battles occured in 1908, in Spokane, Washington, center of much of the hiring of workers for the Pacific Northwest, when members of the Industrial Workers of the World (I.W.W.) protested the establishment of labor agencies which charged workers fees to find them employment, then did little to help. Apparently, there was also collusion between Big Business and the labor agencies who had formed "sweetheart deals"—certain businesses would hire only through labor agencies which, of course, charged fees for searching for employment. With signs proclaiming, "don't Buy Jobs," the workers took to the streets to protest what they saw as corruption and fraud. In response, the labor agencies managed to convince the Spokane City Council to pass an ordinance banning all "street speaking."

The I.W.W. remained calm about a year until the Council exempted religious groups from the ban. In one day, about 150 laborers and labor leaders were arrested; more than four hundred were arrested within a month. The Western Federation of Miners added its strength when it declared it would boycot all products made in Spokane. Faced by an economic retaliation, and with its jails incapable of housing and caring for the picketers, Spokane relented, again allowing freedom of expression and freedom of assembly—both of which the Council had no constitutional right to deny in the first place.

Other Free Speech fights were fought during the next two years throughout the country, as cities attempted to regulate Free Expression and labor organizations tried to exercise their First Amendment rights. In many cities, including San Diego, attempts to speak out against Big Business and the government resulted in not only jailings, but also physical attacks against laborers by "persons unknown." When the ordinances were challenged in court, the courts had no choice but to declare that the Constitution of the United States always took precedence over local ordinances; the I.W.W. never lost a case in court; however, the battles had cut the union energy and resources.

Chapter 24

The First Amendment: Sedition From Peace to War

Just as the Civil War brought out the sentiments and fears on both sides of the debate, the years leading up to and including World War I provided ample opportunity for radicals and socialists to square off with capitalists and conservatives. The first twenty years of the twentieth century experienced some of the most dramatic changes the United States had ever experienced. The United States was extensively involved in external politics and expansion as reflected in President William McKinley's (1843-1901; president, 1897-1901) statement in Buffalo, New York, in 1901, that "the period of exclusiveness is past." McKinley could not have anticipated his death only a few days later and the effect the unexpected rise of Theodore Roosevelt to the presidency at the age of forty-two would have on the nation's expansionism. Roosevelt hoped for war with foreign states so that the United States could conquor and gain power. To back his interest in foreign power, Roosevelt added ten new battleships by 1905, and the fleet continued to grow until the nation completed the Panama Canal in 1914. But Roosevelt was concerned with all social problems and soon became one of the most active of all U. S. presidents in domestic affairs.

While the United States might be looking outside its borders for more power, the domestic changes leading up to World War I were of equally much consequence. The major population migration was the continued movement from the country to cities. About one third of the population lived in cities in 1900; over one half lived in cities by 1920.

The new laboring class in the cities organized itself into unions to protect itself against the giant corporations that had emerged during the late nineteenth century. The farmers organized themselves into small unions to protect their own needs—and to fight the trusts. Some of the labor-trust fights became bloody and much property was destroyed. While the trusts became more greedy, the governmental bosses in the nation's cities were no better; they felt no remorse for taking money from the public treasury, selling franchises to the highest bidder, or overlooking crime—for a price.

But the middle classes and small business people had no organizational sturcture to protect themselves against labor, corporate, or governmental corruption. The essentially conservative urban middle class found itself in need of action, but for a long time did not want to depart from the *laissez faire* approach to

167

politics fearing that they might lose what success they had gained. But the attitude began to change, partly because of the writings of the muckrakers and partly because a group of social reformers including Robert M. La Follette, Charles Evans Hughes, Hiram W. Johnson, and James Cox appeared to lead the middle class into the Progressive Era—all politicians who made their record on reform platforms.

The climate of fear existing before World War I opened the way for legislation that repressed the right of free expression. Many states, including New York, developed their own sedition laws largely out of the fear aroused by the assassination of President William McKinley (1901) and fear of the anarchists, socialists, and radicals—a recurrence of supression not seen since the lapse of the Sedition Act of 1798 a century earlier.

Controlling Aliens

The Immigration Act of 1903 showed how fearful and authoritarian the nation had become. The Congress had passed a few immigration acts during the nineteenth century (after the lapse of the Alien Act of 1798) for administrative purposes and to keep out people who might end up on the public welfare. But the act of 1903 went further and declared that epileptics, individuals who had suffered insanity in the past five years or had suffered two attacks at any time, professional beggers, and "anarchists, or persons who believe in or advocate the overthrow by force or violence of the Government of the United States, or of all government, or of all forms of law, or the assassination of public officials" could legally be excluded from entry to the United States. The law provided a three year period during which the aliens could be forced out of the United States. The United States again had a criterion based on the attitudes of an individual for deciding if an alien could enter the nation or should be deported after entry. While Congress was active passing its own law to control aliens, the courts were involved in their own controls.

When Kaoru Yamataya appealed to the Supreme Court [*Kaoru Yamataya* v. *Thomas M. Fisher, Immigrant and Chinese Inspector* (1903)] complaining over the decision of inspector Fisher to exclude her from the United States because he had decided she was a pauper and probably would become a public charge, the Supreme Court refused to overturn the decision and decided that Yamataya's "due process of law" protections had not been abused. Existing law allowed the exclusion of the entire class of people who were considered to be paupers.

The decision of the Supreme Court only a year later, in *United States ex rel John Turner* v. *William Williams* (1904), decided that the Immigration Act of March 3, 1903, was within the constitutional power of Congress, even when the act provided for the deportation of a person judged to be an anarchist by the government. Turner was not arrested because of questionable entry, but because of views he held and discussed. Although John Turner was imprisoned and would be deported if his appeal failed because he expressed views supporting anarchy in a lecture delivered in New York on October 23, 1903, speech, he committed no violent actions. Chief Justice Melville W. Fuller (1833-1910) could see no conflicts with the First Amendment in ordering the deportation of any person who advocates views contrary to the statute:

> It is said that the act violates the 1st Amendment, which prohibits the passage of any law "respecting an establishment of religion, or prohibiting the free exercise thereof; or abridging the freedom of speech, or of the press; or the right of the people peaceably to assemble, and to petition the government for a redress of grievances."
>
> We are at a loss to understand in what way the act is obnoxious to this objection. It has no reference to an establishment of religion, nor does it prohibit the free exercise thereof; nor abridge the freedom of speech or of the press; nor the right of the people to assemble and petition the government for a redress of grievances. It is, of course, true, that if an alien is not permitted to enter this country, or, having entered contrary to law, is expelled, he is in fact cut off from worshipping or speaking or publishing or petitioning in the country; but that is merely because of his exclusion therefrom.

The lengths to which the government would go in seeing that alien laws were enforced can be seen in *Chin Low* v. *United States* (1908). Low was citizen born in the United States of Chinese heritage, who was detained at the port of San Francisco when he tried to re-enter the United States after a trip abroad. He was not granted opportunity to prove American citizenship. Thus, due process of law was denied. Writing for the majority, Justice Oliver W. Holmes, Jr. (1841-1935) rejected the Department of Commerce and Labor's position and granted a writ of *habeas corpus* to Low. Holmes noted Low's right to a court trial in which to prove citizenship, a case decidedly more liberal than earlier cases.

The Court was afforded the opportunity to show how the law applies to shipping companies carrying certain types of aliens. In *Oceanic Steam Navigation Company* v. *Nevada N. Stranahan* (1909), the Supreme Court agreed that the provision against the entry of an alien with "a loathsome or dangerous contagious disease" could be used to refuse entry of a ship carrying a alien with such a disease. The significant points of this case were that the court would allow an administrative officer (not a court of law) to determine "whether the defined crime has been committed, and, if so, to inflict a punishment." An administrative officer using an official medical examination at the port of entry to reach the determination to refuse entry and impose a fine was not a violation of of the Fifth Amendment prohibition of taking property without due process of law according to Justice Edward D. White (1845-1921). Although not the specifics of this case, the enforcement of the immigration rules raises the possibility for denying entrance to the United States when a person's political or religious views differ from those of the American majority without the applicant having the protections of the Fifth Amendment.

War and Suppression

War imposes special circumstances on a nation's need to protect itself from menaces within and without its borders—as many theorists say. World War I was no exception. The climate of fear that had pervaded much of the nation since 1900 continued into the war, and Congress, as well as American citizens, exhibited a willingness to suppress the freedoms protected in the First Amendment to the Constitution.

Congress, fearful of the preservation of the country, had an opportunity to demonstrate its authoritarian instincts when World War I became a reality for the United States. The legislature declared war on April 6, 1917, and, less than two months later, created the Selective Service Act (May 18, 1917) to help raise an army. Most of the public supported the need for the United States to enter the conflict that was tearing Europe apart, and few disagreed with the law authorizing the draft. This law had little to do with the suppression of free expression in the United States during the war, but too many remembered the outspoken nature of the press during the Civil War and, fearing the German propaganda machine, demanded laws dealing with treason. Most people believed that the courts using the existing conspiracy laws could not handle the problems of outspoken citizens.

President Woodrow Wilson expressed his support of anti-espionage legislation, but he also promised not to use the law to conceal his own acts from political scrutiny. In a letter of April 25, 1917, he wrote, "I approve of this legislation but . . . I shall not expect or permit any part of this law to apply to me or any of my official acts, or in any way to be used as a shield against criticism." Congress passed the Espionage Act of [June 15] 1917* designed, "To punish acts of interference with the foreign relations, the neutrality, and the foreign commerce of the United States, to punish espionage, and better to enforce the criminal laws of the United States, and for other purposes." Most of the law concerned itself with the substantive issues of a war such as real espionage, protection of military information, and matters between countries, but Section 3 of Title 1 went further:

> Whoever, when the United States is at war, shall willfully make or convey false reports or false statements with intent to interfere with the operation or success of the military or naval forces of the United States or to promote the success of its enemies and whoever, when the United States is at war, shall willfully cause or attempt to cause insubordination, disloyalty, mutiny, or refusal of duty, in the military or naval forces of

---

*Before the Espionage Act was passed, the United States had at its disposal other laws to prosecute people engaged in activities that might injure the United States. These laws included conspiracy to overthrow the United States and treason. See 18 U. S. C. A. Sections 1, 2, 4, 6, 88, 550. Beyond any laws, the Constitution in Article III Section 3 prescribes: "Treason against the United States, shall consist only in levying War against them, or, in adhering to their Enemies, giving them Aid and Comfort." The federal government, therefore, had ample statutory and constitutional controls without the espionage statute it desired.

the United States, or shall willfully obstruct the recruiting or enlistment service of the United States, to the injury of the service or of the United States, shall be punished by a fine of not more than $10,000 or imprisonment for not more than twenty years, or both.

The next section (4) orders punishment under section 3 when "two or more persons conspire to violate the provisions [of 3 if] one or more of such persons does any act to effect the object of the conspiracy, each person shall be punished." Congress included letters, writings, circulars, postal cards, pictures, prints, and many other forms of communication in the list of censorable media.

The Espionage Act did not provide enough power to suit Attorney General Thomas W. Gregory, and eleven months later Congress amended the law to include provision for dealing with sedition, the first time since 1798. The Report of the Attorney General of the United States (1918) suggested that individual complaints about the war were creating a national clamor for a tighter law:

These individual disloyal utterances, however, occuring with considerable frequency throughout the country, naturally irritated and angered the communities in which they occurred, resulting sometimes in unfortunate violence and lawlessness and everywhere in dissatisfaction with the inadequacy of the Federal law to reach such cases. Consequently there was a popular demand for such an amendment as would cover these cases.

The law, often called the Sedition Act, gained Congressional approval on May 16, 1918; it added nine new offenses as well as adding "attempts to obstruct" to the existing "willfully obstruct[ing] the recruiting . . . " found in the original act. The following offenses were declared to be illegal:
1. Saying things that might obstruct the sale of war bonds;
2. Saying or printing that [which] might bring contempt or scorn to the United States government;
3. the Constitution;
4. the flag;
5. [the] military uniform;
6. or anything that might cause resistance to the United States or promote causes of enemies;
7. supporting curtailment of military production;
8. "advocating, teaching, defending, or suggesting the doing of any of these acts;" and,
9. communication or action supporting a country with which the United States was at war.

This amendment lasted only until 1921 when it was repealed by Congress, but the original act of 1917 remained in force. Because the act of 1918 came late during World War I, most of the prosecutions occured under the 1917 law.

Using one or both laws, the government gained conviction of more than 1,900 persons and approximately a hundred newspapers, some of which had done little more than urge people, "Don't enlist," or "Resist your superior officers." The application of the law seemed directed at the radicals, socialists, independent farmers, and others who disagreed with the war, without regard for whether they actually committed treason. Many types of books and pamphlets came under the strong hand of the government.

Although sedition generally can mean all forms violent acts designed to interfere with the security of the state, it usually refers to less dangerous activities leading to more serious acts. Seditious libel, therefore, is writing encouraging violence towards the state, and it was the least offensive type of communication the Act of 1918 seemed designed to curtail.

More Cancellations of Free Expression

Other laws at the state and federal level appeared in this climate of fear. One of the most famous was the Trading-with-the-Enemy Act. The prosecutions could be direct or could simply ban the offender's publications from the mails. In the latter regard, Postmaster General Albert S. Burleson (1863-1937) became a most vigorous censor. He proposed no mercy for offending publishers as had been the case in the Civil War, and he made clear that criticism of governmental actions would be offensive:

> [Any printer who published] that this government got in the war wrong, that it is in it for wrong purposes, or anything that will impugn the motives of the Government for going into the war [will be prosecuted]. They can not say that this Government is the tool of Wall Street or the munitions-makers. That kind of thing makes for insubordination in the Army and Navy and breeds a spirit of disloyalty through the country . . . There can be no campaign against conscription and the Draft Law.

During 1917, U. S. District Court Judge Learned Hand, of the Southern District of New York, was given the opportunity to express his view on one application of the Espionage Act of 1917. In *Masses Publishing Co.* v. *Patten* (1917), the Postmaster of New York prevented the mailing of the August issue of *The Masses*, a journal proclaiming revolutionary concepts. When asked just which parts of the journal violated the provisions of the Espionage Act, the postmaster cited four cartoons named, "Liberty Bell," "Conscription," "Making the World Safe for Capitalism," and "Congress and Big Business"; a poem praising Emma Goldman and Alexander Berkman who were convicted for conspiracy to resist the draft; and three articles favorable to conscientious objectors. The *Masses* case became a test, not of the Espionage Act of 1917, but the extent to which Congress might have intended the criminal provisions of the law to be taken.

The law required the postmaster to specifically identify offending materials that led to the decision to deny access to the mails; the postmaster complied by citing several articles, cartoons, and a poem; but he declared that the items were were generally subversive or had a seditious effect, rather than point to specific words or sentences. Judge Hand responded: "It is difficult and often impossible to meet the charge that one's general ethos is treasonable."

Masses Publishing Co. v. *Patten* (1917) permitted Hand to reject the concept that all propaganda and hostile criticism could be prosecuted under a treason law that Congress appeared to apply only to communications that interfered with military affairs. Judge Hand saw no reason for limiting speech to polite conversation; he did not want to permit the Espionage Act to become a device for reversing the liberty of the press and speech through considerations of the decency or propriety of an argument. Rather, he noted, "the standard for judgment should be the strong danger that it will cause injurious acts." In his decision, Hand defined the limits of free speech:

> Words are not only the keys of persuasion, but the triggers of action, and those which have not purport but to counsel the violation of law cannot by any latitude of interpretation be a part of that public opinion which is the final source of government in a democratic state.

Hand also made clear the belief that citizens could discuss how existing laws are mistaken or unjust as long as they do not urge the belief that the laws must be violated. Hand would allow such discussion even if illegal conduct resulted from the communications, as long as violation of the law was not urged:

> Political agitation, by the passions it arouses or the convictions it engenders, may in fact stimulate men to the violation of law. Detestation of existing policies is easily transformed into forcible resistance of the authority which puts them in execution, and it would be folly to disregard the causal relation between the two. Yet to assimilate agitation, legitimate as such, with direct incitement to violent resistance, is to disregard the tolerance of all methods of political agitation which in normal times is a safeground of free government. The distinction is not a scholastic subterfuge, but a hard-bought acquisition in the fight for freedom . . . If one stops short of urging upon others that it is their duty or their interest to resist the law, it seems to me one should not be held to have attempted to cause its violation. If that be not the test, I can see no escape from the conclusion that under this section every political agitation which can be shown to be apt to create a seditious temper is illegal.

Hand's statement was the clearest and strongest pronouncement on freedom of expression that appeared during World War I. Hand would limit convictions to the objective test of the words themselves—did the words advocate violation of the law?

In reacting to Hand's decision, Zechariah Chafee, Jr. (1885-1957), Langdell Professor of Law at Harvard University and author of *Free Speech in the United States* (1941), observed:

> No one should have been held under clauses 2 and 3 of the Espionage Act of 1917 who did not satisfy these tests of criminal attempt and

incitement . . . "It is a question of degree." We can suppose a series of opinions, ranging from "This is an unwise war" up to "You ought to refuse to go, no matter what they do to you," or an audience varying from an old women's home to a group of drafted men just starting for a training camp. Somewhere in such a range of circumstances is the point where direct causation begins and speech becomes punishable as incitement under the ordinary standards of statutory construction and the ordinary policy of free speech, which Judge Hand applied. Congress could push the test of criminality back beyond this point, although eventually it would reach the extreme limit fixed by the First Amendment, beyond which words cannot be restricted for their remote tendency to hinder the war. In other words, the ordinary tests punish agitation just before it begins to boil over: Congress could change those tests and punish it when it gets really hot, but it is unconsitutional to interfere when it is merely warm. And there is not a word in the 1917 Espionage Act to show that Congress did change the ordinary tests or make any speech criminal except false statements and incitement to overt acts.

But Hand's concepts were overturned by the U. S. Circuit Court of Appeals on several points. First, there was the administrative point that the postmaster should not be overturned unless the decision was clearly wrong. More importantly, the Court of Appeals rejected Hand's objective test of reading the words themselves and substituted the view that speech was punishable "if the natural and reasonable effect of what is said is to encourage resistance to law, and the words are used in an endeavor to persuade to resistance." Whereas Hand had held the view that direct advice to action was the only test for violation of the Espionage Act of 1917, Judge Charles Merrill Hough (1858-1927) used the Sermon on the Mount to observe:

It is at least arguable whether there can be any more direct incitement to action than to hold up to admiration those who do act . . . The Beatitudes have for some centuries been considered highly hortatory, though they do not contain the injunction: 'Go thou and do likewise.'

The real effect of the final appeal in the *Masses* v. *Patten* case was to re-establish the old standard "of remote bad tendency" for district court judges. The result was that most of the free expression concepts laid down by Hand were rejected by judges throughout the nation.

Hand's test that the words must very nearly induce people to violate the law—criminal attempt as the test of guilt; that is, the communicator must instruct the audience to violate the law—was displaced by the new standards. The appeals court did keep one view, however—"bad intention," the motivation of the communicator in speaking or writing about the war. Most federal district court judges came to agree with the test that words "need only have a tendency to cause unrest among soldiers to make recruiting more difficult." Intention became the key test because judges could examine intention from indirect effects. Constructive intent, in the absence of the first two elements, became the primary standard for judging the guilt of writers and speakers. The courts added the standard of bad tendency—do the words have the tendency to induce people to violate the law?

The bad statements with ill intention has an administrative flaw—how can one be certain that the person uttering negative criticism with bad motives is going to be punished and the person making similar remarks with good intentions will be set free? Chafee, quoting an unnamed English judge, pointed out the problem with attempting to determine motivation—"The thought of man is not triable: for the Devil himself knoweth not the mind of man."

There followed a period when the two doctrines, bad tendency and constructive intent, became the core of nearly two thousand district court cases. These cases treated opinions like statements of fact. When the opinion differed from that of the President or the Congress, the courts concluded that they were false. Most of the convictions arose regarding opinions about the conduct of the war or the fact that the United States was engaged in the war. Among the opinions adjudged criminal was the suggestion that heavier taxation rather than bond issues was the way to finance the war. Criticisms of the Red Cross and the YMCA also became criminal. One law, the Minnesota Espionage Act, led a court to determine that it was a crime to say "No soldier ever sees these socks," thereby discouraging women from knitting socks for the American Red Cross.

In one case of the era, *United States* v. *Rose Pastor Stokes* [Mo. Dist 1918, App. Ct. 1920], the court decided that it was criminal to say to women, "I am for the people and the government is for the profiteers," because the statement might be taken as antiwar and cause the wives, mothers, and sweethearts to lose their enthusiasm for the work of "our armies in the field and our navies upon the seas [which] can operate and succeed only so far as they are supported and maintained by the folks at home." As a result of her statement, Stokes was convicted and sentenced to ten years in prison (the conviction was later set aside). In the Stokes decision, the judge permitted the admission of speeches or letters not part of the original indictment. Other cases considered remarks made before the beginning of the war in determining the intent of those on trial.

The setting in which a person uttered a criminal statement seemed did not limit the will of the courts to punish: cases developed out of communications in a hotel lobby, at a boarding house table, and on a train car. In one case, *United States* v. *J. Harshfield* (1919), a farmer found himself being convicted for words said at his dinner table. Two strangers had come to Harshfield's door to ask for gasoline because their car had stalled. Being friendly, the farmer provided the gasoline and offered the two strangers dinner. At the table, an argument broke out and Harshfield expressed strong attitudes about the military and the conduct of the war. The guests reported his conduct, and he was convicted for attempting to create disloyalty, insubordination, and mutiny. Eventually, the case was reversed; but it showed the lengths to which the government was willing to go.

Robert Goldstein, a filmmaker who had been involved with D. W. Griffith's now classic production of *The Birth of a Nation* (1915), was forced into bankruptcy for creating a film entitled *The Spirit of '76*, a work that included Patrick Henry's speech and other events surrounding the establishment of the United States. The film, however, contained scenes in which British soldiers murdered children and women in the Wyoming Massacre. Because the United States and England were allies, the film was confiscated and Goldstein was sentenced to ten years (later reduced to three years) in prison. In deciding the case, *United States* v. *Motion Picture Film The Spirit of '76* (1917), the Court observed:

> No man should be permitted, by deliberate act, or even unthinkingly, to do that which will in any way detract from the efforts which the United States is putting forth or serve to postpone for a single moment the early coming of the day when the success of our army shall be a fact.

Goldstein lost $100,000, his profession, and his freedom— for portraying the origin of his country on film.

Goldstein's sentence shows the lengths to which district judges during World War I went to punish violators of the Espionage Act. At least ten other people received ten year sentences, six received fifteen year sentences, and twenty-four got twenty year sentences. Although many writers have compared prosecutions using the Espionage Act to sedition actions under George III, most violators in England received only four-year sentences with the maximum being fourteen years. The English limited their punishment to relatively short terms while American judges imposed long sentences.

Citizens of high esteem in the community frequently became involved in the effort to seek out and stop treason as they saw it. As John Lord O'Brian (1874-1973), an assistant to the Attorney General during the prosecution of Espionage Act cases, observed:

> Throughout the country a number of large organizations and societies were created for the purpose of suppressing sedition. All of these were the outgrowth of good motives and manned by a high type of citizens. The membership of these associations ran into the hundreds of thousands. One of them carried full page advertisements in leading papers from the Atlantic to the Pacific, offering in substance to make every man a spy chaser on the payment of a dollar membership fee. These associations did much good in awakening the public to the danger of insidious propaganda, but no other one cause contributed so much to the oppression of innocent men as the systematic and indiscriminate agitation against what was claimed to be an all-pervasive system of German espionage. ["Civil Liberty in War Time," *New York Bar Association Journal*, 1919.]

The societies spent much time collecting evidence against people who supposedly engaged in sedition, worked as informers, or criticized government, and they had virtually as much power as the Department of Justice in finding critics of government.

Although lawyers in the U. S. Attorney General's office had prosecuted a number of cases under the 1917 law, many appeals for legal action could be refused because the publication or speech had no connection with securing an army—a requirement of the first law. But the 1918 amendment changed that by taking away any requirement that communication be related to the raising of an army. Now the small staff of the Justice Department could hardly handle the workload imposed upon them.

Espionage Laws: Disagreement in the Supreme Court

Most of the prosecutions under the Espionage statute were decided in the lower courts of the United States. Not until *Schenck* v. *United States* (1919) did the Supreme court have a chance to review actions. Charles T. Schenck, general secretary of the Socialist party, had overseen the publication of 15,000 leaflets be mailed to young men eligible for induction into the military services.

The leaflets used strong language to urge readers not to submit to conscription, which he called the worst form of despotism. According to the writer:

> Do not submit to intimidation . . . Assert Your Rights . . . [Recognize] your right to assert your opposition to the draft . . . If you do not assert and support your rights, you are helping to deny or disparage rights which it is the solemn duty of all citizens and residents of the United States to retain.

There followed a claim that arguments for conscription came from of the capitalist press and cunning politicians, the belief that resisting conscription was a constitutional duty, and an appeal to exert one's rights—"You must do your share to maintain, support, and uphold the rights of the people of this country."

The attorney for Schenck claimed the constitutional protection of the First Amendment as a reason for permitting the publication of the leaflet; however, the unanimous Supreme Court was not persuaded. Said Justice Oliver W. Holmes, Jr. (1841-1935) in writing the opinion:

> We admit that in many places and in ordinary times the defendants, in saying all that was said in the circular, would have been within their constitutional rights. But the character of every act depends upon the circumstances in which it is done . . . The most stringent protection of free speech would not protect a man in falsely shouting fire in a theater, and causing panic. It does not even protect a man from an injunction against uttering words that may have all the effect of force . . . The question in every case is whether the words used are used in such circumstances and are of such a nature as to create *a clear and present danger that they will bring about the substantive evils* that Congress has a right to prevent [italics added for emphasis]. It is a question of proximity and degree. When a nation is at war many things that might be said in time of peace

are such a hindrance to its effort that their utterance will not be endured so long as men fight, and that no court could regard them as protected by any constitutional right. It seems to be admitted that if an actual obstruction of the recruiting service were proved, liability for words that produced that effect might be enforced . . . We perceive no ground for saying that success alone warrants making the act a crime.

This case involved defendants who had printed circulars with language urging readers to resist the draft; therefore, the language appeared to violate the Espionage Act of 1917 and the relationship of the First Amendment to the law came under consideration. The "clear and present danger" test was the full court's first major attempt to spell out a clear, precise, and objective test for determining the dividing line between writings and speech protected under the First Amendment to the Constitution and what the state has the proper right to punish in an effort to preserve itself. The principal characteristic of the test is found in the conviction that writings and speech can not be punished unless it is extremely likely to produce major violence before additional speech can restore order. This test would have overturned many of the convictions of the lower courts had it existed throughout World War I; in fact, the standard was much more liberal than any test that the courts had used up to that time. Moreover, the standard had the effect of restricting the "prior restraint"—punishment before the communication is disseminated—standard that had been frequently adopted by courts drawing from the thinking of Blackstone. The test was to become the standard guiding many future Supreme Court decisions.

Although Holmes did not require that the words lead to action, he declared that their content must pose a strong chance of success. The test included both circumstance of communication as well as the specific content or nature of the message. Schenck was the first, and most influential, of six cases decided by the Supreme Court during the Spring of 1919 and the following winter.

Espionage Act: More Tests

A second in the series of 1919-1920 cases before the Supreme Court, *Frohwerk* v. *United States* (1919), provided the Supreme Court another opportunity to assess its attitudes towards the Espionage Act. Jacob Frohwerk had published in the *Missouri Staats-Zeitung* several articles about the constitutionality of the draft and the reasons for World War I. Department of Justice lawyers were uncertain if they had a case that would stand up to the comparison with the law, but filed the case nevertheless. The resulting case record was so weak that Justice Holmes thought if the record were clearer, there might be grounds for reversal. The court allowed the conviction to stand, but the decision resulted primarily from sloppy defense at the trial court level—the record upon which the Supreme Court makes its decision; consequently, *Frohwerk* is of less importance to the history of free expression than the other cases.

The third case during the spring, *Debs* v. *United States* (1919), led to a Supreme Court decision that allowed the conviction of Eugene V. Debs because he had engaged in a lecture about socialism on June 16, 1918, in Canton, Ohio, during which he supposedly urged the audience to be insubordinate, disloyal, and mutinous. Debs was accused of using the speech to obstruct the recruiting and enlistment of soldiers in the military of the United States.

Although Debs appeared to stop short of actually urging people to resist the draft, his speech, mostly on the history and growth of socialism in the United States, did focus kind remarks on Kate Richards O'Hare, a person convicted of obstructing the enlistment service, and Rose Pastor Stokes (case discussed elsewhere). According to the Supreme Court opinion written by Justice Holmes:

> The defendant spoke of other cases, and then, after dealing with Russia, said that the master class has always declared the war and the subject class has always fought the battles,—that the subject class has had nothing to gain and all to lose, including their lives; that the working class, who furnish the corpses, have never yet had a voice in declaring war and have never yet had a voice in declaring peace.

In addition to the specific remarks during the speech, Debs had also spoken highly of the "Antiwar Proclamation and Program" adopted by the socialists at St. Louis in April 1917; but these remarks were made before the speech, not as part of it.

The jury seemed to decide against Debs because the general tone of his discourse encouraged resistance to the draft, although it stopped short of a specific call to actively oppose the draft. This case provided the clear evidence of the problems associated with rejecting Judge Learned Hand's objective test for determining violations of the Espionage Act of 1917.

In Justice Holmes' opinion, the Court reviewed the liklihood of error in instructing the jury on the rules that should guide its decision process. The Court found that jury instructions had been delivered properly consistant with historical practice. The jury was instructed:

> ... they could not find the defendant guilty for advocacy of any of his opinions unless the words used had as their natural tendency and reasonably probable effect to obstruct the recruiting service, etc., and unless the defendant had the specific intent to do so in his mind.

The opinion did not attempt to use the clear and present danger test constructed only a week earlier in *Schenck* (March 3) in this March 10 decision, but focused on the nature of the evidence admitted to the trial and the process of instructing the jury—both of which met the requirements for sustaining guilt.

At the election of 1920, while Debs was confined to prison, the electorate gave him 919,799 votes for the presidency, a larger number of votes than he had received in any previous attempt to win the presidency. The three decisions disappointed civil liberterians who had believed that the Supreme Court would invalidate the Espionage Act of 1917 in the face of the First Amendment. The decisions were particularly distressing because Justice Holmes had the reputation of being the most liberal member of the court at the time.

THE HYPOCRISY OF
THE UNITED STATES AND HER ALLIES

Our Our President Wilson, with his beautiful phraseology, has hypnotized the people of America to such an extent that they do not see his hypocrisy.

Know, you people of America, that a frank enemy is always preferable to a concealed friend. When we say the people of America, we do not mean the few Kaisers of America, we mean the "People of America." You people of America were deceived by the wonderful speechs of the masked President Wilson. His shameful, cowardly silence about the intervention in Russia reveals the hypocrisy of the plutocratic gang in Washington and vicinity.

The President was afraid to announce to the Ameican people the intervention in Russia. He is too much a coward to come out openly and say: "We capitalistic nations cannot afford to have a proletarian republic in Russia." Instead, he uttered beautiful phrases about Russia, which, as you see, he did not mean, and secretly, cowardly, sent troops to crush the Russian Revolution. Do you see how German militarism combined with allied capitalism to crush the Russian Revolution?

This is not new. The tyrants of the world fight each other until they see a common enemy—WORKING CLASS—ENLIGHTMENT as soon as they find a common enemy, they combine to crush it.

In 1815 monarchic nations combined under the name of the "Holy Alliance" to crush the French Revolution. Now militarism and capitalism combined, through not openly, to crush the Russian revolution.

What have you to say about it?

Will you allow the Russian Revolution to be crushed? You: Yes, we mean YOU the people of America!

THE RUSSIAN REVOLUTION CALLS TO THE WORKERS OF THE WORLD FOR HELP.

"The Russian Revolution cries: WORKERS OF THE WORLD! AWAKE! RISE! PUT DOWN YOUR ENEMY AND MINE!"

Yes friends, there is only one enemy of the workers of the world and that is CAPITALISM.

It is a crime, that workers of America, workers of Germany, workers of Japan, etc., to fight the WORKERS' REPUBLIC OF RUSSIA.

AWAKE! AWAKE, YOU
WORKERS OF THE WORLD!
REVOLUTIONISTS

P. S. It is absurd to call us pro-German. We hate and despise German militarism more than do your hypocritical tyrants. We have more reasons for denouncing German militarism than has the coward of the White House.

WORKERS — WAKE UP.

The preparatory work for Russia's emancipation is brought to an end by his Majesty, Mr. Wilson, and the rest of the gang; dogs of all colors!

America, together with the Allies, will march to Russia, not, "God Forbid," to interfere with the Russian affairs, but to help the Czecho-Slovaks in their struggle against the Bolsheviki.

Oh, ugly hypocrites; this time they shall not succeed in fooling the Russian emigrants and the friends of Russia in America. Too visible is their audacious move.

Workers, Russian emigrants, you who had the least belief in the honesty of our government must now throw away all confidence, must spit in the face the false, hypocritic, military propaganda which has fooled you so rentlessly, calling forth your sympathy, your help, to the prosecution of the war. With the money which you have loaned or are going to loan them, they will make bullets not only for the Germans but also for the Workers Soviets of Russia. Workers in the ammunition factories, you are producing bullets, bayonets, cannon, to murder not only the Germans, but also your dearest, best, who are in Russia and are fighting for freedom.

You who emigrated from Russia, you who are friends of Russia, will you carry on your conscience in cold blood the shame spot as a helper to choke the Workers Soviets? Will you give your consent to the inquisitionary expedition to Russia? Will you be calm spectators to the fleecing blood from the hearts of the best sons of Russia?

America and her Allies have betrayed (the workers). Their robberish aims are clear to all men. The destruction of the Russian Revolution, that is the politics of the march to Russia.

Workers, our reply to the barbaric intervention has to be a general strike! An open challenge only will let the government know that not only the Russian Worker fights for freedom, but also here in America lives the spirit of revolution.

Do not let the government scare you with their wild punishment in prisons, hanging and shooting. We must not and will not betray the splendid fighers of Russia. Workers, up to fight.

Three hundred years had the Romanoff dynasty taught us how to fight. Let all rulers remember this, from the smallest to the biggest despot, that the hand of the revolution will not shiver in fight.

Woe unto those who will be in the way of progress. Let solidarity live!

THE REBELS.

Justice Holmes, however, had permitted the cases to pass because they did not provide the framework within which he could make the strongest statements regarding the Espionage Act of 1917.

In *Abrams v. United States* (1919), the 1918 amendment to the Espionage Act of 1917 was tested. and Justice Holmes with Justice Louis D. Brandeis (1856-1941) agreed on the limits of suppression.

The case began with the throwing of pamphlets—one in English, the other in Yiddish—from a window into the intersection of Houston and Crosby streets in New York City the morning of August 23, 1918. The leaflets protested U. S. intervention in the Bolshevik Revolution, and called for a strike in the munitions industry.

Military Intelligence Police searched the building from which the leaflets had been thrown until they found a young Russian Jew who led the police to five other Russians including Jacob Abrams, Molly Steimer, S. Lipman, H. Lachowsky, and H. Rosansky—the ones ultimately convicted. Although the department had refused to prosecute several Bolsheviks in the past, this group's appeal for a munitions workers' strike seemed serious enough to warrant action.

The defendants had distributed about nine thousand of the ten thousand leaflets they had printed to groups of workers in the streets and at radical meetings, but no one had shown that the publications had influenced anyone to strike in the munitions industry.

The trial for the five defendants began in New York City on October 10, 1918, before Judge Henry De Lamar Clayton. Although Clayton had never tried an espionage case, and his home judicial district was not New York, he received the assignment because other judges with experience had their dockets full. Clayton was from an old Southern family, had served in Congress where he gave his name to the Clayton Antitrust Act, and had retired to the judgeship.

At the trial, the defense argued that the Espionage Act was unconstitutional, that the defendants had not violated the law, and that there was no criminal intent. Most of the debate over the case centered on the fourth and last of the indictments in which the defendants were accused of:

> . . . willfully by utterance, writing, printing, publication, . . . urg[ing], incit[ing], or advocat[ing] any curtailment of production in this country of any thing or things, product or products necessary or essential to the prosecution of the war in which the United States may be engaged [specifically the war with Germany], with intent by such curtailment to cripple or hinder the United States in the prosecution of the war.

Clearly, the pamphlets contained sentences designed to discourage the action in Russia. But the United States was not at war with Russia; therefore, any suggestion that the action be stopped could not be interpreted as criminal.

An announcement from the government on August 3 declared that the United States was sending a few troops to the Soviet Union to aid Japan, which also had troops in the nation. This statement led to the Abrams publication, because the pamphlets resulted from the publication.

There were only two theories upon which a conviction could have been gained. First, the leaflets might have been designed to interfere with the action of the United States in Russia; but, since Russia was a neutral country with which the United States was not at war, any publications about military actions in Russia could not be considered a criminal violation of the Espionage Act unless the Russian action was planned by the United States government as part of the overall battle plan against Germany (for which no conclusive evidence existed). Second, the pamphlets were directed specifically at the American drive to defeat Germany; but there was nothing in the language to indicate any interest in keeping the United States out of Germany—if anything, the opposite is suggested.

On September 15, before the case went to trial, the United States Committee on Public Information* published statements suggesting that the Germans had hired the Bolshevik government, lending substance to the belief that fighting the Russians was fighting the Germans. This information was so widely published, it must have come to the jury's attention and probably influenced attitudes on the case.

The opinion of the Supreme Court does not claim that the conviction was based on the first theory—an indefensible theory as already noted; the Supreme Court majority view concluded that the grounds for upholding the lower court rested on the second theory.

Neither the English nor the Yiddish leaflets showed any passages directed at Germany or the war with Germany. But the court admitted hand- and type-written pages found in the apartments of the defendants—information upon which no indictment had been issued—to conclude that there might be some hidden purpose regarding the German army. Even here the evidence had to rest on a few scattered statements and no systematic evidence. Finally, in the testimony from the defendants, one finds that the defendants declared most emphatically that they were opposed to German militarism.

In the end, five of the six defendants were convicted and sentenced to prision terms ranging from three to twenty years and fined $500 to $1,000—punishment that could not have been much greater had they succeeded in closing all the munitions plants in the United States through strikes.

Seven of the justices of the Supreme Court agreed with the convictions in an opinion delivered by Justice John H. Clarke (1857-1945), but Justices Holmes strongly dissented and Justice Louis D. Brandeis (1856-1941) concurred.

Holmes believed that the only form of speech or publication present in the writings of the Russians in the United States upon which the majority could conclude a conviction were opinions; but Holmes believed that the First Amendment forbade any conviction of opinion under the free speech provision.

---

*One week after entering World War I, President Wilson created the Committee on Public Information to produce and disseminate information about the war to the media. To head the committee, Wilson appointed George Creel, a newspaper editor who had worked in New York, Kansas City, and Denver. The CPI created a voluntary censorship code, published an *Official Bulletin* (1917), and distributed over 6,000 news stories. The CPI developed an excellent record for honesty. CPI and other government public relations agencies are discussed in chapter 50.

The Final Espionage Cases of 1919-1920

After *Abrams*, the Supreme Court had two more opportunities to declare their unreserved support for the First Amendment in *Schaefer* v. *United States* (1920) and *Pierce* v. *United States* (1920).

In the first case, five officers of *Philadelphia Tageblatt* were convicted of espionage, based on fifteen articles that criticized the United States war effort and glorified German actions during the war. The poorly-financed German newspaper could do little more than republish edited versions of articles found in other sources. The same articles had not led to similar convictions for the original sources. Six members of the Supreme Court voted for the convictions of all but two members of the *Tageblatt* (the two had had nothing to do with the selection and publication of the articles). Justice Brandeis dissented in the strongest words:

> To hold that such harmless additions to or omissions from news items, and such impotent expressions of editorial opinion, as were shown here, can afford the basis even of a prosecution, will doubtless discourage criticism of the policies of the Government.

In the last opinion, *Pierce* v. *United States* (1920), a conviction ensued for the distribution of *The Price We Pay*, a pamphlet by St. John Tucker, an Episcopal clergyman. Seven members agreed with the conviction, but Justices Brandeis and Holmes dissented. According to the majority, three statements in the pamphlet were false and merited punishment. The majority were offended at one comment:

> Our entry into it [the war] was determined by the certainty that if the allies do not win, [multimillionaire] J. P. Morgan's loans to the allies will be repudiated, and those American investors who bit on his promises would be hooked.

Since this statement is only an opinion, the Supreme Court had to conclude that the expression of opinion could be proved sufficiently false to support a conviction.

Free Speech—A View of the Supreme Court's Work

The thinking of Justices Brandeis and Holmes gave new and more precise boundaries to the limits of free expression, defined by the "clear and present danger" test and continual improvements of the concept over the years following. Outside the courtroom, Zechariah Chafee, Jr., first wrote an extensive treatise on the First Amendment and concepts of free expression in 1920, later updated and rethought in some aspects in 1941 entitled, *Free Speech in the United States*. Chafee's goal was to review the relevant court cases, the history of the First Amendment, and comparisons that some authors have made to English law and legal thinking to determine the proper limits of free expression. Chafee, in *Free Speech in the United States* (1941), expressed his own view and:

reject[ed] both extreme views of the Bill of Rights: [that] the Bill of Rights is a peace-time document and consequently freedom of speech may be ignored in war . . . [and] the belief of many . . . that the First Amendment renders unconstitutional any Act of Congress without exception "abridging the freedom of speech, or of the press," that all speech is free, and only action can be restrained and punished.

While Chafee believed in a strict interpretation of the First Amendment and the limits on government sanctions, he would not permit all unrestrained expression. It became necessary for Chafee to find what he considered the proper boundary between protected and unprotected speech.

Chafee rejected the thinking of Sir William Blackstone, the great English legal scholar, as irrelevant to the Ameican First Amendment. Blackstone had believed "the liberty of the press . . . consists in laying no previous restraints upon publications and not in freedom from censure for criminal matter when published".

[Chafee in *Free Speech in America* believed] this Blackstonian theory dies hard, but it ought to be knocked on the head once for all. In the first place, Blackstone was not interpreting a constitution, but was trying to state the English law of his time, which had no censorship and did have extensive libel prosecutions. Whether or not he stated that law correctly, an entirely different view of the liberty of the press was soon afterwards enacted in Fox's Libel Act . . . so that Blackstone's view does not even correspond to the English law of the last hundred and twenty-five years. Furthermore, Blackstone is notoriously unfitted to be an authority on the liberties of American colonists, since he upheld the right of Parliament to tax them, and was pronounced by one of his own colleagues to have been "we all know, an anti-republican lawyer."

Chafee went on to detail his constraints and purposes for free expression:

. . . The essential question is not, who is judge of the criminality of an utterance, but what is the test of its criminality . . . The real issue in every free speech controversy is this: whether the state can punish all words which have some tendency, however remote, to bring about acts in violation of law, or only words which directly incite to acts in violation of law . . .

The meaning of the First Amendment did not crystalize in 1791. The framers would probably have been horrified at the thought of protecting books by Darwin or Bernard Shaw, but "liberty of speech" is no more confined to the speech they thought permissible than "commerce" in another clause is limited to the sailing vessels and horsedrawn vehicles of 1787. Into the making of the constitutional conception of free speech have gone, not only men's bitter experience of the censorship and sedition prosecutions before 1791, but also the subsequent development of the law of fair comment in civil defamation, and the philosophical speculations of John Stuart Mill. Justice Holmes phrases the thought with even more than his habitual felicity. The provisions of the Constitution are not mathematical formulas having their essence in their form; they are organic living institutions transplanted from English soil.

It is now clear that the First Amendment fixes limits upon the power of Congress to restrict speech either by a censorship or by a criminal statute, and if the Espionage Act exceeds those limits it is unconstitutional . . . The First Amendment is just as much a part of the Constitution as the war clauses, and . . . that the war clauses cannot be invoked to break down freedom of speech. The truth is that all provisions of the Constitution must be construed together so as to limit each other. In a war as in peace, this process of mutual adjustment must include the Bill of Rights. There are those who believe that the Bill of Rights can be set aside in war time at the uncontrolled will of the government . . . The Third and Fifth Amendments expressly apply in war. A majority of the Supreme Court declared the war power of Congress to be restricted by the Bill of Rights in *Ex parte Mulligan* . . . [The First Amendment] must apply to those activities of government which are most liable to interferewith free discussion, namely, the postal service and the conduct of war.

The true meaning of freedom of speech seems to be this. One of the most important purposes of society and government is the discovery and spread of truth on subjects of general concern. This is possible only through absolutely unlimited discussion, for, as Bagehot points out, once force is thrown into the argument, it becomes a matter of chance whether it is thrown on the false side or the true, and truth loses all of its natural advantage in the contest. Nevertheless, there are other purposes of government, such as order, the training of the young, protection against external aggression. Unlimited discussion sometimes interferes with these purposes, which must then be balanced against freedom of speech, but freedom of speech ought to weigh very heavily in the scale. The First Amendment gives binding force to this principle of political wisdom.

Or to put the matter another way, it is useless to define free speech by talk about rights. The agitator asserts his constitutional right to speak, the government asserts its constitutional right to wage war. The result is a deadlock. Each side takes the position of the man who was arrested for swinging his arms and hitting another in the nose, and asked the judge if he did not have a right to swing his arms in a free country. "Your right to swing your arms ends just where the other man's nose begins." To find the boundary line of any right, we must get behind rules of law to human facts. In our problem, we must regard the desires and needs of the individual human being who wants to speak and those of the great group of human beings among whom he speaks. That is, in technical language, there are individual interests and social interests, which must be balanced against each other, if they conflict, in order to determine which interest shall be sacrificed under the circumstances and which shall be protected and become the foundation of a legal right. It must never be forgotten that the balancing cannot be properly done unless all the interests involved are adequately ascertained, and the great evil of all this talk about rights is that each side is so busy denying the other's claim to rights that it entirely overlooks the human desires and needs behind that claim . . .

The First Amendment protects two kinds of interests in free speech. There is an individual interest, the need of many men to express their opinions on matters vital to them if life is to be worth living, and a social interest in the attainment of truth, so that the country may not only adopt the wisest course of action but carry it out in the wisest way. This social interest is especially important in war time. Even after war has been declared there is bound to be a confused mixture of good and bad arguments in its support, and a wide difference of opinion as to its objects. Truth can be sifted out from falsehood only if the government is vigorously and constantly cross-examined, so that the fundamental issues of the struggle may be clearly defined, and the war may not be diverted to improper ends, or conducted with an undue sacrifice of life and liberty, or prolonged after its just purposes are accomplished. Legal proceedings prove that an opponent makes the best cross-examiner. Consequently it is a disastrous mistake to limit criticism to those who favor the war . . . If a free canvassing of the aims of the war by its opponents is crushed by the menace of long imprisonment, such evils, even though made public in one or two newspapers, may not come to the attention of those who had power to counteract them until too late.

Chafee wrote perhaps the best defense of the clear and present danger limitation on free speech as he gave ringing defenses to the arguments of Justice Holmes.

Chapter 25

Changing Concepts:
World War I to World War II

Just because World War I had ended, there was no indication that the nation was prepared to restore free expression to its peacetime condition. During 1919-1920, a number of acts of violence occured, including explosions that damaged Attorney General A. Mitchell Palmer's house. On May Day 1919, there was fighting in the streets of Boston and Cleveland. Members of the Industrial Workers of the World (IWW), a group opposed to the American war effort, and the American Legion clashed in Centralia, Washington, resulting in the death of five ex-members of the armed services.

Into this environment, Palmer, through a letter circulated to leading magazines, spoke of his own fears:

> The Department, as far as existing laws allow, intends to keep up an unflinching war against this movement no matter how cloaked or dissembled. We are determined that this movement will not be permitted to go far enough in this country to disturb our peace or create any widespread distrust of the people's government.
>
> There is a menace in this country ... My one desire is to acquaint people like you with the real menace of evil-thinking which is the foundation of the Red movement.

Members of Congress proposed a number of bills to provide stronger legislation to censor or prosecute people engaged in actions that might constitute sedition, including one draft submitted by the Attorney General during the 1919-1920 period. Both the Department of Justice and various congressional committees became actively involved in trying to come up with new laws to protect the nation form the menace they felt was spreading. Meanwhile, the press was filled with stories about the arrests of Reds or the destruction of Red headquarters.

Suppressing Socialists: The Post Office Still at Work

Suppression of freedom of speech during World War I also involved the U.S. Post Office. As the result of a hearing on September 22, 1917, the second class permit of the publisher of the *Milwaukee Leader* was revoked because the newspaper had violated the Espionage Act of 1917. The hearing followed quickly after the passage of the Espionage Act on June 15, 1917.

The *Leader*, under the editorship of Victor L. Berger, founder of the Socialist Party in the United States and a member of Congress (1911-1913), published the "Proclamation and War Program" of April 14, 1917, a document that criticized the entry of the United States into World War I. The Proclamation had been passed by the Socialist Convention in St. Louis that year and represented the group's views. After publishing the proclamation, Berger published a steady stream of critical essays, editorials, and cartoons about the United States' war effort. But the *Leader* did not try to persuade anyone not to sign up for military service. Indeed, registration in Minnesota and Wisconsin indicated that the two states were contributing large numbers of personnel to the war services. The evidence, therefore, suggested that the *Leader* had no effect on registration or service, despite the wide distribution of the publication.

The newspaper, believing that its rights had been abridged, appealed through the courts, to the Supreme Court of United States which rendered an opinion in 1921 written by Justice John H. Clarke (1857-1945) in *United States of America ex. rel. Milwaukee Social Democratic Publishing Company v. Albert S. Burleson, Postmaster General of the United States* (1921).

In its statement against the newspaper, the Postmaster General quoted from more than fifty excerpts from editorial and articles that appeared in the newspaper between April 14 and September 13, 1917, the first five months of World War I. Some of the complaints about the war included statements that the war, which:

. . . denounced the draft law as unconstitutional, arbitrary, and oppressive, with the implied conunsel that it should not be respected or obeyed.

The publisher contended that the Espionage Act was unconstitutional because it did not provide for a trial by a court, it destroyed the newspaper's right of free speech, and it deprived the newspaper of property without due process of law.

Clarke's opinion referred to earlier cases in refusing to reconsider the validity of the Espionage Act, the right of the postal authorities to revoke second class permits, or the constitutionality of the statute granting the Post Office the authority to establish classifications.

The opinion also supported the right of the Postmaster General to withdraw the second-class privilege and to review character before conferring the right for future publications. In the order, the Postmaster had withdrawn the privilege only until the publisher could show that it has restored itself to worthiness to enjoy the privilege—acceptable in the eyes of the majority of the court.

The problem with the case was that the Postmaster General had used two statutes to reach his conclusion, the Mail Classification Act of 1879, and the Espionage Act of 1917. The first law provided the framework for estabishing the rate to be changed to users of the mail. The second class rate, created especially for publishers who regularly send their printed product through the mails, provided a rate as much as ninety percent lower than the next lowest postal class. Thus, a publisher excluded from the second class rate would be at a competitive disadvantage to other organizations enjoying the lower rate.

Justices Brandeis and Holmes disagreed with the majority (with Brandeis writing the dissent and Holmes agreeing) by noting that nothing in the Classification Act provides the postmaster with the right to exclude all future publications from the mails without regard for their content. At best, the postmaster can review each edition and stop the mailing of only those that contain statements in violation of the law. Any other course of action would be in violation of the "prior restraint" concept of censorship—keeping all future publications out of the mails. Brandeis also objected to the majority combining two statutes, the Classification and the Espionage acts, to come up with the right to exclude the newspaper from using the second class permit without concerning itself with the relationship of the other classifications and their relation to the right of the Postmaster General to exclude.

To support his view, Brandeis quoted from an order of the Attorney General:

> "It must be premised that the Postmaster General clearly has no power to close the mails to any class of persons, however reprehensible may be their practices or however detestable their reputation; if the question were whether the mails could be closed to all issues of a newspaper, otherwise entitled to admission, by reason of an article of this character in any particular issue, there could be no doubt that the question must be answered in the negative."

> If such power were possessed by the Postmaster General, he would, in view of the practical finality of his decisions, become the universal censor of publications. For a denial of the use of the mail would be, for most of them, tantamount to a denial of the right of circulation.

Despite the reasoning of Brandeis and Holmes, the majority decided that revocation of the second class permit was not a form of punishment or suppression.

Gitlow—State Suppression: Enter the 14th Amendment

Benjamin Gitlow was the business manager of *Revolutionary Age* when it printed the Left Wing Manifesto. The Communist Labor Party and the Communist Party had separated from the Socialist Party in September 1919, a division that caused many of the left-wing socialists to abandon their former party organization. The Left Wing Manifesto became their guiding document.

The Lusk Committee objected to the socialist writing and took on the responsibility of putting Gitlow and his friends out of business. The Lusk committee was a legislative group committed to protecting New York State residents from revolutionary ideas, and it compiled a four volume report for the New York State Legislature in 1920, *Revolutionary Radicalism . . . Report of the Joint*

Legislative Committee Investigating Seditious Activities; it pressed legislation through the New York State legislature, and it initiated the prosecutions against socialists. Among the Lusk bills were proposals to set up a staff of investigators to search out and question revolutionaries and another designed to get teachers with objectionable ideas fired. Other laws would regulate schools and courses to insure protection from revolutionary thoughts. Although Alfred E. Smith (1873-1944), governor of New York (1919-1921, 1923-1929), vetoed all the Lusk bills, he was defeated and spent a term out of office, only to see the Lusk bills passed and signed. But in 1923, Smith returned to the Governor's office and oversaw the repeal of the Lusk laws. In 1928, he was the Democratic nominee for President.

To prove their charges of seditious activities, the committee published the complete manifesto as it appeared in *Revolutionary Age*. The document had been worded in traditional socialist rhetoric, language familiar to most readers and too boring for most to read—not a document that was likely to gain much hostile action from any group of socialists, unless, perhaps a demand to stop the dreary reading—although the words were strong.

Nevertheless, the jury considered the manifesto to be dangerous and in violation of the law, and they held Gitlow guilty of violating New York State law. The court imposed a five to ten year sentence, of which three years had been served before the case came before the Supreme Court of the United States. The conviction was based on a seldom used New York statute passed in 1902, after William McKinley's assassination, dealing with criminal anarchy prohibiting "advocacy, advising or teaching the duty, necessity or propriety of overthrowing or overturning organized government by force or violence."

There is an important distinction between the Gitlow case and cases treated earlier regarding free expression—the earlier cases rested on the First Amendment to the Constitution and interpretations of statutes passed by Congress regarding the provisions; but, in *Gitlow* v. *New York* (1925), Gitlow was convicted under the New York State Criminal Anarchy Act. The First Amendment did not apply to the states, only to laws passed by Congress. The Supreme Court had to consider the question of similar First Amendment protections against repressive state laws. The Court used the Fourteenth Amendment which prescribes, "Nor shall any state deprive any person of . . . liberty . . . without due process of law," to say that this Amendment passes First Amendment protections regarding free expression to state laws, *i.e.* free expression standards used in evaluating federal laws could be used to judge the constitutionality of New York's Criminal Anarchy Act. (The First Amendment had applied only to statutes enacted by Congress, not the states prior to this decision.)

In the majority opinion prepared by Justice Edward T. Sanford (1865-1930), the Supreme Court ruled against Gitlow and for the New York State law; but the court made a pronouncement on the Fourteenth Amendment that is of much importance:

> For present purposes we may and do assume that freedoms of speech
> and of the press—which are protected by the First Amendment from

abridgment by Congress—are among the fundamental personal rights and "liberties" protected by the due process clause of the Fourteenth Amendment from impairment by the States . . .

We cannot hold that the present statute is an arbitrary or unreasonable exercise of the police power of the State unwarrantably infringing the freedom of speech or press; and we must and do sustain its constitutionality.

The majority concluded that the statute was not unconstitutional, nor was the use of the statute in Gitlow's case improper, affirming the lower court's conviction. While Gitlow lost, the nation gained an affirmation that the rights of free speech extended through the Fourteenth Amendment to the states.

Justice Holmes, with the concurrence of Justice Brandeis, dissented with the majority opinion and stood by the "clear and present danger" test:

The general principle of free speech, it seems to me, must be taken to be included in the Fourteenth Amendment, in view of the scope that has been given to the word "liberty" as there used, although perhaps it may be accepted with a somewhat larger latitude of interpretation than is allowed to Congress by the sweeping language that governs or ought to govern the laws of the United States. If I am right then I think that the criterion sanctioned by the full Court in Schenck v. United States, applies:

"The question in every case is whether the words used are used in such circumstances and are of such a nature as to create a clear and present danger that they will bring about the substantive evils that [the State] has a right to prevent. . . ."

It is said that the manifesto was more than a theory, that it was an incitement. Every idea is an incitement. It offers itself for belief and if believed it is acted on unless some other belief outweighs it or some failure of energy stifles the movement at its birth. The only difference between the expression of an opinion and an incitement in the narrower sense is the speaker's enthusiasm for the result. Elequence may set fire to reason. But whatever may be thought of the redundant discourse before us it had no chance of starting a present conflagration.

Not everything of importance regarding free expression occured with the Supreme Court. Smith used his considerable power to support people who held to unpopular causes. When the Supreme Court allowed Gitlow's conviction to stand, Governor Smith immediately pardoned him—Smith had already pardoned Gitlow's left- wing friends from prison. Indeed, Governor Smith was so anxious to pardon Gitlow, his friends had to restrain the governor until the Supreme Court acted.

Freedom of speech via 14th A. = clear + Present Danger—Test

Criminal Syndicalism

The successful passage and use of the Espionage Act of 1917* in punishing political opinion unpopular with the majority of the citizens at the federal level led quickly to a series of new state laws called criminal syndicalism statutes, defined in California law as:

> . . . any doctrine or precept advocating, teaching or aiding . . . the commission of crime, sabotage . . . or unlawful acts of force and violence or unlawful methods of terrorism as a means of accomplishing a change in industrial ownership or control, or effecting any political change.

Thirty-three states passed similar laws, but only California became an active prosecutor of people engaged in violating the new laws.

The Supreme Court had the opportunity to express its view on criminal syndicalism statutes in a case involving Anita Whitney (*Whitney* v. *California*, 1927). A woman almost sixty years old, Whitney had graduated from Wellesley College and had devoted her life to philanthropic endeavors; she had joined the Socialist Party and, for a time, the Communist Labor Party of California. As a member of the Communist Party, she had participated in an open meeting in Oakland during which the Communist party organized itself. Whitney, at the convention, supported a motion to seek power through the political process. Attendees were unaware of any legal violations in which they might be engaged.

When an agent of the federal government described Whitney's correspondence, the agent concluded that Whitney had done nothing indicating she intended to urge the overthrow of the government through violence. Yet, in January 1920, Whitney was convicted of violating the Criminal Syndicalism Act.

At the Supreme Court, the majority upheld Whitney's conviction, but the important part of the decision was the concurring opinion of Justice Brandeis, with the agreement of Justice Holmes. Brandeis took the opportunity to clarify the "clear and present danger" test and to analyze the constitutional protection for free expression. The analysis provides an eloquent defense for free expression:

> . . . Those who won our independence believed that the final end of the state was to make men free to develop their faculties, and that in its government the deliberative forces should prevail over the arbitrary. They valued liberty both as an end and as a means. They believed liberty to be the secret of happiness and courage to be the secret of liberty. They believed that freedom to think as you will and to speak as you think are means indispensable to the discovery and spread of political truth; that

*Although this book is not specifically about individual state laws, most states created statutes regarding freedom of speech and press. Most states have, or have had, laws dealing with opposition to war, the display of the red flag, conspiracy, incitement to crime and, specifically, acts of violence, sedition, criminal anarchy, criminal syndicalism, unlawful assembly, preventing certain radicals from voting, scandalous newspapers and regulations of teachers, public officials, and schools. In addition, some cities passed their own laws limiting free expression.

without free speech and assembly discussion would be futile; that with them, discussion affords ordinarily adequate protection against the dissemination of noxious doctrine; that the greatest menace to freedom is an inert people; that public discussion is a political duty; and that this should be a fundamental principle of the American government. They recognized the risks to which all human institutions are subject. But they knew that order cannot be secured merely through fear of punishment for its infraction; that it is hazardous to discourage thought, hope and imagination; that fear breeds repression; that repression breeds hate; that hate menaces stable government; that the path of safety lies in the opportunity to discuss freely supposed grievances and proposed remedies; and that the fitting remedy for evil counsels is good ones. Believing in the power of reason as applied through public discussion, they eschewed silence coerced by law—the argument of force in its worst form. Recognizing the occasional tyrannies of governing majorities, they amended the Constitution so that free speech and assembly should be guaranteed.

Fear of serious injury cannot alone justify suppression of free speech and assembly. Men feared witches and burnt women. It is the function of speech to free men from the bondage of irrational fears. To justify suppression of free speech there must be reasonable ground to fear that serious evil will result if free speech is practiced. There must be reasonable ground to believe that the danger apprehended is imminent. There must be reasonable ground to believe that the evil to be prevented is a serious one. Every denunciation of existing law tends in some measure to increase the probability that there will be a violation of it. Condonation of a breach enhances the probability. Expressions of approval add to the probability. Propagation of the criminal state of mind by teaching syndicalism increases it. Advocacy of lawbreaking heightens it still further. But even advocacy of violation, however reprehensible morally, is not a justification for denying free speech where the advocacy falls short of incitement and there is nothing to indicate that the advocacy would be immediately acted on. The wide difference between advocacy and incitement, between preparation and attempt, between assembling and conspiracy, must be borne in mind. In order to support a finding of clear and present danger it must be shown either that immediate serious violence was to be expected or was advocated, or that the past conduct furnished reason to believe that such advocacy was then contemplated.

Those who won our independence by revolution were not cowards. They did not fear political change. They did not exalt order at the cost of liberty. To courageous, self-reliant men, with confidence in the power of free and fearless reasoning applied through the process of popular government, no danger flowing from speech can be deemed clear and present, unless the incidence of the evil apprehended is so imminent that it may befall before there is opportunity for full discussion. If there be time to expose through discussion the falsehood and fallacies, to avert the evil by the process of education, the remedy to be applied is more speech, not enforced silence. Only an emergency can justify repression. Such, in my opinion, is the command of the Constitution. It is therefore always open to Americans to challenge a law abridging free speech and assembly by showing that there was no emergency justifying [it] . . .

Prohibition of free speech and assembly is a measure so stringent that it would be inappropriate as the means for averting a relatively trivial harm to society . . . Among free men, the deterrents ordinarily to be applied to prevent crime are education and punishment for violations of the law, not abridgment of the rights of free speech and assembly.

Justice Brandeis concurred with the majority that the rights protected in the First Amendment to the Constitution are not absolute, and he went to great pains to declare where the protection ceases and the right of government to curb expression begins. The "clear and present danger" test is more clearly defined when Brandeis concludes that speech must be protected unless there is indication that insufficient time exists to counteract the potential violent effects of statements. Just the possibility of minor consequences is not enough to permit government to repress expression. The limit for Brandeis and Holmes is just short of major violence in an emergency where opportunity for counteracting arguments is not possible.

A free press can, of course, be good or bad. But, most certainly, without freedom it can never be anything but bad.

—Albert Camus

The 1930s: A New Court Attitude

As the 1930s began, a change took place in the Supreme Court of the United States with the appointment of Chief Justice Charles Evans Hughes (1862-1948). Hughes had views similar to Holmes and Brandeis; add two other swing votes, and the majority might include Holmes and Brandeis, which would be the case on many free expression cases during the next few years.

The first evidence of the change in the voting patterns of the Supreme Court came when the court was called upon to decide *Stromberg* v. *California* (1931), another criminal syndicalism law, involving Yetta Stromberg, a young woman of nineteen who worked at a summer camp for children. She had been convicted under California law for running a red flag with the Soviet hammer and sickle on it up a flagpole. It was also the flag for the Communist Party in the United States, and she asked campers to pledge allegiance to that flag—"I pledge allegiance to the worker's red flag and to the cause for which it stands, one aim throughout our lives, freedom for the working class." A number of convictions

Clear + Present Dager = it has to be big danger

involving the Red flag had been upheld in state courts, and, now, the Supreme Court had to decide on this case that started in a camp for children ten to fifteen years of age in the San Bernardino Mountains.

In writing the majority opinion, the new Chief Justice declared that the vagueness of part of the California statute under which Stromberg had been convicted made that portion of the statute unconstitutional:

> The maintenance of the opportunity for free political discussion to the end that government may be responsive to the will of the people that changes may be obtained by lawful means, an opportunity essential to the security of the Republic, is a fundamental principle of our constitutional system. A statute which upon its face, and as authoritatively construed, is so vague and indefinite as to permit the punishment of the fair use of this opportunity is repugnant to the guaranty of liberty contained in the Fourteenth Amendment.

The Stromberg case extented the liberty of speech beyond the speaking of words to actions, such as the raising of a flag, and held unconstitutional laws that were so indefinite that they might be construed as limiting proper free expression, the case often with sedition laws. For the first time, Brandeis and Holmes found themselves comfortably voting with the majority.

In 1937, the Supreme Court had another opportunity to render its view on the criminal syndicalism laws, in this case involving the law of Oregon. Dirk De Jonge was charged with assisting in the conducting of a meeting under the auspices of the Communist Party on July 27, 1934, in Portland, Oregon, attended by 150 to 300 persons. The Communist Party was believed to be an organization that advocated criminal syndicalism. De Jonge's lawyers argued that the meeting was public, orderly, and held for legal purpose. The defense stated that there was no teaching or advocating of criminal syndicalism at the meeting.

Although the trial and appeal in lower courts violated procedures the Supreme Court considered necessary, the Court took the case and considered the criminal syndicalism aspects. De Jonge had been convicted solely because he helped conduct a lawful public meeting held under the leadership of the Communist Party, and it was on this charge that the Supreme Court acted. There was no attempt to incite violence against the United States Government or to engage in any other illegal act. Chief Justice Hughes did not like the conviction:

> The greater the importance of safeguarding the community from incitements to the overthrow of our institutions by force and violence, the more imperative is the need to preserve inviolate the constitutional rights of free speech, free press and free assembly in order to maintain the opportunity for free political discussion, to the end that government may be responsive to the will of the people and that changes, if desired, may be obtained by peaceful means. Therein lies the security of the Republic, the very foundation of constitutional government . . .

The holding of meetings for peaceable political action cannot be proscribed. Those who assist in the conduct of such meetings cannot be branded as criminals on that score . . .

Nothwithstanding [the] objectives [of the Communist Party], the defendant still enjoyed his personal right of free speech and to take part in a peaceable assembly having a lawful purpose, although called by that Party.

In *Herndon* v. *Lowry* (1937), the Supreme Court also took the opportunity to strenthen the Fourteenth Amendment's application of freedom of expression concepts to state laws.

From Conscience to the Unconscionable

On May 25, 1931, a week after the Stromberg decision, the Supreme Court rendered a decision in the case of Yale Divinity School professor Kenneth Macintosh who had been denied citizenship because he was unwilling to swear "that I will support and defend the Constitution of the United States against all enemies, foreign and domestic . . ." Macintosh, a Canadian, had served in France during World War I and was willing to serve in future wars as long as he believed them to be morally acceptable, but he would not swear that he would serve in any war. On this ground the lower court had denied citizenship, and the majority of the Supreme Court sustained the conviction; but Hughes dissented:

> Much has been said of the paramount duty to the State, a duty to be recognized, it is urged, even though it conflicts with convictions of duty to God. Undoubtedly that duty to the State exists within the domain of power, for government may enforce obedience to laws regardless of scruples. When one's belief collides with the power of the State, the latter is supreme within its sphere and submission or punishment follows. But, in the forum of conscience, duty to a moral power higher than the State has always been maintained. The reservation of that supreme obligation, as a matter of principle, would unquestionably be made by many of our conscientious and lawabiding citizens. The essence of religion is belief in a relation to God involving duties superior to those arising from any human relation. One cannot speak of religious liberty, with proper appreciation of its essential and historic significance without assuming the existence of a belief in supreme allegiance to the will of God. Professor Macintosh, when pressed by the inquiries put to him, stated what is axiomatic in religious doctrine. And, putting aside dogmas with their particular conceptions of deity.

Hughes argued that religious liberty, the right to practice one's beliefs, and the exclusion of the state when no damage was being inflicted on the state, had been decided long before the Macintosh case. Congress had sought to avoid any conflict between conscience and public duty. Hughes agreed that the state had the right to protect the public order, to raise an army when needed, but he did not believe that this was at issue in the Macintosh case.

A First Amendment Landmark

Stromberg and *Macintosh* held a hint of how the court might decide in a decision of great importance to newspapers, *Near* v. *Minnesota* (June 1, 1931), in which Chief Justice Hughes delivered the opinion of the majority. The decision rested on an interpretation of a Minnesota law that allowed the state to take action against people engaged in the publishing or distribution of newspapers of "obscene, lewd[,] . . . lascivious . . . malicious, scandalous and defamatory newspaper, magazine or other periodical."

The county attorney in Hennepin County had brought suit against *The Saturday Press*, a sleezy newspaper cited for being "malicious, scandalous and defamatory" because of articles about a number of local citizens, the *Minneapolis Tribune*, the *Minneapolis Journal*, the Jewish people, and members of a Hennepin grand jury. Jay M. Near—manager, owner, and proprietor of the newspaper—had allowed the publication to engage in attacks on community citizens, and had created a situation in which he clearly, in the view of Minnesota courts, had overstepped the law of the state. The publications had claimed that a Jewish gangster controlled gambling, bootlegging, and racketeering in Minneapolis; and that the mayor, county attorney, the chief of police, and police officers were failing their duty. Near represented the worst of journalism, with his vicious and unsubstantiated attacks on community citizens, ethnic groups, and institutions. If the often repeated conviction, "Freedom of speech is of no value unless it protects the right of the community's vilest citizen" meant anything in the law, the court was now called upon to show its courage. Could the Supreme Court justices ignore the distaste they must have had for Near and protect the right of free expression? The case provided one of the most serious and difficult tests of the right to print and speak freely.

The Minnesota law provided that "truth . . . with good motives and for justifiable ends" was a defense against conviction in the case of the law. The statute provided that a person found guilty "in and by such judgment, such nuisance [violation] may be wholly abated [stopped]." The statute also provided for fine and imprisonment. The effect of this provision was that the law could deal not just with a particular article or statement, but with the entire life of the publication.

Hughes delivered a long opinion in which he dealt with the history of the First Amendment and free expresson provisions conferred through the Fourteenth Amendment:

> It is no longer open to doubt that the liberty of the press and of speech is within the liberty safeguarded by the due process clause of the 14th Amendment from invasion by state action. It was found impossible to conclude that this essential personal liberty of the citizen was left unprotected by the general guaranty of fundamental rights of person and property.

Although Hughes maintained the right of free expression, he stopped short of suggesting that the right transended all state rights:

> In maintaining this guaranty, the authority of the State to enact laws to promote the health, safety, morals and general welfare of its people is necessarily admitted . . .
>
> [Moreover] liberty of speech and of the press is also not an absolute right, and the state may punish its abuse.

To focus the intent of the Court's opinion on the precise problem being addressed, Hughes first described what was not part of the case. For example, he pointed out that the case had nothing to do with traditional libel provisions. The injunction sought to supress the future publication of newspapers, came without any need to prove the falsity of the statements—a condition of personal libel cases. "This law is not for the protection of the person attacked nor to punish the wrongdoer. It is for the protection of the public welfare."

Secondly, Hughes observed the statute dealt with the publication of charges of corruption against public officials, and with their performance in office. "Such charges by their very nature create a public scandal," he wrote. His other arguments were:

> Third.   The object of the statute is not punishment, in the ordinary sense, but suppression of the offending newspaper or periodical. The reason for the enactment, as the state court has said, is that prosecutions to enforce penal statutes for libel do not result in "effecient repression or suppression of the evils of scandal . . ."
>
> This suppression is accomplished by enjoining publication and that restraint is the object and effect of the statute.
>
> Fourth.   The statute not only operates to suppress the offending newspaper or periodical but to put the publisher under an effective censorship.   When a newspaper or periodical is found to be "malicious, scandalous and defamatory," and is suppressed as such, resumption of publication is punishable as a contempt of court by fine or imprisonment. Thus, where a newspaper or periodical has been suppressed . . . it would seem to be clear that the renewal of the publication of such charges would constitute a contempt and that the judgment would lay a permanent restraint upon the publisher . . . [Yet,] the law gives no definition except that covered by the words "scandalous and defamatory, and publications charging official misconduct are of that class . . ."
>
> If we cut through mere details of procedure, the operation and effect of the statute in substance is that public authorities may bring the owner or publisher of a newspaper or periodical before a judge upon a charge of conducting a business of publishing scandalous and defamatory matter— in particular that the matter consists of charges against public officers of official dereliction—and unless the owner or publisher is able and disposed to bring competent evidence to satisfy the judge that the charges are true and are published with good motives and for justifiable ends, his newspaper or periodical is suppressed and further publication is made punishable as a contempt. This is of the essence of censorship.

The question is whether a statute authorizing such proceedings in restraint of publication is consistent with the conception of the liberty of the press as historically conceived and guaranteed. In determining the extent of the constitutional protection, it has been generally, if not universally, considered that it is the chief purpose of the guaranty to prevent previous restraints upon publication.

Hughes proceeded with an extensive study of the developing thought of free expression, censorship, and previous restraint beginning with Blackstone's concepts in England and adding the corresponding development in the United States. He concluded the discussion with the observation that common law rules provided standards for dealing with libel, criminal libel, and contempt of court, and methods for awarding damages, matters not under consideration in the case of J. M. Near. Thus, Hughes went to considerable lengths to insure that the limits of the interpretation were understood:

The objection has also been made that the principle as to immunity from previous restraint is stated too broadly, if every such restraint is deemed to be prohibited. That is undoubtedly true; the protection even as to previous restraint is not absolutely unlimited. But the limitation has been recognized only in exceptional cases, [for example, when a nation is at war] . . . No one would question but that a government might prevent actual obstruction to its recruiting service or the publication of the sailing dates of transports or the number and location of troops. On similar grounds, the primary requirements of decency may be enforced against obscene publications. The security of the community life may be protected against incitements to acts of violence and the overthrow by force of orderly government. The constitutional guaranty of free speech does not "protect a man from an injunction against uttering words that may have all the effect of force." These limitations are not applicable here. Nor are we now concerned with questions as to the extent of authority to prevent publications in order to protect private rights according to the principles governing the exercise of the jurisdiction of courts of equity.

Then Hughes followed with a resounding defense of free expression and the rights of publishers to espouse unpopular causes. He began by quoting a letter.

In the letter sent by the Continental Congress (October 26, 1774) to the Inhabitants of Quebec, referring to the "five great rights," it was said: "The last right we shall mention, regards the freedom of the press. The importance of this consists, besides the advancement of truth, science, morality, and arts in general, in its diffusion of liberal sentiments on the administration of government, its ready communications of thoughts between subjects, and its consequential promotion of union among them, whereby oppressive officers are shamed or intimidated, into more honourable and just modes of conducting affairs." Madison, who was the leading spirit in the preparation of the 1st Amendment of the Federal Constitution, thus described the practice and sentiment which led to the guaranties of liberty of the press in state constitutions:

"In every state, probably, in the Union, the press has exerted a freedom in canvassing the merits and measures of public men of every description which has not been confined to the strict limits of the common law. on this footing the freedom of the press has stood; on this footing it yet stands . . . Some degree of abuse is inseparable from the proper use of everything, and in no instance is this more true than in that of the press. It has accordingly been decided by the practice of the states, that it is better to leave a few of its noxious branches to their luxuriant growth, than, by pruning them away, to injure the vigour of those yielding the proper fruits. And can the wisdom of this policy be doubted by any who reflect that to the press alone, chequered as it is with abuses, the world is indebted for all the triumphs which have been gained by reason and humanity over error and oppression; who reflect that to the same beneficent source the United States owe much of the lights which conducted them to the ranks of a free and independent nation, and which have improved their political system into a shape so auspicious to their happiness? Had Sedition Acts, forbidding every publication that might bring the constituted agents into contempt or disrepute, or that might excite the hatred of the people against the authors of unjust or pernicious measures, been uniformly enforced against the press, might not the United States have been languishing at this day under the infirmities of a sickly Confederation? Might they not, possibly, be miserable colonies, groaning under a foreign yoke?"

The fact that for approximately one hundred and fifty years there has been almost an entire absence of attempts to impose previous restraints upon publications relating to the malfeasance of public officers is significant of the deep-seated conviction that such restraints would violate constitutional right. Public officers, whose character and conduct remain open to debate and free discussion in the press, find their remedies for false accusations in actions under libel laws providing for redress and punishment, and not in proceedings to restrain the publication of newspapers and periodicals. The general principle that the constitutional guaranty of the liberty of the press gives immunity from previous restraints has been approved in many decisions under the provision of state constitutions.

The importance of this immunity has not lessened. While reckless assaults upon public men, and efforts to bring obloquy upon those who are endeavoring faithfully to discharge official duties, exert a baleful influence and deserve the severest condemnation in public opinion, it cannot be said that this abuse is greater, and it is believed to be less, than that which characterized the period in which our institutions took shape. Meanwhile, the administration of government has become complex, the opportunities for malfeasance and corruption have multiplied, crime has grown to most serious proportions, and the danger of its protection by unfaithful officials and of the impairment of the fundamental security of life and property by criminal alliances and official neglect, emphasizes the primary need of a vigilant and courageous press, especially in great cities. The fact that the liberty of the press may be abused by miscreant purveyors of scandal does not make any the less necessary the immunity of the press from previous restraint in dealing with official misconduct. Subsequent punishment for such abuses as may exist is the appropriate remedy, consistent with constitutional privilege.

In attempted justification of the statute, it is said that it deals not with publication per se, but with the "business" of publishing defamation. If, however, the publisher has a constitutional right to publish, without previous restraint, an edition of his newspaper charging official derelictions, it cannot be denied that he may publish subsequent editions for the same purpose. He does not lose his right by exercising it. If his right exists, it may be exercised in publishing nine editions, as in this case, as well as in one edition. If previous restraint is permissible, it may be imnposed at once; indeed, the wrong may be as serious in one publication as in several. Characterizing the publication as a business, and the business as a nuisance, does not permit an invasion of the constitutional immunity against restraint. Similarly, it does not matter that the newspaper or periodical is found to be "largely" or "chiefly" devoted to the publication of such derelictions. If the publisher has a right, without previous restraint, to publish them, his right cannot be deemed to be dependent upon his publishing something else, more or less, with the matter to which objection is made.

Nor can it be said that the constitutional freedom from the previous restraint is lost because charges are made of derelictions which constitute crimes. With the multiplying provisions of penal codes, and of municipal charters and ordinances carrying penal sanctions, the conduct of public officers is very largely within the purview of criminal statutes. The freedom of the press from previous restraint has never been regarded as limited to such animadversions as lay outside the ranage of penal enactments. Historically, there is no such limitation; it is inconsistent with the reason which underlies the privilege, as the privilege so limited would be of slight value for the purposes for which it came to be established.

The statute in question cannot be justified by reason of the fact that the publisher is permitted to show, before injunction issues, that the matter published is true and is published with good motives and for justifiable ends. If such a statute, authorizing suppression and injunction on such a basis, is constitutionally valid, it would be equally permissible for the legislature to provide that at any time the publisher of any newspaper could be brought before a court, or even an administrative officer (as the constitutional protection that he has on mere procedural details) and required to produce proof of the truth of his publication, or of what he intended to publish, and of his motives, or stand enjoined. If this can be done, the legislature may provide machinery for determining in the complete exercise of its discretion what are justifiable ends and restrain publication accordingly. And it would be but a step to a complete system of censorship. The recognition of authority to impose previous restraint upon publication in order to protect the community against the circulation of charges of misconduct, and especially of official misconduct, necessarily would carry with it the admission of the authority of the censor against which the consitutional barrier was erected. The preliminary freedom, by virtue of the very reason for its existence, does not depend, as this court has said, on proof of truth . . .

Equally unavailing is the insistence that the statute is designed to prevent the circulation of scandal which tends to disburb the public peace and to provoke assaults and the commission of crime. Charges of reprehensible conduct, and in particular of official malfeasance, unquestionably create a public scandal, but the theory of the constitutional guaranty is that even a more serious public evil would be caused by authority to prevent publication. "To prohibit the intent to excite those unfavorable sentiments against those who administer the government is equivalent to a prohibition of the actual excitement of them; and to prohibit the actual excitement of them is equivalent to a prohibition of discussions having that tendency and effect; which, again, is equivalent to a protection of those who administer the government, if they should at any time deserve the contempt or hatred of the people, against being exposed to it by free animadversions on their characters and conduct." There is nothing new in the fact that charges of reprehensible conduct may create resentment and the disposition to resort to violent means of redress, but this well-understood tendency did not alter the determination to protect the press against censorship and restraint upon publication. As was said in *New Yorker Staats-Zeitung* v. *Nolan*, "If the township may prevent the circulation of a newspaper for no reason other than that some of its inhabitants may violently disagree with it, and resent its circulation by resorting to hysical violence, there is no limit to what may be prohibited." The danger of violent reactions becomes greater with effective organization of defiant groups resenting exposure, and if this consideration warranted legislative interference with the initial freedom of publication, the constitutional protection would be reduced to a mere form of words.

Door to Door—Free Expression includes Distribution

Beginning in the late 1930s, a series of cases involving the right to distribute "circulars, handbills, advertising, or literature of any kind" were decided by the Supreme Court. Involved were municipal ordinances that required solicitors to secure a license, or written permission, from a city before taking the literature to people's homes. The Jehovah's Witnesses were most frequently involved in the cases because of their active canvassing program. Municipal officials justified the ordinances partly on the grounds that they served the community purpose of keeping the streets clean, but the cases raised the more fundamental question of licensing expression.

The first case, *Lovell* v. *City of Griffin* (1938), began in Griffin, Georgia, which had a local law prohibiting the distribution of literature in the community without permission from the city manager. Alma Lovell, a Jehovah's Witness, went from door to door in Griffin, was arrested under the provisions of the law, and was convicted and sentenced to imprisonment for fifty days because she did not pay the $50 fine. Her case went to the Supreme Court, where Chief Justice Charles E. Hughes (1862-1948) held the ordinance invalid because:

> Whatever the motive which induced its adoption, its character is such that it strikes at the very foundation of the freedom of the press by subjecting it to license and censorship. The struggle for the freedom of the press was primarily directed against the power of the licensor. It was against that power that John Milton directed his assault by his "Appeal for the Liberty of Unlicensed Printing." And the liberty of the press became initially a right to publish "*without* a license what formerly could be published only with *one*" . . .
>
> Legislation of the type of the ordinance in question would restore the system of license and censorship in its baldest form.
>
> The liberty of the press is not confined to newspapers and periodicals. It necessarily embraces pamphlets and leaflets.

Other handbill cases strengthened the position first expressed in *Lovell* and include *Schneider* v. *Irvington* (1939), with the following grouped with *Schneider*: *Young* v. *California*, *Snyder* v. *Milwaukee*, and *Nichols* v. *Massachusetts*. The ordinances being tested in these four cases included one that required fingerprinting and photographing of solicitors. The other local laws absolutely prohibited distributing handbills. No attempt was made to balance the civic interest in clean and safe streets with the freedom of expression. Handling litterers could be done by punishing those who litter; freedom of speech and press is supreme over other local laws.

The freedoms that this first case insured received a boost in the opinion written by Justice Owen J. Roberts (1875-1955) in *Cantwell* v. *Connecticut* (1940), a decision based on the fact that Jehovah's Witnesses were going from house to house asking for contributions, and trying to play a record attacking Roman Catholics to people themselves Catholics. The unpopularity of the ideas being promoted led to a court case and ultimately to a strongly worded opinion from the Supreme Court defending the right to unpopular ideas:

> In the realm of religious faith, and in that of political belief, sharp differences arise. In both fields the tenets of one man may seem the rankest error to his neighbor. To persuade others to his own point of view, the pleader, as we know, at times, resorts to exaggeration, to vilification of men who have been, or are, prominent in church or state, and even to

false statement. But the people of this nation have ordained in the light of history, that, in spite of the probablility of excesses and abuses, these liberties are, in the long view, essential to enlightened opinion and right conduct on the part of the citizens of a democracy.

Although other cases followed in the 1940s, this group of cases established the main theme of Supreme Court views—the right of free expression is so important that concern over clean streets or of invasion of one's
personal values can not overcome the need to protect free speech.

Freedom of Assembly

Jersey City, New Jersey, had an ordinance created in 1908 that amounted to a peace-time sedition law. Mayor Frank Hague of Jersey City used that early law and every other administrative power he could find to create the closed city as a means for combating the closed shop and labor unions.

When called upon to consider the local laws, the Supreme Court held the Jersey City law to be invalid (*Hague* v. *Committee for Industrial Organization,* 1939). One of the most important clauses under test was:

The Director of Public Safety is herby authorized to refuse to issue said permit [for assembly] when, after investigation of all of the facts and circumstances pertinent to said application, he believes it to be proper to refuse the issuance thereof; *provided, however, that said permit shall only be refused for the purpose of preventing riots, disturbances or disorderly assemblage.*

Mayor Hague used the ordinance to exclude anyone whom he did not approve from using public parks and streets. The power was used against organized labor and other groups experiencing the mayor's disfavor, but, on appeal to the Supreme Court, the ordinance was held to be invalid. In deciding the case, Justice Roberts applied a balancing analysis:

Wherever the title of streets and parks may rest, they have immemorially been held in trust for the use of the public and, time out of mind, have been used for purposes of assembly, communicating thoughts between citizens, and discussing public questions. Such use of the streets and public places has, from ancient times, been a part of the privileges, immunities, rights, and liberties of citizens. The privilege of a citizen of the United States to use the streets and parks for communication of views on national questions may be regulated in the interest of all; it is not absolute, but relative, and must be exercised in subordination to the general comfort and convenience, and in consonance with peace and good order; but it must not in the guise of regulation be abridged or denied.

While the interpretation might leave some questions unanswered, the history of Jersey City would suggest that the decision provides for uncensored free assembly and expression.

A case that raised questions regarding just how serious the Supreme Court was in protecting the freedom of expression occured because Walter Chaplinsky was charged with saying, "You are a God damned racketeer" and "a damned Fascist and the whole government of Rochester are Fascists or agents of Fascists."

Chaplinsky was supposed to have made these statements in Rochester, New Hampshire, while distributing literature for the Jehovah's Witnesses. The statements led to a trial and eventually to the Supreme Court in *Walter Chaplinsky* v. *New Hampshire* (1942).

In reviewing the case, Justice Frank Murphy (1893-1949), speaking for the Court, agreed that freedom of expression must be protected and that there was a history of the Supreme Court supporting the First and Fourteenth Amendments, but he noted:

> Allowing the broadest scope to the language and purpose of the Fourteenth Amendment, it is well understood that the right of free speech is not absolute at all times and under all circumstances. There are certain well-defined and narrowly limited classes of speech, the prevention and punishment of which have never been thought to raise any Constitutional problem. These include the lewd and obscene, the profane, the libelous, and the insulting or "fighting" words—those which by their very utterance inflict injury or tend to incite an immediate breach of the peace. It has been well observed that such utterances are no essential part of any exposition of ideas, and are of such slight social value as a step to truth that any benefit that may be derived from them is clearly outweighed by the social interest in order and morality. [A similar view was expressed in *Cantwell* v. *Connecticut*.]

The Supreme Court sustained the law under which the conviction of Chaplinsky had been made because the law limited itself to unprotected speech, and the Court further let stand the conviction of Chaplinsky.

Chapter 26

Burning Books: American Style

During the years between World War I and World War II, the concepts of obscenity and the right of the state to suppress were to undergo some dramatic changes. Many communities had their societies for suppression of vice patterned after the model created by Comstock; in fact, the New York Society was still in operation in the 1920s. A number of cases were taken to court with the result that the publications, publishers, or retailers were punished. For example, Judge Arthur Stone fined Edith Law of Arlington, Massachusetts, $100 for renting Robert Keable's *Simon Called Peter* (1921) published by E. P. Dutton and Company. The case arose from a complaint lodged by the Watch and Ward Society in the Boston area.

Some judges, however, took a more tolerant approach such as the one taken by Magistrate Charles A. Oberwager in the Harlem (New York) court who refused in 1922 to suppress Petronius's *The Satyricon*, a book first written about the first century A.D., and published in the United States by Boni and Liveright. Oberwager did not believe that the legislature of New York intended to censor literary works and felt that suppression would threaten the freedom of expressions and thus the foundations of democracy in the United States.

During the early 1920s, at least ten literary works, plays and novels, were being challenged in the courts, including James Joyce's *Ulysses*, Edouard Bourdet's *The Captive*, Radclyffe Hall's *The Well of Loneliness*, Pierre Louys's *Aphrodite*, Gustave Flaubert's *November*, Upton Sinclair's *Oil!*, William Faulkner's *Sanctuary*, James T. Farrell's *Young Lonigan*, Erskine Caldwell's *God's Little Acre*, and the dramatic version of Caldwell's *Tobacco Road*.

A period of greatest censorship occurred in Boston beginning in 1927 and continuing through 1928 and 1929. During 1928, Boston officials suppressed sixty or more books; during 1928 and 1929, the city banned at least sixty-eight more books. The Watch and Ward society was enjoying its greatest success ever under the Rev. Charles S. Bodwell. Similar societies existed in Chicago, elsewhere in Illinois, and in other communities. Perhaps the beginning of the change in attitude can be traced to a pamphlet designed to instruct in sex rather than serve as a literary work.

In 1930, the question of mailing obscene literature arose because Mary W. Dennett, mother of two boys—ages eleven and fourteen—could find no articles, books, or other published information on sex she considered appropriate for her

209

children. To give her children the frank and fair treatment of sex she believed necessary, Dennett wrote a pamphlet, *Sex Side of Life*. But the publication became popular enough that Union Theological Seminary, Young Men's Christian Association, Young Women's Christian Association, the public schools in Bronxville, New York, and several Public Health Departments adopted the work for their own use.

Dennett included two parts in her essay, an "Introduction for Elders" and "An Explanation for Young People." In the first part, she explained her intentions: "From a careful observation of youthful curiosity and a very vivid recollection of my own childhood, I have tried to explain frankly the points about which there is the greatest inquiry."

Upon the basis of Bennett's publication, and because copies had been sent through the mails, the United States government brought suit in *United States v. Dennett* (1930). In making the charge to the jury, the trial judge instructed that the motives of the defendant could not be considered, only if the words in the pamphlet were "obscene, lewd, or lacivious within the meaning of the statute." The judge added:

> . . .[E]ven if the matter sought to be shown in the pamphlet complained of were true, that fact would be immaterial, if the statements of such facts were calculated to deprave the morals of the readers by inciting sexual desires and libidinous thoughts.

The jury concluded that the publication was obscene under the Comstock Act; Dennett was fined $300.

Dennett appealed to the court of appeals where Judge Augustus N. Hand (1869-1954) wrote the majority opinion. Hand agreed with the district court that the intention of the writer could not be considered in determining if the publication was obscene. Then Hand observed that the Comstock Act did not exclude from the mails medical literature, "Sex Education" pamphlets issued by the United States Public Health Service in 1927, or chaste poetry and fiction.

The district court's conviction was overturned. Judge Hand used the opinion to reject the concept that the risk of the publication exciting lust was reason enough to suppress the pamphlet. Although Hand believed that any treatment of sex might encourage lust in some people, he also thought that education was a better way to deal with the problems of sexual matters, rather than ignorance and mystery or information gained from the ill- informed.

Two years later, in *United States v. O. B. Limehouse* (1932), the Supreme Court reversed a lower court decision that had quashed an indictment based on the mailing of thirty letters containing sexual content that was filthy. The case provided the Court, with Justice Brandeis writing the majority opinion, an opportunity to review an amendment to the Comstock Act (March 4, 1909) which added the words "and every filthy [book]" to the list of "obscene, lewd, or lascivious" publications eligible for exclusion from the mails. Brandeis and the majority concluded that filthy should have a meaning distinct from the other terms and that the letters were indeed filthy, but not "obscene, lewd, or lascivious" and overturned the quash of the indictment.

Brandeis observed that the analysis of the court in *Limehouse* was to be limited to the letters in question and left open alternative interpretations of other communications. The main effect of this decision was to distinguish the meaning of filthy from obscenity, lewdness, or lasciviousness.

Ulysses: A New Direction

A much more important case in determining the direction the courts would take arose in 1934, when the court of appeals looked at *Ulysses*, by James Joyce. The case arose because the book had been seized when it was being brought into the United States. Random House, the American publisher which wanted to publish *Ulysses*, desired the book seized so that a test case could be conducted to determine if the book could be published in the United States. The plan worked, but the publisher had to import two copies before it was successful. The first attempt failed because the copy did not attract the attention of customs officials and passed quietly into the country. Finally, on second attempt the book was stopped by customs inspectors, and the case, *United States* v. *One Book Entitled Ulysses By James Joyce, Random House, Inc., Claimant (1933)*, was decided with an opinion by Judge John M. Woolsey of the District Court for the Southern District of New York, himself a very literate person, who had read the entire book and concluded that it was not obscene, taken in total. Woolsey was an extraordinarily courageous individual because he rejected the "Hicklin" standard and set about to create a new standard for judging literature by looking at the entire book.

On appeal, Judge Augustus N. Hand affirmed the decision of Judge Woolsey and rejected the standard of *Hicklin* by considering the total effect of *Ulysses* rather than looking at isolated passages. The opinion shows that Judge Hand, a widely read and thoughtful man, examined the book with care and judged the entire work. Hand also rejected the views of admirers who praised the book too highly and critics who totally rejected the work. Hand found in *Ulysses* "originality and . . . symmetry and excellent craftsmanship of a sort." The fundamental question, to Hand, was "whether such a book of artistic merit and scientific insight should be regarded as 'obscene' within [the law]."

Judge Hand dealt with the question of selected obscenity:

That numerous long passages in Ulysses contain matter that is obscene under any fair definition of the word cannot be gainsaid; yet they are relevant to the purpose of depicting the thoughts of the characters and are introduced to give meaning to the whole, rather than to promote lust or portray filth for its own sake. The net effect even of portions most open to attack, such as the closing monologue of the wife of Leopold Bloom, is pitiful and tragic, rather than lustful. The book depicts the souls of men and women that are by turns bewildered and keenly apprehensive, sordid and aspiring, ugly and beautiful, hateful and loving . . .

It is settled . . . that works of physiology, medicine, science, and sex instruction are not within the statute, though to some extent and among some persons they may tend to promote lustful thoughts . . . We think the same immunity should apply to literature as to science, where the presentation when viewed objectively, is sincere, and the erotic matter is not introduced to promote lust and does not furnish the dominant note of the publication. The question in each case is *whether a publication taken as a whole has a libidinous effect* [emphasis added] . . .

We do not think that Ulysses, taken as a whole, tends to promote lust, and its criticised passages do this no more than scores of standard books that are constantly bought and sold. Indeed a book of physiology in the hands of adolescents may be more objectionable on this ground than almost anything else.

Thus, Judge Hand chose to examine the questionable literature in total, rejecting the *Hicklin* standard of any part of the work that offended made the entire work offense. Secondly, Hand refused to consider a work obscene if the work might be obscene to some part of the population, such as young people. The standard of *Regina* v. *Hicklin*, and cases based on Hicklin, said Hand,

. . . [W]ould exclude much of the great works of literature and involve an impracticability that cannot be imputed to Congress and would in the case of many books containing obscene passages inevitably require the court that uttered them to restrict their applicability.

It is true that the motive of an author to promote good morals is not the test of whether a book is obscene, and it may also be true that the applicability of the statute does not depend on the persons to whom a publication is likely to be distributed. The importation of obscene books is prohibited generally, and no provision is made permitting such importation because of the character of those to whom they are sold. While any construction of the statute that will fit all cases is difficult, we believe that the proper test of whether a given book is obscene *is the dominant effect*. In applying this test, relevancy of the objectionable parts to the theme, the established reputation of the work in the estimation of approved critics, if the book is modern, and the verdict of the past, if it is ancient, are persuasive pieces of evidence; for works of art are not likely to sustain a high position with no better warrant for their existence than their obscene content.

It may be that Ulysses will not last as a substantial contribution to literature, and it is certainly easy to believe that, in spite of the opinion of Joyce's laudators, the immortals will still reign, but the same thing may be said of current works of art and music and of many other serious efforts of the mind. Art certainly cannot advance under compulsion to traditional forms, and nothing in such a field is more stifling to progress than limitation of the right to experiment with a new technique. The foolish judgments of Lord Eldon about one hundred years ago, proscribing the works of Byron and Southey, and the finding by the jury under a charge by Lord Denman that the publication of Shelley's "Queen Mab" was an indictable offense are a warning to all who have to determine the

Ulyses decision 1934 = look at whole book via a reasonable adult (p 213)

limits of the field within which authors may exercise themselves. We think that Ulysses is a book of originality and sincerity of treatment and that it has not the effect of promoting lust. Accordingly it does not fall within the statute, even though it justly may offend many.

The effect of this decision was fourfold—first, the decision considered the author's reason for writing the book, a way to provide a judicial benefit of the doubt; second, the decision considered the work as a whole, not the isolated passages of the *Hicklin* standard in deterining obscenity; third, the human criterion for obscenity was the effect on reasonable adults, not those most likely to be influenced by questionable passages such as children; finally, the aesthetic merits of the book were balanced against the occasionally obscene passages in the work.

This decision reflected a turning point away from the *Hicklin* standard of earlier years; however, it would not be until the 1950s that the Supreme Court of the United States would devote extended opinions to examining the obscenity question in greater detail using motion pictures as the basis of judgment.

The motion picture business was an industry where the question of censorship frequently arose because of the large body of fiction films available to the American public, the wide audiences including children, young people, adults, and elderly people, and the visual nature of the medium. Just as important as the content of films in leading to the demand for censorship, was the much reported lives of Hollywood actors, actresses, and directors which was at odds with the conservative middle-American ethic. During the 1920s and 1930s, much conflict arose on the proper nature of content for films. In 1922, Will H. Hays, a Presbyterian elder, Postmaster General of the United States, and President Harding's campaign director became president of the Motion Picture Producers and Distributors of America, the Hays Office. Motion pictures were coming under the same public demands as the print media.

Chapter 27

Censorship of Motion Pictures

The history of the censorship of motion pictures in America presents an excellent illustration of the confusion caused by attempting to reconcile an unflagging allegiance to abstract liberty with a traditional desire to censor personal morality.

[The First on-screen kiss, in a film of about a minute in 1898, had scandalized the country, with several organizations calling for restrictions. Later, several American cities and states created film review ordinances; the earliest one was in Chicago, in 1907, and required the city police to pre-screen all movies for acceptability. The last state board, in Maryland, was not abolished until 1982.]

In 1915, the censorship of the motion picture by previous restraint was placed on a firm legal basis by the unanimous decision of the Supreme Court in the case of *Mutual Film Corporation* v. *Industrial Commission*. The case arose under an Ohio statute which created a board of censors for motion pictures, and provided that "all motion picture films to be publicly exhibited and displayed in the state of Ohio" were subject to censorship. The statute further provided that "only such films as are in the judgment and discretion of the Board of Censors of a moral, education or amusing and harmless character shall be passed and approved by such board." Counsel for appellants argued that the statute contravened the First and Fourteenth Amendments to the Federal Constitution, and Section 11, Article I of the Ohio Constitution, providing that "Every citizen may freely speak, write and publish his sentiments on all subjects, being responsible for the abuse of the right; and no law shall be passed to restrain or abridge the liberty of speech, or of the press." Mr. Justice McKenna disposed of this contention in forthright terms, holding that however didactic films may become there is no impediment to their value and effect in the Ohio statute; that the police power is familiarly exercised in granting or withholding licenses for theatrical performances as a means of their regulation, and that the argument is "wrong or strained which extends the guaranties of free opinion and speech to the multitudinous shows which are advertised on the billboards of our cities." "It cannot be put out of view," he said, "that the exhibition of moving pictures is a business pure and simple, originated and conducted for profit, like

---

This chapter is edited and reprinted, with permission, from the *Yale Law Journal*, Volume 49, 1939-1940). Additional comments by the editors are in brackets.

other spectacles, not to be regarded, nor intended to be regarded, by the Ohio constitution, we think as part of the press of the country or as organs of public opinion . . ."

It is difficult to see how these arguments are any less applicable to newspapers and magazines than to motion picture films. Certainly newspapers may be used for evil, but the Supreme Court has struck down a statute making the publication of a scandalous paper punishable as a nuisance [*Near* v. *Minnesota*]. Certainly, furthermore, it cannot be said that the *New York Times* or the *Saturday Evening Post* are "any less a business pure and simple, originated and conducted for profit than is the cinema industry."

[However, by 1952, in *Burstyn* v. *Wilson*, the Court finally ruled that films were protected by the First Amendment.] The recognized power to license and thereby to regulate theatrical exhibitions under the police power very probably originated in an anomaly of English law, the rigorous censorship of the drama which was left unimpaired during the development of the freedom of speech and press. During the 16th and early 17th centuries the stage enjoyed a status comparable to that of the press. But there is and has been a strong tendency in the English middle-class climate of opinion, dating from Cromwellian times, to consider the stage a low form of entertainment and to bracket actors in the same category with vagabonds and beggars. And in 1737 Sir Robert Walpole, to quiet the satire of his administration prevalent in the theatres of London, persuaded Parliament to pass a bill giving the Lord Chamberlain the statutory power of licensing all stage plays. The Theatres Act of 1843, with minor amendments, leaves this power basically unchanged. Had it not been for these two statutes, it is quite possibly that "pulpit, press, and play would today be on a footing of equality." The stifling effect of this censorship is attested by the quality both of the plays banned and of the authors who have fought it. With such a background in English law, and with a Puritan heritage in America which frowned on the stage, it is understandable that the theatre in the early years of this country was regarded as a low form of entertainment to be licensed by each town or city in the interest of morality and decency. Occasionally a court, interpreting a state constitution, declared the drama to be protected from "previous restraint" censorship, but in the vast majority of cases control by license of the theatre was considered an emmimently legitimate use of the police power.

The other probable explanation for the *Mutual* decision lies in the fact that twenty-five years ago, when the case arose, there was a tendency to regard the primitive motion picture as a disreputable form of entertainment.

At the time of the *Mutual* decision, three of the forty-eight states had their own censor boards. Since then, six more have provided for previous restraint censorship. The number of states with censorship boards would not of itself be impressive if the other states were immune from their influence. But the peculiar nature of the industry makes such isolation impossible. There are only a limited number of prints made of each individual film, and these prints are apportioned to some thirty exchanges for distribution in the area served by each exchange. All but six of these exchanges serve territory in more than one state, several of them in as many as five states. Furthermore, to have a film cut or mutilated by any one state means not only a direct material loss to the producer; it carries as well an unappraisable but distinct [diminuation] of the entertainment value of the film in that area. Thus the producers and particularly the administrators of the Production Code, are faced with the problem of producing movies that will meet the individual pecularities of different state boards, operating under different acts. And even where statutory standards are identical, boards in two different states will, in practice, rarely make the same deletions.

The statutes under which these boards operate are so general in their terminology that their interpretation is largely left to the discretion of the members, who are usually three residents and citizens of the state "well qualified by education and experience." Although the examination fees have proved to be a sizeable source of revenue to the state, the primary purpose of these statutes is to protect the inhabitants of the state from unwholesome and indecent motion pictures. Many of them provide that a film or any part thereof may be censored if it falls within the statute, without regard to the theme of the film as a whole. In literature, the courts have lately arrived at the wiser conclusion that a questioned book must be judged as an entity. The boards have yet to realize that they cannot effectively censor the underlying theme.

When challenged, the constitutionality of these boards has been sustained by the courts, which have held that regualtion of the content of all films designed for public exhibition within the state is a proper exercise of the police power. This regulation has been applied alike to newsreels and full-length films. Only once since the *Mutual* case has a court been required to pass squarely on the validity of censoring newsreels. On that occasion the New York courts upheld the censorship on the ground that inasmuch as newsreels are shown in a "public place of amusement," they are not a part of the press. Of the state statutes, only New York, Pennsylvania and Kansas now exempt "current event" films from the operations of censorship. Exemptions are granted under several of the statutes to scientific films for use by the learned professions, if not to be exhibited at any place of amusement, and exemptions are permitted at the discretion of the board for films intended solely for educational, charitable, or religious purposes. Exemptions for news films, however, are the exception, not the rule.

Much of the justification for state censor boards is based on a fear that a relaxation of legal standards would have a markedly deleterious effect on the morals and behavior of movie-going children. The wisdom of such a contention seems open to challenge. The large number of parents groups and other unofficial bodies which classify films according to their suitability for exhibition to the young have gained widespread popular support, and the Hays office has been anxious to cooperate with these groups. This method of meeting the problem seems preferable to the British system of semi-official classification of films for universal or for only adult view.

The records of the boards of censors reveal no lack of hesitancy in exercising their power . . . Ohio and Pennsylvania . . . have banned films and newsreels considered pro-labor. In Kansas a speech by Senator Wheeler opposing the bill for enlarging the Supreme Court was ordered cut from the *March of Time*. A documentary film of the civil war in Spain entitled *Spain in Flames* was banned in Pennsylvania, with the proviso that if the words "Fascist," "Nazi," "Italian," "Rome," "German," "Berlin," and the like be deleted wherever they appear, the picture would be approved. This decision was reversed in the coruts on the ground that the film, being documentary, was one of the current events and therefore allowable in Pennsylvania. In Ohio, *Spain in Flames* was banned with this comment: "The picture itself did not contain any harmful propaganda. However, the dialogue of the narrator made the picture, we consider, very harmful. We suggest that the narrators, in reporting on this subject . . . keep their remarks neutral, or we will find it necessary to make eliminations." A film on sterilization was banned in New York, and the courts would not disturb the decision. Judge Hill, in a strong dissent, said: "It is further argued that the subject of sterilization should not be given publicity. Such an argument presents the issue of whether our people may govern themselves or be governed; whether arguments for and against proposed and impending legislation may be presented direct in the public prints, on the stage and by films, or whether a Commission or Commissioner is to determine the limit and character of the information to be given to the public . . ."

The film *The Birth of a Baby*, presented by the American Committee on Maternal Welfare, to depict maternity in "a clean, dignified and reverent manner," was banned in Virginia and New York. Clearly, under the statutes, a board of censors "may ban as immoral a film dealing with social sex problems, human biology or the procreative function even when not obscene or indecent."

In the event a film is rejected by the board, the statutes specify that the applicant may demand a reexamination, and if the rejection is affirmed, may then appeal to a designated court. Provisions for judicial review, however, give little relief from oppressive decisions. One reason for this is the nature of the industry: a film, especially, if it is a newsreel, loses value rapidly in the time required for a judicial hearing. The other reason is the unanimous refusal of the courts to substitute their judgment for that of the censors unless the examining officials acted in bad faith, capriciously, or arbitrarily. Cases in which the boards have been upheld are legion; cases in which they have been overridden can be counted on the fingers of one hand. So long as some evidence is present upon which the board's action might have been based, so long as it is possible that three citizens of the state may honestly consider a film indecent, the courts will not interfere.

The danger of unlimited municipal control over motion pictures is well brought out when a film which touches on controversial topics appears. The recent movie, *Blockade*, a fictional and reasonably well disguised treatment of the Spanish Civil War, which ventured to condemn the bombing and starvation of women and children, was infuriating to adherents of General Franco [Spanish dictator] who considered it a pro-Loyalist movie. The film was actively boycotted and picketed by the Knights of Columbus and by Catholic groups throughout the country. Attempts to ban or censor the film were made in Boston, Omaha, Kansas City, and elsewhere. The entire film was barred from Somerville, Massachusetts, and a license was refused for second-run showings in Providence although the first-run showing had been uneventful. The final speech of the film, deletion of which was demanded in Kansas City, read: "It's not war. War is between soldiers. It's murder, murder of innocent people. There's no sense to it." It was a rephrasing of an address made by Pope Pius XI on September 14, 1936.

A Russian picture, *Youth of Maxim*, was prohibited by the police in Detroit on the ground that it was "pure Soviet propaganda and is likely to instill class hatred and hatred of the existing government and social order of the United States." The ordinance applied only to immoral or indecent films. The Michigan Supreme Court rejected the contention that the word "immoral" could mean "contra to good order or public welfare" and reversed the order.

The paramount newsreel of the South Chicago strike massacre of Decoration Day, 1937, was banned in Chicago, although it later received nation-wide publicity on being shown before the LaFollette Civil Liberties Committee in the Senate. The *Inside Nazi Germany* issue of the *March of Time* and *Professor Manlock* were also forbidden to Chicago movie-goers, although extensive popular indignation induced reconsideration and reversal of the decisions. In Fall River, Massachusetts, the film, *Heart of Spain*, portraying the modern blood transfusion technique in Loyalist hospitals, was banned by the mayor on the ground that it was "communistic and not for the best interests of this community." These examples are not isolated instances; there are many such actions which receive no record other than casual mention in the daily press.

Federal Regulations and Self-Censorship

Federal regulation of the contents of motion pictures is at present exercised in three ways. A statute of the criminal code, aimed at the men's smoker type of film, forbids the interstate transportation of "any obscene, lewd, or lascivious, or any filthy" motion picture film. Another statute makes unlawful the importation or interstate transporation of "any film or other pictorial representation of any prize fight or encounter of pugilists, under whatever name, which is designed to be used or may be used for purposes of public exhibition." And under Section 305 of the Tariff Act of 1930, the importation of any picture which is obscene or immoral or which advocates treason or insurrection is prohibited.

Numerous attempts have been made to secure the passage of legislation providing for direct federal censorship of motion pictures, but none of the proposed bills has received the approval of Congress. These bills generally fall into two categories: one, those forbidding the interstate transportation of films portraying criminal activities, and two, those setting up a federal motion picture commission, empowered to establish standards for the cinema and to license films as a prerequisite to their entering into interstate or foreign commerce. However, the record of the past twenty years has indicated that censorship by any agency of government impedes both art and expression. Today the industry is effectively demonstrating the superfluity of such control. At present the only comprehensive centralized agency for control comes voluntarily from Hollywood itself. The organization formally entitled the Motion Picture Producers and Distributors of America, Inc. and known to the industry as the Hays office, was organized in March 1922 after a wave of reform agitation. [Director is Will H. Hayes, former Postmaster General] . . .

The Hays policy, and consequently the policy of the M.P.P.D.A., has been to gain and keep the support of the public by whatsoever means seemed necessary.

The idea of regulating the content of films . . . began with a modest list of "don't" and "be carefuls" promulgated in 1927. Three years later, in January and February 1930, these rules were elaborated into a formal production code, written largely by Martin Quigley, publisher of the *Motion Picture Herald*, and by Father Daniel A. Lord, S.J., which was ratified by the members of the Hays organization on March 31, 1930. This fourteen page document, which in some detail enumerated forbidden themes and episodes has been the basis for all subsequent self-regulation in the industry . . .

The administration of this Code was haphazard and not too exacting in the years immediately after 1930. Box office figures were falling, and producers sought an answer in liberal injections of salacity into their pictures. The novelty of talking pictures, and the influx of new producers in their wake, were other factors in the appearance of films of questionable decency. By 1933, the moral tone of the cinema industry had reached its lowest point since 1922. Popular protests snowballed, but the only group to which the industry paid especial heed was an organization of Catholics called the "Legion of Decency." The Legion of Decency attacked the industry on two fronts; it demanded that movies be "made right" at the source, and it advocated a boycott of all films of which it did not approve. The Catholic bishops announced that they would order all Catholics to stay away from unapproved pictures. But by that time the tide had turned in Hollywood.

Faced with a large-scale nationwide boycott, the producers found for the first time that box office meant being decent rather than salacious. And, to insure decency, they voted a $25,000 fine against any member of the Hays organization who violated the Code established Joseph Ignatius Breen at the head of a Production Code Administration. Breen began a system of strict control over the making of motion pictures from the preliminary script to the final print, and enforced the Code to the letter. Between 1934 and 1938 his office wrote 26,808 opinions interpreting the Code. Today what Breen has to say on an embryonic film may make it or break it; his alone is the authority to give the "purity seal" required of every motion picture to leave Hollywood.

Breen has warned the producers that, above all else, they must not offend the Roman Catholic Church, because unlike the Protestants, the Catholics can "keep their people out of the movie houses."

[Among millions of film feet left on the cutting room floor were scenes of a "topless" six-year-old Shirley Temple doing the hula in *Curley Top*, and King Kong crushing and swallowing people in one of Hollywood's greatest terror pictures.

When David O. Selznick was trying to turn *Gone With the Wind*, Margaret Mitchell's epic novel of the Civil War, into an epic film, he had to spend two years fighting with his studio and the internal censorship offices. Among the changes, the studio required Rhett Butler's powerful and now-classic line,

"Frankly, my dear, I don't give a damn," to be replaced by the insipid, "Frankly, my dear, I don't care." The original line was finally allowed to remain; although the line shocked many, audiences applauded Rhett Butler's decision that had led him to leave Scarlett O'Hara and Tara, the plantation now devastated by the war.]

Chapter 28

Radio:
Scarcity Means Suppression

Radio confused the governmental regulators. They did not know how to handle the new medium, so they avoided any form of legislation until Congress passed the Wireless Ship Act of 1910 requiring that radio equipment be on "certain ocean steamers"; the Congress gave power to the secretary of commerce to create regulations. Only two years later, Congress decided that the first law was inadequate and passed the Radio Act of 1912 requiring that operators be on ships and that they stand ready to operate the radio equipment. Congress created no new laws until 1927, but the government did not leave the act of regulating wireless.

World War I and Radio Censorship

Prior to the issuing of licenses to several stations including KDKA, East Pittsburgh, Pennsylvania; and WWJ, Detroit, Michigan, in 1920-1921, all radio transmitting was conducted by amateurs and the government—regular broadcasting did not exist, but many amateurs were experimenting with limited broadcasting. Although not much is made of censorship of wireless during World War I, one of the most severe forms of censorship did occur—a form of censorship that often goes unnoticed and might have influenced all succeeding generations. Gleason L. Archer documents the events in his well-researched book, *History of Radio to 1926* (1938):

> Upon the outbreak of war, however, all amateur wireless stations had been ordered dismantled ... To be sure, rebellious individuals still continued to maintain amateur stations here and there throughout the country, yet they did so at their own peril. Wartime zeal of military and police forces left little opportunity for successful evasion.

An article in *Wireless Age* of October, 1917, urged amateurs and others using radio for experimental, short broadcasts, to comply with the federal order suppressing all radio transmissions during the war and giving the military total control over the radio waves:

It has come to the notice of the Navy Department that the President's Executive Order which called for the dismantling of private radio stations has been misinterpreted by many experimenters, publishers and amateurs. By dismantling is meant the *complete disconnection of all pieces of apparatus and antennae, and the sealing and storing of same.* Apparatus which is not dismantled as outlined above is subject to confiscation . . .

According to Archer:

By proclamation on the day following the declaration of war in April, 1917, President Wilson directed the Navy to take over all wireless stations in the United States and its possessions that were not already under the control of the Army. With patriotic zeal, wireless officials complied wholeheartedly with the proclamation and turned over to the Government not only their physical equipment but all available talent, technicians and research workers.

When the war ended, two bills were submitted to Congress to continue the government monopoly of radio communication. The House of Representatives bill, H.R. 13159, known as the Alexander Bill, appeared on November 21, 1918, with a similar bill appearing in the Senate, S. 5036. The National Wireless Association lodged a strong protest against the proposed legislation in the January 1919, issue of *Wireless Age*, declaring—"The individual worker, in a phrase, is to be suppressed." Other protests followed in newspapers and magazines, and Congress took up the debate with partisans on both sides. Some of the opposition at the congressional hearings came from Edward J. Nally, vice-president and general manager of Marconi Wireless Telegraph Company of America, and Hiram Percy Maxim, president of the American Radio Relay League. Representative William B. Bankhead's (Alabama) resolution to table the motion received a unanimous vote on January 16, 1919.

After the War—Chaos

Although radio narrowly missed permanent censorship by the United States military establishment through a congressional act, the government continued to award or reject broadcast licenses.

Broadcasters and radio interests knew that the present system of regulating broadcasting was not working because stations were interfering with each other, too many stations were on the air, and many stations broadcast using inferior equipment. Secretary Herbert Hoover (1874-1964) also thought that something had to be done, and on February 27, 1922, called the first national radio conference to determine what action should be taken. Among the participants were executives from the Radio Corporation of America, American Telephone and Telegraph Company, General Electric Corporation, and Westinghouse Electric and Manufacturing Corporation. The industry had been invited in to tell the government what should be done to control the new medium. Hoover was pleased to observe "this is one of the few instances where the country is unanimous in its desire for more regulation." That first conference was followed by three other conferences, one each year through 1925.

Although the radio conferences produced a number of recommendations on legislation, Congress failed to pass anything. During the sixty-seventh Congress (1921-1923), twenty bills were considered; in the sixty-eighth (1923-1925), another thirteen bills appeared; in the sixty-ninth (1925-1927), eighteen more were sponsored. Finally, the last bill, the Radio Act of 1927, passed both houses of Congress, but for reasons quite beyond the debates going on in Congress.

The courts slowly took away Secretary Hoover's power to regulate radio under the existing 1912 law starting with *Hoover* v. *Intercity Radio Co., Inc.*, (1923) when Hoover discovered he had to award licenses to all qualified applicants, but that he could prescribe time, power, and frequency of operation for the station. In *United States* v. *Zenith Radio Corporation* (1926), Hoover was told: "There is no express grant of power in the Act to the Secretary of Commerce to establish regulations." Hoover could not prescribe any regulations for operating stations, but neither could he refuse licenses. Chaos followed.

President Calvin Coolidge acted quickly to urge Congress to pass a law; in his message to Congress on December 7, 1926, the President pleaded:

> The Department of Commerce has for some years urgently presented the necessity for further legislation in order to protect radio listeners from interference between broadcasting stations and to carry out other regulatory functions. Both branches of Congress at the last session passed enactments intended to effect such regulation, but the two bills yet remain to be brought into agreement and final passage.
>
> Due to decisions of the courts, the authority of the department under the law of 1912 has broken down; many more stations have been operating than can be accommodated within the limited number of wave lengths available; further stations are in course of construction; many stations have departed from the scheme of allocation set down by the department, and the whole service of this most important public function has drifted into such chaos as seems likely, if not remedied, to destroy its great value. I most urgently recommend that this legislation should be speedily enacted
>
> . . .

The legal philosophy upon which Congress could assume the right to enact legislation to regulate radio, a medium of expression, is found in these brief remarks when Coolidge observed, "Many more stations have been operating than can be accommodated within the limited number of wave lengths. . ." The radio channels were scarce, and the scarcity doctrine has frequently been used by the government as justification for taking over the resource and regulating it "in the public interest."

In Congress, the justification for regulating radio was articulated most effectively by Rep. Wallace White of Maine when working for the passage of the Radio Act:

We have reached the definite conclusion that the right of all our people to enjoy this means of communication can be preserved only by the repudiation of the idea underlying the 1912 law that anyone who will may transmit and by the assertion in its stead of the doctrine that the right of the public to service is superior to the right of any individual . . . The recent radio conference met this issue squarely. It recognized that in the present state of scientific development there must be a limitation upon the number of broadcasting stations and it recommended that licenses should be issued only to those stations whose operation would render a benefit to the public, are necessary in the public interest, or would contribute to the development of the art. This principle was approved by every witness before your committee. We have written it into the bill. If enacted into law, the broadcasting privilege will not be a right of selfishness. It will rest upon an assurance of public interest to be served. [67 Cong. Rec. 5479].

Many years later, the Supreme Court would reaffirm the doctrine in *Red Lion Broadcasting Co.* v. *Federal Communications Commission* (1969):

Before 1927, the allocation of frequencies was left entirely to the private sector, and the result was chaos. It quickly became apparent that broadcast frequencies constituted a scarce resource whose use could be regulated and rationalized only by the Government. Without government control, the medium would be of little use because of the cacophony of competing voices, none of which could be clearly and predictably heard. Consequently, the Federal Radio Commission was established to allocate frequencies among competing applicants in a manner responsive to the public "convenience, interest, or necessity" . . .

When two people converse face to face, both should not speak at once if either is to be clearly understood. But the range of the human voice is so limited that there could be meaningful communications if half the people in the United States were talking and the other half listening. Just as clearly, half the people might publish and the other half read. But the reach of radio signals is so incomparably greater than the range of the human voice and the problem of interference is a massive reality. The lack of know-how and equipment may keep many from the air, but only a tiny fraction of those with resources and intelligence can hope to communicate by radio at the same time if intelligible intelligence can hope to communicate by radio at the same time if intelligible communication is to be had, even if the entire radio spectrum is utilized in the present state of commercially acceptable technology.

It was this fact, and the chaos which ensued from permitting anyone to use any frequency at whatever power level he wished, which made necessary the enactment of the Radio Act of 1927 and the Communications Act of 1934.

Scarcity became the justification for censorship of the new medium of communication or, as Congress said when granting licensing stations powers, the new commission was to grant permits in "the public interest, convenience, or necessity." The Congress resorted to its authoritarian instincts in finding a way to solve the problem of interference on the radio waves.

Congress acted quickly to create the Radio Act of 1927 as a temporary measure that would continue in operation only so long as was necessary to serve the needs of radio. The new law created a five member commission to award licenses, fix terms of licenses, and prescribe regulations. The law allowed the new commission to consider technical, financial, legal, character, citizenship, and public interest matters in deciding to award a license, and the statute permitted the FRC to consider *past programming practices* of existing licenses in deciding upon renewals.

Congress wanted to clean up the air waves, but it wanted to be sure that there was no violation of the First Amendment to the Constitution, so it added:

> Nothing in this act shall be understood or construed to give the licensing authority the power of censorship over the radio communications or signals transmitted by any radio station, and no regulation or condition shall be promulgated or fixed by the licensing authority which shall interfere with the right of free speech by means of radio communications.

Not included in the protection was anything that was "obscene, indecent, or profane." Although the law ordered the FRC to stay out of the censoring business, its decision to award or reject a license application amounted to authoritarian restraints on a medium of communication.

The Radio Act of 1927 was continued with its five member commission until 1934 when the Federal Communication Commission was created as a permanent body with substantially the same powers over broadcasting as the FRC had. The issue of whether the First Amendment prohibited the creation of either commission or if the extensive set of regulations promulgated has not been seriously questioned by a majority of the Supreme Court since, although Justice William O. Douglas (1898-1980) has raised serious questions.

The regulation of radio differed markedly from that of motion pictures and print media. When Congress enacted laws that dealt with print and cinema, they were laws enforced through action in the courts as was the case with the Espionage Act of 1917 and the postal laws prescribing classes of mail. No special agency was established to police these media, and, as the law developed in the twentieth century, the standard against which obscenity, mail permit, and sedition was tested was the First Amendment to the Constitution. But with radio, Congress established a separate agency, the FRC, to award licenses, revoke licenses, insure the public interest was protected, etc. Although the courts and many thinkers have justified the need for a federal regulator of broadcasting, the agency reflects a real difference in the handling of two media of public expression. The most serious problem is that many of the cases tested the decisions of the FRC and later the FCC against the statute. Although most cases suggested a constitutional basis, the linkage was not always clear.

Chapter 29

Struggles for Domination

In 1940, Congress passed the Smith Act, the first peace time sedition statute since the Sedition Act of 1798. The new law joined the Espionage Act of 1917 (war time powers) as active statutes of the United States. However, during World War II* the government did not suppress any periodicals except *Social Justice*, published by the Rev. Charles E. Coughlin (1891-1979), the outspoken, racist pastor of the Roman Catholic Shrine of the Little Flower in Royal Oak, Michigan; many people protested that suppression. The Supreme Court under Hughes had built up a strong record supporting freedom of expression. Consequently, the American people during World War II did not experience the rampant attack on the First Amendment that was seen during World War I. An observer in 1945 might have concluded that the problems of suppression had passed from the American landscape. But there lingered a number of indications that all might not be perfect, including the fact that the Congress and state legislatures were abridging freedoms.

The most devastating civil rights action during World War II was the decision by President Franklin D. Roosevelt (1882-1945, President: 1933-1945) to remove 117,000 Japanese-Americans from their homes along the Pacific coast to ten relocation centers in the interior of the nation. About two-thirds of the people moved were American citizens who should have enjoyed the same legal protections afforded to other citizens. Although Roosevelt, with the support of public opinion, took action against so many American citizens violating their rights, and forcing sale of their property, 17,600 Americans of Japanese heritage fought, often with great bravery, for their homeland, the United States, during World War II.†

First, the Smith Act provided virtually everything that Attorney General A. Mitchell Palmer (1872-1936), might have wanted to stamp out the "Red

---

*During World War II, Franklin D. Roosevelt created the Office of War Information (OWI) to disseminate news to broadcasters and print media and placed it under Elmer Davis, formerly of the *New York Times* and CBS. Byron Price, executive news editor from AP, headed the Office of Censorship which screened overseas communications and formed a *Code of Wartime Practices for the American Press* (1942). See full discussion in Chapter 50.

†There was no relocation of Italian-Americans or of German-Americans, and Roosevelt's orders can only be interpreted as being racist.

229

Menace" when he was alive and working twenty-two years earlier. Secondly, a new committee in the House of Representatives came into being in 1938 known as the House Committee on Un-American Activities. And, thirdly, the American fear of the Soviet Union flared again after the Second World War.

of course
it did
Why !??

When Congress began considering an alien registration law, numerous people including representatives of the American Federation of Labor (AFL), of the American Newspaper Association, and the National Association for the Advancement of the Colored People (NAACP) appeared to oppose the bill, but later, in 1939, when the formal hearing occured, few showed up to testify.

Rep. Howard W. Smith (1883-1976) of Virginia introduced the first bill (H.R. 5138), but it would go through a series of amendments before it became the Alien Registration Act of June 28, 1940 (the Smith Act). This law had its origins in hearings first conducted in 1935 when the United States had no major conflict with any other nation. The primary debates regarding the bill took place in the House of Representatives during July 1939 before Germany entered Poland. Little discussion took place during 1940 when the bill was finally passed, with no debate at all regarding what was happening in Europe. Nothing in the congressional debates lends the slightest indication that the bill was intended for war protections. It was simply a peacetime measure.

The name of the law suggests nothing about sedition, but the purposes listed by the Senate Judiciary Committee (1940) suggest otherwise:

(1) To prohibit the advocacy of insubordination, disloyalty, mutiny, or refusal of duty in the military or naval forces of the United States.

(2) To prohibit the advocacy of the overthrow or destruction of any government in the United States by force or violence.

(3) To add several additional grounds for the deportation of aliens to those already provided . . .

(4) To permit the suspension, subject to congressional review, of deportation of aliens in certain "hardship cases" when the ground for deportation is technical in nature and the alien proves good moral character.

(5) To require the registration and fingerprinting of aliens.

The Smith Act illustrates the concern the Congress had over teachings that might injure the nation. Sections 2 and 3 read:

Sec. 2. It shall be unlawful for any person—

(1) to knowingly or willfully advocate, abet, advise, or teach the duty, necessity, desirability, or propriety of overthrowing or destroying any government in the United States by force or violence, or by the assassination of any officer of any such government;

(2) with the intent to cause the overthrow or destruction of any government in the United States, to print, publish, edit, issue, circulate, sell, distribute, or publicly display any written or printed matter advocating, advising, or teaching the duty, necessity, desirability, or propriety of overthrowing or destroying any government in the United States by force or violence;

(3) to organize or help to organize any society, group, or assembly of persons who teach, advocate, or encourage the overthrow or destruction

Smith Act created ~ 1940!?

of any government in the United States by force or violence; or to be or become a member of, or affiliate with, any such society, group, or assembly of persons, knowing the purposes thereof . . .

Sec. 3. It shall be unlawful for any person to attempt to commit, or to conspire to commit, any of the acts prohibited by the provisions of this title. Despite the problems created by the Smith Act, the American Civil Liberties Union (ACLU) in its 1943 annual report found much to comfort them. They reviewed the record of World War I and World War II and found that the laws were not being used against dissenters nearly as much as had been the case in World War I—there seemed to be less need to resort to the two sedition laws.

Although World War II saw little in the way of direct suppression of newspapers, radio stations, magazines, or public speeches in the U. S., the removal and interment of the Japanese-Americans was a severe blight on the character of American law during that period. Other countries were undergoing their own problems.

Suppression by Death: Hitler

While in power, Adolf Hitler (1889-1945) saw to the systematic killing of between 4,500,000 and 6,000,000 Jews in Germany, Poland, and the Soviet Union—all in the name of dealing with the Jewish "problem." Even in the Ukraine, Hitler murdered citizens who might have supported his campaign if their nationalistic feelings had been encouraged. While the Jews suffered more than other people, many other groups felt the suffering inflicted by Hitler. The destruction of Jews and other groups served Hitler in two ways—it helped rid Hitler of the intellectuals who were critical of his actions, and it provided a propaganda rallying point for the idealized blond image that Hitler told the German people would dominate the world. Hitler was successful in appealing to German patriotic pride, but he also appealed to economic interests by creating jobs.

Violence, death, and sex became significant parts of the Nazi scheme for keeping the organization growing. A *Sturmabteilungen*—an army organized under Ernst Rohm—brawl in a beer hall garnered much coverage in the Nazi press. Ritual murder was combined with sex, violence, and anti-Semitism to raise emotions.

But persuasion and murders were not enough to achieve the long-term goals of the Nazi party; repression had to be used to control dissident writers, editors, and reporters. On February 27, 1933, fire damaged the *Reichstag* building, which the Nazis claimed was the result of a communist plot. When, one week later, elections were to be held at Hitler's urging, the propaganda value of the fire helped elect Hitler. Hermann Goring (1893-1946) took control of the police force and used his power to purge it of any dissidents and to prevent this regular police force from interferring with intimidation the SA was carrying out in the streets.

The Nazis used all of the media of communication to promote their interests in the election set for March 5, 1933. The combination of the *Reichstag* fire on

February 27, intimidation by the SA, extensive propaganda, and with the help of the Nationalists, Hitler gained a bare majority guaranteeing success for his programs.

Although the Nazis failed to gain a majority without the help of the Nationalists, Hitler was able to create the third *Reich* (empire) by getting the newly elected members to vote an Enabling Act which provided the basis for Hitler's new government. As needed, Hitler got new laws passed. Over the next few months a number of decrees leading up to the Law for the Reconstruction of the *Reich* (Jan. 30, 1934) transferred all control to the *Reich* under Hitler's control.

Suppression became wide-spread with a law passed on April 7, 1933, barring all Jews from service in government, making marriages between Jewish and German-blood individuals illegal, and depriving Jews of all civil rights; with the abolishing of labor unions in May 1933; through widespread acts of intimidation by the SS forces; by the "voluntary" dissolution of political parties during the summer of 1933; with the institution of state control of schools, universities, newspapers, magazines, radio, theater, and motion pictures; through the creation of the Hitler Youth to train the young; by the arrest of dissident Protestant pastors; through interference and persecution of the Catholic citizens; and by the declaration of the Nazi party as the only political organization in Germany on July 14, 1933, and through it all, there were few protests from the Germans.

The Nazi SA troops became the defenders of the state by arresting thousands of people and sending them to concentration camps, systematically removing critics, intellectuals, and independent editors. Josef Goebbels (1897-1945), now firmly seated in power as propaganda chief, set out to destroy all sources of information contrary to the Nazi line. In just over one year, 1933-1934, Goebbels increased Nazi control from 121 small dailes and periodicals to 436 newspapers and indirectly to all of the 4,700 German newspapers. Although many of the newspapers continued to carry information similar to content before Goebbels' control, there was a slow erosion of independence.

One of the devices used to control the press was to create an image of the ideal editor—a person who was a good journalist; but also one who fought for the ideals of the Nazi party. This institutionalizing of the ideal newspaperman in the minds of editors and reporters was designed to bring everyone in line voluntarily. The media would be a part of the State to represent the State to the people.

But persuasion was not enough and in the Fall of 1933, legislation passed decreeing the position of "official editor." These editors had to be German citizens, neither Jewish nor married to a Jew, and not a German who had lost citizenship rights. The law described the content that these editors could and could not print, thereby removing all editorial independence.

To Goebbels, free expression might injure the state, and thus the individual liberties of citizens. Although Goebbels believed the Germans might enjoy the same freedom the English had, they would have to wait until the nation reached the same level of maturity—in about one hundred years. After the *Reichstag* fire, 1,500 publishers lost their businesses; by 1944, the Nazis ran eighty-two percent of the newspapers. They had also driven many publishers out of businesses. The Nazi suppression worked hand-in-hand with the propaganda arm to insure that Hitler's goals were achieved.

Hitler, after his people had destroyed so much of the world, finally, in the face of a final allied offensive, killed himself.

Italy: Mussolini and Fascism

In Italy, Benito Mussolini (1883-1945) was engaging in his own means of suppression. Early in his life, Mussolini developed the concepts that would later guide his work. He became a member of the Italian socialist movement and edited a socialist paper, *La lotta di classe*, where with his study of Nietzsche and experiences with the socialist movement, he evolved the concept that "Socialism is war; and in war woe to those who have humanitarian feelings."

During World War I, Mussolini began organizing the working classes and threatened the government with an uprising, but he was expelled from the Socialist party over his conviction that war and violence were the path to social revolution. He then turned on March 23, 1919, to forming his own *Fasci de Combattimento*, or Fascist organization.

After World War I, Italy remained in a state of unrest with a workers' movement that took over factories for a time before returning them to their owners, but the fear created by the movement remained, and Mussolini exploited that concern. He secured funds from industrialists and landowners who were fearful of loosing their property to support the formation of armed squads, *squadre d'azione*, which destroyed many organizations such as the Communists, Republicans, and Socialists. The success of the organization led to the election on May 15, 1921, of thirty-six Fascists, including Mussolini, to Parliament.

The Fascist dictatorship gained new power with the passage in 1923 of a bill givings two-thirds of the seats in Parliament to the party gaining the largest number of votes in an election; the remaining third went to all other parties. This success insured Mussolini open passage to full dictatorship; in April 1924, the Fascists, using the support of the police and their armed squads, gained two-thirds of the recorded votes.

The need for press censorship appeared to Mussolini after the June 1924 murder of Giacomo Matteotti, an outspoken Socialist deputy who objected to the new regime. The event cost Mussolini support, but he decided to suppress opposition newspapers such as *Popolo, Avanti*, and *Mondo* that had tried to get him impeached, then ordered, a new press law passed in July 1924 that permitted the confiscation of "seditious" newspapers. The police were given the right to take any issues of any newspaper they thought to be seditious.

The suppression also led to the removal or forced resignation of members of Parliament who disagreed with Mussolini during 1925. When the military protested Mussolini's defense posture, he took over the department and installed his own friends in leadership positions.

Meanwhile, the major national newspapers became pro-Fascist in editorial tone under threat of violent attack. Since Mussolini had once been a journalist, he recognized the power of the press and often sent anonymous articles to newspapers promoting his views. One of Mussolini's controls was the promise of wealth to his friends, who exchanged their independent decision-making functions for the chance to acquire assets.

By 1925, most of the opposition had been destroyed and little suppression was needed; however, before that time, the squads of soldiers had used rubber truncheons (the short sticks carried by police) to discipline independent thinkers. In 1925, there was an "antifascist manifesto" pubished with the signatures of intellectuals on it, but by 1926, a new law dissolved all national parties. Mussolini became an absolute power in Italy when all opposition activities were prohibited on November 6, 1926.

Nevertheless, a number of suppressive controls were instituted after 1926, including a tribunal that judged political crimes *in camera*, insulated from public exposure, the death penalty for those who disagreed with the state, the abolishment of trial by jury, and the formation of a police force as a branch of the Fascist party independent of State controls. Funds for security rose by tenfold expenditures over previous governments.

But the Fascist government of Mussolini returned some form of stability and economic well-being to the nation—a carrot and stick encouragement to stay with the Fascists; as in Germany, the people came to love their leader, and opposition was destroyed in the interest of unity.

As Mussolini drew closer to Hitler (1937), Italy assumed a stance more like that of Germany. In 1938, the Grand Council proposed policies that limited the professional activities of Jews; rules also excluded them from the military and civil services. The new laws provided more interference in the private lives of all citizens through fixed prices for commodities, the power of the state to take all the crops it wished, and the dismissal of a number of prominent Italians from their posts in government, industry, and research. Many scholars, scientists, and dissidents escaped to other countries including the United States. Meanwhile, Mussolini told members of Parliament how to vote and what to demand, and then he told Parliament to disband itself.

By 1943, Mussolini was voted out of office, then put into internal exile. He was rescued by Hitler's troops, returned to govern Italy with German troops, and allowed the wholesale execution of "traitors" in 1944 and 1945. He was eventually killed by Partisans.

Japan

The interest Japan took in World War II came from forces quite different from Germany and Italy. After 1900, Japan's population became so large that the nation became an importer of food. There was a growing interest in heavy industry and a shifting of populations to the cities. The traditional government repressed the labor movement which blocked attempts to organize the work force.

The rural, agricultural population experienced considerable economic problems during the early twentieth century because of rising tenet problems and a fragmented system of agriculture.

The cities, meanwhile, began to westernize; western music, sports, and dancing becoming popular. Women began going to work; and a feminist movement appeared. But the liberalizing tendencies in Japan did not go far and frustration developed. At home, Japan was experiencing social and economic problems; internationally, matters were not much better.

Although a number of Japanese citizens had moved to the United States to get away from the problems of Japan, they found discrimination in the San Francisco schools (especially when in 1906 Japanese-American students were excluded from many schools) were ill-treated by immigration authorities, and were discriminated against by a federal law passed in 1924 and by many state laws. Australia excluded the Japanese altogether. Japan appealed to the League of Nations, but it was not of much help, and so the argument that the nation could get ahead only by embarking on a military campaign gained popularity. Japan was the subject of international discrimination, and the nation began to believe that it had but one solution—military conquests. The Depression of 1929 sped the conviction.

Military officers—at least many of the young rural officers—fed the growing conviction over a military solution, and many Japanese, as they adopted western ideas of government, began to distrust the traditional leaders and seemed willing to listen to the militarists. Officers sympathic to the revolutionary causes ignored orders from the civilian government, and finally a terrorist attack in Tokyo caused the death of at least one high ranking official. The unrest in Japan further isolated it from the United States and the Soviet Union and strengthened German-Japanese ties—although they were never strong. The final setback with the United States came when the U. S. refused to negotiate with Japan over oil exports to Japan after the United States froze Japanese assets and oil shipments because Japan occupied Indochina.

Thus, while there was little censorship in Japan—the unity of the people reduced the need— the rest of the world isolated Japan through its racist attitudes at a time when the nation wanted and needed to be a part of the world community.

By 1941, Tojo, having crushed his enemies and reducing Emperor Hirohito to a "puppet status," while letting the people believe war was the will of the emperor and the people, was ready to launch the world into its "Day of Infamy." Five years later, Tojo, who had suppressed all freedoms of exppression, was hung following trial by Americans.

In France, Leon Blum, came to power in the election of 1936 as the Socialist candidate, but he had trouble keeping his government together and was forced to take action against right-wing forces including the Croix de Feu, Col. François de la Rocque's league, and the Cagoulards or Comité Secret d'Action Re'-volutionaire during the late 1930s. During the 1940s France was concerned less with domestic problems than the advancing German troops. Many countries found it necessary to engage in some degree of suppression to keep control over their governments. And in other countries, suppression—even torture and murder—became common.

Back in the United States as the war was coming to an end, the Postmaster General was engaging in actions that would test the long-standing censorship power found in the second class permit.

ACLU Annual Report (1943)

The striking contrast between the state of civil liberty in the first eighteen months of World War II and in World War I offers strong evidence to support the thesis that our democracy can fight even the greatest of all wars and still maintain the essentials of liberty. The country in World War II is almost wholly free of those pressures which in the first World War resulted in mob violence against dissenters, hundreds of prosecutions for utterances; in the creation of a universal volunteer vigilante system, officially recognized, to report dissent to the F.B.I.; in hysterical hatred of everything German; in savage sentences for private expressions of criticism; and in suppression of public debate of the issues of the war and the peace.

No such atmosphere marks the present war. We experience no hysteria, no war-inspired mob violence, no pressure for suppressing dissent, no activity of a secret political police, no organization of virtuous partiots seeking out seditious opinion, and no hostility to persons of German or Italian origin. Hostility to persons of Japanese ancestry, while painfully in evidence, is largely confined to the Pacific Coast and smaller communities in the west.

The government has not resorted to prosecution or censorship on any appreciable scale. War-time prosecutions brought by the Department of Justice for utterances, and publications barred by the Post Office Department as obstructive, have so far numbered about forty-five, involving less than two hundred persons, compared with over a thousand persons involved in almost as many cases in World War I. Even though some of the proceedings were hardly justified by any reasonable interpretation of the "clear and present danger" test laid down by the Supreme Court the Department of Justice has on the whole shown commendable restraint.

A striking test of our progress in war-time tolerance is the much more favorable attitude to Jehovah's Witnesses, whose anti-war propaganda and public activities are calculated to provoke partiotic opposition. Yet in contrast with World War I, when their leaders were jailed and their propaganda curbed, and with outbursts against them in 1940, they have been accorded by the courts and by public opinion even greater liberties than in time of peace.

Conclusions as to our comparative freedom are supported not only by observation of the larger national aspects, but by local observers all over the country. A check-up early in 1943 with 112 correspondents of the Union in 41 states showed remarkable unanimity on the almost complete absence of repressive tendencies, and a surprising freedome of debate and criticism of war mearsures.

Many of them reported the general climate of freedom in their localities as much better than even a year ago.

The record of violations of civil liberties shows that extraordinary fact that more issues and cases have arisen from the normal conflicts in our democracy than from the pressures of war, though some have been accentuated by war-time strains. In that continuing field, the record, particuarly in May and June with the agitation over the miners' strikes and the outbreaks of racial mob violence, has been far from encouraging.

The causes of the heartening contrast with World War I in war-inspired issues are to be found in the comparatively slight opposition to the war,—concealed and unorganized,—against a vigorous radical and pacifist opposition then; in the widespread opposition to the Administration from powerful sources acting in the conventional democratic pattern, which tends to keep open the channels of debate and criticism; in the concentration of public attention not on attitudes to the war but on the debate as to what kind of a post-war world we are in process of creating; in the liberal policies of the Administration; and in the much firmer foundations put under the Bill of Rights in the last decade by numerous Supreme Court decisions.

The measures taken by the government to intern dangerous enemy aliens, to denaturalize the disloyal who acquired citizenship by fraud, to control espionage and sabotage—virtually nonexistent,—the centralization of controls in Washington, have all tended to allay fear and to create the conviction that any movements obstructive of the war e well in hand.

But this encouraging war record is not without its inevitable exceptions. From the viewpoint of both the numbers affected and the seriousness of the rights violated, undoubtedly the worst single invasion of citizens' liberties under war pressures was the wholesale evacuation from the Pacific Cost of over 70,000 Americans of Japanese ancestry and their subsequent confinement in what are virtually concentration camps. The evils and injustices of that desparate move, dictated by race prejudice and military precaution, have been somewhat relieved by permitting those found to be loyal to leave the centers and resettle outside the military zones; by recently accepting into the army volunteers of Japanese ancestry after excluding them from Selective Service, and even by permitting soldiers in uniform to return to the evacuated area. But none of the measures are as yet nearly adequate to restore the rights of American citizens nor to offer a long-range solution . . .

In the larger arena of communication an exception to the excellent record of war-time control of press and radio under voluntary codes must be recorded in the censorship of non-military news cabled to allied nations. Undue caution as to what news and opinion might feed the Axis propaganda machines led to unreasonable restraints, particularly on news of race conflicts, and to frequent complaints by foreign corresondents.

The treatment of conscientious objectors, so much better in principle than in World War I, has nevertheless resulted in imprisoning more than three times as many, in large part because of a narrow interpretation of "religious training and belief" and reluctance to parole men to useful occupations. The administration of the Selective Service law has resulted in jailing hundreds of Jehovah's Witnesses, who demand a status as ministers although they are not employed full-time in that occupation and who, when that status is denied, prefer jail to any form of compulsory war service. The Supreme Court has, however, agreed to review one case in which draft boards denied the ministerial status. More Jehovah's Witnesses are in prison today for their particular brand of conscience than any other minority in the country.

Although the government has generously freed all Italian enemy aliens of war-time restrictions, it has not yet moved to free a class with an even greater claim on our democracy—the anti-Nazi German refugees who are still under the same restrictions as apply to all enemy aliens.

In addition to these exceptions to the generally favorable administration of war-time controls, apprehension is expressed in many quarters over the effects on our liberties of the vastly expanded war-time powers of government. Many, indeed, profess to see in measures already taken the outlines of a totalitarian state. But these measures largely concern economic controls which do not directly affect freedom of opinion and debate, nor the right of opposition or of criticism. Apprehension is also expressed over the prospects of the passage of a civilian compulsory war-service act, and its presumed effects in regimenting the entire population. But fear for the future of our democracy does not negate the plain facts of a record so far generally encouraging.

This survey of the record justifies, we believe, our opening assertion that "our democracy can fight even the greatest of all wars and still maintain the essentials of liberty." Indeed, this is not the whole of the story, for we witness in this war not only the substantial maintenance of our rights but vigorous campaigns to strengthen and extend them. Thus, even with a conservative Congress, the movement for abolition of the poll tax makes headway; the attacks on the various censorships yield results; campaigns waged by Negroes, by labor, and by other minority groups register advances; court decisions have considerably enlarged constitutional guarantees; and the executive departments of the government have on the whole shown a growing response to the protection of minority rights.

But in the midst of so vast a conflict, with uncertain shifts in national and international policy in the war and post-war periods, it would be folly to let any encouragement lead to complacency. Dangers remain great. Undue prolongation of the war, reaction from war weariness or the growth of reaction in other fields, a sudden change in the public temper, might easily reverse the record of these months.

Today, as always, only "eternal vigilance" and activity protects our liberties. Sensitive and alert awareness by all liberal forces, instant and determined resistance to every encroachment, and the foresight to anticipate and effectively to meet whatever new forces of repression and reaction may appear—these will alone preserve the democratic process of change.

Chapter 30

A New Media Control:
Making the Journalists Responsible

With the end of World War II, there emerged a Cold War between the United States and the Soviet Union. The failure of the Soviet Union and the United State to come to agreement on East and West Germany, the U.S.S.R. blockade of land and water routes between Berlin and East Germany—with President Truman's corresponding military air lift in June 1948—the Communist defeat of Nationalist troops in China, the generally conservative attitude of the American electorate, the existence in the U.S.A. of the most powerful weapons the world had ever known and the fear that the Soviet Union might gain the tools for use against the United States, and the failure of the Yalta conference to gain a compromise between the U.S.A. and the U.S.S.R. in (1945) led to a conviction that the nation had to constantly work to stay ahead of the Russians. The result was the Cold War and the Red Scares of the late 1940s and 1950s. Other nations, however, feared the United States because it *did* possess the atomic bomb and such great power.

The extent to which the United States would go to protect against the real and imagined fears can be seen by the fact that Congress voted $400 million in April 1948 to aid Chiang Kai-shek in China rebuild his country and fight communism. The government was also active in the creation of the North Atlantic Treaty Organization (NATO), authorized through the Vandenberg Resolution in June (1948). Negotiations brought twelve nations into NATO in April 1949; two additional nations joined later. The Truman Doctrine "to support free peoples who are resisting attempted subjugation by armed minorities or by outside pressures" provided contributions of $400 million and led to the creation of The Marshall Plan designed to aid economic rehabilitation in Europe.

Stamping Censorship on Esquire

While the nation had survived World War II without much suppresion, the years after 1945 saw the rise of peacetime censorship that duplicated or exceeded that of the years before and after World War I. In 1946, Postmaster General Robert E. Hannegan (1903-1949) suppressed the "smoking room" humor that appeared in *Esquire*, by revoking the second-class mailing permit of the magazine, an action that would cost the magazine $500,000 in additional postage per year at the time.

In the postmaster's decision there was no finding that *Esquire* contained obscene material, only "indecent, vulgar, [or] risque." According to Hannegan's decision:

> A publication to enjoy these unique mail privileges and special preferences is bound to do more than refrain from disseminating material which is obscene or bording on the obscene. It is under the positive duty to contribute to the public good and the public welfare.

Although he did not say, presumably Hannegan intended to be the censor who decided what was socially good enough to merit the second class permit. Hannegan did not object to most of what was in the magazine; but he did complain about the jokes, cartoons, pictures, articles, and poems that became known as "the smoking-room type of humor, featuring, in the main, sex." In the hearing on depriving *Esquire* of the mailing permit, Hannegan got a wide variety of testimony from witnesses, including some who thought the information to be non-offensive and others who thought it to be very offensive.

Hannegan had ample precedent for his action with the number of censorship cases that went in his favor and with the power that the Post Office had built up in the years since the passage of the Comstock Act. Consequently, from the perspective of the 1940s, Hannegan must have thought he was not in violation of the First Amendment, established judicial opinion, or statute. The Supreme Court of the United States was to change all that.

Speaking for the majority in *Hannegan* v. *Esquire* (1946), Justice William O. Douglas (1898-1980) rejected Hannegan on the following grounds:

> It is plain . . . that the favorable second-class rates were granted periodicals meeting the requirements of the Fourth condition [periodical issued at regular intervals], so that the public good might be served through a dissemination of the class of periodicals described. But that is a far cry from assuming that Congress had any idea that each applicant for the second-class rate must convince the Postmaster General that his publication positively contributes to the public good or public welfare. Under our system of government there is an accommodation for the widest varieties of tastes and ideas. What is good literature, what has educational value, what is refined public information, what is good art, varies with individuals as it does from one generation to another . . . A requirement that literature or art conform to some norm prescribed by an official smacks of an ideology foreign to our system. The basic values implicit in the requirements of the Fourth condition can be served only by uncensored distribution of literature. From the multitude of competing offerings the public will pick and choose. What seems to one to be trash may have for others fleeting or even enduring values. But to withdraw the second-class rate from this publication today because its contents seemed to one official not good for the public would sanction withdrawal of the second class rate tomorrow from another periodical whose social or economic views seemed harmful to another official.

Postal Fraud

The decision of the Supreme Court in *Hannegan* dealt with information that might be of limited social value in the mind of the postmaster general, but it did not concern itself with mailings that might be fraudulant. In *Donaldson* v. *Read Magazine* (1948), the Court concluded that a contest carried on by the magazine in which advertising misled contestants on the real costs of the contest was fraud and not protected by the First Amendment. The postmaster issued a mail fraud order to insure that the public was not exploited. The Supreme Court held that as long as there was sufficient evidence to support the conclusion that fraud was present, freedom of the press was not violated, since the First Amendment does not include "a right to raise money to promote circulation by deception of the public."

These two cases indicate that the Supreme Court was willing to support the media, and, more importantly, protect the availability of diversity in communications, even when it could not determine the social worth of the publication, but the Court wanted to hold publishers responsible for some actions. Others agreed.

'Oppose Privileged Class and Public Plunderers'

The history of journalism suggests that many reporters and editors believed they have a responsibility to their readers that transcends anything that the government may have to say about legal duties. A compact exists between reader and editor, these people think, that says something like, "I, the reader, have enough confidence in you as an editor to provide me with accurate, complete, and timely news, and as long as I feel this way I will continue to subscribe to your newspaper." Meanwhile, the editor and the newspaper's reporters seem to promise, "We will provide you with the best coverage of which we are capable. We do not promise that we will cover every event or even that we will be absolutely objective; but we will do the best to provide news that will give you the information upon which to make sound judgments." This kind of thinking has appeared in the writing of many in the past.

As early as 1817, editors at the *Richmond* (Va.) *Compiler* proposed to Hezekiah Niles (publisher of the *Niles' Register*) a "depot of facts":

> In the first place, we *want*, what we may call, *cannons for the management of the press*, a sort of "*codification*," as Jeremy Benthan calls it, of those rules, which ought to guide the conductor of the press—to regulate its *liberty*, and restrain its *licentiousness*. Not rules enacted by the laws of the land; but rules, drawn from the sound principles of discussion, and forming a sort of moral legislation for the press; rules, which every editor ought to observe, and which none should violate without an offense to decency and good taste. These rules will prescribe the rights and duties which one editor owes to another, or which editors and correspondents own to each other. They would teach us the species of *manner* which editors ought to use towards each other; the *species of matter*, which they

ought to publish, and those which they ought not; in other words, what is fit for the public eye, and what is not; the species of evidence they ought to require and furnish for their statements; with other cases, which are apt to occur in the editorial line.

We hold, that the number of well regulated papers is a species of *test* of the state of the public mind; their multiplication, is an indirect proof of the growth of a liberalizing spirit among the people; their declension, of a depreciation of that spirit. Hence we should like to see a Register of the numbers of newspapers; which should notice every newspaper that is set up, or the discontinuance of every old one—with the change of editors . . . Thus you would take notice of every typographical star that rose above or set below the horizon . . .

While no canons of journalism came out of this specific request, the thinking of journalists continued to develop. Almost a century later, Joseph Pulitzer, in retirement and fearing that he could no longer be a significant force in the operation of his newspapers, sent a cable in 1907 to the *New York World* and the *St. Louis Post-Dispatch* declaring his vision of the quality and integrity that should guide every newspaper:

. . . I want to express to you and the editors, managers and entire staff my sincere appreciation for the integrity and ability with which the Post-Dispatch has been so successfully conducted. My grateful thanks are also due to the people of St. Louis for their generous approval of the principles and character of the paper. I know that my retirement will make no difference in its cardinal principles, that it will always fight for progress and reform, never tolerate injustice or corruption, always fight demagogues of all parties, never belong to any party, always oppose privileged classes and public plunderers, never lack sympathy with the poor, always remain devoted to the public welfare, never be satisfied with merely printing news, always be drastically independent, never be afraid to attack wrong, whether by predatory plutocracy or be afraid to attack wrong, whether by predatory plutocracy or predatory poverty.

Some reporters, meanwhile, were spending their time looking for the problems they thought were plaguing newspapers and magazines. For example, articles by Will Irwin in *Collier's* (1911) observed that newspapers no longer devoted much effort to the editorials but concentrated more on the news sections. Irwin suggested that the commercial nature of newspapers dictated the change.

Just as earlier theorists had believed that government control suppressed the free flow of ideas and information, in the twentieth century some writers concluded that advertising made newspapers "beholden" to the companies who purchased space with a newspaper. Upton Sinclair (1878-1968) explained this views in *The Brass Check: A Study of American Journalism* (1919). The term, "brass check" came from the brass medallion that patrons of brothels received showing that they had paid for services and were waiting. The medal often had the name of the person who was to perform services written on it and was to be used as an "admissions ticket." After a detailed analysis of how publishers have failed to publish in the public interest, he concluded *The Brass Check* with a scathing rebuke:

> What is the Brass Check? The Brass Check is found in your [the reporters and editors] pay-envelope every week—you who write and print and distribute our newspapers and magazines. The Brass Check is the price of your shame—you who take the fair body of truth and sell it in the market-place, who betray the virgin hopes of mankind into the loathsome brothel of Big Business. And down in the counting- room below sits the "madame" who profits by your shame; unless, perchance, she is off at Palm Beach or Newport, flaunting her jewels and her feathers.

Sinclair, thus, boldly pointed out that journalists had become prostitutes of big business.

Sinclair was active in in the socialist party and received much of his support through socialist organizations, having been employed by the Socialist weekly newspaper, *Appeal to Reason,* which sent him to Chicago to look into the stockyards.

Although Arthur Brisbane (1864-1936) had earlier thought little of Sinclair's ability to cover the Chicago meat packers, he ran an editorial in the New York *Evening Journal* on May 29, 1906. The *Times* coverage had converted Sinclair into a credible authority. Said the *Evening Journal*:

> Mr. Sinclair traces the career of one family. It is a book that does for modern INDUSTRIAL slavery what "Uncle Tom's Cabin" did for black slavery. But the work is done far better and more accurately in "The Jungle" than in "Uncle Tom's Cabin."

Others, like Walter Lippmann (1899-1974) the philosopher-journalist who believed that there were problems with some of the underlying institutions of democracy, concluded that the press had some difficulties, but he saw hope. Lippman noted in *Public Opinion* (1922):

> It is possible and necessary for journalists to bring home to people the uncertain character of the truth on which their opinions are founded, and by criticism and agitation to prod social science into making more usable formulations of social facts, and to prod statesmen into establishing more visible institutions. The press, in other words, can fight for the extension of reportable truth. But as social truth is organized today, the press is not constituted to furnish from one edition to the next the amount of knowledge which the democratic theory of public opinion demands. This is not due to the Brass Check, as the quality of news in radical papers shows, but to the fact that the press deals with a society in which the governing forces are

so imperfectly recorded. The theory that the press can itself record those forces is false. It can normally record only what has been recorded for it by the working institutions. Everything else is argument and opinion, and fluctuates with the vicissitudes, the self-consciousness, and the courage of the human mind.

[The press] is too frail to carry the whole burden of popular sovereignty, to supply spontaneously the truth which democrats hoped was inborn. And when we expect it to supply such a body of truth we employ a misleading standard of judgment. We misunderstand the limited nature of news, the illimitable complexity of society; we overestimate our own endurance, public spirit, and all-round competence. We suppose an appetite for uninteresting truths which is not discovered by any honest analysis of our own tastes . . .

Acting upon everybody for thirty minutes in twenty-four hours, the press is asked to create a mystical force called Public Opinion that will take up the slack in public institutions. The press has often mistakenly pretended that it could do just that . . .

Writing a few years later in the Yale Review (1931), Lippmann described the conditions that make for a press that can serve the needs of society without falling under the undue influence of any one interest. He seemed more convinced of the ability of the press to perform important functions. His remarks were titled, "Two Revolutions in the American Press":

The popular commercial press of the second half of the nineteenth century and down to our own times has had as its central motive the immediate satisfaction of the largest number of people . . .

I have heard this type of journalism defended eloquently on the ground that in a democracy the press . . . should give the pubic what it wants. A sounder justification for it can . . . be found which is that if the publication of news and opinion was ever to be genuinely freed of control by the ruling powers of the State, it had to find its first support in powers which were a match for the ruling powers. The popular commercial press . . . has finally broken the ancient monopoly of intelligence, and has at least opened the way to much more substantial liberties.

It could be demonstrated, I think, that however much laws may seem to grant political freedom, they are ineffective until a country has for some considerable time accustomed itself to newspapers which are highly profitable and immediately powerful because of their skill in enlisting, in holding, and in influencing a great mass of readers. When there is no prosperous and popular press the liberty of publication is precarious . . .

Largely because our population provides the broadest base of this kind in the world, the American press has, I believe, become freer from hidden control than any in the world. This is the great service performed by what I have called the popular commercial press, otherwise known as yellow journalism . . . It is the first politically independent press which the world has known . . .

Other people besides Lippmann had their views of the press and its failings. George Seldes another observer and reporter, in *Freedom of the Press* (1935), reminded the reader of the conventional wisdom that had developed through the cycle of depression and prosperity and the continual predictions in newspapers of good times "around-the-corner" that left people convinced, "You can't believe a thing you read in the papers nowadays."

Seldes believed that editors and publishers were so concerned with the attitudes of their advertisers that they would censor news items to match the advertisers' perspective. Seldes used an example from his early days at the *Pittsburgh Leader* where the editor deleted a reference to the Silver Top Brewing Company in a story involving an injured driver of one of the company's delivery wagons, fearing the brewer might dislike the adverse publicity. (Silver Top was one of the newspaper's larger clients.)

After chronicling a number of examples of how the news was suppressed, Seldes observed:

> The suppression of news in America and its corollary, the dissemination of propaganda, to which a large part of this book is devoted, are the pragmatic necessities of our social and economic system. Some of the powers which control the press are known to everyone, others are secret and their work is subtle, and there is, moreover, an atmosphere in every newspaper office which defeats all the high hopes and idealism of the young reporter. It breaks him and brands him as a colt is broken and branded on the prairies.

Seldes spent much space dealing with question of advertiser influence:

> . . . The *New York World* went to a ludicrous extreme when it rejected O. Henry's famous *The Unfinished Story* because it dealt with a department-store girl who got seven dollars a week and who planned to sacrifice what in those days was euphemistically known as "her virtue." This story, the supposedly fearless *World* thought, might harm its relations with all department stores.

Department stores, of all industries, exerted the greatest influence over news, because their owners purchased the largest share of local advertising. Consequently, a boycott from them could be fatal to a publisher.

Seldes found many examples of news suppression to protect the interest of political advertisers also. In Pittsburgh, political parties and organizations purchased so much advertising, newspapers there willingly supported candidates. For example, the Pittsburgh *Leader* supported the sheriff in power. In return Allegheny County placed official notices in the *Leader* at high rate.

Editors enjoyed special benefits from affiliation with political organizations. Republican National Committee members would visit the editor where Seldes worked to give the editor market "tips" and to let him in on the "ground floor" of new corporations.

Some newspapers were "bought," such as 400 foreign language newspapers which received advertising from a bureau underwritten by wealthy corporations. The advertising was purchased to insure that the foreign language newspapers would support the correct candidates. The subsidized bureau existed from 1919 to 1924.

Not only were publishers bought out by advertisers and wealthy corporations, many publishers were themselves wealthy corporate owners. Some gained their wealth through the acquisition of many newspapers and other media properties while others owned both newspapers and non-media companies. According to Seldes:

Among the fifty-nine men who rule America, in the table made by former Ambassador Gerard, appear the names of five newspaper publishers and most important among them, in my opinion, is William Randolph Hearst.

The *Times* is the most influential newspaper in America but its owner, [Adolph] Ochs, was a conservative gentleman not given to whims or a desire to arouse mob hysteria; Messrs. [Robert R.] McCormick and [Joseph Medill] Patterson of the *Chicago Tribune* and *New York Daily News* permit their hopes or prejudices considerable play but no complete domination of the news; Roy Howard and the twenty-four papers he directs have a known program of mild liberalism. But William Randolph Hearst, now in his seventies, remains the unpredictable playboy of American journalism. He is a collection of egotisms, ideals, whims and prejudices, which are translated daily into news read by some ten million people.

Above everything else, Hearst proves for our time the fact that news is largely a matter of what one man wants the people to know and feel and think. With Hearst . . ., news is a means to an end, the end being whatever ideal, idea or *ide'e fixe* may arise at the breakfast table or in a dream or nightmare. Reputed masters of mass psychology, men of this type endeavor to become dictatorial leaders without putting in a public appearance; they stir nations, send millions marching, influence history, and unseen and unheard gloat over thier victories in their private chambers, far from the crowd they have maddened. They have Napoleonic complexes. They rejoice in being secret, intramural Napoleons.

Seldes objected to the newspaper establishment because he believed that it protected only its interests, suppressed news that the public needed to have, and had too few people making decisions about which news should reach the people. But Seldes believed the Associated Press was just as bad as the newspapers.

Seldes, however, was hardly the only person criticizing editors and publishers for selling out to the business interests that seemed to control their publication. James Rorty (1890-1966), who wrote *Our Master's Voice: Advertising*, found that advertising in newspapers was one of the twelve largest industries in the United States. Most of that advertising was crooked—because, thought Rorty, misleading advertising sells products better than truthful messages.

Only four years later, Harold Le Claire Ickes (1874-1952), secretary of the interior under Pres. Franklin D. Roosevelt from 1933-1946, completed *America's House of Lords*. In his book, Ickes pointed out that newspapers have become big business with about 150,000 workers employed full-time and annual sales exceeding one billion dollars in 1930. Ickes saw frightening bonds between business and publishing, pointing to Harry Chandler, publisher of the Los Angeles *Times*, who not only owned the newspaper, but had extensive holdings in real estate, agriculture, and other industries. Chandler was an officer or director in thirty-five California companies.

Ickes reported that other publishers had interests in unrelated industries, including J. R. Knowland, of the *Oakland Tribune*, who was president of Franklin Investment Company; Harris M. Crist (*Brooklyn Daily Eagle*) who was a trustee of the Fulton Savings Bank and involved with Manufacturers' Trust Company; and Robert Fiske Marden (*Lowell*, Mass., *Courier-Citizen*) who was also president of the Morris Plan Bank.

Business considerations, thought Ickes, influenced the content of newspapers. Chandler, for example, was extremely conservative and opposed the many plans of President Franklin Roosevelt to help the unemployed. Ickes objected to "interlocking directorates" fearing that no director would want his company treated negatively in the news media:

> According to its report, in 1928 a huge merger took place between the International Paper Company and the International Power Company, when "the stockholders of International Paper Company exchanged their stock in International Paper Company for stock of the International Paper & Power Co." This combination was as extraordinary as it was gigantic, for International Paper in the words of *Fortune* (May 1930), was the "world's chief producer of newsprint," while International Power was "one of the world's largest producers of power." The assets of this octopus, as made known in 1933, amounted to the stupendous sum of $887,283,254.
>
> This enormous corporation soon began to acquire control of a number of newspapers. Since this is a matter of great complexity and one that has been the subject of recriminations and denials, let me again quote from *Fortune* (May 1930, p. 72), that Boswellian journal of Big Business: "It was suddenly discovered that I. P. & P. had been quietly dickering with the press. Something more than $10,000,000 had been lent to publishers notably to Mr. Frank E. Gannett, owner of a dozen papers in New York and Connecticut. A half interest had been bought in two Boston papers, the *Herald* and the *Traveler,* and there were efforts to purchase other papers, such as the *Cleveland Plain Dealer*."

Later, when the facts of the interlocking relationships between paper, power, and newspaper companies came to light, Gannett sold his interests in the power company, while the paper company disposed its stock in the newspaper company. In a *Time* (May 1, 1939) "Letters," Gannett denied any involvement with the Paper & Power company.

Whatever the ultimate truth in the Gannett situation, a rising number of writers were criticizing the mass media for their affilation with other media and for their decreasing interest in the concerns of the working people.

Ferdinand Lundberg, in *Imperial Hearst: A Social Biography* (1936), developed a picture of Hearst in much the way that Ickes had portrayed all of the news media—big business people with interests similar to those of any big business. By the 1940s, most critics realized that newspaper publishers as business people might have the same interests and attitudes as any other business person, and with the declining number of daily newspapers, critics began wondering if there were enough independent voices to insure that all shades of opinion would be heard.*

Breaking Media Monopolies

Even the government, under the administration of Franklin D. Roosevelt, was concerned over the growing number of media outlets owned by a single organization. The Department of Justice, the agency charged with enforcing the antitrust laws, looked with disfavor on the vertical ownership patterns existing in motion pictures—organizations that owned the means of production, distribution, and retailing of media products. The large motion picture producers distributed their films through wholesale arms, and exhibited the movies in company-owned theaters. In July 1938, the Department of Justice began suits against several of the major motion picture companies—cases that would be solved through the break up of several companies that owned production facilities, wholesale distributers, and exhibitors in *U. S. v. Paramount Pictures Corp.* (1948) and consent decrees that followed with other motion picture houses. Involved were Paramount, RKO, Twentieth Century-Fox, Warner Brothers, Loews including MGM, and three companies that did not own chains of theaters—Columbia Pictures, Universal, and United Artists.

Roosevelt's interest in monopolistic and restraint of trade practices within the mass media led him to appoint James Lawrence Fly (1898-1966) chairman of the Federal Communications Commission (September 1, 1939-November 13, 1944). Fly pressed forward an investigation that led to the creation of a rule preventing broadcasters from affiliating with a network that served more than one station in a market (NBC's Red and Blue networks each provided programming to stations that were often in the same market.) A second rule prevented radio stations from giving up any control over their time to network organizations—the effect of the CBS contract.

The United States Supreme Court decision, *NBC* v. *U.S.* and *CBS* v. *U.S.* (1943), upheld the FCC's regulations regarding networks. The effect of the decision was to force CBS to revise its contract and force NBC to sell one of its television networks to Edward J. Noble with the FCC's approval on October 12, 1943; the new network became ABC.

---

*Orson Welles, the actor and director, produced a devastating portrait that was usually believed to be about the life of Hearst in the picture *Citizen Kane* (1941).

Elsewhere, the government was showing interest in activities of publishers that might be construed as violations of the antitrust laws. The government was concerned with the possible influence large companies might have on the free flow of information. That many thinkers wanted publishers and broadcasters to be free from governmental restraint did not mean that these people wanted to give the media right to engage practices that would inhibit the free flow of communications.

In *Associated Press et al.* v. *United States* (1945), the Supreme Court concluded there was no conflict between the First Amendment and the application of antitrust laws to the mass media. The AP case reflected the view that as communication companies had changed and were now large businesses that happened to be engaged in the finding and reporting of news and information. This recognition by the Supreme Court was realized by others in society including Arthur Hays Sulzberger (1891-1968), publisher of *The New York Times* who talked about the ethics of journalism before the American Society of Newspaper Editors:

> As I see it we, as a newspaper, have one paramount responsibility and that is to the public. I, in turn, as the publisher, have a second great responsibility and that is to the staff.
>
> As a newspaper we live under certain guarantees of freedom, and it is important to point out that there is no *quid pro quo* written into the Constitution. Freedom is granted—responsibility is not required. Despite that, more and more of us have come to recognize that responsibility is the Ruth to freedom's Naomi.
>
> I would define a responsible press as one which admits that the manner in which it covers and presents the news is a matter of legitimate public concern.
>
> It seems to me that the public has a right to demand this. It has a right to protection from unscrupulous advertising; it has the right to demand as accurate, full and impartial a news service as the public itself is prepared to support. It has this right because freedom of the press is one of its own fundamental freedoms which, in effect, it vests with a relatively small number of its citizenry. And the press suffers, and freedom everywhere suffers, where a community fails to demand and receive its rights in this respect.

As Sulzberger was encouraging journalists to assume a public responsibility and limit their freedom of expression, another group was reviewing the performance of the press. Their review would lead to a major new theory in press-State relationships.

Chapter 31

Formalizing Responsibility

By 1947, a number of criticisms had been leveled against the press by people inside and outside the profession. According to Theodore Peterson, dean of the College of Journalism and Communications at the University of Illinois, who wrote about the times leading up to the Commission on the Freedom of the Press ["The Social Responsibility Theory of the Press," *Four Theories of the Press*, 1956] that criticism fell into seven catagories:

1.   The press has wielded its enormous power for its own ends. The owners have propagated their own opinions, especially in matters of politics and economics, at the expense of opposing views.

2.   The press has been subservient to big business and at times has let advertisers control editorial policies and editorial content.

3.   The press has resisted social change.

4.   The press has often paid more attention to the superficial and sensational than to the significant in its coverage of current happenings, and its entertainment has often been lacking in substance.

5.   The press has endangered public morals.

6.   The press has invaded the privacy of individuals without just cause.

7.   The press is controlled by one socioeconomic class, loosely the "business class," and access to the industry is difficult for the newcomer; therefore, the free and open market of ideas is endangered.

Speaking about the environment in which journalism functioned, Jay W. Jensen in "Toward a Solution of the Problem of the Freedom of the Press," summarized the conditions that would have confronted the commission, as well as all of modern society:

> It is clear that the philosophical foundations of the traditional concept of freedom of the press have been precipitously undermined by the revolution in contemporary thought. The static and timeless World-Machine of Newton has been wrecked by the idea of evolution and the dynamic concepts of modern physics. Locke's doctrine of natural rights has been subverted not only by Romantic philosophy but also by present-day social science. Classical *laissez-faire* economics has been repudiated by most contemporary economists, and in practice by almost every modern industrial nation. Moreover, the Miltonian doctrine of the "self-righting process" has lately become suspect. [*Journalism Quarterly* (Fall 1950)].

With an awareness of these views, the Commission on the Freedom of the Press was formed in December 1942. Henry R. Luce (1898-1967), of Time, Inc., proposed the study to Robert M. Hutchins, president of the University of Chicago (1929-1945; chancellor, 1945-1951), who became the chairman of the commission. Hutchins selected the members of the commission who were scholars, government officials and others not employed in the media. The first meeting occurred a year after the initial meeting with Luce. Although Luce provided a grant of $200,000 to assist the commission in its work, he refused to pay the final part of the cost, and an additional $15,000 came from Encyclopaedia Britannica, Inc. (Hutchins became the chairman of the Board of Editors of *Encyclopaedia Britannica* in 1943).

In its review of the status of the news media, the commission included radio, newspapers, motion pictures, magazines, and books. The group concentrated on matters related to the role of the media in educating people in public affairs.

The commission produced its reports out of information collected from fifty-eight people connected with the press appearing before the commission, staff interviews with two hundred and twenty-five representatives of industry, government, and private agencies, and seventeen meetings of two or three days each. Besides the testimony and meetings, the staff and members of the commission reviewed 176 documents.

The Commission on Freedom of the Press, therefore, did not conceive its own ideas in a vacuum, but drew heavily upon the thinking of many scholars,

---

Members of the Commission on Freedom of the Press

Robert M. Hutchins, Chairman, Chancellor, The University of Chicago; Zechariah Chafee, Jr., Vice-Chairman, Professor of Law, Harvard University; John M. Clark, Professor of Economics, Columbia University; John Dickinson, Professor of Law, University of Pennsylvania, and General Counsel, Pennsylvania Railroad; William E. Hocking, Professor of Philosophy, Emeritus, Harvard University; Harold D. Lasswell, Professor of Law, Yale University; Archibald MacLeish, Former Assistant Secretary of State; Charles E. Merriam, Professor of Political Science, Emeritus, The University of Chicago; Reinhold Niebuhr, Professor of Ethics and Philosophy of Religion, Union Theological Seminary; Robert Redfield, Professor of Anthropology, The University of Chicago; Beardsley Ruml, Chairman, Federal Reserve Bank of New York; Arthur M. Schlesinger, Professor of History, Harvard University; George N. Shuster, President, Hunter College. Foreign Advisors John Grierson, Former General Manager, Wartime Information Board, Canada; Jacques Maritain, President, Free French School for Advanced Studies; Hu Shih, Former Chinese Ambassador to the United States; Kurt Riezler, Professor of Philosophy, New School for Social Research.

The Commission had a staff of Robert D. Leigh, director; Llewellyn White, assistant director; Ruth A. Inglis; and Milton D. Steward.

reporters, editors, publishers, and other thinkers; however, the commmission's work drew all of these concepts together and produced a document that has become the focus for modern thinking regarding the role of the press.

Publishers themselves already believed that they had an obligation to serve their community. Codes of conduct appeared many years earlier. Journalism had its Canons of Journalism, established by the American Society of Newspaper Editors in 1923; the National Association of Broadcasters, through its code authorities, formed the Radio Code (1937) and later the Television Code (1952). Even the motion picture makers created a code (1930) and, later, a rating system. Yet, many of these codes were written to prevent state regulation, not out of a sense of civic responsibility.

The commission tried to review the role of the mass media as part of the means whereby people gather information about their society, and it tried to describe the role of mass communication in "the education of the people in public affairs." Members wanted to identify the responsibilities that the owners and managers of the media should assume in formulating public opinion.

An Alternate View

Vitaly Petrusenko, a Communist writer, discussed his view of the Commission on the Freedom of the Press in *The Monopoly Press: Or How American Journalism Found Itself In The Vicious Circle Of The "Crisis Of Credibility"*:

Henry Luce, of the Time-Life empire, had originally provided support for a commission that studied the status of press freedom. Out of the report Luce had apparently wanted a report that said the press was responsible only to God in its gathering and presentation of news . . .

Those who had testified declared that the Press had been free and would continue to be free. The report had, in muted terms, spoken about the problems of a press monopoly—a thought that enraged Luce. Also, the report proposed the formation of a ten year commission to review press performance. Luce could not tolerate the thought of any outside organization reviewing his performance, and he refused to provide any funds beyond the $200,000 already spent.

The commission, without financial help, let the report sit on a shelf for a time. No other organization would step in where Henry Luce had refused to continue support until William Benton, a Yale University friend of Hutchins and now owner of Encyclopedia Britannica, invested an additional $15,000 to bring the report to conclusion.

The final report, issued in 1947, reflected serious content perhaps, because it was produced by serious men who had ambitions of joining the list of serious thinkers in the United States. Among the people were Arthur Schlesinger, later a close associate of President Kennedy, Hutchins, himself to become president of Ford Foundation, and others already established such as Harold Lasswell, a well known writer on mass media issues.

The commission issued a unanimous report on December 10, 1946, (published 1947) *A Free and Responsible Press: A General Report on Mass Communication: Newspapers, Radio, Motion Pictures, Magazines, and Books* detailing the problems, requirements, performance, and self-regulation of the media.

According to the commission's report, with the development of inexpensive newspapers, magazines, books, and a national system of broadcasting and film distribution, people throughout the nation had come to rely upon the media more than any previous generation had done. Gone were the convenient entertainments such as vaudeville. Even the weekly picnics sponsored by religious organizations and the comfortable town meetings seemed to be unavailable, or, at least, people were attending these events less.

In this environment, the Commission on Freedom of the Press concluded:

> First, the importance of the press to the people has greatly increased with the development of the press as an instrument of mass communication. At the same time the development of the press as an instrument of mass communication has greatly decreased the proportion of the people who can express their opinions and ideas through the press.
>
> Second, the few who are able to use the machinery of the press as an instrument of mass communication have not provided a service adequate to the needs of society.
>
> Third, those who direct the machinery of the press have engaged from time to time in practices which the society condemns and which, if continued, it will inevitably undertake to regulate or control.

The failure of the press to be responsive to the needs of modern society was one of the principal dangers. Although the Commission did not believe the freedom of expression would vanish immediately, the members thought an insidious trend would be more likely. In this, they saw great danger. Totalitarian governments strike first at freedom of expression. Yet, said the commission, "as freedom of the press is always in danger, so is it always dangerous."

As part of its work the commission set out to define and explain the principles underlying its findings:

Parties at Interest. Three parties have an interest in the production, distribution, and consumption of news. The first and most obvious party is the producer or "issuer" of news—the newspapers themselves. Because the producers of news copy want a receiver or customer for their product, the subscriber or listener, the audience, is a party at interest. There is a third party at interest: the community, or the larger group of people consisting of those who do not read newspapers or listen to broadcasts.

Freedom of Parties. While freedom of the press implies the right to publish, uninhibited by governmental interventions, the same freedom "must imply freedom of the consumer not to consume any particular press product." The press cannot compel a consumer to receive information; the consumer cannot force someone to publish.

The consumer's interest is protected when the interests of the purveyor is protected because the audience will tune out or refuse to buy unsatisfactory products; in time, the medium not responsive to the public interest will fail economically—and other providers will take the place of the unsatisfactory one. The consumer's interest, however, might not be protected if the number of "voices" declined—as was happening through the growing media concentrations and the declining number of newspapers. Under these special conditions some action might be needed to insure the protection of the consumer's interest. The commission approved of the anti-trust actions designed to maintain independent voices.

The Commission wanted the media to remain under private ownership, but it acknowledged that the classical views of a completely free private press might not work—never in its writing did the Commission totally rule out government intervention.

Issuer Freedom. Modern society depends on ideas. Ideas, however, by their very nature can not meet the approval of every person or institution. Inevitably, there will be someone or some organization that wishes to restrict the flow of ideas. The Commission believed that unpopular ideas, and hostile responses needed to be protected. "[The commission's] intention is that the *level of social conflict shall be lifted from the plane of [physical] violence to the plane of discussion.*" The Hutchins Commission did not propose that the purveyor of an unpopular argument would be free from loss of audience, contempt, or suffering; but that he would be free for open violence such as bombing the printing shop or threating employees or patrons.

Government's Need to Promote Free Expression. Since extended discussion of public issues sometimes turns from argument and dialogue to violent exchanges, especially after long periods of discussion, the Commission felt that government's police power was a powerful agent for enhancing discussion by maintaining public order. This police protection provides the major means by which government can promote free expression. When participants know that government will provide physical protection, debaters probably would be more willing to particpate.

The commission cautioned:

> Freedom of the press to appeal to reason is liable to be taken as freedom to appeal to public passion, ignorance, prejudice, and mental inertia. We must not burke the fact that freedom of the press is dangerous. But there is no cure for bad argument either in refusing to argue or in substituting irrelevant pressures upon, or repression of, the free critic for the patient attempt to reach the elements of reasonableness of the mass mind, as long as the belief persists that such elements are there. The only hope for democracy lies in the validity of this belief and in the resolute maintenance, in that faith, of the critic's freedom.

Government Protecting against Government. If government can protect the freedom of the press, it also has the power to infringe that freedom. All governments have a vested position—a philosophy upon which the government is founded. Both totalitarian and democratic governments wish to protect their interests fearing the power of popular opinion to overturn their authority; therefore, they must:

> . . . set limits upon [their] capacity to interfere with, regulate, control, or suppress the voices of the press or to manipulate the data on which public judgment is formed . . . [Among the rights that must be most carefully protected are] free thought, free conscience, free worship, free speech, freedom of the person, free assembly . . . [and] freedom of the press.

Expression, A Right. Although the commission saw freedom of expression as a moral right, it believed the right was not absolute and rested on the morality of the person claiming the right:

> Since all rights, moral or legal, make assumptions regarding the will of the claimants, there are no unconditional rights. The notion of rights, costless, unconditional, conferred by the Creator at birth, was a marvelous fighting principle against arbitrary governments and had its historical work to do. But in the context of an achieved political freedom the need of limitation becomes evident. The unworkable and invalid conception of birthrights, wholly divorced from the condition of duty, has tended to beget an arrogant type of individualism which makes a mockery of every free institution, including the press. This conception has concealed the sound basis of our liberal polity, the one natural right, the right to do one's human task.

The Right to Err. Although there is a duty associated with the right of free expression, the right is not lost when the person expressing controversial thoughts errs, inadvertantly. Deliberate error, however, the commission did not include in this protection.

Abuse is not reason for legal intervention. Some members of the press might use their powers to lie or to be abusive, but the fact that some are in the wrong does not provide grounds for government to step in and take legal action. Courts cannot determine the inner motivation of the critic, and if they set out to make such judgments, they might chill other critics. The commission sided with letting deliberate abuses go unpunished to some extent, in the interest in protecting press freedoms.

The limits, therefore, of governmental intervention should be held to communications that invade in a "serious, overt, and demonstrable" way *private rights* or *vital social interests.* The first category provides protection against invasion of privacy and libel. Limits also are placed on misbranding, obscenity, sedition (using clear and present danger test), and inciting to riot.

Press and the Public Interest. The Commission pointed out that in modern society concentration of ownership has limited the variety and structure of news. The new environment requires that the press take on a character somewhat like that of a common carrier, a public trustee or, better yet, private educator in which the purveyor has the right to experiment and the obligation to provide a certain level of content. This public accountability led the commission to call for "an over-all social responsibility for the quality of press service to the citizen . . . This means that *the press must now take on the community's press objectives as its own objectives.*"

Self-correction, thought the commission, would be superior to external controls, and privately owned media better than government ownership.

Government's involvment should stop at improving the distribution of newspapers to achieve a more universal access, adding new legal remedies to curb the excessive abuses when necessary, and promoting the public debate. Government should be involved in the process of supplying news and comment to the press.

The Commission's version of a free press. The press no longer is a private enterprise operated for the private interest of its owners—in modern society the press has become a private enterprise that must be operated for the public interest. "There is a point beyond which failure to realize the moral right will entail encroachment by the state upon the existing legal right, noted the commission."

None of the commission's recommendations urged the FCC to remove itself from the act of regulating radio, television, or facsimile, but it suggested that the industry fight the government in court when the rights guaranteed in the First Amendment were being violated by government. The FCC should cooperate in these efforts.

The Commission did not recommend that the FCC lose its power to review a licensee's performance or that it be prevented from using the "public interest" standard in awarding licenses.

Improving Press Performance

The Commission believed that three avenues existed for improving the performance of the press—through the press itself, through the public, and through the government.

The press should develop a professional spirit just as the professions of law, medicine, and dentistry have done argued the commission. Because of professional integrity, members of those professions do not do some things. The profession, as a whole, accepts voluntarily the responsibilities that society might otherwise impose upon it. The press should assume its own responsibilities— the complete dissemination of the news as a common carrier. The press should take on the common carrier responsibility of its own free will—not through legal requirement.

An independent agency should be set up to compile reports on the status of the press each year. This information could guide the public in its decision making processes.

Some Concluding Remarks

The social responsibility, libertarian, and authoritarian theories are but part of a common concept—characterized by private ownership of the media, but with differing views on just how much intervention government should take in the daily workings of the media. Throughout history, the three concepts have coexisted to varying degrees. In authoritarian England, occasional moments of freedom came to printers and writers. In the United States, government officials and courts have imposed restrictions on the press on a number of occasions. Even the Commission on the Freedom of the Press kept the prospect of government intervention in the background as a limitation on the excesses of the media.

All three theories fear the power of the media and the injury they believe the media can inflict on social order. Words are powerful instruments in the hands of skilled craftspeople; words can strike fear to the heart of administrators and governmental officials; words can incite violent action not only in the minds of mobs but also in the minds of the pillars of the community; words can expose secret acts, bribes, agreements, and errors; words can cause the powerful to loose their power. No one with power or status, therefore, seems willing to give the press completely free reign to engage in any communication it chooses.

The private ownership theory of the media holds that the media should not come under government ownership, for any reason. Authoritarians would maintain strict control over the media using licensing, torture, threats, frequent court cases, and government censors to keep the undisciplined press in order, but they would not assume the ownership of the media. The authoritarian concepts ruled the handling of information from the earliest times. For centuries, no government official apologized for suppressing a writer, editor, or speaker or for persecuting the outspoken.

Then thinkers proposed giving the media liberty to say some things without licensing, suppression, or oversight while maintaining control in other areas; but the growth of the libertarian theory was not so much new theory as it was a loosening of the restraints of authority. Libertarians would give the press freedom to discuss many political issues, but controls over defamation, obscenity, contempts of court, sedition, and unethical advertising must be controlled. Even the most broad-minded libertarian imagined the need for a number of restraints to protect children, the state, and personal reputations. All that had changed was the boundary of authority.

The social responsibility of the press theorists suggested that the media must exercise restraint within the customary moral values of their society, or else the government, under pressure from the citizens, would step in and impose order. Although the Commission on Freedom of the Press acknowledged the market might refuse to support media whose views deviated too far from society's, the Commission did not accept economic restraint as sufficient regulatory power. The theorists required that the press earn its freedoms through responsible reporting, writing, and presentation. The theory seeks to transfer some of the authoritarian restraints from the government to the individual newspaper, radio or television station, motion picture producer, or magazine.

While those who held to the social responsibility theory did not like government exercising too much control, they did not trust the media enough to set
them completely free to do anything they wanted. Consequently, the combination of threat and flattery was used to bring order. The threat of government
regulation was always present when the media could not control themselves,
but the commission hoped the flattery that reporters and editors had gained with
a resulting professional stature would force journalists to impose strict limitations upon themselves that would make them accept conventional community
standards, thus removing the need for direct authoritarian restraints from the
hand of a government censor.

. The libertarian, authoritarian, and social responsibility theories all rest on two
common principles: private ownership of the media and some form of restraint
to control excesses. The only differences are who exercises the control and to
what extent repression is exercised.

The Press and Public Opinion

by Zechariah Chafee, Jr.

Although [my] survey shows a predominance of trends toward governmental
interference with mass communications, these trends will be inevitably prevail.
The chances for successful resistance depend greatly on the existence of a
healthy public opinion. It is when society and the press are in a bad way
that despotism finds its golden opportunity. Consequently, we need to concern
ourselves about the preservation of the essential conditions of healthy public
opinion. Two main conditions, somewhat interrelated, may be called the two-
way process and the self-righting process.

1. *The two-way process.*—Communication is a two-way process of mutual
response between the members of the community. The right to speak implies
a readiness to listen and give consideration to what the other man says. A
community is a universe of discourse in which the members participate by
speaking and listening, writing and reading. In a free community the members
establish and re-establish, examine and re-examine, in response to one another,
their formulations of man's ultimate ends, the standards of their behavior, and
their application to concrete issues. Thus, the society in a continuous enterprise
of inquiry and discussion gropes its way through changing tasks and conditions;
the individual, even if not free from the pressures of his own circumstances,
can feel "free" by participating in that enterprise. The First Amendment takes
the universe of discourse for granted. It is doubtful whether and to what extent

Reprinted from *Government and Mass Communications* by Zechariah Chafee, Jr., by permission
of The University of Chicago Press. Copyright 1947 by the University of Chicago.

it can be taken for granted under the conditions of life in a modern industrial society. Hence it must be defended.

In Germany during the Hitler regime there was a significant change in the process of communication from two-way discussion to one-way propaganda. As Goebbels formulated it: "We no longer want the formation of public opinion, but rather the public formation of opinion." The universe of discourse had broken apart—no discussion or argument was permitted to the Nazis by their leaders. A public opinion which thus is *made* is to be distinguished from one which *grows*.

Therefore, it is not enough to have the right of a free press on parchment in the Constitution. As we look toward the future of this freedom, it is important to know the extent to which this two-way process is working actively. The country is not without dangers in this respect. One danger, already mentioned, is the way we are divided into racial, religious, and economic groups. In every industrial society of large size, forces arise that tend to separate sections of the community from the universe of discourse and thus split the community into parts between which discussion dies out. Workers, farmers, racial minorities, the *gens bien nés* or *bien pensant*, the members of the Union League Club, may finally move in separate worlds.

Fortunately, the process of growth of opinion is still rather strong in the United States (though too little studied in comparison with the manipulation of opinion). Discussion in this country is still vigorous and alive, and the universe of discourse has not yet been shattered. Consequently, the dangers just indicated can still be met by a deliverate and consistent effort of the national community. The possibilities of action must be constantly explored.

2. *The self-righting process.*—This is the process by which in the long run truth is to emerge from the clash of opinions, good and bad. Milton described it in a famous passage: "And though all the winds of doctrine were let loose to play upon the earth, so Truth be in the field, we do injuriously by licensing and prohibiting to misdoubt her strength. Let her and Falsehood grapple; who ever knew Truth put to the worse, in a free and open encounter?"

The importance of the satisfactory operation of this process for the freedom of the press was constantly stressed at meetings of the Commission. One member said: "A free society presupposes a self-righting process, some sort of ballast. The assumption is that free action in rational minds will result in self-correction, social as well as individual. Now the problem is not whether freedom is good, but whether, given freedom, the self-righting process is in good order, whether the above assumption is being realized. Discussion is not self-correcting in a society which does not use the criteria of a serious search for truth. It is like a cattle ship with the cattle broken loose from their halters. Perhaps we are getting like that. What we want therefore [in our inquiry] is a formulation of the dangers arising from failure to understand and to realize in practice the assumptions which are essential to the workings of a democratic society."

Expressions of similar ideas by others were: "It is material to consider how much immunity to harmful lies the public possesses. This immunity may vary with education and other qualities of readers." And, again: "It is important to determine the level at which public discussion is carried on. How far can we count on society to take care of itself?"

That this self-righting process is not working well at the present time was plain to the Commission. It was unquestionably demonstrated to us that the output of the press includes an appallingly large quantity of irresponsible utterances and even deliberate lying. Consequently, some members feared that it is a matter of manipulation or luck what conclusions will emerge from such a tangle. They came to regard Milton's vision of victorious Truth as an illusion. The natural inference was that the government must step in as an umpire in the contest of conflicting opinions and allegations.

Although others were less pessimistic, we were all gravely concerned. To be more specific, the Commission was disturbed by three obstacles to the satisfactory operation of the self-righting process today:

First and foremost is the drift toward concentration of power which has already by mentioned and is fully set forth in *A Free and Responsible Press*. This is exemplified by the large number of cities with only one newspaper, the common ownership of newspapers and radio stations, and the growth of newspaper chains. Now, diversity in the effective communication of facts and opinions is a fundamental presupposition of the self-righting process. That point is stressed by Judge Learned Hand in the recent case which prevented the Associated Press from denying its services to competing newspapers:

> . . . The newspaper industry . . . serves one of the most vital of all general interests: the dissemination of news from as many different sources, and with as many different facets and colors as is possible. That interest is closely akin to, if indeed it is not the same as, the interest protected by the First Amendment; it presupposes that right conclusions are more likely to be gathered out of a multitude of tongues, than through any kind of authoritative selection. To many, this is, and always will be folly: but we have staked upon it our all.

And Justice Black in the Supreme Court said of the First Amendment:

> That Amendment rests on the assumption that the widest possible dissemination of information from diverse and antagonistic sources is essential to the welfare of the public . . .

This fundamental presupposition is seriously weakened by concentration of power. Instead of several views of the facts and several conflicting opinions, newspaper readers in many cities, or, still worse, in wide regions, may get only a single set of facts and a single body of opinion, all emanating from one owner.

A second obstacle lies in the present prevalence of sales talk in American life, so that it naturally flows into the press. There is a significant distinction between discussion, which tries to uncover the facts, and sales talk, which is interested in the facts only so far as they further the sale. If the spirit of sales talk prevails over the spirit of discussion, talk can no longer be met with talk. Freedom of speech loses its self-regulating power.

Thirdly, the public reads unfavorable news and opinions about people and policies with more appetite than the favorable. Hence, an unfavorable item may be insufficiently counteracted because the opposing item (*a*) will not be printed or (*b*) will not be read. As one informant said about news from government departments and business: "Peace, harmony, and brotherly love are not news; a fight is." And we were told that, even when an editor requests an abundant flow of information about Latin America from the Associated Press, he does not print what he gets unless it is unfavorable to the particular country; then he gobbles it up. This inclination of the public to hear about quarrels and excitement and the unusual makes it hard for them to get a well-rounded understanding of important situations at home and abroad. Often it is the long-run facts which really matter. In the pithy words of one of our number: "The fact that no more dogs are biting men should be bigger news than 'Man bites dog.' "

One existing remedy for this partial presentation of life is that longer articles do get favorable and constructive information to interested readers. The monthly magazines and books are a better vehicle for this than the daily press. Even so, is there adequate counteraction to untrue or lopsided derogatory news?

For such reasons the Commission became critical of the principle of laissez faire, according to which the solution for problems of freedom is more freedom. The following attitude of one of our members fairly expressed our apprehensions: The press fails to bring about the kind of communication of fact and idea which leads to a rational discussion of ends and means. Our society rests upon the assumption that, through the freedom of one to speak and the readiness of others to listen and consider, any divagation of our people from a just course will be corrected by themselves. Today there is reason to suppose that this self-correcting process, although commonly considered to function fully, does not in fact function, to our danger. The eighteenth-century champions of liberty assumed *human* nature to be like the rest of nature, with an inner tendency toward harmony, but today men cannot be so complacent. Human society knows no limits to its desires, hence any value can become a peril— even liberty. An analysis of the problem of democracy in general and of the free press in particular proves that there are no such natural harmonies and balances in a community as democratic theory used to assume. Whatever harmony exists at a particular moment may be disturbed by the emergence of new factors and vitalities. Our people have put too much trust in the automatic tendencies of our society to right itself. We have found that we cannot depend on unmanaged processes, whether in economics or in communications. We need more effective methods of self-correction. We cannot rely merely on automatic action. The unity of a society is partly the fruit of moral and political contrivance and is not the inevitable consequence of freedom per se. Since purely political contrivance is bound to destroy freedom for the sake of unity, it follows that the preservation of both unity and freedom depends partly upon the achievement of self-control and a sense of high responsibility on the part of the forces which direct the instruments of a society. But the preservation of such unity also depends partly upon the careful and discriminating establishment of such public and political controls as are least inimical to the value of freedom.

The repeated insistence in the foregoing passages on some sort of management of discussion does not necessarily require the government to predominate in the managing, but it implies that, if others do not manage, the government will. . . There are alternative private influences such as the will of individuals, and schools and colleges, and the press itself, which are capable of raising the level of discussion if they are sufficiently intelligent and vigorous. Even though the self-righting process clanks along pretty jerkily, I am far from ready to abandon the case against abridging the freedom of speech and of the press. How self-righting was England when Milton wrote the *Areopagitica* in 1644?

Some reflections I wrote five years ago still represent my own beliefs:

"Speech should be fruitful as well as free . . . Lack of interference alone will not make discussion fruitful. We must take affirmative steps to improve the methods by which discussion is carried on. Of late years the arguments of Milton and Mill have been questioned, because truth does not seem to emerge from a controversy in the automatic way their logic would lead us to expect. For one thing, reason is less praised nowadays than a century ago; instead, emotions conscious and unconscious are said to dominate the conduct of men . . ."

"Nevertheless, the main argument of Milton and Mill still holds good. All that this disapointment means is that friction is a much bigger drag on the progress of Truth than they supposed. Efforts to lessen that friction are essential to the success of freedom of speech. It is a problem, not for law, but for education in the wide sense that includes more than schools and youngsters. . . ."

"Reason is more imperfect than we used to believe. Yet it still remains the best guide we have."

The foregoing discussion has brought out many reasons why the impulse toward governmental activity in the field of communications will grow stronger in the near future. If that impulse is allowed free play, very great dangers will arise, not only to the press, but also to the continuance of democracy.

So much stress has been laid of late on various economic pressures and forces which warp mass communications that there is some risk that the American people will lose sight of the evils of a government-controlled press. It is right to emphasize these economic influences, as the general report of the Commission does. Immunity from state action is not enough; the press should also be independent of private forces which prevent it from giving society the kind of mass communications which society needs. Yet nobody should fall into the opposite error of assuming that economic obstacles are the only impairments of freedom or that a press which is dominated by the state is free merely because it is dissevered from all capitalistic controls. The meaning which our ancestors gave to liberty of the press, namely, freedom from the will of legislators and officials, is just as vital today as it was in 1791. It is constantly important for the public to realize the indispensability of freedom of the press from governmental control so that they can fight for it with a clear idea of what they must defend.

This does not mean that all state activity in the field of communications is necessarily bad . . .

The point is that unwise state activity must be steadily resisted, because otherwise it is likely to come to pass in response to numerous conditions of the United States today. The First Amendment is a gun behind the door which must never be allowed to rust.

Chapter 32

'I Have a List of Communists'

Although the Commission on the Freedom of the Press issued a call for more independence for the press and a challenge to the press to serve the public interest through responsible and well trained practitioners, only a few years passed before many were questioning if the United States would allow its media to have the freedom that is necessary in a democratic society.

The Cold War that began with the failure of the United States and the Soviet Union to agree on the division of Germany grew into full blown fear of each other. The Soviet Union, fully aware of the Nazi power and threat, had no interest in restoring the German might of pre-World War II years, while the western nations wanted a unified state. Western nations, which saw the obstinate attitude of Russia as a threat, immediately began questioning the U.S.S.R.'s motivations. The fact that Poland became part of the Soviet camp worsened matters.

One statute, the Smith Act, would be used by the nation in trying to stamp out Communists during the Cold War. In *Eugene Dennis* v. *United States* (1951), the Supreme Court reviewed the 1948 conviction of Communists under the Smith Act. The case gave the Supreme Court an opportunity to determine if the Smith Act violated the First and Fifth amendments to the Constitution. The Court held that the Smith Act was not unconstitutional because it was "directed at advocacy, not discussion." Discussion was to be protected under the First Amendment, but advocacy was not to enjoy the same shelter. The Court used the "clear and present danger" standard:

> We hold that . . . the Smith Act [does] not inherently, or as construed or applied in the instant case, violate the First Amendment . . . Petitioners intended to overthrow the Government of the United States as speedily as the circumstances would permit. Their conspiracy to organize the Communist Party and to teach and advocate the overthrow of the Government of the United States by force and violence created a "clear and present danger" of an attempt to overthrow the Government by force and violence.

The interest of the Soviet Union in the Korean War and the United States participation created another reason for fearing the Soviet Union and its motivations. North Korea invaded South Korea on June 25, 1950, starting the war; but the

265

Soviet Union and China had been supporting a build up in Korea for most of the years since the end of World War II, and the North Koreans had a strong army with 130,000 armed men.

In this arena of fear, the Congress decided to enact the the Internal Security Act of 1950, known as the McCarran Act after Senator Pat McCarran of Nevada, to provide more protections than previous laws had. Thinking it was unnecessary and objectionable President Harry Truman (1884-1972; president, 1945-1953) vetoed the bill, but the bill was passed again on September 23, 1950, over the veto. Truman said about the bill:

> Legislation with these consequences is not necessary to meet the real dangers which communism presents to our free society. These dangers are serious and must be met. But this bill would hinder us, not help us, in meeting them. Fortunately, we already have on the books strong laws which give us most of the protection we need from the real dangers of treason, espionage, sabotage, and actions looking to the overthrow of our Government by force and violence. Most of the provisions of this bill have no relation to these real dangers.

Truman objected to the bill on other grounds, and he made these points in his veto message of noting his concern over laws that punished opinions:

> In a free country, we punish men for the crimes they commit, but never for the opinions they have. And the reason this is so fundamental to freedom is not . . . that it protects the few unorthodox from suppression by the majority, [but that to] permit freedom of expression is primarily for the benefit of the majority because it protects criticism and criticism leads to progress.

Despite the many repressive measures to be found in the law, Congress included in the early part of the act the following statement that seemed to lose its meaning later in the act:

> Nothing in this Act shall be construed . . . in any way to infringe upon freedom of the press or of speech as guaranteed by the Constitution.

The new law had three major portions: the Subversive Activities Control Act as part of Title I; a criminal sedition law also found in Title I; and the Emergency Detention Act. The new law defined a Communist-action organization as one which (i) is substantially directed, dominated, or controlled by the foreign government or foreign organization controlling the world Communist movement . . . and (ii) operates primarily to advance objectives of such world Communist movement. A second definition of Communist-front organization also can be found in the act which (A) is substantially directed, dominated or controlled by a Communist-action organization, and (B) is primarily operated for the purpose of giving aid and support to a Communist-action organization, a Communist foreign government, or the world Communist movement.

The new law created a Subversive Activities Control Board which could review conduct of an organization to determine if it was a Communist-action or a Communist-front organization, and, if the board found the organization fell in either category, it was required to file a registration statement. Registered organizations had to keep extensive records of funds received and spent including sources and amounts, lists of officers (and members in the case of Communist-action) and addresses, and logs of printing and duplicating equipment.

Belonging to a registered organization meant that the member could not apply for a passport (the application was considered criminal) and was labeled a traitor who owed allegiance to a foreign country—regardless of any action or inaction the person might take beyond membership in the organization; thus, it was criminal to be a member of a Communist-front organization. Members could not hold a non-elective job working for the United States government.

The registered organizations fared no better. The government monitored record keeping so carefully that the slightest infraction was prosecuted and the organization was forced out of business. Most ceased operation or went under-ground. Penalties could be imposed without any showing that the organization or person had engaged in violence, advocated violence or force, or performed any illegal action. Section 4(a) of the new law went further by making it illegal for any person:

> . . . knowingly to combine, conspire, or agree with any other person to perform any act which would substantially contribute to the establishment within the United States of a totalitarian dictatorship . . . the direction and control of which is to be vested in, or exercised by or under the domination or control of, any foreign government, foreign organization, or foreign individual.

No force or violence needed to occur to invoke the provisions of this section; the person had only to engage in peaceful membership.

The detention provision could only be invoked in the case of an emergency or declaration of war, but when in force the Attorney General of the United States could detain

> each person [where] . . . there is reasonable ground to believe that such person probably will engage in, or probably will conspire with others to engage in, acts of espionage or of sabotage.

In November 1950, the attorney general filed a petition to have the Communist Party investigated and registered. The Subversive Activities Control Board acted on the petition and conducted hearings that involved thousands of pages of testimony and exhibits and finally issued its report in April 1953; the decision was appealed to the Court of Appeals several times, then to the Supreme Court twice. Consequently, the Supreme Court did not issue its decision until 1961 in *Communist Party* v. *Subversive Activities Control Board* when it upheld the Board.

The attorney general filed petitions regarding twenty-three organizations taking years to review—through most of the 1960s. By the time of *DuBois Clubs of America* v. *Clark* (1967), the last case still before the Subversive Activities Control Board, the Board was concerned only with testing administrative procedures. The Supreme Court majority felt that any short-cuts in administrative procedures would have "the effect . . . that important and difficult constitutional issues would be decided devoid of factual context and before it was clear that appellants were covered by the Act."

Speaking at the Four Freedoms Foundation in the Fall of 1953, Harry S Truman noted that freedom is not just the responsibility of the courts at a time when the Subversive Activities Control Board was considering registrations that would shortly be taken up by the Supreme Court and upon which in 1961 the Court would render a verdict that was suppressive:

> The good life is not possible without freedom. But only the people, by their will and by their dedication to freedom, can make the good life come to pass. We cannot leave it to the courts alone, because many of the invasions of these freedoms are so devious and so subtle that they cannot be brought before the courts.
>
> The responsibility for these freedoms falls on free men. And free men can preserve them only if they are militant about freedom. We ought to get angry when these rights are violated, and make ourselves heard until the wrong is righted. . . . There are times when the defense of freedom calls for vigorous action. This action may lead to trouble, and frequently does. Effective effort to preserve freedom may involve discomfort and risk. It takes faith, unselfishness and courage to stand up to a bully; or to stand up for a whole community when it has been frightened into subjection. But it has to be done, if we are to remain free.
>
> We have to start wherever we can—in the family, the lodge, the business community, the union, our local government, party, church— and work outward; asserting, demanding, insisting that the most unpopular persons are entitled to all the freedoms, to fundamental fairness. Almost always, the issues are raised over unpopular people or unpopular causes. In the case of freedom, we have to battle for the rights of people with whom we do not agree; and whom, in many cases, we may not like. These people test the strength of the freedoms which protect all of us. If we do not defend their rights, we endanger our own.

Truman spoke these words while the McCarthy Communist scare tactics were being practiced by many throughout the government. Only a few months later the Congress would pass another law designed to suppress unpopular organizations.

In 1954, Congress tried to handle internal security through another law, the Communist Control Act of 1954. Section 3 of "Proscribed Organizations" declared that the Communist Party in the United States and related groups "are not entitled to any of the rights, privileges, and immunities attendant upon legal bodies created under the jurisdiction of the laws of the United States or any political subdivision." Section 4 simply said that members of the Communist Party or organizations that subscribe to the views of the Communist Party would be punished under the Internal Security Act of 1950.

Although there were virtually no prosecutions under the Communist Control Act, the law shows the lengths to which Congress was willing to go at the time in finding and punishing Communists.

President Dwight D. Eisenhower (1890-1969; president, 1953-1961) objected to making all information in the Executive Branch of government available to Congress; therefore, he prepared a memorandum to the Secretary of Defense, dated May 17, 1954, in which he laid down the rights of the Executive to withhold information:

> Dear Mr. Secretary: It has long been recognized that to assist the Congress in achieving its legislative purpose every executive department or agency must, upon the request of a congressional committee, expeditiously furnish information relating to any matter within the jurisdiction of the committee, with certain historical exceptions—some of which are pointed out in the attached memorandum from the Attorney General. This administration has been and will continue to be dilligent in following this principle. However, it is essential to the successful working of our system that the persons entrusted with power in any one of the three great branches of Government shall not encroach upon the authority confided to the others. The ultimate responsibility for the conduct of the executive branch rests with the President.
>
> Within this constitutional framework each branch should cooperate fully with each other for the common good. However, throughout our history the President has withheld information whenever he found that what was sought was confidential or its disclosure would be incompatible with the public interest or jeopardize the safety of the Nation.
>
> Because it is essential to efficient and effective administration that employees of the executive branch be in a position to be completely candid in advising with each other on official matters, and because it is not in the public interest that any of their conversations or communications, or any documents or reproductions, concerning such advice be disclosed, you will instruct employees of your Department that in all of their appearances before the subcommittee of the Senate Committee on Government Operations regarding the inquiry now before it they are not to testify to any such conversations or communications or to produce any such documents or reproductions. This principle must be maintained regardless of who would be benefited by such disclosures.
>
> I direct this action so as to maintain the proper separation of powers between the executive and legislative branches of the Government in accordance with my responsibilities and duties under the Constitution. This separation is vital to preclude the exercise of arbitrary power by any branch of the Government.

By this action I am not in any way restricting the testimony of such witnesses as to what occured regarding any matters where the communication was directly between any of the principals in the controversy within the executive branch on the one hand and a member of the subcommittee or its staff on the other.

This document reflected Eisenhower's belief that some information was private within the executive branch and it showed that he objected to the breadth of some of hearings that Sen. Joseph R. McCarthy was engaging in his Senate committee to find security risks. Eisenhower, however, did not directly interfere with the senator's work.

The Senator from Wisconsin

A senator from Wisconsin, Joseph McCarthy (1908-1957), took up the anti-Communist issue in 1950 when he came to the Congress and demonstrated just how far the zeal of a member of Congress could go in the crusade sometimes known as the "Red Scare" as he claimed to purge the nation of criminals when in reality he was destroying civil liberties.

McCarthy used publicity as much as official investigations to find Communists. Sometimes he would conduct a news conference with a sheaf of papers in his hand proclaiming, "I have a list of 1,500 [or other number] Communists," and he would hold up a stack of papers to convince his audience. He never, however, released the papers to the press for their examination. The papers might have been blank, have contained discarded memos, or have been what the Senator claimed.

McCarthy investigated alleged Communists in the Department of State, the Voice of America, the Federal Communications Commission (FCC), other governmental agencies, and the mass media. Actors, directors, and writers— as well as other people—lost their jobs as the result of McCarthy's accusation. As author Richard H. Rovere observed in his detailed account, *Senator Joe McCarthy* (1959), mass entertainment and much of the press were dominated by people who concentrated on keeping anything offensive to McCarthy out and by vice-presidents in charge of censorship. The result was little room for creative freedom.*

Some news figures became close to McCarthy such as Fulton Lewis, Jr., of Mutual Broadcasting System (MBS) and George Sokolsky of American Broadcasting Company (ABC). *Red Channels* and *Counterattack* were established to publish the names of people who were Communists, or at least believed to be Communists. McCarthy was having success with the Eisenhower administration by getting people favorable to his position appointed to the Federal Communications Commission and to work for John Foster Dulles (1888-1959), Secretary of State; Dulles hired Scott McLeod as director of personnel and security at the urging of McCarthy.

---

*Among those who testified about alleged communists was Ronald Reagan, liberal President of the Screen Actors Guild.

The Eisenhower administration, like previous administrations, developed its own plan for dealing with employees who were disloyal or a security risk. While President Truman had separated the two categories, Eisenhower combined loyalty and security risks into a single category called security risks. During the first months in office, Eisenhower removed 1,456 people from jobs on the ground of security considerations. Later a presidential lawyer declared that "1,456 subversives have been kicked out of government jobs." The *New York Times*, reporting on the speech, noted that "1,456 Reds" had been found and removed. Most of the people were only security risks based on the sensitive nature of the work they had to perform—hardly Communists.

The organization Aware, Inc., formed in 1953, devoted itself to finding actors and other people in the entertainment business suspected of being Communists and getting them fired. Aware was effective because it would write sponsors of programs employing the actor, writer, or director and explain why the person was an offense to the nation. If the person remained employed, Aware's letters would take a more strident tone implying actions that might influence sales. The message usually got action.

Although a number of stories had appeared in the *New York Herald*, *New York Times*, *Washington Post*, and many newspapers owned by chains about McCarthy, nothing seemed to have stopped the senator's drive. Prominent journalists including Drew Pearson, Walter Lippmann, Joseph and Stewart Alsop, and Thomas L. Stokes frequently engaged in thoughtful and critical analyses, but McCarthy seemed to keep his power. Then on March 9, 1954, Fred Friendly and Edward Murrow broadcast a news program made up of film clips of McCarthy's public statements and statements by Murrow on CBS's *See It Now* series. Besides the Murrow-Friendly broadcast, many citizens were becoming aware of the real McCarthy, and on December 2, 1954, the Senate, now under Democratic control, declared, 67-22, that the senator had engaged in conduct "contrary to Senate traditions." McCarthy never regained his former power.

The Supreme Court began rethinking its attitude towards Communists in *Yates* v. *United States* (1957). Fourteen petitioners, all Communists, including Oleta O'Connor Yates, Henry Steinberg, and Loretta Stavus Stack, had been tried and convicted under the Smith Act. The Supreme Court went to considerable length to distinguish the intended limits of the statute:

> . . . The statute was aimed at the advocacy and teaching of concrete action for the forcibile overthrow of the Government, and not of principles divorced from action . . .
>
> In failing to distinguish between advocacy of forcible overthrow as an abstract doctrine and advocacy of action to that end, the District Court appears to have been led astray by the holding in *Dennis* that advocacy of violent action to be taken at some future time was enough.

The Court went on to examine the evidence and found it inadequate to secure a conviction, but let stand the conviction of nine petitioners subject to possible later action by the government, action that never came. The decision erected new barriers against governmental intervention in expression issues.

Broadcasting's Own Problems

Television broadcasting from 1955 through the end of the decade fell in love with quiz shows. Walter Craig, a partner at the Norman, Craig & Kummel advertising agency, heard about the concept for *The $64,000 Question* and got sponsorship. It helped Revlon, the cosmetic manufacturer and sponsor, increase sales so much the company could not keep up with demand. Other programs copied the successful format, including *The Big Surprise* (1955), until quiz shows were the most popular and one of the most pervasive shows on television.

The very popularity of the shows raised questions about their honesty, and rumors began to appear in articles in *Look* and *Time*. Finally, another contestant, Charles Van Doren, appeared before a congressional oversight committee under the chairmanship of Rep. Oren Harris during the Fall 1959 to read a long statement in which Van Doren explained how *Twenty-One*, the show on which he had appeared, was rigged. The information was met with consternation by everyone and Congress passed an amendment to the Communications Act of 1934 as Section 509 to control quiz shows:

> It shall be unlawful for any person, with intent to deceive the listening public—
>
> To supply to any contestant in a purportedly bona fide contest of intellectual knowledge or intellectual skill any special and secret assistance whereby the outcome of such contest will be in whole or in part prearranged or predetermined.

During 1959, another problem surfaced called "payola" or bribing disk jockeys (DJs) to play certain records. Stan Richards, a disk jockey at Station WILD, Boston, Massachusetts, admitted that he had been accepting money and gifts from record companies which wanted him to play their records. Investigations by a congressional subcommittee found that one person had received as much as $36,050.

Congress found the practice of payola widespread and amended the Communications Act of 1934 again to cope with the problem through Section 508.

> Any employee of a radio station who accepts or agrees to accept from any person . . . who pays or agrees to pay such employee, any money, service or other valuable consideration for the broadcast of any matter over such station, shall, in advance of such broadcast, disclose the fact of such acceptance or agreement to such station.

During these years Congress was dealing with the problems of the broadcast media by passing more authoritarian statutes and by ordering the FCC to enforce the new laws.

The Profession to Blame

Sometimes critics have declared that the irresponsibilities of the press are the source of much of the suppression that occurs. They have believed that there is a lack of professionalism. Those who subscribed to this theory had their view supported by the Warren Commission, a committee headed by Chief Justice Earl Warren (1891-1974) of the Supreme Court which had as members Sens. Richard B. Russell of Georgia and John Sherman Cooper of Kentucky, Reps. Hale Boggs of Louisiana and Gerald R. Ford of Michigan, and two private citizens, Allen W. Dulles, former director of the Centeral Intellegence Agency and John J. McCloy, former president of the International Bank for Reconstruction and Development. The commission was set up by President Lyndon B. Johnson (1908-1973; President 1963-1969) on November 29, 1963 to investigate the circumstances associated with the assassination of President Kennedy (1917-1963; president, 1961-1963) the Warren Commission, (report issued in September 1964), reviewed how the news media handled the assassination of President John F. Kennedy (November 22, 1963) and found problems with the way reporters did their job. Lee Harvey Oswald (1939-1963), the alleged assassin, was shot to death on November 24, 1963, as he was being moved to the Dallas county jail by Jack Ruby (1911-1967). Much publicity surrounded the event from police, bystanders, and reporters.

Publicity as a form of trial became an issue to be explored. Since everyone knew the opinions of police and prosecutors, could an unbiased jury be found to try Oswald? The Commission found the police and the news media guilty of error. They suggested the news media should seek to establish a code for professional conduct to help avoid the same problems in the future. The findings of the commission were particularly significant because, in *Irvin* v. *Dowd* (1962), a conviction was overturned because of publicity:

> The Commission believes . . . that a part of the responsibility for the unfortunate circumstances following the President's death must be borne by the news media. The crowd of newsmen generally failed to respond properly to the demands of the police. Frequently without permission, news representatives used police offices on the third floor, tying up facilities and interfering with normal police operations. Police efforts to preserve order and to clear passageways in the corridor were usually unsuccessful. On Friday night the reporters completely ignored [Police Chief] Curry's injunction against asking Oswald questions in the assembly room and crowding in on him. On Sunday morning, the newsmen were instructed to direct no questions at Oswald; nevertheless, several reporters shouted questions at him when he appeared in the basement.

The commission found other errors in the way the news media handled the coverage of Oswald, including "a regrettable lack of self-discipline by the newsmen." As a result, the Commission assigned blame to both the news media and police; and it suggested methods to prevent similar events from happening in the future:

The promulgation of a code of professional conduct governming representatives of all news media would be welcome evidence that the press had profited by the lesson of Dallas.

[But the Commission wanted more.] The burden of insuring that appropriate action is taken to establish ethical standards of conduct for the news media must also be borne, however, by State and local governments, by the bar, and ultimately by the public. The experience in Dallas during November 22-24 is a dramatic affirmation of the need for steps to bring about a proper balance between the right of the public to be kept informed and the right of the individual to a fair and impartial trial.

Vietnam

The widespread dissent against the involvement of the United States in the Vietnam war included many respected citizens including a group of 320 ministers, writers, professors, and other professionals who signed "A Call to Resist Illegitimate Authority" in September 1967. Signers approvingly recounted a number of forms of resistance to the war-effort and said: "We believe that each of these forms of resistance against illegitimate authority is courageous and justified." Besides the public statement, the group promised to raise money and engage in other means to resist the war. The statement included an affirmitive call: "Now is the time to resist."

The first document was followed within a few weeks with another statement by eighteen Jewish, Protestant, and Roman Catholic leaders and fifty delegates of the United States Conference on Church and Society declaring: "We hereby publicly counsel all who in conscience cannot today serve in the armed forces to refuse such service by non-violent means." Many other groups issued their own statements.

Some groups provided instruction or advice on methods for avoiding the draft. Among the techniques were the following: feigning insanity, claiming homosexuality, and exhibiting the signs of chronic illness.

Besides the calls to resist the war and the draft, other forms of protest called symbolic speech appeared during the Vietnam era. The best known forms included draft card burinings, blocking entrances to draft boards, and lying in front of troop convoys. Some even poured blood over military files. The purpose of these visual activities was to get exposure from the mass media, especially television, because the protestors did not have the funds to purchase time to discuss their cause.

Government response to the protests was predictable. President Johnson declared he was "dismayed by the demonstrations and [have given my] full endorsement to the Justice Department's investigation of possible Communist infiltration of the antidraft movement." The Federal Bureau of Investigation (FBI) and the Department of Justice investigated many groups for Communist involvement including the Students for a Democratic Society (SDS). Not to be outdone one congressional committee issued its *Senate Committee on the Judiciary, Subcommittee to Investigate the Administration of the Internal Security Act and Other Internal Security Laws, the Anti-Vietnam Agitation and the Teach-In*

Movement: The Problem of Communist Infiltration and Exploitation (1965). The House Committee on Un-American Activities produced a report on Vietnam Week (1967) examining its own concerns and suggesting: "The real objective of Vietnam Week is not the expression of honest dissent to promote the best interest of the American people and their Government, but to do injury and damage to the United States and to give aid and comfort to its enemies."

Some of the harrassment from the government was physical and brutal, including intervention of the police in marches that might otherwise have been peaceful. Draft boards, meanwhile, sped the process of inducting demonstrators into service. The American Civil Liberties Union (ACLU) in "The Vietnam War and the Status of Dissent" issued in June 1967 was convinced that official intimidation and harrassment was so widespread the nation might enter a new era of McCarthyism.

President Richard M. Nixon (1913- ; president 1969-1974) used his own techniques to deal with the media and its handling of Vietnam and his own Watergate problems. By June 1970, Nixon had agreed to a plan to establish a domestic security group made up of representatives from the Central Intelligence Agency (CIA), and FBI to secure information on disloyal American citizens. FBI Director J. Edgar Hoover, however, refused to go along with the plan. Nevertheless, Nixon agreed to wiretaps on government officials and newsmen using FBI agents. By 1971, the Nixon administration wanted more, and initiated its own surveillance group to find leaks in national security—it became known as the "Plumbers."

One White House aide, Charles Colson, in 1971, produced a list of "political enemies." Eventually, the list grew to include well-known figures in journalism, politics, entertainment, and business. One of the tasks of Nixon's security group was to interfere with the Democratic Party and the campaigning of Senator Edmund Muskie who was a candidate for the Democratic nomination for a time in 1972.

Reagan and the Media

Ronald Reagan (1911-) came to the presidency in 1981 after the Supreme Court of the United States had decided that Frank Snepp 3rd, a former CIA employee who had written *Decent Interval*, had to give all of his earnings from his book to the government and that CIA regulations requiring all former employees to secure approval prior to getting anything published was legal. The case, *Snepp* v. *United States* (1980), left open considerable freedom for government to extend the Court's opinion to other branches of government. To prevent this from happening, Attorney General Benjamin R. Civiletti (in President Jimmy Carter's administration) prepared guidelines to prevent the First Amendment rights from being abused. A new attorney general, William French Smith, revoked most of Civiletti's regulations during 1981.

A year later, on April 2, 1982, Reagan reversed another President Carter initiative, this time signed in 1978, that limited the quantity of information the government could withhold from the public. The policy required that government officials planning to classify anything consider the right of the public to know the information. With the new Reagan regulations, officials no longer had to consider the public's right to know.

Then on March 11, 1983, Reagan, through executive order, directed that present and past governmental officials secure review of materials they intended to publish that might have been classified. The order relied on *Snepp* for justification.

Press-government relations took another turn for the worse when the Reagan Administration on August 25, 1983, released a contract that all government officials who had access to highly classified information were required to sign. The contract bound the officials for the rest of their lives—whether in or out of government—to secure approval for anything they intended to submit for publication. The contract required the officials to submit the writings for review *prior to publication* of any information that fell into the new category of "sensitive compartmented information" (SCI).

The new order covered letters to the editor, pamphlets, scholarly writings, books, and magazine and newspaper articles. Although the order appeared to be directed at publication of the most sensitive classified information, the Justice Department explanations included classified and unclassified information of a sensitive nature.

The Reagan administration has used systematic attempts to limit the free flow of information in other ways by limiting the Freedom of Information Act, slowing the movement of television films across U. S. borders, including an ABC documentary, "The Killing Ground," which dealt with toxic waste, and extending the reach of the federal military classification system.

The president also took steps to limit the freedom of universities to discuss, lecture, or publish unclassified information. For example, the administration tried to declare that teaching certain subjects containing technological information (regardless of its classified nature) might be considered exporting of technology, placing teaching under constraints never before experienced by U. S. higher education. Federal law prohibited the export of secret technology; therefore, universities engaged in their regular teaching function might be taken to court for violating the law.

In addition to the direct actions that limited the flow of information to the news media, Reagan used the McCarran Act to keep speakers with whom he disagreed, or who had political philosophies different from the majority of Americans, out of the United States. Included were Hortensia Allende, the widow of former President Salvador Allende of Chile, the deputy cultural minister of Cuba, Julio Garcia Espinosa; and a spokesman for the radical Protestant group in Northern Ireland, the Rev. Ian Paisley.

Reagan's wish to stop the flow of anything that might project a message contrary to his own became ludicrous when he tried to get three films made by the prestigious National Film Board of Canada labeled propaganda. *If You Love This Planet*, one of the films his administration attempted to stigmatize, eventually won an Academy Award.

Grenada

On October 25, 1983, the first news regarding an American invasion of the small island nation of Grenada could be found in the newspapers and on radio and television. The story Americans got regarding that invasion said that 3,000 troops had landed on the island and that they were protecting some 1,000 United States citizens living there. All information reaching the public came not from reporters covering the story, but from governmental sources; Reagan had prevented any United States journalists from entering the nation.

Not until after the invasion did representatives of the news media get to enter Grenada, and only then did they discover that the Reagan Administration had manipulated the facts. Instead of the 3,000 troops, the actual number of was 6,000. Although the invasion had been to stop a Russian-backed Cuban push, only 700 Cubans were on the island, and 600 were construction workers. The American journalists could find no evidence of a terrorist training base. Reagan had declared the presence of this base to be much of the reason for the invasion.

During this invasion, the president of the United States had censored the news media by denying them access to the fighting area and the result was inaccurate information reaching the public. By the time journalists were reporting facts, Grenada had become less significant, no longer occupying front pages and lead stories on newscasts. Consequently, many people learned only the government story.*

For other cases regarding censorship of information by the government during the latter half of the twentieth century, see Part II, especially chapters 36-43.

The Reagan administration's concern over security and the integrity of the military classification system led the Department of Defense to order an investigation of procedures for controlling sensitive information at the 14,000 contractors with access to the secrets in 1984. The investigation arose when the government discovered that James D. Harper, Jr., had been stealing classified documents from a military contractor in California and had sold copies of them to Polish intelligence officers. He was arrested and sentenced to life in prison.

The 250 page Harper report, as it became known and announced by the Defense Department on June 29, 1985, found that contractors were not controlling sensitive information, that too many people had security clearances, and that the military should make wholesale changes in its procedures to insure that spying became more difficult. The study found that part of the problem was the sheer size of the classification system in the United States which includes 1.5 million civilians with clearances and over 16 million documents stored at military contractors. The report suggested the need to reduce the number of people with clearances.

On June 29, President Reagan used the release of the report to call for a reduction of foreign espionage agents working in the United States "to a more manageable size." The President called the United Nations a "spy's nest," and

---

*For other cases regarding censorship of information by the government during the latter half of the twentieth century, see Part II, especially chapters 36-43.

he suggested the nation needed to exercise better control over the organization. He also wanted a bigger counter-intelligence operation. Although the report dealt with spying and espionage, it pointed out the overwhelming number of secrets the United States tries to keep from its foes and the nation's desire to exercise tight control over military information.

Although it is sometimes convenient to believe that the United States no longer practices censorship or other forms of restraint on the flow of news and information, forces are still willing to restrict the free flow of information and are working just as hard in the mid 1980s as they were throughout the entire history of the United States. The theorists who have thought about the need for free expression have explored various means for achieving what they consider a reasonable balance between restraint and freedom.

Chapter 33

Free Expression and Suppression: Defining the Limits

The limits of free expression have stimulated perhaps as much debate as any social issue, considering the number of cases that have been argued in the courts, books that have been published, and symposia that have been conducted.

One view on the theories that have governed the regulation of expression was written by Fredrick Siebert, dean-emeritus of the College of Communication Arts at Michigan State University, in *Freedom of the Press in England 1476-1776* (1952):

> One basic assumption appears to be common to all theories of liberty of the press, whether it is the theory of the Tudors, or of the eighteenth century as stated by Blackstone and Mansfield, or the theory of the late eighteenth- and early nineteenth-century libertarians. This assumption is that freedom of the press is not and never can be absolute. All agree that some forms of restraint are necessary and that the government has a legitimate function to define the limitations. They differ only as to the nature and number of these limitations.
>
> Government must necessarily exert some control over the press as it must over all other types of institutions operating in society. All agree that it is the function of government to protect private reputations, to control to some unspecified degree the distribution of obscene matter, and to regulate to a still more vague degree publications which undermine the basic structure of organized society. Henry VIII, John Milton, John Locke, [Sir Horace] Walpole, George III, and even Lord Erskine agree that some government control of the press is necessary. The principal disagreements arise over the standards to be applied in devising and administering controls designed to protect the third objective mentioned above, the preservation of the basic structure of organized society. With this assumption in mind, the following proposition [is] advanced:
>
> The extent of government control of the press depends on the nature of the relationship of the government to those subject to the government. This relationship, which in its nature provides for a greater or lesser degree of accountability, has been identified under such general terms

as Monarchy (absolute or enlightened), Democracy (more or less direct), and Totalitarianism (Communist or Fascist).

With this starting point, eleven major theories of media-State relations can be described. Although each theory—except one— seems to allow a different degree of freedom, there is an underlying unwillingness to allow the media complete freedom. Most of the theories have strong authoritarian roots, and, therefore, set out to describe just how much latitude they wish to permit from total authoritarian control. If one considers the theories as a rational for granting some freedom, the areas of restraint show where the theorists fear the media, and thus cannot bring themselves to grant unrestrained freedom. Each theory is authoritarian minus some degree of freedom—a statement that can even be said about authoritarian England which sometimes gave its printers a degree of freedom.

Theory 1: Absolute Government Control of Expression

The Theory.   The absolute control of expression concerns all types of communication, both private and public, and empowers secular and religious authorities to license, censor, punish, or grant favors to the press to control the flow of information to the public in order to protect the public.   Authorities can protect against seditious communications, defamation, obscenity, unethical commercial publications, defendant trial rights, and anything authorities remotely damaging to church, State, or the people running these institutions. The theory rests on the conviction that only the rulers know everything and only they are wise enough to understand what the public should know.   The underlying principle is that rulers fear the masses and to maintain their power, they have to control the available knowledge.   The theory has controlled information flow since earliest human government and is still practiced in much of the world today.   It does not allow government ownership, but requires government control.

Theory 2: No Previous Restraint

The Theory.   The theory of no previous restraint defines censorship of the press as government exercising its authority to prevent the publication of information it deems dangerous; it applies to all types of public and private communications.   The theory holds that government should not censor—prevent publication—but the government could punish the publisher of "irresponsible" messages after-the-fact. The theory rests on the belief that the public needs to have information, but there are two underlying fears—the government would censor too much, preventing the public access to information it needed and thus should be restrainted; and, second, the press would become capricious and could not be given too much freedom—the threat of punishment for words printed had to be there always.

The Background. The great English legal authority, Sir William Blackstone* (1723-1780), in *Commentaries* (1765-1769), defined the liberty that the press should have as the unlimited right to publish anything it wished (the absence of prior restraint); if the press was irresponsible, it should be punished.

During nineteenth century United States, the post office suppressed the mails of obscenity under the Comstock Law, but although Blackstone's definition of free expression has appeared in American law, very few twentieth century examples can be found. One example was when a district attorney in Minnesota censored an offensive paper under a state statute, but the Supreme Court overturned the action in *Near* v. *Minnesota* (1931).

One of the most famous censorship cases occurred in 1971 over the classified study, "History of U. S. Decision-Making Process on Viet Nam Policy" (popularly known as the Pentagon Papers), when the *New York Times* published portions between June 12 and 14, 1971, and the *Washington Post* published parts on June 18. The Government tried to restrain publication of the document and asked two district courts and two appeals courts for injunctions between June 15 and 23. Because of the seriousness of the matter, the Supreme Court issued opinions—six concurring and three dissenting opinions—on June 30, 1971, upholding the right of both the *New York Times* and the *Washington Post*** failed to prove its case. to publish the Pentagon papers and concluding that the Government had failed to prove its case.

The conflicting views expressed in the Pentagon Papers case raised as many questions as the Court resolved, and the Supreme Court had another opportunity to express its views in the *Nebraska Press Association* v. *Stuart* (1976) case arising from a gag order imposed by a Nebraska state trial judge on "any testimony given or evidence adduced" at a preliminary hearing considering testimony for an alleged mass murderer, Simants. The gag order prevented the broadcast and print media from reporting confessions or other statements made by Simants. The case brought two rights into conflict, the Sixth Amendment guarantee for a "trial by an impartial jury" and the Fourteenth Amendment protection for free expression.

In its review of the case, the Supreme Court did not find that pretrial publicity automatically led to an unfair trial; but, regarding the previous censorship cases, the Supreme Court said:

---

*Much of modern censorship has been the result of states attempting to control obscene materials. In *Kingsley Books, Inc.* v. *Brown* (1957), the Supreme Court affirmed a decision that found fourteen booklets obscene and enjoined their publisher from further distribution of the publications. Four justices, however, dissented. The Supreme Court has not allowed all forms of censorship, especially when it is too broad or vague; see *Freedman* v. *Maryland* (1955) and *Bantam Books, Inc.* v. *Sullivan* (1963) when the Supreme Court held the work of a administrative commission to be censorship.

**For other views on the burden that the government must bear in proving the need for censorship see *Organization for a Better Austin* v. *Keefe* (1971), and a clarification in *Pittsburgh Press Co.* v. *Pittsburgh Commission on Human Relations* (1973), and *United States* v. *Progressive, Inc.* (1979).

The thread running through [*Near*, *Keefe*, and *Pentagon Papers*] is that prior restraints on speech and publication are the most serious and the least tolerable infringement on First Amendment rights. A criminal penalty or a judgment in a defamation case is subject to the whole panoply of protections afforded by deferring the impact of the judgment until all avenues of appellate review have been exhausted. [But] a prior restraint [has] an immediate and irreversible sanction. If it can be said that a threat of criminal or civil sanctions after publication "chills" speech, prior restraint "freezes" it at least for the time . . .

Regardless of how beneficent-sounding the purposes of controlling the press might be, [we] remain skeptical about those measures that would allow government to insinuate itself into the editorial rooms of this Nation's press. In this case, the Court found that it was virtually impossible for a judge to show reason for preventing newspapers or broadcasters from publishing pretrial information,* leading the Department of Justice to move to dismiss the case. The article was published by *The Progressive*. The case was an example of censorship "in the national interest."

As the *Pentagon Papers* case showed, the problem of dealing with the suppression of information that the government considers sensitive has created special problems for the courts. The problem arose again in *United States* v. *Progressive, Inc.* (1979) over an article written by a freelance writer Howard Moreland, "The H-Bomb Secret—How We Got It, Why We're Telling It." The article relied on public documents, but when the editor of *The Progressive* sent a copy to the Department of Energy for technical verification, the department found that some of the information was restricted. When the magazine proceeded with plans to publish the article, the government secured a restraining order and the Court decided that the article contained information that would "irreparably harm the national security of the United States."

The case might have continued had another magazine, *The Press Connection* (Madison, Wisconsin) not printed a similar article leading the Department of Justice to move to dismiss the case. The article was published by *The Progressive*. The case was an example of censorship "in the national interest".**

---

*Other cases involving pretrial suppressions include *WXYZ, Inc.* v. *Hand* (1981); *Smith* v. *Daily Mail Publishing Co.*, (1979); *United States* v. *Layton* (1981); *United States* v. *Sherman* (1978); *Chicago Council of Lawyers* v. *Bauer* (1975), *cert.* denied, (1976).

**The Supreme Court has upheld the right of the CIA to require former employees to secure approval from the Director of the CIA when they intend to publish information acquired while employed by the CIA, see *Snepp* v. *United States* (1980); see also, *Alfred A Knopf* v. *Colby*, *cert.* denied, rehearing denied (1975).

Prior restraint = most dangerous

Theory 3: Bad Tendency and Constructive Intent

The Theory. "Bad tendency" means that the words someone says may have the *tendency* to cause bad actions immediately or at some future time. It is not necessary that the actions have taken place, so the jury only has to decide if the communication might cause some bad action. Implicit in the phrase is interest in the audience. If any member of the audience might have been in a position to take action on the words, then an adverse judgment would have to be rendered. Intent allows the jury to decide what the writer's motivations are—an impossible task. These two tests revived the standards of the Alien and Sedition Acts of 1798 during World War I through interpretations of the Espionage Act of 1917. The theory applies primarily to seditious utterances, rather than to private publication.

The theory rests on the belief that journalists are irresponsible and have be watched at every turn. The only truly responsible authority is believed to be government, and all statements are tested against the "truth" of government. This theory was only slightly different from the absolute government control theory.

The Background. The district court cases during World War I regarding the Espionage Act of 1917, with the exception of *Masses Publishing Co.* v. *Patten* (1917), relied on the doctrines of bad tendency and constructive intent. In the nearly two thousand Espionage Act cases handled by district courts of the United States, opinions were accepted as statements of fact and reviewed to see if they differed from the views Congress expressed in its resolutions or statements made by the President. If they did, the trial went against the defendant. The standard allowed the conviction for saying World War I was contrary to the will of Christ and for criticizing the YMCA or the Red Cross. *Bad tendency* and *constructive intent* had the effect of suppressing all public discussion because it was a subjective standard that changed with different judges and juries. A change began when the Supreme Court reviewed convictions under the Espionage Act.

Theory 4: "Clear and Present Danger"

The Theory. This theory displaced the constructive intent and bad tendency views of the district courts with an objective standard for determining what words might be suppressed. The test was that there "must be a clear and present [immediate] danger" of serious action taking place before more communications could occur. The theory conceded that government had to have the right to suppress some communication to protect the safety of its citizens, but the communication must meet a rigid and objective test. The theory related primarily to political or public communication rather than private publication in its earlier development, but it began to take on a wider perspective later.

The theory relies on the belief that in a democracy as much communication as possible is necessary to insure that the nation reaches the best judgments—even to the point of saying or writing some offensive things. The theory trusts discussion and the mass media more than government and places a narrow limit on government restraint, but the theory did not give publishers unlimited freedom.

The Background. This new concept on the limits of expression was articulated by Justice Oliver W. Holmes in his landmark opinion, *Schenck* v. *United States* (1919). However, a similar objective test had been articulated by Judge Learned Hand in *Masses Publishing Co.* v. *Patten* (Southern District, New York, 1917).

The test substituted an objective test for the subjective standard of the district courts—expression that had an obvious and immediate chance of leading to dangerous actions could be suppressed. This concept was given considerable intellectual support by Zechariah Chafee, Jr., in his landmark book, *Free Speech in the United States* (1920). Holmes was to draw a tighter line on the meaning of "clear and present danger" in *Abrams* v. *United States* (1919).

A series of cases involving the state criminal syndicalism laws and the right of citizens to distribute literature door to door and to assemble in public places began testing the limits of what could be said. The Supreme Court sustained the conviction of Anita Whitney in *Whitney* v. *California* (1927), but a more strict protection of free expression emerged under the Charles Evans Hughes Court, beginning with *Fiske* v. *Kansas* (1927), the overthrowing of a decision suppressing the use of the red flag in *Stromberg* v. *California* (1931), and the support of the right to peacefully assemble in *De Jonge* v. *Oregon* (1937) and *Herndon* v. *Lowry* (1937). The door-to-door solicitation cases, including *Lovell* v. *Griffin* (1938) and *Cantwell* v. *Connecticut* (1940), further provided protection for free speech that was not directly leading to violence. Special support came in *Near* v. *Minnesota* (1931), which rejected prior restraint doctrine except in a "clear and present danger" situation, applying the First Amendment protections to state laws.

The freedom of assembly cases provided another avenue for the Supreme Court to insure that people had the right to gather in public places to peaceably discuss their interests. These cases included *Hague* v. *Committee for Industrial Organization* (1939) and *Milk Wagon Drivers Union* v. *Meadowmoor Dairies* (1941).

In *American Communications Association, C.I.O.* v. *Douds* (1950), the Supreme Court upheld the non-Communist affidavit provision of the Labor Management Relations Act of 1947 which directed the National Labor Relations Board (NLRB) not to recognize a labor organization unless all officers filed affidavits saying that they were not members of the Communist Party or supported its views. The Court saw no conflict with the "clear and present danger" interpretation of the First Amendment freedoms.

The "clear and present" danger standard underwent extensive analysis by the Supreme Court in the advocacy of unlawful conduct cases beginning with *Dennis* v. *United States* (1951). The case arose because Dennis and eleven of his associates in the Central Committee of the Communist party were indicted in July 1948, for violations of the Smith Act provisions against advocacy and organizing. The petitioners according to the Court of Appeals belonged to a party that:

clear + present Dan[g]er test created — 1919

... is a highly disciplined organization, adept at infiltration into strategic positions, use of aliases, and double-meaning language; that the Party is rigidly controlled; that Communists, unlike other political parties, tolerate no dissension from the policy laid down by the guiding forces; ... that the literature of the Party and the statements and activities of its leaders, petitioners here, advocate, and the general goal of the Party was, during the period in question, to achieve a successful overthrow of the exiting order by force and violence.

The majority opinion delivered by Chief Justice Fred M. Vinson (1890-1953) rested the case on the Holmes-Brandeis "clear and present danger" test and held that government did not have to wait on the sidelines until a group advocating the overthrow of the government was about to take its action. The Court "reject[ed] the contention that success or probability of success [was] the criterion" and concluded by upholding the Smith Act:

We hold that . . . the Smith Act [does] not inherently, or as construed or applied in the instant case, violate the First Amendment and other provisions of the Bill of Rights . . . Petitioners intended to overthrow the government of the United States as speedily as the circumstances would permit. Their conspiracy to organize the Communist Party and to teach and advocate the overthrow of the Government of the United States by force and violence created a "clear and present danger" of an attempt to overthrow the Governent by force and violence. They were properly and constitutionally convicted.

Justices William O. Douglas and Hugo Black dissented from the majority. Douglas was appalled by the majority and said, "[N]ever until today has anyone seriously thought that the ancient law of conspiracy could constitutionally be used to turn speech into seditious conduct.   Yet that is precisely what is suggested."

A few years later, in *Yates* v. *United States* (1957), fourteen individuals who were leaders in the California Communist Party were accused of conspiring to advocate the overthrow of the Government of the United States.   They were convicted in the United States District Court for the Southern District of California; the Court of Appeals supported the district court's decision.

The majority of the Supreme Court, in an opinion delivered by Justice John M. Harlan (1899-1971), considered *Yates* substantially different from that of *Dennis* in that *Dennis* involved a situation where advocacy of an immediate concrete action was involved— different from some abstract advocacy of an action at some future time. *Yates*, said the Court, was an abstract future-time matter. Thus, the Court distinguished between *advocacy of abstract doctrine* and *advocacy of action*:

We are thus faced with the question whether the Smith Act prohibits advocacy and teaching of forcible overthrow as an abstract principle,

Dennis (1951) treated differently from Yates (1957)

divorced from any effort to instigate action to that end, so long as such advocacy or teaching is engaged in with evil intent. We hold that it does not.

As a result of its review, the Court ordered the acquittal of five petitioners and allowed the retrial of nine; but the government decided it could not meet evidence tests required by the Supreme Court, and requested dismissal. Justices Black and Douglas objected to the decision in part, wishing all of the defendants to be acquitted because they believed that the Smith Act was a violation of the First Amendment.

Theory 5: Syndicalism and "Clear and Present Danger"

The Background. The question of state criminal syndicalism laws came to the attention of the Supreme Court in *Brandenburg* v. *Ohio* (1969). Brandenburg was leader of a Ku Klux Klan group that was covered in some television film clips in which speakers claimed that the group would march on Congress and had made defamatory comments about Jews and Blacks. The majority of the Supreme Court overturned Ohio's Criminal Syndicalism Act because it failed to distinguished between "mere advocacy . . . [and] incitement to imminent lawless action." The Supreme Court used the decision also to reverse the findings of *Whitney*.

Later, the Supreme Court used loyalty oath decisions to further clarify the limits of constitutional protections. In *Cole* v. *Richardson* (1972), the Court decided:

> Since there is no constitutionally protected right to overthrow a government by force, violence, or illegal or unconstitutional means, no constitutional right is infringed by an oath to abide by the constitutional system in the future. Therefore there is no requirement that one who refuses to take the Massachusetts oath be granted a hearing for the determination of some other fact before being discharged.

A contempt of court case, *Wood* v. *Georgia* (1962), started in Bibb County, Georgia, over an allegation that a large bloc of the Black vote had been bought. The judge conducting a grand jury review in the case had held a news conference with reporters to give them information regarding the case. The sheriff of Bibb County was offended and issued his own news release, calling the news conference "race agitation." The Sheriff was cited on July 7, 1960, for contempt because of his statement. On appeal to the Supreme Court, the Court was told:

> If a State is unable to punish persons for expressing their views on matters of great public importance when those matters are being considered in an investigation by the grand jury, a clear and present danger to the administration of justice will be created. [But the Supreme Court was not persuaded.] We find no such danger in the record before us.

Theory 6: Preferred Position

The Theory. The preferred position theory suggests that freedom of expression was the most important of the human rights guaranteed by the First Amendment to the Constitution because expression makes the processes of a democratic society function properly. The theory held when another right was in conflict with the right of free expression, expression was considered the more important right in all but the most exceptional cases. The theory rests on the conviction that public debate is the most likely avenue to resolving issues and on a fear of too much governmental intervention in human affairs. The theory applied primarily to public communication, but also applied to private publication as in the Jehovah's Witnesses cases when members of the organization were protected in their right of expression.

The Background. A number of cases during the 1930s and 1940s developed the concept of a "preferred position" for the First Amendment protections of free expression. These cases provided some foundation for the absolute interpretations of Justices Black and Douglas. The important cases in this progression included *Herndon* v. *Lowry* (1937): "The power of a state to abridge freedom of speech and of assembly is the exception"; *United States* v. *Carolene Products Co.* (1938), which rephrased *Herndon* and *Schneider* v. *Irvington* (1939) in which the Court noted:

> Mere legislative preferences or beliefs respecting matters of public con-
> venience may well support regulation directed at other personal activities,
> but be insufficient to justify [actions that diminish] the exercise of rights
> so vital to the maintenance of democratic institutions. In another case,
> *Bridges* v. *California* (1941) the court observed:
> What finally emerges from the "clear and present danger" cases is
> a working principle that the substantive evil must be extremely serious
> and the degree of imminence extremely high before utterances can be
> punished.

The Jehovah's Witness cases discussed earlier gave strong position for ex-
pression, but the first time the term "preferred position" was used was in *Jones* v. *Opelika* (1942). Other cases to subscribe to the preference for the First Amendment include *West Virginia State Board of Education* v. *Barnette* (1943) and *Thomas* v. *Collins* (1945):

> [A]ny attempt to restrict those liberties must be justified by clear public
> interest, threatened not doubtfully or remotely, but by clear and present
> danger. The rational connection between the remedy provided and the evil
> to be curbed, which in other contexts might support legislation against
> attack on due process grounds, will not suffice. These rights rest on
> firmer foundation . . . Only the gravest abuses, endangering paramount
> interests, give occasion for permissible limitation.

Freedom of expression = most important, overrides all

This strong language was a minority view of four of the justices. In this case, the majority had concluded that a union organizer who had refused to secure a required registration card (that a government official had no right to withhold) had lost his right to engage in organizing efforts without the card.

Theory 7: Public Speech v. Private Speech

The Theory. This theory was first expressed in 1948 by Alexander Meiklejohn (1872-1964), founder of the San Francisco School of Social Studies (1938), in *Free Speech And Its Relation to Self-Government* (1948), as a way to separate publication of private communication such as defamation and obscenity, for which Meiklejohn believed there must be restrictions, and public speech for which there must be no restrictions. The theory rests on the view that truth can prevail in political discourse only when all views are given non-threatening expression. This means that government could not censor public communication at any level. The theory proposes the need for free and open discussion and rests upon a fear that government will repress the dialog. However, there is another conviction—the rights of individual citizens have to be protected because of their fraility. The defamed need a way to recover damages to reputation; children require protection from obscenity; and the gullible have to be protected from unethical advertisers. Thus, the theory applies different standards to public and private speech using the First Amendment for public and the Fifth Amendment for private communication.

The Background. One of the problems that has plagued those wishing to grant greater freedom of expression has been that there are two broad categories of expression. One form deals with public matters such as civil rights, taxation, foreign policy, and public budgets. Most libertarians have argued for wide latitude for public speech—such as the "clear and present danger" test. But the second form of publication, more private in nature, has created problems for those wanting to grant as much freedom to expression as possible.

Meiklejohn developed an argument to deal with the problem by dividing speech into an absolute form of expression in the case of public speech protected under the First Amendment, ("Congress shall make no law,") and less freedom to private speech protected under the Fifth Amendment.

Meiklejohn developed his argument because he was unable to free all forms of speech from some limitations—a liberalizing for which he could find no justification. He saw three underlying principles that must be considered in the interpretation of the First Amendment and free expression:

> Let it be noted that, by those words, Congress is not debarred from all action upon freedom of speech. Legislation which abridges that freedom is forbidden, but not legislation to enlarge and enrich it. The freedom of mind which befits the members of a self-governing society is not a given and fixed part of human nature. It can be increased and established by learning, by teaching, by the unhindered flow of accurate information, by giving men health and vigor and security, by bringing them together in

activities of communication and mutual understanding. And the federal legislature is not forbidden to engage in that positive enterprise of cultivating the general intelligence upon which the success of self-government so obviously depends. On contrary, in that positive field the Congress of the United States has a heavy and basic responsibility to promote the freeedom of speech.

And second, no one who reads with care the text of the First Amendment can fail to be startled by its absoluteness. The phrase, "Congress shall make no law . . . abridging the freedom of speech," is unqualified. It admits no exceptions. To say that no laws of a given type shall be made means that no laws of that type shall, under any circumstances, be made. That prohibition holds good in war as in peace, in danger as in security. The men who adopted the Bill of Rights were not ignorant of the necessities of war or of national danger. It would, in fact, be nearer to the truth to say that it was exactly those necessities which they had in mind as they planned to defend freedom of discussion against them. Out of their own bitter experience they knew how terror and hatred, how war and strife, can drive men into acts of unreasoning suppression. They planned, therefore, both for the peace which they desired and for the wars which they feared. And in both cases they established, an absolute, unqualified prohibition of the abridgment of the freedom of speech. That same requirement, for the same reasons, under the same Constitution, holds good today.

Against what has just been said it will be answered that twentieth-century America does not accept "absolutes" so readily as did the eighteenth century. But to this we must reply that the issue here involved cannot be dealt with by such twentieth-century a priori reasoning. It requires careful examination of the structure and functioning of our political system as a whole to see what part the principle of the freedom of speech plays, here and now, in that system. And when that examination is made, it seems to me clear that for our day and generation, the words of the First Amendment mean literally what they say. And what they say is that under no circumstances shall the freedom of speech be abridged. Whether or not that opinion can be justified is the primary issue with which this argument tries to deal.

But, third, this dictum which we rightly take to express the most vital wisdom which men have won in their striving for political freedom is yet—it must be admitted—strangely paradoxical. No one can doubt that, in any well-governed society, the legislature has both the right and the duty to prohibit certain forms of speech. Libellous assertions may be, and must be, forbidden and punished. So too must slander. Words which incitement to crime are themselves criminal and must be dealt with as such. Sedition and treason may be expressed by speech or writing. And, in those cases, decisive repressive action by the government is imperative for the sake of the general welfare. All these necessities that speech be limited are recognized and provided for under the Constitution. They were not unknown to the writers of the First Amendment. That amendment, then, we may take it for granted, does not forbid the abridging of speech. But, at the same time, it does forbid the abridging of the freedom of speech. It is to the solving of that paradox, that apparent self-contradiction, that we are summoned if, as free men, we wish to know what the right of freedom of speech is . . .

Meiklejohn went on to explain the difference he saw between two types of communication—one that provided extensive freedom, and one that provided limited freedom.

. . . [I]t may be asserted that our civil liberties, in general, are not all of one kind. They are of two kinds which, though radically different in constitutional status, are easily confused. And that confusion has been, and is, disastrous in its effect upon our understanding of the relations between an individual citizen and the government of the United States . . .

As an instance of the first kind of civil liberty I would offer that of religious or irreligious belief. In this country of ours, so far as the Constitution is effective, men are free to believe and to advocate or to disbelieve and to argue against, any creed. And the government is unqualifiedly forbidden to restrict that freedom. As an instance of the second kind, we may take the liberty of an individual to own, and to use the income from, his labor or his property. It is agreed among us that every man has a right, a liberty, to such ownership and use. And yet it is also agreed that the government may take whatever part of a man's income it deems necessary for the promoting of the general welfare. The liberty of owning and using property is, then, as contrasted with that of religious belief, a limited one. It may be invaded by the government. And the Constitution authorizes such invasion. It requires only that the procedure shall be properly and impartially carried out and that it shall be justified by public need.

Our Constitution, then, recognizes and protects two different sets of freedoms. One of these is open to restriction by the government. The other is not open to such restriction. It would be of great value to our argument and, in fact, to all attempts at political thinking in the United States, if there were available two sharply defined terms by which to identify these two fundamentally different kinds of civil liberty . . .

If, however, as our argument has tried to show, the principle of the freedom of speech is derived, not from some suppposed "Natural Right," but from the necessities of self-government by universal suffrage, there follows at once a very large limitation of the scope of the principle. The guarantee given by the First Amendment is not, then, assured to all speaking. It is assured only to speech which bears, directly or indirectly upon issues with which voters have to deal—only, therefore, to the consideration of matters of public interest. Private speech, or private interest in speech, on the other hand, has no claim whatever to the protection of the First Amendment. If men are engaged, as we so commonly are, in argument, or inquiry, or advocacy, or incitement which is directed toward our private interests, private privileges, private possessions, we are, of course, entitled to "Due Process" protection of those activities.

But the First Amendment has no concern over such protection. That pronouncement remains forever confused and unintelligible unless we draw sharply and clearly the line which separates the public welfare of the community from the private goods of any individual citizen or group of citizens.

—*Free Speech and the Relation to Self-Government* (1949)

Meiklejohn presented an argument for dividing two classes of speech so that the specific wording of the First Amendment would not be tampered by the prosecution of libel, slander, and obscenity which he placed under the Fifth Amendment; however, Meiklejohn's argument has not been adopted in modern judicial interpretations nor has it received wide acceptance among legal scholars. Consequently, one must look elsewhere in trying to clarify currently accepted positions on free expression.

Theory 8: An Absolute Right

The Theory. This theory was a creation largely of Justices William O. Douglas and Hugo L. Black of the Supreme Court who believed that nothing should restrain any form of communication, private or public, and that publications should not be punished after the fact. The theory rested on the belief that the best way to solve political problems was through discussion, but it went further by believing that all communication should enjoy free reign from any form of government restraint. The only limitation, according to the theory, should be people's independent right to refuse any communication they do not wish to consider. The theory relied on the conviction of the value of all communication, upon a fear of any government interference, and upon a confidence in the ability of people to select that which is best for them. The theory has not been widely adopted by the Supreme Court.

The Background. Ten years after Meiklejohn wrote his dual rights theory, Justice William O. Douglas (1898-1980) proposed that free expression under the First Amendment to the Constitution should be very nearly absolute in *The Right of the People* (1958). Douglas made no attempt to differentiate betweeen public and private speech as Meiklejohn had done:

In the totalitarian State there is freedom of expression in a limited sense. In Russia there are great debates concerning the course to follow, the choice of procedures, the policy that should be adopted in factories or on farms. Criticism fills the papers and magazines of Russia. But this criticism and debate do not challenge communism as a system. Rather,

Absolute right = no restraint (Block) via ability of the
masses to choose
= both to public and private speech

they assume that communism is the ideal state. Once that postulate is express or implied, discussion and debate go on apace. The same seems to be true in Red China, where the communist regime recently approved a new slogan derived from the Chinese classics: "Let hundreds of schools crow in competition." Yet in both Soviet Russia and Red China, if the discussion goes so far as to question the premise on which communism rests, it is condemned as counterrevolutionary.

My thesis is that there is no free speech in the full meaning of the term unless there is freedom to challenge the very postulates on which the existing regime rests. It is my belief that our First Amendment must be placed in that broad frame of reference and construed to permit even discourse or advocacy that strikes at the very foundation of our institutions. The First Amendment was a new and bold experiment. It staked everything on unlimited public discussion. It chose among conflicting values, selecting freedom to talk, to argue, and to advocate as a preferred right. It placed us on the side of free discussion and advocacy, come what may . . .

The First Amendment does not say that there is freedom of expression provided the talk is not "dangerous." It does not say that there is freedom of expression provided the utterance has no tendency to subvert. It does not put free speech and freedom of the press in the category of housing, sanitation, hours of work, factory conditions, and the like, and make it subject to regulation for the public good. Nor does it permit legislative restraint of freedom of expression so long as the regulation does not offend due process. All notions of regulation or restraint by government are absent from the First Amendment. For it says in words that are unambiguous, "Congress shall make no law . . . abridging the freedom of speech, or of the press . . ."

This guarantee plays a unique role. The compact of the Constitution is a compact of We The People. The ultimate political power is in the people. They can alter, revise, or undo what they created any time they choose. While the compact lasts, the various agencies of government are responsible to the people. The people elect their law-makers and their Chief Executive for limited terms only. Those who exercise authority must have it recurringly renewed at the hands of the people. The people are, indeed, the final repository of all power . . .

Every majority tends to acquire a vested interest in the *status quo*. The values represented by their economic, political, racial, or religious interests seem to them to be the expression of the ultimate. They cling tenaciously to them and look on the minority with antagonism and suspicion. In a State under the domination of the church, the teaching of evolution might be deemed subversive. In a State ruled by atheists, religion might be deemed subversive . . .

When sovereignty rests in a man or in a majority, suppression of a minority may be necessary to protect and safeguard the *status quo*. But when sovereignty is in the people, it is distributed equally and indivisibly

should be restricted (not even overthrow)

among every member of the group. The conformists and the noncon-formists alike can claim the privilege. So can the reactionaries and the revolutionaries, those who believe in *laissez faire* and those who believe in the dictatorship of the proletariat. That, at least, is the theory. And freedom of expression is as integral a part of the rights of sovereignty as running for office or voting.

Freedom of expression is a necessary political right once the people have the full right of sovereignty. It is indeed the only guarantee that the people will be kept adequately informed to discharge the awesome responsibilities of sovereignty. Without freedom of expression, only some public issues might be canvassed. Without it, the nation might drift to a pattern of conformity that loses all relation to the world and its large affairs . . .

Freedom of expression must cover the entire public domain. The public domain includes more than election issues. . . . If the people are to be wise sovereigns, there must be no restraints or limits on cultural, scientific, artistic, or intellectual endeavor . . .

Yet in practice, Justice Douglas' concept of First Amendment protections was not absolute. When he was called on to react to the registration of the Communist Party in *Communist Party* v. *Subversive Activities Control Board* (1961), he agreed that the registration was valid because:

. . . more than debate, discourse, argumentation, propaganda, and other aspects of free speech and association are involved. An additional element enters, *viz.*, espionage, business activities, or the formation of cells for subversion, as well as the use of speech, press and association by a foreign power to produce on this continent a Soviet satellite.

Douglas seemed to see the element of action besides speech in the case of the Communist Party of the United States. Nevertheless, many of his opinions reflected an absolute view of the First Amendment, and at least one Supreme Court Justice went further than Douglas.

Justice Hugo L. Black (1886-1971) was remarkably consistant in his adoption of an absolutist approach to the First Amendment. Speaking at the James Madison Lecture at New York University (1960), Justice Black observed: "It is my belief that there are 'absolutes' in our Bill of Rights, and that they were put there on purpose by men who knew what words meant and meant their prohibitions to be 'absolutes.'" He added:

The whole history and background of the Constitution and Bill of Rights, as I understand it, belies the assumption or conclusion that our ultimate constitutional freedoms are no more than our English ancestors had when they came to this land to get new freedoms. The historical and practical purposes of a Bill of Rights, the very use of a written Constitution, indigenous to America, the language the Framers used, the kind of three-department government they took pains to set up, all point to the creation of a government which was denied all power to do some things under any and all circumstances, and all power to do other things except precisely in the manner described.

Justice Black remarked in 1962:

I learned a long time ago that there are affirmitive and negative words. The beginning of the First Amendment is that "Congress shall make no Law."

Of course, some will remark that that is too simple on my part. To them, all this discussion of mine is too simple, because I come back to saying that these few plain words actually mean what they say, and I know of no college professor or law school professor, outside of my friend, Professor [Edmond N.] Cahn [professor of law at New York University] here, and a few others, who could not write one hundred pages to show that the Amendment does not mean what it says.

Black's First Amendment views appeared in his dissent in *Communist Party* v. *Communist Control Board* (1961):

The enforcement of [the Alien and Sedition Acts of 1798], particularly the Sedition Act, constitutes one of the greatest blots on our country's record of freedom. Publishers were sent to jail for writing their own views and for publishing the views of others. The slightest criticism of government or policies of government officials was enough to cause biased federal prosecutors to put the machinery of Government to work to crush and imprision the critic . . . Members of the Jeffersonian Party were picked out as special targets so that they could be illustrious examples of what could happen to people who failed to sing paeans of praise for current federal officials and their policies . . .

I feel impelled to recount this history of the Federalist Sedition Act because, in all truth, it must be pointed out that this law—which has since been almost universally condemned as unconstitutional—did not go as far in suppressing the First Amendment freedoms of Americans as do the Smith Act and the Subversive Activities Control Act.

Black's position of providing as much latitude for expression as possible was reflected in his dissent to *Dennis* v. *United States* (1951) and his reiteration in *Yates* v. *United States* (1957) in which he and Justice Douglas believed that the Smith Act prosecutions of the two cases violated the First Amendment protections. Justices Black and Douglas could find no reason for the "clear and present danger test" in their concurring opinions in *Brandenburg* v. *Ohio* (1969).

In a series of cases called "loudspeaker cases" because they involved sound trucks driving through communities with their equipment blaring loud sounds, Justice Black had the opportunity to develop his attitudes towards free expression. Justice Douglas wrote the majority opinion in *Saia* v. *New York* (1948) with Justice Black joining. They held that a sound amplification ordinance was "previous restraint" on free speech because the ordinance was a standardless law. Then, in *Kovacs* v. *Cooper* (1949), Justice Black, with concurrence from Justices Douglas and Rutledge dissented, from the majority by objecting:

> [T]he court denies speech amplifiers the constitutional shelter recognized by our decisions and . . . goes beyond a mere prior censorship of all loud speakers . . . [and] wholly bars the use of all loud speakers mounted upon any vehicle in any of the City's public streets . . . The basic premise of the First Amendment is that all present instruments of communication, as well as others that inventive genius may bring into being, shall be free from governmental censorship or prohibitions.

In the loyalty oath case, *Cole* v. *Richardson* (1972), Justice Douglas, dissenting from the majority, agreed that serious danger might give the government the right "to compel citizens to do things which would ordinarily be beyond their authority to mandate." But he thought, "Perhaps we have become so inundated with a variety of these oaths that we tend to ignore the difficult constitutional issues they present." Black held to similar views in the Bar Admission cases, *Konigsberg* v. *State Bar* (1957), and *Konigsberg* II (1961), and in *American Communications Association, C.I.O.* v. *Douds* (1950): "Never before has this Court held that the Government could for any reason attaint persons for their political beliefs or affiliations."

Justice Black did not limit his objection to the "clear and present danger" test. He dissented *In Re Anastaplo* (1961) with the concurrence of Chief Justice Earl Warren (1891-1974) and Justices Douglas and William J. Brennan (1906-):

> If I had ever doubted that the "balancing" test comes close to being a doctrine of governmental absolutism—that to "balance" an interest in individual liberty means almost inevitably to destroy that liberty—those doubts would have been dissipated by this case. [The] effect of the Court's "balancing" here is that any State may now reject an applicant for admission to the Bar if he believes in the Declaration of Independence as strongly as Anastaplo and if he is willing to sacrifice his career and his means of livelihood in defense of the freedoms of the First Amendment.

In *Columbia Broadcasting System, Inc.* v. *Democratic National Committee* (1973), Justice Douglas, in a concurring opinion, took the opportunity to say that he was totally opposed to the Fairness Doctrine, the federal statute allowing the FCC to take action against stations that did not give balanced treatment to important public issues. He said he saw the doctrine as a weakening of the First Amendment protection from government interference; he claimed the doctrine "puts the head of the camel inside the tent." Similarly, both Justices Douglas and Black had earlier opposed the censorship that had occured in *New York Times Co.* v. *United States* (1971)—the Pentagon Papers case.

When Paul Branzburg, a Louisville, Kentucky, reporter, refused to tell a grand jury the names of those whom he had seen possessing marijuana, he was tried and convicted of contempt of court; *Branzburg* v. *Hayes* (1972), but the Supreme Court reviewed the case sustaining the Kentucky Court of Appeals which rejected a First Amendment privilege. Justice Douglas believed there was no compelling need for the government to know the information that Branzburg had so long as the reporter had not committed a crime; therefore, "His immunity . . . is . . . quite complete."

In *New York Times Co.* v. *Sullivan* (1964), which established the "public official" interpretation, Justice Black with Justice Douglas concurring wanted the record to show that in his opinion the First and Fourteenth Amendments prohibited public figures from recovering damages.

The views of Justices Black and Douglas helped shape the concept that the First Amendment provided an absolute freedom, but the view did not persuade a majority of the Court.

A ringing defense of the need for unlimited freedom of expression came from John C. Merrill while, professor of journalism at the University of Missouri, in his book *The Imperative of Freedom: A Philosophy of Journalistic Autonomy* (1974), disagreed with the underlying premise of the social responsibility theorists:

> It is interesting that these persons recognize that it is not yet quite the time to drop the term "free" from their catechism, and so they plunge ahead brainwashing others (even themselves, evidently) into believing that a press can be both "free" and "responsible" in some kind of collective, monolithic or commonly-accepted way. This, of course, is a myth and a logical contradiction: if a newspaper, for example, must be "socially responsible" according to some *outside* standard, then quite logically, its editorial freedom is curtailed. It need not accept this-or-that as its responsibility if it is an autonomous and freely acting agent. This is what is interesting about such journalistic cliches as the press "being a fourth branch of government" or a "watchdog on government"; a free press (or units thereof) has no reason to consider itself either of these. Press units of a free journalistic system are *whatever* they want to be; they might even decide to be government supporters and apologists.

To Merrill, the ideal system is one of "[p]ress libertarianism . . . pure . . . uncontrolled, full, unregulated *laissez-faire* journalism—with a separation of State and press." Although no such system has ever existed, he suggests that journalists should dedicate themselves to keeping the system as "pure" as possible *by keeping control of their own journalistic decisions* and by thwarting as vigorously as possible any *outside* power or control.

Theory 9: Balancing of Rights

The Theory. The Bill of Rights and the Constitution contain a number of rights that are to be protected. The theory of balancing of rights holds that all rights are of equal weight and have to be balanced on a situation by situation basis so that the greatest good would be achieved. The judgment, of course, rests with legislatures and the judicial branch of government. The theory started with the fear that any right given unbounded supremacy would eventually injure the government or its citizens. The belief that the goverment has the right to protect itself against too much expression dominates the theory; underneath the theory is the fear of the public found in classical authoritarianism. The theory has been applied to all types of communication.

The Background. The concept that the Bill of Rights protects several rights that must be balanced has gained some favor among a legal scholars and some justices of the Supreme Court. Laurent Frantz discussed the concept in a *Yale Law Review* article, "The First Amendment in the Balance" (1962):

> We are discussing the theory that the first amendment has no hard core, that it protects not rights but "interests," that those "interests" are to be weighed against "competing interests" on a case-to-case basis and protected only when not found to be outweighed.
> This theory would seem to reduce the problem to one of expediency rather than principle since to weigh freedom of speech against considerations of mere expediency would be impossible if one could not treat the two as commensurable. One's need for a new car may be balanced against the other uses to which the same money might be put, but not against "Thou shalt not steal." But the theory, though it characterizes freedom of speech as always expendable, does not, per se, say anything about the position it should occupy on the value scale of expediencies. Accordingly, it is conceivable that a court might apply the balancing test, yet attach so high a value to freedom of speech that the balance would nearly always be stuck in its favor. It is even conceivable that a balancer who attached a very high value to freedom of speech might decide in its favor more often than a definer who applied a narrow definition . . .

The major proponent of a balancing theory of the First Amendment was Justice Felix Frankfurter (1882-1965) who wrote in his concurrence in *Dennis* v. *United States* (1951):

> The demands of free speech in a democratic society as well as the interest in national security are better served by candid and informed weighing of the competing interests, within the confines of the judicial process, than by announcing dogmas too inflexible for the non-Euclidian [scholar] . . .
> But how are competing interests to be assessed? Since they are not subject to quantitative ascertainment, the issue necessarily resolves itself

into asking, who is to make the adjustment?—who is to balance the relevant factors and ascertain which interest is in the circumstances to prevail? Full responsibility for the choice cannot be givem to the courts. Courts are not representative bodies. They are not designed to be good reflex of a democratic society . . .

Primary responsibility for adjusting the interests which compete in the situation before us of necessity belongs to the Congress . . . We are to set aside the judgment of those whose duty it is to legislate only if there is no reasonable basis for it . . . Free-speech cases are not an exception to the principle that we are not legislators, that direct policy-making is not our province. How best to reconcile competing interests is the business of legislatures, and the balance they strike is a judgment not to be displaced by ours . . . A survey of the relevant decisions indicates that the results which we have reached are on the whole those that would ensue from careful weighing of conflicting interests.

The concept of balance was given support by the majority in *Barenblatt* v. *United States* (1959), a case involving congressional interrogation of a teacher who was cited for contempt of Congress for refusing to answer questions. The majority agreed:

> . . . the balance between the individual and the governmental interests here at stake must be struck in favor of the latter, and that therefore the provisions of the First Amendment have not been offended. (Justice Black, with whom Chief Justice Warren and Justice Douglas agreed, dissented from the majority.)

As Frantz observed, the balancing test allowed the Court to side first one way and then the opposite way on the same question, as in *Gibson* v. *Florida Legislative Investigation Committee* (1963) and *NAACP* v. *Alabama* (1968), when the Court held that the Florida committee could not have access to the membership list of the NAACP. In *Uphaus* v. *Wyman* (1959), the Supreme Court sustained a contempt of court citation for Uphaus, executive director of World Fellowship, for refusing to produce a list of guests at the camp run by the organization in New Hampshire. Based on this, Frantz observed:

> Accordingly, the only difference between a balancing first amendment and none at all is that it permits the balance to be struck twice, first by Congress and then again by the courts.
>
> If a balancing test is applied to the first amendment, it is hard to see why it should not be applied to the entire Constitution. If the first amendment, and only the first amendment, can be balanced away, then that amendment is assigned a status inferior to the rest of the Constitution. Thus the Court has, for the moment, achieved an ironic inversion of the old theory that the first amendment has a *preferred* status.

Balancing of these rgiht belongs to Congress

Wallace Mendelson disagreed with Frantz in "On the Meaning of the First Amendment: Absolutes in the Balance" (*California Law Review*, 1962):

> Above all, the open balancing technique is calculated to leave "the sovereign prerogative of choice" to the people—with the least interference that is compatible with our tradition of judicial review . . .
>
> My point is that liberals appreciate the political processes far too little, and expect far more from judicial review than it has ever been able to deliver. Conservatives no longer make this mistake. They know the cost and fraility of a preferred place in the court . . .
>
> Sooner or later libertarians will have to face it—the real victories are won in legislatures and at the polls. Man after all is a political, not a legal, animal.

The theory received continuing support in Justice Harry A. Blackmun's (1908-) opinion in *New York Times Co.* v. *United States* (1971) when he said:

> The First Amendment, after all, is only one part of an entire Constitution . . . Each provision of the Constitution is important, and I cannot subscribe to a doctrine of unlimited absolutism for the First Amendment at the cost of downgrading other provisions . . . What is needed here is a weighing.

The debate, continues while the courts try to establish the proper line between expression that is protected and that which is not.

Theory 10: Expression and Action: The Dividing Line

The Theory. The theory of free expression is very clear: expression must not be touched by government action; action could be prosecuted. The theory is, in effect, an absolute First Amendment interpretation and applies to all forms of publication, public and private. The theory differs little from that held by Justice Black, except that it tries to systematically analyze all possible types of situations where the question of limiting free expression might arise and reach a solution to the legal questions raised.

The Background. Some years later, Thomas I. Emerson, Lines Professor of Law at Yale University School of Law, constructed his theory of the First Amendment, culminating in *The System of Freedom of Expression* (1970). Emerson set out to develop a framework in which all questions regarding expression could be answered, including creating and performing music, protesting against societal ills, remaining silent, expressing opinions, publishing pornography, and arguing for the overthrow of government. The theory must define the limits, if any, that must be imposed on the dissemination of ideas.

The fundamental concept of Emerson's theory is a distinction between expression and action—different standards apply to each.

Emerson recognized that belief precedes expression and he held that his theory insured the right to hold a belief:

> Considering the problem within the confines here outlined, the right to freedom of belief falls readily within the coverage of the First Amendment. Coercion of belief plainly constitutes an "abridgment" of freedom of expression.
>
> The basic theory that governmental regulation must be directed specifically to action, and may not control action through control of expression, is fully applicable . . . The legal doctrine . . . should be that the holding of a belief is afforded complete protection from State coercion.

But what happens when opinion appears as unpopular political views or views that urge the overthrow of the government?

> The principle that the government cannot restrict expression in order to coerce conformity to social norms means that freedom of expression must receive full protection in this context. No matter how deviant the expression may be—how obnoxious or intolerable it may seem— the expression cannot be suppressed. The First Amendment extends . . . to fundamental challenges to the basic premises of the society. And the protection must be afforded even though the unwanted expression is injected into a sensitive situation where the need for unity may be, or may appear to be, urgent. In times of stress pressures to abandon the principle of full protection mount. It is argued that a small amount of repression will restore consensus and save the community. But such a course of action would probably be self-defeating. It would be more likely to bottle up the frustrations, hide the underlying grievances, and ultimately end in explosion. Of one thing we may be sure: it would not bring back the consensus. . . . The rule of full protection for all expression applies without qualification.

When Emerson applied his system to war, he distinguished between military and civilian populations. The military must work under a structure that inhibits certain forms of expression, and Emerson dealt with those separately. But he believed that his system applied to the civilian population. Espionage, however, was where the problem arises. Emerson saw espionage as stealing military information and giving it to the enemy; consequently, espionage was action rather than just expression. Secondly, espionage was the transmission of military information to a foreign power and would come under the federal government's right to regulate matters with another nation.

Treason, which is prohibited by the Constitution and which has traditionally been interpreted as a combination of action and expression, was not protected under Emerson's theory.

Emerson addressed the question of those who opposed the nation's participation in war by agreeing with the interpretation of the Supreme Court in *Bond* v.

Floyd (1966). Julian Bond was an elected member of the House of Representatives in Georgia. Bond, however, was one of the signers of a statement critical of United States involvement in the Vietnam War, and he thought that people could substitute work in the civil rights movement in place of work service in the military. Bond, a Black, observed:

> I don't think that I as a second class citizen of the United States have a requirement to support [the Vietnam] war . . . I'm against all war. I'm against that war in particular, and I don't think people ought to participate in it. Because I'm against the war, I'm against the draft.

Because of his statements, the Georgia House of Representatives challenged Bond's right to be seated in the legislature. A hearing was held that led to a vote of the Georgia House refusing to seat Bond.

A unanimous decision of the Supreme Court of the United States held that Bond's right of free expression had been violated. Said the Court:

> [W]e do not quarrel with the State's contention that [the oath's provisions] do not violate the First Amendment. But this requirement does not authorize a majority of state legislators to test the sincerity with which another duly elected legislator can swear to uphold the Constitution.

Regarding the treatment of the Smith Act, Emerson believed any ideological discussion of overthrowing the government, Communism, or other anti-government ideas should be allowed as long as the instruction did not get into the mechanics of violence—the making of bombs, training in para-military operations, *i.e.*, the preparation for physical actions.

In dealing with sedition laws in general, Emerson believed them unnecessary to the protection of free expression and that they have been contrary to the First Amendment and to his theory.

Regarding obscenity, Emerson classified the portrayal of erotic material in books, magazines, films, and pictures to be expression. Generally, the theory rejected obscenity laws. In specific terms restrictions on the dissemination of obscenity was permitted only when the material was being thrust on unsuspecting adults against their wills and when the publication was being distributed to children.

Even in the case of libel—laws set up to protect the individual—Emerson believed, the rule of "unconditional privilege," the right of all people to say anything they wish without concern for defamation prosecutions. Emerson believed that truth would ultimately prevail.

Emerson's interests in other areas such as loyalty oaths, right to belong to associations, and taxation were based on the same views. In each case he evaluated the issue on the basis of if it were expression or action.

Theory 11: Social Responsibility

The Theory. The social responsibility theory of the media rests on two fears—that the government would become too powerful in its suppressive measures; and that the media might also become too powerful. Neither, therefore, should enjoy absolute freedom. The underlying philosophy of this theory might be described by Lord John Emerich Edward Dalbert Acton (1834-1902), the English historian and philosopher, who observed that "Power tends to corrupt; absolute power corrupts absolutely." The theory held that the best way to regulate the media was for journalists and other workers in the mass media to be driven by a spirit of professional responsibility. Thus, the theory does not trust the government. But neither does it trust the media, so it holds up the specter of government intervention if the media are not responsible. The theory applies to all types of publication.

The Background. This theory of media control is held to last, not because it is the last theory to be developed—it has its roots in the early nineteenth century—but because it differs from the other theories which address primarily the degree of governmental intervention in the process of regulating the media. Because they remembered the suppression that governmental control of the media created, the social responsibility theorists wanted to keep government out as much as possible, yet keep it available to force the responsibility of the media. In their search for a better way, they turned to the same regulatory forces that guided the professions of medicine, dentistry, and law for their concepts. The theory is a hybrid of authoritarian controls used as a last result and of internal controls imposed by journalists themselves.)

The Supreme Court: All the Views

Although the Supreme Court has generally rejected the older arguments of prior restraint, bad tendency and constructive intent, and preferred position, no single view can be said to cover all of the Supreme Court's decisions. The generally conservative courts during the 1980s have tended to move away from absolute standards for free expression and have often balanced interests; but to characterize the Court in a single mold would be inappropriate. Thus, free expression in the United States, rather than being protected by a single theory or philosophy, is decided on the basis of the justices on the Court, the nature of the issue being considered, and the relationship of other public interests. Just as important are the statutes that Congress passes which the Court reviews. It would be, therefore, incorrect to say that the Court follows either a totally authoritarian or libertarian view in its decisions.

For this reason, the freedom of expression that exists at any time is always a frail freedom, a freedom that must be protected. Moreover, although the United States believes itself to be a libertarian nation, all of the theories of free expression are defined by the extent to which they deviate from authoritarian principles, not as purely libertarian guidelines. Most of the theories are explained on the basis of how much more liberty is granted by the theory than

Lord Acton : give absolute power to no one (gov' or press)

authoritarians provided, and there is no apology that the theory deviates from pure libertarian freedom for expression.

Many journalists, recognizing the delicate situation and being aware that few subscribe to total freedoms for the media, have devoted much time to arguing the need for an alert electorate. The loss of freedom can be achieved just as easily by inaction or unconcern as it can by fighting. Fear drives those with power to attempt to control the media; fear also motivates the public to demand book burnings, censorship, and boycotts.

The First Amendment: An Absolute Right

by Hugo L. Black and Edmond Cahn

[On April 14, 1962, Justice Black appeared before the biennial convention of the American Jewish Congress in New York City where a banquet was held in his honor. At that time, Edmond Cahn interviewed Black about his views on the First Amendment. Black did not see the questions or edit the resulting transcript. The interview was printed in the New York University Law Review (1962). Black provided much insight into his views:]

PROF. CAHN: Let me start by explaining the purpose of this interview. Two years ago, when you delivered your James Madison Lecture at New York University, you declared your basic attitude toward our Bill of Rights. This was the positive side of your constitutional philosophy. Tonight I propose we bring out the other side, that is, your answers to the people who disagree with and criticize your principles. The questions I will ask, most of them at least, will be based on the criticisms. As you know, I consider your answers so convincing that I want the public to have them.

Suppose we start with one of the key sentences in your James Madison Lecture where you said, "It is my belief that there *are* 'absolutes' in our Bill of Rights, and that they were put there on purpose by men who knew what words meant and meant their prohibitions to be 'absolutes.'" Will you please explain your reasons for this.

BLACK: My first reason is that I believe the words do mean what they say. I have no reason to challenge the intelligence, integrity or honesty of the men who wrote the First Amendment. Among those I call the great men of the world are Thomas Jefferson, James Madison, and various others who participated in formulating the ideas behind the First Amendment fot this country and in writing it.

Reprinted by permission from 37 (1962) N.Y.U.L. Rev. 549.

I learned a long time ago that there are affirmative and negative words. The beginning of the First Amendment is that "Congress shall make no law." I understand that it is rather old-fashioned and shows a slight naivete to say that "no law" means no law. It is one of the most amazing things about the ingeniousness of the times that strong arguments are made, which *almost* convince me, that it is very foolish of me to think "no law" means no law. But what it *says* is "Congress shall make no law respecting an establishment of religion," and so on.

I have to be honest about it. I confess not only that I think the Amendment means what it says but also that I may be slightly influenced by the fact that I do not think Congress *should* make any law with respect to these subjects. That has become a rather bad confession to make in these days, the confession that one is actually for something because he believes in it.

Then we move on, and it says "or prohibiting the free exercise thereof." I have not always exercised myself in regard to religion as much as I should, or perhaps as much as all of you have. Nevertheless, I want to be able to do it when I want to do it. I do not want anybody who is my servant, who is my agent, elected by me and others like me, to tell me that I can or cannot do it. Of course, some will remark that that is too simple on my part. To them, all this discussion of mine is too simple, because I come back to saying that these few plain words actually mean what they say, and I know of no college professor or law school professor, outside of my friend, Professor Cahn here, and a few others, who could not write one hundred pages to show that the Amendment does not mean what it says.

Then I move on to the words "abridging the freedmon of speech or of the press." It *says* Congress shall make no law doing that. What it *means*— according to a current philosophy that I do not share—is that Congress shall be able to make just such a law unless we judges object too strongly. One of the statements of that philosophy is that if it shocks us too much, then they cannot do it. But when I get down to the really basic reason why I believe that "no law" means no law, I presume it could come to this, that I took an obligation to suport and defend the Constitution as I understand it. And being a rather backward country fellow. I understand it to mean what the words say. Gesticulating apart, I know of no way in the world to communicate ideas except by words. And if I were to talk to great length on the subject, I would still be saying—although I understand that some people say that I just say it and do not believe it—that I believe when our Founding Fathers, with their wisdom and patriotism, wrote this Amendment, they knew what they were talking about. They knew what history was behind them and they wanted to ordain in this country that Congress, elected by the people, should not tell the people what religion they should have or what they should believe or say or publish, and that is about it. It says "no law," and that is what I believe it means.

CAHN: Some of your colleagues would say that it is better to interpret the Bill of Rights so as to permit Congress to take what it considers reasonable steps to preserve the security of the nation even at some sacrifice of freedom of speech and association. Otherwise what will happen to the nation and the Bill of Rights as well? What is your view of this?

BLACK: I fully agree with them that the country should protect itself. It should protect itself in peace and in war. It should do whatever is necessary to preserve itself. But the question is: preserve what? And how?

It is not very much trouble for a dictator to know how it is best to preserve his government. He wants to stay in power, and the best way to stay in power is to have plenty of force behind him. He cannot stay in power without force. He is afraid of too much talk; it is dangerous for him. And he should be afraid, because dictators do not have a way of contributing very greatly to the happiness, joy, contentment, and prosperity of the plain, everyday citizen. Their business is to protect themselves. Therefore, they need an army; they need to be able to stop people from talking; they need to have one religion, and that is the religion they promulgate. Frequently in the past it has been the worship of the dictator himself. To preserve a dictatorship, you must be able to stifle thought, imprison the human mind and intellect.

I want this Government to protect itself. If there is any man in the United States who owes a great deal to this Government, I am that man. Seventy years ago, when I was a boy, perhaps no one who knew me thought I would ever get beyond the confines of the small country county in which I was born. There was no reason for them to suspect that I would. Be we had a free country and the way was open for me. The Government and the people of the United States have been good to me. Of course, I want this country to do what will preserve it. I want it to be preserved as the kind of Government it was intended to be. I would not desire to live at any place where my thoughts were under the suspicion of government and where my words could be censored by government, and where worship, whatever it was or wasn't, had to be determined by an officer of the government. That is not the kind of government I want preserved.

I agree with those who wrote our Constitution, that too much power in the hands of officials is a dangerous thing. What was government created for except to serve the people? Why was a Constitution written for the first time in this country except to limit the power of government and those who were selected to exercise it at the moment?

My answer to the statement that this Government should preserve itself is yes. The method I would adopt is different, however, from that of some other people. I think it can be preserved only by leaving people with the utmost freedom to think and to hope and to talk and to dream if they want to dream. I do not think this Government must look to force, stifling the minds and aspirations of the people. Yes, I believe in self-preservation, but I would preserve it as the founders said, by leaving people free. I think here, as in another time, it cannot live half slave and half free.

CAHN: I do not suppose that since the days of Socrates a questioner ever got answers that were so cooperative.

In order to reserve the guaranteed freedom of the press, are you willing to allow sensational newspaper reports about a crime and about police investigation of the crime to go so far that they prejudice and inflame a whole state and thus deprive the accused of his right to a fair jury?

BLACK: The question assumes in the first place that a whole state can be inflamed so that a fair trial is not possible. On most of these assumptions that are made with reference to the dangers of the spread of information, I perhaps diverge at a point from many of those who disagree with my views. I have again a kind of an old-fashioned trust in human beings. I learned it as a boy and have never wholly lost that faith.

I believe in trial by jury. Here again perhaps I am a literalist. I do not think that trial by jury is a perfect way of determing facts, of adjudicating guilt, or of adjudicating controversies. But I do not know of a better way. That is where I stand on that.

I do not think myself that anyone can say that there can be enough publicity completely to destroy the ideas of fairness in the minds of people, including the judges. One of the great things about trials by jury in criminal cases that have developed in this country—I refer to criminal cases because there is where most of the persecutions are found in connection with bringing charges against unpopular people or people in unpopular causes—we should not forget that if the jury happens to go wrong, the judge has a solemn duty in a criminal case not to let an unfair verdict stand. Also, in this country, an appellate court can hear the case.

I realize that we do not have cases now like they had when William Penn was tried for preaching on the streets of London. The jury which was called in to send him off quickly to jail refused to do so and suffered punishment from the judge because they would not convict a man for preaching on the streets. But that is a part of history, and it is but one of thousands of cases of the kind. Those people had publicity; that is why they would not convict William Penn. They knew, because the people had been talking, despite the fact that there was so much censorhsip then, that William Penn was being prosecuted largely because he was a dissenter from the orthodox views. So they stood up like men and would not convict. They lost their property, some of them their liberty. But they stood up like men.

I do not myself think that it is necessary to stifle the press in order to reach fair verdicts. Of course, we do not want juries to be influenced wrongfully. But with our system of education we should be in better condition than they were in those days in England, when they found that the jury was one of the greatest steps on their way to freedom. As a matter of fact, [James] Madison placed trial by jury along with freedom of the press and freedom of conscience as the three most highly cherished liberties of the American people in his time.

I do not withdraw my loyalty to the First Amendment or say that the press should be censored on the theory that in order to preserve fair trials it is necessary to try the people of the press in summary contempt proceedings and send them to jail for what they have published. I want both fair trials and freedom of the press. I grant that you cannot get everything you want perfectly, and you never will. But you won't do any good in this country, which aspires to freedom, by saying just give the courts a little more power, just a little more power to suppress the people and the press, and things will be all right. You just take a little chunk off here and a little bit there. I would not take it off anywhere. I believe that they meant what they said about freedom of the press just as they meant what they said about establishment of religion, and I would answer this question as I have answered the other one.

CAHN: Do you make an execption in freedom of speech and press for the law of defamation? That is, are you willing to allow to sue for damages when they are subject to libel or slander?

BLACK: My view of the First Amendment, as originally ratified, is that it said Congress should pass none of these kinds of laws. As written at that time, the Amendment applied only to Congress. I have no doubt myself that the provision, as written and adopted, intended that there should be no libel or defamation law in the United States under the United States Government, just absolutely none so far as I am concerned.

That is, no federal law. At that time—I will have to state this in order to let you know what I think about libel and defamation—people were afraid of the new Federal Government. I hope that they have not wholly lost that fear up to this time because, while government is a wonderful and an essential thing in order to have any kind of liberty, order, or peace, it has such power that people must always remember to check them here and balance them there and limit them here in order to see that you do not lose too much liberty in exchange for government. So I have no doubt about what the Amendment intended. As a matter of fact, shortly after the Constitution was written, a man named St. George Tucker, a great friend of Madison's, who served as one of the commissioners at the Annapolis Convention of 1786 which first attempted to fill the need for a national constitution, put out a revised edition of [Blackstone's Commentaries]. In it he explained what our Constitution meant with reference to freedom of speech and press. He said there was no doubt in his mind, as one of the earliest participants in the development of the Constitution, that it was intended that there should be no libel under the laws of the United States. Lawyers might profit from consulting Tucker's edition of Blackstone on that subject.

As far as public libel is concerned, or seditious libel, I have been very much disturbed sometimes to see that there is present an idea that because we have had the practice of suing individuals for libel, seditious libel still remains for the use of government in this country. Seditious libel, as it has been put into practice throughout the centuries, is nothing in the world except the prosecution of people who are on the wrong side politically; they have said something and their group has lost and they are prosecuted. Those of you who read the newspaper see that this is happening all over the world now, every week somewhere. Somebody gets out, somebody else gets in, they call a military court or a special commission, and they try him. When he gets through sometimes he is not living.

My belief is that the First Amendment was made applicable to the states by the Fourteenth. I do not hesitate, so far as my own view is concerned, as to what should be and what I hope will sometime be the constitutional doctrine that just as it was not intended to authorized damage suits for mere words as distinguished from conduct as far as the Federal Government is concerned, the same rule should apply to the states.

I realize that sometimes you have a libel suit that accomplishes some good. I practiced law twenty years. I was a pretty acive trial lawyer. The biggest judgment I ever got for a libel was $300. I never took a case for political libel because I found out that Alabama juries, at least, do not believe in political suits and they just do not give verdicts. I knew of one verdict given by a big newspaper down there for $25,000, and the Supreme Court of Alabama reversed it. So even that one did not pan out very well.

I believe with Jefferson that it is time enough for government to step in to regulate people when they do something, not when they *say* something, and I do not believe myself that there is *any* halfway ground if you enforce the protections of the First Amendment.

CAHN: Would it be constitutional to prosecute someone who falsely shouted "fire" in a theater?

BLACK: I went to a theater last night with you. I have an idea if you and I had gotten up and marched around that theater, whether we said anything or not, we would have been arrested. Nobody has ever said that the First Amendment gives people a right to go anywhere in the world they want to go or say anything in the world they want to say. Buying the theater tickets did not buy the opportunity to make a speech there. We have a system of property in this country which is also protected by the Constitution. We have a system of property, which means that a man does not have a right to do anything he wants anywhere he wants to do it. For instance, I would feel a little badly if somebody were to try to come into my house and tell me that he had a constitutional right to come in there because he wanted to make a speech against the Supreme Court. I realize the freedom of people to make a speech against the Supreme Court, but I do not want him to make it in my house.

That is a wonderful aphorism about shouting "fire" in a crowded theater. But you do not have to shout "fire" to get arrested. If a person creates a disorder in a theater, they would get him there not because of *what* he hollered but because he *hollered*. They would get him not because of any views he had but because they thought he did not have any views that they wanted to here there. That is the way I would answer: not because of what he shouted but because he shouted.

CAHN: Is there any kind of obscene material, whether defined as hardcore pornography or otherwise, the distribution and sale of which can be constitutionally restricted in any manner whatever, in your opinion?

BLACK: I will say it can in this country, because the courts have held that it can.

CAHN: Yes, but you won't get off so easily. I want to know what you think.

BLACK: My view is, without deviation, without exception, without any ifs, buts, or whereases, that freedom of speech means that you shall not do something to people either for the views they have or the views they express or the words they speak or write.

There is strong argument for the position taken by a man whom I admire very greatly, Dr. Meiklejohn, that the First Amendment really was intended to protect *political* speech, and I do think that was the basic purpose; that plus the fact that they wanted to protect *religious* speech. Those were the two main things they had in mind.

It is the law that there can be an arrest made for obscenity. It was the law in Rome that they could arrest people for obscenity after Augustus became Caesar. Tacitus says that then it became obscene to criticize the Emperor. It is not any trouble to establish a classification so that whatever it is that you do not want said is within that classification. So far as I am concerned, I do not believe there is any halfway ground for protecting freedom of speech and press. If you say it is half free, you can rest assured that it will not remain as much as half free. Madison explained that in his great Remonstrance when he said in effect, "If you make laws to force people to speak the words of Christianity, it won't be long until the same power will narrow the sole religion to the most powerful sect in it." I realize that there are dangers in freedom of speech, but I do not believe there are any halfway marks.

CAHN: Do you subscribe to the idea involved in the clear and present danger rule?

BLACK: I do not.

CAHN: By way of conclusion, Justice Black, would you kindly summarize what you consider the judge's role in cases arising under the First Amendment and the Bill of Rights?

BLACK: The Bill of Rights to me constitutes the differences between this country and many others. I will not attempt to say most others or nearly all others or all others. But I will say it constitutes the difference to me between a free country and a country that is not free.

My idea of the whole thing is this: There has been a lot of trouble in the world between people and government. The people were afraid of government, they had a right to be afraid. All over the world men had been destroyed—and when I say "government" I mean the individuals who actually happened to be in control of it at the moment, whether they were elected, whether they were appointed, whether they got there with the sword, however they got there—the people always had a lot of trouble because power is a heady thing, a dangerous thing. There have been very few individuals in the history of the world who could be trusted with complete, unadulterated, omnipotent power over their fellowmen.

Millions of people have died throughout the world because of the evils of their governments. Those days had not wholly passed when the Pilgrims came over to this country. Many of them had suffered personally. Some of them had their ears cut off. Many of them had been mutilated. Many of their ancestors had. Some of our ancestors came here to get away from persecution. Certainly, mine did.

There had been struggles throughout the ages to curb the dangerous power of governors. Rome had a sound government at one time. Those who study it carefully will find that, except for the slave class, they had, so far as most of the people were concerned, a good form of government. But it turned, and then they had Augustus and the other Caesars, and the Neros and the Caligulas and Tiberiuses.

One of the interesting things about Tiberius is that in all the history I have read he is about the only man of great prominence who ever defended informers.

He made the statement that the informers were the guardians of Rome. Recently I have heard that said here once or twice.

When our ancestors came over here and started this country, they had some more persecutions of their own. It was not limited to any one religion. A lot of my Baptist brethren got into trouble; a lot of the Methodist brethren got in trouble; a lot of the Episcopal Church got in trouble, the Congregational Church—each of them in turn. A lot of the Catholics got in trouble. Whichever sect was in control in a state for a time, they would say that the others could not hold office, which is an easy way of getting rid of your adversaries if you can put it over. Even for half a century after the Constitution was adopted, some of the states barred the members of certain faiths from holding office.

Throughout all of this—as the Jewish people know as well as any people on earth—persecutions were abroad everywhere in the world. A man never knew, when he got home, whether his family would be there, and the family at home never knew whether the head of the family would get back. There was nothing strange about that when Hitler did it. It was simply a repetition of the course of history when people get too much power.

I like what the Jewish people did when they took what amounted to a written constitution. Some of the states did it before the time of the Federal Constitution; they adopted written constitutions. Why? Because they wanted to mark boundaries beyond which government could not go, stripping people of their liberty to think, to talk, to write, to work, to be happy.

So we have a written Constitution. What good is it? What good is it if, as some judges say, all it means is: "Government, you can still do this unless it is so bad that it shocks the conscience of the judges." It does not say that to me. We have certain provisions in the Constitution which say "Thou shall not." They do not say, "You can do this unless if offends the sense of decency of the English-speaking world." They do not say that. They do not say, "You can go ahead and do this unless it is offensive to the universal sense of decency." If they did, they would say virtually nothing. There would be no definite, binding place, no specific prohibition, if that were all it said.

I believe with Locke in the system of checks and balances. I do not think that the Constitution leaves any one department of government free without there being a check on it somewhere. Of course, things are different in England; they do have unchecked powers, and they also have a very impressive history. But it was *not* the kind of history that suited the people that formed our Constitution. Madison said that explicitly when he offered the Bill of Rights to the Congress. Jefferson repeated it time and time again. Why was it not? Because it left Parliament with power to pass such laws as it saw fit to pass. It was not the kind of government they wanted. So we have a Bill of Rights. It is intended to see that a man cannot be jerked by the back of the neck by any government official; he cannot have his home invaded; he cannot be picked up legally and carried away because his views are not satisfactory to the majority, even if they are terrible views, however bad they may be. Our system of justice is based on the assumption tht men can best work out their own opinions, and that they are not under the control of government. Of course, this is particularly true in the field of religion, because a man's religion is between himself and his Creator, not between himself and his government.

I am not going to say any more except this: I was asked a question about preserving this country. I confess I am a complete chauvinist. I think it is the greatest country in the world. I think it is the greatest because it has a Bill of Rights. I think it could be the worst if it did not have one. It doest not take a nation long to degenerate. We saw, only a short time ago, a neighboring country where people were walking the streets in reasonable peace one day and within a month we saw them marched to the back of a wall to meet a firing squad without a trial.

I am a chauvinist because this country offers the greatest opportunities of any country in the world to people of every kind, of every type, of every race, of every origin, of every religion—without regard to wealth, without regard to poverty. It offers an opportunity to the child born today to be reared among his people by his people, to worship his God, whatever his God may be, or to refuse to worship anybody's God if that is his wish. It is a free country; it will remain free only, however, if we recognize that the boundaries of freedom are not so flexible; they are not made of mush. They say "Thou shalt not," and I think that is what they mean.

Now, I have read that every sophisticated person knows that you cannot have any absolute "thou shall nots." But you know when I drive my car against a red light, I do not expect them to turn me loose if I can prove that I thought I was going across that red light, it was not offensive to the so-called "universal sense of decency." I have an idea there are some absolutes. I do not think I am far in that respect from the Holy Scriptures.

The Jewish people have had a glorious history. It is wonderful to think about the contributions that were made to the world from a small, remote area in the East. I have to admit that most of my ideas stem basically from there.

It is largely because of these same contributions that I am here tonight as a member of what I consider the greatest Court in the world. It is great because it is independent. If it were not independent, it would not be great. If all nine of those men came out each Monday morning like a phonograph speaking one voice, you can rest assured it would not be independent. But it does not come that way. I want to assure you that the fact that it does not come that way does not mean that there is not a good, sound, wholesome respect on the part of every justice for every other justice.

I do hope that this occasion may cause you to think a little more and study a little more about the Constitution, which is the source of your liberty; no, not the source—I will take that back—but a protection of your liberty. Yesterday a man sent me a copy of a recent speech entitled "Is the First Amendment Obsolete?" The conclusion of the writer, who is a distinguished law school dean, was that the Amendment no longer fits the times and that it needs to be modified to get away from its rigidity. The author contends that the thing to do is to take the term "due process of law" and measure everything by that standard, "due process of law" meaning that unless a law is so bad that it shocks the conscience of the Court, it cannot be unconstitutional. I do not wish to have to pass on the laws of this country according to the degree of shock I receive! Some people get shocked more readily than others at certain things, I get shocked pretty quickly, I confess, when I see—and this I say with trepidation because it is considered bad to admit it—but I do get shocked now and then when I see some gross injustice has been done, although I am solemnly informed that we do not sit to administer justice, we sit to administer law in the abstract.

I am for the First Amendment from the first word to the last. I believe it means what it says, and it says to me, "Government shall keep its hands off religion. Government shall not attempt to control the ideas a man has. Government shall not attempt to establish a religion of any kind. Government shall not abridge freedom of the press or speech. It shall let anybody talk in this country." I have never been shaken in the faith that the American people are the kind of people and have the kind of loyalty to their government that we need not fear the talk of Communists or of anybody else. Let them talk! In the American way, we will answer them.

Expression and Action:
The Dividing Line

by Thomas I. Emerson

The system of freedom of expression in a democratic society rests upon four main premises. These may be stated, in capsule form, as follows:

First, freedom of expression is essential as a means of assuring individual self-fulfillment. The proper end of man is the realization of his character and potentialities as a human being. For the achievement of this self-realization the mind must be free. Hence suppression of belief, opinion, or other expression is an affront to the dignity of man, a negation of man's essential nature. Moreover, man in his capacity as a member of society has a right to share in the common decisions that affect him. To cut off his search for truth, or his expression of it, is to elevate society and the state to a despotic command over him and to place him under the arbitrary control of others.

Thomas I. Emerson is professor emeritus of law, Yale University. He received A.B., M.A., and LL.B. degrees from Yale. After two years in private practice, he began a thirteen year government career, serving in senior levels with the National Recovery Administration, National Labor Relations Board, Social Security Board, the U.S. Department of Justice, and the Office of Economic Stabilization. In 1946, he was appointed to the law faculty at Yale. Emerson is author of *Toward a General Theroy of the First Amendment* (1966), *The System of Free Expression* (1970), and co-author of *Political and Civil Rights in the United States* (1952). He was a Guggenheim and Fulbright fellow, and president of the National Lawyers Guild. [Edited and reprinted from *The System of Freedom of Expression*; reprinted by permission of the University of Chicago Press. ©1970.]

Second, freedom of expression is an essential process for advancing knowledge and discovering truth. An individual who seeks knowledge and truth must hear all sides of the question, consider all altneratives, test his judgment by exposing it to opposition, and make full use of different minds. Discussion must be kept open no matter how certainly true an accepted opinion may seem to be; many of the most widely acknowledged truths have turned out to be erroneous. Conversely, the same principle applies no matter how false or pernicious the new opinion appears to be; for the unaccepted opinion may be true or partially true and, even if wholly false, its presentation and open discussion compel a rethinking and retesting of the accepted opinion. The reasons which make open discussion essential for an intelligent individual judgment likewise make it imperative for rational social judgment.

Third, freedom of expression is essential to provide for participation in decision making by all members of society. This is particularly significant for political decisions. Once one accepts the premise of the Declaration of Independence—that governments "derive their just powers from the consent of the governed"—it follows that the governed must, in order to exercise their right of consent, have full freedom of expression both in forming individual judgments and in forming the common judgment. The principle also carries beyond the political realm. It embraces the right to participate in the building of the whole culture, and includes freedom of expression in religion, literature, art, science, and all areas of human learning and knowledge.

Finally, freedom of expression is a method of achieving a more adaptable and hence a more stable community, of maintaining the precarious balance between healthy cleavage and necessary consensus. This follows because suppression of discussion makes a rational judgment impossible, substituting force for reason; because suppression promotes inflexibility and stultification, preventing society from adjusting a changing circumstances or developing new ideas; and because suppression conceals the real problems confronting a society, diverting public attention from the critical issues. At the same time the process of open discussion promotes greater cohesion in a society because people are more ready to accept decisions that go against them if they have a part in the decision-making process. Moreover, the state at all times retains adequate powers to promote unity and to suppress resort to force. Freedom of expression thus provides a framework in which the conflict necessary to the progress of a society can take place without destroying the society. It is an essential mechanism for maintaining the balance between stability and change.

The theory rests upon a fundamental distinction between belief, opinion, and communication of ideas on the hand, and different forms of conduct on the other. For shorthand purposes we refer to this distinction . . . as one between "expression" and "action." . . . In order to achieve its desired goals, a society or the state is entitled to exercise control over action—whether by prohibiting or compelling it—on an entirely different and vastly more extensive basis. But expression occupies an especially protected position. In this sector of human conduct, the social right of suppression or compulsion is at its lowest point, in most respects nonexistent. A majority of one has the right to control action, but a minority of one has the right to talk.

This marking off of the special status of expression is a crucial ingredient of the basic theory for several reasons. In the first place, thought and communication are the fountainhead of all expression of the individual personality. To cut off the flow at the source is to dry up the whole stream. Freedom at this point is essential to all other freedoms. Hence society must withhold its right of suppression until the stage of action is reached. Secondly, expression is normally conceived as doing less injury to other social goals than action. It generally has less immediate consquences, is less irremediable in its impact. Thirdly, the power of society and the state over the individual is so pervasive, and construction of doctrines, institutions, and administrative practices to limit this power so difficult, that only by drawing such a protective line between expression and action is it possible to strike a safe balance between authority and freedom . . .

Finding the Limits

It is necessary to recognize the powerful forces that impel men towards the elimination of unorthodox expression. Most men have a strong inclination, for rational or irrational reasons, to suppress opposition. On the other hand, persons who stand up against society and challenge the traditional view usually have similarly strong feelings about the issues they raise. Thus dissent often is not pitched in conventional terms, nor does it follow customary standards of polite expression. Moreover, the forces of inertia within a society ordinarily resist the expression of new ideas or the pressures of the underprivileged who seek a change. And the longer-run logic of the traditional theory may not be immediately apparent to untutored participatants in the conflict. Suppression of opinion may thus seem an entirely plausible course of action; tolerance a weakness or a foolish risk.

Thus it is clear that the problem of maintaining a system of freedom of expression in a society is one of the most complex any society has to face. Self-restraint, self-discipline, and maturity are required. The theory is essentially a highly sophisticated one. The members of the society must be willing to sacrifice individual and short-term advantage for social and long-range goals. And the process must operate in a context that is charged with emotion and subject to powerful conflicting forces of self-interest.

These considerations must be weighed in attemting to construct a theory of limitations. A system of free expression can be successful only when it rests upon the strongest possible commitment to the positive right and the narrowest possible basis for exceptions. And any such exceptions must be clear-cut, precise, and readily controlled. Otherwise the forces that press toward restriction will break through the openings, and freedom of expression will become the exception and suppression the rule.

A second major consideration in imposing restrictions upon expression is the difficulty of framing precise limitations. the object of the limitation is usually not the expression itself but its feared consequences. Repression of expression is thus purely a preventive measure and, like all preventive measures, cuts far more widely and deeply than is necessary to control the ensuing conduct.

Moreover, the infinite varieties and subtleties of language and other forms of communication make it impossible to construct a limitation upon expression is brought within reach of the limitation and enormous discretionary power placed in the hands of those who administer it.

Again, the apparatus of government required for enforcement of limitations on expression, by its very nature, tends towards administrative extremes. Officials charged with the duties of suppression already have or tend to develop excessive zeal in the performance of their task. The accompanying techniques of enforcement—the investigations, surveillance, searches and seizures, secret informers, voluminous files on the suspect—all tend to exert a repressive influence on freedom of expression. In addition, the restrictive measures are readily subject to distortion and to use for ulterior purposes.

Finally we must take into account the whole impact of restriction upon the healthy functioning of a free society. Limittions are seldom aplied except in an atmosphere of public fear and hysteria. This may be deliverately aroused or may simply be the inevitable accompaniment of repression. Under such circumstances the doctrines and institutions for enforcing the limitations are subjected to intense pressures. Moreover, while some of the more hardy may be willing to defy the opposition and suffer the consequences, the more numerous are likely to be unwilling to run the risks. Similarly, persons whose cooperation is needed to permit the full flow of open discussion—those who own the means of publication or the facilities for communication—are likely to be frightened into withholding their patronage and assistance.

The lesson of experience, in short, is that the limitations imposed on discussion, as they operate in practice, tend readily and quickly to destroy the whole structure of free expression. They are very difficult to keep in hand; the exceptions are likely to swallow up the principle. Maintenance of a system of free expression, therefore, is not an easy task. This is especially true as we confront the conditions of today. We have tended over the years to refine and delineate more carefully the restrictions we seek to impose. But the new problems arising out of modern industrial society make the issues more delicate and troublesome than at any other time in hour history.

Role of the First Amendment

The major source of legal doctrine supporting the system of freedom of expression is the First Amendment. That constitutional guarantee is: "Congress shall make no law . . . abridging the freedom of speech, or of the press, or the right of the people peacably to assemble, and to petition the Government for a redress of grievances." The precise meaning of the First Amendment at the time of its adoption is a matter of some dispute. In the broadest terms, however, the provision was plainly intended to assure the new nation the basic elements of a system of free expression as then conceived. As our constitutional law has developed over the years the First Amendment has come to have the same broad significance for our present, more complex, society. The fundamental meaning of the First Amendment, then, is to guarantee an effective system of freedom of expression suitable for the present times.

Other constitutional provisions also have an important bearing upon the system of freedom of expression. The Fourth Amendment's protection against unreaonable searches and seizures, the Fifth Amendment's privilege against self-incrimination, and the due process rules against vagueness and overbreadth in legislation all play a significant role in maintaining the system. In fact, the courts have come to give these constitutional guarantees a substantially different meaning when invoked in behalf of First Amendment rights. Thus the First Amendment has an umbrella effect, drawing within its shelter doctrines from many other areas of the law. Equally pertinent are various procedural rules, such as those providing judicial relief by injunction; other legal doctrines, such as those governing Federal control over State action; the operation of various institutions, such as the prosecutor's office; and innumerable practices and policies, such as those of the Federal, State, and local police.

A Comprehensive Standard

Our main effort, . . . is to apply a comprehensive and effective theory of the First Amendment to the various problems that arise in the operation of the free expresion system. That theory, . . . needs the distinction between "expression" and "action." The line in many situations is clear. But at some points it becomes obscure. All expression has some physical element. Moreover, a communication may take place in a context of action, as in the familiar example of the false cry of "fire" in a crowded theater. Or a communication may be closely linked to action, as in the gang leader's command to his triggerman. Or, the communication may have the same immediate impact as action, as in instances of publicly uttered obscenities which may shock unforewarned listeners or viewers. In these cases it is necessary to decide, however artificial the distinction may appear to be, whether the conduct is to be classified as one or the other. This judgment must be guided by consideration of whether the conduct partakes of the essential qualities of expression or action, that is, whether expression or action is the dominant element. And the concept of expression must be related to the fundamental purposes of the system and the dynamics of its operation. In formulating the distinction there is a certain leeway in which the process of reconciling freedom of expression with other values and objectives can remain flexible. But the crucial point is that the focus of inquiry must be directed toward ascertaining what is expression, and therefore to be given the protection of expression, and what is action, and thus subject to regulation as such.

The definition of "abridge" is not difficult in most situations in which the government seeks to limit expression in order to protect some other social itnerest. But it is likely to become more complex when the government controls undertake to regulate the internal operations of the system of freedom of expression itself, or when the status of an individual in an organization imposes obligations different from those of the ordinary citizen to the general community. In any case the decision as to whether there has been an "abridgment" turns on the actual impact of the regulation upon the system . . .

Different legal doctrines, derived from the definition of the foregoing terms, apply to different kinds of protection which legal institutions must provide for a system of freedom of expression. Most of the issues fall into three categories:

(a) First is the protection of the individual's right to freedom of activities, of the activities of children, and of communication with foreign countries. This does not mean that the First Amendment has no application in these sectors. It simply recognizes that the functions of expression and the principles needed to protect expression in such areas are different from those in the main system, and that different legal rules may therefore be required.

Bibliography
Chapters 1-33

Alexander, James, *A Brief Narrative of the Case of John Peter Zenger* (edited by Stanley N. Kotz), Harvard University Press (Cambridge, Mass.), 1963.

Archer, Gleason, L. *History of Radio to 1926.* The American Historical Society (New York), 1938.

Bailey, C. (ed.), *Legacy of Rome,* Oxford University Press (New York, N.Y.), 1956.

Barnouw, Erik, *A Tower in Babel: A History of Broadcasting in the United States to 1933.* Oxford University Press (New York, N.Y.), 1966.

_____, *The Golden Web: A History of Broadcasting in the United States 1933-1953.* Oxford University Press (New York, N.Y.), 1968.

_____, *The Image Empire: A History of Broadcasting in the United States from 1953,* Oxford University Press (New York, N.Y.), 1970.

_____, "The Reaprotionment Cases: One Person, One Vote", 1964 *Sup. Ct. Rev.,* pp. 156, 1442, 1445, 1450, 1463.

Baron, Salo, *A Social and Religious History of the Jews,* Columbia University Press (New York, N.Y.), 1937.

Beard, Charles A.; Mary Beard, *The Rise of American Civilization,* Macmillan (New York, N.Y.), 1930.

Becker, Carl, *The Eve of the Revolution,* Yale University Press (New Haven, Conn.), 1918.

_____, *Freedom and Responsibility in the American Way of Life,* Alfred A. Knopf (New York), 1945.

_____, *New Liberties for Old,* Yale University Press (New Haven, Conn.), 1941.

_____, *Progress and Power.* Alfred A. Knopf (New York), 1949.

Berns, Walter. *The First Amendment and the Future of American Democracy.* New York: 1976.

Blagden, Cyprian, *The Stationers Company,* Allen & Unwin (London, England), 1960.

Bleyer, William G., *Main Currents in the History of American Journalism*, Houghton-Mifflin (Boston, Mass.), 1927.

Bollan, William, *The Freedom of Speech and Writing Upon Public Affairs*, S. Baker (London, England), 1766.

Boton, Lord, *Essays and Freedom and Power*, Meridian Books (New York, N.Y.), 1955.

Brigham, Clarence S., *History and Bibliography of American Newspapers, 1690-1820*, American Antiquarian Society (Worcester, Mass.), 1947.

Broun, Heywood and Margaret Leech, *Anthony Comstock: Roundsman of the Lord*, Albert & Charles Boni (New York), 1927.

Bury, J.B.,*A History of Freedom of Thought*, Oxford University Press (New York), 1913.

Carter, Thomas F., *The Invention of Printing in China, and Its Spread Westward*, Ronald Press (New York, N.Y.), rev. ed. by L. Carrington Goodrich, 1955.

Channing, Edward, *History of the United States*, Macmillan (New York, N.Y.), 1927.

Clark, Grenville, ; "The Limits of Freedom of Expression," *United States Law Review*, vol. 73 (June 1939).

Covert, Cathy, "'Passion Is Ye Prevailing Notice': The Feud Behind the Zenger Case," *Journalism Quarterly*, Spring 1973.

Cockburn, Henry C.*Examination of the Trials for Sedition Which Have Hitherto Occurred in Scotland,*, David Douglas(Edinburgh, Scotland), 1888.

Cranfield, G.A., *The Press and Society*, Longmans (London, England), 1978.

Davidson, Philip, *Propaganda and the American Revolution*, University of North Carolina Press (Chapel Hill, N.C.), 1941.

Duniway Clyde A., *The Development of Freedom of the Press in Massachusetts*, Longmans, Green (New York, N.Y.), 1906.

Eaton, Clement. *The Freedom-of-Thought Struggle in the Old South*, Harper & Row (New York, N.Y.), 1964.

Eisenstein, Elizabeth, *The Printing Press as an Agent of Change*, Cambridge University Press (Cambridge, England), 1980.

Emery, Edwin; Michael Emery, *The Press in America*, Macmillan (New York, N.Y.), 5th ed., 1984.

Fogel, Howard H. "Colonial Theocracy and a Secular Press," *Journalism Quarterly*, Autumn 1960.

Foner, Eric, *Tom Paine and Revolutionary America*, Oxford University Press (New York, N.Y.), 1976.

Ford, Edwin H., "Colonial Pamphleeteers," *Journalism Quarterly*, March 1936.

Ford, Worthington C., *Jefferson and the Newspaper, 1755-1830*.

Frank, Joseph, *The Beginnings of the English Newspaper*, Harvard University Press (Cambridge, Mass.), 1961.

Frankfort, Henri. *The Birth of Civilization in the Near East*, Indiana University Press (Bloomington, Ind.), 1951.

Gerald, J. Edward, *The Press and the Constitution, 1931-1947*, University of Minnesota Press (Minneapolis), 1948.

Greeley, Horace, *Recollection of a Busy Life*, Ford (New York, N.Y.), 1868.

Griffith, Robert. *The Politics of Fear: Joseph R. McCarthy and the Senate*. University Press of Kentucky (Fraankfurt, Ky.), 1970.

Hadas, Moses. *A History of Rome*, Anchor Books (New York, N.Y.), 1956.

Hanson, Laurence, *Press, 1695-1763*. Oxford University Press (London, England), 1936.

Harrison, Jane Ellen, *A Study of the Social Origins of Greek Religion*, Cambridge University Press (Cambridge, England), 1912.

Hentoff, Nat. *The First Freedom: The Tumultuous History of Free Speech in America*. Delacorte Press (New York, N.Y.), 1980.

Hocking, William Ernest. *A Free and Responsible Press*, University of Chicago Press (Chicago, Ill.), 1948.

———. *Freeodm of the Press: A Framework of Principle*. University of Chicago Press (Chicago, Ill.), 1947.

Jensen, Merrill, The American People and the American Revolution, *Journal of American History*, June 1970.

Juergen, George, *Joseph Pulitzer and the New York World*, Princeton University Press (Princeton, N.J.), 1966.

Kahn, Frank J. *Documents of American Broadcasting*, 3rd Ed., Prentice-Hall (Engelwood Cliffs, N.J.), 1978.

———. *Freedom of the Press from Hamilton to the Warren Court*, Bobbs-Merrill (Indianapolis, Ind.), 1967.

Kobre, Sidney, *Develoment of American Journalism*, William C. Brown (Dubuque, Iowa), 1969.

———, *The Development of the Colonial Newspaper*, The Colonial Press (Pittsburgh, Pa.), 1944.

Lee, Alfred McCLung, *The Daily Newspaper in America*, Macmillan (New York, N.Y.), 1937.

Levy, Leonard, *Emergence of a Free Press*, Oxford University Press (New York, N.Y.), 1985.

———, *Freedom of the Press From Zenger to Jefferson*, Bobbs-Merrill (Indianapolis, Ind.), 1966.

———, *A Legacy of Suppression*, Harvard University Press (Cambridge, Mass.), 1960. (2nd ed., 1985).

Lichty, Lawrence H.; Malachai C. Topping, *American Broadcasting; A Sourcebook on the History of Radio and Television*, Hastings House (New York, N.Y.), 1975.

Middlekauff, Robert, *The Glorious Generation, 1763-1789*, Oxford University Press (New York, N.Y.), 1982.

Miller, John C., *Crisis in Freedom: The Alien and Sedition Laws*, Little, Brown (Boston, Mass.), 1951.

———, *Sam Adams: Pioneer in Propaganda*, Little, Brown (Boston, Mass.), 1936.

Milsson, Martin P., *A History of Greek Religion*, Oxford University Press (London, England), 1925.

Moordian, Karlen, *The Dawn of Printing*, Journalism Monographs, June 1972.

Moran, James, *Printing Presses: History and Development From the Fifteenth Century to Modern Times*, University of California Press (Berkeley, Calif.), 1973.

Morgan, Edmund S., Helen M. Morgan, *The Stamp Act Crisis*, University of North Carolina (Chapel Hill, N.C.), 1963.

Morison, Stanley, *The English Newspaper From 1622*, Cambridge University Press (Cambridge, England), 1932.

Mott, Frank Luther, *A History of American Magazines*, 4 vols., Harvard University Press (Cambridge, Mass.), 1930.

————, *American Journalism: A History, 1690-1960*, Macmilan, 3rd ed. 1962.

Muller, Herbert J., *Freedom in the Ancient World*, Martin Secker & Warburg (London, England), 1962.

Murphy, Paul L., *The Meaning of Freedom of Speech: First Amendment Freedoms From Wilson to FDR*, Greenwood Press (Westport, Conn.), 1972.

Murray, Robert K., *Red Scare: A Study in National Hysteria, 1919-1920*. McGraw-Hill (New York, N.Y.), 1964.

————, *Freedom of the Press from Hamilton to the Warren Court*, Bobbs-Merrill (Indianapolis), 1967.

————, "Seditious Libel in Colonial America," *American Journal of Legal History*, April 1959.

Nelson, Harold, *Freedom of the Press From Hamilton to the Warren Court*, Bobbs-Merrill (Indianapolis, Ind.), 1967.

————, "Seditious Libel in Colonial America," *American Journal of Legal History*, April 1959.

Nixon, Raymond B., *Henry W. Grady, Spokesman of the New South*, A.A. Knopf (New York, N.Y.), 1943.

Parrington, Vernon L., *Main Currents in American Thought*, Harcourt Brace (New York, N.Y.), 1927.

Pfeffer, Leo, *Church, State, and Freedom*, The Beacon Press (Boston, Mass.), 1953.

Preston, William, Jr. *Aliens and Dissenters: Federal Suppression of Radicals, 1903-1933,* Harvard University Press (Cambridge, Mass.), 1963.

Rich, Wesley E., *The History of the United States Post Office to the Year 1829*, Harvard University Press (Cambridge, Mass.), 1963.

Rostovtzeff, M.I., *A History of the Ancient World*, Oxford University Press (London England), 1926.

————, *The Social and Economic History of the Hellenistic World*, Oxford University Press (London, England), 1941.

Rovere, Richard H. *Senator Joe McCarthy*, Harcourt, Brace, Jovanovich (New York), 1959.

Schlesinger, Arthur M., *Prelude to Independence; The Newspaper War on Britain, 1764-1776*, Alfred A. Knopf (New York, N.Y.), 1958.

Schuyler, Livingston, *The Liberty of the Press in American Colonies, Before the Revolutionary War*, Thomas Whittaker (New York, N.Y.), 1905.

Siebert, Fred S., Theodore Peterson, and Wilbur Schramm, *Four Theories of the Press*, University of Illinois Press (Urbana, Ill.),1956.

——, *Freedom of the Press in England 1476-1776*. University of Illinois Press (Urbana, Ill.), 1952.

Siebert, Frederick Seaton, *Freedom of the Press in England, 1476-1776*, University of Illinois Press (Champaign, and Urbana, Ill.), 1952.

Smith, James M, *'Freedom's Fetters' For Aliens and Sedition Laws and American Civil Liberties*, Cornell University Press (Ithaca, N.Y.), 1956.

Smith, Page, *A New Age Now Begins: A People's History of the American Revolution*, McGraw-Hill (New York, N.Y.), 1976.

Sterling, Christopher, and John M. Kittross, *Stay Tuned: A Concise History of American Broadcasting*, Wadsworth (Belmont, Calif.), 1978.

Stevens, John D., and Hazel Dicken Garcia, *Communication History*, Sage (Beverly Hills, Calif.), 1980.

Stewart, Kenneth, and A. John Tebbell, *Makers of Modern Journalism*, Prentice-Hall (New York, N.Y.), 1952.

Stone, Candice, *Dana and the Sun*, Dodd, Mead (New York, N.Y.), 1938.

Sweet, William W., *Religion in Colonial America*, Charles Scribner's Sons (New York, N.Y.), 1942.

Tebbell, John, *A History of Journalism in America*, R. R. Bowker (New York, N.Y.), 4 Vols., 1972-1981.

——, *The Media in America*, Thomas Y. Crowell (New York, N.Y.), 1975.

Teeter, Dwight L., *A Legacy of Expression . . . 1775—1783*, doctoral dissertation, University of Wisconsin (Madison, Wisc.), 1966.

Thomas, Isaiah, *The History of Printing in America*, Self-Published, 1810.

Whipple, Leon, *The Story of Civil Liberties in the United States*, American Civil Liberties Union (New York, N.Y.), 1927.

Van Tyne, Claude H., *The War of Independence: American Phase*, Houghton-Mifflin (Boston, Mass.), 1929.

Chapter 34

Communist and Socialist Theories of Mass Communication

The earliest known socialistic thinking may be traced to the philosophy of Plato who described a communistic and naturalistic form of government. Plato apparently thought a classless form of government, which he described in the *Republic*, to be the ideal government, but rejected the form as unworkable and went on to conceive a "second best" government.

Plato, of course, can hardly be regarded as the founder of modern socialism, nor can other authors who contributed thoughts here and there in more modern times, but their efforts can not be overlooked. Sir Thomas More (1478-1535), English humanist who was Lord Chancellor from 1529 to 1532 and who held a number of other government offices, wrote *Utopia* (1516), in which he described a state ruled by reason with citizens living in a communistic (communal) state.

Tommaso Campanella (1568-1639), the Italian utopian philosopher and author of *La Citt'a del Sole* (1602), developed views regarding the ideal society in which everyone enjoyed benefits, not just the landed classes. Campanella's society was to be ruled by pure reason and provided some thinking for later socialist thinkers.

The later social critic Gerrald Winstanley (1609-1660) who was the leader of the Diggers, a group of English farmer-communists, helped establish a communist colony on St. George's Hill in Surry. According to Winstanley's philosophy, the rich owed their wealth to the poor who produced it; and commercial transactions were the source of oppression, poverty, and bondage because they benefitted the trader more than the producer.

Gabriel Bonnot de Mably (1709-1785), writer of *Entretiens de Phocion Sur le Rapport de la Morale Avec la Politique* (1763), was a critic of French social and economic institutions and prepared the intellectual climate for the French Revolution. None of these people, however, formed a school of socialistic thinking, largely, perhaps, because the industrial revolution had not yet reached its height with the concurrent growth of a worker class of poorly paid people.

With the emerging economic power conferred by the industrial revolution, factory workers and others wanted a share of accumulating wealth. The beginning of the modern socialist movement may be traced to François Noel (Gracchus) Babeuf (1760-1797). Babeuf, who led the Societe des Egaux, tried to

323

overthrow the Directory government in 1796 (French Revolution). Babeuf's followers wanted to complete the Revolution of 1789 by having the land and industry socialized so that the worker would benefit. Although they failed, Babeuf's views widely influenced other thinkers in France and England.

The first formal use of the terms *socialist* and *socialism* appeared in Great Britain and France around 1825. *Co-operative Magazine*, 1826, seemed to have used the word socialist first—a term applied to the followers of Robert Owen (1771-1858). Owen was a socialist and reformer who operated a cotton mill at Manchester that was one of the best managed mills in England. Owen used his power and wealth to improve housing, open a store, and provide training for the workers. He also proposed a cure for pauperism that he hoped all of England would adopt.

Owen observed that contemporary factory owners often exploited the work of their employees, giving them little in return for their contribution. He wanted to show that a manufacturer could profit while treating employees well. Owen opposed competition and favored a cooperative system of communal villages in which people lived peaceably together while each enjoyed the result of labor in farm and factory.

Owen explained his views in two works, *New View of Society* (1813-14) and *Report to the Country of Lanark* (1821). While Owen's views attracted much positive attention from the working class in England, most of his attempts to establish a society based on his views had failed by mid-century.

The French magazine *Globe*, 1832, used *socialiste* to describe the followers of Claude Henri de Rouvroy, comte de Saint-Simon (1760-1825). Socialistic thinking developed in England and France; in England because it was the most advanced industrial nation in Europe at the time—creating great wealth for owners while leaving factory workers in poverty and dissatisfied with their condition; and in France because the tradition of radical thinkers in that nation encouraged new ways for looking at economic and social conditions.

The industrial revolution, with its realigning relationships between worker and owner, produced the impetus for rethinking the relationship of classes. The comte de Saint-Simon understood that the developing political and scientific changes required the creation of new means for social organization and called for planned organization in the interest of all citizens. He, however, stood for the rights of the producers against the non-producers because he believed that property ownership provided the basis for maintaining overall social order. de Rouvroy developed the view that a new Christianity sould be created which would rest on a faith in the sciences (*Nouveau Christianisme*, 1825). The state would be responsible for keeping abreast with scientific discovery and promote means for planning and using production most efficiently.

A contemporary of De Rouvroy, Charles Fourier (1772-1837), developed his own views on socialism, with the concept of the *phalanstere*—a cooperative composed of 1,500 to 1,600 people as the centerpiece. Members would work coopcratively togethei and enjoy the benefits of their labors. However, while members pooled their efforts and lived in a single large building, Fourier believed in property ownership and proposed that income be divided based on work, property ownership, and talent. His thinking influenced some of the most influential newspaper editors and publishers during the nineteenth century, including Charles A. Dana and Horace Greeley in the United States.

Because Germany was more backward industrially than England or France, the nation lagged behind others in the development of a socialist movement. The writings of philosopher Georg Wilhelm Friedrich Hegel (1770-1831) assisted in the development of socialism in Germany, partly because of his critical writings on religion and partly because he provided strong discussion and logic for the dialectic—a device that Marx later adopted.

Hegel also provided a clear analysis on freedom of expression matters. In *Naturrecht und Staatswissenschaft im Grundrisse* and *Grundlinien der Philosophie des Rechts* (Natural Law and Political Science in Outline: Elements of the Philosophy of Right—a book published under two titles in 1821; English translation, 1952) Hegel explained his views:

> Of the two modes of communication, the press and the spoken word, the first exceeds the second in range of contact but lags behind it in vivacity—satisfaction of the goading desire to say one's say and to have said it, is directly assured by the laws and by-laws which control or punish its excesses . . .
>
> To define freedom of the press as freedom to say and write whatever we please is parallel to the assertion that freedom as such means freedom to do as we please. Talk of this kind is due to wholly uneducated, crude, and superficial ideas.

The early socialists did not devote any attention to Hegel's concepts of press limitations and freedoms; however, his thinking was available to later thinkers.

Karl Marx (1818-1883) was one of the followers of Hegel that included Bruno Bauer (1809-1882), Moses Hess (1812-1875), and Karl Grun (1817-1887)—a German group that helped shape Marx's early thinking. Marx was a student of Hegel. However, Marx developed his communistic ideas after moving to France where he became close friends with Friedrich Engels (1820-1895), and the thinking of Hegel only helped establish an intellectual attitude which opened the way to later thinking.

Another influence in Marx's life was Ludwig Feuerback (1804-1872), who aided the German socialist movement through his views on religion as a humanistic activity and who rejected the concept of a god. Feuerback assisted the socialistic movement mainly because his views encouraged the struggle between church and state, capital and labor.

Marx's early life was more as a liberal than as a socialist or communist. He attended the University of Jena where he received a doctorate in philosophy in 1841. Upon graduation, the liberal-thinking Marx became the editor of the *Rheinische Zeitung* in 1842 published at Cologne where he fought censorship and for the right of newspapers to cover what they chose.

During this period, Marx married Jenny von Westphalen, a close friend since childhood and the daughter of a prominent government official. That marriage, which lasted a lifetime, gave Marx the strength to continue with his controversial writing in times of adversity.

Shortly after his marriage, the *Rheinische Zeitung* became the focus of government suppression. With the shortlived career in journalism at an end for the moment, Marx moved to Paris where he developed close contact with the French socialist writers. Later, in London, he became a correspondent for Horace Greeley's *New York Tribune*.

Friedrich Engels (1820-95), became Marx's closest and life- long friend; he greatly influenced the direction of his thinking—from this time Marx spent most of his time developing his theory of history and the conflict between the working and owner classes. In exile from his homeland, Marx wrote the first of his throughts on economic socialism as a response to P. J. Proudhon's book, *Philosophie de la misere* (Philosophy of Poverty), and entitled it *Misere de la philosophie* (1847)—the English translation is *Poverty of Philosophy*. This first book developed the basis upon which later works would grow. Marx had a strong interest in economics and history, and he tried to create a theory of history that would provide a complete and systematic view of human progress, a theory based on four major components:

1. Historical progress or social development is determined by economic developments, which are the foundation of social, religious, political, and artistic institutions.

2. All great progress or change is the result of total conflict between a new and an old concept or principle, Marx believed the dialectic: "Each stage or condition (thesis) contains contradictions (antithesis) which struggle to compose a synthesis."

3. Social classes are in real conflict—the rich against the poor, the owner against the worker, big business against small business, political leadership against the citizen.

4. Labor Value Theory. This concept says that the amount of work or labor put into the production of a commodity establishes the value of that product. To Marx, profit came from the "exploitation of labor"—not paying it properly for its work.

The Communist Manifesto

Marx and Engels enjoyed some recognition within the Communist League, a group of socialists who replaced the League of the Just (1836-47) as the dominant socialist organization in France in 1847. The congress of the Communist League authorized Marx and Engels to draft the *Communist Manifesto* (November 1847). Working together they produced the *Manifesto* in January 1848 which spelled out the essentials of the socialist movement.

To Marx, the enemy was the ruling class; he included the czarist government of Russia, Napoleon III in France, and the Bismarck government of Germany. Marx believed that once the source of conflict—the oppression imposed by the rulers—disappeared, harmony would replace discord and conflict. The Communists proclaimed the year, 1848, the "year of revolutions." The new document first described the revolutionary role of the working class—the proletariat:

A spectre is haunting Europe—the spectre of Communism. All the powers of old Europe have netered into a holy alliance to exorcise this spectre; Pope and Czar, Metternich and Guizot, French Radicals and German police-spies . . .

The history of all hitherto existing society is the history of class struggles.

Freeman and slave, patrician and plebeian, lord and serf, guild-master and journeyman, in a word, oppressor and oppressed, stood in constant opposition to one another, carried on uninterrupted, now hidden, now open fight, a fight that each time ended, either in a revolutionary re-constitution of society at large, or in the common ruin of the contending classes.

Our epoch, the epoch of the bourgeoisie, possesses, however, this distinctive feature; it has simplified the class antagonisms. Society as a whole is more and more splitting up into two great hostile camps, into two great classes directly facing each other: Bourgeoisie and Proletariat . . .

In the conditions of the proletariat, those of the old society at large are already virtually swamped. The proletarian is without property; his relation to his wife and children has no longer anything in common with the bourgeois family relations; modern industrial labor, modern subjection to capital, the same in England as in France, in America as in Germany, has stripped him of every trace of national character. Law, morality, religion, are to him so many bourgeois prejudices, behind which lurk in ambush just as many bourgeois interests . . .

After a long description of the state of the proletariat, Marx and Engels ended the manifesto with a challenge:

Finally, they labor everywhere for the union and agreement of the democratic parties of all countries. The Communists disdain to conceal their views and aims. They openly declare that their ends can be attained only by the forcible overthrow of all existing social conditions. Let the ruling classes tremble at a Communistic revolution. The proletarians have nothing to lose but their chains. They have a world to win. Working men of all countries unite!

Marx believed that humanity was communal in nature, and when people failed to recognize this fact, they became self-alienated. The creation of wage-labor class made inevitable this alienation. Capitalism, therefore, denied the natural characteristics of the human spirit. It was natural that Marx would see communism as consistant with the human need:

> Communism is the positive abolition of private property and thus of human self-alienation and therefore the real reappropriation of the human essence by and for man. This communism as the complete and conscious return of man—conserving all the riches of previous development for man himself as a social, i.e. human, being. Communism as completed natualism is humanism and as completed humanism is naturalism.

Marx's writing in Paris was to establish the base upon which some of his later works would be founded. This writing focused on class struggles, historical conflicts, and economic considerations. Marx also devoted some time to the role of criticism in creating new thought.

Some have thought that Marx and Engels interpreted everything in history in context with the dialectic, but this is not the case. Only the major social revolutions, the great turning points in human history and institutions, fell under the interpretation of their theory. The daily activities were mere random events. In fact, Marx believed that "Man always makes his own history." Marx hoped his analysis of history would bring order to the study of history—a means for identifying a pattern, rather than seeing history as a random set of unrelated events.

Speaking about Marxist concepts, Andrei Vyshinsky, a student of communism observed:

> "Pre-Marxian sociology" and historiography at best presented a desultory assemblage of crude facts and a portrayal of separate sides of the historic process. Marxism pointed the way to an all-embracing, omnifarious study of the process of emergence, development, and decay of social-economic formulations. It contemplates the totality of all contradictory tendencies and reduces them to precisely defined conditions of the life and production of the various classes of society. It eliminates subjectivism and arbitrariness in choosing or interpreting "master" ideas. It exposes, without exception, the roots of all ideas and all different tendencies in the condition of material production forces.

Marx and the Media

One of Marx's beliefs held that when the working class gained control, and the oppressor classes were defeated, a complete unity and peace would reign in the world. This concept had implications for press freedoms. If the supremacy of the working class satisfied every human need and created a condition of happinesses for everyone, there would be no need for the media to engage in criticism of the foundations of communism. Any published criticism need be limited only to trying to refine an imperfect communistic system until it met the ideal laid down by Marx. Marx, however, never indicated that he felt that way about the freedom of expression—it was for later thinkers to add this limit on the media. Indeed, as a journalist, his several comments or actions regarding the press give no reason to be convinced that he would suppress all anti-communist writing.

In 1848, Marx with a number of other radical members started the *Neue Rheinische Zeitung* in Cologne intended to be a national newspaper concentrating not only on what was going on in Germany, but also on events in France and England. The newspaper supported universal suffrage, creation of a state banking organization, state underwriting of unemployment, some forms of capitalism, and direct elections. The primary goal, however, was to support worker or proletarian causes; however, the newspaper went to considerable length to see that the proletariat remained associated with its natural allies.

On March 2, 1849, two members of the military called on Marx to complain about an article carried in the newspaper and to ask for the name of the author of the report. In describing the event, Marx felt no need to suppress the two men's right of speech, but he pointed out that they had recourse against the newspaper if they wished:

> I answered the gentlemen (1) that the article had nothing to do with me as it was an insertion in the non-editorial part of the paper; (2) that they could be provided with free space for a counterstatement; (3) that it was open to them to seek satisfaction in the courts. When the gentlemen pointed out that the whole of the Eighth Company felt itself slandered by the article, then I replied that only the signatures of the whole of the Eighth Company could convince me of the correctness of this statement which was, in any case, irrelevant. The [noncommissioned officers] then told me that if I did not name "the man," if I did not "hand him over," they could "no longer hold their people back," and it would "turn out badly." I answered that the gentlemen's threats and intimidation would achieve absolutely nothing with me. They then left, muttering under their breath.

The newspaper continued until May 18, 1849, when 20,000 copies were sold on the last day of publication.

Although Marx appeared to tolerate the contrary attitudes of others as in the case of the noncommissioned officers, a statement issued by Marx and five other communists during April 1850, while forming the Universal Society of Communist Revolutionaries, suggests an intolerant attitude:

> The aim of the society is the overthrow of all the privileged classes, and to submit these classes to the dictatorship of the proletariat by maintaining the revolution in permanence until the realization of communism, which will be the last organizational form of the human family.

While Marx continued the struggle for communism, he also helped support himself through journalistic writing. Charles Dana, managing editor of the *New York Daily Tribune*, had offered Marx the opportunity to serve as a foreign correspondent for the newspaper, a task he began in 1852, despite his contempt for the wide mix of causes the newspaper adopted. Marx saw the newspaper supporting both the "industrial bourgeoisie of America" and those of the working classes. However, the income kept him from starving and provided a base from which he could develop his theory.

The later years of Marx's life were devoted to completing his major three volume work, *Das Kapital* (1867, volumes two and three posthumously in 1885 and 1894) and to participation in communistic activities; consequently, his newspaper and magazine writing declined significantly despite periodic attempts to write. He had little reason, therefore, to participate in any debate over press freedoms during the later years, and never made any definitive statements on his attitudes towards press-state matters. Marx's influence on free expression matters arises out concepts laid down for the society generally and on the application of his writings.

Occasionally, Marx would engage in criticism of the writings of others whom he did not believe reflected the true socialist spirit. He objected, for example, to the publication in August 1877 of *Die Zukunft*, a theoretical journal designed to provide intellectual analysis to the movement, which brought "a bourgeois into the party." The cost of the publication was underwritten by Karl Hochberg, son of a wealthy bootmaker. Marx did not, himself, provide the framework for suppression through any systematic statements or practices in his life. It was for later generations to establish concepts for socialist-communistic press freedoms.

Later Party Actions

Not until the German Social Democratic Party adopted Marxist views in 1891 did a party that subscribed to Marxism gain a large vote in an election. The party gained power until it could boast 4,250,000 votes in the election of 1912, a third of all votes cast that year. The party wanted a social redevelopment of society along the lines proposed by Marx. Elsewhere in Europe, socialist parties were formed near the end of the nineteenth century. For example, Marx's son-in-law, Paul Lafargue (1842-1911), formed the Marxist Parti Ouvrier Francais in 1880; in Belgium, the followers of Cesar de Paepe (1842-1890) formed a party allied with the trade unions and cooperative societies, in 1885; and in Spain, Pablo Iglesias (1850-1925) created a Marxist party in 1879.

Although the socialist movement in Europe gained considerable support from the working class citizens, it had trouble defining its own goals or intellectual foundation. The Parti Ouvrier split in France in 1882 into the Guesdists and Possibilits, and the Possibilists split again in 1890, each group following the thinking of a prominent socialist thinker. Similar splits took place in Germany because of the 1899 work, *Die Voraussetzungen des Sozialismus*, by Eduard Bernstein. Bernstein wanted a fundamental revision in the Marx theory.

Not until the Bolshevik Revolution in 1917 did the socialist movement have a chance to implement its philosophies. However, Russian socialism, itself, was practiced by four parties—Socialist Revolutionairies, Left Socialist Revolutionaries, Bolsheviks, and Mensheviks, each with its own attitudes on what the word meant.

Russian socialism followed its own course, borrowing from the western views, but adding nationalistic elements. Russia had much less industry than did the rest of Europe, and had a large peasant class clustered in small villages that had long been subjected to repression. These fundamentally different conditions led Peter Lavrov (1823-1900) and other socialist leaders to develop their views.

By 1895, Vladimir Ilyich Ulyanov (Lenin) (1870-1924) had organized several parties. Eventually, the Social-Democratic Workers' Party (Minsk, 1898) came into being representing the communistic view of which Lenin approved, but in time Lenin came to disagree with the revisionist attitude of many in the party.

The party held a conference in Brussels and London in 1903 and adopted the revolutionary program of Lenin. Lenin wanted land reform, national self-determination, and a dictatorship of the proletariat, and he wanted party discipline—a very strict control. Although Lenin was opposed by much of the party's membership, his views prevailed. However, the split led to the party developing two wings—the Bolsheviks ("those of the majority") who supported Lenin and the Mensheviks ("those of the minority").

Lenin and the Media

Lenin shaped the form of press-state relationships after the revolution that brought the communist state into being. Lenin saw a special role for newspapers and their staffs, a view which he expressed while he was editor *Iskra* [*The Spark*]. He saw journalists as activist participants in the development of a better society, rather than objective reporters of events:

> [Newspaper staffs] would become part of an enormous pair of Smith's bellows that would fan every spark of the class struggle and of popular indignation into a general conflagration. Around what is in itself a very innocuous and very small, but regular and common, effort, in the full sense of the word, a regular army of tried fighters would systematically gather and receive their training. On the ladders and scaffolding of this general organizational structure there would soon develop and come to the fore [leaders] who would take their place at the head of the mobilized army and rouse the whole people to settle accounts with the shame and the curse of Russia.

Lenin spent considerable time before the 1917 Revolution writing out his concepts for a new political order in *The State and Revolution* (1917); *The Proletarian Revolution and Kautsky the Renegade* (Eng. trans., 1920). Lenin's thinking before the Revolution became the foundation for the development of institutions in the new Republic.

Lenin had strong views on the role of criticism which he saw as a bourgeoisie concept designed to keep the poor and working citizens from seeing reality. He observed:

> The capitalist (and with them, wittingly or unwittingly, many Socialist Revolutionaires and Mensheviks) define as "freedom of the press" a state of affairs under which censorship is abolished and all parties freely publish all kinds of newspapers. In reality, this is not freedom of the press, but freedom to deceive the oppressed and exploited masses of the people by the rich, by the bourgeoisie.

One of the people Lenin most criticized was French socialist Alexander Millerand (1859-1943) who eventually became a French cabinet minister in 1899, selling out to the establishment and proving Lenin's accusations to be "true." Lenin observed that Millerand had turned the corner to become a bourgeoise social reformer with the following consequences for Millerand and others who turn from revolutionary thinking:

> Thus, the demand for a decisive turn from revolutionary Social-Democracy to bourgeoise social-reformism was accompanied by a no less decisive turn towards bourgeois criticism of all the fundamental ideas of Marxism. In view of the fact that this criticism of Marxism has long been directed from the political platform, from university chairs, in numerous pamphlets and in a series of learned treatises, in view of the fact that the entire younger generation of the educated classes has been systematically reared for decades on this criticism, it is not surprising that the "new critical" trend in Social-Democracy should spring up, all complete, like Minerva from the head of Jove. The content of this new trend did not have to grow and take shape; it was transferred bodily from bourgeois to socialist literature.

In 1917, Lenin was openly criticizing the bourgeois press, declaring that the socialist press was the "free" press; on August 30 and 31, he observed, the proletariat "will close down the bourgeois newspapers after openly declaring by law, by government decree, that the capitalists and their defenders are enemies of the people." Lenin used the opportunity to say that the old tyranny of Russia was returning and that "the government of 'free Russia' could not, and did not, do anything of the kind." To Lenin there was no middle ground:

> Since there can be no talk of an independent ideology formulated by the working masses themselves in the process of their movement, the *only* choice is—either bourgeois or socialist ideology. There is no middle course (for mankind has not created a "third" ideology and, moreover, in a society torn by class antagonisms there can never be a non-class or an above-class ideology). Hence, to belittle the sociologist ideology *in any way, to turn aside from it in the slightest degree*, means to strengthen bourgeois ideology.

Having established to his satisfaction that capitalism was a repression of the working class person, Lenin had no difficulty concluding that only the socialist view should receive exposure in the media.

In 1917, just before the revolution, Lenin argued that true freedom of expression meant that all citizens must have access to the press, but since the capitalist press was controlled by money, advertisers who purchased space had their influence, while people without money had no access to the press. To remedy the problem, Lenin called for a state monopoly over advertising and free or low cost distribution of newspapers to the peasants. His call was for the state to take "*all* the printing presses and *all* the newsprint and distribute them *equitably*: the state should come first—in the interests of the majority of the people."

Lenin's new plan would provide freedom of the press for rich and poor alike. The plan was in direct conflict with that of those who called for private ownership of the media with some limited press controls. By October 25, 1917, Lenin had proposed a three-point program for handling newspapers: (1) He would suppress all counterrevolutionary newspapers, (2) establish a government controlled monopoly on advertising, and (3) place the press under the control of the government. Beginning on October 26, 1917, the Military Revolutionary Committee (MRC) of Petrograd Soviet began closing down newspapers, including seven of the largest circulation papers in Petrograd on that day. The suppressions continued throughout November and December and into 1918 despite some resistance from local revolutionary groups.

Many of Russia's best known writers protested the actions and some newspapers continued to publish after being suppressed. Lack of staff members and supplies imposed by the suppressions, however, crippled many of the papers.

On July 10, 1918, the Constitution of the Russian Soviet Federative Socialist Republic provided:

> To ensure for the toilers genuine freedom to express their opinions, the Russian Soviet Federative Socialist Republic puts an end to the dependence of the press upon capital and transfers to the working class and peasant poor all the technical and material resources necessary for the publication of newspapers, pamphlets, books and other printed matter, and guarantees their unobstructed circulation throughout the country.

The constitutional proclamation occurred just after Lenin had completed the suppression of the bourgeois press, and he asked if there was any other place on earth where the proletariat "enjoys anything approaching *such* liberty . . . of using the largest printing plants."

Years later, the new constitution of the U.S.S.R. (1936) provided for civil liberties as follows:

> In conformity with the interests of the working people, and in order to strengthen the socialist system, the citizens of the U.S.S.R. are guaranteed by law:

a) freedom of speech;
b) freedom of the press;
c) freedom of assembly, including the holding of mass meetings;
d) freedom of street processions and demonstrations.

These civil rights are ensured by placing at the disposal of the working people and their organizations printing presses, stocks of paper, public buildings, the streets, communications facilities.

Despite the language of the Soviet Constitution, the heritage before the Revolution of czarist suppressions and the attitudes of Lenin in his interpretation of Marx created an environment in which freedom of expression was limited to the extent permitted by the Party's will. Describing political freedoms in the U. S. S. R., George Kennan, a student of the Soviet condition observed:

Their particular brand of fanaticism, unmodified by any of the Anglo-Saxon traditions of compromise, was too fierce and too jealous to envisage any permanent sharing of power. From the Russian-Asiatic world out of which they had emerged they carried with them a skepticism as to the possibilities of permanent and peaceful coexistence of rival forces. Easily persuaded of their own doctrinaire "rightness," they insisted on the submission or destruction of all competing power. Outside of the Communist Party, Russian society was to have no rigidity. There were to be no forms of collective human activity or association which would not be dominated by the Party . . . And within the Party the same principle was to apply. The mass of Party members might go through the motions of election, deliberation, decision and action; but in these motions they were to be animated not by their own individual wills but by the awesome breath of the Party leadership and the overbrooding presence of "the world."

The new Soviet Republic established bureaus and agencies to perform every task. The military protected the state from the enemies outside the nation, police kept counterrevolutionary sentiment from gaining expression, and the media were:

. . . not only [to be] a collective propagandist and a collective agitator, [but] also a collective organizer . . . With the aid of the newspaper, and through it, a permanent organization will naturally take shape that will engage, not only in local activities, but in regular general work, and will train its members to follow political events carefully, appraise their significance and their effect on the various strata of the population, and develop effective means for the revolutionary party to influence those events.

The media in the new Soviet republic were to function as a department of the government; they were owned by the state, and it was their job to serve the goals of the state just as the military was to preserve the security of the nation.

No private ownership was permitted; therefore, management and control of the media was through direct chain of command from the central party through the lines of bureaucracy to the working editor and reporter.

Since, as Marx said, humanity was a communal being that would be happy and satisfied in a communistic state, and since capitalism was the source of all discontent and human misery, the ideal state for people could only be achieved by establishing a media system owned by the proletariat through its central party. The media would then be given absolute power to discuss anything they wished within the limits of the socialist philosophy. Since capitalism was destructive, there was no reason to give exposure to capitalistic views.

Stalin

The concepts of Lenin received further expression and support by the tyrannical Joseph Vissarionovich Stalin (1879-1953), who eventually became leader of the Communist Party in the Soviet Union after Lenin's death in January 1924:

> [T]he state [is to] acquire the function of protecting Socialist property from thieves and pilferers of the people's property. The function of defending the country from foreign attack fully remained; consequently the Red Army and the Navy also fully remained, as did the punitive organs and the intelligence service, which are indispensable for the detection and punishment of the spies, assassins, and wreckers sent into this country by foreign espionage services. The function of economic organization and cultural education by the state organs also remained, and was developed to the full. Now the main task of our state inside the country is the work of peaceful economic organization and cultural education. As for our army, punitive organs and intelligence service, their edge is no longer turned to the inside of our country but to the outside, against the external enemies.

Just as Stalin believed that the military had to continue to serve the needs of the proletariat and republic, he had strong views on what constituted press freedom, a view tied to the social condition of the nation's citizens. He believed freedom started with the meeting of basic human needs for employment, food, and comforts—there could be no freedom for the person who was hungry and who could not find employment. Consequently, he saw the American mass media as lacking freedom since nothing was done to insure that the poor had adequate housing, clothing, and food. The poor could not concentrate their intellectual energies to analyzing societal problems, and for them freedom was an illusion.

Stalin found himself constantly in conflict with his opponents; he successfully suppressed any freedom of expression that might have remained in the Party. Ultimately, the Communist Party became a "monolithic" organization. Finally by 1929, Stalin had expelled all opposition leaders from the U.S.S.R., or had forced any remaining to "recant" and became the sole leader of the nation.

Stalin did not become more tolerant, and in 1936 conducted the purge trials of the Bolsheviks and anyone who might stand in his way. During the trials people were forced to "confess" their guilt of treason, terrorism, or espionage. The mass purges created a terroristic environment in which freedoms died out as millions were imprisoned or murdered.

Mass Media and the Soviet State

Wilbur Schramm, then director of the Institute for Communication Research at Stanford University, observed in 1956, the Soviet media served six major functions:

> 1) Mass communications are used instrumentally—that is, as an instrument of the State and the Party.
> 2) They are closely integrated with other instruments of State power and Party influence.
> 3) They are used as instruments of unity within the State and the Party.
> 4) They are used as instruments of State and Party "revelation."
> 5) They are used almost exclusively as instruments of propaganda and agitation.
> 6) They are characterized by a strictly enforced responsibility.

In 1979, the Soviet Communist Party Central Committee indicated that the media were still to be used to promote the goals of the party, and directed the media:

> . . .to eradicate ugly vestiges of the past—vestiges hostile to socialism— that frequently are still present in our life, such as money-grubbing and bribery, the desire to grab whatever one can from society without giving it anything in return, mismanagement, wastefulness, drunkenness, hooliganism, red tape, a callous attitude toward people and violations of labor discipline and public order.

To perform its role in Soviet society, the nation produces approximately 8,000 newspapers, of which 640 are dailies, and 6,000 journals and other periodicals. There were two general types of newspapers—regional or municipal newspapers of general circulation, and newspapers serving specialized audiences. Although most of the newspapers are local or regional in nature, there are several all-Union newspapers, including the Communist Party newspaper, *Pravda*; the national youth newspaper, *Komsomolskaya Pravda*; and the government newspaper, *Izvestia*.

Publications that concentrate on interest groups include *Krasnaya Zvezda* (Red Star) from the Ministry of Defense, papers for youth, and others for laborers in various industries. All newspapers and journals supported the party—directed views. To maintain necessary controls, censorship agencies, referred to as GLAVLIT, review content; the most important organization is the Chief Administration for the Preservation of State Secrets in the Press. Besides the formal censorship chain, editors are punished or removed from their posts for missteps. To insure that they are instructed in the will of the party, editors regularly receive information of party goals and views.

The Agitprop staff of Central Committee maintains direct supervision of the all-Union publications, and each republic and other political subdivision provides its own Agitprop-like unit to insure that publications are managed properly.

Each of the fourteen republics in the U.S.S.R. by law have made political communication contrary to the Party dictates illegal. The laws prohibit propaganda that might weaken the power of the Soviet authority, and it is the party that decides when the laws of the republic have been violated.

Most of the content of U.S.S.R. newspapers is planned days and weeks ahead of time and is discussed by editors in regular meetings. Little current news ever appears in newspapers, as in the case in Western newspapers where currency and superficiality are considered most important. The long lag time between event and report provides the state censors time to decide what should be released.

The controls insure that negative information such as accidents, crime, drug problems, alcoholism, and epidemics receive little coverage in the media. Press controls insure that newspapers and magazines contain political stories and tales of corrupt petty officials—pages that might bore most Western readers; yet, circulation figures for *Pravda* has reached 11 million in 44 cities, and other national newspapers have similar huge circulations in the 1980s.

Just as an army can not successfully fight without weapons, so the Party can not successfully carry out its ideological work without such a sharp and militant weapon as the press.

—Nikita Khrushchev

One aspect of the Soviet press merits special attention. The Party encourages letters of complaint from readers—a drive that has led to a flood of 360,000 letters yearly to *Pravda* and 500,000 to *Izvestia*. *Pravda* had 50 people working in the letter department in the mid 1980s.

During recent years, the Soviet Union has provided electricity to most parts of the nation, and, with the growth of low cost radio equipment, the nation experienced a dramatic increase in the number of people with their own receivers. The U.S.S.R., prior to this growth, had invested in an extensive network of wired communication media that provided the Soviet authorities with total control over sound communications—a network still existing in the mid-1980s. A number of broadcast services also exist, including Radio Moscow and the central radio service, which broadcast eight separate program services on FM and three different AM bands for a total of over one thousand hours of programming weekly.

Estimates place the number of television sets in operation in the Soviet Union at seventy million. To serve the demand, programs are distributed by satellite and microwave to most parts of the nation. The number of channels available vary from six in Moscow to three Leningrad, and only two in most other cities.

News is gathered and distributed by TASS (Telegraphic Agency of the Soviet Union) formed in 1935, and Agentstvo Pechati Novesti (formed in 1961). Besides the information provided for publication, TASS also sends bulletins to officials that was not made available for publication.

Even in Soviet society, it became impossible to promulgate only the type of information consistant with party desires. As a large state with world-wide influence, the Soviet Union requires vast quantities of accurate information to function, just as any other nation. Consequently, the party tolerates, or encourages, the "full and comprehensive elucidation of the work of party and government organs."

The major newspapers and media in the Soviet society are owned and operated by the Communist Party. The Party is the representation of the workers' will; it stands in place of the population. The Party, therefore, is the only organization qualified to manage and operate the media in the interest of *all* of the nation's citizens. Any other form of organization would take the media out of the hands of the people and would fail to serve the greater need.

Because the media are operated by the Party, they receive their support from Party funds and need not worry about economic considerations that constantly concern Western media. Party philosophy holds that this freedom from economic problems frees the media from influence of advertisers. Communist leadership believes they have created the freest, most objective journalistic establishment in the world.

Eastern Europe

Similar patters of media exist in Czechoslovakia, East Germany, Poland, Romania, Hungary, Bulgaria, Yugoslavia, and Albania when they first became Communist countries; but, with time, changes have developed. According to John C. Merrill (1983), Albania, for example, has left the Soviet bloc, but it remains committed to Communism. The central committee in each nation maintains its own official newspaper.

Nation	Central Committee Papers Newspaper	Circulation
Bulgaria	*Rabotnichesko Delo*	850,000
Czechoslovakia	*Rude Pravo*	900,000
East Germany	*Neues Deutschland*	800,000
Poland	*Trybuna Ludu*	970,000
Romania	*Scinteia*	1,300,000
Hungary	*Nepszabadsag*	810,000
Albania	*Zeri i Popullit*	110,000

(Source: John C. Merrill, *Global Journalism: A Survey of the World's Mass Media*, New York: Longman, 1983.)

Assignment 4.5

MCOM 4150

Media and Government

Assignment #5

To date we have dealt with whatever controls were instituted to "protect" – to "determine the appropriate limitation of the independence" to be allowed the media "in the interest of the 'greater' societal or individual rights."

Now, turn your attention to the independent thinkers – these persons and/or acts which attempted to loosen those controls – whatever was in conflict with the status quo – that posture which exhibited the most authoritarian restraints. Select what you feel was an exemplary philosophy arguing for free expression in the first section of the text, pp. 3-317.

1. Identify the work and any specific person(s) involved.

2. Briefly state the intent/issue(s)/consequences.

3. Indicate the ultimate disposition/outcome of your choice.

Submit your response on one side of one piece of 8½x11" paper, typed, double-spaced. Use the above headings and partition your paper accordingly - to be presented at the next class meeting.

Like the Soviet Union, the bloc nations have newspapers devoted the the youth, sports, and special interests. They also have weekly newspapers, journals, and magazines.

Discussing the controls that one Communist nation exercises, Paul S. Underwood, former reporter for the Associated Press and *The New York Times* who later became a professor at Ohio State University, observed:

> How tight and detailed the controls on the media are was evidenced by the Polish government's instructions to the press of that country on the occasion of the visit of Pope John Paul II to his homeland in 1979. Ten pages of instructions were issued (later published in the West). Among other things, most newspapers were told that on the first day of the visit, they were to print a picture of the Pope, an item reporting his arrival, a profile of the man, and a commentary. The commentary was prepared by the national news agency PAP. Nothing more was to appear.

Even more limitations were imposed on the official party newspapers, and newspapers published by the Catholic Church had to secure clearance on everything before publication.

General control over the media in Poland starts with the Central Committee Press Department, which sets policy and sees that the media cover major events consistant with the party goals. Reporting to the Press Department is the Main Office for Control of Press, Publications and Public Performances (GUKPPiW) and serves as Poland's principal censor. GUKPPiW produces and maintains thorough and accurage records of all official acts to insure that censors could be instructed in the way to perform their tasks. Most Poles do not view the GUKPPiW with much respect, and the people who went into its employment often did so because they could not get another job—thus, the need to provide comprehensive training to insure that the censors would do their job correctly.

The Main Office for Control in Warsaw oversees the tasks of branch offices that regulates almost everything. Sheet music, dramas, exhibitions, concerts, even business cards and rubber stamps come under the watchful eye of the official censor. Other people review imported matter, including motion pictures, books, and television programs. Programs in all media have to be monitored and some had to be cleansed. Censors typically demand changes about 10,000 times each year.

All of the censorship of Poland is guarded by extensive secrecy so that even the editors, reporters, producers, and directors often do not know the extent to which the government has gone in the management of the media. The job of the censors extend to 56 daily newspapers, two radio and two television stations, 595 magazines, 220 specialized and local newsletters, *Przyjaciólka*, a women's weekly, a variety of specialized journals, and the Catholic weekly *Tygodnik Powszechny*.

During the late 1970s, some newspapers and periodicals began enjoying limited freedom from the censors as was evidenced when *Zycie Gospodarcze* published articles that caused censors to issue a memorandum on July 6, 1976, objecting to two articles that went beyond the limits of what was considered acceptable, but the document observed:

> In the event the editorial leadership does not agree with the censor's reservations and does not wish to adopt our suggestions, and the difference of opinion concerns less important questions, such a publication is permitted to be printed, provided that the editor-in-chief assumes personal responsibility for printing unchanged the formulations or excerpts questioned by us.

Seemingly, the censors would allow the publication of some questionable articles if the editors would take responsibility. Other papers, however, did not enjoy so much freedom, falling between the outer limits of the intellectual papers and the tight controls on the party papers. Censorship in Poland reached such a level that most editors simply decided to comply with the censors' demands—often before the demands came.

The growing freedom may have contributed to the assertive spirit of Solidarity, the group of tradespeople who demanded the right to form an independent union at the Gdansk shipyards in August 1980. Their freedom was short lived because the government declared "war" on the workers on December 13, 1981, and a new wave of censorship appeared to control unrest rather than any attempt to confront the real problems. The new repression affected journalists, editors, union leaders, and workers.

China

In September 1949, at the Chinese People's Political Consultative conference in Peiping, members met to organize a new nation, and, in October 1949, the People's Republic of China came into being with the capital to be at Peiping, renamed Peking.

The organization exercised central control over the new government including all aspects of the mass media and education. By the mid-1960s, the media to be controlled included an extensive network of telegraph lines to every part of the nation, telephones with 90,000 miles of lines, radio broadcasting that completely covered the country, and loudspeakers in most villages and community centers.

The Chinese viewed their form of communism to be more in the intellectual tradition of Marx and Mao Tse-Tung (1893-1976), the revolutionary statesman, and Communist Party leader, believed to be the proper heir of Marx. Yet, China patterned its mass media after that of the Soviet Union. The Communist Party exercised strict control over all of the media and had its party newspaper, *Renmin Ribao* (*People's Daily*, 1948); and 382 newspapers, with a circulation over seventy million, serve the nation. Letters coming into the newspapers provide feedback. The newspaper prints an eight page edition each day with no sports, entertainment, comics, or contrary political opinion.

China maintains the Central People's Broadcasting Station with four services for internal audiences. Two of the stations provide news, culture, and policy statements; another concentrates on art, literature, and music. The fourth is organized for ethnic minorities. Radio Peking has forty stations across the nation and is a major international service. Although television is spreading across China with the growth of Peking Television, by 1980, the nation had only about ten million receivers which could reach about one-third of the population—that number may have risen to 33 million in 1986.

Although television is controlled by the Central Committee of the Communist Party, the stations are carrying some commercials in the 1980s, and the previously uninteresting programs have been taking on improved production values—especially since the end of the Cultural Revolution. Some world news is taken from Western agencies and rebroadcast to the audiences.

The hierarchy for publishing news insures that the Central Party's releases receives first priority, while other news is submitted to officials before publication. The nation also operates the Xinhau News Agency news service.

The actual organization that controls the media varies by the nature of the publication. For example, the Department of Propaganda supervises science related *Kwang Ming Daily*, while the Ministry of Defense's General Political Department oversees the *Liberation Army Daily*.

While China is one of the nations in the Asia-Pacific region that subscribes to the Communist philosophy, others include Afghanistan, Kampuchea, Laos, Vietnam, and North Korea. In all of these countries the role of the mass media is to support the goals and policies of the Communist Party.

According to Mao Tse-tung, the role of the mass media is four fold:

1) Distribute information on policies,
2) Educate the people,
3) Organize the masses, and
4) Mobilize the masses.

In recent years, the role of the mass media has been to support the modernization of China while the class struggle of past generations has been deemphasized. The result has been an increasing quantity of news and features and the development of a more lively style of writing. To promote the new goals, journalism education has received standing in the university.

Other regions of the world

In Africa, a number of nations have Communist or socialist media establishments, including Angola, Benin, Cape Verde, Ethiopia, Guinea, Guinea-Bissau, Mozambique, Sao Tome and Principe, Somalia, Tanzania, and to some extent Madagascar and Mali.

During the 1980s in Latin America, Cuba is the principal government that subscribes to the Marxist concept of the media. The constitution of Cuba (1975) documents the nation's concept of media-government relationships:

The press, radio, television, and cinema are the instruments of ideological education for creation of a collective society.

Only Nicaragua, besides Cuba, subscribes to some form of Communistic government, but does so without officially acknowledging the fact.

Although variations occur in the handling of the media in Communist countries, in every case the nation's central Communist Party exercises final control over the freedoms that media within the nation enjoy. The central committee usually appoints an arm with censorship powers to insure that information contrary to the official policy is not printed and to provide news for publication about the activities of the party, goals for the state, and official interpretations of domestic and foreign news.

The model after which most Communist countries have patterned their media is the U.S.S.R. which established a central press censor reporting to the Central Committee to execute the standards set by the Central Committee. Spreading out in a pyramid are regional and local censorship units which take their lead from the next committee above.

All of the media are owned and controlled by the party and exist to promote the goals of the state, just as the military exist to function under the direction of the government. The media enjoy freedom only within the guidelines established by the central committees, and they are never free to criticize the foundations of the state.

While all Communist governments use a similar organizational structure, China has developed its own way of managing its media. Principally, this means that the media can use better production and writing values; they can enlarge the scope of programs somewhat, and can use some foreign news and programming.

The media-State relationship is closest in the socialist-communist theory of the media where journalists enjoy no freedom to use their independent judgement in newsgathering beyond that permitted by the state. They function as civil servants would in any other agency of government—they are hired to do the job they are assigned.

Besides the nations that have declared themselves to be Communist, many countries have Communist parties that function like other political organizations although the nation is not considered to be practicing the U.S.S.R model. For example, most Western European countries have Communist parties whose members cast votes in elections just as any other person would, but the party does not control the media or establish the pattern for ownership and control.

Concepts of the Socialist Press: Selected Writings

by Georgi Dimitrov

The press is a great force in building up a new society; the newspaper must inform, orient and educate masses; the journalist should be deeply devoted to the people, should be a vertitable patriot of complete honesty and indomitable faith in the power of the popular masses. When the journalist is writing, his foremost duty should be to have the image of the reader before his eyes . . . [Address to Union of Bulgarian Journalists, May 30, 1945.]

. . .At the time of the former governments the newspapers were generally the property of individual capitalists and capitalist trusts or were financed by suspicious sources and were in the service of the propaganda of an anti-national policy. Progressive newspapers and magazines were oppressed. The people [were] deprived of the right to express their own opinion by special draconian laws and barbarous censorship. In the time of our people's democracy, however, the principle of press freedom found its brilliant application. Our nation's democratic political organizations, its mass cultural organizations obtained the right to have their own periodicals and express freely their opinion on all state and policital problems. ["Report to the Second Congress of the Fatherland Front," February 2, 1948; Published in *Rabotnichesky Delo*, No. 28, February 5, 1948.]

We should create a press in the service of the people, of truth, which should be the voice of the victorious revolution . . .

You should discuss the truth about Bulgaria and arm with it the journalists from Western countries, from France, England, the United States, the small European countries. Your fight should be conducted on a broad battlefield. . .

The opposition employs lies and demogogy while our weapon is the truth, but this truth must be stated clearly and convincingly. It is not enough to tell the truth, one must expose lies and demogogy. And this is the secret of it all.

Georgi Mikhailovich Dimitrov (1882-1949), a journalist and labor leader, was one of the founders and leading philosophers of the Communist party in Europe. From 1905 through much of 1923, he was a leader of the Revolutionary Trade Union Federation. During that time, he was also a member of the Central Committee of the Bulgarian Communist Party and a deputy in the parliament. In 1923, he fled Bulgaria for Russia after leading an anti-fascist movement that was crushed. In 1933, he was one of those arrested in Nazi Germany on charges of starting the fire at the Reichstag building, probably caused by Nazis hoping to turn world attention against communism. In an elegant defense, he was acquited. During the next decade, he became a deputy of the Lenningrad Soviet, general secretary of the executive committee of the Communist International (1935-1943), deputy of the Supreme Soviet (1937-1945), and the guiding force behind the Bulgarian revolution. In 1945, after being awarded the Order of Lenin, Dimitrov returned to Bulgaria, became general secretary of the Communist party, and the architect of a popular-democratic constitution.

[A newspaper] should be written with inspiration for the children. They must be taught to love their people, the Party, the fatherland, labour and science, peace and friendship.

The fatherland should appear every day on the pages of the newspaper in the same way as it changes its appearance, its landscape, with its citizen busy at their daily work, and with its people who decides everything all over the country.

The proletarian revolution frees the masses from exploitation, opens for them the doors to a rapid advance, enhances the domination of man over nature by way of technology mastered by the people and thus creating the prerequisite for an unprecedented unfolding of their creative forces.

. . . In agitation and propaganda activity the press is one of the most powerful instruments, it leaves the most lasting traces on the life and struggles of our Party. The press will help us best in expanding the circle of adherents to our ideas . . . [Memoirs]

We need re-educate the backward strata of the people in a new, democratic and progressive spirit. We need grow up ourselves, develop—from the biggest to the smallest group in our political and economic life, in the state apparatus, in the administration, in the social organizations. We should not remain at the level we are at present because if we remain here, we would not only stop moving forward but would start moving backwards, for life is in constant evolution. We need printed words as a powerful weapon for increasingly stronger unity of the people's forces against our internal and external enemies.

Systematic work is necessary through the press, radio, the cinema and all other possible means in the re-education of the nations, of the people in towns and villages, in the re-education and education in the spirit of the people's democracy, of fraternity among the nations, of frank international cooperation, on the basis of equality between small and big nations, between great and small states.

And, finally, the feeling of national dignity, the faith in our own popular forces, in our just cause must be cultivated so that we can eliminate in time all wavering, every weakness and disbelief among the people during periods of very great stress and during the most severe storms. [Rabotnichesko Delo, No. 14, 20 January, 1948.]

. . . Journalism is a serious matter. When a Party journalist writes, he is obliged to think continuously of whether the fact he is going to state in the newspaper contributes or brings harm to the Party. Speed and resourcefulness are good enough qualities for a journalist but we have no intention of replacing the bourgeois press in the privilege of using cheap sensations.

So many bright names, such talented journalists have been given us by our Party: Georgi Kirkov, Khristo Kabakchiev, Todor Petrov, all of them used to be journalists of passionate pens, of high erudition and complete devotion to the Party. The Party journalists should be trusted by the Party. Otherwise he cannot fulfil his highly responsible duty. [Kirkov, Kabakchiev, and Petrov— three of the world's journalists—were founders and leaders of the Bulgarian Socialist Workers Party.]

No limitations should exist for the Party journalist. He should be admitted everywhere when the tasks of the newspaper demand this.

You may be a Minister or a chief of any kind, and you expect a journalist to come and speak with you on a couple of important points. He must not be left to wait in the waiting room or with your secretary because in the meantime the newspaper will already be printed and your explanations will be of no use afterwards.

A newspaper requires the strict and accurate utiliation of each minute. Time is allocated and coordinated with a lot of things: train departure, technical facilites, etc. There cannot and must not exist a closed door to a journalist; he enters without waiting with the secretary . . .What is more, if the telephone rings late at night because an editor from the Party periodical would like to visit you for the elucidation of a problem, you are obliged to get up and meet him politely and explain what might interest him in a calm and patient tone.

This is necessary, for when the journalist makes a mistake, it will go into the newspaper, it will go into the Party periodical . . . Any misunderstanding or wrong information brings about confusion, while any correction afterwards will not be read by all of us in the first place, and in the second place, those who have read it, will be left embarassed, confused; they will start protesting against the editorial board for lack of seriousness. Unfortunately, our newspapers still carry a lot of mistakes and this is the reason why we must help journalists by all means! [*Memoirs*]

Preservation of a Culture

In the sphere of culture there are no small and big nations with respect to capabilities. There are no nations of full values and of small values. Each nation, no matter how small it is, is able to add its own share of values to the common treasury of culture. Our nation is small but we are also a small country. We are the more interested in our further qualifications because we cannot possess even in ten years the enormous industry which the big countries have, those riches the other countries have. However, we can and must be proud of the culture we carry in ourselves, of the ability to create highly qualified pieces of art, and works in the field of science in general, and our people can also serve as an example to many other peoples. We should make such efforts hand in hand—statesmen, Party leaders, men of art and science—that in the course of a couple of years the Bulgarian people will be regarded and pointed to everywhere as an able, talented, erudite and exemplary people of experts who are taking in active part in the creation of a world socialist culture with the great Soviet Union at the helm and in cooperation with our brothers from the other People's Democracies [*Works*]

The revolutionary press fights for the preservation of the people's culture, for its liberation from the chains of the perishing monopolistic capital . . .Only the proletarian revolution can prevent the culture from perishing, can raise it to the loftiest level as a genuine people's culture, national in form and socialist in content . . .

Art should be decisively pressed into the service of the proletarian revolution, against fascism and capitalism, for the mobilization and revolutionary upbringing of the masses.

Any piece of art should revolutionize millions of non-Party members by popularizing socialist construction and the great accomplishments of the Soviet Union. Art should be placed at the service of the great revolutionary ideal of millions of people. [*Literature, Art, and Culture*]

. . .Our people need gunuine popular literature as they do bread and air, such a literature that by its profound justice and lofty emotions will raise their cultural and ideological level, will develop devotion and love for the people and the fatherland, will intensify hate for fascism and for all people's enemies, will lash everything that is rotten and that decomposes the integral organism of the people . . . will clear the Bulgarian air from the ulcers of great-Bulgarian chauvinisma and obscurantism, will disseminate love for real science, will encourage the heroic deeds in the field of labour and culture, in the struggle for the protection of the people's freedom and rights, will develop the feeling of . . . international solidarity and eternal friendship with our liberator, the great Soviet people.

The wonderful heroism of our national partisans, both men and women, and the underground activists in the struggle against fascism, the brave participation of the Bulgarian Army in the final victorious blow against fascist Germany, the militant activity in the rear in support of the front and the nation, all that is waiting for artistic treatment by the creative pen of the real people's writers. Moreover, millions of childrena and juveniles need good children's and juvenile literature. [*Works*]

We look at art in all its aspects above all as a means of mobilizing the moral, spiritual, and physical efforts of our people and youth for constant creative work, for enduring love for the fatherland, for readiness to overcome difficulties, for steeling its will and faith in its own forces. Our nation, though small, has such potentialities, that, if brought out, and we are convinced they are going to be, will compete with the biggest nations in the field of culture and art. We have already now individual artists who are by no means worse than artists in the other civilized countries. If these artists of ours obtain better conditions for work, some of them could compete with the most remarkable artists the world over. [*Works*]

Fascism cut down the lives and trodded over the talents of many a gifted man; the Ministry of today has an important task, to find our talented children and juveniles. Writers, artists, musicologists, actors and people of art in general must help schools in encouraging and supporting such children, if necessary financially as well, in bringing up the future talents of socialist Bulgaria that are to raise its culture to a higher level. [*Memoirs*]

We dearly wish our talented artists to draw inspiration from their Soviet colleagues, those great masters, and, naturally, without simply copying them, but mastering their creative pathos, high artistry and mainly the national spirit and nature of their works, to create art in service of the people, of truth, of Socialism! [*Works*]

The Trade Press

There is a close, rather organic relationship between the history of the working-class trade union movement in our country and the *Rabotnicheski Vestnik*. There is not a single episode in the movement that could be considered at present without bearing in mind the active, valuable and ultimately beneficial participation of the newspaper . . .

In the first stage of the workers' trade union movement in our country when the bourgeoisie, profiting widely from the favours of the "right-wing" socialists, made all possible efforts to turn the workers' syndicates into "neutral bodies" in order to divert them from the road of the class struggle and transform them into its own tool, "Rabotnicheski Vestnik" carried out a brilliant campaign against the bourgeois neutrality of the trade union workers' organizations and protected the fledgling movement against the great danger threatening it.

We have to be grateful to the "Rabotnicheski Vestnik" largely for the fact that the workers' trade union movement in Bulgaria is at present an entirely class proletarian movement, that it is united, that in industry, transport, the crafts and agriculture outside the General Workers' Syndicate trade unions, there are no other trade union organizations and that within its ranks there is neither ground for the treachery of opportunism nor place for the adventurous sneaking ambitions of anarchism.

That, unlike the trade unions in many other countries, our workers' trade union movement in the course of the World War had not been led astray by the imperialist and military storm and had remained faithful to the liberation ideas and internationalism of the proletariat, and that after the war, it had oriented itself quickly and properly in the ensuing revolutionary epoch is due to the "Rabotnicheski Vestnik", a fact for which we should be very much obliged.

But the Syndicate Union organ was not only the first pioneer in the trade union organization of the Bulgarian workers engaged in the consolidation and class education of the proletariat in our country. It used to be and is the irreplaceable champion and guide of the trade unions in the complex social and political circumstances which are now developing.

And this is not all. By its lashing and revealing criticism which is daily rubbing the necks of the workers' exploiters, by its constant and energetic support of the vital demands, interests and rights of the working masses, the "Rabotnicheski Vestnik" is actively involved in all trade union actions and struggles and is closely cooperating in their successful outcome.

Having in mind the numerous victories our trade unions have won so far and the enormous difficulties they have managed to overcome, we should express our deep gratitude and stress that the "Rabotnicheski Vestnik" has a great share in this respect. [*Rabotnicheski Vestnik*]

The agitation [to establishing more trade unions] will be obviously the more effective the more it is accompanied by wide dissemination of our trade union and Party periodicals, "Rabotnicheski Vestnik" in the first place. Those who think that reliable and lasting successes in this respect can be obtained without the powerful support of the socialist press, and particularly of our daily, will be bitterly disappointed. The experience we have had so far shows irrefutably that each step forward in the number of trade unions is closely related to the stabilization and dissemination of the "Rabotnicheski Vestnik" and the remaining periodicals we have. If we therefore want to have 10,000 organized workers as soon as possible with the complete assurance that our movement will go rapidly forward, we must work hard and without any interruption or slackening whatsoever to recruit 10,000 subscribers and regular readers of our "Rabotnicheski Vestnik"! [*Works*]

In the course of nearly twenty years since the date of the foundation of the General Workers' Syndicate in Bulgaria (August, 1904), the "Rabotnicheski Vestnik" has been a reputable organ of the Union, the Bulgarian Communist Party central organ, and a favorite paper of the working people, and its contributions to the workers' trade union movement in our country have been immense.

When at present, owing to the growing needs and the new big and complex tasks of the trade union movement, the Syndicate Union sets out to publish a special weekly of its own; this, of course, will by no means diminish the need for and significance of the "Rabotnicheski Vestnik" for the organized workers and employees and to the entire trade union movement, the great champion and faithful leader of the militant proletariat.

"Trud" comes forward only to continue, promote and enhance in response to the new requiremnts and conditions of the struggle the same cause that has been so magnificently furthered by the "Rabotnicheski Vestnik" in the course of decades in the formation and development of the workers' trade union movement and in the proper fulfilment of its own tasks.

Trud will be the brave and indefatigable advocate and defender of the idea of a United Front in the economic struggle, of the syndicate unity in every field of labour and of the federation of all trade unions and organizations, no matter how insignificant some of them are, into a General Federation of the proletariat of manual and intellectual labour, fighting mercilessly against any separation and preserving the syndicate movement as the apple of the eye.

But as afterwards too, when the organizational unity of the trade union movement will be completely restored, not an inconsiderable number of workers and employees with a less militant conscience will still remain outside the ranks of the united trade unions, *Trud* will advocate the formation and setting up of workers' commissions in enterprises and committees in offices, and it is only these commissions and committees that will be able, under any conditions, to unite the entire staff of workers and employees regardless of their cultural and intellectual level, and to maintain their solidarity and united actions. *Trud* will elucidate the practical tasks of these class organs uniting the entire proletariat, will throw light on their difficult path and will help them in their advance to the status of institutions which will be able to take over successfully the performance of workers' control over the production, banking affairs, and trade, as a countermeasure against the chaos in economic life brought about by capital, and for the welfare of the working masses.

Being a militant organ of the Syndicate Union and the entire trade union movement against exploitation, arbitrariness and injustice, to which the workers and employees are subjected, *Trud* will work constantly for maintaining the essential unity between the economic and political struggle of the proletariat, continuously explaining that with such unity alone the economic struggle will gain with the smallest exertion of effort and means the greatest possible practical results at this time.

By writing about and clarifying the everyday conditions and struggles of the workers and employees and their trade union organizations against capitalist exploitation and in protection of the vital interests and rights of the workers, *Trud* will always point to the existing close and inseparable relationship between these everyday efforts and struggles and the great struggle for the final elimination of capitalist exploitation and for the liberation of labour from the chains of capitalism.

By propagating the principles, ideas and methods of the revolutionary trade union movement and the program of the Red Syndicate International, *Trud* will expose the full inconsistency of reformist syndicalism on the one hand, that turns the trade unions into tools in the hands of capital and the bourgeoisie, and of the anarchist syndicalism on the other hand, that pushes the syndicates along the road to adventures and light-headed romanticism shifting the gravitation centre from the mass workers' organizations and actions to the field of individualistic but very often irrational steps which are harmful to the workers' cause and initiatives.

Finally, *Trud* will be a geniune mirror of the sufferings and hopes, of the life and struggles of all workers of manual and intellectual labour in the field of the economy. It will be a pioneer for the awakening of the slumbering working strata and for organizing them in trade unions, it will encourage and stimulate the weak, will uplift those who sunk into despondency and scepticism, will provide hopeful wings for those striving forward and will be a guide for the proletariat in its difficult economic struggle along the steep and thorny road to freedom and happiness. [*Trud*, September 1923.]

Trud [on the occasion of its one hundredth number has justified] its existence and purpose. It should continually improve in order to become a completely truthful expression of the social opinion of our working class, a powerful stimulator of working heroism of our people engaged in physical and rational labour, and of the advance of the material and cultural standard, of the progress of our nation.

In my opinion, the *Philosophic Thought* magazine in our country is highly needed. It can even be claimed to have come into life a little late. It is expected to play a big role. In my modest opinion as far as I realize its tasks, particularly in the immediate future, beside it fundamental and permanent task of forming a solid bridge between advanced philosophy and the nation and its intelligentsia, of turning the accomplishments of philosophic thought into national property by taking philosophy out of the study rooms and into the living, practical life of our country, all these tasks of the *Philosophic Thought* can be briefly formulated as follows:

First: It should expose and contribute by all means to the ultimate eradication of fascism ideology (racism, the theory of the "upper" class domination over the "lower" classes, the Fuehrer's principle, the superman doctrine, the Bulgarian chauvinistic ideas). We should not forget that without elimination of racist ideology, against which the ideological struggle is still in progress in our Universities, in our literature and culture, we cannot annihilate completely all remnants of the fascist regime in the social and political life of our country. Fascist ideology has grown deep roots in the heads of a part of the Bulgarian intelligentsia in particular and this poison cannot be so easily removed.

Second: It should disclose and castigate the fascist falsifications of history in general and of our own Bulgarian history in particular. Our historical literature and educational aids which students use to study our people's history are full of extremely harmful misrepresentations and crude falsifications. *Philosophic Thought* is expected to do some very desirable creative and critical work in this respect. Scientific, Marxist criteria for the proper elucidation of the important periods and great events in our people's history, particularly during the last decade, must be laid down and popularized as soon as possible, in a clear and convincing way and on the basis of scientific analysis of the historical facts. It is not being underlined in vain that our best teacher at present and in the future is our properly understood history and the utilization of its rich treasury of valuable lessons. We need our own Marxist philosophy for our history just as we need bread and air.

Third: The *Philosophic Thought* should help the people's intelligentsia, and above all the working-class and rural intelligentsia, their young people, in the formulation of a strong, scientific, Marxist point of view, in mastering the essence of Marxist philosophy in its newest form, Leninism, the Marxist dialetical method, not only as the safest means for the correct explanation of the past and present, but as a guide for action in the solution of the big and complex tasks of the present and in the continuing development of our country. The overall experience of the international workers' movement, and particularly the experience from the Second World War, shows clearly the enormous significance the dissemination of the general ideas of the dialectical method has in studying social life, social history and social laws of evolution, the enormous significance these ideas have especially in the practical activity of the working class and its Party.

Fourth: The *Philosophic Thought* would have to render an important contribution to the struggle against the various rotte, retrograde idealistic philosophical school and trends which are serving the restoration of fascism and are ideological weapons of reaction against the advance of our people's democracy. The magazine must also castigate in concrete terms and with solid arguments every attempt to deviate from live and creative militant Marxism as well as to treat accurately from the Marxist point of view the new problems on the ideological front connected with the present Fatherland Front era in our country and its trends and development prospects. In this respect the *Philosophic Thought* magazine also faces the development of basic methodological problems of all individual sciences and of those in particular which are more directly related to the economic, social and cultural construction of the people's republic.

Fifth: The *Philosophic Thought* magazine faces yet another task. It should methodically encourage in our country interest in the problems of philosophy, love for this science and by its entire activity stimulate the studious working youth to persistent and searching self-education assisting it in all possibl ways directly and efficiently in the same direction.

A very important condition for the successful fulfilment of these tasks, of course, that the *Philsophic Thought* should be written in a popular, comprehensible way for its average readers, i.e. for those readers with no secondary or higher education. It is not true that one cannot write in a simple, clear and comprehensible way on philosophical and other theoretical problems. The best example in this respect is provided by the great classics of Marxism. But to achieve this purpose the authors should constantly self-educate themselves and work harder, and while writing they should have the image of their readers they write for before their eyes. They must especially throw away the harmful routine of the bourgeois philosophers who, in general, in an effort to impress as scholars, are deliberately writing in a language not accessible to the average reader and address their "works" to "experts", to the "selected" elitist spiritual aristocrats.

I also think that the *Philosophic Thought* editorial board should cherish the noble ambition to become in the course of time a laboratory, no matter how modest, of scientific philosophical thinking in our country, rallying round itself for the most able and faithful scientific minds, becoming a school for the advance and education of new, young Marxist experts in Bulgarian science so indispensable for our new Bulgaria.

I cannot but mention that the role of the *Philosophic Thought* is an extremely difficult and responsible one. This role imposes serious requirements on both the editorial board and the contributors for knowledge, skill, enormous methodical work and severe self-criticism aiming at the further improvement and perfection of the magazine. [*Philosophic Thought*]

A View of Censorship

While the government was subjecting the strikers, the entire proletariat and its associated organizations to a military, police and bandit terror that had not been experienced even during the most gruelling moments of the past, the bourgeois press, both party and non-party, was continuously firing broadsides and pouring out calumnies, lies, intrigues, low insinuations and furious provocations against militant workers and the Communist Party. And in order to have the masses more easily deceived by this abominable bourgeois press, the censorship kept the mouth of the workers' press closed with ninety nine keys, it did not even allow the publication of the bulletins of the Central Strike Committee and carefully sealed off every opportunity for disclosing before the world the truth about the progress of the struggle and the general state of affairs. [*Works*, v.5, pp. 326-328]

To the Union of Publishers and Booksellers. The book-marker is kept overstocked with sensational literature of doubtful quality, sometimes even pornography. Our publishers and booksellers should consider themselves and their work as that of people's educators, social workers, pioneers of the dissemination of good progressive scientific, socio-political and fiction books among our people and particularly our youth, and not acting as ordinary peddlers and even profiteers who, we must admit, may still be encountered in the new Bulgaria. Each kilogram of the scanty amount of paper available should be used for the advancement of our people's culture and not for personal enrichment. The noble ambition of both publishers and booksellers will be to apply all their efforts to purging Bulgarian literature of the malignant weeds that threaten to suffocate the crop of healthy books in the service of the people. It is therefore necessary to turn your serious attention to the improvement of the technical quality and good appearance of the printed editions, features that would promote the lasting utilization of any good book and would increase the love of the readers for our literature and would also help to provide eventually most reasonable prices of the books for the reading public. Our people will show their love, gratitude and appreciation to those of our publishers and booksellers who are duly performing their patriotic duty on the cultural front of the new Bulgaria. [*"Rabotnichesko Delo"*, *No. 157, July, No. 1946.*]

A New Revolution

Bulgarian newspapers and Bulgarian journalists are facing very serious and responsible tasks indeed. To fulfill them, Bulgarian journalists should be first of all completely devoted to the people; they should be genuinely patriotic and wholeheartedly loyal, should believe unshakably in the people's power and the future of the fatherland, should be inseparably linked to the popular masses, know their needs, demands and hopes; they themselves must study hard and improve their qualifications as journalists, know how to write in such a way that every literate reader can, without much difficulty, comprehend and use the newspaper. When the journalist is writing, he must have the image of the reader before his eyes in the first place, the reader he is writing about, and should always think whether the average reader can understand properly what is written there.

The newspaper should provide information, orientation and education for its readers in the spirit of the irreconcilable struggle against facist obscurantism, against all internal and external enemies of the people, against all overt and covert enemies of the Fatherland Front unity. It must throw light on most significant topics, as well as on home and foreign political events, and not deal with cheap sensations and verbosities devoid of any content.

The interests of our nation require that all those remnants of the mercenary press of the past should be once and for all eliminated. It should not be forgotten that up to the present day not all journalists are immune against the temptations of bribes of different kinds offered on the part of the agents of our enemies.

The sharpest vigilance and determined resistance to this great evil are all the more needed.

The press is a great power. I wish you with all my heart that the honest patriotic Bulgarian journalists should master well this power and place it in the full service of the new, free, democratic Bulgaria of the Fatherland Front. [May 30, 1945]

All those working in the press and political propaganda institutions are facing a lot of responsible work in the forthcoming election campaign. It should be taken into consideration that beside the mean splitters and deceivers of the people, there are numerous patriotic voters, men and women, in the towns and particularly in the villages, who being insufficiently informed and with no political experience whatever, can fall victims to various demagogues and rogues. These people should be helped in realizing the truth, in recognizing true friends and masked enemies; they have to be freed of any kind of hesitation and doubt and shown the right course of unconditional support for the ideas and candidates of the Fatherland Front.

The election campaign should be carried out politically and on grounds of principle, while at the same time it should be straightforward and accessible to the most ordinary voters. We should not forget that the issue is not confined to the mere casting of votes for the Fatherland Front candidates, which is, of course, of great importance from the point of view of the consolidation of the Fatherland Front and the future development of our country, but what is also particularly important is that the present electoral campaign is a vertable political school for our nation and especially for the new categories of voters, the youth, women and soldiers. The press, the workers in the political propaganda institutions, the Fatherland Front candidates and agitators must remember that the greater the amount of truth they bring over to the people, the better and more convincing their explanation of the true nature and purpose of the Fatherland Front ideas and policy will be, the clearer their proof of the harmful role played by the enemies of our unity and perfidious intentions of foreign hostile agencies, the stronger the anti-fascist patriotic unity of our nation, the more easily we shall overcome the difficulties inherited from the fascist regime, the more certain and speedier the annihilation of the remnants of doomed fascism, the more confident and successful the progress of the construction of a new, free, democratic and powerful Bulgaria a will be. [August 1, 1945; Published in *Robotnichesko Delo*, No. 269, August 2, 1945.]

The Role of Mass Media
in a Developed Socialist Society

by Valerij Semenovich Korobeinikov

The mass media system including press, cinema, radio and TV is one of the important elements of the Soviet society. As a socialist society develops, there grows the significance of spiritual communication through mass media, which in Marx's words are "speaking bonds connecting an individual with the state and the whole world."

The social role of press, cinema, radio and television is connected first of all with the development of consciousness of wide masses, of every member of a socialist society. Lenin's principle according to which the strength of the socialist state is in the consciousness of masses, and the state is strong when the masses know everything, can judge everything and do everything consciously, becomes especially urgent under the mature socialism conditions. Presently, as it was pointed out in the resolution of the CPSU Central Committee of April 26, 1979, *On Further Improvement of Ideological and Political Educational Work*, "Press, television, radio, verbal propaganda and agitation must increasingly assist The Soviet man to be well oriented in the internal life and in international events, arouse aspirations to contribute to a maximum to the common cause, to the construction of communism."

Mass Media Relationships

The most important social tasks of the mass media systems are, as it is stressed in the CPSU's documents, the profound interpretation of such issues as increasing effectiveness and improving work in all fields of social life, accelerating scientific and technical progress, active participation in further development of socialist competition and of the movement for the communist attitude to work, the propaganda of Marxism-Leninism and of the historical experience of the CPSU, the struggle for the eradication of survivals of the past enimical to socialism in the life of our society, systematic presentation of the experience of socialist countries, the exposure of imperialist propaganda.

Thus, the mass media activities are not connected with a separate field or with a separate level but with the social life as a whole. The functioning of these social institutions is also rightly connected with the realization of social, economic, political and individual rights and freedoms of Soviet citizens, particularly with the realization of freedoms of speech and press.

According to Article 50 of the Constitution of the U.S.S.R., "The realization of these political freedoms is provided for by making available to the working

Dr. Valerij Semenovich Korobeinikov is head of the Public Opinion Sector of the Institute for Sociological Research, Academy of Sciences, U.S.S.R., and president of the mass media and public opinion research section of the Soviet Sociological Association. [This article is edited and reprinted with permission from *The Social Role of Mass Communication*, published by the University of Tampere (Finland), 1982; ©1982, University of Tampere.]

people and to their organizations public buildings, streets and squares, by the wide distribution of information, by rendering it possible to use press, television and radio."

At the developed stage of socialism, the Soviet society has at its disposal a powerful information complex, equipped by modern technology, an integrated system of mass media. By the beginning of the 1980s in this country there were published nearly eight thousand papers, including twenty-nine central ones four weeklies in their number), 153 republican ones, 370 territorial and regional ones, over 3,500 district, city and area ones, nearly four thousand papers of mass circulation and over 5,200 magazines and editions of the magazine type. The population of this country possessed over seventy million television sets, nearly as many radio sets and nearly seventy-four broadcasting stations. Television reaches almost eighty-five percent and radio almost ninety-seven percent of the whole population. 85,000 titles of books and pamphlets totalling nearly 1.9 billion copies are published annually in the U.S.S.R. There are 110,000 journalists working for radio, press, and television in this country.

"Our party," said L.I. Brezhnev at the twenty-sixth congress of the CPSU, "has great confidence in [the] . . . strong force of Soviet journalists; it highly appreciates their [difficult] . . . work. Naturally, we are all interested in our mass media and propaganda means which are always a genuine tribune [to] . . . the party and people's opinion."

Media and Soviet Life

An important feature of Soviet mass media activities is its orientation towards strengthening the high prestige of the man of labor. Sociological research on Soviet mass media materials, describing various professions, testify to the fact that press, cinema, radio and television focus the main attention to the representatives of separate, quite concrete professions. To a lesser degree, they describe production collectives and still more rarely—professionals as such, irrespective of man. In the majority of materials, concrete representatives of various social and professional groups are described as people engaged in creative work.

Mass labour enthusiasm, initiative and creation, high prestige of the man of labour, reflected in the materials of press, cinema, radio, and television, reveal the humanistic nature of socialism.

Another direction of mass media activities, conencted with the development of an individual's spiritual activity is of the same character. It refers primarily to the problems of perfecting socialist type relations among people, establishing a socialist way of life, communist norms of community life and morals. Socialism provides for the propaganda bodies an audience which is thinking creatively and is socially active. Numerous studies, for example, of Soviet leading newspapers' readers show, that the majority of their audience consists of collectively minded people concerned not only with the problems and interests of their nearest environment but with those of the country as a whole and of the progressive world. Thus, over three quarters of *Pravda's* readers indicated international life problems to be among the particularly interesting subjects, and sixty-nine percent questions of morals and education . . .

In spreading and establishing the norms of communist morality, Soviet mass media appeal first of all to positive examples, striving to connect individual's moral substance with deep comprehension of his social duty, with the principled attitude towards immoral and anti-social phenomena. The materials of this kind, as sociological research proves, influence Soviet people deeply . . .

The Soviet way of life is inseparable from the population's high activity in the fields of culture. This elevated cultural activity, which is so characteristic of a socialist society, manifests itself particularly at the stage of mature socialism. As the volume of free time grows, Soviet wage and salary earners most highly appreciate the possibilities of its use in the following way: "One can read more and watch television," "There are more possibilities for visiting cinemas and theatres," "Conditions for combining work with study are improving." Research has shown that people have supported their opinion with the corresponding behavior in the field of culture. Thus, among the workers constituting the majority of the population, the number of visits to cinema, theatre, and sports events grows. Soviet people began reading more, the volume of the reading matter being distributed more evenly among various population groups . . .

Actually, the formation of a personality actively determining one's attitude towards one's spiritual development is not a spontaneous process. The education of a spiritually rich personality is a component of the formation of a new man.

Soviet mass media activites are closely connected with spreading such materials, which would make Soviet people spiritually richer, would raise their cultural level, would free them from poor taste and shallowness.

The CPSU continuously follow the state of affairs in this field. For example, in its resolution *On Further Development of Soviet Television* (1960), the Central Committee of the CPSU suggested to provide [time for the better] amateur groups for regular appearance on television, declared it expedient to organize the preparation of performances, concerts, stage versions and of other television programs by amateur groups and recommended to public, creative and scientific associations to render television practical assistance in preparing programmes and in involving authors and performers.

The same resolution included the principle which bears clear testimony to the fact that the distribution of cultural values under socialism is not connected with commerical profit: "Theatre performances, films, concerts, circus performances, sports events and other open entertainments are broadcasted by television without *special* payment."

The requirements of man's cultural growth and of his spiritual development always have priority over financial interests of mass media and propaganda. The discussion which has taken place some time ago in the Soviet press is very significant in this respect. Some Soviet cinema managers' decision to put on thrillers under any pretext in order to fulfill the financial plan with ease was challenged. This tendency was sharply criticised by public opinion and by specialists. The following point of view was expressed: "Excessive quantity of thrillers in the repertoire does not contribute to the cause of education, especially that of the youth. In some cases it is necessary to reduce the number of performances of such films to a certain extent. Material loss can not be put on a level with the losses of moral nature, with the damage to the spiritual development of personality."

This point of view coincides with the preferences of the audience itself. Active and conscious members of the audience do not demand empty thrillers, they demand films, which can provide food for thoughts and feelings. As a result of generalizing extensive empirical material, a Ural sociologist, for example, came to the following conclusion: "The basic trend of the development of aesthetic consciousness of our society shows that [as the] Soviet people's demands towards art grow, their spiritual requirements and interests become more varied, their attitude to shallow themes, to the lack of progressive ideas, to light minded ness and banality which sometimes do penetrate films becomes more and more irreconcilable."

The social role of mass media manifests itself not only in the field of influencing an individual, but also in the sphere of interrelations among social groups including classes. In exploiting societies propaganda is called upon to fix class barriers, to substantiate "the natural character" of dividing people in to separate groups, those ruling and subordinate . . .

The formation of a historically new social and international community— the Soviet people—is an important indicator of the Soviet society's growing homogenity. In this connection, mass media contribute to the inculcation of the idea that at the mature socialism stage "general features of the Soviet peoples behavior, character and outlook independent of social and national distinctions gradually acquire" a decisive importance.

The press, cinema, radio and television . . . widely present the achievements of all Union republics, festivals and exhibitions of fraternal peoples, the youth tours of people's glory sites and many other events developed with the Soviet people the awareness of their belonging to a united socialist mother-country, deep esteem of all nations and nationalities.

Internationalist consciousness is brought about primarily in collaboration which is directed towards a common goal. That is why the socialist competition of workers of various union republics of the Soviet Union becomes a genuine school of internationalism and patriotism. Information bodies undertake the role of a mediator and organizer of a labour dialogue among the workers of all republics. Both central and local mass media describe e.g. a labour dialogue between Ukranian Donbass miners and miners of Karaganda in Siberia, between textile workers of the Russian city of Ivanovo and their colleagues in the capital of Uzbekistan—Tashkent—and of many other collectives in various regions of this country.

Socialist patriotism and proletarian internationalism include organically the involvement of people into the affairs of both of their country and of the socialist community as a whole.

The necessary ideological element of socialist integration is an accurate and possibly fullest notion of the peoples of the socialist community of each other. The widening of the volume and the improvement of the quality of information of the life in other socialist countries is a characteristic feature of the mature socialism stage.

There is no information channel in the Soviet Union which does not *regularly* to some extent acquaint the Soviet people with the life and problems of individual countries of socialism and of the socialist community as a whole.

The realization of the Integrated Program of the Council for Mutual Economic Assistance makes it possible to propagate socialist patriotism and internationalism through the demonstration of forms and methods of socialist countries co-operation. Thus, Soviet journalists in co-operation with their colleagues from the leading GDR newspaper, *Neues Deutschland*, repeatedly prepared reports and other materials on the main problems of economic integration. Reporters from some socialist countries went went for a trip along the international pipe line "Druzhba" in order to prepare materials which would create awareness of the audience's belonging to the whole socialist community.

The Soviet . . . who is being educated in the spirit of internationalism is most interested in obtaining various kinds of information of the life in fraternal socialist countries. This is convincingly supported by the results of sociological research. For example, the following question was suggested to respondents in the course of studying the audience of the newspaper *Pravda* and of other Soviet mass media: "What aspects of life in fraternal countries draw your particular attention and create the desire to receive fuller information?"

It appeared that the respondents are particularly interested in propaganda's presentation of every day life of the population's culture, arts, literature, recreational problems, health services, agricultural development and service sector. This data testify to the fact that the significance of mass media in creating the basis for establishing truly fraternal relations between the peoples going along the path of socialism is growing.

Thus, at the stage of mature socialism there increases the role of press, cinema, radio and television in the mechanism of social management whose aim is to provide for the steady rise of material and cultural levels of people's life, the creation of better conditions for the comprehensive development of a personality on the basis of further improvement of all public production, the increase of labour productivity, the growth of social and labour activity of the Soviet people.

Bibliography

Asia Research Center, *The Great Cultural Revolution in China*, Asia Research Center (Hong Kong), 1967.

Chai, Winberg (ed.), *Essential Works of Chinese Communism*, Bantam (New York, N.Y.), 1969.

Eckstein, Alexander, Walter Galenson, and Ta-chung Liu (eds.), *Economic Trends in Communist China*, Edinburgh University Press (Edinburgh, Scotland), 1968.

Erdei, Ferenc, Ed., *Information Hungary*, Pergamon Press (New York, N.Y.), 1968.

Great Soviet Encyclopedia, Translation of 3rd ed., Macmillan (New York, N.Y.), 1973-1981.

Harrington, Michael, *Socialism*, Saturday Review Press (New York, N.Y.), 1970.

Hollander, Gayle Durham, *Soviet Political Indoctrination, Developments in Mass Media and Propaganda Since Stalin*, Praeger (New York, N.Y.), 1972.

Hopkins, Mark W., *Mass Media in the Soviet Union*, Pegasus (New York, N.Y.), 1970.

Lazitch, Branko, and Milorad M. Drachkovitch, *Lenin and the Comintern* (Vol. 1), Hoover Institution Press (Stanford, Calif.), 1972.

Lendvai, Paul, *The Bureaucracy of Truth: How Communist Governments Manage the News*, Westview Press (Boulder, Colo.), 1981.

Lenin, Valdimir Ilyich, *What is to be Done?* Foreign Languages Publishing (Moscow, USSR), n.d.

Lowenstein, Ralph, *World Press Freedom, 1966*, Freedom of Information Center, Publication no. 181, May 1967.

Martin, L. John and Anju Grover Chaudhary, *Comparative Mass Media Systems*, Longman (New York, N.Y.), 1983.

MacBride, Sean, *Many Voices, One World*, Kogan Page (London, England), 1980.

McLellan, David, *Karl Marx: His Life and Thought*, Harper & Row (New York, N.Y.), 1973.

———, *The Thought of Karl Marx: An Introduction*, Harper & Row (New York, N.Y.), 1971.

Merrill, John C., *Global Journalism: A Survey of the World's Mass Media*, Praeger (New York, N.Y.), 1981.

Mickiewicz, Ellen Propper, *Media and the Russian Public,* Praeger (New York, N.Y.), 1981.

Mond, G., "Press Concentration in Socialist Countries," *Gazette*, no. 3, 1974.

———, Carter R. Bryan, and Marvin Alisky, *The Foreign Press*, Louisiana State University Press (Baton Rouge, La.), 1970.

Paulu, Burton, *Radio and Television Broadcasting in Eastern Europe*, University of Minnesota Press (Minneapolis, Minn.), 1974.

Yu, Frederick T.C., *Chinese Knowledge of the United States as Reflected in Mass Communication*, (Washington, D.C.) USICA, 1980.

Also p. 482, 489-500

Chapter 35

The New World Information Order
by Anantha S. Babbili

Political, social, economic, and cultural realities of nations, particularly in the Third World, are being confronted with profound changes never before experienced in their turbulent histories. These changes were triggered by the process of decolonization in many developing countries during the post-World War II period. During this period, many countries, free from burdensome and generally exploitative colonial rule, hoped for and attempted a rapid process of economic development. These expectations, however, proved fruitless. During the last three decades, the developing countries saw their position steadily worsening in relation to economically advanced countries. The present system of world trade and economics dominated by the powerful Western transnational corporations and the state of balance of power in international relations work inherently against the development efforts of many Third World countries. A United Nations declaration in 1974 noted that it has proven impossible to achieve "an even and balanced development of the international community under the existing economic order. The gap between the developed and developing countries continues to widen in a system which perpetuates inequality."

The developing nations, in response to this problem, issued a formal call for a New International Economic Order (NIEO), with specific proposals to implement changes which will eradicate such perceived inequality. In 1974, the developing countries launched a united front to stress a need for a comprehensive approach with all countries having equal input into global policy-making. The NIEO demands also included the transfer of resources for developing countries and the restructuring of many existing international organizations. The call for a new order in international economic system also contained new and much-

Dr. Anantha Babbili, the 1985 recipient of the National Teaching Award from The Poynter Institute for Media Studies, teaches journalism at Texas Christian University. He received bachelors degrees in biological sciences and journalism from India's Osmania University, an M.A. in journalism from the University of Oklahoma, and a Ph.D. in mass communication, with emphasis in international press systems, from the University of Iowa. He worked as a journalist in his native India. He is a newspaper columnist and author of several published studies on media professionalism, media ethics, newspaper readership, and communication technology. Dr. Babbili is research chair of the International Communication Division of the Association for Education in Journalism and Mass Communications (AEJMC).

debated elements—emphasis on national sovereignty over resources and the right to nationalization according to domestic laws as a basis for self-reliance.

Such proposed changes in international economic order set the tone for the New World Information Order (NWICO). The embryonic term later evolved into the New World Information and Communication Order (NWICO)—to include the related concerns of cultural sovereignty and social values of a given society which will be impacted by the communication satellite, and the transborder data flows.

History and Context of NWICO

International communication today has completely transformed international relations. International misunderstandings arise not only from the inadequacy of communication between different regions of the world, but also from a lack of understanding between peoples, their ways of life, and different political ideologies. Improving the quality and quantity of information flow between countries and regions could contribute, to some extent, to a decrease in world tensions.

During the last three decades, especially in the early 1970s, basic communication problems, (e.g., The imbalance in the flow of information between nations, particularly through major world news agencies) have become the subject of the continuing international debate. The topic of information itself has raised vital questions in foreign policy and international conduct. Widely differing opinions are held regarding the present "dominance" of transnational news agencies and the proposed solutions concerning the underlying principles of the concept of the "free flow of information." The Third World's growing interest in the process of international communication is being nourished by increasing awareness of communication as an indispensable element of social organization and nation-building among developing countries. UNESCO, the specialized agency of the United Nations which deals with world politics regarding information flow, has witnessed careful scrutiny by its members of the concept of "free flow." At the same time, innovations in the technology and understanding of communication are bringing about profound changes so that expressions such as the "communications revolution," the "information explosion," and the "communication era" have gained common usage among developing nations.

Besides communication technology, several other factors have become important during the past several decades in setting the context for the debate on NWICO and for the evolution of new and expanded concepts to regulate international communication. These include the emergence of the Third World nations as a collective political power, increasing recognition of the interdependence of issues facing those nations and the rest of the world, and awareness of the role of international organizations dealing with global communication practices and regulations. Developing countries have come to reassess the concept of the free flow of information with a view to including the idea of free and balanced flow, both in principle and in practice, between all nations, and to place the concept within the framework of access to information technology and information. Similarly, developing nations see a need to transcend the traditional concept of freedom of information in the limited sense of institutional rights—now perceived as the cause of the bias favoring the advanced nations in international communication. These nations favor an emerging concept called the "Right to Communicate," which emphasizes access, participation, feedback, and multi-way processes of communication, and is now regarded as essential for individuals, groups, and nation-states.

Sean MacBride, the Irish statesman who headed the UNESCO-initiated International Commission for the Study of Communication Problems, notes, "A one-way or even two-way communication system reflects and supports autocratic and paternalistic structures. A multi-way information flow is indispensable for democratization, for wider mass participation in the decision-making process, as well as mutual respect in international relations." [*Irish Broadcasting Review*, Spring, 1977]. MacBride's observation typifies the Third World criticism about monopolies and the imbalance in information flow and the principles underlying those conditions.

Moreover, underlying the debate on NWICO is the basic difference in outlook between the Western nations and the Third World countries as to the nature of information and of news. To the West, information is a commercial commodity. On the other hand, most Third World nations see information as a basic resource—a resource to be used for nation-building, shaping a consensus at home, and presenting a favorable image abroad because the developing countries are highly sensitive to world opinion. They want to project the image of the culture they are rightfully proud of; the image is also vital in securing economic pacts with the Western countries and banks and other monetary agencies. Hence, the information flow between East and West has been treated by the developing countries as an essential element in the creation of both the new economic order and the new information order. Their fears about imbalance and one-sidedness in information flow reflect their concern over West's "cultural imperialism." These nations also maintain that the ability to dominate the international gatekeeping of information may well serve countries with power with technological advantage.

This concern is not baseless. Information is power and a vital need in a changing world. Information makes alternatives known, reduces uncertainty about their implications, and facilitates such implications. Broad agendas for national development are viewed in this context. Consequently, information, appropriately applied in the pursuit of well-defined objectives, becomes central to decision-making. On the political level, while developing countries generally recognize the value of communication and information resources for advancing their efforts of industrialization, they are equally cognizant of the potentially negative aspects associated with acquiring these technologies from abroad. Much concern exists in the Third World that it will simply move from one form of dependency to another through increased reliance on foreign technology and information services. Some nations fear that this new type of dependence could possibly result in vulnerability to foreign control, loss of employment opportunities, infringements on national sovereignty, and cultural erosion. The fact that the information hardware, telecommunication, and computer resources in a developing country may be available solely through foreign enterprises often raises further concerns that an important basis for national decision-making is now extra-territorially located with some private firms or transnational corporations. There is a recognition that modern communication and information technologies bring with them new opportunities for jobs and the growth of new sectors of teh economy. As long as these technologies and related services are delivered from abroad, however, hopes for increased domestic employment largely remain unfulfilled. Also, developing countries guard national sovereignty with an obsession. However, there is also a growing concern that the lack of information to permit adequate preparation for intergovernmental negotiations makes the bargaining process unworkable.

The debate on NWICO is often clouded with multiplicity of voices from the Third World. However, there are some basic issues in the NWICO debate. The primary concerns of the Third World and the West are the following:

Third World Concerns
● Domination of international news flow by Western media
● Biased reports about the Third World in Western media
● Disinterest in Third World's positive news in Western media
● Communication hardware control by the West leading in some cases to implicit control over software

Western Concerns
● Government control of Third World media
● Limited access to news sources in the Third World
● Need to upgrade hardware in the Third World
● Need for training of journalists in the Third World
● Taxes/restrictions on the media in the Third World

The perception of the best and the worst of NWICO has been cited in a report discussed by a U.S. Senate sub-committee in 1977. At its worst, NWICO could mean:
● Sanctioning State control of all media and other information that comes into or leaves any nation;
● A dramatic loss in the amount of information about the world available too governments and people;
● Loss of parts of the electonic spectrum used by Western space satellites as well as loss of frequencies used by military surveillance technology.

At its best, NWICO could mean:
● A much greater flow of news, movies, television programs, books, scientific and cultural information;
● Closer relations and better understanding among societies and individuals of the world breaking through stereotypes created and nurtured by the Western media;

- Less change of war;
- More chances of increased wealth and education, health and worldwide well-being;
- A friendly, rather than hostile, climate for international business and investment.

The conflict thus embraces several major areas of concern. Political leaders, development strategists, researchers, and communication practitioners are questioning the structure, operations, financing, ideology, and influence of certain international communication organizations; and challenging traditional concepts of communication rooted in the context of the developed countries and, until recently, accepted by the developing nations. In the former area, the role of international news agencies, Television and film exporters, and trasnational advertisers is being "condemned as a key tool for external domination." In the latter area, the classic concepts of "press freedom," "communication rights," and "free flow of information," as well as standard definitions of "news" are also regarded as instrumental in the domination process.

Except for the messages that are exchanged between governments, notes U.S. scholar Glen Fisher, the flow of news stands out as having the most significant consequences of any element in the entire international communication system. He observes:

> Such factors as just what is chosen as "news," how it is interpreted and conceptualized, to whom it is disseminated, and how credibly it is received determine the data base for interacting in international society. It becomes part of the fundamental "knowledge"—whether accurate and complete or not—by which the psychological processes of the mind turn out perceptions, judgements, reactions, and decisions. It is to international life as the city newsroom is to community affairs; possibly more significant, for a local community has more alternative ways to know about local affairs. [*American Communication in a Global Soceity*]

In the 1950s, the London-based International Press Institute (IPI) undertook one of the earliest studies on flow of news "because of the importance of foreign news not merely as 'news' but as information upon which the people of free countries base certain vital decisions... Foreign news is not only important today, it is increasingly complex. The importance of news as information has increased at a time when it is more difficult to make foreign news completely informative." The importance of information for the conduct of international relations can be seen in IPI's observation in 1953:

> Relations between governments are now more than ever strongly influenced by the people's view of their own interest; this view is itself largely shaped by the people's information.

NWICO as a Press Concept

The differing perceptions about the nature and role of news are rooted in a combination of political philosophies and historical traditions. These philosophies, reflecting the changes the world has been witnessing for the last three decades, has added other roles to the press in a given social order. These functions came to be embedded in additional concepts of the press— Revolutionary, Developmental, Paternalistic, Democratic-Participation, Public-Philosophy, and others. For example, the NWICO often takes on the semblance to social responsibility concept of the press, albeit, with differing interpretations as to what such responsibility constitutes. Does the press serve the State, the party, or efforts in nation-building? In whom shall the power be vested? Ironically, too, the debate carries liberal sprinklings of authoritarianism and libertarianism. Nevertheless, the bottom line in the Third World arguments in the NWICO debate seems to be this: if self-regulation of journalists does not work to cater to the needs of nation-building, then the State has to step in to enforce regulation on press conduct. We see that happening in many developing countries today. A direct product of the NWICO debate has been the ideology of developmental journalism. As yet, this concept is a curious mixture of political thetoric, ideas and grievance of the Third World. Some notable Third World journalists have articulated the central concerns of Developmental concept of the press. According to them, the concept reflects partly the frustrations and anger of poor nations of the Third World; it is also a critique of and reaction against the West and its transnational media. The Developmental concept as synthesized by William Hachten is:

● All the instruments of mass communication—newspapers, radio, television, films, etc.—must be mobilized by the central government to aid in the great tasks of nation-building: fighting illiteracy and poverty, building a political consciousness, assisting in economic development. Implicit here is the social responsibility view that the government must step in and provide adequate media service when the private sector is unable to do so.

● The media, therefore, should support authority, not challenge it. There is no place for dissent or criticism, in part because the alternative to the ruling government most probably would be chaos.

● Information (or truth), thus, becomes the property of the State; the flow of power (and truth) between the governors and the governed works from the top down. Information or news is a scarce national resource; it must be utilized to further the national goals.

● Implied, but not often articulated, is the view that individual rights of expressions and other civil liberties are somewhat irrelevant in the face of the overwhelming problems of poverty, disease, illiteracy, and ethnicity that face a majority of these nations.

● This concept of a guided press further implies that in international news, each nation has a sovereign right to control foreign journalists and the flow of news back and forth across its borders.

It is this concept of journalism—the concept tantamount to the concept of a *guided press*—that has to be studied in the context of press theory. The Third World nations, through internaitonal organizations like the UNESCO, are seeking worldwide responsibility for the concept. Some journalists in the Third World support the concept; but the advocacy for the concept comes mainly from government representatives and their political leaders. However, journalists in India, Nigeria, Kenya and Pakistan insist on self-regulation and attempt to practice journalism that is independent of State control. Some hournalists also perceive develomental journalism as a transitional phase until a stable and participant society is established.

Time for a New Order

In the larger context, the issues in NWICO have become problems in international relations. During the 1950s, developing countries began to see that their economic and political spheres were so dominated by the developed countries that it was detrimental to national development. In the 1970s, the developing nations' concern over cultural domination reinforced their belief that communication was central to all three types of domination—economic, political, and cultural. A South American scholar, Luis Beltran, notes:

> Third World countries are not struggling today only to bring about a real end to colonialism by obtaining fair treatment in trade and aid. They are simultaneously and relatedly pursuing the establishment of a "New International Economic Order" and a "New International Information Order." As both these attempts are being actively resisted by the most developed countries, communication has now come to lie neatly in the domain of international conflict. [*Communication*, 1980]

During the last ten years, manifestations of this conflict occurred at several public discussions. In 1976, an inter-governmental conference was held in Costa Rica under the auspices of UNESCO. Out of this meeting, specific recommendations to lessen dependence on Western news agencies and to develop their own infrastructure for new dissemination were derived in the Latin American context. These recommendations were adopted to achieve balance in the international flow of information and to endow the region with an independent news agency capable of filling the perceived gaps in AP and UPI coverage, which historically have been quasi-monopolies in that region.

The 20th UNESCO General Conference's approval of a declaration on international communication in 1978 on the role of the press in human rights promotion, countering racism and apartheid also witnessed this conflict. The eventual compromise was the product of a long and lively debate between those who considered the statement an expression of a will to totalitarian control of communication and those who saw it as an expression of the will to democratize communication. The meetings of the nonaligned countries and the conferences and seminars of media and academic organizations are additional arenas where the conflict is conspicuous.

Need for New Regulations

The problem of news flow can be dissected into two distinct, yet inextricably linked, concerns in the NWICO. At issue are factors which are *structural* in nature—the appropriate technology of news transmission, the Third World's dependence on the four Western news agencies, and the question of access to these transmitting facilities. The structural concerns include technological factors and the question of basic tenets or principles which, in the view of the Third World, encourage Western dominance in news transmission. These technological factors and principles which, in the view of the Third World, encourage Western dominance in news transmission. These principles are rooted in the Universal Declaration of Human Rights (UDHR), the United Nations Charter, and the Constitution of UNESCO. These technological factors and principles are quantitative and qualitative in nature—quantitative when we consider the Third World's dependence on, and lack of access to, the information transmission technology; qualitative when we take into consideration the perceived potency of the existing principles in view of the changing nature of contemporary international relations.

The second concern, one of which occupies the largest part of the debate, is that of the *content* of news flowing through the four Western news agencies. This concern encompasses both the quantitative and qualitative nature of the content and has raised specific disagreements over news values.

Third World dissatisfaction over the free flow concept became particularly evident in the early 1970s. The concept itself had been the heart of an international communication system supported by Article 19 of UDHR. Article 19 provided the basis for the notion of free flow:

> Everyone has the right to freedom of opinion and expression; this right includes freedom to hold opinion without interference and to seek, receive and impart information and ideas through any media and regardless of frontiers.

Implications of NWICO

While most Western countries subscribe to the concept of free flow, UNESCO's Nairobi Conference in 1976 saw a surprisingly strong resistance from the Third World participants to the present international structures and patterns of news flow. In response to these growing concerns, UNESCO itself shifted from its support of the free flow concept to a "free *and balanced*" flow concept. In this process, UNESCO has also been examining the evolvoing "Right to Communicate" as a possible framework to solve the problems of imbalance in information flow and related issues such as diversification of international communication channels, dependency relationships, lack of communication resources, media and cultural imperialism, and concern over communication rights being vested mostly with the economically powerful.

The heavy flow of information from the U.S. to Asian countries veils the fact that there is only a very slight trickle of information flowing from Asia to the

U.S. Even where there may appear to be a substantial return flow, the apparent reciprocity merely disguises the fact that people who handle or manage this return flow are primarily the agents of major Western media systems, whose criteria of choice are determined above all by their domestic market needs. The second feature is the small number of "source" countries accounting for a substantial share of all international information flow across the world. These countries are primarily the United States, Great Britain, France, and the Soviet Union. The sources identified only by country of origin also may obscure the fact that the real sources are even more limited, located as they are in a handful of giant Western media conglomerates. The biggest single source of information, evidently, is the news agency. Consequently, many national media systems have little choice but to depend on it for international news. The major news agencies which gather news from most of the countries and sell or distribute it widely are the AFP (Agence France Presse), AP, UPI, and Reuters. (Distributing news to the Communist countries is TASS; distributing to the billion-population China is the New China News Agency.)

Illustrating the extent of news flow dependency, a British researcher, Oliver Boyd-Barrett, notes:

> The services of the "Big Four" agencies eventually affect, to a greater or lesser degree, to a total world daily newspaper circulation in excess of 450 million (readership would be much higher) and a world broadcast audience well in excess of [a billion] persons. The extent of media dependence on the world agencies has been documented in dozens of academic and professional studies over the past quarter century. Dependence takes a variety of forms. The most visible is the qualitative extent to which media around the world depend on the world agencies *not only for general world news but also for news of their own geopolitical regions.*

The IPI study noted that the means for collection and dissemination of foreign news for developing countries like India "are under foreign—specifically Western—control." The study recommended that foreign news should be dispatched to the Indian press by journalists with knowledge and interpretation of Indian needs. The study also suggested that dominant news agencies should cover more extensively the Asiatic neighbors of India, "not through British or American eyes but through India." Dependence on the four agencies is also illustrated by a 1977 study done by U.S. researchers. This study on Third World news coverage of fourteen Asian newspapers found that a little over three-quarters of all non-local Third World news came from the "Big Four."

One aspect of the NWICO debate was succinctly stated in 1978 on behalf of the Third World by Narenda Aggarwala, an Indian journalist, now with the U.N. Development Program:

> The Third World's complaint against the international news media is twofold. First, that only a quarter of the news that goes on the wires of the four major Western news agencies emanates from, or deals with,

the developing countries, although they constitute nearly two-thirds of humanity. Second, most of the Third World news is negative and deals with such subjects as shortages, famines, natural disaster, and political and military intrigues. The news disseminated by the four transnational news agencies is meant primarily for users in the developed countries and has a very strong northern orientation. What the developing countries want is world news by the Third World journalists for developing country media use. There is a genuine need for creating a channel through which developing nations can get news about each other, and the industrialized world, from their own perspective.

In light of these issues surrounding cultural bias and objectivity in journalism, the transnational news agencies have become a central part of the NWICO debate. Of course, the challenge may have been raised with different political motives. Yet, the underlying unity among the Third World representatives and some media professionals is evident. There has been a consensus, too, behind the charge that AP, UPI, AFP, and Reuters, are primarily interested in advancing the economic, political, and cultural interests of their respective countries. They are charged with reporting mainly disasters and calamities of the developing countries. Constructive analyses of development problems of these countries is rarely done. The criticism, in other words, is that Western journalists covering the Third World countries for their entire clientele devote too little attention to developmental constructive news—and when they do, their stories focus on "negative" events.

The result, as Aggarwalla pointed out, is typically this: *one Third World country's media system receives news of another Third World country—the news perceived, constructed and disseminated with a Western bias and intended for Western readership.*

Media Imperialism and News Values

The NWICO debate about the free flow concept frequently occurs under the umbrella term of media or cultural imperialism. This thesis has received attention in numerous studies on news agencies, television, broadcasting and satellite communications, advertising, and the press and film. Some scholars conclude that media imperialism is "the process whereby the ownership, structure, distribution or content and media in any one country are singly or together subject to substantial external pressure from the media interests of any other country or countries without proportionate reciprocation of influence by the country so affected." Some others suggest that the absence of reciprocity of media influence by the affected country and the element of imbalance of information resources between the countries concerned contributes to this imperialistic tendency. These two elements, these scholars argue, justify the use of the term "media imperialism" by the Third World.

A major question involves the determinants of the international flow of information and the definition of news values—the criteria used for selection of news events as shaped by journalistic professionalism in a particular social context. For instance, the operation of American agencies, writes British sociologist Jeremy Tunstall, is heavily geared to supplying news to domestic U.S. media. They carry an American flavor. Tunstall concludes that while selling their media output outside the country, the exporters, by nature of this dominance, "also tend to influence and define news values, styles and formats around the world." Even the notions of how a national news agency should operate are strongly influenced by the news which other nations acquire from the Anglo-American news agencies.

The disparity in news value judgement is commonplace among different press systems rooted in a particular political philosophy. The Third World apparently recognizes this factor but they also see the Western newsman as contributing to the "tyranny of taste"—the known or perceived interests of the audience. Nevertheless, there seems to be justification for the Third World criticism that most of the news of events in their neighboring and developing countries is deemed newsworthy or not by professional newspeople of the AP, UPI, AFP, and Reuters, operating under a system of government often different from those of the Third World. The Western sets of values and judgments are deciding what is to be reported from the Third World and even to other nearby developing countries. Developmental news of one Third World nation, largely ignored by existing agencies, may be vital and, indeed crucial, in planning international trade and foreign policy in another Third World nation. It also seems clear that professional ideologies and news values permeate the problem of information imbalance and, indeed, affect international relations in general.

UNESCO and the NWICO Status

As a result of these controversies, the concept of every nation's right to communicate has given a focus to the NWICO. International reaction to the NWICO has been mixed. Developing nations have viewed it favorably while the West, including the United States, has been cautious, even hostile.

The political status of the problem is evident by the increasing responsibility of, and roles played by, international organizations which serve as fora for the continuing debate. Much of the NWICO debate concerning the free flow concept and the discussion of the Right-to-Communicate has been initiated by, or conducted under the auspices of UNESCO, the nonaligned nations conferences, and regional meetings. For example, the debate has been in progress in one form or another since the birth of UNESCO in 1945. The focus sharpened considerably in the early 1970s. In order to understand the issues in NWICO, one has to examine the role of UNESCO in some detail because this forum has been the crystallizing agent of the debate.

As an organization with a statutory purpose of guiding world communications, UNESCO has shifted from an idealistic to a pragmatic outlook and halfway back because of changing international relations and ideological positions pursued by major nations like the U.S., the Soviet Union, and the collective stance of the non-alligned nations. The agency has had to meet the challenges of the Cold War, the emergence of the Third World, and a less than whole-hearted acceptance of development aid, communication technology and facilities by receiving countries. These conditions have impeded UNESCO's ability to deal constructively with the NWICO.

Despite the adaptability of UNESCO to the changing political scene, it has not always met with success. Stalemates are common-place, but this should come as no surprise for an organization in which more than 150 nations are represented. Many of these stalemates occur on the East-West ideological basis. At least three main positions are represented—the free flow concept (supported by the U.S.), the government's control of information flow (backed by the Soviet Union), and the moderate and compromising stand (taken by Third World nations such as Yugoslavia and India.) Some of these views surfaced sharply at the 1975 Helsinki Conference on Security and Cooperation, and reached a crescendo at the Nairobi Conference. The Nairobi Conference of UNESCO in 1976 was crucial in that a proposal (by the Soviet Union) calling for State control on information flow was defeated. The vote indicated that the Third World nations were pressing for access to information outlets, rather than for control of information content.

UNESCO has staunchly upheld Article 19 of the UDHR as a guiding principle for the regulation of international communication. The free flow concept is endorsed by the UNESCO Constitution and several international agreements. However, the Third World movement for revision of these agreements resulted in the 1976 General Conference's adoption of "free and balanced flow of information." The question of its actual implementation in terms of access and participation, however, has been left in limbo.

The recommendations of NWICO encompass several broad areas of concern for the Third World. They include initiatives to embark on constructing national and regional networks of news collection and dissemination; training of Third World journalists in developmental journalism; coherent and unified national information policies to resist cultural synchronization, and to encourage diversity of autonomous cultural systems; and an international code of professional ethics and a possible licensing scheme to protect journalists in dangerous situations or in armed conflict. (The Western press has been particularly fearful of the licensing prospects; UNESCO and several Third World journalists also share the concern that licensing may pose dangers to freedom of information).

Conclusion

The logistics of translating these recommendations into reality are overwhelming. However, the Third World leaders are not about to discontinue their efforts for these changes through NWICO. They also expect the Western nations to play an active role in the process of realigning the flow of international communication. In a highly interdependent world, the Western nations cannot afford to be mere spectators. Neither can they reject everything alien. All cultures must develop by free choice and without imposition from other cultures. International mechanisms must be devised to bring about the desired changes. Self-regulation of communication industry and journalistic conduct must be fully explored in international dialogues as a means to realize every one's right to communicate.

Bibliography

Beltran, Luis Ramiro, "A Farewell to Aristotle: Horizontal Comunication," *Communication*, 1980.

Boyd-Barrett, Oliver, "Media Imperialism: Toward an International Framework for the Analysis of Media Systems," in *Mass Communication and Society*, edited by James Curran, published by Edward Arnold (London), 1977.

Desmond, Robert W., *The Information Process: World News Reporting to the Twentieth Century*, University of Iowa Press (Iowa City, Iowa), 1978.

Fisher, Glen, *American Communication in a Global Society*, Ablex (Norwood, N.J.), 1979.

Ghorpade, Shailendra, "Foreign Correspondents and the New World Information Order," *Gazette*, 1984.

Gurback, Thomas H., *The International Film Industry: Western Europe and America Since 1945*, Indiana Univesity Press (Bloomington, Ind.), 1969.

Hachten, William A., *The World News Prism: Changing Media, Changing Ideologies*, Iowa State University Press (Ames, Iowa), 1981.

Horton, Philip C., Ed., *The Third World and Press Freedom*, Praeger (New York, N.Y.), 1978.

International Commission for the Study of Communal Problems, UNESCO, *Final Report. Many Voices, One World*, UNESCO (Geneva, Switzerland), 1980.

International Press Institute, *UNESCO and the Third World Media: An Appraisal*, IPI (London, England), 1978.

Lee, Chin-Chuang, *Media Imperialism Reconsidered*, Sage (Beverly Hills, Calif.), 1980.

MacBride, Sean. "NWICO," *Irish Broadcasting Review*, Spring, 1977.

Martin, L. John; Anju Grover Chaudhary, *Comparative Media Systems*, Longman (New York, N.Y.), 1983.

Renaud, Jean-Luc, "A Revised Agenda for the New World Information Order: The Transborder Data Flow Issue," *Gazette*, 1984.

Richstad, Jim; Michael H. Anderson, *Crisis in International News: Policies and Prospects*, Columbia University Press (New York, N.Y.), 1981.

Schiller, Herbert, *Mass Communications and American Empire*, Beacon (Boston Mass.), 1969.

Sommerlad, E. Lloyd, *The Press in Developing Countries*, Sydney University Press (Sydney, Australia), 1966.

Sussman, Leonard R., "A New World Information Order?" *Freedom at Issue*, November-December 1978.

Part II

The Framework for the Media: Contemporary Perspectives

"Whenever any Form of Government becomes destructive . . . it is the Right of the People to alter or abolish it."

—Declaration of Independence

Section 1

The State as Suppressor:
Arguments for Limiting Expression

"Throughout their history, Americans have been strangely intolerant libertarians, often suppressing individual liberties in the name of a more trnascendent freedom."

—David Paul Nord, 1985

Those who enjoy the good life wish to keep it from others who might take it away; politicians with power wish to protect it from the weak; religious leaders desire to maintain their organizations, and, if possible, expand them to acquire more followers; in short, people who have something want to protect their possessions from others.

Others, with a sense of self-justifying morality, want to protect the naive from decadence—the young or the inexperienced adult from pornography.

The state, and its politicians, wish to preserve the sate from those who would overthrow it.

The protectionist instinct of the authoritarian leads governments to restrain free expression in four categories, first, the morality must be produced. For that reason, pornography laws are enacted. Second, an people's right to their creative enterprises must be preserved (copyright). Third, the state must be saved from those who would advocate its immediate and forcible overthrow, or use state information against the government (seditious libel and confidential information). Fourth, certain parts of a person's life belong only to the individual and should remain in tact (defamation, privacy, and fair trial).

President Jimmy Carter, desiring to keep some information from the public, invoked "executive privilege" when he refused to release eighteen documents prepared as part of governmental action against a Texas anti-proverty organization in 1978. According to Carter, release of the information would injure the confidentiality needed for the decision-making practices of government. On other occasions, Carter used executive privilege to keep information regarding actions aimed at the Israeli settlement question, data developed over unemployment research, and deliberations in Cabinet meetings from the public.

President Ronald Reagan, with his concern over leaking information, tightened procedures for handling people with access to classified information, including initiating lie detector tests, required signing of "non-disclosure pledges," and mandatory review of manuscripts written by present and former administration personnel. Reagan has also sought to "reduce the opportunity for negligent or deliberate disclosures of classifed information" by requiring policies regarding contact between government employees with access to classified information and reporters. In another attempt to restrict the flow of ideas, Reagan has tried to limit the flow of foreigners into the United States with "dangerous" ideas, and the travel of American scholars to foreign conferences.

All of these practices are in direct conflict with the concept of a "liberal democracy" which holds that all ideals should be given free exposure in the public forum. Yet, fear and the need prevents authorities from opening the gates to all thinkers—and their authority permits them to institute authorization measures to control expression.

Chapter 36

Preservation of the State

The Liberty of the Press is essential to the security of the State.

—Massachusetts Constitution, drafted by John Adams

It is one of the fundamental rights and most essential responsibilities of government to do everything it can to protect the State and, thus, the people, from destruction, whether by invasion or insurrection. To protect itself, the State creates a military or "home defense" force of uniformed citizens; civilian executive, administrative, and support staff; and diplomats. In countries with a history of unstable governments, the ratio of military to non-military population is often closer than in countries with stable populations. The State also creates myriad regulations, ordinances, acts, and laws to preserve to orderly movement of society—and enforces them with myriad law enforcement agencies at all levels of government. In addition, in many countries, including the United States, all federal cabinet departments have bureaus, branches, or divisions with investigatory and arrest powers. However, the responsibilities and rights of the State are often in conflict with the inherent rights of the people. By imposing fear upon the people, allowing them to believe that the existence of the State is in jeopardy, the State can often modify, suspend, or quash the rights of the people, usually with their compliance. Raymond Japhet of the London *Daily Express* argues:

> If there is anybody to blame for press restrictions, the press is partly responsible, because if it gives in tamely and too easily to requests in the interest of national security which do not affect national security, then we are going to be of great disservice to the country. It is up to us. We ourselves must put over the very best service we can to the public by giving the news truthfully and fearlessly and also explaining how we are hampered and how there is constant tampering with the machinery used.

The history of the United States, like the history of every country, includes a history of oppression in the name of security for the State—and a press that has not always been as aggressive in sorting out the difference between matters of security and matters of politics.

Numerous municipal, county, and state governments hve used authoritarian doctrine to justify reasons for various suppressions of free expression, each petty government claiming that its own security was threatened by "inaccurate reporting." The instances at the federal level have been fewer, but far more significant for at that level it *is* the State, not some functionary of the State, that has taken action. Although George Washington was furious over the media's inaccurate and vitriolic reporting of his administration, and especially his handling of foreign affairs, he did not consider the press a sufficient threat to the nation's security. Nevertheless, Washington, as president, cited "executive privilege" to deny documents to the House of Representatives which was investigating conduct of a military campaign against the Indians.

By signing the Alien and Sedition Acts, 1798-1801, John Adams declared that there were sufficient threats to American security to justify the imposition of such laws that were later declared to be unconstitutional.

I would observe, that the more we understand of the science of government, the less necessity we find for governmental secrets. State-craft and priest-craft are fond of hidden mysteries: they delight in their esoteric and exoteric doctrines and measures; but hidden motives are always suspicious in a republican government. In such a government, so far as we have experienced, secrecy is the child of misconduct and the parent of mischief . . . Where a statesman chooses to conceal his motives, it is at least an equal chance that he is afraid to disclose them, as that he ought not to disclose them.

The cases where secrecy is expedient are very few: they occur but rarely; and unless there be something apparently wrong, or some good reason for previous distrust, the people generally (far too generally) acquiesce without suspicion. The objection, therefore, amounts at the most to an exception only of small extent, to a general rule. Nor can a right of so much consequence as the right contended for, be overthrown by a few cases of possible inconvenience, and even these of so dubious a complexion.

—Thomas Cooper, *Political Essays* (1800)

During the Mexican-American War, 1846-1848, the American government claimed that the security of the United States was in jeopardy—at the same time its armies, under Gen. Zachary Taylor (1784-1850), had invaded northern and central Mexico, pillaged its towns, raped and slaughtered its people. Taylor, who would become U.S. president, 1849-1850, had proclaimed that he believed in the freedom of the press—then suppressed a dozen Mexican newspapers which had written articles opposing the American invasion. Even American newspapers agreed with Taylor's decisions. According to media historian Dr. Tom Reilly, in the Summer 1977 issue of *Journalism Quarterly*:

There was little press comment in the States regarding Taylor's action, and what there was supported him. The *Baltimore Sun* [of August 9, 1846] reported:

In judging this matter [of the censorship of the Mexican press], we must not view it as a restriction of the liberty of the press—it is a restriction of the press from an abuse of privilege. There is no such thing as liberty of the press in Matamoras, [Mexico,] by civil law, and certainly it cannot have existence under the general despotism of military rule.

Any American war newspaper which did not limit itself to only reporting news would be in danger to the success of the invasion, the *Sun* argued, adding Taylor's army could not tolerate the "nuisance" of newspaper critics. Otherwise, the *Sun* pointed out, "Every dissatisfied soldier would rush to its columns to pour out his complaints, parties would be formed, strife engendered, insubordination ensue and the commanding officer soon find himself in an [intolerable] plight . . ." Regarding Mexican newspapers, the *Sun* complained of the "pretty free language" they were allowed to use, considering they were operating in "captured cit[ies], governed by martial law." A Washington correspondent of the *Sun* carried the point further: "That the Mexican press must be crushed every reasonable man will at once understand . . . We must deprive them of everything that can lend to union of action."

The Polk Administration's newspaper, the *Washington Union*, strongly supported this position. It argued that if any American newspaper in Mexico took an anti-war stand it would be the commanding general's duty to "silence" such organs of flagrant treason on grounds they'd be protracting the war by giving "aid and comfort to the enemy."

The Mexican-American War, although supported by a significant majority of Americans, was also a controversial war, one in which numerous persons were arrested for protesting American imperialism. Among those jailed was Henry David Thoreau who, like many others, refused to pay taxes to a government that invaded another country. Many other dissenters were jailed on various charges related to "giving aid and comfort to the enemy," even if that "aid" was merely writing or speaking against the war.

Abraham Lincoln had a different problem. In a war fought within the country, many northern newspapers not only wrote vicious reports against Lincoln, but also supported southern philosophies and reported, in detail, northern troop movements, thus giving substantial aid to the Confederacy. Although there was some suppression of newspapers in both the north and south, the American press remained relatively free, compared to the press in many countries that were not torn apart by a civil war.

Very few people really care for liberty; what they crave is merely security.

—H. L. Mencken

To promote American views and keep the people informed, while also preserving State and military secrets, the United States established the Committee on Public Information in World War I, and the Office of War Information in World War II. Most media recognized the actual jeopardy that threatened the existence of the country, and submitted to voluntary censorship guidelines. During World War II, the *Chicago Tribune*, on June 7, 1942, published Stanley Johnston's story that American Naval forces were prepared for the Japanese "surprise" attack on Midway Island the day before. A careful reading of the story revealed that the Navy had broken the Japanese radio codes, and could now monitor most Japanese battle strategies; such information was properly classified as "top secret," and not meant for public dissemination. The U.S. Office of Censorship cited the *Tribune* for violation of the nation's Voluntary Censorship Code. The Departments of Justice and Navy had brought charges to a federal grand jury which chose not to indict the *Tribune* for violation of the Espionage Act.

During the "Cold War" era following World War II, numerous State actions restricted the rights of American citizens. First it was the re-emergence of required loyalty oaths for anyone working for a public agency; those working for foreign governments signed the oaths, many of those who were loyal Americans but disagreed with either the principle of a loyalty oath or of a specific kind of American government, refused to sign, were not hired or were removed from their employment, and subjected to large-scale investigation. Then, it was the "witch-hunts" of the various "anti-communist" organizations, including the House Committee on Un-American Activities. And then it was the domestic surveillance by the Army, the FBI, the IRS, and numerous intelligence-gathering agencies which established elaborate spy networks to keep files on "anti-American suspects." Included in various files were Sen. Adlai E. Stevenson III, son of a popular presidential candidate and grandson of a vice-president; the Rev. Martin Luther King; Sen. Eugene McCarthy, presidential candidate; and numerous persons who were either members of certain organizations, or who had views that were contrary to the established views of the government in power. Many presidents, including Eisenhower, Kennedy, and Johnson, used the FBI to track down "leaks" among administration employees that could have embarrassed certain actions of their superiors. President Nixon used the IRS to harrass unfriendly reporters, and brought in both the FBI and CIA to help block aspects of what became known as the Watergate investigations. President Carter was also concerned about "leaks," but did not use federal powers to stop them; President Reagan established strict administrative procedures that restricted freedom of government employees from talking with the press.

And all the spying, and all the files, and all the various arrests, whether on specific charges that stood up in the courts, or on spurious charges that were nothing more than harrassment, was done in the guise of protecting the national security.

Free Speech, The Military, and The National Interest

by Felix F. Moran

The First Amendment to the Constitution of the United States provides, in part, that "Congress shall make no law . . . abridging the freedom of speech, or of the press; or the right of the people peaceably to assemble . . ." Despite the almost unquestioned acceptance of this principle within American society, there remains a great deal of misunderstanding as to its application to members of the military forces.

Much of this misunderstanding is voiced in highly publicized comments of senior military officials and prominent legal commentators. The recent experiences of Major General John K. Singlaub, USA (Ret), are a case in point. Recalled from his post in Korea after making critical comments concerning President Carter's decision to withdraw United States ground forces from that country, General Singlaub has, with much fanfare and a great deal of publicity, made many references to the suppression of senior military officers' tactical, strategic, and political opinions. From his perspective, free speech does not exist in the military.

Lt. Col. Felix F. Moran is director of anti-terrorism and deputy chief of staff/security police for the headquarters of the Military Airlift Command, Scott Air Force Base, Illinois. A command pilot with over 4800 flying hours, including 680 in combat, Lt. Col. Moran earned the Distinguished Flying Cross, the Air Medal with twelve oak leaf clusters, and the Meritorious Service Medal with two oak leaf clusters, and the Air Force Commendation Medal with one oak leaf cluster. He received a B.S. in police science and administration from Washington State University, and an M.A. in criminal justice from California State University at Sacramento. [This article is reprinted, with permission, from the *Air University Review*, May-June 1980.]

Likewise, freedom of expression by lower-ranking personnel is thought not to exist. Melvin Wulf of the American Civil Liberties Union has commented that free speech in the military is opposed by "those who enjoy the picturesque spit and polish of traditional military life, as well as its predictability, security and class structure. They recognize that those features of their life are threatened by unfamiliar political ideologies and cultural habits. . ."

Free speech, as guaranteed by the First Amendment, does exist in the military. There are curbs placed on free expression, but they are not as restrictive as they appear on the surface, and they are not without counterparts in civilian life. There are, after all, few wholly free agents in our society. For example, a judge is not free to practice civil disobedience from the bench but must conform to the rulings of the Supreme Court; nor is an employee of a private company protected by law from dismissal for expressing opinions distasteful to management. The situation is much the same in the armed forces.

Freedom of speech, press, and assembly as secured by the Constitution does not mean that the right to speak or publish one's convictions may be practiced without responsibility or without consideration for other factors. Justice Oliver

---

Striking the BBC

More than three thousand radio and television journalists struck the British Broadcasting Co. (BBC) for twenty-four hours, August 6-7, 1985, to protest cancellation of a forty-five minute documentary about Northern Ireland. It was the first time that journalists ever struck the fifty-three year old BBC, widely recognized as one of the most prestigious media networks. The documentary profiled two men, one a member of the Irish Republican Army (IRA) which is attempting to force England out of Northern Ireland, and one of whom was a member of the Democratic Union Party which supports England's continued presence. Both men, members of the Northern Ireland Assembly, said they would use violence to further their political opinions on England's role in the country in which more than 2,500 persons have died since 1969.

The journalists struck when the BBC Board of Governors refused to allow the transmission of the documentary, which it claimed favored the outlawed IRA. BBC journalists claimed that the Board of Governors yielded to governmental pressure. Ray McGuigan, president of the National Union of Journalists, noted that "Journalists need to take this kind of action to ensure that that censorship does not take place again."

However, many journalists did not see the issue as one of censorship, but one of preservation of the State. Peregrine Worsthorne, editor of the [London] *Daily Telegraph* said that he believes that "if one takes the view that we are at war with the IRA [then] a program like that should not be put on. We couldn't have done such a program about the Nazis and we shouldn't do one about the IRA. I wouldn't have banned it, but I wouldn't have made it."

Wendell Holmes stated in *Schenck* v. *United States*: "The most stringent protection of free speech would not protect a man in falsely shouting fire in a theater, and causing a panic." As concluded in the *Schenck* opinion, the right to free speech is dependent on the circumstances surrounding its exercise. In considering these circumstances, the question becomes one of outcome. Again, Justice Holmes provided a guideline in the *Schenck* opinion: "the question in every case is whether the words are used in such circumstances and are of such nature as to create a clear and present danger that they will bring about the substantive evils that Congress has a right to prevent."

By 1950, the clear and present danger test was well established. In that year, however, a new requirement was forecast by the dissenting opinion of Justice William O. Douglas in *Dennis* v. *United States*. He argued that for speech to be punishable some immediate injury to society must be likely. This requirement was adopted outright nineteen years later in *Bradenburg* v. *Ohio*. The Supreme Court observed that statements must go beyond mere advocacy and be directed toward "inciting or producing imminent lawless action."

In a military context, that standard forces us to ask whether or not free expression represents an imminent threat to the national interest. The national interest can take many forms, but for our purposes here it is generally synonymous with the ability of the armed forces to perform their wartime military mission. Senior officials, both military and civilian, agree that unlimited free speech is inconsistent with command, control, and military authority on which the armed forces are based and, therefore, must be restricted in some degree if the military is to maintain its capability for immediate and unified action. An army or navy whose members are allowed to spread internal dissension and disorder constitutes a hazard with perhaps as great a potential for danger to the country as a hostile foreign power. Thus, as Detlev F. Vagts states, "The national defense brooks no opposition and overrides many freedoms . . . even in peace time the military must act as if war were imminent, for new habits cannot be established on the day the balloon goes up . . ." It is a true paradox that the soldier, under certain circumstances, must sacrifice some of the liberties that he is called on to protect.

This suggested relationship is a balancing between the free speech rights of the individual military man on one side and the national interest on the other. As suggested by Justice Holmes, the balance is never even, nor is it always tipped in favor of one side only. The circumstances of the particular situation provide additional weight to one side, and the balance shifts in favor of the individual or the national interest.

United States v. Voorhees

One of the earliest First Amendment cases decided by the USCMA, *United States* v. *Voorhees* [1954], had involved a lieutenant colonel who wrote an account of his war service in Korea. He submitted the manuscript for review, as required by military regulation, but refused to delete certain passages as requested by the reviewing authority. Ignoring an order to withdraw the manuscript, Lt.

Col. Voorhees went ahead with publication. He was convicted by court-martial of five violations of the UCMJ for publishing his work without proper clearance. A board of review reversed all the findings of guilty except one but upheld the sentence of dismissal and total forfeiture of all pay and allowances.

On appeal, the USCMA concluded that a regulation requiring security review was valid and, therefore, did not violate the military member's First Amendment rights, noting that the right to free speech is not an indiscriminate right and is qualified by the requirements of reasonableness in relation to time, place, and circumstances. Although the court failed to address the issue of policy review, Judge George W. Latimer, in a separate opinion, concluded that the First Amendment does not guarantee any expression that would jeopardize the efforts of the armed forces. He wrote:

> A few dissident writers, occupying positions of importance in the military, could undermine the leadership of the armed forces, and if every member of the service was, during a time of conflict, or preparation therefor, permitted to ridicule, divide, deprecate, and destroy the character of those chosen to lead the armed forces, and the cause for which this country was fighting, then the war effort would most assuredly fail.

Judge Latimer further observed: "Undoubtedly, we should not deny to servicemen any right that can be given reasonably. But, in measuring reasonableness, we should bear in mind that military units have one purpose justifying their existence: to prepare themselves for war and to wage it successfully. That purpose must never be overlooked . . ."

The unrestricted application of First Amendment rights by servicemen could seriously jeopardize this single purpose by undermining discipline and morale. Judge Latimer succinctly noted in his *Voorhees* opinion, "A war cannot be won in the halls of debate, and conditions do not permit meeting lies with truth . . . In times of peace, those who voluntarily or involuntarily work to protect our nation should not be required to toil in contention and strife engendered from within."

Thus, the *Voorhees* decision clearly supports the military's authority to limit free speech with respect to both the security and policy interests of the armed forces.

It has been clearly established, beginning with the *Schenck* decision, that restraints which reasonably protect the national interest do not violate the constitutional right guaranteed in the First Amendment. Within the armed forces, the restraints take the form of regulations that require review and clearance for release of information by military members and prior approval for the distribution or posting of written material on a military installation. They also prohibit personnel stationed overseas from participating in demonstrations.

Enforcement of these regulations, policy restraints, and traditional restrictions affecting discipline is accomplished through seven articles of the Uniform Code of Military Justice (UCMJ). Specific articles prohibit:

1. Commissioned officers from using contemptuous words against the President and other senior civilian government officials.

2. Any person from behaving with disrespect toward a superior commissioned officer.

3. Insubordinate conduct (speech) toward a warrant officer, noncommissioned officer or petty officer.

4. Willful disobedience of an order or regulation.

5. Persons from making provoking or reproachful speeches or gestures towards other persons subject to the UCMJ.

6. Conduct unbecoming an officer.

7. Conduct prejudicial to the good order and discipline of the armed forces, or that will bring discredit upon the service.

Within the framework of regulations and the UCMJ, the basic elements of the limitations imposed depend on the time, place, and circumstances associated with the particular expression made by the military member. The final authority in determining whether the application of these limitations denies the serviceman his basic constitutional rights rests with the United States Court of Military Appeals (USCMA) and, collaterally, the Supreme Court of the United States.

United States v. Howe

A significant and much publicized military First Amendment case of recent times was *United States* v. *Howe* (1967). Howe, a second lieutenant stationed at Fort Bliss, Texas, was convicted of using contemptuous words against the President and conduct unbecoming an officer and gentleman, in violation of articles 88 and 133, Uniform Code of Military Justice. Specifically, he had participated in a demonstration in downtown El Paso and was observed by military police while carrying a sign reading: "Let's have more than a choice between petty ignorant fascists in 1968," and, on the reverse side, "End Johnson's fascist aggression in Vietnam." Lieutenant Howe appealed his conviction to the Court of Military Appeals, arguing, in part, that the charges against him violated his first amendment rights.

In affirming the conviction, the military high court answered the First Amendment question by relying on the principle of civilian control over the military. Traditionally, members of the armed forces, particularly officers, have been restricted from using contemptuous words against or otherwise maligning the policies of the civilian leadership. Beginning with the adoption of the first Articles of War in 1775, Congress and other civilian leaders have sanctioned this restriction in order to prevent the possibility of a military coup. In applying this principle to the Howe case, the court stated:

True, petitioner is a reserve officer, rather than a professional officer, but during the time he serves on active duty, he is, and must be, controlled by the provisions of military law. In this instance, military restrictions fall upon a reluctant "summer soldier"; but in another time, and differing circumstances, the ancient and wise provisions insuring civilian control of the military will restrict the "man on the white horse."

The rationale offered by the USCMA in its *Howe* decision traces the necessity of civilian supremacy over the military and the intent, from our earliest history, to use article 88 and its precursors to ensure that supremacy. Actual practice has not followed that intent, however. Past applications of Article 88 have usually been confined to political activists, enemy sympathizers, and various types of malcontents. When civilian supremacy has actually been at stake, administrative actions, such as removal, reassignment, and forced retirement have been taken against the errant officer.

Parker v. Levy

[In 1974], *Parker* v. *Levy* further defined the limits of military free speech. Dr. Levy was convicted for making disloyal and disrespectful comments to enlisted personnel intended to promote disaffection among the troops, in violation of articles 133 and 134, and for failure to obey a lawful order, in violation of article 92.

Although the issue on appeal was the vagueness and overbreadth of articles 133 and 134, the Supreme Court's decision has considerable application to the issue of military free speech rights. The Court said that while members of the armed forces were not excluded from the protection of the First Amendment, a different application was required because of the fundamental need for obedience and discipline. Stressing this uniqueness, the Court stated that civilian First Amendment standards do not automatically apply to the military.

In reaching its decision, the Court relied on the Court of Military Appeals to explain the unique need of the military. The latter court stated in *United States* v. *Priest*:

> In the armed forces some restrictions exist for reasons that have no counterpart in the civilian community. Disrespectful and contemptuous speech, even advocacy of violent change, is tolerable in the civilian community, for it does not directly affect the capacity of the Government to discharge its responsibilities unless it both is directed to inciting imminent lawless action and is likely to produce such action . . . In military life, however, other considerations must be weighed. The armed forces depend on a command structure that at times must commit men to combat, not only hazarding their lives but ultimately involving the security of the Nation itself. Speech that is protected in the civil population may nonetheless undermine the effectiveness of response to command. If it does, it is constitutionally unprotected.

This endorsement of the *Priest* decision clearly demonstrates the Supreme Court's application of the balancing test, weighing the peculiar needs of the armed forces as but one factor to determine the extent of military free speech rights.

United States v. Priest

The case, *United States* v. *Priest* [1972], resulted from the publishing activities of a navy journalist convicted of two specifications of printing and distributing issues of a publication which contained statements disloyal to the United States, in violation of Article 134. The paper encouraged desertion and gave the names of groups in Canada [which] would aid deserters. It made references to assassinating the President, taking over the government, and bombing the United States.

In affirming the conviction, the USCMA rejected the *Bradenburg* requirement that there be an incitement to imminent lawless action, holding that the clear and present danger test outlined by Justice Holmes in *Schenck* was the proper standard for determining the extent of free expression within the military services. The court further stated:

> The danger resulting from an eroding of military morale and discipline is too great to require that discipline must already have been impaired before prosecution for uttering statements can be sustained. As we have said before, the right to free speech in the armed services is not unlimited and must be brought into balance with the paramount consideration of providing an effective fighting force for the defense of our country.

Navy v. Avreck

A final notable publication case is that of the *Secretary of the Navy* v. *Avreck* [1974]. Avrech, a Marine Corps private stationed in Vietnam, was convicted of attempting to publish disloyal statements with the intent to promote disaffection among the troops, in violation of articles 80 and 134. He had not actually published or distributed the material since he was apprehended while carrying the typed stencil.

The case eventually reached the Supreme Court and was decided as a companion case to *Parker* v. *Levy*. The value of the *Avrech* decision is that it indicates that, while in a war zone, the balance is shifted almost exclusively in favor of the need to protect the national interest.

There have been two notable cases concerning the serviceman's right to assemble peaceably, as guaranteed by the first amendment. In the first, *Dash* v. *Commanding General* (1969), the commanding general of Fort Jackson, South Carolina, denied petitioners permission to distribute unofficial material on post and to conduct an open public meeting to discuss the war in Vietnam. The petitioners, twelve enlisted men, sought declaratory relief from the United States District Court in South Carolina, challenging the commander's authority to deny them the right to hold on-post meetings. The district court upheld the commander's power to deny such meetings when it was reasonably determined that their purpose was to produce discontent, disorder, and dissension.

In another case, *Culver* v. *Secretary of the Air Force* [1977], the federal appeals court upheld the conviction of an Air Force captain for participating in a demonstration in a foreign country, as prohibited by AFR 35-15, in violation of articles 92 and 133. In reaching its decision, the court reasoned that the military must be given wide latitude for the prevention of political activities that might embarrass the host country. From this decision, it is clear that under certain circumstances first amendment guarantees must yield to the interest of the government in maintaining cordial relations with the host country.

Unique Position of Senior Officers

The discussion of free speech to this point has centered on the balance between the national interest, as manifested in the morale and discipline of the armed forces, foreign policy and security considerations, and the individual military member's rights. Another frequently used justification for the suppression of First Amendment freedoms, however, is the issue of civilian control of the Department of Defense. The ultimate prupose of civilian supremacy is, of course, to prevent the military take-over of the government, a possibility that seems quite remote in our time. A more likely goal for restricting the content of statements by military officials, particularly flag officers, is to prevent excessive influence of the military in the formulation of government policy.

In our democracy, formulation of policy is constitutionally vested in the civilian authorities of government. The professional military man merely executes policy in a nonpartisan manner. Prussian General Karl von Clausewitz explained this situation, stating: "The subordination of the political point of view to the military would be unreasonable, for policy has created war; policy

---

A Probability of Deception

Every radio station in the United States has a secret packet of sealed instructions, complete with code words, of what to do during a military attack upon the country. By law, most stations will run a signal and direct listeners to one or two authorized Emergency Broadcast Service (EBS) stations for further information.

In Dade County, Florida, there was a twist to the accurate information that is supposed to be broadcast. The Civil Defense organization, in cooperation with the EBS, had prepared a tape that told the country the enemy force "struck the first blow," adding, "Our Strategic Air Command and naval units have devastated many of the major cities and industrial centers. Our defense forces have retaliated with tremendous effectiveness, and probability of victory is good."

The tape was later destroyed when the media learned of the deliberate attempt to deceive the people. The reason the tape was originally made, said civil defense officials, was because they didn't want to create a mass panic which could have not only destroyed the public morale but would have probably interfered with military operations against an enemy; thus, they argued, the public's right to know accurate information was secondary to the preservation of a country.

is the intelligent faculty, war only the instrument, and not the reverse. The subordination of the military point of view is, therefore, the only thing which is possible."

Throughout our history some senior military officers have been unable to accept this concept and have challenged its traditions, but most have recognized the wisdom of civilian supremacy and reconciled any differences they may have had with their government. The Continental Congress insisted in 1774 on civilian control of the military. Gen. Washington made it clear that he would bow to the congressional will, even if he was personally opposed to its policy. Gen. U.S. Grant, while commanding federal troops during the Civil War, expressed his feelings on the subject by stating, "So long as I hold my present position, I do not believe I have the right to criticize the policy or orders of those above me, or give utterance to views of my own, except to the authorities in Washington." Gen. George C. Marshall, perhaps the greatest soldier-statesman in our history, recalling his differences with President Franklin D. Roosevelt, hastened to add, "But I didn't make any public speeches." General Marshall appproved of Gen. Douglas MacArthur's removal from command, [in Korea], saying that the situation of a local theater commander publicly voicing his displeasure and disagreement with the foreign policy of the nation was "wholly unprecedented."

This view is shared equally by the civilian leadership within the government. The Senate Armed Services Committee, in a report released in October 1962, concluded that "once the decision has been made by the properly constituted authorities the military man must support it . . . If, in good conscience, he cannot live with a decision, he should divest himself of his uniform and carry on his fight in a civilian status."

Continuing this tradition, guidelines [were] clarified and reinforced by Secretary of the Army Clifford L. Alexander, Jr., in his address at West Point in 1977. Alexander outlined three distinct forums for opinion by the military professional:

> *Within the military:* Opinions can be voiced freely within the chain of command. Once a final decision has been made, however, the soldier's responsibility is to work in a creative and dedicated manner to execute the decision.
>
> *Before Congress:* A military man can freely express personal opinion when asked. Once policy has been established, it is his duty to cite the policy and his intent to follow it. If asked, he can state an opinion at odds with the policy, so long as the opinion is so identified.
>
> *Dealing with the media:* The officer must be aware that even before policy is established, expressing personal opinion may be contrary to the national interest. On the other hand, in some cases, discussion may be helpful in the formulation of policy. The official must be sure to state that policy has not been established or is subject to final review by military or civilian authority. Alexander further noted that, "in almost no instance will the national interest be served by a military person

voicing disagreement with established policy . . . Attempts to achieve outside the chain of command what one could not achieve inside the chain of command are out of keeping with this tradition [of the President as Commander-in-Chief] and inconsistent with military professionalism."

It is important to note that the general officer is just as susceptible to prosecution as a result of . . . expressed thoughts as the enlisted man, even though a general officer has not been prosecuted since the court-martial of Billy Mitchell in 1925. . . These . . . officers are usually dealt with through the use of administrative sanctions such as removal from command, reassignment, or forced retirement . . .

Servicemen do, in fact, have the same First Amendment rights as their civilian brothers. They are, however, not absolute. But, then, neither are these rights absolute in civilian law. The difference is that the military has peculiar needs and interests apart from those of the civilian community it serves, and they preclude the exercise of the right of free speech on as broad a basis as is the practice in the civilian community. As Judge Latimer wrote: . . . "No officer or man in the armed forces has a right, be it constitutional, statutory or otherwise, to publish any information [or make any statement] which will imperil his unit or its cause."

The President and the Press: Restraints of National Secruity

by John F. Kennedy

[John F. Kennedy (1917-1963), a former reporter, had a warm relationship with the media, but he, like all presidents, was deeply concerned about national security issues. During his administration, significant problems arose over the withholding of information about both the attempted invasion of Cuba by CIA-trained former Cubans living in the United States, and of the Cuban missile crisis. In a speech given April 27, 1961, to the American Newspaper Publishers Association, and reprinted in *Vital Speeches* (May 15, 1961), Kennedy warned of the right of a nation to suspend certain other rights in order to preserve itself.]

The very word "secrecy" is repugnant in a free and open society and we are as a people inherently and historically opposed to secret societies, to secret oaths and to secret proceedings. We decided long ago that the dangers of excessive and unwarranted concealment of pertinent facts far outweighed the dangers which are cited to justify it.

Even today, there is little value in opposing the threat of a closed society by imitating its arbitrary restrictions. Even today, there is little value in insuring the survival of our nation if our traditions do not survive with it. And there is a very grave danger that an announced need for increased security will be seized upon by those anxious to expand its meaning to the very limits of official censorship and concealment.

That I do not intend to permit to the extent that it's in my control. And no official of my Administration, whether his rank is high or low, civilian or military, should interpret my words . . . as an excuse to censor the news, to stifle dissent, to cover up our mistakes or to withhold from the press and the public the facts they deserve to know.

It is very important for a president to maintain up until the moment of decision his options, and for someone to speculate days or weeks in advance that he is going to do thus and thus is to deny the President the latitude he needs to make, in the light of existing circumstances, the best possible decision.

—Bill Moyers, press secretary to Lyndon B. Johnson
(quoted in the *Washington Post*; March 30, 1967)

But I do ask every publisher, every editor and every newsman in the nation to reexamine his own standards, and to recognize the nature of our country's peril. In time of war, the Government and the press have customarily joined in an effort, based largely on self-discipline, to prevent unauthorized disclosures to the enemy. In times of clear and present danger, the courts have held that even the privileged rights of the First Amendment must yield to the public's need for national security.

Today no war has been declared—and however fierce the struggle may be [in Vietnam] it may never be declared in the traditional fashion. Our way of life is under attack. Those who make themselves our enemy are advancing around the globe. The survival of our friends is in danger. And yet no war has been declared, no borders have been crossed by marching troops, no missiles have been fired.

If the press is awaiting a declaration of war before it imposes the self-discipline of combat conditions, then I can only say that no war ever posed a greater threat to our security. If you are awaiting a finding of "clear and present danger," then I can only say that the danger has never been more clear and its presence has never been more imminent.

It requires a change in outlook, a change in tactics, a change in mission by the Government, by the people, by every business man or labor leader and by every newspaper. For we are opposed around the world by a monolithic and ruthless conspiracy that relies primarily on covert means for expanding its sphere of influence—on infiltration instead of invasion, on subversion instead of elections, on intimidation instead of free choice, on guerrillas by night instead of armies by day.

It is a system which has conscripted vast human and material resources into the building of a tightly knit, highly efficient machine that combines military, diplomatic, intelligence, economic, scientific and political operations.

Its preparations are concealed, not published. Its mistakes are buried, not headlined. Its dissenters are silenced, not praised. No expenditure is questioned, no rumor is printed, no secret is revealed. It conducts the cold war, in short, with a wartime discipline no democracy would ever hope or wish to match.

Nevertheless, every democracy recognizes the necessary restraints of national security—and the question remains whether those restraints need to be more strictly observed if we are to oppose this kind of attack as well as outright invasion.

For the facts of the matter are that this nation's foes have openly boasted of acquiring through our newspapers information they would otherwise hire agents to acquire through theft, bribery or espionage; that details of this nation's covert preparations to counter the enemy's covert operations have been available to every newspaper reader, friend and foe alike, that the size, the strength, the location and the nature of our forces and weapons, and our plans and strategy for their use, have all been pinpointed in the press and other news media to a degree sufficient to satisfy any foreign power; and that, in at least one case, the publication of details concerning a secret mechanism whereby satellites were followed required its alteration at the expense of considerable time and money.

The newspapers which printed these stories were loyal, patriotic, responsible and well-meaning. Had we been engaged in open warfare, they undoubtedly would not have published such items. But in the absence of open warfare, they recognized only the tests of journalism and not the tests of national security. And my question tonight is whether additional tests should not now be adopted.

That question is for you alone to answer. No public official should answer it for you. No governmental plan should impose its restraints against your will. But I would be failing in my duty to the nation in considering all of the responsibilities that we now bear and all of the means at hand to meet those responsibilities if I did not commend this problem to your attention, and urge its thoughtful consideration.

On many earlier occasions, I have said—and your newspapers have constantly said—that these are times that appeal to every citizen's sense of sacrifice and self-discipline. They call out to every citizen to weigh his rights and comforts against his obligation to the common good. I cannot now believe that those citizens who serve in the newspaper business consider themselves exempt from that appeal.

I have no intention of establishing a new Office of War Information to govern the flow of news. I am not suggesting any new forms of censorship or new types security classifications. I have no easy answer to the dilemma I have posed, and would not seek to impose it if I had one. But I am asking the members of the newspaper profession and the industry in this country to reexamine their own responsibilities—to consider the degree and the nature of the present danger—and to heed the duty of self-restraint which that danger imposes upon us all.

Every newspaper now asks itself, with respect to every story: "Is it news?" All I suggest is that you add the question: "Is it in the interest of national security?" And I hope that every group in America—unions and business men and public officials at every level—will ask the same question of their endeavors, and subject their actions to this same exacting test.

And should the press of America consider and recommend the voluntary assumption of specific new steps or machinery, I can assure you that we will cooperate wholeheartedly with those recommendations.

Perhaps there will be no recommendations. Perhaps there is no answer to the dilemma faced by a free and open society in a cold and secret war. In times of peace, any discussion of this subject, and any action that results, are both painful and without precedent. But this is a time of peace and peril which knows no precedent in history.

It is the unprecedented nature of this challenge that also gives rise to your second obligation—an obligation which I share. And that is our obligation to inform and alert the American people—to make certain that they possess all the facts they need, and understand them as well—the perils, the prospects, the purposes of our program and the choices that we face. No President should fear public scrutiny of his program. For from that scrutiny comes understanding; and from that understanding comes support, or opposition, and both are necessary. I am not asking your newspapers to support an Administration. But I am asking your help in the tremendous task of informing and alerting the American people. For I have complete confidence in the response and dedication of our citizens whenever they are fully informed.

I not only could not stifle controversy among your readers—I welcome it. This Administration intends to be candid about its errors; for, as a wise man once said: "An error doesn't become a mistake until you refuse to correct it." We intend to accept full responsibility for our errors; and we expect you to point them out when we miss them.

Without debate, without criticism, no Administration and no country can succeed—and no republic can survive. That is why the Athenian lawmaker Solon decreed it a crime for any citizen to shrink from controversy. And that is why our press was protected by the First Amendment—the only business in America specifically protected by the Constitution—not primarily to amuse and entertain, not to emphasize the trivial and the sentimental, not to simply "give the public what it wants"—but to inform, to amuse, to reflect, to state our dangers and our opportunities, to indicate our crises and our choices, to lead, mold, educate and sometimes even anger public opinion.

This means greater coverage and analysis of international news—for it is no longer far away and foreign but close at hand and local. It means greater attention to improved understanding of the news as well as improved transmission. And it means, finally, that government at all levels, must meet its obligation to provide you with the fullest possible information outside the narrowest limits of national security and we intend to do it.

It was early in the seventeenth century that Francis Bacon remarked on three recent inventions already transforming the world; the compass, gunpowder and the printing press. Now the links between the nations first forged by the compass have made us all citizens of the world, the hopes and threats of one becoming the hopes and threats of us all. In that one world's effort to live together, the evolution of gunpowder to its ultimate limit has warned mankind of the terrible consequences of failure.

And so it is to the printing press—to the recorder of man's deeds, the keeper of his conscience, the courier of his news—that we look for strength and assistance, confident that with your help man will be what he was born to be: free and independent.

Classification and Obfuscation: A Review

by Muriel Akamatsu, Karen M. Brown, and Maura Christopher

Classification [of documents] has been used to conceal political mistakes, embarrassment, and bureaucratic confusion. There has been over-classification, random stamping of innocuous documents and a lack of an orderly and effective declassification system.

One unnamed CIA official, who testified in the *Pentagon Papers* case, has said "most of what is classified is political secrets." While some documents dealt with such legitimate concerns as sensitive codes, the "rest is a bunch of baloney; it's policy-posturing," the official said.

Former CIA agent Victor Marchetti [in *The CIA and the Cult of Intelligence*] underscored the account of witnesses who said classification concealed more embarrassments and blunders than State secrets . . .

Presidents and other officials have regularly leaked classified documents to suit partisan political goals.

The authors were graduate students in journalism when they wrote their articles about classification. Dr. Muriel Akamatsu received a B.A. in art, and an M.S.J. from the University of Missouri, and an Ed.D. in education from West Virginia University. She is a computer analyst and consultant in industrial safety, and a former public relations professional for both government and industry. Karen M. Brown received a B.A. in geography from Victoria University (Wellington, New Zealand), a diploma in journalism, Canterbury University (New Zealand), and an M.A. in journalism, University of Missouri. She was the Washington, D.C., correspondent for the *Yakima* (Wash.) *Herald Republican*, *Coalfield* (Va.) *Progress*, and the *Colorado Transcript*. She has also been a general assignment, science, diplomatic, and parliament reporter for the *Wellington Evening Post*, and is currently a sub-editor. Maura Christopher received a B.S. in public administration and an M.S.J. from the University of Missouri. She is currently associate editor of *Scholastic Update*. [This article has been edited, revised, and reprinted from Freedom of Information Center reports nos. 271 (1982), 469 and 482 (1983), published by the School of Journalism, University of Missouri.]

An ironic example of declassification being used to suit political purposes was offered by the *Press Censorship Newsletter*, which reported the CIA's finding that "by declassifying additional sensitive files relating to prior events—mainly the Bay of Pigs, the Cuban Missile Crisis, and the fall of the Diem Government in South Vietnam—it [the White House] sought to obtain material helpful in neutralizing critics . . . "

One result of such political control over information says the Louisville *Courier-Journal and Times Magazine*, is an American public that is less-informed than our nation's purported enemies:

> The North Vietnamese, the Chinese and the Russians knew all about the CIA war in Laos; only the American Congress and electorate were kept in the dark. It is also true that the secrecy system has been a fertile source of blunder and folly in foreign policy.

Secrecy is a necessary function of government [since] bureaucrats move up the ladder by a knowledge not accessible to others.

—Max Weber

Classification succeeds in barring public access to massive amounts of gover-nemnt information. The House Committee on Government Information, disclosed that in 1976 the executive branch classified 4.5 million documents, totalling an estimated 45 million pages. Said David Wise, a reporter specializing in intelligence activities:

> At a conservative estimate, there would be 100,000,000 classified documents in government files. The Pentagon's chief classifier has testified that the Defense Deprtment has more than one million cubic feet of classified documents, the equivalent, if stacked, of 2,297 Washington monuments. [*Center Magazine*, July-August 1977.]

One reason asserted as causing such over-classification is its tendency toward randomness. Asked in court how he classified documents, Leslie Gelb said: "The only instruction I had was a movie, the theme of which was, 'beware of blonds who may be excessively friendly—they may be Russian spies.' " . . .

Arthur Schlesinger, Jr. [in 1972] . . . concluded that the classification system is hopelessly out of control because the only control present has been exercised through executive orders. He says Congress has the authority to control classification, but has not chosen to exercise that power . . .

The Early Years of Secrecy

"From the start, the American government has been into secrecy," commented . . . Schlesinger in 1972. The founding fathers who drafted the Constitution in 1787 met in secret. James Madison, who drafted the First Amendment in 1789, said that no constitution would have been adopted if the Constitutional Convention's debates had been public.

The Federalist, a series of conservative articles published beginning 1787, specified two areas—diplomatic negotiations and intelligence—in which secrecy seemed essential to uphold the executive branch's right to conduct certain affairs without an immediate obligation to supply Congress with full details.

Meeting privately is one form of government secrecy. Restricting access to government documents is another.

Classification is a system used by the Executive branch to, in part, protect national security and foreign policy interests. The system offers several degrees of protection for documents—"confidential," "secret," and "top secret" being the most commonly used. The use of such labels has been traced back to the War of 1812.

The next step in the development of the classification system was the issuance of a series of general orders, the first of which appeared April 1869. That order banned the taking of photographs of Army posts and coastal military installations in the United States. Another general order, issued twenty-eight years later, limited visiting privileges on U.S. military posts to military personnel and members of Congress.

The Rise of Twentieth Century Secrecy

The systematic use of classification markings with precise definitions was established during World War I. The system was patterned after British and French procedures.

Several modifications of the system were incorporated in 1917, 1921, 1935 and 1936. The classification procedures applied only to military information and were found in Army and Navy regulations. Executive agencies, including the State Department, relied upon a 1789 housekeeping statute to withhold information from the public.

Since 1936, major changes in the field of government secrecy have originated with presidents in the form of executive orders, with President Franklin D. Roosevelt's 1940 Executive Order #8381 being the first such use of an executive order in the classification field. That order applied classification designations and procedures to military and naval installations, equipment, maps, photographs, documents, designs and similar items.

During World War II, the Office of War Information established a government-wide clasification system . . . The military had its own system based upon the 1940 order.

—Karen M. Brown

Truman: Control Through Classification

One of the most upsetting [actions of Harry Truman] in the eyes of the press occurred September 25, 1951, when he issued an unprecedented order greatly tightening controls on the outflow of information.

Executive Order 10290 granted the tight security exercised by the State and Defense departments to all government agencies handling military information.

For the first time in U.S. history, all agencies of the Executive were given official permission to classify information. It was the first instance in which these kinds of controls were used in peacetime, and it was the first permanent system for safeguarding defense information.

Robert McLean, then president of Associated Press, said the order invited "a creeping censorship of a kind never before established in this country in time of peace or even in time of war." . . .

Later, after a few months of the order's existence, James S. Pope, of American Society of Newspaper Editors, said there was " . . . a dangerous trend toward the suppresion of official public records by federal, state and municipal officials" and that classifying for "national security" had been "seriously abused." [March 4, 1952] . . .

I would observe, that the more we understand of the science of government, the less necessity we find for governmental secrets. State-craft and priest-craft are fond of hidden mysteries: they delight in their esoteric and exoteric doctrines and measures; but hidden motives are always suspicious in a republican government. In such a government, so far as we have experienced, secrecy is the child of misconduct and the parent of mischief . . . Where a statesman chooses to conceal his motives, it is at least an equal chance that he is afraid to disclose them, as that he ought not to disclose them. The cases where secrecy is expedient are very few: they occur but rarely; and unless there be something apparently wrong, or some good reason for previous distrust, the people generally (far too generally) acquiesce without suspicion. The objection, therefore, amounts at the most to an exception only of small extent, to a general rule. Nor can a right of so much consequence as the right contended for, be overthrown by a few cases of possible inconvenience, and even these of so dubious a complexion.

—Thomas Cooper, *Political Essays*, 1800, pp. 77-78.

Erwin D. Canham, editor of the *Christian Science Monitor*, said access to news had been "under widespread attack recently in the United States . . . There has been more refusal of access to the public records in the last five years than in the preceding century."

Eisenhower: Military-Industrial Secrecy

Dwight Eisenhower incurred the wrath of the "Fourth Estate" when it seemed that he was treading too heavily on the press' right of access to executive information.

On May 16, 1954, Eisenhower issued an order suppressing information on the nature of executive consultations. It was an attempt to avoid the infamous publicity coming out of the McCarthy-Army hearings.

Clark Mollenhoff [a Pulitizer Prize-winning investigative reporter] condemned the action as one of the greatest threats to press freedom in history:

> . . .[executive privilege] looms as the biggest obstacle to a free press and an informed Congress . . . [the order] started this precedent that is the greatest threat to press freedom in history . . . This doctrine has the seeds for executive dictatorship. The extreme executive privilege theory should be destroyed before it falls into the hands of some group that would use it to destroy our system of government.

Although defending the administration for doing better than it appeared with regard to press relations, [columnists] Joseph and Stewart Alsop observed that the administration had lost its believability by being "less than frank in explaining its policies." [May 30, 1954].

The American Society of Newspaper Editors saw the trend toward executive secrecy as a threat to a participatory democracy:

> The criticism of some recently released material has left officials, the press, and the public without any standard of release upon which they can rely to defend the disclosure of any technical information. Unless this attitude is clarified, it is bound to have a profound and paralyzing effect upon the flow of information to the American public. [May 15, 1955]

In September 1955, another uproar of a similar nature occurred when the Defense Department asked defense industries to "exercise considerble caution" in publicizing economic and technical information.

J. E. Wiggins, then executive editor of the *Washington Post*, wrote that the magnitude of the statement's restrictions "threaten the access of American citizens to the facts about the nation's defense and menace the democratic process." . . .

By 1957, Sigma Delta Chi's (SDX) Freedom of Information Committee reported that "Bureaucratic secrecy attained new heights in the federal government during 1957." SDX attributed this problem to Order 10501, 5 USC 22,

5 USC 1002 and especially to the May, 1954 defense directive. SDX reported comments by Pentagon correspondents:

> A million people wield the stamp of secrecy; 500,000 do the stamping; the other 500,000 check on the stampers . . . Somewhere along the line somebody always stamps 'for official use only' on it . . . It's all due to fear—fear of reprimand and loss of job—and to just plain stupidity.

All correspondents agreed that much legitimate information never became available to the press.

James R. Wiggins and Francis E. Rourke listed specific criticisms of the 10501 directive:

1. It provided no appeal to review an agency classification;
2. It provided procedures for withholding information not classified at all;
3. It promoted a tendency to overclassify in order to keep information from the public;
4. Declassification was long and burdensome . . .

By April, 1959, even Stewart Alsop was concerned:

> The American government these days is rather frequently cast in the role of Daddy of us all, telling us that Daddy knows best and not to ask questions. And Daddy's warning is often implied or explicit—"or Daddy spanks" . . .

Windscale and Hot Air

The concrete had been poured wrongly [for the atomic reactors at Windscale in 1950] and the main walls were porous to radioactivity. It was a national scandal but the chief civil servant in the ministry involved contacted the then-editor and warned him that if we printed the story we should be prosecuted. That was enough. A year later when the walls had been repaired at huge cost, the ban on the story was reluctantly removed. The civil servant concerned later told me—with some hilarity—that we could never have been prosecuted. He was astonished that the paper had given in so easily.

[In another instance], in 1958 I learned that work on a brilliant swing-wing aeroplane developed by Dr. Barnes Wallis had come to a stop because the Government had cancelled the contract. Attempts to prevent publication of the news were made at the highest level accompanied by the usual dark hints of prosecution. I successfully argued that the plane could hardly be secret when it had been abandoned. There was no prosecution.

—Chapman Pincher, *The Daily Express* (London), 1967

Kennedy: The Cuban Capers

· John F. Kennedy employed diverse tactics to keep the press in line. When Walter Winchell stopped distributing his column through the Hearst syndicate it came to light that the President had threatened antitrust action to the chain if criticism of his administration continued. And he was also not above using the FBI to harrass reporters, government officials and Pentagon personnel in an effort to discover where reporters got certain news items.

James Reston attempted perspective on Kennedy's handling of information:

> The reflex action of the press is to howl like a scalded dog every time it catches the government tinkering with the truth, but it can scarcely apply normal procedures to actions of the first American government ever engaged in facing up to the possibility of nuclear war. And it is palpable nonsense to talk about these distortions as being 'unprecented'! [*New York Times*, November 2, 1962]

Kennedy's press relations took on what was by then a familiar trend:

> President Kennedy had a lot of fine things to say about freedom of information in the federal government just before and right after his inauguration in 1961. But these fine resolutions have slowly eroded away during his nearly three years in office, and . . . genuine freedom of information is at its lowest ebb today in the history of our federal government. [SDX Freedom of Information Committee 1963 report]

Several events led to this castigation by SDX. The President was barely installed in the White House when an editorial in *Editor and Publisher* referred to the handling of information by government officials as constituting a "disturbing trend."

This "trend" was borne out in the credibility crisis occurring in the Cuban Bay of Pigs incident. The President [had] stated in an April 12, 1961 news conference that no U.S. armed forces would be in Cuba. But on April 27, 1961, in the interests of the Cold War, Kennedy asked the press to exercise voluntary censorship on the affair in the interests of national security and public safety.

The *New York Times* was uncertain:

> For the preservation of our democratic society in this time of 'clear and present danger' it is more essential that ever that the people be fully informed of the problems and of the perils confronting them. This is a responsibility of the press as it is of the President . . . But the terrible difficulty arises in the twilight zone where that revelation of militant secrets might effect immediately and adversely the security of the country, and yet where the withholding of information might involve deception of the public. [April 28, 1961]

However, in a latter editorial, the *Times* seemed to have taken a position:

> . . . Not only is it unethical to deceive one's own public as part of a system of deceiving an adversary government; it is also foolish. Our executive officers and our national legislators are elected on stated days, but actually they must be reelected day by day by popular understanding and support. This is what is signified by a government by consent. [May 10, 1961]

This view [had earlier been] shared by the St. Louis *Post-Dispatch:*

> "This [request] we believe would undermine the essential mission of the press, which is to inform, interpret, and criticize." [April 30, 1961]

A year later, in October, 1962, Kennedy blocked information on events connected with Soviet missile bases in Cuba, saying full information of government activities would constitute a "clear and present danger" and that even the protection of the First Amendment "must yield to the public's need for national security."

Assistant Secretary of Defense Arthur Sylvester defended the move, contending that managed news was "part of the arsenal of weaponry that a President has . . . the government's inherent right to lie, if necessary."

The New York *Times* said:

> There is no doubt that 'management' or 'control' of the news is censorship described by a sweeter term. There is no doubt that it restricts the people's right to know. [October 31, 1962] . . .

Clark Mollenhoff wrote:

> For a period of several days in late October our knowledge and our coverage were largely limited to the facts that were fed us by the White House. There was no power to go behind the self-serving declaration of the White House. There was no power to go behind the self-serving declaration of the Kennedy administration, and for the time being most of us were willing to put up with it. [*Nieman Reports*, December 1962]

Mollenhoff tempered his resentment in his last sentence. The Washington *Post* was less kind:

> The consequences are serious enough. The statements of government will have a diminished credibility in any crisis hereafter and citizens will wonder if they are being told what is the truth or what the government thinks will favorably influence events. The American press, which is made by this means an unwilling servant of the government, will also have a reduced credibility at home and abroad. [November 1, 1962] . . .

Still, other papers defended the executive position. The president of ASNE referred to the papers clamoring for military secrets as indicative as "an all but traitorous tipping-off to the enemy of our defense secrets."

Time wrote:

> For all the goofs, for all the reportorial grumbling by the Washington press corps, the fact remained that the Cuban crisis was an unprecedented situation—even in the cold war. It demanded the most careful handling of information that might affect the nation's security. [November 2, 1962]

Johnson: Credibility Gap

Kennedy's untimely death seemed to portend a temporary lull in government secrecy cries by the press. Johnson enjoyed several months' grace before resuming the presidential war with the press.

But in 1964, SDX reported "a vague uneasiness has begun to be felt among some Washington correspondents," and the St. Louis *Globe-Democrat* complained ". . . he has maintained a virtual silence on such major topics as politics at home and crises abroad." [June 19, 1964]

The Washington *Post* reported:

> Increasingly of late, complaints have been heard in press and television circles about the President's fascination with secrecy and about the altered nature—some would say diminuation—of the presidential press conference in his administration. [December 28, 1964]

The *New York Times* said Johnson's annoyance with news leaks "is of historic proportions." The article [pointed] out Johnson's extreme dislike of "forecasts" before he made official announcements. The *New York Times* asked, "But if

---

Despite many courageous and expensive court fights by some news organizations, much of the press, including some of its most powerful representatives, acquiesce in the worst restrictions on their own freedom. They continue to exhibit incredible naivete about the realities of government manipulation of information and hypocrisy in "national security" secrecy.

—Ben Bagdikian, professor of journalism, University of California; former assistant managing editor, The *Washington Post*

---

publication is withheld for this reason, does not that effect an indirect censorship and news management which is an even greater disservice to the national interests?" [January 24, 1965]

James Dakin of the St. Louis *Post-Dispatch* said Johnson was "blaming the messenger who brings the bad news," and columnist Marquis W. Childs warned of a danger in the press-presidential "fuss" becoming a "feud." Doris Fleeson [of the St. Louis *Post-Dispatch*] noted " . . . unhappy echoes of presidential secretiveness resound in editorial offices." And in the same article: "Even men of standing are reluctant to see printed the legitimate news, legitimately gathered, about them or their programs, lest the President be offended."

U.S. News and World Report quoted a Washington correspondent as saying:

> The censorship in Washington is serious. There is more under Johnson than under any other Democratic President to my knowledge. He has clamped down on everybody in government. [March 2, 1965]

Joseph Alsop saw an "almost hysterical intensification of the secretiveness which the Johnson administration has for months been carrying to extremes." Walter Lippmann concurred: "[The President] just barely stopped short of denying their [the press's] right to disagree with him."

SDX's 1965 report said the President had tried to "warp the proposed federal public records legislation into an almost unlimited authority for the President to establish secrecy practices."

Rowland Evans and Robert Novak in *Lyndon B. Johnson: The Exercise of Power* (1966)] cite the war effort as leading to greater secrecy:

> The president's obsession with the criticism embarked him on the most blatant personal campaign to see the intervention to the country through the White House press corps that any President in history had ever undertaken. It was this campaign . . . that brought about the crisis in credibility that was to heighten, not lessen tensions.

SDX quoted a Pentagon reporter: "There is a mistrust of reporters and a fear that anyone caught talking will be punished."

Even in 1967, the year the Freedom of Information Act was implemented, SDX's annual report's introduction read, ". . . high officials consistently employed inaccurate and misleading statements that contradicted most of the fine words [issued by Johnson on press freedoms]" and:

> In Washington, news correspondents struggled with an information problem which has grown increasingly difficult in the last few years . . . Secrecy, lies, half-truths, deception—this was the daily fare of the correspondents as they attempted to play the historic role intended for the press in our democratic system.

1968 brought no improvements in the press-presidential tensions. William McGaffin in the Kansas City *Times* mentioned that Johnson continued the

Kennedy tradition of sending out "investigators" for uncooperative reporters (e.g., FBI, security agents). [April 29, 1968]

The Progressive [in June 1968] said newsmen wore "chains" which were "worn around the neck, and from them are suspended the White House press cards issued by the Secret Service."

SDX reported that Johnson's secrecy policies "have periodically intereferred with the operations of the Freedom of Information Law," and that the "credibility gap" had reached "awesome proportions."

On the other hand, some members of the press were not upset by Johnson's maneuvers. *Saturday Review* intimated that "misleading" information may often be due to the minute-to-minute changes in any situation and went on to say of Johnson, "There is no attempt to mislead the press ever." [May 8, 1965]

Harpers suggested that Washington correspondents overreacted to Johnson's press policies and, "events are steadily outpacing our capacity to understand them." [July 1965]

In a *U.S. News and World Report* article surveying the problem, reporters gave as a justification for Johnson's actions the naturalness of press-President "conflict." One report said:

> . . . all politicans are sensitive to criticism, and the more skilled the politican the more sensitive he is. Any politician is also in conflict with the press because the press is a rival power, and a good politican senses that. [March 22, 1965]

Classification Under Nixon

Herbert Klein, the administration's director of communciations, said, prior to Nixon's assuming office, that, "Truth will be the hallmark of the Nixon administration." And, as usual, the press seemed genuinely pleased with Nixon's initial adherence to this theme.

[By the end of the year, however, things were different.] The conflict began with . . . Vice-President Spiro T. Agnew's criticism of television's instant analysis of Nixon's November 3 speech. [Agnew had not only criticized the media, but argued that the media no longer represent the view of the people.] The reaction from the press was swift and dramatic . . .

A New York *Times* editorial on November 15, 1969, noted:

> Agnew is in effect putting extreme pressure on communications media that are under direct control through federal regulation of the airways of the United States Government. This is a transparent form of intimidation foreshadowed by the extraordinary action of Dean Burch, newly appointed chairman of the FCC, in personally phoning the presidents of the three national networks to ask for transcripts of their commentator's remarks following Mr. Nixon's speech . . .

War coverage, especially the Cambodian "incursion," was another fly in the ointment for reporters. John Chancellor said in a NBC newscast:

We haven't been able to tell the whole story because we are not allowed to. The American government put so many restrictions on coverage of those battles that we were put in the position of trying to cover the football game from the infirmary and the locker room. [March 1971] . . .

—Muriel Akamatsu

[Nevertheless, President Nixon did establish solid procedures to eliminate many of the problems associated with the classification of documents.] Nixon's Executive Order #11652 was designed to remedy defects already apparent in the classification system. His order replaced the Eisenhower order on June 1, 1972, and was the result of more than a year's work by a special interdepartmental committee.

Under his order, guidelines for classification were made more restrictive. Officials in certain executive agencies and departments were authorized to classify information if they believed its "unauthorized disclosure could reasonably be expected to cause damage to the national security." Said then-National Security Adviser Henry Kissinger, "If the classifier has any substantial doubt as to which security classification is appropriate, or as to whether the material should be classified at all, he should designate the less restrictive treatment."

New timetables envisaged automatic declassification after between six and ten years, with exemptions for particularly sensitive material. Documents exempt from automatic declassification could be reviewed after ten years. Any documents classified for thirty years or more would be declassified, with limited exceptions. Materials exempted from declassification could be reviewed after ten years.

In 1971, . . . 59,316 officials had the authority to classify documents. Nixon's order reduced the number with the authority to stamp materials "top secret" to 1,860. His order also provided for greater individual responsibility by requiring classifiers to sign their names whenever they stamped materials. Sanctions—basically a strong reprimand—for abuse of the system also were included . . .

Continued monitoring of the system was to be done by the National Security Council and an Interagency Classification Review Committee. Established after the June 1971 publication of the Pentagon Papers—many of which were clearly improperly classified—the ICRC was seen as a direct response to charges of excessive secrecy in government . . . The committee's task was to limit the number of documents classified and to implement a speed-up in the declassification of documents, many of which dated from World War II.

Although the Nixon order generally was regarded as one permitting greater access to information than was previously possible, criticisms still were expressed. Access to documents, critics charged, was an unduly burdensome task. People seeking access, it was said, had to know exactly what documents they wanted, had to get the department concerned and the original classifier of the information to agree to access, and had to be prepared to contest the matter through the federal courts.

Nixon's order also was faulted for not establishing specific criteria for determining what documents should be protected and for failing to ensure that classified information was deserving of such protection.

Secrecy in the Ford and Carter Administrations

On October 7, 1976, President Gerald R. Ford amended a May 17, 1972, National Security Council directive on the classification, declassification and safeguarding of national security information. Ford required that each department submit its proposed security regulations to the ICRC for approval . . .

Each department also had to submit semiannual reports of its actions on classification requests, classification abuses, and unauthorized disclosures. Lists of the people having classification authority no longer needed to be submitted to the ICRC.

As a candidate for the presidency, Jimmy Carter promised to conduct an open administration if elected. On June 19, 1978, [he] issued Executive Order #12065, designed to increase openness in government by tightening the ground rules for the classification of documents.

The order was initiated by CIA Director Adm. Stansfield Turner and National Security Advisor Zbigniew Brzezinski, whom Carter aides said believed that government was so overwhelmed with intelligence information that it was difficult to distinguish between truly sensitive and less-important material.

Carter's order attempted to increase protection for national security information while allowing public access to documents through a strong declassification program. For the first time, an executive order dealing with classification was circulated to agencies, congressional committees and interested government groups prior to its release.

Also for the first time, broad categories were established for information that could be classified if disclosure would cause "identifiable damage" to national security. Information could not be classified unless it concerned foreign government information; intelligence activities, sources or methods; foreign relations or foreign activities in the United States; scientific, technological or economic matters relating to national security; U.S. government programs for safeguarding nuclear materials or facilities; and other categories of information the president or his designate decided warranted protection.

Carter's order said that, except as provided in the Atomic Energy Act of 1954 as amended, it was now the only documentary basis for the classification of documents.

Nixon's three classification labels were retained and a new one—"royal"—was added, reportedly in an effort to stop the disclosure of national secrets.

The new designation was to be applied to information stemming from the most sensitive of methods and sources. The information was to be distributed only to about twenty-four senior aides and to less than ten members of Congress.

It was reported that other members of Congress as well as military officers and government officials with "top secret" clearance were unaware of the label's existence. Washington *Post* correspondent Jack Taylor quoted one source as saying, "When you establish something this restrictive, you in effect deny access to the minority party, which could have an effect on policy."

. . . Royal label aside, the label of "top secret" was to be applied only to information the unauthorized disclosure of which could be expected to cause exceptionally grave damage to national security. The "secret" label was for information the disclosure of which would be expected to cause serious damage, and a "confidential" label referred to information whose disclosure could be expected to cause identifiable damage to national security.

If the classifier had a reasonable doubt about which designation was appropriate, or whether the material should be classified at all, the less restrictive designation was to be used, if at all.

Under Carter's order, the declassification process was [used] for the first time, to include a test that balanced the public's interest in disclosure against the government's need for secrecy. Documents were to be declassified as early as national security considerations permitted, typically after six years, instead of the previous six to ten years. Documents granted long-lasting classification were to be declassified after not more than twenty years, rather than the previous deadline of thirty years.

In addition, the classification of documents was to take place on a section-by-section basis so the restriction of portions of a document would not preclude declassification of non-sensitive sections.

Carter's order also stripped eleven agencies—including the Department of Health, Education and Welfare, and the Departments of Agriculture and Labor—of their classification authority. Five other departments or agencies had their authority reduced.

A new government office—the Information Security Oversight Office—was established to provide overall supervision for the classification system and to report regularly to the National Security Council and the president about the sytem's operation. ISOO was given the authority to review agencies' procedures, files, regulations and decisions on the classification of documents.

Carter's order made it clear that classification itself was not necessarily a sufficient reason to deny access sought under the Freedom of Information Act. Agencies had to examine the requested document to determine if its release would cause identifiable harm to national security.

Finally, Carter's order included sanctions of up to ten years imprisonment or a fine of up to $10,000, or both, for the unlawful disclosure of classified information . . .

The National Archives, for its part, estimated that the speedier declassification process requried by the order would remove the secrecy stamp from an extra 250 million documents within the decade.

The Reagan Years

With the issuance of President Ronald Reagan's Executive Order #12356, that estimate by the National Archives may not come to pass.

Gone is the presumption of the Carter order that a document must likely cause identifiable damage to national security before it could be classified. Gone is the practice of opting for a lower-security classification in times of doubt, for Reagan's order says:

If there is reasonable doubt about the need to classify information, it shall be safeguarded as if it were classified pending a determination by an original classification authority . . . If there is reasonable doubt about the appropriate level of classification, it shall be safeguarded at the higher level of classification pending a determination by an original classification authority . . .

Gone is the Carter order's balancing test that required the government to weigh the public interest against national security concerns.

The Reagan order did retain the standard "top secret," "secret," and "confidential" labels. It also added three additional categories of information qualifying for classification.

The three new categories are for material on "the vulnerabilities or capabilities of systems, installations, projects or plans relating to the national security"; cryptology; and information in government records that was obtained from confidential sources.

Reagan's order also continued the Carter policy of protecting basic scientific information from classification. Strong lobbying efforts by post-secondary education and scientists' groups helped to reinstate that protection of basic research data, which had been eliminated in an early draft of the order.

However, Reagan's order sharply departed from Nixon and Carter-era policy by eliminating specific time limits for the declassification of materials. Reagan's order states, "Information shall be classified as long as required by national security considerations."

In addition, Reagan's order permitted the classification of material after a request for the information had been made under either the Freedom of Information Act or the Privacy Act of 1974.

The Center for National Security Studies' Allan Adler said the removal of a time limit for declassification until the National Archives—which is up to forty years behind its acquisitions—reviews the documents will pose special problems for historians: "It means that what's classified remains classified. There are no broad lines being drawn to indicate to a scholar, or journalist, or scientist, or anyone else, when he can anticipate when material will be declassified."

The director of records declassification for the National Archives, Edwin A. Thompson, said Reagan's order would halt the declassification program begun by previous administrations: "The whole program is, for all intents and purposes, dead. Systematic review as we've known it since 1972 will essentially wither and become a thing of the past."

Adler said that by dropping the Carter requirement that declassification policies be given comparable emphasis with classification policies, Reagan's order has rendered declassification the "stepchild" of the two. Adler wondered why that change was necessary, since budget cuts at the National Archives would have hindered that process anyway:

I think this administration basically has made a decision that . . . particularly in the areas of national defense and foreign policy, it has found
itself truly wading in areas of extreme public controversy. It wants to
have the choice of how much should be released to the public and when.

Basically, they've decided when they're doing things that are very controversial, it [access] doesn't help.

Fears were expressed, particulary by press organizations, that the new classification system would effectively allow the administration to eviscerate the Freedom of Information Act. Those fears were based, in part, on the FOIA exemption for information classified under separate statutes.

Adler said such an undermining of the FOIA is especially serious because it is tantamount to a signal to the executive branch, agencies and the courts that they do not have to be specific in their reasons for denying access to information: "The courts are going to have to be pulling teeth from agencies as to why particular information, if disclosed, would harm national security."

Virtually all CIA operations, it was feared, would be exempt from disclosure under the FOIA because the Act exempts materials classified under criteria established by executive order.

—Karen M. Brown

Control of Sources

[Reagan's executive order also] requires government officials with access to classified information to sign a "nondisclosure agreement" before they are permitted access. The nondisclosure form requires that the official agree to take lie detector tests at the request of any supervisor. Most importantly, the official must agree to a prepublication review . . . All future writing must be submitted to the official's former agency for review and censorship. The order's sweep includes books, articles, editorials and the texts of speeches and newscasts, even if the official believes that no classified material is included.

Approximately 100,000 government employees are affected, and the government has conferred upon itself the right to seize the profits from the writing of any who fail to comply. The American Society of Newspaper Editors has called the act "peacetime censorship of a scope unparalled in this country since the adoption of the Bill of Rights in 1791."

The order covers all officials, including former presidents, for the rest of their lives, even after the material becomes unclassified. In effect, it suppresses the voices of the government's most able critics. Political candidate Walter Mondale, for example, would [have been] required to submit the text of all of his campaign speeches to the White House for review. The order exempts material that does not contain or imply any statement of fact. It would be difficult, however, to express an opinion without at least implying a statement of fact.

Enforcement procedures have the potential to be used selectively to achieve political objectives. The Central Intelligence Agency currently operates the only censoring system in the government. Their example may illustrate how the system will operate. The CIA has an office particularly designed for review. Its legitimacy was upheld in 1980 by the Supreme Court decision, *Snepp* v. *United States*. Each year the office reviews 800 manuscripts. Often, reviewers delete material that the author did not consider classified . . .

The president's order also permits agencies to reduce their media contacts, in one of a series of actions that discourage officials from talking to reporters.

An administrative study group during 1982 proposed that the administration enact an anti-leak statute that would impose criminal penalties on anybody caught passing unauthorized information. These actions are to ensure, in the words of chief of staff, James Baker, that national security information is disseminated "with one voice and in a coordinated way."

On January 9, 1982, the White House issued a directive to agency heads restricting government officials from discussing any national security issues with the media. A week later, the directive was changed to forbid any major press conferences with either print or broadcast journalists on any subject without a supervisor's clearance. The directive also required that a memorandum be prepared directly after an interview detailing the subjects discussed and the information provided. The directive provided no guidelines as to what constituted a major interview, and resulted in a flood of requests to the White House. Agencies as far removed from national security considerations as the Department of Agriculture reduced the volume of information provided to the public as a result of this directive.

The Pentagon has taken the directive one step further. Assistant Secretary of Defense Frank Carlucci released an internal memorandum tying the disclosure of information, intentional or unintentional, to violations of espionage laws and wrote:

> Even classified infomation should be treated with circumspection, when it relates to sensitive internal deliberations . . . Disclosures tend to make our work more difficult by stimulating inquiries about the subject matter revealed. I am particularly concerned that there be no wounds of this type inflicted by members of this office. [June 1983]

The Pentagon is backing up its threat with action. They hired one hundred polygraph-test operators and have authorized them to administer lie detector tests to any of the Pentagon's more than 15,000 civilian and military personnel on short notice. In addition, the Pentagon has announced that telephones may have to be wiretapped.

Such tactics should silence any employees predisposed to releasing information. For example, on January 8, 1982, Richard DeLouer, head of civilian weapons procurement, told the Chiefs of Staff at a closed meeting that the president's five-year arms program could cost up to fifty percent more than the originally projected $1.5 trillion. The information was subsequently leaked to a *Washington Post* reporter . . .

All of the people who attended the secret meeting were subject to lie detector tests. John Tillison, civilian director of manpower, was accused of leaking the unclassified information. Five Congressional committees which require this information to make budgetary decisions also had to obtain the information through the leak.

The material was unclassified because it was supposed to be for public knowledge, but Tillison was threatened with the loss of his job for passing "official information" to "adversaries."

Other leaks and unauthorized disclosures have contributed to administrative suppression. The disclosure in January of President Reagan's agreement to permit Taiwan to purchase certain supersonic fighters, but not the advanced FX fighter, also created a frantic attempt within the administration to placate Chinese officials who were upset to read about the decision in the newspapers.

Other Measures

The Intelligence Identities Protection Act is one manifestation of the administration's belief that if reporters cannot gather news, they cannot report it. The act makes it illegal to identify an undercover agent even if the information is public knowledge or unclassified. The law was initiated as an effort to stop the publication of several counter spy magazines that were printing the names of intelligence officers.

The act creates a dire problem for journalists. The most common question journalists ask at the end of an interview is, "who else should I talk to?" If an official answers "Go see so-and-so, he worked in this area," the official would be breaking the law. This law chills sources, and discourages newspapers from naming any questionable sources.

CIA Director William Casey recommended further chilling action. He requested legislation allowing the CIA and the FBI to conduct surprise searches of newsrooms. These measures stifle the ability of journalists to investigate agencies and creates an atmosphere of intimidation.

The administration in August 1983 initiated efforts to control material about the production and shipment of nuclear weapons, even if the information is unclassified. Release of the "unclassified, controlled information" would incur a $100,000 fine. This act was widely disputed by civil and environmental groups who believe the public has a right to the information that will affect their health and safety.

Foreign visitors with views unpalatable to the administration are finding it more difficult to enter the country. For example, the widow of Salvador Allende, a Communist and former Chilean President, was denied entrance. Japanese who came to join the nuclear weapons protest during the summer of 1982 were also denied visas.

Perhaps the actions most distasteful to the world scientific community are government efforts to restrict scientific discussions. In 1982, the government prevented the publication of 100 unclassified scientific papers at a conference on optical engineering. The administration's actions undercut basic academic freedom. Ultimately, scientific advancement will suffer from a curtailed interchange of information.

Representative Glenn English, chairman of the Information subcommittee, summed up the administrative motives as "politics, nothing but pure and simple politics." He continued, "All administrations try to control information for their own political purposes. The difference with the Reagan team is the degree of effort being put into reaching this goal."

In April 1981, President Reagan through the Office of Management and Budget placed a moratorium on government pamphlets and publications. Later, another directive was issued which requires agencies to submit their pamphlets to the office for approval or cancellation. Six months later, more than 900 items had been cancelled. Many of them were concerned with health, energy, social welfare or nutrition.

Former President Carter had led the reduction with his Paperwork Reduction Bill in December 1980. The goal of the bill was to reduce the amount of information by twenty-five percent by 1983. Under the Reagan administration, elimination of reports seem to be based on political [not security] considerations. For example, the results of the government's auto safety and mileage tests were compiled in *The Car Book*. More than 1.5 million people requested copies. It was called "anti-industry" by Secretary of Transportation Drew Lewis and was eventually cancelled . . .

The House Government Operations Committee released a report in September 1982 showing that the administration had eliminated or decreased at least fifty major statistical programs containing information about such matters as oil imports, medicare expenditures, fertility and nursing home care.

—Maura Christopher

An Inherent Right to Lie

by Arthur Sylvester

[In October 1962, the United States government determined that based upon photographs taken by pilots in U.S. Air Force reconaissance planes, not only did Cuba have some offensive missiles that were either operational or close to being operational, but that the Soviet Union was shipping additional missiles. These missiles posed an immediate and grave threat to the security of the United States. During the week that President Kennedy and his advisors were preparing a course of action, the people were fed a number of "cover stories" and outright lies to disguise the fact that the United States knew there were missiles in Cuba and was preparing to respond to the threat. The President's reponse, about a week after learning of the threat, was firm—the United States was establishing a Naval blockade of Cuba; any attack upon any country in the Western Hemisphere would be considered by the United States to be an attack upon it by the Soviet Union. Eventually Premiere Nikita Khrushchev recalled the missiles, reducing the possibility of a nuclear war.

The person given the responsibility for keeping the press from learning about the situation until such time that the President announced the country's response was Arthur Sylvester, assistant secretary of defense for public information. Sylvester (1901-1979), for thirty-five years, had been a journalist for the *Newark* (N.J.) *Evening News*, including eight years as city editor and fifteen as chief of the Washington bureau, a position in which he had dug up numerous stories that the government had wished not to be released. Now, as a government official, he saw a different side to the release of information that could threaten the existence of a nation. About six weeks after the initial crisis had passed, Sylvester told members of the New York chapter of Sigma Delta Chi, national professional journalism fraternity (now the Society of Professional Journalists):

> [I]t would seem to be basic, all through history, that a government's right—and by a government I mean a people since in our country, in my judgment, the people expressly have the right to express, and do express every two and four years what government they want—that it's inherent in that government's right, if necessary, to lie to save itself when it's going up into a nuclear war. This seems to me basic. Basic.

Reaction from the nation's media, politicians, and the general public was swift—they were furious that a public official would dare to say, even if he believed it, that a lie was permissible in order to save a country; afterall, they reasoned, doesn't this then lead to myriad abuses as to what the threats to national security are?

In extensive testimony before a subcommittee of the House of Representatives, Sylvester, who in less than two years in the position had opened up numerous lines of communication to the people, explained his comments:

> Obviously, the remarks as quoted would disturb anybody. But I would like to put them in context because they were in effect a shorthand of a basic point of view, and that is that any nation has the right of survival, self-preservation, particularly in this time when it can be faced almost overnight with a nuclear holocaust.
>
> In our country, the government representatives of this people whom they elect and dispose of have a duty to take whatever means in their judgment or in the judgment of the top people is necessary when that people faces nuclear disaster. This is what I was trying to say and what I did say was a sort of shorthand way of saying it . . .
>
> During war, it is accepted that the United States has a duty to its people to withhold information, such as the extent of damage to our military capabilities immediately following Pearl Harbor, and to take active steps to mislead our enemies, such as the activities of the Allies just before D-Day in 1944.
>
> This is necessary, not only to protect the civilian population in this country, but also to protect the lives of men and women who are in our Armed Forces.

While most frequently the enemy is misled by action, there are occasions—and I am speaking of times when the very survival of their country is at stake and where the spectre of a nuclear holocaust is an imminent possibility—when it can become necessary to mislead the enemy by statements issued by public officials.

A few months after leaving office in 1967, having served six years, longer than any other person in that position, Sylvester reviewed the Cuban missile crisis and his own opinions about his by-now much-quoted statement about an "inherent right to lie":]

If I had been living in the early 19th century in what was then our country's West, and had been a religious man, I am sure I would have taken my stand with the Lying Baptists against the Truthful Baptists.

The issue that created the two sects arose at Long Run, Ky., in 1804, and posed the question whether a man with three children captured by marauding Indians was justified in lying to the savages to conceal the presence nearby of a fourth child. The Lying Baptists argued that under the circumstances he had the right, indeed the duty, to lie. But the Truthful Baptists shook their head, uh-uh: Tell the truth and sacrifice the child.

The sects have long since disappeared. But during six years as Assistant Secretary of Defense for Public Affairs I often found the self-righteous descendants of the Truthful Baptists wandering in the same old moral fog.

As the Defense Department's spokesman I espoused the thesis that the indisputable requisite of a government-information program was that it be truthful. But I also stated that on occasions (such as the Cuban missile crisis) when the nation's security was at stake, the Government had the right, indeed the duty, to lie if necessary to mislead an enemy and protect the people it represented. For months the news industry, and others, distorted my remarks beyond recognition, howling that they were proof the Government was not to be believed under any circumstances. How hypocritical can you get? I know that it's axiomatic that fog hangs longest over the low places, but I can't bring myself to believe that fog alone accounts for the misinterpretation, misrepresentation and down-right lying that tarnish the American news industry, written and electronic. I don't know a newsman who has served the Government as an Information Officer who hasn't been dismayed at the evidence of shabby performance by what he used to think of with pride as his profession.

If, as the news industry properly insists, the Federal Government has a complete obligation for truth, you would think the newsmen would abide by that rule for their own first principle. But they don't. As a wit has said, their motto is: "Don't get it right, get it written." Add to this a handout psychology, an incurable desire to prophesy and interpret, plus a failure to ask the right questions. Is there any surprise that much information about Government is misinformation?

Currently the news industry likes to explain its shortcomings by blaming the Johnson Administration for a "credibility gap." Every sophisticated newsman knows the Federal Government puts its best, not its worst, foot forward; after all, the newsman's best friend, his club, his business, his city, county and state government all do things that way. That being so, it is his function to penetrate this protective coloration behind which all men attempt to mask their errors. If there is a credibility gap, it measures the failure of newsmen to do their job.

I was the Defense Department's spokesman during the Cuban missile crisis. President Kennedy was to make the fateful decision to force the Soviet Union to remove its missiles from Cuba, come what may. The overriding requirement was surprise.

During that momentous week of Oct. 15-22, 1962, President Kennedy interrupted a political tour in Chicago and returned to Washington. The reason given was that he had a cold. I didn't know whether the President had a cold or not, but on the basis of my thirty-seven years' experience as a reporter and news executive, I doubted it. But because the explanation was simple and not easily refutable—who is going to say to the President of the United States, "No, you don't have a cold"?—it was as good as any and better than most of the cover stories I heard in Government. I shudder to think of the flimsy explanations held in reserve to cover some current and vital activities of our Government. But I could be wrong. For six years I watched cover stories go down smooth as cream when I had thought they would cause a frightful gargle. It was well that some, dealing with intelligence, did survive, but some others should have been exposed.

Certainly President Kennedy could not, and should not, have informed news representatives of the true reason he was returning to Washington: that for the first time the United States had proof positive—pictures, plenty of pictures—that contrary to their denials the Soviets had installed offensive missiles in Cuba, and that he was returning to Washington to consult with his advisers on how to counter the nuclear threat. President Kennedy was not dealing with some Indians about the life of a child, but with the lives of millions of his countrymen. If he thought the first step in fulfilling that obligation required him to contract a cold, he was joining the Lying Baptists, and so did I, and so be it.

On October 19, after consultation, I authorized a Defense Department release responding to questions about Cuba. The release read:

> A Pentagon spokesman denied tonight that any alert has been ordered or that any emergency military measures have been set in motion against Communist-ruled Cuba. Further, the spokesman said, the Pentagon has no information indicating the presence of offensive weapons in Cuba.

A case can be made that the first sentence was technically correct. But the second sentence was untrue. The man who issued the release did not know that. I did. I knew that some of the Soviet missiles were operational. That meant that nearly the entire U.S. soon would be vulnerable to a sudden strike. I knew the President and the Executive Committee of the National Security Council had decided on a confrontation with Premier Khrushchev and were completing plans for it. I had been alerted that within seventy-two hours President Kennedy, in a report to the American people, would publicly demand that the Soviets withdraw the missiles and that he would announce the imposition of a blockade.

Newsmen, insisting they speak for the public, have argued that a response of "no comment" can avoid such untruths as our denial of knowledge that the Soviet missiles were in Cuba. But like all general statements, the assertion that Government information must always be truthful requires qualification, because these programs do not and should not operate in a vacuum. Government information may be addressed to the American people, to their adversaries, their friends, to the neutrals, or to any combination of them or to all of them at once. The newsmen's argument that the Government can easily say "no comment" is disingenuous because "no comment" is not a neutral term. Under the circumstances of the missile crisis, any good reporter would have been correct in interpreting "no comment" as a confirmation that we knew the Soviet missiles were in Cuba. An alternative would have been to take the inquirer aside and acquaint him with the facts on the understanding that nothing would be printed. Unfortunately that system works only sometimes. Without reflection

---

The Lost H-Bombs

In March 1966, a B52 and a KC135 while on a refueling mission off the coast of Spain collided. The B52 was carrying four H-Bombs. An immediate secrecy was clamped onto the rescue efforts. Three of the bombs were soon recovered. However, the fourth H-Bomb remained lost. For almost two months, search operations continued. Soon, several nations learned, by their own means, that the bomb, which the U.S. claimed was not activated, was missing. Although public information officers at both the Departments of State and Defense wanted the information released to the American people, the U.S. respected Spain's demand that no information of any kind—even *if* there had been a missing bomb—be released. Finally, the U.S. did release information, with the permission of Spain, that claimed that there had been no radiation leak, and that there was no health hazard. During the next few months, long after the bomb had been recovered, it was learned that there had been some contamination on land; and fish had absorbed some radiation, presumably from the bomb that "didn't leak."

Two years later, another H-Bomb was lost off the coast of Greenland. Because Greenland was part of the Danish realm, and because Denmark had refused nuclear flights over its territories, the situation became a diplomatic and military nightmare. The United States, Denmark, and Greenland refused any comment; the U.S. even refused to acknowledge that there was a flight or that there was an airplane that was down. Finally, Canada noted the crash, the Associated Press reported it, and the U.S. finally acknowledged that it was true that another H-Bomb had been temporarily lost.

on the inquirer's patriotism, it was decided not to risk the country's safety, in the name of the people's "right to know" and the Government's duty to "tell the truth." After all, newsmen *are* gabby.

It is really not the missile-crisis type of event that causes credibility problems. Nor does the refusal to discuss intelligence activities or new weapons systems, although holding the line on the latter is always difficult due to both industry and military pressures. It is the problems created in the Vietnam war by the absence of censorship and the presence of television that produce difficulties. I have often wondered whether critics think we should have called a press conference on certain tense Vietnam situations that have never before come to light. For example, early in 1964, with Vietnam already a very hot war, more than 600 Air Force F-105 fighter planes were temporarily grounded due to deficiencies in their propulsion system. My guess is that if questions had been raised we would have taken the gamble and leveled with newsmen and asked them to lay off. My experience is that in those circumstances the Pentagon reporters would have honored the request. But some itinerant newsman on the scene might have written the story, just as some itinerant newsmen damaged their country's interest by revealing U.S. Air Force combat planes were flying out of Thailand against North Vietnam at a time when the Thai government threatened to deny us the bases if any publicity developed. Newsmen in Saigon who had been briefed honored the request for silence, only to be beaten by the blabbermouths.

Government officials as individuals do not have the right to lie politically or to protect themselves, but they do always have the duty to protect their countrymen. Sometimes, even apart from military considerations, a program may be too tentative to reveal or there may be a question of timing the announcement. Sometimes, and those times are rare indeed, Government officials may be required to fulfill their duty by issuing a false statement to deceive a potential enemy, as in the Cuban missile crisis. I believe the Bay of Pigs was also such a time. But the fact is that this operation was carried on with such ballyhoo that the news media later accused the Government of Madison Avenue publicity tactics. So sensitive to the charge was the Kennedy Administration that it went to the other extreme in the missile crisis.

My personal notoriety as an alleged exponent of the Government's "right to lie" developed as a result of distorted reporting of my answer to one question

A Non-Rescue

The first U.S. soldiers captured by the Viet Cong were given a heavy dose of propaganda and sent back to their units in May 1962. The South Vietnamese army, however, claimed to have "rescued" the soldiers from the Viet Cong. The United States Information Agency, misled by South Vietnam, put out the "rescue" version. Only when the former prisoners returned to their units, were debriefed, explained that there was no rescue attempt, and a suitable time passed—while political affairs officers tried to determine the effect of recanting the Vietnamese story—did the truth come out.

put to me December 6, 1962, at the end of a two-hour give-and-take dinner meeting of the New York chapter of Sigma Delta Chi, a national journalism society of which I am a member. The news industry, even after six weeks, was still angry over the shutdown of news during the height of the missile crisis, and Jack V. Fox, a United Press-International reporter, asked, in view of my assertion that "the people must be able to depend on what the Government says," what I thought about half-turths, citing President Kennedy's "cold." My answer seemed to uncap hidden, foolish furies; the newsmen mostly flocked to the Truthful Baptists. Mr. Fox's story read: "He [Sylvester] said that the Government must not put out false information, but later added, 'I think the inherent right of the Government to lie to save itself when faced with nuclear disaster is basic.'" I haven't found another reporter who coupled the rule with the exception as he did. Certainly *The New York Times* didn't. Its headline next morning read, U.S. AIDE DEFENDS LYING TO NATION, and its story began: "'When a nation's security is threatened . . . that nation's leaders are justified in telling lies to its people,' Arthur Sylvester, Assistant Secretary of Defense for Public Affairs, told a press gathering here last night." One need not be surprised at this from a paper that didn't hesitate to attribute faked quotations to a U.S. official in a page-one story of a meeting that hadn't taken place (I happen to know about the fakery since I was the official who did not hold the reported meeting); or put a phony date on a letter that the management tried to suppress because it nailed the paper on one of its untruthful reports from Vietnam (I know about this because I wrote the letter and checked on it later). The *Times* was not alone in distortion. It has had newspaper, magazine, electronic and congressional company across the nation, all adding to the "credibility gap."

In a world of nuclear weapons we can stand more candor and less hypocrisy about the relationship between press and Government. Unfortunately the news industry hasn't caught up with its changed role, much less acknowledged it.

The late Gen. George C. Marshall, who served as both Secretary of State and Secretary of Defense, and was known for his probity, once gave an enlightening dissertation to newsmen on the strategic advantage to the military of confusing the enemy by deliberate leakage of misleading information to the press. Former President Eisenhower expressed the idea in simple form during a TV interview with Walter Cronkite who, referring to me, asked General Eisenhower what he thought about the thesis that the Government had a right to lie on behalf of its people when facing a nuclear threat. The former President replied that in times of crisis "you develop elaborate systems of deceit . . . So you can't just say that in such situations the truth, the whole truth, must be given instantly, because that would be terrible."

President Kennedy got to the heart of the matter when he told a meeting of publishers: "Every newspaperman now asks himself with respect to every story: 'Is it news?' All I suggest is that you add the question: 'Is it in the national interest?'" I would add only that when there is uncertainty whether the national interest is involved, the question to ask is: "Is this something that you, if you were on the enemy's side, would like to know?" I know from reading the Defense Department mail that most citizens—despite all the lamenting about the credibility gap and the Government's right to lie—upbraid the Department for releasing information they fear is helpful to our antagonists. They don't want their children surrendered to the savages merely so that the Government could boast it always told the truth, the whole truth, and nothing but the truth.

Wartime Censorship

by George Creel

The initial disadvantages and persistent misunderstandings that did so much to cloud public estimation of the [Committee on Public Information] had their origin in the almost instant antagonism of the metropolitan press. At the time of my appointment in 1917 [as director], a censorship bill was before Congress, and the newspapers, choosing to ignore the broad sweep of the Committee's functions, proceeded upon the exclusive assumption that I was to be "the censor." As a result of press attack and Senate discussion, the idea became general and fixed that the Committee was a machinery of secrecy and repression organized solely to crush free speech and a free press.

As a matter of fact, I was strongly opposed to the censorship bill, and delayed acceptance of office until the President had considered approvingly the written statement of my views on the subject. It was not that I denied the need of some sort of censorship, but deep in my heart was the feeling that the desired results could be obtained without paying the price that a formal law would have demanded. Aside from the physical difficulties of enforcement, the enormous cost, and the overwhelming irritation involved, I had the conviction that our hope must lie in the aroused patriotism of the newspaper men of America.

With the nation in arms, the need was not so much to keep the press from doing the hurtful things as to get it to do the helpful things. It was not servants we wanted, but associates. Better far to have the desired compulsions proceed from within than to apply them from without. Also, for the first time in our history, soldiers of the United States were sailing to fight in a foreign land, leaving families three thousand miles behind them. Nothing was more important than that there should be the least possible impairment of the people's confidence in the printed information presented to them. Suspicious enough by reason of natural anxieties, a censorship law would have turned every waiting heart over the fear that news was being either strangled or minimized.

Aside from these considerations, there was the freedom of the press to bear in mind. No other right guaranteed by democracy has been more abused, but even these abuses are preferable to the deadening evil of autocratic control. In addition, it is the inevitable tendency of such legislation to operate solely

[Reprinted from *How We Advertised the War*, by George Creel, Published by Harper & Bros., 1922.]

against the weak and the powerless, and . . . the European experience was thick with instances of failure to proceed against great dailies for bold infraction.

Censorship laws, too, even though they protest that the protection of military secrets is their one original object, have a way of slipping over into the field of opinion, for arbitrary power grows by what it feeds on. "Information of value to the enemy" is an elastic phrase and, when occasion requires, can be stretched to cover the whole field of independent discussion. Nothing, it seemed to me, was more dangerous, for people did not need less criticism in time of war, but more. Incompetence and corruption, bad enough in peace, took on an added menace when the nation was in arms. One had a right to hope that the criticism would be honest, just, and constructive, but even a blackguard's voice was preferable to the dead silence of an iron suppression.

My proposition, in lieu of the proposed law, was a voluntary agreement that would make every paper in the land its own censor, putting it up to the patriotism and common sense of the individual editor to protect purely military information of tangible value to the enemy. The plan was approved and, without further thought of the pending bill, we proceeded to prepare a statement of the press of America that would make clear the necessities of the war-machine even while removing doubts and distrusts. The specific requests of the army and the navy were comparatively few, and were concerned only with the movements of troops, the arrival and departure of ships, location of the fleet, and similar matters obviously secret in their nature.

The European press bureaus have also attempted to keep objectionable news from their own people. This must be clearly differentiated from the problem of keeping dangerous news from the enemy. It will be necessary at times to keep information from our own people in order to keep it from the enemy, but most of the belligerent countries have gone much farther. In one of the confidential documents submitted to us there is, under Censorship Regulations, a long section with the heading, "News likely to cause anxiety or distress." Among the things forbidden under this section are the publication of "reports concerning outbreaks of epidemics in training-camps," "Newspaper articles tending to raise unduly the hopes of the people as to the success" of anticipated military movements. This sort of suppression has obviously nothing to do with the keeping of objectionable news from the enemy.

The motive for the establishment of this internal censorship is not merely fear of petty criticism, but distrust of democratic common sense. The officials fear that the people will be stampeded by false news and sensational scare stories. The danger feared is real, but the experience of Europe indicates that censorship regulations do not solve the problem. A printed story is tangible even if false. It can be denied. Its falsity can be proven. It is not nearly so dangerous as a false rumor.

The atmosphere created by common knowledge that news is being suppressed is an ideal "culture" for the propaganda of the bacteria of enemy rumors. This state of mind was the thing which most impressed Americans visiting belligerent countries. Insane and dangerous rumors, some of obvious enemy origin, were readily believed, and they spread with amazing rapidity. This is a greater danger than printing scare stories. No one knows who starts a rumor, but there is a responsible editor behind every printed word. But the greatest objection to censoring of the news against the home population is that it has always tended to create the abuse of shielding from public criticism the dishonesty or incompetency of high officials. While it certainly has never been the policy of any of the European press bureaus to accomplish this result, the internal censorship has generally worked out this way. And there are several well-established instances where the immense power of the censor has fallen into the control of intriguing cliques. Nominally striving to protect the public from pernicious ideas, they have used the censorship to protect themselves from legitimate criticism . . .

Our European comrades in arms viewed the experiment with amazement, not unmixed with anxiety, for in every other belligerent country censorship laws established iron rules, rigid suppressions, and drastic prohibitions carrying severe penalties. Yet the American idea *worked*. And it worked *better* than any European law. Troop-trains moved, transports sailed, ships arrived and departed, inventions were protected, and military plans advanced, all behind a wall of concealment built upon the honor of the press and the faith of the individual editor. Yet while the thing itself was done there was no joy and pride in the doing. Never at any time was it possible to persuade the whole body of Washington correspondents to think of the voluntary censorship in terms of human life and national hopes. A splendid, helpful minority caught the idea and held to it, but the majority gave themselves over to exasperation and antagonism, rebelling continuously against even the appearance of restraint. Partisanship, as a matter of course, played a larger part in this attitude, but a great deal of it proceeded from what the French call "professional deformation." Long training had developed the conviction that nothing in the world was as important as a "story," and not even the grim fact of war could remove this obsession.

In face of the printed card [guidelines for self-censorship], with its simple requests unsupported by law, the press persisted in spreading the belief that I *was* a censor, and with mingled moans and protests each paper did its best to make the people believe that the voluntary censorship was *not* voluntary, and that the uncompelled thing the press was doing was not really uncompelled at all.

When one paper violated the agreement, as many did in the beginning, all the others were instant in their clamor that the Committee should straightway inflict some sort of "punishment." This was absurd, for we had no authority, and they knew that we had none, yet when we made this obvious answer, a general cry would arise that the "whole business should be thrown over." Never at any time did it occur to the press to provide its own discipline for the punishment of dishonor.

All through the first few months it was a steady whine and nag and threat. Every little triviality was magnified into an importance, and the manufacture of mole-hills into mountains was the favorite occupation . . .

This voluntary agreement, having no force in law, and made possible only by patience, infinite labor, and the pressure of conscience upon the individual, was the Committee on Public Information's one and only connection with censorship of any kind. At no time did the Committee exercise or seek authorities under the war measures that limited the peace-time freedom of individuals or professions. Not only did we hold aloof from the workings of the Espionage law, operated by the Postmaster-General and the Attorney-General, but it was even the case that we incurred angers and enmities by incessant attempt to soften the rigors of the measure.

What the Government Asks of the Press

The desires of the government with respect to the conealment from the enemy of military policies, plans, and movements are set forth in the following specific requests. They go to the press of the United States directly from the Secretary of War and the Secretary of the Navy and represent the thought and advice of their technical advisers. They do not apply to news dispatches censored by military authority with the expeditionary forces or in those cases where the government itself, in the form of official statements, may find it necessary or expedient to make public information covered by these requests.

For the protection of our military and naval forces and of merchant shipping it is requested that secrecy be observed in all matters of—

1.   Advance information of the routes and schedules of troop movements. (See Par. 5.)

2. Information tending to disclose the number of troops in the expeditionary forces abroad.

3. Information calculated to disclose the location of the permanent base or bases abroad.

4. Information that would disclose the location of American units or the eventual position of the American forces at the front.

5. Information tending to disclose an eventual or actual port of embarkation; or information of the movement of military forces toward seaports or of the assembling of military forces at seaports from which inference might be drawn of any intention to embark them for service abroad; and information of the assembling of transports or convoys; and information of the embarkation itself.

6. Information of the arrival at any European port of American war-vessels, transports, or any portion of any expeditionary force, combatant or non-combatant.

7. Information of the time of departure of merchant ships from American or European ports, or information of the ports from which they sailed, or information of their cargoes.

8. Information indicating the port of arrival of incoming ships from European ports or after their arrival indicating, or hinting at, the port at which the ship arrived.

9. Information as to convoys and as to the sighting of friendly or enemy ships, whether naval or merchant.

10. Information of the locality, number, or identity of vessels belonging to our own navy or to the navies of any country at war with Germany.

11. Information of the coast or anti-aircraft defenses of the United States. Any information of their very existence, as well as the number, nature, or position of their guns, is dangerous.

12. Information of the laying of mines or mine-fields or of any harbor defenses.

13. Information of the aircraft and appurtenances used at government aviation-schools for experimental tests under military authority, and information of contracts and production of air material, and information tending to disclose the numbers and organization of the air division, excepting when authorized by the Committee on Public Information.

14. Information of all government devices and experiments in war material, excepting when authorized by the Committee on Public Information.

15. Information of secret notices issued to mariners or other confidential instructions issued by the navy or the Department of Commerce relating to lights, lightships, buoys, or other guides to navigation.

16. Information as to the number, size, character, or location of ships of the navy ordered laid down at any port or shipyard, or in actual process of construction; or information that they are launched or in commission.

17. Information of the train or boat schedules of traveling official missions in transit through the United States.

18. Information of the transportation of munitions or of war material.

Photographs.—Photographs conveying the information specified above should not be published.

These requests to the press are without larger authority than the necessities of the war-making branches. Their enforcement is a matter for the press itself. To the overwhelming proportion of newspapers who have given unselfish, patriotic adherence to the voluntary agreement the government extends its gratitude and high appreciation.

Committee on Public Information,
by George Creel, *Chairman.*

Bay of Pigs:
More Than Just a Military Fiasco

by E. Clifton Daniel

[In April 1961, Cuban exiles, trained by Americans in Guatamala and in Florida, attempted to invade Cuba and overthrow the government of Fidel Castro, who had overthrown the dictatorship of Fugluencia Batista in 1959, and replaced it with the Communist government. The invasion quickly failed—and the Bay of Pigs became an American fiasco. However, its implications stretched far beyond just the diplomatic and military failures, but into the profession of journalism. On June 1, 1966, before the members of the World Press Council, meeting in St. Paul, Minnesota, Clifton Daniel, managing editor of the New York Times, discussed many of the ethical concerns surrounding decisions by the *Times* not to publish some information about the invasion.]

The Bay of Pigs was not only important in the history of United States relations with Latin America, the Soviet Union and world Communism; it was also important in the history of relations between the American press and the United States Government . . .

Late in March and early in April, 1961, we were hearing rumors that the anti-Castro forces were organizing for an invasion. For example, the editor of *The Miami Herald*, Don Shoemaker, told me at lunch in New York one day, "They're drilling on the beaches all over southern Florida."

Tad Szulc, a veteran correspondent in Latin America with a well-deserved reputation for sniffing out plots and revolutions, came upon the Miami story quite accidentally.

He was being transferred from Rio de Janeiro to Washington and happened to stop in Miami to visit friends on his way north. He quickly discovered that an invasion force was indeed forming and that it was very largely financed and directed by the C.I.A. He asked for permission to come to New York to discuss the situation and was promptly assigned to cover the story.

His first article from Miami . . . began as follows: "For nearly nine months Cuban exile military forces dedicated to the overthrow of Premier Fidel Castro have been in training in the United States as well as in Central America. An army of 5,000 to 6,000 men constitutes the external fighting arm of the anti-Castro Revolutionary Council, which was formed in the United States last

---

E. Clifton Daniel was assistant managing editor of *The New York Times* at the time of the Bay of Pigs. His newspaper career, after receiving an A.B. from the University of North Carolina, includes serving as associate editor of the *Dunn* (N.C.) *Bulletin*, 1933-1934; reporter, Raleigh (N.C.) *News and Observer*, 1933-1937; and reporter/foreign correspondent, *Associated Press*, 1937-1943. With *The New York Times*, he was a reporter and foreign correspondent, 1944-1956; assistant to the managing editor, 1956-1959; assistant managing editor, 1959-1964; managing editor, 1964-1969; associate editor, 1969-1975. Mr. Daniel was recipient of the Overseas Press Club Award for best reporting abroad, 1955.

month. Its purpose is the liberation of Cuba from what it describes as the Communist rule of the Castro regime."

His article, which was more than two columns long and very detailed, was scheduled to appear in the paper of Friday, April 7, 1961. It was dummied for Page 1 under a four-column head, leading the paper.

While the front-page dummy was being drawn up by the assistant managing editor, the news editor and the assistant news editor, Orvil Dryfoos [the publisher of *The New York Times*] came down from the 14th floor to the office of Turner Catledge, the managing editor.

He was gravely troubled by the security implications of Szulc's story. He could envision failure for the invasion, and he could see *The New York Times* being blamed for a bloody fiasco.

He and the managing editor solicited the advice of [James] Reston, who was then the Washington correspondnet of The New York Times and is now an associate editor . . . the managing editor told Mr. Reston about the Szulc dispatch, which said that a landing on Cuba was imminent.

Mr. Reston was asked what should be done with the dispatch.

"I told them not to run it," Mr. Reston says.

He did not advise against printing information about the forces gathering in Florida: that was already well known. He merely cautioned against printing any dispatch that would pinpoint the time of the landing.

Others agree that Szulc's dispatch did contain some phraseology to the effect that an invasion was imminent, and those words were eliminated.

Tad Szulc's own recollection, cabled to me from Madrid the other day, is that "in several instances the stories were considerably toned down, including the elimination of statements about the 'imminence' of an invasion."

"Specifically," Mr. Szulc said, "a decision was made in New York not to mention the C.I.A.'s part in the invasion preparations, not to use the date of the invasion, and, on April 15, not to give away in detail the fact that the first air strike on Cuba was carried out from Guatemala."

After the dummy for the front page of *The Times* for Friday, April 7, 1961, was changed, Ted Bernstein, who was the assistant managing editor on night duty at *The Times*, and Lew Jordan, the news editor, sat in Mr. Bernstein's office fretting about it. They believed a colossal mistake was being made, and together they went into Mr. Catledge's office to appeal for reconsideration.

Mr. Catledge recalls that Mr. Jordan's face was dead white, and he was quivering with emotion. He and Mr. Bernstein told the managing editor that never before had the front-page play in *The New York Times* been changed for reasons of policy. They said they would like to hear from the publisher himself the reasons for the change.

Angry at Intervention

Lew Jordan later recalled that Mr. Catledge was "flaming mad" at this intervention. However, he turned around in his big swivel chair, picked up the telephone, and asked Mr. Dryfoos to come downstairs. By the time he arrived, Mr. Bernstein had gone to dinner, but Mr. Dryfoos spent ten minutes patiently explaining to Mr. Jordan his reasons for wanting the story played down.

His reasons were those of national security, national interest and, above all, concern for the safety of the men who were preparing to offer their lives on the beaches of Cuba. He repeated the explanation in somewhat greater length to Mr. Bernstein the next day . . .

Mr. Bernstein and Mr. Jordan now say, five years later, that the change in play, not eliminating the reference to the imminence of the invasion, was the important thing done that night.

"It was important because a multi-column head in this paper means so much," Mr. Jordan told me the other day.

Mr. Reston, however, felt that the basic issue was the elimination of the statement that an invasion was imminent.

Ironically, although that fact was eliminated from our own dispatch, virtually the same information was printed in a shirttail on Tad Szulc's report. That was a report from the Columbia Broadcasting System. It said that plans for the invasion of Cuba were in their final stages. Ships and planes were carrying invasion units from Florida to their staging bases in preparation for the assault.

When the invasion actually took place ten days later, the American Society of Newspaper Editors happened to be in session in Washington, and President Kennedy addressed the society. He devoted his speech entirely to the Cuban crisis. He said nothing at that time about press disclosures of invasion plans.

Appeal by President

However, a week later in New York, appearing before the Bureau of Advertising of the American Newspaper Publishers Association, the President asked members of the newspaper profession "to re-examine their own responsibilities."

He suggested that the circumstances of the cold war required newspapermen to show some of the same restraint they would exercise in a shooting war.

He went on to say, "Every newspaper now asks itself with respect to every story, 'Is it news?' All I suggest is that you add the question: 'Is it in the interest of national security?'"

If the press should recommend voluntary measures to prevent the publication of material endangering the national security in peacetime, the President said, "the Government would cooperate wholeheartedly."

Turner Catledge, who was the retiring president of the A.S.N.E., Felix McKnight of *The Dallas Times-Herald*, the incoming president, and Lee Hills, executive editor of the Knight newspapers, took the President's statement as an invitation to talk.

Within two weeks, a delegation of editors, publishers and news agency executives was at the White House. They told President Kennedy they saw no need at that time for machinery to help prevent the disclosure of vital security information. They agreed that there should be another meeting in a few months. However, no further meeting was ever held.

That day in the White House, President Kennedy ran down a list of what he called premature disclosures of security information. His examples were mainly drawn from *The New York Times*.

He mentioned, for example, Paul Kennedy's story about the training of anti-Castro forces in Guatemala. Mr. Catledge pointed out that this information had been published in *La Hora* in Guatemala and in *The Nation* in this country before it was ever published in *The New York Times*.

"But it was not news until it appeared in *The Times*," the President replied.

While he scolded *The New York Times*, the President said in an aside to Mr. Catledge, "If you had printed more about the operation you would have saved us from a colossal mistake."

Sorry You Didn't Tell It

More than a year later, President Kennedy was still talking the same way. In a conversation with Orvil Dryfoos in the White House on Sept. 13, 1962, he said, "I wish you had run everything on Cuba . . . I am just sorry you didn't tell it at the time."

Those words were echoed by Arthur Schlesinger when he wrote, "I have wondered whether, if the press had behaved irresponsibly, it would not have spared the country a disaster."

They are still echoing down the corridors of history. Just the other day in Washington, Senator Russell of Georgia confessed that, although he was chairman of the Senate Armed Forces Committee, he didn't know the timing of the Bay of Pigs operation.

"I only wish I had been consulted," he said in a speech to the Senate, "because I would have strongly advised against this kind of operation if I had been."

It is not so easy, it seems, even for Presidents, their most intimate advisers and distinguished United States Senators to know always what is really in the national interest. One is tempted to say that sometimes—sometimes—even a mere newspaperman knows better.

My own view is that the Bay of Pigs operation might well have been cancelled and the country would have been saved enormous embarrassment if *The New York Times* and other newspapers had been more diligent in the performance of their duty—their duty to keep the public informed on matters vitally affecting our national honor and prestige, not to mention our national security.

Perhaps, as Mr. Reston believes, it was too late to stop the operation by the time we printed Tad Szulc's story on April 7.

"If I had it to do over, I would do exactly what we did at the time," Mr. Reston says. "It is ridiculous to think that publishing the fact that the invasion was imminent would have avoided this disaster. I am quite sure the operation would have gone forward."

"The thing had been cranked up too far. The C.I.A. would have had to disarm the anti-Castro forces physically. Jack Kennedy was in no mood to do anything like that."

Prelude to Graver Crisis

The Bay of Pigs, as it turned out, was the prelude to an even graver crisis—the Cuban missile crisis of 1962.

In Arthur Schlesinger's opinion, failure in 1961 contributed to success in 1962. President Kennedy had learned from experience, and once again *The New York Times* was involved . . .

In the Cuban missile crisis, things were handled somewhat differently than in the previous year. The President telephoned directly to the publisher of *The New York Times*.

He had virtually been invited to do so in their conversation in the White House barely a month before.

That conversation had been on the subject of security leaks in the press and how to prevent them, and Mr. Dryfoos had told the President that what was needed was prior information and prior consultation. He said that, when there was danger of security information getting into print, the thing to do was to call in the publishers and explain matters to them.

In the missile crisis, President Kennedy did exactly that.

The President called me [Reston remembers]. "He understood that I had been talking to Mac Bundy [National Security Advisor] and he knew from the line of questioning that we knew the critical fact—that Russian missiles had indeed been emplaced in Cuba."

"The President told me," Mr. Reston continued, "that he was going on television on Monday evening to report to the American people. He said that if we published the news about the missiles Khrushchev could actually give him an ultimatum before he went on the air. Those were Kennedy's exact words."

"I told him I understood," Mr. Reston said this morning, "but I also told him I could not do anything about it. And this is an important thought that you should convey to those young reporters in your audience."

"I told the President I would report to my office in New York and if my advice were asked I would recommend that we not publish. It was not my duty to decide. My job was the same as that of an ambassador—to report to my superiors."

"I recommended to the President that he call New York. He did so." . . .

The President telephoned the publisher of *The New York Times*; Mr. Dryfoos in turn put the issue up to Mr. Reston and his staff

And the news that the Soviet Union had atomic missiles in Cuba only 90 miles from the coast of Florida was withheld until the Government announced it . . . information is essential to people who propose to govern themselves. It is the responsibility of serious journalists to supply that information—whether in this country or in the countries from which our foreign colleagues come.

Still, the primary responsibility for safeguarding our national interest must rest always with our Government, as it did with President Kennedy in the two Cuban crises.

Up until the time we are actually at war or on the verge of war, it is not only permissible—it is our duty as journalists and citizens to be constantly questioning our leaders and our policy, and to be constantly informing the people, who are the masters of us all—both the press and the politicians.

Two Weeks that Shook the Press

by Jules Witcover

For most of the American people, the story of the Pentagon Papers began on Sunday, June 13, when copies of the *New York Times* appeared on doorsteps and newsstands bearing an unsensational two-line, three-column headline that read: *Vietnam Archive: Pentagon Study Traces 3 Decades of Growing U.S. Involvement.* To the left was a particularly handsome picture of President Richard M. Nixon, his smiling daughter Tricia on his arm, at her Saturday afternoon White House wedding. The chances are that most readers saw that before they noticed the story that was to trigger one of the major government-press confrontations in American history.

Nineteen months earlier, however, readers of the *Times* had been told of the existence of the papers. In an article about former Secretary of Defense Robert S. McNamara in the *New York Times Magazine* of Nov. 9, 1969, Henry Brandon of the *Sunday Times* of London had written:

> McNamara is reluctant to comment on what he believes were his lasting accomplishments in the Department of Defense, but not as reluctant as he is to discuss his role in the Vietnam war. Even with the documents at his disposal, he says, he would not trust himself to write a history of those years. Instead, long before leaving the Pentagon, he ordered detailed historical records to be assembled, and there are now thirty to forty volumes that will be the raw material for a definitive history of that war.

And on Oct. 25, 1970, in the popular Personality Parade column in *Parade* magazine by "Walter Scott," who is Lloyd Shearer, *Parade's* editor on the West Coast, there was this exchange:

Jules Witcover is a political columnist for the *Baltimore Evening Sun*; his column, with Jack Germond, is syndicated nationally by the Tribune Media Services. He also writes a weekly column for the *National Journal* and a monthly article for *Washingtonian* magazine. Mr. Witcover received an A.B. and a M.S.J. from Columbia University, and was employed by the Newhouse Newspapers, 1954-1969; he was a Washington correspondent for the *Los Angeles Times*, and a political reporter for the Washington Post, 1973-1977 and the Washington Star, 1977-1981. Mr. Witcover is the recipient of the Sigma Delta Chi award for distinguished Washington reporting, 1962; and is the author of eight books on national politics. [This article is edited and reprinted, with permission, from *The Columbia Journalism Review*, September-October 1971; ©1971, School of Journalism, Columbia University: ©1986, Jules Witcover.]

Q. There is a belief in this community that most quietly President Nixon has ordered a top-secret, exhaustive report on the U.S. involvement in Vietnam dating from World War II. Is there in fact such a report in the works? If so, will it be made available to the public so that we may finally learn the truth about the origin of the war? B. T. Clancy, Washington, D.C.

A. President Nixon has ordered no such report. Robert McNamara, Defense Secretary under Presidents Kennedy and Johnson, did, however. Several months before Lyndon Johnson oozed him out of the Pentagon, McNamara assigned a task force under Les Gelb to undertake the most thorough, indepth study of U.S.-Vietnamese relations. The report was finished when McNamara was already out of the government. It runs to thirty volumes, is approximately 10,000 pages. There are relatively few copies in existence. There are no plans to make it public.

Daniel Ellsberg, one of the men who worked on the study, since then has said that he was the source of the material first published in the *New York Times*. He has not said when or how he supplid the documents, and the *Times* has said only that it obtained 7,000 pages through the investigative reporting of Neil Sheehan, a Washington reporter formerly assigned to coverage of the war in Vietnam. Sheehan obtained the papers sometime in March [1971] and informed his superiors. From the start, according to *Times Talk*, the paper's internal newsletter, their handling was a matter of utmost secrecy; *Times* employees were informed on the same strict need-to-know principle that guides internal disclosure of highly classified material within the Pentagon itself. Managing editor A. M. Rosenthal assigned foreign editor James L. Greenfield to direct the project, and Gerald Gold, an assistant foreign editor in New York, was told at the end of March he was to work with Sheehan.

Eventually, about seventy-five *Times* employees were brought into the effort and they successfully maintained the secrecy, going to remarkable pains to do so. On May 20, three weeks before publication, Nat Hentoff wrote in the *Village Voice* that the *Times* was working on a "breakthrough unpublished story concerning the White House, Pentagon, and Southeast Asia," and, alluding to an internal debate, he asked: "Is this story going to be published?" Still, most members of the *Times* staff learned about the story when they read it in the paper . . .

In Washington, where the story probably had its greatest impact, reporter Don Oberdorfer of the *Washington Post* had heard some rumblings during the final week before publication, and on Thursday, Philip Geyelin, editor of the editorial page at the *Post*, heard that the project had something to do with Indochina, and that its publication would materially affect U.S. policy on Vietnam, possibly speeding American withdrawal . . .

The editors [of the *Post*] decided to accept a one-day beating on the story by the *Times* in favor of doing a careful description of what the *Times* printed each day, feeding in documentation from the *Times* and other sources to give the reader an intelligible package.

Meanwhile, the *Post*—and the rest of American journalism—started scrambling, either to try to get the Pentagon Papers— a dim prospect, it seemed, at that juncture—or to spin off enterprise and reaction stories based on what the *Times* was printing in New York. For most Washington bureaus, it was a period first of shock and then of frustration, until events and enterprise finally spread the story among a number of papers.

The first development in that direction, ironically, came Sunday morning when U.S. Attorney General John N. Mitchell reached outside his Watergate apartment and picked up his delivered copy of the *Times* at his doorstep. He had received no advance warning . . .

Mitchell's Sunday morning reading was interrupted by a call from Secretary of Defense Melvin P. Laird, who was about to appear on CBS' *Face the Nation*. He was certain to be asked about the *Times*' disclosures. What should he say? Tell them the matter has been referred to the Justice Department, Mitchell growled. Laird went on the panel show with two CBS reporters and one from the *New York Times* but, incredibly, through thirty minutes and twenty-seven questions there was not a single inquiry about or reference to the Pentagon Papers story.

Mitchell, for all his concern, did nothing on Sunday. On Sunday night the *Times* published its second installment. On Monday morning Mitchell and two assistant attorneys general, Robert C. Mardian)for internal security) and William H. Rehnquit)legal counsel), began conferring. Laird called again, to ask what he should tell the Senate Foreign Relations Committee; again he was told to say that the matter had been referred to Justice, and Mitchell asked Laird for a Pentagon memorandum indicating the national security implications of publication. About 7 p.m., Monday, Mardian met Mitchell at Mitchell's Watergate apartment and they agreed on the text of a telegram to Sulzberger asking the *Times* to desist. It was decided to phone him as well.

Mardian placed the call and was told Sulzberger was in London; he talked instead to Harding F. Bancroft, executive vice president. The papers, Mardian said, reading the telegram, contained "information relating to the national defense of the United States" bearing top-secret classification whose publication was "directly prohibited" by the Espionage Law. If the paper did not desist, he told Bancroft, Mitchell would seek an injunction. The *Times*' answer came in a statement read to Mardian two hours later and printed in the *Times* of Tuesday, June 15, along with the third installment. "The *Times* must respectfully decline the request of the Attorney General," it said, "believing that it is in the interest of the people of this country to be informed of the material contained in this series of articles." Later Tuesday, the *Times* was enjoined from further publication, pending a hearing on the Government's plea.

At the *Washington Post*, the paper's Vietnam experts still were rewriting, and scrambling to get a piece of the action on their own . . . The *Post's* editors anticipated that the Government's action against the *Times* would be thrown out in short order and that the *Times* would resume publication on Wednesday. Instead, U.S. District Court Judge Murray I. Gurfein granted a temporary restraining order for four days, until Saturday, June 19, at 1 p.m. Suddenly the *Times* was faced with prior restraint of publication; the scramble among the competition was bound to intensify now—and, as it turned out, segments of the Pentagon Papers soon were to become available to other newspapers. That night, Wednesday, June 16, on a New York radio show, former *New York Times* reporter Sidney Zion identified Ellsberg as the source of the *Times's* stories, and the FBI was on Ellsberg's trail.

On Thursday morning, June 17, [Ben Bagdikian, asistant managing editor, *The Washington Post*,] brought 4,400 unbound pages of the documents [to the home of Ben Bradlee, *Post* executive editor. For the next twelve hours, Bagdikian, Bradlee, several reporters, editors, lawyers, and management discussed whether to publish and, if so, how to handle it]

Basically, according to Bagdikian, it was the lawyers and management on one side, wary about publication, and the editors and writers on the other, zealous to print. The lawyers posed the question of legal tactics and propriety—whether it might be wiser to establish the right to publish by allowing the *New York Times* case to run its course, avoiding indication of any contempt for the court in that case; the editors and writers saw it strictly in terms of freedom of the press and journalistic responsibility to the public—if it is authentic and significant, publish it. The discussion continued through the *Post's* small first edition run, finally ending about 9:30 p.m., in time for the main run. The decision was to publish, [although the lawyers continued to raise objections] . . . The *Post* ran its first story on Friday, June 18.

All Thursday, the *Times* had been preparing its defense. The Justice Department had asked Judge Gurfein to order the *Times* to turn over the documents. While he urged the *Times* do do so, he did not so order. The paper refused to give up the papers but did supply a list of what it had. At the *Times*, its lawyers were busy educating its newsmen about the legal implications; the newsmen were educating the lawyers in the realities of how classified information, as a matter of course, is used and abused by government and press in Washington. Max Frankel now was in New York aiding in preparation of the defense, and he started to write a memo to the lawyers on how use of classification had become a self-serving government tool. It turned out to be a ninety-page affidavit, including seventy-two pages of exhibits . . .

On Friday, June 18, while Government witnesses in New York charged that the *Times'* publication had damaged national security and while Judge Gurfein examined the documents, the *Post* also heard from the Justice Department. Around noon, Rehnquist called Bradlee and "respectfully requested" that the paper halt publication of the study-based stories. Bradlee "respectfully declined." A telegram ensued from Mitchell to [Katherine] Graham [*Post* owner]. Justice then went into the federal district court in Washington seeking a temporary restraining order. Judge Gerhard Gesell in early evening refused to grant it, and the *Post* proceeded with its second installment. But the Government appealed, and two judges ordered Gesell to take a longer look at the case and decide by 5 p.m. on Monday. The *Post* stopped its presses, pulled off the plates containing Marder's story, and was ready to install substitute plates that had been prepared omitting the story. Just then one of the *Post's* lawyers called; he had gone to one of the appellate judges, who said the order permitted the *Post* to complete its Monday night run. The original plates were rushed back onto the press and the full run was completed, with a delay of only about thirty minutes.

On Saturday, June 19, Gurfein ruled for the *Times*, but U.S. Circuit Court of Appeals Judge Irving R. Kaufman quickly extended the restraining order until the next Monday to enable a three-judge panel to hear the case. It was becoming clear now that a historic legal confrontation was under way that doubtless would reach the Supreme Court. *Post* editors and reporters, meanwhile, prepared affidavits of their own like Frankel's . . .

—September-October 1971

On Monday, June 21, the restraining order against the *Times* was extended another day to permit a full eight-judge panel to consider the case, and in Washington Gesell again backed the *Post* but the U.S. Court of Appeals extended the restraining order another day to allow the full nine-man appellate court to consider it.

Meanwhile, in Boston, a segment of the Pentagon Papers had come into the hands of the *Boston Globe*, and a select group of staff members were gathered in a locked room with the papers . . . About . . . 5 a.m., Tuesday, the phone rang in the *Globe* city room. Joseph Dineen, managing editor of the *Evening Globe*, took the call. It was Mardian asking whether the *Globe* would voluntarily cease publication—and griping about having been roused out of bed by news of the *Globe's* stories. *Globe* editors, after conferences, called back and said that it planned to publish more. At 10:10 a.m., the phone rang in

---

[*Columbia Journalism Review:*] What is your response to the charge that you were publishing documents "stolen" from the Government?

[A.M. Rosenthal, managing editor, *The New York Times:*] We are dealing with decisions made in government that affect the people. Can you steal a decision that was made three years ago and that has caused consequences that a country now pays for, good or bad? How can you steal a decision like that? How can you steal the mental processes of elected officials or appointed officials?

As a reporter I was evicted from Poland. They accused me of probing into the internal affairs of the Polish government. From their point of view I was stealing their information. I never thought that Americans would buy the argument that you can steal information on public matters. As a newspaperman you are in search of as much of the truth as you can arrive at. Your basic philosophy in life is that, taken altogether, the truth on important matters—or as much as you can arrive at—is good. That is your occupation in life; that is your belief: that what is harmful is lack of information.

—September-October 1971

Winship's office. This time it was Mitchell himself. "Yes sir, General, Tom Winship here," the young editor said jovially. "Well," Mitchell said, "I see you're in the act." He "respectfully requested" that the *Globe* desist; Winship "respectfully declined." All right, Mitchell said, the Government would have to move against the *Globe*; otherwise the *Times* and *Post* would feel discriminated against.

In this instance, not only was the paper enjoined from further publication of its own stories based on the papers it also was ordered to have the documents and stories impounded at the federal courthouse and was prohibited from printing stories from other newspapers or wire services based on the secret documents. The *Globe's* lawyers swiftly appealed the rulings and won permission to store the papers and unpublished stories in a commercial bank vault, thus retaining possession. Also, after a day, the prohibition against using other stories based on the papers was lifted. Meanwhile, the bans on the *Times* and *Post* continued, amid more legal maneuvering.

The next paper to, in Mitchell's words, "get into the act" was the *Chicago Sun-Times*. About 5 p.m. Tuesday, the day Mitchell had called Winship, the *Sun-Times'* first edition had a story based, according to editor James F. Hoge, on declassified documents and "access to sources who had the papers." It concerned a contingency memorandum by then Assistant Secretary of State Roger Hilsman on the prospects for the overthrow of President Diem in 1963; the declassified memo had been dealt with much earlier in a *New York Times Magazine* article by former Johnson adviser John Roche, and was being offered around Washington by the Vietnam Veterans Against the War. At 1:30 a.m. Wednesday, June 23, a call came to Hoge from the U.S. Attorney's office in Chicago inquiring what the paper had and what it intended to print in the future. Hoge was not there but other editors reported the paper would print what was "relevant and responsible," without indicating whether it had any secret papers. Presumably for this reason, and because the paper ran no documents as such, no Justice action followed, though the paper subsequently did run stories based on the Pentagon study.

That night, as a grand jury in Los Angeles was looking into the matter of the leaked papers, two more news organizations—the Knight newspapers' and the *Los Angeles Times'* Washington bureaus—were preparing stories based on parts of the study. In each case, the same procedure was followed: careful examination of the material by teams of newsmen to determine what was significant and had not yet been published elsewhere. Knight released its story with a statement that the papers at that time did not plan further stories. No one at Justice ever called, though the Knight papers later did obtain more secret papers and did publish again. Mardian tried to call *Los Angeles Times* executives Wednesday night but was unsuccessful. On Thursday, June 24, however, the U.S. Attorney in Los Angeles, Robert Meyer, called the paper's executive editor, William F. Thomas, and was told that the *Times* had no present intention of publishing more. Subsequently, the *Los Angeles Times*, too, obtained more of the papers and ran another story. Neither Knight nor the *Los Angeles Times* was enjoined.

Throughout all this, both the *New York Times* and *Post* cases continued to occupy the courts; the appellate court in New York voted 5 to 3 to send the *Times* case back to Gurfein; the appellate court in Washington voted 7 to 2 for the *Post*, but retained the restraining order to permit the Government to take a further appeal. The *Times* asked the Supreme Court to rule in its case, and the Government appealed the *Post* case there. On Friday, June 25, the cases were consolidated and the Supreme Court voted 5 to 4 to continue the ban and hear evidence. At this juncture, primarily at issue was certain material the Justice Department had listed as damaging to national security. Under the rulings, both papers now were free to publish material not listed, but both declined, partly on principle, partly out of practicality . . .

As the Supreme Court prepared to hear the combined case, still another newspaper published stories and documents from the Pentagon study—the *St. Louis Post-Dispatch*, in its afternoon editions of Friday, June 25. About 9:30 p.m., assistant managing editor David Lipman received a call from U.S. Attorney Dan Bartlett in St. Louis, asking whether the paper planned further stories. If it did, Bartlett told Lipman, or if the paper wouldn't say, the Government was going to seek a restraining order. The paper was going to print more, Lipman said, but not until Sunday; the Saturday paper was thin with small circulation.

Overnight, however, wire stories from Washington quoted the Justice Department as saying the *Post-Dispatch* was desisting pending the outcome of the Supreme Court decision in the *Times* and *Post* cases, then possibly due on Saturday. *Post-Dispatch* officials, learning of this erroneous version, called Bartlett and told him the paper's position had been misrepresented, that it appeared the *Post-Dispatch* was bowing to pressure. Hence, to protect its reputation for independence, the paper had decided to print a study-based story on Saturday. Before it could get another story in print, the *Post-Dispatch* was enjoined.

On Saturday, the Supreme Court heard arguments and then went into seclusion to vote and write opinions. On Monday, June 28, it extended its term, which was to have ended that day, and the final, most tense wait began. A brief and minor diversion came Tuesday morning, June 29, when the *Christian Science Monitor* printed the first of three articles based on the secret study. Shortly before noon, Erwin D. Canham, the paper's editor-in-chief, got a call from Herbert F. Travers, Jr., the U.S. Attorney in Boston. Travers said he was under orders to ask the *Monitor* not to publish further articles based on the study. Travers was told the paper would not voluntarily desist. Then he asked what the future stories would include, and Canham told him in a very broad way the subject mattter. "I was in no sense submitting this or seeking clearance," he said later. "There was no question of clearance. It was the last thing I would have done." But the Justice Department issued a statement saying the *Monitor's* editors "had cooperated by disclosing to [Travers] the contents of the two remaining intallments they propose to publish" and hence there would be no effort to enjoin the paper.

Shortly before the Supreme Court ruling one other paper, *Newsday*, published a story based on the Pentagon study, together with a cloak-and-dagger account of how a reporter had been contacted and led through a treasure-hunt scenario to get the papers, in a shopping bag, in Boston.

Moments after 2 p.m. on Wednesday, June 30, the historic ruling of the Supreme Court finally came. The 6 to 3 verdict in favor of the *Times* and *Post* was flashed to jubilant newsrooms by reporters at the court. Cheers erupted in the *Times* newsroom when a news assistant rushed in from the wire room with a bulletin shouting, "We won!" Nowhere were the cheers louder and lustier than near the foreign news desk where Gerald Gold, who had played the central editing role from the start, sat in anticipation. Sulzberger and Rosenthal hugged each other; at a press conference, Sulzberger expressed "complete joy and delight," and Rosenthal called it "a joyous day for the press and for American society" . . .

A Most Insidious Case

by Ben H. Bagdikian

[Shortly after World War II, the United States, the only country in the world with an atomic bomb, fearful that other countries might acquire the technology, enacted the Atomic Energy Act. The Act provided for the death penalty (reduced more than two decades later to a maximum ten years in prison and/or $10,000 fine) for stealing or disseminating

    . . . all data concerning (1) design, manufacture, or utilization of atomic weapons; (2) the production of special nuclear material [plutonium and enriched uranium]; or (3) the use of special nuclear material in the production of energy, but shall not include data declassified or removed from the Restricted Data category . . .

Ben H. Bagdikian is professor of journalism, University of California at Berkeley. He received an A.B. from Clark University and honorary doctorates from Clark and Brown universities.
Mr. Bagdikian was a reporter for the *Springfield* (Mass.) *Morning Union*; associate editor of Periodical House; reporter, foreign correspondent, and chief Washington correspondent for the *Providence* (R.I.) *Journal*; contributing editor, *Saturday Evening Post*; project director for the Study of the Future of the U.S. News Media, Rand Corp.; assistant managing editor, *Washington Post*; and national correspondent, Columbia Journalism Review. He is the recipient of numerous writing awards, including a Peabody. He is the author of several books, including *In the Midst of Plenty: The Poor in America* (1964), *The Information Machines: Their Impact on Men and Media* (1971), *The Shame of the Prisons* (1972), *The Effete Conspiracy* (1972), *Caged: Eight Prisoners and Their Keepers* (1976), *The Shame of the Prisons* (1972) and *The Media Monopoly* (1983). He is a member of the board of editors, Investigative Reporters and Editors, member of the Committee to Protect Journalists, and member of the board of the National Citizens Committee for Broadcasting. He was a member of the steering committee of the National Prison Project, 1974-1982; trustee, Clark University, 1964-1976, and member of the board of the National Capital Area Civil Liberties Union, 1964-1966. [This article is edited and reprinted, with permission, from *Quill*, June 1969, ©1969 Quill; ©1986 Ben H. Bagdikian.]

Thus, Congress had authorized all data involving nuclear energy to be "classified at birth," and to remain classified until actions were officially taken to declassify the material. Many scientists at the time claimed that nuclear energy secrets, because most involved the natural laws of the universe, were already known, or could become known by scientists throughout the world.

Few arrests were made under the Act since there was strong co-operation among the people of a nation in fear of its existence. Even the news media carefully followed every restriction within the Act; many even refused to write or publish *anything* involving nuclear energy, afraid to violate the provisions of the Act. Then, there was the *Progressive* . . .]

The Progressive is the liberal-left magazine of 40,000 circulation created in 1909 by Robert M. LaFollette, Sr. It has been a persistent opponent of exapnding nuclear armament by any nation and of United states nuclear energy policies. In July of 1978 it assigned a free-lance writer, Howard Morland, a former Air Force pilot interested in nuclear politics, to spend six months attempting to show that much of what arms makers said was classified secret was not secret at all but known to hundreds of thousands of non-governmental people all over the world, but that the aura of secrecy is maintained over most of these data for political reasons. The political reasons of the nuclear establishment are the desire to limit public debate on armaments and nuclear power by making the public dependent on the selected facts that government and industry choose to release. These secrecy policies help prevent release of reliable information of distrubing dangers like unsafe nuclear reactors, careless use of nuclear materials, concealment of injuries and deaths caused by nuclear industry and weapons development, and the dangers of disposing of nuclear wastes. Secrecy makes it easier for the government and the nuclear industry to obtain continuing appropriations (about $59 billion a year for armaments and supplies) without having to disclose negative information.

With the approval of the Department of Energy, successor to the Atomic Energy Commission, Morland visited open portions of nuclear plants, read physics books, encyclopedias, the Congressional Record and other government publications, and interviewed scientists. Morland says he received no classified information.

In January of 1979, the magazine had a draft of the Morland article, including technical material and diagrams. Some of the technical segments were sent to a few of the scientists Morland had interviewed asking if details and concepts were accurate. Some answered with minor corrections. But one of these scientists showed his segment of the article to Dr. George Rathjens of M.I.T. Rathjens, a former government employee and among those interviewed by Morland, had not been sent any portion of the article for checking, possibly because he is a political scientist and not a physicist, and possibly because he is a consultant to the government. Rathjens, with his borrowed portion of the Morland manuscript, called The Progressive to say he was sending it to the Department of Energy and, despite bitter protests by the magazine, did so.

For days there was no response from the government. Erwin Knoll, editor of The Proressive, consulted the magazine's lawyer. The lawyer, telling Knoll of the vague and severe criminal provisions of the Atomic Energy Act, advised him to send the entire article to the Department of Energy in order to permit the placement of the government-held portion in the whole context. It was a serious mistake for a publication that believed it was exercising its First Amendment rights. (Knoll now says he has serious reservations about the wisdom of his move.)

Energy's Message to The Progressive

The Department of Energy informed The Progressive that it had three choices: 1. don't publish the article; 2. let the Department of Energy rewrite the entire article (the government said it could not inform the editor which portions were sensitive because that information itself is sensitive); or 3. publish the article and face prosecution. The magazine informed the government that it intended to publish the article as it stood, and the government obtained a restraining order to prevent publication.

U.S. District Judge Robert Waren in Milwaukee accepted the government's arguments and, without reading the article, issued a temporary restraining order against the magazine and, later, issued an injunction which has been appealed.

The performance of the press in reporting the case was careless, and some of the stories may have contributed to hostile editorials. Most stories, including accounts by AP and UPI, said the magazine article was entitled, "How a Hydrogen Bomb Works," which is how the government characterized the article, though that was only the label on a diagram accompanying the piece. The working title was always, "The H-Bomb Secret," and finally, "The H-Bomb Secret: How We Got It and Why We Are Telling It."

A journalist owes nothing to those who govern his country. He owes everything to his country.

—Vermont Royster, editor *The Wall Street Journal*, 1968

Time and *Newsweek* both reported that the magazine sent the article to the Department of Energy "to check for accuracy" (*Newsweek*) and "for verification of the facts" (*Time*). Neither said that the Department of Energy had received part of the article beforehand against the *Progressive's* wishes.

The bad reporting led to worse headlines, as it always does. The *Lansing State Journal's* headline read: "You, Too, Can Build H-Bomb". Hostile editorials repeated the nonsense. One particularly simple-minded one in the *San Francisco Chronicle* referred to the article as "a handy guide to building your own H-bomb." Or the *Times News* of Twin Falls, Idaho: " . . . the magazine's intent is sensationalism. The author has latched on to some hot information . . ."

High in most stories of the judge's decision was his catchy phrase: "I want to think a long, hard time before I'd give a hydrogen bomb to Idi Amin. It appears to me that is just what we're doing here." In his acknowledgment of the historic inhibition he was placing on the First Amendment, he said, "You can't speak freely when you're dead."

What was not reported at all in many news stories, or more obscurely in others, was the judge's conclusion that the article was not, in fact, a "do-it-yourself" guide to building a hydrogen bomb and that the bomb could not be built by any nation or group that did not have as the judge agreed, "a large sophisticated industrial capability, coupled with a coterie of imaginative, resourceful scientists and technicians."

One might be forgiven for wondering how the judge could have said what he did about Idi Amin and also the need for a large industrial-scientific establishment. And wonder, as many scientists and the more thoughtful journalists did, why any country or group with the huge industrial, scientific and engineering complex needed to build a hydrogen bomb, the atomic bomb needed to trigger the hydrogen bomb, the half-billion to one billion dollars needed to build a bomb after the decision is made, and the desire to commit such resources to that enterprise, would depend on *The Progressive* magazine of Madision, Wisc., to get the idea and then implement it.

The Press Chooses Sides

Some news organizations responded with a clear view of the First Amendment and an understanding of the true nature of government secrecy. Major papers supporting *The Progressive* editorially were the *Chicago Tribune*, *St. Louis Post-Dispatch*, *Minneapolis Tribune* and *The New York Times*. Larry Jinks, editor of the *San Jose Mercury-News*, and H. L. Stevenson, editor-in-chief of UPI, said they supported the magazine, as did editors of some other magazines.

Condemnation of *The Progressive* and support for the government came from some prestigious press organizations. John Hughes, president of the American Society of Newspaper Editors, expressed his personal view that the magazine was wrong to accept the judge's offer to have an outside committee of one judge, two scientists and two lay persons rewrite the article. The *Chicago Sun-Times* agreed. *The Washington Post* editorially advised *The Progressive* to "forget about publishing" the article because the magazine might lose the case in the Supreme Court. Jack Landau, head of the Reporters Committee for Freedom of the Press, agreed that the magazine should not pursue its case to the high court.

Other papers said *The Progressive* should have announced that it had learned how a hydrogen bomb works by referring only to open sources but then not published the article.

Editor & Publisher, the newspaper trade magazine, said the case "will prove to be detrimental to the cause of a free press no matter which way the court or courts decide." This is not surprising. It was *Editor & Publisher*, that editorialized in the Dan Schorr case that Schorr should not have permitted publication of something the House of Representatives did not want published, a bizarre view of the proper relationship of a free press to government . . .

The argument that the magazine should have accepted the judge's offer to have the article rewritten by an outside committee appointed by a judge comes strangely from the head of the American Society of Newspaper Editors. How many editors would permit this for major stories critical of government? And if they did permit this, what do they think the response would be in the future whenever government wished to alter an article it disliked?

The idea of announcing that the "secret" of the hydrogen bomb was found from open sources, but not printing it, would be as convincing as Woodward and Bernstein announcing that they have found a link between the White House and the burglary of Democratic National Committee headquarters but would not print the evidence . . .

In an important respect there is more at stake in The Progressive case than in the Pentagon Papers. Application of the Espionage Act to the printing of classified information has always been on shaky legal grounds. The intent has to be to harm the United States or to passdocuments to a Communist nation. Precedent has demanded that there be a "clear and present danger" to justify inhibition of the freedom to publish. The government has had to show that damage will be immediate, grave, and irreparable.

The Progressive case is more insidious. It is saying that even if the information is not secret and is available to all, anyone who gets ideas about nuclear matters the Department of Energy or the Department of Justice consider dangerous may be censored or punished.

Remember Why the Bill of Rights

"Dangerous thoughts" (including diagrams) have been known before in history . . . Punishment for "dangerous thoughts" in totalitarian societies has been a standard indictment in official American propaganda to the rest of the world. These suppressions in other societies are usually printed as the work of cold cynics. Most often they are not. They are most often the work of people in power who genuinely believe that what they are doing is best for everyone. The Federalists thought they were passing the Alien and Sedition Acts not only to prevent foreigners from taking over the government but to keep the Jeffersonians from permitting that dangerous act. The desire to suppress for what is perceived to be good purposes is not unique to totalitarian states but is a desire of most people of power in any society. That is why the Bill of Rights was written in the first place.

None of the arguments submitted by the government in The Progressive case claimed a clear and present danger. The arguments spoke in the subjunctive mood, of speculations of distant events, though, of course, fearsome ones. More influential than the official statements was one by Dr. Jeremy Stone of the Federation of American Scientists who claimed that The Progressive article would accelerate the spread of hydrogen bombs "by decades, let alone years." This is more than anything the government claimed and it came from a more scientific source. But it sounded strange to many people familiar with the magnitude of U.S. production of the essential ingredient of a hydrogen bomb, plutonium, the country's aggressive exportation of plutonium to other countries, and the knowledge and inclination of some nations with a greater scientific-industrial complex and more knowledge than Howard Morland . . .

There was a significant Catch-22 in the fate of some affidavits issued in defense of The Progressive [arguments that all information in the article had been published.] Morland gave the court affidavits, inches thick, showing where he obtained his information. The government succeeded in having some of these affidavits kept secret from the court record. One was Morland's college physics book in which, in 1961, he had underlined some sentences when he was a student in Emory College in Atlanta. Others were copies of articles from encyclopedias describing the sun and comets, underlined by Morland during his research. The government said the underlining violated security and the court accepted the government assertions.

[While the courts had restrained The Progressive from publishing its article, several newspapers, using information already public ran short articles about the H-Bomb. Eventually, the Department of Justice dropped its suit—more than a year later, and with The Progressive faced with legal costs of more than $250,000.]

Since Hiroshima, since creation of the military classification system, since the Atomic Energy Act, and since the mutual involvement of government, industry and universities in weapons development, we have, almost without noticing it, drifted toward a more closed society. We have accepted what was never accepted before, the decision by government that in the area of public policy with maximum risk and expense, that the public shall have a right to know only what the policy-makers decide to tell it. We have had historical periods when the policy-makers didn't bother telling the electorate what they were doing, and others when much of the public was not enfranchised to know. But we have not had a period in which the right to know was officially denied as a permanent prerogative of government.

This background makes more understandable the steady attrition on freedom of the press. It is a difficult time in which to challenge censorship. But there is more at stake than a bad court decision. Every time an infringement of the right of expression is accepted, either because some of the press feels more comfortable in alliance with the authorities or because the fight seems too difficult, it adds legitimacy and power to the revisionists of the First Amendment and to the larger growth of secrecy in society.

The Campaign Against
the Underground Press

by Geoffrey Rips

The freedom of expression and the freedom of the press have always been relative freedoms. A government intent on controlling the economic and social realities of a country must understandably become involved in the manipulation of the written perception of those realities, even at the expense of legal and moral principles held to be the cornerstone of that government . . .

Government surveillance of political and cultural expression has existed here not only for decades but for centuries. The re-affirmation of these freedoms by one generation seems to be either taken for granted or forgotten by the next. The suppression of press freedom during the McCarthy era was not an aberration of the 1950s as some recent films and articles suggest.

Now, once again, revelations about government interference are awakening a new awareness of a need for vigilance. During the 1960s and 1970s, the U.S. Government, through its police and surveillance agencies, made a full-scale effort to silence dissident writing and publishing. Under at least three administrations, it developed highly sophisticated techniques to intimidate the press that spoke for the popular liberative movements of recent decades.

In the 1960s, investigative journalists, poets, novelists, political activists, community organizers, and artists [had] formed an unprecedented alliance for change in the vigorous underground press movement that flourished in the United States. This network of counterculture, campus, and other alternative media brought larger political issues into communities, awakening citizens to their own power to influence national policy . . .

The dramatic decline of the underground press has been attributed to many things. The end of the war and a changing economy were critical factors; and the inexperience, bad management, self-indulgence, and political naivete that plagued many alternative journals cannot be overlooked. But most of these analyses omit one ominous fact: the withering of the underground press was not entirely a natural decline. Alternative presses, whether serious journals of adversary politics or counterculture avant-garde papers, were targets of surveillance, harrassment, and unlawful search and seizure by U.S. government agencies. Operating with pragmatic immorality, these agencies were mobilized to crush the constitutional rights of a large sector of the American populace which had found it necessary to dissent.

Geoffrey Rips is editor of the *Texas Observer* (Austin). In 1985, the *Observer* received the Playboy Foundation's First Amendment Award for outstanding contributions to the cause of free expression in the United States. Prior to assuming the editorship in 1982, Mr. Rips was director of the Freedom to Write Committee of the PEN American Center, New York City. He has a B.A. from Wesleyan University, and an M.A. from Indiana University. [This article is edited and reprinted, with permission, from *The Campaign Against the Underground Press*, published by City Lights Books, 1981; ©1981 by Geoffrey Rips.]

. . . With the sheer mass of information available to media, censorship has come to operate by simply excluding what is aberrant. The marginal economic nature of underground newspapers and the "marginal news" they carried—often considered not "fit to print" by established dailies—rendered them particularly vulnerable to government persecution because they were considered outside the limits of polite society and, therefore, not "worthy" of the constitutional guarantees afforded established writers and publications.

Small journals began springing up all over the country. They had much in common: they opposed the Vietnam war, advocated sexual and artistic freedoms, and urged critical consciousness towards conventional authority and power relations. Some called for communal or cooperative living; and many warned of the dangers of uncontrolled technology, especially nuclear power. Poetry, prose, graphic arts, and coverage of folk and rock music thrived in the underground. And these popular arts swelled the rising tides of dissent

Political information supplied by independent news services, such as the Liberation News Service and the Underground Press Syndicate, usually differed greatly from that offered by establishment media, which often relied heavily on government and Pentagon sources. Just as alarming to Washington may have been the close connections between alternative media and independent community action. Many of the underground papers worked closely with daycare centers, free medical clinics and food cooperatives. Others were connected with movements to extend social democracy and with insurgent political parties. The Black Panther Party, for example, initiated school breakfast and neighborhood defense programs . . .

Grass Roots "Anti-Social" Journalism

Both the independent newspapers and organs of political parties encouraged a relationship between reader and publisher that challenged the one-way transmission of news and information characteristic of the establishment press. Most staff members worked on a volunteer basis, and financially supported the papers, rather than the other way around, proving how vital publication was to the growing counterculture and how closely readers and newspapers could cooperate to meet social needs. These connections between expression and action looked dangerous to those who feared changes in the status quo. Community participation bent on alternative ways of doing things provoked suspicion. The government perceived in these grass roots relationships "anti-social" threats.

The new journalism, it seemed, was partly responsible for the increased political power of the hippies, New Left and anti-war movements. The government move against the underground press was clearly intended to blunt a potential force for political and social change. Official police agencies, however, rarely admitted they were prosecuting alternative papers for their political positions, but alleged that press offices were used as meeting places to plan illegal, even terrorist activities. They hunted for marijuana, arrested editors for obscenity, and quibbled over street vending rights.

At the same time, most underground journals regarded the publication of erotic art, four-letter words, and discussions about drugs and alternative living to be acts of cultural enlightenment. They viewed arrests for drug violations, distribution of "pornographic" literature, and unlicensed vending as political arrests while government agencies worked to dissociate these forms of harassment from any notion of political repression. In fact, the government rarely attempted to prosecute any underground newspaper for its open political statements and *never obtained a conviction on a political charge*. Often the real issues of freedom of the press never came to light. Faced with the prospect of trials on petty charges, and unable to meet court costs, underground papers were ruined. Fourth Amendment rights were violated in searches and seizures of equipment by police agents. Records were lost, typewriters destroyed, and staffs disbanded as a result of police raids. When they failed to find drugs, agents nevertheless ransacked equipment and files. In other cases, where drugs were found, police brought publication to a halt by arresting an entire staff rather than charging an individual offender.

The Establishment Responds

Neither the severity nor the scope of this outrageous campaign of harassment against alternative media was reported by major American news organizations. Equating partisanship with a failure to tell the truth, most establishment journalists did not see, in the move against vanguard and counterculture presses, a more general threat to constitutional guarantees of free expression and seldom looked behind the scenes to investigate harassment as a deliberate attempt to silence an adversary voice. There was no eagerness to cover an underground press that often vociferously criticized establishment media.

Most of the time, government interference with underground writing was reported in an uncoordinated and local manner. The sudden refusal of a printer to continue printing a paper, an overnight doubling of a journal's office rent, advertising cancellations, or shipping losses fostered a not unjustified suspicion of large-scale interference by government agencies. Officials dismissed such complaints as "paranoid."

Given the bizarre nature of some of these cases, established media and even some sectors of the underground were inclined to agree.

The frequent failures of alternative newspapers and the many arrests of staff members were greeted in some quarters as an indication of the tenuous, "off the wall," and irresponsible nature of underground journalism. The failures and arrests bred an insecurity among staff members that itself contributed to the failure of several publications . . .

The Government Responds

Because military intelligence maintained close ties with the FBI, it often acted as the FBI liaison abroad, insinuating agents into United States civilian and military groups. Between 1972 and 1975, Army and Navy intelligence closely monitored and attempted to infiltrate staffs of underground newspapers published by United States citizens in Japan and West Germany . . .

During the last twenty years, military intelligence has played an ominous role in the affairs of civilian writers at home as well. On January 14, 1969,

Army intelligence took part in an FBI search of the offices of the *Free Press*, a Washington, D.C., underground newspaper. The Army agents kept the documents they found in the search. Throughout the 1960s, Army intelligence and the Chicago Police Department regularly exchanged intelligence information. When restrictions placed on military intelligence in 1971 called for destroying files on civilians, Army agents in Chicago, Cleveland, Pennsylvania, and Washington, D.C., gave the files instead to local and state police.

In 1956, in the wake of the McCarthy era, the FBI initiated its vast counterintelligence program (COINTELPRO) "to disrupt, expose, discredit, and otherwise neutralize the United States Communist Party and related organizations."

Under COINTELPRO, the FBI planted stories about "subversives" in the media, wrote scurrilous letters from fictional sources, opened mail, forged public documents, pressured universities and employers to dismiss targeted workers, encouraged "friendly" organizations and local police to harass dissidents, exploited IRS tax records, and infiltrated legal organizations. Expanding well beyond harassment of Communist Party members, the FBI operation soon included any group with a left, socialist, pacifist, or minority rights position the agency arbitrarily judged "subversive."

The FBI viewed underground writing in the 1960s and 1970s as one part of a concentrated political movement threatening the security of this country. The authority of COINTELPRO expanded to include the monitoring of putative "foreign infiltration" of newly-formed domestic political movements. No proof ever appeared that the underground press was under foreign influence, and the Church Report found that the FBI failed to provide a shred of evidence of it. As in so many other cases, this "infiltration" proved to be pure fiction. In fact, much of the vigor of the U.S. underground press arose from its indigenous spontaneity and cantankerous nature. At the same time, the FBI was able to exploit this rather uncoordinated obstreperousness for its own ends.

COINTELPRO was directed against New Left, anti-war and women's groups, Black Liberation and civil rights organizations, as well as individuals such as Martin Luther King, Jr. The way was opened for a full-scale FBI program against constitutionally guaranteed rights of free speech. The FBI interpreted a Presidential instruction from the 1950s as a mandate to disrupt by any means all political activity not in agreement with current official policy. Lists of "subversives" were drawn up, along with new definitions of threats to national security. This led the agency to participate in illegal break-ins as well as to create a new monitoring bureau—the Interdivisional Information Unity (IDIU), a data bank of all information collected by a number of agencies . . .

On November 5, 1968, the day Richard Nixon was elected president, J. Edgar Hoover sent to FBI offices around the country a memo zeroing in on "New Left Movement Publications." He requested an immediate "detailed survey concerning New Left-type publications being printed and circulated in your territory on a regular basis." He additionally asked for information on each paper's publisher, printer, sources of funds, identity of editorial staff, subversive connections, and possible foreign ramifications.

The FBI [also created] two mock underground publications, *Armageddon News* in Indiana and *Longhorn Tales* in Texas, to promote the view that most students were not participating in protest movements. The FBI believed that one of its best weapons against the New Left was the "shocking" writing and art in underground publications. The agency found ideas about sexual and political liberation in these journals to be decadent and depraved. The moral indignation the Bureau expressed in COINTELPRO memoranda was used to rationalize and exercise unmandated powers against independent publications. The older crusade against "Communist" influence became a crusade against the emerging counterculture. The campaign against alien subversion became a campaign against dissent and alternative strategies for living.

Kudzu

Kudzu, produced in Jackson, Mississippi, served as a major organizational center for the New Left and counterculture in that area. The tenacity of the paper and its allies can be gauged by the fact that by 1968 the newspaper had survived a conviction on obscenity charges, the arrest of salespeople, the confiscation of cameras, and even eviction from its offices. On October 8, 1968, eighteen staff members and supporters of *Kudzu* were attacked and beaten by Jackson deputy sheriffs. At the same time, the FBI was planting information with one of its "friendly" media contacts at the Jackson *Daily News* for an article condemning the New Left. COINTELPRO documents record the fact that this article was made into a pamphlet to be distributed to local schools by the American Legion. In 1970, *Kudzu* was put under direct surveillance by the FBI. For more than two months, FBI agents made daily searches without warrants, claiming to be looking for SDS leader Mark Rudd and for Brandeis students accused of robbing a bank. On October 24 and 25, *Kudzu* sponsored a Southern regional conference of the Underground Press Syndicate. The night before the conference the FBI and Jackson detectives searched the *Kudzu* offices twice. During the search, an FBI agent threatened to kill *Kudzu* staffers. On the morning of October 26, FBI agents again searched the offices. That evening, local police entered the building, held its eight occupants at gunpoint, produced a bag of marijuana, then arrested them. After conflicting police testimony, the eight were released. This intimidation followed the appearance of a series of articles in *Kudzu* concerning the police shooting of students at Jackson state College the previous May. Moreover, in October, *Kudzu* had exposed an FBI provocateur, who had bombed a building at the University of Alabama. A *Kudzu* staff member commented, "The FBI used to be fairly sophisticated, but lately they have broken one of our doors, pointed guns in our faces, told us that 'punks like you don't have any rights,' and threatened to shoot us on the street if they see us with our hands in our pockets."

—Geoffrey Rips

The Central Intelligence Agency, on the other hand, did not rely on a moralistic position to justify action against underground writing and the counterculture. Instead, it saw itself as a highly professional agency whose purpose was to carry out, overtly and covertly, the wishes of the executive branch. Yet, CIA agents soon took on powers that were often illegal and unknown to those they served. The CIA's domestic mail-opening program, which ran from 1952 through 1973, was hidden from Presidents Truman, Eisenhower, Kennedy, and possibly Johnson. So secret were these machinations that not only was the Postmaster General kept in the dark, but even CIA directors John McCone and Admiral William F. Raborn, Jr. claimed ignorance . . .

Even though the "dirty tricks" of the Counter-Intelligence branch began to dominate operations, the agency still regarded its effort as a skilled professional campaign against a political enemy in which questions of public morals or legality were irrelevant. Thus it did not, like the FBI, become histrionic over sex and drugs in the underground. The CIA's public rationale was that the counterculture and its publications were giving comfort and support to the North Vietnamese and the Viet Cong, and that, therefore, its actions against them were a domestic front in the Vietnam war effort.

The CIA, FBI, and military intelligence were not the only conspirators in the manipulation of underground writing. The Special Services Staff and the Intelligence Division of the Internal Revenue Service used their powers to audit tax returns and collect confidential information to harass and spy on allegedly dangerous writers. The Special Services Staff Director, for example, asked the Detroit District Office of the IRS to investigate the Radical Education Project as part of the IRS's participation in "an effort to save the country from dissidents and extremists." At the request of the CIA, the IRS audited Victor Marchetti in 1972, while he was writing a critique of the CIA. It investigated *Ramparts* magazine in 1967, following its publication of an article detailing CIA connections with the National Student Association. Not only useful to the CIA, the IRS also served the Nixon administration as an instrument to stifle dissent. In a 1970 memorandum, a Nixon aide stated: "What we cannot do in a court room via criminal prosecutions to curtail the activities of some of these groups, IRS could do by administrative action."

The National Security Agency, with a high-tech electronic spying apparatus and a "watch list" (compiled with the help of the CIA, FBI, Secret Service, and the Bureau of Narcotics and Dangerous Drugs) had the power to monitor the communications of over 75,000 Americans. The data they gathered illegally went into a vast information storage system, for purposes of future control of free speech . . .

While alternative media were only one aspect of a general social, political, and cultural movement, their importance to a pluralistic counterculture was not lost on entrenched interests. In time, the network of government control was to touch every writer, editor, publisher, printer, and distributor of underground writing. A coast-to-coast juggernaut was mobilized to keep tabs on every American who could be labeled "extremist," "communist," "socialist," "dissident," or sometimes even "liberal." Most small, independent underground publications could not withstand the pressures applied by the various agents of government.

According to the Underground Press Syndicate, there were, in 1971, over 400 underground publications in this country. By 1978, there were only 65, and more than a third of these had been founded after 1973. This extraordinary rate of attrition was largely due to the pitched battle for survival these journals were forced to fight. The UPS reported that sixty per cent of its members had experienced a great deal of government interference, ranging from distribution interruption, customer and printer harassment, to wiretaps, legal costs, infiltration by agents, and even bombings and bomb threats.

By using narcotics and obscenity statutes as a pretext, police found it easy to attack the new media on grounds which reflected a traditional, puritanical morality distinct from any notion of political rights . . .

Street Corner Justice

Preventing distribution was an effective disruption tactic. For the most part, underground papers were sold on the street. By exploiting the vague wording of vagrancy and pornography laws, the police frequently rounded up street vendors. After *The San Diego Free Press* published an investigative report in 1969 exposing a corrupt local businessman, the paper's street sellers were arrested at the rate of two a week. A single round-up brought in twenty-five vendors at one time. In most cases, charges against vendors arrested for loitering were subsequently dismissed. This kind of tactic dissipated staff energy, made it difficult to recruit vendors, and meant lost revenues for the papers. Political activists became wary of selling papers on the street because arrests took time and money away from other projects. The editors of Spokane's *Natural* were arrested on vagrancy charges while trying to sell their paper. In New Orleans, people selling *NOLA Express* were arrested many times, in one case for "carrying a dangerous weapon"—the seller's umbrella. FBI intent to stop distribution of the *Black Panther Party Paper* surfaced in a COINTELPRO memorandum sent by the Newark office to J. Edgar Hoover, proposing that newspapers be sprayed with Skatole, a foul-smelling chemical. The Detroit office sent a similar request to the Director for "a solution capable of duplicating the scent of the most foul-smelling feces available . . . along with a dispenser capable of squirting a narrow stream for a distance of approximately three feet . . ." A flurry of memoranda followed, but the idea was never acted on.

The FBI often used intimidation against distributors as well as journals: simple persuasion worked form time to time, as when the FBI convinced a New York shipper for the *Black Panther Party Paper* to make his rates prohibitive. After a visit by FBI agents, the distributor of the New York-based *Rat* refused to continue doing business with the paper. In their vendetta against *Rat*, the FBI, according to a postal worker, ran a "cover" on the paper's mail, spying on all correspondence the editorial board received. The FBI documents also reveal that the Bureau owned subscription lists of the *East Village Other* and the *Yipster Times* and interviewed many of the subscribers.

When twelve vendors from *NOLA Express* were arrested in a three-month period in 1969, the editors obtained an injunction against further arrests. The paper was banned from college campuses in the area. College authorities across the country banned the campus distribution of much underground journalism: in both Austin, Texas, and Madison, Wisconsin, papers like *The Rag* and *Kaleidoscope* were forbidden on campus. It took a three-judge federal panel to find this ban unconstitutional, ruling, "First Amendment freedoms are not dependent upon the will of an administrator."

Love Not War

Obscenity laws gave the police a tool that appealed to citizens disturbed by turbulent changes in the sexual mores of a large youthful population. While underground papers were describing napalming, bombing, and defoliation in Vietnam and Cambodia as government-sponsored obscenities, police agents were prosecuting alternative journalists for printing four-letter words, "lewd" pictures, or depicting people making love. When the underground press transgressed conventional ideas of public decency, the government exploited the possibilities of clouding the issue of free expression.

Miami, Florida, was the scene of a nefarious campaign against *The Daily Planet*. Its editor was arrested twenty-nine times in 1969 and 1970 for selling obscene literature on the streets. Although he was acquitted twenty-eight times, he still had to pay nearly $93,000 in bail bonds. When poet Allen Ginsberg came to Miami to give a benefit reading for *The Daily Planet*, the police broke up his reading of "Pentagon Exorcism." It took an appeal to the federal courts to prove that the reading was, in fact, constitutionally protected. The court ordered city officials to give *The Daily Planet* the municipal auditorium to complete the interrupted reading of his poem.

In March, 1969, *Open City* in Los Angeles was forced to pay court costs and a $1,000 fine on an obscenity conviction. This paper was later vindicated by a higher court, but the punitive defense fees forced *Open City* out of business. The street vendors of *Kaleidoscope* in Madison, Wisconsin, were repeatedly arrested for selling obscene literature to minors. As reported in the *New York Times*, this was only part of a campaign that included the publisher's arrest for obscenity, an editor's arrest for refusing to reveal sources, and the fire-bombing of the offices of the paper and an editor's car.

After one newsstand in New York City was fined for selling the *East Village Other*, which allegedly contained obscentiy, other newsstands and bookstores were afraid to carry the paper. After the newspaper had successfully won state and local obscenity cases in federal court, an entire printing of *Great Speckled Bird* of Atlanta was seized by the U.S. Postal Service in 1972 for printing abortion referral information. The same abortion advertisements had appeared in the *New York Times*. In one case, authorities had prosecuted *Great Speckled Bird* under an Atlanta city ordinance prohibiting the "use of any derogatory words relating to the methods of sexual intercourse with relatives or strangers."

Generally, alternative presses won legal battles against government agencies. However, it often took years for judgments to be handed down, and the expenses of appealing often meant that the newspaper couldn't survive, even if it won its case . . .

Hoping to eliminate the alternative media, the city of Milwaukee passed a tough, new obscenity law. It was immediately used to arrest John Kois, the editor of *Kaleidoscope*. He was fined $2,000 and given two years probation. Probation was an indirect means of censorship because the writer or editor became liable for any printed material that the court might construe as a probation violation.

A Milwaukee COINTELPRO memo of February 14, 1969, outlined how the FBI suggested exposing two teachers at the University of Wisconsin, Milwaukee, for writing articles in a paper which the agency called "extremely pornographic in nature." The FBI proposed arousing public outrage for "permitting instructors at that school to engage in this type of activity." The editor, publisher, and cartoonist at the University of Hartford *Liberated Press* were all arrested for violating a Connecticut obscenity statute after they published a caricature of Nixon as a large, erect [middle] finger.

Police often used charges of pornography or obscenity to dismantle an entire publishing operation. In Dallas, the vice squad raided the offfice of *Dallas Notes* twice in the fall of 1968. The publisher was arrested, and two editors were intimidated into quitting. Armed with search warrants for "pornography," the police confiscated typewriters, cameras, darkroom and graphic equipment, business records, a desk, a drafting table, and all the copy for the next issue. The police never had to demonstrate how a drafting table could be considered "pornographic." . . .

Sabotage of News Services

The FBI and its allies also concentrated on underground news services. COINTELPRO documents reveal that the FBI constantly spied on the Underground Press Syndicate and the Liberation News Service, which sent information bulletins and news stories with a radical perspective to subscribing journals. The FBI directed the IRS to investigate the tax records of Liberation News Service . . .

The Alternative Press Syndicate (formerly the Underground Press Syndicate), an underground information and advertising clearing-house, was another victim of government suppression. It helped establish new papers, organized the defense of member papers against government action, and maintained an extensive library of underground literature. In 1969, UPS served a combined readership of twenty million. Cindy Ornstein and Thomas Forcade, Project Coordinator for UPS, were under constant surveillance. They were arrested while covering the 1972 Miami convention. In 1969, the Phoenix office of UPS, run by Forcade and *Orpheus* magazine, was infiltrated by a narcotics agent, who worked on the staff for six months. After he quit, local police raided the office with a warrant for illegal drugs. A thorough search, however, failed to turn up any drugs. In the course of the search, the police stole UPS subscription lists, destroyed files, and damaged the UPS library. Among the destroyed files were the legal records from underground papers which were being given legal aid by the UPS. When Forcade and UPS moved to New York, they continued to be harassed by FBI agents. On one occasion, Cindy Ornstein was arrested for violating a firearms act, and UPS material was confiscated in the process.

In 1970 after repeated disruptions by government agencies, Thomas Forcade published a passionate open letter to the President's Commission on Obscenity and Pornography, to which he added a list of forty-five underground papers that had been victims of censorship.

Intimidation of Printers

Many underground newspapers had difficulty finding a willing printer. Local political pressure, the threat of boycotts by advertisers and customers, and the printer's own political orientation often resulted in a refusal to do business with underground newspapers. In some cases, printers' unions dictated that members could not handle the work of underground publications. There is evidence that the FBI was behind some of these obstructions. *Orpheus* was refused by thirty printers; the *East Village Other* and *Rat* were turned down by countless printers on the East Coast. A New Jersey printer who originally had an agreement with *Rat* later reneged after the state's attorney general threatened prosecution for obscenity. Some papers were forced to cross state lines to find a printer. A printer agreed to accept the *Seattle Helix* only if the work was done secretly. After a visit from the FBI, the regular printer of the *Los Angeles Free Press* refused to continue. *The Rag* was turned down by several print shops in Austin. One printer who did accept its business delivered an issue with blank pages and black boxes masking sections he thought were obscene. COINTELPRO documents later revealed that at least one of *The Rag's* printers was persuaded to stop printing the paper after a visit by San Antonio FBI agents. A memorandum of October 13, 1970, from the Detroit FBI office proposed "the disruption of the physical plant of the Radical Education Project," a publisher of New Left documents.

In Port Washington, Wisconsin, William F. Schanen, Jr., of the *Ozaukee Press* took on the publication of dozens of midwestern underground newspapers, refusing to comply with FBI and local advertiser demands that he keep away from allegedly subversive projects. He lost nearly $200,000 per year in printing business and advertising in his three establishment papers because he brought out *Kaleidoscope* and other alternative papers. A local industrialist and the American Legion retaliated by leading a boycott of Schanen's papers and of his advertisers. By 1970, Schanen was printing papers from as far off as Omaha, indicating the difficulty these papers had in securing printers . . .

The FBI also approached advertisers and investigated progressives who provided financial backing for underground papers. The agency wrote spurious letters when it was convenient. In 1969, the Detroit FBI office sent a letter to local advertisers signed "Disgusted Taxpayer and Patron" objecting to the content of one paper. In December 1970, the FBI in Alabama sent an anonymous letter to a university administrator and threatened to expose two instructors who were providing money for a student counterculture newspaper. This action was intended to make the journal "fold and cease publication," to "eliminate what voice the New Left has in the area." The two instructors were put on probation.

Housing Interference

COINTELPRO memoranda also reveal that the FBI pressured landlords to evict journalist tenants. The Los Angeles FBI field office reported its measures to get two New Left papers evicted in 1968. The same year, in New York, the FBI persuaded the landlord of *Rat* to double the office rent, forcing the paper to move. In Austin, Texas, the city condemned *whatever* building *The Rag* rented for its office. Fearing condemnation, landlords refused to rent to the paper . . .

Continued Violations of Human Rights

A state-of-siege atmosphere prevailed in many alternative newspaper offices. In 1968, the St. Louis *Daily Flash* printed a series of articles critical of police chief Walter Zinn. An undercover police officer was assigned to infiltrate the *Flash*. A short time later the police agent arrested an editor, Pete Rothchild, for suspected possession of marijuana. The Ann Arbor *Argus* ceased publication in 1970 when the entire staff was arrested on charges of drug possession, following an editor's arrest on an obscenity charge. The two-year-old paper had a circulation of 15,000. The editors of *Rat* and the Minneapolis *Free Press* were arrested, the *Free Press* editor sentenced to five years in prison for the possession of marijuana. After being arrested twice on pornography charges, then convicted for inciting riot, Stoney Burns, art director and founder of *Iconoclast*, was sentenced in Dallas, in 1972, to ten years and one day in prison for the possession of less than one-tenth of an ounce of marijuana. The extra day in the sentence prevented eligibility for parole. Within a year, public protest freed editor Burns.

Perhaps the best known case in which drug laws were used to silence radical writing was that of John Sinclair and the Artists' Workshop in Detroit . . .

Fifty-six members of the workshop, including Sinclair, were arrested on testimony by two undercover narcotics agents who had infiltrated the Workshop. The charges against most Workshop members were dropped. Sinclair, however, was found guilty of possessing two joints' worth of marijuana. Although his arrest was protested by many writers and literary groups, including PEN American Center, he was sentenced to ten years imprisonment, the longest term ever given in Michigan for a similar offense. He was denied bail during the appeals process. At the time of his imprisonment, Sinclair was editor of the *Sun*, a writer for the Ann Arbor *Argus* and *Fifth Estate*, minister of information of the White Panther Party, and was a widely published poet.

Stoney Burns, editor of *Dallas Notes*, was charged with inciting a riot after his arrest in 1970 during a confrontation between young people and the police in a Dallas park. Shouting, "There's the one we want, right there," Dallas policemen grabbed Burns, clubbed him, and took him to jail. The riot charge was later changed to "interfering with an officer during a civil disturbance." Burns was convicted and sentenced to three years. This was not the first time Dallas police had clashed with the editor. In two earlier raids, police had confiscated *Dallas*

Notes' property. Incoming mail addressed to staff members was often marked "Opened by mistake by U.S. Marshal's Office." *Dallas Notes* was banned on the Southern Methodist University campus, and students at North Texas State University in Denton were arrested for distributing an election issue. Before raiding *Dallas Notes*, police had Southwestern Bell Telephone disconnect the telephones. The paper's offices were twice attacked by organized vigilantes, who destroyed typewriters and printing equipment. At least three times shots were fired at Stoney Burns' car. Dallas police repeatedly stopped and searched automobiles owned by the workers. A Fort Worth man told Burns he had been hired to assault Burns physically. In view of the fact that Burns was later sentenced to ten years imprisonment for a minor drug offense, the charge of terrorist activity—inciting riot—proved to be just one of several tactics used to stop him and *Dallas Notes*. In filing suit on Burns' behalf, the Dallas Civil Liberties Union charged that ". . . the conduct on the part of the Dallas police is part of a conspiracy having as its object prohibiting the expression of ideas that are alien to the defendants, and having as its ultimate goal the abolition of *Dallas Notes*."

The persistent persecution of Burns stemmed in part from Burns' 1967 investigative report in *Dallas Notes* about Texas Congressman Joe Pool's arrest for drunken driving, after his car hit a carload of soldiers at a red light. Pool was released and the arrest records destroyed after police realized who Pool was. The story did not appear in the big Dallas daily newspapers. In fact, the Dallas *Morning News* and *Times Herald* responded to the *Dallas Notes* report by reporting Pool's statement that the underground newspapers would "slander and libel everyone who opposes these traitors [the underground press] in their attempts to destroy American government." COINTELPRO documents petitioned by the Underground Press Syndicate reveal that Pool, a member of the House UnAmerican Activities committee, called for an investigation of underground newspapers. These official records . . . state that Pool "has already made a major plank of his re-election campaign in Dallas the harassment of 'Notes from Underground' (*Dallas Notes*)."

Articles exposing wrongdoing by political officials triggered attacks on underground newspapers in Philadelphia, including the use of terrorist charges against them. In 1968, after publishing several articles critical of the Philadelphia Police Department and it commissioner, Frank Rizzo, the *Distant Drummer* was charged by Rizzo with solicitation to commit murder. The District Attorney refused to prosecute, claiming that printing these articles did not constitute a crime. When the Philadelphia *Free Press* published damaging information about Rizzo and the police department, Rizzo vowed to destroy the *Free Press* just as he had the local Students for a Democratic Society (SDS) and the Student Nonviolent Coordinating Committee (SNCC). Between February and August, 1970, the Philadelphia Police Department assaulted one *Free Press* staff member, held several others in detention without charge, searched four staff members' homes without warrants, broke into their locked cars, confiscated political literature on narcotics warrants, and opened mail. At least six police cars tailed

Free Press staff members. In addition, police agents visited employers, advertisers, and the paper's printer. As a result, one staff member lost his outside job, the paper's printer refused to continue, and many advertisers withdrew their business. On July 28, 1970, the Philadelphia *Evening Bulletin* ran a major story on the *Free Press*, calling staff members "violent" and "hardcore revolutionaries." Material for the article came from Philadelphia police and FBI files and from Selective Service records. The story gave confidential financial, family, and employment information about people who worked for the *Free Press* and attempted to link them with Weather Underground bomb factories and the Cuban government. This portrayal of the *Free Press* as an advocate of violence and murder threatened to drive the paper out of business. More people were fired from their regular jobs, and because no new advertisers replaced those lost, the paper's free distribution was jeopardized . . .

Police harassment of underground newspapers certainly encouraged groups intent on carrying out their own vendettas. These groups often assumed that their actions would either be condoned by the local police or, at the very least, that they would not be prosecuted. In fact, there were very few arrests made in connection with attacks on underground newspapers. When offices were firebombed, officials rarely intervened to protect the victims or to apprehend the perpetrators.

When the Los Angeles *Free Press* was bombed three times, police made no effort to investigate the crime. While *Dallas Notes* was under heavy police surveillance, it was raided twice by right wing groups. In Houston, *Space City News* was bombed in 1969 during a systematic campaign of violence against white political activists and black liberation groups in the area. The Ku Klux Klan was believed to be responsible for the bombing. The Houston Police Department conducted only lax, inconclusive investigations of the bombings and shootings. Ironically, the same police agencies were accusing left progressive groups of engaging in "terrorist" activities and subverting American "law and order." In fact, much of the right wing terror was generated by FBI provocateurs working in groups like the Ku Klux Klan.

Information released since 1970 reveals that the Chicago Police's Red Squad also worked in close cooperation with the Army's 113th Military Intelligence Group. The Red Squad's accomplices in the Legion of Justice received money, tear gas, mace, and electronic surveillance equipment from the 113th. Several times, material stolen in Legion burglaries found its way to the Military Intelligence Group. This included defense documents stolen from the attorneys in the Chicago Conspiracy trial. Army agents acted as observers in that burglary. Chicago police, in testimony before the Senate Committee on Intelligence, disclosed that a fire had destroyed Red Squad files, housed in police headquarters, during a probe of that intelligence unit. The CIA (through the Law Enforcement Intelligence Unit) also worked with the Chicago Red Squad and the Legion of Justice. The CIA and the Chicago Red Squad exchanged surveillance information through LEIU. In addition, the CIA trained spies for the LEIU. A CIA memorandum of February 8, 1973, listed some of the briefings and training seminars held for LEIU agents. Between October 6 and October 8, 1967, Chicago police participated in "demonstrations of explosive devices, an exhibit of foreign weaponry, air operations, and paramilitary displays . . ." The CIA trained them in "surreptitious and nonsurreptitious entry" and in electronic surveillance. In several instances, the CIA provided the police departments with the equipment required for these operations.

The Milwaukee and Madison *Kaleidoscope*, which together had a circulation of 30,000, were the objects of violent attacks that seem related to simultaneous legal prosecution. An FBI COINTELPRO memorandum of February 14, 1969, proves that the Milwaukee *Kaleidoscope* was under FBI surveillance. While editor John Kois was on probation in the late 60s for his obscenity conviction, his car was bombed and shot at. The newspaper office also was bombed and its windows shattered by gunfire. *Kaleidoscope*, more than other alternative journals, seems to have been persecuted more for exercising normal press freedoms than for the content of the material printed. Photographer Gary Ballsieper was arrested four times for disorderly conduct while taking pictures for the journal. He and Kois were arrested in Chicago covering the antidraft trial of the Chicgo 15. They were jailed with the defendants and temporarily charged with conspiring in their case . . . In May, 1972, Ron Ridenour, of the Los Angeles *Free Press*, was arrested while covering an anti-war demonstratin in front of CREEP (Committee to Re-elect the President) headquarters. Two police officers pushed Ron Kovic, a paraplegic Vietnam veteran, from his wheelchair and began to beat him. When Ridenour shot pictures of the incident, from fifteen feet away, the police confiscated his camera and arrested him for unlawful assembly and interfering with a police officer. He was convicted and sentenced to a year in jail. When his camera was returned, the film had been exposed.

In 1971, Tom Miller, a freelance writer for the Underground Press Syndicate, *Rolling Stone*, and other journals, was subpoenaed by a federal grand jury to testify in its Tucson hearings on the Weather Underground. The Justice Department refused to allow Miller the exemption customarily allowed reporters because he was a freelance writer and an activist. Before this issue could be resolved, the original grand jury disbanded . . .

The U.S. government saw the Black Panther Party as the center of black liberation struggles in the country, and the FBI kept it under constant surveillance. It was a prime target of COINTELPRO operations; documents show that 233 of 295 authorized COINTELPRO actions against black groups were directed against the Panthers. Among the crimes committed by the government in dealing with the Party were spying, wiretaps, forged defamatory letters, disruptions ·of meetings, provocation of dissension, and gang wars . . .

The *Black Panther Party Paper* was harassed by the government because it was the Party's chief means of circulating information and bringing in income. The *Paper's* salespeople were arrested repeatedly by Buffalo police for violating a state criminal-anarchy statute. The FBI forged anonymous letters and sent them to school officials protesting the presence of the paper in the library and classrooms. In 1969, a federal grand jury ordered Sherry Bursey and Brenda Joyce Presley, Panther newspaper staff members, to disclose confidential information about the management of the newspaper. The two refused, and [their refusals] were later upheld by an appeals court. In 1970, a House subcommittee investigating the Black Panthers asked Frank B. Jones, a former managing editor of the paper, to furnish details about circulation, distribution and finances.

Not only was the Black Panther Party destroyed by government agents, but underground papers were not allowed access to report the trial of Party members in New Haven in 1971. A group of writers formed an Ad Hoc Committee for a Public Trial to protest their being denied access to the trial by a "conspiracy" of the Nixon administration, the Federal Bureau of Investigation and the State of Connecticut.

Silencing the Press in San Diego

A classic example of government efforts to muzzle an underground newspaper is the case of the San Diego *Free Press and Street Journal*, founded in 1968 by The People's Commune. The commune also operated a retail store, Peoples' Dry Goods, which sold works by local artists and craftspeople, published handbooks and pamphlets, supplied office space to the Movement for a Democratic Military, and provided five-cent dinners for San Diego citizens in need. All this was going on in a community dominated by a large U.S. Navy presence, a strong John Birch Society, two daily papers owned by conservative James S. Copley, and a business community headed by financier D. Arnholdt Smith, a major fundraiser for Richard Nixon and Ronald Reagan.

The *Street Journal's* troubles began after one of the first issues exposed the corrupt, Mafia-related deals of a prominent businessman, who was later imprisoned for his crimes. In October, 1969, the newspaper picked up a story reported in the *Wall Street Journal* (but unreported in the Copley papers) concerning the large profits made by D. Arnholdt Smith at the expense of other stockholders in transactions with public companies he directed. Smith was reported to have reacted to the *Street Journal's* story by saying, "I wish there was some way to bomb them clear to the other side of the Coronados." Soon afterward, the bombing began.

A suit filed by the *Street Journal* and the Peoples's Commune in 1970 against the San Diego Police Department, the City of San Diego, and officers of both lists attacks on the newspaper between November 1, 1969, and February 24, 1970.

In a single month, twenty street vendors were arrested for "obstructing the sidewalk." Vendors of other publications, in the same locations, were not arrested. In December, 1969, a municipal court ruled the obstruction ordinance to be unconstitutional, but police continued to make arrests on the same charge. On November 18, 1969, bullets were shot through the windows of the paper's editorial offices. The incident was reported to the police, but they took [minimal] action on it. On November 23, five San Diego squad cars surrounded the offices of the paper and police searched the office twice without a warrant, arresting seven members of the Peoples' Commune on various charges. The charges were later dropped.

On November 29, 1969, the glass door to the *Street Journal's* editorial office was smashed and 2,500 copies of the current edition stolen. This occurred during the period San Diego police were keeping watch on the commune. When staff formally reported the incident, the police once again did not investigate. On December 1, the *Street Journal's* landlord received telephone calls demanding the paper's eviction. Through this period, commune members and other tenants of the building received bomb threats. The police were informed and did not investigate. The newspaper was forced to find new offices and reached an agreement with Billy Joe Reeves. On December 14, a San Diego police officer asked Reeves to cancel the lease as "a personal favor." Reeves refused but he agreed two weeks later after being arrested on a murder charge. He was detained for an hour, and his offices were searched. Commune members later learned that the murder suspect being sought was five feet, eight inches tall, weighing 175 pounds, while Reeves was five feet, three inches tall, and weighed 114 pounds.

On December 11, 1969, two police officers, without a search warrant or consent, entered and searched the *Street Journal* and arrested a friend of the commune members on suspicion of burglary. The victim was handcuffed and taken away, then released without being booked. On December 25, hood-lums invaded the editorial offices, stole business and subscription records, and destroyed expensive typesetting equipment. The police were informed and did not investigate. On January 3, 1970, a car belonging to a *Street Journal* writer was fire-bombed. When informed, the police threatened to impound the car at the paper's expense if it were not removed from the street. On January 9, police impounded another automobile, owned by a commune member and legally parked, for remaining in the same location for seventy-two hours. The day before, a driver of that same car had received a ticket for a traffic violation in another part of San Diego. The next day a *Street Journal* staffer got a ticket for an invalid driver's license, even though he had, in fact, shown the officer a valid license. On January 15, 1970, six police officers and four United States Navy Shore Patrolmen entered the newspapers's premises without a search warrant or consent. They interrogated people from the commune, opened envelopes, files, and address books, copied information, confiscated personal property, and threatened physical violence if the victims attempted to communicate with a lawyer. On January 6 and 15, street sellers were arrested for violating non-existent laws. On January 17, a commune member, just discharged from the Navy, was arrested for wearing a military jacket. He was held for fourteen hours and interrogated before charges were dropped. On January 18 and 25, three vendors were arrested for littering and held on $1,500 bail. On February 4, San Diego police and Shore Patrolmen again illegally searched newspaper offices and arrested staff members on phony charges, later dropped. On February 8, they attacked the Peoples' Commune again, threatening residents and searching the premises. They smashed in the door and seized and dragged one person outside, though he was never accused of wrongdoing. Throughout the period of harassment, police routinely confiscated coin-operated vending machines owned by the *Street Journal* and held them at the police department.

The *Street Journal's* suit ends with the charge: "During the latter part of 1969 and 1970 to date, plaintiffs are informed and believe and therefore allege that officers of the said San Diego Police Department have kept plaintiffs under almost constant surveillance, in violation of plaintiff's rights of privacy, and that, included in such surveillance have been the use of wiretaps, hidden microphones, and infrared photography, and that said surveillance has been conducted without any warrants or orders of the courts, or any reasonable, legal or probable cause whatsoever."

Harassment did not end when the lawsuit was filed. The searches continued, automobile tires were slashed, and the windows of stores selling the paper were smashed. A federal grand jury was convened in an attempt to indict the *Street Journal* on charges of "criminal syndicalism," a law used to crush organization and publication by the Industrial Workers of the World in San Diego in 1919. The law had been declared unconstitutional in 1950. Finally, the pressure of constant surveillance and intimidation forced the *Street Journal* to close down. It took nearly a year for the suit filed by the paper to be heard, by which time most of the plaintiffs had moved, and the suit was dropped.

Having annihilated the *Street Journal*, the San Diego right-wing coalition then turned to the San Diego *Door*. When it followed the path of the *Street Journal*, it too was attacked. Cars were firebombed, and office windows shot out. On one occasion, arsonists set the newspaper's office on fire, destroying typesetting equipment and almost killing a staff member. During this period, the two established daily newspapers in San Diego made almost no mention of the attacks on underground papers.

On June 21, 1971, a movie theatre showing X-rated movies was bombed while two San Diego police officers were sitting in the audience. An investigation found William Francis Yakopek to be the bomber and a member of the Secret Army Organization (SAO), the militant wing of the Minutemen, a far-right paramilitary group. The investigation also exposed Howard Berry Godfrey as a leader of the SAO and an FBI informant. Subsequently, Godfrey was called on to testify before the Senate Select Committee on Intelligence concerning the relationships among the SAO, the FBI, and the San Diego Police Department (SDPD). Godfrey told how the FBI and SDPD organized, trained, and equipped the Minutemen and SAO. Godfrey said he instructed the SAO in guerrilla warfare, locksmithing, propaganda techniques, and security and intelligence procedures. He gave information to the FBI in exchange for funds for SAO activities. Godfrey admitted that his group was responsible for firing on the *Street Journal* offices, smashing the windows of a store selling the *Street Journal* and *Door*, and stealing 2,500 copies of the *Journal*. In collaboration with a San Diego police officer who had infiltrated the *Street Journal* staff, the SAO destroyed the typesetting equipment and stole the newspapers's records.

Information released over the years provides a disturbing picture of a coordinated effort to silence the *Street Journal* and other underground publications.

In San Diego, local business leaders, the city police force, the district attorney, the U.S. Navy, the FBI and a paramilitary group all conspired against the constitutional rights of the free press. Long before this conspiracy was brought to light, however, its object had been accomplished.

Bibliography

Abrams, Floyd, "The Pentagon Papers a Decade Later," *The New York Times Magazine*; June 1981.

Atkins, Jeanni; Belvel J. Boyd, *Classification Reexamined*, Freedom of Information Center (Columbia, Mo.), January 1975.

"After the Pentagon Papers: The First Amendment on Trial," (special section), *Columbia Journalism Review*; September-October 1971.

Antieau, Chester, "'Clear and Present Danger'—Its Meaning and Significance," *Notre Dame Lawyer*, 1950.

Auerbach, Carl A., "The Communist Control Act of 1954: A Proposed Legal-Political Theory of Free Speech," *University of Chicago Law Review*, 1956.

Bagdikian, Ben H., "A Most Insidious Case," *The Quill*; June 1979.

Bernstein, Carl, "The CIA and the Media," *Rolling Stone*; October 20, 1977.

Burkett, Warren, "The Progressive Case Revisited," *The Quill*; September 1979.

"CIA Wins Case Against Snepp But Damages Are Not Awarded," *FOI Digest*, March-April 1979.

Cohen, Bernard C., *The Press and Foreign Policy*, Princeton University Press (Princeton, N.J.), 1957.

Committee on the Judiciary, *Army Surveillance of Civilians*, U.S. Government Printing Office (Washington, D.C.), February and March 1971.

"Court Upholds Prior Restraint Law; Indiana Paper Challenges on Appeal," *FOI Digest*, September-October 1983.

Frank, L.J., "U.S. Navy v. The Chicago Tribune," *Historian*; February 1980.

Frankel, Max, "The State Secrets Myth," *Columbia Journalism Review*; September-October 1971.

Feld, Barbra, "Just Two Deletions and Let The Progressive Publish," *The Quill*; June 1979.

Florence, William G.; Ruth Mathews, *Executive Secrecy: Two Perspectives*, Freedeom of Information Center (Columbia, Mo.), April 1975.

"Former CIA Analyst Ordered to Submit Magazine Articles for Agency Review," *FOI Digest*, September-October 1978.

Friedman, Robert, "The United States v. The Progressive," *Columbia Journalism Review*; July-August 1979.

Glessing, Robert J., *The Underground Press in America*, Indiana University Press (Bloomington, Ind.), 1970.

Goulding, Phil G., *Confirm or Deny: Informing the Public on National Security*, Harper & Row (New York, N.Y.), 1970.

Guback, Thomas H., "General Sherman's War on the Press," *Journalism Quarterly*; Spring 1969.

Hunter, Howard O., "Toward a Better Understanding of the Prior Restraint Doctrine: A Reply to Professor Mayton." *Cornell Law Review*, (1982).

"Justice Department Files Suit Against Ex-CIA Agent Who Broke Security Oath," *FOI Digest*, March-April 1978.

Kessler, Lauren, *Against the Grain: The Dissident Press in America*, Sage (Beverly Hills, Calif.), 1984.

Knoll, Erwin, "If . . ." *The Quill*; June 1979. "La. Paper Files For Review in Cases Involving Prior Restraint, *FOI Digest*," May-June 1973.

Lewis, Jerome X., "Freedom of Speech—an Examination of the Civilian Test for Constitutionality and its Application to the Military," *Military Law Review*, July 1968.

Medow, Jonathan, "The First Amendment and the Secrecy State: *Snepp* v. *United States*" *University of Pennsylvania Law Review*.

Merrill, John C., *Global Journalism*, Longman (New York, N.Y.), 1983.

McGaffin, W.C.; Erwin Kroll, *Anything But the Truth*, G.P. Putnam's Sons (New York, N.Y.), 1968.

Moffett, Meri West, "Open Secrets: Protecting the Identity of the CIA's Intelligence Gatherers in a First Amendment Society." *Hastings Law Journal*.

Morland, Howard, "The H-Bomb Secret; How We Got It, Why We're Telling It," *The Progressive*; November 1979.

Moyer, Homer E., *Justice and the Military*, Public Law Education Institution (Washington, D.C.), 1972.

"Paper is Convicted for Revealing Judges Being Investigated by State," *FOI Digest*, January-February 1976.

"Prior Restraint Permissible in Some Cases, Court Rules," *FOI Digest*, May-June 1975.

Reilly, Thomas, "Newspaper Supression During Mexican-American War," *Journalism Quarterly*, Summer 1977.

Relyea, Harold C., *The Evolution of Government Information Security Classification Policy: A Brief Overview*, 1775-1973, Library of Congress (Washington, D.C.), 1974.

Rourke, Francis E., *Secrecy and Publicity: Dilemmas of Democracy*, The Johns Hopkins Press (Baltimore, Md.), 1961.

Rosenthal, A.M., "Why We Published," *Columbia Journalism Review*, September-October 1971.

Stevens, Jean, *Classification: Threat to Democracy*, Freedom of Information Center (Columbia, Mo.), October 1971.

Stohl, Michael and George A. Lopez (eds.), *The State as Terrorist: The Dyanamics of Government Violence and Repression*, Greenwood Press (Westport, Conn.), 1984.

Stone, Jeremy, "Giving Away the Secret of the First Amendment," *The Quill*, June 1979.

Strong, Frank P., "Fifty Years of Clear and Present Danger;" *Supreme Court Review*, 1969.

"Supreme Court Denies Hearing on Army Restraint of GI Paper," *FOI Digest*, November-December 1972.

Ungar, Sanford J., *The Papers and the Papers: An Account of Legal and Political Battle Over the Pentagon Papers*, Dutton (New York, N.Y.), 1972.

Vagts, Detlev F., "Free Speech in the Armed Forces," *Columbia Law Review*, February 1957.

Whalen, Charles W., Jr., *Your Right to Know*, Random House (New York, N.Y.), 1973.

Wiggins, James Russell, *Freedom or Secrecy*, Oxford University Press (Oxford, England), 1964.

Williams, Allen, Jr., *Tolerance of Nonconformity*, Jossey-Bass (San Francisco, Calif.), 1978.

Wilson, Quintus, *A Study and Evaluation of the Military Censorship During the Civil War*, master's thesis, University of Minnesota, 1945.

Wulf, Melvin L., "Commentary: A Soldier's First Amendment Rights: The Act of Formally Granting and Practically Suppressing," *Wayne Law Review*, March-April 1972.

Zenger, Sanford J., *The Papers and the Papers*, Dutton (New York, N.Y.), 1972.

Chapter 37

Licensing:
Improving the Profession,
Destroying Their Freedom

In almost every country of the world, printers and journalists have found guilds to improve their working conditions and to exchange knowledge of their profession. Some guilds were informal, with limited membership; some guilds were established and controlled by the state. The first guild in England, the Stationers Company, was formed about 1357, and consisted entirely of writers. Later, booksellers and printers were admitted to membership. In 1555, Queen Mary brought the Stationers Company under further state control by "allowing" it to establish rules of conduct to "improve" the profession and prevent licentiousness, and to determine qualifications for membership. Because membership was required in order for a printer to open a shop, the Stationers Company of existing printers could establish a stateapproved monopoly, excluding those who could threaten them financially-or who could threaten the state. It was not necessary for Mary to keep the Stationers Company under her direct control-the Stationers Company itself, in exchange for its privileges, which it thought were merely standards for the improvement of its profession, did nothing to upset the crown, while believing it was independent. Under the reign of Queen Elizabeth I, the benefits and responsibilities of the twenty members of the Stationers Company increased, while the noose tightened around the freedom of the press.

Contemporary Licensing

Thirteen Latin American countries have established *collegios*, associations of journalists. The purpose of the *collegio* is to improve the working conditions of journalists, advance the interests of the journalism profession, while also establishing standards for membership, and codes of conduct. All journalists must be members of the *collegio*. Membership usually requires graduation from an accredited school of journalism-usually the only accepted schools are within the country issuing the license; those who graduate from non-national schools (e.g., a school in the United States) may still be licensed if they pass certain examinations. As such, they are little different from various non-journalistic professionsal and vocational licensing agencies within the United States which

465

require graduation from approved schools and passing examinations prior to licensing. American licensing boards, composed primarily of members of that profession or vocation, have frequently come under attack for representing only "establishment" interests. For example, most state licensing boards for lawyers are attacked for including large sections on corporate and civil law, but not much on consumer law; thus, because law schools create those programs which have the greatest possibility of guaranteeing their students the knowledge to pass bar exams, many areas are emphasized, certain areas neglected. It is no different in *collegios*—what is important is what the establishment says is important. The degree of press freedom in countries with *collegios* is dependent upon the amount of freedom the state gives the *collegio*. The most liberal policies appear to be in Ecuador and Venzuela; the most oppressive appear to be in Bolivia, Costa Rico, Haiti, and Panama. Other Latin American countries with *collegios* are Chili (a dictatorship, but with membership voluntary; most journalists are members), Colombia, Dominican Republic, Guatamala (as of late 1985), Honduras, and Peru. Brazil has the *syndicato*, a variation of the *collegio*. The *syndicato* is more of a labor union; however, the state has intervened at times, especially when Brazil was under a military dictatorship.

Like in renaissance England, it makes little difference if the state has a direct hand in imposing its philosophies—as long as it has that authority to create agencies that will do its work.

The collegios are unique to the Latin American countries, but numerous other countries have licensing, each one with its own variations. In October 1949, under Mao TseTung, China required the registration of all newspapers. Those that were determined to be "politically unacceptable" were denied permits; as a result, several hundred non-Communist newspapers were terminated. In Taiwan, which claims it is for freedom and that the People's Republic of China is for oppression, the press must be registered, each newspaper, periodical, radio or television station required not to discuss the People's Republic of China favorably; forfeiture of registration and criminal penalties are attached to those who do. In Malyasia, the government can revoke or refuse to renew or to revoke the required annual license if the reporter has stirred "community unrest." In Communist countries, however, there is no licensing; since all media are owned by the state, and since all reporters are government employees, there is no need to license.

Licensing: American Style

Every now and then, a civic official, politician, member of a licensed profession, or even a journalist, will propose licensing for the United States. The usual reasons for wanting licensing are to improve the quality of the press and "benefit" journalism by giving it professional status.

In 1971, U.S. Sen. Jack Miller, Iowa, called for examinations of all journalists prior to allowing them to practice their profession:

A reporter or . . . editor whose words can inform or misinform thousands of people has no examination to take. He can be hired . . .

without even having to read . . . the canons of journalism . . . Why shouldn't he have to pass an examination by his peers to demonstrate his capability? Why shouldn't he have to live up to the canons of ethics of his profession? Why shouldn't he be subject to having his privilege . . . to practice his profession revoked for unethical conduct?

Robert K. Schwartz also came out for licensing of journalists, presenting an argument similar to those for establishing the *collegios*-or any of a hundred different kinds of licensing boards already functioning in the United States:

I suggest that a national journalism association be formed . . . which would designate those colleges qualified to teach "professional" journalism. The association would take an active role in setting up curriculums and final examinations. Once established, the association would be the mentor and monitor of journalism performance and ethics. Graduates would have to serve one-year interships on newspapers determined by the journalism schools. Journalists would be licensed only after satisfactory completion of both the schooling and the internship.

Before being licensed, the thousands of already-established journalists today, regardless of academic background and experience, would still have to successfully pass the same examinations, including any "character" test the national journalism association might require. Enforcement of the licensing . . . should come from a state or federal agency whose statutory power is limited solely and simply to making sure that anyone engaged by any newspaper of general circulation in the writing, editing, or managing of news be licensed. The agency would in no way have any authority to regulate news.

Yet if all this were done, it would still be only half the solution to publishing fully responsible newspapers. Our typical new journalist, like the starting physician, would be tremendously proud of the license for which he worked so hard to earn; . . . his commitment to professionalism would be even more reinforced in him than it is generally in today's journalism school graduate. Quite naturally, he wouldn't stay long with any publisher whose newspaper was self-serving or who forced him to compromise his journalism code. This weakness among publishers is far too common among newspapers today; it forces good journalists to abort their career, leaving many publishers with inferior journalists who are also willing to compromise or who don't know the difference.

If Schwartz was just another citizen upset with the modern licentiousness of the press, his words would have been given little credence, probably filed then forgotten, among journalists. However, Schwartz had been a journalist for nineteen years, working for the Chicago City News Bureau (CNB), on daily newspaper in Texas, Arkansas, and Alaska, as managing editor of community newspapers near Chicago, and, at the time of his statement, as executive editor of the Des Plaines Publishing Company, publisher of several suburban newspapers near Chicago. In 1970, the *Park Ridge* (Ill.) *Herald*, of which he was managing editor, was named first place award winner for general excellence, and winner of the Loomis Trophy for outstanding editorial achievement from the Illinois Press Association. The profession did listen to him, recovered from the shock of a journalist advocating licensing, then dismissed Schwartz's arguments as "nonrepresentative" of the profession.

During the next few years, a number of journalists spoke out against licensing. One of the strongest arguments against licensing was given by John C. Merrill at the October 12, 1978, meeting of the Inter-American Press Association. Merrill, one of the nation's leading media scholars, and a libertarian who believes there must be absolutely no governmental controls in the media, outlined several arguments opposing licensing:

> . . . As dangerous as I see licensing . . . to be, I realize that authoritarian governments can control the press without such professional bodies if they want to. However, licensing and the drift toward professionalization may well add another facet to press control, giving governments a more subtle way to control the press and to escape taking responsibility for it. The specific objections to licensing are:
>
> (1) Licensing would exclude many writers from participation in journalism, thereby causing a richness and diversity to disappear;
>
> (2) Licensing would grant only a small elite group of journalists press freedom, thereby revoking the spirit of a libertarian press;
>
> (3) Licensing would sooner or later grant the government an entre into the business of journalism, for in order to make licensing work, non-licensed journalists who practiced would be taken to court; this implies legal action which in turn implies legislative procedure which implies *Government*;
>
> (4) Licensing would lead to a restriction of pluralism of journalists and points of view. The professional association can do much to foster restriction, and it should be remembered that the danger to press freedom does not come only from government;
>
> (5) Licensing might result in a scarcity of journalists in many countries-if only graduates from schools of journalism are free to practice; . . .
>
> (6) Licensing would cause a press system to become ever more conformist and monolithic-with recalcitrant, eccentric, or non-conformist journalists being excluded. It will also put undue importance on those university students with journalism degrees. (As much as I am in favor of journalism education, I would hate to see only journalism school graduates practicing journalism in the United States.)

Sylvia Porter, syndicated columnist, in 1979, wrote:

> Licensing would kill our free society just as surely as Soviet-type dictatorship would kill it. Instead of spurring a rise in our standards, it would invite arbitrary controls through intimidation by those in power.

The American Society of Newspaper Editors (ASNE) argued that, "In licensing lies control, and a controlled press is not-for it cannot be-independent and free."

Nevertheless, despite the profession's greatest concerns against licensing, the United States does have a licensing of reporters; however, the American version is called "credentialing"-and it is done with the knowledge, approval, and assistance of the journalism profession.

Licensed to Cover Government

Almost every municipality, county, and state issues "press passes" to reporters. These may be "passes" issued by the police or fire departments, the state legislatures (both lower and upper houses), and various county and state executive departments. Sometimes, even private corporations that have substantial "public business" issue press cards. No matter how "democratic" the process is, every governmental agency or private corporation that issues press passes has the ability-and right-to deny certain reporters from getting the passes, or to suspend or revoke passes that were issued. Frequently, governmental bodies have denied press credentials to "underground" or "alternative" publications, such as the *Los Angeles Free Press*, which had a long-running battle to be given certain police passes. Many news organizations supported the *Free Press*'s rights to be credentialled; however, many newspapers and journalism associations claimed that the "Freep" wasn't *really* a newspaper and didn't practice *serious* journalism-like the establishment newspapers. Further, others in the profession kept pointing out myriad "abuses"-the *"Freep"* reporters weren't "properly trained"; they insulted and embarrassed the media by their appearance. (Most reporters didn't wear the same kind of clothes as the establishment press); besides, sniffed some of the establishment reporters, some of the *"Freep"* reporters "did" drugs, practiced free love, and were *anti-establishment*. Thus, not only did government already rule what was and was not "acceptable" as a reporter and news organization, they were backed up by many persons who already had press credentials.

Almost every American reporter who covers the Congress will reject the concept of licensing. And yet, every one has a form of a license, something they readily apply for, accept, and obey the rules of the people who issue and enforce the provisions of the license. The House and Senate each have four media galleries-press (daily newspapers); periodical press (magazines and non-daily newspapers); radio-television; and photographers. These galleries are essentially associations of journalists, and membership gives access to covering most activities in either the House or Senate.

The Congress-much like the English monarchs three and four centuries earlier, and not too unlike some of the governments that created *collegios*-have delegated administrative responsibility, including determination of membership and of enforcement of codes of conduct, to those who are already members of the galleries. Each gallery establishes rules for the election of members to serve as standing committees. But the government-in this case each of the houses of Congress-also retains both direct and indirect control. The rules of each gallery, enforced by the standing committees of journalists, are "subject to the approval and supervision" (periodicals; Radio-TV), or "review and approval" (press, photography) of the Speaker of the House of Representatives and the Senate Committee on Rules and Administration. The rules are signed not by journalists, but approved by the Speaker and the chair of the Senate committee.

Each gallery establishes its own requirements for membership, but every gallery requires the applicant to be a "bona fide" correspondent or newsgatherer of "repute in their profession" (press, photography), or of "reputable standing" (periodicals, radio-TV). The potential for abuse, including the denial of credentials for journalists who work for alternative media, is strong when such vague terms as "repute" and "reputable" are used. Among many other requirements is the provision that the reporter is not "engaged in" "the prosecution of claims or the promotion of legislation pending before the Congress." Thus, a strict interpretation of this provision would prohibit any reporter from becoming involved with any legislation that could directly benefit or hinder American journalism; reporters who helped draft clauses in the federal sunshine act, for example, could be forbidden from covering Congress.

Persons who do not meet the requirements for permanent membership in the galleries are allowed to apply for temporary credentials on a "day-only" basis or, occasionally, on a "week-long" basis, subject to renewal; the reporter must still agree to all restrictions imposed by the galleries. And, temporary credentials can be denied for any reason-to anyone.

Another form of government control is in staff employment. Each of the eight galleries employs a superintendent, assistant superintendent, and, for the larger galleries, assistants-all of them hired by a committee of journalists, all of them paid by the House or Senate. The journalists may argue that because the staff is hired, promoted, and fired by the standing committees composed entirely of journalists, they are employees of the journalists, not the government. Yet, almost every journalist will readily agree that in *other* matters, it is who signs the paycheck that determines employment and potential abuse of conflict of interest ethics canons.

Just as the press credentials in the House and Senate are laminated cards, worn on chains around the neck, so are the press credentials for the White House. The rules for covering the White House are just as strict as for covering the Capitol; however, the rules have a much more practical reason-most are designed for security, and the reporter must first pass a security clearance. Press credentials are also required for all federal departments, as well as for the Supreme Court.

Membership Requirements for Reporters:
U.S. House and Senate

Daily Press

. . .[T]he Standing Committee of Correspondents shall admit to the galleries no person who does not establish to the satisfaction of the Standing Committee all of the following:

(a) That his or her principal income is obtained from news correspondence intended for publication in newspaper entitled to second-class mailing privileges.

(b) That he or she is not engaged in paid publicity or promotion work or in prosecuting any claim before Congress or before any department of the government, and will not become so engaged while a member of the galleries.

(c) That he or she is not engaged in any lobbying activity and will not become so engaged while a member of the galleries.

Periodical Press

Persons eligible for admission to the Periodical Press Galleries must be bona fide resident correspondents of reputable standing, giving their chief attention to the gathering and reporting of news. They shall state in writing the names of their employers and their additional sources of earned income; and they shall declare that, while a member of the Galleries, they will not act as an agent in the prosecution of claims, and will not become engaged or assist, directly or indirectly, in any lobbying, promotion, advertising, or publicity activity intended to influence legislation or any other action of the Congress, nor any matter before any independent agency, or any department or other instrumentality of the Executive Branch; and that they will not act as an agent for, or be employed by the federal, or any state, local or foreign government or representatives thereof; and that they will not, directly or indirectly, furnish special or "insider" information intended to influence prices or for the purpose of trading on any commodity or stock exchange; and that they will not become employed, directly or indirectly, by any stock exchange, board of trade, or other organization or member thereof, or brokerage house or broker engaged in the buying and selling of any security or commodity. Applications shall be submitted to the Executive Committee of the Periodical Correspondents' Association and shall be authenticated in a manner satisfactory to the Executive Committee.

Applicants must be employed by periodicals that regularly publish a substantial volume of news material of either general, economic, industrial, technical, cultural, or trade character. The periodical must require such Washington coverage on a continuing basis and must be owned and operated independently of any government, industry, institution, association, or lobbying organization. Applicants must also be employed by a periodical that is published for profit and is supported chiefly by advertising or by subscription, or by a periodical meeting the conditions in this paragraph but published by a nonprofit organization that, first operates independently of any government, industry, or institution and, second, does not engage, directly or indirectly, in any lobbying or other activity intended to influence any matter before Congress or before any independent agency or any department or other instrumentality of the Executive Branch. House organs are not eligible.

Radio and Television

. . . Applicants shall state in writing the names of all radio stations, television stations, systems, or news-gathering organizations by which they are employed and what other occupation or employment they may have, if any. Applicants shall further declare that they are not engaged in the prosecution of claims or the promotion of legislation pending before Congress, the Departments, or the independent agencies, and that they will not become so employed without resigning from the galleries. They shall further declare that they are not employed in any legislative or executive department or independent agency of the Government, or by any foreign government or representative thereof; that they are not engaged in any lobbying activities; that they do not and will not, directly or indirectly, furnish special information to any organization, individual, or group of individuals for the influencing of prices on any commodity or stock exchange; that they will not do so during the time they retain membership in the galleries. Holders of visitors' cards who may be allowed temporary admission to the galleries must conform to all the restrictions of this paragraph . . .

. . . The Executive Committee of the Radio and Television Correspondents' Galleries who shall see that the occupation of the galleries is confined to bona fide news gatherers and/or reporters of reputable standing
. . .

. . . Persons engaged in other occupations, whose chief attention is not given to-or more than one-half of their earned income is not derived from-the gathering or reporting of news for radio stations, television stations, systems, or news-gathering agencies primarily serving radio stations or systems, or news-gathering agencies primarily serving radio stations or systems, shall not be entitled to admission to the Radio and Television Galleries.

Photography

. . . The Standing Committee of Press Photography shall limit membership in the photographers' gallery to bona fide news photographers of repute in their profession and to Heads of Photographic Bureaus.

Provided, however, that the Standing Committee of Press Photographers shall admit to the gallery no person who does not establish to the satisfaction of the Committee all of the following:

(a) That any member is not engaged in paid publicity or promotion work or in prosecuting any claim before Congress or before any department of the Government, and will not become so engaged while a member of the gallery.

(b) That he or she is not engaged in any lobbying activity and will not become so engaged while a member of the gallery.

Licensing: Some American Problems

by Leslie C. Henderson

Perhaps the most dramatic attempt at licensing reporters occurred in 1979 in Massachusetts. A bill requiring investigative reporters to be licensed as private detectives was passed in the Massachusetts Senate and gained the preliminary approval of the House of Representatives before it was declared unconstitutional by a joint judiciary committee of the two houses.

The bill, S. 1093, would have required reporters and photographers to pay a $750 licensing fee, renewable annually for $400. The bill required that print and electronic investigative reporters be 25 years of age, have three years experience and post a $5,000 bond. The licensing fee was payable to the state Department of Public Safety. The legislation was designed to cover any person employed by "newsgathering organizations" who poses as someone else while gathering the news or who conducts "secret surveillance of a person from a hidden vantage point by means of a camera, telescope or any other manner, or at night uses a specially adapted camera for such observation."

The bill cleared the Senate after being amended to include the electronic news media and was passed by voice vote on the first reading in the House.

The licensing legislation was introduced by Sen. Denis L. McKenna, who was miffed at a *Boston Globe* investigation that turned up evidence revealing one of his aides was drawing a full-time salary for a part-time job.

McKenna also sponsored a bill that would require statehouse reporters to file financial disclosure statements. The senator said he saw no reason to put reporters "in a special class. They are no better or worse than politicians." McKenna added that, "Reporters have a sensitivity to the public. They should be able to say 'I have no other source of income other than the newspaper I'm working for'" [*Boston Globe*, March 18, 1979] . . .

Leslie Henderson is a copyeditor for the *Colorado Springs Gazette-Telegraph*. She received a B.A. in Latin American Studies from George Washington University, and an M.A. in journalism from the University of Missouri. [This article is edited and reprinted, with permission, from Freedom of Information Center Report No. 440, 1981, School of Journalism, University of Missouri.]

Arthur Miller, a constitutional law professor at Harvard Law School, [observed]:

> The bill reflects latent anxieties regarding some of the practices of such groups (investigative reporters). If it is passes, it would probably be declared unconstitutional. But there is some concern that the press is behaving more like police than the police do. It's inevitable that some politician would try to something like this.
>
> "The First Amendment does not afford [reporters] the privilege they claim, which they have been getting away with for 300 years," McKenna said in the *Boston Globe*. "I think it is wrong that members of the media have greater rights than our law enforcement officials." [April 18, 1979]

From Reporters to Chimney Sweeps

A 1980 ordinance in Granite City, Illinois, a suburb of St. Louis, called for the licensing and collecting of fees from more than 650 businesses, including reporters for newspapers, television and radio stations. The remainder of the business ranged from public libraries, fraternal organizations, and nursing homes to church furnishing firms and chimney sweeps.

The proposal was drawn up by City Inspector Emerald Dawes, who used a telephone book to make certain the ordinance would be as inclusive as possible. Yet, neither Dawes nor anyone else remembered including news reporters in the licensing ordinance. Someone else must have added the news reporters, said Dawes . . . although he did remember including a category that covers "court and convention reporters."

A $25 a year licensing fee was recommended for all reporters covering events in Granite City. The ordinance [was] considered "unconstitutional and in conflict with the freedom of speech."

12¢ or $1,200

In Pittsburgh, Pennsylvania, in 1971 . . . a public safety director referred to the news press passes-issued at a $12 fee-as licenses. News media executives adamantly protested the fee, forcing Mayor Peter F. Flaherty to revoke the $12 "service charge."

Frank Hawkins, editor of the Pittsburgh *Post Gazette*, wrote:

> If the city can charge $12 for a press card, which it might require for access to public events, it can charge 12 cents or $1,200-or any amount. It could through that device attempt to bar newsmen from coverage of events vitally affecting the lives of the citizens of this community.

Other news executives joined the protest, sending up a communal howl. "We will not submit to the city's licensing system for newsmen . . . We shall proudly continue to play the role of news hounds, but will not submit to being licensed like dogs," wrote John Troan, editor of the *Pittsburgh Press*.

Following the uproar raised by the media, Mayor Flaherty agreed to review the "service charge." The cards cost the city about $2 to process, and although many cities charge a nominal fee for press cards, Mayor Flaherty said the loss of revenue from the press cards would not significantly alter the budget . . .

The Pittsburgh uproar subsided when the mayor announced that a new press card would be prepared free of charge to those who requested it.

Licensing of Newspaper Carriers

Attempts to license the press take forms other than requiring a license or permit for reporters or photographers.

In Providence, Rhode Island, a 47-year-old ordinance requiring the licensing of persons who sell newspapers on the street suddenly was enforced in late 1969.

The ordinance (which applied to bootblacks as well), dated back to 1922 and stated:

> No person known as a bootblack or as a newsboy shall ply his trade or business in any of the streets, avenues or other public places in the city without a permit from the bureau of licenses issued as herinafter provided.
>
> No permit shall be issued to a bootblack or newsboy until the parent or guardian of the applicant for such permit, if the applicant is a minor, or some other person approved by the chief of police, if the applicant is an adult, shall give to the chief of police satisfactory assurance of the good character of such applicant.

A $1.25 deposit fee was required for the identifying badges, which were to be worn on the front of the newsboys' caps. The deposit fee was refundable when the badges were returned. The ordinance also contained a clause that allowed the newsboys' licenses to be revoked for the usage of "indecent language."

In a case brought by the Providence underground newspaper *Extra*, Judge Raymond J. Pettine ruled that the ordinance was unconstitutional because it called for the chief of police to make a judgement about the "good character" of the applicants. The U.S. District Court in Providence declared the ordinance an infringement on the First Amendment guarantee of a free press.

In his Jan. 13 ruling, Pettine said the language of the ordinance set it apart from other laws becuase "it allows a discretionary judgment of the 'good charac-ter' of the permit applicant as a condition precedent to the granting of the per-mit." The judge further declared, "The Providence newsboy permit ordinance [is] unconstitutional as an impermissible direct restraint upon freedom of press and as a licensing scheme which vests overly broad and vague discretionary powers in the chief of police and the members of the licensing bureau."

Arguing for the *Extra* against the newsboy permit was First Amendment lawyer Hayden C. Covington who stated . . . "If a newspaper boy can be required to wear a badge, then a minister or priest can also be required to wear a badge before he enters a pulpit or visits a parishoner."

Also involved in the case was the contention by the *Extra* that [it] had been singled out for harassment by the police. Covington told the court, "The truth of the matter is that the plaintiffs in this case have been arrested and harassed because of their much hated attitude [against] the war in Vietnam."

The judge described the staff of the weekly underground newspaper as "a group of young people with a lifestyle unique to the accepted norms of society." He added that "the personnel are overwhelmingly of an obvious different culture to that which most of us have embraced."

Covington claimed the ordinance had been selectively enforced against the underground newspaper, saying, "There are a great multitude of newsboys who are not required to have the permit and badge. This great multitude compared to the few that are compelled to have it by the City of Providence proves discrimination."

In his ruling, the judge said the only evidence of selective enforcement was statistical-while there were 28 to 30 vendors of the *Providence Journal*, there were only 12 outstanding licenses. Thus, while some vendors didn't have permits and had not been arrested, Judge Pettine said there was nothing in the record "showing a purposeful or intentional discrimination against the plaintiffs by the defendants [the city]."

Financial Disclosures

A law requiring reporters to disclose their financial holdings and win accreditation from an ethics commission before being allowed to cover state government was signed . . . into effect by Alabama Gov. George Wallace on Sept. 14, 1973.

The law . . . would have barred reporters who failed to comply with the legislation from covering "the state government in any way." Anyone found guilty under the law was subject to a $10,000 fine and 10 years in jail. A reporter who violated the law also was required to pay the state treasury three times the amount of his financial gain.

The same law required public officials to disclose their finances. The public officials, however, needed only to list . . . outside sources of income under the heading of "legal fees" or "tax-exempt bonds," while reporters were required to make specific disclosures.

A class action suit claiming the law violated the First and Fourteenth Amendments was filed by the *Birmingham Times*, the *Eagle Eye* (publication of the Alabama Democratic Party), and the state chapter of Sigma Delta Chi, a professional journalism society.

The three-judge court ruled in a 2-1 decision that the legislature could not single out an individual profession and require its members to disclose their finances . . .

Professional Writer's License

In California during the early sixties [Charles] Carson led a successful one-man protest against an ordinance requiring all professional writers to purchase a $25 writer's license. The Manhattan Beach ordinance threatened writers with a $500 fine and/or a six-month jail sentence if they wrote without taking out a license.

"Of itself, this little incident does not mean very much. I am a relatively obscure writer in a city that most Americans never heard of. What difference does it make if I pay $25 for a license to write?" asked Carson in a *New York Times* article. "But," continued Carson, . . . a novelist, magazine writer and ghost writer:

> I have read a great deal about the Bill of Rights and I think this involves an important principle of freedom. When legislators start passing these laws in one place, the laws tend to spread from one town to another. They can be extended until they affect the freedom of all writers and the freedom of the people. I think this is a clear violation of the freedom of the press. Any writer could be taxed out of existence by legislators. [*New York Times*, April 6, 1964]

Walter Anderson, then city attorney for Manhattan Beach, took a different view:

> What is so special about a writer? This is an occupational tax. Writing is an occupation. We are not discriminating against writers or anyone else. As a lawyer, most of my work is a product of the mind, just as a writer's. But I pay my licensing tax.

Two days after a 16-paragraph story discussing Carson's crusade appeared in the *New York Times*, the Manhattan Beach City council met and ended the tax on writers.

Journalists Relinquish Passes

In various instances, reporters in the United States and Canada have turned in press passes issued by the police, saying that it is not up to the police any more than it is to any other group to choose the journalists that cover its activities.

The Quebec Federation of Professional Journalists protested a decision by the Montreal urban community to permit only journalists with a council pass to cover police news. Under the plan, journalists would receive the pass only after having been approved by a four-member committee.

In Madison, Wisconsin, members of the Madison Newspaper Guild turned in their police department-issued passes [in 1971], saying the cards represented a "form of license."

"The power to license implies the power to withdraw the right. [The members of the Guild] do not believe reporters should be licensed by the police to protect their constitutional rights," Guild chairman Matt Pomme [said].

The Guild also protested the "repeated police use in this country of undercover agents using press cards."

Other journalists have protested the use of press cards by non-media personnel. After an outcry by the regional chapter of the Sigma Delta Chi in Des Moines, the Iowa state legislature agreed not to issue press credentials to Republican and Democratic party members . . .

Bibliography

"Are Journalists Professionals? Not According to the NLRB," *FOI Digest*, May-June 1975.

"City's New Ordinance Requires Fees & Licensing of Reporters," *FOI Digest*, March-April 1980.

"Creation of State Boards to License Newsmen Suggested Again; Need for Standards Cited," *FOI Digest*, January-February 1970.

Leahigh, Alan Kent, *Press Passes: Patent or Privilege?*, Freedom of Information Center (Columbia, Mo.), June 1971.

"License Plans Increase U.S. Foreign Concern," *FOI Digest*, May-June 1981.

Luebke, Barbara F., *When Is a Reporter Not a Reporter?*, Freedom of Information Center (Columbia, Mo.), January 1978.

"Mass. Lawmakers Nix Licensing Reporters as Private Detectives," *FOI Digest*, March-April 1979.

"Militant Socialist News Service Denied Press Cards in New York," *FOI Digest*, May-June 1975.

Orr, Eloise, *Challenges to TV License Renewals*, Freedom of Information Center (Columbia, Mo.), December 1970.

"Reagan Administration Order Newsman to License or Face Expulsion," *FOI Digest*, January-February 1984.

Saddler, Owen, *FCC Hearing in Omaha*, Freedom of Information Center (Columbia, Mo.), May 1963.

"Secret Service Must Explain Request Denials for Press Passes," *FOI Digest*, July-August 1976.

"Senator Miller Tells NY Lawyers Newsmen Should Be Licensed," *FOI Digest*, July-August 1971.

"Underground Paper Fights to Obtain Press Cards," *FOI Digest*, September-October 1970.

Chapter 38

Censorship and Human Needs

Within the human spirit is the essential need to suppress information which is believed to be unfavorable, threatening, or untrue. It makes no difference whether or not the people claim to be libertarian and democratic, the essential human trait of fear will dictate how people respond to information. Even those who claim to oppose all forms of censorship will allow certain items (*e.g.*, pornography or racial defamation) to be suppressed for the sake of the "public good."

To maintain the "public good," numerous institutions of the state have enacted many specific laws to suppress information. In some countries, as in Iran under the religious leader, the Ayatollah Khomeini, the penalties for violation of a strict religious code include torture and death. In other countries, such as the United States, the penalties are imposed only for civil law violations, but can include confiscation of printing equipment, fines, and imprisonment.

Censorship reflects a society's lack of confidence in itself.
It is the hallmark of an authoritarian regime.

—Potter Stewart, U.S. Supreme Court Justice

At one time, censorship was narrowly defined as official governmental action to suppress information *prior* to its publication. Later, the concept of censorship included any governmental action to suppress information. In many instances, suppression is not by overt action of a governmental body, but by the writers, editors, and publishers themselves, afraid of what "might" happen. For example, continual law suits and arrests, whether spurious or not, against a publication will force the writers and editors to self-censor their articles, perhaps deciding against writing something because of what "might" happen, yet being able to justify, often in elaborate detail, why they chose not to write or publish something. With radio and television, the fear is magnified. The Federal Communications Commission (FCC) does not need to issue formal specifications or impose heavy fines in most instances. The concept of the "raised eyebrow," a seemingly innocuous question or request, will often be enough to give stations an idea of what "might" happen. In many instances, the sanctions the radio and television stations impose upon themselves, in fear of "what might happen" are usually greater than what the FCC would impose had it decided to do so.

World Press Freedom

by Dana R. Bullen

It is significant that national leaders everywhere want uncensored, straight news about the world, their region, and their countries.

If it is useful to them, it seems this would be useful to everyone.

But too often these leaders combine efforts to ensure they know what is going on with equally vigorous efforts to be sure that others don't.

The guiding statement is Article 19 of the 1948 Universal Declaration of Human Rights. Some call this the "First Amendment of the World."

Article 19 provides that:

> Everyone has the right to freedom of opinion and expression; this right includes freedom to hold opinions without interference and to seek, receive and impart information and ideas through any media and regardless of frontiers.

How are these principles being carried out around the world? Not well. In some places, the situation is desperate. Problems facing journalists range from fear for their lives to more subtle pressures to shape what they write to somebody else's agenda.

In two-thirds to three-quarters of the world—the figures, respectively are for print and broadcast media—governments either control news media outright or have a significant or dominant voice in what does or does not appear. According to Freedom House, the New York-based human rights group that grades countries on their level of freedom, this definition does not include regulation such as that practiced in the United States by the Federal Communications Commission. It means control over newspaper or broadcast content—over what

Dana R. Bullen, former foreign editor of *The Washington Star*, has been executive director of the World Press Freedom Committee since 1981. The WPFC joins under one banner thirty-two journalistic organizations on five continents to provide a strong voice against those who advocate state-controlled news media and to provide assistance to those Third World media needing it. During twenty-one years with *The Star*, Bullen served as U.S. Senate reporter, U.S. Supreme Court reporter and assistant news editor. He was a Neiman Fellow at Harvard, 1966-1967; research fellow, Harvard's East Asian Research Center, 1971; and Journalist in Residence at the Fletcher School of Law and Diplomacy, 1980-81. He is the recipient of the Silver Gavel Award, American Bar Association and the Reporting Award of the American Political Science Association. Bullen has journalism and law degrees from the University of Florida. [©1986, Dana Bullen]

people are allowed to know. The situation is not static, and some nations move back and forth between free and unfree categories.

A survey by a broadcasters' organization in June 1985 of the state of press freedom in Latin America, for instance, listed breakthroughs for free expression in Brazil, Argentina, and Uruguay. There also were important steps forward in El Salvador.

In Chile, Paraguay, and Ecuador, though, there were new problems. Terrorism affecting free expression was cited in Bolivia. There was condemnation of lack of freedom of expression in Cuba, Nicaragua, and Haiti.

"This past year has seen a continuous increase in the number of journalists expelled, jailed or murdered," reported Peter Galliner, director of the London-based International Press Institute (IPI) in December 1984. "There have been more cases of newspapers, magazines and broadcasting stations forcibly closed."

The IPI report detailed abuses against journalists, and closings of newspapers for countries from Afghanistan to Zimbabwe. This dismal record took fifty-four columns of fairly small type.

Index on Censorship, a London-based publication, took twenty-four columns of type for its own report on problems facing journalists. Similar reports by others were equally voluminous.

In Indonesia, for instance, censors carefully scan all incoming foreign publications before they reach newsstands or subscribers. According to one account, they blot out offending material with a thick layer of gummy black ink, then affix a flap of paper over the damp blotch to prevent it from blemishing the inoffensive print on the facing page.

In Nigeria, a decree by the government granted itself power to close down newspapers, radio, and television stations deemed to be acting in a manner detrimental to the interest of the government. In the Sudan, three journalists were sentenced to die for publishing a political pamphlet.

A straight-to-the-point, stark report from Uruguay—before the return of democratic government there—had said simply:

> The following publications were shut down by government this week:
> 1) Somos Idea. Weekly. Closed down permanently.
> 2) Busqueda. Weekly. Closed down for 8 editions.
> 3) Cinco Dias. Daily. Closed down permanently.
> 4) La Prensa. Daily. Closed down for 90 editions.
> 5) Tribuna Amplia. Weekly. Closed down permanently.

[In Uganda, Gen. Idi Amin Dada seized power in 1971. During the next eight years, until he was overthrown, Amin suppressed all dissent, bringing about the execution of almost 300,000 people, and the expulsion from Uganda of most of that nation's 45,000 Asians. Freedom of expression, as during the Spainish Inquisition, was limited to the strict adherence to the views of the dictatorship.

In 1986, the "the democratically–elected" dictators Francois Duvalier of Haiti and Ferdinand Marcos of The Phillipines fled their countries amidst charges of looting the treasury and massive violations of human rights.]

Aside from the all-too-natural desire of leaders to hear only good things about themselves, to be constantly reminded of their great wisdom and the high merit of their programs and projects, deep-seated, ideological differences exist on the proper role of news media.

Independent news media in Western nations serve a "watchdog" role that is one of the checks and balances of democratic societies. But there are also numerous "not-so-independent" media in many Third World countries. Zambia's President Kenneth Kaunda once instructed newsmen to:

> . . . reflect the nature of our society, project and defend our philosophy, our values and our interests as a sovereign state. If you do not, you are not with us as a nation . . . Some of you have been the instruments of our enemies . . . Some of you have been preoccupied with the failures of some of our development programs. You must stop it before other measures are taken.

Totally integrated media in the Soviet Union and Communist countries are part of the government. According to *Pravda*, "a journalist is an active fighter for the cause of the party."

Attempting to define their own press-state relationships, a number of the 120 or so nations comprising the Third World of developing countries expanded the "social responsibility" of the 1950s Western theorists into a "national responsibility" that would require journalists to toe the line.

At the big international conferences at which delegates of governmetns argued for a New World Information Order—at UNESCO and elsewhere—one got the impression these officials felt journalism was too important to be left to journalists. You rarely heard what journalists themselves might think. Spokesmen of governments too often demanded that the press perform certain duties. To insure compliance, these same people wanted to control the press. The press, they claim, must support a New World Economic Order. Or it must present more positive news. Or it must back certain so-called liberation movements. Or it must promote development projects. Or it must do something else somebody thinks is a good idea.

There also were lists of things the press must not do.

Journalists were called on to be "responsible." But the troubling question was: Would this be "responsibility" to follow a story wherever it leads? Or would it be "responsibility" to drop a story the instant it seemed to be going in the "wrong" direction?

The countries that make up the long lists kept by Freedom House, by IPI, by *Index on Censorship* devised their own ways to influence journalists and news media.

Writing on Third World press freedom in *Comparative Mass Media Systems* (1983), Sunwoo Nam, a professor at the University of Maryland, gave this list of twenty-one control techniques (ranging from subtle to brutal):

> Constitutional provisions; security laws; press laws; penal laws; bribes, subsidies; special favors; control of newsprint; leverage of official advertising; control of bank loans; denial of access to government information;

ubiquity of press spokesman; licensing, registration; certification of bona fide journalists; self censorship based on broad guidelines; telephone systems by which government agents tell editors what not to print; stationing censors in news organizations; post-publication reprisals; getting recalcitrant journalists fired; arrest, interrogation, torture, often by "extralegal" security forces; bombing and other terror tactics; forced merger or closing of news media; disappearances or killings of journalists.

Instructive on what kind of news it was that leaders feared was this pledge extracted in 1978 from editors in Indonesia:

> We shall not aggravate the situation and will play our part in calming things down if tensions occur in society. We shall restrain ourselves by giving priority at all times to the interests of society and the state above personal interests and the interests of our newspapers. We shall at all times guard the good name and authority of the government and the national leadership and will not engage in slanders of other forms of insult directed towards the national leadership and members of his [sic] family . . ."[Quotation from the Legal Aid Institue's *1980 Report on Human Rights in Indonesia."*]

[In the Republic of South Africa, freedom of expression is limited, by law, to the White population who compose less than one-fifth of the nation's thirty-two million residents. Although there are "advisory councils" of Coloureds (ten percent of the population) and Asians (three percent), Blacks (more than two-thirds of the population) are not represented in Parliament in the nation in which only Whites may vote or run for office. The government restricts the Black population to certain jobs, and even in these, Blacks are paid lower wages than Whites; all housing is segregated; all Blacks must have "internal passports," a

---

Egyptians Nix Pix

Egypt doesn't seem to share America's nostalgia for Anwar Sadat. Columbia Pictures' TV docudrama "Sadat," which aired [Fall 1983 caused] plenty of hard feelings in Cairo. The government [said] it is full of "historical errors" and banned all Columbia films from the country. Some Egyptians had minor objections: camels, not cars, on the streets of Cairo. Other complaints were political: an insulting portrayal of Gamal Abdel Nasser. Some were cultural: too much kissing. And one was racial: Louis Gossett Jr., who played Sadat, happened to be black. That bothered race-conscious Egyptians and wouldn't have pleased Sadat, who was sensitive about his color. The Columbia boycott won't suppress the film. "Sadat" is now playing all over Cairo—in pirated cassettes.

—*Newsweek*; February 13, 1984.

system of registration. White opposition has been curtailed by the government's military and police forces, and thousands—Black, Coloured, Asian *and* White— have been imprisoned for speaking out on the issues of equality for the races.] (In 1984, Bishop Desmond Tutu, for a long history of opposition to apartheid policies, was awarded the Nobel Price in Peace.) In July 1985, South Africa invoked a state of emergency to help it deal earlier with trouble in black areas. One of the first steps was to ensure that news accounts from the affected districts would be "properly validated and properly controlled" by the authorities. An official said that "dramatized versions, slanted truths (and) half-truths—these will obviously not be allowed."

Then there was the physical abuse of newspeople, what Louis Boccardi, president of the AP, has called "censorship by intimidation."

A study prepared for the World Press Freedom Committee entitled *Killed, Wounded, Jailed, Expelled* showed that during 1984 alone there were 211 such incidents involving more than 359 individual journalists.

Twenty-three journalists were killed in twenty-two incidents; more than eighty-one were wounded in forty-four incidents; 205 were jailed in 109 incidents, and more than fifty were expelled in thirty-six incidents. Some journalists were killed or wounded on battlefields, where risks are expected. But more were killed or wounded—a number at their homes or offices—because of who they were and what they did. This was plainly true for all of those who were jailed or expelled.

There is great strength in an idea—the idea of a free press—that can withstand such varied and deadly challenges.

The most effective antidote to the poison of the mindless orthodoxy is ready access to a broad sweep of ideas and philosophies. There is no danger in such exposure. The danger is in mind control.

—Joseph Tauro, Judge, U.S. District Court, 1978

The few studies tha have touched on the subject indicate that freedom, a free press, more successful development, and a better life tend to run together. It is a false choice to say—as many supporters of a NWIO assert—that developing countries must choose between a free press and needed development.

Keith Fuller, former president of the AP, notes

As a fledgling nation in the 18th century, the United States had free speech ... from the beginning. Can one honestly think that was a handicap to our development.

[Although trade routes, natural resources, and the population's historical development and economic philosophies are primary determination of gross national product, in general, those nations with a higher gross national product tend to be those with a higher gross national product.]

Among the many reasons must be these:

1) The best programs flow from a full debate of alternatives, not only behind the closed doors of government offices but throughout a society.

2) The choices developed in such an open debate will draw understanding and support far beyond what leaders might attempt to command.

3) Nobody possesses all wisdom. Independent news media help bring to the surface ideas from many sources that may be better than those under consideration.

4) An independent media will watch the progress of development programs. Such programs will be more effective if problems are exposed than if they are covered up.

5) Often, it is only a free press that allows the voices and needs of the people to be heard by governments or other powerful interests.

Indian journalist Pran Chopra said:

Discovering the truth and stating it is one of the best contributions that newspaper (and other media) people can make toward nation-building . . . if there is any suppression of the truth under any kind of a false notion of the obligations of the media, then very soon you will end up with a situation where you neither have truth nor nation-building.

This leaves the press controllers—and those found even in free societies who hanker for such power—with only the flimsiest of excuses beyond self–aggrandizement for what they are doing to control and distort what others can know about the world around them.

Sovereign Censorship; State
vs Printed Word in the Slavic Lands

by Marianna Tax Choldin

Emperor Alexander II of Russia (1855-1881) once remarked angrily to his minister of education: "Oh, your writers! One cannot rely on a single one of them!" This mistrustful attitude on the part of an absolute monarch—directed, by the way, not only toward those writers living and working within his empire, but toward all writers, everywhere, whose works might enter his empire— was typical of many European monarchs of the time. The royal thinking went something like this: Writing dealing with private, personal concerns or aimed at sheer entertainment of the reader should be encouraged by all means. Unfortunately, some writers also produce books, poems, plays, and articles containing ideas that may be dangerous, and readers may be influenced by these dangerous ideas. Therefore, the state must maintain control over the printing and dissemination of these works in order to protect readers from corrupting influences.

Nowhere has this attitude persisted more doggedly than in Russia, where control of the printed word has been attempted by the government, with varying degrees of success and with only brief interruptions, since at least 1796. Other Slavic lands (including present-day Bulgaria, Czechoslovakia, Poland, and Yugoslavia), ruled before World War I by the Hapsburg and Ottoman empires and the kingdom of Prussia, were subject to similar control. The revolutions of 1848 resulted in significant liberalization for Hapsburg and Prussian subjects but there too, relief was only temporary; one hundred years later the Slavic peoples (and some of their non-Slavic neighbors—Rumanians, Hungarians, East Germans) were to find their reading and writing once again under strict control, now supervised more comprehensively and effectively than ever before by the Soviet Union and governments under the Soviet influence . . .

Early Imperial Censorship

Catherine the Great (1762-1796) established Russia's first official secular censorship agency in September 1796, two months before her death. Thirteen years earlier she had granted approval for private printing presses to be established in the empire, but with the disquieting reports of revolution in France she

---

Mariana Tax Choldin holds concurrent appointments as professor of library science, assistant director of general services, head of the Slavic and East European Library, and research director of the Russian and East European Center at the University of Illinois. She is the author of *A Fence Around the Empire; Russian Censorship of Western Ideas*, (Duke University Press, 1985); and editor of *Access to Information in the 1980s; Proceedings of The First International Conference of Slavic Librarians and Information Specialists* (Russica Publishers, 1982). From the University of Chicago, Dr. Choldin received a B.A. in Russian Language and Literature, an M.A. in Slavic Language and Literature, and a Ph.D. in library science. [This article is a revision of one that appeared in *Censorship in the Slavic World*, published by the New York Public Library, 1984. ©1986, Marianna Tax Choldin]

began to have second thoughts. Police censors had failed to stop Russian publications such as the political travelogue by Alelksandr Radishchev (1749-1802), *Puteshestvie iz Peterburga v Moskvu* (A Journey from Petersburg to Moscow), published in 1790, and dangerous foreign publications were also finding their way into the empire. Accordingly, the 1796 law directed that all private printing presses be shut down and established censorship offices in the two capitals (Moscow and St. Petersburg) and in several port and border cities.

After Catherine's death, her son, Paul, became emperor and continued her censorship policy with increasing vigor (some observers said in part, at least, because of his mental illness) until his death in 1801; in April 1800 he formally banned the importation of all publications and musical scores from abroad. Fortunately for the future of foreign publications in Russia, Paul I was succeeded by his son, Alexander I (1801-1825), who revoked that ban and, in 1804, introduced the first imperial statute dealing with censorship. This, the mildest of Russian censorship, was also considered by some observers to be the best because it is the shortest, consisting of only forty-seven articles! All works intended for the public were to be examined, with the aim of "providing the public with those leading to true enlightenment of the mind and formation of morals and removing those books contrary to that aim." Not a single work was to be printed in the Russian empire, or offered for sale, which had not first been examined by censors [Articles 2 and 3]. Still, the exceptionally benign Article 21 is particularly noteworthy: " . . .in the case of a doubtful passage having a double meaning, it is better to interpret it in the way most advantageous to the author, than to prosecute him."

Quite a different attitude was expressed in the next censorship statute, the infamous "cast-iron statue" of 1826. Nicholas I (1825-1855) was now emperor, and he was as worried about the harmful influences of the printed word as his father Paul and grandmother Catherine had been. One censor observed that if one applied the 1826 statute properly, "it would be possible to interpret 'Our Father who art in heaven' as a Jacobin expression." The 1826 version of the article in the 1804 statute regarding double meanings stated, "Do not permit passages in works and translations to be printed if they have a double meaning and one of the meanings is contrary to the censorship laws." Incidentally, it should be noted that if Russian censorhsip in this period is known for its pettiness and absurdity, the situation in Austria-Hungary and Prussia before 1848 was no better; every Russian anecdote can be matched by at least one from those countries, and no doubt from many other countries as well.

The "cast-iron statute," so rigid as to be totally unworkable, was replaced two years later. The new statute of 1828 established for the first time two separate and parallel committees, one to deal with domestic, the other with foreign, publications. There were special censorship arrangements for the Church, and also a separate postal censorship agency responsible for the control of periodical publications sent to subscribers throught he mail. Isabel Hapgood (1850-1928), the well-known American translator of Russian literature, gives a detailed and amusing account of her dealings with this and other parts of the censorship operation in her 1890 article in *The Nation*. George Kennan (1845-1924) wrote of his travels in Siberia; the series appeared in *Century* magazine beginning in December 1887. Kennan's work, translated into many languages, made a great stir in the West and was greeted with horror by the Russian authorities as it began to make its way into the empire. Also connected with the postal censorship was a secret operation known as the "black office," responsible for the interception and reading of domestic and foreign mail.

The Foreign Censorship Committee reveals clearly the main areas of official concern. Unlike domestic works, which were subject to censorship prior to publication, foreign works had not been tailored to please the Russian authorities. Thus, the Russian response to foreign works shows precisely what was considered objectionable for Russian readers. Indeed, the official position is quite literally visible, thanks to the methods employed by the Committee. Like their colleagues in neighboring Austria-Hungary, the Russian censors were directed to examine each work and decide whether it should be permitted for distribution in its complete form; banned for the general public (accessible, on request, to "qualified" readers); banned in its entirety; or—going beyond the Austrians— permitted for distribution only after objectionable passages had been excised (covered with "caviar," in the censors' lingo) . . .

Constraints on the domestic press were lightened considerably in 1865, when Emperor Alexander II put a new statute into effect. In keeping with a general spirit of reform, Russia was to follow her European neighbors who, after the turmoil of 1848, had largely dispensed with pre-publication censorship and settled down with post-publication systems involving the courts. In retrospect, however, it seems clear that Alexander II and his successors could not quite bring themselves to dispense with prior censorship, although they were willing enough to add a system of judicial measures that could if necessary be taken after publication. It was not until 1906, during the reign of the last emperor, Nicholas II (1868-1918, reign 1894-1917), that a new statute freed the domestic press from most of its remaining constraints. As for imported publications, they lumbered along under the old regulations, with some modifications, until the collapse of the empire in 1917. Hindsight proves that the imperial Russian censorship failed in its mision with regard to foreign publications; single lines in obscure poems had been banned, but much of Marx's work had been considered too abstract to be of any danger.

Russia was not the only country to employ brilliant writers and thinkers as censors. Alexander von Humboldt and Johann Gottlieb Fichte served Prussia in that capacity, and Johann Wolfgang von Goethe was a censor in Weimar—but in the course of the nineteenth century the Russian censorship committees had more than their share of great minds (along with some notoriously petty ones, to be sure). There is a common view of censors as hacks, small minds caught up in small questions. But two famous writers—the novelists Ivan Concharov (1812-1891) and Konstantin Aksakov (1817-1860)—were active as censors of domestic publications, and three of Russia's most important poets—Fiodor Tiutchev (1803-1873), Apollon Maikov (1821-1897), and Iakov Polonskii (1819–1898)—

were deeply involved for many years in the foreign censorship committee, as was the poet Valerii Briusov (1873-1924) in the early years of the Soviet regime. (Incidentally, Polonskii was aided in his duties, albeit unofficially, by Ilena Stackenschneider (1836-1897), a cultivated lady from a prominent St. Petersburg family who took much of the work of censoring German publications off his hands. It would be interesting to know whether she was an isolated case, or whether there were other women who volunteered as censors to help male friends.)

Soviet Censorship

The official Soviet view is that "the October Revolution brought an end to censorship—both imperial and bourgeois" . . .

Within days of the Bolshevik seizure of power, Lenin instituted what was said to be only a temporary measure:

> As sooon as the new order becomes stabilized, all administravive restrictions of the press will be lifted and complete freedom of the press will be established, subject only to limitations of legal liability, in accordance with the broadest and most progressive legislation on this problem.

The measure never was revoked. Six years later, in 1923, Lenin's wife, Nadezhda Krupskaia, issued instructions for removing books from Soviet libraries; one model list included biographies of, and works by, Descartes, Kant, Plato, and many others.

After the death of Lenin, Joseph Stalin (1879-1953, dictatorship, 1924-1953) emerged as the Soviet Union's leader. For the first few years of his reign, he exiled opponents and closed or restricted much of the opposition media. Beginning in the early 1930s, his power now solidified, he began a series of "purges" that over the next two decades left millions murdered or exiled. To further guarantee "unification" of the people, Stalin also purged the history of his country creating the "un–person." When a person became an "un-person" all traces of his existence disappeared from printed works, either employing the old technique of applying "caviar" or relying on readers to do their duty by following simple instructions for home exscion by means of razor blade and paste . . .

And what about the censorship of foreign publications? A recent example . . . is a "whited out" ("covered with sour cream"?) 1978 issues of *Science*. Another technique used to excise unwanted material from foreign publications is much harder to spot than "caviar" or "sour cream": the technique of excision via translation, in which undesirable passages are simply edited out of the Russian translation. Since Soviet-made translations are now the only versions of foreign works available to most Soviet readers, this is a highly effective technique . . .

Another old tradition carried on into the present is postal censorship. The imperial Russian system included both open and secret procedures, the latter taking place in what was known as the "black office." (Incidentally, specialists in the "black office" were acknowledged by their colleagues in neighboring

states to be unexcelled in the art of "perlustration," the term used to describe
the clandestine opening, examining, and resealing of letters). The practice
continues today, although, like other forms of censorship, it is not openly
acknowledged. Official concern has been extended in the modern age to other
common forms of communication, such as radio and telephone, and to more
exotic forms such as carrier pigeons. The borders are closed now, preventing all
but a very few Soviet citizens from traveling abroad and making direct contact
with foreign cultures. All in all, the Soviet government has limited access
to foreign publications far more effectively than its imperial predecessor was
capable of doing, even if the ruler had been so inclined.

Webster's Dictionary (third edition) defines "censor" in several ways, two
of which seem relevant here: "an official empowered to examine written or
printed matter (as manuscripts of books or plays) in order to forbid publication,
circulation, or representation if it contains anything objectionable"; and "an
official empowered to examine written or printed matter (as manuscripts of
books or plays) in order to forbid publication, circulation, or representation
if it contains anything objectionable"; and "an officer or official charged with
scrutinizing communications to intercept, suppress, or delete material harmful
to his country's or organization's interests." Both definitions describe fairly
accurately the role of the pre-revolutionary Russian censor—a role that one
might call reactive rather than active. It would seem, however, that his Soviet
counterpart has an additional, active role to play: the contemporary censor must
not merely delete "harmful" material, but must also translate, edit, amend,
and rewrite an author's work. Where foreign publications are concerned, the
author is not personally involved in this process; indeed, it is clear that many
foreign authors are not even aware of unauthorized changes made in the Soviet
translations of their works. Since 1973, when the Soviet Union acceded to
the Universal Copyright Convention, such unauthorized changes are illegal, but
there is ample evidence that the legalities are not always observed.

What is the situation of writers in the Soviet Union? The requirement—in
effect both before and after the Revolution—that authors submit their books
and articles for approval prior to publication has caused writers to practice an
insidious self-censorship dictated by a sense of what is and is not likely to be
tolerated by the authorities. This creates a terrible dilemma for writers now that
censorship has become active rather than merely reactive. After leaving the
Soviet Union writer Anatolii Kuznetzov (1929-1979) described self-censorship
in that country as "an ugly and unavoidable form of self-torment":

> When I was still a "Soviet writer," I once experienced the great pleasure
> of writing without an inner censor, but it required a tremendous effort
> to cast off my chains and completely free myself . . . I would bolt the
> door in the evenings and make absolutely certain that no one could see
> or hear me—just like the hero in Orwell's *1984*. Then I would suddenly
> allow myself to write everything I wanted to. I produced something so
> unorthodox and so "seditious" that I immediately buried it in the ground,

because they used to search my apartment when I was away. I consider what I wrote at that time to be the best of anything I have ever written. But it was so extraordinary, so insolent, that to this very day I have not dared to show it even to my closest friends. The situation in other countries of the region is similar. The workings of Polish censorship have been revealed to Western observers through the publication of the "black book," a two-volume compilation of rules and regulations for censors which was smuggled out of the country and published in London.

It is likely that the "black book" has its counterparts in each of the other countries under consideration. In the Soviet Union it is known as the "Index" or, even more ironically, the "Talmud" (the commentaries on the Hebrew Bible and other Jewish writings).

Other Slavic Censorship

Each of the Slavic countries has its martyrs to censorship, past and present. For imperial Russia, one thinks of Radishchev and the great poet Aleksandr Pushkin, censored personally by Catherine the Great and Nicholas I respectively, and of Aleksandr Herzen (1812-1870), who emigrated to England and published his influential journal *Kolokol*, there, uncensored. Along with these are Andrei Amal'rik, author of *Prosushchestvuet li Sovetskii Soiuz do 1984 goda?* (Will the Soviet Union survive until 1984?); the well-known literary critic Andrei Siniavskii, who was tried and imprisoned for his writing; and Nobel Prize-winner Aleksandr Solzhenitsyn.

Major Baltic, Byelorussian, and Ukrainian writers, whose countries are now within the Soviet Union were also censored, including Janis Plieksans (1876-1925), known as Rainis (Latvia); Bishop Motiejus Valancius (1801-1875) (Lithuania); Lydia Koidula (1843-1886) (Estonia); Yanka Kupala (1882-1942) and Frantzishak Bahushevich (1840-1900) (Byelorussia); and Taras Shevchenko (1814-1861) (Ukraine).

In the west Slavic world, Poland is represented by works of Adam Mickiewicz (1798-1855), arguably the greatest Polish writer of all time; poet and Nobel laureate Czeslaw Milosz, now residing in this country; and contemporary writers such as Adam Michnik, Jacek Kuron, Stanislaw Baranczak, and Bogdan Madej, who have published their works abroad because they could not be published at home uncensored. Four writers who left Czechoslovakia after the brief respite from censorship in 1968—part of the phenomenon known as the "Prague Spring"—are Arnost Lustig, Pavel Kohout, Milan Kundra, and Josef Skvorecky.

In the south Slavic area are Milovan Djilas, who had begun to challenge accepted doctrine during Stalin's reign; and the journal *Praxis*, forced by the government to close down in 1974. Censored Bulgarian writers include Pen'o Penev, a poet who committed suicide in 1959 because his works could not be published; Atanas Slavov, a prolific writer who emigrated to the United States in 1976; and Georgi Markov, who emigrated in 1969 and worked as a broadcaster for the BBC until his assassination in 1978.

The resulting picture of sovereign censorship in the Slavic World is certainly a grim one, but it is not hopeless. After all, the battle here is between a Goliath, the state, and a David, the producers of printed words, and we know that Davids have a way of outwitting Goliaths. Courageous writers in these countries will continue to chafe against the constraints under which they are forced to work, and whether they remain at home or must leave their countries, they will not suffer in silence, but will continue to speak out as best they can against censorship.■

The Profession of Censor

In 1980, with permission of the Censor's Office of Poland, *Tygodnik Solidarnosc* (Solidarity Weekly) published an interview with a former state censor, identified only as K-62. Interviewer was Barbara Lopienska; translator was Nika Krzeczunowicz. The elipses in the interview indicate portions that were censored by the Censor's Office.

Q: Can anyone become a censor?
K-62: Anyone with a college education and the desire to work in this business. Graduates with diplomas in the humanities are in the majority; one girl has studied political economy, another the Polish language, a friend of mine geography. You could find people who studied journalism.
Q: Frustrated journalists?
K-62: Young people with diplomas in journalism take the job because the starting salary is good. Back in 1974, I got 4,000 [zloty], but then the salary does not go up fast. A pal after seven years gets five thousand.
Q: Still, one must have a definite psychological predisposition?
K-62: Honest people also work in censorship—I swear to you, although you will probably find it hard to believe—as well as drunks and loving fathers, good wives, and less honest girls. The image of a censor looking like a PIDE [the secret service police under Salazar] agent is completely off. I did meet a censor like that, though; there are a couple of them who work on their texts with evil smiles, but only a few. The profession is pretty well feminized, because it is a quiet and calm job. On the other haand, there is a big turnover, I don't think more than a quarter work in censorship for longer than a couple of years . . .
Q: What is the mentality of a born-and-bred censor?
K-62: I would not like to create the impression that there is a definite Censor Personality. There is no such thing, albeit there is a type of mentality of professional soldier, guard, or youth activist. Some are guided by a peculiar interpretation of ideology. They think that censorship is the best way to protect Socialism and the Leading Role of the Party. Others think that it is a super game. Like chess players. They enjoy getting the best of a journalist.
Q: Where would you place yourself?

K-62: Among the most numerous, those who take the job with the idea of leaving it in a few years. One keeps looking for one's place in life. It is easier if one has some talent, though . . . I have no feeling of a mission or calling. Even now, I could not tell you what I would really like to do. I know what I would not.

Q: What's that?

K-62: I would not like to work in the police or in the Army. I would not like to be a priest. Today I would not like to be a censor, but then I did.

Q: Why?

K-62: Because I wanted to be a journalist, and I thought that nothing would train my eyes for that line of work like being a censor. If one has a fairly open mind, work in censorship greatly aids radicalism. Unless one is an extreme cynic.

Q: And you are not?

K-62: I think I am one-third cynic. And a man who has no journalistic talent. I would never have been a good journalist, because it means not only having interesting and good ideas, but above all a good style. It is no use being a noble hothead who will finally show the world how it is, if he writes it all in a dead manner.

Q: Did you try?

K-62: I did . . . Some censors manage to write; but not I. I did try at home in the evenings, but as soon as I wrote something the skill that was so useful in my work as a censor would take over and I only thought how I could put it differently. So I gave up . . .Then I met some journalists personally, and I thought Jesus God, that's a zoo. And I would have become one of them, because I was not outstanding.

Q: And were you an outstanding censor?

K-62: I was not the worst, and they were sorry to lose me. My chief, actually, did not want to let me go. And I must tell you that I recall my work in censorship with satisfaction. I would like to add that in my whole career it was the only business that functioned well, notwithstanding what it did. An ideal mechanism. I have never had another chief like that and probably never will. I think back about him, with pleasure; he took me on, and if it weren't for him, I possibly would not have taken the job. Because I am basically a liberal, I behaved with dignity at the university during March 1968; and I was never repressively inclined.

Q: How then, did your chief win you over?

K-62: He was direct and bright. No cant, no slogans. He said that some form of censorship had existed forever, and he was looking for people. And I took the job.

Q: Why?

K-62: Because it was interesting. I could find out what was going on all over Poland and how the repression mechanism worked. It was an observation point, and I treated my work in censorship as learning. I wanted to read papers as one reads them, let us say, in Paris. No more, no less.

Q: And you had no desire for advancement?

K-62: Absolutely not. I had no intention of staying on; I joined to have a look around.

Q: And what were the motives of your colleagues, the other censors?

K-62: I don't know. Apparently in the 1950s human relations in the business were closer. There were parties; people got married; the whole office went to help with the harvest together. Now things have changed. I would not dream of asking anyone: why are you working here? It was not the thing to do.

Q: Why not?

K-62: If you are so torn in two, why do you stay, then? This is a basic question that everyone has to ask himself when he takes the job. Later on, there is no point discussing it, because once a person has made up his mind to work in this business, there is nothing to talk about.

Q: Let's talk about the principles on which the business works.

K-62: There is a chairman, two vice-chairmen and a couple of unit directors: press, books, performances, analysis, and training . . .There was a "sundry printing" unit* too, but it has been closed down now. In all the old voivodship capitals there are branches of the main office, with a similar structure (. . .) Work in branch offices is much easier; what can a censor in Zielona Gora have to do? But in Cracow work is probably as complicated as anywhere, because this is where *Tygodnik Powszechny* [a Catholic weekly] comes out, to my mind the best weekly in the country.

Q: You mean the worst? Or how does one put it in your job?

K-62: I used to say the best. There is a specialized group in the press unit that reads religious publications, and its actions are the outcome of relations between the Office for Religious Denominations and the Episcopate. We call them "the Saints." Another group, called "the Funnies," would attend movie shows, theatres, and cabarets. Work in the theatre was easier, because one could hardly correct Musset or Fredo [an 18th-century Polish playwright]. One had to watch the staging. Actually, I don't recall a bigger showdown than there was for Dejmek's *Dziady* [which led to riots in 1968]. Perhaps I am being unfair to some director here. Censors of posters is an easy job; censors of books, terribly dull. The most noteworthy group, known as the aristocracy of censors, are the press people. The avant-garde. They are the foundation of the business. It is the largest and the brightest unit. The first line of fire.

Q: And where were you in this line?

K-62: I did not work in repression, but in transmission. In the training and analysis unit which published an information bulletin about how a good censor should act in a given case. Instructions were given by example.

Q: Could you show me something of that sort?

K-62: One could not take it from the office! Everything was numbered. I did not remove a thing, although in my time one could have taken everything. Only after that fellow from Cracow ran off with the stuff [to Sweden], did things become tougher. I did not take out anything because it would have been

---

*All printed matter, including visiting cards, letterheads, and death announcements, had to be submitted to the censor—Ed.

disloyal to the business . . . I personally prepared daily information about what had been deleted on a given day, even about the smallest cuts in a text. The unit was like an appeal to our lords and masters to take interest in the stuff that was in the press.

Q: Meaning the stuff that was not.

K-62: They got everything. Nothing was omitted. It was my job to present the text in its fullest detaidl; and all those demands and problems that have now flooded our long-suffering country, all that stuff that you journalists ferreted out and we deleted, went out neatly marked to the Press Department of the Central Committee across the road. So it is an evident untruth that the authorities were not informed. They knew everything. Although one might think that comrades form the voivodships pulled the wool over their eyes, they got it straight from my desk, and on my desk I had everything every day that the censors had removed. I was very well informed indeed!

Q: And what did it do for you?

K-62: I knew. And I could think and talk more sensibly.

Q: Talk? How about your loyalty to the business?

K-62: Discretion was required, and I obviously did not talk about things that were restricted for the sole information of the censor. Otherwise I was most popular at various banquets and parties. The girls' eyes shone; I could not have had it better. Others were out of luck.

Q: So you like making friends and going to banquets?

K-62: I never concealed the fact that I worked in censorship. Never. There is this business; they need people, and there are such people, and I was among them. So what? I should have a hangover about it? There would have been something wrong with me. Perhaps there is? I am capable of defending my work in censorship till I drop, although I do not defend censorship as such. I could function well while working in the business, and I stress once again that I was in contact with people with whom I had studied, with whom I had gone on strike at the university in March 1968. I remain in touch with them now, and none has seriously reproached me.

Q: How about unseriously?

K-62: "Oh, you dog"—stuff like that. And I must emphasize again that I worked in transmission, not repression; in creation, not prevention. (. . .) I am a Social-Democrat at heart and would not like to limit freedom of the press. And anyway, if I were in repression, I would have been deprived of some of the information . . .

Q: How [did] you start in censorship.

K-62: In the beginning one goes through thorough training, being informed about things that others must not be informed about. It is the broadest inter-pretation of our recent history and a couple of other things that they will not let you print anyway and about which it is unseemly for me to talk, because it would be disloyal. The training takes about two weeks and is organized according to needs. There are practical exercises—one compares a text [edited by one's self] with the corrections of a skilled censor.

Q: And they take the person who deletes the most?

K-62: Who crosses out in the cleverest way. I was given *Forum* to train on and I crossed out terribly and my chief told me: "Wrong. This is *Forum*. The texts have already been selected. They can go." I was quite shocked. In general, it is not at all a question of blue-pencilling a lot . . . It is more like a game, where one party tries to get the better of the other. No, but seriously: there was a sort of admiration for the intelligent journalist who wrote his stuff and tried to be cleverer than us.

Q: Meaning that you are fond of those whom you censor most?

K-62: Sure, they are good journalists. And good things were excluded, not bad ones. Kisielewski, for instance, would write a little note to the Censor: "How about letting it through this time, pussy cat? . . ."

Q: And a rank-and-file censor was never tempted to let a thing like that through?

K-62: No, it would be a betrayal of skill. A good rank-and-file censor crosses out what's required and understands what he's reading.

Q: For us, he is the one who does not understand.

K-62: A contrary approach. In my times, the principle on Mysia Street [location of the Censorship Office] was that if a censor did not understand what he was reading, the article might be let through as such, because the reader wouldn't understand either. We think that we are more intelligent than the average reader. Fools are not employed there. If your article was confiscated and you said: 'Oh, God, how idiotic?' it was not us censors. Now let me make a statement explaining censors. People think that censorship is all-powerful; but it is only the arm of the press department [of the Central Committee], and the harder the times, the smaller the censor's role. It is a very fine sieve. First, the day-worker reads it, then the department head, and if the interference is to be maintained, it may go all the way up to the chief. Sometimes, if the matter was tricky, the article would go further up, to the chairman or even to the Committee. But if the text is not marked by the low-level censor, it goes to the printer unread. Because there can always be trouble, the rank-and-file censor keeps crossing out . . .Yet, the belief prevails, as among the army engineers, that men are fallible. It was the chairman who sometimes got into trouble. I remember Jaroszewicz would ring up with complaints; but the lowly censor would not get into trouble.

Q: So why did you not let things slip through?

K-62: . . .you seem to forget that the business does not exist in order to let things through, but in order to ban them. If you hold down this job, you should act correctly (or, as you would put it, incorrectly). You have the choice: Either you work here or you don't. If a rank-and-file censor let something through— "what the hell, let the people find out!"—then he would be doing a poor job and letting down the business. And in the business everything depends on good human relations and it is an unusually close-knit crowd; the work requires it. Pretty tough articles would appear, but I don't think that it was the censor's decision. He may have been tempted but would decide against it, so as not to be taken in the business for one of those who have such tendencies. Such guys are OK in the high echelons. And quite frequently, the higher up you go, the more liberal it gets. A censor crosses something out, and the chief restores it. My chief was very favourably inclined toward the outspoken papers, and he would save all he could. He always spoke about *Wiez* [a Catholic magazine] in the highest terms and said that it would be a great pity if it should get into trouble (there have been such intentions) because *Wiez* offered a super approach to our national history. Among the outspoken papers, there were the incomparable *Tygodnik Powszechny, Polityka, Kultura, Literatura, Zycie Literackie*, and *Zycie Gospodarcze*. And among the dailies, the best were *Slowo Powszechne, Glos Pracy*, and the materials issued by the Polish Press Agency. The illustrated weeklies, in principle, suffered very little intervention.

Q: Does a censor get satisfaction from his work?

K-62: I was pleased when I prepared my report, and the chief told me I did a good job and nothing should be changed . . . But it is easier to be satisfied being a journalist than being a censor. A journalist would write something— we would remove it—but he had the feeling that he had tried. A censor also thought: fine, the guy goes to the bottom with honour. But satisfaction is not a normal feeling for a censor. he can speak of a job well done, that, yes.

Q: After he has crossed something out?

K-62: Well, look here, Miss; he is there to cross things out. He works in a crossing-out business. So what do you want him to do, write?

Q: It has been done.

K-62: Oh, cosmetic improvements. Adding a "now and then," or "sometimes." As you know, a censor has no contact with the author. But in fact, I do remember a text about Watergate in which there had been so many changes that the author came to the office and rewrote the text altogether with the censor. In general, towards the more renowned citizens, the attitude of the censors was, how shall I put it, more elegant . . .

Q: What does a chief expect from a rank-and-file censor?

K-62: Intelligence and loyalty.

Q: Have there been cases where a censor has behaved disloyally?

K-62: In my opinion, the fellow from Cracow who took out all this stuff to Sweden.[A former censor smuggled out major papers regarding the censorship office.] I am not convinced about his motives. He wrote later that his eyes had been opened and that he only awaited an opportunity to take this stuff out and publish it. If that is so—okay. But I have this feeling that he simply took advantage of an opportunity to make some cash and create some trouble for the business.

Q: Only some?

K-62: This is a very resilient business, Miss, and I don't remember any stronger reaction than some giggling. Perhaps upstairs, but among the blue-pencil crowd the incident was treated as funny. In the 1960s, he would have had a much harder time taking anything out. Censorship was much less bureaucratized . . . A lot of things were settled by telephone. Various high-placed people telephoned and gave word-of-mouth instructions, leaving no traces.

Q: You surely won't tell me that there were no word-of-mouth instructions in the 1970s. There are some even now.

K-62: If some Minister wanted to get something, in my time he had to do it through the Prime Minister or the Party's press department. And then we would get a written telephone message from the department. The message would go to the appropriate unit with a number and a date, so that it could be found and annulled when necessary. If there had been any word-of-mouth instructions I knew nothing about them. Apart from the Press department, instructions were sent down by the Minsitry of Foreign Affairs, the Government spokesman, and Minister Wieczorek. The Minsitry of Foreign Affairs would send lots of topical instructions. For instance, when Idi Amin put up a statue of Hitler, we were not allowed to write about it, because we had friendly agreements with Amin.

A censor works on the basis of a very thick instruction book and generally-stated but not fully-detailed principles of censorship. Each week we had a conference for the press censors on censorship-editing in the coming week. Some student festival was coming up, for instance, or a film such as *The Man of Marble* was opening in the cinemas. The directive was "look out, consult, don't trust yourselves too much, act collectively, because each censor has his intuition but it is highly individualized." A "feeling," an internal voice, "Hey, there is something there"—and then it is better to go and see the chief. The chief says either, "Well, yes," or else "It's all right, let it go."

Q: Did you ever get a text so horribly positive that a censor could not stand it and threw out this saccharin?

K-62: If a journalist wrote it in good faith, because he was stupid, and there are innumerable stupid journalists, then the censor did not feel obliged to teach him wisdom. But if he wrote in order to jeer, to build himself up, then he was stopped. We could distinguish there.

Q: Did you, as a censor, ever wonder what dictated this-or-that instruction or directive?

K-62: One takes it as it comes, because thinking is sterile. After all, what might lie behind the order not to mention that construction materials are full of poisons, or that it is a wonder that the people in Tomaszow Mazowiecki are alive at all? Must we discuss the face that it is a bloody shame, and then work in the business and take money for it? One must not think too much about such things, because it interferes with work. A journalist who is not absorbed in his job is a poor one. A censor could end up in a madhouse . . . I think that a modern-day censor is rather Kafkaesque, unreal.

Q: Except that the effects of his work are pretty real.

K-62: You will not make me admit to a bad conscience, moral scruples, or catharsis. There ain't no such thing. No way. I did approach my work in a double fashion, though. I am basically a good and honest guy, and I was doing something that was pretty nasty, objectively and subjectively.

Q: A split personality?

K-62: Do I really look like that? I treated my work in censorship as an episode in my life, nothing shocking. I never had nightmares about censorship.

Q: Yet, [someone] working in censorship must somehow rationalize what he is doing. You told me, for instance, that your work, which was not in prevention, but in creation (as you put it), informed you about what was going on in the country.

K-62: You won't get me to say it. I never pretended that by working in censorship, I was doing a good deed. It was not like that.

Q: Like what, then?

K-62: I wanted to know. And the longer I worked, the more papers I had on my desk, not just because there was an escalation of instruction but because the journalists were getting madder and madder. One had to react more and more strongly, according to the general principle of censorship, so that the authorities would feel good and the population would maintain the belief that everything was fine. More and more texts were rejected as a whole. And they were lovely to read.

Q: Lovely to read? You really had such a detached attitude?

K-62: Well, possibly I became somewhat cynical . . . I even had on my desk a text written by [someone] from my old sociology department. She worked hard on it, and then I worked hard, and in the end the whole thing was thrown out. It was an article on the language of official Party documents. A super piece . . .

Q: We talk pleasantly in the past tense, but all this is still going on.

K-62: Much more liberally, you will admit. One can see that the boys are working differently now. I believe that there is a deep conviction in this profession that it is necessary. The model of censorship may change; it may become even more liberal; but it is a most durable institution.

Q: Were the recent events a shock to the office?

K-62: I went to visit the office in September and asked them, can you feel the wind of history? And they said, of course, in the streets—in the papers—but not in the business. It was not shaking in its foundations. A shock in censorship, talked about to this day, was the year 1956 when the censorship department wanted to dissolve itself, and 1968 when very many Jews left work. I don't know what December 1970 was like. Nothing special happened in 1976; I don't remember any state of alert. The press struck one note, condemned troublemakers, and meetings were called. You did the job for us, although we were on the lookout and ready.

Q: How did the censors react to the appearance of uncensored publications?

K-62: They didn't. It was not a matter for consideration.

Q: Why did you leave the business?

K-62: Certainly not because my eyes were opened, as that fellow who took out the censorship material said. It was not a case of "at first I did not know, and then I did, and was shocked." As I have said, I was first interested and then I got bored . . . I came back in September [from abroad] and found myself out on the street once more. It is another country and, in the spirit of renewal, finding work is tough. One place I looked I as told, and I quote: "You may be a good man in private, and your references are pretty good, but it would be careless of us to employ you at this stage. You understand, we have nothing against you personally, but when people find out where you worked for a time, there might be trouble. So why start it?" All in all, I agreed with him . . .

Q: And what do other former censors do?

K-62: One is a director of a sanatorium; another is with the KAW publishing house. A [woman] I know is in the Main Chamber of Control. A couple of them became journalists. But I really don't know what I can do . . . I am getting married in three days time, and I put my trust in friends. I have invited 120 people. It may not be much as a goal in life, but I have no other idea.

Q: May we use your name in this interview?

K-62: It would not bother me. You could have my picture on Page One, too; but my wife asked me not to, and my mother would not be happy. Anyway, don't you think it would be neater to give a number? Because in the business there are no names. There are numbers.

Q: Why did you agree to this interview at all?

K-62: I am a helpful person. And, furthermore, I wanted people to find out how it functioned or, rather, how I think it did. Because a mountain of myths has grown up about the business—that it is all-powerful, almighty, staffed by demons.

Q: The question arises, will they find out? What do you think, as a professional?

K-62: I told a friend who works there. He laughed himself sick. He said that if it were up to him, he would let the whole damn thing through.

Q: What would he delete, though?

K-62: Miss, here you can delete nothing. You can only ban it completely.

[Suppression of free expression in Poland has a long history, dating from the Middle Ages during which Jews were confined to ghettoes. During the late eighteenth century, Poland was divided by conquering armies which imposed strict adherence to their own political philosophies. The country was overrun by German armies in World I, declared its independence in 1919, lost much territory to Russia in 1922, then fell under Nazi occupation in 1939. During World War II, the Nazis killed six million Poles, most of them Jews, Gypsies, and Gays. In 1947, Poland came under Soviet domination, during which the Stalinist puppet government confiscated private land and abolished all opposition. The government in 1953 required all higher level appointments in the Catholic church to be approved by the government. Three years later, however, the government, following massive rioting by a nation disgusted by economic conditions, approved a "liberalization" that included the restoration of religious liberty provided the church stayed out of politics. General riots in 1970 led to a revocation of massive price increases. Then, in mid-1980, workers began a series of strikes that crippled the country and led the government to recognize the independent trade union, Solidarity, with the right to strike. Among the demands of Solidarity was full and complete access to the nation's mass media. By the end of the year, however, under fear of Soviet invasion, the Polish government revoked the concessions it had previously made, clamped a tighter restricition on all media, and arrested Lech Walesa, Solidarity leader.]

Skokie: Protecting a Principle

[When the history of the American Republic is finally written, it will probably not be the war of revolution nor the Civil War, not westward expansion, industrialization, nor Franklin D. Roosevelt's "Fair Deal" or Lyndon Johnson's Great Society that identifies the American people. It will probably be Skokie, a town in Illinois in which the principles of libertarianism came into direct conflict with many of the principles of authoritarianism and social responsibility. It would be a case that would find Jews torn by their personal beliefs forced to defend Nazis against Jews, with the stakes being no less than a defense of the principles established by the First Amendment.]

Early in 1977 Frank Collin, leader of the National Socialist Party of America (commonly called the Nazis) wrote to a number of suburban park districts seeking permits to stage public assemblies in various suburban parks. It is our understanding that the Skokie Park District responded to his request by passing an ordinance which requires the posting of $350,000 insurance prior to any rally. (At the time, no similar insurance requirement was in effect for the streets or sidewalks of the Village of Skokie.)

Collin responded with a letter stating his intention to march in the Village of Skokie with his organization outside the Village Hall in protest of the Skokie park's ordinance insurance requirement. Collin's letter to Skokie stated that the march would last for half an hour on Sunday, May 1. The letter further stated that the demonstration would not feature either speeches aimed at particular ethnic or racial groups or the distribution of literature. The Nazis also indicated their intention to carry signs proclaiming "Free Speech for Whites" and similar slogans and their intention to appear in uniform and to display the swastika emblem. On April 27, 1977, several weeks after the letter was received, the Village of Skokie filed suit to enjoin the May 1st march. The Village scheduled an emergency hearing on April 28, 1977, a day after the filing of the suit, and sought an injunction against display of the uniforms or the swastika, and also sought to enjoin the dissemination of any Nazi literature. Frank Collin was served with notice of the April 28 hearing the night before that hearing. He thereupon contacted ACLU Roger Baldwin Fund attorneys. In light of the fact that the dispute was a classic First Amendment confrontation, members of the staff and the President of the organization conferred by telephone and decided to provide representation at the hearing the following morning.

This case study was written by members of the American Civil Liberties Union (ACLU), and distributed by the Illinois CLU. Principal writer was David Hamlin. Hamlin is Development Director for the American Civil Liberties Union of Southern California; he was formerly executive director of the New Hampshire CLU for four years, and the Illinois CLU for four years. Others who contributed were Aryeh Neier, executive director; Edwin Rothschild; Frank Haiman; Margo Krupp; Sheila Meyer; and David Goldberger, staff counsel who was appointed by the ACLU to represent the Nazis in court. Additional coments by Goldberger, taken from a letter to members of the ACLU, are included in parentheses; editors' comments are in brackets.

Skokie's case before the court was simple: the residents of the Village are violently opposed to the beliefs and tenets of the Nazis, and therefore *might* become violent if the Nazis appear and if the Villagers witness the demonstration.

(Skokie's population is predominantly Jewish, and includes a large number of concentration camp survivors. To allow people calling themselves Nazi to parade in that town seemed to many an agony too much to bear.

I share that agony. All of us at the ACLU do.

The Executive Director of the ACLU, Aryeh Neier, is himself a survivor of Nazi Germany. He has more reason than most to despise what people calling themselves Nazis stand for.

But the Nazis are not the real issue. The Skokie laws are the real issue.)

'Heckler's Veto'

Skokie did not contend, and still does not contend, that the marchers would be anything other than peaceful. They did, and do, contend that the audience might violate the law by becoming unruly or agitated. Because the audience is that hostile, Skokie argued, the demonstration should not be allowed to take place as planned. That argument, known as the "heckler's veto," is the core of the dispute.

After a brief hearing before the Circuit Court Judge Wosik, an injunction was issued prohibiting the Nazis from displaying their uniform, swastika, or disseminating literature in Skokie on May 1, 1977. A stay of that injunction was immediately sought from the Illinois Appellate Court, and was summarily denied. Thereafter, the Nazis announced their intention to appear in Skokie to stage their demonstration on April 30, a date which the injunction did not cover. The Village sought, on the morning of April 30, a second injunction to prevent that day's march. Arguing before a Circuit Court Judge who resides in Skokie—and without any notice to either Frank Collin, his group, or his lawyers—the Village obtained an extention of the original injunction covering April 30 and *all* days following.

The basis of the defense argued by ACLU/Roger Baldwin Fund was that an audience response to a demonstration cannot be grounds for censorship. Thus, we argued, the First Amendment protects all ideas, even those which have little or no popular support. We argued that those who disagree with the Nazi positions are free to express that disagreement, using the First Amendment, with a counter-demonstration or some other lawful means; the rights which we seek to protect for the Nazis are the same rights we seek to protect for those who disagree with them. If a hostile audience can ban a demonstration simply by threatening to become agitated or violent, then no demonstration is safe: those opposed to the right to choice in the abortion debate could threaten to half a demonstration by those who favor that right to choice; speeches or marches by Socialists, Republicans, or any political group could be prevented by an openly hostile opposition. No idea in the political spectrum achieves total support, and most ideas generate hostile opposition. If we wanted to listen to, and to debate, only popular ideas we wouldn't need a First Amendment at all—it is there precisely because ideas often meet hostile resistance, and it guarantees that such opposition will not rise to the level of government censorship.

Arguments and Counter-Arguments

In the days following the issuance of the injunction, ACLU/RBF sought direct appeal to the Illinois Supreme Court. That Court refused to accept the case for a hearing, and refused to stay the force of the injunction pending such a hearing. ACLU/RBF therefore appealed to the United States Supreme Court for a stay of the injunction. In a dramatic (and highly unusual) move, the Court treated the petition for a stay as a petition to hear the full procedural case, then granted that petition, and ruled, ordering the Illinois courts to decide the matter of the validity of the injunction expeditiously.

In the meantime, Skokie's Village Council met and passed three new ordinances, creating the same barriers to a Nazi march which the injunction itself created. The first ordinance requires a permit for any demonstration of fifty or more individuals in the streets or on the sidewalks of Skokie. To secure that permit, the applicant must provide $350,000 insurance (this requirement is distinct from the Skokie Park requirement which set the entire case moving). A second ordinance bans "political organizations" from demonstrating in "military-style" uniforms. The third is a dual ban on both the display of "symbols offensive to the community" and on the distribution of literature which says unpleasant things about racially or ethnically identifiable groups. For all of the reasons which led us to oppose the injunction, ACLU/RBF have also challenged the ordinances in Federal District Court. We believe, incidentally, that one of the first groups to be denied a permit to demonstrate in Skokie under the first ordinance was the Jewish War Veterans, who wanted to march in opposition to Collin but who apparently couldn't find the insurance required. (It is crucial that these kinds of laws and requirements be struck down, because there is no way to limit them. If they are not struck down, then *towns everywhere will have the legal power to pass identical laws, and to use them to prohibit whatever they believe is offensive.*

Think of such power in the hands of a racist sheriff, or a local police department hostile to anti-war demosntrators, or the wrong kind of President.)

A number of legal arguments have been raised by friend and foe alike in the Skokie debate. Many of the arguments raised are, by virtue of the law or the facts, inapplicable to Skokie:

1. The Nazi activity in Skokie will be the precise equivalent of shouting "Fire" in a crowded theater. Everyone seems to know that the Supreme Court once said it was beyond First Amendment protection to falsely shout "Fire" in a crowded theater, and a lot of people believe that the Nazi march in Skokie is the equivalent of that shout. The "Fire" doctrine does not apply in Skokie for two crucial reasons.

First, the doctrine covers a captive audience, one which does not expect—and therefore cannot avoid—the message. A public demonstration, announced in advance, does not provide that captive audience—anyone who wishes to avoid the message is absolutely free to do so by simply avoiding the location of the message when it is delivered. Nobody in Skokie is required to go watch the Nazi demonstration.

Second, "Fire" contemplates surprise and panic (and people racing for the exists) in the midst of which a counter message can't be delivered ("Wait, there is no fire."). The doctrine, in other words, speaks to a circumstance in which only *one side* of the debate can be heard. In Skokie, there will be no surprise, for there will be ample, advance warning, which negates the panic element; moreover, the advance notice provides anyone who wants to deliver a counter-message ample time to do so. Where both sides of the issue can be aired, "Fire" does not apply.

2. The Nazi activity is the equivalent of "fighting words." Skokie itself has used this argument, claiming that the swastika, displayed before the Jewish residents of Skokie, is "fighting words" to that audience, and thus beyond First Amendment protection. The "fighting words" doctrine is a rarely used doctrine which says that in personal communications one cannot use words characterizing another under circumstances likely to cause that other to retaliate physically *before* he has a moment for rational reflection.

"Fighting Words" is designed, therefore, to control one-to-one confrontations, and has never been applied, in any other context. It was not written, and has not been applied, in a context involving political demonstrations.

Moreover, one cannot determine in advance whether words are "fighting" or not. Only *after* the words are uttered can a court judge their impact, so that even if Collin is using a symbol as "fighting words," that charge is valid only *after* the demonstration, not as the basis for prior restraint or an injunction.

Finally, it is questionable whether "fighting words" could ever apply where the messenger and the recipient are separated by a line of law enforcement officers, which is likely to be the case in Skokie. The recipient of the "fighting words" will have to go through a police line to physically respond, and presumably the police will restrain that response on the spot.

3. "Obscenity." A surprising number of people seize upon the Supreme Court's obscenity exception to the First Amendment and . . . suggest that because everyone knows Nazism is "obscene," censorship of the Nazi march is justified.

The Supreme Court, whatever one thinks about its work in the obscenity area, has never suggested that obscene can be used to define anything other than *sexually* explicit material. Never has the Court even considered expanding obscenity to include social or political ideas, no matter how offensive.

For obscenity to apply, the Courts would have to judge the content of the Nazi message, and such a judgement would be directly contrary to everything the democratic system and the First Amendment stand for.

4. The Nazi march in Skokie will be "incitement to riot." If the audience actually attacks Collin and his followers in Skokie, won't Collin have commited the crime by inciting that attacks with his mere presence? No.

For incitement to be valid, the speaker must urge upon his audience unlawful conduct which the audience then undertakes to commit in concert with the speaker's advocacy. In Skokie, that circumstance would exist if Frank Collin urged the audience to attack Frank Collin; simple logic suggests that Colin is not going to do that. Collin and his followers have no intention of advocating unlawful conduct in Skokie.

In general, two principles are notably useful in debating the extra-legal arguments. First, Skokie has amply demonstrated a willingness to use any valid method to stop the Nazi march. If any of the arguments used above had merit, Skokie would have adopted them, and they have not done so.

Second, while it is true that the Supreme Court has found on rare occasions exceptions to the First Amendment, it has always done so on the narrowest possible grounds and never in a context which favors prior restraint against speech. The Court's willingness to protect the First Amendment against prior restraint through an injunction extends to a rejection of the United States Government's argument that American lives would be lost as the direct result of publication of the Pentagon Papers. If, in time of war with combat troops in the field, the U.S. Supreme Court rejected censorship, how can Skokie justify narrowing the First Amendment?

The ACLU Mission

Beyond the facts of the case, and beyond the law involving the First Amendment, there are objections to ACLU/RBF involvement in the Skokie matter which go directly to our principles, our mission. These come, in my experience, from those who know us best. It is the audience which knows about civil liberties, which knows where we stand, it is *that* audience which challenges our principles in this matter.

They ask "How can ACLU represent an organization which would eliminate ACLU if it came to power?" The answer is: because the principles we protect serve to protect democracy itself, and we have faith in that system. To permit a court or a legislative body to select ideas on the basis of content, and enjoin those ideas which are unpopular or repugnant, will weaken our basic freedom by opening the doors to censorhsip of any political speech. The risk which accompanies freedom is the risk that people will make bad choices, and the only way to overcome that risk is to eliminate democracy itself by limiting the range of ideas available for debate.

We oppose, in all our organizational willingness to protect all ideas, Nazism and all other totalitarian systems; we are confident that countless organizations and individuals will continue to fight, and to reject, such platforms. If Skokie has taught us nothing else, it has certainly taught us that Nazism has no support in the body politic; thus, the only real fight in Skokie is the censorship fight.

Some protest that ACLU/RBF doesn't *have* to defend Nazis, that the principle could be defended with another, presumably less repugnant, client. ACLU/RBF *must* protect the First Amendment, which in turn protect tha Nazi right to demonstrate in this instance. ACLU and RBF are, first and foremost, protectors of the rights to free expression. We must never turn away a meaningful First Amendment case. We have represented the Nazis before and may well be required, by the actions of another governmental body, to represent them again. Our single most vital purpose (and our most meaningful service to the community) is our willingness to protect the rights of everyone—even the most unpopular, even the most anti-democratic.

We did not create this controversy. It was the Village of Skokie's willingness to remove from the political spectrum which created this case. We take no institutional benefit other than the adherence to principle which is our hall mark from this case. If Skokie had relied upon the judgment of its people, and their ability to respond lawfully to ideas both good and bad, there would have been no litigation. Instead, Skokie's officials decided to remove from the people of Skokie the right to reject a bad idea; Skokie decided to supplant that power with a court order. Courts do not—must not—decide which ideas are good and which are bad; legislative bodies do not decide which ideas are good and which are bad; ACLU does not decide which ideas are good and which are bad—only citizens have that power. When anyone seeks to alter or remove that power, ACLU/RBF steps in.

Similarly, those who argue that ACLU/RBF are *too* blind to the politics of the case fail to recognize our role. We, like the courts, must be blind to the ideas which Skokie wants to censor. We, with the courts, must protect the marketplace for all ideas, leaving to each person the ultimate choices.

We are asked, "Can't this principle be tested in another way?" What good does it do to expend resources on the defense of clients such as these in such an ultimately minor matter? First, the reaction to our work suggests that this is hardly a minor matter. Second, this principle is tested constantly, and we almost inevitably take part in that testing—but on *every* case in the First Amendment part in that testing—but on *every* case in the First Amendment area, not just those we like or feel good about, but in all instances. In the field of free expresion, we take all cases.

Perhaps more importantly, it remains true that from *any* case in the realm of free expression can come precedent which is very important or very dangerous. In the early 1960s, the Supreme Court of the United States laid down the constitutional foundation for the activist phase of the civil right movement with two important decisions. Both cases involved the rights of demonstrators, and in finding for the rights of those demonstrators the Court relied on a previous ruling in the area. The case which the Court used to open the doors to civil rights activism in the streets, at lunch counters, in schoolhouse . . . was *Terminello*, an ACLU/RBF suit involving the rights of an avowed racist. In the right to voice racism, the Court found the right to preach equality. Even unpopular, anti-democratic clients end up protecting the rights of everyone, whether or not the client believes in those rights himself.

Because any case can lead to that sort of protection, and because we are firmly committed to protecting all rights for all citizens, ACLU/RBF really had no choice: we would have been untrue to ourselves, our purposes, and our ultimate promise to the public if we had let Skokie's attempt to censor go without challenge.

It is also true that we are not "house counsel" to the Nazi Party. We represent them on 1st Amendment issues (or other free expression matters) because that's our job. We do not take their cases no matter what—Collin's organization and Collin himself are the objects of close Federal scrutiny for both income tax and gun law violations, and in neither instance do we represent Collin . . .

Finally, in response to all arguments about our motives and our purpose, ACLU and The Roger Baldwin Foundation are above all else dedicated to the protection of those principles which the nation itself places above all else. If we depart from those principles, because public pressure is against our particular client and we are associated with his defense, then we are less than we claim to be, and ultimately not very valuable at all. In the 1950s, as ACLU sought to protect citizens from the Red Scare and its fall-out, there was considerable concern that people would perceive ACLU itself as a "communist" organization because it defended communists. To ward off such hostility, to remove the stigma of "bad" clients, a few members of the ACLU family (without the knowledge of the rest of the organization) sought to cooperate with the FBI to assure that the organization remained "untainted" by "subversives."

To be absolutely *sure* that nobody thought ACLU was just like its clients, those individuals in question passed to a law enforcement agency minutes of meetings and memoranda, tactics, and "inside" information. Many people regard that conduct as shameful, some regard it less harshly; nobody questions the fact that a departure from the principles which guide the organization occured, and nobody questions tha fact that that departure was wrong.

Nobody else would defend Frank Collin and the Nazi Party because nobody else has, as the single, guiding criterion, the principles and integrity which ACLU/RBF bring to every single suit we file.

Attacks Upon the ACLU

(Yet many, understandably, did not see it that way. They felt that the Nazis' views were so reprehensible that they did not deserve the protection of the Constitution.

A few people even made personal threats against me and other members of the ACLU staff.

The effect of all this on the ACLU has been very disturbing to me. Thousands of members have resigned, and its income has plummeted. For the first time in fifty-eight years of serving as a watchdog and enforcer of the Bill of Rights, ACLU is suffering a decline.

All over the country, ACLU offices have had to lay off staff, and financial support for many of its cases is now in jeopardy.

Of the approximately 6,000 cases handled by the ACLU throughout the country, only six—or one-tenth of one percent—are like the Skokie case. But now the others are in danger, too, because there isn't enough money to continue.

What do we say to the woman who has been cut off from Medicaid payments for abortion? Or to the parents of a mentally retarded child rotting in a state institution? What do we say to a former government employee whose book on the CIA is being censored? Or to parents and teachers in a high school that has just banned Kurt Vonnegut and Bernard Malamud from its shelves?

Right now, we may have to say no. We can't help. Too many members have stopped contributing . . .

On May 22, 1978, the United States Court of Appeals struck down all three Skokie laws including the $350,000 insurance requirement. On June

12, 1978 the United States Supreme Court refused a request to bar the Skokie demonstration. In doing so, the Court put an end to 409 days of prior restraint.

We were relieved that the citizens of Skokie were spared yet another reminder of the horrors that Nazis represents. The Nazis chose to rally in Chicago when the ACLU persuaded the U.S. District Court to overrule the Chicago Park District's opposition . . .

In every generation, there is a comparatively small number of people with rare social insight whose thoughtfulness and conscience tip the scales in favor of important human values. Their names are not always recorded in the history books, but the consequences of their deeds are.)

Kanawha County:
Not Just Another Book Burning

by Walter M. Brasch

It's relatively quiet now in Kanawha County, West Virignia. Children are riding school buses, and parents are no longer firebombing the schools.

Many call what happened in 1974 in the 970 square mile, 230,000 population rural county a battle over censorship, a "Battle of the Books." But, what happened was not censorship as much as a philosophy of life that led to a social movement, one which illustrated the breakdown in the traditional concepts of what distinguished authoritarian, libertarian, and social responsibility theories.

It had begun long ago, in Charleston, the state capital and county seat of Kanawha County, and in Alum Creek, Blue Creek, Coal Fork, Sissonville, Frame, Pocotalico, Blakeley, Mammouth, Dawes, Eksdale, Decota, Weyako, and many other small rural villages, some with only a few houses and a store or two. For quite some time, the people in the rural areas of the county had thought that the people in the city, Charleston, were getting all the benefits, the better roads, the jobs. In the rural areas of the state, mining salt and bituminous coal alternated with unemployment, poverty, and Black Lung Disease. The people in Charleston just don't listen to us, complained some of the people of the rural, areas; the people of the rural areas just aren't educated, complained some of the people of the city. For years, the people in the rural county put up with what the people in the state capital ordered. For years, they put up with it, yet tried to assert their independence, their rugged individualism.

The Protest Begins

In 1970, in response to national trends, the state board of education mandated all school districts to include "inter-ethnic textbooks that accurately portray minority and ethnic group contributions to American growth and culture . . . and depict and illustrate the intercultural character of our pluralistic state." For

Nazis won, but chose to go elsewhere, anyway

four years, no major problems surfaced in the 121 public schools of Kanawha County. Then in April, a five-teacher commission recommended a purchase of a total of 96,095 copies of 325 composition and literature titles from the state lists. This time, the Kanawha County School Board decided to look into some of the books. "Trashy, filthy, and too one-sided!" proclaimed Alice Moore, a member of the five-person school board, who had been elected in 1970 for her opposition to sex education in schools. Intelligent, articulate, and respected, Moore would now lead the opposition to the inclusion of most of the new books into district curriculum. She would oppose books that included dialect and Black English, books that included sexual situations, "obscene" or "dirty words"—Arthur Miller's *All My Sons* included the phrase "God damn" thirty-nine times—and books and articles in which characters showed disrespect for authority, protested certain American traditions or ideals. Many would accurately note that some of the writing in the books—most of the editors were public school teachers and university professors—was "poor" or "mediocre." Others would label many of the books as anti-American, Communistic, and both un-Christian and anti-Christian.

In June, the school board, with almost a thousand persons in attendance, voted 3-2 to accept all but eight of teh books recommended by the teachers' committee. The Board did agree that poems by e.e. cummings, Allen Ginsberg, Gwendolyn Brooks, and Lawrence Ferlinghetti, and articles by Sigmund Freud, Germaine Greer, and Eldridge Cleaver, among many others, were not suitable for high school juniors and seniors. The decision to accept all but eight of the books infuriated Moore who took the leadership in a campaign to stop distribution of all books.

By now, she was getting the support of a large majority of the rural population of the county, most of whom believed they saw an erosion in the values and educational levels of their children. Together, they formed Concerned Citizens. When the Rev. Marvin Horan, minister of the Freewill Baptist Church, created Christian-American Parents, most of the congregations of the county's fundamentalist churches became involved. Together, they launched a massive publicity campaign, and prepared for a confrontation.

Boycotting Education

On September 3, 1975, the opening day of school, several hundred angry parents—more than two-thirds of them the mothers of Kanawha County students—threw picket lines around the schools in the eastern half of the county. About half the students in rural areas did not show up for class; absenteeism in the Charleston areas, however, was reported as eight percent, "about normal"; more than eleven thousand students in the 45,000-student district were absent. The next day, the parents picketed not only the schools, but also the mines.

More than 3,500 miners—most of them in sympathy with the aims of the parents' groups, and unwilling to cross any picket line, even if they knew that secondary boycotts were illegal, stayed away in a wildcat strike that would cost coal owners more than $20 million. The leadership of the United Mine Workers (UMW) ordered the membership to return to work; most refused.

The strike quickly spread to four other counties. Soon, nine thousand miners were on strike; thousands of other workers—truckers, businessmen, construction workers, among others—dependent upon the mines, were forced off the job.

Two days after picketing began, the school board and coal operators obtained temporary restraining orders (TROs) against picketing. Concentrating upon keeping pickets from in front of the school buses and out of the entrances to the schools, the Sheriff's Department did not enforce the TROs for several days.

On September 10, the beginning of the second week of the protest, Dr. K. E. Underwood, school superintendent, ordered the county schools closed following extensive violence on the picket line. When the schools reopened a week later, Underwood had removed all offending textbooks from the schools for thirty days, and created, with the school board, an eighteen-member citizens committee to investigate the books. But, this was not enough for many of the parents of Kanawha County who demanded a return of power to the people, no punishment for protestors or children, and the resignation not only of Underwood, but also of Albert Anson, Jr., school board president who had voted with the majority that originally permitted the books in the schools.

And still the strikes and protests continued. By now, parents were blocking entrances to schools, throwing rocks at school buses, and violating court injunctions that required groups of no more than five pickets at any site at any time. Even heavy fines and jail sentences for most of the eleven arrested did not stop picketing or the violence. One minister prayed that God would "strike three members of the Kanawha County Board of Education dead" for having voted to allow the books into the schools. Others sent death threats to Underwood, Anson, and several others who opposed the banning of books.

And now, in large bonfires, in scenes not unlike those throughout the history of mankind, books were being burned, to the cheers of hundreds.

On October 6, more than four thousand people, led by several fundamentalist ministers, attended a rally designed to overthrow the decisions of the school board. Horan defiantly shouted, "No education at all is one hundred percent better than what's going on in the schools now!" He urged a boycott of all schools in a three county area "until all the books are out!" It was a suggestion that was virtually unanimously supported. Monday morning, October 7, hundreds of protestors set up a large scale defiance of the school board and the courts. Nineteen of the protestors were arrested on a variety of charges, including resisting arrest, obstructing traffic, unlawful assembly, failing to obey the lawful orders of a police officer—and littering. The Rev. Ezra Graley, one of the most militant of the leaders, who was fined $250 and sentenced in September to thirty days in jail, was now fined $1,500 and sentenced to an additional sixty days in jail.

Following the sentencing of Graley and several others, violence again struck the county. This time, it went beyond rock throwing and name calling. One man was shot, and an auto firebombed. And then they struck the schools along Cabin Creek; the two dynamite blasts and two firebombings caused damage, but were done when no one was expected to be in the buildings. At subsequent trials, the nine persons who were originally arrested for the violence said that their purpose was to "scare the students" into staying at home. Among those convicted was Horan who was sentenced to a three-year prison term.

Later, Anson and Underwood both resigned in protest of the violence and the mass protests. In mid-October, a delegation of protestors presented their concerns to a White House official who "promised to assist."

Finally, on November 8, the Board, having seen many of its schools under seige since the first week in September, declared that "no student would be required to use a book that is objectionable on moral or religious grounds [and no teacher is] authorized to indoctrinate a student to follow either moral or religious values which are objectionable to either student or parent." By a 4-1 vote, Alice Moore dissenting, the Board allowed the 325 books back into the schools as supplemental reading. But, the fighting was not over. Several hundred parents cheered as the Rev. Avis Hill shouted, "We have just begun to fight! If it comes to it, we'll even set up our own schools!"

A subsequent report by the National Education Association (NEA) avoided the main issues, and put much of the "blame" for the continuation of the protest on "highly-sophisticated, well-organized right-wing extremist groups" who "had infiltrated" the people. The media even had a field day when the Ku Klux Klan came to town in January, at no one's invitation, got four hundred citizens to attend a rally, and proclaimed most of the books not only "dirty," un-American, and un-Christian, but part of a "Communistic plot" to destroy the moral fiber of America. However, the NEA, the American Library Association, the various media organizations, and others who had come into Kanawha County recognized that *they* were also "highly-sophisticated, well-organized . . . outside influences" whom many of the protestors believed had "infiltrated" the people in education and government with philosophies opposed to the common good of the people.

A Descent of Reporters

The cry of censorship, no matter how muffled, will usually arouse even the most apolitical organizations. Some will support the censorship or pre-selection of reading materials, indicating that there is a "higher responsibility" to the community; others will attack any action as a violation of the most basic rights of mankind. For those organizations directly concerned about free expression, it will serve to rally a massive counter-protest, often reflected in news columns as objective reporting—the facts are accurate, the truth may be distorted.

George Weber, who in 1975 was acting editor of the *Council for Basic Education Bulletin*, did not see the controversy as being censorship-caused. "One of the most inane arguments in textbook controversies is the cry of 'censorship,' " Weber wrote in the January 1975 issue. Elaborating, he noted:

> In connection with the Kanawha County episode, [censorship] was raised in defence [sic] of the controversial books by many who should know better. It is not censorship to choose one book rather than another for school use, nor to decide that a book, once chosen, should be dropped

in favor of another. One can only conclude that Americans have had so little experience with censorhsip that many do not know the meaning of the term.

Weber was technically correct, but his views represented only a minority opinion within the media.

The local and regional media had hovered around the story for several months before the April meeting in which Alice Moore had expressed her concern about the kind of textbooks the district was purchasing. As the protest became stronger, and with the beginning of the boycott on September 3, the media now descended into Kanawha County; within three months, stories would appear on the three television networks, in most daily newspapers (some of whom sent their own reporters, others of whom used AP or UPI reports), and in major national magazines, including both *Time* and *Newsweek*. Most newspapers editorialized against what they saw as censorship; some agreed that the protestors were right; and many took no sides at all, either not concerned or not wishing to offend anyone, the same problem most the local and state politicians faced. For his editorials against censorship and the violence of the protest, John D.

Whose Foot Is To Be The Measure . . . ?

One day in 1814, Thomas Jefferson decided he wanted to read a copy of work by M. deBecourt who discussed the creation of the universe. Upon learning that the book was banned in Virginia, he shot off a vitriolic letter that questioned what the United States had become in the three decades after its founding:

I am really mortified to be told that, in the United States of America, a . . . science book can become a subject of inquiry, and of criminal inquiry too, as an offence against religion; that a question about the sale of a book can be carried before the civil magistrate. Is this then our freedom of religion? And are we to have a censor whose imprimatur shall say what books may be sold, and what we may buy? And who is thus to dogmatize religious opinions for our citizens? Whose foot is to be the measure to which ours are all to be cut or stretched? Is a priest to be our inquisitor, or shall a layman, simple as ourselves, set up his reason as the rule for what we are to read, and what we must believe? It is an insult to our citizens to question whether they are rational beings or not, and blasphemy against religion to support it cannot stand the test of truth and reason. If M. deBecourt's book be false in its facts, disprove them; if false in its reasoning, refute it. But, for God's sake, let us freely hear both sides, if we choose . . . [Letter to N.G. Dufief, April 19, 1814]

Maurice of the *Charleston Daily Mail* was awarded the Pulitzer Prize in 1975. Many reporters stayed to learn about the issues; most, however, were "instant anthropologists"—they came into the area, looked around, talked to a few people, picked up a few bits of information, wrote a few stories, then left, never really understanding the complex issues that went beyond book burning.

In the state capital, where the "flatlanders" and city-folk frequently had little to do with those "hillbillies," people took up banners against censorship and the "armies of ignorance," and often talked about "them hillbillies who called up to say what was 'wrote' in the books." The protestors had objected to "bad language" in the textbooks, language that included Black English as well as Standard English "cuss words." The media noted the protestor concerns, then held the "uneducated hill folk" up to public ridicule by printing their exact spoken dialect.

Most frequently, the reporters echoed a "defender of the books" stance, sounded by educators and the "city-folk," that the protestors hadn't read the books; at most they had read isolated passages from several books. But, the reporters also didn't report that few of educators had read more than parts of the books; certainly, not one person in the state had read even a tenth of all 325 books. Combined, the five member textbook selection committee hadn't read all the books.

Most reporters looked at the protest and saw a fusion of church and state, noting that the protest was a moral crusade. The protest is against books that don't hold Christianity up to the best possible light, the media reported, pointing out the supporters are Baptist fundamentalists, and not in the "mainstream" of religion. For justification, the media seemed to delight in pointing out that most of the ministers had other jobs, and that many of the "mainstream" Christian ministers opposed the protestors, noting specifically that the Episcopal clergy in Charleston had noted that the disputed books were "creative and timely." However, most of the protestors were not so upset by stories that reflected alternative religious values, but those they considered either reflected *anti*-Christian values, or did not present Christianity at all.

"Get them nigger books outta our schools!" the reporters heard protestors proclaim, and assumed there was blatant racism in the protest. When people began throwing rocks at school buses, the media often assumed that, like in other cities, it was an attack upon integration. It seemed reasonable—the reporters reasoned. After all, most of the books either dealt with ethnic themes, or were anthologies of literature that included poems and short stories that were written by Blacks, Hispanics, Jews, and other minorities, and often reflected urban bias. But, the protestors, although many undoubtedly were racist, were not protesting the ethnicity as much as the lack of stories about the people of the West Virginia hills. "Aren't we ethnic, too?" they asked. "Shouldn't our children learn about *our* way of life? . . . Certainly, there must be stories by West Virginia authors who wrote about the people of the hills."

But, the exclusion of books was still seen as censorhsip, and many of the national organizations that became involved used the "professional educator" argument to urge a change of attitudes. The Authors League sent a message to President Gerald Ford and Attorney General William Saxbe—"No groups have the right to dictate what particular books may not be used by the schools of their community. The selection of books is the professional responsibility of teachers and school administrators." The Association of American Publishers declared, "Qualified educators should be the ones to decide what instructional teachings should be used."

The National Education Association and the American Library Association, both of which have censorship "watchdog" functions, at the invitation of a local teachers' association, sent a combined eight-member team into Kanawha County for three days. The group determined that, indeed, there was censorship. The protestors countered that they had a right—and a duty—to teach their own children about moral values, sex, religion, and politics. However, the NEA added to the class war by arguing that it must be professional educators, not parents, who determine what children should read. The protestors readily admitted they may not know as much as the educators, but that it was not "anti-intellectualism," as much as the fact they didn't trust the educators. The protestors, led by the fundamental ministers, correctly argued that there were numerous children in the high schools who didn't even have a grasp of the basic fundamentals of learning—they couldn't spell, had trouble with the essentials of arithmetic, and could barely read. Most of the parents did not have as much academic education as the teachers, many didn't even have high school diplomas. But, they knew it was only through education that their children would be able to "get a better break in life" than they had. Why should we trust teachers who couldn't teach, they argued. It was a difficult argument to rebut.

Dr. Terrell Bell, U.S. Commissioner of Education, disagreed that textbook selection must be done entirely by professional educators. Addressing textbook publishers on December 2, 1974, Bell used a classic libertarian argument—and was criticized by many who saw themselves as "liberals" for being not only "conservative," but "reactionary":

> Parents have the ultimate responsibility for the upbringing of their children. When they send their children to school, they delegate some of their authority to administrators and teachers. These professionals should, in turn, respect parental attitudes represented by children in their classrooms.

It's been more than a decade since Alice Moore first argued against the textbooks, and the people of Kanawha County realized how little power and influence they had in their government. But, the revolution did work. Although the books were eventually used by the students, the school board recognized the rights of both students and parents to help determine what kind of education they needed. Eventually, the school district established Parent Advisory committees (PAC), each of them meeting once a month with teachers and school officials. The PACs have no power, but the public officials have realized that the wishes of the people must be taken into consideration in all aspects of their governance.

Textbooks went into use
PAC has no power, but is still useful (→ how?)

Alice Moore became the president of the school board, then moved to Columbus, Ohio, where her husband, a minister, was given a larger congregation. Those sentenced to prison, including the Revs. Graley and Horan, served their time, returned to their communities, and tried to resume their pre-boycott lives. The revolution was over.

The Breakdown of Theoretical Distinction

The Kanawha County textbook case illustrates the failure of the authoritarian, libertarian, and social responsibility theories to clearly identify and differentiate political and media philosophy. If one assumes that the protestors represent authoritarian theory, then the school board majority, and numerous anti-censorship forces, would have to represent libertarian theory. The authoritarian theory would argue that the protestors had the right—even the responsibility—to remove the books from the schools. If the books inlcuded obscenity, blasphemy, heresy, or showed a disrespect for authority, as determined by the dominant religion in the area, then the books must be banned as not being in the public interest; when read by children, the books most likely would be harmful to them. The libertarian theory would argue that, with the exception of obscenity, defamation, excessive sexual situations, seditious libel, and treason, all books must be available to the people and that the school board, by allowing all views, was giving the people, a rational creature in God's image, the choice. Thus, the school board, by presenting alternative literature, was acting within the tenets of the libertarian theory. But, the authoritarian theory also argues that the purpose of the media and, thus, the people, is to support the government, itself composed of the people; attacks upon government are attacks upon the people. Thus, the attacks by the protestors were attacks against lawful authority. Traditionally, those in power became more authoritarian-like in their actions; those our of power became more libertarian-like in their actions.

If some of the doctrines of the libertarian theory are applied to the protestors, then the actions of the school board are seen as being authoritarian. Because many libertarians would also have excluded obscenity, defamation, indecency and excessive sexual matter, treason and wartime sedition from the media, the protestors could argue that they were libertarian for they were excluding that which the basic theory argued could be, even should be, excluded.

However, the central issue of the Kanawha case was not the books themselves, although the books had been part of the controversy. The issue was the right of the people to determine their own government and to decide what kind of education they wanted. They had believed that they were excluded from the decision-making process in all areas of government. They saw others imposing taxes upon them, but not listening to how the people wanted those taxes spent. They tried, but few listened. And, always, it was as if the school board or the "government," was telling them, "You're good people, but *we're* the experts. We'll make the decisions that affect your lives." Certainly, the NEA and all the teachers groups' and all the teachers' groups supporters did little to alleviate the class war; their tactics were to argue against censorship, but for the right of a small minority, the "educated," to make the decisions. In defense of textbook selection policies, the various groups would point to how many years of education they had, how much knowledge and experience they had acquired—and, thus, widened the gulf. Yet, while thinking they were libertarian, they were truly authoritarian, for as Plato argued, decision-making should be by those "philosopher-kings" who were specially-selected by divine providence to rule. Once in power, whether by nature a conservative or revolutionary, people tend to argue that because they have been exposed to "another side," and because they now have a lot of information that the average person does not have, they now can see many different aspects to an issue and, thus, know what is best. The teachers' groups would see the war as a battle that also involved academic freedom. But, even here the teachers themselves were constrained—no teacher could select a book that was not already approved by an even smaller group of the "elite" or "educated." Thus, there was not even true academic freedom, a situation the teachers, not the protestors, created.

Mankind is *not* rational, the school board and anti-censorship forces argued-afterall, look at what the protestors tried to do to censor books! Certainly, book burning and violence against dissenters is authoritarian, not libertarian. But, in arguing for the irrationality of the protestors, the school board was really presenting a basis of the authoritarian theory. Further, if there was true libertarianism, it would not make any difference if the protestors won at first, or the school board won—the "self-righting process" would eventually allow truth to emerge. It might take awhile, but at some point it would be apparent that the people were right to protest the books, or the school board was right to force certain books into the curriculum.

The social responsibility theory, which has almost as many elements of authoritarianism as libertarianism in it, argues that mankind *is* rational, but that it is essentially lazy, and needs continual assistance, that conflict must be raised to the "plane of discussion." Thus, each side could claim that it was, by its actions, putting a spur to society. The Board could argue it was forcing the people to see other cultures, other values; the protestors could argue they were forcing the people to recognize how their freedoms had been eroded by governmental action, that by a massive boycott, a revolution of the people, they were forcing the issues to the public.

The media should be controlled not only by professional ethics, but also by community opinion and the actions of the people, the theory propounds; each side could argue that the theory met its needs. The protestors could argue that they were the community—maybe not the Charleston community, but certainly the "hills" community of rural West Virginia—that their actions were meant for the preservation of the community. The anti-censorship groups could claim that a group of all people—metropolitan and rural—elected a school board to establish policy and, thus, it was the school board, not isolated groups, which represented the community. Whereas the authoritarian theory prohibits sedition and treason, criticism of officials and the accepted majority religiaon, and the libertarian theory forbid defamation, obscenity, sexual indecency, and sedition in times of crises, the social responsibility theory would permit the censoring of books which included a serious attack upon private rights and social concerns. The anti-censorship forces would argue that censoring the books would be the same as denying the people the right to read literature that is regarded as "classic," informative, or challenging, that no one's rights are violated in the presentation of such literature. The protestors would disagree, arguing that the presentation of what is perceived to be blasphemy, obscenity, defamation, and heresy could only serve to hurt individuals who held strong moral convictions, and that as such it could destroy the basic moral fibers of the community. If the media do not assume a social obligation to the people, the theory argues, then the people must assume that responsibility. For the protestors, it was logical that since the books were "irresponsible," then the people who buy the books, the taxpayers, must exert their responsibility to keep the books out of the school system.

What happened in Kanawha County was a microcosm of America. It was not a libertarian vs. authoritarian approach to political and social issues—although those in power tend to accept whatever parts of the authoritarian theory that is comfortable to them, and those out of power tend to accept libertarianism, at least those parts which are beneficial to them. It was not a censorship vs. anti-censorship battle; it was not a gaggle of "crazies" vs. a bureaucracy of "high-brows"; it was not a lot of things that the people and the media said it was. What it was, however, was a traditional struggle against those in power, fighting to retain their professional pride and dignity, and its perceived right to hold that power, fearful of overthrow, against those who were fearful that their own values and worldviews were being eroded, perhaps even destroyed, by those to whom they had delegated their authority for self-determination.

Throughout America are hundreds of thousands of Kanawha counties, from the smallest committee in the smallest village to the federal government. The distinctions of authoritarian, libertarian, and social responsibility theories blur before the greater concept of fear, the one human emotion that tends to override all others.

Books Under Fire

by John Edward Weems

Big winds battered Texas schoolbooks on two fronts in Mid-September
[1961]. On the Gulf Coast thousands of textbooks were destroyed by Hurricane Carla, and in the capital city of Austin, A leader of the Daughters
of American Revolution (DAR) and thirty persons representing an organization called "Texans for America" huffed and puffed at a September 14 State
Textbook Commission hearing against books, mostly history, that they termed
anti-American for a variety of reasons. Of the more than one hundred textbooks
up for adoption, they singled out about fifty.

This was the second such Texans-for-America appearance. The first came
last fall and enjoyed some success.

Leader of Texans for America is ultraconservative J. Evetts Haley, rancher,
writer, sometime-teacher of Canyon, Texas, who crashed into headlines recently
by punching a history teacher at West Texas State Teachers College during a
political dispute. Making lesser headlines again at Austin in September, he
voiced disapproval of a long list of authors—not particularly because of what
they had written, but because they had been cited in textbooks proposed for
Texas schoolchildren.

Haley's stand is explained in his group's manifesto:

The stressing of both sides of a controversy only confuses the young and
encourages them to make snap judgments based on insufficient evidence. Until
they are old enough to understand both sides of a question, they should be
taught only the American side.

This year, as last, Texans for America offered themselves as arbiters of
what represents the American side. At the hearing they appeared in talkative
succession, each of them reviewing individual books and pointing out their most
serious flaws. The hearing went something like this:

Don Riddle, a Paris, Texas, veterinarian who heads the Texans for America
textbook committee, reviewed *A History of the United States*, published by
American Book Company. He objected to a statement in the book that the
Ku Klux Klan is a more enduring blot on the United States history than the
Communist party. And he was not satisfied with a reply sent him by the
publisher that this was so because the Klan was an American product and
communism was not.

John Edward Weems is secretary-treasurer of the Texas Institute of Letters. He is author of fourteen
books, including *Talking Back to the Censors* (1962), and several regional histories. Mr. Weems
received B.J. and M.J. degrees from the University of Texas, and an M.A. from Florida State
University. [This article is edited and reprinted, with permission, from *Publishers Weekly*; October
2, 1961; ©1961, 1986, John E. Weems]

Two books were banned by Indiana school boards in 1982 — "Belly Button Defense," by John Maurice; and "Make It With 'Mademoiselle'." Upon closer investigation, it was learned that the first book was about basketball; the second book was about dressmaking for teens.

Riddle also referred with displeasure to a description of the late Senator [Joseph] McCarthy's activities as reckless red-hunting. "This approaches character assassination of Senator McCarthy," Riddle declared.

Jeannette Farmer, who was formerly a Fort Worth, Texas, schoolteacher, reviewed *America: Land of Freedom* published by D.C. Heath. She asserted that the book resorts to "half-truths" and "distortions", that most of our current trouble with Soviet Russia stems from the diplomatic recognition extended by President Roosevelt "without approval of Congress"—and that the text should say so.

That was only the beginning. Other shortcomings of *America: Land of Freedom* include the following, according to Farmer: The book should have told children that Gen. Douglas MacArthur was not allowed to win in Korea and should have stated positively that the United States is a constitutional republic. (She stated that the word republic had been used just once in the book, and then only in reference to the sinking of a ship by that name. But in a written reply the publisher pointed out the inclusion of a quotation by Benjamin Franklin in which he used the word.) And the book, she said, should have mentioned that social security—being socialistic—is a social evil.

Haley himself reviewed *The Story of Our Country,* published by Allyn and Bacon. "In it Ralph Bunche is listed as a distinguished statesman," Haley said, "but it neglects to say he is reported to have twelve Communist-front citations, or that he is a national director of the N.A.A.C.P." "On the same page it says we are proud of the poet Langston Hughes. Read his poem, 'Goodbye, Christ,' and see how proud it makes you."

Haley interrupted his discussion to read aloud the poem, which he referred to as "strictly antireligious and procommunist." Then he remarked that Hughes' many literary honors, including Guggenheim and National Institute of Arts & Letters fellowships, "do not show his achievement in literature but the degeneracy of those who make these awards."

Lynn Sanders of Corsicana, Texas, said *American History* (Ginn) displayed "left-wing socialistic tendencies."

[Another parent] disliked *Living World History* (Scott Foresman) because, for one thing, it said World War II was caused by "superpatroits." Her objection was based on a concern that patriotism would thus be discouraged.

Joan Slay, Fort Worth, Texas, housewife, objected to *Rise of the American Nation,* (Harcourt, Brace) for declaring George Washington enjoyed hunting, entertaining, and participating in community affairs. "This follows the liberal train of thought," she said. It omits the fact that Washington served his country without pay.

Mrs. William Moler, Dallas housewife, criticized *Story of America* (Holt, Rinehart and Winston) for not mentioning that Alger Hiss helped write the United Nations charter and for not presenting a true picture of the United Nations. (Control of the U.N. military forces, she commented, has always been in the hands of the Russians.)

Mrs. B.W. Woolley, former Dallas schoolteacher, blasted *The Making of Modern America* (Houghton Mifflin) for saying Herbert Hoover was the first president to recognize that government should use its power in the interests of the people to combat recessions and depressions. "The statement," she argued, "is based on the premise that the federal government has the right to interfere and control business and economic conditions."

Haley returned to review *This Is Our Nation* (Webster), of which a co-author is Paul Boller, Jr., professor at Southern Methodist University in Dallas.

"Dr. Boller is soft on communism," Haley said. And he added that just because Boller is not a member of any organization on the attorney general's list does not mean anything, because "the attorney general's list is inadequate." Neither was Haley placated by the fact that Boller had signed a loyalty oath. "He is technically clear," Haley admitted, "but is in contempt of the spirit of the law."

The D.A.R. leader who spoke was Mrs. A.A. Forrester of Texarkana, Texas, head of her organization's textbook selection committee and a teacher for thirty-one years. She listed the criteria used by her committee in judging textbooks, and this loomed important:

> Is sufficient or equal attention given to all the rights of the American citizen—or does the text give a great deal of attention to 'civil liberties' such as freedom of religion, speech, and press, and little or no attention to the right to acquire and hold property, the right to work, the right to engage in free enterprise, the right of a free society to protect itself against subversion?

Forrester then filed a protest against five books that Texans for American had already lambasted.

Still other books were targets of the dart throwers: *The Record of Mankind* (D.C. Heath), *The Adventure of the American People* (Rand McNally), *United States History* (D.C. Heath), and so on.

R. A. Kilpatrick, reviewing the latter—*United States History*—voiced his displeasure at the omission of such heroes as Nathan Hale, Patrick Henry, David Crockett:

> None of the famous sayings or patriotic views of these men are presented in this book. But time and again it does mention men who have been cited for un-American activities.

Kilpatrick [named] some of the cited men: Upton Sinclair, Jack London, Eugene O'Neill. Then: Carl Sandburg, Stephen Vincent Benet. Still later: Pearl Buck, Ernest Hemingway, Sinclair Lewis, Ring Lardner, Jr., Theodore Dreiser, Allan Nevins. And even more.

"Now I know some of you think we're just a bunch of crackpot radicals; that we're scared—which we are," he said. "But I'm not scared of Russia. I'm scared of Americans. If it turns out, I'm wrong, then I'm just a crackpot lawyer. But if it turn out I'm right, think of the eventuality."

He added, in a more humorous vein, "I'm glad my school records are burned, because my instructors would tell you I'm against all textbooks. There's a good deal of truth in it."

Meanwhile, on the Gulf Coast, the textbooks that were destroyed by Hurricane

---

Writers Guides

Today, when writing a book for use in public schools, an author must be aware of:

1. how many Black faces appear in proportion to the number of white faces;

2. the use of names such as Carlos and Juanita in proportion to those of Billy and Sue;

3. the use of pronouns that negate sex bias;

4. putting anyone in a stereotypical role;

5. paying obeisance to mandates of the consumer enlightenment moguls;

6. excluding materials that imply the rape of our natural beauty;

7. any vaguely humorous, satiric, and/or critical treatment of anyone's religious preference;

8. any allusion to stereotypes of ethnic or national origins;

9. statements that may contain political bias;

10. references to the use of drugs, tobacco, alcohol, non-nutritious food, etc.

. . .[B]oth the left and right are getting in their licks on textbook publishing these days. Not suprisingly, both claim to be representing "The People" in their demands. The result is a more powerful and restrictive censorship than we have ever known in American education. Textbook writers are denied latitude in what they can choose as themes and topics, the kinds of allusions they can use, and the way in which they convey their messages. In the emotional concern with individuals' rights, the forgotten people are the authors and text compilers.

—John S. Simmons, from "Productive Censorship: The New Wave,"
English Journal (December, 1981)
[reprinted by permission, National Council of Teachers of English]

Carla had mourners. Culver City, Calif., School Superintendent Jack R. Singer telegraphed Texas Commissioner of Education J.W. Edgar an offer to replace them with used books from his school district. At the same time, J.B. Golden, textbook division director of the Texas Education Agency, immediately began obtaining replacements from Texas stocks.

But in Austin, the textbooks that were huffed and puffed at evoked little sympathy. Newspapers paid but scant attention to the textbook hearing—only two Texas dailies and one weekly sent reporters—and not even the book publishers seemed to be especially concerned, for relatively few defense witnesses spoke—so few that reporter Bob Sherrill of the liberal *Texas Observer*, published in Austin, remarked, "It was about as poor a job of public relations as I've ever seen. The press heard the fanatics' full voice, but heard hardly a chirp from the publishers."

All publishers did submit written replies to the criticisms leveled, but the state-duplicated copies were in numbers sufficient only for distribution to the fifteen members of the State Textbook Commission and to those persons who filed protests against books. Virtually all publishers let these written replies stand as their rebuttals; so persons without copies ever were aware of most of the publishers' arguments.

To the casual observer it seemed (whether true or not) that some publishers must have regarded the hearing as too ludicrous to be taken seriously. Last fall, however, Haley's roughriders were said to have been directly responsible for getting at least three textbooks off the approved list, and probably more, and the hearing was just as ludicrous: One protester contended that a certain book held the Boy Scouts up to ridicule by including the sentence, "There weren't any drowning children to save or any old ladies to help through traffic . . ."

Southwestern folklorist J. Frank Dobie, dean of Texas writers, [noted] that these objectors "are really objecting to the Twentieth Century. They seem unaware of the modern treatment of social history. They want to go back to history writing that consisted mostly of accounts of wars and heroes, and that left out the masses of people."

Radio, Television, Music—and the FCC

Nowhere is the government's direct influence upon the media as overt as in the FCC control of broadcasting. The FCC's congressional mandate to regulate the public airwaves in the "public interest, convenience, and necessity" has provided a wide latitude of discretion and control.

The FCC has established a long list of guidelines on acceptability; but, broadcasters, operating in fear of losing audiences, ratings, or even their lucrative licenses, often exclude a lot more than the public, advertisers, or FCC would suggest.

Words

For its first few years, the television industry forbad visibly pregnant women from appearing on television; even the words "pregnant" and "pregnancy" were forbidden. And then Lucille Ball, star of "I Love Lucy," one of the most popular shows on the air, became pregnant. CBS executives finally swallowed hard, and permitted her to continue on the series—although the forbidden words were never mentioned.

In 1973, WBAI-FM, New York, broadcast, as part of a discussion of the public attitudes about language, comedian George Carlin's monologue, about "dirty words." More than a hundred times, Carlin mentioned the seven words the FCC specifically forbade from the air. In response to a complaint, the FCC noted the violation, recorded it, but issued no fines or threats. WBAI argued that the Supreme Court had never ruled that the specific words were obscene. The FCC argued that although the words were not obscene, they should not be aired at a time when children could be listening. The Supreme Court agreed.

In the mid-1980s, the mood of the people, as reflected in FCC policy, hadn't changed much. The Charlie Daniels Band had to record two versions of the traditional folksong, "The Devil Went Down to Georgia." On the "A" side, the Devil was called a "son-of-a-gun." On the "B" side, the Devil was a "son-of-a-bitch."

Violence

On the radio and in the early 1950s on television, The Lone Ranger never killed the "bad guys"; in extraordinary feats of marksmanship, he usually shot the guns out of their hands. But by the mid- and late-1960s, both television and the movies showed not only the "bad guys" being killed, and also retribution killings. (TV codes—and the audience—didn't permit the "good guys" being killed.) By the end of the 1960s, all three networks, seeing their ratings on Westerns and adventure shows rise, not only scheduled more of the same, but also increased the level of violence. But, even here the networks refused to be realistic—all bullet wounds were clean, all "bad guys" died quickly and on the exact spot they had been standing when first shot—even if killed by a shotgun. The popularity of the "Spaghetti Westerns"—"good guy/bad guy" movies with most of the casts and crews American but filmed in Italy—increased the public acceptance of media violence.

Then in 1969, the National Commission on Causes and Prevention of Violence concluded that "research evidence strongly suggests . . . that violence in television programs can and does have adverse effects upon audiences—especially child audiences." But, the Commission report was not definitive—some researchers also concluded that media violence has little effect upon audiences that are not predisposed to violence.

In 1969, the National Association for Better Broadcasting, various PTAs, and Action for Children's Television (ACT) picked on KTTV-TV, Los Angeles, and got the station to agree to eliminate several children's shows, including *Superman, Batman,* and *Aquaman,* and to either run eighty-one other shows after 8:30 p.m., or to broadcast a "Caution to Parents" notice if the shows were broadcast earlier. With KTTV as the "first domino," numerous groups looked at other stations and networks. The result was mass capitulation by stations and networks, recognizing that it was adults not chidlren who bought the sponsors' toys and cereals. Another result was the inane editing of numerous classic cartoons, including most Bugs Bunny and Roadrunner/Coyote cartoons.

But, there was still violence on television. The FCC noted its "concern"; some violence was diminished. Then a few senators and representatives "suggested" that there was too much violence on television—and if the FCC didn't do too much more to solve the problem, there "could be" severe budget limitations. In a series of speeches, Richard Wiley, FCC chairman, spoke out against violence on television. By the end of 1974, he had talked with members of the National Association of Broadcasters, and the vice-presidents of programming and the presidents of the three major national networks. It didn't take long for the broadcasters to figure out that the government investigations, with possible FCC inquiries, weren't good for the ratings or for levels of security in maintaining their licenses. By the following season, most of the westerns and adventure shows were off the air, the depiction of violence declined significantly, and the government in the role of "protecting the people," once again was satisfied.

The role that a government takes in control of the broadcasting of violence apparently is culturally-based, rather than based upon any broad philosophy of life or the media. In England, social violence is lower than in the U.S., but the level of violence permitted on television is also much lower. In contrast, in Japan, which also has a very low rate of social violence, the depiction of violence on television is much higher in quantity and intensity than in the United States.

During the 1980s, violence again increased on television, as program executives realized the insatiable appetites of the public. Among myriad acts of violence have been the shooting of greedy and amoral J.R. Ewing in "Dallas" (1983); and the terrorist massacre in "Dynasty" (1985)—both shows were watched by more than sixty million people.

Sex

Television stations, not wishing to test the FCC limits of tolerance, reject on-air frontal nudity and partial-nudity in any form, However, in England, the BBC has permitted full frontal nudity, but restricts violence. Often, American-made television shows and films are edited of many violent acts before they can be released in England and many other countries.

During the 1960s and early 1970s, Barbara Eden, star of "I Dream of Jeannie," a thirty-minute prime time situation comedy about a genie and an astronaut, was required to wear her harem dress above the navel; only in the 1980s did TV audiences see female navels.

During the early 1970s, Cher, of the popular singing duo Sonny & Cher, tried to pass many almost-revealing costumes past the CBS censors; although they allowed her to show a little more skin than many TV stars, most of her body remained covered during prime time. The one time she showed her navel, thousands of protests flooded CBS.

Because the movie industry has less restrictive standards for depiction of sex and violence than does the television industry, extensive editing occurs on many movies before they are shown on television. The people at Network Standards and Practices (the internal censors), have been responsible for snipping out twenty minutes of *The Apartment*, among many other classic films.

In an era where pre-marital sex was not widely accepted, many writers were forced to create alternate lyrics so the artists could go on the air. For the Ed Sullivan Show, Mick Jagger and the Rolling Stones changed "Let's Spend the Night Together" to the more innocent, "Let's Spend Some Time Together."

Each year, the television censors, finely attuned to public mores, become a little more convinced that the depiction of human skin is not a mortal sin. However, it isn't primetime television, but the afternoon soaps, desperately finding ways to attract audiences, that have shown everything but sexual organs. Couples in bed, couples in showers, couples swimming nude have all been shown on the soaps—with appropriate camera angles giving the illusion of nudity.

The cable television industry is largely regulated by local ordinances, almost none of them dictating programming. Because Cable is a "wired" not a broadcast medium, and because the argument of the necessity of protecting the public airwaves is not applicable, Cable has gone further in portrayal of sexual situations than has broadcast television. In New York City, the "Blue Channel" programs what others may call "dirty movies." The Playboy Channel frequently shows nudity, but little sex, and other cable companies transmit programs including explicit sex. Even the cable giant, Home Box Office, owned by Time Inc. has programmed nudity into a number of its continuing serials, including *The Hitch Hiker* and *First and Ten*, both of which are network-quality shows which are aimed for family viewing.

The "hot" medium of radio never had to show nudity to be more sexually alluring than television—and to be given sanctions by the FCC. "Topless Radio" probably began in Los Angeles in the early 1970s when DJ Bill Balance turned his morning "two-way radio" into a forum for listeners to talk about their sexual lives. No topic was considered too risque, and Balance soon had a large audience of Southern California women, and a few men. Soon, more than five hundred radio stations throughout America had their own version of "Topless Radio"; a few stations even syndicated thirty- and sixty-minute programs. When Balance moved to San Diego, his audience moved with him. By now, the FCC was receiving thousands of letters from outraged citizens who, apparently unable to tune in other stations or turn off their radios, decided to complain. The FCC investigated. Commissioner Nicholas Johnson, however, refused to listen to the tapes of some of the shows, claiming that to participate in *any* decision was to indicate his approval of governmental censorship. In one of the ironies of governmental regulation, it wasn't Balance or his station that was fined; the FCC fined WGLD, Oak Park, Illinois, $2,000 for its version of

"Topless Radio." Soon after the fine, the "Topless Radio" Fad died out, to be replaced by the safer format of marriage counselors, psychologists, and pseudo-psychologists conducting "two-way talk radio" shows about myriad problems, including sexual problems.

Social Mores

The depiction of mores that the timid television executives didn't think the public was "as yet ready for," led to the television industry restricting certain people or situations from the air. For more than two decades, the only Black stars on the air were those in the CBS "Top 10" comedy show, "Amos 'n' Andy," which the network, now fearful of a growing Black economic and political power, pulled off the air in the 1960s after protests by the NAACP. It wasn't until almost two decades after television became a mass medium that television permitted a Black, Bill Cosby, to star in a dramatic television serial, "I Spy." For the most part, television families were White, with a father who wore suits and worked at a professional job, and a mother who was a housewife; the children, always cute, sometimes troublesome, were "all-American" types who never ever became involved with any social issues of greater significance than what band to choose for the high school's senior prom.

One instance shows the nature of network timidity—and, for its time, an unusual courage. On a variety show, near the end of a duet, Petula Clark affectionately put her hand on the arm of Harry Bellefonte. The network executives and staff panicked—Clark was White; Bellefonte, Black. After recovering, and significant discussion, they finally, almost reluctantly, allowed that segment to air—and hoped that neither the ratings nor the sponsors fell.

In the July 12, 1969, issue of *Saturday Review*, David Dempsey summarized a major problem within the industry:

> Critics of television, including many of its own creative personnel, point out that the fallacy of playing to these "accepted moral standards" is that they are not the true standards of most communities, but rather those which the community wants to think are true. By eliminating the unpleasant, the controversial, and the "immoral," TV helps to sustain a mass illusion that is false to the society which gives the medium its franchise.

'The Devil's Own Music'

In Cleveland, in the early 1950s, DJ Allen Freed defied conventional wisdom—and his bosses—and played some "rhythm and blues" music of some outstanding Black singer-musicians, among them Chuck Berry and Little Richard. Soon, the "rhythm and blues" sound merged with some country sounds, and Freed gave it a label, "Rock 'n' Roll." When Elvis Presley's first songs were recorded by Sun Records about 1955, most stations refused to play them, believing that Presley was Black. When it was learned that although Presley's singing style was based in the "rhythm and blues tradition," he was a White from Mississippi, a few stations cautiously tried a song or two. How America saw the "threat" of "rhythm and blues" and "rock 'n' roll" music helps explain not only the nation's attitudes about racial, ethnic, and cultural differences, but also its attitudes about free expression.

Numerous cities, in the 1950s, created ordinances banning radio stations from broadcasting "rhythm and blues" music. Among the reasons that both legislators and station managers gave for not broadcasting the music were that it was "nigger music" ("Actually, we really don't have all that many negroes who listen to our station, so it really doesn't pay us to broadcast that kind of music") and citizen groups bemoaned the anti-establishment ways of rock 'n' roll ("That *kind* of music is truning the children against their parents and society.")

And, always, station managers were watching and trying to outguess what the FCC was thinking.

In 1971, the FCC issued a directive to all radio stations suggesting that they might wish to "review" the lyrics of songs they put on the air to avoid innocently broadcasting songs that may have lyrics condoning illegal drug usage. The FCC didn't order any station to remove any song, nor did it establish a list of forbidden songs. It didn't have to. Throughout the country, numerous groups drew up lists of songs they claimed had "drug-related lyrics." Soon, the songs on the list were no longer heard, and several hundred more not on the list, were deliberately kept off the air. Among the songs that didn't have drug-related lyrics, but were banned by the industry as if they advocated drug use, were "Puff the Magic Dragon," written by Leonard Lipton and Peter Yarrow, and recorded by Peter, Paul, and Mary; "Lucy in the Sky With Diamonds," written by Paul McCartney and John Lennon, and recorded by the Beatles; "Rocky Mountain High," written by John Denver and Michael Taylor, and recorded by Denver.

Sooner or later it had to happen. A congressional investigation was eventually launched to look into "hidden meanings," and see what the "teenage music" was doing to the country. Among the songs the sub-committee focused on was Richard Berry's song, "Louie, Louie," with its nonsensical lyrics. The investigation fizzled, and the "hidden meanings"—if any—remained hidden.

Contemporary Social Issues

Songs with "dirty words," sexual situations, and even drug-related lyrics can be tolerated, even if reluctantly, by most of the people. But songs that challenge a contemporary way of life, a majority way of life, are too threatening. A "dirty word" can throw disgust into the mind of a listener; but, a song of social protest throws a fear into the soul. Throughout history, writers have used the medium of music to express their beliefs, their values. And when the values and beliefs are controversial, or attack sacred or beloved institutions, then the people become upset.

In the 1960s and 1970s, anti-war songs and other songs that did not agree with the administration views of life found little or no airplay. Among them were several songs by Phil Ochs, including "I Ain't Marching" and "A Small Circle of

Friends"; P.F. Sloan's "The Eve of Destruction," sung by Barry McGuire, and just about anything Pete Seeger recorded. In one of the interesting statements about the fears of station owners, most of Tom Lehrer's satirical songs were not heard on radio, although many first appeared on television's thirty-minute satire, "That Was the Week That Was."

Television executives were not as tolerant of the Smothers Brothers, however. During the 1960s, CBS gave folk singers Tom and Dick Smothers their own show, profited from the ratings success, then cancelled then, afraid that the Smothers Brothers comedy routines were too controversial for television. Among many "offenses," the Smothers Brothers and their guests had taken satirical looks at the Vietnam War, politicans, and even religion. Among the things that upset CBS executives was a song by Pete Seeger, "Waist Deep in the Big Muddy," an attack upon the Vietnam policies of President Johnson. CBS pulled the segment off the air in 1967; a year later, when the country began to acknowledge that, maybe, there were reasons for American troops not to be in Vietnam, CBS flip-flopped and allowed the song. CBS also censored four minutes of a David Steinberg comedy monologue about Jonah and the Whale. Every show had something cut from the original script. It was the Smothers' vigorous protest against CBS policies that eventually led to their cancellation.

Ghost Resurrected

From the 1950s to the present, the ghosts of licensors past were resurected as thousands of bonfires were lit into which record albums, sheet music, and books were thrown, each fire-building group making its statement for a "better" America. In the vapors that were created from the fire, one can see a history of civilization.

Bibliography

Amiel, Barbara, "The Dangers of Self-Censorship," *Macleans*, September 26, 1983.

"Another Book Ban," *Christian Century*, May 30, 1984.

"Appeals Court Overrules Order Baning TV Series," *FOI Digest*, September-October 1980.

Baldwin, Hanson W., "Managed News; Our Peacetime Censorship," *Atlantic Monthly*, April 1963.

"Ban Against Publication of School Records Lifted," *FOI Digest*, May-June 1981.

Barnouw, Erik, *The Sponsor*, Oxford University Press (New York, N.Y.), 1978.

Becker, Carl, L. *Freedom and Responsibility in the American Way of Life,* William W. Cook Foundation Lectures, University of Michigan (Ann Arbor, Mich.), 1945.

Bemen, Lamar Taney, *Selected Articles on Censorship of Speech and the Press,* (New York, N.Y.), 1930.

"Behind the Move to Ban More Books," *Changing Times,* June 1982.

Bilgrez, Felix J. "Some Questions Concerning Movie Censorship and the First Amendment," *Association of the Bar on New York City. Record,* January 1963.

"Book Banning in the United States, 1957-65," *FOI Digest,* February, 1966.

"Bordello List Printed; Penthouse Ban Lifted," *FOI Digest,* January-February 1981.

Carmen, Ira H., *Movies, Censorship, and the Law,* University of Michigan Press (Ann Arbor, Mich.), 1966.

"Censorship Efforts Increase Against Bookstores, Schools and Libraries," *FOI Digest,* May-June 1982.

"Censorship Threatens School Freedom," *FOI Digest,* September-October 1980.

"City's Refusal to Permit 'Hair' in Theater is Prior Restraint, Supreme Court Rules," *FOI Digest,* March-April 1975.

Clancy, Phyllis, *Obscenity: From the Ginzburg to Stanley,* Freedom of Information Center (Columbia, Mo.), March 1970.

"Court Refuses to Ban Article on Abortion in School Paper," *FOI Digest,* May-June 1981.

Craig, Alec, *Suppressed Books: A History of the Conception of Literary Obscenity,* World Publishing (Cleveland), 1963.

Curry, Jane Leftwich (trans.), *The Black Book of Polish Censorship,* Vintage Books (New York, N.Y.), 1984.

DeGrazia, Edward, *Censorship Landmarks,* R.R. Bowker (New York, N.Y.), 1969.

DeGrazia, Edward; and Roger Newman, *Banned Films,* R. R. Bowker (New York, N.Y.), 1982.

Egertson, Yvonne, *Killed, Wounded, Jailed, Expelled,* American Newspaper Publishers Association (Washington, D.C.), 1985.

Elkin, F., "Censorship and Pressure Groups," *Phylon,* Spring 1960.

Ernst, Morris L. and Alan U. Schwartz. *Censorship: The Search for the Obscene.* New York: Macmillan Co., 1964.

_____, *The First Freedom,* Macmillan (New York), 1946.

_____, "Radio Censorship and the 'Listening Millions'", *The Nation,* April 28, 1926, p. 473.

"Federal Judge Overruled in Attempt to Bar '60 Minutes' Broadcast," *FOI Digest,* January-February 1983.

Friendly, Fred W., *Minnesota Rag,* Random House (New York, N.Y.), 1984.

Froelich, Cliff, "Pressure Groups v. The Movies", *Freedom of Information Center Report,* School of Journalism, University of Missouri, 1980.

Gastil, Raymond D. *Freedom in the World, 1984-1985,* Greenwood Press ( ), 1985.

Geller, Evelyn, *Forbidden Books in American Public Libraries,* 1876-1939: A Study in Cultural Change, Greenwood Press (Westport, Conn.), 1984

Gertz, Elmer, "An End to All Censorship," *The Nation,* July 5, 1965.

Gillett, Charles Ripley, *Burned Books: Neglected Chapters in British History and Literature*, (New York, N.Y.), 1932.

————, *Censored: Books and Their Right to Live*. University of Kansas Library (Lawrence, Kansas), 1965.

Goodman, Paul, "Censorship and Mass Media," *Yale Political Journal*, Autumn 1963.

Gordon, D.E., "Great Speckled Bird," *Journalism Quarterly*, Summer 1979.

Grant, Sidney E. and S.E. Angoff, "Censorship in Boston," *Boston University Law Reivew*, January 1930, April 1930.

Haight, Anne Lyon, *Banned Books*, R. R. Bowker (New York, N.Y.), 3rd ed. 1970.

Hamlin, David, *The Nazi-Skokie Conflict*, Beacon Press (Boston, Mass.), 1981.

Horton, Philip C., ed. *The Third World and Press Freedon*, Praeger (New York, N.Y.) 1978.

Hurwitz, Leon, *Historical Dictionary of Censorship in the United States*, Greenwood Press (Westport, Conn.), 1980.

Inglis, Ruth, *Freedom of the Movies*, University of Chicago Press (Chicago, Ill.), 1947.

International Press Institute, "World Press Freedom Review," *IPI Report*, Decem ber 12, 1984.

Jenkinson, Edward, *Classroom Censorship*, University of Illinois Press (Urbanna).

"Judge Declares Unconstitutional City's Theater Licensing Law,", *FOI Digest*, January-February 1979.

Lendvai, Paul, *The Bureaucracy of Truth*, Westview Press (Boulder, Colorado) 1981.

Lent, John A., "Press Freedom in Asia: The Quiet But Completed Revolution," *The Gazette*, August 15, 1980.

Liston, Robert A., *The Right to Know: Censorship in America*, Franklin Watts 1973.

Luebke, Barbara F., *Textbook Censorship: New Aspects*, Freedom of Information Center (Columbia, Mo., April 1968.

Marshall, Max L., *The Right-to-Read Controversy*, Freedom of Information Center Columbia, Mo.), April 1968.

Merill, John C., *The Imperative of Freedom: A Philosophy of Journalistic Autonomy*, Hastings House (New York, N.Y.), 1974.

Morris, Ernest; Alexander Lindez, *The Censors Marches On*, DaCapa Press New York, N.Y.), 1971.

Muller, Herbert J., *Freedom in the Western World*, Harper & Row (New York, N.Y.), 1963.

Oboler, Eli M., *Defending Intellectural Freedom: The Library and the Censor*, Greenwood Press (Westport, Conn.), 1980.

"Paper is Convicted for Revealing Judges Being Investigated by State," *FOI Digest*, January-February 1976.

Paul, James C.N. and Murray L. Schwartz, *Federal Censorship: Obscenity in the Mail*, Free Press of Glencoe (New York, N.Y.), 1961.

Perry, Marna, "Gauging World Press Freedom," *Presstime*, April 1980.

Pool, Ithiel de Sola. *On Free Speech in an Electronic Age: Technologies of Freedom*. The Belknap Press of Harvard University Press (Cambridge, Mass.) 1983.

Randall, Richard S., *Censorship of Movies*, University of Wisconsin Press (Madison, Wisc.) 1968.

Righter, Rosemary, *Whose News?* Times Books (New York, N.Y.) 1978.

Rucker, Bryce W., *The First Freedom*, Illinois University Press) Carbondale, Ill.) 1968.

Schramm, Wilbur L. ed., *One Day in the World's Press*, Stanford University Press (Stanford, Calif.) 1959.

Simmons, John S., "Proactive Censorship: The New Wave," *English Journal*, December 1981.

Stouffer, Samuel, *Communism, Conformity and Civil Liberties*. Doubleday (New York, N.Y.), 1955.

"Symposium: *Near v. Minnesota*, 50th Anniversary." *Minnesota Law Review*, 1981.

Tedford, Thomas L., *Freedom of Speech in the United States*, Random House (New York, N.Y.), 1985.

Thompson, Fred, *Right-Wing Censorship of Books*, Freedom of Information Center (Columbia, Mo.), January 1968.

———, *Textbooks and Racial Pressure Groups*, Freedom of Information Center (Columbia, Mo.), February 1968.

Wen-Ching, Chou, "Cancellation of the Four Freedoms by the Chinese Communists," *Asian Outlook*, April 1980.

World Press Freedom Committee, *The Media Crises . . . A Continuing Challenge*, Rex Rand Fund, 1982.

Writers and Scholars International, *Index on Censorship*, Vol. 14, 1985.

Chapter 39

Obscenity
by T. Barton Carter

Ours is a society seemingly obsessed with sex. One might argue, however, that there are really two obsessions. Some people are obsessed with obtaining and enjoying access to sexually–explicit or suggestive materials. Others are equally obsessed with denying them access to these materials.

While the never ending battle between these two groups has often spilled over into the courts, it has also been fought in other arenas. Community groups have picketed stores selling sexually– explicit materials. Others have threatened to boycott advertisers who sponsor television shows they find objectionable. A few people have even resorted to violence.

Pornography is what the censor wants to censor, and regulation is an euphemism.

—Hugh Hefner

The complexity and multifaceted nature of this problem is illustrated by the contradictory solutions attempted in Boston and Detroit. Boston decided the best solution was to gather all the pornography-related businesses into one small section of the city, the infamous "combat zone." In that way, those who wanted access could have it while others would not be exposed to it. Detroit, in contrast, passed a zoning law prohibiting adult movie theaters from being located within 1,000 feet of one another. The hope was the dispersing them in this fashion

---

Dr. T. Barton Carter is associate professor of communication, College of Communication, Boston University. He was chair of the Law Division of the Association for Education in Journalism and Mass Communication, 1983-1984, and is co-author, with Marc Franklin and Jay Wright, of *The First Amendment and the Fourth Estate*, 3rd edition (1985), and the *The First Amendment and the Fifth Estate* (1986). Dr. Carter has B.A. in psychology from Yale University, a J.D. from the School of Law, University of Pennsylvania, and an M.S. in mass communication, from Boston University. [©1986, T. Barton Carter]

would prevent them from having a serious impact on any given neighborhood. Neither solution has proven especially satisfactory.

Few "free speech" issues arouse people's emotions the way pornogrpahy does. The debate crosses traditional political lines. Where else would one find feminists allied with fundamentalists?

The problem of pornography has never been satisfactorily resolved and probably never will. The issues are too complex ad the various viewpoints too disparate to allow either a legal or social resolution.

One of the first difficulties encountered in discussing pornography is deciding what it is. To paraphrase Supreme Court Justice John Harlan, "One man's pornography is another man's artform." The attempt to define pornography led Justice Potter Stewart in 1964 to declare that he could not define hardcore pornography, "but I know it when I see it." Unfortunately, this statement holds true for every individual in this country.

The problem of definition alluded to by these Supreme Court justices is illustrated by the number of famous books, plays, and movies that have both been banned as obscene and recognized as great works of art or literature. For example, James Joyce's *Ulysses* was at one time banned from this country. Now there are universities throughout the country offering entire courses on this work.

How is it that something no one can even define can cause such an uproar? Why do some people feel compelled to fight not only to avoid their own exposure to it, but also to deny access for those who desire it? Why do others who profess to hate this material fight so hard to defend the rights of those who wish to disseminate it?

The most common argument made by those wishing to ban pornography—at least what they consider to be pornography—is that pornography affects them even if they are not directly exposed to it. Despite the finding of the 1970 Presidential Commission on Pornography that there was no evidence of a direct link between crime and exposure to pornographic materials, they claim that pornography causes crime.

Others argue that even if it doesn't cause crime, it affects the tone of the community. They believe that just as pollution can harm the physical environment, pornography can harm the social environment. This analogy to pollution is often reflected in the way they discuss the issue. Pornography is always referred to as pollution, garbage, or filth. In essence, the real concern is the moral fabric of the community.

This authoritarian position that the government has the right to restrict the dissemination of pornographic materials in order to safeguard the well-being and moral fabric of the community is opposed by libertarians who fear that the same reasoning can then be used to restrict other ideas and speech "for the good of the community." Although many of them profess to be disgusted by the pornographic materials they are defending, they argue that once the government is given the right to distinguish between "good" ideas and "bad" ideas, then the protections afforded by the First Amendment cease to have any meaning.

There are certainly a wealth of historical examples to support this argument. In the early 1950s, a film titled "The Miracle" was banned in New York for being sacrilegious. Similarly, the film, "Lady Chatterley's Lover," was banned in New York in the mid-1950s because it portrayed adultery in a positive light and, thus, was immoral. (The Supreme Court of the United States overturned both bans.)

More recently, an attempt was made to revoke the license of WGBH-TV, a public broadcasting station in Boston, for broadcasting several "obscene and immoral" programs including the "Masterpiece Theatre" presentation of "I, Claudius." The Federal Communications Commission summarily rejected the petition filed by a conservative citizens group. Other groups have pressed public and school libraries to remove everything from Eldridge Cleaver's *Soul on Ice* to Mark Twain's *Huckleberry Finn*. The reasons given have ranged from objectionable language to the use of demeaning stereotypes.

Children and Women

Even strong free speech advocates have difficulty when the issue of children's access to pornography is raised. Many who are willing to defend the right to disseminate pornographic materials in general balk at the idea of allowing children to be exposed to these materials. In May 1984, President Reagan signed a bill making it a federal crime, punishable by as much as a $200,000 fine or fifteen years imprisonment to reproduce or distribute "kiddie porn." Pornograph's possible damage to the social fabric of a community may not justify limitations on speech, but possible psychological or emotional harm to children presents a very different problem.

Is it then possible to allow access to "consenting adults," but deny it to children? Perhaps such limitations are feasible when applied to movie theaters, but how do you keep a book or videotape sold to a "consenting adult" from subsequently finding its way into the hands of a child? If such restrictions cannot be adequately imposed on obscene materials, does this justify limiting or banning pornographic works for everyone? Many libertarians find qustions such as these especially troubling.

In the last decade a new argument has surfaced as a justificaion for banning pornographic materials. Various women's groups have taken the position that the sexual portrayal of women in many articles, magazines, books, and films encourage sex discrimination and violence against women. Some even define pornography in terms of "graphic sexually explicit subordination of women." Causes for their concern range from pornographic movies' widespread portrayal of women as "sex objects" to the high incidence of rape and vioence towards women in these films. The apparent increase in films with strong sadomasochism themes has also contributed to this movement.

There is, however, a certain irony in their position. To a great extent they are concerned about violence towards women. Yet, the focus is on sexual representations not violent ones. Violence is only an issue in the context of sexual materials. This is, of course, consistent with the country's history. Violence as an issue has never stirred emotions in the same way that sex has.

A strong argument could certainly be made that the "slasher" genre of movies does much more to create an atmosphere conducive to violence than the average hardcore pornographic movie. Yet there is comparatively little outcry against "slice-and-dice films." When is the last time a theater showing such a film was picketed? Advocates of defining pornography in terms of "subordination of women" argue that exposure to materials of that nature make people callous and more willing to accept or tolerate violence towards women. If that is so, wouldn't exposure to films that emphasize violence and gruesome murders make people even more callous and tolerant of violence?

A second question raised by this new approach to the issue of pornography is its emphasis on the ideas conveyed by the films. In essence, they are saying that these films are beyond the protection of the First Amendment because they advocate treating women as second class citizens. While they may indeed advocate this, and while most of the people in this country may believe such an idea is wrong, how do you differentiate between them and films that advocate other ideas not endorsed by the majority of the country?

"Unprotected Speech"

Regardless of their rationale, anyone who wishes to limit or ban any form of speech must first address the problem of the First Amendment. The speech in questions must somehow be determined by the courts to be outside the protections of the First Amendment. This has not proved to be a serious problem with obscenity. Using an approach known as definitional balancing, the courts have consistently defined obscenity as unprotected speech.

Under definitional balancing the court will view an entire class of speech and determine whether the positive value of that speech is outweighed by the harm that it might do. Other classes of speech that have at one time or another been dclared unprotected under this approach are libel, commercial speech, and "fighting words" (words likely to incite an immediate breach of the peace). Libel and commercial speech, however, have now been given limited constitutional protection.

Determining that obscenity is unprotected by the First Amendment has not proven difficult for the courts. Determining what is obscenity has proven almost impossible. The frustration of attempting to define obscenity drove Potter Stewart to make his famous "I know it when I see it" statement.

Although everyone may know it when they see it, very few can agree on the definition. Nevertheless, judges have often attempted this seemingly impossible task.

Historical Precedent

Massachusetts enacted the American colonies' first anti-obscenity act, making it a crime for anyone to "publish any filthy, obscene, or profane song, pamphlet, libel, or mock sermon." By 1792, the fourteen American states had made blaspheny and profanity crimes, although obscenity, widely recognized as a crime during the colonial era, was no longer carried over as a crime. It wasn't until 1815 that Pennsylvania created the nation's first state anti-obscenity law; it wasn't until seven years later that the state convicted a printer-writer on charges of obscenity.

While the Tariff Act of 1842, which prohibited importation of obscene literature, was the first obscenity statute in the United States, the first definition of obscenity used in this country originiated in England more than two decades later. *Regina* v. *Hicklin* (1868), established the following test for obscenity: "Whether the tendency of the matter charged as obscenity is to deprave and corrupt those whose minds are open to such immoral influence and into whose hands a publication of this sort may fall." The test was applied to isolated passages of the work in question. This test, applied to isolated passages, might make most Walt Disney movies obscene.

In the second half of the nineteenth century, other obscenity statutes were passed, most notably the Comstock Act (1873), and later ammended in 1876 to prohibit the mailing of obscene materials. An 1876 amendment to the Act also prohibited the mailing of obscene materials. The Post Office took the amendment very seriously, banning numerous books and periodicals from the mails. This postal censorship continued until the 1940s when several court decisions involving both the Comstock Act and the Administrative Procedures Act forced them to hold hearings prior to seizing any mail. As a result, the Post Office radically reduced its efforts in that area.

Meanwhile, judicial dissatisfaction with *Hicklin* started to develope during the early part of the twentieth century. By the 1930s, most courts requried a book to be judged in its entirety based on the audience it was likely to reach. However, the Supreme Court's failure to address the question left the issue in doubt.

It was not until 1957 that the Supreme Court handed down a clear statement. Declaring obscenity to be unprotected by the First Amendment, the Court defined obscenity according to the following test: "Whether to the average citizen applying contemporary community standards, the dominant theme of the material taken as a whole appeals to prurient interest."

Between 1957 and 1966, the test gradually evolved into a three-part test. As announced in a 1966 case involving John Cleland's *Memoirs of a Woman of Pleasure* (more commonly known as "Fanny Hill"). The three requirements were:

> (a) the dominant theme of the material taken as a whole appeals to a prurient interest in sex; (b) the material is patently offensive because it affronts contemporary community standards relating to the description or representation of sexual matters; and (c) the material is utterly without redeeming social value.

In applying the test, a single, nationwide standard was to be used. The special sensitivities of any community were not supposed to influence the definition of obscenity.

The test, however, created several problems of definition. Much of the language used left great latitude for interpreatation. How offensive is "patently offensive"? What exactly is the prurient interest of the average citizen? Does

THE PRESS AND THE STATE

this mean that the more peculiar one's sexual tastes the less likely that materials directed at them will be held obscene?

Moreover, this was a floating standard. Since it was based on contemporary community standards, it had to change as society changed. On the one hand, this meant that the standards always adjusted to changing moral standards. On the other, it meant that a work could be obscene one year and not the next. Thus, it did not provide much in the way of objective guidance.

From the standpoint of law enforcement officials seeking to prosecute "obscene" materials, the test had another major flaw. There was hardly anything that was obscene under this test. It is very difficult to demonstrate that something is *"utterly without redeeming social value."* This is especially true when the purveyors of allegedly obscene material have also read the law. For example, many "dirty" movies during this time period would open with a man dressed as a doctor discussing how the film could serve as a marital aid. The same man womuld reappear at the end to deliver the same message. Arguably, this would give the movie the tiniest amount of social value and prevent it from being declared obscene.

As a result, the Supreme Court was reduced to viewing movies and declaring them obscene or not without any explanatory opinion. In essence, the legal definition of obscenity had indeed become "I know it when I see it." This approach was known as the *Redrup* rule from *Redrup v. New York* (1967).

Meanwhile, the Court did create an exception to the general obscenity test. Advertising a work in such a way as to create the appearance of obscenity could result in a conviction regardless of the actual content. This was the result of the Court's 1966 decision in *Ginzburg v. United States*. Ginzburg was the publisher of *EROS*, an avant-garde magazine dealing with sexual themes. Although the magazine was not obscene according to the legal definition, Ginzburg promoted it as though it was. For example, he attempted, unsuccessfully, to have it mailed from Intercourse and Blue Ball, Pennsylvania; neither post office which could handle the volume of mail proposed. Ginzburg then secured a permit from the post office of Middlesex, New Jersey. The Court affirmed his conviction because his promotional attempts removed whatever social value the magazine actually had.

A New Definition

In 1973, a markedly more conservative Supreme Court tried once again to define obscenity. *Miller* v. *California* arose when a restaurant manager and his mother received five unsolicited advertising brochures in the mail. The brochures described four books, *Intercourse, Man-Woman, Sex Orgies Illustrated,* and *An Illustrated History of Pornography,* as well as a film "Marital Intercourse." The brochures consisted primarily of sexually explicit pictures. Miller, who had mailed the brochures, was convicted of knowingly distributing obscene material.

The new definition, known as the *Miller* standard, increased the likelihood of obscenity convictions. The *Miller* definition (which is the current definition of obscenity) also relies on a three-part test:

(a) [W]hether "the average person, applying contemporary community standards" would find that the work, taken as a whole, appeals to the prurient interest, (b) whether the work depicts or describes, in a patently offensive way, sexual conduct specifically defined by the applicable state law, and (c) whether the work, taken as a whole, lacks serious literary, artistic, political, or scientific value.

The Court emphasized that it was rejecting the "utterly without redeeming social value" standard. Instead, *serious* literary, artistic, political or scientific value became the key. Of course, determining what constitutes serious value, especially in the fields of art and literature is far from easy. What one critic labels a new masterpiece another will refer to as junk. Besides, how serious is "serious"?

The Supreme Court also declared in *Miller* that the standards to be applied should be local as opposed to national. The Court's reasoning was that differing parts of the country have different tastes and attitudes and that the more liberal areas such as New York and Las Vegas should not set the standards for more conservative areas like Maine and Mississippi.

The problem with the Court's analysis was that it assumed that people would produce different versions of films, books, and magazines for different parts of the country. Unfortunately, producing multiple versions of the same work is seldom economically feasible, leaving publishers and filmmakers two choices. They can either produce works acceptable to all parts of the country or limit their distribution to the more liberal parts of the country. The economic incentive, of course, is to produce the version acceptable to all. Thus, what the Court accomplished was to let the most conservative parts of the country dictate standards for the more liberal.

An extreme example of the problem raised by local standards was a Georgia theater owner who was convicted for showing the film *Carnal Knowledge*. The film starred Jack Nicholson, Art Garfunkel, Ann Margret, and Candice Bergen. It was even nominated for several Academy Awards.

The conviction was upheld by the Georgia Supreme Court. However, the U.S. Supreme Court finally reversed, stating that the jury's verdict went beyond the limits of their decision. *Carnal Knowledge* was obviously not what the justices had in mind when the *Miller* standard was created. However, despite the eventual reversal of his conviction, it was still quite a hardship on the poor theater owner.

The *Miller* definition of obscenity greatly increased the likelihood of successful obscenity prosecutions. Even so it did not go far enough for some. In *Salt Lake City v. Piepenburg* (1977), A.H. Ellett, chief justice of the Utah Supreme Court, in a strong and colorful opinion, expressed his disagreement with the new standard:

However, certain justices of the Supreme Court of the United States have said that before a matter can be held to be obscene, it must be "

. . . when taken as a whole, lacks serious literary, artistic, political, or scientific value."

Some state judges, acting the part of syncophants, echo that doctrine. It would appear that such an argument ought only to be advanced by depraved, mentally deficient, mind-warped queers. Judges who seek to find technical excuses to permit such pictures to be shown under the pretense of finding some intrinsic value to it are reminiscent of a dog that returns to his vomit in search of some morsel in the filth which may have some redeeming value to his own taste. If those judges have not the good sense and decency to resign from their positions as judges, they should be removed either by impeachment or by the vote of the decent people of their constituency.

Ellett did not indicate just how far he would extend the definition of obscenity. Others, however, have gone so far as to argue that even objectionable language, "four-letter words," should be prohibited. In most contexts, however, the courts have not allowed such restrictions. For example, the conviction of a man who wore a jacket with "Fuck the Draft" across the back was overturned by the Supreme Court. *The mere phrase simply did not meet the existing definition of obscenity.*

Conflicting Standards

Radio and television, however, are another story. Even strong free speech advocates are troubled by the possibility of children being exposed to questionable material. This concern has resulted in a different set of standards being applied to broadcasting.

These standards are the ironic result of a New York City radio station playing a comedy monologue of George Carlin's entitled, "Seven words you can't say on television." As WBAI was soon to discover, you can't say them on radio either. (*Pacifica*, 1975).

Acting on a complaint from a man who claimed his young son was exposed to the monologue, the Federal Communications Commission ruled that the playing of such material could subject the licensee to administrative sanction. The Commission's action was based on a federal statute banning the broadcast of obscene, indecent or profane material.

The Supreme Court upheld the statute and the Commission's action as constitutional. The key question was whether indecent as well as obscene material (as defined by *Miller*) could be regulated. The Court relied heavily on broadcasting's greater accessibility to children in finding that objectionable language could be banned from the airwaves.

With new communications technologies come new controversies. The advent of cable television has raised new concerns about pornography and indecency. "Adult" programming services such as the Playboy Channel have met with serious opposition in many communities across the country. Legislation aimed at banning such services has been proposed in most states and in a few cases enacted into law. Usually, these laws take the form of a total prohibition of nudity on cable.

Proponents of programming restrictions argue that cable is like broadcasting—it intrudes into the home and is accessible to children. Therefore, just as dirty words can be prohibited from broadcasting, so can nudity from cable television.

Supporters of the targeted programming services counter by pointing out that one has to subscribe to cable before it enters the home. Furthermore, one can subscribe to some cable services without being forced to take others. Finally, it is possible, by law, to obtain "locking devices" that enable parents to black out individual cable channels during periods when they are not around, eliminating the danger of unsupervised children gaining access to unsuitable programming.

So far, the courts have agreed with the "adult programming" advocates. Finding that cable is more analogous to movie theaters or videotapes, they have consistently struck down laws attempting to ban any programming other than that which meets the *Miller* definition of obscenity.

However, the battle is far from over. Sexually–related communication, whether in magazines, books, or movies, cable or broadcasting, will continue to remain controversial. The issues are too complex and emotions too strong to allow for consensus. Regardless of how the Supreme Court defines pornography, some will view it as too permissive and others as too restrictive. It is truly an area where everyone has his or her own opinion.

Banning Porn: The New Censorship

by Lois P. Sheinfeld

On the evening of July 10, 1884, a 23-year-old Minneapolis woman doused herself with gasoline and set herself aflame to protest pornography. She was taken to the hospital in critical condition. Three days later, the Minneapolis City Council passed a package of antipornography legislation.

The legislation included a censorship ordinance condemning pornography on the theory that it violated the civil rights of women. That ordinance was the product of an intensive antipornography campaign mounted by two feminists, Catharine MacKinnon, associate professor at the University of Minnesota Law School; and Andrea Dworkin, a New York City-based writer. Last year, MacKinnon and Dworkin drafted a similar ordinance and persuaded the City

Dr. Lois Sheinfeld is associate professor of journalism, New York University. Among the courses she teaches are Media and the Law, First Amendment and Free Speech, and Broadcast Cable Regulations and the First Amendment. She formerly taught constitutional law, criminal justice, and the First Amendment at Stanford University where she was also the university ombudsman; she is active in public interest and civil rights law. Sheinfeld has a B.A. in history and political science from Queens College, and a law degree from New York University. [This article is edited, revised, and reprinted form the *Nation*, September 8, 1984; ©1984, 1986 Lois P. Sheinfeld.]

Council to adopt it on December 30, following highly emotional legislative hearings. On January 5, Mayor Donald M. Fraser vetoed that ordinance. "The remedy sought through the ordinance as drafted is neither appropriate nor enforceable within our cherished tradition and constitutionally protected right of free speech," he said.

'Louie, Louie'

A generation of Americans didn't understand the lyrics of "Louie, Louie," and so many of them assumed the words were obscene, and tried to ban it.

"We didn't have too much of a problem with airplay," recalls Max Feirtag, president of Limax Music, publishers of the 1960s rock hit, "but there was a lot of objection from some people. Some claimed the lyrics, which were set to a Calypso beat, were obscene; some claimed that when the lyrics were played backward [backward masking], they advocated use of illegal drugs."

"Louie, Louie" was written by Richard Berry and first recorded by 1957 by Berry and Feirtag on Flip Records. "The lyrics were perfectly understandable," says Feirtag. During the next few years, with no one objecting to the lyrics, "Louie, Louie," became mildly popular in the Northwest, then was recorded in the Fall of 1963 by the Kingsmen. Feirtag recalls that "The sound [on the Kingsmen version] was garbled. We had recorded it in a second-rate studio, with a mike fifteen feet over the head of the lead singer, Jack Ely, who wore braces." It was the Kingsmen version which brought about national recognition and the claims of obscenity. Throughout the country, people knew—they just absolutely, positively *knew*—that "Louie, Louie" was obscene. "We didn't intend to have 'dirty' lyrics," says Feirtag, "but if there are indistinguishable lyrics, you can count on the dirty little minds to assume it's obscene." Some people even created obscene lyrics to go with the music, says Feirtag.

To counter what could have been a national censorship battle, Feirtag placed an ad in *Teen* magazine, offering to send the lyrics for only a dollar to prove that the song wasn't obscene—and thousands of people sent for the lyrics, many of them believing they were going to get obscene lyrics by return mail.

In 1964, with several radio stations becoming concerned about the lyrics, the National Association of Broadcasters (NAB) reviewed the song, and determined it was acceptable for airplay by member stations. But, the protests continued.

Meanwhile, sales topped the charts as "Louie, Louie" became one of the most popular songs of the mid-'60s, an "anthem for the young." Paul Revere and the Raiders, the Beach Boys, David McCallum, and numerous others all recorded versions; but, even with understandable lyrics, the song was still branded obscene.

"Tropic of Cancer": Sea of Storm

It was praised as a realistic portrait of a part of Parisian life. It was condemned as obscene, and banned by most English-speaking countries. With James Joyce's *Ulysses*, James Cleland's *Fanny Hill*, and several other books, *Tropic of Cancer* became not only a part of a literary heritage, but a heritage of suppression.

Tropic of Cancer, Henry Miller's semi-autobiographical story of Bohemian life in Paris after World War I, was banned almost as soon as it was published in Paris in 1934. Several attempts to get the book admitted into the United States failed; a decision against the book by the U.S. District Court in 1948 reinforced the nation's desire to keep the book out of the country. Then in 1961, Grove Press, an American publisher, secured publication rights, and published a hardcover edition. On June 9, 1961, the Post Office banned the book, then lifted the ban four days later.

Nevertheless, sales were not enough to cause widespread concern among the book-banners, although the book was banned in Dallas. Then, on September 28, Grove published a large-run softcover edition. Within weeks, hundreds of police throughout the country, backed by countless district attorneys, removed copies of the book from sale; several booksellers were arrested, others warned. There was no logic to why some cities ordered the ban, why some didn't. In St. Paul, the book was banned; in neighboring Minneapolis, there was no ban. In Rhode Island, the attorney general suggested that booksellers "voluntarily" remove the copies. However, in New Jersey, where several district attorneys and police forces had already confiscated copies of the book, the state attorney general issued a strongly-worded statement indicating that the police and state attorneys can warn booksellers not to display or sell the book, but could take no action without a court order. Even after Customs permitted the book to be imported, and the Post Office permitted it to be mailed, police and prosecutors continued to make arrests.

The magical words, "It's obscene," apparently was enough to trigger the lust in a sizable chunk of the American population. In cities where the book was not banned, booksellers, armed with myriad press clippings, had difficulty keeping the book on the shelves. In cities where there were bans, people bought and sold copies of the book as if there were no other books ever to be manufactured. By January 1962, more than two million copies were in print.

Although sales were streaking through the best-sellers lists, the book continued to be banned throughout the country. For Barney Rosset, owner of Grove Press, and a vigorous proponent of the rights of free expresison, there was a principle to be fought. Rosset began fighting back, suing police departments and eventually bringing the case to the courts. Finally, in June 1962, five members of the supreme Court ruled that under the Roth Test, *Tropic of Cancer* was not obscene.

Assisted by MacKinnon, an unlikely marriage of feminists and members of the Moral Majority secured the passage of corresponding legislation in Indianapolis on May 1, 1984. An hour after Mayor William H. Hudnut signed the measure into law, it was challenged in Federal court on First Amendment and other constitutional grounds . . . [In 1985, the U.S. Court of Appeals affirmed a District Court ruling that such ordinances are unconstitutional.]

Repudiation of the free speech principles of the First Amendment marks the current antipornography campaign as the new censorship. Under the banner of civil rights, its proponents seek to suppress free expresison by state proscription of books, magazines, films, plays and the visual arts . . .

Citizens for Morality

They're not cranks and crazies out to stop sex, but well-organized people who believe, as did Anthony Comstock more than a century earlier, that pornography, if allowed to remain, will be some of the seeds of America's destruction.

Whether in small *ad hoc* village groups or in chapters of Citizens for Decent Literature (CDL) and Morality in Media, Inc., the two major national organizations, they have developed extremely complex and persuasive techniques, have extensive fund-raising campaigns, and are attacking everything from the depiction of the female nude in *Playboy* to hard-core pornography, from "topless" shows to sex shows.

Their campaigns have often taken on the tone of a religious crusade. According to Charles H. Keating, Jr., founder of CDL:

> The question posed by this onslaught of evil is not one involving freedom or censorship. The question is the survival of Judeo-Christian civilization. If the decent citizens of this nation continue lethargic and apathetic in the face ofthis pernicious enemy, the families of Western Civilization will live under the anarchy of the libertine, and "the plum soon thereafter will become ripe for plucking" by Communism.

The leaders of various chapters will tell the people that the Supreme Court allows "community standards" to be a determining factor in pornography cases, that the law enforcement agencies are interested in curbing pornography, and that the battles are those of common people against the multibillion dollar "Big Business" of pornography. But *you* must become involved, they exhort the people, working them into an emotional state of anger and fear that their own values and world views could be destroyed should pornography continue.

CDL will assist local communities, will encourage the use of picketing against "adults-only" bookshops, will advise people how to file complaints against publishers and distributors, and will even file lengthy legal briefs as *amicus curiae* (friends of the court) in trials against those on trial on charges of manufacturing, reproducing, or distributing obscene materials.

Through the First Amendment's guarantees of freedom of speech and of the press, the framers of the Constitution sought to prevent control of thought and expression. "The main purpose of [these] constitutional provisions is to prevent such previous restraints upon publications as had been practised by other governments." So held the Supreme Court more than fifty years ago in *Near v. Minnesota*, striking down a Minnesota law censoring books and magazines.

Unless it can be factually demonstrated that speech causes severe harm, the First Amendment denies to any official the power to decide what people may or may not see and hear. The public, not the government, determines the acceptability and value of ideas. "Fear of serious injury cannot along justify suppression of free speech . . . . Men feared witches and burnt women," warned Justice Louis Brandeis.

While some assert that pornography causes rape and other acts of criminal sexual violence, the existing evidence does not support that view. After extensive investigations, both the President's Commission on Obscenity and Pornography and the British Committee on Obscenity and Film Censorship concluded that there was no reliable evidence connecting pornography and crime. Since the publication of their reports, in 1970 and 1979 respectively, the state of the evidence has not changed. A leading opponent of pornography, Ernest van den Haag, professor at the Fordham University Law School, recently said: "There have been studies on the connection between pornography and sexual agression, but none serious. If I had any statistics, believe me, I would use them."

It is therefore not surprising that the new antipornography ordinances abandon reliance on the serious-harm exception to the First Amendment and instead categorically declare pornography a violation of women's rights. They define pornography as the "graphic, sexually explicit subordination of women, whether in pictures or in words," including pictures of words by which women are presented as sexual objects for domination or conquest, as sexually submissive or as degraded or inferior in a sexual context.

Under those vague, overreaching provisions, a charge of pornography could easily be leveled at the poems of Charles Baudelaire, John Donne, and Anne Sexton; the books and stories of Doris Lessing, Mary McCarthy, John le Carre, and even Andrea Dworkin; many if not all of Marilyn Monroe's films; the plays *Hurlyburly* by David Rabe, *One for the Road* by Harold Pinter, and *Noises Off* by Michael Frayn—and so forth ad infinitum.

And why draw the line at sexually explicit material?

Under a civil rights theory, the requirements of sexual explicitness is superfluous. If these ordinances are constitutional, any material depicting the subordination of women could be labeled discriminatory and could therefore be suppressed. The censorship possibilities are staggering.

Admittedly, other provisions in the ordinances are aimed more narrowly at depictions of violent sexual acts against women. I find such depictions repulsive. But in this country we have witnessed attempts to ban *Ms.* and *A Doll's House* because some people found the feminist views expressed in them repulsive. We cannot permit a popular vote at any particular time or place to override the First Amendment right to free expression.

Censorship is not advocated by everyone who opposes pornography, and antipornography censorship is not supported by all feminists. As a feminist, I am troubled by a campaign that exalts book-burning in the name of women's rights. Official repression of disfavored expression, places all expression and essential liberty in jeopardy. Without fidelity to the constitutional commands that assure open and free discourse, the struggle for sexual equality itself is at risk.

Stifling speech cannot advance women's rights, nor can violent martyrdom. Of the attempted suicide in Minneapolis, Catharine MacKinnon said: "Women feel very desperate about the existence of pornography. This doesn't single her out. People make choices on how [to express their angers]." This pronouncement is simply irresponsible. The young woman's self-immolation was heartbreaking, and I grieve for her. But her "choice" must be unequivocally rejected, lest it encourage other young people to pursue causes—good or bad— by senseless, self-destructive means.

An Obscene Story

by Walter Brasch

And so it came to pass that Sidney Thornacre, a mild-mannered stock clerk from Orange County, Florida, was elected President of the United States without opposition and on a 1-0 vote. It was 1-0 in the popular vote and 1-0 in the electoral college, the first time that anyone was elected president unanimously.

How President Thornacre was elected shall remain an inspiration to all people throughout the world, but the events of many decades ago need to be recounted every now and then.

It all began in 1977 when the Fort Lauderdale, Florida, City Council decided that there had to be laws against obscenity. A noble gesture. But the Supreme Court determined that for laws to be fair, they had to be spelled out—in painstakingly exact detail. According to the Supreme Court, it wasn't good enough just to say that obscenity was bad, the laws had to specify just what was bad.

So, the Fort Luaderdale City Council put its collective research mind to work, read all the appropriate books and magazines, watched all the appropriate television shows and movies, and spelled out a series of ordinances so explicit that they made Hugh Hefner blush.

Naturally, the laws themselves were obscene and all members of the city council were sent to jail. After all, obscenity—"and whomsoever shall be party to obscenity"—must be punished. And that's how the D.A. and his entire staff were prosecuted and sent to jail.

[Reprinted from "Wanderings," ©1977, 1986 by Walter M. Brasch]

Soon, a chain reaction began. One after another, the prosecutor became the prosecuted. Although many recognized what would ultimately happen, they had a duty to perform. After prosecuting the guilty to reading the obscenity statutes, they willingly accepted their own prosecution. America's sense of values had to be preserved. By the end of the year, the entire population of Fort Lauderdale was in jail, victims of rampant obscenity.

From Florida it spread throughout the rest of the country, first throughout the South, then North along the Atlantic coast and New England; next into the Midwest, the Far West and the Pacific Coast. Person after person; jail after jail. Soon, the jails weren't enough, and people were placed under house arrest, leading to the elimination of smog but creating a sudden population explosion.

And then it happened—something everyone feared but no one expected. The President of the United States, hoping to stop the problem, read the Fort Lauderdale ordinance, admitted guilt, then resigned, leaving the country without a President . . . or government—the Congress had been the first ones to read the ordinance. With everyone in jail, a massive campaign was launched to find a replacement president.

And that's how Sidney Thornacre, the only person in the country who hadn't read the Fort Lauderdale ordinance, applied for the Presidency. On that fateful Tuesday in November, he went to his precinct polling place—where he was precinct captain, precinct judge, precinct poll watcher, and precinct election counter—and cast his lone vote. Then, a couple months later he made that vote official by going to the nation's capital and, as the country's only member of the electoral college—and the only one in the country not convicted of a felony,— cast a unanimous vote for himself for president.

On the office wall in the White House, Sidney Thornacre—President of the United States, Commander–in–Chief of the Armed Forces; Secretaries of State, Defense, Agriculture, Commerce and other departments; Chief Justice of the United States; Senate majority leader; and Senior Maintenance Engineer of the Library of Congress—has a framed copy of the Fort Lauderdale anti–obscenity ordinance—with appropriate sections blacked out.

Bibliography

Barton, Richard L., "The Lingering Legacy of Pacifica: Broadcasters' Freedom of Silence," *Journalism Quarterly*.

Bass, Abraham Z. *Ginzburg: Intent of the Purveyor*, Freedom of Information Center (Columbia, Mo.), June 1967.

Bottini, Ronald L., *Regulation of TV Sex and Violence*, Freeodm of Information Center (Columbia, Mo.), July 1966.

Boyer, Paul, *Purity in Print: The Vice-Society Movement and Book Censorship in America*, Charles Scribner's Sons (New York, N.Y.), 1968.

Brown, Dennis, *Dilemmas of Film Classification*, Freedom of Information Center (Columbia, Mo.), December 1967.

Calverton, Victor F., *The Liberation of American Literature*. Charles Scribner's Sons (New York, N.Y.), 1932.

Chandos, John, ed. *'To Deprave and Corrupt . . .'* Association Press (New York, N.Y.), 1962.

Clancy, Phyllis, *Obscenity: From Ginzburg to Stanley*, Freedom of Information Center (Columbia, Mo.), March 1970. "Douglas' Abstention Maintains Ruling on 'I Am Curious (Yellow)'," *FOI Digest*, March-April 1971.

Clor, Harry, *Obscenity and Public Morality: Censorship in a Liberal Society*, University of Chicago Press (Chicago, Ill.), 1969.

Commission on Obscenity and Pornography, *Technical Reports*. (Vol. 1, *Preliminary Studies*; Vol. 2, *Legal Analysis*; Vol. 3, *The Marketplace: The Industry*; Vol. 4, *The Marketplace: Empirical Studies*), Government Printing Office (Washington, D.C.), 1971.

Cullinan, Gerald, *The United States Postal Service*, Praeger Publishers (New York, N.Y.), 1973.

Easterly, Elenora, *CMAA: Experiment in Self-Regulation*, Freedom of Information Center (Columbia, Mo.), April 1967.

"Editor and Publisher Imprisoned for Illustrated Obscenity Report," *FOI Digest*, January-February 1976.

Ernst, Morris; Alexander Lindley, *The Censor Marches On: Recent Milestones in the Administration of Obscenity Law in America*, Doubleday, Doran & Co. (New York, N.Y.), 1940.

Ernst, Morris L. and Alan U. Schwartz. *Censorship: The Search for the Obscene*. New York: Macmillan Co., 1964.

"FCC Attacks Obscene Radio; 'Topless' Shows Condemned," *FOI Digest*, May-June 1973.

"FCC Calls Broadcast Indecent, Issues Warning to Radio Station," *FOI Digest*, January-February 1975.

"FCC Plans Hearing to Probe Alleged Obscenity in Broadcasting," *FOI Digest*, March-April 1973.

Gerber, Albert, *Sex, Pornography, and Justice*, Lyle Stuart (New York, N.Y.), 1965.

Gilfond, Duff, "Arbiters of Obscenity in the Post Office Department," *New Republic*, July 3, 1929.

Gilleland, LaRue, *Obscenity—'Anybody's Guess'*, Freedom of Information Center (Columbia, Mo.), March 1961.

Gilmor, Donald, *Sex, Censorship, and Pornography*, Greenleaf Classics (San Diego, Calif.).

Ginzburg, Ralph, *An Unhurried View of Erotica*, Helmsman Press (New York, N.Y.), 1958.

Goodman, Paul, "Censorship and Mass Media," *Yale Political* (Autumn 1963).

Johnson, W.T., "The Pornography Report; Epistemology, Methodology, and Ideology," *Duquesne Law Review*, Winter 1971.

Kilpatrick, James, *The Smut Peddlers*, Doubleday (Garden City, N.Y.), 1960.

Lacy, Dan, *On Obscenity and Censorship,* Freedom of Information Center (Columbia, Mo.), September 1960.

Murphy, Patricia, *Pornography on the Local Level,* Freedom of Information Center (Columbia, Mo.), November 1973.

Lapham, Lewis H., "The Place of Pornography," *Harper's,* November 1984.

Loth, David, *The Erotic in Literature,* Secker & Warburg (London, England), 1962.

Lewis, F. F., *Literature, Obscenity, and Law,* Southern Illinois University Press (Carbondale, Ill.), 1976.

Murphy, Terrence, *Censorship: Government and Obscenity,* Helicon Press (Baltimore, Md.), 1963.

Oboler, Eli, *The Fear of the World, Censorship and Sex,* Scarecrow Press (Metuchen, N.J.), 1974.

Patton, Lloyd H. Jr., *"Variable Obscenity" Legislation,* Freedom of Information Center (Columbia, Mo.), June 1969.

Paul, James; Murray Schwartz, *Federal Censorship; Obscenity in the Mail,* The Free Press of Glencoe (New York, N.Y.), 1961.

Roote, Betty, *State Regulation of Obscenity,* Freedom of Information Center (Columbia, Mo.), February 1966.

St. John-Stevas, Norman, *Obscenity and the Law,* Secker & Warburg (London, England), 1956.

Schauer, Frederick, *The Law of Obscenity,* the Bureau of National Affairs (Washington, D.C.), 1976.

Schleifer, Bernard, *The Obscenity Report,* Stein and Day (New York, N.Y.), 1970.

Sriburatham, Arry, *The Bangkok 'World',* Freedom of Information Center (Columbia, Mo.), November 1963.

Tickton, S.D., "Obscene/Indecent Programming: The FCC and WBAL," *Communications and the Law,* 1979.

Tuck, George. *Post Office Controls of Obscenity,* Freedom of Information Center (Columbia, Mo.), January 1970.

"White House Rejects Pornography Report; Major Court Case Hinges on Two-Year Study," *FOI Digest,* July-August 1970.

Yeager, Suzanne, *G-GP-R-X:Exercise in Ambiguity?,* Freedom of Information Center (Columbia, Mo.), March 1971.

Yeager, Suzanne, *G-GP-R-X: Forced Self-Regulation?,* Freedom of Information Center (Columbia, Mo.), February 1971.

Chapter 40

Defamation

All people are concerned with their reputation—what other people think about them. Consequently, when someone publishes or speaks negatively about another, most people become offended. Out of this concern for individual image has come the conept of defamation.

Concern over defamation goes back at least to the Jewish law found in *Exodus* 20:16—"Thou shalt not bear false witness against thy neighbor," the eighth commandment, and has been a part of law throughout the world for most of history. Turkish law required that a mark be burned into the forehead of the defamer. In France, the defamer was whipped on the first conviction and sentenced to death on the second offense; and the British have very strict laws punishing defamation.

The authoritarian argues that rules regarding defamation created by the state should exist to protect the powerless private person from the wealthy media and from careless individuals. Rules of defamation provide for financial compensation equal to the damage done by the defamer. In this way, reputation taken is replaced by money—the law thus gives value to reputation—and the legal scales are kept in balance by the payment.

While the argument has considerable appeal, defamation laws are passed only by states, not the federal government, in the Unites States because the First Amendment prohibits Congress from making any law that restricts freedom of expression—the Fourteenth Amendment has not been used to apply the First Amendment standard against state defamation laws. A true libertarian, however, would be at a loss to justify *any* statute prescribing damages for words spoken; however, very few legal authorities, other than Justice Hugo Black, have come out strongly against defamation laws.

Defamation falls into two categories—libel and slander. Libel is the more serious of the two forms in that it is published through newspapers, magazines, books, memos, letters, radio, film, and television. Exposure through the media usually means that more people hear, see, or read the defamation; and the communication is more permanent—printed on paper, recorded on tape or film. Because it is spoken without the aid of a medium of recording or dissemination, slander is the less serious form of defamation, and damages awarded by courts tend to be considerably less.

Law in the United States recognizes four types of individual defamation—communication that leads people to hate the defamed, that causes one's neighbors to shun him or her—claiming that the person has a mental or loathsome disease, that hurts a person's ability to practice one's occupation, or that opens a person to ridicule or contempt. Under some circumstances, a corporation may be defamed, as, for example, when a communication injures a company's credit standing.

Negative comments about a person are not defamatory when the statements are true—truth was the argument made in the John Peter Zenger trial regarding negative statements. Consequently, modern laws of defamation seem to take their standard from the Jewish law regarding "false witness."

Much of the legal battles regarding defamation during the 1960s and 1970s centered on the defenses that would be considered in holding a reporter not guilty of libel. Three traditional defenses against libel include truth, fair comment, and qualified privilege. Truth was the defense used to help acquit John Peter Zenger, but not until the nineteenth century did the defense become widely accepted. This defense says that when a defendant has printed an unkind statement that was true, no defamation occurred. Qualified privilege permits the news media to publish defamatory statements appearing in official proceedings, and fair comment allows critics to perform their work reviewing movies, plays, or sculpture.

Defining the Public Figure

In *New York Times* v. *L. B. Sullivan* (1964), the Supreme Court of the United States reversed a judgment of the Alabama Supreme Court in which Sullivan had been awarded damages for statements appearing in editorial advertising in the *New York Times*. Although the statements contained some errors, the Supreme Court declared that since Sullivan, one of the three elected commissioners of the City of Montgomery, Alabama, was a public figure, his claim of defamation had to stand a stricter test.

The Supreme Court believed that "[i]njury to official reputation affords no more warrant for repressing speech that would otherwise be free than does factual error." The Court stated:

> The constitutional guarantees require, we think, a federal rule that prohibits a public official from recovering damages for a defamatory falsehood relating to his official conduct unless he proves that the statement was made with "actual malice"—that is, with knowledge that it was false or with reckless disregard of whether it was false or not.

This new standard for evaluating public officials effectively prevented people falling in this group from recovering defamation damages, but it failed to define just who should be included in the category of a public official. The question was answered when a private businessman, George A. Rosenbloom, was named on thirteen radio broadcasts as a Philadelphian who was engaged in selling obscene publications. The resulting case, *Rosenbloom* v. *Metromedia* (1971), led to this observation:

> Further reflection over the years since New York Times was decided persuades us that the view of the "public official" or "public figure" as assuming the risk of defamation by voluntarily thrusting himself into the public eye bears little relationship either to the values protected by the First Amendment or to the nature of our society. We have recognized that "[e]xposure of the self to others in varying degrees in a concomitant of life in a civilized community" [is a natural part of membership in society] . . . Voluntarily or not, we are all "public" men to some degree . . . Conversely, some aspects of the lives of even the most public men fall outside the area of matters of public or general concern . . . Thus, the idea that certain "public" figures have voluntarily exposed their entire lives to public inspection, while private individuals have kept theirs carefully shrouded from public view is, at best, a legal fiction.

Because his actions were of a public nature, Rosenbloom had to be judged under the public figure test when he was disseminating questionable materials.

But the Supreme Court began backing away from its expansion of the public figure concept to cover almost everyone to some extent in *Gertz* v. *Robert Welch, Inc.* (1974). The decision specifically restricted the opinion in *Rosenbloom* because the Court believed that the media had gained too much latitude while the good name and reputation of individual citizens had lost some of the necessary protections. The Supreme Court could not find that Gertz was a public official, because he had never held public office. The Court found that Gertz was not a public figure either because he had gained no "such pervasive fame or notoriety" as to merit public figure status, nor had he become famous because of his involvement with a public issue.

In the second case a person would have to "voluntarily inject . . . himself . . . into a particular public controversy and thereby become a public figure."

The result of the case was to considerably restrain the freedom that the media had come to enjoy under the older standards of *New York Times* and *Rosenbloom*. The late 1970s and 1980s would show the result of the new standard.

During the first half of the 1980s more than twenty-five convictions have been decided against defamers with awards of $1 million or more; however, many of the verdicts have been overturned on appeal. Some of the large libel suits include actress Carol Burnett's $1.6 million judgment against the *National Enquirer* for having "acted in reckless disregard in publishing an item concerning Burnett in 1976."

Because of a program CBS aired on January 23, 1982, Gen. William C. Westmoreland, the Vietnam War military leader, filed suit against the network asking for $120 million in damages because the network invaded his privacy and defamed him. The two sides, however, eventually dropped the case in 1985.

The Illinois County Circuit Court, however, awarded a judgment of $9.2 million to James Green, a local builder. Reporters at the *Alton Telegraph* had sent a four-page memo to the U.S. Department of Justice in 1969 to verify connections between Green and organized crime. Although the memo was never published, information reached Green and other residents who were mentioned, and they filed suit. Eventually, the award was overturned.

Thus, the states provide the legal mechanism to try those accused of defamation, although cases are for the most part civil not criminal. The awarding of damages, thus, also serves the states' interest since it helps assure that media which lose such cases are more careful in their reporting—perhaps even thinking several times before attacks against the agents of government.

Bibliography

Cooley, Thomas M., *A Treatise on the Law of Torts*, 2ed., Callaghan and Co. (Chicago, Ill.), 1888.

Fraser, Sir Hugh, *Libel and Slander* 7ed., (London: 1936).

LeBel, Paul A., "Defamation and the First Amendment: The End of the Affair," *William and Mary Law Review* 1983-1984.

Miller, Arthur R., *The Assault on Privacy*, University of Michigan Press (Ann Arbor, Mich.), 1971.

Packard, Vance, *The Naked Society*, David McKay (New York, N.Y.), 1964.

Pember, Don R., *Privacy and the Press*, University of Washington Press (Seattle, Wash.), 1972.

Prosser, William, *Law of Torts*, 3ed., West (St. Paul, Minn.), 1964.

Van Alstyne, William W., "First Amendment Limitations on Recovery from the Press—An Extended Comment on 'The Anderson Solution,'" *William and Mary Law Review*, No. 5, 1983-1984.

Warren, Samuel; Louis D. Brandeis, "The Right to Privacy," *Harvard Law Review*, 1890.

Westin, Alan, *Privacy and Freedom*, Atheneum (New York, N.Y.), 1967.

Cases

Cantrell v. Forest City Publishing Co., 419 U.S. 245, 95 S.Ct. 465 (1975).

Cox Broadcasting Corp. v. Cohn, 420 U.S. 469, 95 S.Ct. 1029 (1975).

Curtis Pub. Co. v. Butts, 388 U.S. 130, 87 S.Ct. 1975 (1967).

Dietemann v. Time, Inc., 449 F.2d 245 (9th Cir. 1971).

Farmers Eductional and Cooperative Union of America v. WDAY, Inc., 360 U.S. 525, 79 S.Ct. 1302 (1959).

Florida Publishing Co. v. Fletcher, 403 U.S. 713, 91 S.Ct. 2140 (1971).

Garrison v. Louisiana, 379 U.S. 64, 85 S.Ct. 209 (1964).

Gertz v. Robert Welch, Inc., 418 U.S. 323 (1974).

Holmes V. Curtis Pub. Co., 303 F.Supp. 522 (DCSC 1969).

New York Times Co. v. Sullivan, 376 U.S. 254, 84 S.Ct. 710 (1964).
Olmstead v. U.S., 277 U.S. 438, 48 S.Ct. 564 (1928).
Pearson v. Dodd, 279 F.Supp. 101 (DCDC 1968).
Rosenblatt v. Baer, 383 U.S. 75, 86 S.Ct. 669 (1966).
Rosenbloom v. Metromedia, 403 U.S. 29, 91 S.Ct. 1811 (1971).
Time, Inc. v. Hill, 385 U.S. 374, 87 S.Ct. 534 (1967).
Time, Inc. v. Firestone, 424 U.S. 448, 96 S.Ct. 958 (1976).

Chapter 41

Free Press v. Fair Trial
by Jay B. Wright

Few communications law issues have generated the sustained controversy which typifies the free press v. fair trial problem. The press cannot be considered entirely "free" if its access to information about crimes and trials is restricted or if it is restrained from publishing or broadcasting some or all of the information it has. On the other hand, individuals may not be able to have an entirely "fair" trial if information about the crime is alleged to have committed is printed or broadcast to the public before trial even begins. The problem is a true dilemma—how does one "compromise" between two seemingly uncompromisable rights—the right of a free press and the right of a fair trial?

The problem is, of course, an old one. It is human nature to talk about, write about, even gossip about crimes and trials. Anyone who might doubt that crimes and trials are entertaining need only look so far as prime-time network television programming to see how insatiable is the public's appetite for such material. When the criminals, the victims, and the trials are real instead of fictional, they can generate even more public interest. Depending on one's point of view, that public interest can be characterized in either a positive or a negative way. Journalists seeking to explain their catering to such public interest with front page stories detailing a crime may say they are fulfilling an appropriate role of the press in giving the public an opportunity to view and evaluate the administration of justice. They will point out that our trials are not secret Star Chamber proceedings and that members of the public have a legitimate need to know what their taxpayer-supported police and judiciary are doing. Attorneys critical of front page attention to crime stories are far more

Dr. Jay B. Wright is professor of journalism, S. I. Newhouse School of Public Communications, Syracuse University, and executive director since 1972 of the New York Fair Trial Free Press Conference, the state's permanent bench-bar-media organization. With Marc Franklin and T. Barton Carter, he is author of *The First Amendment and The Fourth Estate*, 3rd edition (1985) and *The First Amendment and the Fifth Estate* (1986). He was chair of the Law Division, Association for Education in Journalism and Mass Communication, 1982-1983. Dr. Wright received the Bachelor of Science in Journalism (BSJ) and Master of Science in Journalism (MSJ) from Northwestern University, a Master of Studies in Law (MSL) from Yale University, and a Ph.D. in mass communication from Syracuse University. [©1986, Jay B. Wright]

likely to say that the journalist is "pandering" to the baser instincts of human nature by exaggerating the importance of criminal activity. They are likely to add that the media are generally quite profitable businesses and that crime news and sensationalism in court coverage may translate into more dollars in the owners' already well-lined pockets. And, attorneys are likely to say that all this is done at the expense of people deserving of more protection: the defendants (who are entitled to a presumption of innocence until their guilt is established properly in a court of law) and the victims (whose privacy may be irreparably injured).

Choice of vocabulary sometimes says something about the debate. What a journalist calls "news coverage," the lawyer may call "publicity." What a journalist calls "a fact related to the case," the lawyer may call "prejudicial information." Should a judge take the highly unusual step of ordering the press not to print or broadcast information about the case (an act which would normally be considered unconstitutional), the press is likely to characterize that action by the judge as a "gag order," while the lawyer might call it a "judicial restrictive order."

Regardless of which side one is on in the endless debate, virtually no one would deny that the press coverage of some sensational crimes has created some quite real problems. The tempation for lawyers and judges is to blame the press for the "excesses" which lead to those problems. Journalists are much more likely to say that they do not create the news, they only report it. Thus, they will sometimes argue that if police would stop making prejudicial comments, if prosecutors eager to get their names in the media would stop leaking information to reporters, and if judges would keep control of their courtrooms and properly instruct jurors not to look at the media, the problem would take care of itself.

In 1963, when Lee Harvey Oswald was arrested for the assassination of President Kennedy, there followed such immediate and voluminous press coverage that the Warren Commission which investigated the assassination was forced to conclude that it would have been virtually impossible for Oswald to have received a fair trial in the United States.

Creating Guidelines

Seeking to do something about the problem, judges, lawyers, journalists, and police officials in the 1960s—through a committee of the American Bar Association and through a number of state bench-bar-press groups—promulgated guidelines to safeguard against fair trial/free press problems. They met with mixed success, partially because journalists thought lawyers should not tell them how to report the news, but consciousness of the general problem increased. This increased consciousness led to greater caution by police about what they said, fewer newspaper headlines saying "Ex-Convict Arrested," and more care by judges in controlling their courtrooms. But sensational crimes still yielded sensational news accounts—sometimes with sidebars about the fair trial/free press implications.

While voluntary guidelines may serve a purpose, it was inevitable that the Supreme Court of the United States would have to decide some of the critical issues in the fair trial/free press debates. No matter which side of the debate one is on, it is worth pondering the fact that a dispute between judges and journalists was going to be decided by nine judges—not by nine journalists. The cases which the Supreme Court has heard in this area fall into two broad categories—(1) appeals by convicted criminals who claim that their trials were unfair because of prejudicial news accounts and (2) appeals by the news media claiming that their First Amendment rights have been damaged by the courts.

Defendant Rights

Among the cases which decided defendant rights were *Irvin* v. *Dowd* (1961), *Rideau* v. *Louisiana* (1963), *Estes* v. *Texas* (1965), and *Sheppard* v. *Maxwell* (1966). Leslie Irvin was a suspect in six murders committed in and around Evansville, Ind., in 1954-55. The murders were attributed to a "Mad Dog Killer," and Irvin was arrested and brought back to Indiana to stand trial. News accounts announced his police line-up identification, accused him of being a parole violator, and reported that he had confessed to the murders. When potential jurors were questioned, almost 90 per cent of those examined on the point entertained some opinion as to Irvin's guilt. Irvin was convicted at the trial, but the Supreme Court held in 1961 that the trial had been unfair. At a subsequent retrial, he was convicted again.

Wilbert Rideau was accused of a Louisiana bank robbery in which three bank employees were kidnapped and one was killed. After he was apprehended, Rideau was "interviewed" by a sheriff; a sound film was made of Rideau's confession to the crimes, and the film was shown on television. Rideau was convicted of the crimes. Three members of the jury had seen the televised confession before the trial; two members of the jury were themselves deputy sheriffs. The Supreme Court held that the trial had been unfair. At a subsequent retrial, he was convicted again.

Billie Sol Estes was accused of swindling farmers by inducing them to buy fertilizer tanks and other equipment which did not exist. At the time, in 1962, television in courtrooms was exceedingly rare but was sometimes permitted in Texas, where Estes was tried. Approximately 100,000 viewers saw a pre-trial hearing in the Estes case, which had already received great publicity. Estes was convicted. The Supreme Court held that the process had not been fair. At a subsequent retrial, he was convicted again.

In the best known of these cases, Dr. Sam Sheppard, an osteopathic physician, was accused of the brutal slaying of his pregnant wife, Marilyn, at their Ohio home in 1954. Sheppard claimed that he had struggled with a mysterious "bushy haired intruder" who had knocked him unconscious and escaped. The crime and trial attracted national attention, and front page editorials about the crime and trial appeared in Cleveland newspapers. Sheppard was convicted but continued to maintain that he was innocent. Numerous attempts to have the conviction overturned were unsuccessful. In 1966, the Supreme Court of the United States, hearing an appeal of Sheppard's murder conviction, concluded that his trial had been unfair because of the news coverage which surrounded it. Although the Court made clear that it was the trial court judge who had failed to fulfill his responsibility to Sheppard by protecting the fairness of the trial, the implication was clear that the media had acted irresponsibly in their coverage of a sensational crime and trial. At a retrial, Dr. Sheppard—unlike Irvin, Rideau, and Estes—was found *not* guilty of the murder of his wife. He died within a few years of his release from prison.

Faced with precedents like these—and noting the Supreme Court's emphasis on their role—it is not surprising that trial court judges in the 1970s went to new lengths to try to protect defendants. In some instances they tried to block journalists' access to information relating to cases, or to block their entrance into courtrooms. In others, they tried to block journalists' dissemination of news the journalists had already obtained. Despite the fact that some journalists might be inclined to characterize either tactic as a "gag," there are very real conceptual differences between a denial of access and a prior restraint on publication. The fact that they are in pursuit of news stories does not give journalists special rights to barge into the President's oval office in the White House without permission or to attend a confidential board meeting of a corporation or to demand government records not otherwise available to the public. In those examples, at least, a denial of access—while frustrating to the journalist—may be constitutionally acceptable. Prior restraints on publication are another matter; they are typically considered to be unconstitutional.

Rights of the Media

Among the cases decided by the Supreme Court which are appeals by the media of restrictions placed on them by the courts are *Nebraska Press Association* v. *Stuart* (1976), *Gannett* v. *DePasquale* (1979), *Richmond Newspapers* v. *Virginia* (1980), and *Globe Newspaper Co.* v. *Superior Court* (1982).

Nebraska Press involved an attempt by a trial court judge in Nebraska to curtail prejudicial news accounts of the sensational murders of members of a rural Nebraska family. The judge ordered the press not to reveal prejudicial information and to follow the state's bench-bar-press guidelines which had been adopted voluntarily by the parties concerned.

Gannett involved a trial judge's decision to close a pre-trial suppression hearing (a hearing to decide whether certain evidence against the defendants which had been obtained out of state could be used in the trial). Reacting to a request by defense attorneys, the judge had closed his courtroom so that prejudicial information revealed at the pre-trial hearing would not be in the news media prior to the trial. Gannett newspapers appealed the order.

In *Richmond Newspapers*, a trial court had been closed during a murder trial itself—an attempt to try the defendant fairly after problems with earlier trials. Richmond Newspapers appealed the closure order.

Globe Newspapers involved automatic closure of a courtroom during testimony by a child sex crime victim, as then specified under Massachusetts law. Globe Newspapers believed that the media ought at least to have the opportunity to argue for reasons the press and public might observe.

Of these four cases, the press won all but *Gannett v. DePasquale*. In *Nebraska Press*, the court found the judge's order, a form of prior restraint, to be unconstitutional; while the court stopped short of saying *all* prior restraints for fair trial reasons would be unconstitutional, it set up a seemingly unreachable test for such orders. The *Gannett* decision, which provoked considerable outcry from the press, affirmed the trial court judge's right to close a pre-trial hearing for purposes of protecting the defendant's rights; but a year to the day later the high court decided that such a closure would virtually never be acceptable for a trial itself. Lawyers were divided in their interpretations of the two rulings, some believing that *Richmond* eviscerated *Gannett*, and others believing that closures were still acceptable for *pre*-trial closures. In *Globe Newspaper*, the court held that automatic closures of courtrooms by statute—with no opportunity for the media to argue on a case-by-case basis for a need for the public and press to observe—was unacceptable.

From the Supreme Court cases mentioned thus far, one might conclude that when the Supreme Court gets appeals based on prejudicial news coverage, it reverses the convictions and that when the Supreme Court hears cases in which the media allege that their rights have been interfered with, it decides the cases in favor of the media. Those generalizations will not, however, withstand scrutiny. The court does not, by any means, always reverse convictions. Examples are *Murphy* v. *Florida* (1975), in which the court held that Murphy's trial was sufficiently fair despite the fact that he was frequently identified in the press as "Murph the Surf," a jewel thief, prior to his murder trial; and *Chandler* v. *Florida* (1981), in which the court held that Chandler's trial was sufficiently fair despite his objection to television in the courtroom during his trial). How much news coverage, or how bad it has to be for the Supreme Court to consider a trial unfair, will probably continue to be determined on a case-by-case basis, but many observers believe that a Supreme Court populated by Nixon and Reagan appointees will not quickly move to overturn trial court convictions.

The generalization about the press's winning the fair trial/free press cases they begin is also suspect. In *Federated Publications* v. *Swedberg* (1981), for example, a trial court judge tried a new twist by granting admission to his courtroom only to those who agreed to comply with the state's usually-voluntary bench-bar-press guidelines. Despite the media's contention that placing such a condition on access was unacceptable, the Supreme Court declined to review the case.

Debate over fair trial/free press issues will no doubt continue as long as the First Amendment and the Sixth Amendment are part of the Bill of Rights. Judges and lawyers will continue to say that the press must cooperate and, at least in some cases, withhold information from the public, if a defendant's right to a fair trial is to be protected adequately. Journalists will continue to ask why they should withhold information from thousands of readers or viewers just because the court wants to find a dozen unbiased jurors to decide a case. Journalists will point out that the courts have available "remedies" to solve the fair trial/free press problems: change of venue (moving the trial to another location), postponement, sequestering the jurors, telling police and prosecutors to avoid revealing prejudicial information, etc. And judges will continue to point out that these remedies are sometimes expensive, sometimes unfair to the people involved, and often ineffective.

Under scrutiny, many of one's basic assumptions about the free trial/free press conflict tend to break down. Because of decisions in cases like *Irvin*, *Sheppard*, and *Rideau*, one might assume that public attention in the press is inherently bad for the defendant, but that is contrary to the long-held view that the openness or publicness of trials is a *protection* for the accused. Furthermore, there are many examples of accused people who received significant attention in the press and were subsequently acquitted. There may also be a tendency on the part of some people to assume that *most* crimes and trials get a lot of media attention. In fact, in big cities like New York, Chicago, or Los Angeles, there are so many crimes committed that only a small fraction of them ever get even a single mention in the press. Indigent defendants who are unhappy with their court-appointed lawyers and seemingly-hostile judges often wish there *were* cameras in their courtrooms so that the American public could view what the defendants sometimes think are miscarriages of justice.

Regardless of their differences on the way pre-trial and trial news should be handled, lawyers and journalists have similar goals—trying to arrive at the truth. For the lawyer, arriving at the truth requires a trial in a courtroom free from prejudices created by the news media. For the journalist, arriving at the truth may mean obtaining the facts as quickly as possible and then making them known. The two methods can complement one another and need not always lead to conflict, but each side must be sensitive to the needs of the other. ■

Gag Orders—Contempt of Court

The courts, like any other branch of government, have long believed that they must protect their reputation and that of people involved with the courts, as well as protecting the accused's right to a fair trial. The courts often place gag orders on reporters, orders not to publish anything they have heard or seen in the court for a specified period of time.

The real problem arises out of a conflict between three amendments to the Constitution—the First Amendment prohibiting Congress from enacting any laws restricting the right to publish and the Fifth and Sixth Amendments guaranteeing that a person shall not be "deprived of life, liberty, or property, without due process of law" and the assurance that "the accused shall enjoy the right to a speedy and public trial, by an impartial jury." Many judges have feared that publicity will hinder the process of selecting an unbiased jury, or that publicity will otherwise injure the accused's rights.

Clearly, the right to a fair trial must not be compromised; but does this mean that the court, as representative of the state, has the right to censor information reaching the public on all matters? Does the court have the right to interfere with reporters because the reporters say something that offends a judge? Judges have considered this issue many times. In the United States, one of the powers available to control communications regarding the judiciary is contempt of court citation. Harold Nelson and Dwight Teeter in *Law of Mass Communications* (Third ed., 1978) define a contempt as:

> Any act calculated to embarrass, hinder, or obstruct a court in the administration of justice, or calculated to lessen its dignity or authority. Contempts are of two kinds: direct and indirect. Direct contempts are those committed in the immediate presence of the court. Indirect contempts refer to the failure or refusal to obey a lawful order, or otherwise obstruct the court's work outside its presence.

One type of contempt applies to journalists—constructive contempt, contempt committed outside the view of the court, such as might occur when a newspaper publishes something negative about a trial. This concern arose first in England in *Rex* v. *Almon* (1764). Justice Wilmont, who heard the case, prepared an extensive opinion; but the decision was never published because the case had been mistitled *Rex* v. *Wilkes* instead of *Rex* v. *Almon*, and the defendant's counsel would not permit the renaming of the case's record.

In 1802, Justice Wilmont's son published the never-delivered opinion with powerful words on contempt that would later influence courts on both sides of the Atlantic:

> The power which the courts in Westminister Hall have of vindicating their own authority is coeval with their first foundation and institution; it is a necessary incident to every court of justice, whether of record or not, to fine and imprison for contempt to the court, acted in the face of it, [I Ventris I], and the issuing attachments by the supreme courts of justice of Westminister Hall for contempts out of court stands upon the same immemorial usage as supports the whole fabric of the common law; it is as much the *lex terrae* and within the exception of *Magna Charta* as the issuing any other legal process whatsoever. I have examined very carefully to see if I could find out any vestiges or traces of its introduction but can find none. It is as ancient as any other part of the common law; there is no priority or posteriority to be discovered about it and therefore [it] cannot be said to invade the common law, but to act in an alliance and friendly conjunction with every other provision which the wisdom of our ancestors has established for the general good of society. And though I do not mean to compare and contrast attachments with trial by jury, yet truth compels me to say that the mode of proceeding by attachment stands upon the very same foundation and basis as trial by juries do— immemorial usages and practice.

By these words, Justice Wilmont had intended to punish a bookseller by the name of Almon for publishing a criticism of Lord Mansfield, such act being an alleged libel—Justice Wilmont had been raised to his position by an individual under the authority of Lord Mansfield.

Like any other power, the contempt citation can be used by judges to protect the rights of the accused, or to serve the selfish purposes of judges. Questions have arisen over the limits of this power.

U. S. Interpretations of Contempt

The first judicial contempt law in the United States was the Judiciary Act of 1789, which provided federal courts with "the power . . . to punish by fine or imprisonment, at the discretion of said courts, all contempts of authority in any case or hearing before same [court]." In 1809, Pennsylvania passed the first state law regarding contempt, a law that condemned misconduct on the part of judicial officers and other misbehavior in the court.

An early case testing the law of 1798 and the extent to which federal judges could go in issuing contempt orders occured in Missouri regarding Judge James H. Peck. In 1826, Peck delivered an opinion that might adversely affect the claims of land speculators to property in the Upper Louisana territory, property once belonging to Spain but secured by the United States. Luke Lawless, a lawyer interested in owner rights to these claims, wrote a newspaper article critical of Peck's decision.

Peck believed that Lawless had committed constructive contempt of court, invading the rights of the court. After finding Lawless guilty, Peck suspended the lawyer's right to practice for eighteen months.

Lawless protested to Congress and asked that Peck be impeached and convicted. Four years of effort led to articles of impeachment voted by the House of Representatives, but the Senate, 22-21, failed to convict Peck, despite exhaustive work by the five managers of the impeachment proceeding. Both the House and the Senate did not want further constructive contempts beyond the courtroom; however, on March 2, 1831, Congress passed a restrictive contempt of court bill. The bill had been presented by James Buchanan, later the president. The law read:

> The power of the several courts of the United States to issue attachments and inflict summary punishments for contempts of court, shall not be construed to extend to any cases except the misbehavior of any person or persons in the presence of the said courts, or so near thereto as to obstruct the administration of justice, the misbehavior of any of the officers of the said court in their official transactions, and the disobedience or resistance by any officer of the said courts, party, juror, witness, or any other person or persons, to any lawful writ, process, order, rule, decree, or command of the said courts.

The law continues with a section describing the conditions under which punishment can be imposed and the extent of that punishment.

State Contempts

Most courts complied with the law or similar state provisions until 1855, when Chief Judge Elbert H. English constructed his own standard for state courts. English, a state supreme court judge in Arkansas, believed he and his court did not come under the direct powers of the federal statute; consequently, he was free to search Arkansas laws and constitution for standards in establishing his opinion.

English expressed his concept on a legislature's right to establish rules for courts in issuing contempt citations when a reporter published an article regarding the bail set in the case of a murderer. English thought the article had accused the court of accepting bribes and issued a contempt of court citation, much as Peck had done in the Lawless case.

Arkansas had a statute similar to the federal one precluding court judges from imposing contempt of court citations on actions taking place far from the courtroom, passed in 1838. English used the case to express the belief that courts had "immemorial powers" that could not be restrained by a co-equal branch of government; rather, only an amendment to the constitution of Arkansas could limit the court in its administration of justice. English rejected the argument of the counsel for Morrill who had argued that the limits imposed by the state legislature did indeed apply to the state's courts.

Courts in other states looked favorably on English's opinion constructing a successful position for rejecting legislatively established contempt rules limiting the court's ability to impose citations upon individuals outside the court, and many followed the lead thus established. A century would pass before the Supreme Court of the United States would begin to reverse the matter.

Modern Contempts

In a landmark decision [*Irvin* v. *Dowd* (1961)], the Supreme Court overturned a conviction because of the media coverage of the event. That decision provided some guidance in the handling of publicity reaching jurors:

> It is not required . . . that the jurors be totally ignorant of the facts and issues involved. In these days of swift, wide-spread and diverse methods of communication, an important case can be expected to arouse the interest of the public in the vicinity, and scarcely any of those best qualified to serve as jurors will not have formed some impression or opinion as to the merits of the case. This is particularly true in criminal cases. To hold that the mere existence of any preconceived notion as to the guilt or innocence of an accused, without more, is sufficient to rebut the presumption of a prospective juror's impartiality would be to establish an impossible standard . . . It is sufficient if the juror can lay aside his impression or opinion and render a verdict based on the evidence in court.

Justice Felix Frankfurter concurred with the majority opinion and pointed out his own concern over the relationship of the media to fair trials:

Not a term passes without this Court being importuned to review convictions had in states throughout the country in which substantial claims are made that a jury trial has been distorted because of inflammatory newspaper accounts . . . exerting pressures upon potential jurors before trial and even during the course of trial thereby making it extremely difficult if not impossible to secure a jury capable of [hearing] evidence [free from prior bias]. Indeed, such extraneous influences, in violation of the decencies guaranteed by our constitution, are sometimes so powerful that an accused is forced, as a practical matter, to forego trial by jury.

With the assassination of President John F. Kennedy in 1963 and the subsequent [Earl] Warren Commission report on the handling of the coverage of that assassination, the judiciary began confronting the problems of excessive media coverage of pretrial events and the potential impact of that coverage on the rights of defendants. The Warren report criticized the media and police officials for their handling of the events following the assassination.

In 1962, the Supreme Court of the United States had an opportunity to consider the effect statements made in the public media on an accused's right to a fair trial. The case [Wood v. Georgia (1962)] involved James I. Wood, sheriff of Bibb County, Georgia, who was held in contempt of court for expressing his thoughts on a hearing being conducted by a grand jury. The investigation involved the alleged sale of the votes of Blacks in the sheriff's county.

Wood was convicted of contempt by the courts in Georgia, and the case was taken to the Supreme Court of the United States which reversed the conviction citing the "clear and present danger" test in the administration of justice. The court concluded that the statements made by Wood, "did not present a danger" to the administration of justice that should vitiate his freedom to express his opinions in the manner chosen.

The problem of pretrial publicity became especially acute in the case of Wilbert Rideau who was convicted in Calcasieu Parish, Louisiana, for murder, robbery, and kidnapping and sentenced to death, a case where the trial judge could not issue a gag order.

Although Rideau's attorneys asked that the trial be conducted in another location, because of adverse media coverage, the court refused. In overturning the conviction, the Supreme Court observed:

> The kangaroo court proceedings in this case involved a more subtle but no less real deprivation of due process of law [than physical brutality]. Under our Constitution's guarantee of due process, a person accused of committing a crime is vouchsafed basic minimal rights. Among these [is] . . . the right to be tried in a courtroom presided over by a judge. Yet in this case the people of Calcasieu Parish saw and heard, not once but three times, a "trial" of Rideau in the jail, presided over by a sheriff, where there was no lawyer to advise Rideau of his right to stand mute.

Television had become the medium for disseminating the improper "trial" to the citizens of the Parish.

The issue of publicity came before the Supreme Court of the United States again in 1966 over a case originating in Cuyahoga County, Ohio, when Dr. Samuel H. Sheppard was accused of murdering his wife.

The Court made no attempt was made to keep the jurors away from the media during the trial, and they regularly read newspapers or watched television news reports. Seven of the twelve jurors had home delivery of newspapers.

The defense attorney asked for a change in location for the trial on the grounds

---

Direct and Indirect Contempt

The distinction between direct and indirect contempt is not always made. Upon the classification hinges such important privileges as the right to a jury trial and the right to be heard before a court which is not involved in the contempt itself, as well as the protection of the First Amendment. But even here, the courts have had problems of classification which are confusing and at times procedurally expensive to the contemnor. Very generally, this distinction was based upon the immediacy and location of the contemptuous act. Direct contempts were spontaneous, aggressive offenses expressly aimed at the court, itself, or at parties to the judicial process, which were committed in the presence of the court, and which tended to physically obstruct the administration of justice. The prime example would be misconduct in the view of the court . . . Examples are myriad and run the gamut from striking a judge, juror, attorney, or witness to failing to produce a witness or to testify in a manner properly before the court. The conduct itself was offensive without proof of what was precisely the actual obstruction or interference with justice.

Indirect contempts were acts of misconduct, apart from the immediate proceeding in time or location, which by implication tended to interfere with the administration of justice. Bribing a juror or a witness at a distant place or publishing prejudicial statements about a pending case are obvious examples of this offense. The title indirect contempt was originally used synonymously with the terms consequential or constructive contempt, but in substance meant the same thing. Nowadays, the term indirect contempt is used to include all nondirect contempts with one usual exception. Contempts by publications in the press have now the term constructive contempt as almost one of special connotation, reserved usually for press contempt cases. There is no special reason for this except commonly accepted practice and habit.

There is little essential difference between direct and indirect contempts. Both are contempts in the historical sense of the word. Both are implied offenses to the workings of judicial government. There are no special causes or reasons for the distinction other than the historical . . . Unfortunately, there has been some confusion in these cases.

—Ronald L. Goldfarb. *The Contempt Power* (1963).

that local citizens had seen so much news and pseudo-news regarding Sheppard that a fair trial could not be attained, a request that was denied.

The Supreme Court set aside the conviction noting that the trial court had made an error: "The court's fundamental error is compounded by the holding that it lacked power to control the publicity about the trial."

The Supreme Court then criticized the court for failing to insulate the witnesses from the sensational coverage and to control the release of information including leads and gossip, but it noted that limits could be imposed on the participants in the trial—jurors, witnesses, police, and counsels:

> The fact that many of the prejudicial news items can be traced to the prosecution, as well as the defense, aggravates the judge's failure to take any action . . . Effective control of these sources—concededly within the court's power—might well have prevented the divulgence of inaccurate informtion, rumors, and accusations that made up much of the inflammatory publicity, at least after Sheppard's indictment.

That the Supreme Court authorized restrictions on the communication of participants in the trial opened the way for other cases to be considered on what judges could do or not do in restraining the dissemination of information adverse to the defendant.

In 1976, the Supreme Court had the opportunity to speak in *Nebraska Press Association* v. *Hugh Stuart*, a case that has become a landmark in the development of judicial attitudes towards the news media. Stuart, judge of the District Court of Lincoln County, Nebraska, had ordered that that the petitioners (members of a news organization) could not publish or broadcast accounts of confessions or other information that "strongly implicat[ed]" the accused.

The crime centered on the murder of six members of the Henry Kellie family, found by police on October 18, 1975, at their home in Sutherland, Nebraska. Local, regional, and national broadcasters and newspapers immediately became interested in the crime, and sent reporters to the scene. Meanwhile, police had a suspect, Erwin Charles Simants, whom they announced to the media and provided pictures.

Both the defense and county attorney asked for a gag order limiting the information the media could disseminate because of the "reasonable likelihood of prejudicial news which would make difficult, if not impossible, the impaneling of an impartial jury and tend to prevent a fair trial." The County Court listened to the arguments for the two sides with no one present for the news media, and on October 22, the next day, granted an order prohibiting:

> [E]veryone in attendance from "releas[ing] or authoriz[ing] the release for public dissemination in any form or manner whatsoever any testimony given or evidence adduced;" the order also required members of the press to observe the Nebraska bar-press guidelines.

One day later, a number of broadcast associations, reporters, and publishers asked that the restrictive order be vacated. This request was directed to the District Court, which issued its own restrictive order on October 27. The new order concluded that there was "a clear and present danger that pre-trial publicity could imfringe upon . . . a fair trial." The order was limited extending only until the jury was impaneled and it dealt with five subjects.

(1) the existence or contents of a confession Simants had made to law enforcement officers, which had been introduced in open court at arraignment; (2) the fact and nature of statements Simants had made to other persons; (3) the contents of a note he had written the night of the crime; (4) certain aspects of the medical testimony at the preliminary hearing; and (5) the identify of the victims of the alleged sexual assault and the nature of the assault. It also prohibited reporting the exact nature of the restrictive order itself.

Like the County Court order, the District Court drew upon the Nebraska bar-press guidelines. It was the District Court's order that *Nebraska Press Association* v. *Stuart* (1976) tested.

Chief Justice Warren Burger, writing for the majority, began with an extensive treatment of the history of media excesses, including the Bruno Hauptmann trial involving the abduction and murder of the infant son of Charles and Anne Lindbergh.

In analyzing the case at hand, Chief Justice Burger concluded that means available to the trial judge other than "prior restraint" on the news media would have served the needs of the defendant for a fair trial, including sequestration of the jurors. In the view of the majority, prior restraint of the news media was not necessary.

The Court turned its attention to the benefits and problems of a limitation on what the news media could publish. One problem with the gag order, or any other gag order, is the gray zone of information that might not be in violation of the order, but might disseminate prejudicial information. No gag order can so limit the scope of information flow that it can protect the defendant from all possible events. Secondly, in the community where the trial was to take place there lived only 850 people—a town of such small size that rumors would fly with or without news coverage. Finally, the Court was concerned with the impact of the District Court's order on the right conferred by the First Amendment.

The Court found fault with the restraining order against the news media because (1) it limited the right of the press to report events taking place in the courtroom—in violation with settled principle, and (2) it was too broad and vague to "survive the scrutiny we have given to restraints on First Amendment rights."

The opinion concluded with a strong statement regarding restraining orders:

Of necessity our holding is confined to the record before us. But our conclusion is not simply a result of assessing the adequacy of the showing made in this case; it results in part from the problems inherent in meeting the heavy burden of demonstrating, in advance of trial, that without prior restraint a fair trial will be denied. The practical problems of managing and enforcing restrictive orders will always be present. In this sense, the record now before us is illustrative rather than exceptional. It is significant that when this Court has reversed a state conviction because of prejudicial publicity, it has carefully noted that some course of action short of prior restraint would have made a critical difference . . .

We reaffirm that the guarantees of freedom of expression are not an absolute prohibition under all circumstances, but the barriers to prior restraint remain high and the presumption against its use continues intact. We hold that, with respect to the order entered in this case prohibiting reporting or commentary on judicial proceedings held in public, the barriers have not been overcome; to the extent that this order restrained publication of such material, it is clearly invalid. To the extent that it prohibited publication based on information gained from other sources, we conclude that the heavy burden imposed as a condition to securing a prior restraint was not met and the judgment of the Nebraska Supreme Court is therefore reversed.

One year later, in *Oklahoma Publishing Co.* v. *District Court in and for Oklahoma County* (1977), the Supreme Court reaffirmed its view of *Nebraska Press Assn.* when it overturned an order preventing the publication of the name and picture of an eleven-year-old child who had been charged with deliquency for the second-degree murder of a railroad switchman.

These two cases brought to an end restraining orders imposed against the news media for the publication of information regarding trials. The Supreme Court has, however, permitted limitations on the conduct of attorneys, witnesses, court officials, and others involved in judicial proceedings. The Supreme Court has tried to protect the First Amendment and the rights of defendants without stretching the limits of either too far through this procedure. The courts continue to impose the requirement that there must be a showing that a "clear and present danger" exists to the rights of the accused. ■

Cameras in the Courtroom

Journalists and judges have always looked upon each other with discomfort. Judges feared that reporters would engage in activities that would jeopardize the judicial process, while news people feared that the court would conceal

---

See, for example, *United States* v. *Sherman* (1978), *United States* v. *Marcano Garcia* (1978), *Hirschkop* v. *Snead* (1979), *Central SC Chapter, Society of Professional Journalists* v. *Martin* (1978), and *Gulf Oil Co.* v. *Bernard* (1981).

information of public interest. That concern became especially apparent in the Bruno Richard Hauptmann case, when Hauptmann was arrested for the kidnapping and murder of the nineteen-month-old son of Charles Lindbergh, the famous aviator who was the first to fly across the Atlantic (*New Jersey* v. *Hauptmann*, 1935).

Between the time that Hauptmann was arrested in September 1934, and his trial in January 1935, statements appeared in the press that were inflammatory in nature. Over seven hundred reporters flocked to Flemington, New Jersey, where the trial occurred, and the courtroom was packed with 150 journalists during virtually every session of the more-than-a-month trial. Hauptmann was executed for the murder of the child.

Many judges and lawyers, as well as a number of editors and publishers, were appalled at the journalists' behavior, and a committee of 18 lawyers, editors, and publishers issued a report, *Report of Special Committee on Cooperation between Press, Radio and Bar*, in 1937 calling the trial "the most spectacular and depressing example of improper publicity and professional misconduct ever presented to the people of the United States in a criminal trial."

The American Bar Association adopted Canon 35 into its Canons of Professional Ethics in 1937 forbidding the taking of photographs in the courtroom. Later, in 1952 the canon was amended to prohibit broadcasting in court proceedings by saying that it "detract[s] from the essential dignity of the proceeding, distract[s] the participants and witnesses in giving testimony, and create[s] misconceptions."

During the early 1960s several events occurred that caused the courts to reconsider their view on television and radio coverage of a trial. In 1962, television footage gathered from a defendant was released to the news media without the defendant's agreement in *Rideau* v. *Louisiana* (1963), and the Supreme Court later found the action violated the due process clause of the Fourteenth Amendment.

In another case, involving a prominent Texas financier, Billie Sol Estes, whose case came to trial in Smith County, Texas, after it was moved from Reeves County, 500 miles west, television and radio equipment was to play an important part. Eleven volumes of newspaper clippings were collected regarding the trial, and every seat in the courtroom was taken when the case started.

Although the defense requested that radio and television broadcasting and the taking of news photos be prevented in the courtroom, the initial two day hearing appeared live on both radio and television. To get the broadcast coverage, twelve camera people were stationed in the courtroom taking pictures, and cables and wires were draped throughout the room. Microphones were placed in the jury box, at the judge's bench, and at the counsel table. The media disrupted the pretrial hearing so much that the event was to become subject of a Supreme Court decision.

In his statements, Justice J. Clark writing for the majority of the Court observed:

The free press has been a mighty catalyst in awakening public interest in governmental affairs, exposing corruption among public officers and employees and generally informing the citizenry of public events and occurrences, including court proceedings. While maximum freedom must be allowed the press in carrying on this important function in a democratic society its exercise must necessarily be subject to the maintenance of absolute fairness in the judicial process.

The majority of the Supreme Court overturned the conviction of Estes because television had, in their opinion, interfered with the judicial process, the right of the defendant Estes to a fair trial with a decision based on the evidence, not on the extraneous factors created by the telecasting of the trial. Despite the apparent setback for television coverage of trials, only five of the nine justices voted for the reversal of the judgment. One of the five took a much more limited view than the other four; therefore, the opinion was sanctioned by the slimest of margins.

In 1972, the American Bar Association replaced its Canons of Judicial Ethics with the Code of Judicial Conduct when the ABA reinforced its views regarding radio, television, and photo journalists in the courtroom in Canon 3A(7) encouraging judges to "prohibit broadcasting, televising, recording, or taking photographs in the courtroom and areas immediately adjacent thereto during sesssions of court or recesses between sessions." But the Canon did permit the judge to make exceptions in situations in which the technology did not distract from the proceedings and parties agreed to the coverage. After the 1972 changes, a majority of the states adopted the provisions of the ABA Code, including the State of Florida which accepted the following:

A judge should prohibit broadcasting, televising, recording, or taking photographs in the courtroom and areas immediately adjacent thereto during sessions of court or recesses between sessions, except that a judge may authorize:

(a) the use of electronic or photographic means for the presentation of evidence, for the perpetuation of a record, or for other purposes of judicial administration;

(b) the broadcasting, televising, recording, or photographing of investitive, ceremonial, or naturalization proceedings;

(c)the photographic or electronic recording and reproduction of appropriate court proceedings under the following conditions:

(i) the means of recording will not distract participants or impair the dignity of the proceedings;

(ii) the parties have consented, and the consent to being depicted or recorded has been obtained from each witness appearing in the recording and reproduction;

(iii) the reproduction will not be exhibited until after the proceeding has been concluded and all direct appeals have been exhausted; and

(iv) the reproduction will be exhibited only for instructional purposes in educational institutions.

The American Bar Association Committee on Fair Trial-Free Press proposed, in 1978, a further revision in the rules covering courtroom electronic media coverage that would have allowed the broadcasters to cover trials if they were unobtrusive in their work. The recommendation, however, was rejected in 1979 by the House of Delegates.

The media were themselves trying to get the rules changed as was evidenced in 1977 when the Associated Press Managing Editors Association produced its "Cameras in the Courtroom: How To Get 'Em There," pointing out that the aid of the courts was necessary to overcome the walls erected around courtrooms.

The Supreme Court's decision, *Chandler* v. *Florida* (1981), began to suggest a change. The history of the case began in January 1975 when the Post-Newsweek Stations of Florida asked the Supreme Court of Florida to consider changing Canon 3A(7). The Court, as a result of the request and its own actions, initiated an experimental program permitting the televising of two trials. That experiment did not work out, so the Supreme Court in Florida started a one year pilot program.

At the end of the year, the Court received briefs, reports, and other information that led it to conclude that more was to be gained from broadcast coverage than was lost, and in 1979 the Court created a revised Canon authorizing electronic media and still photography coverage, but left administration of the matter to the presiding judge.

Florida's experience was similar to that of other states, because, by 1980, nineteen states permitted coverage of trial and appellate court proceedings; three other states allowed coverage of trial courts; six authorized coverage of appellate court coverage; and twelve other states were considering the matter.

The case considered by the Supreme Court, *Chandler* v. *Florida* (1981), addressing the rules covering cameras in the courtroom began when two Miami policemen, Noel Chandler and Robert Granger, were charged with conspiracy to commit burglary and other crimes in 1977. The case interested the media because it involved policemen and because an amateur radio operator, John Sion, had heard and recorded radio conversations between the two appellants planning their burglary.

Counsel for Granger and Chandler asked that the Florida Supreme Court suspend Canon 3A(7), but lost that fight. A camera placed in the courtroom for an afternoon produced footage, a two minute and 55 second segment of which was aired. The two men claimed that they had not had a fair and impartial trial because of the televised portion.

Since the two policemen had cited *Estes* v. *Texas* as the precedent for rejecting electronic media coverage of trials, the Supreme Court in *Chandler* extensively reviewed that case. The Supreme Court, however, did not see *Estes* as announcing a constitutional standard:

> [W]e conclude that Estes is not to be read as announcing a constitutional rule barring still photographic, radio, and television coverage in all cases and under all circumstances. It does not stand as an absolute ban on state experimentation with an evolving technology, which, in terms of modes

of mass communication, was in its relative infancy in 1964, and is, even now, in a state of continuing change.

Additional *amici* briefs were filed by the Conference of Chief Justices and the Attorneys General of seventeen states asking the Supreme Court not to stop the experimentation with television, radio, and still photography in courtrooms; and the Court gave considerable attention to these briefs.

Since the Supreme Court could find no evidence of errors in due process, nor was there the circus atmosphere of *Estes*, it held "that the constitution does not prohibit a state from experimenting with the program authorized by revised Canon 3A(7)."

State courts have held that coverage of trials by television might be acceptable, but hearings should be held to determine if covering all or part of the trial will interfere with fair trial concepts; if the electronic media will make it impossible for the accused to stand trial; if witnesses will be injured physically; or if victims and their relatives will be affected adversely.

Courts in the 1980s have come to recognize the electronic media as part of the news establishment, and they have been willing to give the media consideration; but the courts still give general consideration to the rights of the accused. Although courts appear to be more tolerant of electronic media coverage in the 1980s, it would be incorrect to say that this sensitive issue is fully solved— there is no guarantee that television and radio reporters can cover every trial they might wish. ■

Bibliography

"ABA Gag Order Guidelines Get Little Media Backing," *FOI Digest*, November-December 1975.

"ACLU Calls 'Gag Rules' Unfair; One-sided Use Hampers Defense," *FOI Digest*, July-August 1971.

Advisory Committee on Fair Trial and Free Press. "Standards Relating to Fair Trial and Free Press." American Bar Association (New York, N.Y.), 1966.

American Bar Association, *Code of Professional Responsibility and Code of Judicial Conduct*. ABA (Chicago, ILL.), 1976.

———, "Report of Special Committee on Cooperation between Press, Radio and Bar," Annual Report, 1937.

---

*See *State* v. *Green* (Fla., 1981); *State ex rel Miami Valley Broadcasting Corp.* v. *Kessler* (Ohio, 1981); *State* v. *Palm Beach Newspapers, Inc.,* (Fla., 1981); *State* v. *Williams* (Ga. Supreme Ct., 1981).

American Newspaper Publishers Association. "Free Press and Fair Trial."
    American Newspaper Publishers Association (New York, N.Y.,), 1967.
"Appeal to Supreme Court Fails, Gag Order Challenge Held Moot," *FOI Digest*,
    March-April 1975.
Brechner, Joseph L., *New Media and the Courts*, Freedom of Information
    Center (Columbia, Mo.), June 1967.
"Calif. High Court Upholds Appellate Bans on Gag Rules, Prior Restraint
    Orders," *FOI Digest*, March-April 1973.
"Code Amendment Would Benefit Reporter Violating Gag Order," *FOI Digest*,
    November-December 1977.
Crow, Peter, *Fair Trial-Free Press Case Study*, Freedom of Information Center
    (Columbia, Mo.), April 1966.
"Federal Agencies Imposing Gag on Employees, Officers," *FOI Digest*, March-
    April 1971.
"Free Press-Fair Trial Conflict Grows as Gag Order Rulings Add to Confusion,"
    FOI Digest, July-August 1974.
Gillmore, Donald M., *Free Press and Fair Trial*. Public Affairs Press
    (Washington, D.C.), 1966.
Hachten, William A., *The Supreme Court on Freedom of the Press: Decisions
    and Dissents*. Iowa State University Press (Ames, Iowa), 1968.
"Hearing Has Opened With Condition, N.H. Court Rules Prior Restraint," *FOI
    Digest*, September-October 1979.
"Judge Sentences Reporter for Violating Gag Order," *FOI Digest*, July-August
    1979.
"Judges Call News Reports Prejudicial, Blames Media in Criminal Suit Dismis-
    sal," *FOI Digest*, May-June 1974.
"Judges Continue to Issue Gag Orders Despite Recent Supreme Court Ruling,"
    FOI Digest, July-August 1976.
"Kansas Judge Will Consult Media Before Issuing Gag Restrictions," *FOI
    Digest*, May-June 1977.
Kingsley, Robert G., *Press-Bar Cooperation*, Freedom of Information Center
    (Columbis, Mo.), July 1967.
"Landmark North Carolina Law Prohibits Restraining Orders," *FOI Digest*,
    March-April 1978.
Marler, Charles, *Sequester the Country*, Freedom of Information Center
    (Columbia, Mo.), February, 1972.
McLauchlan, William P., Richard M. Westerberg, "Allocating Broadcast
    Spectrum," *Telecommunications Policy*, June 1982.
"Newspapers Battling Libel Suit Appeal Order Not to Discuss Case," *FOI
    Digest*, July-August 1975.
Pool, Ithiel de Sola, *On Free Speech in an Electronic Age: Technologies of
    Freedom*. The Belknap Press of Harvard University Press (Cambridge,
    Mass.), 1983.
"Press Challenges Gag Rules in Continuing Press-Bar Controversy," *FOI
    Digest*, November-December 1970.
"Press-Bar Coalitions Combine Forces to Challenge Gag Order Restrictions,"
    FOI Digest, September-October 1972.

Report of the President's Commission on the Assassination of John F. Kennedy. Government Printing Office (Washington, D.C.), 1964.

Rivkin, Steven, *A New Guide to Federal Cable Television Regulations.* MIT Press (Cambridge, Mass.), 1978.

Ruane, Don, *The ABA and Gag Guidelines,* Freedom of Information Center (Columbia, Mo.), January 1976.

"S. Carolina Press Fights Gag on Trial Participants, Witnesses," *FOI Digest,* July-August 1977.

Samuels, Deby K., *Judges and Trial News Challenges,* Freedom of Infomration Center (Columbia, Mo.), December 1973. "Senate Passes Criminal Code; Gag Orders to be Affected," *FOI Digest,* January-February 1978.

"Supreme Court Decision Strikes Down Gag Order Issued by Nebraska Judge," *FOI Digest,* May-June 1976.

"Supreme Court Delays Making Decision on Controversial Nebraska Gag Order," *FOI Digest,* November-December 1975.

"Supreme Court Deliberates Constitutionality of Gag Orders," *FOI Digest,* January-February 1976.

"Supreme Court Issues Final Ruling in Oklahoma Gag Order Case," *FOI Digest,* March-April 1977.

"Supreme Court Overturns Gag Order in Okla. Juvenile Manslaughter Case," *FOI Digest,* November-December 1976.

Tans, Mary Dee; Steven H. Chaffee, "Pretrial Publicity and Juror Prejudice," *Journalism Quarterly,* Winter, 1966.

"Task Force Report on Restrictions Proposes 'Model Statute' to Limit Gags," *FOI Digest,* March-April 1976.

"Three-Judge Panel Strikes Down Harsh South Carolina Gag Order," *FOI Digest,* September-October 1976.

"Two Reno Papers Seek Injunction; Want to Publish Names of Jurors," *FOI Digest,* May-June 1971.

"U.S. Appeals Court Overturns Pretrail Discovery Gag Order," *FOI Digest,* January-February 1979.

"Unprecedented Gag Order Issued by California Judge," *FOI Digest,* July-August 1972.

Cases

Angelico v. Louisiana, 593 F2d 585 (5th Cir 1979).
California v. Strobble, 36 Cal 2d 615, 226 P2d 330 (1951).
Chandler, *et al.* v. Florida, 449 US 560, 66 LEd 2d 740, 101 SCt 802 (1981).
Cromer v. Superior Court, 109 Cal App 3d 728, 167 Cal Rptr 671, 6 Media L Rep (BNA) 1821 (1980).
Cox v. Louisiana, 379 US 559, 13 Led 2d 487, 85 SCt. 476.
Delaney v. United States, 199 F2d 107 (CA 1st Cir 1952).

Estes v. Texas 381 US 532, 14 Led 2d 543, 85 SCt. 1628 (1965).

In re Farber, 78 NJ 259, 394 A2d 330; cert denied, 439 US 997 (1978).

Houchins v. KQED, Inc., 438 US 1 (1978).

Irwin v. Down 366 US 717, 6 Led 2d 751, 81 S.Ct. 1639.

Maryland v. Baxter, 7 Media L Rep (BNA) 1374 (Md Cir Ct 1981).Mazzetti v. United States, 518 F2d 781 (19th Cir 1975).

Miami Valley Broadcasting Corp. v. Kessler, 64 Ohio St 2d 165, 413 NE2d 1203, 6 Media L Rep (BNA) 1884 (1980).

New Jersey v. Hauptmann, 115 NJL 412, 180 Atl. 809 (Ct. Err. & App. 1935).

Richmond Newspapers, Inc. v. Virginia, 448 US 555, 6 Media L Rep (BNA) 1833 (1980).

Rideau v. Louisiana, 373 US 723, 10 Led 2d 663, 83 SCt. 1417.

Seymour v. United States, 373 F2d 629 (5th Cir 1967).

Sheppard V. Maxwell, 384 US 333, 16 Led 2d 600, 86 S.Ct. 1507 (1966).

United States v. Kleinman, 107 FSupp 407 (DCDC 1952).

U.S. v. Caldwell et al. (1972).

Chapter 42

The Double Standard: Print and Broadcast

Almost every citizen of the world has access to some form of broadcasting, usually radio, although an increasing number may view television as well. While the electronic media may be found almost everywhere, and they provide a major means for delivering news to semi-literate as well as literate people, most nations grant broadcasting considerably less freedom from governmental intervention than newspaper, magazine, and book publishers enjoy.

Each nation has its own pattern for the management and ownership of the media, but most patterns involve some form of state control or ownership. England owns and operates British Broadcasting Corporation (BBC), radio and television, but it also authorizes privately-owned commercial broadcasting. Broadcasting in England is not directly controlled by political parties, but the French which operate Radio Television Francaise (RTF) somewhat like the BBC, manage the organization through a cabinet-level office, the Minister of Information, a political official.

In the United States, broadcasting began with stations owned by both commercial organizations, including Westinghouse, RCA, AT&T, and newspapers and educational institutions, including the University of Wisconsin, one of the first broadcasters. The federal government had no broadcast stations, but it operated a large number of military transmitters. (Later, the federal government built international transmitters.)

Most of the nation accepted the new commission as a necessary instrument for the policing of broadcasting. While the concept that an agency of government was needed to keep the airwaves clear, many of the individual ideas in the new law were tested in the courts.

Tiers of Regulation

In recent years, concern over federal management of the radio spectrum has become especially troublesome as newspapers have begun delivering their product to homes over cable lines using teletext (one-way transmission of text, graphics, and pictures for viewing on a home television set) and videotex (two-way communication between user and the source of information so the viewer may select only the information desired).

579

Ithiel de Sola Pool, in *Technologies of Freedom: On Free Speech in an Electronic Age* (1983), concluded that the United States has developed a three tiered system of communication law.

According to Pool, print is the first tier of expression law, and is the freest with laws limited to covering copyright, obscenity, defamation, privacy, and seditious libel.

The second tier follows a common carrier concept and includes telephones, point-to-point communications (taxi and airplane transmissions), the telegraph, and the postal system. Common carrier designation requires the communications system owner to serve all who can afford to pay for the service without discrimination. State public service agencies regulate rates and routes for this class of carrier on a local and state level. The Federal Communications Commission (FCC) regulates common carriers on an interstate basis and when the service crosses one of the borders of the United States. No one can be refused access to the service and, ideally at least, neither the carrier nor the regulatory commissions interfere in the content of messages.

The third of Pool's tiers is broadcasting. Broadcasting is distinguished from the other media since broadcasters must secure a license before they are permitted to operate, which includes regulations that control the content of a broadcast; among these are the Fairness Doctrine and the political equal opportunities provisions of the Communications Act of 1934 prescribing the treatment of controversial public issues and political candidates. At various times, the FCC has considered imposing a "license fee" on broadcasters; enforcing a "Blue Book" of program regulations; and deleting licenses for what it called "smut," different from obscenity.

Creating a Regulatory Agency

The wireless media in the United States operated largely without a law, except for a statute passed in 1912 requiring ships to have operators and wireless equipment. With the growth of broadcasting between 1920 and 1927, interference developed on the airwaves; and broadcasters began demanding that Congress take some action.

A series of events removed all federal control over wireless, beginning with *Hoover* v. *Intercity Radio Co., Inc.* (1923) when the court told Herbert Hoover, secretary of commerce, he had no authority to refuse a radio license to anyone who asked. Three years later, in *United States* v. *Zenith Radio Corporation* (1926), Hoover lost all power to dictate time of operation, channel, or transmitter power to stations. The court told Hoover that the Radio Act of 1912 gave him no power to issue any regulations. When Hoover asked the attorney general for an opinion on the case, the reply pointed out the problem: "The power to make general regulations is nowhere granted by specific language to the Secretary."

In 1927, Congress decided that there was a need to create an organization to regulate the use of channels, as much to protect broadcasters from themselves—broadcasters often tried to "overpower" or "jam" other stations on their frequencies—and to reserve some channels for military uses as to serve the public good.

In 1934, Congress replaced the Federal Radio Commission with a new Federal Communications Commission (FCC) through the Communications Act of 1934. The Communications Act of 1934 was clear in its prescription of the powers of the new commission. It could "classify radio stations" (radio includes television); regulate the type of service offered by each station; select channels for the classes of stations; establish locations for types of stations; control the type of equipment and quality of transmitted signals; create regulations to insure stations comply with the FCC's wishes as long as those desires did not violate the Communications Act of 1934; "study new uses for radio"; designate the area each station could serve; impose special regulations on stations affiliated with networks; make general "rules and regulations" regarding record-keeping; treat radio stations on railroad cars differently from other stations; establish the qualifications for license holders; license individual operators (technicians and engineers); suspend operator licenses for various reasons; inspect stations; "designate call letters"; dictate when and how the call letters should be broadcast; and order painting and lighting of broadcast towers.

The philosophy of federal regulation is that because there were a limited number of available frequencies, determined not by governments but by the laws of nature, it was the responsibility of the state to regulate those finite number of frequencies in the "public interest, convenience, and necessity."

Since the Communications Act of 1934 envisioned radio frequencies owned by the government to be lent to broadcasters, each prospective user of a channel had to sign a waiver agreeing that it did not own the frequencies. Since the channel space was being provided to broadcasters on a temporary basis, the FCC could not award a license for longer than three years, later extended to five years. At each renewal the FCC, until the 1980s, reviewed program performance before awarding a renewal license.

Because the government wanted to keep foreigners out, foreign governments, corporations, individuals, or representatives of foreign concerns could not own broadcast stations—although some limited access was permitted.

When the FCC concluded that broadcasters had erred, it could fine, grant short term licenses (at renewal time), and revoke licenses. Revoking a license because the FCC objected to some aspect of the programming of the station appears to constitute censorship or prior restraint, although the courts have decided differently.

Surveying the problem, Pool concluded:

> The electronic modes of twentieth century communication, whether they be carriers or broadcasters, have lost a large part of the eighteenth and nineteenth century constitutional protections of no prior restraint, no licenses, no special taxes, no regulations, and no laws. Every radio spectrum user, for example, must be licensed . . . Congress . . . imposed licensing on transmitters, thereby breaching a tradition that went back to John Milton against requiring licenses for communicating . . .

The erosion of traditional freedoms that has ocurred as government has striven to cope with problems of new communications media would not have surprised [Alexis de] Tocqueville, for it is a story of how, in pursuit of the public good, a growing structure of controls has been imposed.

Part of the problem with regulating the electronic technologies, was that government had no model to follow when it established the first law requiring licensing of wireless transmissions in 1912. As regulation moved forward, the government, and the courts, looked to other areas of regulation for guidance.

Granting and Revoking Licenses

The first major test of the Federal Radio Commission came in how the courts viewed the actions of the agency. The courts, for example, might have concluded that because broadcasting was a form of expression, it should enjoy exactly the same protections as the print media. Such a conclusion would dictate that broadcasting should not be regulated by a federal commission. The Court of Appeals of the District of Columbia in a series of cases concluded that broadcasting was a business, and, therefore, subject to "reasonable regulation of Congress" as were other businesses including some that were not engaged in broadcasting (*Technical Radio Lab.* v. *Federal Radio Commission*; *Campbell* v. *Galeno Chemical Company*).

In the case of KFKB Broadcasting Association operated by Dr. John R. Brinkley, the court of Appeals in Washington noted that Brinkley had the "burden" of proving that his past programming practices were of sufficient quality to merit a renewal:

> This being an application for the renewal of a license, the burden is upon the applicant to establish that such renewal would be in the public interest, convenience, or necessity . . . and the court will sustain the findings of fact of the commission unless "manifestly against the evidence."

Prior licensee performance was a criterion for determining if a licensee could engage in future broadcasting. In the Brinkley case, the license was not renewed. This attitude differed from that expressed in *Near* v. *Minnesota* (1931) in which the Supreme Court decided that past performance of an offensive newspaper publisher could not be used as a reason for denying the publisher any right to publish in the future, prior restraint or censorship.

The standard applied in *KFKB Broadcasting Ass'n., Inc.* v. *Federal Radio Commission* (1931), however, was quite different:

> In the present case, while the evidence shows that much of appellant's programs is entertaining and unobjectionable in character, the finding of the commission that the station "is conducted only in the personal interest of Dr. John R. Brinkley" is not "manifestly against the evidence" . . .
>
> Appellant contends that the attitude of the commission amounts to a censorship of the station contrary to the provisions of . . . the Radio

Act of 1927 . . . This contention is without merit. There has been no attempt on the part of the commission to subject any part of appellant's broadcasting matter to scrutiny prior to its release.

Later, in *Trinity Methodist Church, South* v. *Federal Radio Commission* (1932), the Court of Appeals specifically spoke of the libertarian history, but supported the FRC's refusal to renew the license:

> We need not stop to review the cases construing the depth and breadth of the first amendment. The subject in its more general outlook has been the source of much writing since Milton's Areopagitica, the emancipation of the English press by the withdrawal of the licensing act in the reign of William the Third, and the Letters of Junius. It is enough . . . to say that the universal trend of decisions has recognized the guaranty of the amendment to prevent previous restraints upon publications, as well as immunity of censorship, leaving to correction by subsequent punishment those utterances or publications contrary to the public welfare. In this aspect it is generally regarded that freedom of speech and press cannot be infringed by legislative, executive, or judicial action, and that the constitutional guaranty should be given liberal and comprehensive construction.

The court also declared that all citizens had the right to speak or write what they wished, but that punishment could come for improper statements. In sustaining the FRC, the court did not see the refusal to renew a license because of past programming practices to be censorship, only proper governmental action.

When the Supreme Court had the opportunity to consider its position on the FRC in *FRC* v. *Nelson Brothers Bond & Mortgage Company* (1933), Chief Justice Charles Evans Hughes, delivering the majority opinion, declared:

> In view of the limited number of available broadcasting frequencies, the Congress has authorized allocation and licenses. The Commission has been set up as the licensing authority and invested with broad powers of distribution in order to secure a reasonable equality of opportunity in radio transmission and reception . . .
>
> That the Congress had the power to give this authority to delete stations, in view of the limited radio facilities available and the confusion that would result from interferences, is not open to question.

These words were written by the same Hughes who had written the strong anti-censorship opinion in *Near* v. *Minnesota*, but apparently believed a different standard permitting the licensing and deleting of licenses, thus preventing a licensee from ever broadcasting again, to be appropriate in light of the limited nature of broadcasting.

---

*The refusal of many daily newspapers to give advertis-
ing space to the [National Recovery Act, developed under
Franklin D. Roosevelt in 1933] was brought to the attention of the American people by Gen. [Hugh] Johnson over
the radio. True, it was subtly done and it was only an
incident, but the fact should be recorded that any government in Washington may, if it wishes, use the radio—a
channel of communication subject to federal license—to
build a backfire in American homes against any individual,
business, or institution, even though the First Amendment
of the Constitution guarantees the freedom of opinion [and]
speech . . .*

—Dean Ackerman, *Report on the NRA, 1933*

Fairness and Political Opportunity

In 1959, the Congress added the Fairness Doctrine to the Communications Act
of 1934. The Fairness Doctrine was a creation of the FCC after the broadcast
industry expressed dissatisfaction with the Mayflower Doctrine (*The Mayflower
Broadcasting Corporation and the Yankee Network, Inc.*, 1941) in which the
FCC had declared that broadcasters had no right to engage in editorializing.
The new doctrine (*Editorializing by Broadcast Licensees*, 1949) was intended
to respond to the issue of a licensee's right to editorialize and the relationship
to the need for a licensee to engage in "a fair and equal presentation of all sides
of controversial issues." While the doctrine did authorize editorializing, it also
told broadcasters that they had to offer a balanced presentation of controversial
issues of public importance.

The commission concluded its statement with:

> We fully recognize that freedom of the radio is included among the
> freedoms protected against governmental abridgment by the first amend-
> ment . . . But this does not mean that the freedom of the people as a
> whole to enjoy the maximum possible utilization of this medium of mass
> communication may be subordinated to the freedom of any single person
> to exploit the medium for his own private interest.

In 1969, the constitutionality of the Fairness Doctrine was tested before
the Supreme Court of the United States in *Red Lion Broadcasting Co., Inc.,
v. Federal Communications Commission, et al.* In supporting the Fairness
Doctrine, the Court specifically noted that different media required different
interpretations of the First Amendment:

Although broadcasting is clearly a medium affected by a First Amendment interest . . . differences in the characteristics of new media justify differences in the First Amendment standards applied to them . . . For example, the ability of new technology to produce sounds more raucous than those of the human voice justifies restrictions on the sound level, and on the hours and places of use, of sound trucks so long as the restrictions are reasonable and applied without discrimination.

The Court then used the scarcity of channels for broadcasting as the justification for imposing special regulations on broadcasting, and on permitting licensing: "Congress unquestionably has the pwoer to grant and deny licenses and to eliminate existing stations."*

Many have questioned the validity of a Fairness Doctrine, as noted in *Brandywine-Main Line Radio, Inc.* v. *FCC* (1972), when Chief Judge Bazelon, dissenting from the majority opinion, took the opportunity to present a strong statement regarding the doctrine. He observed:

In this case I am faced with a *prima facie* violation of the First Amendment. The Federal Communications Commission has subjected Brandywine to the supreme penalty: it may no longer operate as a radio broadcast station. In silencing WXUR, the Commission has dealt a death blow to the licensee's freedoms of speech and press. Furthermore, it has denied the listening public access to the expression of many controversial views. Yet, the Commission would have us approve this action in the name of the fairness doctrine, the constitutional validity of which is premised on the argument that its enforcement will *enhance* public access to the marketplace of ideas without serious infringement of the First Amendment rights of individual broadcasters . . .

A re-examination of the value, purposes and effects of the fairness doctrine raises for me such serious doubts about the constitutionality of its application here that I am compelled to withhold my affirmance . . .

The entire field of governmental regulation of broadcast communication is so fraught with competing interests and uncertain results, and the shifting balance of First Amendment freedoms offers so few definite guidelines in this area, that there is no easy answer to this question.

Many other people have opposed the Fairness Doctrine, and by the 1980s, even the chairman of the FCC, Mark S. Fowler, wanted the doctrine revoked. In an interview in the *Washington Times* in August 1985, Fowler observed, "If anything, the doctrine is chilled water on the flames of robust debate."

Although Fowler wanted the doctrine revoked, he and the FCC believed that Congress had to make the changes, because the doctrine had been enacted

---

*After *Red Lion*, a number of organizations sought access to the airwaves through the Fairness Doctrine, including *CBS* v. *Democratic National Committee* (1973) in which the Supreme Court accepted the FCC's refusal to grant limited access for paid access, and *Patsy Mink and O. D. Hagedorn* v. *Station WHAR* (1976).

into statute by the Congress. The commission, in a 4-0 vote, asked Congress to take action, but Rep. John D. Dingell (D-Mich.) chairman of the House communication sub-committee, believed that the doctrine was "absolutely fundamental" to insure that issues are treated fully.

The concern over the Fairness Doctrine had led the FCC to initiate an inquiry into the need for, and role of the Fairness Doctrine in 1984. By the conclusion of the proceeding, more than a hundred people had testified before the FCC, and the Commission had issued an extended report urging Congress to repeal the doctrine. The FCC's statement, published August 30, 1985, informed broadcasters that it would continue to enforce the Fairness Doctrine until it was repealed, but added:

> We believe that the same factors which demonstrate that the fairness doctrine is no longer appropriate as a matter of policy also suggest that the doctrine may no longer be permissible as a matter of constitutional law.

The chairman of the FCC, Mark S. Fowler, added his own strong comment:

> This very week the British Broadcasting Corporation experienced a walk-out of its journalists. They did not strike over wages or seniority, but over the matter that concerns us today: their freedom of the broadcast press to cover a controversial issue of public importance in the manner they saw fit. Justice Douglas was right: there is a difference amongst the nations of this world that have a constitutional protection against restraints on press that those that, unhappily, do not.
>
> So it is freedom, then, that is at the heart of this exemplary example of draftsmanship from the Mass Media Bureau. I have made the advancement of First Amendment rights an uppermost objective of my Chairmanship . . .
>
> Today's report is an indictment of a misguided government policy . . . The First Amendment dictates : Choose between the right of the press to criticize freely and the authority of the government to channel that criticism . . . Free speech and free government thrive together or they fail together. John Peter Zenger said that. William O. Douglas said that. And today, so do we.

In the mid-1980s the Fairness Doctrine remains controversial, in force, and an example of the distinction between governmental relationships to broadcast and print media.

Another related regulation is the equal opportunities provisions of Section 315 of the Communications Act of 1934 which requires a broadcaster who sells time to one legally qualified political candidate for public office to offer an equal amount of time of the same quality for the same price to all other legally qualified candidates for the same office in the same election. A number of specialized FCC interpretations have grown up around the requirement leading the FCC to issue several guidelines on how to apply the law. The National Association of Broadcasters (NAB) has its own primer for its members further explaining the doctrine.

Programming Statements

Over the years, the FCC has produced statements indicating how broadcasters should handle various programming matters. In 1946, the FCC issued its Blue Book on programming practices, a document that was never enforced because of broadcaster outcries. Then in 1960, the agency prepared a shorter statement that covered the areas it believed stations should consider in programming. They were: (1) local self expression; (2) use of local talent; (3) children's programs; (4) religious programs; (5) educational programs; (6) public affairs programs; (7) editorialization; (8) political broadcasts; (9) agricultural programs; (10) news programs; (11) weather and market reports; (12) sports; (13) minority programs; and (14) entertainment. Although the FCC was not requiring that every broadcaster carry programs in each category, it was another attempt to encourage balanced programming.

In 1971, the FCC issued a new *Ascertainment Primer*, spelling out requirements to be imposed on stations in determining just what they should be carrying based on their community needs. The procedure required interviews with members of the community's leadership, the public, business, and education.

In 1979, the FCC concluded that all of this regulation might not be achieving the desired goal and it published a *Notice of Inquiry and Proposed Rulemaking in the Matter of Deregulation of Radio*:

> The Commission is proposing rule and policy changes that would remove current requirements in nontechnical areas including nonentertainment programming, ascertainment, and commercialization. This represents a clear departure from our present involvement in such matters
> . . .
> In sum, there have been three major, ongoing structural changes in radio: (1) competition has increased substantially, especially in the larger markets, with many markets enjoying the benefits of a large number of viable, competing stations; (2) radio's role among the various media has shifted from being the major mass medium to being more of a secondary and often specialized medium; and (3) the . . . community has changed in recognition of the diversity of American society, and radio has been responsive to this change.

Twenty thousand comments and two thousand replies to those comments flooded into the FCC as a result of the *Notice*. Eventually, the FCC issued a *Report and Order* (1981) declaring that it would no longer provide advertising and nonentertainment guidelines, and that it was abolishing ascertainment requirements. The FCC also removed the rule requiring stations to keep logs of their programming.

The United Church of Christ went to court against the FCC, but the court accepted all of the FCC's new deregulation policies except for the logging matter, demanding that the FCC reconsider that issue (*United Church of Christ v. FCC*, 1983).

Ownership

The FCC still has rules that limit the ownership of media. While these regulations are designed to fulfill the intent of the anti-trust laws of the United States, they go somewhat beyond laws that apply to print media. The rules include the one-to-a-customer policy that allows *new* licenses to hold television or radio permits, but not both in a market; the "duopoly" rule limiting a licensee to one station of a class (AM, FM, or television) in a market; and the rule of twelve (formerly the rule of seven) retricting a licensee to a total of twelve stations in each class (e.g., twelve AM, twelve FM, and twelve television stations.) The FCC also discourages extensive cross-media ownership of broadcast and cable, or broadcast and newspapers in the same community.

Although deregulation in the field of radio has changed the picture somewhat, Congress has not rethought the differences in how government handles the three levels of media—relatively-free print media; common carrier telephone, data, and telegraph media; and broadcast media with program regulations.

Regulation Through Intimidation:
The Case of "The Selling of the Pentagon"

From 10 to 11 p.m., Tuesday, February 23, 1971, CBS-TV broadcast "The Selling of the Pentagon," written and produced by Peter Davis. After the opening "teaser" and a commercial break, journalist Roger Mudd set the focus of the show:

> Nothing is more essential to a democracy than the free flow of information. Misinformation, distortion, propaganda all interrupt that flow. They make it impossible for people to know what their government is doing, which, in a democracy, is crucial. The largest agency in our government is the Department of Defense, and it maintains a public relations division to inform the people of its activities. In December, Congress cut the appropriations for this division, but, according to the Pentagon, it will still spend $30 million this year on public affairs, an amount more than ten times what it spent to tell people about itself just twelve years ago. Even this figure may be only the tip of the public relations iceberg. A special, still unpublished report from the prestigious 20th Century Fund estimates the real total at $190 million. The combined news budgets of the three commercial networks—ABC, CBS, NBC—are $146 million.
>
> Whatever the true cost at the Pentagon, there have been recent charges in the press and in Congress that the Department is using these public relations funds not merely to inform but to convince and persuade the public on vital issues of war and peace.

The documentary, initially seen by about 9.6 million people, was praised for having brought vital information to the public attention; however, it was also condemned for some of the same things it accused the Pentagon—selective editing, distorting and manipulating the facts, and taking comments of public officials out of context. Rep. F. Edward Herbert, chair of the House Armed Services Committee, called it, "the most misleading and damaging attack on our people over there that I have ever heard of," and asked the FCC to investigate. Vice-President Agnew called it a "disreputable program." On March 23, CBS re-ran the program, and added twenty-two minutes of additional comments by supporters and critics of the documentary. More than 14.1 million people saw the re-run.

On April 8, following closed-door hearings, the Special Subcommittee on Investigations of the House Interstate and Foreign Commerce Committee, issued a subpoena to Frank Stanton, CBS president, requiring him or a CBS representative to turn over to the committee certain information about the program. In response, Dr. Stanton indicated:

> We will comply with that part of the subpoena which calls for a film copy and written transcript of the material actually broadcast.
>
> The subpoena also demands all outtakes and other materials used in connection with preparing the broadcasts, but not actually broadcast. It therefore raises an unprecedented issue in the history of the relationship between the Federal government and the press in this nation. No newspaper, magazine or other part of the press could be required constitutionally to comply with such a subpoena with respect to material gathered by reporters in the course of a journalistic investigation but not published.
>
> Unlike other instances in which a Committee of the Congress has subpoenaed broadcasters' materials, this subpoena appears to involve no question of alleged violation of criminal law on the part of the broadcaster and no question of any government interest in whether the broadcaster has evidence pertinent to the criminal prosecution of third persons. Rather, the sole purpose of this subpoena, so far as we can ascertain it, is to obtain materials which will aid the Committee in subjecting to legislative surveillance the news judgments of CBS in preparing "The Selling of the Pentagon."
>
> The fact that television and radio stations are licensed by the government does not deprive the broadcast press of First Amendment protection, and the courts have so held. The protection does not depend upon whether the government believes we are right or wrong in our news judgment.
>
> We will respectfully decline to furnish the Committee the outtakes and other materials used in connection with preparing the broadcast, but not actually broadcast.

On April 18, CBS opened an hour of its evening time for a balanced discussion of the controversy being created around the documentary; CBS made innumerable efforts to get Pentagon officials on the show, but none chose to accept the invitation.

By now, several newspapers and magazines which had earlier raised serious and significant questions about the fairness of the CBS documentary, were concerned about the government's reaction to the documentary. Both of the other two major national networks, ABC and NBC, vigorously supported CBS. The American Society of Newspaper Editors noted that the subpoena was nothing less than "an open attack on the First Amendment." Among other organizations which supported the CBS refusal to fully comply with the Subcommittee's subpoena were Sigma Delta Chi, national professional journalism fraternity (now the Society of Professional Journalists); the Authors League of America; the American Newspaper Guild; the Associated Press Broadcasters Association; the American Association of Schools and Departments of Journalism; the American Civil Liberties Union; and the American Friends Service Committee.

On July 1, 1971, the Subcommittee recommended to the House that CBS and its president be held in contempt of Congress. Following extensive debate, the full House on July 13 voted 226-181, with only twenty-eight representatives abstaining or not present to vote, to send the contempt citation back to the subcommittee; CBS would not be held in contempt of Congress.

Can a Licensed Press be Free?

by Richard W. Jencks

. . . It would be easy for me to bask in the warm glow created by this virtual unanimity of support for our position [on "The Selling of the Pentagon"] among critics, competitors and others. But the issue of freedom of the broadcast press is not just a case of identifying the white hats and arraying them against the black hats.

You should not suppose, for example, from the list of those who have supported us in this controversy, that the liberal establishment has been consistently in favor of First Amendment freedom for broadcasters or that conservatives have uniformly wished to curtail that freedom. For the plain fact is that the vulnerability of broadcasting to governmental attacks on its independence has

Richard W. Jencks, currently a member of the Board of Directors, RKO International, was president of CBS/Broadcast Group, 1969-1971; and vice-president, CBS/Washington, 1971-1976. Other positions he held in the telecommunications industry were as assistant to the general counsel for the National Association of Broadcasters, 1948-1950; CBS attorney, 1950-1959; president, Alliance TV Film Producers, 1959-1965; vice-president, Association of Motion Picture and Television Producers, 1963-1965; deputy general counsel, 1965-1967; general counsel, 1967-1968; and executive vice-president, Television, 1968-1969. He was a member of the Board of Directors of the National Association of Broadcasters, 1971-1976. Mr. Jencks was a Naval officer during World War II, then received A.B. and LL.B. degrees from Stanford University. [This article is an edited version of a speech Richard W. Jencks delivered to the Association of American Publishers, April 28, 1971.]

been created as much, if not more, by liberals as by conservatives. Both can say, with Pogo: "We have met the enemy and they are us."

Chairman [Harley] Staggers got to the heart of the problem shortly after the issuance of the subpoena when a reporter for *Television Digest* queried him and reported the following colloquy:

Q. Do you have the power to subpoena my notes from this interview?

A. No.

Q. What if I were a reporter for TV talking to you on the phone?

A. Well, then, that would be different. The Committee could subpoena your notes.

Q. Why?

A. TV is different. It's very important that the networks be accurate.

Chairman Staggers is a decent, honorable and representative American, and this informal expression of his views, if reported correctly, illustrates the dilemma faced by television and radio in seeking full recognition of First Amendment protection. By referring to the importance of *network* accuracy, he seems to imply that the print media, being less powerful, are to be permitted to be less accurate, though doubtless he would like to make them more accurate if he could. But what he misses—and what I'm afraid most people miss—is that the reason the First Amendment commands that the press be left alone is not because we don't care whether or not it is accurate. The reason we let them alone is because we think they will be *more accurate* that way than under government surveillance.

As James Reston wrote recently in *The New York Times*: "The basic assumption of the First Amendment was that people in a democratic society had a better chance to get a fair presentation of news from a multitude of free reporters than from reporters regulated by the government. The Founding Fathers had no illusions about the infallibility of the press. Their comments about our stupidity, inaccuracy and bias make [Vice-President] Spiro Agnew's [attacks] sound almost genial. But they were persuaded that the risks of freedom were less than the risks of legal strictures or government control, and it is hard to argue that this protection for the newspaper reporters should not now be guaranteed to the radio and television stations, which now supply a majority of the American people with their first reports of the news."

It is the fact that this sentiment is now so forthrightly expressed by so many in the print media that makes the present moment so unique—and so hopeful. One of the leading constitutional scholars in the First Amendment area, Professor Harry Kalven of the University of Chicago, not long ago referred to "the anomaly of having at the moment in the United States two traditions of freedom of the press in this country—that of the written and spoken word and that of the broadcast word."

Until now, many in the print media have been concerned about the consequences of conceding full freedom to the broadcast media. Ten years ago, accepting the Lovejoy Award at Colby College, Bernard Kilgore, president of *The Wall Street Journal*, explained why:

... [W]e are going to get the issue of freedom of the press obscured dangerously if we try to stretch it to fit the radio and television industries that operate and apparently must operate for some time in the future under government licenses ... It seems to me that no matter how loose the reins may be ... the argument that freedom of the press protects a licensed medium from the authority of the government that issues the license is double talk ...

I think if we try to argue that freedom of the press can somehow exist in a medium licensed by the government we have no argument against a licensed press.

Mr. Kilgore was right in perceiving that the habit of regulating a licensed medium is well nigh irresistible and can spread. A few years ago the National Convention of the American Civil Liberties Union foreshadowed Mr. Kilgore's worst fears by urging the imposition of the FCC's "fairness doctrine" upon the nation's newspapers. But he was wrong, I think, in assuming that press freedom could long survive if broadcast freedom were denied. An increasing number of print journalists now realize that we are all in the same boat, and that the way to keep that boat afloat is to find a way to preserve freedom in a licensed medium.

This is not going to be easy. Many who now have come to our support, where the issue is government interference with "The Selling of the Pentagon," have helped make that interference possible by vociferous demands for greater government control over broadcast content.

The New York Times, for example, has strongly supported us in this controversy, but over the years its editorial voice has been perhaps the nation's most influential advocate of increasing government control over broadcast content. The same can be said of the ACLU and the National Citizens Committee for Broadcasting ...

All of this goes to illustrate that at least some of our current support in the subpoena issue is coming from people who quite simply see CBS, in their judgment, "doing its best" and want to support that effort. I am afraid, however, that that kind of support is not enough to establish freedom of the press for broadcasters.

The question needs to be asked: If a Congressional committee dominated by doves, had subpoenaed outtakes of a CBS documentary which was *supportive* of the Pentagon, how many of these organizations and individuals would have opposed such a subpoena?

Yet, if we are to have First Amendment freedom, we need support from individuals and organizations whether they think our documentaries to be right or wrong, careful or sloppy, well- or ill-intentioned.

For if a large part of the motive force backing us in this controversy is only that we should be let alone while we are *doing good*, we are in a dreadful case. If that is so, many of these same individuals and groups will call upon the government to chastise us when we are not—in their view—doing good.

The late Professor Zechariah Chafee of Harvard once wrote of a possible way to deter that impulse. "Whenever anybody," he wrote, "is inclined to look to the government for help in making the mass media do what we desire of them, he had better ask himself one antiseptic question: 'Am I envisaging myself as the official who is going to administer the policy which seems to me so good?'. . ."

Among many who, in the past, have been enthusiastic for government surveillance of the broadcast press, it is my hope that some are beginning to understand the force of Professor Chafee's remarks. At least they perceive that neither the Staggers Committee—good and decent Americans though they be—nor any other Congressional committee or Administrative body is likely to fit the description of "splendid fellows in our crowd" who should be entrusted with making television more accurate and impartial.

Let me express the hope that out of the current controversy will come the realization of two important propositions.

One is that freedom of the press *is* indivisible. It is no longer possible in this country to consider the print media as being free if the broadcast press is not. There are simply too many intimations, on the part of too many people, of a desire to subject the print media to controls which have been exercised over the broadcast press.

The other is that it is not possible to consider the freedom of the press as being available only to the weak and not to the powerful. The three national networks are concededly powerful and pervasive media of communication. But is is difficult, as our own Eric Sevareid remarked last year at the Elmer Davis Memorial Lecture, "to see the logic in a legal situation which holds that the most pervasive, if not necessarily the most persuasive, medium of information and ideas is not protected by the First Amendment while less pervasive media are so protected."

In any event, pervasive as the networks are, their news broadcasts together account for less than one-third of the public's total viewing of television news. All the rest of the public's news viewing is through the locally produced news broadcasts of individual television stations. Many a local newspaper has occupied a relatively more powerful position in its community than has any of the three networks, or indeed all three networks together, in the national community.

In [Franklin D. Roosevelt's] time it was fashionable to say that we should not be concerned about "big government in the hands of free men." But if you are going to have big government—and you can hardly avoid it—you must also have powerful media—and they must also be in the hands of free men.

It will not be easy to establish a firm tradition of freedom for a broadcast press which, as is frequently said, uses "the public's airwaves." But such an effort is not entirely without successful precedent. If broadcasters rely upon the use of "the public's airwaves," so news and other magazines, to take one example, use the public postal system. This has not prevented us from developing a robust legal tradition which has frustrated government efforts to supervise the content of magazines.

In the current controversy there are really no villains. Those who berate the press from left and right and seek governmental intervention to correct abuses are almost always sincere, well-motivated [people] who believe deeply that what they propose will advance the public good.

As in all human situations there may be some confusion about the root cause of our present difficulties. Lincoln Steffens, the famous muckraking journalist, when asked who was at fault for a system which permitted corruption and evil-doing, once remarked that it was like finding the fault for original sin. "Most people," he said, "say it was Adam. But Adam, you remember, he said it was Eve . . . And Eve said, no, no it wasn't she; it was the serpent. And that's where (the) clergy have stuck ever since. (They) blame that serpent, Satan. Now I come and I am trying to show you it was, it is, the apple."

The apple in our situation is a licensing process which tempts unsatisfied partisans to seek governmental intervention. We must build a tradition which will remove that temptation . . .

Full Freedom of Expression for the Media

by Bob Packwood

When the publisher and editors . . . decided to print this article, the decision was theirs alone. They do not have to worry about how the government reacts to their editorial judgments. No Federal agency can review the contents . . . and order that material be added or deleted, much less order that the [operation] be shut down entirely. The First Amendment protects [all print media] from those kinds of infringements. It says, "Congress shall make no law . . . abridging the freedom of speech, or of the press . . ." It is concise and emphatic, and it forms the foundation upon which all of our other freedoms are built.

If, however, I were speaking these words to you over radio or television, we would face an entirely different situation. The station's management, in deciding whether to broadcast these words, would be deeply concerned about possible government reactions. Broadcasters *are* regulated by a Federal agency which reviews their programming decisions. It can bring them before its commissioners or before a court of law to justify their actions. It can shut a station down altogether by revoking its government license. For the electronic media, the First Amendment might well read, "Congress shall make no law . . . abridging the freedom of speech, or of the press (except in matters involving the electronic media.)"

Bob Packwood is a U.S. senator from Oregon, first elected in 1969. In the Senate, he is a member of the Commerce, Science, and Transportation Committee; chair of the Finance Committee; and vice-chair of the Joint Committee on Taxation. He was a member of the President's Committee on Population Growth and the American Future, 1972; and chair of the National Republican Senatorial Committee, 1977-1978, 1981. Sen. Packwood is recipient of the Anti-Defamation League Brotherhood Award, 1970; Torch of Liberty Award, of the B'nai B'rith, 1971; and the Richard L. Newberger Award of the Oregon Environmental Council. He received an A.B. from Willamette University, and an LL.B. from New York University. [This article is edited and reprinted, with permission, from *USA Today*; March 1984; ©1984, Society for the Advancement of Education.]

Thus, our nation's media are divided into a two-class society. The print media are fully protected, but the electronic media are subjected to content regulations. Here are just a few examples:

- Broadcasters are licensed for limited terms and may have these licenses suspended, revoked, or not renewed if they do not operate in the government-defined "public interest."
- Stations must devote a substantial amount of time to the discussion of "public issues."
- A station which presents one side of an issue must provide opportunity for the presentation of contrasting views on that issue.
- The FCC limits the ability of broadcasters to editorialize.
- Broadcasters' licenses can be revoked if they deny airtime to Federal candidates; once a candidate obtains airtime, other candidates for the same office must receive equal time.
- Rates for political airtime are regulated.

None of these regulations could be applied to the print media, and all of them violate the fundamental premise of the First Amendment—our government has no business determining *who* is permitted to say *what*. I believe that premise holds true whether a message is shouted from a soapbox, printed on a pamphlet, broadcast over a radio, or beamed from a satellite. I believe further that we must act to ensure that electronic speech receives the protection which it deserves.

A Historical Overview

The history of this two-class society can be traced back to the earliest days of commercial radio broadcasting. In the 1920's, more and more radio stations crowded onto the broadcasting frequencies then available. The result was increasing interference among stations. Everyone agreed that some kind of government control was needed to end the growing anarchy in radio.

Because of the technological confines of that era, a primary concern of the Congress was "spectrum scarcity"—the notion that radio frequencies were severely limited. These concerns were reflected in the Radio Act of 1927, which established the public ownership and control of the airwaves. Broadcasters who were allotted spectrum space were licensed; in return for the license, they were required to act in the public interest. The Federal Radio Commission was created to administer this scheme and ensure that broadcasters fulfilled their obligations.

Seven years later, the Congress passed the Communications Act of 1934 and transformed the Federal Radio Commission into the Federal Communications Commission. However, Congress did not alter the basic regulatory framework. The retention of the "public interest" concept is especially significant, for that is the source of all of the government's content regulations.

That regulatory scheme remains essentially intact to this day. Thus, a statute which originated in the days of the crystal radio set is still the guide that the FCC, the Congress, and the courts follow when they must deal with microwave transmissions and digital signals from geostationary satellites. The act was designed for AM radio broadcasting, but it is now the procrustean bed into which all of the newer technologies have been fit—including FM broadcasting, VHF television, UHF television, cable television (even though it is *not* delivered into your homes over the supposedly scarce airwaves), and direct broadcasting from satellites.

The content regulations which stem from the act's public interest standard have been attacked by broadcasters, but they have withstood court challenges. The broadcasters' claims to full First Amendment protections were shattered in 1969, when the Supreme Court handed down the *Red Lion* decision.

The case arose when an author named Fred Cook attacked Barry Goldwater in a book. The Rev. Billy James Hargis, a Goldwater supporter, then attacked Cook in a broadcast carried by a small radio station licensed to the Red Lion Broadcasting Company. Red Lion offered to sell Cook air time for $25, after he learned of the broadcast, but Cook demanded the *free* reply time to which he was entitled by FCC regulations. When Red Lion Broadcasting refused to give him time, Cook took the case up to the Supreme Court and won. The Court upheld the FCC's "Fairness Doctrine" regulations, ruling that these content regulations did not violate the First Amendment rights of broadcasters: "Because of the scarcity of radio frequencies, the Government is permitted to put restraints on licensees in favor of others whose views should be expressed on this unique medium . . . It is the right of the viewers and listeners, not the right of the broadcasters, which is paramount."

A case decided just five years later highlighted the subordinate status of the broadcasters' First Amendment rights. In 1974, the Supreme Court was faced with another challenge to a right of reply rule—only this time, the rule was applicable to newspapers. The facts leading up to this *Miami Herald* case were remarkably similar to those of *Red Lion*, but the Court's holding could not have been more different.

The Florida legislature had passed an "equal space" statute which applied to the print media. The *Miami Herald* had published several editorials attacking Pat Tornillo, a candidate for local office. Tornillo demanded free reply space in the *Herald*. When the paper refused, Tornillo took the case up to the Florida Supreme Court and won a unanimous decision. The Florida State Supreme Court utilized the electronification rationale in upholding the right of reply statute which Tornillo used against the *Miami Herald*. The paper then appealed the case to the U.S. Supreme Court and the Court struck down the statute because it violated the First Amendment rights of *newspapers*. They stated: "the Florida statute fails to clear the barriers of the First Amendment because of its intrusion into the function of editors . . ." It has yet to be demonstrated how government regulation of this crucial process can be exercised consistent with First Amendment guarantees of a free press as they have evolved to this time.

Remember that the Florida Supreme Court unanimously decided that the principles established for broadcasters in the *Red Lion* case could apply to newspapers as well.   Because the *Miami Herald* would "perish" without electronic communications, the Florida court said, this government intrusion into its editorial affairs did not violate the First Amendment.

The Florida Supreme Court used this reasoning over 10 years ago, when the *Miami Herald* was much less dependent upon electronics than today's press people are. When tomorrow's printed materials can be delivered more easily on video screens than in mailboxes, the courts will be even more likely to follow the existing precedents and permit the government to regulate *any* information which moves electronically.

Impending Danger

The subordinate First Amendment status of broadcasters should be troubling to the print media. Communications technology is moving in directions which are making even the most complacent in the press wake up to the impending danger. The print media and the electronic media are converging in ways which may soon undercut pleas for the First Amendment protection for publishers.

What will [our publications] look like ten or twenty years from now? In the not so distant future . . . printed material could be available in several different formats, each based on *electronic* distribution.

Printed versions of [newspapers, magazines, and books] will probably always be available, but it may be edited in a central location, with the page layouts beamed by satellite to regional printing presses. (The *Wall Street Journal* and other papers use this technology today.) You also may be printing your own copy of [the daily newspaper] in your home. The magazine could be transmitted via telephone or cable lines, or by terrestrial or satellite signals to your home terminal's printer. For some readers, [the daily newspaper] may never be on paper at all. You may choose to browse among totally electronic "pages" which are "printed" on your video screen.

How will the government handle that kind of "press?" Will the First Amendment protect [the newspaper, magazine, or book] of the future from content regulations? Or will it, like the broadcasters, be subject to government regulations merely because it utilizes electronic methods of distribution?

Technological forces are making freedom of expression issues especially timely and these same forces are making old fears about scarcity obsolete. We must not continue down the path on which tradition, complacency, unthinking application of precedent, and outright error have led the U.S.

We are living in an era of rapid and explosive communications development. Scarcity may have been a reasonable concern during the 1920s and 1930s, but today's problem is keeping track of communications abundance.

Radio broadcasting, of course, has grown far beyond the confines of its infancy, and newer methods of communication seem to be appearing at an ever-increasing rate. Our nation now has over 9,000 radio stations and over 1,000 television stations. Cable systems using coaxial cable can provide hundreds of channels; future systems utilizing optical fibers could provide even more. Low-power broadcasting, microwave channels, and direct satellite-to-home broadcasting will further expand communications options.

Communications technology is advancing at such a rapid rate that even experts can not predict what the future will bring. They stress, however, that scarcity is no longer an issue. Any limitations on our communications abundance will be caused by economic constraints or by government regulation itself, not by technological shortcomings. Spectrum scarcity simply can not be used to justify government controls which fly in the face of our First Amendment rights.

The diversity of electronic voices which the government's content regulations were intended to provide (but never did) can be achieved by opening up all of these new methods of communication to freedom. If these technologies are allowed to be free, they can be as diverse as the world of print—all to the benefit of the public. Some electronic outlets, like some papers and magazines, will appeal to a wide, national audience. Others will aim for local or specialized markets. All of them will be able to seek their fair share of the interested public, if they are freed from stifling governmental obligations.

Ensuring Full Protection

How can we best ensure that the electronic media gain full protection? Our nation's founders surely would have guaranteed full protection if they could have foreseen these technological advances.

The FCC is the logical place to begin, for that is the agency created to deal directly with communications. However, the FCC can not provide lasting protection for the media. First, the FCC can not overturn regulations which are required by Congress in the Communications Act. Second, any protections established by the FCC would be impermanent—future commissions, the Congress, and the courts can easily reimpose regulation.

We could turn to the Congress. It could eliminate regulations by amending the Communications Act. Yet, as a member of that body, I must tell you that Congressional relief is equally impermanent. A future Congress which is angered or frightened by the media could reenact these regulations by a mere majority vote of both houses.

Finally, there is the Supreme Court. It could free the media by finding these regulations unconstitutional. That, however, is an uncertain and shifting solution. First, the Court would have to wait for the "right case"—it can not set policy in a vacuum. Second, any protections won for the media in one case can be altered or chipped away in later decisions.

I belive that the only effective and permanent solution is a constitutional solution. I have proposed that we add an amendment to our Constitution which would guarantee that electronic communications are protected from government regulation after we have exhausted statutory relief. While this could be a long and arduous process, the goal is certainly worth while. We have no other means of guaranteeing a permanent right—freedom of expression—which is as important. I believe it is a cause worth fighting for, a cause which would guarantee freedom of expression well into the future.

Bibliography

Barrow, R. L, "Fairness Doctrine: A Double Standard for Electronic and Print Media," *Hastings Law Journal*, 1976.

Barton, Richard L., "The Lingering Legacy of Pacifica: Broadcasters' Freedom of Silence," *Journalism Quarterly*, Winter 1976.

Berns, Walter, *The First Amendment and the Future of American Democracy.* New York: 1976.

———. *Freedom, Virtue and the First Amendment.* Louisiana State University Press (Baton Rouge, La.), 1957.

Bernstein, Marver H., *Regulating Business by Independent Commission*, Princeton University Press (Princeton, N.J.), 1966.

Besen, Stanley M.; Robert W. Crandall, "The Deregulation of Cable Television," *Law and Contemporary Problems*, Fall 1981.

Chamberlin, B. F., "The FCC and the First Principle of the Fairness Doctrine: A History of Neglect and Distortion," *Federal Communications Law Journal*, 1979.

Cole, Barry, *Reluctant Regulators: The FCC and the Broadcast Audience*, Addison-Wesley (Reading, Mass.), 1978.

Coons, John E., ed., *Freedom and Responsibility in Broadcasting*, Northwestern University Press (Evanston, Ill.), 1961.

Emery, Walter B., *Broadcasting and Government.* Michigan State University Press (East Lansing, Mich.), 1961.

Friendly, Fred, *The Good Guys, the Bad Guys and the First Amendment: Free Speech vs. Fairness in Broadcasting*, Random House (New York, N.Y.) 1976.

"General Fairness Doctrine Obligations of Broadcast Licensees," *Federal Register*, August 30, 1985.

Head, Sydney W.; Christopher H. Sterling, *Broadcasting in America: A Survey of Television, Radio, and New Technologies*, Houghton Mifflin (Boston, Mass.), 1982, 4th ed.

Kahn, Frank J., *Documents of American Broadcasting* Prentice-Hall (Engelwood Cliffs, N.J.), 1978.

Krasnow, Erwin G.; Lawrence D. Longley, *The Politics of Broadcast Regulation*, St. Martin's (New York, N.Y.), 1973.

Levin, Harvey J., *Fact and Fantasy in Television Regulation.* Russell Sage Foundation (New York, N.Y.), 1980.

Labunski, Richard E., *The First Amendment Under Siege: The Politics of Broadcast Regulation,* Greenwood Press (Westport, Conn.), 1981.

Levin, Harvey J., *Fact and Fantasy in Television Regulation.* Russell Sage Foundation (New York, N.Y.), 1980.

Pool, Ithiel de Sola, *On Free Speech in an Electronic Age: Technologies of Freedom*, The Belknap Press of Harvard University Press (Cambridge, Mass.), 1983.

Rivkin, Steven, *A New Guide to Federal Cable Television Regulations*, MIT Press (Cambridge, Mass.), 1978.

Ulloth, Dana R., *The Supreme Court: A Judicial Review of the Federal Communications Commission*, Arno Press (New York, N.Y.), 1979.

Chapter 43

Economic Restraints

Because the media are part of the society that has created the State, anything that alters the economic stability of the State must also alter the economic stability of the media.

A strong economy with low interest rates will allow newspapers to expand as its advertising and circulation base expands. However, a recession will cause both advertisers and subscribers to divert funds to other areas.

Although a national recession will affect all media, a local recession has a more significant impact. If a major industry, for example, reduces its workforce, or goes out of business or moves to a better economic climate, all media in the marketing area will be directly influenced. In small communities with one or two large industries, the effect will be greater than in larger communities with several large industries. But, in either case, the lower circulation base, will force the media to initially lower their advertising rates to reflect the fewer number of readers, initially giving advertisers more advertising space for their budget. The media then raises the rates in an attempt to maintain revenue. The increase in rates will force advertisers either to increase their budgets or to maintain the same or lower budgets, redistributing the placement of advertising to reduce overlapping circulation. Thus, in a recession, the newspaper in first circulation position in a market should be able to hold or possibly increase its position, while other newspapers in the market will lose advertising revenue. For regional advertisers, more of the budget may go to television which usually has a greater rate but a lower cost per thousand (cpm); as with newspapers, radio or television stations not leading the ratings race may lose revenue as advertisers try to "target" their audiences. For local advertisers, whose primary business is in a community or several small communities, it becomes important to advertise in local general circulation newspapers in order to avoid wasting advertising on larger regional audiences that listen to radio or watch television.

The socialist press argues that it is free—freer than the Western press—since it is economically free, given that freedom by the State. However, the State also requires that in exchange for the freedom, the press must also be politically "responsible" to the people. And, in some countries which are not socialist, the State also imposes quotas on production, reasoning that not only are supplies (*e.g.*, ink and newsprint) limited, but that by restricting a newspaper's

601

or magazine's circulation, the State can prevent a monopolization of the media; this, of course, theoretically allows a greater diversity of opinion, but also guarantees the State that no one newspaper or magazine can become so large as to become powerful enough to challenge the State and existing government.

In a capitalist society, how the State deals with recession, inflation, unemployment, and other major economic problems will determine how the media, as an industry, adapt to the changing economic base—or if they stay financially strong at all. Nevertheless, it makes no difference whether the State was established as a dictatorship, oligarchy, republic, or democracy, every government determines the levels it will support the economic survival of the media; all media, no matter which system they are a part of, understand that one of the primary functions is for economic survival. By excessive taxation, economic based laws and subsidies, and favorable treatment to competitors, the State can force the media's compliance.

Taxation

Although recognized as a restraint, taxes are the primary financial means for the State to implement its policies. By excessive and selective taxation, the State has historically limited free expression its leaders arguing that a press capable of printing anything it wishes is also capable of the overthrow of the State; thus, taxation has traditionally been used to constantly remind the press that the State not only has the power to control the media, but that the State must be preserved at all costs.

Recorded instances of taxation date to the dawn of history in which communal societies provided for each unit to contribute a portion of income to a communal leader or group of leaders. The taxes were usually a crop or slain animal, sometimes a tool, such as a flat rock. The Biblical requirement to "Render unto Caesar that which is Caesar's" provides for many of the world religions to recognize that there are secular requirements, not under control of the church, that provide for the continuance of the State.

In 1712, Queen Anne established a stamp tax upon the media in England; the tax also required all newspapers to publish the name of the printer or editor, effectively suppressing freedom of expression. In 1765, George III imposed a stamp tax upon all newspapers and legal documents in England and her colonies. The tax had originally been enacted to help England pay for her military campaigns in the French and Indian wars in North America. However, the radical Colonial press, at that time a minority, used the imposition of the tax as a brace for its desire for political autonomy, arguing that taxation without representation is tyranny. Behind the leadership of Sam Adams, radical colonials raided British ships, throwing tea into Boston harbor, then forcing all newspapers in the colonies to disregard the tax by threatening violence against any newspaper that either paid the tax or put their own names in the newspaper, as required by British law.

Even after the American Revolution, discriminatory taxes were applied against American newspapers. In 1785, four years before the First Amendment was adopted, the Massachusetts legislature enacted a stamp tax upon all newspapers and magazines. However, the public outrage was so strong tat the stamp tax against newspapers was repealed the following year; two years later, the tax against magazines was repealed.

It wasn't until 1935, however, that the Supreme Court of the United States declared discriminatory taxes against the media to be unconstitutional. On July 12, 1934, the Louisiana legislature, upon request of U.S. Sen. Huey Long, enacted a two percent tax on the gross advertising receipts of all newspapers with circulations more than 20,000. Known as the "Kingfish," Long was the most powerful person in Louisiana, a former governor who was elected to the Senate in 1930, and who now had visions of the presidency. Long was a populist who cared about the rural community and who, as governor, had steamrolled needed improvements in the state's roads and health care, often in violation of several already-enacted laws. As his popularity increased, he became politically greedy, and eventually gained a virtual stranglehold on Louisiana.

Opposing him were most of the "big city" dailies, especially the *New Orleans Times-Picayune*; it was these newspapers, whom Long accused of representing "big city interests" at the expense of the rural areas, that Long sought to punish. Of the thirteen Louisiana newspapers with circulations more than 20,000, twelve were political opponents of Long. The other "big city" newspaper, and most of the 124 newspapers with circulations under 20,000 were a very influential base of support for the maintenance of Long's political power.

The Louisiana legislature argued that by English common law, taxation of newspapers was acceptable. In striking down the state law, the Supreme Court ruled that the imposition of a discriminatory circulation number (20,000) would force newspapers to try to stay below that figure in order to avoid the two percent tax; the tax, therefore, not only benefitted the rural newspapers, but also reduced the dissemination of opinion. Justice George Sutherland (1862-1942), probably assisted by Justice Benjamin Cardoza, wrote the opinion of the unanimous Court, noting:

> The tax here involved is bad not [just] because it takes money from the pockets of the appellees. If that were all, a wholly different question would be presented. It is bad because, in the light of its history and of its present setting, it is seen to be deliberate and calculated device in the guise of a tax to limit the circulation of information to which the public is entitled in virtue of the constitutional guarantees. A free press stands as one of the great interpreters between the government and the people. To allow it to be fettered is to fetter ourselves.

> In view of the persistent search for new subjects of taxation, it is not without significance that, with the single exception of the Louisiana statute, so far as we can discover, no state during the one hundred and fifty years of our national existence has undertaken to impose a tax like that now in question.

> The form in which the tax is imposed is in itself suspicious. It is not measured or limited by the volume of advertisements. It is measured alone

by the extent of the circulation of the publication in which the advertisements are carried, with the plain purpose of penalizing the publishers and
curtailing the circulation of a selected group of newspaper . . .

[T]he act is unconstitutional under the due process of law clause because
it abridges the freedom of the press . . . [*Grosjean* v. *American Press*]

The decision did not exempt the media from all taxes, however; subsequent
court cases allowed taxation of the media provided that the taxes were not
discriminatory, and that similar businesses were equally and fairly taxed.

The next major constitutional issue on taxation was fought in Minnesota when
the legislature exempted the state's newspaers from paying "use" taxes on the
first $100,000 in newsprint and ink purchased each year. In 1971, the state had
imposed a general "use" tax on all newspapers, but when the smaller newspaper
complained, the state raised the minimum to $100,000, effectively imposing the
tax on ink and paper on the thirteen larger dailies. In March 1983, the Supreme
Court of the United States, in an 8-1 decision, ruled the tax discriminatory and
unconstitutional. In her majority opinion, Justice Sandra Day O'Connor pointed
out:

[The tax] violates the First Amendment not only because it singles out
the press, but also because it targets a small number of newspapers.

The effect of the $100,000 exemption enacted in 1974 is that only a handful
of publishers pay any tax at all, and even fewer pay any significant amount of
tax. The state explains this exemption as part of a policy favoring an "equitable"
tax system, although there are not comparable exemptions for small enterprises
outside the press . . .

Even if we were willing to accept the premise that large businesses are
more profitable and therefore better able to bear the burden of the tax, the
state's commitment to this "equity" is questionable, for the concern has
not led the state to grant benefits to small business in general.

And when the exemption selects such a narrowly defined group to bear
the full burden of the tax, the tax begins to resemble more a penalty for a
few of the larger newspapers than an attempt to favor struggling smaller
enterprises . . .

A tax that singles out the press, or that targets individual publications
within the press, places a heavy burden on the state to justify its actions.

Anti-Trust Laws

In a truly libertarian society, there would be no antitrust laws, for survivability
would be determined by economic factors in an open marketplace in which all
business competes. However, the State often assumes an obligation to assure
that there is an equal opportunity for survival by requiring certain minimal
standards of compliance. By establishing certain laws that prohibit monopolies
and monopolistic tendencies, the State reasons that it is giving a greater base
for the dissemination of all views; in its self-interest, it is also preventing
any organization or system of organizations from becoming large enough to

threaten the security of the State. However, it was not until some "muckraking" reporters in the late 1890s and early 1900s began investigating the avaricious greed of the trusts, with their "public be damned attitudes," that the federal government, which had largely represented the Big Business interests, but now pushed by a handful of large circulation newspapers and magazines, finally enacted antitrust legislation. Ironically, some of the court decisions, based upon both the Constitution and the antitrust legislation, were directed against the Associated Press, itself a monopolistic giant. In 1900, an Illinois court ruled that the AP, by its own bylaws could be interpreted as a public utility and, thus, had no right to discontiue service to any newspaper which had both AP and another news service. After a reorganization, the AP continued to refuse service to newspapers subscribing to competitors. In 1915, the U.S. attorney general advised the AP that such actions on its part were monopolistic. During the mid-1930s, the Associated Press Managing Editors agreed that AP services should not be extended to radio stations, except as brief bulletins. The immediate result was that radio initiated full-scale news operations in direct competition to the AP—and the AP eventually recognized the economic advantage of selling its services to radio.

By the end of the decade, the AP lost another antitrust battle, this one which would establish a major precendent. In *Associated Press* v. *National Labor Relations Board*, the Supreme Court that ruled the media were not exempt from federal laws on business practices. In a 5-4 decision, Justice Owen Roberts wrote:

> The business of the Associated Press is not immune from regulation because it is an agency of the press. The publisher of a newspaper has no special immunity from the application of general laws. He has no special privilege to invade the rights and liberties of others.

The case arose when the AP fired a reporter who was trying to organize a chapter of the American Newspaper Guild. The NLRB had ordered the reporter reinstated; AP appealed, taking the case to the Supreme Court. After losing the case at the Supreme Court, the AP then fired for "incompetence" a very competent reproter.

In 1941, the FCC created a regulation that prevented stations from affiliating with organizations operating two or more networks serving the same area. To support its action, the FCC pointed out that NBC, with its two networks (Red and Blue), dominated the airwaves, that the networks required five year contracts with affiliates (although FCC licenses were for only three years), and that affiliates were not allowed to carry programs from any other source. NBC countered that it was protected by the First Amendment guarantees against governmental intrusion. However, the Supreme Court, citing *AP* v. *NLRB*, disagreed, pointing out that there was no conflict between antitrust legislation and the First Amendment since the First Amendment does not deal with the "business" of communication. The Supreme Court decision forced NBC to sell one of its networks if it wanted any affiliates. In 1943, following the Supreme Court ruling, RCA retained the Red Network and sold the Blue Network, to Edward J. Noble who renamed it American Broadcasting Co.

The NBC/CBS case served as a precedent for the destruction of AP's monopolistic agreements with member newspapers. In its bylaws, AP had allowed any newspaper to obtain its services—as long as a competing newspaper with AP services did not object; if there was an objection, the newspaper could still receive the service if four-fifths of all members agreed; the bylaw essentially shut off the smaller newspapers from receiving the nation's largest wire service. In 1941, the newly-founded *Chicago Sun* challenged the AP rule, after the *Chicago Tribune* vetoed the request. Two years later, Judge Learned Hand of the U.S. District Court for the Southern District of New York, proposed that federal antitrust laws and the principles of the First Amendment were "closely akin" to each other, for the antitrust laws would help bring about a greater dissemination of information. In his opinion, Judge Hand ruled:

> However, neither exclusively, nor even primarily, are the interest of the newspaper industry conclusive; for that industry serves one of the msot vital of all general interests: the dissemination of news from many different sources, with as many different facets and colors as is possible. That interest is closely akin to, indeed if it is not the same as, the interest protected by the First Amendment; it presupposes that right conclusions are more likely to be gathered out of a multitude of tongues, than any kind of authoritative selection . . .

In 1945, the Supreme Court of the United States affirmed the lower court's rulings and dismissed AP's argument that it was protected by the First Amendment and could, therefore, conduct business without government interference. In his majority opinion, Justice Hugo Black, one of the Court's most vigorous defenders of a free press, rejected application of the "clear and present danger" test providing a special avenue of protection, noting:

> The [First] Amendment rests on the assumption that the widest possible dissemination of information from diverse and antagonistic sources is essential to the welfare of the public, that a free press is a condition of a free society. Surely a command that the government itself shall not impede the free flow of ideas does not afford non-governmental combinations a refuge if they impose restraints upon that constitutionally guaranteed freedom. Freedom to publish means freedom for all and not for some. Freedom to publish is guaranteed by the Constitution, but freedom to keep others from publishing is not.

Three years later, in *United States* v. *Paramount Pictures*, the Supreme Court declared that block booking was a violation of federal antitrust laws. For more than four decades, most major film studios either had owned their own theaters or had exclusive contracts with independent theaters. The studios often required the theaters—whether studio-owned or independent—to book a "B" film or a weak "A" film in order to get a better quality film; further, the studios established minimum ticket prices for all films. Although the Supreme Court ruling broke up the "stranglehold" the studios held on production and distribution of films, it also forced several smaller studios out of business, unable to grarantee adequate distribution of their films.*

In 1951, the Supreme Court further tightened the antitrust noose around the media. Between 1933 and 1948, the *Lorain* (Ohio) *Journal* and *Times Herald*, a morning-afternoon combination, had a news and advertising monopoly in Lorain, reaching about ninety-nine percent of all homes, When WEOL-AM was established in Elyria, about eight miles form Lorain, the management of the newspapers told advertisers that the newspapers would no longer accept any advertising from any business which advertised on the radio station. The Department of Justice sued, arguing that the monopolistic practices of the *Journal* and *Times-Herald*, by forcing a boycott of a legally conducted business also restricted interstate commerce. The newspapers argued that publishers can accept or reject any advertising, and that the First Amendment protected the media from governmental incursion. The Supreme Court disagreed. The majority opinion, written by Justice Burton, argued:

> The publisher claims a right as a private business concern to select its customers and to refuse to accept advertisements from whomever it pleases. We do not dispute that general right . . .
> The right claimed by the publisher is neither absolute nor exempt from regulation. Its exercise as a purposeful means of nonpolizing interstate commerce is prohibited by the Sherman Act. The operator of the radio station, equally with the publisher of the newspaper, is entitled to the protection of that Act.
> . . . *The injunction [by the Department of Justice] does not violate any guaranteed freedom of the press.* The publisher suggests that the injunction amounts to a prior restraint upon what it may publish . . . We find in it no restriction upon any guaranteed freedom of the press. The injunction applies to a publisher what the law applies to others. [In the case of *Associated Press* v. *The United States*, The Supreme Court ruled that] the publisher may not accept or deny advertisements in an "attempt to monopolize . . . any part of the trade or commerce among several states."

In a related case, the Supreme Court ruled that it was not a violation of the Constitution or of federal laws if the publisher of two newspapers, in a

---

*In 1962, the Supreme Court, in *United States* v. *Loew's, Inc.* extended its arguments to television stations. The case had resulted from an industry-wide practice to rent a package of films to a television station; in order for the station to show a better quality film or one with a potentially large audience, it was required to rent films of lesser quality or lesser audience potential.

market that supports additional media, requires advertisers to advertise in one newspaper in order to secure advertising in the other (*Times Picayune Publishing Co.* v. *United States*, 1953, 5-4 decision).

But, in 1957, the Supreme Court ruled that the Star Co., publishers of the *Kansas City Star*, the *Kansas City Times*, the *Sunday Star*, and licensee of WDAF-AM/FM and WDAF-TV, engaged in monopolistic practices by requiring persons who wished to subscribe to one newspaper to subscribe to all three, and forcing advertisers to buy space in all three newspapers; advertisers who chose not to buy space in the newspapers, but wished to advertise on either the radio or television stations, received less favorable treatment. In its ruling, the Court noted that the company's media dominated the market with more than ninety-four percent coverage and that the "ruthless" disregard for the public by the company threatened less favorable news coverage for advertisers who did not follow the company's advertising restrictions—would not be tolerated. In a subsequent action, the Star Co. agreed to sell its radio and television stations and no longer requrie "tie-in" advertising.

By the time of the sale of the WDAF stations, the right of the FCC to create situations that allowed the broadest dissemination of views had been established. In 1953, the FCC had issued what became known as the "7-7-7 Rule"* —no individual, partnership, or company could hold the licenses for more than seven AM radio stations, seven FM stations, and seven television stations, no more than five of the TV stations could be in the VHF band. The rule was challenged, and the Supreme Court, in 1956, upheld the FCC's right to impose limits of ownership in order to increase dissemination of information.

However, the FCC saw no antitrust violation when it approved, in 1965, the merger of ABC and the International Telephone and Telegraph (ITT), a two billion dollar conglomerate that, among other things, leased telephone lines to some radio and television stations and networks. This time, the Department of Justice cited direct violations of antitrust law and was successful, through a two year series of tactical delays, in blocking the merger.

The year that the ABC-ITT proposed merger was finally dissolved was the year that the U.S. District Court for the Central District of California ruled that the purchase, in 1964, of the *San Bernardino Sun* and the *Telegram*, a morning-afternoon combination, by the Times Mirror Co., publisher of the *Los Angeles Times*, violated federal law since it resulted in the creation of a monopoly of ownership. The Court cited the diminishing number of competing newspapers in San Bernadino county, adjacent to Los Angeles County. There were only three other daily newspapers in the county. The third had begun in 1967. All three had smaller circulations than the *Sun*, which at that time had a circulation of about 37,000; the *Telegram's* circulation was about 19,000. It was found that the ownership of the *Sun* by the company which published the *Los Angeles Times*, which had a large circulation in San Bernardino County,

---

*In 1984, the FCC adopted a "12-12-12 Rule"

would create an economic monopoly and further restrict the dissemination of news by an independent news medium—two of the other three dailies were owned by chains. In 1968, the Supreme Court of the United States affirmed the lower court's ruling. The Times Mirror Co. subsequently sold the newspaper to the Gannett Co., a large chain with headquarters in New York.

Within a few years, newspapers learned that not only could they not own newspapers in overlapping circulation areas, they couldn't even own radio or television stations. In 1970, the FCC ruled against one individual or firm from holding the licenses for two competing stations in the same market—two AM stations or two FM stations or one AM or FM stations and a TV station. The concept was extended against ownership of a newspaper *and* a radio or television station in the same community. Because of a vigorous opposition, the FCC allowed that proposal to die, finally implementing the rule in 1975 after a probe from the Department of Justice. The new rules required the breaking up of sixteen newspaper/radio or TV combinations, mostly in smaller communities with no competing media; most other combinations were "grandfathered" in, allowed to remain in place until the sale of the newspaper or radio/TV license.

At the same time the FCC was looking into cross-media ownership, the Department of Justice was probing network programing practices. In 1974, it refiled a suit charging that ABC, CBS, and NBC television networks had created a monopolization of the airwaves because of their extensive domination of prime time programming. The Department had argued that by producing a large amount of primetime programming, then requiring affiliates to purchase that programing, the networks had created a monopoly. Three years later, NBC agreed, in an our-of-court settlement, to limit the number of hours of programming it produced; in 1980, ABC and CBS also agreed. The consent decree specifically exempted all news and documentary programing. The result was an increase of programming by independent producers, some of whom had strong ties to the network.

Joint Operating Agreements

In 1933, the *New Mexico State Tribune* and the *Albuquerque Journal*, competing newspapers, merged their business, distribution, and production areas, while retaining separate administrative and editorial identities. The agreement permitted a more efficient operation that resulted in higher profits for both newspapers. During the next three decades, more than twenty other pairs of newspapers, most in large cities, formed Joint Operating Agreements. For the most part, the creation of the agreements was between a stronger and a weaker newspaper. The absence of state or federal intervention was a tacit understanding that in some cases the creation of what may be monopolistic practices was acceptable in order to maintain a diversity of opinion. Then, in 1965, the Department of Justice took a look at the practice; in 1969, the Supreme Court, in *Citizen Publishing Co.* v. *United States* affirmed lower court opinions that the agreements amounted to violations of the Shaeman Act. Through Congressional action, however, a Failing Newspaper Act, later replaced by the Newspaper

Preservation Act, was created; the philosophy underwriting the acts was that the preservation of newspapers was of such importance to the State that situations that could be considered monopolistic in other businesses needed to be tolerated within the media to assure the widest dissemination of news. However, many media and legal scholars had argued that instead of assuring a wider range of information diffusion, what existed was that a couple newspapers, by their monopolistic tendencies, shut off outside competition.

Legislative Controls and Freedom of Expression: The FTC and Commerical Advertising

Proponents of increased government regulation argue that users of mass media, particularly the broadcast media, exert a disproportionate amount of influence and even control on the thoughts, values, and behavior of the American public. Accordingly, they see a need for legislation to "protect" the public.

On the other hand, opponents argue, as did the drafters of the First Amendment, that the public has "nothing to fear" from the exercise of free speech regardless of the degree to which it may be abused. Instead, they hold that what the public should fear is any attempt by government to infringe on this freedom. In this view, public protection does not require the outlawing of certain ideas or opinions because a basic belief that in the free flow of ideas and opinions, truth will eventually prevail.

Most of the first hundred years of the United States was based largely on a *laissez faire* economics given intellectual support by Adam Smith (1723-1790), the Scottish political economist and philosopher, in his book, *The Wealth of Nations* (1776). Smith advanced two ideas: First, there is a "natural order of things" which is derived from the "natural liberty" of people to pursue their own self-interests. Second, when the natural order is left free, it operates for the general good. Although some attempts to regulate business at the state level occured, notably in Pennsylvania, Massachusetts, New Jersey, and Virginia, before the Civil War, govenmental regulation was not widespread.

The great economic growth of the United States after the Civil War converted the nation from a nation of states with small businesses serving limited geographic areas into a national system of commerce.

During the early years of the twentieth century, the federal government passed legislation that created independent regulatory agencies, largely at the urging of

Portions of the section on "Legislative Controls and Freedom of Expression: The FTC and Commercial Advertising" were written by John G. Myers, professor of business, Graduate School of Business, University of California at Berkeley.

reformers in the Progressive Movement (1906-1917), to oversee the emerging commerce. Many states were involved in the movement with the formulation of public utility commissions (such as in New York and Wisconsin in 1907). In addition, the federal government passed the Hepburn Act of 1906 giving the Interstate Commerce Commission power to set railroad rates. Also created were the Pure Food and Drugs Act (1906), forbidding the manufacture or preparation of adulterated foods, medicines, and drugs, and providing for federal inspection of meats; and the Federal Reserve System (1913).

Progressives believed regulation of business should be by an agency separate from the president and Congress because both were too political to handle the problems of regulating business, and from the courts because they lacked the necessary knowledge to handle business problems, and they were too slow to be efficient. The solution was an "independent commission" not directly under any of the traditional branches of government headed by a committee of "experts."

Opposition to the concept came from prominent people, including Justice Oliver Wendell Holmes of the Supreme Court; however, Justice Louis Brandeis was a strong supporter of the commission idea. Brandeis advised President Wilson that the Sherman Anti-Trust Act was a sound idea, but that it required supplementary legislation, and that it needed a federal board to assist in the execution of the Act's provisions. Brandeis hoped that the commission would have members who had comprehensive, up to date knowledge. Holmes, by comparison, observed (1910): "I don't disguise my belief that the Sherman Act is a humbug based on economic ignorance and incompetence." Since Holmes opposed the antitrust law, he opposed an agency designed to carry out some of its provisions. He also opposed the Interstate Commerce Commission as unfit to regulate.

A series of cases under the Sherman Act, including *Northern Securities Co.* v. *U.S.* (1904), *Standard Oil Co. of New Jersey* v. *U.S.* (1911), and *U.S.* v. *American Tobacco Co.* (1911) convinced many that corporations were engaging in illegal activities, and government must take stronger actions.

The Federal Trade Commission (FTC) was created in 1914 by the Federal Trade Commission Act which transferred the investigatorial functions of the Bureau of Corporations from Department of Commerce and Labor to the new FTC. The powers conferred on the FTC included investigatorial responsibilities to gather evidence to be presented to Congress and enforcement functions against industries violating the law the FTC was created to oversee. The act specifically prohibited unfair methods of competition (Section five of the FTC Act).

In *FTC* v. *Raladam Co.* (1931), the Supreme Court decided that there could be no "unfair method of competition" without a competitor against whom the violation occured. The case arose because the FTC was trying to change the old *caveat emptor*, "let the buyer beware," practice of advertising and selling. *Caveat emptor* placed the entire burden on the buyer to determine if the product being purchased was any good and if it was safe. The effect of the Supreme Court's decision to reject the FTC's position was to decide that the consumer had no standing under the FTC law, returning *caveat emptor* to its historic standing.

Congress passed the Wheeler-Lea Act in 1938 to give the consumer standing, thus giving the FTC the right to regulate in the consumer's interest. The Act revised Section 5 of the FTC statute to add the italicized phrase: "Unfair methods of competition in commerce, *and unfair or deceptive acts or practices in commerce*, are hereby declared unlawful." The FTC now had two legal positions upon which to take action: (1) if an activity injured another business, and (2) if the activity injured consumers.

The new law gave special attention to advertising:

> It shall be unlawful for any person, partnership, or corporation to disseminate, or cause to be disseminated, any false advertisement . . . by United States mails, or in [interstate] commerce by any means, for the purpose of inducing, or which is likely to induce, directly or indirectly, the purchase in commerce of food, drugs, devices or cosmetics . . .
>
> The term false advertising" means an advertisement, other than labeling, which is misleading in a material respect . . ."

Until recently, the courts have generally upheld the advertiser's right to use exaggeration or puffery in commercial transactions. The claim that Blatz is Milwaukee's finest beer may or may not be true. With puffery permissible, it doesn't have to be true. Advertisers have long known that they can freely make such claims, with no attempt to prove that they are true or that anyone believes them.

Puffery, however well established, is also thoroughly vulnerable. The spirit of *caveat emptor*, predominant in these early court decisions, has given way in recent times to a spirit of consumer protection. The consumerism movement of the late 1960's has produced a wide variety of legislative proposals and new control mechanisms, many of which directly or indirectly affect advertisers and advertising practice.

Solving a Dilemma

How does one bring a measure of control on the *content* of speech (in this case, advertising or "commercial speech") without at the same time abrogating the free speech provisions of the First Amendment? Simply declaring certain statements or linguistic-artistic forms in adversiting illegal involves the State in the impossible task of deciding what those forms shall be. Setting up a panel of government experts to review advertisements and advertising campaigns poses an equally impossible task of monitoring hundreds of thousands of such "messages." Either alternative is susceptible to attack as an infringement of free speech because each implies governmental interference and the imposition of governmental judgments and values on the interchange of ideas, opinions or "speech." This regulatory dilemma is not unique to advertising. It occurs in any area of comunications where the impositions of some measure of control on what the sender says is under consideration.

Making the sender directly responsible to the receiver for the accuracy, reliability or "truth" of the sender's statements is the alternative. In effect, it called for a law that gives the receiver the right to challenge any statement the sender makes. Among the virtues of this alternative is that it lies within the bounds of the First Amendment. Moreover, it places no reliance on government monitoring, review boards or the imposition of governmental standards.

The first application of this imaginative idea—which may be used in many areas of mass communications in the future—exists in the field of commercial advertising. The consumer-regulatory concept underlies advertising legislation introduced by Sen. Frank E. Moss and Sen. George McGovern in April 1971: The Truth in Advertising Act of 1971.

By 1911, many states had created "Truth in Advertising" laws, first proposed by *Printer's Ink*, a trade publication. In 1952, the National Association of Broadcasters created regulations for the acceptance of commercials, then retali ated and eliminated all actions when a federal district court looked into matters of length and number of commercials during stated time periods.

The Truth in Advertising Act was the first attempt by the government to apply the principle of making the sender directly responsible to the receiver for reliability, accuracy, and fairness of product claims. The goals are to provide the consumer with more and better information, reduce the incidence of dishonest and misleading advertising, and to help expose and counterbalance unfound claims.

The Requirement of Proof

The requirement that a sender must "prove" his statements or allegations to the satisfaction of the receiver has profound implications for rights of free speech set down in the First Amendment. A loose interpretation of citizen protection under the First Amendment contends that, so long as many or all senders are allowed to "speak," truth will eventually conquer ignorance. It does not mean that senders have the right to speak only if capable of proving what they are saying. Drafters of the First Amendment put much credence in the capacity of the citizen to sort out "right" from "wrong" as long as everyone was allowed a voice, rather than imposing on speakers the requirement that they speak only the "truth." The commercial analogy, of course, rests on the high value that has historically been placed on the maintenance of fair competition. Citizen protection has long been based on the concept of "many available products" and "many available ideas" from which to choose. It implies that protection lies in having many advertisers (many senders) bidding for the same consumer patronage, using a wide variety of appeals and persuasive techniques.

The Truth in Advertising Act instituted a fundamental change in this version of consumer-receiver control. Projected to other spheres of persuasive or mass communications, it has a major impact on both the volume and content of "free speech."

The Act requires substantial documentation of all facts or alleged facts within an ad. The Act did not interfere with the advertiser's use of subjective judgment, opinion and puffery in referring tohis product. Nor would it appear to include the most extreme forms of puffery in which sujective opinion is carried to the point of outright spoof (e.g. the male fending off the attacks of females aroused by his Hai Karate aftershave).

Nevertheless, the FTC soon began looking into numerous advertisements. Among its actions, it required the Milk Council to change its slogan, "Every*body* needs milk" to "Milk has something for every*body*." FTC logic was that not *every* body needs milk, and that milk can be harmful to some.

In 1975, the FTC, three decades after its first investigations, required "corrective advertising" for Listerine claims. The Warner-Lambert Co., manufacturers of the mouthwash, Listerine, claimed that it helped reduce colds and sore throats. Medical evidence disagreed; not only didn't Listerine do as it was supposed to do, but *no* mouthwash could be effective against colds which are caused by viruses rather than bacteria. The FTC required Warner-Lambert to conduct a $10 million ad campaign, designed by the FTC, to let the consumers know that Listerine was effective only as a mouthwash. The following year, in *Virginia State Board of Pharmacy* v. *Virginia Citizens Consumer Council*, the Supreme Court of the United States ruled that not only is commercial speech different from other forms of free expression, it fell under regulation in certain cases. However, Justice Harry Blackman also noted, "Speech is not stripped of First Amendment Protection merely because it appears in the form of a paid advertisement." The FTC had gained the power to regulate the nature or content of advertising and the size of companies in the interests of the public or competing business. But the judgment of what constituted the public or competing business interests was established by the FTC, often without a significant part of the public involved in the decision-making process. When the FTC, after extensive pressure from Action for Children's Television (ACT), began exploring possibilities of reducing or eliminating TV ads directed to younger children, the various self-interest groups (*e.g.*, toy companies) felt that they had been pushed too far.

The Congress agreed; in 1978, the House of Representatives failed to approve creation of an Agency for Consumer Representation; in 1980, the Congress ordered that all FTC regulations be subjected to a congressional veto.

Advertising today is regulated under more than twenty federal agencies, and several industry codes, each regulation designed in the "Public interest"; each regulation the result of a combination of authoritarian and social responsibility philosophies.

Bibliography

Barnett, Stephen R., "Monopoly Games: Where Failures Win Big," *Columbia Journalism Review*, May-June 1980.

Bernstein, Marver H., *Regulating Business by Independent Commission*, Princeton: Princeton University Press, 1966.

Compaine, Benjamin M., *Who Owns the Media?* Knowledge Industries (White Plains, N.Y.), 1979.

Dreier, Peter; Steven Weinberg, "Interlocking Directorates," *Columbia Journalism Review*, November-December 1979.

Stempel, Guido H. III, "Effects on Performance of a Cross-Media Monopoly," *Journalism Quarterly*, June 1973.

Udell, Jon G. ed., *The Economics of the American Newspaper*, Hasting House (New York, N.Y.), 1978.

Section 2

The State as Facilitator: Arguments for Promoting Expression

"In proportion as the structure of government gives force to public opinion, it is essential that public opinion should be enlightened."

—George Washington,
Farewell Address, 1783

Sometimes government assists in the flow of information to the public. For example, the *Madison* (Wisc.) *Capital Times* won a suit against the University of Wisconsin-Madison in 1983 granting the newspaper access to University records. Judge Robert Pekowsky became the force securing the newspaper's, and thus the public's, right of access to records including faculty evaluation data. Pekowsky's decision reflected a sincere appreciation for the need for access—"Nondisclosure raises unfounded suspicions of illegitimate activities."

In *Wald* v. *Regan* (1983), another court ruled that the Ronald Reagan administration did not have the authority to ban travel to Cuba unless there was a national emergency.

Some legislative bodies were showing an interest in letting the public see what they were doing by admitting cameras to their halls. The U.S. House of Representatives installed its own television system, and then provided a feed of pictures and sound to interested media. Many state courts have also opened their doors to television coverage, as did the Arkansas Supreme Court for the first time on May 16, 1983; Oregon began an experiment with cameras in its courts on June 3, 1983.

Other governmental actions assisting the flow of communication include sunshine laws, and opening administrative and legislative proceedings to reporters and members of the public.

Sometimes, government even provides economic benefits to help the disseminators of information, such as the second-class mail permit allowing periodicals to send their products throught the mails at a greatly reduced rate—rates that have saved many from failure.

Although the principal theory motivating government in its relationship with the media is an authoritarian control of information, many officials recognize that some access to ideas and state records is necessary if government is to function in a pluralistic society. It is, therefore, in the enlightened self-interest of the most fearful administrator to reduce the bonds on the freedom of expression some of the time.

Chapter 44

Economics of Assistance

The state that can tax a press can also subsidize the press. Throughout history, governments have used financial susidies to assure both a vigorous and a compliant press. In England, Sir Robert Walpole (1676-1745, prime minister, 1721-1742), one of England's most respected politicans, used patronage, bribery, subsidies, and threats to force a compliant press. His most famous victims were John Trenchard and Thomas Gordon, writing under the name Cato. When Cato's attacks upon Walpole and the government became intolerable, Walpole bribed the editor of the *London Journal* to suspend publication of the column, forcing Trenchard and Gordon to move to the less-influential *British Journal*.

In the American colonies, as in most countries, the various colonial governments provided direct subsidies to printers of tracts, pamphlets, and official announcements. When the Colonies' second newspaper was initiated in 1704—the first one was suppressed in 1690 after one issue—the Commonwealth of Massachusetts provided financial independence. As postmaster, John Campbell received not only free postage for his *Boston News–Letter*, but also direct payments and legal advertisements. Twice during the first fourteen years, the Commonwealth provided additional funds to keep the three-hundred-circulation newspaper from bankruptcy. To get the state's assistance, Campbell had only to make sure that nothing in his newspaper offended the state.

However, the State that provides the subsidies can also take them away, and in 1719, with a new government, Campbell lost his postmastership—and, thus, his free mailing privileges, the subsidies, and the official notices which he had faithfully printed the previous fourteen years. The governmental assistance would now go to William Brooker's *Boston Gazette*. (The *News–Letter*, a Tory newspaper, would continue until 1776 when the Sons of Liberty shut it down.) Nevertheless, during the first seven decades of the eighteenth century, most printers received some form of subsidy; most printers although not subjected to any licensing laws, didn't print much that could be interpreted as harmful to the state.

Following the Revolutionary War, subsidies to the press were disguised within the newly-emerging political party structure.

Alexander Hamilton and the Federalists provided the economic stability for *The Gazette of the United States*, edited by John Fenno. The *Gazette* was first published in New York, the nation's capital, in 1789, then moved to Philadelphia two years later when that city became the capital.

To counteract the semi-official *Gazette*, Thomas Jefferson and the Anti-Federalists (Republicans, later called Democrats) created the *National Gazette*, edited by Philip Freneau. Freneau had been a Radical, a prisoner of the British, and the poet/propagandist of the Revolution. After the Revolution, Freneau unleashed his hatred against the Federalists whom he believed had, by their own counter-revolution, stopped the ideals of the Revolution from developing. Now, in 1791, Thomas Jefferson, secretary of state, gave Freneau a stipend and a position as translator, requiring only that Freneau edit the Anti-Federalist newspaper. After a few months of relatively innocuous objectivity, Freneau unleashed the fury of Anti-Federalist sentiment, prompting Hamilton to argue that those paid by the government owe their allegiance to the government. During the next few years, the nation's colleges, most of them Federalist, stopped teaching their students Freneau's poetry.

Other editors received governmental subsidies, but none had the power that Amos Kendall and Francis P. Blair had during the Andrew Jackson administration, 1829-1837. Kendall and Blair were two of Jackson's closest friends and political advisors. Before Jackson was elected to the presidency, Kendall was editor of *The Argus of Western America*, the political newspaper of the newly-formed Democratic party. After the election, Kendall moved to Washington, and Blair became editor of the party newspaper. Within two years of Jackson's election, Blair became editor of the *Washington Globe*, an official newspaper backed by party funds and governmental printing contracts. Even if the adminsitration had not channeled funds into a newspaper—as every previous administration had done—the economic stability of the newspaper would have been assured since few advertisers or subscribers, themselves ruled by fear as much as by personal greed, would want to be "out of favor" with a popular administration.

Newspapers became more independent after the Jackson era, but publishers still traditionally aligned their papers with a political party, arguing that they could be editorially independent although keeping a political philosophy.

Many of the world's media still accept subsidies and governmental grants, without believing they are being compromised, or fearing governmental intrusion. Their governments reason that the subsidies are not to force political, econopmic, or social compliance, but to assure that freedom of the pres is *not* diminished because of economic reasons. A reality of contemporary business practice in capitalistic countries is that in a two-or three-newspaper town, the newspaper with the largest circulation also gets most of the advertising revenue. The libertarian philosophy argues that the marketplace of opinion is what should determine the survivability of a newspaper, and that governmental intervention is neither acceptable nor desired. However, the state has a responsibility to the people to provide for the base that allows competing newspapers, a multiplicity of voices, to exist.

In 1971, the Swedish government, recognizing the financial difficulties of many newspapers, imposed a six percent tax on advertising in all daily newspapers, a ten percent tax on advertising in all non-daily newspapers; later, the tax was raised to ten percent for all newspapers. The income was then used to provide low cost and interest-free loans, production grants, and to assist publishers to achieve financial stability of newly-created newspapers. To assure that there was a "multiplicity of voices" in Sweden, the government restricted most of the assistance to newspaperw which were not the leading circulation newspapers in any market.

When other capitalistic Western countries began experimenting with similar subsidies, the American media reacted with fright. Robert U. Brown, publisher of *Editor & Publisher*, a weekly magazine for the newspaper industry, presented the American point of view:

> All of these things are being done ostensibly to maintain the diversity of the press. But the disease is virulent. No government in history has been able to grant funds for the press without a quid pro quo. There is no reason to believe that governments or the humans who run them will ever change. [May 11, 1974]

Nevertheless, although the American media do not accept cash payments, they do accept indirect subsidies. In addition to accepting the numerous and substantial tax deductions that all businesses are entitled to, many newspapers qualify for low-interest government loans through the Small Business Administration or low-interest mortgages and tax-deferred benefits on land and property which many municipalities provide to attract industry to the area. Newspapers also don't pay inventory taxes on unopened printing supplies, including imported newsprint. Recent IRS rulings, however, now require book publishers to pay taxes on all inventory; as a result, many companies are publishing books that may have substantial "early" sales, while remaindering, or trashing, books sooner than before, and not publishing as many quality "risk" books that may take awhile to prove themselves.

Although almost all business are required to withhold municipal, state, and federal taxes, social security, workman's compensation/disability, and unemployment taxes from employee paychecks—and to make business contributions to social security, workman's compensation/disability, and state unemployment—newspapers are exempt from doing so for their carriers, avoiding many kinds of liabilities by being allowed to claim that the carriers are "independent contractors." In most municipalities, newspapers do not pay business license fees for the public property on which they place their newsstands, nor are they requried to collect municipal and state sales taxes on subscriptions or on advertising. The printed media are also granted a special second-class mailing privilege that provides for lower mailing costs.

For the non-print media, there have also been numerous business advantages. For several years, investors could receive a tax credit for investing in films; sales taxes are not collected on radio and television advertising, many producers and on-air talent are classified, like newspaper carriers, "independent contractors," and thus, able to receive lump-sum salaries while the station avoids paying the business share of several kinds of taxes.

All media are also able to take advantage of government-funded training for journalists and production staffs. In most occupations, the employer pays for the employee to learn a job task, often by paying a lower starting wage in exchange for the training, or the employee went to a trade-tech school, paying full costs, to learn the skills necessary to enter that occupation. Students attending public colleges and universities are subsidized by the state; although seemingly an enormous burden at times, tuition and fees do not cover the full cost of education. State funding, coupled by a school's investment portfolio (which is usually tax-exempt) and alumni contributions (which are tax-deductible) contribute the other costs. For many of the larger schools of journalism and telecommunications, the media, through tax-exempt foundations or by tax-deductible contributions, also contribute to the programs. Students also qualify for low-interest and deferred loans, as well as cash grants. While the benefits apply to all schools and all students, in varying amounts, the media are still able to avoid initial extensive training programs, assuming that the student who majors in journalism or telecommunications has received a minimal basic education in those areas. Because almost all persons entering journalism now have college degrees, and because most of them have been trained in journalism in college, the public support for journalism training has reduced the financial obligation of newspapers and other media.

Second Class Mail Privileges

by Tonda Rush, Terry Maguire, and Claudia M. James

When the Republic was established, Congress inherited a well-established system of post roads and post offices. Busy with weightier matters, it was content with the status quo, making only appropriations and minor adjustments until it finally established a national Post Office in 1792. It commended newspapers in the mail for "circulation of political intelligence" and permitted a newspaper to travel any distance for 1.5 cents, while a letter traveling 450 miles would cost 25 cents. At the time, the *Federalist Papers* of Alexander Hamilton were competing through the *Gazette of the United States* with Thomas Jefferson's Anti-Federalists in Philip Freneau's *National Gazette*. The linguistic lessons of Noah Webster traveled through the mails, along with Thomas Paine's *Rights of Man* as readers of both persuasions followed the battles in Europe of the French Revolution.

The postage rate discussions in Congress came to be a wedge between the larger city newspapers and small local ones, the former wishing for a low

American Newspaper Publishers Association, [*Amicus curiae* brief, *The Enterprise, Inc.*, v. William F. Bolger, et. al., 1985. Edited]

uniform rate to encourage national circulation and the latter seeking a rate based upon distance to discourage the larger competitors from invading local fiefdoms.

In 1794 new postal legislation maintained the rates but added a new penny postage rate for newspapers circulating anywhere in their states of publication. It also recognized for the first time the existence of pamphlets and magazines, which drew a slightly higher rate.

Those rates remained for nearly fifty years. In the meantime, [by] the War of 1812, . . . newspapers [constituted] half the volume of the mails. The Louisiana Purchase of 1803 [had] opened huge new territories in which the first to set up shop was usually the printer-editor, who depended upon larger newspapers for material to reprint and circulate locally.

In 1852, postage rates were revised. A newspaper could send up to three ounces anywhere for a penny. Each additional ounce was charged a penny. A newspaper mailing within the state had an even lower rate: 1.5 ounces for a half cent. Newspapers mailing within their own counties could travel for free. At the time, fifteen pounds of *Journal of Commerce* newspapers, which were primarily delivered by mail, could be sent for 45.5 cents. Fifteen pounds of letters would cost $14.40.

By 1855 a class of transient mail, created in 1825, was atracting many advertising circulars for which the recipient was to call at the post office, pay the postage and receive the mail, a practice then also followed for newspapers. Many circulars, however, were left at the Post Office, depriving the government of the price of carrying them. Congress remedied the problem that year by requiring prepayment of postage for the circulars.

[During the Civil War], the importance of . . . newspapers to the nation was dramatic. Horace Greeley's *Weekly Tribune* [was] circulated by mail to nearly 200,000 subscribers, many of whom were Middle Western farmers troubled by the issues of slavery and war. Greeley soundly denounced slavery, urged support of the Union, and forged the national unity that President Lincoln so desperately needed to recruit soliders for the war effort. Readers on the frontier loyally read the "Try-bune," though they may have disagreed with it, and relied upon it to learn where their sons, husbands and fathers were meeting enemy forces in the fractious war.

Establishing Classifications

[In 1863] the three mail classes were first defined; first class, correspondence: second class, regular periodicals; and third class, all other mail, including books, seedlings, advertising, and engravings. The definition of second-class mail was "all mailable matter exclusively in print, regularly issued at stated periods without additions by writing, mark or sign."

In 1874 rates went up as the country struggled with post-war depressions. Newspapers could mail anywhere in the country for two cents per pound if they published weekly or more frequently. Other second-class mail was charged three cents per pound. In-country newspapers remained free, but recipients were obliged to call for them at the post office.

Free circulation or "regular publications designed for advertising purposes" were for the first time subdivided into a special, higher rate than the subscriber newspapers (one cent for every two ounces, or eight cents per pound) but remained within second-class.

The new subdivision apparently failed to distinguish sufficiently between the second-class mail which Congress intended to enjoy and the lowest rates. In the 45th Congress, the matter arose in the context of a bill to establish post roads. Sen. Ferry introduced a bill to sharpen the class distinctions, complaining that the low rates were being exploited by advertising publications:

> We are now losing at the rate of about a half million dollars a year by the transportation of periodicals, as they are claimed to be, but issued for advertising purposes for individual interest.

Ferry's efforts failed that year, but the following year the House took up the cause when Rep. Waddell introduced a bill which he said had the broad support of New York publishers anxious to improve the situation and to preserve the class for newspapers. His proposal was to create a fourth class of mail for the shipping of merchandise, which would leave the third class solely for "miscellaneous printed matter." To limit the second class solely to bonafide periodicals, he suggested a system of registration with the post office and, following registration, a flat rate for all registered matter.

However, the registration proposal was too like a government license for some and it was deleted from the new classification scheme in final passage. Among the foes of registration was Rep. Cannon, who found the existing law already quite clear on the divisions needed between classes:

> The house will observe that the law as it now is marks plainly the difference between a newspaper which has a regular list of subscribers and between an advertising sheet which is issued primarily as an advertising sheet and supplied free or at nominal rate; and I say again I doubt if the English language can make the distinction plainer than it now is made in the law.

Moreover, Cannon objected to the flat rate for all periodicals, which were, he noted, paying only one-seventeenth of the cost of transportation and delivery. He supported the continued low rate for newspapers, arguing:

> As to the matter of revenue when compared with the expenditures which this matter involves, I will say that the rate of postage on both classes is too low, but I apprehend that you cannot raise the postage in this country.
> And it is no good argument because two cents a pound is too low and three cents a pound is too low to say you should reduce it all to two cents a pound. That is one reason. Now for another. The newspapers published weekly or more frequently than once a week go to the masses of people throughout the country, to the poor people, to the laboring people;

everybody takes them. It is the exclusive few as the rule who take the monthlies. The same argument would apply in this case that would apply in favor of supporting the common schools at public expense, but not the colleges.

In final enactment, the Act of March 3, 1879, drew up important criteria for second-class publications which survive to this day in U.S. Postal Service regulations. It required a publication to publish regularly from a known office of publication, to print unbound material and, the all-important fourth criterion:

> . . . The publication must be originated and published for the dissemination of information of a public character, or devoted to literature, the sciences, arts, or some special industry and have a *legitimate list of subscribers* [emphasis added]; provided, however, that nothing herein contained shall be so construed as to admit to the second-class rate regular publications designed primarily for advertising purposes or for free circulation at nominal rates.

As notable as the congressional colloquy in this matter is the state of American journalism at the time. The country was bursting forth with new western settlements at a tremendous rate, and demand for the news was burgeoning. Between 1870 and 1900, the U.S. doubled its population and quadrupled its daily newspapers. The numbers of copies increased sixfold. The newspapers clamoring for postal carriage were not the New York dailies of Horace Greeley or James Gordon Bennett; as Rep. Money noted on the House floor, many metropolitan newspapers had already left the mails so they could meet the Congressman's demand for a newspaper on his breakfast table. The *Journal of Commerce* had already invented the Pony Express to deliver its news from Philadelphia to New York.

Rep. Cannon said, on the House floor, it was the small town reader, the western reader, the common person, who depended upon the post for news.

Another Series of "Reforms"

In 1896, Congress was once again chasing "abuses of second-class mail, accused of costing the government $18 million a year."

The Loud Postage Reform bill in the 54th Congress would have maintained the paid subscriber rule and severely restricted sample copies. It would have excluded so-called "advertising journals" which maintained nominal lists of subscribers and then built circulation by sending as many as a million "sample copies" to patrons who had not requested them. It would have prohibited newspapers from sending sections or parts alone, a practice then regularly followed by Sunday newspapers. It would have curtailed the widespread practice of luring subscribers with bonuses, premiums and clubbing rates. Loud believed the bill would save as much as $15-20 million a year. ANPA endorsed the bill even though in doing so its member newspapers would have surrendered the sample copy (unrequested mail) privilege.

Loud's reforms were . . . opposed by the advertising publications and some businesses, though the National Board of Trade endorsed it. The bill died in the 55th Congress. Nevertheless, it was a stepping stone to a more intense examination of postal reform.

Congress began a thorough investigation of the second-class controversy in 1906. The investigation led to a re-endorsement of the rule by the Joint Commission of Congress on Second-Class Mail Matter, led by Sen. Boies Penrose of Pennsylvania and Rep. Jessee Overstreet of Indiana. The commission was to explore whether or not revenue should cover costs in all classes of mail; if not, how to define that matter to be carried at a loss to the government, and (after a decade of legislative frustration), how the existing law could be changed to carry out the recommended policy.

The Commission . . . concluded:

> First.   That the class of objects intended to be given the second-class privilege are instrumentalities for the dissemination of the current knowledge of the world, whether relating to public affairs, literature, art, or science.
>
> Second.   That in order to get the benefit of this special rate this instrumentality must exist in response to a general public demand.
>
> Third.   That the instrumentality of public enlightenment so privileged shall not be perverted to a commercial purpose.
>
> While no one, perhaps, of these ideas is explicitly expressed in the statute, they are all involved so to speak in its texture . . .
>
> The idea that the thing must be issued in response to public demand was embodied principally in the requirement that it must have a legitimate list of subscribers, but it lies equally at the root of the requirement that the publication shall not be for free circulation, or for circulation at nominal rates.
>
> The idea that the publication must be kept true to its educational function in the dissemination of useful information and not commercially exploited is expressed with some distinctness in the proviso against its being designed primarily for advertising purposes.

The Commission recommended retention of the paid subscriber rule and stringent enforcement of it by postal officials. Less objective criteria would be unmanageable by the govenment if the goal was to weed out advertising publications:

> If the existence of a public demand can be guaranteed by the amendments already suggested, the question of primary advertising design will very largely solve itself . . .   It has been the experience of the postal administration, that it is much safer, where there is a strong suggestion of advertising purpose, to proceed to ascertain the fact by an inquiry into the nature of the circulation rather than to attempt to pass directly upon the design itself.

The Commission noted that the Post Office Department was operating in the black for once, siphoning off the urgent need to raise second-class rates, but it also found continuing value in those low rates, in the educational value of the press, even though it mused that the goal had been only partially met because of the difficulties in enforcement. Still, it noted, the Congress had created the rates for a historic purpose, which it wished to continue. But subjective judgment based upon the content of the publication rather than the objective paid subscriber rule, "would be to set up a censorship of the press."

The paid subscriber rule continued to be regarded with favor through the twentieth century in various ways, through Congressional reaffirmation in laws on nonprofit mail and citations in various court reviews on other matters, without questioning its validity. On the contrary, the right of a mail recipient to reject offensive, unrequested mail further affirms the Congressional intent to give the recipient ultimate control over his mailbox. In upholding that statute, Chief Justice Burger expressed concern over a proliferation of unrequested material in the mailbox:

> Today's merchandising methods, the plethora of mass mailings sub-sidized by low postal rates and the growth of the sale of large mailing lists . . . have changed the mailman from a carrier of primarily private communications . . . and have made him an adjunct of the mass mailer who sends unsolicited and often unwanted mail into every home. It places no strain on the doctrine of judicial notice to obseve that whether measured by pieces or pounds, Everyman's mail today is made up overwhelmingly of material he did not seek from persons he does not know. And all too often it is matter he finds offensive.

With postal reorganization in 1970, the long tradition of newspapers and magazines traveling through the mails at less than their direct costs to the government—at least arguably so—came to an end. With the exception of the phased assumption of costs by the in-county newspapers, all mail must bear its own attributable costs. Also, with the exception of the in-county newspaper mail, each class must contribute a share of the institutional or overhead costs of running the Postal Service.

Even with the new rate-setting mechanisms, second-class mail is generally less expensive than third-class mail largely because of the statutory requirement that cultural value must be considered in rate-making. In this way, and through the revenue foregone appropriation, Congress continues to signify its intention to encourage the dissemination of news and information through the mail.

Congress has explored many times the method for determining which mail belongs in the "newspaper class" of mail and many times has settled upon a reader demand test as the most effective criterion in the class.

It is not, of course, the only criterion for second-class mail. Were it in-validated, a publication would still be judged by whether it is regularly issued, has a known office of publication and is not designed for advertising purposes, which, by postal regulation, means it must not carry more than 75 percent advertising in more than half of its issues.

Those criteria could be easily met by a publication that is a "shopper" today, but would find it easy to insert so-called canned promotional copy touting particular products or other commercially oriented copy. Sparing itself the tremendous overhead of the newspapers in paying news reporters, photographers and editors, such a publication could fill with copy from retail catalogs, reprint the ubiquitous public relations firms' press releases, or borrow liberally from food manufacturers' recipe books to make up 25 percent of its content. Could the Postal Service determine that the "news" in these publications did not meet the criteria intended to delimit the intended recipients of second-class mail? It could not do so without judgments on the inherent value of the material, which would be unconstitutionally invasive beyond tolerance.

If the long-standing tradition of encouraging the circulation of mailed news and literature through second-class mail is constitutionally valid itself . . .the rules governing its manifestation must prevent the government from imposing its cultural taste upon the readers. The rules must be devoid of content judgment [and] political preference . . . ANPA believes the paid subscriber rule has been fashioned by Congress with the First Amendment in mind as a valid way of encouraging distribution of news and literature for the benefit of an informed and educated public. To remove the rule would be to open the second class to any unrequested publication that would take the trouble to reprint the grist of the press release mill or the puff pieces of commerce without engaging in reportage at all. To leave the rule in place is to tell the appellee that it may use the government's mail carriers to deliver its product, but to enjoy the second-class rate and service endowed by Congress, it must let the recipients of the mail prove that it is entitled to the rate. This test was devised and refined over a period of years to perform a legitimate public purpose. Years of debate have failed to produce a practicable and viable alternative.

Joint Operating Agreements: An Overview

by Marie Parsons

A joint operating agreement is a business arrangement peculiar to U.S. newspapers under which two or more separately owned newspapers may conduct their business affairs as partners while they maintain independent news

Marie Parsons is instructor of communication, University of Alabama; co-ordinator of High School/Minorities Activities, University of Alabama; and director of the Alabama Scholastic Press Association. She was a reporter for the *Morning Democrat* (Davenport, Iowa), the *Southern Illinois* in (Carbondale, Illinois), the *Tuscaloosa* (Alabama) *News*, and correspondent for the *Birmingham* (Alabama) *News*. She was awarded first place, news, in 1984, in competition sponsored by the National Federation of Press Women. Parsons received a B.A. in journalism from the University of Minnesota and an M.A. in communication from the University of Alabama. [©1986, Marie Parsons]

and editorial operations. There are twenty-three such partnerships, involving forty-six daily newspapers, which are permitted to jointly operate under special exemption from antitrust laws which restrict monopolistic ventures in industry in general. The special exemptions are allowed by the Newspaper Preservation Act of 1970 in which Congress approved twenty-two existing agreements and gave the U.S. Department of Justice authority to sanction additional partnerships and to supervise changes in existing joint operating agreements.

The Newspaper Preservation Act exempts from the antitrust laws "certain combinations and arrangements necessary for the survival of failing newspapers." In the NPA Declaration of Policy, Congress states:

> In the public interest of maintaining a newspaper press editorially and reportorially independent and competitive in all parts of the United States, it is hereby declared to be the public policy of the United States to preserve the publication of newspapers in any city, community, or metropolitan area where a joint operating arrangement has been hereto fore entered into because of economic distress or is hereafter effected in accordance with the provisions of this Act.

The act defines a joint newspaper operating arrangement as a contract between two or more newspaper owners for the publication of two or more newspapers in which they agree to operate together in one or more of the following areas: printing; time, methods and field of publication; allocation of production facilities; distribution; advertising solicitation; circulation solicitation; business department; establishment of advertising rates; establishment of circulation rates; and revenue distribution. At the same time, the act forbids any merger, combinations or amalgamations of editorial or reportorial staffs and demands that editorial policies be set independently by each newspaper.

The act defines a failing newspaper as "a newspaper publication which, regardless of its ownership or affiliations, is in probable danger of financial failure." Under the antitrust exemption section of the act, newspapers already in joint operation may continue such activity, provided only one publication is financially sound and they may amend their contracts provided they file the new terms with the Department of Justice. New joint operating agreements require the approval of the attorney general who must agree that only one of the newspapers involved is financially sound before he signs the consent. The act also permits reinstatement of any joint operating agreement which the courts had previously held unlawful under any antitrust law.

While some newspaper operations had been jointly managed since the 1930s, their legality was not questioned until the mid-1960s when the U.S. Department of Justice focused attention on a partnership in Tucson, Arizona, and challenged it in court for monopolistic activities, demanding that the relationship be severed. That move apparently signaled owners involved in similar agreements that their business arrangements were in jeopardy for they banded together to propose to Congress that the Tucson newspapers and all others jointly operating be permitted to continue activities under an umbrella of protection from the law and the justice department. After more than five years, the newspaper owners won congressional and presidential approval which overrides the courts' decision that the Tucson arrangement defied the laws of antitrust.

Since the enactment of the Newspaper Preservation Act, the Department of Justice has approved four new agreements, one of which has since dissolved; the Department also has stricken from the original list of twenty-two, one operation which did not qualify. In St. Louis, the *Globe-Democrat* ended its associaiton with the *Post-Dispatch* in 1984 and continued independently. Weak members of other agreements have been warned that their partnerships may be terminated when contracts expire. There remain fewer than thirty cities with competing dailies operating separately which could eventually wish to join operations. Since 1980, more than thirty competing newspapers have elected to merge, while only three chose to apply for joint operation approval. None of those were turned down. Of about 1,500 U.S. cities with daily newspapers, about one hundred have two newspapers under the same ownership; three cities have two newspapers separately owned but jointly operating; and about twenty-seven cities have two newspapers owned and separately operating. About 1,400 newspapers, of a total 1,700, are in one-newspaper cities.

A Brief History

The pattern of newspaper ownership was once that of small, family-owned enterprises, operating from their own shops and determining business and editorial policy within the parameters of family and community. In 1910, there was an all-time high of 2,202 English-language dailies in the United States. More than half of the cities with newspapers had more than one newspaper, and it was unusual to find a small town without its own daily. Ninety-seven percent were independently owned. A rising standard of living in the early twentieth century brought the daily newspaper into more American homes, with some households buying more than one newspaper per day. The ratio of newspaper circulation to households peaked in 1930 with about 1.3 newspapers per home. Then the number of newspapers per household dropped in the early stages of the Great Depression to 1.1. Many private owners of newspapers, pressured by a tightening economy, sold out to newspaper chains in the decade after the stock market crash; by 1930, nearly 250 newspapers were chain owned, up from about fifty-four twenty years earlier. The number of newspapers, on a slow decline during the 1920s, dipped drastically during the 1930s and stabilized halfway into the following decade at about 1,750, down about twenty-two percent from the peak in 1910. Three out of four American towns had no daily of their own. By 1960, almost one-third of U.S. dailies were owned by chains.

It was during the decline in newspaper prosperity in the early 1930s, when there were many failures and mergers, that the newspaper industry itself developed the joint operating agreement to reduce costs. Under the arrangements, two competing newspapers, one of which was in financial difficulty, combined their production and business operations, substantially reducing costs by eliminating duplication of equipment and manpower and especially by efficient utilization of expensive plant facilites. At the same time, each maintained its editorial independence. The first joint operating agreement was signed in 1933 by the *New Mexico State Tribune* (now the *Albuquerque Tribune*), and the *Albuquerque Journal*. E.W. Scripps, owner of the distressed *State Tribune*, and T.M. Pepperday, owner of the *Journal*, brought their newspapers together in one plant and combined advertising, circulation, sales, and distribution, and agreed to share profits. By the end of the decade, newspapers in three other cities had signed operating contracts.

The cause for newspaper preservation and the will to safeguard the institution were at their strongest in the days of the first agreement, when broadcast media were not yet a threat, when innovative survival techniques were a necessity of a depressed economy, and when government control was relatively undeveloped. At mid-century, newspapers began to feel the effects of audience loss as postwar dollars were paid down on television sets in millions of homes and an expansive and relieved American public welcomed entertainment in the media to replace the absence of frontline dispatches. A steady stream of joint operations (at the rate of one per year) were arranged by the newspaper industry as government and society went about their own adjustments to peace and prosperity. And then came the sixties, a period when tradition declined in value and its spokesman, the daily newspaper, lost clout, too. Big industry was under early attack for everything from discrimination to pollution to unfair trade practices and by the middle of the decade the attack hit the newspaper industry in the form of a challenge to its growing use of the joint operation as a management strategy.

While the newspaper industry had been as ready to adopt competitive practices as other businesses, the Department of Justice had initiated very few proceedings against newspapers, probably because of government sensitivity to infringement of press freedom. Before 1963, only eight major suits had been filed against newspapers charged with antitrust violations, and only five of those were instigated by government. In 1963, however, the antitrust division of the Department of Justice increased the number of its actions against the newspaper industry; in 1965, it filed its first challenge to a joint operating agreement. Suit was filed against the *Tucson Daily Citizen* and the *Arizona Daily Star* (also published in Tucson), questioning the recent purchase of the *Star* by the *Citizen* as well as their old (1940) joint operating agreement, which another prospective buyer had wanted to continue. The U.S. District Court ruled that the merger "virtually eliminated the likelihood of renewed competition" between the two papers in violation of the Sherman Anti-trust Act, and it ordered divestiture. (The order was affirmed later by the Supreme Court.) At the same time, the district court found that the joint operating agreement also violated the Sherman Act; in its affirmation, the Supreme Court opinion stated: "The purpose of the agreement was to end any business or commercial competition between the two papers and to that end three types of controls were imposed . . . price fixing . . . profit pooling . . . market sharing." The court did allow for joint operation by the two newspapers under terms that would eliminate the illegal price/market/profit controls. The Supreme Court further stated that to be complete the defense must satisfy three criteria: 1) the company must face liquidation; 2) it must have attempted reorganization under the Bankruptcy Act; and 3) it must have attempted to sell to someone other than the local competitor. The court found that the burden of proving those conditions had not been satisfied.

It was at that point that a major campaign was begun to make joint operating agreements legal by the initiation of federal legislation. The moving force behind the proposed legislation was the newspaper publishers who owned the papers which were jointly operating. Representatives of the newspaper industry said the proposal only asked for limited exemption from antitrust statutes so publishers could conduct businesses as single-ownership papers can with respect to pricing, marketing, and profits. They would not be able to engage in predatory practices aimed at killing existing competition or driving out new competition. Leading the opposition were the Department of Justice and the Federal Trade Commission, newspaper unions, and small publishers. They said the proposal would give the newspapers monopoly power and permit them to choke off competition and enhance their profits beyond reason.

William A. Small, Jr., owner of the *Tucson Daily Citizen*, called the joint operation with the *Arizona Star* successful both commercially and in terms of newspaper quality: "Both newspapers are today (1967) on a sound financial footing . . . the *Daily Citizen* now costs the reader less per page than it did in 1940 . . . Advertising rates have increased a lesser amount than did those of 93 percent of the other newspapers in its circulation category." He said that without the joint economics of joint operation and solicitation of advertising and circulation, the *Citizen* would fail. He continued, "Separate staffing in these commercial areas would eliminate many of the economies which brought the paper together in the first place." The *Citizen* would suffer from a weaker competitive position since it did not have a Sunday paper, he added.

The hearings also yielded statements from owners and publishers who opposed passage of the bill. Eugene Cervi, editor and publisher of the *Rocky Mountain Journal*, a spirited business and public, affairs weekly, called the proposal an "unabashed attempt to legalize practices now prohibited by laws rarely enforced . . .This bill would shut down in time the market place of ideas and ultimately see this significant means of communication gravitate into the hands of a dictatorial elite." Bad newspapers, he argued, ought to die.

Elmer Brown, president of the International Typographic Union, which led the opposition of union interests, said workers were concerned for the envelopment of the industry by monopolistic forces interested in profit rather than in journalism and public service: "They are preoccupied with operating statements and balance sheets. It is for this reason that chain newspapers are notably absent from lists of the best newspapers in the United States."

Ben Bagdikian, currently of the University of California, Berkeley, a former reporter, and a press critic, opposed the bill and favored an alternative offered by the American Newspaper Guild that proposed that failing papers be offered at a fair market price before being merged or killed. "I would prefer an honest, outright merger to an inhibited hybrid that comes from combined business and advertising operations," Bagdikian said. He charged that the act would, at best, give temporary relief for business problems which were genuine; at its worst, it would encourage support for newspaper failures arising from a failure to keep up with technology and good management practices. Once caught in the downward spiral, a term used often during the hearings, failure is inevitable he added. Bagdikian said the joint operations would prevent new independent operators from starting new newspapers and that two newspapers operating jointly would eventually adjust to each other editorially as well.

William J. Farson, executive vice–president of the American Newspaper Guild, which represented 32,000 reporters, photographers, and commercial department employees, said the bill would place the entire newspaper industry outside the reach of antitrust laws and still not accomplish its aim of preserving the historic independence of the press. "Senate Bill 1312 would actually encourage and accelerate the trend toward monopoly and chain-owner dominance of the nation's newspaper industry by legitimatizing certain business practices that are used to discourage or squelch competition, and which are now properly forbidden under antitrust laws," Farson said.

The House of Representatives passed the Act, 292–87; the Senate passed it, 64-13.

The Newspaper Preservation Act sanctioned the joint operating agreements concept when it passed in 1970, but it did not remove the controversy surrounding the concept. Newspapers which have sought the shelter of the act have met with resistance in obtaining approval and have not always enjoyed the success and relief the agreements gave the newspapers which opted for joint operation in pre-NPA days. Even those papers which were already jointly operating when the act passed are now facing financial problems that the strategy may not be powerful enough to solve. Of the four pairs of newspapers which have applied for protection since 1970, two weathered fierce battles to gain approval and one dissolved after severe internal disagreement within the partnership. At least two of the pre-existing agreements have been seriously and repeatedly challenged by competing media and two others have ended. Others with expiration dates in the near future appear to be in jeopardy of cancellation.

In 1974, U.S. Attorney General William B. Saxbe approved the operating agreement in Anchorage, Alaska, of the *Anchorage Daily News* and the *Anchorage Daily Times*. The *News*, with a circulation of 15,000 gave up its Sunday publication to the *Times* which had a daily circulation of 43,000.

The smaller *Daily News*, published by Katherine Fanning, filed a $16.5 million suit in early 1977 charging that the *Times* was managing circulation to the detriment of the *News* and that by taking over the *News's* biggest asset, the city's only Sunday paper, it had damaged it irreparably. The *Times* paid the *News* $750,000 when the parties agreed to terminate, and Fanning raised capital to build her own printing plant by selling a majority interest in the paper to C.K. McClatchy, head of a Sacramento-based chain. Within two years of the split, the *News* had almost tripled its circulation to 39,000 and added a Sunday edition nearly that big to challenge the *Times* for circulation.

In 1977, a request for joint operation in Ohio was submitted to public hearing in a quasi-judicial process with an administrative law judge presiding. Combination of the *Cincinnati Post* and the *Cincinnati Enquirer*, subject of the hearing, was strenuously opposed by the unions and suburban weeklies which charged that the *Post* had been intentionally bled by its owner, Scripps-Howard, so that it could qualify as a failing newspaper and enter into operation with the stronger *Enquirer*, a Gannett paper. Evidence was introduced at the hearing that the *Post* had paid overcharges to Scripps-Howard for use of stories (an allegation which the judge presiding at the hearing found to be true); failed to explore starting a Sunday edition as recommended by its consultants and business manager to forestall further decline; did not raise subscription prices in 1977 to match an increase by the *Enquirer*, although this had been the practice for twenty years; and did not pursue survival by offering the paper for sale. Stephen Barnett, professor of law at the University of California, charged the

Joint Newspaper Operating Arrangements

City	Signed	Newspaper	Approx. Daily Circ.	(as of Jan. 1, 1986) Owner
Albuquerque, N. Mex.	1933	Journal(mS)	93,000	Independent
		Tribune(e)	44,000	Scripps-Howard
El Paso, Texas	1936	Times(mS)	55,000	Gannett
		Herald-Post(e)	32,000	Scripps
Nashville, Tenn.	1937	Tenessean(mS)	124,000	Gannett
		Banner(e)	72,000	independent
Evansville, Ind.	1938	Courier(m)	64,000	independent
		Press(e)	41,000	Scripps
Tucson, Ariz.	1940	Daily Star(mS)	81,000	Pulitzer
		Citizen(e)	61,000	Gannett
Chattanooga, Tenn.	1942	News-Free Press		independent
(terminated)	1946	Times		independent
Tulsa, Okla.	1941	World(mS)	134,000	independent
		Tribune(e)	77,000	independent
Madison, Wis.	1948	State Journal(mS)	76,000	Lee
		Capital Times(e)	30,000	independent
Bristol, Tenn.	1950			
Lincoln, Neb.	1950	Journal(e)	45,000	independent
		Star(m)	33,000	Lee
Fort Wayne, Ind.	1950	News-Sentinel(e)	63,000	Knight-Ridder
		Journal-Gaz.(mS)		independent
Birmingham, Ala.	1950	New (eS)	165,000	Newhouse
		Post-Herald	60,000	Scripps-Howard
Salt Lake City, Utah	1952	Tribune(mS)	110,000	independent
		Deseret News(eS)	64,000	independent

Post's "handsome losses were produced" so that it could claim failure and enter into a joint agreement with the blessing of the Department of Justice.

The Department of Justice, after a seven-week hearing, acepted the recommendation of its antitrust division and the presiding officer, and approved the agreement. It found the overcharges by Scripps were insignificant and that the proposal for a Sunday edition came too late to save the paper. The *Post* was required to open its financial records in support of its losses, something that had not happened before, not even during the hearings for the NPA bill. The court also ruled that a failing newspaper does not have to try to sell the paper to an outside buyer before it resorts to joint operation.

Attorney General Benjamin R. Civiletti confirmed the Cincinnati finding that the failing paper need not seek to sell outside when he approved the joint agreement in 1980 between the *Chattanooga Times* and the *Chattanooga News-Free* Press in Chattanooga, Tennessee, and added the stipulation that a publisher

Shreveport, La.	1953	Times(mS)	79,000	Gannett
		Journal(e)	26,000	independent
Franklin/Oil City, Pa.	1956-	Derrick(m)	17,000	independent
(terminated)	1985	News-Herald(e)	9,000	independent
Knoxville, Tenn.	1957	News-Sentinel(eS)	98,000	Scripps-Howard
		Journal(m)	59,000	Gannett
St. Louis, Mo.	1957	Globe-Democrat(m)	210,000	Newhouse
(terminated)	1984	Post-Dispatch(eS)	236,000	Pulitzer
Charleston, W.Va.	1958	Gazette(mS)	54,000	independent
		Daily Mail(e)	54,000	Clay
Columbus, Ohio	1959	Dispatch(eS)	276,000	independent
	1985	Citizen-Journal(m)	119,000	Scripps-Howard
		(killed on 12/31/85)		
Pittsburgh, Pa.	1961	Press(eS)	260,000	Scrips-Howard
		Post-Gazette(m)	120,000	Block
Honolulu, Hawaii	1962	Star-Bulletin(e)	112,000	Gannett
		Advertiser(mS)	83,000	
San Francisco, Calif.	1964	Chronicle(mS)	536,000	independent
		Examiner(eS)	148,000	Hearst
Miami, Fla.	1966	Herald(mS)	420,000	Knight-Ridder
		News(e)	63,000	Cox
Anchorage, Alaska	1974	Daily News(mS)	190,000	McClatchy
(terminated)	1984	Daily Times(eS)	45,000	independent
Cincinnati, Ohio	1979	Enquirer(mS)	190,000	Gannett
		Post(e)	130,000	Scripps-Howard
Chattanooga, Tenn.	1980	News-Free Press(eS)	55,000	independent
		Times(m)	44,000	independent
Seattle, Wash.	1982	Times (all day S)	223,000	independent
		Post-Intelligencer	192,000	Hearst

who refuses to entertain offers to buy must show that new owners could not materially improve the newspaper's financial condition. The Antitrust division had originally recommended against approval of the joint agreement on grounds that the *Times* was not failing and again later because the *Times* had allegedly consummated the deal without approval, but then, in a supplemental report, recommended approval of the request, citing the *Times'* contention that it could operate only four to six more weeks without approval.

The decision by Attorney General William French Smith to approve a joint operating agreement between the *Seattle Post–Intelligencer* and the *Seattle Times* became the subject of court case. The attorney general's decision was rejected by the district court, but on appeal, the court of appeals reversed the lower court decision and concluded that the attorney general's ruling fulfilled the intent of the Newspaper Preservation Act. The court concluded that while a newspaper had to prove there were no buyers and no alternatives, the *Times*, a Hearst newspaper, had satisfied the burden. The Supreme Court of the United States sustained the appelate court's opinion. The main point of the Seattle case was the court's decision that the financial condition of the parent company, Hearst, was irrelevant to the failure of the newspaper in question.

In 1982, the *Honolulu Star-Bulletin* and the *Honolulu Advertiser* were cleared of a threat to their joint operating agreement when the Honolulu City Council dropped its antitrust suit filed four years earlier. The suit had charged that the agreement was monopolistic and anti-competitive and unfairly controlled charges for legal advertising the city did in the papers. After a five-week trial which ended in a hung jury, a district court judge dismissed the suit on the grounds that the city had waited too long—seventeen years—to file suit against the 1962 arrangement.

An Overview of Current JOA Trends

Joint operating contracts still resemble one another as they did in the early days when one was often almost copied from the last or from others in a chain; however, the sharing plans are being reassessed as old contracts expire. Most of the contracts allot expenses and profits to each publisher based on circulation, advertising linage, or other means of measuring the business activity of each. In several cases, especially prior to the Department of Justice surveillance and when two papers were relatively matched in strength, profits were shared equally. Several agreements accomplish equal sharing by assigning half ownership of the intermediate agency to each publisher. One pact, since terminated, shared profits by assigning half ownership of each paper to the other partner.

"Five or ten years ago, the stronger paper in Philadelphia or Washington or Cleveland might have jumped at the chance to form a JOA," says newspaper consultant Bruce Thorp. "But, five or ten years ago, the competition from suburban papers was not as intense, and papers that were losing money weren't losing a lot. What's happening now is that papers are losing a lot if they are losing. The *Washington Post* was not interested in a JOA to save the *Star* because it would have had to absorb all the losses from the *Star*. The joint revenue would not have been enough to offset the losses." Most analysts agree. Dwight Teeter, professor of journalism at the University of Texas, notes, "If it is clear that the second paper will go out of business, it makes more sense for the bigger paper to back off and let it fail. But if there is a second newspaper that is weak but still drains away some advertising the big paper would like to have, then a joint operating agreement to corner 100 percent of the market may make some sense."

Joint operations may become a moot issue. Two of the last four applications for exemption have been seriously challenged in long and financially exhausting battles for newspapers; litigation is expensive. Small papers in partnerships are becoming smaller and at least one-fourth of those face termination before the end of the decade. Failing newspapers eligible for joint operation are passing up that option and are instead folding.

Proponents of joint operation look at the bright side—only one newspaper in fifty involved has failed in fifty years compared with an overall attrition of twelve in fifty. The one failure and the several weakenings are indicator enough that joint operation is not an all-powerful tool the industry is using to produce unfair profits, they add. Even if a newspaper fails, its survival for an average of twenty-eight years has served the public during the grace period.

Opponents point to some of the same facts in support of their position. If newspapers are no longer turning to joint oepration, it affirms their stance that the strategy does not save failing newspapers; the continued weakening of the several smaller papers confirms it, they say. A newspaper which could not survive under a joint arrangement can still survive under independent operations and even thrive, given the opportunity to escape the contract. Nevertheless, the rate at which chains are buying the smaller papers under joint operations indicates to opponents that joint management is merely a technique to build up an unattractive buy until a buyer comes along.

JOAs: Protection From Competition; Preservation of Monopoly Profits

by Stephen R. Barnett

[Supporters of this bill argue that] the bill's professed objective of stemming the trend toward local newspaper monopoly, of preserving two newspaper voices within a city—especially a city within their constituency—is so important and beneficial as to outweigh whatever harm the bill might do, for example, to the principles of the antitrust laws . . .

This seems a reasonable point of view, and if that were really the choice presented—a choice between preserving the second newspaper and insisting on particular forms of business organization in the newspaper industry—I would not be here today . . . But, this bill, quite apart from the harm it would do, would not do any good. Its artful name notwithstanding, this legislation is not needed to "preserve" the two newspapers in Madison, Wisconsin. There is nothing in the Supreme Court's decision in the Tucson case, or in the list of papers that have failed in the past that poses any serious threat to the continued existence of second newspaper voices in the cities where they now exist.

This bill is . . .the most effective means imaginable to abort and throttle the new newspaper voices that can realistically be expected to appear in the future. If preservation and encouragement of diverse newspaper voices is the overriding consideration, the bill should be defeated.

What is the evidence offered in support of the claim that the bill is needed to preserve second newspapers in Madison and other cities? Certainly not financial statements of the allegedly weak papers. What is offered, basically, is the fact that many daily newspapers in American cities have failed during recent decades, and that the nubmer of two-publisher cities has decreased to approximately 63. As Senator [Everett] Dirksen put it at the Senate hearings on June 12, 1969, "that would indicate that there is a progressive mortality in this business and . . . so the ultimate end is no communities with two papers."

Throughout the hearings already held, and doubtless in these hearings as well, the supporters of the bill will toll the list of defunct metropolitan dailies, leading up to their prize relic, the New York *World Journal Tribune*.

Stephen R. Barnett is professor of law, Boalt Hall School of Law, the University of California. He is a specialist in communication law, copyrights, and torts. At Harvard College, he was president of the *Harvard Crimson*, the student newspaper; and was elected to Phi Beta Kappa, graduating magna cum laude, with highest honors, in slavic languages and literature. He received his law degree in 1962 from the School of Law, Harvard University, where he was notes editor of the *Harvard Law Review*. Mr. Barnett was law clerk for both Judge Henry Friendly, U.S. Court of Appeals, 1962-1963; and Supreme Court Justice William O. Brennan, 1963-1964. He was in private law practice, 1964-1967, and has been on the faculty of the University of California since then, with the exception of 1977-1979 when he was Deputy Solicitor General, U.S. Department of Justice.[This article is excerpted, then edited, from the September 1969, hearings before the Anti-Trust Subcommittee of the Committee on the Judiciary, House of Representatives, ninety-first Congress, on matters relating to HR 279, proposal to establish anti-trust exemptions for Joint Operating Agreements.]

The list is admittedly long and sad, and I do not propose to get involved in the questions other witnesses have raised concerning why these papers may have failed, and whether it may not have been due to poor management, especially in the case of the many Hearst papers . . .

With only a very few exceptions, the papers whose deaths the publishers toll—the *Chicago American, Detroit Times, San Francisco News, Los Angeles Examiner, Cleveland News, Philadelphia Ledger, New York World Journal Tribune*, and so forth—were not second newspapers in their cities, but at least third papers. Their passing did not reduce their cities to a single newspaper voice; those cities in fact still have two publishers. And the deaths of those papers don't necessarily evidence a trend that will continue, unless stopped, until the number of publishers in each city is further reduced from two to one. The failure of third or fourth newspapers—newspapers competing with at least two others, and with at least one other in the same morning or afternoon market— tells us nothing about the likelihood of failure after the number of papers has been reduced to two, *each of which has a monopoly of its morning or afternoon market* . . .

The conclusion that the bill is not needed to preserve newspaper voices in the cities with joint-operating agreements is also verified by a simple fact of economic behavior. If the less successful of the two papers in town was on the way to failure—as supporters of the bill contend must be the case—it would be irrational for the more successful publisher to agree to split his profits with the other, rather than waiting for the monopoly profits that would eventually accrue to him alone. The willingness of the stronger of the two papers to enter into a profit-sharing agreement demonstrates that, at least in the publisher's opinion, the alternative would not be monopoly, but competition. The argument made to the Congress by the joint-operating publishers is thus belied by their own business judgment . . .

The facts show no recent trend towards the disappearance of second voices in cities larger than 50,000, and certainly none in cities larger than 200,000. And this takes account, of course, not only of the joint-agreement cities, but also of cities where two competing papers operate independently of each other— including cities no larger than Little Rock (243,000) and Colorado Springs (144,000), and Champaign-Urbana (132,000).

One must then take account of the fact—which the supporters of this legislation have consistently ignored—that the two papers need not bear the high costs of operating independently of each other. The Supreme Court made clear in the Tucson case that joint operating agreements are not illegal as such, but only if they involve price fixing, profit pooling, or compacts not to compete. The two newspapers in Madison or elsewhere are thus free, without any need for this bill, to enter into joint operating agreements providing for a wide variety of joint functions and thus far large cost savings compared to independent operation. The Justice Department, too, has consistently taken this position, and has never suggested that all joint-operating agreements are illegal. In the statement it recently filed concerning the joint-operating plan now proposed by the Tucson newspapers to comply with the Supreme Court's decree, the Department has agreed to provisions for joint printing, and joint distributions, and joint administrative, accounting and business functions not related to sales efforts, and a combination advertising rate (so long as the discount is based on the cost savings), and (subject to a hearing) a joint circulation department. And the Department has further stated, with respect even to a joint advertising sales force, that it does not regard this as a *per se* violation of the Sherman Act, and would consider it permissible if the papers could demonstrate that the resulting economies were in whole or part essential to the preservation of one of the papers.

Until the negotiations in the Tucson case have been concluded and the resulting arrangement examined, and until at least some publishers have tried to operate in the cost-saving manner that would be legal under the existing law, how can the Congress responsibly honor the publishers' claim that they could not afford to do so? . . .

In an editorial on July 2, 1969, the [*Wall Street*] *Journal* opposed this legislation, and stated: "If a newspaper needs more help than the economies of a joint printing and circulation setup, there is a real question as to just how well it is and has been serving its market.". . .

But even the newspaper that does need "more help," and that in the *Journal's* view probably deserves to die and be replaced by a better paper, could get the help under the existing law. The Justice Department has consistently stated that it will evaluate each case on an individual basis, and has taken a position in the Tucson case, as I just noted, that even a joint sales force may be permitted if necessary to preserve one of the papers. Further, the Supreme Court in its Tucson decision made clear—exposing as a red herring another argument previously relied on by supporters of the bill—that the "failing company" doctrine is no less applicable to joint-operating agreements than to mergers. So if a paper is truly "failing," it could still get, under the present law, all the otherwise illegal advantages that the publishers seek to get on a wholesale, permanent basis through enactment of this bill.

It becomes clear, then, that what the publishers really want is not relief from financial hardship, not preservation of the second newspaper, and not an economic situation in which the paper can make a decent profit. All these advantages are available under present law. What the publishers want is protection from competition, and the right to pile up monopoly profits.

In sum, I submit that the publishers who want this bill passed have failed to demonstrate any need for it. Second newspapers have not been failing in the class of cities affected by the bill, and the cost savings realizable through legitimate joint-operating agreements make the failure of well-managed papers even less likely. The worthy public objective of preserving newspaper voices simply has nothing to gain from enactment of this bill.

Its enactment would, however, damage the public interest in a number of important ways . . .

First, . . . the anti-trust laws do embody an important national policy. This bill would dishonor that policy in the most fundamental of ways. We are dealing here not with the Robinson-Patman Act, not with some technicality about relevant markets or the like, and not with an industry subject to other forms of regulation.

We are dealing with price-fixing, agreements not to compete, and collusively created monopoly—the most fundamental violations imaginable of the competitive principles underlying our economy. Given the fact that so many aspects of joint-operating agreements are permissible under present law, the entire purpose of this bill is to legalize those that the Supreme Court condemned—the price-fixing, profit-pooling, and market-controlling agreements whose purpose is, in the Court's words, "to end any business or commercial competition between the two papers."

To enact special legislation legalizing this conduct and encouraging its proliferation would be, in my view, an indefensible elevation of private over public interest . . .

Second. Enactment of this legislation, purportedly designed to nurture newspaper competition, would in fact cripple such competition. Joint-operated agreements of the type approved by this bill constitute the highest barriers possible, short of a government-granted monopoly, to the entry of new competing papers into the metropolitan market . . .

In San Francisco, the joint-operating agreement there has killed one competitor within the past year. The fact is that technological developments are now creating once again the possibility of new competition in the metropolitan newspaper markets.

It is no coincidence, I suggest, that just as the prospect of new competition arises, the metropolitan publishers have mounted such an all-out effort to get this bill passed. What they want is protection not from failure, but from competition.

Especially misleading is the publishers' argument that the bill would simply allow separately owned papers to operate in the same way as a single publisher owning two papers. First, of course, the publishers have failed to show that the alternative to their joint-operating agreements is indeed single-publisher monopoly. But even if it were, such a monopoly would be much less of a barrier to the new competition.

As Assistant Attorney General [Richard W.] McLaren told the Senate Subcommittee—and as the *Wall Street Journal*, in its July 2 editorial, agreed: "It can be assumed that new competition will be more likely to enter a newspaper market occupied by one publisher, even though he publishes morning and evening papers, than it will a market with separate and ostensibly independent publishers bound together in an agreement to eliminate comercial competition . . ."

Third, and perhaps most important: If you enact this bill you will not be "maintaining the historic independence of the American press," as claimed by the declaration of policy in H.R. 279. You will be tampering with that independence in a most fundamental way.

Assistant Attorney General McLaren made part of the point in his Senate testimony. As he stated, it is essential to the independence and freedom of the press, and to the vital role of the press in our democratic society, that "newspapers . . . remain independent of government and deal with it at arm's length, affording government no immunity and seeking none from it." And he expressed his disbelief that, in the long run, "government promotes newspapers independence by granting newspaper special favors."

One aspect of the problem, is, thus, that enactment of this special-interest legislation for newspaper publishers would compromise the independence of the press vis-á-vis the government. It would undermine the vital ability of newspapers to report and criticize the activities of government without concern for favor or reprisal.

There is the additional point, also noted by McLaren, that the granting of this exemption for newspapers, on the theory of preserving voices of information and opinion, would surely invite pleas for comparable treatment from financially pressed broadcasters, book and magazine publishers, movie producers, and others likewise engaged in the business of expressing and disseminating views. And indeed, if this bill is passed on, what basis will the Congress deny those pleas?

But the bill's impact on the role of newspapers in this country would go much further. A joint-operating agreement such as the bill would approve makes it more difficult, at best, for competing newspapers to stay in business; at worst, it drives them out of business, and it also prevents new competing papers from getting started. The First Amendment provides that "Congress shall make no law abridging the freedom of . . . the press." This bill, in its impact on competing publishers, actual or potential, might well be held to abridge the freedom of the press.

The Supreme Court has stated, and it repeated in the Tucson case: "Freedom to publish means freedom for all and not for some. Freedom to publish is guaranteed by the Constitution, but freedom to combine to keep others from publishing is not." . . . In the recent *Red Lion* case upholding the FCC's "fairness doctrine" for broadcasters, the Supreme Court also declared: "It is the purpose of the First Amendment to preserve an uninhibited marketplace of ideas in which truth will ultimately prevail, rather than to countenance monopolization of that market, whether it be by the Government itself of a private license." By enacting this bill, the Congress would expressly sanction combinations to keep others from publishing; it would "countenance monopolization" of newspaper markets. The First Amendment quite possibly forbids such a law . . .

Perhaps the status of newspapers in this country should be changed so that, in place of the traditional independence of the press, certain publishers receive a special Congressional favor—almost a charter—which establishes and protects them as the daily newspaper monopoly in their particular city. And perhaps the government should asume—as it would then have to—the function of regulating the content of newspapers to assure, in the words of the Communications Act, "reasonable opportunity for the discussion of conflicting views on issues of public importance." I do not propose to discuss the merits of those questions.

The point I wish to make is simply that these are questions this Committee should consider. For this issue of a basic change in the role of America newspaper, of a coming together between newspapers and government, is squarely raised by the proposed "Newspaper Preservation Act."

. . .The objective of preserving newspapers is a worthy one indeed, but that no case has been made for the proposition that this legislation is needed to save any of the papers it is supposed to save. And while the bill would not do any good, it would do a lot of serious harm—by exempting some powerful corporations from basic free-enterprise principles designed to protect the public, by foreclosing daily newspaper competition forever from the metropolitan markets, and by tampering fundamentally with the historic independence of the press.

Types and Number of Intervention by Nations

	Tax Rates	Postal Rates	Tele. Rates	Trans. Rates	Educ./Research	Grants/Subsidies	Loans	Gov't. Ads	Agency Aid	Party Aid	Owner. Reg.	Price Reg.	NO. OF TYPES	PERCENTAGE
Austria	✓	✓	✓	✓		✓		✓					6	50
Belgium	✓	✓	✓	✓	✓	✓		✓				✓	8	66
Canada	✓	✓			✓	✓		✓			✓		6	50
Denmark	✓	✓	✓		✓		✓	✓					6	50
Finland	✓	✓	✓	✓	✓	✓		✓	✓	✓	.		9	75
France	✓	✓	✓	✓	✓	✓		✓	✓		✓	✓	10	83
Germany	✓	✓	✓		✓		✓	✓			✓		7	58
Iceland	✓						✓	✓		✓		✓	5	42
Ireland	✓				✓	✓		✓					4	33
Italy	✓	✓	✓	✓		✓	✓	✓	✓		✓	✓	10	83
Netherlands	✓	✓	✓	✓	✓	✓	✓	✓			✓	✓	10	83
Norway	✓	✓	✓	✓	✓	✓	✓	✓	✓	✓			10	83
Sweden	✓	✓	✓	✓	✓	✓	✓	✓	✓	✓	✓		11	92
Switzerland	✓	✓	✓		✓			✓					5	42
United Kingdom	✓	✓						✓			✓	✓	5	42
United States	✓	✓			✓			✓			✓		5	42
Frequency of Intervention	16	14	11	8	12	10	7	16	5	4	8	6	-	-
Percentage	100	87.5	68.9	50	75	62.5	43.8	100	31.3	25	50	37.5	-	-

(Source: Robert G. Picard,
Mass Comm Review;
Winter/Spring 1984)

Bibliography

Bagdikian, Ben J., "The Myth of Newspaper Poverty," *Columbia Journalism Review*, March/April 1979.

Barnett, Stephen R., "The Anchorage Failure," *Columbia Journalism Review*, May/June 1980.

———. "Combination Ad Rates," *Columbia Journalism Review*, May/June 1980.

———, "Fast Shuffle in Chattanooga," *Columbia Journalism Review*, November/December 1980.

———, Carlson, John H., "Newspaper Preservation Act: A Critique," *Indiana Law Journal*, 1970-71.

Coulson, David C., "Antitrust Law and the Media: Making Newspapers Safe for Democracy," *Journalism Quarterly*, Spring, 1980.

Holder, Dennis., "Joint Operating Agreements," *Washington Journalism Review*, November 1982.

"JOA—A 50-Year Record of Newspaper Life-Saving," *Editor and Publisher*, March 13, 1982, p. 14-15, 45.

Jones, Alex S., "Plight of the Weaker Nespapers," *The New York Times*, Nov. 12, 1983.

Newspaper Preservation Act, U.S. Public Law 91-353 (1970).

Oppenheim, S. Chesterfield, *Newspapers and the Antitrust Laws*, Michie (Charlottesville, Va.) 1981.

Stout, Richard T. and Tinkelman, Joseph. "Death in the Big City," *The Quill*, October 1981.

United States Senate Committee on the Judiciary, subcommittee on Antitrust and Monopoly, hearings on S. 1520, The Newspaper Preservation Act, June 12, 13, and 20, 1969.

———, hearings on S. 1312, The Failing Newspaper Act, Part I, July 12, 13, 14, 18, 19, 25, and 26, 1967.

———, hearings on S. 1312, The Failing Newspaper Act, Part II, July 27 and 28, Aug. 7, 8, 14, and 15, 1967.

———, hearings on S. 1312, The Failing Newspaper Act, Part III, Appendix.

———, hearings on S. 1312, The Failing Newspaper Act, Part IV, Articles, Miscellaneous Documents and Cases.

———, hearings on S. 1312, The Failing Newspaper Act, Part V, Excerpts from hearings on concentration of ownership in news media before the antitrust subcommittee of the Judiciary Committee of the House of Representatives, March 13, 14, and 15, April 9, 1963.

———, hearings on S. 1312, The Failing Newspaper Act, Part VI, Feb. 27 and 28, March 18, 19, 26, 27, April 16, 1968.

———, hearings on S. 1312, The Failing Newspaper Act, Part VII, Feb. 27 and 28, March 18, 19, 26, 27, April 16, 1968.

United States Senate, Report No. 91-535 from the Committee on the Judiciary, Nov. 18, 1969.

United States House of Representatives, Report No. 91-1193 from the Committee on the Judiciary, June 15, 1970.

Wollert, James A., "Antitrust and the Media: the NCCB Decision," an unpublished paper, University of Iowa.

Bottine, Ronald L., *Group Ownership of newspapers*, Freedom of Information Center (Columbia, Mo.), November 1967.

Brown, Dennis, *S., 1312: The Failing Newspaper Bill*, Freedom of Information Center (Columbia, Mo.), February 1968.

Lewels, Joe Jr., *The Newspaper Preservation Act*, Freedom of Information Center (Columbia, Mo.), January 1971.

Ruttle, Margaret, *Limiting Media Ownership*, Freedom of Information Center (Columbia, Mo.), November 1972.

Stevens, Jean, *The Free Market Place Dilemma*, Freedom of Information Center (Columbia, Mo.), May 1971.

Chapter 45

Sunshine Laws: A Right to Know
by Donna Lee Dickerson

James Madison noted that "A popular government, without popular information or the means of acquiring it, is but a prologue to a farce or a tragedy; or perhaps both. Knowledge will forever govern ignorance. And a people who mean to be their own governors, must arm themselves with the power knowledge gives."

In a society as complex as that of 20th Century America, no citizen can be expected to gather all of the information necessary to make rational political decisions.

We have come to expect the media not only to provide us with the information government wants us to have, but also with the information government may not want us to know.

By taking upon itself the role of "watchdog," the media ensure a free flow of information of public importance.

There is little question that the press in America is free to publish the information which it gathers, and may not be forced to publish information which it does not wish to.

A changing society and increased stores of information require that freedom of the press move beyond the traditional meaning to include a duty on the part of government to provide access to information when demanded. If such a duty does not exist, then government is allowed too much influence over the quality and quantity of information that is available to the public.

The process of balancing the broad societal goals of self-government against other interests results in a system of qualified rather than absolute access. Society demands some accommodations to personal rights; without such a recognition, the individual becomes secondary to the system and personal worth is subordinated to accommodate the state.

Dr. Donna Lee Dickerson is associate professor of mass communications, University of South Florida. She is the author of *Typestick: A Texas History* (1972) and *Florida Media Law* (1983), and co-author of *College Student Press Law* (1979, 2nd edition). The Association for Education in Journalism and Mass Communication presented her its first Baskett Mosse Award for Faculty Development, 1984. Dickerson received a Bachelor of Journalism (B.J.) and M.A. in journalism from the University of Texas, and a Ph.D. in journalism from Southern Illinois University. [©1986, Donna Lee Dickerson]

The necessary balancing and accommodations are achieved, at least in the minds of legislatures and courts, by looking at the more specific needs of government in terms of citizen input. One Florida judge, in trying to reach an appropriate accommodation in an open meetings case, likened government agencies, boards, commissions, etc. to a marketplace of ideas where the people and the agency gather to exchange ideas and information. If the agency is going to take action which will subsequently affect the citizens, then the citizens must be allowed input into that decision-making process.

Openness also reinforces in the public mind that our system of self-government continues to work. A willingness on the part of government to share its views and information with the public and to listen to the public, instills stability and confidence in the system. Not only does openness reassure the public, but it also ensures the public that government functions as a genuine participatory democracy.

Openness acts as a reminder to the governing bodies that they are being scrutinized by those who entrusted the government's business to their hands. This checking effect on government abuse or inaction better prepares the public to evaluate their officials at election time.

A Right to Know

Why leave such an important issue as the public's access to government to the discretion of legislators who are so vulnerable to political pressure and special interests? The answer can be found not in *what* the U.S. Constitution says, but in what it does *not* say. Nowhere in the Constitution is there a stated Right to Know. Not only is it absent from the wording, it is also absent from Supreme Court interpretation of that document.

Such a guarantee would not only ensure public access to the people's business, but would prohibit legislatures from placing any restrictions or limitations on that right. A constitutionally recognized Right to Know would place an affirmative obligation on government to conduct all its business in the open with the fullest degree of candor, immune from political pressure to do otherwise.

The federal Freedom of Information Act was passed in 1967, and most states today have some type of open meetings law and more than half have open records laws.

Some of these state laws are strong; others are weakened by hundreds of exceptions; the broader a state's open government law is, the more access it will provide. Ideally, an open meetings law should provide that all meetings of state agencies, including the legislature, state universities, public schools, city and county agencies be open. The law should also provide the public a means of enforcing openness, including penalties for those who close meetings and methods of declaring actions taken in secret to be void.

The best open records law would provide that all records kept by public state bodies be open to the public. It would also provide for redress against those who refuse to provide records and a penalty for those who violate the law.

To enforce the concept of open government, some state legislatures have adopted policy statements about the necessity of openness, leaving no doubt that the preference of the state is for openness and any closure is the exception. Such policies place the burden on the state agency to prove the necessity of closure rather than placing the burden on the citizen to prove the need for openness.

Most states allow citizens to appeal directly to a court where they can claim that an agency has violated the law and their rights under that law. In the case of a closed meeting, by the time a lawyer is found and an appeal made, the meeting will be over. Therefore, the law should allow citizens to see the transcript of the proceedings. If any official action, such as a vote, was taken at the closed meeting, the law should specify that such an action is null and void.

Additionally, the law should specify that anyone who knowingly closes an open meeting is guilty of a misdemeanor punishable by fine and/or imprisonment.

There are going to be numerous meetings and records exempted from any open government law. These exceptions are required in order to protect health, safety and privacy. For example, most states prohibit disclosure of adoption records, certain active law enforcement records, records of hospital patients or personnel.

However, as the number of exemptions grows, access becomes more frustrating, time-consuming and, for many, an empty promise of openness to their government.

Federal Sunshine

On March 12, 1977, the federal "Government-in-the-Sunshine Act" became law, six months after President Gerald Ford reluctantly signed it. President Ford had claimed that the act—which would require about fifty federal agencies to conduct meetings in the open—could upset the proper functioning of government by not only inhibiting discussion among those elected or appointed to such agencies, but could conceivably lead to federal agencies, faced by the intense light from the public, doing what they thought the public wanted rather than what the people needed in order to exist and advance in a representational democracy.

Nevertheless, the President pointed out, almost to underscore his arguments, that if he vetoed the legislation, he would face the enmity of the American people. The President, like most in government, was trapped between what he thought best for the people and what he thought the people thought best.

Open Meeting Laws: An Analysis

by Jack Clarke

The rationale underlying open meeting legislation is a complex of concepts: that government is the people's business, that the people control their government through the electoral process and that rational use of the electoral franchise requires an informed voter. Direct evidence of the rationale may be found in several acts' declarations of public policy.

Indirectly, the rationale is established by the functional effect of an open meeting act coupled with usual limitations. A necessary effect of every open meeting act is to open to public scrutiny one or more meetings of a public agency. Opening government to public view clearly indicates a determination that government is the public's business, but open meeting acts do not replace representational voting with popular voting nor do they even provide a popular right to speak. Open meeting statutes create the right to listen and evaluate governmental processes. Open meeting legislation is completely compatible with representative government; such statutes provide the environment wherein citizens can exercise their electoral franchise based on a rational evaluation of incumbents' performances.

Evaluation

Governmental openness improves the quality of decision-making by providing a broader range of perspectives on any given problem. Any public agency is composed of individuals with collectively limited experiences. Opening the decision-making process provides motivation for persons with other perspectives and experiences to suggest solutions. At a minimum, an observer may foresee undesirable results from agency-suggested solutions. While openness cannot prevent stupid decisions, it will facilitate their quickly being recognized as such.

Open meetings encourage honest government. In a fully open, democratic government, illegal behavior is observable and can flourish only if a voting majority chooses not to be informed or, being informed, approves. In the absence of electorate ignorance, personnel in an open government will behave at least as honestly as the majority of the electorate expect them to; behavior below that standard will result in removal.

Open government is necessary to establish popular confidence in government. "Watergate" and other scandals involving public officials have greatly shaken popular faith in governmental processes. Secrecy itself adds to the disbelief. Secrecy is assumed to be purposeful, and without a clear explanation to the contrary, it is assumed that secrecy hides the illegitimate or inept. Only by

Jack Clarke is an attorney in Tuscaloosa, Alabama, currently specializing in labor arbitration. He is a former Naval submarine officer, 1961-1969; and associate professor of law, University of Alabama, 1971-1976. He received a B.S. and a J.D. from the University of New Mexico. [This article is edited and reprinted, with permission, Freedom of Information Center Report No. 338, 1975; School of Journalism, University of Missouri.]

widely opening governmental processes can the beliefs that government is full of hanky-panky, personal advantage or simple incompetence be dispelled.

Opening governmental meetings facilitates accurate reporting of what occurs. Even when meetings are closed, some reports may be leaked to the public, but such reports are often slanted to favor the views of the informant.

The effects of openness on the quality of government may not be entirely positive. Requiring open meetings places limits on the behavioral standards of participants. As discussed above, dishonesty is discouraged. Similarly, some humanitarian behavior will be discouraged because of divergence from the electorate's prejudices. Granting a higher budget per pupil to predominantly minority schools would be considerably more difficult in an open meeting than behind closed doors, for example. The answer to this criticism is simply that in a democracy it is appropriate for the people to establish norms, subject, of course, to constitutional limitations.

It is widely believed that open meetings will discourage the free exchange of ideas, that participants will feel inhibited from expressing their views and that any ultimate decision will be less reasoned as a consequence. Clearly a participant in a public meeting would be reluctant to express certain perceived results of possible decisions. Specifically it is highly unlikely that an official participant would indicate that his preference for one alternative is based on personal benefit; it is highly unlikely that dishonest alternatives would be seriously considered. The absence of these factors from public decision-making would be welcome.

Other considerations, however, may also be lost to the public debate. Unfortunately, there is little hard evidence regarding the effect of openness on free and frank discussion. Nevertheless, many persons associated with governmental meetings are apparently convinced that the quality of debate would suffer. It is not a sufficient answer to point to situations wherein open debate is the norm, e.g., a courtroom, and note the apparent lack of inhibition on the part of participants, for the effects of selective participation cannot be ruled out. That is, it is impossible to determine whether all persons would be as uninhibited as some are. Perhaps participants in normally oepn forums are cut from a different psychological cloth than some participants in typically closed forums. If some persons are incapable of being frank in an open forum, requiring open meetings will have the effect of denying their wisdom to the decision. While the existence of such a possibility cannot be ignored, it must not be determinative. On balance, the advantages of openness far outweigh the disadvantages in most instances.

In some specific situations there may be special factors favoring secrecy. For example, in hearing charges against an employee, protection of that employee's reputation from false accusations may be sufficiently important to allow secrecy. Those situations, however, are uncommon enough to be dealt with as exceptions from the general rule favoring open meetings. They do not constitute adequate justification for closed meetings generally . . .

Inclusion

Three criteria [should] include all public agencies while excluding private ones. Coverage should extend to any agency which satisfies one or more of the following criteria: (1) it is supported in whole or in part by public funds, (2) it is authorized to expend public funds or (3) it performs a public function per governmental authority . . .

In general existing open meeting statutes provide one of two answers to the question of to what extent the operations of an agency subject to the act should be opened to public view: (1) only the final decision need be made public or (2) the final decision and preceding deliberation must be open. The latter type is supposed to provide a voter with an opportunity to view the entire decision-making process from beginning to end. Information received, alternative solutions perceived and expressed motivations will be observable. The ability of participants to reason logically is exposed. A decision-only statute, on the other hand, provides an observer with only a final answer; reasons for adopting a particular solution are unknown, and the logical processes of the decision makers are unknown . . .

Exclusions

The state legislature and its committees are excluded from the application of open meeting acts in several states. The state legislature is the highest legislative body within a state and should set an example of openness for lesser ones. Its decisions may be presumed to be of greater importance and impact, and the public should have an opportunity to know the factors influencing them. Its members are elected; indeed, individual members represent a constituent's most direct control of his or her government. A citizen must be able to learn how well his legislator functions. Through election of legislators and governors the public exerts democratic control over state governments. If the legislature's operations are clouded in secrecy, openness by lesser nonelected state agencies becomes less significant. Secrecy "at the top" creates the potential for a legislator's claiming to do one thing about a state agency while in fact doing something quite different; in terms of democratic control the significance of openness at the lower level is greatly reduced. Therefore, a state legislature should not be excluded from an open meeting act.

It is obvious that an open meeting act can have no application to the governor individually; no statute can cause the governor to *think* publicly, but it is unrealistic to perceive a modern governor as running the executive branch single-handedly. The executive branch of a state government consists of a large number of people, and their communications with one another can be subjected to an open meeting statute. The impact of the governor's office on state government is so great that its operations should be open. Exclusion would leave a very large hole in the statute and greatly reduce the potential for reasoned democratic control. Because of a governor's capacity to appoint and terminate executive officials, knowledge of his treatment of their performance is essential to rational popular control. Citizen control of the executive branch is usually exercised through election of the governor—not by voting directly for lesser officials. To vote rationally, the citizen must know if the governor's perception of lesser executives' decisions is consistent with his own.

The judicial branch of a state government is commonly excluded from operation of its open meeting act. One result is that whatever discussion occurs among appellate justices regarding a pending case is closed to the public. This cannot be rationalized on the bases of unimportance or that the justices are simply applying law. Fundamental changes in our legal framework have been accomplished by judicial decisions; new norms have been established and old ones dropped. Closing judicial deliberations also prevents disclosure of logical errors before commitment to a decision. Public knowledge and correction is impossible until after publication of a decision, by which time changing minds will be more difficult. Furthermore, the nature of the appellate process limits public input before a decision is reached. Participation by non-parties is at the discretion of the court. Nonetheless, it is appropriate that the judiciary be excluded from an open meeting statute. Other devices hve been developed to protect the judiciary from error. The adversary system is designed to ensure that strengths and weaknesses of both sides of a question are presented to a court before it reaches a decision. A well developed ethical code is designed to ensure impartiality and prevent personal interest in a case by any judge.

Grand and petit juries have traditionally worked in secret and are routinely exempted from open meeting statutes. Such an exemption is consistent with popular governmental control, for both types of juries exemplify direct popular control of government. Jury members are not professional jurists; they give citizen's duty. Unlike governmental employees, jury members may not elect not to participate; absent specified excuses jury duty is mandatory.

In order to protect an officer's or employee's reputation and to limit any invasion into such person's private life and to provide for governmental efficiency, several open meeting acts exclude meetings concerned with personnel matters. An exclusion which extends to all personnel decisions may affect precisely what it is designed to avoid, and, at least in some instances, less extreme measures will accomplish the same ends.

The interests of three parties must be balanced—the employee, the agency, and the people. Recognition of the employee's interests requires that hiring and promotion be distinguished from termination and discipline discussions. In the latter instance, the interests of the employee are heightened; the employee has limited means of reputation protection. The employee has a position and is dependent on it for livelihood. A discussion of the employee's performance can be avoided only by voluntary giving up of that position. In the case of hiring, however, the applicant's livelihood is dependent on some other source, and he can avoid discussion of his record simply by not seeking public employment. Inquiry can be avoided at a much lesser cost. In some situations, however, the employee will prefer inquiry and maximum public disclosure. If untrue charges are brought, maximum publicity of all the evidence may be the optimum technique for clearing a reputation. The interests of the agency and the public do not vary with the situation nor do they differ from one another's. In all situations, the agency and public are interested in good and efficient government. And in all situations the probability for good and efficient government will be maximized by public discussion. The interests can be optimally accommodated by providing for hiring and promotion discussions to be conducted publicly and granting the employee the power to determine whether or not a termination or disciplinary proceeding will be secret.

Similarly deliberations by school authorities of alleged student rule infractions and student placement should be secret only if the student or his or her parent(s) request(s) a closed meeting. It is the interest of the student which is supposedly being protected by secrecy; the student or parent is in a much better position to decide if secrecy will in fact be beneficial.

Quasi-judicial bodies have been exempted from some open meeting acts. The exemption is apparently based on that granted to the judiciary—it falls within the exemption of the judicial branch. An agency outside the judiciary is from a very different tradition and may not be subject to the protections surrounding the judiciary. Many quasi-judicial bodies also have rule-making power. Only when exercising the latter would they be subject to the act, although the alternatives and supporting rationales would be identical in both situations. The technique chosen by one agency to make law is not a rational basis to separate closed and open meetings. If the work of a particular agency or narrow class of agencies requires secrecy, that agency or class should be specifically excluded.

Boards with power to pardon and/or parole prisoners have been exempted, apparently in order to prevent reprisals by prisoners against adverse witnesses. At a minimum, a blanket exemption is much broader than necessary. If deemed necessary, certain evidence could be received in secret while the remainder of the proceedings were open. But even such a limited exemption should be avoided. Secret testimony not only protects the speaker, it also absolutely prevents the prisoner from impeaching the speaker. A prisoner who feels he has been treated unfairly will be a difficult subject for rehabilitation.

Exemption of meetings between a public agency and its attorney to discuss pending or probable litigation is designed to prevent the agency's being placed at a tactical disadvantage. In a suit between public and private parties application of the statute would reveal the public agency's intentions while the private party worked in secrecy. Clearly the public agency and through it the public might be placed at a disadvantage. But the potential disadvantage is clearly outweighed by the benefits to the public of openness. Public business—including litigation—is the public's business and the people should have an opportunity to observe and judge decisions regarding litigation. For example, it has been suggested that secrecy is necessary when discussing compromise solutions. But it is in precisely those situations that valuable public rights may be given up— may be compromised away. In those situations policies may be adopted for the handling of similar situations in the future.

Similarly the potential for inflated price is an insufficient reason for exempting meetings wherein future real estate acquisitions are discussed. Closing such meetings does not really prevent owners of desired land from inflating the price; closing such meetings merely limits the potential private benefactors to those "in the know." Opening all such meetings avoids the suggestions of personal enrichment by members of public bodies. The value of public confidence in government cannot be quantified but it is certainly greater than any small increase in land prices that might be caused by early announcement of a public agency's intention to buy.

The exemption of meetings wherein labor negotiation strategy is discussed is similar in purpose to the attorney exemption—to prevent the private employee group from gaining an advantage over a public agency employer. And the labor negotiation exemption may be analyzed like that for attorney meetings; the result of such an analysis would be that the benefits of openness outweigh the increased labor costs. But such an analysis is seriously deficient in that it ignores the common perception that labor negotiations cannot succeed in open meetings. Requiring labor negotiations to be conducted in public is thus viewed as a device to impede collective bargaining by public employees. Because this movement is still in its infancy and needs a supportive environment to survive, labor negotiation by public agencies should be exempted from an open meeting act.

The discussion of distribution of forces to cope with public safety emergencies —such as riots, tornadoes or hurricanes—may be exempted in order to preclude individuals from thwarting the plans being made. Rioters and looters knowledgeable of police placement would change their locale accordingly. The result would be increased damage. The emergency exemption should be little used. The need to prevent the spread of erroneous rumors will pressure officials into providing maximum information consistent with the public's safety during emergencies.

Meetings of licensing and examining boards should be exempt to the extent necessary to prevent premature disclosure of examination materials. To do otherwise is to render many examinations meaningless.

Deliberation regarding the bestowing of honorary degrees should be exempt to prevent unnecessary embarrassment to rejected nominees. Unlike a public employee, a nominee is not in a position to withdraw voluntarily as he is unaware of being considered.

An open meeting act should provide that public agencies may comply with a request for anonymity made by a donor in a gift or bequest to the agency. Insistence on disclosure will discourage giving and will not result in a better informed public.

Open meeting statutes frequently exempt meetings wherein federal law requires secrecy. The same result is mandated by the supremacy clause of the U.S. Constitution. The redundancy, however, does no harm. And expressing the exemption in the open meeting act provides an opportunity to clearly establish that it extends only so far as is necessary to comply with the federal law and to set forth devices to guard against abuse.

An exemption for meetings expressly authorized by state law to be conducted in executive session will avoid problems of inferential repeal. Like the federal law exemption the state law exemption should be limited to minimum scope and circumscribed by abuse-avoiding protections.

Devices used to avoid abuse of exemptions include requirements that any executive session be announced in open meeting, that the subject matter of the closed meeting be announced in open meeting and that no other matters be discussed in such a meeting. The requirements are reasonable; they place no great burden on a public agency yet are adequate to prevent abuse of specified exemptions.

Remedies

One or more of the following remedial devices are commonly found in open meeting statutes: voiding of action taken, placing criminal liability on participants in unauthorized meetings and civil remedies. Used alone, voiding action taken is a very limited remedy, for it presupposes that some action capable of being voided has been taken. Deliberation without a vote cannot be voided; it is beyond the limits of judicial power to erase the participants' memories. In conjunction with other remedies, the potential for voiding action taken is of questionable value. The very existence of the remedy casts a pall over all action taken by public bodies, for there exists a possibility suit will be brought to nullify the action. The remedy places too much power in an individual willing to bring spurious suits. The remedy itself could become a tool whereby a minority would force otherwise undesirable concessions. Where third parties are involved, they will certainly be reluctant to rely on the action taken.

Voiding action taken by a public body can have one or two results: (1) the decision voided may never again be reached by that body or (2) the body must follow appropriate procedures before making the decision again. The former result is rational in its recognition that once the decision-making is tainted, it remains tainted. But it is totally unacceptable because highly desirable action may be forever prohibited. The second result is undesirable because it is essentially a requirement for a *pro forma* open meeting. The public agency is free to hold an open meeting and rubber-stamp its earlier decision. There is no requirement for honest public debate. On balance the voiding action remedy is more harmful than beneficial and should be avoided.

Imposing criminal liability for failure to comply with an open meeting statute is viewed as an extreme response. It may be so extreme that prosecutors are reluctant to seek it. Proof problems limit the utility of the criminal remedy; the standard of proof is higher than in civil cases, and it is necessary to prove intent. Narrow construction of criminal statutes has been argued in an attempt to limit the applicability of open meeting statutes. But legislative declaration of the remedial nature of the statute and of an intention that the statute be broadly construed to effect its goals is sufficient to avoid the problem. Although the criminal remedy may be used infrequently, its retention is valuable for willful repeating violators. Requiring proofs of multiple violations also protects public officials from overly zealous prosecutions.

Removal from office is valuable for repeat violators. Because it focuses more directly on a violator's public capacity than does criminal liability, it is a more appropriate device to ensure compliance with an open meeting statute.

Civil remedies—including civil fines—provide the best tools to ensure compliance with an open meeting act. They can be fashioned to operate prospectively as well as retroactively. The impact of a civil remedy is more closely related to the magnitude of the harm being avoided than that of the other remedies; the impact is not so great as to discourage its use. Principal reliance on civil remedies avoids subjecting all action taken by an agency to a period of doubtful validity. The remedies can be used to prevent or correct violations at any stage in the decision-making process.

To fully maximize the utility of civil remedies, an open meeting act should encourage their use. Establishing a reasonable civil penalty to be paid to a successful plaintiff and providing that successful plantiffs will be awarded court costs and reasonable attorney fees will encourage individuals to enforce an open meeting act. Conversely, disallowing civil penalities, costs and attorney fees is to place a significant financial cost on an individual's statutory right; the right becomes a right for the wealthy only. Encouraging the use of civil remedies will put meaningful teeth into an open meeting act without impeding worthwhile decisions. And the techniques suggested here are such as to be valuable only to a successful plaintiff. They do not constitute an invitation to initiate unfounded suits . . .

Bibliography

"Access Problems on the Local Level," *FOI Digest*, October 1968.

"Access Laws: Defeats," *FOI Digest*, November 1962.

"Access Laws: Development," *FOI Digest*, October 1962.

"Access Laws: Interpretations," *FOI Digest*, November 1962.

"Bill-Drafting Sessions Open by Unanimous Senate Vote," *FOI Digest*, November-December 1975.

Brenner, J.D., *Covering Local Government*, Freedom of Information Center (Columbia, Mo.), August 1963.

"Broadcast Access to Legislatures," *FOI Digest*, May 1967.

"Capitol Hill Sunshine Beamed at Executive-Legislative Secrecy," *FOI Digest*, January-February 1973.

"Center Implements Federal Sunshine Law," *FOI Digest*, July-August 1978.

"Carter, Powell Plan for More Open Government," *FOI Digest*, November-December 1976.

"Congress Maintains Committee Secrecy: Chiles Introduce National 'Sunshine' Bill," *FOI Digest*, November-December 1972.

"Court Says Meeting Not Required for FCC Vote on Routine Matter," *FOI Digest*, January-February 1979.

"Courts Rebuke Federal Agencies for Skirting Sunshine Act," *FOI Digest*, November-December 1980.

Crow, Peter, *Access to News: Gray Areas*, Freedom of Infomation Center (Columbia, Mo.), October 1965.

"Dismissal Expected in First Suit Under Federal Sunshine Act," *FOI Digest*, January-February 1978.

"Environmental Council Faces Suit Charging Sunshine Act Violations," *FOI Digest*, March-April 1979.

Featherer, Esther, *Electronic Access to Public Meetings*, Freedom of Information Center (Columbia, Mo.), December 1963.

"Federal Agencies Ignore and Sidestep the Sunshine Act," *FOI Digest*, November-December 1981.

"Ford Signs Federal Sunshine Law, Bringing Public Scrutiny to Agencies," *FOI Digest*, September-October 1976.

"Government in Sunshine: Litigation and Reform Attempts to Reveal Need for Improvement," *FOI Digest*, March-April 1981.

"Government Sunshine Bill Draws Bureauratic Fire," *FOI Digest*, July-August 1975.

"Government Sunshine Bill Passes House by 390 to 5," *FOI Digest*, July-August 1976.

"Governmental Sunshine: Agencies Prepare to Comply," *FOI Digest*, January-February 1977.

Higgenbotham, Robert, *The Case Law of Open Meetings Laws*, Freedom of Information Center (Columbia, Mo.), May 1976.

"House Panel Gives Approval to Federal Sunshine Bill," *FOI Digest*, March-April 1976.

"Implementation of Sunshine Law Brings Varied Agency Reactions," *FOI Digest*, March-April 1977.

"Interpretation Creates Difficulties With D.C.'s Controversial FOI Act," *FOI Digest*, July-August 1975.

Johnson, Kathryn, "How Lawmakers are Dodging Those Sunshine Rules," *U.S. News & World Report*, February 20, 1984.

Keefe, Pat, *State Open Meetings Activity*, Freedom of Information Center (Columbia, Mo.), September 1977.

Kelly, Frank K., *Communication in a Free Society*, Freedom of Information Center (Columbia, Mo.), June 1961.

Miller, Susan, *City Council Executive Sessions*, Freedom of Information Center (Columbia, Mo.), March 1964.

Morgan, Earnest, *Informal Methods of Combating Secrecy in Local Government*, Freedom of Information Center (Columbia, Mo.), May 1976.

"New Rules Enacted to Let Sunshine In," *FOI Digest*, September-October 1979.

"New Teller Vote Procedure Ends Congressional Secrecy," *FOI Digest*, March-April 1971.

"Press Given Responsibility for Open Meetings," *FOI Digest*, May-June 1977.

"Senate Approves Federal Sunshine Bill, Measure Sent to House for Consideration," *FOI Digest*, November-December 1975.

"Senate Committee Opposes 'Sunshine Bill' Legislation," *FOI Digest*, September-October 1975.

"State Access Statutes," *FOI Digest*, June 1968.

"State Access Statutes: A Comparison," *FOI Digest*, June 1970.

"Sunshine Act Study Cites Seven Agencies for Record of Secrecy," *FOI Digest*, September-October 1978.

"Supreme Court Declines Review of Sunshine Act's Applications," *FOI Digest*, March-April 1980.

Thompson, William M., *Attitudes Toward Open Meetings*, Freedom of Information Center (Columbia, Mo.), August 1976.

Thompson, William M., *Sunshine and Public Pension Plans*, Freedom of Information Center (Columbia, Mo.), October 1977.

Van Gerpen, Maurice, *Privileged Communication and the Press: The Citizen's Right to Know Versus the Laws's Right to Confidential News Source Evidence*, Greenwood Press (Westprot, Conn.), 1979.

Chapter 46

Freedom of Information Act (FOIA): Access and Denial

by J. David Truby

Despite the grandiose scope of the written and interpreted First Amendment, there is no common law or constitutional guarantee of a right to gather and report news. Despite our being a representative democracy founded by people who believed it was the right of the people to govern themselves, they provided no provisions in our Constitution that mandates the public's business being conducted by government in public. Politicians and their attendant bureaucrats have a natural inclination toward secrecy, often expressed by the career governmentalist as "They [the public] wouldn't understand, so let's not worry them with the details of what we're doing or spending in their name."

Thus, public access to its government has never been a basic right. Between 1789 and 1966, public access to its government and records was not a basic right. Most of the laws passed by Congress between those years dealt with ways to withhold and suppress information rather than give people free access to it.

In 1954, Sigma Delta Chi, now the Society of Professional Journalists, had a Freedom of Information (FOI) Committee draft a model FOI bill, then urged local chapters to push for passage in their state legislatures. By 1957, about half the states had open-record laws; today, all fifty states have such laws on the books, giving the public access to most government information.

Despite the start in the middle 1950s, it was not until 1966, after years of testimony, much debate and journalism-interest lobbying, plus writing and

Dr. J. David Truby is an editor for National News Service (NNS) and professor of journalism at Indiana University of Pennsylvania. His journalistic specialties include the political, military and intelligence operations beats. His most recent assignment for NNS was in Latin America. He is the author of fourteen books and several hundred national newspaper and magazine articles done on a freelance basis. Truby has also testified during FOIA hearings and served on several FOIA seminars. His writing and photography have won several national awards, including those from Sigma Delta Chi, the Society of Professional Journalists; The Watchdog Society; The Washington Foreign Council; and the Keystone Press Awards of Pennsylvania. He has served as a contributing editor for several professional and trade publications, including *Eagle*, *TVI Journal*, *The Journalist* and *The Military Journal*. He was a combat intelligence NCO with the U.S. Army. Truby holds a B.A. in advertising, an M.A. in journalism, and a Ph.D. in communication from The Pennsylvania State University. [©1986, J. David Truby]

rewriting, that Congress finally passed the Freedom of Information Act (FOIA). The act said that basically all government records were open to public inspection, access, and use, except for those in nine specific categories of exemption. Congress, however, wrote itself outside the coverage of the FOIA.

The new law went into effect on July 4, 1967, and was amended in 1974 and 1976. There was another attempt to amend the law in 1984.

A 1984 congressional review of selected government agencies and their processing of FOIA requests documented that a large number of requests are handled and the majority are granted, at least in part. However, only fifteen to twenty percent of all requests came from journalists; the rest came from attorneys, business, and prisoners, among others.

The review noted that the Department of Defense handled 72,534 inquiries in 1983 and granted ninety-two percent in whole or in part. The Department of Health and Human Services had 82,488 FOIA requests in 1983 and granted ninety-eight percent. By contrast, the Department of Justice granted slightly less than half of its 24,372 requests.

One reason for this high rate of refusal was given by Deputy Attorney General Carol E. Dinkins, who said the FBI reported that fifteen percent of all its FOIA requests came from federal prisoners. An Official of the Drug Enforcement Agency said that fifty-eight percent of its FOIA requests were from prisoners in federal jails. Law enforcement agencies fear the use of FOIA by dangerous felons will result in dead witnesses and/or blown prosecutions. On the other hand, there is legitimate use of the FOIA by persons incarcerated under less than just situations.

Many people involved with journalism believe the FOIA may be one of the most important tools a reporter will use when covering Federal government stories. Currently, it is a matter of daily Standard Operating Procedure in many newsrooms to make formal FOIA requests. Elaine P. English, director of the Freedom of Information Service Center, Washington, D.C., notes, "All reporters must know how very important this Act is and how useful it can be for working journalists. For example, the Act can be used to get documents to support the allegations made by government personnel in whistleblowing situations or to document the information leaked by government sources."

The FOIA is used widely and well. Harold Relyea of the Congressional Research Service notes, "The press is making better use of FOIA. Journalism students are learning that federal agencies are repositories of records bearing upon a variety of state and local matters, too."

Use of the FOIA by journalists turned up evidence that J. Edgar Hoover had used the FBI to illegally spy on and discredit Dr. Martin Luther King and other civil rights leaders. Use of the FOIA brought out uncontestable facts that dissident ex-CIA contract agents were actively involved in the conspiracy to murder President John F. Kennedy. The FOIA was used to discover the hazards of radiation, plus the effects of Agent Orange in Vietnam. Journalists using the FOIA reported on secret and illegal American involvement in the Bay of Pigs invasion and in dozens of civil wars and revolutions all over Asia, Latin America, and Africa.

The FOIA was used by news organizations to get details about a CIA assassination manual in 1984, President Nixon's plans to illegally bomb Cambodia in the '70s, government coverup of unsafe prescription drugs, plus hundreds of examples of other vital issues and problems our government tried to keep secret from its citizens.

Athan Theoharis, a history professor at Marquette University, obtained documents detailing FBI collusion with Sen. Joseph McCarthy in spying on President Eisenhower to get embarrassing information to blackmail the President into supporting McCarthy's innane witchhunt. He also learned that J. Edgar Hoover had ordered illegal break-ins to link Eleanor Roosevelt with Communist groups.

When Penn Kimball, Columbia University journalism professor, used the FOIA to learn what the FBI had on him in its files he was shocked at the amount of outrageous misinformation and disinformation. One report described him as a "Communist sympathizer." He said wryly, "Maybe Mr. Hoover was confused because I have been an active, longtime Democrat."

Use of the FOIA has created some additional clerical and legal responsibility within the government. Personnel and budget are needed to perform this public service. For example, in 1984, the FBI had assigned forty law-trained special agents plus 360 clerical and support personnel to FOIA duties. They estimate an annual expenditure of $13 million on FOI and Privacy Act services.

The FOIA has worked so well, in fact, that in the first four years of the 1980s, more than 30 major bills were proposed to Congress that would weaken or destroy the Act. None passed. The pressure continues, though, as several groups, most notably the CIA and the FBI, try mightily to wiggle out of the public spotlight under the FOIA.

However, the FOIA is not perfect—it does not cover all federal information, nor does it always result in the public receiving all requested information, even if the information is not protected by exemptions.

FOIA Exemptions

The nine specific exemptions are:

1. Materials that have been properly classified to protect national security or foreign policy.

Major examples of this type of material include classified documents like the Pentagon Papers, CIA after-action reports of covert operations, or a presidential executive order properly classifying a treaty agreement.

2. Material relating to internal personnel rules and practices of agencies.

This exemption generally covers routine internal management or housekeeping records like cafeteria regulations, parking lot assignments, vacation schedules, etc. Also covered are agency manuals where public disclosure could cause circumvention of the law. For example, an exemption would stop a prisoner from using a law enforcement agent handbook to escape detection in some criminal situation. However, there are also many times when such records may well be of legitimate public and press interest, e.g., incidents involving improper utilization of official time and records.

   3.   Material specifically exempted from public exposure by other statutes.

The only challenges to this broad set of exemptions have been on a piecework appeal basis through the courts. Some of the more important exemptions to the FOIA under this listing include certain Census Bureau records, most Federal Trade Commission materials generated from the business sector, materials from the Consumer Product Safety Commission, Social Security records, information gained by the Department of Energy from investigation of public utilities, most of the "sources and methods . . . communication intelligence activity" of the CIA, plus bank records, tax records, patent applications, veterans' benefits and virtually all information from and about the National Security Agency.

   4.   Trade secrets and certain other financial and commercial information gathered by government agencies from individuals or companies.

This exemption deals primarily with two concerns, trade or proprietary secrets and sensitive financial information about companies. The exemption attempts to prevent use of the FOIA as a method of industrial espionage.

   5.   Inter-agency and intra-agency materials involving the internal decision-making process.

Generally called the "executive privilege" exemption, this is designed to protect working papers, studies, non-final drafts or reports from disclosure. It does not cover the final decision drafts or studies, reports, papers and other materials, however. The rationale for this exemption is to encourage open discussion and free thinking among agency personnel during their planning sessions before final decisions are reached. This exemption also incorporates the attorney-client privilege which protects most communication between an agency and its counsel or, for example, the Justice Department acting as official attorney for other government agencies.

This exemption incorporates several privileges commonly recognized in civil and criminal discovery. There is a privilege for commercial information generated by the government for witness statements given as part of a military aircraft defect investigation, for example.

   6.   Personnel and medical files, plus similar documents that must be kept confidential to protect individual privacy.

The nature of this exemption is to protect almost all personal information files of individuals from unwarranted intrusion. However, courts have ruled that this exemption is not automatic. The courts have also held that this exemption allows a judicial balancing of the right of personal privacy versus the public right to know, the critical element to any decision in this area.

   7.   Investigatory records kept for law enforcement purposes.

This exemption is designed to protect the confidentiality and security of documents related to law enforcement activity. There are six so-called "harms" in which the statute holds unwarranted disclosure could impede necessary law enforcement:

   Interference with present or pending enforcement proceedings. . .

Deprivation of the right to a fair trial or an impartial adjudication. . .

An unwarranted invasion of personal privacy,

Disclosing the identity of a confidential source, and in the case of a record compiled by a criminal law enforcement authority in the course of a criminal investigation, or by an agency conducting a lawful national security intelligence investigation, confidential information furnished only by the confidential source,

Disclosing investigative techniques and procedures, or

Endangering the life or physical safety of law enforcement personnel.

This specific exemption, though, covers investigatory records only when the enumerated harms can be demonstrated by the government agency involved.

8. *Materials used by agencies to regulate banks and other financial institutions.*

The eighth exemption is known as the Bank Reports loophole. It applies mainly to reports prepared by federal agencies about the conditions of banks and other federally-regulated financial institutions.

9. *Geological and geophysical materials related to oil and gas exploration data.*

Designed primarily to prohibit speculators from obtaining information about profitable energy sources, this exemption also has some national security ramifications, i.e. possible terrorism and sabotage.

Many of these nine exemptions are so broad as to allow massive secrecy and almost total denial of FOIA requests. In addition to the nine formal exemptions, there is another, unwritten yet equally strong, one called "I don't want you to have it." It's born of the obstinate governmentalist's desire to operate in secret without the meddling of the media and the public. During the Carter years, reporters were accustomed to prompt and unprecedented access to previously classified documents. The Reagan reign shut off the flow, as reporters found themselves generally treated with hostility, and even routine historical requests were often denied in whole or part.

Mary Hargrove, staunch FOIA supporter and a reporter for the *Tulsa Tribune*, says all too often government officials drag out FOIA requests with their "Slow Boat to China" routine, or they "baffle you with bullshit" about delays or refusals.

Denying Requests

After an agency receives an FOIA request, it has ten working days to either provide the request or to deny the request with an explanation of why it did so.

If the request is denied, the user may appeal the denial through the agency's own appeals process. However, in most appeal cases, the courts have been very lenient about allowing agencies more than ten days to respond. One reporter encountered a two year delay from the Department of Justice.

In another instance, after dilly-dallying around with an informal request for a routine laboratory report and photos from a well-publicized federal case in which the defendant had pleaded guilty, the Bureau of Alcohol, Tobacco and Firearms required a journalist to file a formal FOIA letter. He requested a waiver fee.

Their disclosure officer denied the waiver unless the journalist could submit letters from publishers indicating that the material would be published. The letters were written. Finally, after a month's time, the Director of the Bureau denied the entire request, then pronounced the issue as "moot as there are no such photos in any ATF files."

If the journalist does take the litigation route, however, Robert L. Shaloschin, a Washington attorney who was head of the Justice Department's FOIA office, reports that the government often loses in FOIA appeal cases. The FOIA also requires the government to reimburse victorious plaintiffs for all legal costs.

If the FOIA requester files suit in federal court, a judge is empowered to review the requested materials *in camera*, then rule on the agency's decision to deny the request.

A major controversy arose in 1982 when many agencies began charging search fees for requested data. Agencies had been allowed by law to charge search fees since 1974. What had actually changed in 1982 was the policy whereby agencies began to charge and collect "estimated" search fees in advance of their processing requests. Often, the FOIA filer was told that this search fee was due and payable even if nothing turned up later in the search. Some individuals and reporters claimed the fees were very high. The agencies claimed they were simply making the FOIA pay its own way, as allowed by law. Critics said it was an attempt to tighten access by the Reagan administration, or that the information was already public property and thus belonged to the people.

Although one of the 1974 FOIA amendments did allow agencies to charge search and copy fees for requests, any user may request a fee waiver if he or she can demonstrate that the documents will inform, educate or otherwise be in the public interest. Most FOIA users routinely got fee waivers, until 1982. Sometimes, the results were ludicrous.

Syndicated columnist Jack Anderson charged "Under the Reagan administration federal agencies have done their best to take the 'free' out of the Freedom of Information Act." Among Anderson's examples was the U.S. Forest Service

---

Detrimantal to Survival

Rusty Martin, student body president at the University of Northern Iowa (Cedar Falls, Iowa), learned that use of the Freedom of Information Act could be detrimental to one's survival.

Martin, in 1980, had spoken out against several U.S. government policies, and had advocated resisting the draft. Thinking that the FBI might have a file on him, he requested the Bureau to allow him to see his records. It wasn't too long before Selective Service arrested him for resisting the draft, having been given his address by the FBI which learned about it from a return address on the envelope Martin sent to the FBI. Ironically, after July 1980, when Martin requested the information, he wasn't required to register for the draft.

billing him $673.90 for sending public documents about the agency's billion dollar bailout of the large lumber corporations in 1983. He returned the materials unopened.

In another instance, the FBI responded to my request for two fairly common bits of data in the John F. Kennedy murder for an investigative story I was doing. I was told by official letter that it would take 609 hours to search for these data at a cost to me of $4,872, payable in advance and non-refundable even if the data were not found. Any competent researcher could have located the materials inside of an hour, and that's what I told an FOIA official at the Bureau. Shortly after, another FOIA officer at the Bureau called to apologize for the "administrative oversight" and to tell me that my request had been filled with less than an hour's work and at no charge.

About the charging of excess fees, Penn Kimball noted, "Not only does the fox guard the hen house, but collects a bounty for every chick."

President Reagan went on record before the American Society of Newspaper Editors in 1984 as favoring the further restriction upon the FOIA. It was his keynote to a major effort toward "reform" of the FOIA. His idea of "reform" chilled advocates of open, democratic government. Reform was his euphemism for doing away with as much of the FOIA as possible. As journalists pointed out with justifiable alarm, this massive and involuntary surgery was being planned by a media-hostile Reagan administration as a major gutting of the Act. Under intense lobbying pressure by various media groups, led by the Society of Professional Journalists, the so-called "reform" proposals failed.

One of the press freedom's congressional friends, Rep. Glenn English, has championed both the form and intent of the existing law, saying in 1984, "Disclosures made as a result of FOIA requests have documented government waste and abuse, identified threats to health and safety and exposed violations of law. Some disclosures have resulted in many millions of dollars savings for the government."

Rep. English said during FOIA hearings in 1984, "We would like to make the FOIA simpler for agencies to administer and faster and easier for people to use. But, we do not want to jeopardize the flow of information to the thousands who use the FOIA. Any amendments must preserve the Act's effectiveness."

Despite beating back the oppression of 1984 and saving the FOIA, freedom continues to face major opposition from the Reagan government. By 1985, it was a very open secret that the word had gone out directly from the White House to "Stall, deny, ignore and otherwise do not disclose. If you must disclose, refuse to waive fees, then charge outrageous fees as a means of discouraging requests."

In 1985, Secretary of State George Shultz said, "We need a crackdown to prevent such disclosures," after the *New York Times* had published news of American contigency plans to deploy nuclear depth charges in some countries. Despite the fact that these plans had been in public print and discussion in at least two of the targeted nations, Shultz testified to a Senate committee examining U.S. espionage laws that the *Times* should never have published the story anyway "in the interest of national security."

As *Editor & Publisher* noted in a lead editorial on the matter, "Secrecy begets secrecy. When an important official of our government contends that certain information should not be published in spite of its knowledge and publication elsewhere it is not too much to suppose that this government may go to extreme lengths to insure that the American people are told only what the government wants them to know."

The Reagan administration's fear about press independence has created the very same police state mentality common to the nations whose communist dictatorships we abhor. As former Deputy Secretary of State George W. Ball said during House hearings on Mr. Reagan's controversial National Security Decision Directive 84, "Our current obsession with the Soviet Union should not lead us to imitate the very Soviet methods and attitudes our leaders most insistently deplore."

Every journalism student knows of the watchdog of government role assigned by tradition to the news media. Government by the people is a noble thought, while government by professional governmentalists is more the norm. It's also true that too many governmentalists favor turning that aggressive media watchdog into a toothless, silent, old lapdog.

In an arrogant bit of Catch 22, the CIA asked the Congress in 1984 to exempt it completely from having to search and disclose from their operational files for FOIA requests on the grounds it never released anything from those files anyway. About this, Kimball noted, "This illustrates the compelling need for more, not less, independent oversight." Despite heavy criticism from media critics, this bill passed Congress that year and is now law.

The U.S. government has become a secretive and frightening anti-champion, an administration with a sophisticated information managing operation and sharply curbed access to public information.

Yet, Elaine English, of the Freedom of Information Service Center, says, "My basic concern is to encourage the use of the FOIA by journalists. The more requesters there are and the more sophisticated they become in the Act and in law, generally, I believe the better chance they, and the public, have to counter these agency secrecy practices. Only by increasing the pressure on the agencies and Congress to keep the Act intact will we ever succeed in preventing further erosion. One good way to keep the Act safe is to use it often and use it well."

Additional support from the journalism industry came in the Spring of 1985, when the Society of Professional Journalists opened a First Amendment Center in Washington. Funded by a generous grant from the Pulliam newspaper family, the Center was established to improve public understanding and appreciation for the First Amendment. Among the initial action efforts of the Center were grants to various task forces groups to establish and support Freedom of Information hotlines in a number of states.

Press revelations about the horrors of Watergate are probably forgotten with the newer generations of Americans—more than a pity. The reality of misuse of power, even to the point of murder, for personal and political gain should frighten every thinking citizen.   Telling the FOIA-gained stories of misdeed 25 years after the fact is history; journalism must be concerned with what is happening today or with what will happen tomorrow.   That's why we must never surrender our FOIA key to government's locked door.   That the use and encouragement of a strong FOIA is vital to continued freedoms for all Americans has never been more clear.

The major sources of professional support and aid in FOIA matters are:
The Freedom of Information Center
University of Missouri School of Journalism
P.O. Box 858
Columbia, MO 65201
(314) 882-4856

FOI Service Center
Reporters Committee for Freedom of the Press
Room 300
800 18th Street NW
Washington, DC 20006
(202) 466-6313 (24-hour hotline)

The First Amendment Congress
The Newspaper Center
Box 17407
Dulles International Airport
Washington, DC 20041

In addition, many states now have FOI hotline centers, working in conjunction with state press associations and the Society of Professional Journalists.

Bibliography

Adler, Allan, *Litigation Under the Amended Freedom of Information Act*, 3rd ed., American Civil Liberties Union (Washington, D.C.), 1985.
American Civil Liberties Union, *Free Speech*, 1984, ACLU (Washington, D.C.), 1984.
"Appellate Court Says FOI Act Doesn't Compel FAA to Identify Questioner of Pilot Fitness," *FOI Digest*, September-October 1971.
"Army Uses FOI Provisions to Deny Access to Report," *FOI Digest*, March-April 1975.
Baldwin, Judith M., *Access Laws; Interpretations*, Freedom of Information Center (Columbia, Mo.), November 1962.

Cardwell, Richard W., *Access to State Committees Survey*, Freedom of Information Center (Columbia, Mo.), April 1970.

Cross, Harold. *The People's Right to Know*, Columbia University Press (New York, N.Y.), 1953.

Demac, Donna, *Keeping America Uninformed*, The Pilgrim Press (New York, N.Y.), 1984.

Dorsen, Norman; Stephen Gillers, eds., *None of Your Business: Government Secrecy in America*, Viking Press (New York, N.Y.), 1974.

"Editorial: FOI Requests by Journalists Inadequately Counted," *FOI Digest*, May-June 1981.

Federal Bureau of Investigation, *Impact of the FOIA Upon the FBI*, Department of Justice, 1981.

"Freedom of Information Act Comes Under Fire as a Misused Law; Officials Call for Legislative Revision," *FOI Digest*, May-June 1981.

"GAO Finds Weakness in Feds' FOIA Conduct," *FOI Digest*, May-June 1983.

"Groups Secretly Watched by IRS and FBI Spy Units," *FOI Digest*, November-December 1974.

"Guide Available to Explain Use of FOI, Privacy Acts," *FOI Digest*, November-December 1977.

"Has the FOIA Backfired? Submitters of Information Use Reverse Suits to Withhold Their Information from the Public," *FOI Digest*, November-December 1980.

Helm, Lewis M., *Informing the People*, Longman (New York, N.Y.), 1980.

Horton, Forest W., *Understanding U.S. Information Policy*, Information Industry Association (Washington, D.C.), 1982, 4 vols.

Hudson, Robert V., "FOI Crusade in Perspective," *Journalism Quarterly*, Spring 1973.

Kelly, Frank K., *Communication in a Free Society*, Freedom of Information Center (Columbia, Mo.), June 1961.

Kielbowicz, Richard B., "The Freedom of Information Act and Government's Corporate Information Files," *Journalism Quarterly*, Fall 1978.

Landau, Jack C., *How to Use the Federal FOI Act*, FOI Service Center (Washington, D.C.), 1984.

"Press Use of the Freedom of Information Act is Criticized Unduly," *FOI Digest*, July-August 1971.

"Privacy Act and FOIA Exemptions Are Conflicting," *FOI Digest*, July-August 1984.

Relyea, Harold C., *The Presidency and Information Policy*, Center for the Study of the Presidency (New York, N.Y.), 1984.

Rosenfeld, Seth, "FBI Fools With FOIA," *Mother Jones*, February 1983.

Rourke, Francis E., *Secrecy and Publicity*, Johns Hopkins Press (Baltimore, MD.), 1961.

Society of Professional Journalists, *Freedom of Information: 1984-85*, Society of Professional Journalists (Chicago, Ill.), 1984.

U.S. Congress House Committee on Government Operation, *A Citizen's Guide on How to Use the Freedom of Information Act. . .*, USGPO (Washington, D.C.), 1977.

Chapter 47

Shield Laws
by Tonda Rush

A group of journalism students were relaxing after a vigorous evening of classroom debate over the journalist's privilege against compulsory testimony. The question was to what degree there should be such a privilege, in light of society's interest in hearing the testimony. The differences of opinion were surprisingly intense, for a group whose interests might have seemed somewhat similar.

The hypothetical problem had been this:

A man is on death row, scheduled to die for a robbery-murder. A free man who claims he was with the defendant on the night of the murder in a town fifty miles away from the crime scene holds the key to the condemned man's freedom. In succession, the free man makes his confession to the following:

—his lawyer, because he fears the convict will spill the beans about another robbery that night which the two did commit, but in which there was no injury;

—his wife, because she is in the room when he talks with his lawyer;

—his pastor, because he is remorseful over his long silence;

—a journalist, because he wants his story to be told to spare his friend's life. He relies on the journalist's promise of confidentiality in telling the story and he understands that the confession will be printed without his name.

The next day, as the story breaks, he drops from sight. The district attorney, furious at the implication that he has prosecuted the wrong man, announces a new investigation. The condemned man is spared.

Now, assuming that the prosecutor learns of the existence, if not the content, of all of these conversations, who should be required under subpoena to tell what they know?

Tonda Rush is counsel for government affairs for the American Newspaper Publishers Association. She is former director of the Freedom of Information Service Center, a project of the Reporters Committee for Freedom of the Press, and has written and lectured on the First Amendment and other legal principles. She is a contributing author to *Everywoman's Legal Guide* (1983). Before entering law school, she was a newspaper reporter for the *Lawrence* (Kan.) *Daily Journal-World* and other midwest newspapers. She is a former journalism instructor at the William Allen White School of Journalism at the University of Kansas and a graduate of the University of Kansas School of Law. [©1986, Tonda Rush]

The students had learned the principle that the law has a right to everyone's evidence. But they also knew that many exceptions have been made to the rule to preserve relationships considered more important to society than the testimony.

Their willingness to accord a privilege to each confidant of the secretive robber seemed to mirror their degree of respect for the relationships represented.

Begrudgingly, for instance, they granted an attorney-client privilege, although several swore distrust of the legal profession. Nevertheless, they finally did acknowledge the importance of legal representation and the confidentiality necessary to it.

The clergy-penitent privilege was granted more readily, to preserve the value of the theology. Even those who claimed no religious faith thought that was important.

The spousal privilege was in doubt, and only reluctantly allowed as the women in class were horrified to learn the origin of the privilege: that the husband and wife were considered one person in the law (that person being the husband, of course) and a person couldn't be compelled to testify against himself. The antediluvian origins were finally overlooked and the privilege was justified simply by the need for trust in marriage.

When they came to the journalist, however, consensus was lost.

Some objected to putting the reporter on a social or professional level with the pastor or lawyer. Still others thought that if too many exceptions were thoughtlessly created, the law eventually would come up dry in its investigations, and crime would run amok. Finally, one or two (who planned careers in public relations, ironically) thought the media were so untrustworthy and contemptible that no special privilege ought to be doled out to them—ever.

The journalist's privilege seemed to have no friends at all—until one student spoke up timidly. The reporter was the only one of the group whose conversation led to the sparing of the convicted man's life, she pointed out. Without the promise of confidentiality, would that story have been told?

And it was on that note that they adjourned to a local cafe to see whether they could arrive, during a long night of undoubtedly schorlarly discourse, at a piece of the truth that continues to divide legal experts—should the state permit a journalist's privilege? If so, how should it be described and when should it be respected?

The issue has raged for more than a century in various forums. It is often intertwined with general disagreement over First Amendment freedoms or the value of a free press or, sometimes, arguments over the power of various institutions.

Although virtually all judges and politicians pay homage to the First Amendment, along with apple pie and the Fourth of July, many find themselves loving the concept more than its realities when it means they can't get at the information they want. In such cases, it is usually said that while the First Amendment is important, it must be balanced against other equally important values.

Perhaps still another source of disagreement is the unanswered question in the robbery story—does the promise of confidentiality enable this story to be told or would it have been told anyway, despite a possibility of the source's exposure? And, of course, since the answer will never be known, each side is free to answer as it wishes. So the debate goes on.

The journalist's privilege is neither new nor old. American journalists have insisted upon it since John Peter Zenger refused a £50 bribe to reveal sources critical of Gov. William Cosby. Yet, it is still growing, developing and being refined as few areas of the law are. It is far better established in the law than it was, say, in 1900 or even 1960, but the rights of journalists from state to state vary widely. And journalists continue to go to jail in some states in defense of a principle that judges, lawyers, and citizens often do not understand—or sometimes simply reject. Even among journalists themselves, there is wide and sometimes fatal disagreement about the need for a privilege from testimony.

The press subpoena's earliest recorded use in this country was as a tool of investigation in the Congress. In the nineteenth century, more than one journalist was sentenced in the well of the House of Representatives, which holds contumacy powers similar to those of judges in court, for a refusal to expose their sources in stories of official corruption. One *New York Times* writer spent nineteen days in jail in 1857 for refusing to reveal the sources for his story that congressmen were selling their votes for as much as $1,500. He argued that exposing his sources would deprive him of information in the future; not surprisingly, the members of Congress were unsympathetic.

Congress has continued to affront a journalist's privilege in modern times. In 1971, Rep. Harley Staggers of West Virginia sought to prove through CBS subpoenas that "The Selling of the Pentagon," a television documentary, was inaccurate. CBS president Frank Stanton agreed to provide copies of the aired film, but refused the transcripts, outtakes and other background material. He said:

> We recognize that journalists can make mistakes, that editing involves the exercise of judgment, and that we and other journalists can benefit by criticism. But I respectfully submit that where journalistic judgments are investigated in a Congressional hearing, especially by the Committee with jurisdiction to legislate about broadcast licenses, the official effort to compel evidence about our editing processes has an unconstitutionally chilling effect.

More recently, the House Ethics Committee threatened in 1984 to subpoena a newspaper reporter for writing about the committee's decision to overrule staff advice on disciplinary action against Vice Presidential candidate Geraldine Ferraro. The newspaper revealed that staff investigators had been rebuffed by the Democratically-controlled committee in recommendations for harsh sanctions. Rep. Louis Stokes, D-Ohio, the committee chairman, was outraged at the staff report's leak and sought in vain to learn its origin. Contempt charges were averted only when the committee could not muster a quorum between legislative sessions to recommend jail for the reporter.

Today the struggle of officialdom to learn what journalists know is played out in the courts more frequently than in Congress. In courtrooms, the privilege has been claimed on a variety of theories. Some journalists have based a refusal to testify upon their personal codes of ethics. Others have claimed testimony would lead to a loss of livelihood either through a damaged reputation or dismissal for violation of an employer's regulations. None of these arguments has been successful.

It was in a libel lawsuit by actress Judy Garland against CBS that the journalists' privilege was first argued as a constitutional matter. Garland sought from columnist Marie Torre the name of a CBS executive who had been quoted in the column as saying that Garland thought of herself as "terribly fat." The actress claimed that if discovery of the source's name were barred, her libel suit would be thwarted. Torre asserted a First Amendment right to protect her source—and lost. But the case led to a ground-breaking recognition by a federal appeals court that forced disclosure might have a negative impact upon the free press. The possible harm was outweighed by the interests of justice in that case, but the development of a constitutional argument for protecting sources was conceived in the process.

Precedent Cases

Similar arguments erupted sporadically around the country for more than a decade until the issue finally reached the Supreme Court in a 1972 trilogy of subpoena challenges captioned under *Branzburg* v. *Hays*. The cases grew from attempts by law enforcement to break a veil of secrecy around various 60's era counter-culture activities that reporters had probed in confidence.

The lead case had stemmed from a series of stories by Paul Branzburg, reporter for the *Louisville Courier-Journal*, into a hashish operation in the Kentucky hills. Branzburg had observed the operation as part of an investigation into the flow of illicit drugs into Louisville. When he was subpoenaed to tell a grand jury what he had seen, he claimed a First Amendment right to silence. He said the public benefit from his stories would have been lost unless his sources had been promised anonymity. The courts denied his claim, and Branzburg was found in contempt. He appealed.

Joining Branzburg at Supreme Court were two investigative reporters who had gained the confidence of Black Panthers organizers. One, Earl Caldwell, was a black *New York Times* reporter who had developed sources within the militant group that white reporters had been unable to cultivate. To gain their trust, Caldwell had labored for months to prove he was not working with the police. He claimed his confidential relationships led to stories that no one in the country could have written without promises of anonymity. Also before the Court was Paul Pappas, a Massachusetts television reporter who had visited with Panthers in New Bedford during civil disorders. He was invited to their headquarters where he waited for three hours for an anticipated police raid. The

to materialize, and Pappas kept his promise that he would write no story and discuss no conversations he heard at the headquarters.

Pappas was subpoenaed by a state grand jury; Caldwell was subpoenaed by a federal grand jury. Both asserted that the First Amendment allowed them to protect their sources. The Massachusetts Superior Court rejected Pappas's claim outright.

In California, Caldwell fared somewhat better. A federal judge recognized the potential impact upon newsgathering abilities if reporters were forced to testify; the judge issued a protective order requiring Caldwell to testify but shielding "confidential associations that impinge upon the effective exercise of his First Amendment right to gather news . . ."

Kaleidoscope

Kaleidoscope was instrumental in one of the most important tests of press freedom. It was probably attacked because it made a policy of exposing undercover agents working in the area. The January 20, 1970, issue of the [alternative] paper published the names, addresses, and photographs of three military intelligence officers conducting surveillance around Madison, [Wisc.]. In late August, the paper printed a statement by the New Year's Gang claiming responsibility for the August 24 bombing of the Army Mathematics Research Center on the University of Wisconsin campus. A grand jury subpoenaed *Kaleidoscope* editor Mark Knops, asking him to disclose the source of the New Year's Gang statement. Knops refused on the grounds that the press could not be required to reveal its sources. Judge Erwin Zastrow sentenced Knops to six months in jail for contempt of court, stating, "What has to give is the First Amendment privilege—in the interest of justice." Knops served one month and was released when he agreed to answer six questions unrelated to the source of his story. One hour after his release he was subpoenaed again and this time ordered to reveal all his news sources. On refusing, he was sent back to jail. In December, after having served four months, Knops was released on bond by a federal judge pending appeal. The reaction of the established dailies to this case was mixed. A September 4, 1970, editorial in the Chicago *News* took the position that the contempt charge was correct, citing Attorney General John Mitchell's "temporary guidelines" for certain circumstances. The Chicago *Sun Times*, on the other hand, defended Knops' right to withhold his sources. The *Milwaukee Journal* initially sided with the contempt charge, but after the second subpoena and Knops' return to jail, the paper backed Knops, saying a demand for all sources was a threat to all reporters and an illegal use of grand jury powers. On November 7, the Milwaukee chapter of the professional journalist society, Sigma Delta Chi, issued a resolution condemning Knops' imprisonment.

—Geoffrey Rips

Caldwell was not satisfied with the protective order. Because grand jury proceedings are secret, he feared the super-sensitive Panthers would note his mere appearance and assume he was talking to authorities. He appealed the order to the U.S. Court of Appeals for the Ninth Circuit.

Out of the Ninth Circuit's decision to spare Caldwell from the witness stand came the framework for a First Amendment privilege that would gradually be developed in other courts over the next 15 years—but not without setbacks and considerable controversy. The court held that Caldwell need not testify until the government had proven: 1) the relevance of the information sought; 2) a compelling public need for the information; and 3) lack of alternative sources. The court ruled:

> To convert news gatherers into Department of Justice investigators is to invade the autonomy of the press by imposing a governmental function upon them. To do so where the result is to diminish their future capacity as news gatherers is destructive of their public function. To accomplish this where it has not been shown to be essential to the Grand Jury inquiry simply cannot be justified in the public interest. Further, it is not unreasonable to expect journalists everywhere to temper their reporting so as to reduce the probability that they will be required to submit to interrogation. The First Amendment guards against governmental action that induces self-censorship.

When *Caldwell, Pappas,* and *Branzburg* reached the U.S. Supreme Court together, however, the 9th Circuit's concern for the journalist's plight found too few friends. In an opinion by Justice Byron White, the Court in a 5-4 decision, found no First Amendment right for journalists to refuse to testify before a grand jury. The Court, however, was severely split in its approach to the case.

Four justices joined White in denying the notion that irreparable damage would be done to the reporter's newsgathering abilities if confidences could not be kept. White was not persuaded that sources would be lost and the public's access to information diminished by the subpoenas. He found such fears too speculative to be trusted. To the reporters' argument that informants would talk to the press rather than officialdom where job security, personal safety, or peace of mind would be threatened by public exposure, White questioned whether informants would trust the press over public officials who have experience in protecting confidential informants. And to the argument that the public would be ill-informed if confidential sources were lost, White responded:

> We cannot seriously entertian the notion that the First Amendment protects the newsman's agreement to conceal the criminal conduct of his source, of evidence thereof, on the theory that it is better to write about crime than to do something about it . . .

Justice Lewis Powell expressed reservations about White's words. Nevertheless, in a concurring opinion he held out the possibility that some constitutional protection might be available to defeat a grand jury called to harass the news gatherer or to seek information having only a remote relationship to an investigation. Courts, he said, would be available to protect legitimate First Amendment claims in those cases.

Four dissenting justices sided with the reporters. Justice William O. Douglas took a hard line and found a total immunity from testimony except where the news gatherer was implicated in a crime himself. Three others joined Justice Stewart in recommending the three criteria for reporters' testimony written for Caldwell by the Ninth Circuit. Stewart scoffed at White's belief that informants would necessarily trust authorities as readily as the press:

> An office holder may fear his superior; a member of the bureaucracy, his associates; a dissident, the scorn of majority opinion. All may have information valuable to the public discourse, yet each may be willing to relate that information only in confidence to a reporter whom he trusts, either because of excessive caution or because of a reasonable fear of reprisals or censure for unorthodox views. ●

The Court's decision was handed down to a glum press which feared a flood of investigative subpoenas across the country. Most believed that the First Amendment should protect the confidences of reporters and were shocked to find that it did not—at least where grand juries were concerned.

They found a ray of hope in a little-noticed passage from White's opinion. White said the creation of a privilege, while not constitutionally-mandated, was possibly a matter for legislatures to write into state laws. In addition, he noted:

> At the federal level, Congress has freedom to determine whether a statutory newsman's privilege is necessary and desirable and to fashion standards and rules as narrow or broad as deemed necessary to address the evil discerned . . .

Legislative Action

White seemed to be drawing a roadmap for the press to take its arguments to the Congress. Organized press groups followed it directly to Capitol Hill. Model legislation was drafted. Bills were introduced by Sens. Walter Mondale and Sam Ervin. A press alliance led by the American Newspaper Publishers Association was formed to campaign for a federal reporter's privilege, or shield, law. Exhaustive hearings were held in the House and Senate of the 93rd Congress.

But problems immediately arose. How should the press be defined? Were student reporters included? How about the lonely pamphleteer? Could any citizen evade a subpoena by claiming to be a reporter? What about ex-reporters? Should the privilege include only confidential sources? Or only information for which a specific promise of confidentiality was given? Should scholarly research be protected? Could information be withheld in a criminal case where the right to a fair trial might be at stake?

Extensive efforts were made to resolve these questions. But the biggest question of all divided the press as well as the Congress. If Congress offered a privilege could it take the privilege away? The specter of ceding to politicians a right that many still believed was protected by the constitution led many journalists to withhold their support and doggedly insist upon constitutional protection or none at all.

Ultimately, the divided ranks of the Fourth Estate and opposition in Congress to various proposals caused the effort to be abandoned by the press. To this day, no federal shield law exists to protect the press from federal subpoenas.

Federal prosecutors are free to subpoena reporters to reveal their sources, supply their notes or turn over their tapes for grand jury investigations. They are deterred only by internal guidelines that sometimes are no deterrence at all. In the absence of a clear legal right to object, journalists sometimes surrender their materials.

In state investigations, the law is somewhat more clear. Passage of statutory shield laws in smaller, less complex environments came more easily than on Capitol Hill. More than half the states now have shield laws. Some protect only sources of information. Others also protect the information itself. Many qualify the protection by the three-point test in Caldwell's case. In states where no legislation has emerged, court decisions have filled the void, again often relying upon the three-point test or variations of it. Some states have found a journalist's privilege within the parameters of the free press rights in their state consititutions.

Despite state laws, the drama over confidential sources continues to play, like a bad soap opera whose themes are the same as the characters change. Every year, it seems, news of a reporter behind bars for insisting upon his right to protect sources reaches the front pages. The six months spent in a New Jersy jail by *New York Times* reporter Myron Farber for declining to testify in the trial of a physician accused of murder was a graphic demonstration of the paper-thin protection reporters really have. New Jersey has a shield law, relied upon by Farber. But the court refused to recognize it, saying the right to a fair trial was more important. Since then, New Jersey's law was rewritten and Farber was pardoned by the governor, but judges continue to put aside laws that interfere with the court's ability to gather evidence where they believe more important rights are at stake.

Where no other constitutional rights fall into the mix of a court's concerns, the adamant reporter sometimes wins—with one exception. Where the case in court is a suit against that reporter or his publication for invading privacy or defaming the subject of a story, courts may make the defendants choose between revealing a source or losing the case. The List of Protecting the Principles of Confidentiality in these cases may be $1 million or more if the court rules against the reporter because of the obsence of unidentified source. Whether the newsroom rules for taking on controversial and difficult stories have been affected seems tautological.

The press has abandoned, by and large, an insistence upon absolute immunity from testimony. It tends to be satisfied with assurances that testimony will not be sought unless it is necessary to an investigation or a lawsuit, is unavailable elsewhere and is not the object of a fishing expedition by lawyers. Often, application of those principles voids the subpoena and frees the reporter from testifying. However, even where a reporter takes the witness stand just to verify the truth of a published or broadcast story, some colleagues will claim he has become a tool of the state, to the detriment of a rightful role in society.

Possibly the right balance is struck in the Caldwell test, despite the fact that some subpoenaes will pass the test and some reporters will testify. It is clear that the duty of citizens to testify must be maintained. It is also clear that justice has wheeled safely into the 20th century without the ready testimony of lawyers, priests, and spouses.

Many scholars have argued that comparing reporters to other professionals is meaningless because their roles are different. Others say the acceptance of a privilege goes hand-in-hand with the imposition of duties, such as the lawyers' Codes of Professional Responsibility by which shamans may be barred from practice. Whether journalists, like clergy, could enjoy a privilege based upon constitutional protection and use the constitution as a shield against regulation as well is roundly rejected by the most independent of their ranks.

But many reporters, from both the print and broadcast businesses, have decided to fear the invasive subpoena far more than the prospect of licensing by the government, as lawyers are licensed. Their problem is a harder one yet. If courts will not recognize the First Amendment as a reporter's shield, must reporters beg relief from the politicians in the statehouse? Must they ask the very public officials who are often on the receiving end of the reporter's lancet for this favor? And what will they have to give in return?

If public tolerance for this journalist's right must stem from its respect for journalism, as its tolerance of the lawyer's privilege grew with the status of lawyers—or the physician's privilege with the fairly modern elevation of the medical profession to respectability—all may be lost. The free-wheeling, David-and-Goliath battles that the press will fight in pursuance of its duties will call into controversy the "professionalism" as long as they occur. Most reporters would choose the slingshot over the three-piece suit. But in so choosing, they relinquish reasonable expectations that the legal system will be content to let them tell their stories without accounting to anyone.

The debate returns to a question of values. Which is more important, from the public's point of view? Enjoying the possibly ephemeral stores of knowledge in the journalist's notebook—until the information will no longer find its way to the notebook? Or adding to the law's list of important relationships the one between reporters and their sources? Searching the constitution for an answer, the Supreme Court so far has said only that the notebook will continue to be filled. If the Court is wrong—and most journalists say it is—the tougher question becomes not whether the Court will answer differently next time but whether there will be a question to ask.

Rejecting the Shield Law

by Jesse Helms

I reject the notion that a so-called "shield law" for newsmen is either needed or desirable.

In fact, the news people who are now crying for such special treatment would do well to ponder whether they are not asking for the handcuffs at some point down the road.

I cannot buy the assumption that such a protective umbrella is necessary to continued press freedom.

Before becoming a Senator in January, I spent most of my life in the field of journalism. I worked as a reporter, a city editor and a TV editorialist. Now this doesn't qualify me as any sort of expert in the field, but I do have a personal knowledge of the work-a-day world faced by today's reporters.

In all these years, I have done my share of investigative reporting. I have not, however, encountered the so-called dilemma of some newspapermen today who are asking for a special exemption. I never found a need for a shield to get the facts.

I have dealt with confidential sources all my working career and I have been subpoenaed before grand juries.

On one occasion, I declined to identify a source. The incident dealt with a story I had written disclosing malfeasance in public office. I explained to the grand jury that my source was completely innocent and that identification could endanger this person's well-being. Once explained, I had no trouble at all. I was not, in any manner, arrogant about it.

I have a hunch, really without knowing definitely, that some of these people in trouble with grand juries have been self-serving newsmen and it has gotten to be a personal thing. I believe the reporters recently jailed for contempt in the much-publicized cases could have avoided such trouble.

I would never make any commitment of secrecy to a criminal. I have had people, who were at least questionable in character, give me information, but rather than go around protecting them, I made an effort to learn whether they were telling me the truth.

In short, during my years as a newsman the crisis to press freedom some see today never materialized.

Sen. Jesse Helms has been a U.S. senator since 1972. He graduated from Wake Forest College, then became an editor of the *Raleigh* (N.C.) *Times*, 1941-1942; a Naval officer, 1942-1945; news and program director, WRAL, 1948-1951; administrative assistant to Senators Willis Smith and Alton Lennon, 1951-1953; executive director, North Carolina Bankers Association, 1953-1960; and executive vice-president of Capitol Broadcasting (Raleigh, N.C.), 1960-1972. He is a member of the Senate Foreign Relations and Ethics committees. Sen. Helms is the recipient of several awards, including the Freedoms Foundation award for Best TV editorial 1962; and newspaper article, 1963; Southern Baptist National Award for Service to Mankind, 1972; the VFW Gold Medal; Liberty Award of the American Economics Council, 1978; and Legislator of the Year Award, National Rifle Association, 1978. [This article is reprinted from the *Congressional Digest*, May 1983.]

It is rare when responsible reporters, using sound judgment in dealing with secret sources, are faced with such a so-called crisis. In my view, skillful newsmen can oftentimes relate their story without indicating the source. It is the few irresponsible writers who act without corroborating evidence who leave the profession open to public criticism.

In a desire to gain a scoop, too many reporters and editors rush to the trough to feed without knowing the exact contents or the aftermath effects. Deadlines, far too often, are allowed to pull rank over cautiousness. Before making a special social order of journalists, we need to rethink some fundamental questions. I simply cannot favor giving newsmen any right, protection, privilege, or immunity not enjoyed by all other citizens.

The few isolated arrests of reporters for refusing to divulge their confidential sources have brought on a falling-sky hysteria among some media people. The threat they see just doesn't exist. The danger lies in the singling out of any segment of our society for special treatment. Every citizen has a duty under our laws and the Constitution to give testimony in criminal and civil proceedings. Like butchers, bakers, and candlestick makers, the press should be no exception.

Promisingly, some media people are beginning to have second thoughts on this question of immunity. They realize there is an inherent danger in governmental intrusion. Past experiences show that with legislative goodies come regulatory strings.

While this reexamination by some newsmen offers some reassurances, it is currently overshadowed by a mass of shield law bills already introduced in the Congress. The threat of panic is obvious. Opposing a shield law is, in the mind of some, akin to being against motherhood and apple pie.

It must, nevertheless, be opposed. For 197 years, the First Amendment has been adequate in affording the free press guarantee. That seaworthy ship has carried us across much troubled water, and while at times it may appear to be imperfect, it is a far better vessel than the frail, plastic boat of legislative shield.

If we allow the law to decide who can write, how soon will come the day when the laws tell us what we can write? Under a shield law, someone must define a newsman and someone must legally describe the media. Do we want a committee of the Congress, the press, or the private sector to make such decisions?

What are the mechanics of such proposals? Would it be fair to grant the same canopy to a budding high school journalism student as given to a full-time major media editor? Would a mimeographed pamphlet demand the same treatment as a large metropolitan daily newspaper?

The unanswered questions are endless. So, too, are the pitfalls.

Considering the opportunity for chicanery, the possibility of extremism, and the likelihood of abuse, the wiser course is to leave well enough alone. Any meddling with the First Amendment is a foolhardy expedition into a dark forest.

I would, therefore, counsel my fellow newsmen that if the Government protects you against performing the duties of citizenship, one day it will control you.

Search of the Newsroom:
A Philosophical Inquiry

by Walter B. McCormick, Jr.

The resolve of the press to advance claims of constitutional immunity to subpoenas and the presence of shield laws protecting the confidentiality of news sources have led law enforcement officials to seek new ways of acquiring information from uncooperative journalists. One resort has been to the *ex parte* search warrant process. This procedure, which permits police to seize now and litigate later, was upheld by the United States Supreme Court against First and Fourth amendment challenges in *Zurcher* v. *Stanford Daily*.

The case arose in 1971 when four police officers, pursuant to a warrant, searched the premises of a Stanford University student newspaper for photographs of a clash between police and demonstrators. Nine officers had been injured in the fray, and police hoped that pictures taken by a *Daily* photographer would help identify the assailants. Photographic laboratories, desks, filing cabinets and waste paper baskets were searched, and although locked drawers and rooms were not opened, the officers had the opportunity to read confidential notes and correspondence. They found only photographs which had already been published, and left empty-handed.

The *Daily* and members of its staff sued for injunctive and declaratory relief under 42 U.S.C. §1983, alleging that the search had deprived them, under color of state law, of rights secured by the first, fourth and fourteenth amendments to the United States Constitution. The district court denied the injunction, but granted declaratory relief. It held that where material is sought from a third party—one not suspected of criminal activity—a search is unreasonable per se unless a magistrate has before him an affidavit showing that the material sought is likely to be destroyed, or that a subpoena *duces tecum* is otherwise "impractical." Furthermore, since first amendment interests in newsgathering, editing and dissemination are involved, the court ruled that a media search should only be permitted in the "rare" situation where there is "a *clear showing* that 1) important materials will be destroyed or removed from the jurisdiction; *and* 2) a restraining order would be futile." The Court of Appeals for the Ninth Circuit affirmed *per curiam*, adopting the district court opinion.*

---

*"Every person who, under color of any statute, ordinance, regulation, custom, or usage, of any State or Territory, subjects, or causes to be subjected, any citizen of the United States or other person within the jurisdiction thereof to the deprivation of any rights, privileges or immunities secured by the Constitution and laws, shall be liable to the party injured in an action at law, suit in equity, or other proper proceeding for redress." 42 U.S.C. §1983 (1976).

Walter B. McCormick, Jr. is general counsel, U.S. Senate Committee on Commerce, Science, and Transportation. He earned a bachelor of journalism degree and a law degree from the University of Missouri. He was in private law practice, then became a legislative assistant to U.S. Sen. John C. Danforth before accepting his current position. [This article is reprinted, with permission, from the *Missouri Law Review*, Spring 1979.]

In an opinion by Justice Byron White, the Supreme Court of the United States reversed. The Court held that valid warrants may be issued to search any property, whether or not occupied by a third party, when there is probable cause to believe that fruits, instrumentalities or evidence of crime may be found there. When First Amendment interests are involved, it said that courts need do no more than apply the warrant requirements with "particular exactitude . . ."

More is involved in press search and seizure than a simple confrontation between the First Amendment and society's need to protect itself from crime . . .

At least four distinguishable interests are involved in searches of the news media: (1) the right of the press, both as individuals and as an institution, to an expectation of privacy under the Fourth Amendment; (2) First Amendment freedom to gather, edit and disseminate information; (3) the government's need for the power of search and seizure to provide for the security of its citizens; and (4) the need of society's dispute-resolving forums, the courts, to be furnished with relevant information.

The Fourth Amendment broadly secures the right of the poeple "against unreasonable searches and seizures." Although historically the amendment has been primarily concerned with persons suspected of wrongdoing, it is clear that its protection extends to innocent and quilty alike since the sanctity of a person's privacy is the controlling consideration.

But despite this paucity of discussion, third party searches, and particularly those of newspaper offices, raise serious fourth amendment questions. The principal remedy afforded the victim of an unreasonable search and seizure— the exclusionary rule—is not available to a third party. Neither the individual searched nor the party against whom the seized evidence is introduced at trial has standing to contest the legality of the intrusion. The result is that an innocent, law-abiding citizen has less protection against invasions of his privacy than does a person suspected of criminal behavior. Furthermore, because of their necessarily broad scope, it has been argued that searches of newsrooms and reporters' files violate the Fourth Amendment's specific prohibition against general searches.*

Faced with these issues in *Zurcher* v. *Stanford Daily*, the Supreme Court held that "[n]othing on the face of the Amendment suggests that a third-party search warrant should not normally issue." Arguing that search warrants are not directed at persons, but at "places and things", it reasoned that probable

---

*The problems connected with a general search arise when police enter premises with a search warrant that fails to describe with particularity the materials sought. As a result, police rummage about, seizing any item which seems relevant to the investigation. The Framers of the Constitution were familiar with the problem of the general search, and it has been said that the case of *Entick* v. *Carrington*, 19 How. St. Tr. 1029 (1765), which held that English officers could not break into a citizen's house pursuant to a general arrest warrant and search for evidence of libel, had a tremendous impact on the founding fathers and served as the basis for the Fourth Amendment. *Boyd* v. *United States*, 116 U.S. 616, 626-27 (1886). The Supreme Court, in turn, has sought to limit the power of law enforcement officials to rummage by holding that the scope of a search must be reasonable in light of the circumstances that warrant the initial intrusion . . .

cause to believe incriminating evidence will be found on the property to which entry is sought justifies the invasion of privacy. The Court discounted what it perceived to be the premise of the district court holding—that issuance of a warrant is dependent upon a reasonable belief in the culpability of the party to be searched—indicating that, if anything, "a less stringent standard of probable cause is acceptable where the entry is not to secure evidence of crime against the possessor." The Court rejected the argument that additional protection is required to safeguard the constitutional rights of third parties because of the unavailability of the exclusionary rule as a deterrent. It further disagreed that general searches would be a problem "if the requirements of specificity and reasonableness are properly applied, policed and observed."

The opinion may be a Pandora's box. As pointed out by Justice Stevens in dissent, it exposes [c]ountless law-abiding citizens "to unannounced searches, and requires no consideration of whether the offensive invasion of privacy is justified by the law enforcement interest it is intended to vindicate." Applied to the press, the principle is particularly reprehensible. Two considerations need be noted. First, police acting pursuant to a valid search warrant may seize evidence of other crime that is inadvertently found. Second, police may enter and search a news office under warrant when reporters and editors are absent.

Journalists must rely at times on confidential sources for information. During the production of a story notes and correspondence are filed in their offices. No matter how specifically a warrant describes the material sought, a search through all the journalist's papers until the documents sought are found will often be necessary. During the course of such a search, perusal of confidential information is likely. If evidence of crime is uncovered—whether or not related to the subject of the search—it may be seized. Moreover, since police need not make the search in the reporter's presence, the journalist may not have the opportunity to provide his sources with even limited protection by cooperating with law enforcement officials and delivering relevant materials to them. The practical effect is that the press is left remediless. Post-seizure access to the courts for return of the materials is essentially futile—the confidential cat is out of the bag.

For this reason, searches of news media offices interfere with the First Amendment right of the press to gather, edit and disseminate information. A source who had wished to remain anonymous and whose identify was disclosed as the result of a police search is going to be reluctant to give information in the future. Other potential sources who learn of the disclosure will be reluctant to come forward as well. Furthermore, premature disclosure, even when not damaging to the source, could damage the developing story by putting targets on guard. A pragmatic publisher might well decide to kill a number of important, but relatively minor, investigative stories in order to avoid the chance of a police search that could expose the subject matter of a major story currently under production. And, especially among smaller newspapers and broadcast stations operating on limited budgets, editors might discourage investigative work by their reporters in order to avoid the expenses of litigation and disruption to the news facility so often associated with searches and seizures. The net result, of course, would be a diminution in the flow of information to the public.

Because of the importance of freedom of expression, the Supreme Court has ruled that the First Amendment modifies the fourth amendment to require additional protections when both are involved in the same case. It has found constitutional violations where government regulations fell short of prohibiting the exercise of First Amendment rights but nevertheless "chilled" those rights by discouraging their practice. Furthermore, the Court has indicated that where the state has a variety of effective means to achieve a legitimate end, it must choose the alternative which least interferes with first amendment freedoms . . .

The government has a responsibility to provide for the safety of its citizens and to provide its adjudicatory bodies with evidence . . .

Judicial supervision and procedural safeguards prevent the subpoena from requiring the press indiscriminately to disclose its sources. For example, a subpoena must be "reasonable." It may require only the production of documents that are relevant to the investigation, it must specifically describe the materials sought, and it may only order records covering a reasonable period of time. A subpoena is subject to prior challenge. If a reporter believes that the information being sought bears only a remote and tenuous relationship to the investigation, or would expose confidential sources without a legitimate need of law enforcement, he has access to the court on a motion to quash. If appropriate, a protective order may be issued. Finally, the characteristic secrecy of grand jury proceedings is a further protection against the undue invasion "of First Amendment rights."

Contrast this with the search warrant procedure. In at least four ways it more seriously infringes First Amendment interests than the subpoena process . . .

First, a search is a more serious invasion of the citizen's right to privacy than the subpoena. Police are not bound to secrecy, and in executing a warrant they may break, enter and even ransack if necessary. Second, the inhibiting effect of searches on the willingness of informants to make disclosures to newsmen, and the concomitant burden on newsgathering, is far greater than that which Justice White found consequential, but uncertain in *Branzburg*. A search renders a journalist's pledge of confidentiality impotent. If he tries to block the search, he may be lawfully forced aside. Since the search need not be made in his presence, he may be unable to limit its scope by voluntarily surrendering the materials. While the warrant must describe with reasonable specificity the place to be searched and the things to be seized, this limitation allows significant access if the item is small and capable of concealment. Officers may rummage through files, scrutinize their contents, and seize evidence of unrelated criminality inadvertently found. Informants whose names or confidential information might be on record may justifiably fear exposure. Third, searches affect not only newsgathering, but the media's editing and disseminating functions as well. A search may disrupt a newsroom for several hours, impede timely broadcast or publication, and impose extra costs in the form of salaries paid to employees made idle or required to put things back in order. As a result, the mere threat of a search may chill newsgathering and editorial policy.

Finally, search warrants lack the judicial supervision and procedural safeguards relied upon by the Court . . . Although there is judicial administration to the extent that only a "neutral and detached magistrate" may authorize a search, upon examination the apparent protectiveness of this requirement fades. Magistrates who are approached for search warrants often have a symbiotic rather than a supervisory relationship with the police. In some jurisdictions they need not even be attorneys . . . The probable cause standard, while in theory more protective than the reasonableness requirement of the subpoena, is in practice somewhat less protective. While a grand jury must show a legitimate need for the information sought in order to withstand a motion to quash, a mere showing that an item is relevant to a criminal investigation will justify seizure under a search warrant. But most importantly, search warrants are issued in *ex parte* proceedings lacking the adversarial engagement that assures consideration of competing interests in the subpoena process. When confronted with a search warrant, the journalist is left with only the insufficient *post facto* remedy of seeking return of the materials seized.

On the other hand, there are societal needs which only the search warrant can serve that must be balanced against its more severe infringement of First Amendment interests. While police have myriad alternative means of obtaining information, when swift action is necessary to acquire crucial evidence and the possessor will not cooperate, a search may be imperative. It is, however, only in this limited situation where police fear imminent destruction or loss of vital evidence that the search becomes as essential to the police as is the subpoena to the grand jury.

Justice Potter Stewart argued in dissent that the concurring opinion of Justice Powell in *Branzburg* properly interpreted the First Amendment to require a careful balancing of "vital constitutional and societal interests." Since a subpoena would normally serve the legitimate needs of government . . . without infringing freedom of the press, "Justice Stewart would have required a showing of probable cause to believe a subpoena" impractical before permitting a warrant to issue.

The majority, however, refused to engage in a new balancing of interests. In the words of Justice White:

> The Fourth Amendment has itself struck the balance between privacy and public need, and there is no occasion or justification for a court to revise the Amendment and strike a new balance by denying the search warrant in the circumstances present here and by insisting that the investigation proceed by subpoena *duces tecum*, whether on the theory that the latter is a less intrusive alternative, or otherwise.

Noting that the Framers of the Bill of Rights did not forbid warrants where the press was involved, the Court said that prior cases do no more than insist that the courts apply the warrant requirements with particular exactitude when First Amendment interests would be endangered by the search. It held that so long as they are properly administered, the warrant requirements themselves "should afford sufficient protection against the harms that are assertedly threatened by searches of newsrooms." The Court was unconvinced that confidential sources would disappear or that the press would suppress news because of fear of warranted searches, and argued that a warrant to search newspaper offices for criminal evidence involves no "realistic threat of prior restraint since even presumptively protected materials are not necessarily immune from seizure under warrant for use at a criminal trial." Finally, the Court said it could see no reason for requiring a prior adversary hearing because if the evidence is sufficiently connected with the crime to satisfy the probable cause requirement it will very likely be sufficiently relevant to justify a subpoena and withstand a motion to quash.

Perhaps Justice Powell's concurring opinion limits the holding somewhat. As in *Branzburg*, Powell's was the swing vote, and his concurrence sets out factors that a magistrate should take into account in determining whether to authorize a third party search. Powell said the magnitude of the proposed search, together with the nature and significance of the material sought are "properly considered" as bearing upon the reasonableness and particularlity requirements of the warrant process. Furthermore, Justice Powell said, "there is no reason why police officers executing a warrant should not seek the cooperation of the subject party in order to prevent needless disruption." While he agreed that there is no justification for the establishment of a separate Fourth Amendment procedure for the press, the Justice did say that a magistrate asked to authorize a news media search "should take cognizance of the independent values protected by the First Amendment."

Before closing, the Court noted that "the Fourth amendment does not prevent or advise against legislative or judicial efforts to establish nonconstitutional protections against possible abuses of the search warrant procedure." The statement has been received as a virtual call to action at both the state and federal level. California has already enacted an amendment to its shield law dealing with the search situation. Similar protective legislation is pending in other states. Eighteen bills restricting the issuance of search warrants were introduced into the second session of the Ninety-Fifth Congress, and the House of Representatives Committee on Government Operations has issued a report recommending that legislation be enacted "to curtail the effects of the decision in *Zurcher* v. *Stanford Daily*." The President of the United States, after requesting the Justice Department to review all proposed legislation for the purpose of constructing procedures to safeguard First Amendment rights, announced his own proposal for remedying what the White House termed "a serious threat to the ability of the press to gather information and to protect confidential sources."

However, there are difficulties in drafting appropriate legislation. One is trying to determine what parties should be protected. Should federal law protect all persons not suspected of involvement in the crime under investigation? If so, would it be encouraging criminals to conceal evidence in the "sanctuaries" of third parties? Should it protect only the press? If so, how should "the press" be defined? Should professinal journalists have special legal protections or should the same rights extend to authors, academicians, freelance writers and pamphleteers? Another difficulty is trying to determine what jurisdictions should be covered. While Congress could restrict the use of search warrants by federal law enforcement agencies, such legislation would affect only a small percentage of warrants issued throughout the country. It is an open constitutional question whether the federal government can impose limitations on the activities of states and municipalities where there is arguably no commerce clause relationship. Since civil rights are involved, the fourteenth amendment may imbue Congress with some authority in this area.

President Carter's proposal sidesteps a few of these problems by prohibiting, with limited exceptions, searches and seizures of materials produced in connection with any form of public communication "in or affecting interstate commerce." The legislation would afford protection to newspaper reporters, broadcasters, authors of books, and academicians—in effect, anyone preparing information for dissemination to the public. As for other third parties, because of the "complexities" involved, the administration believes "that further study is necessary."

While the *Zurcher* v. *Stanford Daily* holding may be an unfortunate one, it should be remembered that often the federal Constitution, as interpreted by the United States Supreme Court, is not the only applicable standard. Free speech and search warrant provisions in state constitutions may give broader protection, and could provide the advocate with a valuable tool in this area.

Bibliography

"ANPA, ASNE Ask Court for Opinion on Privilege," *FOI Digest*, January-February 1976.

"Anderson Won't Identify Sources; Lawsuit Against Nixon Dismissed," *FOI Digest*, May-June 1978.

Baker, Nancy, *Reporters' Privilege Worldwide*, Freedom of Information Center (Columbia, Mo.), February 1984.

"Brooklyn Judge Rejects Research Journal Confidentiality Plea," *FOI Digest*, March-April 1984.

"CBS Told to Release Subpoenaed '60 Minutes' Tapes," *FOI Digest*, November-December 1983.

"California Appeals Court Ruling Ends Farr's Battle with Court," *FOI Digest*, November-December 1976.

"California High Court Shuns Test of Shield Act in Fresno Bee Case," *FOI Digest*, November-December 1975.

"Cases (State and Foreign) Bearing on the Question: Need a Reporter Reveal to a Court the Source of His Information?" *FOI Digest*, July 1963.

"Clamor for Federal Shield Law Cools; Qualification Argument Slows Action," *FOI Digest*, May-June 1973.

Cohen, Marla, *Shield Legislation in the United States*, Freedom of Information Center (Columbia, Mo.), November 1968.

Colcord, Herbert, *Nebraska's Shield Law*, Freedom of Information Center (Columbia, Mo.), February 1975.

"Contempt Conviction of Fresno Newsman May Produce Shield Law Repercussions," *FOI Digest*, May-June 1975.

"Court Gives Film Makers Right to Protect Confidential Sources," *FOI Digest*, September-October 1977.

"Court Rejects Farr's Appeal of Court Order to Name Sources," *FOI Digest*, July-August 1977.

"Court Rule Favors No Naming of Sources," *FOI Digest*, November-December 1983.

"Courts Rule on Reporters' Privilege: U.S. High Court May Hear Kansas Case," *FOI Digest*, November-December 1978.

"Courts Seek Definition of Reporters' Privilege; Justice Department Appeals Caldwell Decision," *FOI Digest*, January-February 1971.

"Denial of Right to Protect Sources on the Increase Despite Shield Laws," *FOI Digest*, November-December 1983.

"Federal Court Upholds Shield Law; TV Station Allowed to Protect Sources," *FOI Digest*, May-June 1976.

"Federal Shield Litigation Introduced; State Judges Reject Privilege Claims," *FOI Digest*, January-February 1979.

"Fifth Amendment Privilege Protects Reporters Against Disclosing Source," *FOI Digest*, May-June 1981.

"First Amendment Pleaded by Television Newsman," *FOI Digest*, September-October 1970.

"Fresno Reporters and Editor Sentenced for Shielding Source of Jury Information," *FOI Digest*, March-April 1975.

Gilliam, Thomas B., *Newsmen's Sources and the Law*, Freedom of Information Center (Columbia, Mo.), March 1971.

Gordon, David, *Newsman's Privilege and the Law*, Freedom of Information Center (Columbia, Mo.), August 1974.

"High Court Refuses to Hear Shield Case; States Vary on Disclosure of Sources," *FOI Digest*, March-April 1979.

"Idaho High Court Rulings Bolster Newsmen's Shield," *FOI Digest*, September-October 1980.

"Illinois Shield Bill Becomes Law; Libel and Slander Cases Excluded," *FOI Digest*, September-October 1971.

"Individual States Clarify Shield Law Application," *FOI Digest*, November-December 1979.

Jumpp, James A., *Branzburg, Caldwell and Pappas Cases*, Freedom of Information Center (Columbia, Mo.), May 1974.

"Justice Renquist Faces Conflict in Positions Taken on Shield Law," *FOI Digest*, March-April 1972.

"Lewis Refuses Under Calif. Shield to Give SLA Document to Jury," *FOI Digest*, November-December 1975.

"Los Angeles Court Says Reporters Must Reveal Sources," *FOI Digest*, November-December 1982.

"N.M. Supreme Court Upholds Order for Disclosure of Confidential Sources," *FOI Digest*, September-October 1976.

"N.Y. Times Gives Up Jascalevich Files, Reporter Myron Farber Is Still In Jail," *FOI Digest*, July-August 1978.

"National Shield Legislation Divides Reporters' Groups," *FOI Digest*, May-June 1975.

"New Jersey Supreme Court Repeals Ruling; Shield Law Protects Reporters' Data," *FOI Digest*, May-June 1980.

"New Mexico Court Ruling Criticizes Disclosure Law," *FOI Digest*, July-August 1976.

"New York Appeals Court Rules Shield Law Protects Reporter," *FOI Digest*, May-June 1984.

"New York Supreme Court Rules Shield Laws Protect 'Name Withheld at Request' Letters," *FOI Digest*, March-April 1973.

"New York Supreme Court Says Law Applies Only When Confidentiality Granted," *FOI Digest*, March-April 1984.

"Newsman Refuses to Reveal Sources for *Times* Story," *FOI Digest*, July-August 1970.

"Newsman's Privilege Still Undecided Despite Caldwell Ruling; Commissions Study Problem," *FOI Digest*, March-April 1971.

"Newsmen's Privilege Goes to Supreme Court While Lower Courts Debate Its Constitutionality," *FOI Digest*, September-October 1971.

"Newspaper Orders Reporters to Disclose Sources," *FOI Digest*, November-December 1983.

"Reporter Refuses to Yield Tape in Minnesota Privilege Law Test," *FOI Digest*, November-December 1975.

"Reporter Shield Statutes Provide Uncertain Protections," *FOI Digest*, January-February 1982.

"Reporters Across the Nation Confront Problem of Protecting Their Sources," *FOI Digest*, September-October 1978.

"Reporters' Shielding of News Sources Gets Varied Treatment from Courts," *FOI Digest*, January-February 1978.

"Reporters Struggle to Protect Sources in Court Cases Throughout the States," *FOI Digest*, January-February 1980.

"Scholars Request Immunity in Pentagon Papers Inquest," *FOI Digest*, November-December 1971.

"Selective Biography of Recent (1958 to Present) Articles Concerning the Reporters' Right to Keep Secret His Sources of Information," *FOI Digest*, July, 1963.

"Source Protection Right Upheld in Washington," *FOI Digest*, November-December 1983.

"South Carolina Paper, Reporters Feel Effects of Privilege Ruling," *FOI Digest*, July-August 1972.

"State Courts Deal Favorbly With Confidentiality of News Sources," *FOI Digest*, May-June 1977.

"State Legislatures and Courts Active in the Area of Reporters' Privilege," *FOI Digest*, May-June 1979.

"State of Florida Challenges Protection for Journalists," *FOI Digest*, September-October 1975.

"States Lose Fight for News Sources; Federal Judge Upholds Shield Privilege," *FOI Digest*, May-June 1982.

"Supreme Court Decides Against Press, Newsmen, Legislators to Name Sources," *FOI Digest*, March-April 1972.

"Supreme Court Hears Shield Law Arguments on Branzburg, Caldell, Pappas Cases," *FOI Digest*, May-June 1971.

Chapter 48

Public Radio, Public Television: The State as Restraint or Facilitator?

Public broadcasting in the United States has always had difficulty finding its place in the broadcasting media. Overshadowed by its larger cousin, commercial broadcasting, non-commerical television and radio seem unimportant to many. The problem is illustrated by the response from the FCC, the agency designated to regulate all of broadcasting, when it responded to a conference on Telecommunications Policy Research in 1975.

> While this topic [public broadcasting] does not appear to have any particular relevance to this commission's activities, it is fascinating, and probably merits consideration.

The history of public broadcasting has been one of uncertainty as Douglas Cater (1976), founder of the Aspen Institute Program on Communication and Society, has observed:

> It is not easy to trace a coherent plan for the development of public broadcasting in America. In 1952, Commissioner Freida Hennock and her colleagues on the FCC set aside a number of TV channels and radio frequencies to serve vaguely specified "educational needs of the community." A few universities, school systems and community associations, supported by a few private philanthropies, responded to this opportunity; but more than a decade later, educational radio and television had still made little impact.

The Kennedy Administration decided to provide facility funds, and set loose a station building boom throughout the country. But, then, in just a few more years, educational broadcasting found itself teetering on bankruptcy; the Carnegie Corporation responded to the urgent appeals of the system by setting up a study commission under the chairmanship of James Killian. Early in 1967, the Carnegie Report came forth with an ambitious design for noncommercial broadcasting, (henceforth to be designated "public") and President Johnson and the Congress pushed through legislation which created a nongovernmental corporation, Corporation for Public Broadcasting, CPB to help chart the future.

The passage of the Public Broadcasting Act of 1967 gave public broadcasting a big boost, but a crisis came in 1972 when, as Saundra Hybels and Dana Ulloth wrote in *Broadcasting: An Introduction* (1978):

> . . . Despite overwhelming Congressional support for CPB appropriations, Richard M. Nixon, then president, vetoed the bill. Basically, Nixon had two objections to CPB: he felt that it was supporting news and public affairs programs that were biased, and that it was becoming too powerful and centralized. Nixon believed that CPB was creating a fourth network whose power was centered in the Eastern cities—particularly New York and Washington. Instead he favored grassroots participation; a system in which all local stations would participate in the programming and decision-making process.

The problems of public broadcasting did not go away, even when, as Ulloth, Peter Klinge, and Sandra Eels noted in *Mass Media: Past, Present, and Future* (1983):

> In 1975, Congress passed for the first time a long-term, five-year educational broadcasting funding bill; previously, funding had been on a year-to-year basis. Although some of the funding for public television stations comes from federal sources, other funding sources include local boards of education, local governments, state boards of education, state governments universities, foundations, businesses, and industries, subscriptions, and auctions. Because they operate on such limited sources of funds, a significant drop in any area can lead to near disaster for public broadcasting stations. Moreover, their ties to sources of funds are quite frail.

The broadcast stations are not owned or operated by the federal government; rather, state governments, universities, school districts, local governments, and nonprofit organizations hold the licenses. The purpose for owing public stations varies as much as the nature of the owners, but some of the reasons include to disseminate instructional programs, provide an outreach for school districts and colleges, serve as a training ground for students, and to provide for direct instruction to classrooms from central locations.

Ideally, the public service should enhance free expression, but concerns over funding and political pressure often make achievement of this goal impossible.

National Public Radio:
Regulated and Assisted

by William A. Storer

National Public Radio is the only broadcast center that keeps alive the eastern establishment liberal idea of the Kennedy administration. It is a socially conscious organization, and essentially separate from its sister television equivalent, PBS, as well as free of intimidation or censorship by one of its largest sources of funds, the federal government.

National Public Radio, NPR, which should not be confused with American Public Radio or any state system, such as Minnesota Public Radio (the home of APR), has since its inception in the early 1970s, been an intricate part of the Washington, D.C., scene. NPR's first president, Frank Mankewicz, was press secretary to Sen. Robert Kennedy, and presidential campaign manager for Sen. George McGovern.

Such stories as NPR broadcasts are listened to by congressmen and a generally upscale audience including a majority of reporters in the United States. Nevertheless, the effect of NPR on public policy is virtually nil.

National Public Radio is also a program distribution center as well as a producer of programs. Not only does it produce such award-winning news programs as "All Things Considered" and "Morning Edition" from its Washington, D.C., studios, but also extensive arts, educational and cultural programming. Many cultural events are done as co-productions, such as the Santa Fe chamber music series, NPR's World of Opera, the Pittsburgh and St. Louis symphonies, and NPR Playhouse. Further, NPR distributes programs produced by member stations, such as WFMT Chicago, WGBH Boston, or WSCI Charleston, S.C.

NPR is partially funded by the Corporation for Public Broadcasting (CPB) which, like NASA, is a public corporation, not a department of the Federal government. However, CPB is funded directly by Congress, though its board is composed of presidential appointees who are a mixture of broadcast professionals and non-broadcast persons who represent geographical, national, or political interests. In fiscal year 1984, CPB supplied $10.4 million of the $22.9 million NPR budget.

CPB, which also funds PBS television programming, directly supports some NPR station affiliates, of which there were 325 in August 1985. Their support goes only to production centers, stations with full staffing, not satellite repeaters.

Dr. William A. Storer is currently president of MindAlive, an organization concerned with management training and research on learning processes. Storer has written extensively on the mass media and the new communication technologies—writing that has appeared in publications throughout the world. In addition, Storer has written what *The New York Times* called the definitive catalog of Frank Lloyd Wright's work. Storer has been an invited lecturer and instructor on interactive media for national conventions. Storer holds a Ph.D. from Ohio University (1968), the M.F.A. from Boston University (1962), and an A.B. from Harvard University (1959). [©1986, William A. Storer.]

For instance, South Carolina has seven broadcast facilities, each with its own call letters, but only two of these maintain production facilities.

A second source of funds for NPR is annual membership dues and distribution interconect fees, $1.42 million and $2.26 million of the 1984 budget, respectively. Each of the 325 affiliated stations pays NPR an annual membership fee for the right to use programming, plus fees for some specific programs. The interconnect charge is payment for the downlink from the NPR satellite. This specific fee, for the most part, is commonly paid indirectly through the NPR member stations by CPB. Production stations also need an uplink to the satellite, and this is charged on a "per use" basis.

Another major source of funding for NPR is the grants and contributions from foundations, corporation, associations, government agencies and individuals. Energy (oil) companies in particular have been lavish in their support of public broadcasting, and their images are well-known particularly on the PBS television network. Among the sponsors are Exxon for Lincoln Center programs, Texaco (radio and TV) for the Metropolitan Opera broadcast, Gulf for National Geographic specials, and Mobil for Masterpiece Theatre. In the 1984 fiscal year, 432 funders provided $4.01 million, all of them exerting a powerful, though indirect control.

There are two other main sources of funding for NPR–underwriting by commercial sponsors and fund raising by local stations. An underwriter usually pays all production costs. NPR and PBS member stations may have these programs free of any specific fee. Local stations or their state networks have fund raising usually twice a year; before Christmas and before Easter. Pledges are taken on phone lines, with normal programming "interrupted" by announcements related to the fund raising and its progress. These funds are kept by the individual stations, and used for purchase of programming rights, purchase of new recordings, but not usually for general operating expenses.

All this could change in 1987 when CPB financing may no longer go directly to NPR for its determination of use and sharing with member stations. Instead, it has been proposed, CPB funding will go only to the local NPR affiliates. Each may then determine to use these monies to purchase NPR supplied programming and other services or not, as each sees fit. Each may choose to originate more programing locally, or to buy from American Public Radio (from which originates the very popular "The Prairie Home Companion") or other sources. The delay to 1987 is related to the paying off of an enormous operating deficit incurred in the last years of the late 1970s and early 1980s.

Bibliography

Krawetz, Leah, *Public Television: Quo Vadis?*, Freedom of Information Center (Columbia, Mo.), July 1968.

Lynn, Harlan C., *Public Television in Transition*, Freedom of Information Center (Columbia, Mo.), April 1973.

Williamson, Mary E., *PTV — Good Guys and Gadflies*, Freedom of Information Center (Columbia, Mo.), January 1969.

Chapter 49

Copyright

Novelists, poets, dramatists, journalists, photographers, musicians, painters, television and film directors, scientists, and critics may product their creative works partly for the aesthetic satisfaction they derive from the experience; but they also work to receive payment for their efforts. It is not the desire of these creative individuals to give their work away, or to have others benefit financially from the produce without some income being paid to the originator. The creator wishes to restrict the free use of the work—an authoritarian concept. A conflict arises between the completely free exchange of information envisoned by the libertarian and the producer's desire to keep control over his or her work for profitable purposes.

The first known attempt to promote copyright legislation came from Noah Webster who wanted to protect his *American Spelling Book* and asked the colonial congress for action. The colonial congress had no power to enact copyright legislation; therefore, on May 2, 1783, it recommended to the colonies that they produce their own laws. By the time the United States Constitution was ratified in 1788, only Delaware had not adopted its own copyright legislation.

Recognizing this desire of writers to enjoy a return on the time invested, the writers of the Constitution of the Unied States incorporated as Article I, Section 8 (8) the provision:

> The Congress shall have Power to . . . promote the Progress of Science and useful Arts, by securing for limited Times to Authors and Inventors the exclusive Right to their respective Writings and Discoveries.

This provision provided the avenue by which Congress could create copyright laws to protect rights to creative output, but the concept of copyright predated the United States, with England passing a copyright statute in 1710 as "Statue of 8 Anne." Earlier, in 1556, Queen Mary I chartered the Stationers Company giving it a monopoly on book printing. The Stationers Company developed its own concept of common law copyright, believing that a writer or printer had rights to a work into perpetuity. In time, authors and printers urged Parliament to pass a formal statute of copyright, which became the Statue of 8 Anne in 1709. That law gave an author fourteen years of exclusive rights to a book with the provision that it could be renewed for a second fourteen years if the author was alive at the time. Authors and printers were unhappy with the new statue, and tried to get copyright in perpetuity reestablished. Their desires led to the House of Lords action in 1774, *Donaldson* v. *Beckett*, that established two forms of copyright, *statutory* and *common law*. Common law copyright applied only to unpublished works, protecting them in perpetuity; statutory copyright covered published works and was limited to twenty-eight years. This interpretation became the basis of law in the United States.

The first United States copyright law, in response to constitutional provisions, was passed in 1790 and gave the federal government *statutory* copyright authority; common law copyright was reserved to the state courts. The new law also provided protection for charts, maps, and books, and authors could enjoy the protection for fourteen years, with a renewal for a second fourteen year period. Not until 1891, however, did the copyright law extend to works by foreign authors. The law frightened publishers in the United States who saw considerable competition from less expensive foreign publishers, but the law included a requirement that published works had to be printed in the United States for distribution in the nation.

A new law, repealing all former copyright legislation, was passed in 1909 as a comprehensive act; however, the law omitted photoplays and motion pictures—an error that was corrected in 1912. The works that could be copyrighted included "all writings of an author," including addresses, lectures, periodicals, books, reproductions of works of art, photographs, prints, scientific and technical drawings, and dramatic compositions. But the law did not provide any protection for phonograph and other sound recordings.

The publication of the work gave the owner copyright, but copies of the work along with a registration of copyright form had to be sent to the United States copyright office for the author to be able to enjoy an enforcable claim. The certificate of registration from the copyright office was prima-facia evidence of ownership. The 1909 law provided twenty-eight years of protection with an additional twenty-eight years if the owner applied for the renewal.

Since the copyright law had undergone only slight revision since 1909, in 1955, the copyright office initiated an extensive study of the statute and eventually completed thirty-five studies leading to a recommendation for a revised bill in 1961. During the 1960s, a number of bills were introduced in Congress, but none were enacted into statute.

A new law was finally passed by Congress in 1976, becoming effective in 1978. The new law preempted common law copyright at the state level, leaving only the statutory form of copyright, and it attempted to deal with the problems of copyrighting works done in new media such as television, audio recordings, and video cassette; the law includes a clause covering unanticipated media. The new copyright law covers creative production in a number of media:

> Copyright protection, subsists . . . in original works of authorship fixed
> in any tangible medium of expression, not known or later developed, from

which they can be perceived, reproduced, or otherwise communicated, either directly or with the aid of a machine or device. Works of authorship include the following categories:

(1) literary works;
(2) musical works, including any accompanying words;
(3) dramatic works, including any accompanying music;
(4) pantomines and choreographic works;
(5) pictorial, graphic, and sculptured works;
(6) motion pictures and other audiovisual works; and
(7) sound recordings

Under the new law the duration of a copyright lasts for the life of the owner plus fifty years.

The copyright statute represents a real conflict between the desire to permit free use of thoughts by the media by limiting the right of dissemination to the holder of the copyright or to persons authorized. Yet, without copyright protections, most people would be unwilling to devote the time and energy to creating the music, fiction, journalism, motion pictures, and other works most people have come to expect as part of life.

The emergence of a number of new communication technologies during the late 1970s and early 1980s left the picture clouded regarding the effectiveness of the new copyright law to deal with the problems being raised. One area of special conflict arose because of the sale of home videotape recorders permitting the owner to cop programs from the air in presumed violation of copyright laws. Universal Studios, Inc. and Walt Disney Productions objected to the sale of Betamax videocassette recorders (VCRs), a product of Sony Corporation, because the machines could be used for the unauthorized copying of licensed television programs and movies from cable television and broadcast sources.

Universal and Disney initiated action against Sony in 1976 before the United States District Court for the Central District of California saying that Sony was liable for copyright infringements committed by customers who had bought Betamax recorders. Disney and Universal believed that the sale of videocassette machines would reduce their receipts for the movies and television programs they were producing.

The problem was not clear-cut because viewers could use their VCRs for time shifting, that is record a program for viewing at a more convenient time and then erase the tape for reuse—an action not considered illegal under the copyright act. The Supreme Court, however, refused to hold Sony responsible for the uses made of recorders it sold:

Sony demosntrated a significant likelihood that substantial numbers of copyright holders who license their works for broadcast on free television would not object to having their broadcast time-shifted by private viewers. And . . . respondents failed to demonstrate that time-shifting would cause any likelihood of non-minimal harm to the potential market for, or the value of, their copyrighted works. The Betamax is, therefore, capable of substantial noninfringing uses. Sony's sale of such equipment to the general public does not constitute contributory infringement of respondent's copyright.

But the problems of copyright and technological innovations did not disappear as the final paragraph of the Supreme Court opinion observed:

It may well be that Congress will take a fresh look at this new technology, just as it so often has examined other innovations in the past. But it is not our job to apply laws that have not yet been written.

Other areas where technological innovation have raised questions about copyright infringement include pay-television networks which distribute their programs to cable systems through satellites. One example is Home Box Office (HBO). HBO earns its revenues from sales made to subscribers by cable companies. Owners of satellite antennas can view HBO programs without cost. Effective 1986, HBO began use of a scrambling system to prevent unauthorized use. But what happens when someone discovers a method for putting the signal back into good order? And, people argue that the State has no right to enforce what is in "the atmosphere." Nevertheless, copyright exists throughout the world, as created by the State, to protect the people from what it considers unwarranted freedom.

Bibliography

"Arguments Over Copyright of Ford's Memoirs Concluding," *FOI Digest*, March-April 1982.

"Court Allows Government to Hold Copyrights," *FOI Digest*, March-April 1982.

Crow, Peter, *Toward a New Copyright Law*, Freedom of Information Center (Columbia, Mo.), March 1966.

DeWolf, R.C., *Outline of Copyright Law*. John W. Luce (Boston, Mass.), 1925.

"Facts in Book Research Not Covered by Copyright," *FOI Digest*, July-August 1981.

"High Court Decides to Hear Copyright Case Over Ford's Memoirs," *FOI Digest*, May-June 1984.

"High Court Refuses Review of Copyright Infringement Cause," *FOI Digest*, January-February 1978.

Kaplan, Benjamin, and Ralph S. Brown, Jr., *Cases on Copyright*, Foundation Press (Brooklyn, N.Y.), 1960.

Nimmer, Melvinne E. *Nimmer on Copyright* (Brooklyn, N.Y.), Matthew Bender (New York, N.Y.), 1963-1976, (2 vols.).

"Copyright Law Revision." United States House of Representatives Report No. 94-1476.

Solberg, Thorvald. *Copyright Enactments of the United States, 1783-1906* (Washington, 1906).

Title 17, United States Code, amended by Public Law 94-553, 94th Congress, 94 Stat. 2541 (1976).

Section 3

The State as Manipulator:
The Right to Influence

"[The First] Amendment rests on the assumption that the widest possible dissemination of information from diverse and antagonistic sources is essential to the welfare of the public."

—Justice Hugo Black

From mountains of press releases come avalanches of facts, enough to smother any reporter. In almost all cases, there are no factual errors. But, it is not necessary to lie to the American people in order to manipulate them. The selection and ordering of facts for a press release, combined with what is left out, is enough that it can be factual but not truthful. It makes no difference if the press release originates in the local PTA or in General Motors, in the neighborhood flower society or the Department of Defense, each organization, under the veil of giving information to the public, wishes to manipulate the public to do something, even if it's only to attend the local flower show. Underlying all apparent messages is the one true message—please have a better impression of us; every organization, no matter how impersonal it seems, has a fear that people will not think kindly of it; this fear, of course, translates into a fear not only of a lost image but in lost sales.

To preserve their access to the news media, the special-interest groups give journalists benefits not ordinarily available to the general public. Included could be something as innocuous as complimentary admissions, although many journalists and news organizations refuse "comps," as well as all gifts. Nevertheless, the organizations don't care, for there are numerous other ways to assure the reception of the message. For example, cub reporters usually have greater access to high-level executives than do four-decade employees of the corporation. Thus, the bonds tend to be formed between reporter and management than between reporter and worker. Organizations also provide "leaks" and "Exclusives" to selected journalists. Many organizations, from the Los Angeles Rams to Disneyland to the Congress, provide special work areas for the media. Few recognize that they are being manipulated by complimentary admissions, accompanied by pounds of press releases to be digested after they digest the lavish spread of gourmet food and liquor available to them—but not available to the masses of the public—in sports press boxes, amusement parks, or a special reception (for a new car, a new movie, a top-level promotion . . .). While the reporters are drinking their favorite liquors and eating prodigious meat-filled sandwiches or even prime rib, the masses are drinking watered-down soft drinks and eating two-ounce hamburgers—all at inflated prices. Fewer journalists will claim that the opulent press lounges and "press-only" elevators in Congress, the almost-instant access to governmental leaders, occasional parties with the "movers and shakers," among numerous other benefits, influence their stories, but no one can know what messages are being received by the subconscious.

Although journalists will often brag that they verify all press releases before revising them for publication, the truth is that not even the most careful editorial staff, even if given unlimited budget and personel, can check out every fact of every press release it plans to use. Even the largest news staffs not only can't check out all the facts, they can't even get half the stories on their own that are made known to them through the press release. Thus, it is the not the editorial staffs who contribute the most information to the public, but the country's special interests.

It's usually a fairly symbiotic relationship—reporters get the stories they need and the attention they enjoy (to make their difficult jobs easier), and the various self-interest groups get the stories *they* need; in the world of publicity, "some ink," even if unfavorable, is often better than "no ink" at all. Nevertheless, without the public relations professionals, the amount of news in print and on the air would decrease significantly, while increasing the public's basic fears and anxieties magnified by rumor carried through the medium of interpersonal communications.

Chapter 50

The Agencies of American Government

The leaders of the State, who have been given inherent responsibilites for the preservation of the State and the maintenance of public order, inject a fear into the people, but also live in fear of overthrow. Thus, the State also has an inherent *need* to be seen in the best possible light. A population that is given no information or even minimal information about its existence is likely to be a population that is oppressed; as levels of oppression increase, levels of resistance increase, leading to a threat to the security of the State itself. Therefore, even the most oppressive State has established formal channels to give information to the people.

According to Scott Cutlip and Allen Center, in *Effective Public Relations*:

> Long before the complexities of communication, there was acknowledged need for a third party to facilitate communication and adjustment between the government and the people. So it was with the church, tradesmen, and craftsmen . . . The communication of information to influence viewpoints or actions can be traced from the earliest civilizations. Archeologists found a farm bulletin in Iraq that told the farmers of 1800 B.C., how to sow their crops, how to irrigate, how to deal with field mice, and how to harvest their crops—an effort not too unlike today's distribution of farm bulletins by the U.S. Department of Agriculture. What is known today of ancient Egypt, Assyria, and Persia comes largely from recorded material intended to publicize and glorify the rulers of that day. Much of the literature and art of antiquity was designed to build support for kings, priests, and other leaders. Vergil's *Georgics* was written to persuade urban dwellers to move to the farms to produce food for the growing city. The walls of Pompeii were inscribed with election appeals. Caesar carefully prepared the Romans for his crossing of the Rubicon in 49 A.D. by sending reports to Rome on his epic achievements as governor of Gaul, and historians believe he wrote his *Commentaries* as propaganda* for himself . . .

---

*The modern interpretation of the word *propaganda* originated in 1662 when Pope Gregory XV established the *Congregatio de Propaganda Fide* (Congregation for Propagating the Faith) as a missionary program to train priests to spread Catholicism and to counter the emerging Protestant Reformation.

In seventeenth-century England, public opinion manifested itself in a victory over Stuart absolutism and showed rulers the need for cultivating good relationships with the public. Louis XIV of France engaged in his own type of public relations. He struck medals and sent ambassadors to various countries to enhance French prestige.

Perhaps the most successful propagandist in modern history were the American Radicals who had to change the attitudes of the overwhelming mass of citizens, as well as convince them that the Radical concepts of government were sound and not threatening to their existance. Without qeustion, it was the direction that Sam Adams gave to the Movement—which included almost all the techniques of propaganda currently used by contemporary society's most competent professionals—that eventually led not only to the Revolution, but also to the successful overthrow of an established government. Following the Revolution, Alexander Hamilton and James Madison, against significant opposition, but using many of the same tactics Sam Adams had successfully used for two decades, led the fight to have at least nine of the thirteen states ratify the proposed Constitution which called for a strong central government and, thus, was regarded with suspicion by most Americans, including Adams.

The Agencies of Information

Because of the inherent need to inform and influence the people, the State creates agencies and official channels for the dissemination of information. Although communications systems existed in the United States for almost a century, it wasn't until the Civil War that the United States created a formal system to disseminate information. In 1862, the United States created the Organic Act which directed federal agencies to "acquire and diffuse among the people of the United States, information on agriculture in the most general and comprehensive sense of the word." From that directive has come a flood of newsletters, flyers, pamphlets, books, films, and videotapes of interest not only to farmers, but also to most Americans.

Within a half-century, the dissemination of information had become a political issue, with the administration claiming that it needed to inform the people of the workings of its government, and the opposition claiming that the administration was using government employees and public information channels for propaganda. In 1913, the Congress reacted, creating the Gilbert Amendment which provided that "appropriated funds may not be used to pay a public relations expert unless specifically appropriated for that purpose." The result has been that *no* government agency has a "public relations expert" on its staff—however, there are several thousand "public affairs specialists," "public information specialists," "press secretaries," and "communications specialists."

During World War I, the United States created the Committee on Public Information. Heading the Committee was George Creel, one of the country's most respected journalists. The Committee responsibilities included establishing guidelines for voluntary censorship by the media, informing the people about the war effort, and boosting morale. Serving the government were numerous distinguished journalists and historians. However, after the war, historians Carl Becker, Guy Stanton Ford, and James Shotwell, among many others who had worked for the government, had to face the arrogance and pomposity of their colleagues who sanctimoniously charged them with having violated professional ethics by working for the government.

Nevertheless, several thousand writers, journalists, artists, and historians served in the government, many of them in the Federal Writers Program, a part of the Works Progress Administration (WPA), established by Franklin D. Roosevelt during the Depression. Many of them focused upon oral history projects, writing about the people of America, as seen through the eyes of the people. From WPA workers came *The Plow That Broke the Plains* (1936), a highly successful film story of Midwestern farmers. The film was shown in more than three thousand American theaters. The following year, the government produced the critically-acclaimed, *The River*.

Carl Byoir and Edward L. Bernays, two of the nation's leading public relations specialists, helped teach the government the necessity of a vigorous public relations program; writers Archibald Macleish and Robert Sherwood gave the government a foundation for the establishment of a massive propaganda system which emphasized truth as a basis of influence.

During World War II, the United States resurrected the Committee on Public Information, named it the Office of War Information, gave it some different responsibilities, then named Elmer Davis its director. Davis had been a reporter for *The New York Times* and CBS Radio news anchor. Although Davis and the OWI were often attacked, they conducted a responsible operation.

Truth, however, was not a necessity for the information/disinformation programs in Nazi Germany. Joseph Goebbels, who frequently noted that "Whoever says the first word to the world is always right," established the world's most complex, efficient propaganda system by directing his campaigns at mankind's emotions, rather than its rationality. By directing their messages to mankind's most essential emotion, fear, and using an underlying blanket that included a scattering of facts, Hitler and Goebbels were able to convince Germans—and much of the world—that the Jews had plans to take over industry, education, adn the arts. By the beginning of World War II in 1939, Goebbels and Hitler had succeeded in convincing much of Germany and the world of the existence of an invincible military machine that would help Germany reclaim its losses and embarassment from World War I while leading the new country into a "Thousand Year Reich."

"We no longer want the formation of public opinion, but rather the public formation of opinion."

—Joseph Goebbels, Nazi Propaganda Minister

After World War II, the United States expanded the role of the United States Information Agency, and gave it broad responsibilities for disseminating information about America. However, Congress, fearful that the USIA could be used for political purposes, forbid any of the USIA messages from being distributed within the United States. Within its vast program, the USIA currently publishes fifteen magazines in thirty-one languages, transmits more than twenty-five thousand words of news and features every day, produces several films each year, organizes exhibits and cultural affairs shows in most countries in the world, and operates more than two hundred world information centers, in addition to its comprehensive broadcast services.

The Individual Agencies of Government

Within the United States, the creation of channels for the dissemination of information has led to every federal agency, virtually all state governments and agencies, and many municipal governments and departments to have public information specialists either on consulting contract or on staff; some of the larger agencies have public information departments as well as several consultants. In

---

The great mass of people is not composed of diplomats or even teachers of political law, nor even of purely reasonable individuals who are able to pass judgment, but of human beings who are as undecided as they are inclined towards doubts and uncertainty. As soon as by one's own propaganda even a glimpse of right on the other side is admitted, the cause for doubting one's own right is laid. The masses are not in a position to distinguish where the wrong of the others ends and their own begins. In this case they become uncertain and mistrusting, especially if the enemy does not produce the same nonsense, but, in turn, burdens their enemy with all and the whole guilt. What is more easily explained than that finally one's own people believe more in the enemy's propaganda, which proceed more completely and more uniformly, than in one's own? This, however, may be said most easily of a people which suffers so severly from the mania of objectivity as the German people does. For now they will take pains not to do an injustice to the enemy, even at the risk of the severest strain on, or destruction of, his own nation and State.

—Adolph Hitler, *Mein Kampf*

---

addition, every U.S. Senator and governor, most representatives, and numerous other elected and appointed officials have public information staffs. No matter how professional, how objective a public relations professional is, there is still the underlying conflict—public relations personnel, most of them trained as journalists, often are torn between the necessity of informing the people and the reality of pleasing a boss, perhaps even being required to make the boss "look good." It's no different if the boss is in private industry or is a cabinet secretary to the President.

A report in *U.S. News and World Report* indicated "The federal government spends more money each year trying to influence the way people think than it spends altogether for disaster relief, foreign military assistance, energy conservation, and cancer research." Each year, attempting to inform the people, while making the boss look good, the federal government spends $1-2 billion—no one knows how much. The Department of Defense, the largest employer in the United States, spends over $45 million a year in advertising, operates a news bureau, a radio-television network, and a film studio, oversees more than 1,500 newspapers, several hundred magazines and yearbooks, and creates numerous shows, exhibits, and special teams, including the Navy's Blue Angels, the Air Force's Thunderbirds, and the Army's Golden Knights parachute team. To train its public information specialists and officers, the armed forces created the Defense Information School (DINFOS) at Fort Benjamin Harrison, Indiana. The curriculum compares favorably to that of most accredited schools of journalism.

The second largest public information program is that of the U.S. Department of Agriculture. The USDA specializes in publishing pamphlets and brochures of general interest to the public. However, it also produces films and radio and television shows and public service announcements.

National Media

In socialist and communist countries, all the media are owned by the State; in other forms of government, a small number of the media, perhaps only one newspaper, one radio and television station, are owned by the government. The most common ownership is of newspapers.

In the United States, the most respected, and most influential, newspaper was the *Washington Globe*, edited by Francis P. Blair (1791-1876) during the adminsitrations of Andrew Jackson (1767-1845, presidency, 1829-1837), and Martin Van Buren (1782-1862, presidency, 1837-1841). The early American official newspapers were assisted by official State subsidy; the *Globe* prospered on its editorial, circulation, and advertising strength—combined with a fear. Many persons read the *Globe* not because they agreed or disagreed with administration policies, but out of fear that by not reading it, they would miss the important news of Washington; businessmen often bought ads not only because their customers were Jackson supporters, but to support the administration's official newspaper and, quite possibly, because they thought that buying ads in the *Globe* would help them gain the favor of the administration.

After Van Buren and the Democrats lost the election of 1840, replaced by Whigs William Henry Harrison for one month, and John Tyler for the remainder of the term, the *Globe* lost much of its influence, becoming a general circulation newspaper with no official ties to the administration. In 1845, James K. Polk forced Blair to sell the *Globe*. With the exception of the Pacific and European editions of *Stars and Stripes*, relatively-independent military newspapers, there would be no other general circulation "official" newspapers in American history, although every president could count on at least a few newspapers to give him almost unqualified editorial support. Although there are no longer official newspapers to keep the people informed of a president's activities, the wire services and Washington-based newspaper and broadcast media bureaus now provide to clients a seemingly limitless log of the President's activities, announcements, and proclamations—even if it's only for something like National Pickle Day.

In many countries, especially those in the Third World and nations with low to moderate literacy levels, the State creates national radio and television stations. In almost all cases, the official broadcast stations are directed by the government to their own people. However, several countries have created broadcast systems directed to the people of other countries. The countries with the most broadcast hours are (in approximate order) the Soviet Union, the United States, the People's Republic of China, England, West Germany, North Korea, Albania, Cuba, Egypt, and East Germany.

The Voice of America (VOA), a part of the United States Information Agency, itself a part of the Department of State, was created in 1942. It currently broadcasts in forty languages, the signals carried by more than a hundred transmitters. VOA news broadcasts are reasonably objective and factual, although distinctly from an American perspective; VOA which broadcasts everything from opera and drama to Rock 'n' Roll "D.J." shows, reflects American cultural values.

In addition to the VOA, there are three semi-official operations. After World War II, the National Committee for a Free Europe created Radio Free Europe; the American Committee for Freedom for the Peoples of the USSR created Radio Liberty. Both the committees were fronts for the Central Intelligence Agency to permit funding for the stations. Additional funds came from public subscription drives. In 1973, after the CIA connection became widely known, Congress removed the stations from CIA domination, created the Board for International Broadcasting, and merged Radio Free Europe and Radio Liberty. Almost all funding is from Congressional budgets. Unlike VOA broadcasts, RFE/RL broadcasts are created as if the station were in the target country, broadcasting without restriction. In 1985, funding was approved for Radio Marti, directed to the people of Central America, and focused upon Cuba.

The American Forces Radio and Television Service (AFRTS) which includes shows broadcast on commercial radio and TV stations, is directed primarily to American military personnel on ships andnon-American bases, but the signals are often picked up by the people in other countries.

Although VOA is praised for its credibility, the British Broadcasting Company (BBC) is considered to be the most accurate of all external services. Part of the international credibility is based upon the relation of the BBC to the government. Although funding is provided by the Foreign Office, there are no government employees on BBC payrool, and BBC maintains a firm independent status.

How We Advertised America
by George Creel

The war was not fought in France alone. Back of the firing-line, back of armies and navies, back of the great supply-depots, another struggle waged with the same intensity and with almost equal significance attaching to its victories and defeats. It was the fight for the *minds* of men, for the "conquest of their convictions," and the battle-line ran through every home in every country.

It was in this recognition of Public Opinion as a major force that the Great War differed most essentially from all previous conflicts. The trial of strength was not only between massed bodies of armed men, but between opposed ideals, and moral verdicts took on all the value of military decisions. Other wars went no deeper than the physical aspects, but German *Kultur* raised issues that had to be fought out in the hearts and minds of people as well as on the actual firing-line. The approval of the world meant the steady flow of inspiration into the trenches; it meant the strengthened resolve and the renewed determination of the civilian population that is a nation's second line. The condemnation of the world meant the destruction of morale and the surrender of that conviction of justice which is the very heart of courage.

The Committee on Public Information was called into existence to make this fight for the "verdict of mankind," the voice created to plead the justice of America's cause before the jury of Public Opinion . . .

In no degree was the Committee an agency of censorship, a machinery of concealment or repression. Its emphasis throughout was on the open

---

George Creel, (1876-1953), one of the nation's most respected journalists was appointed by President Wilson in 1917 as director of the Committee on Public Information. He was editor of the *Kansas City Independent*, 1899-1909; *Denver Post*, 1909-1910; and *Rocky Mountain News*, 1911-1913. Among his books are *Quatrains of Christ* (1907), *Children in Bondage*, with Edwin Markham and B. B. Lindsey (1913), *Wilson and the Issues* (1916), *Ireland's Fight for Freedom* (1919), *How We Advertised America*, (1920), *The War, the World and Wilson*, (1920), *Uncle Henry*, (1923), *The People Next Door* (1926), *Sons of the Eagle* (1927), *Sam Houston* (1928), *Tom Paine—Liberty Bell* (1931), *War Criminals* (1944), *Rebel at Large* (1947), *Russia's Race for Asia* (1949) and *White House Physician* (collaborator). He was chair of the National Advisory Board of the Works Progress Administration, 1935. [This article has been edited and reprinted, with permission, from *How We Advertised America*, published by Harper & Bros., 1920. R1920, 1938, Harper & Bros.]

and the positive. At no point did it seek or exercise authorities under those war laws that limited the freedom of speech and press.

In all things, from first to last, without half or change, it was a plain publicity proposition, a vast enterprise in salesmanship, the world's greatest adventure in advertising.

Under the pressure of tremendous necessities an organization grew that not only reached deep into every American community, but that carried to every corner of the civilized globe the full message of America's idealism, unselfishness, and indomitable purpose. We fought prejudice, indifference, and disaffection at home and we fought ignorance and falsehood abroad. We strove for the maintenance of our own morale and the Allied morale by every process of stimulation; every possible expedient was employed to break through the barrage of lies that kept the people of the Central Powers in darkness and delusion; we sought the friendship and support of the neutral nations by continuous presentation of facts. We did not call it propaganda, for that word, in German hands, had come to e associated with deceit and corruption. Our effort was educational and informative throughout, for we had such confidence in our case as to feel that no other argument was needed than the simple, straightforward presentation of facts.

There was no part of the great war machinery that we did not touch, no medium of appeal that we did not employ. The printed word, the spoken word, the motion picture, the telegraph, the cable, the wireless, the poster, the signboard—all these were used in our campaign to make our own people and all other peoples understand the causes that compelled America to take arms. All that was fine and ardent in the civilian population came at our call until more than one hundred and fifty thousand men and women were devoting highly specialized abilities to the work of the Committee, as faithful and devoted in their servie as though they wore the khaki.

While America's summons was answered without question by the citizenship as a whole, it is to be remembered that during the three and a half years of our neutrality the land had been torn by a thousand divisive prejudices, stunned by the voices of anger and confusion, and muddled by the pull and haul of opposed interests. These were conditions that could not be permitted to endure. What we had to have was no mere surface unity, but a passionate belief in the justice of America's cause that should weld the people of the United States into one white-hot mass instinct with fraternity, devotion, courage, and deathless determination. The *war-will*, the will-to-win, of a democracy depends upon the degree to which each one of all the people of that democracy can concentrate and consecrate body and soul and spirit in the supreme effort of service and sacrifice. What had to be driven home was that all business was the nation's business, and every task a common task for a single purpose.

Starting with the initial conviction that the war was not the war of an administration, but the war of one hundred million people, and believing that public support was a matter of public understanding, we opened up the activities of government to the inspection of the citizenship. A voluntary censorship agreement safeguarded military information of obvious value to the enemy, but in all else the rights of the press were recognized and furthered. Trained men, at the center of effort in every one of the war-making branches of government, reported on progress and achievement, and in no other belligerent nation was there such absolute frankness with respect to every detail of the nation war endeavor.

As swiftly as might be, there were put into pamphlet form America's reasons for entering the war, the meaning of America, the nature of our free institutions, our war aims, likewise analyses of the Prussian system, the purposes of the imperial German government, and full exposure of the enemy's misrepresentations, agressions, and barbarities. Written by the country's foremost publicists, scholars, and historians, and distinguished for their conciseness, accuracy, and simplicity, these pamphlets blew as a great wind against the clouds of confusion and misrepresentation. Money could not have purchased the volunteer aid that was given freely, the various universities lending their best men and the National Board of Historical Service placing its three thousand members at the complete disposal of the Committee. Some thirty-odd booklets, covering every phase of America's ideals, purposes, and aims, were printed in many languages other than English. Seventy-five millions reached the people of America, and other millions went to every corner of the world, carrying our defense and our attack.

The importance of the spoken word was not underestimated. A speaking division toured; great groups like the Blue Devils, Pershing's Veterans, and the Belgians arranged mass-meetings in the communities, conducted forty-five war conferences from coast to coast, co-ordinated the entire speaking activities of the nation, and assured consideration to the crossroads hamlet as well as to the city.

The Four Minute Men, an organization that will live in history by reason of its originality and effectiveness, commanded the volunteer services of 75,000 speakers, operating in 5,200 communities, and making a total of 755,190 speeches.

With the aid of a volunteer staff of several hundred translators, the Committee kept in direct touch with the foreign-language press, supplying selected articles designed to combat ignorance and disaffection. It organized and directed twenty-three societies and leagues designed to appeal to certain classes and particular foreign-language groups, each body carrying a specific message of unity and enthusiasm to its section of America's adopted peoples.

It planned war exhibits for the state fairs of the United States, also a great series of interallied war expositions that brought hom to our millions the exact nature of the struggle that was being waged in France. In Chicago alone two million people attended in two weeks, and in nineteen cities the receipts aggregated $1,432,261.36

The Committee mobilized the advertising forces of the country—press, periodical, car, and outdoor—for the patriotic campaign that gave millions of dollars' worth of free space to the national service.

It assembled the artists of America on a volunteer basis for the production of posters, window-cards, and similar material of pictorial publicity for the use of various government departments and patriotic societies. A total of 1,438 drawings was used.

It issued an official daily newspaper, serving every department of government, with a circulation of one hundred thousand copies a day. For official use only, its value was such that private citizens ignored the supposedly prohibitive subscription price, subscribing to the amount of $77,622.58.

It organized a bureau of information for all persons who sought direction in volunteer war-work, in acquiring knowledge of any administrative activities, or in approaching business dealings with the government. In the ten months of its existence it gave answers to eighty-six thousand requests for specific information.

It gathered together the leading novelists, essayists, and publicists of the land, and these men and women, without payment, worked faithfully in the production of brilliant, comprehensive articles that went to the press as syndicate features.

One division paid particular attention to the rural press and the plate-matter service. Others looked after the specialized needs of the labor press, the religious press, and the periodical press. The Division of Women's War Work prepared and issued the information of peculiar interest to the women of the United States, also aiding in the task of organizing and directing.

Through the medium of the motion picture, America's war progress, as well as the meanings and purposes of democracy, were carried to every community in the United States and to every corner in the world. "Pershing's Crusaders," "America's Answer," and "Under Four Flags" were types of feature films by which we drove home America's resources and determinations, while other pictures, showing our social and industrial life, made our free institutions vivid to foreign peoples. From the domestic showings alone, under a fair plan of distribution, the sum of $878,215 was gained, which went to support the cost of the campaigns in foreign countries where the exhibitions were necessarily free.

Another division prepared and distributed still photographs and stereopticon slides to the press and public.

Over two hundred thousand of the latter were issued at cost. This division also conceived the idea of the "permit system," that opened up our military and naval activities to civilian camera men, and operated it successfully. It handled, also, the voluntary censorship of still and motion pictures in order that there might be no disclosure of information valuable to the enemy. The number of pictures reviewed averaged seven hundred a day.

Turning away from the United States to the world beyond our borders, a triple task confronted us. First, there were the peoples of the Allied nations that had to be fired by the magnitude of the American effort and the certainty of speedy and effective aid, in order to relieve the war-weariness of the civilian population and also to fan the enthusiasm of the firing-line to new flame. Second, we had to carry the truth, we had to get the ideals of America, the determination of America, and the invincibility of America into the Central Powers.

Unlike other countries, the United States had no subsidized press service with which to meet the emergency. As a matter of bitter fact, we had few direct news contacts of our own with the outside world, owing to a scheme of contracts that turned the foreign distribution of American news over to European agencies. The volume of information that went out from our shores was small, and, what was worse, it was concerned only with the violent and unusual in our national life. It was news of strikes and lynchings, riots, murder cases, graft prosecutions, sensational divorces, the bizarre extravagance of "sudden millionaires." Naturally enough, we were looked upon as a race of dollar-mad materialists, a land of cruel monopolists, our real rulers the corporations and our democracy a "fake."

Looking about for some way in which to remedy this evil situation, we saw the government wireless lying comparatively idle, and through the close and generous co-operation of the navy we worked out a news machinery that soon began to pour a steady stream of American information into international channels of commnication. An office [was opened] in every capital of the world outside the Central Powers.

For the first time in history the speeches of a national executive were given universal circulation. The official addresses of President Wilson, setting forth the position of America, were put on the wireless always at the very moment of their delivery, and within twenty-four hours were in every language in every country in the world. Carried in the newspapers initially, they were also printed by the Committee's agents on native presses and circulated by the millions. The swift rush of our war progress, the tremendous resources of the United States, the Acts of Congress, our official deeds and utterances, the laws that showed our devotion to justice, instances of our enthusiasm and unity—all were put on the wireless for the information of the world.

Through the press of Switzerland, Denmark, and Holland we filtered an enormous amount of truth to the German people, and from our headquarters in Paris went out a direct attack upon [German] censorship. Mortar-guns, loaded with "paper bullets," and airplanes, carrying pamphlet matter, bombarded the German front, and at the time of the armistice balloons with a cruising radius of five humdred miles were ready to reach far into the Central Powers with America's message.

This daily news service by wire and radio was supplemented by a mail service of special articles and illustrations that went into foreign newspapers and magazines and technical journals and periodicals of special appeal. We aimed to give in this way a true picture of the American democracy, not only in its war activities, but also in its devotion to the interests of peace. There were, too, series of illustrated articles on our education, our trade and industry, our finance, our labor conditions, our religions, our work in medicine, our agriculture, our women's work, our govenment, and our ideals.

Reading-rooms were opened in foreign countries and furnished with American books, periodicals, and newspapers. Schools and public libraries were similarly supplied. Photographs were sent for display on easels in shop windows abroad.

Window-hangers and news-display sheets went out in English, French, Italian, Swedish, Portuguese, Spanish, Danish, Norwegian, and Dutch; and display-sheets went to Russia, China, Japan, Korea, parts of India and the Orient, to be supplemented with printed reading-matter by the Committee's agents there.

To our representatives in foreign capitals went, also, the feature films that showed our military effort-cantonments, shipyards, training-stations, war-ships, and marching thousands-together with other motion pictures expressing our social and industrial progress, all to be retitled in the language of the land, and shown either in theaters, publid squares, or open fields. Likewise we supplied pamphlets for translation and distribution, and sent speakers, selected in the United States from among our foreign-born, to lecture in the universities and schools, or else to go among the farmers, to the labor unions, to the merchants, etc.

Every conceivable means was used to reach the foreign mind with America's message, and in addition to our direct approach we hit upon the idea of inviting the foremost newspaper men of other nations to come to the United States . . . that they might report truly to their people as to American unity, resolve, and invincibility . . .

From being the most miunderstood nation, America became the most popular. A world that was either inimical, contemptuous, or indifferent was changed into a world of friends and well-wishers. Our policies, America's unselfish aims in the war, the services by which these policies were explained and these aims supported, and the flood of news items and articles about our normal life and our commonplace activities—these combined to give a true picture of the United States to foreign eyes. It is a picture that will be of incalculable value in our future dealings with the world, political and commercial. It was a bit of press-agenting that money could not buy, done out of patriotism by men and women whose services no money could have bought.

In no other belligerent nation was there any such degree of centralization as marked our duties. In England and France, for instance, five to ten organizations were intrusted wiht the tasks that the Committee discharged in the United States . . .

[It was a] world-fight for the verdict of mankind—a fight that was won against terrific odds—and all for less than five million [dollars]—less than half what Germany spent in Spain alone!

It is the pride of the Committee, as it should be the pride of America, that every activity was at all times open to the sun. No dollar was every sent on a furtive errand, no paper subsidized, no official bought. From a thousand sources we were told of the wonders of German propaganda, but our original determinations never altered. Always did we try to find out what the Germans were doing and then we did not do it . . .

What was needed, and what we installed, was official machinery for the preparation and release of all news bearing upon America's war effort—not opinion nor conjecture, but facts—a running record of each day's progress in order that the father and mothers of the United States might gain a certain sense of partnership. Newspaper men of standing and ability were sworn into the government service and placed at the very heart of endeavor in the War and Navy departments, in the War Trade Board, the War Industries Board, the Department of Justice, and the Department of Labor. It was their job to take deadwood out of the channels of information, permitting a free and continuous flow.

A more delicate and difficult task could not have been conceived, for both the press and the officials viewed the arrangement with distrust, if not hostility. On the side of government there was the deep conviction that necessary concealments were being violated, and even when this antagonism was overcome there developed the assumption that only "favorable news" should be given out for publication. It was for our insistence that the bad should be told with the good, failures admitted along with the announcements of success, and that the representatives of the Committee should have the unquestioned right to exercise their news sense and to check up every statement in the interest of absolute accuracy . . .

On the part of the press was the fear, and a very natural one, that the new order of things meant "press-agenting" on a huge scale. This fear could not be argued away, but had to be met by actual demonstration of its groundlessness. Our job, therefore, was to present the facts without the slightest trace of color or bias, either in the selection of news or the manner in which it was presented. Thus, in practice, the Division of News set forth in exactly the same colorless style the remarkable success of the Browning guns, on the one hand, and on the other the existence of bad health conditions in three or four of the cantonments. In time the correspondents realized tha we were running a government news bureau, not a press agency, and their support became cordial and sincere. The Division of News kept open the whole twenty-four hours. Every "story," on the moment of its completion, was mimeographed and "put on the table" in the press-room where the news correspondents came regularly. These "stories" were "live news," meant for the telegraph-wire, and the method employed assured speedy, authoritative, and equitable distribution of the decisions, activities and intentions of the government in its war-making branches.

Not only this, but the Division of News was the one central information bureau. Before its creation, Washington correspondents, running down a "story" or tracking a rumor, were compelled to visit innumerable offices, working dealy to overburdened officials, or else telephoning endlessly, even dragging department heads out of their beds at ungodly hours. Our desk men, in touch with every happening at every hour of the day and night, were able to confirm or deny, so that one visit or one telephone-call met the need of the correspondent, saving his time and likewise the time of the officials.

No attempt was made, however, to prevent independent news-gathering or to interfere with individual contacts. It was our insistence and arrangement that correspondents should have daily interviews with all executive heads, and in every case where a correspondent, feature-writer, or magazine-writer had an idea for a "story" either we supplied him with the facts, information, and statistics desired or else cleared the way for him to get his material first hand.

When we found that the rural press was experiencing a sense of neglect, in that it had neither wire service nor Washington correspondents, we secured the services of a capable "country editor" from the state of Washington, and had him prepare a weekly digest of the official war news that went to the country weeklies in galley form. Country dailies also asked to be put on this list, which grew to more than twelve thousand. Atg any intimation that this matter was not desired the paper was removed from the mailing-list, and by this and other checking we were able to keep a more or less careful watch on the extent to which the service was used. It ran as high as six thousand columns a week.

There can be no question as to the value of the Division of News to the government itself. Through its news-gathering machinery it gave to the people a daily chronicle of the war effort so frank, complete, and accurate that in time it developed a public confidence that stood like iron against the assaults of rumor and the hysteria of whispered alarm . . .

The Committee, while safeguarding the interests of the government and upholding the rights of the press, felt that its true responsibility was to the people of the United States. As a consequence of this belief, which put us between the press and the government as an independent, impartial force, the Committee met with almost constant attack from either one side or the other. When we supported the contentions of the correspondents, the admirals and generals declared that we wanted "to run the war in the interest of the newspapers," and when we accepted censorship rulings as sound and reasonable, the press talked wildly of gags and muzzles. Sometimes it was the case that both sides joined in the attack, forgetting differences in the joy of a common irritation.

Information, Culture, and Public Diplomacy: Searching for an American Style of Propaganda

by Lois W. Roth and Richard T. Arndt

From the beginning, American ambivalence about the practice of international propaganda has been manifest. Doubts about its appropriateness and relevance to the American self-image have continued to haunt discussion of the issue. Clear functional definitions of information, of cultural affairs, and of "propaganda"—the three elements subsumed under Edmund Gullion's catchy euphemism "public diplomacy"—have consistently been avoided by canny bureaucrats, wise congressmen, busy academics, and a media world with its own discomforts. Each administration since 1945 has devised rhetoric to suit its perceptions of need, but these formulae have met with little informed criticism, nor have they often been confronted by the contradictions of institutional memory. Periodically, some public figure will commit an article or a book to print, but even these ephemeral attacks on "the USIA problem" share no common vocabulary.

Yet, since 1950 more than thirty-five separate major studies of the question, in one form or another, can be counted; thirty-one of these took place in the twenty-five year period 1951-1977, a serious attempt to understand the proper role of overseas "information" and "educational-cultural" programs within the context of a democratic American society. Indeed, almost half of the sixty-five-odd public policy studies on foreign affairs reorganization in the same period dwell on what we now call "public diplomacy." Since 1977, however, public discussion has faded, except for five annual reports (1980, 1982, 1983, 1985, 1986)

Lois Roth, before her sudden death in January 1986, was a senior foreign service officer who had served abroad as Cultural Affairs Officer in Tehran, Rome, and Paris. In her last assignment, she directed the United States Information Agency's (USIA) Arts America office, concerned with the overseas outreach of American visual and performing arts. She received her B.A. from Columbia and after graduate work there went as a Fulbright Fellow in sociology to Uppsala University in Sweden. Before joining USIA, she worked for ten years with the American–Scandinavian Foundation in New York. Her husband, Richard Arndt, retired from USIA in the Fall of 1985 after nearly a quarter–century of service. After teaching at Columbia University, he became cultural attache at the American Embassies in Beirut, Colombo, Tehran, Rome, and Paris. In 1972–1974, he directed the Office of Youth, Student, and Special Programs in the State Department Bureau of Educational and Cultural Affairs. Beginning in 1980, he held several senior positions in USIA's newly–acquired Bureau of Educational and Cultural Affairs, most importantly that of Director of Policy, Plans, and Evaluation, before moving to the Office of Near Eastern, South Asian, and North African Affairs as program coordinator. He took his B.A. at Princeton and his Ph.D. at Columbia in French literature. He was a Fulbright Fellow at the University of Dijon in the first year of the French program and later spent a year as Mid-Career Fellow at the Woodrow Wilson School of Public and International Affairs, Princeton University. At present he is teaching a seminar on American cultural diplomacy at the University of Virginia. [This article derives from the groundbreaking, "Public Diplomacy and the Past: The Search for an American Style of Propaganda (1952-1977)," by Lois W. Roth, and published in the *Fletcher Forum*, Summer 1984. This version was prepared by Dr. Arndt with her full cooperation in the Fall of 1985.]

by the United States Information Agency's Advisory Commission. Meanwhile, the Reagan administration has added a new dimension to the discussion by launching a program in "public diplomacy" out of the State Department rather than USIA, with no functional definition as yet made public.

An excursion into history, along with a bit of semantics, is useful in placing these studies, highly visible milestones in the American search for our own way of doing propaganda, into a context that focuses the issues. On the one hand, how was the national antipathy for the art overcome sufficiently to allow propaganda programs to be developed into permanent bureaucratic structures? On the other, how can we explain the persistent longing for international propaganda programs in Washington and the recurrent resurgence of hard-sell policy crowding out proven soft-sell techniques? And, how have these issues fared in the last decades in the face of a shift in national values, as the precariously balanced idealist-internationalist world view of the forties, fifties and sixties has tipped towards a realist-nationalist consensus? How have the issues been shaped in a period marked by a rise in the militarized rhetoric of national crisis?

Early History

Prior to World War I, diplomacy was regarded by all nations, and certainly by Americans, as the formal relationship between governments. With rare exceptions, it was deemed neither necessary nor proper to attempt to reach the people of other nations over or around their governments.

The exceptions came in time of war, even in the U.S. One week after the United States entered World War I, President Wilson instituted the first official U.S. government propaganda office, appointing journalist George Creel to direct it. Its mandate was to make U. S. war aims widely known throughout the world. Creel was sensitive to the pejorative meaning that the Latin gerund "propaganda" had acquired since its origins in 17th-century Rome, when the Committee of Cardinals was established to direct the propagation of the faith. He insisted that the word "information" be used to describe his activities. His office was named euphemistically the Committee on Public Information, marking the opening of a long quest for new American forms of activity in this domain, for a style that would overcome an American distaste for tinkering with the truth. As befitted the President of a democratic nation now at peace, Wilson abolished the Creel Committee in 1919.

If Creel was nervous about propaganda in 1917, what might he have thought if he had known then what the Soviets and the Axis powers would soon make of it? The Soviet hierarchy in the early 1920s, following Lenin's lead, viewed propaganda dispassionately. Their attempt to reach mass foreign audiences directly through propaganda techiques, based on their success at manipulating domestic audiences, went well beyond the niceties of traditional diplomacy. By the thirties, the international propaganda programs of Italian Fascism and later of Nazi Germany, also designed originally to consolidate their domestic positions began to reach abroad.

At first, these developments posed little threat to the United States. But as the European crisis deepened and the tempo of world propaganda increased, the U.S. reacted. In 1938, responding first to the appeal of the universities and the great foundations, but mindful as well of the spread of Axis propaganda, Franklin D. Roosevelt created an Interdepartmental Committee for Scientific Cooperation and a Division of Cultural Cooperation. Although the philanthropists, the universities, and earlier the American missionaries had long practiced cultural relations abroad, these offices in the Department of State marked the beginning of *official* U.S. cultural relations with foreign countries (Frank Ninkovich has documented the period from 1938 to 1950 in his remarkable critical record of these early years, *The Diplomacy of Ideas*). The French had formalized cultural relations as part of diplomacy in the twenties and the British Council was founded in 1935 in response to Axis programs. Now the U.S. government, the last of the great powers to do so, formally entered the arena of intergovernmental cultural relations, previously left to its private sector.

The U.S. did so for important political reasons which were not long in becoming overwhelming. It is significant that in the initial phase these programs built only a cultural relations structure; despite major political imperatives, there emerged nothing more than a benign coordinating function for overseas educational exchanges, a function long sought by the universities and the great foundations and designed to leave most of the decisions in non-governmental hands. But by 1941, these programs had turned activist, especially in Latin America under Nelson Rockefeller's dynamic Office of Inter-American Affairs. The program under Roosevelt's Good Neighbor Policy, which contained the seeds of every government technique in information and cultural affairs we know today, was created in peacetime as a means of countering hostile propaganda. But the title of this effort contained neither the word "information" nor "propaganda."

With the onset of World War II, the situation changed radically. In 1941, President Roosevelt established an Agency for Foreign Intelligence and Propaganda (the one time the word was ever used in the name of a U.S. government agency). One of its divisions, the Foreign Information Service, operated without sanction of Congress until subsumed in 1942 under the Office of War Information (OWI), a name reviving Creel's euphemism. The cultural programs with Latin America, like those initiated with China and the Near East at the same time, were kept separate from the OWI; a carefully articulated policy decision saw information programs as different from the cultural and educational effort, in part because information programs were aimed primarily at enemy and occupied territories, while cultural and educational affairs were directed toward neutral and friendly areas.

At the end of the war, Harry Truman, responding to perceptions of the popular mood, ordered the dismantling of the wartime agencies, including both the OWI and Rockefeller's Office; but he kept Archibald MacLeish's Office of Public and Cultural Affairs (the title is a prescient linkage of functions). With the Cold War clouding the distinction between war and peace, Truman established in the Department of State an Office of Information and Cultural Affairs within MacLeish's old office. "Information" and "cultural affairs" finally joined hands.

Ad-man William Benton, Truman's undersecretary for public and cultural affairs, had jurisdiction over the Office. He proceeded energetically to plan for a long-term peacetime operation, eliminating those wartime functions deemed unnecessary. Benton unveiled his new plan in January 1946 in a speech calling for "a dignified information program, as distinguished from propaganda," adding that President Truman wanted the U.S. to "continue to endeavor to see to it that other peoples receive a full and fair picture of American life and of the aims and policies of the U.S. government." So began the first official peacetime program in the now-linked information and cultural affairs; it was aimed squarely at "other peoples," not governments; and it was based on the notion of a "full and fair picture," a phrase that would live on. The United States had entered a new era of diplomacy—never again would American conduct of foreign affairs take place solely between governments.

Confusion arose early from the lack of a strong rationale for information activities. One group, epitomized by the "Cold Warriors," argued that the U.S. needed an activist program, including a strong if covert "disinformation" component. They saw the need for the kind of propaganda and counter–propaganda activities that the war had proved valuable; they believed that the Cold War required the same kind of tools, adjusted for peacetime. This theme—the need for an unabashed propaganda effort—would recur until today, particularly during periods of heightened international tension, and was usually followed by upswings both in Congressional appropriations and increased scrutiny into these programs.

Others saw the need, as they had in 1938, for a benign and coordinative educational and cultural diplomacy designed to facilitate the extension abroad of the powerful U.S. private sector. They assumed that most nations, most of the time, are friendly, and they set about constructing an agenda for peaceful relationships. This position found a new champion in Senator J. William Fulbright, and an ill-defined slogan in "mutual understanding." Fulbright's amendment to the Surplus Property Act of 1946, the authorizing legislation for the pathfinding Fulbright Program of academic exchanges, and later the broader Smith-Mundt Act of 1948, used this phrase without defining it. Together, these two Acts launched the most imaginative effort ever in U.S. foreign relations; yet, they permitted divergent definitions and interpretations. As specified by Smith-Mundt, for fourteen years the omnibus legislation for overseas information and cultural activities, the purpose of both programs was "to promote better understanding of the United States in other countries, and to increase mutual understanding between the people of the United States and the people of other countries."

Ironically, although its language reflected peaceful assumptions, the Smith-Mundt Act owed its passage to the Cold War. The debate surrounding the passage of the bill focused sharply on the distinction between information and educational activities; there was much insistence that the two be kept separate. The information program, in the debates, was variously described as the "psychological approach," "propaganda," or "public relations," designed to gain acceptance of U.S. policies abroad. Educational exchanges on the other hand were described as "cooperative," "reciprocal," a "dialogue." They were seen in a framework of more general and longer–range, though surely no less political, objectives.

In April 1948, to reflect the intent of the new law, the State Department's Office of International Information and Educational Exchange was divided, creating an Office of Educational Exchange and another Office of International Information. A 1950 task force on government reorganization modified the new organization—a director was appointed, under the assistant secretary of state for public affairs, to supervise both information and educational activities.

Meanwhile, the rapid pace of international events—including the coup d'etat in Czechoslovakia, the defeat of Nationalist forces in China, the Berlin Block-ade, the detonation of the first Soviet atomic bomb in late 1949, and growing anti-communist sentiment in the United States—led to President Truman's call in April 1950 for a "Campaign of Truth," a phrase he specifically preferred to "propaganda campaign." When the Soviet Union's disinformation efforts boomed following North Korea's invasion of the South, Congress tripled pro-gram funds for international information activities. By now, the National Security Council (NSC) was defining the primary mission of the information program as the deterrence of the Soviet war effort. In January 1952, yet another reorganization turned the U.S. International Information Administration (IIA) into a semi–autonomous unit, still within the Department of State.

The new unit, freed from its former colleagues in Public Affairs and their concerns with a domestic audience, was now solely responsible for overseas information activities and educational exchange programs, and the grave doubts often expressed in Congress about a U.S. agency which might propagandize the American people were laid aside. This office remained intact until August 1953, when the U.S. Information Agency (USIA) was separated entirely from the State Department (though without educational and cultural affairs, which remained in State until 1977). Now the United States was set firmly on a course where information concerns dominated educational and cultural affairs, a path from which this nation has not strayed. More than any other single issue, the insistence on including the educational and cultural affairs dimension under the same roof may have frustrated attempts to conceptualize an approach to propaganda in a distinctive American way, while feeding the endless debate on the "integrity" of cultural relations.

Concepts and Issues

From the beginning, the U.S. had only the vaguest conceptual idea of what was expected in peacetime from its overseas information and cultural programs. The lack of precision in concept, questionable analogies with the worlds of advertising and public relations, the loosely-written legislation, capricious Con-gressional oversight, and American ambivalence about foreign policy goals—these combined with the national allergy to "propaganda" to leave USIA's iden-tity more to the whim of its directors than that of most federal agencies.

Part of the conceptual confusion was semantic. Dictionaries may be banal sources, but they are good indicators of the perceived meaning of words at given moments, part of our concern in this paper. *Webster's Unabridged Dictionary* of 1955 defines "propaganda" as any organized or concerted group effort to spread a particular doctrine or system of doctrines or principles, as a scheme or plan for the propagation of a doctrine or system of principles. Harold Lasswell's classic definition of propaganda is also useful for our purposes—it is the attempt to use language to influence mass attitudes on controversial issues, implying that the speaker takes one side or another. On the other hand, "information," according to the 1955 Webster, has a different complex of meanings—it is neutral knowledge communicated by others or obtained by personal study and investigation. The era of "information science" was not yet upon us, even if by 1955 Webster's had noted the work of Claude Shannon and Warren Weaver.

By the fifties, the professionals had begun to make distinctions between *black propaganda*, or information falsely attributed; *grey propaganda*, or unattributed information; and *white propaganda*, information clearly attributed either directly or by inference. Disinformation, the dissemination of false information methodically and purposefully calculated to mislead, was not yet a theme for the average person except in the practice of totalitarian powers and in novels of espionage.

On the information side, it might have been assumed that different conceptual approaches were required for friendly as opposed to enemy targets, but it was not. One analyst, in an early study of overseas information activities, thought information should be less closely linked to controversial issues; U.S. information materials should be selected for the purpose of reinforcing favorable impressions of the United States in allied, neutral, or liberated (i.e. friendly) territories. But, in a Cold War climate, with a battle to be waged midst foreign friends as well as against the Soviet Bloc, the Agency in its search for self-definition tended to describe its methods in the same terms for both ends.

With "educational and cultural affairs," on the other hand, there was an ample diplomatic tradition, a virtual canon established by the French and British, with subtle variations for friends or enemies. Moreover, the universities and the American intellectual world, in the great European humanist tradition, knew precisely what they wanted from the programs remaining in State; so there was less uncertainty (or more traditionalism, depending on the viewpoint) in the definition of the cultural functions.

These three terms—propaganda, information, educational and cultural affairs—define three separate if sometimes overlapping functions in the everyday world. But the language of officialdom tends to be less precise so as to be more operational, and words take on new lives within a bureaucracy. Reading the vague language of the Fulbright Amendment of 1946, it is impossible to foresee what the administrative imagination would later create under its authority. It is not unique to U.S. government officials that they tend to describe functions actually being fulfilled with the rhetoric that comes to hand; their genius lies in doing what they believe needs to be done, under whatever authority.

The vocabulary of American-style propaganda needed omnibus words, so new phrases began to creep into government terminology. "Public affairs," a post-World War II concept borrowed from PR-genius Edward Bernays and used in MacLeish's title as early as 1944, represented a stage beyond "public information" or "public relations." Public affairs people actually participate in policy decisions, getting in on "the takeoffs as well as the crash-landings," in Edward R. Murrow's famous phrase. Quickly "public affairs" came to be defined operationally, encompassing what USIA did—a mix of information, educational and cultural activities aimed directly at foreign audiences. To this day, all USIA field posts are headed by a Public Affairs Officer (PAO).

The portemanteau phrase "public affairs" was enlarged upon in 1965 by Edmund Gullion, who coined "public diplomacy" to cover non-governmental, private-sector and direct people-to-people programs as well as what USIA did on its own. "Cultural diplomacy" emerged later, as a working concept for the Stanton Panel's 1975 report, connoting overseas programs in a broad range of intellectual, artistic, and educational activities which, while also transmitting information about the attainments of a nation, were designed to forge the kind of links that bind nations together.

In short, this mosaic of terminology has not helped much over the years, in the American attempt to define goals for its information and cultural activities. Indeed the conceptual Babel probably reflected, then in turn exacerbated a series of wasteful turf-wars over programs in these fields.

In bureaucracies without strong concepts, issues proliferate. Returning to the 30 studies devoted to information and cultural affairs before 1977, we find that issues hang on recurrent themes. Three basic questions arise repeatedly:

(1) Does the U.S. government need propaganda programs as part of its foreign policy arsenal?

(2) Should the U.S. government operate information and cultural programs as part of its foreign policy?

(3) Are the purposes of such programs clearly articulated and understood?

These then give rise to other questions:

(4) What means should be employed to carry out these programs? Should they tell the whole truth ("full and fair picture") or should they present only favorable information about the United States? Should they be generally informative, or should they be targeted to countering both honest misunderstandings about the United States and distortions spawned by the propaganda of others? Should our programs attack other nations (e.g. the Soviet Union)?

(5) Should these programs be designed to serve long-range strategic goals of "mutual understanding," or should they be used in the service of more specific, tactical foreign policy objectives?

(6) Are short-term objectives and long-range goals best met by the same, or by different programs? Is information a short-range and culture a long-range game? Can these two functions live together within the same organization? If so, how should the optimal mix between long and short, cultural and informational, hard and soft sell, be determined for each country program?

These macro-issues have concerned students of U.S. information and cultural programs. Certain areas of micro-concern have repeatedly preoccupied those who examine the USIA and its predecessor organizations:

(a) *Advisory role*: Should the head of U.S. information programs assume an active advisory role to the President and the NSC on the public affairs implications of U.S. policy decisions?

(b) *Audiences*: Should programs be targeted toward "opinion leaders" and elites, or should a broader-based audience be sought for these programs?

(c) *Voice of America*: How closely should the VOA be tied to U.S. foreign policy? Is retaining its credibility, based on complete truthfulness, a worthwhile goal? Or should it broadcast only information directly supportive of foreign policy objectives?

(d) *Evaluation*: How effectively can the results of U.S. overseas information and cultural programs be measured?

(e) *Attribution*: To what extent and under what circumstances should materials distributed by U.S. information programs be attributed to the U.S. government?

(f) *World-wide or country-targetted media products*: Are world-wide materials effective or would specific media products for individual countries better accomplish the purpose?

(g) *Public vs private sector*: Should U.S. government programs supplant, or should they supplement private-sector initiatives? Should USIA do things, help things get done, or both?

(h) *Personnel*: Should the personnel administering overseas programs be information specialists, cultural-educational specialists or foreign affairs generalists? It is possible for them to be specialists in both branches? Should they be integrated into the Foreign Service personnel system?

These questions cannot be side-stepped in any discussion of public diplomacy. Some sort of consensus on these questions among various branches of government, and among those parts of the private sector with which these programs are closely involved, must lie at the base of any sound thinking about overseas information and cultural programs. Yet the innumerable studies and reports, to cite only one set of sources, suggest that such a consensus has never taken place.

USIA: Founded in Controversy (1952-1953)

The year 1952, an election year in which high partisanship helped intensify attacks on the Department of State and the International Information Administration, found support for the new I I A waning and Senator Joseph McCarthy on the rise. McCarthy's team, acting on the assumption that IIA's sole purpose was a short-term frontal attack on the Soviet menace, would drive many experienced professionals out of overseas information and cultural work, on grounds of their alleged failures or disloyalty. Truman's attempt to win bipartisan support for the information program failed to keep the agency out of the election arena. In a West Coast campaign address in October 1952, Dwight Eisenhower stated his determination to make the program an effective instrument of national policy. Then, in his State of the Union address, he promised to "make effective all activities related to international information because it is essential to the security of the United States." Six days into office he appointed William H. Jackson to head the President's Commission on International Information Activities and nominated a distinguished educator to head I I A. Meanwhile, Senator McCarthy's Committee on Government Operations in its investigation of the IIA was coming as near to destroying its programs as would any other event in its embattled history.

With Jackson in the chair, the President's Committee on International Information Activities enlisted eight distinguished citizens and a high-powered staff. Viewing its mandate as broadly as possible, the Committee tackled all aspects of U.S. government information programs, including covert activities. After reviewing the information programs at State, Defense, the Mutual Security Agency, and the CIA, the Committee concluded that propaganda is effective only as an auxiliary, creating a climate of opinion in which U.S. national goals can be accomplished; to be effective, "propaganda" must be dependable, convincing and truthful [sic]. Assessing the U.S. foreign information program, the Committee recognized that it "suffered greatly from confusion regarding its mission."

The Jackson Committee considered three reorganizational options:

(1) The separation of IIA from the Department of State and its establishment as an independent agency, under the National Security Council, adding the information activities of the Mutual Security Agency and the Technical Cooperation Administration;

(2) Retention in the State Department of most of the educational exchange programs; and establishment of an independent agency for all "fast media" (radio, press, films), books and periodicals, and aid to libraries and information centers;

(3) Retention of IIA in State, but with higher rank for the director and with effective provision for autonomy in the selection, assignment and management of personnel and in the control of appropriations.

The Committee concluded that the third option best solved the problem of locating and properly organizing the foreign information program, arguing that it would facilitate policy guidance and provide the necessary program unity because all media would be contained within a single structure. But the Committee reversed itself, acquiescing to Secretary of State John Foster Dulles, who preferred an agency independent of State (but under its policy control) on the grounds that State should not be burdened with operational responsibilities.

The Jackson Committee was little concerned with the culture-information paradox. After describing the extensive exchange-of-persons program, the Committee admitted there had been differences of opinion among its administrators.

It touched on selection criteria and on short–range and long–term objectives; it suggested that candidates should be chosen less for their academic or technical merit than for their potential usefulness to U.S. policy. Out of 59 recommendations, only one dealt with educational and cultural programs. The relationship between educational–cultural and information programs was dodged.

A far more exhaustive study of U.S. information and cultural programs, over two thousand pages, began at the same time and was produced by the Senate Foreign Relations Committee in early 1954. In the summer of 1952, the Subcommittee on Overseas Information Programs of the United States of the Committee on Foreign Relations began work under the chairmanship of Sen. Fulbright, replaced by Sen. Bourke Hickenlooper in 1953. (Parallel to this effort, five other studies of the U.S. information and cultural programs were under way. All would agree that it was worthwhile for the U.S. government to maintain overseas information and cultural programs, but there was no clear vision as to their ultimate objectives, specific roles in foreign policy, the structure of the organization or organizations which should administer them, or the methods they should employ.)

Senate Resolution 74 of the 82nd Congress, a document ringing with Cold War rhetoric, triggered the Fulbright–Hickenlooper hearings. The final report was delayed until February 1954, in part because of its thoroughness but also because of the turmoil created by the McCarthy investigations. This report stresses the overall value of U.S. overseas information and cultural programs. But there was little consensus on other major points.

Executives of the programs decribe them as foreign policy support mechanisms, in the direct and short-range sense. But others saw the situation quite differently. Various members of the U.S. Advisory Commission on Educational Exchange and of the Board of Foreign Scholarships expressed their concerns. Martin R.P. McGuire, a member of both bodies, said that it was "most unfortunate" that exchange programs and information programs were in the same division: "The long-range foreign policy objectives of international understanding through educational exchange are different psychologically from political persuasion as carried out by the mass media. The two together weaken exchange and make it seem to be but a part of short-range propaganda activities." Historian Walter Johnson testified that he was uneasy that the I I A administered both information and educational exchange programs; he feared that the "Campaign for Truth," while necessary and admirable, already overshadowed long-range programs. Robert Stozier, dean of students at the University of Chicago, urged that IIA's "vague objectives" be clarified. He suggested, "If the program is to be pursued in the adventuresome American tradition that ideas and learning are the source of our material greatness, then we must conduct it free from contradictory political pressure and conduct it as an educational enterprise."

McGuire described the high prestige of the educational exchange programs overseas: "Most countries are allergic to propaganda . . . many are now weak economically and militarily but not culturally." He asked why the government had avoided the word "culture," saying it was time to understand that education is a part of culture, part of our total accumulated achievements in literature, the arts, technology and general know-how. He argued that the phrase "cultural exchange" should be substituted for "educational exchange."

The Hickenlooper Subcommittee, straightforward in its condemnation of propaganda, noted the "lack of common understanding of the objective of the information program on the part of the Administration, Congress, and the American people." Its final recommendation was to "adhere to the terms of Public Law 402 and maintain a tone in the program worthy of the United States and its citizens," a reference to the Smith-Mundt Act's stress on mutual under-standing. It opposed separating out the information and cultural functions from the Department of State and putting them in USIA since that would tend to give exchange programs a "propaganda flavor." If information operations were to be vested in a new independent "information and propaganda agency," the educational exchange programs should remain in State.

The end result was a compromise. The Department of State was freed of having to operate overseas information programs, and the proponents of a new and separate Agency prevailed. But cultural and ecucational programs would stay in the Department of State until April of 1978.

The birth of USIA was less than propitious. Staggering under the weight of scrutiny, exhausted from responding to requests for reports and information, depressed, demoralized, and resentful of the McCarthy investigations, the United States Information Agency began on August 1, 1953, taking with it some forty percent of the Department of State's total personnel. President Eisenhower, on the recommendation of the NSC, issued in October 1953 a directive which established the Agency's first set of objectives, stimulated by the Jackson Report. USIA was to "submit evidence to peoples of other nations . . .that the objectives and policies of the United States are in harmony with and will advance their legitimate aspirations for freedom, progress and peace." The Eisenhower directive called for explaining and interpreting U.S. government objectives and policies; stressing the relation between U.S. policies and other peoples' "legitimate" aspirations; unmasking and countering hostile attempts to frustrate U.S. policies; and delineating those aspects of American life and culture which facilitate understanding of U.S. government policies. For all the research and discussion, this directive contained within it the old contradictions; they would continue to plague the new Agency and its successor.

The Search for Consensus: USIA'S Early Years (1953-1960)

Even with a new mandate, the Agency faced formidable problems in its first year. But a piece of turf had come into existence in Washington; there would be no shortage of warriors to defend it.

In the mid-fifties, Director George Allen, career diplomat and former assistant secretary of state for public affairs, emphasized those aspects of the informa-tion program which he called "cultural activities" (English-language teaching programs, libraries, book translations, and bi-national center activities). With the temporary relaxation of international tensions following Stalin's death, the end of the Korean War, and the Soviet "peace offensive," it was natural that more stress would fall on longer-range aspects of the information program. During Allen's three-year tenure, the USIA reached out for the longer view, for programs in culture and ideas, part of an effort to provide people abroad with an opportunity better to understand the American people, their character and institutions. In a period of relative stability and freedom from controversy, USIA began to build a cadre of professionals, techniques, practices, and overseas installations to stand the test of time.

Still, the USIA was scrutinized again and again in the fifties. The most important of these studies was Eisenhower's Commission on Activities Abroad, headed by New York industrialist Mansfield Sprague. In December 1960, the Sprague Commission submitted a report remarkable in its breadth of vision. It drew three general conclusions:

(1) U.S. information systems and efforts to integrate psychological factors into policy had become increasingly effective;

(2) the evolution of world affairs, the effectiveness of the communist apparatus, and the growing role of public opinion internationally made continued improvement necessary;

(3) U.S. activities demanded substantially greater resources, better training of personnel, further clarification of the role of information activities, more competence on the part of government officials to deal with informational and psychological matters, and improved coordination.

The Commission foresaw a protracted non-military conflict between the free world and the communist system and believed that the eventual outcome of the struggle would depend on the extent to which the United States would be able to influence attitudes abroad. On the information side, there were recommendations for strengthening U.S. covert facilities, for using more unattributed materials, for developing in-depth training in psychological factors for all officers dealing with foreign affairs, for seeking more knowledge about foreign opinion-molders, and for establishing "overall themes, armatures for words and actions."

On the other side, educational exchange programs and cultural activities were convincingly stressed. Long-term foreign educational assistance was recommended. The Report commended existing English-language teaching programs and urged their expansion. Sprague and his colleagues had reservations about "wholesale mobilization of private American international activities"; but they proposed an expanded international role for private foundations and the establishment of a quasi-independent Foundation for International Educational Development.

As for State's educational exchange programs, the Commission urged that they be extended outside Western Europe and suggested that exchanges concentrate on "leaders," recognizing long-range as well as immediate objectives in order to operate for "net political gain." One surprising recommendation, given the climate of a few years before, called for facilitating visits to the United States by leaders from the political left by revising cumbersome visa procedures. Finally, the Commission urged that a single government agency work with American universities to coordinate long-range policy; it suggested that the Department of State's Bureau of Educational and Cultural Affairs was the right body.

Given the timing of the report, six weeks after the election of John F. Kennedy, it is not surprising that few of its recommendations were heeded. Kennedy immediately set up three new task forces to examine information and cultural programs. The three recommended, among other things:

1) that a Committee on Information and Exchange Policy be established under the NSC to provide greater coordination of psychological objectives in all foreign affairs agencies;

2) that the cultural and exchange-of-persons programs in the Department of State be transferred to USIA; and

3) that USIA be renamed the International Exchange Agency or the United States Cultural Agency.

Each tried to clarify USIA's role as a psychological tool for U.S. foreign policy. One called for greater emphasis on programs designed to present a clear image of U.S. national goals, another underlined the importance of presenting U.S. achievements abroad, and the third urged that the Agency persuade, not just inform.

All three recommended that persons of stature head USIA; and in 1961 Kennedy appointed the consummate media pioneer, Edward R. Murrow, to the task. Meanwhile, rejecting the idea of integrating USIA and State's Bureau of Educational and Cultural Affairs (CU) programs into one, Kennedy elevated the Bureau and appointed Philip H. Coombs, Williams College manpower economist and Ford Foundation official, as Assistant Secretary. In the tradition of Archibald MacLeish, Coombs would be succeeded by a line of distinguished men, among them Lucius Battle, Charles Frankel, and John Richardson, until CU came to an end in 1978.

Kennedy's Statement of Mission for the U.S. Information Agency focused on achieving U.S. foreign policy objectives by influencing public attitudes in other nations. Never officially sanctioned by Congress, this Statement served the Agency, with adjustments, until 1978. It moved away from the Eisenhower emphasis on evidence that the policies of the United States harmonized with other nation's aspirations. The new statement, aimed first at the peaceful world community of free and independent nations, included the now-standard admonition to unmask and counter hostile attempts to distort perceptions of U.S. objectives and policies. But its primary emphasis fell on projecting those aspects of American life and culture which would facilitate sympathetic understanding of U.S. policies.

The shift was of degree not kind. USIA now was to "influence public attitudes," not merely to "submit evidence." The Kennedy Statement did not chart a new course but sought merely to clarify and upgrade USIA's role in foreign affairs decision-making and to provide a rationale for the information programs then underway.

Respite From Examining Eyes (1961-1972)

The Mutual Educational and Cultural Exchange Act of 1961 (Fulbright-Hays) consolidated the various educational and cultural exchange programs previously contained in other laws, including the Smith-Mundt Act. It still provides the legislative basis for all overseas educational-cultural and information activities. The Act, in authorizing a number of new activities, emphasized "mutuality," the latest noun for all seasons. New programs were provided for, even if all were not implemented by appropriations; among these were a "reverse flow" of foreign fine and performing arts to the United States, establishing new centers for technical and cultural exchange, financing U.S.-sponsored international scholarly meetings, and supporting private research on problems of educational exchange. A U.S. Advisory Commission on Educational and Cultural Affairs replaced the earlier Commission and its membership was sharply upgraded, under the chairmanship of John Gardner. This omnibus bill was for the most part created in conference by staff aides, since there was little communication between the bill's two sponsors.

The Fulbright-Hays Act was designed to facilitate the use of virtually any and all reasonable means "to increase mutual understanding between the people of the United States and the people of other countries." Lest any of its aims be misconstrued, Fulbright made them explicit in a statement before the Senate in June 1961— "I utterly reject any suggestion that our educational and cultural exchange programs are weapons or instruments with which to do combat . . . there is no room and there must not be any room, for an interpretation of these programs as propaganda, even recognizing that the term covers some very worthwhile and respectable activities." The bill passed both the House and Senate by extremely wide margins.

Meanwhile the persuaders were practicing their art and Murrow's prestige and good relations with Congress translated into increasing appropriations for USIA. Operating funds rose by twenty-five percent in the 1961-1964 period. When Carl Rowan, former journalist, Deputy Assistant Secretary for Public Affairs, and Ambassador to Finland, succeeded Murrow in 1964, operating funds continued to increase. But the large 1965 appropriations increase included ominous demands on the USIA program in Vietnam.

The emergence of new national preoccupations was already bringing other emphases. Lyndon Johnson's "Great Society" programs and civil rights issues focused world attention on U.S. domestic concerns. The communications revolution was already permitting the rest of the world to pay close attention to the internal U.S. scene. A second generation of overseas audiences, in part shaped by USIA's earlier efforts, was more sophisticated than its predecessors and the need for more depth in information was already apparent. The emphasis in USIA began to move beyond information to explanation, but not yet to the "explication" of the seventies. Rowan also helped focus the necessity of addressing the growing concerns of the developing or "Third" world.

While study commissions and reorganization proposals were relatively few in these years, Charles Frankel, Columbia University professor of philosophy, later assistant secretary of state for CU, did a major study for The Brookings

Institution in 1965, published under the title *The Neglected Aspect of Foreign Affairs*. Frankel called for raising educational and cultural programs "to a level consonant with their significance for the relations of the American people and other nations." He urged a more cooperative and more binding relationship between the government and that part of the private sector involved in educational and cultural activities. He recommended that CU leadership be raised to the Undersecretary level, allowing the same access to the President that the Director of USIA enjoyed and providing greater authority over the State Department's assistant secretaries. He also suggested transferring responsibility for the corps of "Educational Attachs," still working for USIA in the field, to CU.

Frankel concluded that, if no change in the structure of the State Department were possible, a semi-autonomous foundation for educational and cultural affairs, similar to the structure of the Smithsonian, could receive support from both private and public sectors. The programs could then be insulated from short-term political demands and freed to do their vital long-range work.

In 1965, President Johnson appointed Leonard Marks, a lawyer specializing in communications, as USIA's new director. At Marks' swearing-in ceremony, Johnson stressed the central role of truth in USIA's mission: "The United States has no propaganda to peddle . . . We are neither advocates nor defenders of any dogma so fragile or doctrine so frightened as to require it." The words at least were proud.

Marks articulated a major new concept, "nation building," meaning the bilateral sharing of information for the purpose of achieving mutual goals. Assisting other nations in their development through information and education programs was Marks' answer to the preoccupations of the developing world. He recognized, as had Rowan before him, that vast Third World audiences and energies meant different challenges for the Agency. It is perhaps a predictable trade-off that, under Marks, the Murrow-Rowan emphasis on persuasion diminished.

Meanwhile, discussion on Capitol Hill continued. In December 1968, just after the election of Richard Nixon, the Subcommittee on International Organizations and Movements of the House Committee on Foreign Affairs, chaired by Rep. Dante Fascell, issued its Report 6 on "Winning the Cold War: The U.S. Ideological Offensive." With admirable forbearance this report resisted the game of proposing organizational change. But it called for a "thorough systematic reappraisal of the entire information policy of the U.S. government," in view of "a disheartening picture of the U.S. image abroad." It found the activities of USIA "sadly lacking."

Richard Nixon in early 1969 named CBS executive Frank Shakespeare to direct USIA. Shakespeare triggered a resurgence of Congressional and private discussion of the Agency in the early 1970s, marked by the familiar persistent questions about USIA's mission and purpose. A management study conducted for USIA by the Arthur D. Little company in June 1970 recommended that the Kennedy Statement of Mission be either revalidated or revised. Agency officials discussed the matter but issued no new statement.

When Shakespeare was replaced by former *Time* editor James Keogh in 1973, the stage was set for another round of scrutiny. USIA, after twenty years of existence, had achieved one major victory: the agency had become an accepted reality. Now debate centered on its mission, objectives, and methods, as contrasted with the more general discussion of the issues in the past. And the quiet in-fought battles over turf, which thrived on obfuscation of issues, mounted as the Agency entered its third decade.

The Debate Rejoined (1973-1977)

By now, the question of whether the United States needed overseas information and cultural programs had disappeared. But, concerns about the relative value of short-term and long-range goals and the proper methods of achieving them still weighed heavily on members of Congress and the Executive, particularly when they turned to organizational issues. At least seven studies grappled with these problems between 1973 and April 1978 when, under President Jimmy Carter, the newly-created International Communication Agency would meld USIA and CU into one agency.

The Senate Foreign Relations Committee, reporting on the USIA authorization bill for 1972, put it this way: "What is needed today is a more mature, confident approach to the world; making information about ourselves available but not trying to foist it off on people. We may be far better served if we remove our information and cultural efforts from the realm of sales and return them to the realm of diplomacy." The Committee, still chaired by Senator Fulbright, questioned the validity of a separate information agency. Suggesting that USIA's "cultural activities" return to State, the Committee considered abolishing the press, motion picture, and television services and retaining the Voice of America as a quasi-independent government agency. While no legislation to this effect was drafted, the committee announced its intention to continue its review of USIA activities.

In 1973, at the request of both the Director of USIA and the Assistant Secretary for Educational and Cultural Affairs, Barbara White, a respected senior USIA officer and later president of Mills College, examined U.S. information and cultural programs, though her phrase was "overseas *communication* programs." Seeking to identify the needs for these programs given a new world communications environment and the requirements of U.S. foreign policy in the seventies, she concluded that the U.S. should offer services that are wanted and are in the U.S. interest to provide. She argued that these programs must increasingly be conceived and executed in the framework of "mutuality." She proposed a number of internal reorganizations to strengthen USIA. Her study, concurrent with the annual report of USIA's Advisory Commission, favored the retention of USIA as a separate entity "for the seventies."

White concluded her study with another suggestion "for the eighties." Noting that "the difference between cultural and information functions would become even more buried because, 'information' programs would concentrate increasingly on information in depth about the United States and its institutions—a function that many now regard as 'cultural,' " she saw advantage in placing information activities in one agency and major U.S. educational, cultural and scientific programs in another. Recognizing that an organization responsible for both international information and cultural relations could not easily be focused on unilateral advocacy of U.S. foreign policy objectives, she envisioned three separate entities:

(1) a Public Affairs Office in the Department of State, containing the traditional overseas press and media functions of USIA, to support U.S. foreign policy positions and advise the Executive branch on the implications of foreign opinion for its policies;

(2) another agency for educational, cultural, and scientific affairs, comprising the State Department's educational exchange and cultural programs, USIA's cultural activities, the Department's Science Office, and programs of other government agencies, such as the Department of Health, Education and Welfare and the National Science Foundation, whose main purpose was overseas exchange;

(3) a separate Voice of America.

This proposal, not unlike Frankel's, was originally posited for the then-distant eighties. But in her remarks before the Stanton Panel only a year later, White advanced the timing of her proposal. She said her suggestions for the eighties should instead "be attained as rapidly as possible." The prominence of these questions in the mind of an experienced USIA professional is as revealing as the inaction which ensued.

In a statement to the chairman of the Murphy Commission in October 1973, USIA Director Keogh proposed a new solution that Shakespeare before him had publicly mentioned only in jest: that USIA be retained as an independent information agency but that it absorb CU. He based his proposal on the "successful integration of these programs in the field," arguing that their separation in Washington was artificial. Keogh's proposal was based on his own elastic definitions of "information" and "cultural" activities: he considered the two to be complementary parts of the total communications effort and saw very little difference between them in view of their "common objectives."

Others did see differences and disagreed as to "common objectives." Under John Richardson, assistant secretary of state for educational and cultural affairs, CU articulated its objectives in a long-meditated Concept Paper, finally issued in March 1974:

"We seek to increase mutual understanding, cooperation and community between people of the United States and other peoples by direct and indirect efforts to: (1) enlarge the circle of those able to serve as influential interpreters between this and other nations; (2) stimulate institutional development in directions which favorably affect mutual comprehension and confidence; and (3) reduce structural and technical impediments to the exchange of ideas and information."

Prompted by growing criticism from both public and private institutions, by the 1973 recommendations of the Senate Foreign Relations Committee for redistribution of USIA functions, and by repeated calls for an in-depth examination from the Advisory Commission on Information, the Advisory Commission on Educational and Cultural Affairs, chaired now by former USIA director Leonard Marks, decided in the summer of 1973 to study ways in which USIA and CU might rearrange their functions, on the grounds that the separation was not working well. The Commission turned to Wayne A. Wilcox, professor of political science on leave from Columbia University and serving as cultural attache in London, who agreed to do a three-month study, on the condition that it have the support of both USIA's and CU's advisory commissions. This plan failed to materialize but triggered the Advisory Committee on Information's later acceptance of the idea of an independent panel on International Information, Education, and Cultural Relations.

Frank Stanton, former CBS President, who had served for nine years as chairman of the Advisory Commission on Information, was named Chairman. Georgetown University's Center for Strategic and International Studies agreed to sponsor the study and Peter Krogh, dean of the Georgetown School of Foreign Affairs, was named Vice-Chairman. Walter Roberts, an associate director of USIA, resigned to take on the task of project director. All members of both Advisory Commissions were appointed members of the panel, and they were supplemented by several other distinguished private citizens. No panel had ever gathered such a collection of informed professionals. In its ten-month study, this potent group would reach the most controversial conclusions of the decade.

By its own admission, the Stanton Panel did not set out to alter official information and cultural programs radically; instead it sought ways to improve the government's capacity to conduct them. It pin-pointed three major problems:

> "(1) the division of one program between two agencies, USIA and the Department of State; (2) the assignment, to an agency separate from and independent of the State Department, of the task of interpreting U.S. foreign policy to the world and advising in its formulation; and (3) the ambiguous positioning of the Voice of America at the crossroads of journalism and diplomacy."

Making the fundamental distinction that some activities of these programs were directly related to the formulation and execution of foreign policy while others were more removed from day-to-day tactical issues, it isolated four functions: exchange of persons, general information, policy information, and advisory role. This distinction at the heart of the Panel's thinking drew the members to a simple conclusion. Although Marks and Edmund Gullion for different reasons dissociated themselves from the opinion, the rest of the panel agreed that the last two functions could not be performed without a close relationship to those who formulate policy and therefore recommended that they be fully integrated into the State Department. The first two functions, on the other hand, with their close dependency on the private sector, could best be performed in an autonomous institution, related to the Department of State. Thus, the Panel proposed:

(1) abolishing the USIA and creating a new, quasi-independent Information and Cultural Affairs Agency, whose director would report to the Secretary of State, and which would combine the cultural and "general information" programs of both USIA and the State Department's Bureau of Educational and Cultural Affairs;

(2) establishing a new State Department Office of Policy Information, headed by a deputy undersecretary, to administer all programs which articulate and explain U.S. foreign policy;

(3) setting up the Voice of America as an independent federal agency under its own board of overseers.

The originality of the Stanton Report lay in a single incandescent idea—that policy information should not be persuasively disseminated by the same institution which handles general information and cultural relations. The Panel's solution offered a means by which policy advocacy, information, and cultural affairs could be successfully structured and implemented, consonant with the American system and style.

Reform and Counter-Reform

The Stanton report caught the attention of a new Presidential team, one which dreamed of reforming the federal government, and Jimmy Carter's White House staff soon produced Reorganization Plan 2, approved by Congress in November 1977. The discussion that produced this merger of USIA and CU, according to some of the participants, appeared to have centered largely on the name of the new agency. As an insight into the lofty tone of the debate, one staffer recalls being laughed out of the room when he proposed a name reflecting the legislation, i.e., the Agency for International Understanding. Some sort of unprecedented name—International Communication Agency (USICA), as it turned out—was deemed necessary, to mark the new presence in the old USIA of the Bureau of Educational and Cultural Affairs and to declare the President's intentions to preserve the integrity of these educational programs. The new name, thus, was a commitment to respect the cultural relations dimension of the new agency. (Such critical distinctions were forgotten by 1982, when the name reverted to USIA. At that time many rejoiced at the demise of a clumsy name; those who contended that the covenant protecting educational and cultural programs had been violated were quietly overlooked.)

The bright light of the Stanton Report had dimmed, even before the creation of USICA. The "two distinct but related goals" outlined in Carter's message transmitting the Plan to Congress had undergone a transmutation; they now read: (1) "to tell the world about our society and policies—in particular our commitment to cultural diversity and individual liberty," and (2) "to tell ourselves about the world, so as to enrich our own culture as well as to give us the understanding to deal effectively with problems among nations." This new view of things was expanded on in March 1978 in the President's Memorandum to USICA Director John Reinhardt, a former cultural attaché and the first career USIA officer to head the agency. The memo used the word "information" only three times, in

Stanton's context of general information; "culture" and "cultural" are sprinkled throughout, nine times in all. And "propaganda" is eschewed as bluntly as it can be, with the new Agency enjoined from undertaking any activities that are "covert, manipulative or propagandistic." The functional simplicity of the Stanton Report's concept is gone, confusion has returned.

The issue had been specifically joined in the Fascell Committee hearings, prior to the creation of USICA, in 1977. Stanton read into the first day's proceedings a ringing plea that the Committee understand the conceptual distinctions which lay at the heart of the Panel's recommendations and avoid faling victim to the turf-owners, specifically those who defended "USIA's vested interests." Shortly after, Ambassador William Tyler noted:

> It is absolutely essential to distinguish between information relating to national policies and objectives on the one hand, and information relating to the infinitely varied aspects of national life on the other. I believe that if this basic distinction is defined and accepted, much of the existing semantic and conceptual confusion will be dispelled and certain principles of organization will suggest themselves logically and naturally ... I think it is a mistake to lump all information and cultural activities under a common catch phrase such as "public diplomacy," which obscures the vital distinction to which I have referred.

Ambassador Tyler and the Stanton Panel's argument lost out in the hearings to contentious turf-warriors and longstanding mindsets, despite the impressive array of statements by experienced and prominent students of these issues. For forty years, Americans had groped towards a way of doing propaganda, a way which was compatible with a parallel effort in cultural relations, but by now all was forgotten. The calibre of the discussion is perhaps best represented by these remarks from a prominent Congressman:

> It might be useful if we just dropped from our lexicon the word 'propaganda' and I don't know that you need persuasion. Is pure news propaganda? Is pure news persuasion? Pure news, whatever that is, certainly has a fantastic impact on society, and to that extent, it becomes part of the cultural milieu in which we live and is therefore propagandistic because it is a basis for me to make decisions. And yet, I am relying upon another man's judgment as to what is pure news or what the facts are. I don't make an independent investigation, so I don't know that we should get hung up on the semantics of what the thing is. I think, we need to say what we need to do and just do it.

In short, USIA/USICA was left once more to figure things out for itself.

One important indirect consequence of the Stanton Commission hearings was the VOA Charter. The Voice of America had been operating, since the middle of 1959, on an informal and internal self-definition, fostered by then-Director of VOA Henry Loomis, later under Frank Shakespeare, deputy director of USIA.

In March 1975, in USIA's Authorization Bill for 1977, Senator Charles Percy placed this "Charter" into law, embodying three principles:

(1) VOA will serve as a consistently reliable and authoritative source of news. VOA news will be accurate, objective and comprehensive;

(2) VOA will represent America, not any single segment of American society, and will therefore present a balanced and comprehensive projection of significant American thought and institutions;

(3) VOA will present the policies of the United States clearly and effectively, and will also present responsible discussion and opinion on these policies.

The decision to turn the VOA Charter into law probably stemmed from a lengthy discussion in hearings between Sen. Percy and USIA Director Keogh, stimulated by the Stanton group, about VOA coverage of the Vietnam withdrawal. The Charter's language and preoccupations show that the "full and fair picture" idea was still very much alive. At the same time, Congressional action in mandating the Charter shows the continuing concern for vigilance against the hard-sell propagandists.

By the fall of 1980, partisan calls were once more heard throughout the land for more vigor in fighting the Soviets. Foreign policy became a key election issue, as the Reagan campaign thrived on national perceptions of weakness in the Carter period. USICA, afterwards, was singled out for special attention and received more than its share of media coverage. A flamboyant director with unusually close White House connections would raise the USIA budget substantially, for a whole menu of programs and purposes. A prophetic taped discussion printed in the *The Washington Quarterly* ("The Telling of America: U.S. Public Diplomacy in the Reagan Years," Winter 1982) along with the threatened cuts in the Fulbright Program that fall, revealed the tilt—a renamed USIA was returning to the hard sell.

The Congress countered. It imposed a second charter, modeled after VOA's, that guaranteed the "integrity" (without defining the word) of USIA's Bureau of Educational and Cultural Affairs and its programs; and it doubled exchange budgets over the next four-year period, in an attempt to keep the balance. But USIA leadership, in its numerous self-descriptions, continued to emphasize only its role as a weapon in the war against the Soviets and their proxies. No new statement of mission emerged, at least into the the the light of public scrutiny. A variety of new programs took wing, some highly innovative, all unprecedented, and some of high value: the Central American Initiative launched the first extensive scholarship program in history for foreign undergraduates, some with little or no English; "Worldnet" began direct television transmissions into friendly nations; Radio Martí was created to broadcast into a single nation, Cuba; a Youth Initiative enlisted private funding to augment exchanges among high school students and young people outside the university track; and a far-reaching cooperative agreement was signed with a private publisher to produce television tapes and allied materials for teaching English abroad through the public media.

Meanwhile, in the Department of State, various offices geared up their own program in "Public Diplomacy," to all appearances designed to counter foreign propaganda and disinformation within the United States and to gain American public support for the administration's foreign policies. Some saw the genesis for this effort in frustration over the historical and legal constraints against propagandizing Americans, imposed on USIA by legislative history and the spirit of the authorizing legislation, and tried to object. Others, advocates of this newest definition of "public diplomacy," argued that the United States was in a crisis situation equivalent to a state of war and brushed aside the accumulated concerns of half a century.

Conclusion

As long as politics in the United States can move forward only through compromise, questions about our American way of doing propaganda will never be answered with the kind of clarity that trained intellect expects. American foreign policy will never be a pure version either of realist nationalism or idealist internationalism; the U.S. approach to foreign affairs has always teetered between the two positions. American propaganda will probably remain a fluid and expedient mixture of education, culture, and information, of soft-sell and hard-sell, of loud-talk and soft-speak, of short-range tactics and long-range strategies.

Yet, it may be permissible to wonder whether America is getting its money's worth. With the greatest media and communications system the world has ever known, what could we not achieve by an effort geared to extending the reach, through this powerful informing resource, of the American dialog with other nations? With the world's greatest collection of universities, research institutions, libraries, hospitals, enlightened businesses, museums, theatres, and concert halls, and with the professionals to fill them, how far could America go if we focused all efforts on the outreach of American intellect and knowledge, science and know–how, of information and culture, while strengthening our own cultural heritage through dialog with all the cultures of the world? How long could certain of the world's technical problems—e.g., hunger—resist an American–fed multilateral attack? If we set out through dialog not to dominate but to help, through information and education generously shared, could there be a truer agenda for world peace? Could there be a better, a more American style of "propaganda?"

The debate over the relation between cultural relations and propaganda in America has gone on for many years, even if since 1977 it seems to have retired from public view, first out of a commitment in the new Agency to "making it work." More disturbing, since 1980, has been the politicization of the discussion: the acrimony of the new ideologized politics, the anti–professional attitudes engendered by "populist" attacks on professionalism in government and on government itself, the unprecedented number of underqualified outside appointments to USIA, the silencing of career officers, the inexplicable non-interest of the media and the universities—all this has helped dull the edge of debate. A democracy thrives when the contending blades of its intellectual shears are sharp enough to cut the clean line of truth. Without informed debate, the search for an American way to maximize our educational, cultural, and informational contributions to life on this planet can only continue to lend confusion to discussions of public diplomacy, cultural relations, and propaganda.

RFE/RL: Objective Advocates

by James L. Buckley

Quite clearly, international broadcasting is serious business. We of the West are committed to the concept that human beings have an inherent "right to know"; the right to "seek, receive, and impart information and ideas through any media and regardless of frontiers," to use the words of the Universal Declaration of Human Rights of which the Soviet Union is a signatory.

Moreoever, we regard this right as more than an abstraction. We see its exercise as a fundamental stabilizer in human affairs, the best guarantee against the threats to peace that can occur from wholesale distortions of the truth . . .

[A]lthough funded by the U.S. Congress, Radio Free Europe and Radio Liberty are essentially independent entities with a mission defined by their role as surrogate home services for the twenty-one nationalities in Eastern Europe and the Soviet Union to which they broadcast. It is indicative of their success that they are often referred to by their listeners as "our" radios. Their primary job is to report on events in the countries to which they broadcast and to provide programs that address the particular interests of their citizens . . .

We are, in short, our listeners' most reliable source of news and analysis, and they have come to know it. Moreover, our programs serve to frustrate official attempts to distort history or induce cultural amnesia. We air the works of banned authors, place historical events in perspective, provide extensive religious programming, and remind our listeners of the national and spiritual heritage that predated Marx by more than a thousand years and link them to the rich cultural life of the Western and Islamic worlds.

Finally, we provide dissidents with a forum. We report their activities and quote from their underground publications, thus helping maintain some semblance of debate of important public issues.

It is this unique identification with each of our audiences, and our reputation for accuracy, that gives us such special access to them. Given the attacks

James L. Buckley is president of Radio Free Europe/Radio Liberty. He received the B.A. and L.L.B. from Yale University, was an associate of Wiggin & Dana, 1949-1953; vice-president of Catawba Corp., 1953-1971; a United States senator, 1971-1977; business consultant, 1977-1980; and undersecretary for security assistance, U.S. Department of State, 1980-1982. He is author of *If Men Were Angels* (1975). [This article is a revision of a speech delivered to the Overseas Press Club, New York City, September 22, 1983; ©1983 James L. Buckley]

levelled at Radio Free Europe and Radio Liberty by the Soviet and East European regimes, let me stress the word "accuracy." I think it fair to say that few, if any, journalistic enterprises today exercise as great care as we do in determining what we can broadcast as fact. We have what we call the "two source rule" which requires corroboration of a story before we put it on the air

For our purposes, truth exists at two levels. The first deals with facts, and our job is to describe them accurately and objectively—what might be described as the classic "who, what, when, and where" school of journalism. But RFE and RL are not merely journalistic enterprises, and our commitment to objectivity in reporting the news is not to be confused with neutrality where human values are concerned. To the contrary, we are committed by our charter to a respect for human dignity, to the rule of law, and to the principles of political, social, economic, and religious freedom that undergird democracy. In short, it is part of our brief to act as advocates for, or perhaps more accurately as witnesses to, the values that are central to the Western experience . . .

[A]lthough political and moral truths may not be capable of clinical proof, they are subject to the tests of human experience and intuition . . .

[O]ppression cannot destroy the human power to evaluate alternatives, provided they are known. It is therefore an essential part of our role to make sure they are. When we are not broadcasting the news or filling informational voids created by the censorship of literature or the rewriting of history, we describe both the alternatives to life under communism as well as its stark realities. In serving as spokesmen for the human values in which we so deeply believe, we offer our audiences what their rulers would deny them, namely intellectual choice.

It is this, I suspect, that causes those regimes such fury; because they fully understand we need do no more, in our commentaries and programs, than simply state the case for freedom with meticulous attention to the accuracy of every fact we cite in its support and then leave it to our audiences to determine for themselves where the truth lies.

There is . . . an infinite variety of ways in which facts can be presented in support of a position, ranging from the insipid to the misleading or inflammatory.

Information will inevitably shape events. Collective action requires collective knowledge. The initial strikes that led to the formation of Solidarity were assiduously ignored by the Polish media. It was largely because of RFE reporting of seemingly isolated actions that the emerging leadership of Solidarity realized the nationwide dimensions of the protests that were taking place. As one writer put it, "Without these programs, Poles certainly would not have been informed of the momentum of the Solidarity workers' movement, nor would other East Europeans have known of its existence."

It is equally true that Radio Free Europe's Polish broadcasts have served as agents of stability. By laying out the situations that confronted our listeners— thoroughly and responsibly, without exaggeration or omission—and by countering rumor and distortion with hard facts, RFE broadcasts have provided listeners with the kind of full information needed for sound judgment and responsible action . . .

Some, I know, would argue that as the mere reporting of facts to people living in a totalitarian society can prove provocative, Western broadcasters should in effect indulge in self censorship. But to fail to broadcast legitimate news on the grounds that listeners might choose to act on that knowledge is to cooperate with and therefore condone the internal suppression of news. That we have proven indispensible in keeping our listeners informed of what is happening in their own countries is an indictment not of RFE and RL but of a system that requires citizens to rely on outside sources for information of the most vital importance to them.

We reject the notion that our listeners should not be trusted to make their own decisions as to how they should act and what risks, if any, they should be willing to take in attempting to bring about change. Where we draw the line is in presuming to tell them what to do. It is they after all, not we, who must live with the consequences of their actions.

Abolish the VOA

by Walter Lippmann

The Rockefeller Committee has advised the President to take the Voice of America and the rest of the propaganda apparatus out of the State Department, and to create a new agency, which might be called the United States Information Service, to direct the government's overseas information activities.

This will work better, I would argue, only if, along with the transfer to the new agency, there is a radical change in the theory of what the government can and should do in the field of information and propaganda.

My own view is that for any government agency to call itself the Voice of America is an impertinence, and that in a democratic government like ours a propaganda department must in the very nature of things cause confusion at home and abroad. In a society where opinions are free, a government propaganda, which is a monopoly, is an inherent contradiction and practically unworkable.

Walter Lippmann (1889-1974) is one of America's most distinguished journalists, the recipient of the Pulitzer Prize special citation, 1957; the Pulitzer Prize, 1962; the Gold Medal for essays and criticism, National Institute of Arts and Letters; the Presidential Medal of Freedom, 1964; and several national awards from European countries. Mr. Lippmann received an A.B. from Harvard College and did graduate work in philosophy. He was associate editor of the The New Republic, reporter and editor of the New York World, reporter of The New York Herald-Tribune, and a nationally-syndicated columnist. Among his twenty-five books are The Stakes of Diplomacy, 1915; The Political Scene, 1919; Liberty and the News, 1920; Public Opinion, 1922; American Inquisitors, 1928; A Preface to Morals, 1929; The Method of Freedom, 1934; The Good Society, 1927; U.S. Foreign Policy; Shield of the Republic, 1943; The Cold War, 1947; Isolation and Alliances, 1952; The Public Philosophy, 1955; The Communist World and Ours, 1959; and The Coming Test with Russia, 1961. [This article is reprinted from the New York Herald Tribune; April 27, 1953.]

The best thing to do, it seems to me, is to abolish the Voice of America as much such, to dissolve the whole organization concerned with interpretation and comment, with reviews of books and of the arts, with the discussion of manners and morals—and then to have broadcast through the government's facilities a selection of the regular American domestic news broadcasts. The people overseas should have available to them substantially the same news that we have available to us. Since, as a practical matter there must be selection, the selection should, I believe, be entrusted to men chosen by our own broadcasting companies and the press services.

While this sounds like a very drastic reform, it is no more than the undoing of what was no doubt a well intentioned but none the less a most serious mistake of the Truman administration.

The story of how the State Department got into the propaganda business in the first place is, as things have turned out, a joke even if it is not very funny. At the end of the war the government propaganda agency was, as any propaganda agency was, as any propaganda agency is bound to be, suspect and unpopular in Congress. On the other hand, the Administration did not wish to liquidate it. The problem was how to induce an unfriendly Congress to go on making the necessary appropriations. The leaders on the Hill were consulted, and the word that came back was that the only executive department which Congress trusted, the only one which was not overrun with New Dealers and what not was—believe it or not—the Department of State. I know the young men and the newcomers in Washington won't believe that. But that was the way it was in 1945 when James F. Byrnes was the secretary of state.

The propaganda organization with its multitude of employees was not taken into the State Department because Secretary Byrnes wanted to do propaganda. It was taken in by him because he was a compassionate Democrat, who alone could provide a refuge and asylum for the displaced persons of the war-time propaganda services.

When the transfer had been carried out, the propagandists, who were now working for the secretary of state, began to think of new worlds to conquer. So they baptized themselves the "Voice of America" and began broadcasting throughout the world, to all the races of mankind in all the languages, their selections of the news and their opinions and comments and interpretations of the foreign policy of the United States and of all other countries.

Thus the Voice of American, as heard day by day throughout the world, was not the President of the United States or the Secretary of State speaking with their own authority. It was a miscellaneous collection of people who could speak various languages. What they were saying from hour to hour in Albanian, in Arabic, in Bulgarian, in Hebrew or Korean, was certainly never known to the secretary of state or to the assistant secretary nominally in charge. For even if some official of the department read what was to be said before it was said, let us say in Albanian, he read it in the English text. There was no way he could know or check on what it would sound like when it was translated, or what it would mean when it had been read. Nothing is easier, as we all know, than to say that "Susie is a nice girl," and make it mean several different and contradictory things about Susie.

I do not mean to say that this happened in the Albanian broadcasts, about which I know as little and yet as much as any secretary of state. But it must have happened again and again since the propaganda to foreign countries was bound to be put in the hands of men speaking their languages, and almost invariably passionately involved, themselves in their affairs and their destinies. The State Department could never know what was really going on. There was no way by which it could control all the people who were impersonating the Voice of America. For the whole conception of the operation was wrong. It put the employees of the Voice of America in a false position, tempting them with power they should not have, subjecting them to attacks which they cannot answer. The false conception created a situation where Congress could never trust the propaganda agency, and yet could never reform it.

And the net effect abroad can, I believe, be described fairly as self-defeating.

To set up an elaborate machinery of international communication and then have it say, "We are the Voice of America engaged in propaganda to make you like us better than you like our adversaries," is—as propaganda—an absurdity. As a way of stimulating an appetite for the American way of life, it is like serving castor oil as a cocktail before dinner.

Foreigners are in more ways than one a good deal like Americans, and certainly like us in that they do not wish to feel that they are being manipulated and made fools of by someone with something to sell. Any one, therefore, who says he is a propagandist is incapacitated to be one. Furthermore, any one suspected of being a propagandist, as all government-paid "voices" are and should be, is a lame duck from the beginning.

This suspicion cannot be removed as long as the government serves up to the foreigner different information than is being served up to the American people. In principle, the foreigner should not be asked to listen to the United States government speaking. He should be enabled to overhear what the American people are hearing. He will then have the same protection against being made the victim of propaganda that we have—namely, the right in our free society to challenge the validity of a news report and to criticize the handling of it. This is the only way, and it is the best way, to create confidence abroad in the integrity of the information that we offer them.

It will be said, I know, that if we abolish the Voice of America, if we limit our overseas broadcasts to straight news, that we shall "lose the battle for men's minds" to the Communists who conduct incessant propaganda. I do not think there is any evidence that the Voice of America has been winning that battle. On the contrary, there are all sorts of reasons, I believe, for thinking it does much more harm than good to our influence abroad. And that was true, I should say, before, Sen. McCarthy took it over and the impression spread that it would now be the Voice of McCarthy or else.

Wasting the Propaganda Dollar

by John Spicer Nichols

Since its inception, the Reagan administration has viewed U.S. propoganda as an important weapon in America's struggle against Soviet power. Responding to the president's determination for the United States to fight the international war of ideas more effectively, new U.S. Information Agency (USIA) Director Charles Wick began early in 1981 to formulate plans to give his agency "the velocity of a projectile" in countering Soviet propaganda. And to mobilize support for escaalating the combat on the world's airwaves, administration officials have repeatedly used terms such as "broadcast barrage" as if they were counting missiles and tanks.

Yet the Reagan administration's habit of describing propaganda efforts in military terms indicates a basic misunderstanding of how international propaganda works. The processes by which bullets and words have their effects are very differnt. In fact, during both world wars virtually all propaganda was based on a simplistic and outmoded communication theory known as the bullet theory, which assumed that foreign audiences could be easily manipulated if the propagandist had good aim and the right ammunition. Communication researchers now know that such international media campaigns have little impact on audiences' attitudes on important topics such as family values, cultural norms, nationalism, and ideology.

Nonetheless, the Reagan administration has embraced the bullet theory. As a result, in 1984 Washington [spent] more than three-quarters of a billion dollars on propaganda, much of it on overtly persuasive programming that, for the most part, will fall on deaf ears. At the same time, President Ronald Reagan's policy has been slighting the more information-oriented programs that can better promote U.S. interests abroad.

A Change in Emphasis

Two of the three U.S. government radio networks broadcasting to foreign audiences have long based their programming strategies entirely on the discredited bullet theory. Radio Free Europe (RFE) and Radio Liberty serve as surrogate home services for listeners in Eastern Europe and the USSR, respectively. Their broadcasts concentrate on the domestic affairs of the Soviet bloc countries, emphasizing information and cultural material not carried on the State media. Only a tiny percentage of the programming deals with the United States. Both stations were covertly backed by the Central Intelligence Agency until

Dr. John Spicer Nichols is associate professor of journalism, Pennsylvania State University. During the 1985-1986 academic year, he was a fellow, Gannett Center for Media Studies, Columbia University. He was a newspaper reporter and Army public information officer. Dr. Nichols received B.A., M.A., and Ph.D. degrees in mass communication from the University of Minnesota. With Larry Soley, he is author of *Clandestine Radio* (Praeger Publishers, 1986). [This article has been edited and reprinted with permission, from *Foreign Policy*; Fall 1984; ©1984 Foreign Policy.]

Congress took over responsibility for their financing in 1971. They now are supervised by the Board for International Broadcasting, a government-appointed citizens' panel.

The third network is the Voice of America (VOA), a division of the USIA; [VOA] broadcasts worldwide, featuring news and entertainment from the United States as well as world news and official commentaries are not for the most part directed at any specific national or ethnic audience. VOA's programming is intended to generate good will toward the United States by providing news-hungry audiences wiht informational programs and by showing American society in a positive light with its cultural features. RFE and Radio Liberty, by contrast, emphasize persuasive programs intended to undermine public support for the communist regimes of Eastern Europe and the Soviet Union. Indeed, the Reagan administration has claimed that RFE played an important role in encouraging the emergence of the now-banned independent trade union Solidarity in Poland in 1980 and the Prague Spring in Czechoslovakia in 1968.

As dissimilar as the VOA's approach is from that of the other two networks, it is difficult for any radio system to maintain a complete distinction between information broadcasting and more persuasive propaganda. It is true, for example, that the widely admired objective news reports of the British Broadcasting Corporation's (BBC) World Service frequently place the British government in a negative light. During the war over the Falkland Islands, the BBC questioned government decisions and reported the Argentine perspective. Yet this service also has the task of maintaining links with and influence over British nationals abroad, former colonial subjects, and other important international audiences.

In addition, there is more to communication than radio broadcasting; the USIA also disseminates information abroad through public affairs officers attached to U.S. embassies and binational centers abroad, numerous periodicals, overseas libraries, and tours by American artists, academicians, and opinion leaders.

Congress recognized the two-way nature of communication (from the latin *communicare*,"to share") when it passed the Foreign Relations Authorization Act of 1979 which directed the USIA to improve Americans' understanding of the history, culture, and attitudes of other peoples and countries in addition to enhancing foreign audiences' understanding of the United States. The Carter administration responded by combining the USIA and the State Department's Bureau of Educational and Cultural Affairs into the U.S. International Communication Agency and promoted foreign visitor programs, educational and cultural exchanges, and audience research. But during the Carter years, stagnant constant-dollar appropriations for these efforts in an inflationary period steadily reduced their reach. Moreover, despite the importance of interpersonal communication in persuasive campaigns, these types of programs have suffered especially sharp cutbacks in recent years. As a result, sixty-eight per cent of all USIA overseas libraries established since World War II have been closed for budgetary reasons. During the past decade, the number of USIA representatives stationed overseas has declined twenty-seven per cent while the total number of VOA employees has declined less than four per cent.

Reagan has reduced emphasis on these person-to-person programs in favor of expanding more aggressive, less effective mass-media compaigns. Thus, the administration has recently established Radio Marti, a VOA surrogate home service directed at Cuba, while at the same time prohibiting almost all U.S. citizens from visiting Cuba and barring Cuban intellectuals and officials from U.S. cultural and educational meetings. Indeed, the administration has successfully boosted agency funding, but it has earmarked most of the new appropriations for programming involving one-way dissemination of propaganda. This change in emphasis on propaganda has been symbolized by the president's decision to change the agency's name back to the U.S. Information Agency.

The administration's efforts to make the USIA a more aggressive tool of U.S. foreign policy have not gone unchallenged. They have met stiff resistance from members of Congress who question the wisdom and cost of a bloated international propaganda budget, as well as criticism from the U.S. Advisory Commission on Public Diplomacy, the citizen's committee responsible for watching over the agency. In fact, Phillip Nicolaides, a newly appointed deputy program officer, decided to resign after his 1981 memo uring VOA to "destablize the Soviet Union and its satellites by promoting disaffection between peoples and rulers" created a furor inside and outside the station.

During these times of astronomical deficits and cutbacks in domestic programs, it is especially important to know what, if any, benefits the increased propaganda expenditures are bringing. Incredibly, the cost effectiveness of these multimillion-dollar programs has never been documented. In appropriations requests and congressional hearings, administration officials have simply asserted that U.S. propaganda is effective. Yet, results from limited research on foreign audiences and domestic propaganda research, interpreted in the light of modern communication theory, cast serious doubt on such claims.

Analyses of World War II propaganda efforts, for example, reveal that German soldiers were unaffected by the supposedly masterful Allied propaganda campaigns until they began to suffer defeats late in the war. Even then, the troops responded not to exhortative propaganda but to promises of good treatment for prisoners of war. And out of concern for their personal survival they paid close attention to broadcasts and leaflets describing surrender procedures. Communication researchers have demonstrated what should have been obvious all along: For propaganda to be effective, a message must not only be received and accepted by the audience. International audiences are not passive recipients of clever propaganda messages. Rather, they actively select material that conforms to their preconceived notions or can somehow improve their lives. Audiences actively avoid messages that create inner tension or conflict with those around them.

U.S. health officials, for example, have learned that mass-media campaigns that harp on the danger of cigarette smoking are notoriously ineffective, reaching mostly nonsmokers. Even when smokers cannot avoid such warnings, they tend to filter out the information or twist it to reduce the psychological stress. This is not to say that media messages are never persuasive. Consumers who need laundry soap can be persuaded to buy one brand instead of an essentially interchangeable competitor. But while the millions of dollars worth of brand advertising purchased annually can increase market shares and introduce new products, it is generally not effective in creating consumer demand or significantly changing other aspects of consumer behavior.

Broadcast Effectiveness

People's basis opinions, attitudes, and understanding of issues and events are not as easily manipulated as the bullet theory assumes. The effects of international propaganda are largely the product of audience needs and motivations rather than the intent and methods of the propagandists.

But none of this knowledge prevented Kenneth Adelman, now director of the U.S. Arms Control and Disarmament Agency, from arguing in the Spring 1981 issue of *Foreign Affairs* that the United States should step up its international propaganda efforts to support U.S. foreign policy. He emphasized the role that hard-sell propaganda can play, contending, for example, that "for the past two years, an impressive fifty-five percent of adults in Poland . . . tuned in RFE at least once a week." Yet even though Polish audiences are unusually receptive to U.S. propaganda, not even Radio Free Europe claims that kind of success. According to statistics from the Board for International Broadcasting, Adelman's figure should have been [for] once a month.

In fact, any statistics purporting to show the effectiveness of Radio Free Europe or Radio Libertry broadcasts should be viewed with skepticism. The figures for Polish listenership are based on interviews with Poles who travel to the West—hardly a representative group. And their responses are extrapolated by computer simulation to cover the entire Polish population. Moreover, people are counted as listeners no matter how short or infrequent their exposure to RFE during the month. Further, assumptions of success of RFE in Poland cannot simply be extended to other countries, as the Reagan administration has claimed. Audiences with different political, socioeconomic, and cultural backgrounds will respond to the same message from the same source in vastly different ways. Consequently, listenership to RFE in the other East European countries varies considerably.

Not only do many Poles view the Polish media as stooges of an illegitimate government, but the Polish people have also traditionally held very positive, almost romantic, attitudes towards the United States. Before RFE began to experience the most intense jamming in its history in late 1981, an estimated sixty-five percent of Polish adults (14 years and older) listened at least once a month. In Czechoslovakia, however, where opposition to the government is less intense and where audiences can easily receive commercial radio and television signals from West Germany and Austria, RFE listenership has been steadily declining and is now about half that of neighboring Poland, located too far east to receive commercial signals from the West. The comparable figures for Bulgaria, Hungary, and Romania are pegged at thirty-two, fifty-six, and sixty-three percent in a 1982 survey by the Board of International Broadcasting.

In the Soviet Union, where the government enjoys greater legitimacy and people are generally distrustful of the U.S. government, only about 9.7 per cent of adults listened to Radio Liberty once or more a month in 1983. Significantly, though, about twice as many Soviets listen to the Voice of America which broadcasts less provocative U.S.-oriented programming in addition to some Soviet domestic news. It is true that the VOA signal is less intensely jammed than the Radio Liberty signal, but even during years when both stations were heavily jammed, VOA audiences in the USSR greatly exceeded Radio Liberty listenership. Similarly, the BBC reaches as many Soviet listeners as Radio Liberty even though it broadcasts less than ten percent as many program hours to the USSR.

Further, many—perhaps most—people who listen to a U.S. government station are interested primarily in the entertainment programs. The best-known American in the Soviet Union after Reagan is Willis Conover, host of VOA's popular "Music USA." All international propagandists broadcast long hours of sports, music, soap operas, and other entertainment to attract large audiences who, it is hoped, will also listen to and accept the political messages sprinkled throughout the fluff. Many foreign listeners simply tune out the propaganda in the same way that approximately half of U.S. television viewers leave the room, change channels, or simply ignore commercials. During World War II, for example, American GIs in the Pacific enjoyed the music played by Tokyo Rose but generally ridiculed her efforts to ruin their morale.

In addition, those who do not listen to foreign radio propaganda are not necessarily political dissenters. In Cuba, for example, most government officials and party cadres regularly tune in VOA for information about U.S. policy so that they can better rebut American charges and arguments in their own organizations and media.

The average citizen usually views foreign radio messages, especially ones from a hostile power, with suspicion. Ralph White wrote in *International Behavior: A Social-Psychological Analysis* (1965) that during the Cuban missile crisis most Soviets clung to the belief that the Soviet Union was a peace-loving country responding to U.S. agression—despite harsh political and economic conditions in the USSR and despite compelling evidence that Moscow had installed offensive nuclear weapons in Cuba. The average person in Moscow reacted the same way to the Soviet attack on a South Korean passenger jet in September 1983. Following the incident, the VOA increased its often simultaneous Russian-language transmissions by about ninety hours a day, employing multiple frequencies and doubling the normal number of transmitters. Yet, despite indications that many Soviets heard these Western broadcasts, the *New York Times* reported September 14, 1983, the "widespread endorsement of their Government's justificaion for the airliner's destruction." Indeed, the U.S. propaganda blitz probably only heightened Soviet xenophobia by adding to the already strong conviction that the Soviet Union is a country under siege by foreign enemies.

The administration has also erroneously claimed that over time U.S. propaganda stations can build ever larger audiences in communist countries that can be persuaded to press their governments for domestic reforms. This claim is wrong on two counts. First, Board for International Broadcasting statistics indicate that except for the steady decline in Czechoslovakia listenership, RFE listenership in Eastern Europe has remained remarkably constant since 1966, the first year for which figures were publicly reported. Only during crises did listenership briefly rise. Second, propaganda research indicates that radio programs generally cannot turn people against their governments. Rather, dissidents first become alienated from their governments independently and afterward seek out foreign propaganda that reinforces their new attitudes. In other words, contrary to administration claims, RFE and Radio Liberty are probably preaching to the converted.

Clearly, many people around the world living under repressive regimes turn against their governments and search out alternatives tot he government-controlled domestic media, particularly during times of crisis. People are selective, however, and tend to avoid highly politicized, confrontational, and thus heavily jammed foreign stations in favor of more credible and accessible stations.

If U.S. propaganda is ineffective in manipulating the opinions of Soviet and East European audiences, why is the U.S. government annually spending hundreds of millions of dollars to broadcast to these countries? It is possible either that U.S. foreign-policy officials are entirely unaware of decades of communication research that discredits the bullet theory or that they feel a sense of moral obligation to reach foreign dissidents. The U.S. government, however, may also value international broadcasting primarily as a way to harass the Soviet Union and its satellites.

And U.S. radio broadcasting is a relatively cheap and easy method of angering the Kremlin. Thus, U.S. propaganda can tie up considerable Soviet resources. Because the Soviet government seems to regard even one dissenting voice as a threat to its credibiliqy, Moscow [believes] it has no choice but to try to jam as much Western broadcasting as it can.

Western societies, which prize alternative voices, do not feel as vulnerable to political harassment and need not jam Soviet propaganda. Worse for the Kremlin, effective jamming is far more costly than broadcasting; Western intelligence sources reportedly estimate that the Soviets currently spend about twice as much on jamming as Washington spends on broadcasting to the Eastern bloc.

Yet Soviet jammming is not necessarily proof that Western radio broadcasts could win or are indeed winning over Soviet audiences. The Soviets may be reacting in essentially the same way that victims of obscene telephone calls seek to prevent recurrences.

An Effective Base

Clearly, the U.S. government should try to communicate its perspective on issues and events to world audiences. And it has an obligation to supply information to inhabitants of repressive societies. But the United States can more effectively further American interests abroad by basing its programs on an accurate understanding of modern communciation theory.

The USIA should reinvigorate its highly effective but underfunded audience-based programs. USIA libraries, book fairs, and educational and cultural exchanges allow people to act on their individual needs and aspirations. International radio braodcasting, which has been taking large share of U.S. propaganda funds, should be de-emphasized. It is far less effective than person-to-person programs because the audiences have no chance to participate actively in the communication process. Personal contacts between U.S. citizens and foreign opinion leaders should be increased by Washington. This new focus would also dovetail with the results of communication research; for example, teenagers who ignored antismoking appeals in the mass media stopped smoking in significant numbers after speaking with peers who had quit.

USIA research activities are also grossly underfunded and should be substantially increased to determine which agency programs are effective. While the overall USIA budget was growing rapidly between 1981 and 1983, the research budget, which amounts to less than three per cent of total USIA expenditures, suffered a sixteen percent cut. In 1982, only forty-nine of the 8,184 USIA employees were engaged in research, eleven fewer than during the previous year. Of the agency is going to spend hundreds of millions of tax dollars on information programs, the least it can do is try to gauge their effectiveness. U.S. propaganda programs should concentrate on quality instead of quantity. In its latest appropriations requests, the administration has called for building more radio transmitters with greater power and broadcasting for more hours during each day, but it has paid little attention to staff professionalism, quality control of content, and audience research. About two-thirds of USIA's 1983 budget increase was earmarked for construction of radio transmitters. Yet, international communication cannot be assessed like military arsenals: Ten hours of propaganda broadcasting does not have the predictable effect on a variety of targets that a ten-megaton bomb has.

A Change of Philosophy

The United States should reduce its lopsided emphasis on broadcasting to communist countries, where propaganda is least effective in changing opinions, and focus instead on friendly, neutral, or undecided audiences. Currently, virtually all of the new radio transmitter construction underway is intended to increase coverage of communist countries. Since the major effect of international propaganda is to reinforce existing opinions, greater stress should be placed on communicating with allied countries. In 1983, the United States broadcast only 17.5 hours per week to Western Europe. In comparison, Voice of America, Radio Free Europe, and Radio Liberty broadcast over 1,300 hours of programming per week to the Eastern bloc. Many Third World audiences, who hold less antagonistic political views might be influenced favorably by foreign broadcasters—at least in theory. But in 1983, VOA beamed only 107 hours of programming per week to sub-Saharan African, 171.5 hours to Asia and the Pacific area, and 52.5 hours to Latin America. Further, the Soviet bloc propaganda efforts—including their less heavy-handed programs—are concentrated where the U.S. efforts are weakest. Eastern bloc countries gave scholarships to almost 5,000 students from the Caribbean Basin in 1981, while the United States funded only 748—14 by the USIA.

In reaching out to world audiences, the United States should favor VOA informational programming over the aggressive propaganda of surrogate home services. In 1983, Radio Liberty broadcast 483 hours a week to the Soviet

Union; but VOA, broadcasting only 201 hours, attracted a much larger audience with its less confrontational tone. Policymakers should thus resist recent pressure to transform VOA into a surrogate home service by attaching to it additional special services to communist countries such as Radio Marti. In encouraging VOA to produce more confrontational and overtly persuasive programming, the Reagan administration overlooks the simple fact that the effectiveness of U.S. propaganda is directly related to foreign audiences' support of U.S. positions. Publicizing those positions to foreign audiences is important, but no amount of persuasion will change world opinion if U.S. positions are deemed to be beyond the pale.

Finally, U.S. broadcasts should go on a low-sugar diet. Music, culture, and entertainment programs play an important role in U.S. propaganda efforts. They can reflect favorably on the country by introducing foreign audiences to American culture. But using entertainment programming as sugar coating to lure foreign audiences into swallowing political messages is a waste of taxpayers' money. As they mull plans to broadcast Venezuelan radio soap operas over Radio Marti to attract Cuban listeners, USIA officials should remember that every day countless people around the world listen to news programs without being baited by entertaiment programming. If U.S. news programming must be sugar-coated, it will probably never be swallowed anyway.

In some respects, aggressive propaganda is like the shouting between a husband and wife during a domestic squabble. The shouting usually reflects deeper marital problems and is not likely to change the opinion of either party; if anything, it will polarize their opinions. Yet international hostilies cannot be solved by one party moving out of the house.

In a perilous nuclear world, where neither the Soviet Union nor the United States is likely to submit to the other or disappear from the world stage, there is a danger that U.S. propaganda will drive the Soviets into an even more defensive and inflexible position. To minimize this danger and to promote U.S. interests effectively by reaching important audiences abroad, a re-evaluation of U.S. propaganda policy is essential.

Bibliography

Anderson, Jack, "PR and the Press," *Washington Post*, September 26, 1982.

Bagdikian, Ben H., "Congress and the Media: Partners in Propaganda," *Columbia Journalism Review*, January-February 1974.

Barnes, Joseph. "Fighting with Information: OWI Overseas," *The Public Opinion Quarterly*, 1943.

Bean, Walton E., *George Creel and His Critics: A Study of the Attacks on the Committee on Public Information, 1917-1919*, doctoral dissertation, University of California (Berkeley, Calif.), 1941.

Blanchard, Robert, *Congress and the News Media*, Hastings House (New York, N.Y.), 1974.

Brown, David H., "Government Public Affairs—Its Own Worst Enemy," *Public Relations Review*, Summer 1976.

_____, "Information Officrs and Reporters: Friends or Foes?" *Public Relations Review*, Summer 1976.

Brock, H.I., "Uncle Sam Hires a Reporter," *The New York Times Magazine*, June 1942.

Bruner, Jerome S., "OWI and the American Public," *The Public Opinion Quarterly*, (1943).

Columbia Broadcasting System, "The Selling of the Pentagon," documentary, 1970.

Cowley, Malcolm, "The Sorrows of Elmer Davis," *The New Republic*, May 3, 1943.

Cutlipp, Scott, "Public Relations in Government," *Public Relations Review*, Summer 1976.

Davis, Elmer, "The Power of Truth," *Vital Speeches of the Day*, November 1, 1942.

Ensley, Philip Chalfant, *The Policital and Social Thought of Elmer Davis*, doctoral dissertation, Ohio State University, 1965.

Franz, Laurent, "The First Amendment in the Balance," *Yale Law Review*, 1962.

_____, "Is the First Amendment Law: A Reply to Mr. Mendelson," *California Law Review*, 1963.

Friendly, Fred. *The Good Guys, the Bad Buys and the First Amendment: Free Speech vs. Fairness in Broadcasting.* Random House (New York, N.Y.), 1976.

Fox, Frank W., *Advertising and the Second World War: A Study in Private Propaganda.* Ph.D. dissertation, Stanford University, 1973.

Gerald, J. Edward. *The Press and the Constitution, 1931-1947.* University of Minnesota Press (Mineapolis, Minn.), 1948.

Goldstein, Stephnie, "Hi, I'm From the Government and I Want to Help You," *Public Relations Journal*, October 1981.

Greenfield, Meg, "Not Everything is Propaganda," *Newsweek*, March 21, 1983.

Heise, Juergen Arthur, *Minimum Disclosure: How the Pentagon Manipulates News*, Norton (New York, N.Y.), 1979.

Hook, Sidney. *Paradoxes of Freedom.* University of California Press (Berkeley, Calif.), 1962.

Jensen, Dwight Wm. "Toward a Normative Theory of Freedom of the Press," Unpublished paper presented at AEJMC Convention, 1985.

Jensen, Jay W., "Toward a Solution of the Problem of Freedom of the Press," *Journalism Quarterly*, Fall 1950.

Johnson, George C. "The Press as an Institution of the Constitution: Justice Potter Stewart's Approach to the First Amendment," Unpublished paper presented at AEJMC Convention, 1985.

Jones, David Lloyd. *The U.S. Office of War Information and American Public Opinion During World War II, 1939-1945*. Ph.D. Dissertation, State University of New York at Binghamton, 1976.

Lasswell, Harold D., *Propaganda Technique in the World War*, Alfred A. Knopf (New York, N.Y.), 1927.

Koppes, Clayton R. and Gregory D. Black, "What to Show the World: The Office of War Information and Hollywood, 1942-1945." *The Journal of American History*, Fall 1977.

———, "What the OWI Is Doing." *The Saturday Review of Literature*, December 5, 1942.

———, "War Information," *In War Information and Censorhsip*, by Elmer Davis and Byron Price. American Council on Public Affairs (Washington, D.C.), n.d.

———, "The War and America." *Harper's Magazine*, April 1940.

Landry, Robert J. "The Impact of OWI on Broadcasting." *The Public Opinion Quarterly*, 1943.

Lewis, Christopher. "The Voice of America," *The New Republic*, June 25, 1945.

MacLeish, Archibald. *American Opinion and the War: The Rede Lecture Delivered before the University of Cambridge of 30 July 1942*. Macmillan (New York, N.Y.), 1942.

Marks, Barry Alan, *The Idea of Propaganda in America*, doctoral dissertation, University of Minnesota, 1957.

Mayton, William T. "Toward a Theory of First Amendment Process: Injunctions of Speech, Subsequent Punishment, and the Costs of the Prior Restraint Doctrine." *Cornell Law Review*, 1982.

Menefee, Selden C., "Propaganda Wins Battles," *The Nation*, February 12, 1944.

Mock, James R. and Cedric Larson. *Words that Won the War: The Story of the Committee on Public Information, 1917-1919*. Princeton University Press (Princeton, N.J.), 1939.

Morgan, David, *The Flacks of Washington: Government Information and the Public Agenda*, Greenwood Press (Westport, Conn.), 1986.

Rabin, Kenneth H., "Government PIOs in the '80s," *Public Relations Journal*, December 1979.

Rivers, William L., *The Adversaries: Politics and the Press*, Beacon Press (Boston, Mass.), 1970.

Rosten, Leo, *The Washington Correspondents*,

Shapiro, Walter, "Pentagon versus Press," *Newsweek*, December 31, 1984.

Small, William J., *Political Power and the Press*, Norton (New York, N.Y.), 1972.

Squires, James D., *British Propaganda at Home and in the United States From 1914-1917*, Harvard University Press (Cambridge, Mass.), 1935.

Steeler, Richard W., "Preparing the Public for War: Effort to Establish a National Propaganda Agency," *The American Historical Review*, 1970.

Steinberg, Charles S., *The Information Establishment: Our Government and the Media*, Hastings House (New York, N.Y.), 1980.

Wise, David, *The Politics of Lying; Government Deception, Secrecy, and Power*, Random House (New York, N.Y.), 1973.

Chapter 51

The Presidency

Presidents Washington, Adams, Jefferson, Madison, Monroe, and John Quincy Adams recognized the necessity of keeping the people informed while also trying to create a favorable impression of the state. However, it was Andrew Jackson's "Kitchen Cabinet," a small circle of friends, most of them journalists, who advised him on almost all personal and presidential matters, and which became the basis for a more formalized political structure that included a wide-scale public relations mission. The most influential of Jackson's advisors was journalist Amos Kendall (1789-1869) whose title of fourth auditor of the treasury, 1829-1835, hid his true influence. In 1835, Kendall became postmaster general, the most politically powerful position in the President's cabinet. According to journalist Fred Endres:

> . . . Kendall performed most, if not all, public relations tasks associated with White House personnel today. He wrote stirring speeches for Jackson; authored highly important state papers and messages; penned early versions of press releases; and performed some rudimentary straw polling. He also served as a political "advance man" for presidential trips, and he was tremendously influential in establishing, implementing, and publicizing political policy. Beneath all these duties was the constant attempt to build and reinforce a favorable image of Jackson as the bold, resourceful, democratic, honest, military hero-president.

Theodore Roosevelt added the press conference to the nature of news reporting; Calvin Coolidge and Warren G. Harding used a professional public relations consultant; Franklin D. Roosevelt added a "personal" touch with his "Fireside Chats," seemingly informal "chats" broadcast by radio, and Harry S Truman won an eletion partly on the strength of a "Whistle-Stop" campaign that took him throughout the country. By the mid-twentieth century, presidential staffs, which once numbered fewer than ten a century earlier, now numbered in the hundreds; included, in an age of media explosion, were a press secretary, deputies, assistants, and *their* staffs.

The intricate and complicated sociological and psychological relationships between the president and the reporters is not confined to just one president and one set of reporters, but is easily extended to all rulers and all members of the

761

media, from tribal chiefs and village mayors to heads of state, from the dawn of history to the final holocaust. The good rulers know the human condition, how to manipulate the media and the public without being obvious about it; the weak leaders often do not know the principles or, if they do know them, are blatantly "heavy-handed" in using them. But, it makes no difference, for all rulers, to be effective, learn the principles of manipulation; and all reporters, especially those who spend much of their time denying that anyone can manipulate them, are, in fact, manipulated.

The President and Popularity

by Elmer E. Cornwell, Jr.

. . . In the absence of constitutionally provided means of enforcing his role as chief legislator, the president (presidents over the history of the office) has developed his prime extra-constitutional resource: his ability to shape, lead, and focus public opinion. Broad public sympathy for what a president is trying to do will impress itself upon Congress; and an aroused public demanding action the Legislative branch finds irresistible [can force action; thus,] the American presidency's power is essentially "plebiscitary" in its basis. That is, the chief executive must rely on his direct linkage with the public and the support he can thus engender and channel, for his influence over policy . . .

Thus, the most important "capital" a president has to invest in his efforts at policy leadership is his ability to mass and lead his national constituency. Obviously, this depends upon his popularity; . . . Without the channels of access to this constituency which the news media represent, and given the fact that American democracy has rarely tolerated direct governmental propaganda efforts through media it controlled, he would have no means of leading. Yet he cannot command access to the privately controlled news channels, save to a limited degree with radio and television. His access ultimately depends on a trade-off with the proprietors of the media.

Newspapers, newsmagazines, networks, and the rest exist to sell news. Government in general, and the presidency in particular, provide them with

Dr. Elmer E. Cornwell, Jr., is professor of political science at Brown University, and parliamentarian of the Rhode Island House of Representatives. He was an alternate delegate to the 1960 and 1964 Democratic presidential nomination conventions, and is former president of the Northeast Political Science Association. He is the author of several major articles and books on the American government and the presidency; for *Presidential Leadership of Public Opinion* (Indiana University Press, 1965), a pioneering work, he was awarded the Frank Luther Mott Award of Kappa Tau Alpha, national journalism scholarship fraternity, for the outstanding research work in journalism. Dr. Cornwell received a B.A. in political science from Williams College, and the A.M. and Ph.D. in political science from Harvard University. [This article is edited and reprinted, with permission, from the *Annals of the American Political Science Society*, September 1976; ©1976, Elmer E. Cornwell, Jr.]

important sources of raw material for their purveying of news to their customers. And the president is *the* outstanding news source. News about him and his activities combines governmental information with human interest. He is both a public institution and a person, with foibles, weaknesses, human involvements, and the rest, as well as policy positions and philosophies. Congress, the courts, and the departments are essentially dehumanized abstractions, whose actions are as newsworthy as the president's but whose human interest can rarely be isolated or identified.

Every president, when he first enters the White House, promises an "open administration." He swears he likes reporters, will cooperate with them, will treat them as first-class citizens. The charade goes on for a few weeks, or months, or even a couple of years. All the while, the President is struggling to suppress an overwhelming conviction that the press is trying to undermine his Administration, if not the Republic. He is fighting a maddening urge to control, bully, villify, persecute, or litigate against every free-thinking reporter and editor in sight . . . Every president, from Washington on, came to recognize the press as a natural enemy, and eventually tried to manipulate it and muzzle it.

—Timothy Crouse, *The Boys on the Bus,* 1977

The press, thus, needs the president as much, probably, as he needs them. Yet mutual dependence characteristically has rarely bred mutuality of interest or cooperation. The use the president wants to make of the press is, of course, self-serving. He wants to control timing, mode of presentation, and, if possible, reaction to his moves. The press has both a professional and, let us be frank, an economic interest in presenting the news in its most complete, unvarnished, and hence salable form. This means that they want to control timing and presentation, for maximum impact. To the extent that they succeed, they may affect reaction as well. Thus, there is a constant struggle between the two, at times muted and masked by apparent camaraderie, at other times open and bitter . . .

[Thus,] the president governs through the media. His effectiveness, his entree with the public, depends on the extent to which he can win and retain public approval. His stock in trade is measured in his popularity. Even casual observation of presidential careers suggests that popularity is related to success in governing. Further, observation also suggests that presidential popularity begins high, and, with fluctuations, seems to trend downward as an administration progresses.

Portraying the President

by Michael Baruch Grossman
and Martha Joynt Kumar

The Stakes of the Relationship

The President of the United States ordinarily is brought to you by the news media. Images of the White House produced by strategists who advise the President reach their audience after they are processed in the great news factories and fine craft shops of print, broadcast, and television journalism. Reporters, editors, and producers regularly communicate messages from and about the President to workers, businessmen, farmers, ethnic groups, religious groups, and similar segments of the population—all of whom once received them primarily from their own leaders. The President, the news media, and the people have an enormous stake in the critical relationship between the White House and news organizations. Both White House officials and reporters work to capture a national audience that demands information about the presidency. Since each uses the other's prestige to add to its own, the relationship between the two sides is often cooperative. Tensions occur because partisans of the President and partisans of the news media compete to gain the most benefits from the relationship. Both argue that their side speaks for the people.

The Stakes for the President

White House publicity operations evolved from the organizational world of a White House bureaucracy that had been established to get the President's image and message into the media. The present White House activities of the media, developed in response to the enlarged prominence of the presidency, are possible because of the economic and technological expansion of publishing and broadcasting enterprises. By the late nineteeth century, several essential features emerged that continue to affect the relationship between the President and the press: (1) news about the White House was transmitted to the public by independent nonpartisan news organizations; (2) these organizations were heavily dependent on the White House staff for most of the information they received about the President's activities and policies; (3) the transition from

Dr. Michael Baruch Grossman and Dr. Martha Joynt Kumar are professors of political science, Towson State College (Towson, Md.) Dr. Grossman received a B.A. from Oberlin College, and a Ph.D. from Johns Hopkins University, both in political science. He was employed at the *Washington Post* and the American Association of University Professors (AAUP). Dr. Kumar received a B.A. from Connecticut College, and an M.S. and Ph.D. from Columbia University, all in political science. She was employed by the National Broadcasting Co. several years as a researcher and consultant on congressional elections. Drs. Grossman and Kumar are also the authors of *Washington Politics and the News Media* (Random House, 1987). [This article is edited and reprinted with permission from *Portraying the President*, published by Johns Hopkins University Press, 1979; ©1979 by Johns Hopkins University Press.]

an episodic to a regular relationship between the President and the press required the development of procedures to provide reporters with information on a regular basis; (4) the increase in both the amount and the diversity of White House publicity activities made it necessary for the President to seek specialized assistants with skills as promoters and with knowledge of the press.

In the following decades the continuing expansion of the resources of both news organizations and the White House staff made the relationship between president and press a recognizable feature of the Washington landscape. Today, several important White House officials administer publicity operations comprising one of the major functions and perhaps the central preoccupation of the President's men and women, while the presidency has become the central concern of major news enterprises and their leading journalists.

Since the 1930s, the White House and news organizations have established institutions that function best in an atmosphere of continuity and stability. Self-perpetuating organizational routines, characteristic of complex organizations, have made the relationship less flexible than participants on either side believe it is or wish that it would be. Each side reacted to technical changes by emphasizing matters of behavior that reinforce the need for continuing cooperation. Consequently, important aspects of the relationship continue over long periods . . .

Because publicity is often an inseparable component of policy, many White House officials, especially those who think it is always inseparable, believe that their political power depends on the public perception that the President is providing strong leadership. They believe that his image as an effective leader is as important to the success of his administration as the substantive appeal of his programs . . .

White House officials decided to create a structure for news operations in response to the growing organizational and technological complexity of the news media as well as to their own ongoing publicity requirements. In his pioneering work on the subject, *Presidential Leadership of Public Opinion*, Elmer Cornwell . . . demonstrated that since the administration of Theodore Roosevelt, an increasingly important factor in determining the success of a president's communications strategies has been the sophistication with which White House officials approached the job of creating and coordinating White House offices that have responsibilities for communicating the President's image and messages to the public. The roots of these White House offices and the origins of some of these White House publicity activities may be traced back as far as the administration of Grover Cleveland, although a large and effective operation was not introduced until the 1930s.

Thus, over a period of almost a century, the organizational world of the White House evolved in a manner that has made it possible for the President to maintain, stabilize, and at times exploit his relations with the media. During the fifty years beginning with Grover Cleveland's administration and ending at Franklin D. Roosevelt's, the evolving White House institutionalized a number of ad hoc roles performed by the President's secretary and other assistants into the permanent position of press secretary, whose most conspicuous role is as the President's spokesman. In the following years, roughly from 1933 to the present, an expanded White House staff began to provide even more publicity resources for the President. A third development, which began in the late 1960s, involved the establishment of permanent institutions that administer and coordinate administration publicity . . .

A contemporary president uses his numerous advantages as occupant of the White House to obtain favorable coverage in the media. The large, well-organized and well-financed White House staff makes elaborate and extensive preparations for the President's appearances at press conferences, public addresses, and ceremonies. It sets the ground rules and picks the locations for appearances by him or other White House officials. Although administrations differ considerably in their attitudes toward news organizations, they use the advantages of incumbency in similar ways to project their version of the President's personal qualities, leadership skills, and policy preferences. Thus each administration attempts to develop a positive image of the President by focusing the attention of the media on the man and his family. Each presents the President as a vigorous and capable leader. Each emphasizes that the President is an advocate of policies and a political philosophy that reemphasize traditional values while directing the country toward a better future . . .

The White House is a vast political communications center that sends messages to Congress, foreign governments, interest groups, bureaucrats, and the American public. Although White House advisers want to publicize most of these messages, they know that even those directed to specific groups or small segments of the public ultimately will be picked up by the mass media. Efforts to keep the contents of the messages private usually fail in a cauldron-like setting in which most items eventually boil to the surface. "They call this place the bubble machine," a Ford administration official reflected. "You see it that way; it literally is that." Staff members may succeed in fine-tuning the reports spread by news organizations about the President, but they find it difficult to keep information secret when it has a high street value . . .

---

*I really look with commiseration over the great body of my
fellow citizens, who, reading newspapers, live and die in
the belief that they have known something of what has been
passing in the world in their time.*

—Harry S Truman

Publicity operations are the central White House activity that link the President's direct appeals for support with his staff's efforts to assist him by lobbying interest groups, Congress, and the bureaucracy. White House officials know that the same news organizations that amplify the President's messages also provide their audiences with information and images harmful to the administration. By influencing what appears as news, the staff hopes to win the media's listeners, readers, and viewers for the President. "Along this line, the President is going to want your creative and sustained thinking about the overall problem of communicating with the American people," Bill Moyers [one of President Johnson's press secretaries] wrote to Robert Kintner of NBC News shortly before the latter came to work at the White House. "Some call it the problem of 'the President's image'," Moyers continued. "It goes beyond that to the ultimate question of how does the President shape the issues and interpret them to people—how, in fact, does he lead." . . .

The Nature of the Apparatus

White House officials command resources that provide important public relations services for the President. Highly visible operations, such as those carried on by the press secretary and his staff, are coordinated with less well-known activites that also play important roles in the formation and execution of White House media policies, such as scheduling, an activity that involves most of the President's senior advisers as well as the twelve persons listed in the White House telephone directory as working for the appointment and scheduling offices. One of President Ford's principal advisers stated that his central consideration in arranging the President's schedule had been the White House's desire to attract, or occasionally to avoid, media coverage. Another high-level aide in that administration called scheduling a "propaganda machine." . . .

Newly-elected presidents and their advisers know that their ability to acquire political influence often depends on their ability to use the tools of image-building. White House officials learn quickly that using these tools to bolster their reputation in the Washington community, as well as with the larger public, contributes to the success of their administration. "Presidential leadership is as much a matter of intangibles, as much shadow as substance," wrote Patrick Anderson [in *The President's Men*]—who has observed the office as chief speechwriter for Jimmy Carter's 1976 presidential campaign, as a national political reporter, and as a White House aide during the Johnson administration—noted, "What a President does may matter less than what the people think he is doing."

A president requires popular support to obtain political influence because his office's constitutional and institutional prerogatives are insufficient for him to achieve many important objectives. Although his powers to command are considerable, effective leadership requries his ability to use a variety of political skills. A president must be able to persuade Congress, the bureaucracy, his political party, lobbyists for interest groups, state and local officials and an army of influentials in the private sector that it is in their interest to support his programs. In order to influence and persuade these groups, presidents have found it increasingly necessary to demonstrate their effectiveness as leaders of public opinion. The mass media is the principal vehicle through which they influence public opinion.

A president needs news organizations because, as communicator of most of his political messages, they determine his credibility with major public officials and the leaders of the most powerful interest groups. His 600 White House subordinates organize his relations with a long list of crucial individuals including most congressmen, important officials of state and local governments, key figures among the diffuse layers in the domestic and foreign policy bureaucracies, the officers and lobbyists for interest groups, and the leading figures of party organizations. In meetings with them, the President or his aides impart vital specialized information and shape the personal elements in the relationship. Since these contacts take place in a society in which, like the public at large, influential leaders get most of their messages about the White House from the news media, organizing the President's relations with news organizations is an important element of all the relationships. "There is no way to do this job as president if you are not willing to think about the media as part of the process in the same way that Congress is part of the process," Richard Cheney, White House chief of staff for Gerald Ford reflected shortly before that administration left office. "Consciously or unconsciously, the press often becomes an actor in the scenario." . . .

The Stakes for the Media

Reporting at the White House takes place at the tips of the media's tentacles. The tentacles extend from news organizations that represent publishing and broadcasting enterprises of diverse size, power, and interest. The needs of these organizations determine what appears as news. The reporters, photographers, and technicians assigned to cover the President and his activities on a regular basis must interpret these needs every time they decide how to get a story at the White House. Reporters, the most important group among these news gatherers, define news according to a mix of professional values, the demands of their organizations, the activities of other reporters, and their reaction to efforts by the President and his advisers to reach the public through them.

Unlike the tentacles, the regular White House reporters are quite visible. They show up at events scheduled for them such as briefings and news conferences and follow the President on his public and private travels. They are visible because of the large amount of time they spend waiting for something to happen—for the briefing to start, for the President to appear for a ceremony in the White House Rose Garden, for a visitor to arrive, for a statement or transcript to be released. A few correspondents wait because they know that eventually there will be an unscheduled announcement or event. . . .

News organizations need to cover the President because he represents the focal point in the American political system for their staffs and audience. For many reporters, a White House assignment represents the high point of a career. They know that the stories they prepare are virtually guaranteed a leading position in the daily or weekly editions of their publications or programs. The White House assignment also gives reporters high visibility with the public, which sees their faces, hears their voices, or reads their bylines. For print media editors and broadcast media producers, maintaining a regular correspondent at the White

House is an important aspect of the prestige of their publication or programs. They want their organizations to reflect the aura of the presidency.

Because the Chief Executive is an individual, presidential activities can be portrayed more dramatically by the media than can those of Congress or the bureaucracy. The news media presents the President in its columns, telecasts, and broadcasts as an embodiment of national authority. John Herbers, deputy chief of the *New York Time's* Washington bureau and a former White House correspondent, gave the following explanation for the predictable manner in which the media lavishes time and space to present the President to the public: "It's the way the whole process operates. If you have an institution [the presidency] in which an enormous amount of power is invested, an enormous amount of prestige, an enormous amount of publicity in the past has been centered on, then you get into a situation which is difficult to break out of. . . . It's a matter of habits in people's minds all the way from the reporting staff through the editors. I think it's true of most news organizations. They're conditioned to think in these terms."

News organizations regard themselves as surrogates for the public; this is another reason why they place so much importance on their relationship with the President. This role found support even from a White House official for the Nixon administration, which was not known for expressing such thoughts during the incumbency of its leader. Gerald Warren, deputy press secretary during parts of the Nixon and Ford administrations, provided the unlikely testimonial: "If you don't assume that, then the whole process breaks down. They are the best representatives our system has been able to find. It's an entirely different subject if you want to discuss how well they represent the American people. But what other representatives do the American people have? . . . On a daily basis, the White House press corps must be assumed to be the people's representatives."

Until recently, working correspondents at the White House were reluctant to define their roles as political actors. They maintained that they merely portrayed events for their viewers and readers. They would speak about getting the story for their news organization or, in general terms, of finding out what's going on and reporting it to the public. They tended to resist analysis of their influence by others and did not offer any themselves. Because of the high level of antagonism between the White House and the news media during the Johnson and Nixon administrations, however, and possibly because the media has been attacked from a variety of political positions during recent years, some reporters are now more inclined to reflect on the critical nature of their role in the relationship that connects the people to the government. Peter Lisagor, one of the most widely respected reporters in Washington during his twenty years there, linked the stakes in the relationship for the President, for the public, and for news organizations when he reflected on his reaction to a tense moment that occurred during the Vietnam War: "Once when Dean Rusk got angry at reporters' questions he yelled, 'Who the hell elected you?' Someone shouted back at him, 'Who the hell ever elected you?' What I would have said is that we represent the public interest. Nobody elected us to do this, but since we don't have a parliamentary system in which the President can be questioned on the floor of Congress, the press acquired that role by custom and tradition. We can't make a strong case for it though. We're used to being challenged all the time." . . .

Responding to the Power of the Media

Perhaps the most important continuing pressure on White House officials to become sources comes from the media itself. The President and his staff respond to media requests, including those they would prefer to avoid, because they believe that they could be badly damaged and lose important channels to the public if they refused. They believe that they have no alternative to meeting with reporters. Their reasons are personal as well as institutional. For example, members of the White House staff often are asked to confirm or deny stories that reporters have uncovered. If they don't respond they fear they will damage their personal relations with the media. Since White House officials, like others in government, regard their relations with reporters as being important to their careers, most form new friendships with reporters after they take office and build on old ones. They regard reporters as part of the Washington establishment, a part that is as important to them as the legislative branch or the bureaucracy.

A person's perception of presidential power changes when he becomes president. From the outside the presidency appears to be an all-powerful position. Once a president takes office, however, he becomes more aware of the power of those outside the White House, especially those he perceives as his antagonists. The media form one of the powers surrounding and restraining the presidency, as incumbents see it.

Frequently the press secretary and others on the White House staff would prefer not to respond to reporters, yet they do so because they believe that avoiding them would harm their long-term relationship with the media. There is an unwritten White House rule that if a reporter has all the facts about a story and asks the press secretary for confirmation, the press secretary will let him know if it is correct or if there is something wrong, even though the White House might prefer to make its own announcement.

The Stakes for the Public

The ultimate significance of the relationship between the White House and news organizations is that most segments of American society depend on what appears in the media for their information about the President. . . .

The highest stakes involve two major aspects of the political system: first, that the President be able to communicate with the public; second, that the people get an accurate assessment of his conduct and activities. Because the media is the main intermediary between White House officials and news organizations over which messages will appear, what information will be available, and which activities reporters will be permitted to cover. The outcome affects whether the public response will be to provide support for the President or to demand that his policies change.

Other important consequences occur when the relationship becomes too cooperative or too competitive. Once probable outcome of a cozy relationship is that reporters, editors, or producers will gloss over official mistakes and thus fail to inform the public who was responsible for a bad decision. . . .

When news organizations are too sensitive to White House needs, they fail to report important aspects of the character of a president. Most reporters did not

is that reporters, editors, or producers will gloss over official mistakes and thus fail to inform the public who was responsible for a bad decision. . . .

When news organizations are too sensitive to White House needs, they fail to report important aspects of the character of a president. Most reporters did not report the strange developments that took place in the White House during the final days of both the Johnson and Nixon administrations. Later it was revealed that President Johnson was convinced that his critics were subversives plotting with the country's enemies, while Nixon was so beset by his problems that he was often unable to function as president. Some critics of the media's role during this period believe that because news organizations later did report many stories of this type, public confidence in the president has been undermined, which makes it harder for him to serve public needs. Alternatively, the failure to report this information at the time may have led to the deep suspicions that are currently prevalent in public opinion that the same types of events may be going unreported now.

There are a number of important consequences for the public when the relationship becomes highly competitive. During the [1970s], the media made it difficult for the President to transmit important messages to the public; at the same time, the White House used manipulative methods to prevent unfavorable stories from appearing. Each side appeared to assault the other. The public, the President, and the media all have a large stake in a final unraveling of these activities that figured so prominently in recent history . . .

Predictable Phases in the White House-News Media Relationship

Every newly-elected president promises to be accessible, to speak frankly, and to make available all information that the public needs to form an adequate assessment of his administration . . . Their tactics and strategies, which are intended to influence the way they are portrayed in the media, include managing the flow of news, wooing reporters with ingratiating approaches, using their control over access to avoid reporters, and attacking the credibility of the media.

The way in which a president employs these tactics depends on his view of the press. Presidents who view news organizations as members of another interest group are likely to use tactics of news management or ingratiation. Those who think their responsibility toward the press ends when they release their public communiques will use the tactics of avoidance or attack. Presidents who want the press to channel the ideas and images of their administrtion are inclined to use tactics of ingratiation.

These tactics bring about predictable reactions from diverse news organizations that have learned how to protect themselves against the methods used by White House officials. As both the White House publicity apparatus and the organizational structure of publishing and broadcasting enterprises have become more complex, features of cooperation and rivalry seem to have occurred at regular intervals during the history of each new administration. There is a period at the beginning of an administration when the White House and news organizations appear to be allies in producing and disseminating news. This is followed by clashes over news and information so great that the two sides appear to be adversaries. In a third stage the intensity of the competition burns out and is replaced by a relationship that is more structured and less intense than that in either of the first two periods. The second and third periods alternately occur and recur after the initial period of cooperation, and there may be a brief return of the first period if a president is reelected, but the long-term trend through either a four- or an eight-year presidency is for rivalry to be characteristic of the middle portion of an administration and the more formal relationship to dominate at the end. The names given to these periods or phases are "alliance," "competition," and "detachment." . . .

Phase One: Alliance

During the phase of alliance, a silent partnership exists between White House officials and representatives of news organizations assigned to cover the presidency. The partnership is based on two elements: the common definition by both parties of newsworthy items; and the willingness of reporters to provide an unfiltered conduit on which the White House can convey messages to the public.

Reporters assigned to cover the presidency on a daily basis need the cooperation of White House officials, particularly those in the Press Office. This is especially true at the beginning of an administration. Reporters are more dependent on White House-sponsored arrangements such as briefings and press releases then than they will be later, when some of them acquire techniques to verify the official line. Because this phase usually coincides with the euphoric early weeks of a new administration, it is commonly but inappropriately referred to as the President's "honeymoon" with the press. The term is inappropriate because it implies the suspension of normal self-interest, thus conveying the impression that the President is being given a chance by reporters to get to know his job and relish the fruits of his newly–won office for a few weeks before reporters and White House officials resume their traditional role as adversaries. Although the relationship is more easygoing at this time, neither officials nor reporters would hold back from non–newlywed treatment of the other if it suited their purpose. The point is that during this period both sides have more to gain by cooperation. They both want to obtain maximum media exposure for the new administration, its people, and its proposed policies. As long as they hold the same definition of news, it makes sense for them to cooperate.

If a president changes his policies and his assistants at the beginning of a second term and provides reporters with easy access to himself and his new aides, there may be a brief reprise of the period of alliance . . . After a four year term, the basic tenor of the relationship between President and press will have been set. The duration of the phase of alliance at the beginning of a second term is likely to be much shorter than that at the beginning of the first term.

Newsworthy Items

The first item on reporters' agendas is to profile interesting personalities—to provide the "people" stories that news editors demand. The most newsworthy person in the new administration is the President. Reporters are interested in three types of stories about the Chief Executive: human interest stories about the man and the people closest to him; stories about the President as policy-maker, focusing on the way he conducts himself while deciding which policy positions he will choose and emphasize; and stories about his goals and plans. All three types of stories are likely to be reported in a manner that is favorable to the President, in large part because of the habits and traditions of reporters in dealing with what they consider to be newsworthy items at this time.

"The President himself is a story, regardless of what he does," said George Reedy, who served as [one of] Lyndon Johnson's press secretaries. A Ford White House official observing the Carter administration getting ready to take office predicted that reporters would be very interested in "personality" stories about President Carter during the early days of his term. The reporters would want to find out "First, who is Jimmy Carter? What is his personality? Does he get mad? Does he golf? Does he fish in a pond? How do you find out who somebody is? You look at his friends, his habits, his manner, his character, his personality."

The stories that result from these personal glimpses invariably are friendly to the President, as are stories that deal with the new president as he attempts [to manage the office.]

Reporters who cover [a] new president when he was a candidate have a somewhat different perspective on the new administration from those whose assignment began after the election. They got to know the White House staff during a period when they were especially anxious to be accessible to the press. These reporters may have established a relationship with the candidate, and they can use their campaign experience as a backdrop for their coverage of the administration.

Some of the earliest critical stories of Jimmy Carter as president were produced by reporters who had covered the Carter campaign. An example of this kind of story—one to which the administrtion took exception—is a *New York Times* article written by James Wooten that appeared on April 25, 1977, and that seemed to characterize Carter as being "aloof" and a "recluse," terms that brought back unhappy memories of the Nixon administration. But members of this group of reporters are constrained from getting too far in front of their colleagues with critical stories. They too work for news organizations that want personal glimpses of the new leaders. It is a situation that the White House can use to its advantage. "I have seen reporters 'co-opted' by the simple device of giving them private photographs taken by the White House photographer," said George Reedy. "No single one of these pictures could be classified as 'news' in the ordinary sense. Most of them merely show the President stolling through the mansion; drinking a cup of coffee; or playing with his dogs. The reporter who got the pictures, however, received very favorable treatment from his editors thereafter and naturally he reciprocated with stories about the President that actually fawned."

*It is an essential truth of this profession that White
House reporters do not like to fight the gods, particularly
Presidents' gods, and they do not cherish an adversary
relationship . . . Their unwillingness to engage in an adversary relationship with the White House is exceeded only
by that of most of their editors and publishers, men by
and large of remarkable timidity who are made intensely
nervous by any digression from the norm, no matter how
terrible the norm.*

—David Halberstam, "Press and Prejudice,"
Esquire; April 1974, p. 110.

A newly inaugurated president also may receive favorable publicity when he announces such general goals as cutting back unemployment or curbing inflation. Reporters are not likely to prepare critical stories in response to this type of announcement because of two deeply ingrained habits common to most of them in their production of news stories. First, when reporters present criticism, they do so in the form of a comparision between the President's rhetoric and his record. Since the President has no record at this time, his rhetoric is presented as news. Second, critical stories seldom are written by reporters on their own authority—they prefer to pluck critical words from the mouths of public figures. At this early stage of an administration, however, most public figures are unwilling to criticize the President in strong and newsworthy terms because it is not yet clear in which direction he is moving. He may be on their side, and they do not want to antagonize him prematurely. Even columnists and analysts who are not constrained by these habits and practices are likely to hold back at this time because they are still developing their sources. Consequently, in the early months of his term, a president is spared critical news stories of the type that become common later . . .

During this phase of alliance, White House officials provide reporters with the best access that they will have at any time during the administration. The flow of information is least restricted, and reporters have their greatest opportunities to get information about the administration at public interchanges and in inter-views. Of course, there are significant differences among administrations as to how available and accessible the information and officials will be. President Kennedy's press secretary, Pierre Salinger, maintains that he did not monitor the contacts between reporters and the White House staff, and the memories of White House reporters from that era bear out his contention. During the Nixon administration both access and information were more difficult from the start, although some reporters recall that the offices of White House aides were opened to them in the early months of the administration.

The promise of an open presidency is an echo of Woodrow Wilson's call for a government "which is all outside and no inside." Although no such sweeping claims have been made by recent presidents, similar, if lesser, assertions are common to all incoming administrations. The new press secretary usually reflects this commitment, especially when he is contrasted against his successors . . .

There is a cordial atmosphere during this period. Most presidents are optimistic about the future when they take office. They forget earlier harsh encounters with the media in the ebullience of their accession to office. Leo Rosten reminded his readers in 1937 that Franklin Roosevelt had had bad press relations before his election. According to Rosten, he "offended newsmen" as assistant secretary of the navy, irritated them in his vice-presidential campaign of 1920 "by denying remarks which the newspapermen recalled his having made," and "threatened reporters" as governor of New York on at least one occasion. As a consequence of all of these incidents, in Albany "some reporters avoided his conferences altogether."

In practical terms, the open presidency means that reporters are more likely to have their phone calls answered, to be granted interviews, and to get information that has not been specifically restricted. The President is more likely at this time to hold regular and frequent press conferences; important administration officials will be made available for questioning by reporters; and more of the information given to reporters will be on the record . . .

Most presidents do not regard the media as overly obtrusive, as did President Eisenhower, or as hostile, as did President Nixon. Especially during their first months in office they recognize the tremendous benefits of conducting an open administration. Because in most cases the outgoing administration had developed abrasive relations with some news organizations, reporters are glad to have the opportunity to make contacts with a new group of officials. More important from the administration's point of view, . . . most of the stories that reporters prepare at this time are likely to be favorable. Consequently, the "open presidency" is a good tactic. The president's personal relations with reporters tend to be most constant during this period. President Kennedy gave private interviews to reporters most frequently during 1961 and early 1962. By 1963 he saw them less frequently and on a more formal basis. Press conferences also are most likely to be scheduled frequently and regularly during this early period. Lyndon Johnson met with reporters thirty-five times during his first thirteen months in office. In 1965, however, his second full year, he held only sixteen press conferences.

Because of their large audiences, the [wire services] and networks are particularly important to the White House during this phase. The common view in the last five administrations that television is the most important contemporary medium has produced a common thread in them. "You pitch everything you have toward television," said one high-level member of President Ford's White House staff. Jody Powell [Jimmy Carter's press secretary] also commented on the importance of presenting material that can be used by television. Powell remarked that Theodore Roosevelt's appraisal of the presidency as a bully pulpit was essentially true today, "only now the pulpit is [the TV networks], and to some extent the wires."

Phase Two: Competition

An end comes to the alliance between the White House and the news media when reporters become interested in the administration's involvement in conflicts among personalities and controversies over policies. An activist president who has made clear policy commitments lends himself to stories about conflicts with his adversaries over policy as well as to stories about disputes among his supporters over which tactics should be used to win the policy battle. In the case of less active presidents, reporters are provided with stories leaked by advisers who want the President to take a stand and speak out and stories about which adviser or cabinet official is currently on top of the White House pecking order. The shared definition of newsworthy items that led to stories supportive of the President and his policies during the alliance phase dissolves in [this] phase of competition. Presidents find that their reaction to press coverage becomes, as John F. Kennedy put it, one of "reading more and enjoying it less."

During this phase, the President and White House officials become unhappy with the media for, from their perspective, focusing on either the wrong aspect of the story or the wrong story entirely. In order to deal with what they see as critical stories, the president and his staff can confront the source of the criticism, its messenger, or both. If the sources have spoken in public, they can be answered; if they are unknown, then the leaks must be traced . . .

[This] phase of competition is characterized by the Chief Executive's attempts to manipulate his relations with the news media. There is a retrenchment from the open presidency; the White House specifies the conditions under which officials may talk to reporters and seeks to curb unauthorized disclosures of information. White House officials usually opt for three approaches during this phase: news management, ingratiation, and attack.

News Management

News management involves manipulation by the President and his advisers of the kinds of information that will be made available to reporters and of the forums in which information is given to them. The president and his staff try to recapture through manipulative tactics what the media had done for them without prodding in the period after the inauguration. Manipulation involves strategies of initiation, in order to direct reporters to some people and events, and of reaction, in order to steer them away from others.

Manipulation of access. A major technique of news management is the manipulation of access. During the competition phase White House officials asked to arrange contacts with reporters are more likely to evaluate what they will get out of a story or whether the reporter's news organization is friendly or hostile to them.

Because the President is the official most in demand, officials ration his media contacts in ways that maximize favorable news coverage. Even celebrated correspondents working for powerful news organizations may accept preconditions when it is important to them to interview the President. On October 12, 1976, during president Ford's campaign trip through New York and New Jersey, Walter Cronkite appeared on the press bus. Not coincidentally, the President had given an interview to Barbara Walters, who had just begun her new career as a rival anchorperson to Cronkite on ABC News. "I was fairly sure that he wanted to talk to Ford," Ronald Nessen recalled. According to Nessen, when he asked the correspondent why he wanted to see the President, Cronkite replied, "You know the name of the game." Cronkite did get his interview, Nessen said, after he agreed that he was "paying a courtesy call" and would not ask the President substantive questions . . . That same day on another news program, John Dean had suggested that Ford had cooperated with the Nixon White House in squelching an early Watergate investigation. Nevertheless, since Cronkite had agreed to the gorund rules, the interview was limited to questions that Ford and his staff thought he could handle easily.

Monitoring staff contacts with the media. Since the source of most news about the White House is the staff rather than the President, regulating the contact between officials and reporters is an important technique of news management. This can be done positively in these ways: by fostering contacts between officials and designated reporters and columnists; by coordinating White House publicity resources between the Press Office and the senior staff so that officials at key points will present the same picture to reporters; and by emphasizing indirect resources, such as those provided by Public Liaison or Congressional Liaison, so that when reporters talk to interest groups or congressmen they get the same message they would by talking to the White House staff . . .

Planting and plugging leaks. Leaks are unofficial disclosures of information provided by sources who make anonymity part of their price for the story. In a minority of cases, what the White House regards as leaks actually are stories reporters have pieced together after assiduous detective work. Others are obtained by socially well-placed reporters who have access to the table talk and private musings of important or knowledgeable officials, and who pass on the stories through the inadvertent disclosures reporters make while trading information. But the vast majority of leaks are deliberately planted. Joseph Krafts's general comments on newsgathering in Washington are particularly applicable to White House operations: "In the typical Washington situation, news is not nosed out by keen reporters and then purveyed to the public. It is manufactured inside the government, by various interested parties for purposes of their own, and then put out to the press in ways and at times that suit the source. That is how it happens that when the President prepares a message on crime, all the leading columnits suddenly become concerned with crime."

The President and his top aides admit that they give policy information privately to selected reporters as part of a coordinated effort to build policy support. Both authorized and unauthorized leaks flow in profusion in Washington . . . When the person who "leaks" is the President himself, the opportunities to control the resulting story are tremendously enhanced. This was the case in 1962 when John Kennedy provided a complete account of the Cuban missile crisis to two reporters who were also his personal friends, Charles Bartlett and Stewart Alsop. The article that the two reporters wrote for the *Saturday Evening Post* depicted the President and his colleagues as great heroes of a major confrontation with America's chief adversary, the Soviet Union. The story, which was disseminated throughout the media, related the events as viewed by the President and his advisers, without a sense of critical detachment. The article included, at Kennedy's insistence, the appraisal of a high-level official that United Nations Ambassador Adlai Stevenson "wanted a Munich." Thus the president was able to provide the script for the major news story about the missile crisis, insist on the details that would appear, and cut down to size an aide and former rival who made him uncomfortable.

Manipulation of settings. News management also involves the attempt to manipulate the settings in which information is given—press conferences, briefings, backgrounders, and interviews—by holding them less frequently, by changing the ground rules, or by providing less information . . .

Ingratiation

Ingratiation is the attempt to manipulate reporters by doing favors for them. Sometimes this may involve reporters as a group, as when a White House official provides them with secret information that they are told is usually provided only to those officials who have a need to know. It also may mean looking after the material needs of reporters, both on the job and as they travel with the President. Usually ingratiation involves rewarding some reporters with exclusive information. At times this may take the form of an exclusive interview with the President granted to a reporter who presumably gets stories "straight" from the White House perspective . . . Such rewards are intended to have the concurrent effect of punishing those reporters who "distort" the White House's position and actions.

The most ingratiating favor that can be done for reporters is to give them information. Its payoff comes because reporters are members of a competitive group that can be divided easily when the members vie for exclusive stories, particularly those concerning the President. Ingratiation as a technique to gain favorable coverage has not been used with the same frequency by all recent administrations. Unlike news management and the open presidency, which have been used by all, ingratiation has been used more frequently by Democratic than by Republican administrations . . .

Courting the elite. Ingratiation works most effectively with journalists whose status is such that they believe their own message is as important as that of the President and with those who work for highly regarded news organizations that demand that their correspondents obtain access to the president. No individual correspondent had more authority or higher status during his professional career than Walter Lippmann. All presidents were interested in getting Lippmann on their side, but no one cultivated him as assiduously as Lyndon Johnson. The esteem in which Johnson held Lippmann was indicated in a handwritten note to Robert Kintner, the staff and cabinet secretary who had been a colleague of Lippmann's on the *Herald Tribune*. Kintner had sent Johnson a memorandum telling him that Lippmann had asked to have lunch with him. Johnson replied in the margin of Kintner's note, "I count him my friend and one of America's great citizens. I'm sorry he disagrees with some of my policies and decisions as I'm sorry that Lady Bird does. The lunch will be good for you and him and me."

Barely a week after Johnson took office he visited Lippmann at his home. In the next months he sought Lippmann's advice on many occasions. According to one White House official, Johnson asked Lippmann to help him prepare several policy statements; Lippmann wrote major portions of Johnson's major Vietnam address at the Johns Hopkins University in 1964. Top administration officials were told to keep their doors open to Lippmann and to provide him with the help he needed.

Chalmers Roberts, diplomatic correspondent for the *Washington Post* for several administrations, commented that Johnson's ingratiating tactics had a detrimental affect on Lippmann who, Roberts believed, "violated the basic rule that reporters should not get too close to public officials . . . [and should not] become captives. I'm sure Walter feels that he was betrayed because he seemed to be taking his advice or asking for it and listening respectfully. It's something from Lippmann's standpoint which was completely contrary. So he'd been double-crossed in effect. This created a real attitude of bitterness there, that kind of thing. From Johnson's standpoint he thought he was being effective but he was being counterproductive." . . .

Presidential friendships. The use or abuse of personal relationships between the President and reporters is an issue that has been raised most frequently about John Kennedy. According to the recollection of aides such as David Powers, because Kennedy's temperament and interests were compatible with those of many journalists, he had little difficulty striking up friendships with them. These relationships were flattering to reporters and useful to the administration. "Kennedy was a more subtle operator [than Johnson]," observed James Reston, columnist for the *New York Times*. "He would see you when you wanted, but because he had been a reporter he knew it was a little dicey to play around with being clumsy in the relationship." Kennedy used selected friends among reporters to channel information; [both] reporters and the President profited. The President got his version of what was happening into the media, while the news people received the professional status and public acclaim that comes from being known as insiders in the administration. Michael Raoul-Duval, an aide in the Ford administration, explained the benefits to Kennedy: "Look how Kennedy used Ben Bradlee. He didn't use him because he was a representative of the public, he used him because he had access to a billboard. Kennedy wanted to effect the message on the billboard, and the billboard happened to be *Newsweek*."

In his book *Conversations with Kennedy*, Bradlee [later executive editor of the *Washington Post*] recalled that Kennedy supplied him with information and met with him on terms that were ultimately beneficial to the White House. Of course, Bradlee was thought to have a clearer picture of Kennedy's plans and thinking than any other journalist. That he was not really privy to important inside information about the administration was less important than his reputation as an intimate of the Kennedys.

It is not surprising that President John F. Kennedy's press relations were unusual. He had been a reporter, an author of a Pulitzer Prize-winning book, had married a press photographer and during his campaign had relied heavily upon both print and broadcast media. For the first time in history, the President of the United States held his press conference live on television and yet made the exclusive interview almost routine. Reporters crowded the White House offices, ballroom and swimming pool. They flocked to Hyannis Port, Miami Beach, fox hunts and church. The faces of the Kennedys dominated television, newspapers, magazines (from Hollywood to household hints), Halloween makeup kits and anything else far removed from the campaign button and poster.

—Esther Featherer, Report No. 120, Freedom of Information Center

In exchange for providing Bradlee with status, Kennedy received from Bradlee useful information about the media. While much of what he received was professional gossip, it was useful to his overall media strategy. For example, he would receive advance word on *Newsweek*'s cover story. Occasionally, Kennedy received information that was important. On one occasion, retold in his book, Bradlee brought to a White House dinner plastic arrows that were part of a newly designed anti–personnel weapon that the *Newsweek* Pentagon correspondent had gotten. Kennedy was furious that such devices could be obtained by journalists from military sources, and he moved to prevent such leaks in the future. Bradlee, by his own account, was eager to win the favor of President Kennedy, whom he provided with information, including intelligence about the President's rivals that Bradlee could obtain from the network of *Newsweek* correspondents. He sought to ingratiate himself with the President, as have other reporters.

Direct favors. Another technique the President and his staff use involves doing favors for reporters. President Johnson spent more time at this than any other recent president. When Associated Press White House correspondent Frank Cormier's parents took a tour of the White House, they attended a bill-signing ceremony in which President Johnson spotted them and came over to meet them. Johnson invited them to his office, where he served refreshments and discussed their son's importance. Johnson said: "Ms. Cormier, your son is in a critical position at a critical time in our nation's history. He's in a job where he could make lots of mistakes—but he doesn't make very many." Cormier recalled: "For myself, I was mindful that it was an election year and that we were being exposed to the vaunted Johnson Treatment. Obviously the President was entertaining us only because I was a White House correspondent whose favor he coveted . . . Yet his hospitality and even his excursion into hyperbole were kindnesses that came easy to him."

Throwing them raw meat. While presidents have been direct in their methods of courting reporters and their organizations, they also can proceed in less visible ways. According to his staff, Lyndon Johnson's motto for reporters he felt were critical was "Throw them a piece of raw meat." This meant that Johnson or other White House officials would feed good information to hostile reporters in an effort to win them over and get them to write stories that reflected his interests. It is a bargain that flatters reporters by making them feel that they are trusted and important correspondents . . .

Attack

Attack, the most explosive weapon in the President's arsenal during the competition phase, is used by White House officials to prevent damage to the President's ability to lead and persuade that they believe is caused by biased or unfavorable media reporting. Attack includes efforts to discredit reporters with their news organizations, to discredit a news organization with the public, and, in the most extreme cases, to challenge the legitimacy of the media's right to reflect points of view that differ from the administration's and the public's and to challenge the authenticity of anything that appears in the media. The attraction that the strategy of attacking the media has had for presidents and their advisers was explained by a Ford administration official:

Inevitably what they are reporting is what somebody [in the opposition] said [that was] critical. If the President is going to discount the criticism, he has only two options: He can say the criticism is wrong, and then say why what he is doing is good for the country. Or he can imply that it is a critical press that is distorting the President's position and exploiting the opposition. In some cases the criticism is highly justified. In that case you have only one option: you have to criticize the press, because you can't criticize the substance of what was reported.

Some manifestations of attack show up in almost every administration, and the implied threat of retaliation by the White House may make some reporters pull in their horns if they see a minor story that is potentially damaging to the president. Some reporters even profit from the widespread paranoia about press enemies that has afflicted so many recent administrations: "A few words of sympathy over the unfair treatment by the 'Eastern press' (or the liberal press or the conservative press) is an effective method of slamming doors against competitors. An important leader who can be persuaded that his journalistic 'friend' is the lone holdout against a 'press conspiracy' can serve as a meal ticket for many years."

Manners of attack. The form of presidential attack varies considerably according to the styles of particular presidents. Some use words, in speeches or in private comments to well-placed audiences, to attack individual reporters and news organizations. Other presidents have attacked reporters by attempting to destroy their status with their news organizations and in the profession, and to damage news organizations through licensing provisions.

Almost all recent presidents have retaliated against some reporters or news organizations at one time during their term, . . . [the result being that] reporters simply did not get what they wanted from the White House. Interviews and access were withheld. On some occasions [a President] would try to get a reporter in trouble with his superiors. [Usually they direct their attacks against] specific reporters and organizations, not against the media as a whole.

The war against the media. The all-out attack on the media, characteristic of the Nixon administration, was well planned and was successful in intimidating large segments of broadcasting and publishing enterprises. Attack obviously struck positive chords among large numbers of citizens, who indicated that their distrust of the media was nearly as great as their distrust of the political leadership. The ultimate impact of the Nixon administration's efforts to exploit popular dissatisfaction with the news media may be a situation in which large segments of the public believe neither the President nor those who report on and analyze the activities of his administration.

There is no doubt that Mr. Nixon feels the adversary relationship with the press more deeply than any of his predecessors. And he is a formidable adversary. I sometimes have the feeling when he walks out of his news conferences he is a little disappointed he did not meet a stiffer challenge. His associations with the press are never casual. They are sometimes social but always guarded. Most newsmen feel they know little about the private Nixon. I think this is unfortunate. The President to me is a fascinating man and has a great deal more charm than is generally known. But he feels—and this is reflected in the attitudes of other top level White House aides—that the press is either incapable or unwilling to accurately reflect his motives and personality. This is a basic distrust of the press over and beyond the normal adversary relationship. It has engendered in many newsmen a mutual feeling of distrust, a feeling that they are being manipulated and not getting an accurate view.

—Eugene V. Risher, UPI White House correspondent, April 1971

Attacks on the media during the Nixon administration were different in scale from those of previous administrations; they constituted a massive and unprecedented assault on the legitimacy of news organizations' activities. The Nixon administration did not recognize the media's claim to act as a surrogate for the public, nor did it view the media as having a legitimate interest in the operations of government. Because they regarded news organizations as political adversaries, administration officials were willing to use their political, legal, and extralegal resources to reduce the profits, power, and public status of news organizations. White House staff members prepared memoranda that raised the specter of the Federal Communications Commission, the Antitrust Division of the Justice Department, the Internal Revenue Service, and the Republican National Committee. Wiretaps were ordered against newsmen who were publishing or broadcasting stories the White House believed should not have appeared. They harassed reporters they regarded as enemies in the hope that they would leave the White House beat or be fired from their posts . . .

In addition to using Executive Office and executive branch institutions in their war against the media, White House officials, including the President, directly confronted their adversaries. President Nixon attacked both the media in general and specific reporters in his news conferences . . . Charges of unfairness and accusations of bias were hurled from lecterns throughout the administration.

Reportorial Responses

To cope with manipulation by the White House, reporters develop manipulative tactics of their own to pry from the White House information that it would prefer to withhold. During the phase of alliance, most reporters adopt the conduit style of reporting. Now, in the competition phase, a reporter may become a friend of the court, an adversary, or a historian-observer. Many reporters do not change their tactics; these more aggressive styles are particularly noticeable on the part of reporters for the major publications.

The friend of the court. This reporter's work depends on information obtained from White House sources in return for supportive articles. In some cases this may involve flattery or ingratiation of a particular official, including the President himself . . .

The adversary. This reporter approaches White House encounters assuming that officials may not be telling the truth or, at the very least, are withholding part of the story. Most White House reporters who take on this role display it only in the combative style with which they question officials in public forums. They argue that this technique pays off because officials do not want to be confronted in public with a lie. A combative style of questioning does not necessarily translate into an accusatory style of writing . . .

The historian-observer and institutional analyst. Some reporters become historian-observers in response to White House manipulation during the competition phase. Those who adopt this style of reporting interpret both the policies and the personalities who make and administer them in terms of the mood of the times. The advantage of this style for reporters is that, because their stories deal with the character of the administration, they are less influenced by the "hard news" that during this phase often consists of "pseudo-events" staged by the White House.

---

*The 'gap' in President Johnson's credibility derives
primarily from his penchant for keeping newspapermen and
the public in the dark until he is ready to turn on the light.*

—Philip Potter, *Baltimore Sun*, 1968

Related to the historian-observer are the institutional analysts, whose beat includes the entire White House staff and the Executive Office of the President. Officials who have worked at the White House during the last sixteen years suggested to interviewers that in their minds this was the best way of finding out what was going on there.

The single greatest problem reporters have in accurately portraying the presidency, according to these respondents, is that they concentrate almost exclusively on the president and those who have contact with him in the Oval Office. They further suggested that reporters could look more profitably at the whole executive process, including the flow of alternative policies as they are sent from office to office before they finally land on the president's desk. This is the part of the story that reporters miss. The manager of this flow of information in the White House during the Ford administration suggested that the people making these important decisions are virtually unknown to reporters because they seldom are visible in conferences with the President and his top advisers.

The success of individual officials and reporters in getting results from manipulative techniques depends in part on relations established during the early days of the administration. More important to the success of the White House is its ability to place the President in dramatic national and international settings and situations, where news organizations seem compelled to follow the agenda set before them. Ultimately, however, White House officials are faced with the fact that manipulating agendas does not restore favorable publicity. Their problem is that the two sides no longer share a definition of news. Consequently the administration finds it more difficult to prevent the media from producing stories that raise issues in ways it doesn't want them raised.

Phase Three: Detachment

The manipulative tactics used by both sides during the phase of competition create antagonisms between White House reporters and officials that are most visible in settings such as the press secretary's daily briefing, which one White House correspondent referred to as the "bear pit." There appears, however, to be a limit to how far conflict may spread. Each side has such fundamental needs for the other that strong elements of cooperation remain at all times.

Consequently, the competition phase is followed by a phase of detachment during which the relationship is carried on in a more structured manner than it was in the previous periods, in almost a formal manner.

The timing of the detachment phase usually is determined by the White House. It occurs soonest in those administrations that have little concern for the need to rally mass support for new policies. Since there is little need to persuade reporters to emphasize the advantages of its policies to a large public, the White House's media policy becomes one of getting maximum exposure with the least risk. It is not surprising to find that in the years since the New Deal detachment has usually occurred sooner and has been employed more successfully in Republican than Democratic administrations.

The most important feature of this period is the tendency of presidents to delegate the management of their relations with the press to surrogates. Although the President may continue to meet reporters regularly, he does so in highly controlled and structured situations. The media strategy that is most characteristic of this phase is avoidance.

Avoidance

Avoidance involves manipulating the schedule so that the President appears only in settings the White House thinks are favorable to him. Other settings might draw questions from reporters that lead the President to say something he does not want to say.

White House officials learn how to ration the President's time by trial and error in the months after a new administration takes office. At the beginning of his term, when the pressures are not as great as they will be later, it is easier for the President to make time for the press. At this stage most presidents want to do so because they like what they read in the press and see on the evening news. It is not long before the president finds better ways to spend his time than on impromptu activities with reporters. Instead, events that communicate the president's message are scheduled.

Tight coordination of the scheduling process is particularly important when a president decides to run for reelection. Because the stakes are now greater, his contacts with reporters are even more likely to be carefully structured and calculated than they were in the middle years of his term. During [Gerald Ford's] 1976 campaign, the Office of Communications was converted into a major decision-making office for campaign publicity. "During the campaign we were selective in the occasions in which we provided press access to the president," an aide explained. "There were themes we wanted to focus on. You wouldn't want to publicize another issue. So you scheduled in such a way that you had the major event. You selected what you wanted to emphasize and controlled coverage to the extent that we determined what was treated." During the campaign the President's staff spends large amounts of time arranging formal activities best suited to project his presidential qualities. In 1980, Jimmy Carter was able to employ the avoidance strategy as president; as a candidate four years earlier he had strongly criticized the same strategy.

Another aspect of the detachment phase is the relatively greater emphasis by the White House on contact with the regional press and with interest groups, without the filter of the Washington press corps. For example, in a two-week period during April 1971, the White House prepared sixteen separate mailings that were sent to 146,000 groups, publications, or individuals. Samples of the mailings indicate that they included environment and reorganization booklets sent to 1,100 reporters and news organizations, a presidential statement opposing abortions sent to 198 Catholic media and organizations, a labor mailing to 1,364 labor and finance writers, a copy of a speech President Nixon made in Williamsburg, Virginia, that was sent in booklet form to 11,094 Republican elected officials, a senior citizens proclamation that was sent to 100,000 groups concerned with issues involving the aged, and a copy of an article by conservative columnist James J. Kilpatrick that was sent to 9,273 academicians and a select group of Republican sympathizers.

The response of some reporters during this phase is to explore the use of independent sources of information in Congress, the Office of Management and Budget, the departments, and among lobbyists. Reporters are also more likely to engage in joint endeavors with other reporters in their own news organizations. They thus reap some of the benefits from the division of labor and specialized expertise in the form of a more thorough analysis of White House plans and actions.

The Phases and the Future

Throughout the terms of all recent presidents the relationship between the President and the news media has been characterized by strong elements of continuity. No recent president has been so dominant over Congress, the bureaucracy, his political party, or private sector leaders that he has been able to downgrade media relations. For their part, no major news organization has been able to find ways of covering the presidency without the cooperation of the President and White House officials. When the needs of both sides converge, as they usually do at the beginning of an administration, the cooperative elements are dominant. Later, when the President's need to use the news media to build a basis of support for his administration conflicts with reporters' interests in producing stories that feature conflict and inconsistency, each side uses manipulative tactics to achieve its goals. Yet the level of conflict that might be engendered by some of these tactics is limited by continuing mutual needs. That is why detachment follows competition in the relationship between the White House and the news organizations. This period of detente lasts until a new president takes office and the process begins again.

Theodore Roosevelt and the Press: Manipulative Openness

by George Juergens

In September 1901, just back from William McKinley's funeral, Theodore Roosevelt called a meeting at the White House that revealed [much] about his view of the presidency and the influence he would have on the office. He instructed his secretary to telephone the Washington managers of the three wire services and ask them to come right over to see him. It was an unusual request in an era when presidents almost never sat down with working reporters, and all the more unusual considering the many demands and pressures on him as he presided over the change in administrations. But Roosevelt clearly regarded a session with reporters as business of the highest priority.

Charles Boynton of the Associated Press, David Barry of the *New York Sun*'s Laffan Agency, and Ed Keen of the Scripps-McRae Press Association (later to become United Press) figured prominently in his plans, both because their dispatches appeared in hundreds of papers across the country, and because they tended to be bellweathers for the rest of the press in deciding how the news would be presented. This president saw news as an instrument of power. It followed that he wanted to waste no time getting his publicity operation in order.

As Barry recalled the conversation, which took place seated around the cabinet table, Roosevelt did most of the talking in laying out how he proposed to deal with the press. He pointed out that since he had known Boynton and Barry for years, and trusted them, they could expect his complete cooperation. "I shall be accessible to [you]," the president said, "I shall keep [you] posted, and trust to [your] discretion as to publication." Keen, on the other hand, whom Roosevelt had never met before, would have to prove he could be relied on. When Boynton and Barry vouched for their colleague, Roosevelt agreed to extend the same terms to him. According to one source, he put Keen to the test right away by using the meeting to deliver a scathing indictment of the old guard in his party. "If you even hint where you got it," Roosevelt warned when he had finished, "I'll say you are a damned liar." He would do more than that. Roosevelt told the wire representatives that a reporter who violated his trust would be mercilessly cut off from further access to news. He would even take steps to deny legitimate news to the paper or agency that employed the offending reporter. The ground rules could not have been made more clear.

Dr. George Juergens is professor of history, Indiana University. He was formerly on the faculties at Dartmouth and Amherst. At Indiana, he received the distinguished Teaching Award in 1970, the Student Alumni Council Distinguished Teaching Award in 1976, and the Amoco Foundation Distinguished Teaching Award in 1982. He is the author of *Joseph Pulitzer and the New York World* (1966), and numerous journal articles and professional papers. Dr. Juergens earned a B.A. from Columbia College, a B.A. and M.A. from Oriel College of Oxford University, and a Ph.D. from Columbia University. [This article is edited and reprinted, with permission, from *News From the White House*, published by the University of Chicago Press, 1981; ©1981, University of Chicago Press; ©1986, George Juergens.]

"All right, gentlemen, now we understand each other," the president said in adjourning the meeting.

Roosevelt proved to be as good as his word over the next seven years. He divided newsmen into distinct groups of insiders and outsiders, and was unforgiving in banishing those that he felt, justifiably or not, had betrayed him. The order went out consigning them to the Ananias Club, named after the New Testament character who, having lied about holding back part of a gift to the Church, was rebuked by Peter and fell dead. Members of the club—and their numbers grew by the years—were dead in the eyes of the White House. On the other hand, for the correspondents who cooperated—which pretty well meant writing sympathetically about Roosevelt's programs as well as respecting his confidences—covering the president suddenly became a reporter's paradise. His accessibility and candor with the insiders almost staggered newsmen who had learned the mechanics of their craft in the gray days of Cleveland and Harrison.

Roosevelt saw reporters almost every day, either individually or in small groups. A favorite occasion was 1:00 in the afternoon, when newsmen made a practice of standing around and asking questions—if they knew how to time the pauses between the president's monologue answers—while a Treasury Department messenger who doubled as his barber gave him his midday shave. It didn't have to be just then, however. He could always manage to squeeze in a few extra minutes during the day for reporters who needed to see him, and often made himself available in the evenings while signing his correspondence before going back to the main house for dinner.

This kind of access to the president of the United States was remarkable enough, but it meant all the more because of Roosevelt's openness when he spoke with the press. Reporters were amazed, and sometimes a bit concerned, at the things he told them. He talked freely about the most delicate matters of state, and seemed at times to be almost courting danger by the bluntness with which he discussed personalities in Washington. The press probably even exaggerated how far down the barriers fell. It is always enticing to be taken into another person's confidence, particularly one who wields power, and the things said can easily distract attention from the many other things consciously left unsaid. To acknowledge as much still does not diminish the fact that Roosevelt went much further than previous presidents in opening up to trusted reporters. He did something else as well. Roosevelt demonstrated through a hundred small gestures that he regarded the journalists in his entourage as friends. He called them by first name; he shared their jokes; he invited them to social functions. For correspondents accustomed to observing presidents only from a distance, and to finding presidential words about as revealing as an oration on the Fourth of July, it was all delightfully unsettling. Little wonder that they came not so much to respect as to revere him . . .

Presidential Television

by Haim Shibi

Television . . . has become today's marketplace of ideas. It has also become the President's medium. The President's prime weapon for influencing policy making is his ability to command and influence a national audience. Television gave him such an ability and in a powerful—some say too powerful—way.

In a Twentieth Century Fund Report, *Presidential Television* (1973), three authors argued that television has seriously tipped constitutional checks and balances in favor of the Executive Branch. Newton Minow (Federal Communications Commission chairman in the Kennedy Administration), John Bartlow Martin, and Lee Mitchell wrote:

> The Constitution established a presidency with limitations upon its powers—the need to stand for reelection every four years, checks that can be exercised by the Congress and the Supreme Court. The evolution of political parties and a strong two-party system provided a rallying point for opponents of an incumbent administration, enhancing the importance of frequent reelection. An intricate set of constitutional balances limiting the powers of each of the three government branches added force to the separation of government functions. These political and constitutional relationships served the country well for many years. Television impact, however, threatens to tilt the delicately balanced system in the direction of the president.

Elmer E. Cornwell, Jr. author of *Presidential Leadership of Public Opinion* (1965) had a different view, [concluding] that the President is limited by "the checks and balances and planned frictions of the American constitutional system, which no degree of mastery of the media nor further expansion of the presidential image can neutralize."

An Awesome Pulpit

Television is an expensive direct line of communication to the national audience and it provides the best message saturation ever. It is used by the nation's Chief Executive whenever and however he wishes, free of charge. Ben Bagdikian, formerly of the Washington *Post*, wrote (*Columbia Journalism Review*, Summer, 1962), what necessarily comes across in live television and radio is what most public figures would like to see of themselves in print if they could manage it—their own words verbatim and without filtration by reporters and editors, intruding comments by others, or editorializing by the medium.

Using this direct channel, a President, as former Sen. J. William Fulbright noted, can "command a national audience to hear his views on controversial

[This article is edited and reprinted, with permission, from two Freedom of Information Center Reports, January 1976; School of Journalism, University of Missouri.]

matters at prime time, on short notice, at whatever length he chooses, and at no
expense to the Federal Government or his party" [Congressional Record, June
2, 1970] . . .

Indirect presidential messages on television (ceremonial events, appearances
on camera before and after meetings with congressmen or public leaders, statements read before and after trips, etc.) as well as direct messages (formal
speeches, press conferences, conversations with the press) are not forced on
the networks. It is custom rather than law that dictates presidential broadcasts.
Sig Mickelson, former president of the Columbia Broadcasting System News,
observed that:

> The office of the President, backed by all the powerful paraphernalia
> of the nation's highest office, has a natural advantage in commanding the
> media. But it frequently isn't necessary to command. The great degree of
> public interest attending virtually every word the President utters, every
> step he takes, every decision he announces, focuses attention on the man
> and the office and make the presidency the most intensely covered office
> in the world. [*The Electric Mirror*, 1972.]

And in the words of Bernard Rubin, School of Public Communication, Boston
University:

> The ability of a Chief Executive to lead the television around is sig-
> nificant. Primarily, this is due to two related facts. First, the televi-
> sion audience accepts *news* much more readily than they accept *views*.
> Second, whatever the President does, even if it is as minor as [when Lyn-
> don Johnson picked] up a beagle by the ears, constitutes *news*. [*Political
> Television*.]

But it is not only the journalistic need that makes television the President's
medium. Television is licensed by the FCC, a part of the federal government,
and the President appoints the members of the FCC. Broadcasting is not a right;
it is a privilege and as such is revocable by the FCC, as former Vice President
Agnew reminded broadcasters . . . Newton Minow, chairman of the FCC in
the Kennedy Administration recalled the following conversation with President
Kennedy:

> KENNEDY: Did you see that goddamn thing on Huntley-Brinkley?
> MINNOW: Yes.
> KENNEDY: I thought they were supposed to be our friends. I want
> you to do something about that. You do something about that [quoted in
> *The Politics of Lying*, by David Wise, p. 370] . . .

Sig Mickelson wrote:

> Nothing strikes terror into the hearts of broadcasters so quickly and
> leaves so profound a hurt as a hint of government action. The threat

of license cancellation, aimed directly at the pocketbooks of licensees. Without a license there can be no broadcast. [*The Electric Mirror*]

White House telecasting started October 5, 1947. The first landmark in White House broadcasting occurred in the summer of 1950 when Harry Truman addressed the nation following the outbreak of the Korean War. Jack Gould, the *New York Times* radio-television critic, wrote:

For the first time in a period of national emergency the person at home not only heard the fateful call for sacrifices to preserve his freedom, but also saw the grave expressions of the president as he explained to the country what it would mean. (New York *Times*, June 20, 1950)

Truman used television in other times of national crisis—a railroad strike, a steel strike, a meat shortage. Although Truman introduced new techniques into presidential television, including the cabinet's first appearance on television in 1950 and allowing newsmen to tape presidential press conferences in 1951 he still approached television essentially in radio terms. Elmer Cornwell noted that:

President Truman and his advisers did not make any special effort to adapt to the peculiar requirements of television . . . Truman used the electronic media in an emergency, "fire-brigade" fashion. [*Presidential Leadership*]

Dwight Eisenhower . . . was the first to allow the telecasting and broadcasting of parts of presidential press conferences. Another innovation was the "keyhole" conversation between Eisenhower and Secretary of State John Foster Dulles, televised in May 1955. As had President Truman, Eisenhower used broadcasting in time of crisis—the Middle East crisis of 1956, the Near East crisis of 1957, the dispatch of federal troops to Little Rock in 1957 and the Berlin crisis of 1959. An informal committee was established in Washington to represent the three television networks, with which James C. Hagerty, White House press secretary, communicated when an address was in the offing. It was Hagerty, not the networks that decided the newsworthiness of a given presidential statement. Jack Gould observed, "The Administration can turn television on or off as it deems expedient." (New York *Times*, February 28, 1958)

President John F. Kennedy was the first to use live television coverage of the presidential press conference. Kennedy relied on negotiations with the informal three-network committee established in the Eisenhower era. "There was . . . no question that TV was willing to preempt millions of dollars in commercial time to carry the pressconferences," wrote Pierre Salinger, Kennedy's press secretary. [*Presidential Television*]

One of the best examples of John Kennedy's use of television to attain political objectives was his crackdown on the steel companies in April 1962 when they attempted to raise steel prices. Kennedy's attack was heard and seen instantaneously on a maximum of thirteen million television sets by a maximum of thirty-five million people, free of editorial comment. Within twenty-four hours the steel companies gave up. As Ben Bagdikian noted:

> Many people were worried by the President's quick victory over steel-people who have no special love for U.S. steel, but who feel that steel, for all its unloveable qualities, was outmatched. The same awesome power of the President to transmit himself electronically into the American living room could be turned on a less powerful adversary. [*Columbia Journalism Review*, Summer 1962]

Kennedy's trips to Europe in 1961 and 1963 were carefully planned for news effect just as Eisenhower's so-called European "peace trip" in 1959 had been. Years later, President Nixon's plane arrived in Peking in prime time and managed to return to Washington in prime time only by sitting on the ground for nine hours in Anchorage, Alaska. Elmer Cornwell's analysis depicts Kennedy as the first television President:

> Far more than his predecessors, he had explored and exploited with skill and imagination the expanding range of possibilities this new medium has to offer to the incumbent in the White House . . . Like F.D.R. before him with radio, he grasped the ultimate significance of television for himself and for the Presidency: the channel it offered for direct, unmediated, instantaneous, and massive access to the public. [*Presidential Leadership*]

Lyndon B. Johnson used television so frequently that he finally asked for, and the networks provided, "hot cameras," manned throughout the day in the White House theater, with crews ready to operate them at a moment's notice. "Once Johnson went on the air so fast," an NBC executive recalled, "that we couldn't put up the Presidential seal. When a network technician said we need a second to put up the seal, Johnson said, 'Son, I'm the leader of the freeworld, and I'll go on the air when I want to.'". [Quoted in *The Politics of Lying*]

Richard M. Nixon took office in 1969 with a rich television experience that included such landmarks as the "Checkers Speech," and the "Great Debates." In office, Nixon used television extensively, helped by the largest staff of television experts ever assembled at the White House, and aimed for the prime time audience. CBS calculated that during his first thirty-nine months in office, President Nixon made thirty-one special prime-time appearances, compared to twenty-four similar appearances by President Johnson in five years, ten by President Kennedy in three years, and twenty-three by President Eisenhower in eight years. Research by CBS concluded that as a result of the move of presidential television to prime time the typical television viewer saw President Nixon almost half again as many times as he saw President Kennedy during the first eighteen months of their respective administrations.

Evaluating the power of presidential television as a propaganda channel, Dr. Stephen Hess said:

Television is not too powerful as a propaganda vehicle, given its present structure; it is simply viewed by a great many people, which is not neces sarily the same thing. Critics of television . . . have tended to measure "power" in terms of numbers, leaving the question of "impact"—or the ability to change political behavior largely unaddressed. [*Congressional Record*, Nov. 13, 1973]

David Wise [in] *The Politics of Lying*, described Nixon's presidential television:

In Nixon's view, television ideally should serve *only* as a carrier, a mechanical means of electronically transmitting his picture and words directly to the voters. It is this concept of television-as-conduit that has won Nixon's praise, not television as a form of electronic journalism. The moment that television analyzes his words, qualifies his remarks, or renders news judgments, it becomes part of the "press," and a political target.

During his twenty-five years in Congress, Gerald Ford was rated . . . by the Sunday network interview shows as a bottom-of-the-barrel choice. He was passed over because producers thought his bland manner, which never seemed to vary either on camera or off, made for poor television. In those congressional years, Ford joined the late Everett McKinley Dirksen in a weekly televised news conference from Capitol Hill popularly known as "The Ev and Jerry Show." The experience, the *New York Times* noted "hardly prepared Ford for the relentless fervor with which television covers a President's every public move." [March 16, 1975]

"When Ford coughs, fifty White House reporters race for the phones," said . . . J. F. terHorst, President Ford's first press secretary. However, with ten televised conferences in his first seven months in the White House, Washington correspondents were beginning to complain . . . that Ford was calling too many and saying too little. The networks refused to broadcast nationwide the four press conferences Ford . . . held away from Washington. Norman Kempster, White House correspondent for the Washington *Star*, observed:

So far, they have aired all of the available Washington conferences but it is an open secret that some network executives are beginning to ask if the shows are worth the time it takes to broadcast them. [March 16, 1975]

President Ford's press conference on October 9, 1975, was not carried live by the American Broadcasting Company. The decision, according to ABC, was based . . . on considerations of news value—the press conference was not expected to have much of it. In the words of Wally Pfister, ABC vice president for special news programming, "We frankly don't feel there'll be anything really big out of this." . . .

[Presidents Carter and Reagan both had good television presence, their populist images enhanced by the nature of television. Carter, wearing a comfortable sweater to emphasize the nation's needs to lower living temperatures to conserve energy, sat in his office, chatting with the people, making it appear that he was talking one-on-one to his audience. It was a technique that Franklin D. Roosevelt successfully used on radio four decades before in his "fireside chats" with the people.

Reagan, for several decades an actor and announcer, was probably the most adaptable to television. As a result, television flattered him, and made even his most controversial policies seem "homespun" by a "nice man" who just wanted to help all the people. Thus, the form of presentation, rather than content, often gave Reagan his political strength and support.] . . .

This is the power of presidential television, and in a system of checks and balances, it is a threat to those who are supposed to check and balance the executive branch of government. "More than ever before in the history of the Republic," wrote Elmer Cornwell in 1965, "the times demand strong Presidents, and more than ever before, the strong President will be the skillful leader of public opinion." But if the presidential leadership of public opinion becomes a monopoly of political communication, it can constitute a danger to democracy.

Congressmen are aware of the role of the press in lightening or increasing their own burdens. Though many blame the press for the poor public image of the typical member of Congress and complain that reporters distort the record and fail to emphasize the important things, few express their unhappiness publicly. Newsmen whom the congressman may despise and fear are given a cordial greeting when they stop by the office. Reporters probably have easier access to the congressman's time than any other group, largely because, despite their shortcomings, they possess the power to advance—or hinder—the congressman's cause.

—Charles L. Clapp,
The Congressman: His Work as He Sees It (1963)

Congressional Exposure: TV in the House

While the president can get air time when he asks for it, at the time of his own choosing and in the format he wants, Congress, supposedly the President's co-equal partner, does not have the same privilege. FCC Commissioner [Nicholas] Johnson has written:

> If one branch of the government increasingly gains effective access to the media of communications, while the other branch is systematically excluded, then the power balance, presumably designed to safeguard our citizenry from the tyrannies and abuses of excessive power, will be upset . . .

The reasons for congressional refusal to give final approval to television coverage are varied . . . Sam Rayburn [while Speaker of the House] once said, "Things are bad enough as they are. Keep the cameras the hell out of here." Other typical reasons find similarly glib expression: Sig Mickelson wrote in . . . The Electric Mirror, "The camera will make actors out of members"; Rep. Jack Brooks (D-Texas) said, . . . "Such coverage for the most part would be confusing and of no interest at all"; and Rep. Clarence Brown (R-Ohio) warned, "A clever editor sitting in New York could change completely the picture of a committee hearing."

As a result of the 1970 Legislative Reorganization Act, the House of Representatives joined the Senate in opening up its committee meetings to the broadcast media, but only with the approval of the committee chairman or a majority of the committee. Sharpening congressional awareness of the advantage the President has by his access to television brought efforts to provide congress with its own communications line to the public.

In 1970, Sen. Fulbright introduced a resolution (S.J. Res. 209) before the Senate Subcommittee on Communications requiring broadcasters to provide network time at least four times a year for broadcast by "authorized representatives" of the Senate and the House. The Fulbright resolution did not specify the method of selecting the "authorized representatives." The resolution, termed by NBC's President Julian Goodman as "regulatory formulas that tell a news medium how it must operate in reporting and analyzing political issues," never went beyond the hearing stage.

The networks were ready to offer congressional leaders the opportunity to present congressional views on television in a way comparable to that always available to the President—but on the networks' own terms. In 1970, NBC offered to produce two programs presenting the views of the majority and minority parties. The Republican congressional leadership made no response at all. The Democrats insisted that only the majority views—their own—should be broadcast.

Elton Rule of ABC told the Joint Committee on Congressional Operations at hearings in March 1972 that ABC would make one hour of prime time available at the beginning of each session for a "State of the Congress" address. This would cover "debates on critical issues" if Congress allowed adequate access to the sessions themselves. ABC would also allow prime time at the end of each session.

The 1974 recommendations of the Joint Committee on Congressional Operations, chaired by Senator Lee Metcalf (D-Mont.), suggested . . . to both houses a one-year trial of continuous live television coverage of floor proceedings of the first session of the 94th Congress.

[In March 1979, the House of Representatives finally allowed floor coverage—under specific limitations. The cameras are permanently placed in a gallery above the floor, are owned by the Congress and operated by crews employed by the Congress. The signal is available to any cable or television system that uses it for news and public affairs. Shortly after the system was introduced, Thomas P. "Tip" O'Neill, speaker of the House, called it "a disaster," and suggested that it be abolished. However, he now agress that although there have been abuses, television coverage "has enhanced the public appreciation and knowledge of the House."

In June 1986, the U.S. Senate finally permitted television coverage.]

Bibliography

Anderson, Patrick, *The President's Men*, Doubleday (New York, N.Y.), 1968.

Bonafede, Dom, "The President's Publicity Machine, . . .   The Press," *Washington Journalism Review*, May 1980.

Crouse, Timothy, *The Boys on the Bus*, Random House (New York, N.Y.), 1973.

Cornwell, Elmer, *Presidential Leadership of Public Opinion*, Indiana University Press (Bloomington, Ind.), 1965.

Hebers, John, *No Thank You, Mr. President*, W.W. Norton (New York, N.Y.), 1976.

Moynihan, Daniel P., "The Presidency and the Press," *Commentary*, March 1970.

Neustadt, Richard E., *Presidential Power: The Politics of Leadership from F.D.R. to Carter*, John Wiley & Sons (New York, N.Y.), 1980.

Pollard, James E., "The Kennedy Administration and the Press," *Journalism Quarterly*, Winter 1964.

———, *The Presidency and the Press*, Octagon Books (New York, N.Y.), 1973.

Porter, William, *Assault on the Media: The Nixon Years*, University of Michigan Press (Ann Arbor, Mich.), 1976.

Reedy, George, *The Twilight of the Presidency*, Mentor (New York, N.Y.), 1970.

Thompson, Hunter, *Fear and Loathing on the Campaign Trail*, Popular Library (New York, N.Y.), 1973.

Truman, David, *The Governmental Process: Political Interests and Public Opinion*, Knopf, (New York, N.Y.), 1951.

Bibliography

Part II

Agee, Warren K., *Mass Media in a Free Society*, University of Kansas Press (Lawrence, Kansas), 1969.

Baron, Jerome A., *Freedom of the Press for Whom?* University of Indiana Press (Bloomington, Ind.), 1973.

Becker, Carl L., *Freedom and Responsibility in the American Way of Life*, Greenwood Press (New York, N.Y.) 1945.

_____, *New Liberties for Old*, Yale University Press (New Haven, Conn.), 1941.

_____, *Progress and Power*, Alfred A. Knopf (New York, N.Y.), 1949.

Belknap, Michael R., *Cold War Political Justice: The Smith Act, the Communist Party, and American civil Liberties*, Greenwood Press (Westport, Conn.), 1977.

Beman, Lamar Taney, *Selected Articles on Censorship of Speech and the Press*; Greenwood Press (New York, N.Y.) 1930.

Berns, Walter, *The First Amendment and the Future of American Democracy*, New York: Regenery-Gateway 1976.

_____, *Freedom, Virtue and the First Amendment*, Louisiana State University Press (Baton Rouge, La.), 1957.

Black, Hugo, "The Bill of Rights," *New York University Law Review*, April 1960.

_____, *A Constitutional Faith*, Alfred A. Knopf (New York, N.Y.), 1960.

Brant, Irving, *The Bill of Rights: Its Origin and Meaning*, Bobbs-Merrill (Indianapolis, Ind.), 1965.

Brenner, Daniel L.; William L. Rivers, *Free But Regulated: Conflicting Traditions in Media Law*, Iowa State University Press (Ames, Iowa), 1982.

Brucker, Herbert, *Freedom of Information*, Greenwood Press (New York, N.Y.) 1951.

Carlyle, Alexander James, *Political Liberty: A History of the Conception in the Middle Ages and Modern Times*; Greenwood Press (London, England) 1941

Carter, Douglas, *The Fourth Branch of Government*, Houghton Mifflin (Boston, Mass.), 1959.

Carwin, Edward Samuel, *Liberty Against the Government: The Rise, Flowering, and Decline of a Famous Judicial Concept*, Louisiana State University Press (Baton Rouge, La.), 1948

Chafee, Zechariah, Jr., *The Blessings of Liberty*, Greenwood Press (Westport, Conn.), 1973.

_____, *Free Speech in the United States*, Harvard University Press (Cambridge, Mass.), 1941.

_____, *Government and Mass Communications*, University of Chicago Press (Chicago, Ill.), 1947.

Chamberlain, Bill, and Charlene J. Brown, *The First Amendment Reconsidered: New Perceptions on the Meaning of Freedom of Speech and Press*, Longman (New York, N.Y.), 1982.

Chenery, William L., *Freedom of the Press*, Greenwood Press (New York, N.Y.), 1955.

Commission on Freedom of the Press, *Government and Mass Communications: A Report*, University of Chicago Press (Chicago, Ill.), 1947.

Commission on Freedom of the Press, *A Free and Responsible Press: A General Report on Mass Communication: Newspapers, Radio, Motion Pictures, Magazines, and Books*, University of Chicago Press (Chicago, Ill.), 1947.

Craig, Alec, *Above All Liberties*, Allen and Unwin (London, England), 1942.

Coons, John E., ed. *Freedom and Responsibility in Broadcasting*, Northwestern University Press (Evanston, Ill.), 1961.

Czitrom, Daniel J., *Media and the American Mind: From Morse to McLuhan*, University of North Carolina Press (Chapel Hill, N.C.), 1982.

Davis, Elmer, *But We Were Born Free*, Bobbs-Merrill (Indianapolis, Ind.), 1954.

Davis, James A., "Communism, Conformity, Cohorts, and Categories: American Tolerance," *American Journal of Sociology*, Vol. 8, 1975.

Dossen, Norman, *Frontiers of Civil Liberties*, Pantheon (New York, N.Y.), 1968.

————, *Political and Civil Rights in the United States*, Little, Brown (Boston, Mass.), 3rd ed., 1967.

Douglas, William O., *The Rights of Mankind*, Random House (New York, N.Y.), 1958.

————, *The Right of the People*, Doubleday (New York, N.Y.), 1958.

Duniway, Clyde A., *The Development of Freedom of the Press in Massachusetts*, Harvard University Press (Cambridge, Mass.), 1906.

Emerson, Thomas I., *The System of Freedom of Expression*, Vintage Books (New York, N.Y.), 1970.

————, *Toward a General Theory of the First Amendment*, Random House (New York, N.Y.), 1966.

————, David Haber, and Norman Dorsen, *Political and Civil Rights in the United States*, 3rd ed., Little, Brown (Boston, Mass.), 1967.

Emery, Walter B., *Broadcasting and Government*, Michigan State University Press (East Lansing, Mich.), 1971.

Finman, Ted, *Toward a General Theory of the First Amendment*, Random House (New York, N.Y.), 1966.

Geller, Evelyn, *Forbidden Books in American Public Libraries, 1876-1939: A Study in Cultural Change;* Greenwood Press (New York, N.Y.) 1948.

Gillett, Charles Ripley, *Burned Books: Neglected Chapters in British History and Literature;* Greenwood Press (New York, N.Y.) 1932.

Konefsky, Samuel J., *The Legacy of Holmes and Brandeis: A Study in the Influence of Ideas*, Macmillan (New York, N.Y.), 1956.

Halpern, Stephen C., *The Future of our Liberties: Perspectives on the Bill of Rights;* Greenwood Press (Westport, Conn.) 1982.

Kallen, Horace Meyer, *A Study of Liberty;* Greenwood Press (Yellow Springs, Ohio) 1959

Kauper, Paul, G., *Civil Liberties and the Constitution;* Greenwood Press (Ann Arbor, Mich.) 1962

Konvitz, Milton Ridvas, *Expanding Liberties: Freedom's Gains in Postwar America;* Greenwood Press (New York, N.Y.) 1966

———, *Fundamental Liberties of a Free People: Religion, Speech, Press, Assembly;* Greenwood Press (Ithaca, N.Y.) 1957

Labunski, Richard E., *The First Amendment Under Seige: The Politics of Broadcast Regulation;* Greenwood Press (Westport, Conn.) 1981

Lacy, Dan, *Freedom and Communications*, 2nd ed., University of Illinois Press (Urbana, Ill.), 1965.

Lippmann, Walter, *An Inquiry into the Principles of the Good Society*, Little, Brown (Boston, Mass.), 1936.

———, *The Public Philosophy*, New American Library (New York, N.Y.), 1956.

———, *Liberty and the News*, Harcourt, Brace (New York, N.Y.), 1920.

Lofton, John, *The Press as Guardian of the First Amendment*, University of South Carolina Press (Columbia, S.C.), 1980.

Meiklejohn, Alexander, *Free Speech and Its Relation to Self-Government*, Harper Bros. (New York, N.Y.), 1948.

———, *Political Freedom: The Constitutional Powers of the People;*, Harper and Row (New York, N.Y.), 1960.

Mendelson, Wallace, "On the Meaning of the First Amendment: Absolutes in the Balance," *California Law Review*, 1962.

———, "The First Amendment and the Judicial Process: A Reply to Mr. Franz", *Vanderbilt Law Review*, 1964.

Merrill, John C., *Imperative of Freedom*, Hastings House (New York, N.Y.), 1974.

———, and Jack Odell, *Philosophy and Journalism*, Longman (New York, N.Y.), 1983.

Morgan, David, *The Flacks of Washington: Government Information and the Public Agenda;* Greenwood Press (Westport, Conn.) 1986.

Mott, Frank Luther, and Ralph D. Casey, *Interpretations of Journalism*, Crofts (New York, N.Y.), 1937.

Murphy, Paul L., *The Meaning of Freedom os Speech: First Amendment Freedoms from Wilson to FDR;* Greenwood Press (Westport, Conn.) 1972.

Oboler, Eli M., *Definding Intellectual Freedom: The Library and the Censor;* Greenwood Press (Westport, Conn.) 1980.

Ogden, August Raymond, *The Dies Committee: A Study of the Special House Committee for the Investigation of Un-American Activities;* Greenwood Press (Washington, D.C.) 1945.

O'Neill, Robert M., *Free Speech: Responsible Communication Under Law*, Bobbs-Merrill (Indianapolis, Ind.), 1966.

O'Neill, Robert M., *Free Speech: Responsible Communication Under Law*, Bobbs-Merrill (Indianapolis, Ind.), 1966.

Phillips, Michael J., *The Dilemmas of Individualism: Status, Liberty, and American Constitutional Law;* Greenwood Press (Westport, Conn.) 1983.

Pierce, Robert, *Keeping the Flame: Media and Government in America*, Hastings House (New York, N.Y.), 1979.

Pool, Ithiel de Sola, *On Free Speech in an Electronic Age: Technologies of Freedom*, The Belknap Press of Harvard University Press (Cambridge, Mass.), 1983.

————, and Wilbur Schramm, eds., *Handbook of Communication*, Rand-McNally (Chicago, Ill.), 1973.

Pound, Roscoe, *The Development of Constitutional Guarantees of Liberty;* Greenwood Press (New Haven, Conn.) 1957.

Rivers, William L., and Michael J. Nyhen, *Aspen Notebook on Govrnment and the Media*, Praeger (New York, N.Y.), 1977.

————, and Wilbur Schramm; Clifford G. Christians, *Responsibility in Mass Communication*, Harper & Row (New York, N.Y.), 1980.

Rome, Edwin P. and Roberts, William H., *Corporate and Commercial Free Speech: First Amendment Protection of Expression in Business;* Greenwood Press (New York, N.Y.) (1985)

Rucker, Bryce W., *The First Freedom*, Southern Illinois University Press (Carbondale, Ill.), 1968.

Sandman, Peter; David Sachsman; David Rubin, *Media*, Prentice-Hall (Engelwood Cliffs, N.J.), 3rd ed., 1982.

Schlesinger, "Freedom of the Press: Who Cares?" *Wall Street Journal*, January 5, 1973.

Siebert, Fred S.; Theodore Peterson; Wilbur Schramm, *Four Theories of the Press*, University of Illinois Press (Urbana, Ill.), 1956.

Steinberg, Peter L., *The Great "Red Menace": United States Prosecution of American Communists;* Greenwood Press (Westport, Conn.) 1984.

Stewart, Potter, "Can We Afford a Free Press?" *American Legion Magazine*, December 1975.

Stohl, Michael and Lopez, George A. (Editors), *The State as Terrorist: the Dynamics of Governmental Violence and Repression;* Greenwood Press (Westport, Conn.) 1984.

Ulloth, Dana R., *The Supreme Court: A Judicial Review of the Federal Communications Commission*, Arno Press (New York, N.Y.), 1979.

————; Peter Klinge; Sandra Eels, *Mass Media*, West (Minneapolis, Minn.), 1982.

Van Gerpen, Maurice, *Privileged Communication and the Press: The Citizen's Right to Know Versus the Law's Right to Confidentail News Source Evidence:* Greenwood Press (Westport, Conn.) 1984

Van Vleck, William C., *The Administrative Control of Aliens: A Study in Administrative Law and Procedure*, De Capo Press (New York, N.Y.), 1971.

Whitney, D. Charles, *Mass Communication Review Yearbooks*, Sage (Beverly Hills, Calif.), 1979-present.

Whipple, Leon, *The Story of Civil Liberty in the United States:* Greenwood Press (New York, N.Y.) 1927

Index

Dudley, Guildford, 33
Dudley, John, 33
Dulles, John Foster, 270
Duvalier, Francois, 481
Dworkin, Andrea, 541, 545
Ed Sullivan Show, 525
Eden, Barbara, 524
Edes, Benjamin, 90, 99
Edward I, King of England, 31
Edward VI, King of England, 33
Eisenhower, Dwight D., 269, 271, 383, 400, 420, 665, 731, 775, 791
Elizabeth I, Queen of England, 33-35, 465
Ellsberg, 434
Ellsberg, Daniel, 432
Emerson v. Board of Education (1947), 49
Emerson, Thomas I., 299-300, 301, 312
Endres, Fred, 761
Engels, 325-327
Epicurus, 13
Epiphanes, Antiochus, 18
Ervin, Sam, 679
Espinosa, Julio Garcia, 276
Estes, Billie Sol, 559, 571-572, 573, 574
Ewing, J. R., 524
FCC, Brandywine-Main Line Radio, Inc. v. (1972), 585
FCC, Red Lion Broadcasting Co. v. (1969), 226-227
FCC, United Church of Christ v. (1983), 588
FTC v. Raladam Co. (1931), 611
Faber, Myron, 680
Fanny Hill, 537
Farmer, Jeannette, 519
Federal Communication Commission, 789, 790
Featherer, Esther, 780
Federal Writers Program, 711
Federated Publications v. Swedberg (1981), 561
Ferdinand, King of Spain, 27
Ferraro, Geraldine, 675
Feuerback, Ludwig, 325
Field, Stephen, 147
Fisher, John, 32
Fisher, Yamataya v. (1903), 168
Fisk, James, 143
Fiske v. Kansas (1927), 284
Florida Legislative Investigation Committee, Gibson v. (1963), 2
Florida, Chandler v. (1981), 561
Floyd, Bond v. (1966), 300-301
Fly, James Lawrence, 248
Ford, Gerald R., 273, 408, 514, 793
Ford, Guy Stanton, 711
Four-Minute Men, 717
Fourier, Charles, 324
Francis I, King of France, 26
Franco, Francisco, 218-219
Frankel, Charles, 736, 737
Frankfurter, Felix, 297

Franklin, Benjamin, 70, 71, 76
Franklin, James, 69, 70
Frantz, Laurent, 297, 298
Fraser, Donald M., 542
Frayn, Michael, 545
Frederick the Wise, H.R.E., 25
Free Press v. Fair Trial, 557-577
Freed, Allen, 526
Freedom of Information Act, 663-671
Freneau, Philip, 622
Freud, S. 509
Friendly, Fred, 271
Frohwerk v. U. S. (1919), 178
Frohwerk, Jacob, 178
Fulbright, J. William, 726, 736
Fulbright Amendment, 728
Fuller, Keith, 484
Fuller, Melville, W., 168
Gag Orders, 562
Gaine, Hugh, 78
Galerius, 19
Galileo, 28
Ganett v. De Pasquala (1979), 560
Gannett, Frank E., 247
Garfunkel, Art, 539
Garland, Judy, 676
Garrison, William Lloyd, 130
Ged, William, 159-160
Gelasius I, Pope, 20, 24
General Electric, 224
Gensfleisch, Johann Gutenberg, 23
George I, King of England, 62, 64
George II, King of England, 78
George III, King of England, 80, 602
Georgia, Wood v. (1962), 286
Germany, 715-723 passim, 724-726
Gerry, Elbridge, 93, 97
Gertz v. Robert Welch, Inc. (1974), 553
Gibson v. Florida Legislative Investigation Committee (1963), 29
Gill, John, 90, 99
Ginsberg, Allen, 509
Ginzburg v. U. S. (1966), 538
Gitlow v. New York (1925), 192
Gitlow, Benjamin, 191, 192
Globe Newspaper Co. v. Superior Court (1982), 560
Goebbels, Josef, 232
Goebbels, Joseph, 711
Goldfarb, Ronald L., 567
Goldstein, Robert, 176
Goldwater, Barry, 596
Gone With the Wind, 220-230
Goodrich, Chauncey, 105
Gordon, Thomas, 64, 68, 621
Goring, Hermann, 231
Gothe, Johann Wolfgang Von, 488
Gould, Jack, 791
Gould, Jay, 143
Grant, U. S., 139
Grassi, Orazio, 28